Third Canadian Edition

Financial Management

Theory and Practice

Eugene F. Brigham
University of Florida

Michael C. Ehrhardt
University of Tennessee

Jerome Gessaroli
British Columbia Institute of Technology

Richard R. Nason
Dalhousie University

NELSON

NELSON

Financial Management: Theory and Practice,
Third Canadian Edition

by Eugene F. Brigham, Michael C. Ehrhardt,
Jerome Gessaroli, and Richard R. Nason

VP, Product and Partnership Solutions:
Anne Williams

Publisher, Digital and Print Content:
Amie Plourde

Senior Marketing Manager:
Alexis Hood

Technical Reviewer:
Ross Meacher

Content Development Manager:
Suzanne Simpson Millar

Photo and Permissions Researcher:
Carrie McGregor

Production Project Manager:
Christine Gilbert

Production Service:
Cenveo Publishing Services

Copy Editor:
Karen Rolfe

Proofreader:
Pushpa V. Giri

Indexer:
BIM Creatives, LLC

Design Director:
Ken Phipps

Managing Designer:
Franca Amore

Interior Design:
Sharon Kish

Cover Design:
Deborah Brock

Cover Image:
J. A. Kraulis/Masterfile

Compositor:
Cenveo Publishing Services

Library and Archives Canada Cataloguing in Publication

Brigham, Eugene F., 1930-, author
    Financial management : theory and practice / Eugene F. Brigham, Michael C. Ehrhardt, Jerome Gessaroli, Richard R. Nason. —Third Canadian edition.

Includes index.
ISBN 978-0-17-658305-7 (bound)

1. Corporations—Finance—Textbooks. I. Ehrhardt, Michael C., 1955-, author II. Gessaroli, Jerome, author III. Nason, Richard Ronald, 1962-, author IV. Title.

HG4026.F53 2016
658.15   C2015-904541-X

ISBN-13: 978-0-17-658305-7
ISBN-10: 0-17-658305-X

Loose Leaf Edition:
ISBN-13: 978-0-17-679471-2
ISBN-10: 0-17-679471-9

brief contents

contents

Chapter 4

Time Value of Money 89

Chapter 5

Financial Planning and Forecasting Financial Statements 130

Web Extensions

Part 3
Projects and Their Valuation 267

Chapter 9

The Cost of Capital 268

Chapter 10

The Basics of Capital Budgeting: Evaluating Cash Flows 299

Appendixes

about the authors

Eugene F. Brigham Dr. Eugene F. Brigham is Graduate Research Professor Emeritus at the University of Florida, where he has taught since 1971. Dr. Brigham received his M.B.A. and Ph.D. from the University of California–Berkeley and his undergraduate degree from the University of North Carolina. Prior to moving to the University of Florida, Dr. Brigham held teaching positions at the University of Connecticut, the University of Wisconsin, and the University of California–Los Angeles. Dr. Brigham served as president of the Financial Management Association and wrote more than 40 journal articles on the cost of capital, capital structure, and other aspects of financial management. The 10 textbooks on managerial finance and managerial economics that he authored or co-authored are used at more than 1,000 universities in the United States, and have been translated into 11 languages worldwide. He has served as a consultant to many corporations and government agencies, including the Federal Reserve Board, the Federal Home Loan Bank Board, the U.S. Office of Telecommunications Policy, and the RAND Corporation. Dr. Brigham continues to teach, consult, and do research, as well as work on textbooks. He spends his spare time on the golf course, enjoying time with his family and dogs, and tackling outdoor adventure activities, such as biking through Alaska.

Michael C. Ehrhardt Dr. Ehrhardt is a Professor in the Finance Department at the University of Tennessee and is the Paul and Beverly Castagna Professor of Investments. He did his undergraduate work in Civil Engineering at Swarthmore College. After working several years as an engineer, he returned to graduate school and received an M.S. in Operations Research and a Ph.D. in Finance from the Georgia Institute of Technology. Dr. Ehrhardt taught extensively at the undergraduate, masters, and doctoral levels in the areas of investments, corporate finance, and capital markets. He is a member of the team that developed and delivered the integrative first year of the MBA program. He was the winner of several outstanding teacher awards. Much of Dr. Ehrhardt's research is in the areas of corporate valuation and asset pricing models, including pricing models for interest-rate sensitive instruments. He teaches in Executive Education Programs and consults in the areas of corporate valuation, value-based compensation plans, financial aspects of supply chain management, and the cost of capital.

Jerome Gessaroli Mr. Gessaroli is on faculty at the British Columbia Institute of Technology's School of Business, teaching courses in corporate finance, security analysis, working capital management, and advanced finance. He has an MBA from the Sauder School of Business at the University of British Columbia. Prior to teaching, he worked in the securities industry, first trading equities and options, and later in corporate finance. Mr. Gessaroli also has international business experience, having worked for one of Canada's largest industrial R&D companies developing overseas business opportunities in London, China, Hong Kong, Singapore, and India. He has also consulted to various organizations, given interviews for newspapers, and served on the board of directors for an industry development association.

Richard R. Nason Dr. Nason is an Associate Professor of Finance at Dalhousie University in Halifax, Nova Scotia, where he teaches corporate finance, enterprise risk management, investments, and derivatives. He has been awarded several teaching awards, including Professor of the Year awards and the A. Gordon Archibald Award for Teaching Excellence. His research interests are in risk management, complexity, and financial education. Dr. Nason has an M.Sc. in Physics from the University of Pittsburgh and an M.B.A. and Ph.D. in Finance from Ivey Business School at Western University.

He is also a Chartered Financial Analyst charter holder. Dr. Nason has an extensive background in the derivatives industry. His experience includes structuring equity derivatives and exotics at Citigroup, starting and heading the credit derivatives business for Bank of Montreal, and being head of training for the Global Markets Group at Bank of America. He is a founding partner of RSD Solutions Inc., a risk management consultancy that specializes in financial risk management for financial institutions and corporations, as well as advanced training seminars on derivatives and financial mathematics.

preface

Financial Management: Theory and Practice, Third Canadian Edition, has four goals:

1. To create a text that would help students make better financial decisions;
2. To provide a book that could be used in an introductory finance course, but one that was complete enough for use as a reference text in follow-on case courses and after graduation;
3. To motivate students by demonstrating that finance is interesting and relevant;
4. To make the book clear enough that students could go through the material without wasting either their time or their professor's time trying to figure out what we were saying.

Valuation as a Unifying Theme

Our emphasis throughout the book is on the actions a manager can and should take to increase the value of the firm. Structuring the book around valuation and cash flows will, we hope, enhance continuity and help students see how various topics relate to one another. Near the beginning of each chapter we provide a corporate valuation framework that explicitly shows how a chapter's material relates to corporate valuation so that students can keep the big picture in mind even as they focus on a chapter's specific topics.

The book begins with fundamental concepts, including background on the economic and financial environment, financial statements (with an emphasis on cash flows), the time value of money, financial forecasting, bond valuation, risk analysis, and stock valuation. With this background, we go on to discuss how specific techniques and decision rules can be used to help maximize the value of the firm. This organization provides five important advantages:

1. Managers should try to maximize the fundamental value of a firm, which is determined by cash flows as revealed in financial statements. Our early coverage of financial statements thus helps students see how particular financial decisions affect the various parts of the firm and the resulting cash flow. Also, financial statement analysis provides an excellent vehicle for illustrating the usefulness of spreadsheets.
2. Covering time value of money early helps students see how and why expected future cash flows determine the value of the firm. Also, it takes time for students to digest TVM concepts and to learn how to do the required calculations, so it is good to cover TVM concepts early and often.
3. Most students—even those who do not plan to major in finance—are interested in stock and bond values, rates of return on investments, and the like. The ability to learn is a function of individual interest and motivation, so *Financial Management*'s early coverage of securities and security markets is pedagogically sound.
4. Once basic concepts have been established, it is easier for students to understand both how and why corporations make specific decisions in the areas of capital budgeting, raising capital, working capital management, mergers, and the like.
5. As its title indicates, this book combines theory and practical applications. An understanding of finance theory is absolutely essential for anyone developing and/or implementing effective financial strategies. But theory alone isn't sufficient, so we provide numerous examples in the book and the accompanying *Excel* spreadsheets to illustrate how theory is applied in practice. Indeed, we believe that the ability to analyze financial problems using *Excel* is absolutely essential for a student's successful job search and subsequent career. Therefore, many exhibits in the book come directly from the accompanying *Excel* spreadsheets.

Intended Market and Use

Financial Management, Third Canadian Edition, is designed primarily for use in an introductory finance course and as a reference text in follow-on case courses and after graduation. There is enough material for either a one- or two-term course, especially if the book is supplemented with cases and/or selected readings.

Features of the Third Canadian Edition

Throughout our work on the third Canadian edition, we have strived for completeness and ease of exposition, with an emphasis on current real-world examples, including the latest changes in the financial environment and financial theory. Below we describe elements used throughout the text as well as features that are specific to individual chapters.

Corporate Valuation Emphasis

Given the text's emphasis on valuation, we have placed a corporate valuation framework in the early pages of each chapter. These diagrams make it clear how the chapter's materials relate to the corporate valuation model. They do so by highlighting the specific parts of the model that are relevant to the chapter. We believe this illustrative framework is a simple yet powerful learning tool.

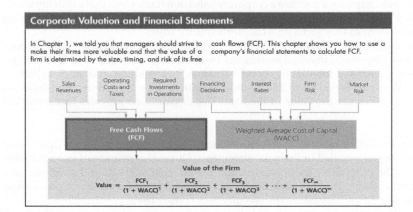

Practical Application of Theory

As happens in most academic disciplines, theory is not always consistent with real life. We realize this and provide students with brief discussions (such as "Capital Structure Theory: Our View" in Chapter 12, and "Current Status of the CAPM" in Chapter 7) on how the theory fits with reality. We also discuss common errors that students may make (such as "Four Mistakes to Avoid" in Chapter 9) when applying financial theory or tools.

Substantial Excel Integration

The application of finance requires extensive use of *Excel*. *Financial Management* has taken the integration of teaching finance and *Excel* to a new level. Illustrations, examples, and formulas are developed using *Excel*, and point-by-point explanations are provided for using *Excel* to model the various concepts. Also, end-of-chapter *Excel* problems provide opportunities to work with finance problems in a much more practical manner than by simply using a calculator. Further information on *Excel* integration is described later on in the "*Excel* Tool Kits" and "Build a Model" sections of this preface.

Canadian Content

We use three criteria for updating the text with Canadian content. (1) Canadian institutions, laws, financial markets, and tax rules are fully reflected in the text. (2) Given the importance of the U.S. markets and institutions to Canada, especially in the area of finance, discussions of key U.S. financial markets and research findings are kept in place where appropriate, along with illustrations. (3) Details with little relevance to Canada, and those of a tertiary nature, have been deleted to maintain focus and clarity.

Corporate Ethics

With corporate ethics and governance issues making headlines throughout the developed economies, we have provided discussions of ethical abuses in Chapter 1 and elsewhere throughout the book. In addition, in Chapter 22, "Corporate Valuation and Governance," we specifically address corporate governance and the actions that both firms and government bodies can take to minimize such events in the future.

Persisting Effects of the 2007–2009 Credit Crisis

At the time of writing this edition, the world's economies are still dealing with the effects of one of the worst financial crises since the Great Depression. It is not an easy story to tell: there are many different opinions about its causes and possible remedies, and there is much that researchers need to learn about those recent events. We do, however, believe it is useful to provide coverage of the credit crisis in a straightforward and readable manner. Our own classroom experience has been that students (whether finance majors or not) are still eager to learn about the credit crisis—including the financial instruments the popular press often refers to—as well as the implications of the crisis for the broader economy. We have provided such a discussion in Chapter 16, "Capital Market Financing: Hybrid and Other Securities." In a number of other chapters, we also discuss specific elements of the financial crisis as they relate directly to the chapter's topic.

Textbook Web Extensions

We have identified specialized topics that are important but not essential for every introductory finance course. We have made this material accessible as chapter Web Extensions, which are provided as Adobe PDF files on the textbook's website at www.nelson.com/brigham3ce or via MindTap. These PDF files are identical in formatting and layout to the text itself. There are 27 Web Extensions from which the instructor and student can choose. We find this an effective way to provide robust coverage without making the actual textbook too large or cumbersome. See the Table of Contents for a complete list of Web Extensions available.

Improvements in the Third Canadian Edition

Throughout the text, we have updated and clarified materials, reviewing the entire book for completeness, ease of exposition, and currency. We have made hundreds of small changes to keep the text up to date, with particular emphasis on updating the real-world examples and including the latest changes in financial theory and the financial environment. We have added more subheadings throughout the book and provided more graphical representations to the data, all of which make the book more readable.

We have made too many small improvements in each chapter to mention them all, but some of the more notable ones are discussed below.

Chapter 1: An Overview of Financial Management and the Financial Environment
A new introduction provides an overview of successful Canadian companies. We have also added a new section on "Separating the Investment and Consumption Decision." The "Economic Conditions and Policies That Affect the Cost of Money" section now includes a graph illustrating the federal government's budget deficits/surpluses and trade balances over time.

Chapter 2: Financial Statements, Cash Flow, and Taxes
The introduction illustrating the different uses of cash by companies has been completely updated. "Cost of goods sold" has been added to the income statement as a separate line item, allowing for easier analysis. This change

is reflected throughout the book. A new vignette titled "Filling in the GAAP" has been added; it describes some key differences between IFRS and U.S. GAAP. A new Challenge Problem has been created for this chapter.

Chapter 3: Analysis of Financial Statements In previous editions, we defined the inventory turnover ratio using sales instead of COGS because some compilers of financial ratio statistics, such as Dun & Bradstreet, use the ratio of sales to inventories. However, most sources now report the turnover ratio using COGS, so we have changed our definition to conform to the majority of reporting organizations and now define the inventory turnover ratio as COGS/Inventories. Also, to be more consistent with many Web-based reporting organizations, we now define the debt ratio as total debt divided by total assets and the debt-to-equity ratio as total debt divided by total common equity, whereas previously we used total liabilities in the numerator.

Chapter 4: Time Value of Money We have added a new vignette on payday lending that discusses the controversy over the high interest rates charged on payday loans. Section 4.17, "Amortized Loans," has been expanded to describe how interest and principal can be calculated for a specific time period. Extra material and four new Intermediate Problems were added at the end of the chapter to allow students to get more comfortable with the math.

Chapter 5: Financial Planning and Forecasting Financial Statements Updates and clarifications have been made to this chapter.

Chapter 6: Bonds, Bond Valuation, and Interest Rates A new vignette on Canadian bond covenant and security provisions has been added.

Chapter 7: Risk, Return, and the Capital Asset Pricing Model The chapter introduction has been rewritten. A graph showing the volatility between the overall TSX index and Canadian government Treasury bills has been added. The current vignette on behavioural finance has been enhanced and moved into the chapter's main body as Section 7.5. This section now also discusses a possible explanation for market bubbles from a behavioural finance perspective. Two new Intermediate Problems and one new Challenge Problem have been created for this chapter.

Chapter 8: Stocks, Stock Valuation, and Stock Market Equilibrium The section "The Market Stock Price versus Intrinsic Value," along with the accompanying diagram, has been revised to improve clarity. Section 8.12, "The Efficient Markets Hypothesis," has been expanded and revised. One new Easy Problem and two new Intermediate Problems have been created for this chapter.

Chapter 9: The Cost of Capital The chapter introduction has been rewritten. A new vignette, "In Search of Capital? Head West," has been added and discusses the cost of capital internationally. A new Challenge Problem has been created for this chapter.

Chapter 10: The Basics of Capital Budgeting: Evaluating Cash Flows The chapter introduction has been rewritten and now uses an oil sands investment example to introduce the chapter material. The section on "Multiple IRRs" has been revised, making it simpler to understand.

Chapter 11: Cash Flow Estimation and Risk Analysis A new introduction expands upon the oil sands example from Chapter 10 and provides context for Chapter 11's discussion on the appropriate cash flows to consider when evaluating a new project's investment potential. The section discussing the various cash flows has been placed earlier in the chapter so it is read before the full analysis of a project example given in Section 11.3. A Web Extension, 11A, which discusses Monte Carlo simulation in capital budgeting, has been added. Three new Easy Problems and one new Intermediate Problem have been added to this chapter.

Chapter 12: Capital Structure Decisions A new vignette discussing capital structures across industries in Canada has been added. We updated Section 12.7 "Capital Structure Evidence and Implications," to include results from the latest empirical tests and reorganized the material and added sub-headings to improve clarity.

Chapter 13: Distributions to Shareholders: Dividends and Repurchases The chapter introduction has been rewritten and now discusses how Apple Computer distributes cash back to shareholders.

Chapter 14: Initial Public Offerings, Investment Banking, and Financial Restructuring The chapter introduction has been completely updated. Two new vignettes have been added, "Crowdfunding and Raising Capital" and "Life in the Fast Lane: High-Frequency Trading!" A new Easy Problem has been created for this chapter.

Chapter 15: Lease Financing The chapter introduction has been rewritten. A new vignette has been added illustrating the use of sale and leaseback agreements by Loblaw and Canadian Tire.

Chapter 16: Capital Market Financing: Hybrid and Other Securities A new vignette on BlackBerry's decision to use convertible debenture financing was added. One new Easy Problem has been created for this chapter.

Chapter 17: Working Capital Management and Short-Term Financing The chapter introduction has been completely updated. Section 17.1, "Overview of Working Capital Management," has been added. Two new vignettes have been added: "Electronic Payments in Canada: What's the Hold-Up?" and "Some Firms Operate with Negative Working Capital!" A new Spreadsheet Problem has also been created for this chapter.

Chapter 18: Current Asset Management The chapter introduction has been rewritten. A new vignette discusses the levels of cash and other current assets held by Canadian companies.

Chapter 19: Financial Options and Applications in Corporate Finance This chapter was shortened by eliminating discussion of the multi-period binomial model. The chapter has an increased focus on the Black-Scholes option pricing model and the factors that affect option prices.

Chapter 20: Enterprise Risk Management We rewrote much of this chapter, changing it from a chapter about derivatives with applications to risk management to a chapter about enterprise risk management with applications of derivatives as one of several tools in managing risk. We adapted the general enterprise risk management framework of the Treadway Commission's Committee of Sponsoring Organizations (COSO) as it is one of the most comprehensive and widely used risk management frameworks.

Chapter 22: Corporate Valuation and Governance We have revised and streamlined this chapter to focus on two major areas: valuation and governance. In doing so, we were able to introduce new material on agency conflicts.

Chapter 23: Mergers, Acquisitions, and Restructuring In Section 23.8, "Setting the Bid Price," we have added new material on "Relative Bargaining Power" and "Cash Offers versus Stock Offers." The existing vignette on "Limits to Foreign Acquisitions" has been expanded and updated based on more recent Canadian events.

Chapter 24: Decision Trees, Real Options, and Other Capital Budgeting Topics This chapter is now available online for flexibility in course offerings.

Walkthrough of Pedagogical Features

Real-World Chapter Introductions
Every chapter starts with a context-setting, real-world example of the material about to be covered. This introduction indicates to students how the material fits in with today's financial environment.

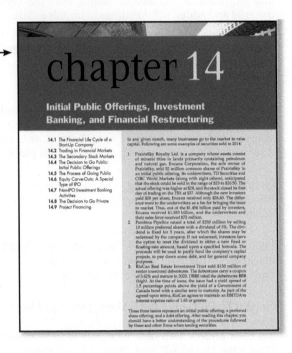

Finance: Small Business Vignettes
Small business accounts for about one-quarter of Canada's GDP. Yet typically, this important sector is scarcely mentioned in most finance texts. Throughout the text we have embedded a number of vignettes discussing the challenges that small businesses face when applying the financial concepts and tools being discussed.

FINANCE: SMALL BUSINESS

Cost of Capital for Small and Privately Owned Businesses

Small and privately owned businesses face unique challenges in calculating their cost of capital. In the previous discussion we have used past stock prices to estimate beta, which in turn was used in the CAPM to calculate the company's cost of equity. But obviously, if shares of a small business don't trade publicly, the required historical stock data are not available. This poses a challenge to smaller businesses. How do they estimate their cost of equity? One method would be to identify one or more publicly traded firms that are in the same industry and that are approximately the same size as the privately owned firm. Betas are then estimated for the publicly traded companies; an average beta is taken and used as an estimated beta for the private company. Note that this is similar to the pure play method for estimating divisional beta that we discussed earlier. With an estimate of beta, the cost of equity can be estimated using the CAPM approach. There is, however, evidence that few small businesses actually calculate their cost of equity. Also, only a minority of small businesses surveyed calculate their WACC. They in fact find it hard to determine their cost of equity.

The liquidity of owning stock in a privately held firm is less than the liquidity of publicly held stock. Just as the yield on a thinly traded bond has a liquidity premium, the required return on stock in a privately held firm should reflect a liquidity premium. An ad hoc adjustment can be made to reflect this lack of liquidity by adding 1 to 3 percentage points to the firm's cost of equity. This "rule of thumb" is not very satisfying theoretically because we don't know exactly how large a liquidity premium to add, but it is very common in practice.

There are also problems in estimating the capital structure weights. Capital structure weights should be based on the target market-value weights. However, a privately held firm can't observe its market value. If a firm doesn't know its current market weights, that makes it difficult for the firm to estimate its target weights. To resolve this problem, many analysts begin by making a trial guess as to the value of the firm's equity. The analysts then use this estimated value of equity to estimate the cost of capital, then use the cost of capital to estimate the value of the firm, and complete the circle by using the esti-

Finance: In Focus Vignettes
A number of vignettes throughout the text provide interesting real-life examples of how the concepts discussed in the chapter at hand are important in today's business environment.

FINANCE: IN FOCUS

Leasing to Unlock Shareholder Value

What do Loblaw and Canadian Tire have in common? Neither of them directly owns the real estate and buildings that drive their operations. Loblaw was the first of the two to sell its properties for $7 billion to Choice Properties real estate investment trust and then lease them back on a long-term basis. Choice Properties then went on to raise $600 million through an IPO, $200 million through the sale of equity to George Weston Limited, and another $800 million through a debenture issue. Much of the funds were used to pay Loblaw for the assets.

More recently, Canadian Tire sold off its stores and land to CT REIT, which also went public soon after. By the two companies separating their real estate assets from their core retail operations, investors were able to value the real estate businesses separately (and higher) than when they were part of Loblaw's and Canadian Tire's overall corporate operations. The sale and leaseback of the properties also freed up cash to either reinvest in operations or to be distributed back to shareholders. While the effect on day-to-day operations was minimal, the effect on its stock price was not. The graph below shows the effect on the companies' share prices when they announced (Day 0) the restructuring. Loblaw's stock closed up over 13% while Canadian Tire's stock climbed about 10%. Over $4.8 billion in shareholder wealth was added by selling their properties to a REIT and leasing them back.

Concept Review questions Students learn specific concepts and understand particular numerical examples best if they work with illustrative questions immediately after they read the applicable section material. Concept Reviews provide this opportunity for immediate reinforcement at the end of most major sections. Numerical questions also include a "check figure" in parentheses, to help students check their work. And for these, fully solved *Excel* worksheets are also available on the textbook's website at www .nelson.com/brigham3ce or via MindTap.

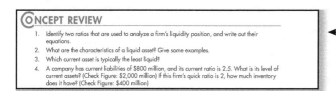

CONCEPT REVIEW

1. Identify two ratios that are used to analyze a firm's liquidity position, and write out their equations.
2. What are the characteristics of a liquid asset? Give some examples.
3. Which current asset is typically the least liquid?
4. A company has current liabilities of $800 million, and its current ratio is 2.5. What is its level of current assets? (Check Figure: $2,000 million) If this firm's quick ratio is 2, how much inventory does it have? (Check Figure: $400 million)

Formulas and Equations Thoroughly explaining finance requires mathematical equations. Whenever a new equation is introduced, it is placed in a shaded box and given a specific equation number. The spacing and shading makes reading the text easy, while the equation numbering makes it straightforward to follow which equation is being referred to in future discussions.

$$r_e = \hat{r}_e = \frac{D1}{P_0(1-F)} + g \qquad (9\text{-}9)$$

Excel Tool Kits We have created *Excel* Tool Kits to enhance student proficiency with spreadsheets. Created for each chapter (except Chapter 1), these models include explanations and screen shots that show students how to use many of the features and functions of *Excel*. We have integrated the Tool Kit models into the text so that many figures and tables in the textbook are drawn right from the *Excel* model, including the *Excel* row and column headings so that students can see exactly how the problem is worked in *Excel*. The Tool Kits are available to students on the textbook's website at www.nelson.com/brigham3ce or via MindTap.

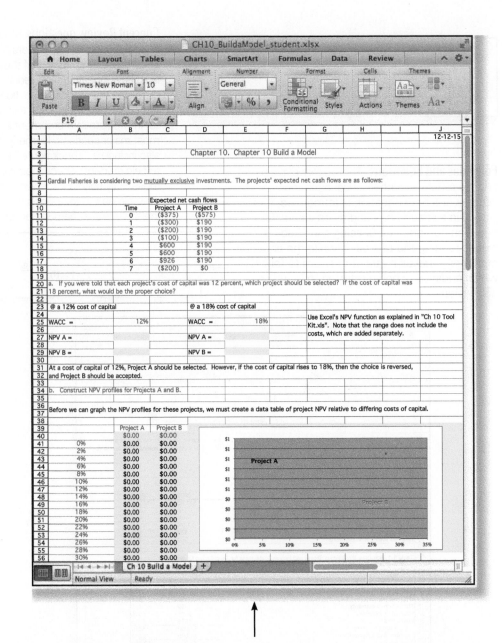

Build a Model Excel Spreadsheets Chapters 2 to 23 include a Spreadsheet Problem. To complement these, *Excel* spreadsheets have been developed. These spreadsheets contain data from the problem, plus general instructions relating to solving it. The problem is partially completed, and the student must "build a model" in order to complete it. These models are available to students on the textbook's website at www.nelson.com/brigham3ce or via MindTap. Fully completed models are available to instructors.

Summary

The main purpose of this chapter was to discuss techniques used by investors and managers to analyze financial statements. The key concepts covered are listed below.

- **Liquidity ratios** show the relationship of a firm's current assets to its current liabilities, and thus its ability to meet maturing debts. Two commonly used liquidity ratios are the **current ratio** and the **quick, or acid test, ratio.**
- **Asset management ratios** measure how effectively a firm is managing its assets. These ratios include **inventory turnover, days sales outstanding, average payable period, fixed assets turnover,** and **total assets turnover.**
- **Debt management ratios** reveal (1) the extent to which the firm is financed with debt and (2) its likelihood of defaulting on its debt obligations. They include the **debt ratio, debt-to-equity ratio, times-interest-earned ratio,** and **EBITDA coverage ratio.**
- **Profitability ratios** show the combined effects of liquidity, asset management, and debt management policies on operating results. They include the **net profit margin, the basic earning power ratio, the return on total assets,** and the **return on common equity.**
- **Market value ratios** relate the firm's stock price to its earnings, cash flow, and book value per share, thus giving management an indication of what investors think of the company's past performance and future prospects. These include the **price/earnings ratio, price/cash flow ratio,** and the **market/book ratio.**
- **Trend analysis,** where one plots a ratio over time, is important, because it reveals

Summary Each chapter includes a bullet-point summary. Each bullet covers a key concept discussed in the chapter. The key terms and/or concepts are bolded both in the body of the chapter and in the summary, making it easy for students to go back into the chapter to review specific materials.

Concept Review Problems At the end of each chapter are comprehensive concept review problems. These problems allow students to test their knowledge of the chapter's primary concepts. Answers are available to students on the textbook's website at www.nelson.com/brigham3ce or via MindTap. Full solutions are available to instructors.

End-of-Chapter Problems

To assist student learning, we have arranged problems by difficulty. The first set of problems is designated "Easy," and most students should be able to work them without much trouble. Then come "Intermediate" problems, which are a bit harder, followed by "Challenging" ones, which are longer and more complex. This ranking procedure reduces students' stress and frustration because they can clearly identify which problems are going to require more effort. Answers to odd-numbered problems appear in Appendix A. Full solutions are available to instructors.

Mini Cases Mini cases are provided for each chapter. These integrated problems are framed in a more realistic manner. Most mini cases have both descriptive and quantitative questions that cover much of the chapter's key content. Instructors can assign the cases in their entirety or utilize only some of the questions. Detailed descriptive and quantitative solutions are available to instructors.

Instructor Resources

The **Nelson Education Teaching Advantage (NETA)** program delivers research-based instructor resources that promote student engagement and higher-order thinking to enable the success of Canadian students and educators. Visit Nelson Education's **Inspired Instruction** website at http://www.nelson.com/inspired/ to find out more about NETA.

The following instructor resources have been created for *Financial Management: Theory and Practice*, Third Canadian Edition. Access these ultimate tools for customizing lectures and presentations at **www.nelson.com/instructor**.

NETA Test Bank

This resource was written by Patrick O'Meara, Southern Alberta Institute of Technology. It includes more than 1,500 multiple-choice questions written according to NETA guidelines for effective construction and development of higher-order questions. Also included are about 500 True/False questions.

The NETA Test Bank is available in a new, cloud-based platform. **Nelson Testing Powered by Cognero®** is a secure online testing system that allows instructors to author, edit, and manage test bank content from anywhere Internet access is available. No special installations or downloads are needed, and the desktop-inspired interface, with its drop-down menus and familiar, intuitive tools, allows instructors to create and manage tests with ease. Multiple test versions can be created in an instant, and content can be imported or exported into other systems. Tests can be delivered from a learning management system, the classroom, or wherever an instructor chooses. Nelson Testing Powered by Cognero for *Financial Management: Theory and Practice* can also be accessed through www.nelson.com/instructor.

NETA PowerPoint

Microsoft® PowerPoint® lecture slides for every chapter have been created by Zhen Wang, Laurentian University. There is an average of 60 slides per chapter, many featuring key figures and tables from *Financial Management: Theory and Practice*. NETA principles of clear design and engaging content have been incorporated throughout, making it simple for instructors to customize the deck for their courses.

Image Library

This resource consists of digital copies of figures and short tables used in the book. Instructors may use these jpegs to customize the NETA PowerPoint or create their own PowerPoint presentations.

Instructor's Solutions Manual

This manual, prepared by authors Jerome Gessaroli and Richard Nason, includes worked-out solutions to all end-of-chapter material. It has been independently checked for accuracy by Ross Meacher.

Build-A-Model Solutions

These downloadable *Excel* spreadsheets integrate with the Spreadsheet Problems at the end of each chapter (excluding Chapter 1). Student versions of these files provide instructions relating to "building the model" and solving the problem. Instructor versions are fully completed models. These solutions have been revised by Shantanu Dutta, University of Ottawa.

Mini-Case Solutions

Mini cases appear at the end of each chapter, and include both descriptive and quantitative questions that cover much of the chapter's content. Solutions for these mini cases have been revised by textbook authors Jerome Gessaroli and Rick Nason, and spreadsheets have been further checked and revised by Shantanu Dutta, University of Ottawa.

Web Extensions

Most chapters in *Financial Management: Theory and Practice* include online "appendices" that provide more detailed coverage of topics addressed in the chapter. Available for students and instructors, these extensions are downloadable PDF files, designed just like the text chapters. An instructor can use any of the extensions to provide deeper coverage of material. We believe that these Web Extensions provide significant flexibility for meeting the variety of needs that finance professors have in the classroom. See the Table of Contents for a full listing.

MindTap

Offering personalized paths of dynamic assignments and applications, **MindTap** is a digital learning solution that turns cookie-cutter into cutting-edge, apathy into engagement, and memorizers into higher-level thinkers. MindTap enables students to analyze and apply chapter concepts within relevant assignments, and allows instructors to measure skills and promote better outcomes with ease. A fully online learning solution, MindTap combines all student learning tools—readings, multimedia, activities, and assessments—into a single Learning Path that guides the student through the curriculum. Instructors personalize the experience by customizing the presentation of these learning tools to their students, even seamlessly introducing their own content into the Learning Path.

Aplia

Aplia™ is a Cengage Learning online homework system dedicated to improving learning by increasing student effort and engagement. Aplia makes it easy for instructors to assign frequent online homework assignments. Aplia provides students with prompt and detailed feedback to help them learn as they work through the questions, and features interactive tutorials to fully engage them in learning course concepts. Automatic grading and powerful assessment tools give instructors real-time reports of student progress, participation, and performance, while Aplia's easy-to-use course management features let instructors flexibly administer course announcements and materials online. With Aplia, students will show up to class fully engaged and prepared, and instructors will have more time to do what they do best—teach. The Aplia problem sets for *Financial Management* were reviewed for consistency with the third Canadian edition by Scott Anderson, Ryerson University.

Student Ancillaries

Companion Website

Nelson Education's Companion Website for *Financial Management: Theory and Practice*, Third Canadian Edition, provides a variety of downloadable material to help students as they work through concepts in the text. Visit **www.nelson.com/brigham3ce** to access this material.

Excel Tool Kits: *Excel* Tool Kits have been developed to enhance proficiency with *Excel*. Created for each chapter, except Chapter 1, these models include explanations and screenshots to show how to use features and functions in *Excel*. A spreadsheet icon in the margin of the text alerts students to when a Tool Kit is available.

Concept Review Worked Solutions: Concept Reviews often appear at the end of a major section, to test your understanding of a concept immediately after you read about it. Numerical questions also include a "check figure" in parentheses, to help check your work. For these, fully worked Concept Review worked solutions (in *Excel*) are available on the textbook's website.

Build-a-Model Spreadsheets: Chapters 2 to 23 include a Spreadsheet Problem. These downloadable *Excel* spreadsheets contain data from the problem, plus general instructions relating to solving the problem. The spreadsheets are partially completed, and the student must "build a model" in order to finalize each one.

Answers to Concept Review Problems: These downloadable PDFs provide answers to the Concept Review Problems at the end of chapters. Use these to help check your progress as you work through the text.

Web Extensions: These chapter "appendices" provide more detailed coverage of topics addressed in the chapter. Presented as downloadable PDF files, they are designed just like the text chapters. See the Table of Contents for a full listing of Web Extensions available.

Calculator Tutorials: These tutorials help acclimatize students to using financial calculators in financial management.

MindTap

Stay organized and efficient with *MindTap*—a single destination with all the course material and study aids you need to succeed. Built-in apps leverage social media and the latest learning technology. For example:

- ReadSpeaker will read the text to you.
- Flashcards are pre-populated to provide you with a jump start for review—or you can create your own.
- You can highlight text and make notes in your MindTap Reader. Your notes will flow into Evernote, the electronic notebook app that you can access anywhere when it's time to study for the exam.
- Self-quizzing allows you to assess your understanding.

Visit http://www.nelson.com/student to start using MindTap. Enter the Online Access Code from the card included with your text. If a code card is *not* provided, you can purchase instant access at NELSONbrain.com.

Aplia

Founded in 2000 by economist and Stanford professor Paul Romer, **Aplia**™ is an educational technology company dedicated to improving learning by increasing student effort and engagement. Currently, Aplia products have been used by more than a million students at over 1,300 institutions. Aplia offers a way for you to stay on top of your coursework with regularly scheduled homework assignments that increase your time on task and give you prompt feedback. Interactive tools and additional content are provided to further increase your engagement and understanding. See http://www.aplia.com for more information. If Aplia isn't bundled with your copy of *Financial Management: Theory and Practice*, Third Canadian Edition, you can purchase access separately at NELSONbrain.com. Be better prepared for class with Aplia!

Acknowledgements

This third Canadian edition of *Financial Management: Theory and Practice* reflects the efforts of a number of diverse contributors.

We would like to thank those reviewers who provided vital insights into their courses and use of textbook resources through their review of the second Canadian edition:

Ian Glew, Memorial University of Newfoundland
Colin F. Mang, Nipissing University
Eloisa Perez, MacEwan University
Mohammad Siddiquee, University of New Brunswick
Thomas Walker, Concordia University
Liyan Yang, University of Toronto

We would also like to thank all those involved in helping us through the entire writing process. Thanks to J. Terry Gordon, who provided very substantial input on the Financial Reporting for Mergers section, Victor Waese, and Patrick Wolfe, all from the British Columbia Institute of Technology and all always ready to share their time and expertise to answer questions and provide valuable feedback. Thank you as well to Jennifer Ziobrowski from Dalhousie University for providing administrative support. Specifically, we also thank our Publisher Amie Plourde and Content Development Manager Suzanne Simpson Millar, who provided answers and direction to countless questions; our Copy Editor, Karen Rolfe, for her thorough efforts; Alexis Hood, Senior Marketing Manager; Christine Gilbert, Production Project Manager; and Ezhilsolai Periasamy, Project Manager. We also are very appreciative of the input, encouragement, and support provided by many others at Nelson, Education, which is a highly professional organization.

Accuracy

At this point, authors generally say something like this: "We appreciate all the help we received from the people listed above, but any remaining errors are, of course, our own responsibility." And in many books, there are plenty of remaining errors. Having experienced difficulties with errors ourselves, both as students and as instructors, we resolved to avoid this problem in *Financial Management*. As a result of our error detection procedures, we are convinced that the book is as free of mistakes as we can make it. We would like to thank Ross Meacher for the detailed accuracy checks on our Problems and Solutions Manual.

Conclusion

Finance is, in a real sense, the cornerstone of the free enterprise system. Good financial management is therefore vitally important to the economic health of business firms, hence to the nation and the world. Because of its importance, corporate finance should be thoroughly understood. However, this is easier said than done—the field is relatively complex and undergoes constant change in response to shifts in economic conditions. All of this makes corporate finance stimulating and exciting, but also challenging and sometimes perplexing. We sincerely hope that *Financial Management: Theory and Practice*, Third Canadian Edition will help readers understand and solve the financial problems faced by businesses today.

Michael C. Ehrhardt
University of Tennessee
Eugene F. Brigham
University of Florida

Jerome Gessaroli
British Columbia Institute of Technology
Richard R. Nason
Dalhousie University

June 2015

part 1

Fundamental Concepts

chapter 1

An Overview of Financial Management and the Financial Environment

What does it take to be one of Canada's "Best Managed Companies"? Well, Deloitte Canada has been assessing companies annually over the past 20 years for this prestigious title. For 2013, a few companies that made the cut included Canadian Tire, CCI Inc., Purdys Chocolatier, and Upside Engineering. What do these companies have that separates them from the rest of the pack?

Deloitte looks at three broad areas: (1) strategy—how well do companies articulate their core competencies and build value; (2) capability—how well do they execute their strategy including customer-focused activities as well as the use of technological solutions; and (3) commitment—how well companies identify, retain, and nurture employees and leaders. Many of these companies operate in highly competitive markets in which they face threats from much larger or even worldwide multinational corporations. How do they thrive and survive in such an environment? Deloitte found one recurring trait is an ability to adapt to a rapidly changing business environment. Adaptability is a necessary skill, particularly in the current climate with its accelerated pace of change driven by technological advances and business globalization. Another enduring characteristic of Canadian business is sustainability. Successful Canadian businesses have plans that are well thought out, and controlled investments that, like all efficient deployments of capital, are seeking the highest rate of return. For example, Toronto-based Spin Master, a toy and entertainment company, places significant emphasis on its information system platforms for building out its international network of product offerings. Newterra, an environmental systems company, maintains its competitive advantage through constant innovation and new product offerings. The company's innovative technologies are created by a combination of internal development, acquisitions, and small continuous improvements. The Great Little Box Company, which produces packaging supplies and services, had grown from just three employees in 1986 to over 250 employees by 2012. Its growth is widely credited due to the company's significant investment in hiring, managing, and workforce management practices.

In a nutshell, these companies succeeded by innovating, applying technology in a clear strategic manner, and fostering a work environment that allows employees to fully utilize their skills and talents. As you will see throughout this book, the resulting cash flows and superior return on capital also create value for shareholders.

Source: Adapted from Peter Brown and John Hughes, *Power of the Best* (Toronto: Penguin Group, 2012), viii–x, 77–81, 145–150, 191–198.

This chapter should give you an idea of what financial management is all about, including an overview of the financial markets in which corporations operate. Before getting into details, let's look at the big picture. You're probably in school because you want an interesting, challenging, and rewarding career. To see where finance fits in, here's a five-minute business degree.

1.1 The Five-Minute Business Degree

Okay, we realize you can't get a business degree in five minutes. But just as an artist quickly sketches the outline of a picture before filling in the details, we can sketch the key elements of a business education. In a nutshell, the objective of a business degree is to provide managers with the knowledge and skills they need to run successful companies, so we start our sketch with some common characteristics of successful companies. In particular, all successful companies are able to accomplish two main goals:

1. They identify, create, and deliver products or services that are highly valued by customers—so highly valued that customers choose to purchase them from the company rather than from its competitors.
2. All successful companies sell their products/services at prices that are high enough to cover costs and to compensate owners and creditors for their exposure to risk.

It's easy to talk about satisfying customers and investors, but it's not so easy to actually do so. If it were, then all companies would be successful, and you wouldn't need a business degree!

Visit the textbook's website. This ever-evolving site, for students and instructors, is a tool for teaching, learning, and financial research. **www.nelson.com/ brigham3ce**

The Key Attributes of Successful Companies

First, *successful companies have skilled people* at all levels inside the company, including leaders, managers, and a capable workforce.

Second, *successful companies have strong relationships* with groups outside the company. For example, successful companies develop win–win relationships with suppliers and excel in customer relationship management.

Third, *successful companies have enough funding* to execute their plans and support their operations. Most companies need cash to purchase land, buildings, equipment, and materials. Companies can reinvest a portion of their earnings, but most growing companies must also raise additional funds externally, by some combination of selling shares and/or borrowing in the financial markets.

Just as a stool needs all three legs to stand, a successful company must have all three attributes: skilled people, strong external relationships, and sufficient capital.

A Business Degree, Finance, and Your Career

To succeed, a company must meet its first main goal: identifying, creating, and delivering highly valued products and services for its customers. This requires that it possess all three of the key attributes mentioned above. Therefore, it's not surprising that most of your business courses are directly related to these attributes. For example, courses in economics, communication, strategy, organizational behaviour, and human resources should prepare you for a managerial role and enable you to manage your company's workforce effectively. Other courses, such as marketing, operations management, and information technology, increase your knowledge of specific disciplines, enabling you to develop the efficient business processes and strong external relationships your company needs. Portions of *this* finance course will address raising the capital your company needs to implement its plans. In short, your business courses will give you the skills you need to help a company achieve its first goal: producing goods and services that customers want.

Recall though, that it's not enough just to have highly valued products and satisfied customers. Successful companies must also meet their second main goal, which is generating enough cash to compensate the investors who provided the necessary capital. To help your company accomplish this second goal, you must be able to evaluate any proposal, whether it relates to marketing, production, strategy, or any other area, and implement only the projects that add value for your investors. For this, you must have expertise in finance, no matter your major. Thus, finance is a critical part of a business education, and it will help you throughout your career.

CONCEPT REVIEW

1. What are the goals of successful companies?
2. What are the three key attributes common to all successful companies?
3. How does expertise in finance help a company become successful?

1.2 The Corporate Life Cycle

Many major corporations had humble origins. Auto parts manufacturer Linamar Corporation started in a garage, while George Weston Ltd. began with two bread routes. How was it possible for these companies to grow into the corporations we see today? No two companies develop in exactly the same way, but the following sections describe some typical stages in the corporate life cycle.

Starting up as a Proprietorship

Many companies begin as a **sole proprietorship**, which is an unincorporated business owned by one individual. Starting a business as a proprietor is easy—one merely begins business operations in one's own name. If doing business under another name, a provincial registration is required. The proprietorship has three important advantages: (1) it is easily and inexpensively formed, (2) it is subject to few government regulations, and (3) its income is not subject to corporate taxation but is taxed only as a part of the proprietor's personal income.

However, the proprietorship also has three important limitations: (1) it is difficult for a proprietorship to obtain the capital needed for growth; (2) the proprietor has unlimited personal liability for the business's debts, which can result in losses that exceed the money he or she invested in the business (creditors may even be able to seize a proprietor's house or other personal property!); and (3) the life of a proprietorship is limited to the life of its founder. For these three reasons, sole proprietorships are used primarily for small businesses. In fact, proprietorships account for only about 13% of all sales, based on dollar values, even though about 80% of all businesses are proprietorships.

More Than One Owner: A Partnership

Some companies start with more than one owner, and some proprietors decide to add a partner as the business grows. A **partnership** exists whenever two or more persons or entities associate to conduct a noncorporate business for profit. Partnerships may operate under different degrees of formality, ranging from informal, oral understandings to formal agreements. Partnerships must also be registered in the province they were formed. Partnership agreements define the ways any profits and losses are shared between partners. A partnership's advantages and disadvantages are similar to those of a proprietorship.

Regarding liability, the partners can potentially lose all of their personal assets, even assets not invested in the business, because under partnership law, each partner is liable for the business's debts. Therefore, in the event the partnership goes bankrupt, if any partner is unable to meet his or her pro rata liability, the remaining partners must make good on the unsatisfied claims, drawing on their personal assets to the extent necessary. It is possible to limit the liabilities of some of the partners by establishing a **limited partnership**, wherein certain partners are designated *general partners* and others *limited partners*. In a limited partnership, the limited partners are liable only for the amount of their investment in the partnership, while the general partners have unlimited liability. However, the limited partners typically have no control—it rests solely with the general partners—and their returns are likewise limited. Limited partners must be aware that they can lose their limited liability status if they become active in managing the business. Limited partnerships are common in real estate, oil, equipment leasing ventures, and venture capital. However, they are not widely used in general business situations because no one partner is usually willing to be the general partner and thus accept the majority of the business's risk, and none of the others are willing to be limited partners and give up all control.

In both regular and limited partnerships at least one partner is liable for the debts of the partnership. However, in a **limited liability partnership (LLP)**, all partners enjoy limited liability with regard to their business partners' professional negligence, and their potential losses are limited to their investment in the LLP. Only lawyers and accountants can form LLPs, though this may broaden to include other professions in the future.

Many Owners: A Corporation

Most partnerships have difficulty attracting substantial amounts of capital. This is generally not a problem for a slow-growing business, but if a business's products or services really catch on, and if it needs to raise large sums of money to capitalize on its opportunities, the difficulty in attracting capital becomes a real drawback. Thus, many growth companies began life as a proprietorship or partnership, but at some point their founders found it necessary to convert to a corporation. Some companies, in anticipation of growth, begin as corporations. A **corporation** is a legal entity created by provincial and federal laws, and it is separate and distinct from its owners and managers. This separation gives the corporation three major advantages: (1) *unlimited* life—a corporation can continue after its original owners and managers are deceased; (2) *easy transferability of ownership interest*—ownership interests can be divided into shares of stock, which can be transferred far more easily than can proprietorship or partnership interests; and (3) *limited liability*—losses are limited to the actual funds invested.

To illustrate limited liability, suppose you invested $10,000 in a partnership that then went bankrupt and owed $1 million. Because the owners are liable for the debts of a partnership, you could be assessed for a share of the company's debt, and you could be held liable for the entire $1 million if your partners were unable to pay their shares. On the other hand, if you invested $10,000 in the shares of a corporation that then went bankrupt, your potential loss on the investment would be limited to your $10,000 investment.[1] Unlimited life, easy transferability of ownership interest, and limited liability make it much easier for corporations than for proprietorships or partnerships to raise money in the financial markets and grow into large companies.

The corporate form offers significant advantages over proprietorships and partnerships, but it also has two disadvantages: (1) Corporate earnings may be subject to double taxation—the earnings of the corporation are taxed at the corporate level, and then earnings paid out as dividends are taxed again as income to the shareholders.[2] (2) Setting up a corporation involves preparing articles of incorporation, writing a set of bylaws, and filing the required provincial and federal reports, which is more complex and time consuming than creating a proprietorship or a partnership.

The articles of incorporation include the following information: (1) name of the proposed corporation, (2) the registered office, (3) the share class description, (4) restrictions on share transfers, and (5) the number of directors. An initial registered office address and first board of directors form must also be completed. This information is filed with Corporations Canada, and when it is approved, the corporation is officially in existence.[3] Once the corporation begins operating, there are requirements to file annual returns and GST/HST reports, along with any changes to directors and the registered office address.

The bylaws are a set of rules drawn up by the founders of the corporation. Included are points such as (1) how directors are to be elected (all elected each year, or perhaps one-third each year for three-year terms); (2) whether the existing shareholders will have the first right to buy any new shares the firm issues; and (3) procedures for changing the bylaws themselves, should conditions require it.

There are actually several different types of corporations. Professionals such as doctors, lawyers, and accountants often form a **professional corporation (PC)**. These types of corporations do not relieve the participants of professional (malpractice) liability. Indeed, the primary motivation behind the professional corporation was to provide a way for groups of

---

[1] In the case of very small corporations, the limited liability may be fiction because lenders frequently require personal guarantees from the shareholders.
[2] The dividend tax credit offers tax relief to Canadian investors receiving dividends from Canadian corporations, partly offsetting the double taxation.
[3] Businesses can be incorporated either provincially or federally. If provincially, the articles must be submitted to the appropriate provincial ministry.

FINANCE: IN FOCUS

The Rise and Fall of Income Trusts

An income trust is an equity investment created to distribute all of a business's free cash flow to investors in a tax-efficient manner. Cash-producing assets such as real estate (real estate investment trusts; REITs) make up the majority of income trusts. Since the goal is to distribute as much free cash flow as possible, businesses that have not required significant capital expenditures in the past have been the best candidates.

Whereas dividends received by investors are taxed at both the corporate and individual level, income trust cash distributions are taxed only in the hands of investors. Since income trusts are taxed preferentially, their value from 1994 to 2007 grew 100-fold, from $1.93 billion to $192 billion. Owing to concerns over tax fairness, the potential for lost government revenue, and lack of reinvested earnings for innovation, in 2011 the federal government eliminated the tax advantage for most income trusts. As a consequence, many income trusts were converted back into corporations, while others were bought out. Certain REITs, such as RioCan and Calloway, were exempt from the tax changes and continue to offer tax-advantaged distributions to investors.

professionals to incorporate and thereby avoid certain types of unlimited liability, yet still be held responsible for professional liability.

Growing and Managing a Corporation

Once a corporation has been established, how does it evolve? When entrepreneurs start a company, they usually provide all the financing from their personal resources, which may include savings, second mortgages, or even credit cards. As the corporation grows, it needs factories, equipment, inventory, and other resources to support its growth. In time, the entrepreneurs usually deplete their own resources and must turn to external financing. Many young companies are too risky for banks, so the founders must sell shares to outsiders, such as friends, family, private investors (often called angels), or venture capitalists. As *shares* and *stocks* are used in Canada and the United States, both terms are used interchangeably in this text. If the corporation continues to grow, it may become successful enough to attract lending from banks, or it may even raise additional funds through an **initial public offering (IPO)** by selling shares to the public at large. After an IPO, corporations support their growth by borrowing from banks, issuing debt, or selling additional shares. In short, a corporation's ability to grow depends on its interactions with the financial markets, which we describe in much more detail later in this chapter.

For proprietorships, partnerships, and small corporations, the firm's owners are also its managers. This is usually not true for a large corporation, which means that large firms' shareholders, who are its owners, face a very serious problem. What is to prevent managers from acting in their own best interests, rather than in the best interests of the owners? This is called an **agency problem** because managers are hired as agents to act on behalf of the owners. Agency problems can be addressed by a company's *corporate governance,* which is the set of rules that control a company's behaviour towards its directors, managers, employees, shareholders, creditors, customers, competitors, and community. We will have much more to say about agency problems and corporate governance throughout the book, especially in Chapters 12, 16, 22, and 23.[4]

⃝ NCEPT REVIEW

1. What are the key differences between proprietorships, partnerships, and corporations?
2. Describe some special types of partnerships and corporations, and explain the differences among them.

---

[4]The classic work on agency theory is Michael C. Jensen and William H. Meckling, "Theory of the Firm, Managerial Behavior, Agency Costs, and Ownership Structure," *Journal of Financial Economics*, October 1976, 305–60. Another article by Jensen specifically addresses these issues; see "Value Maximization, Stakeholder Theory, and the Corporate Objective Function," *Journal of Applied Corporate Finance*, Fall 2001, 8–21. For an overview of corporate governance, see Stuart Gillan, "Recent Developments in Corporate Governance: An Overview," *Journal of Corporate Finance*, June 2006, 381–402.

1.3 The Primary Objective of the Corporation: Value Maximization

Shareholders are the owners of a corporation, and they purchase shares because they want to earn a good return on their investment without undue risk exposure. In most cases, shareholders elect directors, who then hire managers to run the corporation on a day-to-day basis. Because managers are supposed to be working on behalf of shareholders, they should pursue policies that enhance shareholder value. Consequently, throughout this book we operate on the assumption that management's primary objective should be *shareholder wealth maximization*.

The *market price* is the share price that we observe in the financial markets. We later explain in detail how share prices are determined, but for now it is enough to say that a company's market price incorporates the information available to investors. If the market price reflects all *relevant* information, then the observed price is also the *fundamental, or intrinsic, price*. However, investors rarely have all relevant information. For example, companies report most major decisions, but they sometimes withhold critical information to prevent competitors from gaining strategic advantages.

Unfortunately, some managers deliberately mislead investors by taking actions to make their companies appear more valuable than they truly are. Sometimes these actions are illegal, such as those taken by the senior managers at Enron. Sometimes the actions are legal, but they are taken to push the current market price above its fundamental price in the short term. For example, suppose a utility's share price is equal to its fundamental price of $50 per share. What would happen if the utility substantially reduced its tree-trimming program, but didn't tell investors? This would lower current costs and thus boost current earnings and current cash flow, but it would also lead to major expenditures in the future when breaking limbs damage the lines. If investors were told about the major repair costs facing the company, the market price would immediately drop to a new fundamental value of $45. But if investors were kept in the dark, they might misinterpret the higher-than-expected current earnings, and the market price might go up to $52. Investors would eventually understand the situation when the company later incurred large costs to repair the damaged lines; when that happened, the price would fall to its fundamental value of $45.

Consider the hypothetical sequence of events. The company's managers deceived investors, and the price rose to $52 when it would have fallen to $45 if not for the deception. Of course, this benefited those who owned the shares at the time of the deception, including managers with stock options. But when the deception came to light, those shareholders who still owned the shares suffered a significant loss, ending up with shares worth less than their original fundamental value. If the managers cashed in their stock options prior to this, then only the shareholders were hurt by the deception. Because the managers were hired to act in the interests of shareholders, their deception was a breach of their fiduciary responsibility. In addition, the managers' deception damaged the company's credibility, making it harder to raise capital in the future.

Therefore, when we say that management's objective should be to maximize shareholder wealth, we really mean it is to *maximize the fundamental price of the firm's common shares*, not just the current market price. Firms do, of course, have other objectives; in particular, the managers who make the actual decisions are interested in their own personal satisfaction, in their employees' welfare, and in the good of the community and of society at large. Still, for the reasons set forth in the following sections, *maximizing the fundamental share price is the most important objective for most corporations*.

Separating the Investment and Consumption Decision

You may question whether maximizing value is the best investment decision for a company with owners that have different investment preferences. For instance, consider how a company would reconcile one owner's preference for dividend income now versus another owner's preference to forgo dividends currently, but with the prospect for larger dividends in the future. Should the company invest based on the first or second owners' preferences? Either preference could dictate the company's investment decision, but one (or both) may not maximize company value. The **separation theorem** shows that all investors are best off if the company's investment decisions are separate from the owners' (investors') preferences. Companies should invest so as to maximize their fundamental value, while owners

FINANCE: IN FOCUS

Ethics for Individuals and Businesses

Business ethics are a company's attitude and conduct toward its employees, customers, community, and shareholders. A firm's commitment to business ethics can be measured by the tendency of its employees, from the top down, to adhere to laws, regulations, and moral standards relating to product safety and quality, fair employment practices, fair marketing and selling practices, the use of confidential information for personal gain, community involvement, and illegal payments to obtain business.

Ethical Dilemmas

When conflicts arise between profits and ethics, sometimes legal and ethical considerations make the choice obvious. At other times the right choice isn't clear. For example, suppose a railway company's managers know that its coal trains are polluting the air, but the amount of pollution is within legal limits and further reduction would be costly, causing harm to their shareholders. Are the managers ethically bound to reduce pollution? Aren't they also ethically bound to act in their shareholders' best interests?

Ethical Responsibility

An international survey by accounting firm Ernst & Young in 2014 reported that 46% of chief financial officers thought it was acceptable to undertake one or more unethical actions to help a business survive an economic downturn. While such behaviour may be more common in developing economies, Canada too has its share of unethical lapses. The Quebec government has uncovered

significant illegal activities by construction companies bidding on government projects. Montreal-based engineering giant SNC-Lavalin was also caught up in a bribery case worth $56 million, leading to its CEO being "relieved of his duties" and subsequently being charged with fraud.

Protecting Ethical Employees

If employees discover questionable activities or are given questionable orders, should they obey their bosses' orders, refuse to obey those orders, or report the situation to a higher authority, such as the company's board of directors, its auditors, or a prosecutor? Employees who report improper actions are often fired or otherwise penalized, and this keeps many people from reporting situations that should be investigated. To help alleviate this problem, the U.S. Congress in 2002 passed the Sarbanes-Oxley Act, with a provision designed to protect "whistle blowers."

The Canadian response was in two parts. In 2005 the federal government passed the Public Servants Disclosure Protection Act to protect whistle blowers within the federal government. A federal civil servant can now ask the Public Sector Integrity Commissioner to investigate allegations of (a) wrongdoing and (b) retaliation for reporting wrongdoing. To address weaknesses in the regulation of publicly traded companies, the Canadian Securities Administrators have brought forward a number of new rules and guidelines—called National Instruments—which closely follow the rules set by Sarbanes-Oxley and the U.S. Securities Exchange Commission.

can realize their own unique preferences (for current or future dividends) through their own personal investment choices.[5]

Stock Price Maximization and Social Welfare

If a firm attempts to maximize its fundamental share price, is this good or bad for society? In general, it is good. Aside from illegal actions such as fraudulent accounting, exploiting monopoly power, violating safety codes, and failing to meet environmental standards, *the same actions that maximize fundamental share prices also benefit society.* Here are some of the reasons:

1. **To a large extent, the owners of shares *are* society.** Seventy-five years ago this was not true, because most share ownership was concentrated in the hands of a relatively small segment of society, comprising of the wealthiest individuals. Since then, there has been explosive growth in pension funds, life insurance companies, and mutual funds. These institutions now own more than 61% of all stock, which means that most individuals have an indirect stake in the stock market. In addition, 10% of all Canadian households

---

[5]The classic work on separation theorem is Irving Fisher, *The Theory of Interest*, 1930.

now own stock directly. Thus, most members of society now have an important stake in the stock market, either directly or indirectly. Therefore, when a manager takes actions to maximize the share price, this improves the quality of life for millions of ordinary citizens.

2. **Consumers benefit.** Share price maximization requires efficient, low-cost businesses that produce high-quality goods and services at the lowest possible cost. This means that companies must develop products and services that consumers want and need, which leads to new technology and new products. Also, companies that maximize their share price must generate growth in sales by creating value for customers in the form of efficient and courteous service, adequate stocks of merchandise, and well-located business establishments.

   People sometimes argue that firms, in their efforts to raise profits and share prices, increase product prices and gouge the public. In a reasonably competitive economy, which we have, prices are constrained by competition and consumer resistance. If a firm raises its prices beyond reasonable levels, it will lose its market share. Even giant firms such as Dell and Coca-Cola lose business to domestic and foreign competitors, if they set prices above the level necessary to cover production costs plus a "normal" profit. Of course, firms *want* to earn more, and they constantly try to cut costs, develop new products, and so on, and thereby earn above-normal profits. Note, though, that if they are indeed successful and do earn above-normal profits, those very profits will attract competition, which will eventually drive prices down. So again, the main long-term beneficiary is the consumer.

3. **Employees benefit.** There are cases where a stock increases when a company announces a plan to lay off employees, but viewed over time this is the exception rather than the rule. In general, companies that successfully increase share prices also grow and add more employees, thus benefiting society. Note too that many governments around the world, including our federal and provincial governments, are privatizing some of their state-owned activities by selling these operations to investors. Perhaps not surprisingly, the sales and cash flows of recently privatized companies generally improve. Moreover, studies show that these newly privatized companies tend to grow and thus require more employees when they are managed with the goal of share price maximization.

FINANCE: IN FOCUS

Corporate Scandals and Maximizing Share Price

The list of corporate scandals seems to go on forever: Bre-X, Enron, Nortel, WorldCom, Tyco, Hollinger. . . . At first glance, it's tempting to say, "Look what happens when managers care only about maximizing share price." But a closer look reveals a much different story. In fact, if these managers were trying to maximize share price, given the resulting values of these companies, they failed dismally.

Although details vary from company to company, a few common themes emerge. First, managerial compensation was linked to the short-term performance of the share price via poorly designed stock option and stock grant programs. This provided managers with a powerful incentive to drive up the share price at the option vesting date without worrying about the future. Second, it is virtually impossible to take *legal* actions that drive up the share price in the short term without harming it in the long term because the value of a company is based on all of its future free cash flows and not just cash flows in the immediate future. Because legal actions to quickly drive up the share price didn't exist (other than the old-fashioned ones, such as increasing sales, cutting costs, or reducing capital requirements), these managers began bending a few rules. Third, as they initially got away with bending rules, their egos and hubris grew to such an extent that they felt they were above all rules, so they began breaking even more rules.

Share prices did go up, at least temporarily, but as the scandals became public, the shares' prices plummeted, and in some cases the companies were ruined.

There are several important lessons to be learned from these examples. First, people respond to incentives, and poorly designed incentives can cause disastrous results. Second, ethical violations usually begin with small steps; if shareholders want managers to avoid large ethical violations, then they shouldn't let them make the small ones. Third, there is no shortcut to creating lasting value. It takes hard work to increase sales, cut costs, and reduce capital requirements, but this is the formula for success.

Managerial Actions to Maximize Shareholder Wealth

What types of actions can managers take to maximize shareholder wealth? To answer this question, we first need to ask, "What determines a firm's value?" In a nutshell, it is *a company's ability to generate cash flows now and in the future.*

We address different aspects of this in detail throughout the book, but we can lay out three basic facts now: (1) any financial asset, including a company's shares, is valuable only to the extent that it generates cash flows; (2) the timing of cash flows matters—cash received sooner is better; and (3) investors are averse to risk, so all else equal, they will pay more for a firm whose cash flows are relatively certain than for one whose cash flows are more risky. Because of these three facts, managers can enhance their firm's value by increasing the size of the expected cash flows, by speeding up their receipt, and by reducing their risk.

The cash flows that matter are called **free cash flows (FCFs)**, not because they are free, but because they are available (or free) for distribution to all of the company's investors, including creditors and shareholders. You will learn how to calculate free cash flows in Chapter 2, but for now, as shown in Figure 1-1, you should know that free cash flow is:

$$\text{FCF} = \frac{\text{Sales}}{\text{revenues}} - \frac{\text{Operating}}{\text{costs}} - \frac{\text{Operating}}{\text{taxes}} - \frac{\text{Required investments in}}{\text{operating capital}}$$

There are many ways that companies can increase free cash flows. Brand managers and marketing managers can increase sales (and prices) by truly understanding their customers and then designing goods and services that customers want. Human resource managers can improve productivity through training and employee retention. Production and logistics managers can improve profit margins, reduce inventory, and improve throughput at factories by implementing supply chain management, just-in-time inventory management, and lean manufacturing. In fact, all managers make decisions that can increase free cash flows.

One of the financial manager's roles is to help others see how their actions affect the company's ability to generate cash flow and, hence, its fundamental value. Financial managers also must decide *how to finance the firm.* In particular, they must choose what mix of debt and equity should be used and what specific types of debt and equity securities should be issued. They must also decide what percentage of current earnings should be retained and reinvested rather than paid out as dividends. Along with these financing decisions, the general level of interest rates in the economy, the risk of the firm's operations, and stock market investors' overall attitude toward risk determine the rate of return that is required to satisfy a firm's investors. This rate of return from investors' perspectives is a cost from the company's point of view. Therefore, the rate of return required by investors is called the **weighted average cost of capital (WACC)**. The relations among a firm's fundamental value, its free cash flows, and its cost of capital are shown by the equation in Figure 1-1.

FIGURE 1-1   Determinants of a Firm's Value

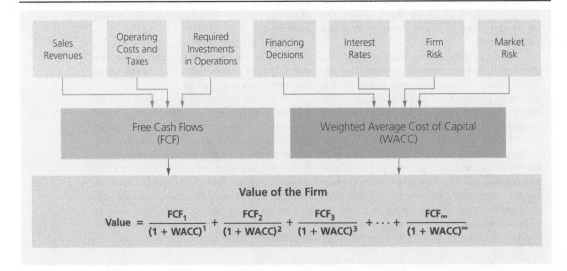

We will explain this equation and how to use it in detail later. But for now, recall that growing firms often need to raise external funds, so the rest of this chapter focuses on financial markets.

CONCEPT REVIEW

1. What should be management's primary objective?
2. How does maximizing the fundamental share price benefit society?
3. What are the three primary determinants of free cash flows?
4. How is a firm's fundamental value related to its free cash flows and its cost of capital?

1.4 An Overview of the Capital Allocation Process

Businesses often need capital to implement growth plans; governments require funds to finance building projects; and individuals frequently want loans to purchase cars, homes, and education. Where can they get this money? Fortunately, there are other individuals and firms with incomes greater than their expenditures. In contrast to William Shakespeare's advice, most individuals and firms are both borrowers and lenders. For example, an individual may borrow money with a car loan or a home mortgage, but may also lend money through a bank savings account. In aggregate, individual households are net savers and provide most of the funds ultimately used by nonfinancial corporations. Although most nonfinancial corporations own some financial securities, such as short-term Treasury bills, nonfinancial corporations are net borrowers in aggregate. It should be no surprise to you that federal, provincial, and local governments are also net borrowers in aggregate. Banks and other financial corporations raise money with one hand and invest it with the other. For example, a bank may raise money from individuals in the form of a savings account, but then lend most of that money to a business customer. In aggregate, financial corporations borrow slightly more than they lend.

Transfers of capital between savers and those who need capital take place in three different ways. Direct transfers of money and securities, as shown in the top section of Figure 1-2, occur when a business sells its shares or bonds directly to savers without going through any type of financial institution. The business delivers its securities to savers, who in turn give the firm the money it needs. For example, a privately held company might sell shares directly to a new shareholder.

FIGURE 1-2 Diagram of the Capital Allocation Process

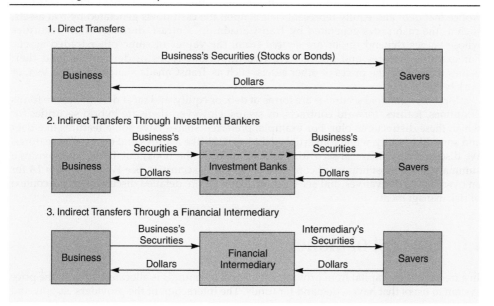

As shown in the middle section, indirect transfers may go through an *investment banking house* such as CIBC World Markets, which *underwrites* the issue. An underwriter serves as a middleman and facilitates the issuance of securities. The company sells its stocks or bonds to the investment bank, which in turn sells these same securities to savers. Because new securities are involved and the corporation receives the proceeds of the sale, this is a *primary market* transaction.

Transfers can also be made through a **financial intermediary** such as a bank or mutual fund, as shown in the bottom section. Here the intermediary obtains funds from savers in exchange for its own securities. The intermediary then uses this money to purchase and then hold businesses' securities. For example, a saver may give dollars to a bank, receiving from it a Guaranteed Investment Certificate (GIC), and then the bank may lend the money to a small business in the form of a mortgage loan. Thus, intermediaries literally create new forms of capital.

There are three important characteristics of the capital allocation process. First, new financial securities are created. Second, financial institutions are often involved. Third, allocation between providers and users of funds occurs in financial markets. The following sections discuss each of these characteristics.

CONCEPT REVIEW

1. Identify three ways capital is transferred between savers and borrowers.
2. Distinguish between the roles played by investment banks and financial intermediaries.

1.5 Financial Securities

The variety of financial securities is limited only by human creativity and ingenuity, and government regulations. At the risk of oversimplification, we can classify most financial securities along two dimensions: (1) time until maturity and (2) debt, equity, or derivatives.

In general, short-term securities are those that mature in less than a year; these are called money market securities. Those that mature in more than a year are called capital market securities.

Financial securities are simply pieces of paper with contractual provisions that entitle their owners to specific rights and claims on specific cash flows or values. Debt instruments typically have specified payments and a specified maturity. For example, a TransCanada Pipelines Limited bond might promise to pay 10% interest for 30 years, at which time it makes a $1,000 principal payment. Equity instruments are a claim upon a residual value. For example, TransCanada's shareholders are entitled to TransCanada's cash flows after its bondholders, creditors, and other claimants have been satisfied. Notice that debt and equity represent claims upon the cash flows generated by real assets, such as the cash flows generated by TransCanada. In contrast, **derivatives** are securities whose values depend on, or are *derived* from, the values of some other traded assets. For example, futures and options are two important types of derivatives, and their values depend on the prices of other assets, such as TransCanada shares, Japanese yen, or pork bellies.

For an overview of derivatives, see **Web Extension 1A** at the textbook's website.

Most conventional securities are forms of debt or equity, and most derivatives are forms of options, futures, forward contracts, or swaps. However, there are hybrid securities for which these distinctions blur. For example, preferred shares have some features like debt and some like equity, while convertible debt has debt-like features and option-like features. We discuss many financial securities in detail later in the book, but Table 1-1 provides a summary of the most important conventional financial securities. See **Web Extension 1A** for an overview of derivatives, and see Chapter 20 for a more detailed discussion in the context of risk management.

1.6 The Cost of Money

In a free economy, capital from providers with available funds is allocated through the price system to users that have a demand for funds. The interaction of the providers' supply and the users' demand determines the cost (or price) of money, which is the rate users pay to providers. For debt, we call this price the *interest rate.* For equity, we call this price the *cost of equity,* and it consists of the dividends and capital gains shareholders expect. Keep in mind that the cost of money from a user's perspective is a return from the provider's point of view, so we often use those terms interchangeably.

Notice in Table 1-1 that a financial security's rate of return generally increases as its maturity and risk increase. We will have much more to say about the relationships among an individual security's features, risk, and return later in the book, but there are some fundamental factors and economic conditions that affect all securities.

Fundamental Factors That Affect the Cost of Money

The four most fundamental factors affecting the cost of money are (1) *production opportunities,* (2) *time preferences for consumption,* (3) *risk,* and (4) *inflation.* By production opportunities, we mean the ability to turn capital into benefits. If a business raises capital, the benefits are determined by the expected rates of return on its production opportunities. If a student borrows to finance his or her education, the benefits are higher expected future salaries (and, of course, the sheer joy of learning!). If a homeowner borrows, the benefits are the pleasure from living in his or her own home, plus any expected appreciation in the value of the home. Notice that the expected rates of return on these "production opportunities" put an upper limit on how much users can pay to providers.

Providers can use their current funds for consumption or saving. By saving, they give up consumption now in the expectation of having more consumption in the future. If providers have a strong preference for consumption now, then it takes high interest rates to induce them to trade current consumption for future consumption. Therefore, the time preference for consumption has a major impact on the cost of money. Notice that the time preference for consumption varies for different individuals, for different age groups, and for different cultures. For example, people in Japan have a lower time preference for consumption than those in Canada, which partially explains why Japanese families tend to save more than Canadian families even though interest rates are lower in Japan.

If the expected rate of return on an investment is risky, then providers require a higher expected return to induce them to take the extra risk, which drives up the cost of money. As you will see later in this book, the risk of a security is determined by market conditions and the security's particular features.

Inflation also leads to a higher cost of money. For example, suppose you earned 10% one year on your investment, but inflation caused prices to increase by 20%. This means you can't consume as much at the end of the year as when you originally invested your money. Obviously, if you had expected 20% inflation, you would have required a higher rate of return than 10%.

Economic Conditions and Policies That Affect the Cost of Money

Economic conditions and policies also affect the cost of money. These include: (1) Bank of Canada policy; (2) the federal budget deficit or surplus; (3) the level of business activity; and (4) international factors, including the foreign trade balance, the international business climate, and exchange rates.

Bank of Canada Policy As you probably learned in your economics courses, (1) the money supply has a major effect on both the level of economic activity and the inflation rate, and (2) in Canada, the Bank of Canada (BoC) controls the money supply. If the BoC wants to stimulate the economy, it increases growth in the money supply. The initial effect will be to cause interest rates to decline. However, a larger money supply can also lead to an increase in expected inflation, which would push interest rates up. The reverse holds if the BoC tightens the money supply.

Budget Deficits or Surpluses If the federal government spends more than it takes in from tax revenues, it runs a deficit, and that deficit must be covered either by borrowing or by printing money (increasing the money supply). If the government borrows, this added demand for funds pushes up interest rates. If it prints money, this increases expectations for future inflation, which also drives up interest rates. Thus, the larger the federal deficit, other

TABLE 1-1 Summary of Major Financial Securities

Instrument	Major Participants	Risk	Original Maturity	Rates of Return on June 11, 2014[a]
Gov't of Canada Treasury bills	Sold by Bank of Canada	Default-free	91 days to 1 year	0.93%[b]
Banker's acceptances	A firm's promise to pay, guaranteed by a bank	Low default risk	Up to 1 year	1.20%[b]
Commercial paper	Issued by firms to large investors	Low default risk	Up to 1 year	1.18%[b]
Money market mutual funds	Invest in short-term debt; held by individuals	Low degree of risk	No specific maturity (instant liquidity)	0.39%[c]
Euro-Canadian market time deposits	Issued by banks outside Canada	Depends on strength of issuer	Up to 1 year	1.22%[b]
Consumer credit loans	Loans by banks, credit unions, finance companies	Risk is variable	Variable	Variable
Commercial loans	Loans by banks to corporations	Depends on borrower	Up to 7 years	Tied to prime (3.00%) or LIBOR (0.23%)[d]
Federal government bonds	Issued by the Government of Canada	No default risk, but price falls if interest rates rise	2 to 30 years	2.34%[e]
Mortgages	Loans secured by property	Risk is variable	Up to 30 years	4.79%[f]
Corporate bonds	Issued by corporations to individuals and institutions	Riskier than Canadian government debt; depends on strength of issuer	Up to 40 years	2.80%[g]
Leases	Similar to debt; firms lease assets rather than borrow	Risk similar to corporate bonds	Generally 3 to 20 years	Similar to bond yields
Common shares	Issued by corporations to individuals and institutions	Riskier than corporate bonds	Unlimited	11.7%[h]

[a]Bank of Canada, "Daily Digest," http://www.bankofcanada.ca, accessed June 12, 2014; *National Post Online*, http://www.financialpost.com and Royal Bank of Canada http://www.rbc.com, accessed June 12, 2014.
[b]T-bill, bankers' acceptances, commercial paper, and euro deposit rates are all 3-month maturity.
[c]Money market return is for 2013.
[d]The prime rate is the rate Canadian banks charge to good customers. LIBOR (London Interbank Offered Rate) is the rate that international banks charge one another in the UK.
[e]The federal government bond rate is based on a 10-year maturity.
[f]The mortgage rate is an average based on a 5-year closed mortgage.
[g]The corporate bond return is based on the DEX Corporate Bond Index.
[h]Arithmetic mean return from 1950–2013 based upon data from the Canadian Institute of Actuaries.

Federal Budget Surplus/Deficit and Trade Balance (Millions of Dollars)

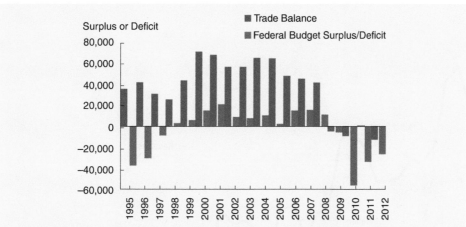

Sources: Statistics Canada. Table 228-0058, "Merchandise imports and exports, customs and balance of payments basis for all countries, by seasonal adjustment and principal trading areas, annual (dollars)," accessed June 12, 2014. Government of Canada, Department of Finance, Fiscal Reference Tables, October 2013.

things held constant, the higher the level of interest rates. As shown in Figure 1-3, Canada's federal government produced surpluses from 1998 to 2008. In response to the financial crisis in 2009, the federal government went back to budget deficits, though it is on track to produce a budget surplus by 2015.

Business Activity Figure 1-4 shows interest rates, inflation, and recessions. Notice that interest rates and inflation typically rise prior to a recession and fall afterward. There are several reasons for this pattern.

Consumer demand slows during a recession, keeping companies from increasing prices, which reduces price inflation. Companies also cut back on hiring, which reduces wage inflation. Less disposable income causes consumers to reduce their purchases of homes and automobiles, reducing consumer demand for loans. Companies reduce investments in new operations, which reduces their demand for funds. The cumulative effect is downward pressure on inflation and interest rates. The Bank of Canada is active during recessions, trying to stimulate the economy. One way it does this is by purchasing Treasury bills that are held by banks. This has two effects. Because they sell some of their bills, the banks have more cash, which increases their supply of loanable funds, which in turn makes them willing to lend at lower interest rates. Also, the BoC's purchases drive up prices, which drives down interest rates. The combined effect of the BoC's activities is to reduce interest rates.

International Trade Deficits or Surpluses Businesses and individuals in Canada buy from and sell to people and firms in other countries. If we buy more than we sell (i.e., if we import more than we export), we are said to be running a *foreign trade deficit*. When trade deficits occur, they must be financed, and the main source of financing is debt. In other words, if we import $20 billion of goods but export only $9 billion, we run a trade deficit of $11 billion, and we will probably borrow the $11 billion.[6] Therefore, the larger our trade deficit, the more we must borrow, and as we increase our borrowing, this drives up interest rates. Also, international investors are willing to hold Canadian debt if and only if the rate paid on this debt is competitive with interest rates in other countries. Therefore, if the Bank of Canada attempts to lower interest rates in Canada, causing our rates to fall below rates abroad (after adjustments for expected changes in the exchange rate), then international investors will sell Canadian bonds, which will depress bond prices and result in higher Canadian rates. Thus, if the trade deficit is large relative to the size of the overall economy, it will hinder the BoC's ability to combat a recession by lowering interest rates.

---

[6]The deficit could also be financed by selling assets, including gold, corporate shares, entire companies, and real estate.

Business Activity, Interest Rates, and Inflation

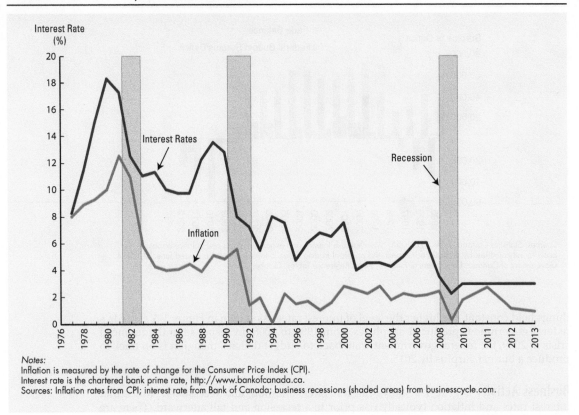

Notes:
Inflation is measured by the rate of change for the Consumer Price Index (CPI).
Interest rate is the chartered bank prime rate, http://www.bankofcanada.ca.
Sources: Inflation rates from CPI; interest rate from Bank of Canada; business recessions (shaded areas) from businesscycle.com.

Figure 1-3 shows Canada running a trade surplus from 1995 to 2008. Note that the trade deficits shown in recent years may be partly attributed to a higher Canadian dollar value relative to the U.S. dollar, which has made our goods and services more expensive to foreigners (and imports from abroad cheaper). Meanwhile, the United States has been running annual trade deficits since the mid-1970s, and the cumulative effect of these deficits is that the United States has become the largest debtor nation of all time.

Country Risk   International risk factors may increase the cost of money that is invested abroad. *Country risk* is the risk that arises from investing or doing business in a particular country. This risk depends on the country's economic, political, and social environment. Countries with stable economic, social, political, and regulatory systems provide a safer climate for investment and therefore have less country risk than less stable nations. Examples of country risk include the risk associated with changes in tax rates, regulations, currency conversion, and exchange rates. Country risk also includes these risks: (1) property might be expropriated without adequate compensation; (2) the host country might impose new stipulations regarding local production, sourcing, or hiring practices; and (3) facilities might be damaged or destroyed as a result of internal strife.

Exchange Rate Risk   International securities usually are denominated in a currency other than the Canadian dollar, which means that the value of your investment depends on what happens to exchange rates. This is known as **exchange rate risk**. For example, if a Canadian investor purchases a Japanese bond, interest will probably be paid in Japanese yen, which must then be converted into dollars if the investor wants to spend his or her money in Canada. If the yen weakens relative to the dollar, then it will buy fewer dollars; hence the investor will receive fewer dollars when it comes time to convert. Alternatively, if the yen strengthens relative to the dollar, the investor will earn higher dollar returns. It follows that the effective rate of return on a foreign investment will depend on both the performance of the foreign security and on what happens to exchange rates over the life of the investment. We will discuss exchange rates in detail in Chapter 21.

CONCEPT REVIEW

1. What four fundamental factors affect the cost of money?
2. Name some economic conditions that influence interest rates, and explain their effects.

1.7 Financial Institutions

When raising capital, direct transfers of funds are more common among individuals and small businesses, and in economies where financial markets and institutions are less developed. While businesses in more developed economies do occasionally rely on direct transfers, they generally find it more efficient to enlist the services of one or more financial institutions when it comes time to raise capital. Here are the major categories of financial institutions:

1. *Investment banks* such as Scotia Capital and RBC Capital Markets in Canada, and JPMorgan and Goldman Sachs, provide a number of services to both investors and companies planning to raise capital. Such organizations (1) help corporations design securities with features that are currently attractive to investors, (2) then buy these securities from the issuing corporation, and (3) resell them to investors. Although the securities are sold twice, this process is really one primary market transaction, with the investment banker acting as a facilitator to help transfer capital from savers to businesses. Most investment banks also provide brokerage services for institutions and individuals (referred to as "retail" customers). In addition to the bank-owned investment dealers, there are a number of smaller firms, such as Canaccord Genuity, GMP Securities, and Peters & Co. These "boutique" companies offer specialized niche services to businesses in sectors such as energy, technology, and mining.
2. *Commercial banks,* such as the Royal Bank of Canada, Toronto-Dominion Bank, Bank of Nova Scotia, Bank of Montreal, and Canadian Imperial Bank of Commerce, are the traditional "department stores of finance" because they serve a variety of savers and borrowers. Commercial banks raise funds from depositors and by issuing shares and bonds to investors. For example, someone might deposit money in a chequing account. In return, that person can write cheques, use a debit card, and even receive interest on deposits. Those who buy the banks' securities expect to receive dividends and interest payments. Banks are providing an ever-widening range of services, from stock brokerage and investment banking, to insurance. This consolidation, which began in the late 1980s, is the reason the big five Canadian banks are now considered "full-service."

    Banks are critically important to a well-functioning economy and for that reason are highly regulated. To provide confidence and ensure stability, bank deposits up to $100,000 are insured by a federal government agency, the Canada Deposit Insurance Corporation (CDIC). Without such insurance, if depositors believed that a bank was in trouble, they would rush to withdraw funds. This is called a "bank run," which can lead to bank failures and an economic crisis. Not all countries have their own versions of the CDIC, so international bank runs are still possible. In fact, a bank run occurred in 2008 at the British bank Northern Rock, leading to its nationalization by the government.
3. *Trust companies* provide a variety of lending, investing, and financial services similar to banks. Although trusts are the only companies allowed to offer trustee services, banks can own trusts to provide this service. Over time the difference between trusts and banks has blurred, and any differences are now regulatory.[7]
4. *Credit unions* and the Quebec-based Le Mouvement des caisses Desjardins are cooperative associations whose members are supposed to have a common bond, such as living in the same community. Credit unions are provincially regulated, have their own deposit

---

[7]Canadian Bankers Association, http://www.cba.ca, accessed October 22, 2008.

FINANCE: IN FOCUS

The 2008 Financial Crisis and U.S. Investment Banks

At one time, most investment banks were partnerships, with income generated primarily by fees from their underwriting, merger and acquisitions (M&A) consulting, asset management, and brokering activities. When business was good, investment banks generated high fees and paid big bonuses to their partners. When times were tough, investment banks paid no bonuses and often fired employees. In the 1990s, however, most large U.S. investment banks were reorganized into publicly traded corporations (or were acquired and then operated as subsidiaries of public companies). In 1994, for example, Lehman Brothers sold some of its own shares to the public via an IPO. Like most corporations, Lehman Brothers was financed by a combination of equity and debt.

A relaxation of regulations in the 2000s allowed investment banks to undertake a wider variety of activities, including taking on more leverage. Basically, the new regulations allowed investment banks to use an unprecedented amount of debt to finance their activities—Lehman used roughly $30 of debt for every dollar of equity. In addition to their fee-generating activities, most investment banks also began trading securities for their own accounts. If you are earning 12% on your investments while paying 8% on your borrowings, then the more money you borrow, the more profit you make. But if you are leveraged 30 to 1 and your investments decline in value by even 3.33%, your business will fail.

This is exactly what happened to U.S. financial institutions Bear Stearns, Lehman Brothers, and Merrill Lynch in the fall of 2008. In short, they borrowed money, used it to make risky investments, and then failed when the investments turned out to be worth less than the amount they owed.

insurance protection, take deposits, and provide loans and financial services to individuals and small businesses. While they are small relative to the banks, credit unions collectively have $163 billion in assets and provide 5 million members with a wide range of financial services activities.[8]

5. *Life insurance companies* take savings in the form of premiums; invest these funds in shares, bonds, real estate, and mortgages; and make payments to beneficiaries. Life insurance companies also offer a variety of tax-deferred savings plans designed to provide retirement benefits. Manulife Financial is Canada's largest insurance company and currently ranks 12th largest worldwide.

6. *Mutual funds* are corporations that accept money from savers and then use these funds to buy financial instruments. These organizations pool funds and thus reduce risks by diversification. They also achieve economies of scale in analyzing securities, managing portfolios, and buying and selling securities. Different funds are designed to meet the objectives of different types of savers. Hence, there are bond funds for those who desire safety, stock funds for savers who are willing to accept significant risks in the hope of higher returns, and still other funds that are used as interest-bearing accounts (the **money market funds**). There are literally thousands of different mutual funds with dozens of different goals and purposes. Some funds are actively managed, with their managers trying to find undervalued securities, while other funds are passively managed and simply try to minimize expenses by replicating a particular market index. Most traditional mutual funds allow investors to redeem their share of the fund only at the close of business. A special type of mutual fund, the *exchange traded fund (ETF)*, allows investors to sell their shares at any time during normal trading hours. ETFs usually have very low management expenses and are rapidly gaining in popularity.

7. Traditional *pension funds* are retirement plans funded by corporations or government agencies for their workers and usually administered by the trust departments of commercial banks or by life insurance companies. Pension funds invest primarily in bonds, stocks, mortgages, and real estate.

8. *Hedge funds* raise money from investors and engage in a variety of investment activities. Unlike typical mutual funds, which can have thousands of investors, hedge funds are limited to a relatively small number of high-wealth individuals or institutional investors.

---

[8]"System Results," 2nd Quarter, 2011, Credit Union Central of Canada, http://www.cucentral.ca, accessed October 31, 2011.

As such, hedge funds are much less regulated than mutual funds. The first hedge funds literally tried to hedge their bets by forming portfolios of conventional securities and derivatives in such a way that they limited their potential losses without sacrificing too much of their potential gains. Recently, though, most hedge funds began to lever their positions by borrowing heavily. During the early and mid-1990s many hedge funds had spectacular rates of return. This success attracted more investors, and thousands of new hedge funds were created. Much of the low-hanging fruit had already been picked, so many hedge funds began pursuing much riskier (and unhedged) strategies. Perhaps not surprisingly (at least in retrospect!), some funds have produced spectacular losses. For example, many hedge fund investors suffered huge losses in 2007 and 2008 when large numbers of U.S. sub-prime mortgages defaulted.

9. *Private equity funds* are similar to hedge funds in that they are limited to a relatively small number of large investors, but they differ in that they own shares (equity) in other companies and often control those companies, whereas hedge funds usually own many different types of securities. In contrast to a mutual fund, which might own a small percentage of a publicly traded company's shares, a private equity fund typically owns virtually all of a company's shares. Because the company's shares are not traded in the public markets, it is called "private equity." In fact, private equity funds often take a public company (or subsidiary) and turn it private. An example was a $6.3 billion privatization of U.S.–based Kinetic Concepts in 2011, by three large investors, including the two investment arms of the Canada Pension Plan Investment Board and the Public Sector Pension Investment Board.

With the notable exception of hedge funds, financial institutions have been heavily regulated to ensure the safety of these institutions and thus to protect investors. Historically, many of these regulations—which have included a prohibition on the types of assets the institutions could buy, ceilings on the interest rates they could pay, and limitations on the types of services they could provide—tended to impede the free flow of capital and thus hurt the efficiency of our capital markets. Recognizing this fact, policymakers took several steps during the 1980s and 1990s to deregulate financial services companies. For example, the barriers that restricted foreign banks from operating in Canada were eased. Likewise, regulations that once forced the strict separation of banking, insurance, and investment banking have been relaxed.

The result of the ongoing regulatory changes has been a blurring of the distinctions among the different types of institutions. Indeed, the trend in Canada today is toward large financial services corporations, which own banks, investment banking arms, insurance companies, transaction processing services, and mutual funds, and which have branches across the country and around the world.

In spite of their size domestically, Canadian banks are not among the world's largest. As of March 2014, two of Canada's largest banks, Toronto-Dominion Bank and Royal Bank of Canada ranked 15th and 17th worldwide respectively, by total share value.

⊙NCEPT REVIEW

1. What is the difference between a pure commercial bank and a pure investment bank?
2. List the major types of financial institutions and briefly describe the primary function of each.
3. What are some important differences between mutual and hedge funds? How are they similar?

1.8 Types of Financial Markets

Financial markets bring together people and organizations needing money with those having surplus funds. There are many different financial markets in a developed economy. Each market deals with a somewhat different type of instrument, customer, or geographic location. Here are some of the major types of markets:

1. *Physical asset markets* (also called "tangible" or "real" asset markets) are those for products such as wheat, autos, real estate, computers, and machinery. *Financial asset markets*, on the other hand, deal with shares, bonds, notes, mortgages, and other *financial instruments*.

2. *Spot markets* and *futures markets* are markets where assets are being bought or sold for "on-the-spot" delivery (literally, within a few days) or for delivery at some future date, such as 6 months or a year into the future.

3. *Money markets* are the markets for short-term, highly liquid debt securities. *Capital markets* are the markets for intermediate- or long-term debt and corporate shares. The Toronto Stock Exchange and New York Stock Exchange are examples of capital markets. When describing debt markets, "short term" generally means less than 1 year, "intermediate term" means 1 to 5 years, and "long term" means more than 5 years.

4. *Mortgage markets* deal with loans on residential, agricultural, commercial, and industrial real estate, while *consumer credit markets* involve loans for autos, appliances, education, vacations, and so on.

5. *World, national, regional,* and *local markets* also exist. Thus, depending on an organization's size and scope of operations, it may be able to borrow all around the world, or it may be confined to a strictly local, even neighbourhood, market.

6. *Primary markets* are the markets in which corporations raise new capital. If Microsoft were to sell a new issue of common shares to raise capital, this would be a primary market transaction. The corporation selling the newly created shares receives the proceeds from the sale in a primary market transaction. The **initial public offering (IPO)** market is a subset of the primary market. Here firms "go public" by offering shares to the public for the first time. Google had its IPO in 2004. Previously, founders Larry Page and Sergey Brin, other insiders, and venture capitalists owned all the shares. In many IPOs, the insiders sell some of their shares plus the company sells newly created shares to raise additional capital. *Secondary markets* are markets in which existing, already outstanding securities are traded among investors. Thus, if you decided to buy 1,000 shares of EnCana stock, the purchase would occur in the secondary market. The Toronto Stock Exchange is a secondary market, since it deals in outstanding, as opposed to newly issued, shares. The TSX Venture Exchange is another Canadian exchange; it trades shares in small, speculative companies. Secondary markets also exist for bonds, mortgages, and other financial assets. The corporation whose securities are being traded is not involved in a secondary market transaction and thus does not receive any funds from such a sale.

7. *Private markets,* where transactions are worked out directly between two parties, are differentiated from *public markets,* where standardized contracts are traded on organized exchanges. Bank loans and private placements of debt with insurance companies are examples of private market transactions. Since these transactions are private, they may be structured in any manner that appeals to the two parties. By contrast, securities that are issued in public markets (e.g., common shares and corporate bonds) are ultimately held by a large number of individuals. Public securities must have fairly standardized contractual features, to appeal to a broad range of investors and also because public investors cannot afford the time to study unique, nonstandardized contracts. Private market securities are, therefore, more tailor-made but less liquid, whereas public market securities are more liquid but subject to greater standardization.

The distinctions among markets are often blurred. For example, it makes little difference if a firm borrows for 11, 12, or 13 months, hence, whether such a transaction is a "money" or "capital" market transaction. You should recognize the big differences among types of markets, but don't get hung up trying to distinguish them at the boundaries.

CONCEPT REVIEW

1. Distinguish between (1) physical asset markets and financial asset markets, (2) spot and futures markets, (3) money and capital markets, (4) primary and secondary markets, and (5) private and public markets.

1.9 The Big Picture

Finance has vocabulary and tools that might be new to you. To help you avoid getting bogged down in the trenches, Figure 1-1 presented the "big picture." A manager's primary job is to increase the company's intrinsic value, but how exactly does one go about doing that? The equation at the bottom of Figure 1-1 shows that intrinsic value is the present value of the firm's expected free cash flows, discounted at the weighted average cost of capital. Thus, there are two approaches to increasing intrinsic value: improve FCF, or reduce the WACC. Observe that several factors affect FCF and that several factors affect the WACC. In the rest of this book's chapters, we will typically focus on only one of these factors, systematically building the vocabulary and tools you will use after graduation to improve your company's intrinsic value. It is true that every manager needs to understand financial vocabulary and be able to apply financial tools, but really successful managers also understand how their decisions affect the big picture. So as you read this book, keep in mind where each topic fits into the big picture.

e-Resources

The textbook's website, at **www.nelson.com/brigham3ce**, contains several items that will be helpful to you:

1. *Excel* files, called *Tool Kits*, provide well-documented models for almost all of the text's calculations. These *Tool Kits* will not only help you with this finance course, but also serve as tool kits for you in other courses and in your career.
2. There are problems at the ends of the chapters that require spreadsheets, and the website contains the models you will need to begin work on these problems.

When we think it might be helpful for you to look at one of the website's files, we will indicate that in a note in the margin like the one that is shown here.

Other resources on the website include Problems, Web Extensions, and the complete solutions to the Concept Review Problems. The Web Extensions are PDF files that cover additional useful material relating to the chapter.

Make sure to check out *MindTap*, available with this text. Stay organized and efficient with *MindTap*—a single destination with all the course materials you need to succeed. Built-in apps leverage social media and the latest learning technology to help you succeed.

In addition to the resources on the textbook's website, your professor has the option of using the Aplia online learning solution (**http://www.aplia.com**) that has been developed for this textbook. Aplia makes finance relevant and engaging with interactive, automatically graded assignments, instant detailed feedback, chapter-specific problem sets, Preparing-for-Finance tutorials, and news analysis articles.

Summary

This chapter provided an overview of financial management and the financial environment. It explained the fundamental determinants of a firm's value and provided an overview of financial securities, financial institutions, and financial markets. The key concepts covered are listed below:

-   The three main forms of business organization are the **proprietorship**, the **partnership**, and the **corporation**.
-   Although each form of organization offers advantages and disadvantages, **corporations conduct much more business than the other forms**.
-   The primary objective of management should be to **maximize shareholders' wealth**, and this means **maximizing the company's fundamental, or intrinsic, share price**. Legal actions that maximize share prices usually increase social welfare.
-   Firms increase cash flows by creating value for **customers**, **suppliers**, and **employees**.
-   **Free cash flows (FCFs)** are the cash flows available for distribution to all of a firm's investors (shareholders and creditors) after the firm has paid all expenses (including taxes) and made the required investments in operations to support growth.
-   The **value of a firm** depends on the **size of the firm's free cash flows**, the **timing of those flows**, and **their risk**.
-   The **weighted average cost of capital (WACC)** is the average return required by all of the firm's investors. It is determined by the firm's **capital structure** (the firm's relative amounts of debt and equity), **interest rates**, the firm's **risk**, and the **market's attitude towards risk**.

- A **firm's fundamental**, or **intrinsic, value** is defined by:

$$\text{Value} = \frac{FCF_1}{(1 + WACC)^1} + \frac{FCF_2}{(1 + WACC)^2} + \frac{FCF_3}{(1 + WACC)^3} + \cdots + \frac{FCF_\infty}{(1 + WACC)^\infty}$$

- Transfers of capital between borrowers and savers take place (1) by **direct transfers** of money and securities; (2) by transfers through **investment banks**, which act as middlemen; and (3) by transfers through **financial intermediaries**, which create new securities.
- Capital is allocated through the price system—a price must be paid to "rent" money. Lenders charge **interest** on funds they lend, while equity investors receive **dividends** and **capital gains** in return for letting firms use their money.
- Four fundamental factors affect the cost of money: (1) **production opportunities**, (2) **time preferences for consumption**, (3) **risk**, and (4) **inflation**.
- There are many different types of **financial securities**. Primitive securities represent claims on cash flows, such as stocks and bonds. **Derivatives** are claims on other traded securities, such as options.
- Major financial institutions include **commercial banks**, **trust companies**, **credit unions**, **pension funds**, **life insurance companies**, **mutual funds**, **hedge funds**, and **private equity funds**.
- One result of ongoing regulatory changes has been a blurring of the distinctions between the different financial institutions. The trend in Canada has been towards firms that offer a wide range of financial services, including investment banking, brokerage operations, insurance, and commercial banking.
- There are many different types of **financial markets**. Each market serves a different region or deals with a different type of security.
- **Physical asset markets**, also called tangible or real asset markets, are those for products such as wheat, autos, and real estate. **Financial asset markets** are for primitive securities and derivative securities.
- **Spot markets** and **futures markets** are terms that refer to whether the assets are bought or sold for "on-the-spot" delivery or for delivery at some future date.
- **Money markets** are the markets for debt securities with maturities of less than 1 year. **Capital markets** are the markets for long-term debt and corporate shares.
- **Primary markets** are the markets in which corporations raise new capital. **Secondary markets** are markets in which existing, already outstanding securities are traded among investors.

Questions

1-1 Define each of the following terms:
   a. Proprietorship; partnership; corporation
   b. Limited partnership; limited liability partnership; professional corporation
   c. Shareholder wealth maximization
   d. Money market; capital market; primary market; secondary market
   e. Private markets; public markets; derivatives
   f. Investment banker; financial intermediary
   g. Mutual fund; money market fund
   h. Production opportunities; time preferences for consumption
   i. Foreign trade deficit

1-2 What are the three principal forms of business organization? What are the advantages and disadvantages of each?

1-3 What is a firm's fundamental, or intrinsic, value? What might cause a firm's intrinsic value to be different than its actual market value?

1-4 The president of Eastern Semiconductor Corporation (ESC) made this statement in the company's annual report: "ESC's primary goal is to increase the value of our common shareholders' equity." Later in the report, the following announcements were made:
   a. The company contributed $1.5 million to the symphony orchestra in Toronto, Ontario, its headquarters' city.

b. The company is spending $500 million to open a new plant and expand operations in China. No profits will be produced by the Chinese operation for 4 years, so earnings will be depressed during this period versus what they would have been had the decision not been made to expand in that market.

Discuss how ESC's shareholders might view each of these actions, and how the actions might affect the share price.

1-5 Edmund Enterprises recently made a large investment to upgrade its technology. While these improvements won't have much of an impact on performance in the short run, they are expected to reduce future costs significantly. What impact will this investment have on Edmund Enterprises' earnings per share this year? What impact might this investment have on the company's intrinsic value and share price?

1-6 Describe the different ways in which capital can be transferred from suppliers of capital to those who are demanding capital.

1-7 What are financial intermediaries, and what economic functions do they perform?

1-8 Suppose the population of Area Y is relatively young while that of Area O is relatively old, but everything else about the two areas is equal.
a. Would interest rates likely be the same or different in the two areas? Explain.
b. Would a trend toward nationwide branching by banks and trust companies, and the development of nationwide diversified financial corporations, affect your answer to part a?

1-9 Suppose a new government was elected in Ottawa and its first order of business was to take away the independence of the Bank of Canada and to force the BoC to greatly expand the money supply. What effect would this have on the level of interest rates immediately after the announcement?

1-10 Is an initial public offering an example of a primary or a secondary market transaction?

1-11 Identify and briefly compare the two primary stock exchanges in Canada today.

MINI CASE

Assume that you recently graduated and have just reported to work as an investment advisor at the brokerage firm of Balik and Kiefer Inc. One of the firm's clients is Sergei Turganev, a professional hockey player who has just come to Canada from Russia. Turganev is a highly ranked hockey player who would like to start a company to produce and market apparel with his signature. He also expects to invest substantial amounts of money through Balik and Kiefer. Turganev is very bright, and he would like to understand in general terms what will happen to his money. Your boss has developed the following set of questions that you must answer to explain the Canadian financial system to Turganev.
a. Why is corporate finance important to all managers?
b. What are the organizational forms a company might have as it evolves from a start-up to a major corporation? List the advantages and disadvantages of each form.
c. How do corporations go public and continue to grow? What are agency problems? What is corporate governance?
d. What should be the primary objective of managers?
   (1) Do firms have any responsibilities to society at large?
   (2) Is share price maximization good or bad for society?
   (3) Should firms behave ethically?
e. What three aspects of cash flows affect the value of any investment?
f. What are free cash flows?
g. What is the weighted average cost of capital?
h. How do free cash flows and the weighted average cost of capital interact to determine a firm's value?
i. Who are the providers (savers) and users (borrowers) of capital? How is capital transferred between savers and borrowers?
j. What do we call the price that a borrower must pay for debt capital? What is the price of equity capital? What are the four most fundamental factors that affect the cost of money, or the general level of interest rates, in the economy?

k. What are some economic conditions (including international aspects) that affect the cost of money?
l. What are financial securities? Describe some financial instruments.
m. List some financial institutions.
n. What are some different types of markets?

chapter 2

Financial Statements, Cash Flow, and Taxes

Even today, $586 million is a lot of money. This is the amount of cash flow that Methanex's operations generated in 2013, up from $416 million in 2012. Cash flow is the lifeblood of a company, and the ability to generate it is the basis of its fundamental value. Methanex used its cash flow for capital expenditures, primarily to expand production, by building two new plants in the United States, as well as investing in its existing facilities, equipment, and locations.

Other companies generated large cash flows from operations in 2013, but they used the money differently. For example, Canadian technology company Open Text generated over $300 million from its operations and invested for the future by making $346 million worth of corporate acquisitions.

Auto parts giant Magna International, which generated $2.6 billion, made some capital expenditures, but returned $1.3 billion to shareholders through share repurchases and dividends.

Stantec Inc., a Canadian consulting and engineering firm, generated about $272 million (up from $181 million the previous year), but made relatively small capital expenditures, acquisitions, and dividend payments to shareholders. Instead, it put over $100 million into cash and short-term financial securities such as Treasury bills.

These four well-managed companies used their operating cash flows in four different ways. Methanex invested in its operations, Open Text made several acquisitions, Magna returned cash to shareholders, and Stantec saved money for a rainy day. Which company made the right choice? Only time will tell, but keep these companies and their different cash flow strategies in mind as you read this chapter.

Source: Cash flow information from 2013 Annual reports for Methanex, Open Text, Magna, and Stantec.

The textbook's website contains an *Excel* file that will guide you through the chapter's calculations. The file for this chapter is ***Ch 02 Tool Kit.xlsx,*** and we encourage you to open the file and follow along as you read the chapter. **www.nelson.com/ brigham3ce**

A manager's primary goal is to maximize the fundamental, or intrinsic, value of the firm's stock. This value is based on the stream of cash flows the firm is expected to generate in the future. But how does an investor go about estimating future cash flows, and how does a manager decide which actions are most likely to increase cash flows? The first step is to understand the financial statements that publicly traded firms must provide to the public. Thus, we begin with a discussion of financial statements, including how to interpret them and how to use them. Because value depends on usable, after-tax cash flows, we highlight the difference between accounting income and cash flow. In fact, it is *after-tax* cash flow that is important, so we also provide an overview of the federal income tax system.

2.1 Financial Statements and Reports

A company's annual report usually begins with the chair's description of the firm's operating results during the past year and a discussion of new developments that will affect future operations. The annual report also presents four basic financial statements—the *balance sheet*, the *income statement*, the *statement of retained earnings*, and the *statement of cash flows*.

The quantitative and written materials are equally important. The financial statements report *what has actually happened* to assets, earnings, dividends, and cash flows during the past few years, whereas the written materials attempt to explain why things turned out the way they did.

When Canada adopted the International Financial Reporting Standards (IFRS) in 2011 for publicly traded companies, Canadian *private* enterprises were given the option to use either IFRS or a simpler standard, modified version of Canadian GAAP, now referred to as the Accounting Standards for Private Enterprises (ASPE). As of 2011, Canadian GAAP ceased to exist. Most private enterprises will use ASPE, but those contemplating an initial public offering; those with international suppliers, customers, and partners; and those that will be expanding globally may wish to use IFRS. While the two standards are based on the same general principles, the application of those principles can be different. To the extent that we deal with specific accounting issues in this text, we will be referring to IFRS.

For illustrative purposes, we use a hypothetical company, MicroDrive Inc., which produces memory components for computers and smartphones.

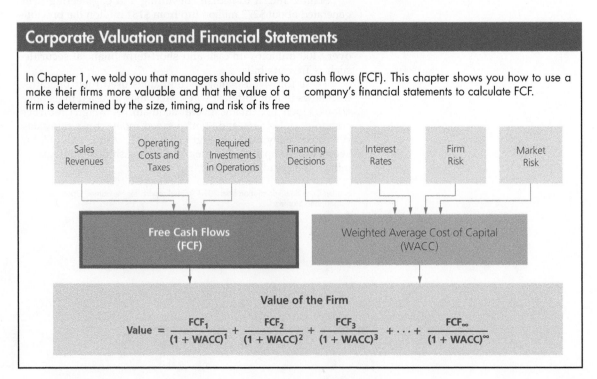

Corporate Valuation and Financial Statements

In Chapter 1, we told you that managers should strive to make their firms more valuable and that the value of a firm is determined by the size, timing, and risk of its free cash flows (FCF). This chapter shows you how to use a company's financial statements to calculate FCF.

Value of the Firm

$$Value = \frac{FCF_1}{(1 + WACC)^1} + \frac{FCF_2}{(1 + WACC)^2} + \frac{FCF_3}{(1 + WACC)^3} + \cdots + \frac{FCF_\infty}{(1 + WACC)^\infty}$$

2.2 The Balance Sheet

Table 2-1 shows MicroDrive's most recent **balance sheets**, (also referred to as statements of financial position), which represent "snapshots" of its financial position on the last day of each year. Although most companies report their balance sheets only on the last day of a given period, the "snapshot" actually changes daily as inventories are bought and sold, as fixed assets are added or retired, or as bank loan balances are increased or paid down. Moreover, a retailer will have much larger inventories before Christmas than later in the spring, so balance sheets for the same company can look quite different at different times during the year.

The left side of a balance sheet lists assets, which are the "things" the company owns. They are usually listed in order of "liquidity," or length of time it typically takes to convert them to cash at fair market values. The right side lists the claims that various groups have against the company's value, listed in the order in which they must be paid. For example, suppliers may have a claim called "accounts payable" that is due within 30 days, banks may have claims called "notes payable" that are due within 90 days, and bondholders may have claims that are not due for 20 years or more.

Shareholders come last, for two reasons. First, their claim represents ownership (or equity) and never needs to be "paid off." Second, they have a residual claim in the sense that they may receive payments only if the other claimants have already been paid. The non-shareholder claims are liabilities from the shareholders' perspective. The amounts shown on the balance sheets are often *book values* since they are based on the amounts recorded by bookkeepers when assets are purchased or liabilities are issued. As you will see throughout this textbook, book values may be very different from *market values*, which are the current values as determined in the marketplace.

The following sections provide more information about specific asset, liability, and equity accounts.

See *Ch 02 Tool Kit.xlsx* for all details.

TABLE 2-1 MicroDrive Inc.: December 31 Balance Sheets (Millions of Dollars)

Assets	2016	2015	Liabilities and Equity	2016	2015
Cash and equivalents	$ 10	$ 15	Accounts payable	$ 60	$ 30
Short-term investments	–	65	Notes payable	110	60
Accounts receivable	375	315	Accruals	140	130
Inventories	615	415	Total current liabilities	310	220
Total current assets	1,000	810	Long-term bonds	754	580
Net plant and equipment	1,000	870	Total liabilities	1,064	800
			Preferred stock (400,000 shares)	40	40
			Common stock (50,000,000 shares)	130	130
			Retained earnings	766	710
			Total common equity	896	840
			Total equity	936	880
Total assets	$2,000	$1,680	Total liabilities and equity	$2,000	$1,680

Assets

Cash, short-term investments, accounts receivable, and inventories are listed as current assets, because MicroDrive is expected to convert them into cash within a year. All assets are stated in dollars, but only cash represents actual money that can be spent. Some marketable securities mature very soon and can be converted quickly into cash at prices close to their book values. Such securities are called "cash equivalents" and are included with cash. Therefore, MicroDrive could write cheques for a total of $10 million. Other types of marketable securities have a longer time until maturity, and their market values are less predictable. These securities are classified as "short-term investments."

When MicroDrive sells its products to a customer but doesn't demand immediate payment, the customer then has an obligation called an "account receivable." The $375 million shown in accounts receivable is the amount of sales for which MicroDrive has not yet been paid.

Inventories show the dollars MicroDrive has invested in raw materials, work-in-process, and finished goods available for sale. MicroDrive uses the *FIFO (first-in, first-out)* method to determine the inventory value shown on its balance sheet ($615 million). It could have used the *LIFO (last-in, first-out)* method. During a period of rising prices, by taking out old, low-cost inventory and leaving in new, high-cost items, FIFO will produce a higher balance sheet inventory value but a lower cost of goods sold on the income statement. (This is strictly used for accounting; companies normally use older items first.) Because MicroDrive uses FIFO, and because inflation has been occurring, (1) its balance sheet inventories are higher than they would have been had it used LIFO, (2) its cost of goods sold is lower than it would have been under LIFO, and (3) its reported profits are therefore higher. In MicroDrive's case, if the company had elected to switch to LIFO, its balance sheet would have inventories of $585 million rather than $615 million, and its earnings (discussed in the next section) would have been reduced by $18 million.[1] Thus, the inventory valuation method can have a significant effect on financial statements, which is important to know when comparing different companies.

Rather than treat the entire purchase price of a long-term asset (such as a property, plant, or equipment) as an expense in the purchase year, accountants "spread" the purchase cost over the asset's useful life.[2] The amount they charge each year is called the **depreciation** expense. Companies have the choice of two methods for reporting property, plant, and equipment (PPE). They may report an amount based on the total cost of the long-term assets they have in place (the cost model), less an another amount called "accumulated depreciation," which is the total amount of depreciation that has been charged on those assets. A company may also periodically revalue its PPE (the revaluation model) and report its fair value, which is its market value, less any accumulated depreciation. MicroDrive reports property, plant, and equipment using the cost method. Also note that no matter which method is used, some companies, such as MicroDrive, show only one line—net plant and equipment, which is the asset amount less accumulated depreciation.[3] Chapter 11 provides a more detailed explanation of depreciation methods for tax purposes.

Liabilities and Equity

Accounts payable, notes payable, and accruals are listed as current liabilities, because MicroDrive is expected to pay them within a year. When MicroDrive purchases supplies but doesn't immediately pay for them, it takes on an obligation called an "account payable." Similarly, when MicroDrive takes out a loan that must be repaid within a year, it signs an IOU called a note payable. MicroDrive doesn't pay its taxes or its employees' wages daily, and the amount it owes on these items at any point in time is called an "accrual," or an "accrued expense." Long-term bonds are also liabilities because they, too, reflect a claim held by someone other than a shareholder.

Preferred stock is a hybrid, or a cross between common stock and debt. In the event of bankruptcy, preferred stock ranks below debt but above common stock. Also, the preferred dividend is fixed, so preferred shareholders do not benefit if the company's earnings grow.

---

[1]LIFO is not allowed in Canada; U.S. GAAP however, does allow it, and since Canadian companies whose shares trade on Canadian and U.S. exchanges are eligible to report using U.S. GAAP, it is fair to say LIFO may still be used by some Canadian companies.

[2]This is called *accrual accounting*, which attempts to match revenues to the periods in which they are earned and expenses to the periods in which the effort to generate income occurred.

[3]The term "amortization" will be used to describe the depreciation of intangible assets, while "depletion" will be used to refer to the depreciation of natural resources such as oil or natural gas.

Most firms do not use much, or even any, preferred stock, so "equity" usually means "common equity" unless the words "total" or "preferred" are included.

When a company sells shares of stock, the proceeds are recorded in the common stock account.[4] Retained earnings are the cumulative amount of earnings that have not been paid out as dividends. The sum of common stock and retained earnings is called "common equity," or sometimes just equity. If a company's assets could actually be sold at their book value, and if the liabilities and preferred stock were actually worth their book values, then a company could sell its assets, and pay off its liabilities and preferred stock, and the remaining cash would belong to common shareholders. Therefore, common equity is sometimes called *net worth*—it's the assets net of the liabilities.

⊙NCEPT REVIEW

1. What is the balance sheet, and what information does it provide?
2. How is the order of the information shown on the balance sheet determined?
3. Why might a company's December 31 balance sheet differ from its June 30 balance sheet?
4. A firm has $8 million in total assets. It has $3 million in current liabilities, $2 million in long-term debt, and $1 million in preferred stock. What is the total value of common equity? (Check Figure: $2 million)

2.3 The Income Statement

Table 2-2 shows the **income statements** and selected additional information for MicroDrive. Income statements can cover any period of time, but they are usually prepared monthly, quarterly, and annually. Unlike the balance sheet, which is a snapshot of a firm at a point in time, the income statement reflects performance during a period.

Net sales are the revenues less any discounts or returns. Depreciation and amortization reflect the estimated costs of the assets that wear out in producing goods and services. To illustrate depreciation, suppose that in 2013, MicroDrive purchased a $100,000 machine with a life of 5 years and zero expected salvage value. This $100,000 cost is not expensed in the purchase year but is instead spread out over the machine's 5-year depreciable life. In straight-line depreciation, the depreciation charge for the full year would be $100,000/5=$20,000. The reported depreciation expense on the income statement is the sum of all the assets' annual depreciation charges. Depreciation applies to tangible assets, such as plant and equipment, whereas amortization applies to intangible assets such as patents, copyrights, and trademarks.

The cost of goods sold (COGS) includes labour, raw materials, and other expenses directly related to the production or purchase of the items or services sold in that period. The COGS includes depreciation, but we report depreciation separately so that analysis later in the chapter will be more transparent. Subtracting COGS (including depreciation) and other operating expenses results in earnings before interest and taxes (EBIT).

Many analysts add back depreciation to EBIT to calculate **EBITDA**, which stands for earnings before interest, taxes, depreciation, and amortization. Because neither depreciation nor amortization is paid in cash, some analysts claim that EBITDA is a better measure of financial strength than is net income. MicroDrive's EBITDA is

$$\text{EBITDA} = \text{EBIT} + \text{Depreciation}$$

$$= \$283.8 + \$100 = \$383.8$$

Alternatively, EBITDA's calculation can begin with sales:

$$\text{EBITDA} = \text{Sales} - \text{COGS excluding depreciation} - \text{Other expenses}$$

$$= \$3,000.0 - \$2,100.0 - \$516.2 = \$383.8$$

---

[4]Companies sometimes break the total proceeds into two parts, one called "par" and the other called "paid-in-capital" or "capital surplus." For example, if a company sells shares of stock for $10, it might record $1 of par and $9 of paid-in-capital. For most purposes, the distinction between par and paid-in-capital is not important, and most companies use no-par stock.

TABLE 2-2	MicroDrive Inc.: Income Statements for Years Ended December 31 (Millions of Dollars, Except for Per-Share Data)		

	2016	2015
Net sales	$3,000.0	$2,850.0
Costs of goods sold except depreciation	2,100.0	2,000.0
Depreciation and amortization[a]	100.0	90.0
Other operating expenses	516.2	497.0
Earnings before interest and taxes (EBIT, or operating income)	283.8	263.0
Less interest	88.0	60.0
Earnings before taxes (EBT)	195.8	203.0
Taxes (40%)	78.3	81.2
Net income	117.5	121.8
Preferred share dividends	4.0	4.0
Net income available to common shareholders	$ 113.5	$ 117.8
Additional Information		
Common share dividends	$ 57.5	$ 53.0
Addition to retained earnings	$ 56.0	$ 64.8
Number of common shares (millions)	50.00	50.00
Common stock price	$ 23.00	$ 26.00
Per-Share Data[b]		
Earnings per share, (EPS)	$ 2.27	$ 2.36
Dividends per share, (DPS)	$ 1.15	$ 1.06
Book value per share, (BVPS)	$ 17.92	$ 16.80

Notes:

[a]MicroDrive has no amortization charges.

[b]Calculations for the 2016 EPS, DPS, and BVPS are shown below:

$$\text{Earnings per share} = \text{EPS} = \frac{\text{Net income available to common shareholders}}{\text{Common shares outstanding}} = \frac{\$113,500,000}{50,000,000} = \$2.27$$

$$\text{Dividends per share} = \text{DPS} = \frac{\text{Dividends paid to common shareholders}}{\text{Common shares outstanding}} = \frac{\$57,500,000}{50,000,000} = \$1.15$$

$$\text{Book value per share} = \text{BVPS} = \frac{\text{Total common equity}}{\text{Common shares outstanding}} = \frac{\$896,000,000}{50,000,000} = \$17.92$$

However, as we show later in the chapter, EBITDA is not useful to managers and analysts as free cash flow, so we usually focus on free cash flow instead of EBITDA.

The net income available to common shareholders, which is revenues less expenses, taxes, and preferred dividends (but before paying common dividends), is generally referred to as *net income*, although it is also called *profit* or *earnings*, particularly in the news or financial press. Dividing net income by the number of shares outstanding gives earnings per share (EPS), which is often called "the bottom line." Throughout this book, unless otherwise indicated, net income means net income available to common shareholders.

IFRS has also introduced the concept of *comprehensive income*, which consists of net income plus *other comprehensive income (OCI)*. While the income statement presents gains and losses from its operations, there may be other gains and losses that a company must show but that have not been realized. For instance, some of the company's assets may be revalued at a higher or lower amount, yet the gains or losses have not been realized since the assets have not been sold. Unrealized gains and losses on certain investments are included as other comprehensive income and are reported either after net income and after earnings per share, or on a separate statement called the *statement of comprehensive income*. Gains or losses on foreign exchange instruments and certain types of hedges are other examples of other comprehensive income.

Just as net income that is not distributed as dividends is added to retained earnings on the balance sheet, other comprehensive income is also added to a shareholders' equity account, called *accumulated other comprehensive income*. OCI is generally a small amount, and some companies may not have any to report, such as in the case of MicroDrive.

For our purposes in this text, net income is the essential figure we will be working with. Also note that *earnings per share is based on net income; it does not include other comprehensive income*.

CONCEPT REVIEW

1. What is an income statement, and what information does it provide?
2. Why is earnings per share called "the bottom line"?
3. What is EBITDA?
4. Regarding the time period reported, how does the income statement differ from the balance sheet?
5. A firm has $2 million in earnings before taxes. The firm has an interest expense of $300,000 and depreciation of $200,000; it has no amortization. What is its EBITDA? (Check Figure: $2.5 million)

2.4 Statement of Changes in Equity

Changes in shareholders' equity during the accounting period are reported in the **statement of changes in equity.** Table 2-3 shows that MicroDrive earned $113.5 million during 2016, paid out $57.5 million in common dividends, and ploughed $56 million back into the business. Thus, the balance sheet item "Retained earnings" increased from $710 million at year-end 2015 to $766 million at year-end 2016.[5] The last column shows the beginning equity, any changes, and the end-of-year equity.

Note that "retained earnings" does not represent assets but is instead a *claim against assets*. In 2016, MicroDrive's shareholders allowed it to reinvest $56 million instead of

TABLE 2-3   MicroDrive Inc.: Statement of Shareholders' Equity, Year Ended December 31, 2016 (Millions)

See **Ch 02 Tool Kit.xlsx** for all details.

	Preferred Shares		Common Shares			
	Shares	Amount	Shares	Amount	Retained Earnings	Total Equity
Balance Dec. 31, 2015	0.40	$40.0	50	$130.0	$710.0	$880.0
Net income					117.5	117.5
Cash dividends					(61.5)	(61.5)
Issuance of stock	–	–	–	–	–	–
Balance Dec. 31, 2016	0.40	$40.0	50	$130.0	$766.0	$936.0

Note: Here and throughout the book, parentheses are used to denote negative numbers.

---

[5]If they had been applicable, then columns would have been used to show "Additional paid-in capital" and "Treasury stock." Also, additional rows would have contained information on things such as new issues of stock, Treasury stock acquired, stock options exercised, and unrealized foreign exchange gains or losses.

distributing the money as dividends, and management spent this money on new assets. Thus, retained earnings, as reported on the balance sheet, does not represent cash and is not "available" for the payment of dividends or anything else.[6]

ⓒNCEPT REVIEW

1. What is the statement of changes in equity, and what information does it provide?
2. Why do changes in retained earnings occur?
3. Explain why the following statement is true: "Retained earnings, as reported on the balance sheet, does not represent cash and is not 'available' for the payment of dividends or anything else."
4. A firm had a retained earnings balance of $3 million in the previous year. In the current year, its net income is $2.5 million. If it pays $1 million in common dividends in the current year, what is its resulting retained earnings balance? (Check Figure: $4.5 million)

2.5 Net Cash Flow

A business's **net cash flow** generally differs from its *accounting profit* because some of the revenues and expenses listed on the income statement were not received or paid in cash during the year. The relationship between net cash flow and net income can be expressed as follows:

$$\text{Net cash flow} = \frac{\text{Net income available to}}{\text{common shareholders}} - \frac{\text{Noncash}}{\text{revenues}} + \frac{\text{Noncash}}{\text{charges}} \qquad (2\text{-}1)$$

The primary examples of noncash charges are depreciation and amortization. These items reduce net income but are not paid out in cash, so we add them back to net income when calculating net cash flow. Another example of a noncash charge is deferred taxes. In some instances, companies are allowed to defer tax payments to a later date even though the tax payment is reported as an expense on the income statement. Therefore, deferred tax payments are added to net income when calculating net cash flow.[7] At the same time, some revenues may not be collected in cash during the year, and these items must be subtracted from net income when calculating net cash flow.

Typically, depreciation and amortization are by far the largest noncash items, and in many cases the other noncash items roughly net out to zero. For this reason, many analysts assume that net cash flow equals net income plus depreciation and amortization:

$$\text{Net cash flow} = \frac{\text{Net income available to}}{\text{common shareholders}} + \frac{\text{Depreciation}}{\text{and amortization}} \qquad (2\text{-}2)$$

We will generally assume that Equation 2-2 holds. However, you should remember that Equation 2-2 will not accurately reflect net cash flow in those instances where there are significant noncash items other than depreciation and amortization.

We can illustrate Equation 2-2 with 2016 data for MicroDrive taken from Table 2-2:

$$\text{Net cash flow} = \$113.5 + \$100.0 = \$213.5 \text{ million}$$

You can think of net cash flow as the profit a company would have if it did not have to replace fixed assets as they wear out.

---

[6]The amount reported in the retained earnings account is *not* an indication of the amount of cash the firm has. Cash (as of the balance sheet date) is found in the cash account, an asset account. A positive number in the retained earnings account indicates only that in the past the firm earned some income, but its dividends paid were less than its earnings. Even though a company reports record earnings and shows an increase in its retained earnings account, it still may be short of cash.

The same situation holds for individuals. You might own a new BMW (no loan), lots of clothes, and an expensive stereo, hence have a high net worth, but if you have only 23 cents in your pocket plus $5 in your chequing account, you will still be short of cash.

[7]Deferred taxes may arise, for example, if a company uses declining balance depreciation (called capital cost allowance) for tax purposes but straight-line depreciation for reporting its financial statements to investors.

Financial Analysis on the Internet

A wide range of valuable financial information is available on the Internet. With just a couple of clicks, an investor can easily find the key financial statements for most publicly traded companies. Here's a partial (but by no means complete) list of places you can go to get started. For information on Canadian companies:

- Try the National Post's finance website, **http://financialpost.com**. Click on markets to bring up TSX market data. Enter a stock's ticker symbol and click GET QUOTE. You will see the stock's current price, along with recent news releases. Along the top are a number of tabs, including "financial," which provides the income statement, balance sheet, cash flow statements, and ratio analysis for the company.
- Other sources for up-to-date market information are **http://finance.sympatico.msn.ca** and **http://globeinvestor.com**. These sites also provide current and recent financial statement information.
- The System for Electronic Document Analysis and Retrieval, at **http://www.sedar.com**, is a central site for obtaining information on any publicly traded company in Canada. Individual company searches can be made to obtain annual reports, prospectuses, information circulars, news releases, financial statements and much more. Sedar contains data going back to 1997.

- The U.S. Securities and Exchange Commission (SEC) requires all companies that wish to trade stock in the United States to file financial reports and other information on EDGAR, a free online database available to all investors. EDGAR is available at **http://.www.sec.gov.**

For information on U.S. companies (and Canadian companies whose shares trade on American exchanges) you can try the following sites:

- Yahoo's finance website is **http://finance.yahoo.com**. Here you will find updated market information along with links to a variety of interesting research sites. Enter a stock's ticker symbol, click GO, and you will see the stock's current price, along with recent news about the company. The panel on the left has links to key statistics, the company's financial statements, and more. The Yahoo site also has a list of insider transactions, so you can tell if a company's CEO and other key insiders are buying or selling their company's stock.
- Two other sources for market data are **http://money.cnn.com** and **http://www.zacks.com**. These sites also provide financial statements in standardized formats.
- Other good places to look are **http://www.bloomberg.com** and **http://www.investor.reuters.com**. Here you can find links to analysts' research reports along with the key financial statements.

CONCEPT REVIEW

1. Differentiate between net cash flow and accounting profit.
2. A firm has net income of $5 million. Assuming that depreciation of $1 million is its only noncash expense, what is the firm's net cash flow? (Check Figure: $6 million)

2.6 Statement of Cash Flows

Even if a company reports a large net income during a year, the *amount of cash* reported on its year-end balance sheet may be the same or even lower than its beginning cash. The reason is that the company can use its net income in a variety of ways, not just keep it as cash in the bank. For example, the firm may use its net income to pay dividends, to increase inventories, to finance accounts receivable, to invest in fixed assets, to reduce debt, or to buy back common stock. Indeed, many factors affect a company's *cash position* as reported on its balance sheet. The **statement of cash flows** separates a company's activities into three categories—operating, investing, and financing— and summarizes the resulting cash balance.

Operating Activities

As the name implies, the section for operating activities focuses on the amount of cash generated (or lost) by the firm's operating activities. The section begins with the reported net income before paying preferred dividends and makes several adjustments, beginning with noncash activities.

Noncash Adjustments Some revenues and expenses reported on the income statement are not received or paid in cash during the year. For example, depreciation and amortization reduce reported net income but are not cash payments.

Reported taxes often differ from the taxes that are paid, resulting in an account called deferred taxes, which is the cumulative difference between the taxes that are reported and those that are paid. Deferred taxes can occur in many ways, including the use of accelerated depreciation for tax purposes but straight-line depreciation for financial reporting. This increases reported taxes relative to actual tax payments in the early years of an asset's life, causing the resulting net income to be lower than the true cash flow. Therefore, increases in deferred taxes are added to net income when calculating cash flow, and decreases are subtracted from net income.

Changes in Working Capital Increases in current assets other than cash (such as inventories and accounts receivable) decrease cash, whereas decreases in these accounts increase cash. For example, if inventories are to increase, then the firm must use cash to acquire the additional inventory. Conversely, if inventories decrease, this generally means the firm is selling inventories and not replacing all of them, hence generating cash. Here's how we keep track of whether a change in assets increases or decreases cash flow: If the amount we own goes up (like getting a new laptop computer), it means we have spent money and our cash goes down. On the other hand, if something we own goes down (like selling a car), our cash goes up.

Now consider a current liability, such as accounts payable. If accounts payable increase then the firm has received additional credit from its suppliers, which saves cash; but if payables decrease, this means it has used cash to pay off its suppliers. Therefore, increases in current liabilities such as accounts payable increase cash, whereas decreases in current liabilities decrease cash. To keep track of the cash flow's direction, think about the impact of getting a student loan. The amount you owe goes up and your cash goes up. Now think about paying off the loan: The amount you owe goes down, but so does your cash.

Investing Activities

Investing activities include transactions involving fixed assets or short-term financial investments. For example, if a company buys new IT infrastructure, its cash goes down at the time of the purchase. On the other hand, if it sells a building or Treasury bill, its cash goes up.

Financing Activities

Financing activities include raising cash by issuing short-term debt, long-term debt, or stock. Because dividend payments, stock repurchases, and principal payments on debt reduce a company's cash, such transactions are included here.

Putting the Pieces Together

The statement of cash flows is used to help answer questions such as these: Is the firm generating enough cash to purchase the additional assets required for growth? Is the firm generating any extra cash it can use to repay debt or to invest in new products? Such information is useful both for managers and investors, so the statement of cash flows is an important part of the annual report.

Table 2-4 shows MicroDrive's statement of cash flows as it would appear in the company's annual report. The top section shows cash generated by and used in operations—for MicroDrive, operations used net cash flows of $2.5 million. This subtotal is in many respects the most important figure in any of the financial statements. Profits as reported on the income statement can be "doctored" by tactics such as depreciating assets too slowly, not recognizing bad debts promptly, and the like. However, it is far more difficult to simultaneously doctor profits and the working capital accounts. Therefore, it is not uncommon for a company to report positive net income right up to the day it declares bankruptcy. In such cases, however, the net cash flow from operations almost always began to deteriorate much earlier, and analysts who kept an eye on cash flow could have predicted trouble. Therefore, if you are

See **Ch 02 Tool Kit.xlsx**
for all details.

TABLE 2-4	MicroDrive Inc.: Statement of Cash Flows for Year Ended December 31, 2016 (Millions of Dollars)

	Cash Provided or (Used)
Operating Activities	
Net income	$117.5
Adjustments:	
Noncash adjustments:	
Depreciation[a]	100.0
Due to changes in working capital:[b]	
Increase in accounts receivable	(60.0)
Increase in inventories	(200.0)
Increase in accounts payable	30.0
Increase in accruals	10.0
Net cash used by operating activities	(2.5)
Investing Activities	
Cash used to acquire fixed assets[c]	(230.0)
Sale of short-term investments	65.0
Net cash used by investing activities	(165.0)
Financing Activities	
Increase in notes payable	50.0
Increase in bonds outstanding	174.0
Payment of preferred and common dividends	(61.5)
Net cash provided by financing activities	162.5
Summary	
Decrease in cash	(5.0)
Cash at beginning of year	15.0
Cash at end of year	$ 10.0

[a]Depreciation is a noncash expense that was deducted when calculating net income. It must be added back to show the correct cash flow from operations.
[b]An increase in a current asset *decreases* cash. An increase in a current liability *increases* cash. For example, inventories increased by $200 million and therefore reduced cash by a like amount.
[c]The net increase in fixed assets is $130 million; however, this net amount is after a deduction for the year's depreciation expense. Depreciation expense would have to be added back to find the increase in gross fixed assets. From the company's income statement, we see that the 2016 depreciation expense is $100 million; thus, expenditures on fixed assets were actually $230 million.

ever analyzing a company and are pressed for time, look first at the trend in net cash flow provided by operating activities, because it will tell you more than any other single number.

The second section shows investing activities. MicroDrive purchased fixed assets totaling $230 million and sold $65 million of short-term investments, for a net cash flow from investing activities of *minus* $165 million.

The third section, financing activities, includes borrowing from banks (notes payable), selling new bonds, and paying dividends on common and preferred stock. MicroDrive raised $224 million by borrowing, but it paid $61.5 million in preferred and common dividends. Therefore, its net inflow of funds from financing activities was $162.5 million.

In the summary, when all of these sources and uses of cash are totalled, we see that MicroDrive's cash outflows exceeded its cash inflows by $5 million during 2016; that is, its net change in cash was a *negative* $5 million.

MicroDrive's statement of cash flows should be worrisome to its managers and to outside analysts. The company had $3 billion in sales but generated only $2.5 million from operations, not nearly enough to cover the $230 million it spent on fixed assets and the

FINANCE: IN FOCUS

Filling in the GAAP

While Canadian companies and those from most other developed nations use International Financial Reporting Standards, or IFRS when preparing financial statements, U.S. companies use Generally Accepted Accounting Principles, or GAAP. The U.S. GAAP system is rules based, with thousands of instructions, or "guidances," for how individual transactions should be reported in financial statements. IFRS on the other hand, is a principles-based system in which detailed instructions are replaced by overall guiding principles.

For example, whereas IFRS provides just four categories of revenue and two overall principles for timing revenue recognition, GAAP provides detailed rules about when to recognize revenue from any conceivable activity. This means that even the most basic accounting measure, revenue, is different under the two standards—total revenue, or sales, under IFRS won't typically equal total revenue under GAAP. Thus financial statements prepared under U.S. GAAP cannot be directly compared to IFRS financial statements, making comparative financial analysis of U.S. and international companies difficult.

Perhaps an even greater issue is that IFRS principles allow for more company discretion in recording transactions. This means that two different companies may treat an identical transaction differently when using IFRS, which makes company-to-company comparisons more difficult. If financial statements are not directly comparable, analyzing companies and raising foreign capital will be more difficult. Dual standards for Canadian companies that rely on U.S. markets or whose stock trades on the New York Stock Exchange (NYSE) or NASDAQ can especially be a problem. In these cases, Canadian companies are given the option to report using GAAP or IFRS.

The U.S. Financial Accounting Standards Board (FASB) and the International Accounting Standards Board (IASB) have both been working to merge the two sets of standards since 2002. While a tentative timetable has been established for U.S. adoption, progress is slow and some in the United States are questioning the process. To keep abreast of developments in IFRS/GAAP convergence, visit the IASB website at **www.iasb.org** and the FASB website at **www.fasb.org.**

$61.5 million it paid in dividends. It covered these cash outlays by borrowing heavily and by liquidating short-term investments. Obviously, this situation cannot continue year after year, so MicroDrive managers will have to make changes. We will return to MicroDrive throughout the textbook to see what actions its managers are planning.

CONCEPT REVIEW

1. What types of questions does the statement of cash flows answer?
2. Identify and briefly explain the three different categories of activities shown in the statement of cash flows.
3. A firm has inventories of $2 million for the previous year and $1.5 million for the current year. What impact does this have on net cash provided by operations? (Check Figure: Increase of $500,000)

2.7 Free Cash Flow: The Cash Flow Available for Distribution to Investors

Thus far in the chapter we have focused on financial statements as they are presented in the annual report. When you studied income statements in accounting, the emphasis was probably on the firm's net income, which is its **accounting profit.** However, the intrinsic value of a company's operations is determined by the stream of cash flows that the operations will generate now and in the future. To be more specific, the value of operations depends on all the future expected **free cash flows (FCF),** defined as after-tax operating profit minus the amount of new investment in working capital and fixed assets necessary to sustain the business. *Therefore, the way for managers to make their companies more valuable is to increase free cash flow now and in the future.*

Notice that FCF is the cash flow *available for distribution to all the company's investors after the company has made all investments necessary to sustain ongoing operations.* How well have MicroDrive's managers done in generating FCF? In this section, we will calculate MicroDrive's FCF.

FIGURE 2-1 Calculating Free Cash Flow

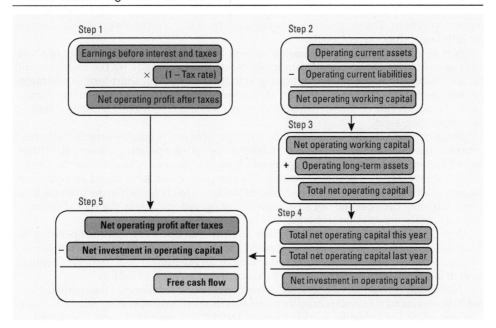

Figure 2-1 shows the five steps in calculating free cash flow. As we explain each individual step in the following sections, refer back to Figure 2-1 to keep the big picture in mind.

Net Operating Profit After Taxes (NOPAT)

If two companies have different amounts of debt, and therefore different amounts of interest charges, they could have identical operating performances but different net incomes—the one with more debt would have a lower net income. Net income is certainly important, but it does not always reflect the true performance of a company's operations or the effectiveness of its operating managers. A better measurement for comparing managers' performance is **net operating profit after taxes** which is the amount of profit a company would generate if it had no debt and held no financial assets. NOPAT is defined as follows:[8]

$$NOPAT = EBIT(1 - Tax\ rate) \tag{2-3}$$

Using data from the income statements of Table 2-2, MicroDrive's 2016 NOPAT is found to be

$$NOPAT = \$283.8(1 - 0.4) = \$283.8(0.6) = \$170.3\ million$$

This means that MicroDrive generated an after-tax operating profit of $170.3 million, a little better than its previous NOPAT of $263(0.6) = $157.8 million. However, the income statements in Table 2-2 show that MicroDrive's earnings per share actually declined. This decrease in EPS was caused by an increase in interest expense, and not by a decrease in operating profit.

Net Operating Working Capital

Most companies need some current assets to support their operating activities. For example, all companies must carry some cash to operate smoothly. Companies continuously receive

---

[8]For firms with a more complicated tax situation, it is better to define NOPAT as follows: NOPAT = (Net income before preferred dividends) + (Net interest expense)(1 − Tax rate). Also, if firms are able to defer paying some of their taxes, perhaps by the use of accelerated depreciation, then NOPAT should be adjusted to reflect the taxes that the company actually paid on its operating income. See P. Daves, M. Ehrhardt, and R. Shrieves, *Corporate Valuation: A Guide for Managers and Investors* (Mason, OH: Thomson South-Western, 2004) for a detailed explanation of these and other adjustments. Also see Tim Koller, Marc Goedhart, and David Wessels, *Valuation: Measuring and Managing the Value of Companies* (Hoboken, NJ: John Wiley & Sons, 2005); and G. Bennett Stewart, *The Quest for Value* (New York: HarperCollins, 1991).

cheques from customers and write cheques to suppliers, employees, and so on. Because inflows and outflows do not coincide perfectly, a company must keep some cash in its bank account. In other words, some cash is required to conduct operations. The same is true for most other current assets, such as inventory and accounts receivable, which are required for normal operations. The short-term assets normally used in a company's operating activities are called **operating current assets.**

Not all current assets are operating current assets. For example, holdings of short-term securities generally result from investment decisions made by the treasurer and not as a natural consequence of operating activities. Therefore, short-term investments are **nonoperating assets** and normally are excluded when calculating operating current assets.[9] A useful rule of thumb is that if an asset pays interest, it should not be classified as an operating asset.

Some current liabilities—especially accounts payable and accruals—arise in the normal course of operations. Such short-term liabilities are called **operating current liabilities.** Not all current liabilities are operating current liabilities. For example, consider the current liability shown as notes payable to banks. The company could have raised an equivalent amount of long-term debt or could have issued stock, so the choice to borrow from the bank was a financing decision and not a consequence of operations. Again, the rule of thumb is that if a liability incurs interest charges, it is not an operating liability.

If you are ever uncertain about whether an item is an operating asset or operating liability, ask yourself whether the item is a natural consequence of operations or a discretionary choice, such as a particular method of financing or an investment in a particular financial asset. If it is discretionary, then the item is not an operating asset or liability.

Notice that each dollar of operating current liabilities is a dollar that the company does not have to raise from investors in order to conduct its short-term operating activities. Therefore, we define **net operating working capital (NOWC)** as operating current assets minus operating current liabilities. In other words, net operating working capital is the working capital required with investor-supplied funds. Here is the definition in equation form:

$$\begin{array}{c} \text{Net operating} \\ \text{working capital (NOWC)} \end{array} = \begin{array}{c} \text{Operating current} \\ \text{assets} \end{array} - \begin{array}{c} \text{Operating current} \\ \text{liabilities} \end{array} \qquad \text{(2-4)}$$

We can apply these definitions to MicroDrive, using the balance sheet data given in Table 2-1. Here is the net operating working capital for 2016:

$$\text{NOWC} = \text{Operating current assets} - \text{Operating current liabilities}$$
$$= (\text{Cash} + \text{Accounts receivable} + \text{Inventories})$$
$$- (\text{Accounts payable} + \text{Accruals})$$
$$= (\$10 + \$375 + \$615) - (\$60 + \$140)$$
$$= \$800 \text{ million}$$

For the previous year, net operating working capital was

$$\text{Net operating working capital} = (\$15 + \$315 + \$415) - (\$30 + \$130)$$
$$= \$585 \text{ million}$$

Total Net Operating Capital

In addition to working capital, most companies use long-term assets to support their operations. These include land, buildings, factories, equipment, and the like. *Total net operating capital* is the sum of NOWC and operating long-term assets:

$$\text{Total net operating capital} = \text{NOWC} + \text{Operating long-term assets} \qquad \text{(2-5)}$$

[9]If the marketable securities are held as a substitute for cash, and therefore reduce the cash requirements, then they may be classified as part of operating working capital. Generally, though, large holdings of marketable securities are held as a reserve for some contingency or else as a temporary "parking place" for funds prior to an acquisition, a major capital investment program, or the like.

Because MicroDrive's operating long-term assets consist only of net plant and equipment, its total net operating capital at year-end 2016 was

$$\text{Total net operating capital} = \$800 + \$1,000$$
$$= \$1,800 \text{ million}$$

For the previous year, its total net operating capital was

$$\text{Total net operating capital} = \$585 + \$870$$
$$= \$1,455 \text{ million}$$

Notice that we have defined total net operating capital as the sum of net operating working capital and operating long-term assets. In other words, our definition is in terms of operating assets and liabilities. However, we can also calculate total net operating capital by looking at the source of funds. **Total investor-supplied capital** is defined as the total of funds provided by investors, such as notes payable, long-term bonds, preferred stock, and common equity. For most companies, total investor-supplied capital is:

$$\begin{matrix} \text{Total investor-supplied} \\ \text{capital} \end{matrix} = \begin{matrix} \text{Notes} \\ \text{payable} \end{matrix} + \begin{matrix} \text{Long-term} \\ \text{bonds} \end{matrix} + \begin{matrix} \text{Preferred} \\ \text{Stock} \end{matrix} + \begin{matrix} \text{Common} \\ \text{equity} \end{matrix} \quad \text{(2-6)}$$

For MicroDrive, the total capital provided by investors at year-end 2015 was $60 + $580 + $40 + $840 = $1,520 million. Of this amount, $65 million was tied up in short-term investments, which were not directly related to MicroDrive's operations. Therefore, we define **total investor-supplied operating capital** as:

$$\begin{matrix} \text{Total investor-supplied} \\ \text{operating capital} \end{matrix} = \begin{matrix} \text{Total investor-supplied} \\ \text{capital} \end{matrix} - \begin{matrix} \text{Short-term} \\ \text{investments} \end{matrix} \quad \text{(2-7)}$$

MicroDrive had $1,520 − $65 = $1,455 million of investor-supplied operating capital.

Notice that this is exactly the same value as calculated above. This shows that we can calculate total net operating capital either from net operating working capital and operating long-term assets or from the investor-supplied funds. We usually base our calculations on operating data because this approach allows us to analyze a division, factory, or work centre, whereas the approach based on investor-supplied capital is applicable only for the entire company.

The expression "total net operating capital" is a mouthful, so we often call it *operating capital* or even just *capital*. Also, unless we specifically say "investor-supplied capital," we are referring to total net operating capital.

Net Investment in Operating Capital

As calculated previously, MicroDrive had $1,455 million of total net operating capital at the end of 2015 and $1,800 million at the end of 2016. Therefore, during 2016, it made a *net investment in operating capital* of

$$\text{Net investment in operating capital} = \$1,800 − \$1,455 = \$345 \text{ million}$$

Most of this investment was made in net operating working capital, which rose from $585 million to $800 million, or by $215 million. This 37% increase in net operating working capital, in view of a sales increase of only 5% (from $2,850 to $3,000 million), should set off warning bells in your head. Why did MicroDrive tie up so much additional cash in working capital? Is the company gearing up for a big increase in sales, or are inventories not moving and receivables not being collected? We will address these questions in detail in Chapter 3, when we cover ratio analysis.

Free Cash Flow vs. Net Cash Flow

Earlier in this chapter, we defined net cash flow as net income plus noncash adjustments, which typically means net income plus depreciation. Note, though, that cash flows cannot be maintained over time unless depreciated fixed assets are replaced, so management is not completely free to use net cash flows however it chooses. Therefore, we now define another term, free cash flow (FCF), which is the cash flow actually available for distribution to investors *after the company has made all the investments in fixed assets and working capital necessary to sustain ongoing operations.*

Calculating Free Cash Flow

Free cash flow is defined as

$$\text{FCF} = \text{NOPAT} - \text{Net investment in operating capital} \qquad (2\text{-}8)$$

MicroDrive's free cash flow in 2016 was

$$\text{FCF} = \$170.3 - (\$1,800 - \$1,455)$$
$$= \$170.3 - \$345$$
$$= -\$174.7 \text{ million}$$

Although we prefer this approach to calculating FCF, sometimes the financial press calculates FCF with a different approach. The results are the same either way, but you should be aware of this alternative approach. The difference lies in how depreciation is treated. To see this, notice that net fixed assets rose from $870 to $1,000 million, or by $130 million. However, MicroDrive reported $100 million of depreciation, so its gross investment in fixed assets was $130 + $100 = $230 million for the year. With this background, the *gross investment in operating capital* is

$$\frac{\text{Gross investment}}{\text{in operating capital}} = \frac{\text{Net investment}}{\text{in operating capital}} + \text{Depreciation} \qquad (2\text{-}9)$$

For MicroDrive, the gross investment in operating capital was:

$$\frac{\text{Gross investment}}{\text{in operating capital}} = \$345 + \$100 = \$445 \text{ million}$$

Because depreciation is a noncash expense, some analysts calculate operating cash flow as

$$\text{Operating cash flow} = \text{NOPAT} + \text{Depreciation} \qquad (2\text{-}10)$$

MicroDrive's most recent operating cash flow is

$$\text{Operating cash flow} = \text{NOPAT} + \text{Depreciation} = \$170.3 + \$100 = \$270.3 \text{ million}$$

An algebraically equivalent expression for free cash flow in terms of operating cash flow and gross investment in operating capital is

$$\text{FCF} = \left(\begin{array}{c}\text{NOPAT}\\ +\text{Depreciation}\end{array}\right) - \left(\begin{array}{c}\text{Net investment}\\ \text{in operating capital}\\ +\text{Depreciation}\end{array}\right)$$

$$= \frac{\text{Operating}}{\text{cash flow}} - \frac{\text{Gross investment}}{\text{in operating capital}} \qquad (2\text{-}11)$$

$$= \frac{\text{Operating}}{\text{cash flow}} - \frac{\text{Gross investment}}{\begin{array}{c}\text{in long-term}\\ \text{operating assets}\end{array}} - \frac{\text{Investment}}{\text{in NOWC}}$$

For MicroDrive, this definition produces FCF of $-\$174.7$, the same value as found earlier:

$$FCF = (\$170.3 + \$100) - \$445$$
$$= -\$174.7 \text{ million}$$

Equations 2-8 and 2-11 are equivalent because depreciation is added to both NOPAT and net investment in Equation 2-8 to arrive at Equation 2-11. We usually use Equation 2-8, because it saves us this step, but you should be aware of this alternative approach.

The Uses of FCF

Recall that free cash flow (FCF) is the amount of cash that is available for distribution to all investors, including both shareholders and debtholders. There are five good uses for FCF:

1. Pay interest to debtholders, keeping in mind that the net cost to the company is the after-tax interest expense.
2. Repay debtholders, that is, pay off some of the debt.
3. Pay dividends to shareholders.
4. Repurchase stock from shareholders.
5. Buy short-term investments or other nonoperating assets.

Recall that the company does not have to use FCF to acquire operating assets since, by definition, FCF already takes into account the purchase of all operating assets needed to support growth. Unfortunately, there is evidence that some companies with high FCF tend to make unnecessary investments that don't add value, such as paying too much to acquire some other company. Thus, high FCF can cause waste if managers fail to act in the best interest of shareholders. As discussed in Chapter 1, this is called an agency cost, since managers are hired as agents to act on behalf of shareholders. We discuss agency costs and ways to control them in Chapter 22, where we discuss value-based management and corporate governance, and in Chapter 12, where we discuss the choice of capital structure.

In practice, most companies combine these five uses in such a way that the net total is equal to FCF. For example, a company might pay interest and dividends, issue new debt, and also sell some of its marketable securities. Some of these activities are cash outflows (e.g., paying interest and dividends) and some are cash inflows (e.g., issuing debt and selling marketable securities), but the net cash flow from these five activities is equal to FCF.

FCF and Corporate Value

FCF is the amount of cash available for distribution to investors, and, as a result, the value of a company depends on the present value of its expected future FCFs, discounted at the company's weighted average cost of capital (WACC). Subsequent chapters will develop the tools needed to forecast FCFs and evaluate their risk. Chapter 22 ties all this together with a model that is used to calculate the value of a company. Even though you do not yet have all the tools to apply the model, it's important that you understand this basic concept: *FCF is the cash available for distribution to investors. Therefore, the value of a firm primarily depends on its expected future FCFs.*

Evaluating FCF, NOPAT, and Operating Capital

Even though MicroDrive had a positive NOPAT, its very high investment in operating assets resulted in a negative free cash flow. Because free cash flow is what is available for distribution to investors, not only was there nothing for investors, but also investors actually had to provide *additional* money to keep the business going. Investors provided most of this new money as debt.

Is a negative free cash flow always bad? The answer is, "Not necessarily; it depends on why the free cash flow was negative." If FCF was negative because NOPAT was negative, that is a bad sign, because then the company is probably experiencing operating problems. However, many high-growth companies have positive NOPAT but negative free cash flow because they are making large investments in operating assets to support growth. There is nothing wrong with profitable growth, even if it causes negative cash flows.

One way to determine whether growth is profitable is by examining the **return on invested capital (ROIC),** which is the ratio of NOPAT to total operating capital. If the ROIC exceeds the rate of return required by investors, then a negative free cash flow caused by high growth is nothing to worry about. Chapter 22 discusses this in detail.

To calculate the ROIC, we first calculate NOPAT and operating capital. The return on invested capital (ROIC) is a performance measure that indicates how much NOPAT is generated by each dollar of operating capital:

$$ROIC = \frac{NOPAT}{Operating\ capital} \tag{2-12}$$

If ROIC is greater than the rate of return investors require, which is the weighted average cost of capital (WACC), then the firm is adding value.

As noted earlier, a negative current FCF is not necessarily bad, provided it is due to high growth. For example, Under Armour's sales grew by 38% in 2011 and its NOPAT grew by 42%; however, it made large capital investments to support that growth and ended the year with a FCF of *negative* $148 million. At some point Under Armour's growth will slow and will not require large capital investments. If Under Armour maintains a high ROIC, then its FCF will become positive and very large as growth slows.

MicroDrive had an ROIC in 2016 of 9.46% ($170.3/$1,800 = 0.0946). Is this enough to cover its cost of capital? We'll answer that question in the next section.

CONCEPT REVIEW

1. What is net operating working capital? Why does it exclude most short-term investments and also notes payable?
2. What is total net operating capital? Why is it important for managers to calculate a company's capital requirements?
3. Why is NOPAT a better performance measure than net income?
4. What is free cash flow? Why is it important?
5. A firm's total net operating capital for the previous year was $2 million. For the current year, its total net operating capital is $2.5 million and its NOPAT is $1.2 million. What is its free cash flow for the current year? (Check Figure: $700,000)

2.8 MVA and EVA

Neither traditional accounting data nor the modified data discussed in the preceding section incorporates stock prices, even though the primary goal of management is to maximize the firm's stock price. Financial analysts have therefore developed two additional performance measures, MVA, or Market Value Added, and EVA, or Economic Value Added. These concepts are discussed in this section.[10]

Market Value Added (MVA)

The primary goal of most firms is to maximize shareholders' wealth. This goal obviously benefits shareholders, but it also helps ensure that scarce resources are allocated efficiently, which benefits the economy. Shareholder wealth is maximized by maximizing the *difference* between the market value of the firm's stock and the amount of equity capital that was supplied by shareholders. This difference is called the **Market Value Added (MVA):**

$$
\begin{aligned}
MVA &= Market\ value\ of\ stock - Equity\ capital\ supplied\ by\ shareholders \\
&= (Shares\ outstanding)(Stock\ price) - Total\ common\ equity
\end{aligned} \tag{2-13}
$$

To illustrate, consider Imperial Oil. In December 2013, its total market equity value was $39.9 billion, while its balance sheet showed that shareholders had put up only $19.5 billion. Thus, Imperial Oil's MVA was $39.9 − $19.5 = $20.4 billion. This $20.4 billion represents

---

[10]The concepts of EVA and MVA were developed by Joel Stern and Bennett Stewart, co-founders of the consulting firm Stern Stewart & Company. Stern Stewart copyrighted the terms "EVA" and "MVA," so other consulting firms have given other names to these values. Still, EVA and MVA are the terms most commonly used in practice.

the difference between the money that Imperial Oil's shareholders have invested in the corporation since its founding—including retained earnings—versus the cash they could get if they sold the business. The higher the MVA, the better the job management is doing for the firm's shareholders.

Sometimes MVA is defined as the total market value of the company minus the total amount of investor-supplied capital:

$$
\begin{aligned}
\text{MVA} &= \text{Total market value} - \text{Total investor supplied capital} \\
&= (\text{Market value of stock} + \text{Market value of debt}) \\
&\quad - \text{Total investor supplied capital}
\end{aligned} \tag{2-13a}
$$

For most companies, the total amount of investor-supplied capital is the sum of equity, debt, and preferred stock. We can calculate the total amount of investor-supplied capital directly from the reported values of these in the financial statements. The total market value of a company is the sum of the market values of common equity, debt, and preferred stock. It is easy to find the market value of equity, since stock prices are readily available, but it is not always easy to find the market value of debt. Hence, many analysts use the value of debt that is reported in the financial statements, the debt's book value, as an estimate of its market value.

Economic Value Added (EVA)

Whereas MVA measures the effects of managerial actions since the very inception of a company, **Economic Value Added (EVA)** focuses on managerial effectiveness in a given year. The basic EVA formula is as follows:

$$
\begin{aligned}
\text{EVA} &= \text{Net operating profit after taxes}\,(\text{NOPAT}) \\
&\quad - \text{After-tax dollar cost of capital used to support operations} \\
&= \text{EBIT}(1 - \text{Tax rate}) - (\text{Total net operating capital})(\text{WACC})
\end{aligned} \tag{2-14}
$$

We can also calculate EVA in terms of ROIC:

$$
\text{EVA} = (\text{Operating capital})(\text{ROIC} - \text{WACC}) \tag{2-15}
$$

As this equation shows, a firm adds value—that is, has a positive EVA—if its ROIC is greater than its WACC. If WACC exceeds ROIC, then new investments in operating capital will reduce the firm's value.

EVA is an estimate of a business's true economic profit for the year, and it differs sharply from accounting profit.[11] EVA represents the residual income that remains after the cost of *all* capital, including equity capital, has been deducted, whereas accounting profit is determined without imposing a charge for equity capital. As we discuss in Chapter 9, equity capital has a cost, because funds provided by shareholders could have been invested elsewhere, where they would have earned a return. Shareholders give up the opportunity to invest elsewhere when they provide capital to the firm. The return they could earn elsewhere in investments of equal risk represents the cost of equity capital. This cost is an *opportunity cost* rather than an *accounting cost*, but it is quite real nevertheless.

Note that when calculating EVA we do not add back depreciation. Although it is not a cash expense, depreciation is a cost since worn-out assets must be replaced, and it is therefore deducted when determining both net income and EVA. Our calculation of EVA assumes that the true economic depreciation of the company's fixed assets exactly equals the depreciation used for accounting and tax purposes. If this were not the case, adjustments would have to be made to obtain a more accurate measure of EVA.

---

[11]The most important reason EVA differs from accounting profit is that the cost of equity capital is deducted when EVA is calculated. Other factors that could lead to differences include adjustments that might be made to depreciation, to research and development costs, inventory valuations, and so on. These other adjustments also can affect the calculation of investor-supplied capital, which affects both EVA and MVA. See Stewart, *The Quest for Value*, cited in Footnote 8.

See *Ch 02 Tool Kit.xlsx* for all details.

EVA measures the extent to which the firm has increased shareholder value. Therefore, if managers focus on EVA, this will help ensure that they operate in a manner that is consistent with maximizing shareholder wealth. Note too that EVA can be determined for divisions as well as for the company as a whole, so it provides a useful basis for determining managerial performance at all levels. Consequently, EVA is being used by an increasing number of firms as the primary basis for determining managerial compensation.

Table 2-5 shows how MicroDrive's MVA and EVA are calculated. The stock price was $23 per share at year-end 2016, down from $26 per share the previous year. Its WACC, which is the percentage after-tax cost of capital, was 10.8% in 2015 and 11.0% in 2016, and its tax rate was 40%. Other data in Table 2-5 were given in the basic financial statements provided earlier in the chapter.

Note first that the lower stock price and the higher book value of equity (due to retaining earnings during 2016) combined to reduce the MVA. The 2016 MVA is still positive, but $460 − $254 = $206 million of shareholders' value was lost during the year.

EVA for 2015 was just barely positive, and in 2016 it was negative. Operating income (NOPAT) rose, but EVA still declined, primarily because the amount of capital rose more sharply than NOPAT—by about 26% versus 8%—and the cost of this additional capital pulled EVA down.

Recall also that net income fell, but not nearly so dramatically as the decline in EVA. Net income does not reflect the amount of equity capital employed, but EVA does. Because of this omission, net income is not as useful as EVA for setting corporate goals and measuring managerial performance.

Intrinsic Value, MVA, and EVA We will have more to say about both MVA and EVA later in the book, but we can close this section with two observations. First, there is a relationship between MVA and EVA, but it is not a direct one. If a company has a history of negative EVAs, then its

TABLE 2-5   MVA and EVA for MicroDrive Inc. (Millions of Dollars)

	2016	2015
MVA Calculation		
Price per share	$ 23.0	$ 26.0
Number of shares (millions)	50.0	50.0
Market value of common equity = Share price × (Number of shares)	$1,150.0	$1,300.0
Book value of common equity	896.0	840.0
MVA = Market value − Book value	$ 254.0	$ 460.0
EVA Calculation		
EBIT	$ 283.8	$ 263.0
Tax rate	40%	40%
NOPAT = EBIT(1 − T)	$ 170.3	$ 157.8
Total investor-supplied operating capital[a]	$1,800.0	$1,455.0
Weighted average cost of capital, WACC (%)	11.0%	10.8%
Dollar cost of capital = Operating capital (WACC)	$ 198.0	$ 157.1
EVA = NOPAT − Dollar cost of capital	$ (27.7)	$ 0.7
ROIC = NOPAT/Operating capital	9.46%	10.85%
ROIC − Cost of capital = ROIC − WACC	(1.54%)	0.05%
EVA = (Operating capital)(ROIC − WACC)	$ (27.7)	$ 0.7

[a]Investor-supplied operating capital equals the sum of notes payable, long-term debt, preferred stock, and common equity, less short-term investments. It could also be calculated as total liabilities and equity minus accounts payable, accruals, and short-term investments. It is also equal to total net operating capital.

Multilateral Instrument 52–109 and Financial Fraud

Investors need to be cautious when they review financial statements. While companies are required to follow IFRS (or GAAP in the United States), managers still have quite a lot of discretion in deciding how and when to report certain transactions. Consequently, two firms in exactly the same operating situation may report financial statements that convey different impressions about their financial strength. Some variations may stem from legitimate differences of opinion about the correct way to record transactions. In other cases, managers may choose to report numbers in a way that helps them present either higher earnings or more stable earnings over time. As long as they follow IFRS (or GAAP in the United States), such actions are not illegal, but these differences make it harder for investors to compare companies and gauge their true performances.

Unfortunately, there have also been cases where managers overstepped the bounds and reported fraudulent statements. Indeed, a number of high-profile executives have faced criminal charges because of their misleading accounting practices. For example, in June 2002, it was discovered that WorldCom (now called MCI) had committed the most massive accounting fraud of all time by recording over $7 billion of ordinary operating costs as capital expenditures, thus overstating net income by the same amount.

WorldCom's published financial statements fooled most investors—investors bid the stock price up to $64.50, and banks and other lenders provided the company with more than $30 billion of loans. Arthur Andersen, the firm's auditor, was faulted for not detecting the fraud. WorldCom's CFO and CEO were convicted and Arthur Andersen went bankrupt. But that didn't help the investors who relied on the published financial statements.

In response to these and other abuses, the U.S. Congress passed the Sarbanes-Oxley Act of 2002. Canadian regulators subsequently introduced a number of similar regulations. Multilateral Instrument (MI) 52–109 requires Canadian CEOs and CFOs to certify that their annual and quarterly reports "fairly present in all material respects the financial condition, results of operations and cash flows of the issuer." Whether this will prevent future financial fraud remains to be seen.

MVA will probably be negative, and vice versa if it has a history of positive EVAs. However, the stock price, which is the key ingredient in the MVA calculation, depends more on expected future performance than on historical performance. Therefore, a company with a history of negative EVAs could have a positive MVA, provided investors expect a turnaround in the future.

The second observation is that when EVAs or MVAs are used to evaluate managerial performance as part of an incentive compensation program, EVA is the measure that is typically used. The reasons are (1) EVA shows the value added during a given year, whereas MVA reflects performance over the company's entire life, perhaps even including times before the current managers were born, and (2) EVA can be applied to individual divisions or other units of a large corporation, whereas MVA must be applied to the entire corporation.

CONCEPT REVIEW

1. A Company's NOPAT is $12 million and its total net operating capital is $100 million. What is its ROIC? (Check Figure: 12%)
2. Define "Market Value Added (MVA)" and "Economic Value Added (EVA)."
3. How does EVA differ from accounting profit?
4. A firm has $100 million in total net operating capital. Its return on invested capital is 14% and its weighted average cost of capital is 10%. What is its EVA? (Check Figure: $4,000,000)

2.9 Taxes

The value of any financial asset (including stocks, bonds, and mortgages), as well as most real assets such as plants or even entire firms, depends on the stream of cash flows produced by the asset. Cash flows from an asset consist of *usable* income plus depreciation, and usable income means income *after taxes*. Because taxes can be a significant cost, they play a critical role in many financial decisions. Tax laws that are administered by the Canada Revenue Agency (CRA) can be changed by the federal government, and in recent years changes have occurred frequently. Thus by the time you read this, tax rates and other factors will almost certainly be different from those we provide. Still, if you understand this section, you will understand the basics of our tax system.

Corporate Income Taxes

Tax rates placed on corporations vary based on their size, location, and type of income being earned. Both the federal and provincial governments tax companies. Table 2-6 shows the 2014 tax rates for small Canadian-controlled private corporations (CCPCs) and all other Canadian corporations. The various tax rates partly reflect governments encouraging the establishment of certain types of businesses (e.g., manufacturing and small businesses). Taxes are calculated on earnings before taxes (EBT) from a company's income statement.

Interest and Dividends Paid by a Corporation A firm's operations can be financed with either debt or equity capital. If it uses debt, it must pay interest on this debt, whereas if it uses equity, it is expected to pay dividends to the equity investors (shareholders). The interest *paid* by a corporation is deducted from its operating income to obtain its taxable income, but dividends paid are not deductible. Therefore, a firm needs $1 of pre-tax income to pay $1 of interest, but if it is in the 26.5% federal-plus-Ontario tax bracket, it must earn $1.36 of pre-tax income to pay $1 of dividends:

$$\text{Pre-tax income needed to pay \$1 of dividends} = \frac{\$1}{1 - \text{Tax rate}} = \frac{\$1}{0.735} = \$1.36$$

Working backward, if a company has $1.36 in pre-tax income, it must pay $0.36 in taxes $(0.265)(\$1.36) = \$0.36$. This leaves it with after-tax income of $1.00.

Of course, it is generally not possible to finance exclusively with debt capital, and the risk of doing so would offset the benefits of the higher expected income. *Still, the fact that interest is a deductible expense has a profound impact on the way businesses are financed—our*

TABLE 2-6 2014 Combined Federal and Provincial Corporate Tax Rates

Province	Active Business Income for a Corporation	Small Business Income up to $425,000 earned by a CCPC
British Columbia	26.0%	13.5%
Alberta	25.0	14.0
Saskatchewan	27.0	13.0
Manitoba	27.0	11.0
Ontario	26.5	15.5
Quebec	26.9	19.0
New Brunswick	27.0	15.5
Nova Scotia[a]	31.0	14.0
Prince Edward Island	31.0	15.5
Newfoundland	29.0	15.0

[a]Nova Scotia's small business threshold is $350,000.

corporate tax system favours debt financing over equity financing. This point is discussed in more detail in Chapters 9 and 12.

Interest and Dividend Income Received by a Corporation Interest income received by a corporation is taxed at its regular corporate tax rate, whereas such income earned by a CCPC is taxed at a higher rate than the CCPC's regular tax rate. If a Canadian company earns dividend income on common stock from another Canadian corporation, those earnings face no taxation.

Depreciation for Tax Purposes For the purposes of calculating taxes, a company is allowed to deduct from earnings a portion of its capital assets that it holds. This depreciation of capital assets for tax purposes in Canada is called **capital cost allowance (CCA)**. While the concepts of depreciation and CCA are the same, their respective calculations differ. Under accounting rules, assets are typically depreciated straight-line. However, the Canada Revenue Agency provides a different and very specific set of rules on how much CCA can be claimed for the purposes of calculating taxes. Assets are typically grouped into asset classes, and each asset class is assigned a CCA rate (percentage). It is that rate of the undepreciated asset value that companies use to calculate the CCA deduction they may claim every year. Since CCA specifies a rate (in most cases), it is a declining balance method for depreciating assets. CCA is a noncash expense, yet it affects the amount of taxes a company pays, and therefore it impacts cash flow. We will look at how to calculate CCA in Chapter 11, along with how it affects a company's cash flows.

Corporate Loss Carryback and Carryforward Ordinary corporate operating losses can be carried back (*carryback*) to each of the preceding 3 years and forward (*carryforward*) for the next 20 years and used to offset taxable income in those years. For example, an operating loss in 2016 could be carried back and used to reduce taxable income in 2013, 2014, and 2015, and forward, if necessary, and used in 2017, 2018, and so on, to the year 2036. After carrying back 3 years, any remaining loss is typically carried forward first to the next year, then to the one after that, and so on, until losses have been used up or the 20-year carryforward limit has been reached.

To illustrate, suppose Apex Corporation had $2 million of pre-tax profits (taxable income) in 2013–2015, and then, in 2016, Apex lost $12 million. Also, assume that Apex's federal-plus-provincial tax rate is 30%. As shown in Table 2-7, the company would use the carryback feature to recompute its taxes for 2013, using $2 million of the 2016 operating losses to reduce the 2013 pre-tax profit to zero. This would permit it to recover the taxes paid in 2013. Therefore, in 2016 Apex would receive a refund of its 2013 taxes because of the loss experienced in 2016. Because $10 million of the unrecovered losses would still be available, Apex would repeat this procedure for 2014 and 2015. Thus, in 2016 the company would pay zero taxes for 2016 and also would receive a refund for taxes paid in 2013, 2014,

See *Ch 02 Tool Kit.xlsx* for all details.

TABLE 2-7 Apex Corporation: Calculation of $12 Million Loss Carryback and Amount Available for Carryforward

	Past Year 2013	Past Year 2014	Past Year 2015	Current Year 2016
Original taxable income	$2,000,000	$2,000,000	$2,000,000	−$12,000,000
Carryback credit	2,000,000	2,000,000	2,000,000	
Adjusted profit	0	0	0	
Taxes previously paid (30%)	600,000	600,000	600,000	
Difference = Tax refund due	$ 600,000	$ 600,000	$ 600,000	
Total tax refund received				$ 1,800,000
Amount of loss carryforward available				
Current loss				−$12,000,000
Carryback losses used				6,000,000
Carryforward losses still available				−$ 6,000,000

and 2015. Apex would still have $6 million of unrecovered losses to carry forward, subject to the 20-year limit. This $6 million could be used to offset future taxable income. The purpose of this loss treatment is to avoid penalizing corporations whose incomes fluctuate substantially from year to year.

Personal Taxes

Individuals pay taxes on wages and salaries, on investment income (dividends, interest, and profits from the sale of securities), and on the profits of proprietorships and partnerships. Income tax must be paid at the federal *and* provincial level. Canadian tax rates are progressive—that is, the higher one's income, the larger the percentage paid in taxes. Tables 2-8 and 2-9 provide the 2014 federal and provincial tax rates and brackets for individuals.

Taxable Income Taxable income is defined as gross income less allowable expenses and deductions that are spelled out in the instructions to the tax forms that individuals must file. Each taxpayer receives a personal tax credit, along with other tax credits such as for charitable donations, caring for a dependent, and so on. All of these reduce taxes. Also, certain expenses such as retirement savings, tuition fees, and union dues are tax deductible, which lowers taxable income.

Let's say Luke, a resident of British Columbia, has taxable income in 2014 of $82,000. In 2015, when Luke prepares his 2014 tax return, he will calculate his total income tax as follows:

Federal Tax Calculation	
$43,953 × 0.15 =$	$6,593
$(82,000 − 43,953) × 0.22 =$	8,370
Total federal tax due	$14,963
B.C. Tax Calculation	
$37,606 × 0.0506 =$	$1,903
$(75,213 − 37,606) × 0.077 =$	2,896
$(82,000 − 75,213) × 0.105 =$	713
Total B.C. tax due	5,512
Total tax due	$20,475

Luke's **marginal tax rate** is 32.5% (federal rate of 22% + provincial rate of 10.5%). For every extra dollar he earns, Luke will pay taxes of 32.5%. However, his **average tax rate** of 25.0% is somewhat lower ($20,475/$82,000 = 0.250). This is the tax rate that Luke pays on all his taxable income.

Taxes on Capital Gains and Dividend and Interest Income Assets such as stocks, bonds, and real estate are defined as capital assets. If you own a capital asset and its price goes up, then your wealth increases, but you are not liable for any taxes on your increased wealth until

TABLE 2-8   2014 Federal Personal Tax Rates

Tax Rates	Tax Brackets
15%	On the first $43,953
22	43,954–87,907
26	87,908–136,270
29	Over 136,270

Source: Canada Revenue Agency, http://www.cra-arc.gc.ca, accessed June 17, 2014.

TABLE 2-9 2014 Provincial Personal Tax Rates[a,c]

Tax Rates	Tax Brackets ($)	Tax Rates	Tax Brackets ($)
British Columbia		**Alberta**	
5.06%	On the first 37,606	10%	All income
7.7	On the next 37,607		
10.5	On the next 11,141		
12.29	On the next 18,504		
14.7	On the next 45,142		
16.8	Over 150,000		
Saskatchewan		**Manitoba**	
11%	On the first 43,292	10.8%	On the first 31,000
13	On the next 80,400	12.75	On the next 36,000
15	Over 123,692	17.4	Over 67,000
Ontario		**Québec[b]**	
5.05%	On the first 40,120	16%	On the first 41,495
9.15	On the next 40,122	20	On the next 41,490
11.16	On the next 433,848	24	On the next 17,985
13.16	Over 514,090	25.75	Over 100,970
New Brunswick		**Nova Scotia**	
9.68%	On the first 39,305	8.79%	On the first 29,590
14.82	On the next 39,304	14.95	On the next 29,590
16.52	On the next 49,193	16.67	On the next 33,820
17.84	Over 127,802	17.5	On the next 57,000
		21	Over 150,000
Prince Edward Island		**Newfoundland and Labrador**	
9.8%	On the first 31,984	7.7%	On the first 34,254
13.8	On the next 31,985	12.5	On the next 34,254
16.7	Over 63,969	13.3	Over 68,508

[a]Source: Canada Revenue Agency, http://www.cra-arc.gc.ca, accessed June 17, 2014.
[b]Source: Revenu Quebec, http://www.revenuquebec.ca, accessed June 17, 2014.
[c]Rates do not include any additional taxes (surtaxes) provinces may have in place.

you sell the asset. If you sell the asset for more than you originally paid, the profit is called a **capital gain**; if you sell it for less, then you suffer a **capital loss**. Capital gains are taxed at one-half the rate of ordinary income. A capital gain on the sale of your principal residence is not subject to any capital gains tax in Canada.

Interest income received by individuals is normally taxed at the same rate as regular income. Because corporations pay dividends out of earnings that have already been taxed, taxing dividends again in the hands of individuals would result in double taxation. In the interest of fairness, the government introduced a dividend tax credit to offset the potential for double taxation of dividends paid by Canadian corporations. The dividend tax credit calculation is somewhat convoluted, consisting of a gross-up of the actual dividend, calculating tax on the grossed-up dividend, and then taking a tax credit on the grossed-up amount. Using our previous example, let's see how much money Luke gets to keep after tax if he receives a capital gain, interest, and dividend income, each of $1,000. We see from Table 2-10 that Luke gets to keep more after-tax dividend income than interest or capital gains income.

TABLE 2-10   Taxation on Capital Gains, Interest, and Dividends

	Capital Gains	Interest Income	Dividend Income
Investment Income	$1,000	$1,000	$1,000
Taxes	163[a]	325[b]	103[c]
After-tax Investment Income	$ 837	$ 675	$ 897

[a]½($1,000) × 0.325 = $163
[b]$1,000 × 0.325 = $325
[c]Dividend tax credit calculation:
   Gross up dividend by 38%, ($1,000 × 0.38) + $1,000 = $1,380
   Tax on grossed-up dividend, $1,380 × 0.325 = $448
   Less Federal and B.C. tax credits, $1,380 × (0.150198 + 0.10) = $345
   Net tax on dividends, $448 − $345 = $103

CONCEPT REVIEW

1. Explain what is meant by this statement: "Our tax rates are progressive."
2. Explain the difference between marginal tax rates and average tax rates.
3. What are capital gains and losses, and how are they taxed?
4. What is the difference in the tax treatment of interest and dividends paid by a corporation? Does this factor favour debt or equity financing?
5. Briefly explain how tax loss carryback and carryforward procedures work.

Summary

The primary purposes of this chapter were (1) to describe the basic financial statements, (2) to present some background information on cash flows, and (3) to provide an overview of the federal income tax system. The key concepts covered are listed below.

- The four basic statements contained in the **annual report** are the balance sheet, the income statement, the statement of retained earnings, and the statement of cash flows.
- The **balance sheet** shows assets on the left-hand side and liabilities and equity, or claims against assets, on the right-hand side. (Sometimes assets are shown at the top and claims at the bottom of the balance sheet.) The balance sheet may be thought of as a snapshot of the firm's financial position at a particular point in time.
- The **income statement** reports the results of operations over a period of time, and it shows earnings per share as its "bottom line."
- The **statement of changes in equity** shows the change in equity between balance sheet dates. Retained earnings represent a claim against assets, not assets *per se*.
- The **statement of cash flows** reports the effect of operating, investing, and financing activities on cash flows over an accounting period.
- **Net cash flow** differs from **accounting profit** because some of the revenues and expenses reflected in accounting profits may not have been received or paid out in cash during the year. Depreciation is typically the largest noncash item, so net cash flow is often expressed as net income plus depreciation.
- **Operating current assets** are the current assets that are used to support operations, such as cash, inventory, and accounts receivable. They do not include short-term investments.
- **Operating current liabilities** are the current liabilities that occur as a natural consequence of operations, such as accounts payable and accruals. They do not include notes payable or any other short-term debts that charge interest.
- **Net operating working capital** is the difference between operating current assets and operating current liabilities. Thus, it is the working capital acquired with investor-supplied funds.

- **Operating long-term assets** are the long-term assets used to support operations, such as net plant and equipment. They do not include any long-term investments that pay interest or dividends.
- **Total net operating capital** (which means the same as **operating capital** and **net operating assets**) is the sum of net operating working capital and operating long-term assets. It is the total amount of capital needed to run the business.
- **NOPAT** is net operating profit after taxes. It is the after-tax profit a company would have if it had no debt and no investments in nonoperating assets. Because it excludes the effects of financial decisions, it is a better measure of operating performance than is net income.
- **Free cash flow (FCF)** is the amount of cash flow remaining after a company makes the asset investments necessary to support operations. In other words, FCF is the amount of cash flow available for distribution to investors, *so the value of a company is directly related to its ability to generate free cash flow.* FCF is defined as NOPAT minus the net investment in operating capital.
- **Market Value Added (MVA)** represents the difference between the total market value of a firm and the total amount of investor-supplied capital. If the market values of debt and preferred stock equal their values as reported on the financial statements, then MVA is the difference between the market value of a firm's stock and the amount of equity its shareholders have supplied.
- **Economic Value Added (EVA)** is the difference between after-tax operating profit and the total dollar cost of capital, including the cost of equity capital. EVA is an estimate of the value created by management during the year, and it differs substantially from accounting profit because no charge for the use of equity capital is reflected in accounting profit.
- Interest income received by a corporation is taxed as ordinary income; however, common stock dividends received by one Canadian corporation from another are excluded from **taxable income.**
- Because interest paid by a corporation is a **deductible expense** while dividends are not, our tax system favours debt over equity financing.
- Ordinary corporate operating losses can be **carried back** to each of the preceding 3 years and **forward** for the next 20 years and used to offset taxable income in those years.
- In Canada, tax rates are **progressive**—the higher one's income, the larger the percentage paid in taxes.
- Assets such as stocks, bonds, and real estate are defined as **capital assets.** If a capital asset is sold for more than its cost, the profit is called a **capital gain.** If the asset is sold for a loss, it is called a **capital loss.**
- A dividend tax credit can be used to reduce the taxes that individuals have to pay on eligible dividends from Canadian corporations. This dividend tax credit partly offsets the double taxation effect that would otherwise occur.

Questions

2-1 Define each of the following terms:
  a. Annual report; balance sheet; income statement
  b. Common shareholders' equity, or net worth; retained earnings
  c. Statement of retained earnings; statement of cash flows
  d. Depreciation; amortization; EBITDA
  e. Operating current assets; operating current liabilities; net operating working capital; total net operating capital
  f. Accounting profit; net cash flow; NOPAT; free cash flow
  g. Market Value Added; Economic Value Added
  h. Progressive tax; taxable income; marginal and average tax rates
  i. Capital gain or loss; tax loss carryback and carryforward

2-2 What four statements are contained in most annual reports?

2-3 If a "typical" firm reports $20 million of retained earnings on its balance sheet, can the firm definitely pay a $20 million cash dividend?

2-4 What is operating capital, and why is it important?

2-5 Explain the difference between NOPAT and net income. Which is a better measure of the performance of a company's operations?

2-6 What is free cash flow? Why is it the most important measure of cash flow?

2-7 If you were starting a business, what tax considerations might cause you to prefer to set it up as a proprietorship or a partnership rather than as a corporation?

Concept Review Problem

Full solutions are provided at www.nelson.com/brigham3ce.

CR-1
Net Income, Cash Flow, and EVA

Last year Custom Furniture had $6,500,000 in operating income (EBIT). The company had a net depreciation expense of $1,000,000 and an interest expense of $1,000,000; its corporate tax rate was 30%. The company has $14,000,000 in operating current assets and $4,000,000 in operating current liabilities; it has $15,000,000 in net plant and equipment. It estimates that it has an after-tax cost of capital of 10%. Assume that Custom Furniture's only noncash item was depreciation.

a. What was the company's net income for the year?
b. What was the company's net cash flow?
c. What was the company's net operating profit after taxes (NOPAT)?
d. Calculate net operating working capital and total net operating capital for the current year.
e. If total net operating capital in the previous year was $24,000,000, what was the company's free cash flow (FCF) for the year?
f. What was the company's Economic Value Added (EVA)?

Problems

Answers to odd-numbered problems appear in Appendix A.

Note: By the time this book is published, Parliament may have changed rates and/or other provisions of current tax law—as noted in the chapter, such changes occur fairly often. Work all problems on the assumption that the information in the chapter is applicable.

Easy
Problems 1–6

2-1
Personal After-Tax Yield

An investor recently purchased a corporate bond which yields 5%. The investor is in the 30% tax bracket. What is the bond's after-tax yield?

2-2
Income Statement

Little Books Inc. recently reported $3.5 million of net income. Its EBIT was $7 million, and its tax rate was 30%. What was its interest expense?

2-3
Income Statement

Pearson Brothers recently reported an EBITDA of $7.5 million and net income of $1.6 million. It had $2.0 million of interest expense, and its corporate tax rate was 30%. What was its charge for depreciation and amortization?

2-4
Net Cash Flow

Kendall Corners Inc. recently reported net income of $3.1 million and depreciation of $250,000. What was its net cash flow? Assume it had no amortization expense.

2-5
Statement of Retained Earnings

In its most recent financial statements, Newhouse Inc. reported $50 million of net income and $810 million of retained earnings. The previous retained earnings were $780 million. How much in dividends was paid to shareholders during the year?

2-6
Cash Flow Statement

Based on the following information, what are Ever Green's cash flows from operations? The company reported profits of $18,000 and claimed amortization of $4,000, while accounts receivable increased by $4,000, inventories decreased by $8,000, and accounts payable increased by $4,000.

Intermediate
Problems 7–11

2-7
Personal After-Tax Return

Karen, a resident of Nova Scotia, has $10,000 to invest for one year. She has found two alternatives: a bond that will provide interest income at year-end of $400, and a common stock whose price is $50 and is expected to increase by $2.00. Ignoring risk and other factors, how much money will Karen have after taxes from each investment? Use Tables 2-8 and 2-9, and assume that Karen has taxable income of $65,000.

2-8
Cash Flows
Companies X and Y are very similar. Both have sales of $5,000,000, and COGS are 65% of sales. Both companies have operating expense of $700,000 and are taxed at 26%. However, X and Y will be claiming $60,000 and $120,000 each respectively in depreciation expense. Calculate each company's net cash flow, and explain specifically the difference in the cash flows.

2-9
Cash Flows
The Moore Corporation has operating income (EBIT) of $750,000. The company's depreciation expense is $200,000. Moore is 100% equity financed, and it faces a 40% tax rate. What is the company's net income? What is its net cash flow?

2-10
Income and Cash Flow Analysis
The Berndt Corporation expects to have sales of $20 million. Costs other than depreciation are expected to be 75% of sales, and depreciation is expected to be $2.5 million. All sales revenues will be collected in cash, and costs other than depreciation must be paid for during the year. Berndt's tax rate is 30%. Berndt has no debt.
a. Set up an income statement. What is Berndt's expected net cash flow?
b. Suppose that Berndt's depreciation expenses doubled. No changes in operations occurred. What would happen to reported profit and to net cash flow?
c. Now suppose that Berndt's depreciation was reduced by 50%. How would profit and net cash flow be affected?
d. If this were your company, would you prefer your depreciation expense to be doubled or halved? Why?

2-11
Free Cash Flow
Financial information on Marine Tech Corporation is presented below. During the year, Marine Tech made a net investment in operating capital of $30 million. If the company's share price is $22, it has 10 million shares outstanding, and its tax rate is 30%, does Marine Tech have sufficient free cash flow to repurchase 10% of its shares?

Marine Tech Corporation Income Statement	($ M)
Sales	$320
Operating costs	220
Depreciation	20
EBIT	80
Interest expense	10
Earnings before tax	70
Tax (30%)	21
Earnings after tax	$ 49

Challenging Problems 12–17

2-12
Free Cash Flow
Using Rhodes Corporation's financial statements (shown below), answer the following questions.
a. What is the net operating profit after taxes (NOPAT) for 2015?
b. What are the amounts of net operating working capital for both years?
c. What are the amounts of total net operating capital for both years?
d. What is the free cash flow for 2015?
e. What is the ROIC for 2015?
f. How much of the FCF did Rhodes use for each of the following purposes: after-tax interest, net debt repayments, dividends, net stock repurchases, and net purchases of short-term investments? (*Hint:* Remember that a net use can be negative.)

Rhodes Corporation: Income Statements for Year Ending December 31 (Millions of Dollars)

	2015	2014
Sales	$11,000	$10,000
Operating costs excluding depreciation	9,360	8,500
Depreciation and amortization	380	360
Earnings before interest and taxes	1,260	1,140
Less interest	120	100
Pre-tax income	1,140	1,040
Taxes (40%)	456	416
Net income available to common shareholders	$ 684	$ 624
Common dividends	$ 220	$ 200

Rhodes Corporation: Balance Sheets as of December 31 (Millions of Dollars)

	2015	2014
Assets		
Cash	$ 550	$ 500
Short-term investments	110	100
Accounts receivable	2,750	2,500
Inventories	1,650	1,500
Total current assets	5,060	4,600
Net plant and equipment	3,850	3,500
Total assets	$ 8,910	$ 8,100
Liabilities and Equity		
Accounts payable	$ 1,100	$ 1,000
Accruals	550	500
Notes payable	384	200
Total current liabilities	2,034	1,700
Long-term debt	1,100	1,000
Total liabilities	3,134	2,700
Common stock (120 million shares)	4,312	4,400
Retained earnings	1,464	1,000
Total common equity	5,776	5,400
Total liabilities and equity	$ 8,910	$ 8,100
Price per share	$ 60	$ 55
WACC	12%	12%

2-13 Using the information from 2-12, calculate the:

MVA and EVA a. Market Value Added in 2015 for Rhodes Corporation.

b. Economic Value Added in 2015.

2-14 Using the information from 2-12, prepare the cash flow statement for Rhodes Corporation.

Cash Flow Statement

2-15 The Bookbinder Company has made $150,000 before taxes during each of the past
Loss Carryback and 15 years, and it expects to make $150,000 a year before taxes in the future. However, in
Carryforward 2015 the firm incurred a loss of $650,000. The firm will claim a loss carryback at the time
it files its 2015 income tax return, and it will receive a cheque from the CRA. Show how
it calculates this loss carryback, and then indicate the firm's tax liability for each of the
next 5 years. Assume a 40% tax rate on *all* income to ease the calculations.

2-16 Financial information on Bristle Brush-Off Corp. is shown below. Calculate the following
Free Cash Flow EVA, MVA for 2016:

a. Free cash flow

b. ROIC

c. EVA and MVA

Bristle Brush-Off Corporation: Income Statements for Years Ended December 31 ($000s)

	2016	2015
Sales	$7,950	$7,000
Cost of goods sold	5,100	4,600
Other expenses	350	500
Depreciation	750	600
Earnings before interest and taxes	1,750	1,300
Interest	654	500
Earnings before taxes	1,096	800
Taxes (25%)	274	200
Net Income	$ 822	$ 600

Bristle Brush-Off Corporation: Balance Sheets as at December 31 ($000s)

	2016	2015
Assets		
Cash	$ 40	$ 60
Short-term investments	0	380
Accounts receivable	2,140	1,950
Prepaid expenses	40	40
Inventory	2,760	2,400
Total current assets	4,980	4,830
Gross plant property & equipment	7,750	6,350
Less: Accumulated depreciation	3,430	2,680
Net plant property & equipment	$4,320	$3,670
Total assets	$9,300	$8,500
Liabilities and Equity		
Accounts payable	$2,890	$2,580
Notes payable	903	1,050
Accruals	85	70
Total current liabilities	3,878	3,700
Long-term debt	500	500
Common stock (400,000 shares)	3,200	3,200
Retained earnings	1,722	1,100
Total equity	4,922	4,300
Total liabilities and equity	$9,300	$8,500
Stock price	$ 20	$18.70
WACC	13%	13%

2-17 Using the information from 22-16, create a cash flow statement for 2016.

Cash Flow Statement

Spreadsheet Problems

2-18

Build a Model:
Financial Statements,
EVA, and MVA;

Start with the partial model in the file *Ch 02 Build a Model.xlsx* at the textbook's website. Cumberland Industries' most recent balance sheets (in thousands of dollars) are shown below and in the partial model in the file:

	2015	2014
Cash	$ 91,450	$ 74,625
Short-term investments	11,400	15,100
Accounts receivable	103,365	85,527
Inventories	38,444	34,982
Total current assets	244,659	210,234
Net fixed assets	67,165	42,436
Total assets	$311,824	$252,670
Accounts payable	$ 30,761	$ 23,109
Accruals	30,477	22,656
Notes payable	16,717	14,217
Total current liabilities	77,955	59,982
Long-term debt	76,264	63,914
Total liabilities	154,219	123,896
Common stock	100,000	90,000
Retained earnings	57,605	38,774
Total common equity	157,605	128,774
Total liabilities and equity	$311,824	$252,670

a. The company's sales for 2015 were $455,150,000, and EBITDA was 15% of sales. Furthermore, depreciation amounted to 11% of net fixed assets, interest charges were $8,575,000, the corporate tax rate was 40%, and Cumberland pays 40% of its net income out in dividends. Given this information, construct Cumberland's 2015 income statement. (*Hint:* Start with the partial model in the file.)

b. Next, construct the firm's statement of shareholders equity for the year ended December 31, 2015, and the 2015 statement of cash flows.

c. Calculate net operating working capital, total net operating capital, net operating profit after taxes, and free cash flow for 2015.

d. Calculate the firm's EVA and MVA for 2015. Assume that Cumberland had 10 million shares outstanding, that the 2015 closing stock price was $17.25 per share, and that its after-tax cost of capital (WACC) was 12%.

e. What will be the retained earnings for year 2015 if the tax rate is 30% and the pay out ratio is 35%? Make necessary changes in the balance sheet.

2-19

Build a Model: Free
Cash Flows, EVA,
and MVA

Begin with the partial model in the file *Ch02 Build a Model.xlsx* on the textbook's website.

a. Using the financial statements shown below for Lan & Chen Technologies, calculate net operating working capital, total net operating capital, net operating profit after taxes, free cash flow, and return on invested capital for 2016. (*Hint:* Start with the partial model in the file and report all dollar figures in thousands to reduce clutter.)

b. Assume there were 15 million shares outstanding at the end of 2016, the year-end closing stock price was $65 per share, and the after-tax cost of capital was 8%. Calculate EVA and MVA for 2016.

Lan & Chen Technologies: Income Statements for Year Ended December 31 (Thousands of Dollars)

	2016	2015
Sales	$945,000	$900,000
Expenses excluding depreciation and amortization	812,700	774,000
EBITDA	132,300	126,000
Depreciation and amortization	33,100	31,500
EBIT	99,200	94,500
Interest expense	10,470	8,600
Pre-tax earnings	$ 88,730	$ 85,900
Taxes (40%)	35,492	34,360
Net income	$ 53,238	$ 51,540
Common dividends	$ 43,300	$ 41,230
Addition to retained earnings	$ 9,938	$ 10,310

Lan & Chen Technologies: December 31 Balance Sheets

	2016	2015
Assets		
Cash and cash equivalents	$ 47,250	$ 45,000
Short-term investments	3,800	3,600
Accounts receivable	283,500	270,000
Inventories	141,750	135,000
Total current assets	$476,300	$453,600
Net fixed assets	330,750	315,000
Total assets	$807,050	$768,600
Liabilities and Equity		
Accounts payable	$ 94,500	$ 90,000
Accruals	47,250	45,000
Notes payable	26,262	9,000
Total current liabilities	$168,012	$144,000
Long-term debt	94,500	90,000
Total liabilities	$262,512	$234,000
Common stock	444,600	444,600
Retained earnings	99,938	90,000
Total common equity	$544,538	$534,600
Total liabilities and equity	$807,050	$768,600

MINI CASE

Jenny Cochran a graduate of the University of Ottawa with 4 years of banking experience, was recently brought in as assistant to the chairman of the board of Computron Industries, a manufacturer of computer components.

The company doubled its plant capacity, opened new sales offices outside its home territory, and launched an expensive advertising campaign. Computron's results were not satisfactory, to put it mildly. Its board of directors, which consisted of its president and vice president plus its major shareholders (who were all local businesspeople), was most upset when directors learned how the expansion was going. Suppliers were being paid late and were unhappy, and the bank was complaining about the deteriorating situation and threatening to cut off credit. As a result, Al Watkins, Computron's president, was informed that changes would have to be made, and quickly, or he would be fired. Also, at the board's insistence, Jenny Cochran was brought in and given the job of assistant to Gary Meissner, a retired banker who was Computron's chairman and largest shareholder. Meissner agreed to give up a few of his golfing days and to help nurse the company back to health, with Cochran's help.

Cochran began by gathering financial statements and other data. Note: these are available in the file *Ch02 Tool kit.xlsx.*

Balance Sheets	2015	2014
Assets		
Cash	$ 7,282	$ 9,000
Short-term investments	20,000	48,600
Accounts receivable	632,160	351,200
Inventories	1,287,360	715,200
Total current assets	1,946,802	1,124,000
Gross fixed assets	1,202,950	491,000
Less: Accumulated depreciation	263,160	146,200
Net fixed assets	939,790	344,800
Total assets	$2,886,592	$1,468,800
Liabilities and Equity		
Accounts payable	$ 324,000	$ 145,600
Notes payable	720,000	200,000
Accruals	284,960	136,000
Total current liabilities	1,328,960	481,600
Long-term debt	1,000,000	323,432
Common stock (100,000 shares)	460,000	460,000
Retained earnings	97,632	203,768
Total equity	557,632	663,768
Total liabilities and equity	$2,886,592	$1,468,800

Income Statements	2015	2014
Sales	$5,834,400	$3,432,000
Cost of goods sold	4,980,000	2,864,000
Other expenses	720,000	340,000
Depreciation	116,960	18,900
Total operating costs	5,816,960	3,222,900
EBIT	17,440	209,100
Interest expense	176,000	62,500
EBT	(158,560)	146,600
Taxes (40%)	(63,424)	58,640
Net income (loss)	$ (95,136)	$ 87,960

Other Data		
Stock price	$ 6.00	$ 8.50
Shares outstanding	100,000	100,000
EPS	$ (0.95)	$ 0.88
DPS	$ 0.11	$ 0.22
Tax rate	40%	40%

Statement of Cash Flows, 2015

Operating Activities

Loss	$ (95,136)
Adjustments:	
Noncash adjustments:	
Depreciation	116,960
Changes in working capital:	
Increase in accounts receivable	(280,960)
Increase in inventories	(572,160)
Increase in accounts payable	178,400
Increase in accruals	148,960
Net cash used by operating activities	(503,936)

Investing Activities

Cash used to acquire fixed assets	(711,950)
Proceeds from sale of short-term investments	28,600
Net cash used by investing activities	(683,350)

Financing Activities

Issue of notes payable	520,000
Issue of long-term debt	676,568
Payment of cash dividends	(11,000)
Net cash provided by financing activities	1,185,568

Summary

Decrease in cash	(1,718)
Cash at beginning of year	9,000
Cash at end of year	$ 7,282

Assume that you are Cochran's assistant and that you must help her answer the following questions for Meissner.

a. What effect did the expansion have on sales and net income? What effect did the expansion have on the asset side of the balance sheet? What effect did it have on liabilities and equity?

b. What do you conclude from the statement of cash flows?

c. What is free cash flow? Why is it important? What are the five uses of FCF?

d. What is Computron's net operating profit (NOPAT)? What are operating current assets? What are operating current liabilities? How much net operating working capital and total net operating capital does Computron have?

e. What is Computron's free cash flow (FCF)? What are Computron's "net uses" of its FCF?

f. Calculate Computron's return on invested capital. Computron has a 10% cost of capital (WACC). Do you think Computron's growth added value?

g. Cochran also has asked you to estimate Computron's EVA. She estimates that the after-tax cost of capital was 10% in both years.

h. What happened to Computron's Market Value Added (MVA)?

i. Given that Computron could have issued preferred shares yielding 6% net of costs, why did the company decide to borrow more from the bank at a rate of 7.5%?

chapter 3

Analysis of Financial Statements

WestJet Airlines announced its first-quarter 2014 results of $0.69 earnings per share (EPS). According to Businessweek.com, WestJet's EPS came in a little higher than analysts' estimates of $0.63. Perhaps not surprisingly, WestJet's stock return during a 2-day period after its announcement date was positive. The company had a return of 3%, much greater than the TSX/S&P Composite Index's negative 0.5% return. While WestJet does not offer earnings guidance, it does forecast overall capacity growth and certain other key variables such as future fuel costs and capital expenditures.

Should a company provide earnings guidance estimates to investors? Virtually no one disputes that investors need as much information as possible in order to accurately evaluate a company, and academic studies show that companies with greater transparency have higher valuations. However, greater disclosure often brings the possibility of lawsuits if investors have reason to believe that the disclosure was fraudulent. Regulators in Canada have introduced rules relating to (a) requirements for timely disclosure, (b) disclosure best practices, and (c) rules about disclosing information to select groups (such as analysts). Canadian companies have since then improved their corporate communications. More firms are providing earnings guidance, mainly through conference calls or media interviews. Firms are also providing additional information as a result of strengthened regulations and the need for greater transparency.

Two trends are now in evidence. First, the number of companies reporting *quarterly* earnings forecasts is falling but the number reporting *annual* forecasts is increasing. Second, many companies are providing other types of forward-looking information, including key operating ratios, as well as qualitative information about the company and its industry. Ratio analysis can help investors use such information, so keep that in mind as you read this chapter.

Sources: Businessweek.com, accessed June 19, 2014; CICA, "Corporate Reporting to Stakeholders," discussion draft, December 2007, http://www.cica.ca; Aline Girard and Paul-Émile Roy, "Canada's Corporate Reporting Getting Better Every Year," *CA Magazine*, January–February 2008, 18–19; Joseph McCafferty, "Guidance Lite," *CFO*, June 2006, 16–17.

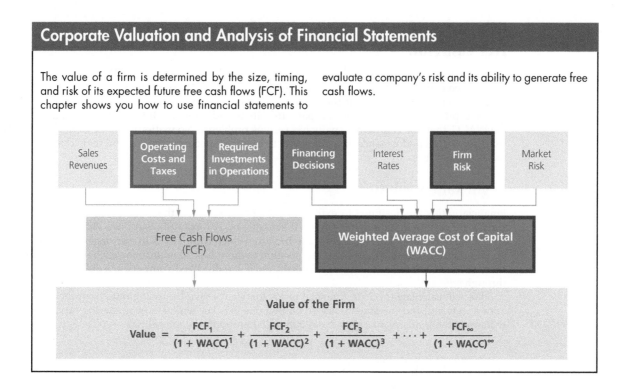

Corporate Valuation and Analysis of Financial Statements

The value of a firm is determined by the size, timing, and risk of its expected future free cash flows (FCF). This chapter shows you how to use financial statements to evaluate a company's risk and its ability to generate free cash flows.

| Sales Revenues | Operating Costs and Taxes | Required Investments in Operations | Financing Decisions | Interest Rates | Firm Risk | Market Risk |

Free Cash Flows (FCF)

Weighted Average Cost of Capital (WACC)

Value of the Firm

$$\text{Value} = \frac{\text{FCF}_1}{(1 + \text{WACC})^1} + \frac{\text{FCF}_2}{(1 + \text{WACC})^2} + \frac{\text{FCF}_3}{(1 + \text{WACC})^3} + \cdots + \frac{\text{FCF}_\infty}{(1 + \text{WACC})^\infty}$$

Financial statement analysis involves (1) comparing a firm's performance with that of other firms in the same industry, and (2) evaluating trends in the firm's financial position over time. Managers use financial analysis to identify situations needing attention, potential lenders use financial analysis to determine whether a company is creditworthy, and shareholders use financial analysis to help predict future earnings, dividends, and free cash flow. This chapter will explain the similarities and differences among these uses.

The textbook's website contains an *Excel* file that will guide you through the chapter's calculations. The file for this chapter is *Ch 03 Tool Kit.xlsx,* and we encourage you to open the file and follow along as you read the chapter. **www.nelson.com/ brigham3ce**

3-1 Financial Analysis

When we perform a financial analysis, we conduct the following steps.

Gather Data

The first step in financial analysis is to gather data. As discussed in Chapter 2, financial statements can be downloaded from many different websites. One of our favourites is Zacks Investment Research, which provides financial statements in a standardized format. If you cut and paste financial statements from Zacks into a spreadsheet and then perform a financial analysis, you can quickly repeat the analysis on a different company by pasting that company's financial statements into the same cells of the spreadsheet. In other words, you do not need to reinvent the wheel each time you analyze a company. While Zacks provides financial data for Canadian companies listed on U.S. markets, Businessweek.com provides information on other publicly traded Canadian companies.

Examine the Statement of Cash Flows

Some financial analysis can be done with virtually no calculations. For example, we always look to the statement of cash flows first, particularly the net cash provided by operating activities. Downward trends or negative net cash flow from operations almost always indicate problems. The statement of cash flows section on investing activities shows whether the company has made a big acquisition, especially when compared with the prior years' net cash flows from investing activities. A quick look at the section on financing activities also reveals whether a company is issuing debt or buying back stock; in other words, is the company raising capital from investors or returning it to them?

Calculate and Examine the Return on Invested Capital and Free Cash Flow

After examining the statement of cash flows, we calculate the free cash flow (FCF) and return on invested capital (ROIC) as described in Chapter 2. The ROIC provides a vital measure of a firm's overall performance. If the ROIC is greater than the company's weighted average cost of capital (WACC), then the company usually is adding value. If the ROIC is less than the WACC, then the company usually has serious problems. No matter what the ROIC tells us about overall performance, it is important to examine specific activities, and to do that we use financial ratios.

Begin Ratio Analysis

Financial ratios are designed to extract important information that might not be obvious simply from examining a firm's financial statements. For example, suppose Firm A owes $5 million in debt while Firm B owes $50 million. Which company is in a stronger financial position? It is impossible to answer this question without first standardizing each firm's debt relative to total assets, earnings, and interest. Such standardized comparisons are provided through *ratio analysis*.

We will calculate the 2016 financial ratios for MicroDrive Inc. using data from the balance sheets and income statements given in Table 3-1. We will also evaluate the ratios in relation to the industry averages. Note that dollar amounts are in millions.

3.2 Liquidity Ratios

See *Ch 03 Tool Kit.xlsx* for details.

A *liquid asset* is one that trades in an active market and hence can be quickly converted to cash at the going market price, and a firm's "liquidity ratios" deal with this question: Will the firm be able to pay off its debts as they come due over the next year or so? As shown in Table 3-1, MicroDrive has current liabilities of $310 million that must be paid off within the coming year. Will it have trouble satisfying those obligations? A full liquidity analysis requires the use of cash budgets, but by relating the amount of cash and other current assets to current obligations, ratio analysis provides a quick, easy-to-use measure of liquidity. Two commonly used **liquidity ratios** are discussed in this section.

Ability to Meet Short-Term Obligations: The Current Ratio

The **current ratio** is calculated by dividing current assets by current liabilities:

$$\text{Current ratio} = \frac{\text{Current assets}}{\text{Current liabilities}}$$

$$= \frac{\$1,000}{\$310} = 3.2 \text{ times}$$

$$\text{Industry average} = 4.2 \text{ times}$$

Current assets normally include cash, marketable securities, accounts receivable, and inventories. Current liabilities consist of accounts payable, short-term notes payable, current maturities of long-term debt, accrued taxes, and other accrued expenses (principally wages).

MicroDrive has a lower current ratio than the average for its industry. Is this good or bad? Sometimes the answer depends on who is asking the question. For example, suppose a supplier is trying to decide whether to extend credit to MicroDrive. In general, creditors like to see a high current ratio. If a company is getting into financial difficulty, it will begin paying its bills (accounts payable) more slowly, borrowing from its bank, and so on, so its current liabilities will be increasing. If current liabilities are rising faster than current assets, the current ratio will fall, and this could spell trouble. Because the current ratio provides the best single indicator of the extent to which the claims of short-term creditors are covered by assets that are expected to be converted to cash fairly quickly, it is the most commonly used measure of short-term solvency.

Now consider the current ratio from the perspective of a shareholder. A high current ratio could mean that the company has a lot of money tied up in nonproductive assets, such

TABLE 3-1	MicroDrive Inc.: Balance Sheets and Income Statements for Years Ended December 31 (Millions of Dollars, Except for Per-Share Data)

Assets	2016	2015	Liabilities and Equity	2016	2015
Cash and equivalents	$ 10	$ 15	Accounts payable	$ 60	$ 30
Short-term investments	–	65	Notes payable	110	60
Accounts receivable	375	315	Accruals	140	130
Inventories	615	415	Total current liabilities	310	220
Total current assets	1,000	810	Long-term bonds[a]	754	580
Net plant and equipment	1,000	870	Total liabilities	1,064	800
			Preferred stock		
			(400,000 shares)	40	40
			Common stock		
			(50,000,000 shares)	130	130
			Retained earnings	766	710
			Total common equity	896	840
			Total equity	936	880
Total assets	$2,000	$1,680	Total liabilities and equity	$ 2,000	$ 1,680

	2016	2015
Net sales	$3,000.0	$2,850.0
Costs of goods sold except depreciation[b]	2,100.0	2,000.0
Depreciation and amortization	100.0	90.0
Other operating expenses	516.2	497.0
Earnings before interest and taxes (EBIT, or operating income)	283.8	263.0
Less interest	88.0	60.0
Earnings before taxes (EBT)	195.8	203.0
Taxes (40%)	78.3	81.2
Net income	117.5	121.8
Preferred share dividends	4.0	4.0
Net income available to common shareholders	$ 113.5	$ 117.8

Additional Information

	2016	2015
Common share dividends	$ 57.5	$ 53.0
Addition to retained earnings	$ 56.0	$ 64.8
Lease payments	$ 28.0	$ 28.0
Bonds' required sinking fund payments	$ 20.0	$ 20.0
Common stock price	$ 23.00	$ 26.00

[a]The bonds have a sinking fund requirement of $20 million a year.
[b]The costs include lease payments of $28 million a year.

as excess cash or marketable securities. Or perhaps the high current ratio is due to large inventory holdings, which might well become obsolete before they can be sold. Thus, shareholders might not want a high current ratio.

An industry average is not a magic number that all firms should strive to maintain—in fact, some very well-managed firms will be above the average while other good firms will be below it. However, if a firm's ratios are far removed from the averages for its industry, this is a red flag, and analysts should be concerned about why the variance occurs. For example, suppose a low current ratio is traced to low inventories. Is this a competitive advantage resulting from the firm's mastery of just-in-time inventory management, or an Achilles' heel that is causing the firm to miss shipments and lose sales? Ratio analysis doesn't answer such questions, but it does point to areas of potential concern.

Quick, or Acid Test, Ratio

The **quick, or acid test, ratio** is calculated by deducting inventories from current assets and then dividing the remainder by current liabilities:

$$\text{Quick, or acid test, ratio} = \frac{\text{Current assets} - \text{Inventories}}{\text{Current liabilities}}$$

$$= \frac{\$385}{\$310} = 1.2 \text{ times}$$

$$\text{Industry average} = 2.1 \text{ times}$$

Inventories are typically the least liquid of a firm's current assets; hence they are the current assets on which losses are most likely to occur in a bankruptcy. Therefore, a measure of the firm's ability to pay off short-term obligations without relying on the sale of inventories is important.

The industry average quick ratio is 2.1, so MicroDrive's 1.2 ratio is low in comparison with other firms in its industry. Still, if the accounts receivable can be collected, the company can pay off its current liabilities without having to liquidate its inventory.

CONCEPT REVIEW

1. Identify two ratios that are used to analyze a firm's liquidity position, and write out their equations.
2. What are the characteristics of a liquid asset? Give some examples.
3. Which current asset is typically the least liquid?
4. A company has current liabilities of $800 million, and its current ratio is 2.5. What is its level of current assets? (Check Figure: $2,000 million) If this firm's quick ratio is 2, how much inventory does it have? (Check Figure: $400 million)

3.3 Asset Management Ratios

The second group of ratios, the **asset management ratios**, measures how effectively the firm is managing its assets. These ratios are designed to answer this question: Does the total amount of each type of asset as reported on the balance sheet seem reasonable, too high, or too low in view of current and projected sales levels? If a company has excessive investments in assets, then its operating assets and capital will be unduly high, which will reduce its free cash flow and its stock price. On the other hand, if a company does not have enough assets, it will lose sales, which will hurt profitability, free cash flow, and the stock price. Therefore, it is important to have the *right* amount invested in assets. Ratios that analyze the different types of assets are described in this section.

Evaluating Inventories: The Inventory Turnover Ratio

The inventory turnover ratio is defined as costs of goods sold (COGS) divided by inventories.[1] The income statement in Table 3-1 separately reports depreciation and the portion of costs of goods sold that does not comprise of depreciation, which is helpful when calculating cash flows.

---

[1] In previous editions, we defined the inventory turnover ratio using sales instead of COGS because some providers of financial ratio statistics, such as Dun & Bradsreet, use the ratio of sales to inventories. However, most sources now report the turnover ratio using COGS, so we have changed our definition to conform to the majority of reporting organizations.

However, we need the total COGS for calculating the inventory turnover ratio. For Micro-Drive, virtually all depreciation is associated with producing its products, so its COGS is:

$$COGS = \text{Costs of goods sold except depreciation} + \text{Depreciation}$$

$$= \$2,100 + \$100 = \$2,200 \text{ million}$$

We can now calculate the inventory turnover:

$$\text{Inventory turnover ratio} = \frac{COGS}{\text{Inventories}}$$

$$= \frac{\$2,200}{\$615} = 3.6 \text{ times}$$

$$\text{Industry average} = 8.0 \text{ times}$$

As a rough approximation, each item of MicroDrive's inventory is sold out and restocked, or "turned over," 3.6 times per year. MicroDrive's turnover of 3.6 times is much lower than the industry average of 8 times. This suggests that MicroDrive is holding too much inventory. Excess inventory is, of course, unproductive, and it represents an investment with a low or zero rate of return. MicroDrive's low inventory turnover ratio also makes us question the current ratio. With such a low turnover, we must wonder whether the firm is actually holding obsolete goods not worth their stated value.

Note that COGS over the entire year, whereas the inventory figure is for one point in time. For this reason, it is better to use an average inventory measure.[2] If the firm's business is highly seasonal, or if there has been a strong upward or downward sales trend during the

FINANCE: IN FOCUS

The Global Economic Crisis

The Price is Right! (Or Wrong!)

How much is an asset worth if no one is buying or selling? The answer to that question matters because an accounting practice called "mark to market" requires that some assets be adjusted on the balance sheet to reflect their "fair market value." The accounting rules are complicated, but the general idea is that if an asset is available for sale, then the balance sheet would be most accurate if it showed the asset's market value. For example, suppose a company purchased $100 million of bonds and the value of those bonds later fell to $90 million. With mark to market, the company would report the bonds' value on the balance sheet as $90 million, not the original purchase price of $100 million. Notice that marking to market can have a significant impact on financial ratios and thus on investors' perceptions of a firm's financial health.

But what if the assets are mortgage-backed securities that were originally purchased for $100 million? As defaults increased during 2008, the value of such securities fell rapidly, and then investors virtually stopped trading them. How should the company report them? At the $100 million original price, at a $60 million price that was observed before the market largely dried up, at $25 million when a hedge fund in desperate need for cash to avoid a costly default sold a few of these securities, or at $0, since there are no current quotes? Or should they be reported at a price generated by a computer model or in some other manner?

The answer to this question has vital implications for many financial institutions. If the price is too low, it could cause investors mistakenly to believe that some companies are worth much less than their intrinsic values, and this could trigger runs on banks and bankruptcies for companies that might otherwise survive. But if the price is too high, some "walking dead" or "zombie" companies could linger on and later cause even larger losses for investors. Either way, an error in pricing could perhaps trigger a domino effect that might topple the entire financial system. So let's hope the price is right!

---

[2]Preferably, the average inventory value should be calculated by summing the monthly figures during the year and dividing by 12. If monthly data are not available, one can add the beginning and ending annual figures and divide by 2. However, most industry ratios are calculated as above, using end-of-year values.

year, it is especially useful to make some such adjustment. To maintain comparability with industry averages, however, we did not use the average inventory figure.

Evaluating Receivables: The Days Sales Outstanding

Days sales outstanding (DSO), also called the "average collection period" (ACP), is used to appraise accounts receivable, and it is calculated by dividing accounts receivable by average daily sales to find the number of days' sales that are tied up in receivables.[3] Thus, the DSO represents the average length of time that the firm must wait after making a sale before receiving cash, which is the average collection period. MicroDrive has 46 days sales outstanding, well above the 36-day industry average:

$$\text{DSO} = \text{Days sales outstanding} = \frac{\text{Receivables}}{\text{Average sales per day}} = \frac{\text{Receivables}}{\text{Annual sales}/365}$$

$$= \frac{\$375}{\$3,000/365} = \frac{\$375}{\$8.2192} = 45.6 \text{ days} \approx 46 \text{ days}$$

$$\text{Industry average} = 36 \text{ days}$$

The DSO can also be evaluated by comparison with the terms on which the firm sells its goods. For example, MicroDrive's sales terms call for payment within 30 days. The fact that 46 days of sales are outstanding indicates that customers, on the average, are not paying their bills on time. This deprives MicroDrive of funds that it could use to invest in productive assets. Moreover, in some instances the fact that a customer is paying late may signal that the customer is in financial trouble, in which case MicroDrive may have a hard time ever collecting the receivable. Therefore, if the trend in DSO over the past few years has been rising, but the credit policy has not been changed, this would be strong evidence that steps should be taken to expedite the collection of accounts receivable.

Evaluating Payables: The Average Payables Period

Average payables period (APP) evaluates how quickly the firm pays off its suppliers and is calculated by dividing accounts payable by average daily operating cost to find the number of days' costs that have not yet been paid. Average daily cost of goods sold can also be used in the denominator. The APP is the average length of time that the firm takes to pay suppliers. MicroDrive has an 8-day average payables period, about the same as the 9-day industry average:

$$\text{APP} = \text{Average payables period}$$

$$= \frac{\text{Payables}}{\text{Average operating cost per day}} = \frac{\text{Payables}}{\text{Annual operating cost}/365}$$

$$\text{or} \qquad\qquad\qquad \text{or}$$

$$\text{Average COGS per day} \qquad \text{Annual COGS}/365$$

$$= \frac{\$60}{\dfrac{\$2,616.2}{365}} = \frac{\$60}{\$7.1677} = 8.4 \text{ days} \approx 8 \text{ days}$$

$$\text{Industry average} = 9 \text{ days}$$

The APP can also be used by comparing it to the credit terms granted by the firm's suppliers. For instance, that suppliers have offered MicroDrive credit terms of 10 days, and that Micro-Drive pays on average in 8 days suggests that its cash flow is sufficient to pay bills on time. If MicroDrive had an APP significantly longer than the credit term provided, it would be at risk of losing those credit terms and having to buy on cash terms only (i.e., cash on delivery, or COD). For a company with cash flow troubles, losing credit terms will make managing cash flows even more difficult. On the other hand, if the APP is significantly lower than the credit terms offered, questions could be raised as to whether the company is taking full advantage of the credit period available (i.e., of the supplier-provided free financing period).

---

[3]It would be better to use *average* receivables, but we used year-end values for comparability with the industry average.

Evaluating Fixed Assets: The Fixed Assets Turnover Ratio

The **fixed assets turnover ratio** measures how effectively the firm uses its plant and equipment. It is the ratio of sales to net fixed assets:

$$\text{Fixed assets turnover ratio} = \frac{\text{Sales}}{\text{Net fixed assets}}$$

$$= \frac{\$3,000}{\$1,000} = 3.0 \text{ times}$$

$$\text{Industry average} = 3.0 \text{ times}$$

MicroDrive's ratio of 3.0 times is equal to the industry average, indicating that the firm is using its fixed assets about as intensively as are other firms in its industry. Therefore, MicroDrive seems to have about the right amount of fixed assets in relation to other firms.

A potential problem can arise when interpreting the fixed asset turnover ratio. Inflation has caused the value of many assets that were purchased in the past to be seriously understated. Under our accounting rules, companies can show plant, property, and equipment (PPE) at their historical cost (book value) *or* at their fair value. Thus, if we were to compare Company A, which chose to show PPE at net book value, with Company B, which showed PPE at fair value, we would probably find that Company A has a higher fixed asset turnover ratio. But this would be more reflective of the differences in accounting policies each company used, rather than of any inefficiency of Company B.

Evaluating Total Assets: The Total Assets Turnover Ratio

The final asset management ratio, the **total assets turnover ratio,** measures the turnover of all the firm's assets; it is calculated by dividing sales by total assets:

$$\text{Total assets turnover ratio} = \frac{\text{Sales}}{\text{Total assets}}$$

$$= \frac{\$3,000}{\$2,000} = 1.5 \text{ times}$$

$$\text{Industry average} = 1.8 \text{ times}$$

MicroDrive's ratio is somewhat below the industry average, indicating that the company is not generating a sufficient volume of business given its total asset investment. Sales should be increased, some assets should be sold, or a combination of these steps should be taken.

CONCEPT REVIEW

1. Identify five ratios that are used to measure how effectively a firm is managing its assets, and suppliers and write out their equations.
2. How might rapid growth distort the inventory turnover ratio?
3. What potential problem might arise when comparing different firms' fixed assets turnover ratios?
4. A firm has annual sales of $200 million, $180 million of cost of goods sold, $40 million of inventory, and $60 million of accounts receivable. What is its inventory turnover ratio? (Check Figure: 5) What is its DSO based on a 365-day year? (Check Figures: 4.5x; 109.5 days)

3.4 Debt Management Ratios

The extent to which a firm uses debt financing, or **financial leverage,** has three important implications: (1) By raising funds through debt, shareholders can maintain control of a firm without increasing their investment. (2) If the firm earns more on investments financed with borrowed funds than it pays in interest, then its shareholders' returns are magnified, or "leveraged," but their risks are also magnified. (3) Creditors look to the equity, or owner-supplied funds, to provide a margin of safety, so the higher the proportion of funding supplied by shareholders, the less risk creditors face. Chapter 12 explains the first two points in detail, while the following ratios examine leverage from a creditor's point of view.

How the Firm is Financed: Debt-to-Assets Ratio

MicroDrive's two primary types of debt are notes payable and long-term bonds, but more complicated companies also might report the portion of long-term debt due within a year, the value of capitalized leases, and other types of obligations that charge interest. For Micro-Drive, total debt is:

$$\text{Total debt} = \text{Notes payable} + \text{Long-term bonds}$$

$$= \$110 + \$754 = \$864 \text{ million}$$

Is this too much debt, not enough, or the right amount? To answer this question, we begin by calculating the percentage of MicroDrive's assets that are financed by debt. The ratio of total debt to total assets is called the *debt-to-assets* ratio or more simply, the **debt ratio**.[4] Total debt is the sum of all short-term debt and long-term debt. It does not include other liabilities. MicroDrive's debt ratio is:

$$\text{Debt ratio} = \frac{\text{Total debt}}{\text{Total assets}}$$

$$= \frac{\$864}{\$2,000} = 43.2 \%$$

$$\text{Industry average} = 30\%$$

Creditors prefer low debt ratios because the lower the ratio, the greater the cushion against creditors' losses in the event of liquidation. Shareholders, on the other hand, may want more leverage because it magnifies expected earnings, as we explain in Section 3.8 when we discuss the DuPont model.

MicroDrive's debt ratio is 43.2%, which is substantially higher than the 30% industry average. The fact that MicroDrive's debt ratio exceeds the industry average raises a red flag and may make it costly for MicroDrive to borrow additional funds without first raising more equity capital. Creditors may be reluctant to lend the firm more money, and management would probably be subjecting the firm to the risk of bankruptcy if it increased the debt ratio by borrowing additional funds.

If you use a debt ratio that you did not calculate yourself, be sure to find out how the ratio was defined. Some sources provide the ratio of long-term debt to total assets, and some provide the ratio of debt to equity, so be sure to check the source's definition.

The **debt-to-equity (D/E) ratio**[5] is another commonly used debt measure. It is simply a transformation of the debt-to-asset ratio:

$$\text{Debt-to-equity ratio} = \frac{\text{Total debt}}{\text{Total common equity}}$$

$$= \frac{\$864}{\$936} = 0.92$$

$$\text{Industry average} = 0.43$$

Ability to Pay Interest: Times-Interest-Earned

The *times-interest-earned (TIE)* ratio, also called the *interest coverage ratio*, is determined by dividing earnings before interest and taxes (EBIT in Table 3-1) by the interest expense:

$$\text{Times-interest-earned (TIE) ratio} = \frac{\text{EBIT}}{\text{Interest charges}}$$

$$= \frac{\$283.8}{\$88} = 3.2 \text{ times}$$

$$\text{Industry average} = 6 \text{ times}$$

---

[4]In previous editions we defined the debt ratio as total liabilities divided by total assets. For better comparability with Web-based reporting sources, we have changed our definition to total debt divided by total assets. As the debt ratio can be calculated differently, each time you use an externally reported debt ratio it is important to check how it has been calculated.
[5]In previous editions we defined the debt-to-equity ratio as total liabilities divided by total equity. For better comparability with Web-based reporting sources, we have changed our definition to total debt divided by total common equity. As the D/E ratio can be calculated differently, each time you use an externally reported D/E ratio it is important to check how it has been calculated.

The TIE ratio measures the extent to which operating income can decline before the firm is unable to meet its annual interest costs. Failure to meet this obligation can bring legal action by the firm's creditors, possibly resulting in bankruptcy. Note that earnings before interest and taxes, rather than net income, is used in the numerator. Because interest is paid with pre-tax dollars, the firm's ability to pay current interest is not affected by taxes.

MicroDrive's interest is covered 3.2 times. Since the industry average is 6 times, Micro-Drive is covering its interest charges by a relatively low margin of safety. Thus, the TIE ratio reinforces the conclusion from our analysis of the debt ratio that MicroDrive would face difficulties if it attempted to borrow additional funds.

Ability to Service Debt: EBITDA Coverage Ratio

The TIE ratio is useful for assessing a company's ability to meet interest charges on its debt, but this ratio has two shortcomings: (1) Interest is not the only fixed financial charge—companies must also reduce debt on schedule, and many firms lease assets and thus must make lease payments. If they fail to repay debt or meet lease payments, they can be forced into bankruptcy. (2) EBIT does not represent all the cash flow available to service debt, especially if a firm has high depreciation and/or amortization charges. To account for these deficiencies, bankers and others have developed the **EBITDA coverage ratio,** defined as follows:[6]

$$\text{EBITDA coverage ratio} = \frac{\text{EBITDA} + \text{Lease payments}}{\text{Interest} + \text{Principal payments} + \text{Lease payments}}$$

$$= \frac{\$383.8 + \$28}{\$88 + \$20 + \$28} = \frac{\$411.8}{\$136} = 3.0 \text{ times}$$

$$\text{Industry average} = 4.3 \text{ times}$$

MicroDrive had \$383.8 million of earnings before interest, taxes, depreciation, and amortization (EBITDA). Also, lease payments of \$28 million were deducted while calculating EBITDA.

FINANCE: IN FOCUS

International Accounting Differences Create Headaches for Companies

Manulife Financial Corp. reported a \$1.28 billion loss for the third quarter of 2011, down from an eye-popping \$2.4 billion loss for all of 2010. Yet if Toronto-based Manulife's headquarters were in the United States, the loss would have turned into a profit of \$2.2 billion, the company's largest. According to Manulife, the discrepancy relates primarily to Canada's new accounting rules, which rely on mark-to-market valuations. Under Canadian rules, assets are carried on the balance sheet at their market value, whereas under the U.S. system the focus is on book value, the purchase price.

In periods of market volatility, the Canadian rules cause asset values to move up or down very quickly, which in turn affects the level of earnings and ultimately the amount of capital the insurance companies report. In the wake of the financial crisis, regulators around the world are looking more closely at financial company capital ratios. If they aren't high enough, companies may be forced to cut dividends or enter the market to raise more capital. In extreme cases, they can be shut down.

Canada has adopted IFRS, which is now used in more than 100 countries. Unfortunately, the United States is not one of those 100. The above example shows the negative effect of not having standardized accounting rules. When will the United States move to IFRS and level the playing field? The U.S. SEC estimates that it will cost \$32 million for a large company to switch over to IFRS. American investors and analysts favour its adoption; however, given the current political environment in the United States, few are betting the U.S. will be converting anytime soon.

Source: Adapted from John Greenwood, "Should Lifecos Just Leave?" *Financial Post*, November 9, 2011.

---

[6]Different analysts define the EBITDA coverage ratio in different ways. For example, some would omit the lease payment information, and others would "gross up" principal payments by dividing them by (1 − T) because these payments are not tax deductions, and hence must be made with after-tax cash flows. We included lease payments because, for many firms, they are quite important, and failing to make them can lead to bankruptcy just as surely as can failure to make payments on "regular" debt. We did not gross up principal payments because, if a company is in financial difficulty, its tax rate will probably be zero; so the gross up is not necessary whenever the ratio is really important.

That $28 million was available to meet financial charges; hence it must be added back, bringing the total available to cover fixed financial charges to $411.8 million. Fixed financial charges consisted of $88 million of interest, $20 million of sinking fund payments, and $28 million for lease payments, for a total of $136 million.[7] Therefore, MicroDrive covered its fixed financial charges by 3.0 times. However, if EBITDA declines, the coverage will fall, and EBITDA certainly can decline. Moreover, MicroDrive's ratio is well below the industry average so, again, the company seems to have a relatively high level of debt.

The EBITDA coverage ratio is most useful for relatively short-term lenders such as banks, which rarely make loans (except real estate–backed loans) for longer than about 5 years. Over a relatively short period, depreciation-generated funds can be used to service debt. Over a longer time, those funds must be reinvested to maintain the plant and equipment or else the company cannot remain in business. Therefore, banks and other relatively short-term lenders focus on the EBITDA coverage ratio, whereas long-term bondholders focus on the TIE ratio.

CONCEPT REVIEW

1. How does the use of financial leverage affect current shareholders' control position?
2. In what way do taxes influence a firm's willingness to finance with debt?
3. In what way does the use of debt involve a risk-versus-return trade-off?
4. Explain the following statement: "Analysts look at both balance sheet and income statement ratios when appraising a firm's financial condition."
5. Name three ratios that are used to measure the extent to which a firm uses financial leverage, and write out their equations.
6. A company has EBITDA of $600 million, interest payments of $60 million, lease payments of $40 million, and required principal payments (due this year) of $30 million. What is its EBITDA coverage ratio? (Check Figure: 4.9)

3.5 Profitability Ratios

Profitability is the net result of a number of policies and decisions. The ratios examined thus far provide useful clues as to the effectiveness of a firm's operations, but the **profitability ratios** go on to show the combined effects of liquidity, asset management, and debt on operating results.

Net Profit Margin

The *net profit margin,* which is also called the *return on sales*, is calculated by dividing net income by sales. It gives the profit per dollar of sales:

$$\text{Net profit margin} = \frac{\text{Net income available to common shareholders}}{\text{Sales}}$$

$$= \frac{\$113.5}{\$3,000} = 3.8\%$$

$$\text{Industry average} = 5.0\%$$

MicroDrive's net profit margin is below the industry average of 5%, but why is this so? Is it due to inefficient operations, high interest expenses, or both?

Instead of just comparing net income to sales, many analysts also break the income statement into smaller parts to identify the sources of a low net profit margin. For example, the **operating profit margin** is defined as

$$\text{Operating profit margin} = \frac{\text{EBIT}}{\text{Sales}}$$

---

[7]A sinking fund is a required annual payment designed to reduce the balance of a bond or preferred stock issue.

The operating profit margin identifies how a company is performing with respect to its operations before the impact of interest expenses is considered. Some analysts drill even deeper by breaking operating costs into their components. For example, the **gross profit margin** is defined as

$$\text{Gross profit margin} = \frac{\text{Sales} - \text{Cost of goods sold}}{\text{Sales}}$$

The gross profit margin identifies the gross profit per dollar of sales before any other expenses are deducted.

Rather than calculate each type of profit margin here, later in the chapter we will use common size analysis and percent change analysis to focus on different parts of the income statement. In addition, we will use the DuPont equation to show how the ratios interact with one another.

Sometimes it is confusing to have so many different types of profit margins. To help simplify the situation, we will focus primarily on the net profit margin throughout the book and simply call it the "profit margin."

Basic Earning Power (BEP)

The **basic earning power (BEP) ratio** is calculated by dividing earnings before interest and taxes (EBIT) by total assets:

$$\text{Basic earning power (BEP) ratio} = \frac{\text{EBIT}}{\text{Total assets}}$$

$$= \frac{\$283.8}{\$2,000} = 14.2\%$$

$$\text{Industry average} = 17.2\%$$

This ratio shows the raw earning power of the firm's assets, before the influence of taxes and leverage, and is useful for comparing firms with different tax situations and different degrees of financial leverage. Because of its low turnover ratios and low profit margin, MicroDrive is not getting as high a return on its assets as the average company in its industry.

Return on Total Assets

The ratio of net income to total assets measures the **return on total assets (ROA)** after interest and taxes:

$$\text{Return on total assets} = \text{ROA} = \frac{\text{Net income available to common shareholders}}{\text{Total assets}}$$

$$= \frac{\$113.5}{\$2,000} = 5.7\%$$

$$\text{Industry average} = 9.0\%$$

MicroDrive's 5.7% return is well below the 9% average for the industry. This low return results from (1) the company's low basic earning power plus (2) high interest costs resulting from its above-average use of debt, both of which cause its net income to be relatively low.

Return on Common Equity

The ratio of net income to common equity measures the **return on common equity (ROE):**

$$\text{Return on common equity} = \text{ROE} = \frac{\text{Net income available to common shareholders}}{\text{Common equity}}$$

$$= \frac{\$113.5}{\$896} = 12.7\%$$

$$\text{Industry average} = 15.0\%$$

Shareholders invest to get a return on their money, and this ratio tells how well they are doing in an accounting sense. MicroDrive's 12.7% return is below the 15% industry average, but not as far below as the return on total assets. This somewhat better result is due to the company's greater use of debt, a point that is analyzed in detail later in the chapter.

CONCEPT REVIEW

1. Identify and write out the equations for four ratios that show the combined effects of liquidity, asset management, and debt management on profitability.
2. Why is the basic earning power ratio useful?
3. Why does the use of debt lower the ROA?
4. What does ROE measure?
5. A company has $200 billion of sales and $10 billion of net income. Its total assets are $100 billion, financed half by debt and half by common equity. What is its profit margin? (Check Figure: 5%) What is its ROA? (Check Figure: 10%) What is its ROE? (Check Figure: 20%) Would ROA increase if the firm used less leverage? (Check Figure: yes) Would ROE increase? (Check Figure: no)

3.6 Market Value Ratios

Market value ratios relate the firm's stock price to its earnings, cash flow, and book value per share. Market value ratios are a way to measure the value of a company's stock relative to that of another company.

Price/Earnings Ratio

The **price/earnings (P/E) ratio** shows how much investors are willing to pay per dollar of reported profits. MicroDrive's stock sells for $23, so with an EPS of $2.27 its P/E ratio is 10.1:

$$\text{Price/earnings (P/E) ratio} = \frac{\text{Price per share}}{\text{Earnings per share}}$$

$$= \frac{\$23.00}{\$2.27} = 10.1 \text{ times}$$

$$\text{Industry average} = 12.5 \text{ times}$$

P/E ratios are higher for firms with strong growth prospects, other things held constant, but they are lower for riskier firms. Because MicroDrive's P/E ratio is below the average, this suggests that the company is regarded as being somewhat riskier than most, as having poorer growth prospects, or both. In the spring of 2014, the average P/E ratio for firms in the Toronto Stock Exchange S&P/TSX 60 Index was 17.30, indicating that investors were willing to pay $17.30 for every dollar of earnings.

Price/Cash Flow Ratio

Stock prices depend on a company's ability to generate cash flows. Consequently, investors often look at the **price/cash flow ratio,** where cash flow is defined as net income plus depreciation and amortization:

$$\text{Price/cash flow ratio} = \frac{\text{Price per share}}{\text{Cash flow per share}}$$

$$= \frac{\$23.00}{\$4.27} = 5.4 \text{ times}$$

$$\text{Industry average} = 6.8 \text{ times}$$

MicroDrive's price/cash flow ratio is also below the industry average, once again suggesting that its growth prospects are below average, that its risk is above average, or both.

Note that some analysts look at multiples beyond just the price/earnings and the price/cash flow ratios. For example, depending on the industry, some may look at measures such as price/sales, price/customers, or price/EBITDA per share. Ultimately, though, value depends on free cash flows, so if these "exotic" ratios do not forecast future free cash flow, they may turn out to be misleading. This was true in the case of the dot.com retailers before they crashed and burned in 2000, costing investors many billions.

Market/Book Ratio

The ratio of a stock's market price to its book value gives another indication of how investors regard the company. Companies with relatively high rates of return on equity generally sell at higher multiples of book value than those with low returns. First, we find MicroDrive's book value per share:

$$\text{Book value per share} = \frac{\text{Total common equity}}{\text{Shares outstanding}}$$

$$= \frac{\$896}{50} = \$17.92$$

Now we divide the market price by the book value to get a **market/book (M/B) ratio** of 1.3 times:

$$\text{Market/book ratio} = \text{M/B} = \frac{\text{Market price per share}}{\text{Book value per share}}$$

$$= \frac{\$23.00}{\$17.92} = 1.3 \text{ times}$$

$$\text{Industry average} = 1.7 \text{ times}$$

Investors are willing to pay relatively little for a dollar of MicroDrive's book value.

The average company in the S&P/TSX 60 Index had a market/book ratio of about 2.10 in the spring of 2014. Since M/B ratios typically exceed 1.0, this means that investors are willing to pay more for stocks than their accounting book values. The book value is a record of the past, showing the cumulative amount that shareholders have invested, either directly by purchasing newly issued shares or indirectly through retaining earnings. In contrast, the market price is forward-looking, incorporating investors' expectations of future cash flows. In June 2014, Dorel Industries, a Canadian juvenile products and bicycle company, had a market/book ratio of only 0.75, reflecting the relatively poor economic conditions in its main market. By contrast, Potash Corporation's market/book ratio was 3.45, indicating that investors expected that demand for its fertilizer products would continue.

Table 3-2 summarizes MicroDrive's financial ratios. As the table indicates, the company has many problems.

CONCEPT REVIEW

1. Describe three ratios that relate a firm's stock price to its earnings, cash flow, and book value per share, and write out their equations.
2. How do market value ratios reflect what investors think about a stock's risk and expected rate of return?
3. What does the price/earnings (P/E) ratio show? If one firm's P/E ratio is lower than that of another, what are some factors that might explain the difference?
4. How is book value per share calculated? Explain why book values often deviate from market values.
5. A company has $6 billion of net income, $2 billion of depreciation and amortization, $80 billion of common equity, and 1 billion shares. If its stock price is $96 per share, what is its price/earnings ratio? (Check Figure: 16) Its price/cash flow ratio? (Check Figure: 12) Its market/book ratio? (Check Figure: 1.2)

TABLE 3-2   MicroDrive Inc.: Summary of Financial Ratios (Millions of Dollars)

Ratio	Formula	Calculation	Ratio	Industry Average	Comment
Liquidity					
Current	$\dfrac{\text{Current assets}}{\text{Current liabilities}}$	$\dfrac{\$1,000}{\$310}$	$=3.2\times$	$4.2\times$	Poor
Quick	$\dfrac{\text{Current assets} - \text{Inventories}}{\text{Current liabilities}}$	$\dfrac{\$385}{\$310}$	$=1.2\times$	$2.1\times$	Poor
Asset Management					
Inventory turnover	$\dfrac{\text{COGS}}{\text{Inventories}}$	$\dfrac{\$2,200}{\$615}$	$=3.6\times$	$8.0\times$	Poor
Days sales outstanding (DSO)	$\dfrac{\text{Receivables}}{\text{Annual sales/365}}$	$\dfrac{\$375}{\$8.2192}$	$=46$ days	36 days	Poor
Average payable period	$\dfrac{\text{Payables}}{\text{operating costs/365}}$ or Annual costs/365	$\dfrac{\$60}{\$7.1677}$	$=8$ days	9 days	OK
Fixed assets turnover	$\dfrac{\text{Sales}}{\text{Net fixed assets}}$	$\dfrac{\$3,000}{\$1,000}$	$=3.0\times$	$3.0\times$	OK
Total assets turnover	$\dfrac{\text{Sales}}{\text{Total assets}}$	$\dfrac{\$3,000}{\$2,000}$	$=1.5\times$	$1.8\times$	Somewhat low
Debt Management					
Total debt to assets	$\dfrac{\text{Total debt}}{\text{Total assets}}$	$\dfrac{\$864}{\$2,000}$	$=43.2\%$	30.0%	High (risky)
Debt-to-equity	$\dfrac{\text{Total debt}}{\text{Total common equity}}$	$\dfrac{\$864}{\$936}$	$=0.92$	0.43	High (risky)
Times-interest-earned (TIE)	$\dfrac{\text{Earnings before interest and taxes (EBIT)}}{\text{Interest charges}}$	$\dfrac{\$283.8}{\$88}$	$=3.2\times$	$6.0\times$	Low (risky)
EBITDA coverage	$\dfrac{\text{EBITDA} + \text{Lease payments}}{\text{Interest} + \text{Principal payments} + \text{Lease payments}}$	$\dfrac{\$411.8}{\$136}$	$=3.0\times$	$4.3\times$	Low (risky)
Profitability					
Net profit margin	$\dfrac{\text{Net income available to common shareholders}}{\text{Sales}}$	$\dfrac{\$113.5}{\$3,000}$	$=3.8\%$	5.0%	Poor
Basic earning power (BEP)	$\dfrac{\text{Earnings before interest and taxes (EBIT)}}{\text{Total assets}}$	$\dfrac{\$283.8}{\$2,000}$	$=14.2\%$	17.2%	Poor
Return on total assets (ROA)	$\dfrac{\text{Net income available to common shareholders}}{\text{Total assets}}$	$\dfrac{\$113.5}{\$2,000}$	$=5.7\%$	9.0%	Poor
Return on common equity (ROE)	$\dfrac{\text{Net income available to common shareholders}}{\text{Common equity}}$	$\dfrac{\$113.5}{\$896}$	$=12.7\%$	15.0%	Poor
Market Value					
Price/earnings (P/E)	$\dfrac{\text{Price per share}}{\text{Earnings per share}}$	$\dfrac{\$23.00}{\$2.27}$	$=10.1\times$	$12.5\times$	Low
Price/cash flow	$\dfrac{\text{Price per share}}{\text{Cash flow per share}}$	$\dfrac{\$23.00}{\$4.27}$	$=5.4\times$	$6.8\times$	Low
Market/book (M/B)	$\dfrac{\text{Market price per share}}{\text{Book value per share}}$	$\dfrac{\$23.00}{\$17.92}$	$=1.3\times$	$1.7\times$	Low

3.7 Trend Analysis, Common Size Analysis, and Percent Change Analysis

Trends give clues as to whether a firm's financial condition is likely to improve or to deteriorate. To do a **trend analysis,** one simply plots a ratio over time, as shown in Figure 3-1. This graph shows that MicroDrive's rate of return on common equity has been declining since 2013, even though the industry average has been relatively stable. All the other ratios could be analyzed similarly.

In a *common size analysis*, all income statement items are divided by sales, and all balance sheet items are divided by total assets. Thus, a common size income statement shows each item as a percentage of sales, and a common size balance sheet shows each item as a percentage of total assets. The advantage of common size analysis is that it facilitates comparisons of balance sheets and income statements over time and across companies.

See ***Ch 03 Tool Kit.xlsx*** for all details.

Common size statements are very easy to generate if the financial statements are in a spreadsheet. In fact, if you obtain your financial statements from a source with standardized financial statements, then it is easy to cut and paste the data for a new company over your original company's data, and all of your spreadsheet formulas will be valid for the new company. We generated Table 3-3 in the *Excel* file ***Ch 03 Tool Kit.xlsx***. This table contains MicroDrive's 2015 and 2016 common size income statements, along with the composite statement for the industry. (*Note:* Rounding may cause addition/subtraction differences in Tables 3-3 and 3-4.) MicroDrive's EBIT is slightly below average, and its interest expenses are slightly above average. The net effect is a relatively low profit margin.

Table 3-4 shows MicroDrive's common size balance sheets, along with the industry average. Its accounts receivable are higher than the industry average, its inventories are significantly higher, and it uses much more debt than the average firm.

In percentage change analysis, growth rates are calculated for all income statement items and balance sheet accounts relative to a base year. To illustrate, Table 3-5 contains MicroDrive's income statement percentage change analysis for 2016 relative to 2015. Sales increased at a 5.3% rate during 2016, while EBIT grew 7.9%. The fact that sales increased faster than operating costs is positive, but this "good news" was offset by a 46.7% increase in interest expense. The significant growth in interest expense caused growth in both earnings before taxes and net income to be negative. Thus, the percentage change analysis

FIGURE
3-1   Rate of Return on Common Equity, 2012–2016

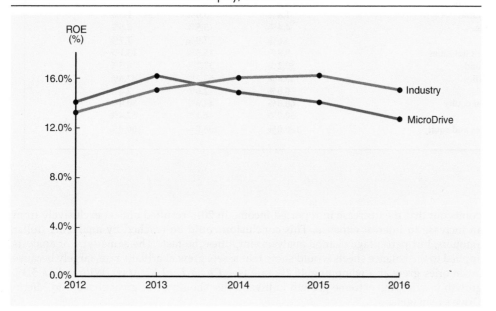

TABLE 3-3   MicroDrive Inc.: Common Size Income Statement

	A	B	C	D	E	F
165				2016		
166				Industry Composite	2016	2015
167	Net sales			100.0%	100.0%	100.0%
168	Costs of goods sold except depreciation			77.6%	70.0%	70.2%
169	Depreciation			2.8%	3.3%	3.2%
170	Other operating expenses			10.0%	17.2%	17.4%
171	Earnings before interest and taxes (EBIT)			9.6%	9.5%	9.2%
172	Less interest			1.3%	2.9%	2.1%
173	Earnings before taxes (EBT)			8.3%	6.5%	7.1%
174	Taxes (40%)			3.3%	2.6%	2.8%
175	Net income			5.0%	3.9%	4.3%
176	Preferred dividends			0.0%	0.1%	0.1%
177	Net income available to common shareholders (profit margin)			5.0%	3.8%	4.1%
178						

TABLE 3-4   MicroDrive Inc.: Common Size Balance Sheet

	A	B	C	D	E	F
187			2016			
188			Industry Composite	2016	2015	
189	*Assets*					
190	Cash and equivalents		1.0%	0.5%	0.9%	
191	Short-term investments		2.2%	0.0%	3.9%	
192	Accounts receivable		17.8%	18.8%	18.8%	
193	Inventories		19.8%	30.8%	24.7%	
194	Total current assets		40.8%	50.0%	48.2%	
195	Net plant and equipment		59.2%	50.0%	51.8%	
196	Total assets		100.0%	100.0%	100.0%	
197						
198	*Liabilities and equity*					
199	Accounts payable		1.8%	3.0%	1.8%	
200	Notes payable		4.4%	5.5%	3.6%	
201	Accruals		3.6%	7.0%	7.7%	
202	Total current liabilities		9.8%	15.5%	13.1%	
203	Long-term bonds		30.2%	37.7%	34.5%	
204	Total liabilities		40.0%	53.2%	47.6%	
205	Preferred stock		0.0%	2.0%	2.4%	
206	Total common equity		60.0%	44.8%	50.0%	
207	Total equity		60.0%	46.8%	52.4%	
208	Total liabilities and equity		100.0%	100.0%	100.0%	
209						

points out that the decrease in reported income in 2016 resulted almost exclusively from an increase in interest expense. This conclusion could be reached by analyzing dollar amounts, but percentage change analysis simplifies the task. The same type of analysis applied to the balance sheets would show that assets grew at a 19.0% rate, largely because inventories grew at a whopping 48.2% rate (see *Ch 03 Tool Kit.xlsx*). With only a 5.3% growth in sales, the extreme growth in inventories should be of great concern to Micro-Drive's managers.

See *Ch 03 Tool Kit.xlsx* for all details.

TABLE 3-5   MicroDrive Inc.: Income Statement Percentage Change Analysis

	A	B	C	D	E
				Percent	
218	Base year = 2015			**Change in**	
219				**2016**	
220	Net sales			5.3%	
221	Costs of goods sold except depreciation			5.0%	
222	Depreciation			11.1%	
223	Other operating expenses			3.9%	
224	Earnings before interest and taxes (EBIT)			7.9%	
225	Less interest			46.7%	
226	Earnings before taxes (EBT)			(3.5%)	
227	Taxes (40%)			(3.5%)	
228	Net income			(3.5%)	
229	Preferred dividends			0.0%	
230	Net income available to common shareholders (profit margin)			(3.7%)	
231					

CONCEPT REVIEW

1. How does one do a trend analysis?
2. What important information does a trend analysis provide?
3. What is common size analysis?
4. What is percent change analysis?

3.8 Tying the Ratios Together: The DuPont Equation

In ratio analysis, it is sometimes easy to miss the forest for all the trees. Managers often need a framework that ties together a firm's profitability, its asset usage efficiency, and its use of debt. This section provides just such a model. The profit margin times the total assets turnover is called the **DuPont equation,** and it gives the rate of return on assets (ROA):

$$\text{ROA} = \text{Profit margin} \times \text{Total assets turnover}$$
$$= \frac{\text{Net income}}{\text{Sales}} \times \frac{\text{Sales}}{\text{Total assets}} \tag{3-1}$$

For MicroDrive, the ROA is

$$\text{ROA} = 3.8\% \times 1.5 = 5.7\%$$

MicroDrive made 3.8%, or 3.8 cents, on each dollar of sales, and its assets were turned over 1.5 times during the year. Therefore, the company earned a return of 5.7% on its assets.

To find the return on equity (ROE), multiply the rate of return on assets (ROA) by the *equity multiplier*, which is the ratio of assets to common equity:

$$\text{Equity multiplier} = \frac{\text{Total assets}}{\text{Common equity}} \tag{3-2}$$

Firms that have a lot of leverage (i.e., a lot of liabilities or preferred stock) have a high equity multiplier—the more leverage, the less the equity, hence the higher the equity multiplier. For example, if a firm has $1,000 of assets and is financed with $800 (or 80%) liabilities and preferred stock, then its common equity will be $200, and its equity multiplier will be $1,000/$200 = 5. Had it used only $200 of liabilities and preferred stock, then its common equity would have been $800, and its equity multiplier would have been only $1,000/$800 = 1.25.

Therefore, the return on equity (ROE) depends on the ROA and the use of leverage:

$$\text{ROE} = \text{ROA} \times \text{Equity multiplier} \qquad (3\text{-}3)$$
$$= \frac{\text{Net income}}{\text{Total assets}} \times \frac{\text{Total assets}}{\text{Common equity}}$$

MicroDrive's ROE is

$$\text{ROE} = 5.7\% \times \frac{\$2,000}{\$896}$$
$$= 5.7\% \times 2.23$$
$$= 12.7\%$$

Now we can combine Equations 3-1 and 3-3 to form the *extended DuPont equation*, which shows how the profit margin, the assets turnover ratio, and the equity multiplier combine to determine the ROE:

$$\text{ROE} = (\text{Profit margin})(\text{Total assets turnover})(\text{Equity multiplier}) \qquad (3\text{-}4)$$
$$= \frac{\text{Net income}}{\text{Sales}} \times \frac{\text{Sales}}{\text{Total assets}} \times \frac{\text{Total assets}}{\text{Common equity}}$$

For MicroDrive, we have

$$\text{ROE} = (3.8\%)(1.5)(2.23)$$
$$= 12.7\%$$

The 12.7% rate of return could, of course, be calculated directly: both Sales and Total assets cancel, leaving Net income/Common equity = $113.5/$896 = 12.7%. However, the DuPont equation shows how the profit margin, the total assets turnover, and the use of debt interact to determine the return on equity.

The insights provided by the DuPont model are valuable, and it can be used for "quick and dirty" estimates of the impact that operating changes have on returns. For example, holding all else equal, if MicroDrive can drive up its ratio of sales/total assets to 1.8, then its ROE will improve to (3.8%)(1.8)(2.23) = 15.25%. For a more complete "what if" analysis, most companies use a forecasting model such as the one described in Chapter 5.

ⓒNCEPT REVIEW

1. Explain how the extended DuPont equation can be used to reveal the basic determinants of ROE.
2. What is the equity multiplier?
3. A company has a profit margin of 6%, a total asset turnover ratio of 2, and an equity multiplier of 1.5. What is its ROE? (Check Figure: 18%)

3.9 Comparative Ratios and Benchmarking

Ratio analysis involves comparisons. A company's ratios are compared with those of other firms in the same industry, that is, with industry average figures. However, like most firms, MicroDrive's managers go one step further—they also compare their ratios with those of a smaller set of the leading computer companies. This technique is called **benchmarking,** and the companies used for the comparison are called *benchmark companies*. For example, MicroDrive benchmarks against five other firms that its management considers to be the best-managed companies with operations similar to its own.

Many companies also benchmark various parts of their overall operations against top companies, whether they are in the same industry or not. For example, MicroDrive has a division that sells hard drives directly to consumers through catalogues and the Internet. This division's shipping department benchmarks against L.L. Bean, even though they are in different industries, because L.L. Bean's shipping department is one of the best. MicroDrive wants its own shippers to strive to match L.L. Bean's record for on-time shipments.

Comparative ratios are available from a number of sources, including FP informart; Financial Performance Indicators for Canadian Business, published by Statistics Canada; *Value Line;* and Dun and Bradstreet (D&B). Table 3-6 reports selected TransCanada Corp. ratios from Reuters.

Each data-supplying organization uses a somewhat different set of ratios designed for its own purposes. For example, D&B deals mainly with small firms, many of which are proprietorships, and it sells its services primarily to banks and other lenders. Therefore, D&B is concerned largely with the creditor's viewpoint, and its ratios emphasize current assets and liabilities, not market value ratios. So, when you select a comparative data source, you should be sure that your emphasis is similar to that of the agency whose ratios you plan to use. Additionally, there are often definitional differences in the ratios presented by different sources, so before using a source, be sure to verify the exact definitions of the ratios to ensure consistency with your own work.

ⓒONCEPT REVIEW

1. Differentiate between trend analysis and comparative ratio analysis.
2. Why is it useful to do a comparative ratio analysis?
3. What is benchmarking?

FINANCE: IN FOCUS

Analyzing the Financials of Small Businesses

While the tools used to evaluate a small business may be quite similar to those used for large companies, small businesses may be structured in ways that distort the analysis. Small companies tend to have high growth rates, so if you are measuring inventory turnover using sales/year-end inventory, your results will be misleading. Inventory is required in order to meet future sales, so if sales are expected to grow, inventory must grow in advance. Calculating inventory turnover based on the past year's sales using year-end inventory will show inventory being turned over more slowly over time. A more accurate way to measure inventory turnover is to use average inventory, which is more closely related to the current year's sales. The same holds true when measuring receivables turnover.

The personal finances of the owner and business are often intertwined. Financial decisions made may be based on the need to protect personal wealth, safeguard secrets, and/or minimize overall personal and corporate taxation. For instance, a small company may use equipment that is not on its balance sheet, but rather is leased from the owner, thus distorting ROE or ROA profitability measures. Profitability may also be affected by the owner's personal aversion to leverage. Little or no debt may be used if the owner is required to personally guarantee the loan, or interest expense may be higher than it ought to be if a bank provides a loan without the owner's guarantee. An owner may show his or her investment in the company as a loan when it is de facto equity. Any or all of these items can affect the debt-to-equity ratio. Without digging deeper, the true picture of a small company's financial health may not be obvious. Questionable assets, expenses, and ratios may well be explained once the company's financials are evaluated, often in conjunction with the owner's personal motivations and wealth.

Source: Adapted from Richard I. Levine and Virgina R. Travis, "Small Company Finance: What the Books Don't Say," *Harvard Business Review*, November–December 1987, 30–32.

<table>
<tr><td>TABLE
3-6</td><td colspan="4">Comparative Ratios for TransCanada Corp.</td></tr>
</table>

Ratio	TransCanada	Oil/Gas Transportation Industry	Energy Sector
P/E ratio	21.56	22.95	15.76
Market to book	2.15	58.22	2.09
Net profit margin	20.24	16.71	9.31
Quick ratio	0.64	0.48	1.43
Current ratio	0.69	0.66	1.63
Long-term debt to equity	126.27	192.22	40.16
Total debt to equity	138.04	204.52	51.42
Interest coverage	4.07	3.82	23.04
Return on assets	3.65	3.13	7.18
Return on equity	10.25	8.64	13.53
Inventory turnover	19.21	8.55	14.23
Asset turnover	0.18	0.23	0.82

Source: From Reuters, http:www.reuters.com, accessed June 20, 2014.

3.10   Uses and Limitations of Ratio Analysis

Ratio analysis is used by three main groups: (1) *managers*, who employ ratios to help analyze, control, and thus improve their firms' operations; (2) *credit analysts*, including bank loan officers and bond rating analysts, who analyze ratios to help ascertain a company's ability to pay its debts; and (3) *stock analysts*, who are interested in a company's efficiency, risk, and growth prospects. While ratio analysis can provide useful information concerning a company's operations and financial condition, it does have limitations that necessitate care and judgment. Some potential problems are listed below:

1. Many large firms operate different divisions in different industries, and for such companies it is difficult to develop a meaningful set of industry averages. Therefore, ratio analysis is more useful for small, narrowly focused firms than for large, multidivisional ones.
2. To set goals for high-level performance, it is best to benchmark on the industry *leaders'* ratios rather than the industry *average* ratios.
3. Inflation may have badly distorted firms' balance sheets—recorded values are often substantially different from "true" values. Furthermore, because inflation affects both depreciation charges and inventory costs, profits are also affected. Thus, inflation can distort a ratio analysis for one firm over time, or a comparative analysis of firms of different ages.
4. Seasonal factors can also distort a ratio analysis. For example, the inventory turnover ratio for a food processor will be radically different if the balance sheet figure used for inventory is the one just before versus just after the close of the canning season. This problem can be minimized by using monthly averages for inventory (and receivables) when calculating turnover ratios.
5. Firms can employ **"window dressing"** techniques to make their financial statements look stronger. To illustrate, a Toronto builder borrowed on a 2-year basis in late December. Because the loan was for more than 1 year, it was not included in current liabilities. The builder held the proceeds of the loan as cash. This improved his current and quick ratios and made his year-end balance sheet look stronger. However, the improvement was strictly window dressing; a week later the builder paid off the loan and the balance sheet was back at the old level.
6. Different accounting practices can distort comparisons. As noted earlier, inventory valuation and depreciation methods can affect financial statements and thereby distort comparisons among firms. Also, if one firm leases a substantial amount of its productive equipment, then its assets may appear low relative to sales because leased assets often

do not appear on the balance sheet. At the same time, the liability associated with the lease obligation may not be shown as debt. Therefore, leasing can artificially improve both the turnover and the debt ratios.

7. It is difficult to generalize about whether a particular ratio is "good" or "bad." For example, a high current ratio may indicate a strong liquidity position, which is good, or excess cash, which is bad (because excess cash in the bank is a nonearning asset). Similarly, a high fixed assets turnover ratio may denote either that a firm uses its assets efficiently or that it is undercapitalized and cannot afford to buy enough assets.

In summary, conducting ratio analysis in a mechanical, unthinking manner is dangerous, but when ratio analysis is used intelligently and with good judgment, it can provide useful insights into a firm's operations and identify the right questions to ask.

CONCEPT REVIEW

1. List three types of users of ratio analysis. Would the different users emphasize the same or different types of ratios?
2. List several potential problems with ratio analysis.

Summary

The main purpose of this chapter was to discuss techniques used by investors and managers to analyze financial statements. The key concepts covered are listed below.

*   **Liquidity ratios** show the relationship of a firm's current assets to its current liabilities, and thus its ability to meet maturing debts. Two commonly used liquidity ratios are the **current ratio** and the **quick,** or **acid test, ratio.**
*   **Asset management ratios** measure how effectively a firm is managing its assets. These ratios include **inventory turnover, days sales outstanding, average payable period, fixed assets turnover,** and **total assets turnover.**
*   **Debt management ratios** reveal (1) the extent to which the firm is financed with debt and (2) its likelihood of defaulting on its debt obligations. They include the **debt ratio, debt-to-equity ratio, times-interest-earned ratio,** and **EBITDA coverage ratio.**
*   **Profitability ratios** show the combined effects of liquidity, asset management, and debt management policies on operating results. They include the **net profit margin,** the **basic earning power ratio,** the **return on total assets,** and the **return on common equity.**
*   **Market value ratios** relate the firm's stock price to its earnings, cash flow, and book value per share, thus giving management an indication of what investors think of the company's past performance and future prospects. These include the **price/earnings ratio, price/cash flow ratio,** and the **market/book ratio.**
*   **Trend analysis,** where one plots a ratio over time, is important, because it reveals whether the firm's condition has been improving or deteriorating over time.
*   The **DuPont equation** is designed to show how the profit margin on sales, the assets turnover ratio, and the use of debt interact to determine the rate of return on equity. The firm's management can use the DuPont system to analyze ways of improving performance.
*   **Benchmarking** is the process of comparing a particular company with a group of similar, successful companies.

Ratio analysis has limitations, but used with care and judgment, it can be very helpful.

Questions

3-1 Define each of the following terms:
a. Liquidity ratios: current ratio; quick, or acid test, ratio
b. Asset management ratios: inventory turnover ratio; days sales outstanding (DSO); average payables period; fixed assets turnover ratio; total assets turnover ratio

c. Financial leverage: debt ratio; times-interest-earned (TIE) ratio; EBITDA coverage ratio
d. Profitability ratios: profit margin on sales; basic earning power (BEP) ratio; return on total assets (ROA); return on common equity (ROE)
e. Market value ratios: price/earnings (P/E) ratio; price/cash flow ratio; market/book (M/B) ratio; book value per share
f. Trend analysis; comparative ratio analysis; benchmarking
g. DuPont equation; window dressing; seasonal effects on ratios

3-2 Financial ratio analysis is conducted by managers, equity investors, long-term creditors, and short-term creditors. What is the primary emphasis of each of these groups in evaluating ratios?

3-3 Over the past year, M.D. Ryngaert & Co. has realized an increase in its current ratio and a drop in its total assets turnover ratio. However, the company's sales, quick ratio, and fixed assets turnover ratio have remained constant. What explains these changes?

3-4 Profit margins and turnover ratios vary from one industry to another. What differences would you expect to find between a grocery chain such as Safeway and a steel company? Think particularly about the turnover ratios, the profit margin, and the DuPont equation.

3-5 How might (a) seasonal factors and (b) different growth rates distort a comparative ratio analysis? Give some examples. How might these problems be alleviated?

3-6 Why is it sometimes misleading to compare a company's financial ratios with those of other firms that operate in the same industry?

Concept Review Problems

Full solutions are provided at www.nelson.com/brigham3ce.

CR-1
Debt Ratio
Argent Corporation has $60 million in current liabilities, $150 million in total liabilities, and $210 million in total common equity. Argent has no preferred stock. Argent's total debt is $120 million. What is the debt-to-assets ratio? What is the debt-to-equity ratio?

CR-2
Ratio Analysis
The following data apply to Jacobus and Associates (millions of dollars):

Cash and marketable securities	$100.00
Fixed assets	$283.50
Sales	$1,000.00
Net income	$70.00
Quick ratio	2.0×
Current ratio	3.0×
DSO	40.55 days
ROE	15%

Jacobus has no preferred stock—only common equity, current liabilities, and long-term debt.
a. Find Jacobus's (1) accounts receivable, (2) current liabilities, (3) current assets, (4) total assets, (5) ROA, (6) common equity, and (7) long-term debt.
b. In part a, you should have found Jacobus's accounts receivable (A/R) = $111.1 million. If Jacobus could reduce its DSO from 40.55 days to 30.4 days while holding other things constant, how much cash would it generate? If this cash were used to buy back common shares (at book value), thus reducing the amount of common equity, how would this affect (1) the ROE, (2) the ROA, and (3) the total debt/total assets ratio?

Problems

Easy
Problems 1–5
Answers to odd-numbered problems appear in Appendix A.

3-1
Days Sales Outstanding
Grey Brothers has a DSO of 27 days. The company's average daily sales are $35,000. What is the level of its accounts receivable? Assume there are 365 days in a year.

3-2
Debt Ratio
Brite-Lite Bulbs has an equity multiplier of 3.2. The company's assets are financed with some combination of long-term debt and common equity. What is the company's debt ratio?

3-3
Market/Book Ratio

A company's stock price is $12 per share, and it has $7 million in total assets. Its balance sheet shows $1 million in current liabilities, $2.5 million in long-term debt, and $3.5 million in common equity. It has 500,000 common shares outstanding. What is the company's market/book ratio?

3-4
Price/Earnings Ratio

A company has an EPS of $1.50, a cash flow per share of $3.00, and a price/cash flow ratio of 8.0 times. What is its P/E ratio?

3-5
Average Payables Period

Davison Truck Repairs has sales of $3,500,000 and cost of goods sold of $2,800,000. The company believes it is possible to delay payment by 6 days and not offend its suppliers. Will the company's accounts payable increase or decrease, and by how much if it takes on average 6 days longer to pay its bills?

Intermediate Problems 6–13

3-6
DuPont Analysis

Gardial & Son has an ROA of 12%, a 5% profit margin, and a return on equity equal to 20%. What is the company's total asset turnover? What is the firm's equity multiplier?

3-7
Current and Quick Ratios

Acme Bearings has current assets of $5 million. The company's current ratio is 2.5, and its quick ratio is 1.4. What is the firm's level of current liabilities? What is the firm's level of inventories?

3-8
Profit Margin and Debt Ratio

Assume you are given the following relationships for the Haslam Corporation:

Sales/total assets	$1.2\times$
Return on assets (ROA)	4%
Return on equity (ROE)	7%

Calculate Haslam's profit margin and debt ratio.

3-9
Current and Quick Ratios

The Nelson Company has $1,312,500 in current assets and $525,000 in current liabilities. Its initial inventory level is $375,000, and it will raise funds from additional notes payable and use them to increase inventory. How much can Nelson's short-term debt (notes payable) increase without pushing its current ratio below 2.0? What will be the firm's quick ratio after Nelson has raised the maximum amount of short-term funds?

3-10
Times-Interest-Earned Ratio

Cayman Auto has $600,000 of debt outstanding, and it pays an interest rate of 8% annually: Cayman Auto's annual sales are $3 million, its average tax rate is 25%, and its net profit margin is 3%. If the company does not maintain a TIE ratio of at least 5 times, its bank will refuse to renew the loan, and bankruptcy will result. What is Cayman Auto's TIE ratio?

3-11
ROE

Selected information is provided for Tiny Bubbles Bath Company:

	2013	2014	2015
Sales	$2,600,000	$3,000,000	$4,000,000
Assets	$2,000,000	$2,250,000	$3,000,000
Net income	$ 207,000	$ 222,000	$ 245,000
Total equity	$ 800,000	$ 800,000	$ 860,000

Calculate ROE from 2013 to 2015 and evaluate whether you think this company's ROE growth is sustainable.

3-12
Current Ratio

ACR Corp. has $1,312,500 in current assets and $525,000 in current liabilities. Its initial inventory level is $375,000, and it will raise funds from additional notes payable and use them to increase inventory. How much can it increase its short-term debt (notes payable) without pushing its current ratio below 2.0?

3-13
TIE Ratio

Maple Leaf Printing has $5 billion in assets, and its tax rate is 30%. Its basic earning power (BEP) ratio is 10%, and its return on assets (ROA) is 5%. What is Maple Leaf Printing's times-interest-earned (TIE) ratio?

Challenging Problems 14–18

3-14
DSO and Accounts Receivable

Rite-on-Time Trucking currently has $750,000 in accounts receivable, and its days' sales outstanding (DSO) is 55 days. It wants to reduce its DSO to 35 days by pressuring more of its customers to pay their bills on time. If this policy is adopted, the company's average sales will fall by 15%. What will be the level of accounts receivable following the change? Assume a 365-day year.

3-15
Balance Sheet Analysis

In the table that follows, complete the balance sheet and sales information for J. White Industries using the following financial data:

Quick ratio: $0.80\times$
Total assets turnover: $1.5\times$
Days sales outstanding: 36.5 days[a]

Gross profit margin on sales: (Sales − Cost of goods sold)/Sales = 25%

Inventory turnover ratio: 3.75×

Average payables period: 89.22 days

^aCalculation is based on a 365-day year.

Balance Sheet

Cash	————	Accounts payable	————
Accounts receivable	————	Long-term debt	50,000
Inventories	————	Common stock	————
Fixed assets	————	Retained earnings	100,000
Total assets	$400,000	Total liabilities and equity	————
Sales	————	Cost of goods sold	————

3-16
Comprehensive
Ratio Calculations
Anvil Metal Works (AMW) had a quick ratio of 1.1, a current ratio of 2.5, an inventory turn-over of 4 times, gross profit margin of 10%, total current assets of $810,000, and cash and marketable securities of $120,000. What were AMW's annual sales and its DSO? Assume a 365-day year.

3-17 Data for Lozano Chip Company and its industry averages follow.
a. Calculate the indicated ratios for Lozano.
b. Construct the extended Du Pont equation for both Lozano and the industry.
c. Outline Lozano's strengths and weaknesses as revealed by your analysis.

Lozano Chip Company: Balance Sheet as at December 31, 2015 (Thousands of Dollars)

Cash	$ 225,000	Accounts payable	$ 601,866
Receivables	1,575,000	Notes payable	326,634
Inventories	1,125,000	Other current liabilities	525,000
Total current assets	2,925,000	Total current liabilities	1,453,500
Net fixed assets	1,350,000	Long-term debt	1,068,750
		Common equity	1,752,750
Total assets	$4,275,000	Total liabilities and equity	$4,275,000

Lozano Chip Company: Income Statement for Year Ended December 31, 2015 (Thousands of Dollars)

Sales	$7,500,000
Cost of goods sold	6,375,000
Selling, general, and administrative expenses	825,000
Earnings before interest and taxes (EBIT)	300,000
Interest expense	111,631
Earnings before taxes (EBT)	188,369
Taxes (30%)	56,511
Net income	$ 131,858

Ratio	Lozano	Industry Average
Current assets/Current liabilities	————	2.0 ×
Days sales outstanding (365-day year)	————	35.0 days
COGS/Inventory	————	6.7 ×
Sales/Fixed assets	————	12.1 ×
Sales/Total assets	————	3.0
Net income/Sales	————	1.2%
Net income/Total assets	————	3.6%
Net income/Common equity	————	9.0%
Total debt/Total assets	————	30.0%
Total liabilities/Total assets	————	60.0%

3-18 The Lee Corporation's forecasted 2015 financial statements follow, along with some industry
Comprehensive   average ratios.
Ratio Analysis   a.   Calculate Lee's 2015 forecasted ratios, compare them with the industry average data,
and comment briefly on Lee's projected strengths and weaknesses.
b.   What do you think would happen to Lee's ratios if the company initiated cost-cutting
measures that allowed it to hold lower levels of inventory and substantially decreased
the cost of goods sold? No calculations are necessary. Think about which ratios would
be affected by changes in these two accounts.

Lee Corporation: Forecasted Balance Sheet as at December 31, 2015

Cash	$ 72,000
Accounts receivable	439,000
Inventories	694,000
Total current assets	1,205,000
Fixed assets	631,000
Total assets	$ 1,836,000
Accounts payable	$ 332,000
Note payable	100,000
Accruals	170,000
Total current liabilities	602,000
Long-term debt	404,290
Common stock	575,000
Retained earnings	254,710
Total liabilities and equity	$ 1,836,000

Lee Corporation: Forecasted Income Statement for 2015

Sales	$ 6,350,000
Cost of goods sold	5,270,000
Selling, general, and administrative expenses	500,000
Depreciation	240,000
Earnings before taxes (EBT)	340,000
Taxes (30%)	102,000
Net income	$ 238,000

Per-Share Data

EPS	$9.52
Cash dividends per share	$1.90
P/E	5×
Market price (average)	$47.60
Number of shares outstanding	25,000

Industry Financial Ratios (2015)[a]

Quick ratio	1.0×
Current ratio	2.7×
Inventory turnover[b]	7.0×
Days sales outstanding[c]	32 days
Fixed assets turnover[b]	13.0×
Total assets turnover[b]	2.6×
Return on assets	9.1%
Return on equity	18.2%
Debt ratio	50.0%
Profit margin on sales	3.5%
P/E	6.0×
P/cash flow	3.5×

[a]Industry average ratios have been constant for the past 4 years.
[b]Based on year-end balance sheet figures.
[c]Calculation is based on a 365-day year.

Spreadsheet Problem

3-19
Build a Model:
Ratio Analysis

Start with the partial model in the file *Ch03 Build a Model.xlsx* from the textbook's website. Joshua & White (J&W) Technologies's financial statements are also shown below. Answer the following questions. (*Note:* Industry average ratios are provided in *Ch03 Build a Model.xlsx.*)

a. Has J&Ws liquidity position improved or worsened? Explain.
b. Has J&Ws ability to manage its assets improved or worsened? Explain.
c. How has J&Ws profitability changed during the past year?
d. Perform an extended DuPont analysis for J&W for 2014 and 2015. What do these results tell you?
e. Perform a common size analysis. What has happened to the composition (that is, percentage in each category) of assets and liabilities?
f. Perform a percentage change analysis. What does this tell you about the change in profitability and asset utilization?

Joshua & White Technologies: December 31 Balance Sheets (Thousands of Dollars)

Assets	2015	2014	Liabilities & Equity	2015	2014
Cash	$ 21,000	$ 20,000	Accounts payable	$ 33,600	$ 32,000
Short-term investments	3,759	3,240	Accruals	12,600	12,000
Accounts receivable	52,500	48,000	Notes payable	19,929	6,480
Inventories	84,000	56,000	Total current liabilities	66,129	50,480
Total current assets	161,259	127,240	Long-term debt	67,662	58,320
Net fixed assets	218,400	200,000	Total liabilities	133,791	108,800
Total assets	$379,659	$327,240	Common stock	183,793	178,440
			Retained earnings	62,075	40,000
			Total common equity	245,868	218,440
			Total liabilities & equity	$379,659	$327,240

Joshua & White Technologies December 31 Income Statements (Thousands of Dollars)

	2015	2014
Sales	$420,000	$400,000
COGS excluding depr. & amort.	300,000	298,000
Depreciation and amortization	19,660	18,000
Other operating expenses	27,600	22,000
EBIT	72,740	62,000
Interest expense	5,740	4,460
EBT	67,000	57,540
Taxes (40%)	26,800	23,016
Net income	$ 40,200	$ 34,524
Common dividends	$ 18,125	$ 17,262

Other Data	2015	2014
Year-end stock price	$ 90.00	$ 96.00
Number of shares (thousands)	4,052	4,000
Lease payment (thousands of dollars)	$ 20,000	$ 20,000
Sinking fund payment (thousands of dollars)	$ 5,000	$ 5,000

MINI CASE

The first part of the case, presented in Chapter 2, discussed the situation of Computron Industries after an expansion program. A large loss occurred in 2015, rather than the expected profit. As a result, its managers, directors, and investors are concerned about the firm's survival.

Jenny Cochran was brought in as assistant to Gary Meissner, Computron's chair, who had the task of getting the company back into a sound financial position. Computron's 2014 and 2015 balance sheets and income statements, together with projections for 2016, are shown in the following tables. The tables also show the 2014 and 2015 financial ratios, along with industry average data. The 2016 projected financial statement data represent Cochran's and Meissner's best guess for 2016 results, assuming that some new financing is arranged to get the company "over the hump."

Cochrane must prepare an analysis of where the company is now, what it must do to regain its financial health, and what actions should be taken. Your assignment is to help her answer the following questions. Provide clear explanations, not yes or no answers.

Balance Sheets	2014	2015	2016E
Assets			
Cash	$ 9,000	$ 7,282	$ 14,000
Short-term investments	48,600	20,000	71,632
Accounts receivable	351,200	632,160	878,000
Inventories	715,200	1,287,360	1,716,480
Total current assets	1,124,000	1,946,802	2,680,112
Gross fixed assets	491,000	1,202,950	1,220,000
Less: accumulated depreciation	146,200	263,160	383,160
Net fixed assets	344,800	939,790	836,840
Total assets	$1,468,800	$2,886,592	$3,516,952
Liabilities and Equity			
Accounts payable	$ 145,600	$ 324,000	$ 359,800
Notes payable	200,000	720,000	300,000
Accruals	136,000	284,960	380,000
Total current liabilities	481,600	1,328,960	1,039,800
Long-term debt	323,432	1,000,000	500,000
Common stock (100,000 shares)	460,000	460,000	1,680,936
Retained earnings	203,768	97,632	296,216
Total equity	663,768	557,632	1,977,152
Total liabilities and equity	$1,468,800	$2,886,592	$3,516,952

Note: "E" indicates estimated. The 2016 data are forecasts.

Income Statements	2014	2015	2016E
Sales	$3,432,000	$5,834,400	$7,035,600
Cost of goods sold except depr.	2,864,000	4,980,000	5,800,000
Other expenses	340,000	720,000	612,960
Depreciation	18,900	116,960	120,000
Total operating costs	3,222,900	5,816,960	6,532,960
EBIT	209,100	17,440	502,640
Interest expense	62,500	176,000	80,000
EBT	146,600	(158,560)	422,640
Taxes (40%)	58,640	(63,424)	169,056
Net income (loss)	$ 87,960	$ (95,136)	$ 253,584

Other Data

Stock price	$ 8.50	$ 6.00	$ 12.17
Shares outstanding	100,000	100,000	250,000
EPS	$ 0.88	$ (0.95)	$ 1.01
DPS	$ 0.22	$ 0.11	$ 0.22
Tax rate	40%	40%	40%
Book value per share	$ 6.638	$ 5.576	$ 7.909
Lease payments	$ 40,000	$ 40,000	$ 40,000

Note: "E" indicates estimated. The 2016 data are forecasts.

Ratio Analysis	2014	2015	2016E	Industry Average
Current	2.3×	1.5×	—	2.7×
Quick	0.8×	0.5×	—	1.0×
Inventory turnover	4.0×	4.0×	—	6.1×
Days sales outstanding	37.4 days	39.6 days	—	32.0 days
Fixed assets turnover	10.0×	6.2×	—	7.0×
Total assets turnover	2.3×	2.0×	—	2.5×
Debt ratio	35.6%	59.6%	—	32.0%
TIE	3.3×	0.1×	—	6.2×
EBITDA coverage	2.6×	0.8×	—	8.0×
Profit margin	2.6%	−1.6%	—	3.6%
Basic earning power	14.2%	0.6%	—	17.8%
ROA	6.0%	−3.3%	—	9.0%
ROE	13.3%	−17.1%	—	17.9%
Price/earnings (P/E)	9.7×	N.M.	—	16.2×
Price/cash flow	8.0×	27.5×	—	7.6×
Market/book	1.3×	1.1×	—	2.9×

Note: "E" indicates estimated. The 2016 data are forecasts.
      "N.M." indicates not meaningful with losses.

a. Why are ratios useful? What are the five major categories of ratios?
b. Calculate the 2016 current and quick ratios based on the projected balance sheet and income statement data. What can you say about the company's liquidity position in 2014, 2015, and as projected for 2016? We often think of ratios as being useful (1) to managers to help run the business, (2) to bankers for credit analysis, and (3) to shareholders for stock valuation. Would these different types of analysts have an equal interest in the liquidity ratios?
c. Calculate the 2016 inventory turnover, days sales outstanding (DSO), fixed assets turnover, and total assets turnover. How does Computron's utilization of assets stack up against that of other firms in its industry?
d. Calculate the 2016 debt, times-interest-earned, and EBITDA coverage ratios. How does Computron compare with the industry with respect to financial leverage? What can you conclude from these ratios?
e. Calculate the 2016 profit margin, basic earning power (BEP), return on assets (ROA), and return on equity (ROE). What can you say about these ratios?
f. Calculate the 2016 price/earnings ratio, price/cash flow ratio, and market/book ratio. Do these ratios indicate that investors are expected to have a high or low opinion of the company?
g. Perform a common size analysis and percent change analysis. What do these analyses tell you about Computron?
h. Use the extended DuPont equation to provide a summary and overview of Computron's financial condition as projected for 2016. What are the firm's major strengths and weaknesses?
i. What are some potential problems and limitations of financial ratio analysis?

chapter 4

Time Value of Money

You have heard the saying "time is money." Deceptively simple, these three words form the basis of some extraordinarily useful concepts for valuing financial assets. In business, the time value of money helps you determine how much a stock is worth, what you should pay for a bond, or whether a company should invest in a new factory. In personal finance, it helps answer questions such as how much you should save in order to retire comfortably and whether you should buy or lease a car. Time value concepts help determine what future cash flows are worth today. In other words, what are the future interest payments (and the principal repaid at maturity) of a bond worth *today*, or—in the case of the factory investment—what are all the future cash flows the new factory is expected to generate worth *today*? Today, virtually all large corporations use time value of money techniques for valuing assets and business opportunities.

Although the economist Irving Fisher is credited with introducing modern present value formulas in the 1930s, present value calculations go back much further in history. In 1202, Leonardo of Pisa, more commonly known as Fibonacci, was the first person to mathematically compare the present value of two differing cash flows. Fibonacci's problem was interesting—he calculated the value of a king paying a soldier two different cash flow streams—a quarterly annuity of 75 bezants (gold coins) versus an annual annuity of 300 bezants for services rendered. Another problem he solved was how to calculate future values from investments made with banking houses. It is possible that Fibonacci's work facilitated the practice of financing government through national debt.

Fibonacci's work on present value calculations formed the basis for Jean Trenchant's writings in the 16th century on interest rate and present value problems. Trenchant wrote about whether King Henry should finance his war (in the 16th century) for the control of Europe! Trenchant was also the first to calculate a table of compound growth. The mathematical tools Fibonacci developed came to serve as the foundation for financial innovation. Anyone who today makes a present value calculation or compares the relative merits of two stocks or bonds owes a debt to Leonardo of Pisa.

Source: Adapted from William N. Goetzmann and K. Geert Rouwenhorst, *The Origins of Value* (Oxford: Oxford University Press, 2005), 125–43.

In Chapter 1, we saw that the primary objective of financial management is to maximize the value of the firm's shares. We also saw that share values depend in part on the timing of the cash flows investors expect from an investment—a dollar expected soon is worth more than a dollar expected in the distant future. Therefore, it is essential for financial managers to have a clear understanding of the time value of money and its impact on share prices. These concepts are discussed in this chapter, where we show how the timing of cash flows affects asset values and rates of return.

The principles of time value analysis have many applications, ranging from setting up schedules for paying off loans to decisions about whether to acquire new equipment. *In fact, of all the concepts used in finance, none is more important than the time value of money,* also called *discounted cash flow (DCF) analysis.* Since time value concepts are used throughout the remainder of the book, it is vital that you understand the material in Chapter 4 and are able to work the chapter problems before you move on to other topics.

4.1 Time Lines

The textbook's website contains an *Excel* file that will guide you through the chapter's calculations. The file for this chapter is *Ch 04 Tool Kit.xlsx*, and we encourage you to open the file and follow along as you read the chapter. **www.nelson.com/ brigham3ce**

The first step in time value analysis is to set up a **time line**, which will help you visualize what's happening in a particular problem. To illustrate, consider the following diagram, where PV represents $100 that is on hand today and FV is the value that will be in the account on a future date:

Periods	0		1	2	3
		5%			
Cash	PV = $100				FV = ?

The intervals from 0 to 1, 1 to 2, and 2 to 3 are time periods such as years or months. Time 0 is today, and it is the beginning of Period 1; Time 1 is one period from today, and it is both the end of Period 1 and the beginning of Period 2; and so on. Although the periods are often years, periods can also be quarters or months or even days. Note that each tick mark corresponds to both the *end* of one period and the *beginning* of the next one. Thus, if the periods are years, the tick mark at Time 2 represents both the *end* of Year 2 and the *beginning* of Year 3.

Cash flows are shown directly below the tick marks, and the relevant interest rate is shown just above the time line. Unknown cash flows, which you are trying to find, are indicated by question marks. Here the interest rate is 5%; a single cash outflow, $100, is invested at Time 0; and the Time 3 value is an unknown inflow. In this example, cash flows occur only at Times 0 and 3, with no flows at Times 1 or 2. Note that in our example the interest rate is constant for all three years. That condition is generally true, but if it were not then we would show different interest rates for the different periods.

Time lines are essential when you are first learning time value concepts, but even experts use them to analyze complex finance problems, and we use them throughout the book. We begin each problem by setting up a time line to show what's happening, after which we provide an equation that must be solved to find the answer, and then we explain how to use a regular calculator, a financial calculator, and a spreadsheet to find the answer.

CONCEPT REVIEW

1. Do time lines deal only with years or could other periods be used?
2. Set up a time line to illustrate the following situation: You currently have $2,000 in a 3-year Guaranteed Investment Certificate (GIC) that pays a guaranteed 4% annually.

4.2 Future Values

A dollar in hand today is worth more than a dollar to be received in the future because, if you had it now, you could invest it, earn interest, and end up with more than a dollar in the future. The process of going forward, from *present values (PVs)* to *future values (FVs)*, is called **compounding.** To illustrate, refer back to our 3-year time line and assume that you plan to deposit $100 in a bank that pays a guaranteed 5% interest each year. How much would you have at the end of Year 3? We first define some terms, after which we set up a time line and show how the future value is calculated.

PV = Present value, or beginning amount. In our example, PV = $100.

FV_N = Future value, or ending amount, of your account after N periods. Whereas PV is the value now, or the *present value*, FV_N is the value N periods into the *future*, after the interest earned has been added to the account.

CF_t = Cash flow. Cash flows can be positive or negative. For a borrower, the first cash flow is positive and the subsequent cash flows are negative, and the reverse holds true for a lender. The cash flow for a particular period is often given a subscript, CF_t, where t is the period. Thus, CF_0 = PV = the cash flow at Time 0, whereas CF_3 would be the cash flow at the end of Period 3.

I = Interest rate earned per year. (Sometimes a lowercase i is used.) Interest earned is based on the balance at the beginning of each year, and we assume that it is paid at the end of the year. Here I = 5%, or, expressed as a decimal, 0.05. Throughout this chapter, we designate the interest rate as I because that symbol (or I/YR, for interest rate per year) is used on most financial calculators. Note, though, that in later chapters we use the symbol "r" to denote rates because r (for rate of return) is used more often in the finance literature. Note too that in this chapter we generally assume that interest payments are guaranteed by the Canadian government; hence they are certain. In later chapters we will consider risky investments, where the interest rate actually earned might differ from its expected level.

INT = Dollars of interest earned during the year = (Beginning amount) × I. In our example, INT = $100(0.05) = $5.

N = Number of periods involved in the analysis. In our example, N = 3. Sometimes the number of periods is designated with a lowercase n, so both N and n indicate number of periods.

Corporate Valuation and the Time Value of Money

In Chapter 1, we told you that managers should strive to make their firms more valuable and that the value of a firm is determined by the size, timing, and risk of its free cash flows (FCF). Recall that free cash flows are the cash flows available for distribution to all of a firm's investors (shareholders and creditors) and that the weighted average cost of capital is the average rate of return required by all of the firm's investors. We showed you a formula, highlighted below, for calculating value. That formula takes future cash flows and adjusts them to show how much those future risky cash flows are worth today. That formula relies on time value of money concepts, which we explain in this chapter.

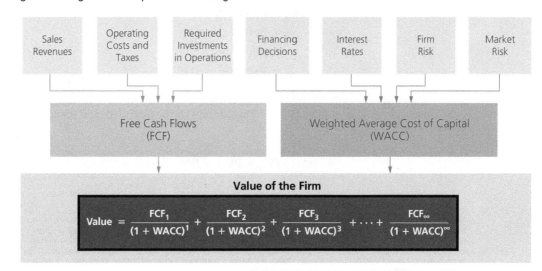

We can use four different procedures to solve time value problems.[1] These methods are described in the following sections.

Step-by-Step Approach

The time line used to find the FV of $100 compounded for 3 years at 5%, along with some calculations, is shown below:

Time	0	5%	1	2	3

Amount at beginning of period $100.00---▶$105.00----▶$110.25----▶$115.76

You start with $100 in the account—this is shown at t = 0. Then multiply the initial amount, and each succeeding amount, by $(1 + I) = (1.05)$.

- You earn $100(0.05) = $5 of interest during the first year, so the amount at the end of Year 1 (or t = 1) is

$$\begin{aligned} FV_1 &= PV + INT \\ &= PV + PV(I) \\ &= PV(1 + I) \\ &= \$100(1 + 0.05) = \$100(1.05) = \$105 \end{aligned}$$

- You begin the second year with $105, earn 0.05($105) = $5.25 on the now larger beginning-of-period amount, and end the year with $110.25. Interest during Year 2 is $5.25, and it is higher than the first year's interest, $5, because you earned $5(0.05) = $0.25 interest on the first year's interest. This is called "compounding," and interest earned on interest is called "compound interest."
- This process continues, and because the beginning balance is higher in each successive year, the interest earned each year increases.
- The total interest earned, $15.76, is reflected in the final balance, $115.76.

The step-by-step approach is useful because it shows exactly what is happening. However, this approach is time consuming, especially if a number of years are involved, so streamlined procedures have been developed.

Formula Approach

In the step-by-step approach above, we multiply the amount at the beginning of each period by $(1 + I) = (1.05)$. Notice that the value at the end of Year 2 is

$$\begin{aligned} FV_2 &= FV_1(1 + I) \\ &= PV(1 + I)(1 + I) \\ &= PV(1 + I)^2 \\ &= 100(1.05)^2 = \$110.25 \end{aligned}$$

If N = 3, then we multiply PV by $(1 + I)$ three different times, which is the same as multiplying the beginning amount by $(1 + I)^3$. This concept can be extended, and the result is this key equation:

$$FV_N = PV(1 + I)^N \tag{4-1}$$

---

[1]A fifth procedure is called the tabular approach. It used tables showing "interest factors" and was used before financial calculators and computers became available. Now, though, calculators and spreadsheets such as *Excel* are programmed to calculate the specific factor needed for a given problem and then to use it to find the FV. This is much more efficient than using the tables. Moreover, calculators and spreadsheets can handle fractional periods and fractional interest rates. For these reasons, tables are not used in business today; hence we do not discuss them in the text. For an explanation of the tabular approach, see **Web Extension 4C** at the textbook's website.

We can apply Equation 4-1 via the formula approach to find the FV in our example:

$$FV_3 = \$100(1.05)^3 = \$115.76$$

Equation 4-1 can be used with any calculator that has an exponential function, making it easy to find FVs, no matter how many years are involved.

Financial Calculators

Financial calculators are extremely helpful when working time value problems. First, note that financial calculators have five keys that correspond to the five variables in the basic time value equations. We show the inputs for our example above the keys and the output, the FV, below its key. Since there are no periodic payments, we enter 0 for PMT. We describe the keys in more detail below the diagram.

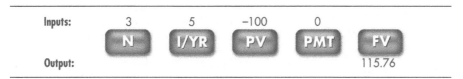

N = Number of periods. Some calculators use n rather than N.

I/YR = Interest rate per period. Some calculators use i or I rather than I/YR.

PV = Present value. In our example we begin by making a deposit, which is an outflow, so the PV should be entered with a negative sign. On most calculators you must enter the 100, then press the $+/-$ key to switch from $+100$ to -100. If you enter -100 directly, this will subtract 100 from the last number in the calculator and give you an incorrect answer.

PMT = Payment. This key is used if we have a series of equal, or constant, payments. Since there are no such payments in our illustrative problem, we enter PMT = 0. We will use the PMT key when we discuss annuities later in this chapter.

FV = Future value. In this example, the FV is positive because we entered the PV as a negative number. If we had entered the 100 as a positive number, then the FV would have been negative. Calculators automatically assume that either the PV, PMT, or FV must be negative.

Spreadsheets

Spreadsheets are ideally suited for solving many financial problems, including time value of money problems.[2] With very little effort, the spreadsheet itself becomes a time line. Figure 4-1 shows how our problem would look in a spreadsheet.

We used *Excel* to create Figure 4-1, which summarizes the four methods for finding the FV. Note that spreadsheets can be used to do calculations, but they can also be used like a word processor to create exhibits like Figure 4-1, which includes text, drawings, and calculations. The letters across the top designate columns, the numbers to the left designate rows, and the rows and columns jointly designate cells.

It is a good practice to put a problem's inputs in the same section. For example, in Figure 4-1, C14 is the cell where we specify the $-\$100$ investment, C15 shows the interest rate, and C16 shows the number of periods.

Drawing a time line is an important step in solving finance problems. When we work a problem by hand we usually draw a time line. When we work a problem in *Excel*, we usually put in a time line. For example, in Figure 4-1 the time line is in Rows 17 to 19. Notice how easy it is in *Excel* to put in a time line, with each column designating a different period on the time line.

In Row 21 we have *Excel* go through the step-by-step calculations, multiplying the beginning-of-year values by $(1 + I)$ to find the compounded value at the end of each period. Cell G21 shows the final result of the step-by-step approach.

We illustrate the formula approach in Row 23, using *Excel* to solve Equation 4-1 and find the FV. Cell G23 shows the formula result, $115.76.

See *Ch 04 Tool Kit.xlsx* for all calculations.

[2]The textbook's website file *Ch 04 Tool Kit.xlsx* does the various calculations using *Excel*. We *highly recommend* that you go through the models. This will give you practice with *Excel*, which will help tremendously in later courses, in the job market, and in the workplace. Also, going through the models will enhance your understanding of financial concepts.

HINTS ON USING FINANCIAL CALCULATORS

When using a financial calculator, make sure it is set up as indicated below. Refer to your calculator manual or to our calculator tutorial on the text's website for information on setting up your calculator.

- **One payment per period.** Many calculators "come out of the box" assuming that 12 payments are made per year; that is, they assume monthly payments. However, in this book we generally deal with problems in which only one payment is made each year. *Therefore, you should set your calculator at one payment per year and leave it there. See our tutorial or your calculator manual if you need assistance.* We will show you how to solve problems with more than one payment per year in Section 4.15.
- **End mode.** With most contracts, payments are made at the *end* of each period. However, some contracts call for payments at the *beginning* of each period. You can switch between "End Mode" and "Begin Mode" depending on the problem you are solving. *Because most of the problems in this book call for end-of-period payments, you should return your calculator to End Mode after you work a problem in which payments are made at the beginning of periods.*
- **Negative sign for outflows.** When first learning how to use financial calculators, students often forget that one cash flow must be negative. Mathematically, financial calculators solve a version of this equation:

$$PV(1 + I)^N + FV_N = 0 \qquad (4\text{-}2)$$

Notice that for reasonable values of I, either PV or FV_N must be negative, and the other one must be positive to make the equation equal 0. This is reasonable because, in all realistic situations, one cash flow is an outflow (which should have a negative sign) and one is an inflow (which should have a positive sign). For example, if you make a deposit (which is an outflow, and hence should have a negative sign) then you will expect to make a later withdrawal (which is an inflow with a positive sign). *The bottom line is that one of your inputs for a cash flow must be negative and one must be positive. This generally means typing the outflow as a positive number and then pressing the +/− key to convert from + to − before hitting the enter key.*

- **Decimal places.** When doing arithmetic, calculators use a great many decimal places. However, they allow you to show from 0 to 11 decimal places on the display. When working with dollars, we generally specify two decimal places. When dealing with interest rates, we generally specify two places if the rate is expressed as a percentage, like 5.25%, but we specify four places if the rate is expressed as a decimal, like 0.0525.
- **Interest rates.** *For arithmetic operations with a non-financial calculator, the rate 5.25% must be stated as a decimal, 0.0525. However, with a financial calculator you must enter 5.25, not 0.0525, because financial calculators are programmed to assume that rates are stated as percentages.*

FIGURE 4-1   Summary: Future Value Calculations

	A	B	C	D	E	F	G
12							
13							
14	Investment	= CF₀ = PV =		−$100.00			
15	Interest rate	= I =		5.00%			
16	No. of periods	= N =		3			
17			Periods:	0	1	2	3
18							
19			Cash Flow Time Line:	−$100 ——→	——→	——→	FV = ?
20							
21	Step-by-Step Approach:			$100 —→	$105.00 —→	$110.25 —▶	$115.76
22							
23	Formula Approach: FVₙ = PV(1+I)ᴺ			FVₙ =	$100(1.05)³	=	$115.76
24							
25			3	5	−$100.00	$0	
26	Calculator Approach:		N	I/YR	PV	PMT	FV
27							$115.76
28							
29	Excel Approach:		FV Function:	FVₙ =	=FV(I,N,0,PV)		
30			Fixed inputs:	FVₙ =	=FV(0.05,3,0,-100)	=	$115.76
31			Cell references:	FVₙ =	=FV(C15,C16,0,C14)	=	$115.76
32	In the Excel formula, the terms are entered in this sequence: interest, periods, 0 to indicate no intermediate cash flows, and then the PV. The data can be entered as fixed numbers or as cell references.						

FINANCE: IN FOCUS

The Power of Compound Interest

Suppose you are 26 years old and just received your MBA. After reading the introduction to this chapter, you decide to start investing in the stock market for your retirement. Your goal is to have $1 million when you retire at age 65. Assuming you earn a 10% annual rate on your stock investments, how much must you invest at the end of each year in order to reach your goal?

The answer is $2,491, but this amount depends critically on the return earned on your investments. If returns drop to 8%, your required annual contributions will rise to $4,185. If returns rise to 12%, you will need to put away only $1,462 per year.

What if you are like most of us and wait until later to worry about retirement? If you wait until age 40, you will need to save $10,168 per year to reach your $1 million goal, assuming you earn 10%, and $13,679 per year if you earn only 8%. If you wait until age 50 and then earn 8%, the required amount will be $36,830 per year.

While $1 million may seem like a lot of money, it won't be when you get ready to retire. If inflation averages 5% a year over the next 39 years, your $1 million nest egg will be worth only $149,148 in today's dollars. At an 8% rate of return, and assuming you live for 20 years after retirement, your annual retirement income in today's dollars will be only $9,618 before taxes. So, after celebrating graduation and your new job, start saving!

Rows 25 to 27 illustrate the inputs and result from using a financial calculator.

The last section of Figure 4-1 illustrates *Excel*'s future value (FV) function. You can access the function wizard by clicking the f_x symbol in *Excel*'s formula bar, or you can go to the menu bar, select Insert, and then select Function from the drop-down menu. Select the category for Financial functions, and then select the FV function. The function is **=FV(I,N,0,PV)**, as shown in Cell E29.[3] Cell E30 shows how the formula would look with numbers as inputs; the actual function itself is in Cell G30. Cell E31 shows how the formula would look with cell references as inputs, with the actual function in Cell G31. We always recommend using cell references as inputs to functions, because this makes it easy to change inputs and see the effects on the output.

Notice that when entering interest rates in *Excel*, you must input the actual number. For example, in cell C15, we input "0.05," and then formatted it as a percentage. In the function itself, you can enter "0.05" or "5%," but if you enter "5," *Excel* will think you mean 500%. This is exactly opposite the convention for financial calculators.

Comparing the Procedures

The first step in solving any time value problem is to understand the verbal description of the problem well enough to diagram it on a time line. Woody Allen said that 90% of success is just showing up. With time value problems, 90% of success is correctly setting up the time line.

After you diagram the problem on a time line, your next step is to pick an approach to solve the problem. Which of the approaches should you use? The answer depends on the particular situation.

All business students should know Equation 4-1 by heart and should also know how to use a financial calculator. So, for simple problems such as finding the future value of a single payment, it is probably easiest and quickest to use either the formula approach or a financial calculator.

For problems with more than a couple of cash flows, the formula approach is usually too time consuming, so here either calculator or spreadsheet approaches would generally be used. Calculators are portable and quick to set up, but if many calculations of the same type must be done, or if you want to see how changes in an input such as the interest rate affect the future value, the spreadsheet approach is generally more efficient. If the problem has many irregular cash flows, or if you want to analyze many scenarios with different cash flows, then the spreadsheet approach is definitely the most efficient.

Spreadsheets have two additional advantages over calculators. First, it is easier to check the inputs with a spreadsheet because they are visible. With a calculator the inputs are buried somewhere in the machine. Thus, you are less likely to make a mistake in a complex problem

See *Ch 04 Tool Kit.xlsx* for all calculations.

---

[3]The third entry in the FV function is zero in this example, to indicate that there are no periodic payments. Later in this chapter we will use the function in situations where we do have periodic payments.

when you use a spreadsheet. Second, with a spreadsheet, you can make your analysis much more transparent than you can when using a calculator. This is not necessarily important when all you want is the answer, but if you need to present your calculations to others, like your boss, it helps to be able to show intermediate steps, which enables someone to go through your exhibit and see exactly what you did. Transparency is also important when you must go back, sometime later, and reconstruct what you did.

The important thing is that you understand the various approaches well enough to make a rational choice, given the nature of the problem and the equipment you have available. In any event, you must understand the concepts behind the calculations and know how to set up time lines in order to work complex problems. This is true for stock and bond valuation, capital budgeting, lease analysis, and many other important financial problems.

Graphic View of the Compounding Process

Figure 4-2 shows how a $1 investment grows over time at different interest rates. We made the curves by solving Equation 4-1 with different values for N and I. The interest rate is a growth rate: If a sum is deposited and earns 5% interest per year, then the funds on deposit will grow by 5% per year. Note also that time value concepts can be applied to anything that grows—sales, population, earnings per share, or your future salary.

Simple Interest versus Compound Interest

As explained earlier, when interest is earned on the interest earned in prior periods, we call it *compound interest*. If interest is earned only on the principal, we call it *simple interest*. The total interest earned with simple interest is equal to the principal multiplied by the interest rate times the number of periods: PV(I)(N). The future value is equal to the principal plus the interest: FV = PV + PV(I)(N). For example, suppose you deposit $100 for 3 years and earn simple interest at an annual rate of 5%. Your balance at the end of 3 years would be:

$$FV = PV + PV(I)(N)$$
$$= \$100 + \$100(5\%)(3)$$
$$= \$100 + \$15 = \$115$$

Notice that this is less than the $115.76 we calculated earlier using compound interest. Most applications in finance are based on compound interest, but you should be aware that simple interest is still specified in some legal documents.

FIGURE 4-2   Growth of $1 at Various Interest Rates and Time Periods

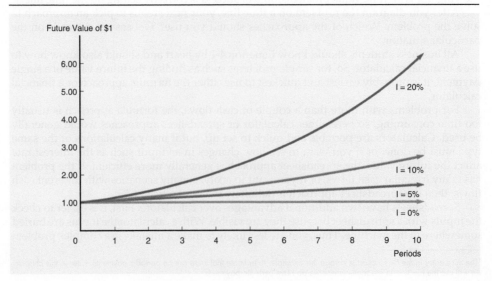

ⓒNCEPT REVIEW

1. Explain why this statement is true: "A dollar in hand today is worth more than a dollar to be received next year assuming interest rates are positive."
2. What is compounding? What would the future value of $100 be after 5 years at 10% *compound* interest? (Check Figure: $161.05)
3. Suppose you currently have $2,000 and plan to purchase a 3-year Guaranteed Investment Certificate (GIC) that pays 4% interest compounded annually. How much will you have when the GIC matures? How would your answer change if the interest rate were 5%, or 6%, or 20%? (Check Figure: $2,249.73; $2,315.25; $2,382.03; $3,456.00) (*Hint:* With a calculator, enter N = 3, I/YR = 4, PV = −2,000, and PMT = 0, then press FV to get 2,249.73. Then, enter I/YR = 5 to override the 4% and press FV again to get the second answer. In general, you can change one input at a time to see how the output changes.)
4. A company's sales in 2015 were $100 million. If sales grow at 8%, what will they be 10 years later? (Check Figure: $215.89 million)
5. How much would $1, growing at 5% per year, be worth after 100 years? What would FV be if the growth rate were 10%? (Check Figures: $131.50; $13,780.61)

4.3 Present Values

Suppose you have some extra money to invest. A broker offers to sell you a security that will pay a guaranteed $115.76 three years from now. Banks are currently offering a guaranteed 5% interest on 3-year Guaranteed Investment Certificates (GICs), and if you don't buy the security you will buy a GIC. The 5% rate paid on the GIC is defined as your **opportunity cost,** or the rate of return you could earn on an alternative investment of similar risk. Given these conditions, what's the most you should pay for the security?

Discounting a Future Value to Find the Present Value

First, recall from the future value example in the last section that if you invested $100 at 5% it would grow to $115.76 in 3 years. You would also have $115.76 after 3 years if you bought the broker's security. Therefore, the most you should pay for the security is $100—this is its "fair price." This is also equal to the intrinsic, or fundamental, value of the security. If you could buy the security for *less than* $100, you should buy it rather than invest in the GIC. Conversely, if its price were *more than* $100, you should buy the GIC. If the security's price were exactly $100, you should be indifferent between the security and the GIC.

The $100 is defined as the present value, or PV, of $115.76 due in 3 years when the appropriate interest rate is 5%. In general, *the present value of a cash flow due N years in the future is the amount that, if it were on hand today, would grow to equal the given future amount.* Since $100 would grow to $115.76 in 3 years at a 5% interest rate, $100 is the present value of $115.76 due in 3 years at a 5% rate.

Finding present values is called **discounting,** and as noted above, it is the reverse of compounding—if you know the PV, you can compound to find the FV, while if you know the FV, you can discount to find the PV. Indeed, we simply solve Equation 4-1, the formula for the future value, for the PV to produce the basic present value equation, 4-3:

See ***Ch 04 Tool Kit.xlsx***
for all calculations.

$$\text{Compounding to find future values: } FV_N = PV(1 + I)^N \qquad \text{(4-1)}$$

$$\text{Discounting to find present values: } PV = \frac{FV_N}{(1 + I)^N} \qquad \text{(4-3)}$$

The top section of Figure 4-3 shows the time line and calculates the PV using the step-by-step approach. When we found the future value in the previous section, we worked from left to right, multiplying the initial amount and each subsequent amount by (1 + I). To find present values, we work backward, or from right to left, *dividing* the future value and each subsequent amount by (1 + I). This procedure shows exactly what's happening, and that can be quite useful when you are working complex problems. However, it's inefficient, especially if you are dealing with a number of years.

With the formula approach we use Equation 4-3, simply dividing the future value by $(1 + I)^N$. This is more efficient than the step-by-step approach, and it gives the same result, as shown in Figure 4-3, Row 73.

See ***Ch 04 Tool Kit.xlsx***
for all calculations.

FIGURE 4-3   Summary: Present Value Calculations

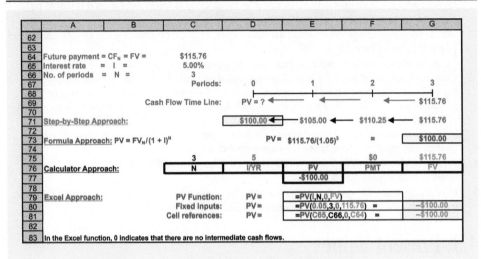

Equation 4-2 is built into financial calculators, and as shown in Figure 4-3, Row 76, we can find the PV by entering values for N = 3, I/YR = 5, PMT = 0, and FV = 115.76, and then pressing the PV key to get −100.

Spreadsheets also have a function that solves Equation 4-2. In *Excel*, this is the PV function, and it is written as **=PV(I,N,0,FV).**[4] Cell E79 shows the inputs to this function. Cell E80 shows the function with fixed numbers as inputs, with the actual function and the resulting −$100 in Cell G80. Cell E81 shows the function with cell references as inputs, with the actual function and the resulting −$100 in Cell G81.

The fundamental goal of financial management is to maximize the firm's value, and the value of a business (or any asset, including stocks and bonds) is the *present value* of its expected future cash flows. Since present value lies at the heart of the valuation process, we will have much more to say about it in the remainder of this chapter and throughout the book.

Graphic View of the Discounting Process

Figure 4-4 shows that the present value of a sum to be received in the future decreases and approaches zero as the payment date is extended further and further into the future, and also that the present value falls faster the higher the interest rate. At relatively high rates, funds due in the future are worth very little today, and even at relatively low rates present values of sums due in the very distant future are quite small. For example, at a 20% discount rate, $1 million due in 100 years would be worth only about 1 cent today. (However, 1 cent would grow to almost $1 million in 100 years at 20%.)

CONCEPT REVIEW

1. What is "discounting," and how is it related to compounding? How is the future value equation (4-1) related to the present value equation (4-3)?

2. How does the present value of a future payment change as the time to receipt is lengthened? As the interest rate increases?

3. Suppose a Canadian government bond promises to pay $2,249.73 three years from now. If the going interest rate on 3-year government bonds is 4%, how much is the bond worth today? How would your answer change if the bond matured in 5 rather than 3 years? What if the interest rate on the 5-year bond were 6% rather than 4%? (Check Figures: $2,000; $1,849.11; $1,681.13)

4. How much would $1,000,000 due in 100 years be worth today if the discount rate were 5%? If the discount rate were 20%? (Check Figures: $7,604.49; $0.0121)

---

[4]The third entry in the PV function is 0 to indicate that there are no intermediate payments in this particular example.

FIGURE
4-4   Present Value of $1 at Various Interest Rates and Time Periods

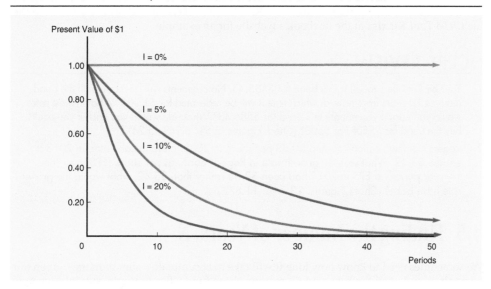

4.4 Finding the Interest Rate, I

We have used Equations 4-1, 4-2, and 4-3 to find future and present values. Those equations have four variables, and if we know three of them, we can solve for the fourth. Thus, if we know PV, I, and N, then we can solve Equation 4-1 for FV, while if we know FV, I, and N we can solve Equation 4-3 to find PV. That's what we did in the preceding two sections.

Now suppose we know PV, FV, and N, and we want to find I. For example, suppose we know that a given security has a cost of $100 and that it will return $150 after 10 years. Thus, we know PV, FV, and N, and we want to find the rate of return we will earn if we buy the security. Here's the solution using Equation 4-1:

$$FV_N = PV(1 + I)^N$$

$$\$150 = \$100(1 + I)^{10}$$

$$\$150/\$100 = (1 + I)^{10}$$

$$(1 + I)^{10} = 1.5$$

$$(1 + I) = 1.5^{(1/10)}$$

$$(1 + I) = 1.0414$$

$$I = 0.0414 = 4.14\%$$

See *Ch 04 Tool Kit.xlsx* for all calculations.

Finding the interest rate by solving the formula takes a little time, but financial calculators and spreadsheets can find interest rates almost instantly. Here's the calculator setup:

Inputs:	10		−100	0	150
	N	**I/YR**	**PV**	**PMT**	**FV**
Output:		4.14			

Enter N = 10, PV = −100, PMT = 0 (because there are no payments until the security matures), and FV = 150. Then, when you press the I/YR key, the calculator gives the answer, 4.14%. Notice that the PV is a negative value because it is a cash outflow (an investment) and that the FV is positive because it is a cash inflow (a return of the investment). If you enter both PV and FV as positive numbers (or both as negative numbers), your calculator will be unable to solve for the interest rate.

In *Excel*, the RATE function can be used to find the interest rate: **=RATE (N,PMT,PV,FV).** For this example, the function would be **=RATE(10,0,−100,150)** = 0.0414 = 4.14%. See the file **Ch 04 Tool Kit.xlsx** at the textbook's website for an example.

ⓒNCEPT REVIEW

1. Your broker offers to sell you a bond for $585.43. No payments will be made until the bond matures 10 years from now, at which time it will be redeemed for $1,000. What interest rate would you earn if you bought this bond for $585.43? What rate would you earn if you could buy the bond for $550? For $600? (Check Figures: 5.5%; 6.16%; 5.24%)

2. Rogers Communications earned $0.83 per share in 2002. Eleven years later, in 2013 it earned $3.42. What was the growth rate in Rogers' earnings per share (EPS) over the 11-year period? If EPS in 2013 had been $2.85 rather than $3.42, what would the growth rate have been? (Check Figures: 13.74%; 11.87%)

4.5 Finding the Number of Years, N

We sometimes need to know how long it will take to accumulate a sum of money, given our beginning funds and the rate we will earn on those funds. For example, suppose we now have $500,000 and the interest rate is 4.5%. How long will it take to grow to $1 million?

Here is Equation 4-1, showing all the known variables.

$$\$1,000,000 = \$500,000(1 + 0.045)^N$$

See **Ch 04 Tool Kit.xlsx** for all calculations.

We need to solve for N, and for this, we can use three procedures: a financial calculator; *Excel* (or some other spreadsheet); or natural logs. As you might expect, the calculator and spreadsheet approaches are easier.[5] Here's the calculator setup:

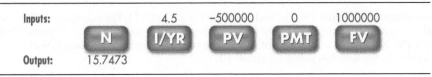

Inputs:		4.5	−500000	0	1000000
	N	I/YR	PV	PMT	FV
Output:	15.7473				

Enter I/YR = 4.5, PV = −500,000, PMT = 0, and FV = 1,000,000. When we press the N key, we get the answer, 15.7473 years.

In *Excel*, the NPER function can be used to find the number of periods: **=NPER(I, PMT,PV,FV).** For this example, the function would be **=NPER(0.045,0,−500000, 1000000)** = 15.7473. See the file **Ch 04 Tool Kit.xlsx** at the textbook's website for an example.

We should also make a comment on rounding. Although our answer of 15.7473 years is technically correct, when calculating for a time period, it often makes sense to round the time period. If we assume interest is paid once a year, we would not actually receive the interest until year-end; therefore, it would make sense to round our answer up to 16 years.

ⓒNCEPT REVIEW

1. How long would it take $1,000 to double if it were invested in a bank that pays 6% per year? How long would it take if the rate were 10%? (Check Figures: 11.9 years; 7.27 years)

2. Rogers' 2013 earnings per share were $3.42, and its growth rate during the prior 11 years was 13.74% per year. If that growth rate were maintained, how long would it take for Rogers' EPS to double? (Check Figure: 5.38 years)

---

[5]Here's the setup for the log solution. First, transform Equation 4-1 as indicated, then find the natural logs using a financial calculator, and then solve for N:

$$\$1,000,000 = \$500,000(1 + 0.045)^N$$
$$2 = (1 + 0.045)^N$$
$$\ln(2) = N[\ln(1.045)]$$
$$N = 0.6931/0.0440 = 15.7473 \text{ years}$$

4.6 Annuities

Thus far we have dealt with single payments, or "lump sums." However, assets such as bonds provide a series of cash inflows over time, and obligations such as auto loans, student loans, and mortgages require a series of payments. If the payments are equal and are made at fixed intervals, then the series is an **annuity.** For example, $100 paid at the end of each of the next 3 years is a 3-year annuity.

If payments occur at the *end* of each period, then we have an **ordinary** (or **deferred**) **annuity.** Payments on mortgages, car loans, and student loans are examples of ordinary annuities. If the payments are made at the *beginning* of each period, then we have an **annuity due.** Rental payments for an apartment, life insurance premiums, and lease payments are examples of annuities due. Ordinary annuities are more common in finance, so when we use the term "annuity" in this book, assume that the payments occur at the ends of the periods unless otherwise noted.

Here are the time lines for a $100, 3-year, 5%, ordinary annuity and for the same annuity on an annuity due basis. With the annuity due, each payment is shifted back (to the left) by 1 year. A $100 deposit will be made each year, so we show the payments with minus signs.

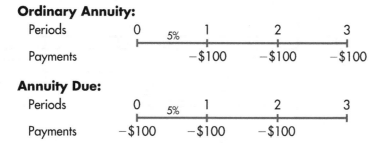

As we demonstrate in the following sections, we can find an annuity's future and present values, the interest rate built into annuity contracts, and how long it takes to reach a financial goal using an annuity. Keep in mind that annuities must have *constant payments* and a *fixed number of periods*. If these conditions don't hold, then we don't have an annuity.

CONCEPT REVIEW

1. What is the difference between an ordinary annuity and an annuity due?
2. Why should you rather receive an annuity due for $10,000 per year for 10 years than an otherwise similar ordinary annuity?

4.7 Future Value of an Ordinary Annuity

Consider the ordinary annuity whose timeline was shown previously, where you deposit $100 at the end of each year for 3 years and earn 5% per year. Figure 4-5 calculates the **future value of the annuity, FVA$_N$,** using each of the approaches we used for single cash flows.

As shown in the step-by-step section of Figure 4-5, we compound each payment out to Time 3, then sum those compounded values to find the annuity's FV, FVA$_3$ = $315.25. The first payment earns interest for two periods, the second for one period, and the third earns no interest at all because it is made at the end of the annuity's life. This approach is straightforward, but if the annuity extends out for many years, it is cumbersome and time consuming.

As you can see from the time line diagram, with the step-by-step approach we apply the following equation, with N = 3 and I = 5%:

$$FVA_N = PMT(1 + I)^{N-1} + PMT(1 + I)^{N-2} + PMT(1 + I)^{N-3}$$

$$= \$100(1.05)^2 + \$100(1.05)^1 + \$100(1.05)^0$$

$$= \$315.25$$

FIGURE 4-5   Summary: Future Value of an Ordinary Annuity

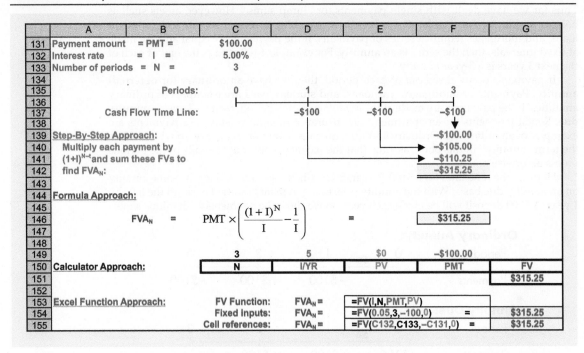

For the general case, the future value of an annuity is

$$FVA_N = PMT(1 + I)^{N-1} + PMT(1 + I)^{N-2}$$
$$+ PMT(1 + I)^{N-3} + \cdots + PMT(1 + I)^0$$

As shown in **Web Extension 4A** at the textbook's website, the future value of an annuity can be written as[6]

$$FVA_N = PMT\left[\frac{(1 + I)^N}{I} - \frac{1}{I}\right] \qquad (4\text{-}4)$$

Using Equation 4-4, the future value of the annuity is

$$FVA_3 = \$100\left[\frac{(1 + 0.05)^3}{0.05} - \frac{1}{0.05}\right] = \$315.25$$

Annuity problems are much easier to solve with financial calculators and spreadsheets. The following formula is built into financial calculators and spreadsheets:

See **Ch 04 Tool Kit.xlsx** for all calculations.

$$PV(1 + I)^N + PMT\left[\frac{(1 + I)^N}{I} - \frac{1}{I}\right] + FV = 0 \qquad (4\text{-}5)$$

When solving an annuity problem with a financial calculator, the presence of recurring payments means that we use the PMT key. Here's the calculator setup for our illustrative annuity:

---

[6]Section 4.11 shows that the present value of an infinitely long annuity, called a perpetuity, is equal to PMT/I. The cash flows of an ordinary annuity of N periods are equal to the cash flows of a perpetuity minus the cash flows of a perpetuity that begins at year N + 1. Therefore, the future value of an N-period annuity is equal to the future value (as of year N) of a perpetuity minus the value (as of year N) of a perpetuity that begins at year N + 1. See **Web Extension 4A** at the textbook's website for details of this derivation.

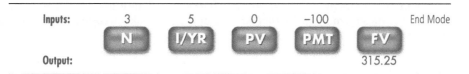

We enter PV = 0 because we start off with nothing, and we enter PMT = −100 because we plan to deposit this amount in the account at the end of each year. When we press the FV key we get the answer, $FVA_3 = 315.25$.

Since this is an ordinary annuity, with payments coming at the *end* of each year, we must set the calculator appropriately. As noted earlier, calculators "come out of the box" set to assume that payments occur at the end of each period, that is, to deal with ordinary annuities. However, there is a key that enables us to switch between ordinary annuities and annuities due. For ordinary annuities, the designation is "End Mode" or something similar, while for annuities due the designator is "Begin," "BGN," or "Due" or something similar. If you make a mistake and set your calculator on Begin Mode when working with an ordinary annuity, then each payment will earn interest for one extra year, which will cause the compounded amounts, and thus the FVA, to be too large.

The last approach in Figure 4-5 shows the spreadsheet solution, using *Excel's* built-in FV function: **=FV(I,N,PMT,PV)**. In our example, we have **=FV(0.05,3,−100,0),** with a resulting value of $315.25.

CONCEPT REVIEW

1. For an ordinary annuity with five annual payments of $100 and a 10% interest rate, how many years will the first payment earn interest, and what will this payment's value be at the end? Answer this same question for the fifth payment. (Check Figures: 4 years, $146.41; 0 years, $100)

2. Assume that you plan to buy a condo 5 years from now, and you estimate that you can save $2,500 per year. You plan to deposit the money in a bank that pays 4% interest, and you will make the first deposit at the end of the year. How much will you have after 5 years? How would your answer change if the interest rate were increased to 6%? Lowered to 3%? (Check Figures: $13,540.81; $14,092.73; $13,272.84)

4.8 Future Value of an Annuity Due

Since each payment occurs one period earlier with an annuity due, the payments will all earn interest for one additional period. Therefore, the FV of an annuity due will be greater than that of a similar ordinary annuity.

If you went through the step-by-step procedure, you would see that our illustrative annuity due has an FV of $331.01 versus $315.25 for the ordinary annuity. See *Ch 04 Tool Kit. xlsx* at the textbook's website for a summary of these calculations.

With the formula approach, we first use Equation 4-4, but since each payment occurs one period earlier, we multiply the Equation 4-4 result by (1 + I):

$$FVA_{due} = FVA_{ordinary}(1 + I) \qquad (4\text{-}6)$$

See *Ch 04 Tool Kit.xlsx* for all calculations.

Thus, for the annuity due, $FVA_{due} = \$315.25(1.05) = \$331.01$, which is the same result as found using the step-by-step approach.

With a calculator we input the variables just as we did with the ordinary annuity, but now we set the calculator to Begin Mode to get the answer, $331.01.

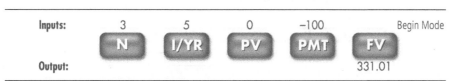

In *Excel*, we still use the FV function, but we must indicate that we have an annuity due. The function is **=FV(I,N,PMT,PV,Type)**, where Type indicates the type of annuity. If Type is omitted, *Excel* assumes that it is zero, which indicates an ordinary annuity. For an annuity due, Type = 1. As shown in *Ch 04 Tool Kit.xlsx* at the textbook's website, the function is = **FV(0.05,3,−100,0,1)** = $331.01.

⊙NCEPT REVIEW

1. Why does an annuity due always have a higher future value than an ordinary annuity?
2. If you calculated the value of an ordinary annuity, how could you find the value of the corresponding annuity due?
3. Assume that you plan to buy a condo 5 years from now, and you need to save for a down payment. You plan to save $2,500 per year, with the first payment made *immediately*, and you will deposit the funds in a bank account that pays 4%. How much will you have after 5 years? How much would you have if you made the deposits at the end of each year? (Check Figures: $14,082.44; $13,540.81)

4.9 Present Value of an Ordinary Annuity and of an Annuity Due

The present value of an annuity, **PVA$_N$**, can be found using the step-by-step, formula, calculator, or spreadsheet methods. We begin with an ordinary annuity.

See **Ch 04 Tool Kit.xlsx** for all calculations.

Present Value of an Ordinary Annuity

See Figure 4-6 for a summary of the different approaches for calculating the present value of an ordinary annuity.

As shown in the step-by-step section of Figure 4-6, we discount each payment back to Time 0, then sum those discounted values to find the annuity's PV, PVA$_3$ = $272.32. This approach is straightforward, but if the annuity extends out for many years, it is cumbersome and time consuming.

FIGURE 4-6

Summary: Present Value of an Ordinary Annuity

	A	B	C	D	E	F	G
196	Payment amount	= PMT =	$100.00				
197	Interest rate	= I =	5.00%				
198	Number of periods	= N =	3				
199							
200		Periods:	0	1	2	3	
201							
202		Cash Flow Time Line:		−$100	−$100	−$100	
203							
204	Step-by-Step Approach:		$95.24				
205	Divide each payment by		$90.70				
206	(1+ I)^t and sum these PVs to		$86.38				
207	find PVA$_N$:		$272.32				
208							
209	Formula Approach:						
210							
211		PVA$_N$ =	$PMT \times \left(\dfrac{1}{I} - \dfrac{1}{I(1+I)^N} \right)$		=	$272.32	
212							
213							
214			3	5		−100	0
215	Calculator Approach:		N	I	PV	PMT	FV
216					272.32		
217							
218	Excel Function Approach:		PV Function:	PVA$_N$ =	=PV(I,N,PMT,FV)		
219			Fixed inputs:	PVA$_N$ =	=PV(0.05,3,−100,0)	=	272.32
220			Cell references:	PVA$_N$ =	=PV(C197,C198,−C196,0) =		272.32

The time line diagram shows that with the step-by-step approach we apply the following equation, with N = 3 and I = 5%:

$$PVA_N = PMT/(1 + I)^1 + PMT/(1 + I)^2 + \cdots + PMT/(1 + I)^N$$

The present value of an annuity can be written as[7]

$$PVA_N = PMT\left[\frac{1}{I} - \frac{1}{I(1 + I)^N}\right] \tag{4-7}$$

*See **Ch 04 Tool Kit.xlsx** for all calculations.*

For our annuity, this present value is

$$PVA_3 = 100\left[\frac{1}{0.05} - \frac{1}{0.05(1 + 0.05)^3}\right] = \$272.32$$

Financial calculators are programmed to solve Equation 4-5, so we merely input the variables and press the PV key, *making sure the calculator is set to End Mode.* The calculator setup is shown below:

Inputs:	3	5		−100	0	End Mode
	N	I/YR	PV	PMT	FV	(Ordinary Annuity)
Output:			272.32			

The last approach in Figure 4-6 shows the spreadsheet solution, using *Excel's* built-in PV function: **=PV(I,N,PMT,FV).** In our example, we have **=PV(0.05,3,−100,0),** with a resulting value of $272.32.

Present Value of Annuities Due

Since each payment for an annuity due occurs one period earlier, the payments will all be discounted for one less period. Therefore, the PV of an annuity due will be greater than that of a similar ordinary annuity.

If you went through the step-by-step procedure, you would see that our illustrative annuity due has a PV of $285.94 versus $272.32 for the ordinary annuity. See ***Ch 04 Tool Kit. xlsx*** at the textbook's website for a summary of these calculations.

*See **Ch 04 Tool Kit.xlsx** for all calculations.*

With the formula approach, we first use Equation 4-7, but since each payment occurs one period earlier, we multiply the Equation 4-7 result by (1 + I):

$$PVA_{due} = PVA_{ordinary}(1 + I) \tag{4-8}$$

Thus, for the annuity due, $PVA_{due} = \$272.32(1.05) = \$285.94$, which is the same result as found using the step-by-step approach.

With a financial calculator, the inputs are the same as for an ordinary annuity, except you must set the calculator to the Begin Mode.

Inputs:	3	5		−100	0	Begin Mode
	N	I/YR	PV	PMT	FV	(Annuity Due)
Output:			285.94			

In *Excel*, we still use the PV function, but we must indicate that we have an annuity due. The function is **=PV(I,N,PMT,FV,Type),** where Type indicates the type of annuity. If Type is omitted, *Excel* assumes that it is zero, which indicates an ordinary annuity. For an annuity

[7]See **Web Extension 4A** on the textbook's website for details of this derivation.

due, Type = 1. As shown in *Ch 04 Tool Kit.xlsx* at the textbook's website, the function for this example is =**PV(0.05,3,−100,0,1)** = $285.94.

ⒸNCEPT REVIEW

1. Why does an annuity due have a higher present value than an ordinary annuity?

2. If you know the present value of an ordinary annuity, how can you find the PV of the corresponding annuity due?

3. What is the PVA of an ordinary annuity with 10 payments of $100 if the appropriate interest rate is 10%? What would PVA be if the interest rate were 4%? What if the interest rate were 0%? How would the PVA values differ if we were dealing with annuities due? (Check Figures: $614.46; $811.09; $1,000.00; $675.90; $843.53; $1,000.00)

4. Assume that you are offered an annuity that pays $100 at the end of each year for 10 years. You could earn 8% on your money in other investments with equal risk. What is the most you should pay for the annuity? If the payments began immediately, how much would the annuity be worth? (Check Figures: $671.01; $724.69)

4.10 Finding Annuity Payments, Periods, and Interest Rates

We can find payments, periods, and interest rates for annuities. Five variables come into play: N, I, PMT, FV, and PV. If we know any four, we can find the fifth. It is not too difficult to solve Equation 4-5 for the payment if you know all of the other inputs. But when trying to find the interest rate or number of periods, Equation 4-5 usually must be solved by trial-and-error. Therefore, we present only the solution approaches using a financial calculator or spreadsheet.

Finding Annuity Payments, PMT

Suppose we need to accumulate $10,000 and have it available 5 years from now. Suppose further that we can earn a return of 6% on our savings, which are currently zero. Thus, we know that FV = 10,000, PV = 0, N = 5, and I/YR = 6. We can enter these values in a financial calculator and then press the PMT key to find how large our deposits must be. The answer will, of course, depend on whether we make deposits at the end of each year (ordinary annuity) or at the beginning (annuity due). Here are the results for each type of annuity:

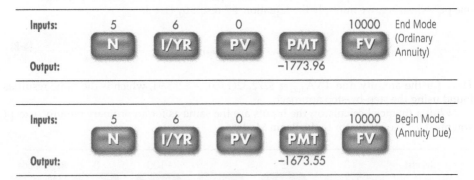

Thus, you must save $1,773.96 per year if you make payments at the *end* of each year, but only $1,673.55 if the payments begin *immediately*. Note that the required payment for the annuity due is the ordinary annuity payment divided by (1 + I): $1,773.96/1.06 = $1,673.55.

See *Ch 04 Tool Kit.xlsx* for all calculations.

Excel can also be used to find annuity payments. To find end-of-year payments, we use the PMT function: =**PMT(I,N,PV,FV)**. In our example, this is =**PMT(0.06,5,0,10000)** = $1,773.96. For the payments of an annuity due (payments at the beginning of the period), the same formula is used, except we must specify the type of annuity, with Type = 1 indicating an annuity due: =**PMT(I,N,PV,FV,Type)** =**PMT(0.06,5,0,10000,1)** = $1,673.55.

Finding the Number of Periods, N

Suppose you decide to make end-of-year deposits, but you can only save $1,200 per year. Again assuming that you would earn 6%, how long would it take you to reach your $10,000 goal? Here is the calculator setup:

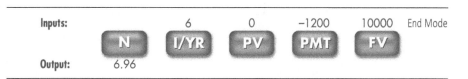

See *Ch 04 Tool Kit.xlsx* for all calculations.

With these smaller deposits, it would take 6.96 years to reach the $10,000 target. If you began the deposits immediately, then you would have an annuity due and N would be a bit less, 6.63 years.

In *Excel*, you can use the NPER function: **=NPER(I,PMT,PV,FV,Type)**. For our ordinary annuity example, Type is left blank (or 0 is inserted) and the function is **=NPER(0.06, −1200,0,10000)** = 6.96. If we put in 1 for Type, signifying an annuity due, we would find N = 6.63.

Finding the Interest Rate, I

Now suppose you can save only $1,200 annually, but you still want to have the $10,000 in 5 years. What rate of return would enable you to achieve your goal? Here is the calculator setup:

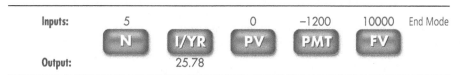

You would need to earn a whopping 25.78%! About the only possible (but risky) way to get such a high return would be to invest in speculative stocks or head to a casino. Of course, speculative stocks and gambling aren't like making deposits in a bank with a guaranteed rate of return, so there's a good chance you'd end up with nothing. We'd recommend that you change your plans—save more, lower your $10,000 target, or extend your time horizon. It might be appropriate to seek a somewhat higher return, but trying to earn 25.78% in a 6% market would require taking on more risk than would be prudent.

In *Excel*, you can use the RATE function: **=RATE(N,PMT,PV,FV)**. For this example, the function is **=RATE(5,−1200,0,10000)** = 0.2578 = 25.78%.

FINANCE: IN FOCUS

Using the Internet for Personal Financial Planning

People continually face important financial decisions that require an understanding of the time value of money. Should we buy or lease a car? How much and how soon should we begin to save for our children's education? How expensive a house can we afford? Should we refinance our home mortgage? How much must we save each year to retire comfortably?

The answers to these questions are often complicated, and they depend on a number of factors, such as projected housing and education costs, interest rates, inflation, expected family income, and stock market returns. Hopefully, after completing this chapter, you will have a better idea of how to answer such questions. Moreover, a number of online resources are available to help with financial planning.

A good place to start is **www.financial post.com** or **www.globeandmail.com**. When you go to the *Financial Post*'s website, click on the section titled "Personal Finance." This section has a number of financial calculators and other descriptive materials that cover a wide range of personal finance issues. When you go to the *Globe and Mail*'s website, click on its "Investing" section. Once there, click on "calculators," where you will find a wide variety of personal finance calculators.

CONCEPT REVIEW

1. Suppose you inherited $100,000 and invested it at 7% per year. How much could you withdraw at the *end* of each of the next 10 years? How would your answer change if you made withdrawals at the *beginning* of each year? (Check Figures: $14,237.75; $13,306.31)

2. If you had $100,000 that was invested at 7% and you wanted to withdraw $10,000 at the end of each year, how long would your funds last? How long would they last if you earned 0%? How long would they last if you earned the 7% but limited your withdrawal to $7,000 per year? (Check Figures: 17.8 years; 10 years; forever)

3. Your rich uncle named you as the beneficiary of his life insurance policy. The insurance company gives you a choice of $100,000 today or a 12-year annuity of $12,000 at the end of each year. What rate of return is the insurance company offering? (Check Figure: 6.11%)

4. Assume that you just inherited an annuity that will pay you $10,000 per year for 10 years, with the first payment being made today. A friend of your mother offers to give you $60,000 for the annuity. If you sell it, what rate of return will your mother's friend earn on the investment? If you think a "fair" return would be 6%, how much should you ask for the annuity? (Check Figures: 13.70%; $78,016.92)

4.11 Perpetuities

In the last section we dealt with annuities whose payments continue for a specific number of periods—for example, $100 per year for 10 years. However, some securities promise to make payments forever. For example, in 1749 the British government issued some bonds whose proceeds were used to pay off other British bonds, and since this action consolidated the government's debt, the new bonds were called consols. Since **consols** promise to pay interest perpetually, they are perpetuities. The interest rate on the consols was 2.5%, so a bond with a face value of $1,000 would pay $25 per year in perpetuity.[8]

A **perpetuity** is simply an annuity whose promised payments extend out forever. Since the payments go on forever, you can't apply the step-by-step approach. However, it's easy to find the PV of a perpetuity with the following formula:[9]

$$\text{PV of a perpetuity} = \frac{\text{PMT}}{\text{I}} \qquad \qquad (4\text{-}9)$$

Now we can use Equation 4-9 to find the value of a British consol with a face value of $1,000 that pays $25 per year in perpetuity. The answer depends on the interest rate. In 1888, the "going rate" as established in the financial marketplace was 2.5%, so at that time the consol's value was $1,000:

$$\text{Consol value}_{1888} = \$25/0.025 = \$1,000$$

The annual payment is still $25 today, but the going interest rate has risen to 5.2%, causing the consol's value to fall to $480.77:

$$\text{Consol value}_{\text{Today}} = \$25/0.052 = \$480.77$$

Note, though, that if interest rates decline in the future, say to 2%, the value of the consol will rise:

$$\text{Consol value if rates decline to 2\%} = \$25/0.02 = \$1,250.00$$

These examples demonstrate an important point: *When interest rates change, the prices of outstanding bonds also change. Bond prices decline if rates rise and increase if rates fall.* We will discuss this point in more detail in Chapter 6, where we cover bonds in depth.

---

[8]The consols actually pay interest in pounds, but we discuss them in dollar terms for simplicity.
[9]See **Web Extension 4A** at the textbook's website for a derivation of the perpetuity formula.

CONCEPT REVIEW

1. What is the present value of a perpetuity that pays $1,000 per year, beginning 1 year from now, if the appropriate interest rate is 5%? What would the value be if the annuity began its payments immediately? (Check Figures: $20,000, $21,000). (Hint: Just add the $1,000 to be received immediately to the value of the annuity.)

2. What happens to the value of a bond if interest rates go up? If rates go down?

4.12 Uneven, or Irregular, Cash Flows

The definition of an annuity includes the term "constant payment"—in other words, annuities involve payments that are equal in every period. Although many financial decisions do involve constant payments, many others involve cash flows that are *uneven* or *irregular*. For example, the dividends on common stocks typically increase over time, and investments in capital equipment almost always generate uneven cash flows. Throughout the book, we reserve the term **payment (PMT)** for annuities with equal payments in each period and use the term **cash flow (CF$_t$)** to denote uneven cash flows, where the t designates the period in which the cash flow occurs.

There are two important classes of uneven cash flows: (1) a stream that consists of a series of annuity payments plus an additional final lump sum and (2) all other uneven streams. Bonds represent the best example of the first type, while stocks and capital investments illustrate the other type. Here are numerical examples of the two types of flows:

1. Annuity plus additional final payment:

Periods	0	1	2	3	4	5
	I = 12%					
Cash flows	$0	$100	$100	$100	$100	$ 100
						$ 1,000
						$1,100

2. Irregular cash flows:

Periods	0	1	2	3	4	5
	I = 12%					
Cash flows	$0	$100	$300	$300	$300	$500

We can find the PV of either stream by using Equation 4-10 and following the step-by-step procedure, where we discount each cash flow and then sum them to find the PV of the stream:

$$PV = \frac{CF_1}{(1 + I)^1} + \frac{CF_2}{(1 + I)^2} + \cdots + \frac{CF_N}{(1 + I)^N} = \sum_{t=1}^{N} \frac{CF_t}{(1 + I)^t} \qquad (4\text{-}10)$$

See **Ch 04 Tool Kit.xlsx** for all calculations.

If we did this, we would find the PV of Stream 1 to be $927.90 and the PV of Stream 2 to be $1,016.35.

The step-by-step procedure is straightforward, but if we have a large number of cash flows it is time consuming. However, financial calculators and spreadsheets speed up the process considerably.

Annuity Plus Additional Final Payment First, consider Stream 1, and notice that it is a 5-year, 12%, ordinary annuity plus a final payment of $1,000. We could find the PV of the annuity, then find the PV of the final payment, and then sum them to get the PV of the stream. However, financial calculators do this in one simple step—use the five TVM keys, enter the data as shown below, and then press the PV key to get the answer, $927.90.

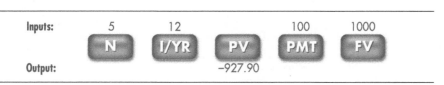

Inputs:	5	12		100	1000
	N	**I/YR**	**PV**	**PMT**	**FV**
Output:			−927.90		

Similarly, we could use the PV function in *Excel*: **=PV(I,N,PMT,FV)**. This is similar to our previous solutions for an annuity, except we now have a nonzero value for FV. Applying the PV function, we get **=PV(0.12,5,100,1000)** = −$927.90.

Irregular Cash Flow Stream Now consider the second uneven stream shown in Figure 4-7. The top section shows the time line and an application of the step-by-step approach.

Because the cash flows do not represent an annuity, you can't use the annuity feature on your financial calculator to find the present value. However, your financial calculator does have a feature that allows you to find the present value. First, you input the individual cash flows, in chronological order, into the cash flow register.[10] Cash flows are usually designated CF_0, CF_1, CF_2, CF_3, and so on upto the last cash flow, CF_N. Next, you enter the interest rate, I. At this point, you have substituted in all the known values of Equation 4-10, so you need to press only the NPV key to find the present value of the stream. The calculator has been programmed to find the PV of each cash flow and then to sum these values to find the PV of the entire stream. To input the cash flows for this problem, enter 0 (because CF_0 = 0), 100, 300, 300, 300, and 500 in that order into the cash flow register, enter I = 12, and then press NPV to obtain the answer, $1,016.35.

Two points should be noted. First, when dealing with the cash flow register, the calculator uses the term "NPV" rather than "PV." The N stands for "net," so NPV is the abbreviation for "Net Present Value," which is simply the net present value of a series of positive and negative cash flows, including the cash flow at time zero.

The second point to note is that repeated cash flows with identical values can be entered into the cash flow register more efficiently by using the Nj key. In this illustration, you would enter CF_0 = 0, CF_1 = 100, CF_2 = 300, Nj = 3 (which tells the calculator that the 300 occurs 3 times), and CF_5 = 500.[11] Then enter I = 12, press the NPV key, and 1,016.35 will appear in the display. Also, note that amounts entered into the cash flow register remain in the register until they are cleared. Thus, if you had previously worked a problem with eight cash flows, and then moved to a problem with only four cash flows, the calculator would simply add the cash flows from the second problem to those of the first problem. Therefore, you must be sure to clear the cash flow register before starting a new problem.

Spreadsheets are especially useful for solving problems with uneven cash flows. Just as with a financial calculator, you must enter the cash flows in the spreadsheet, as shown in Figure 4-7. To find the PV of these cash flows with *Excel*, you can use the NPV function. Put your cursor on Cell G373, click the function wizard, click Financial, scroll down to NPV,

FIGURE 4-7 PV of an Uneven Cash Flow Stream

	A	B	C	D	E	F	G
358	Interest rate	= I =	12%				
359							
360	Periods:	0	1	2	3	4	5
361							
362	CF Time Line:	$0	$100	$300	$300	$300	$500
363	PV of CFs						
364		$89.29					
365		239.16					
366		213.53					
367		190.66					
368		283.71					
369		$1,016.35	= PV of cash flow stream = value of the asset				
370							
371							
372	**Excel Function Approach:**		Fixed Inputs:	NPV =	=NPV(0.12,100,300,300,300,500)		1,016.35
373			Cell references:	NPV =	=NPV(C358,C362:G362)		1,016.35

---

[10]We cover the calculator mechanics in the tutorial, and we discuss the process in more detail in Chapter 10, where we use the NPV calculation to analyze proposed projects. If you don't know how to use the cash flow register of your calculator, you should to go to our tutorial or your calculator manual, learn the steps, and be sure you can make this calculation. You will have to know how to do it eventually, and now is a good time to learn.

[11]On some calculators, instead of entering CF_5 = 500, you enter CF_3 = 500, because this is the next cash flow *different* from 300.

and click OK to get the dialog box. Then enter C358 (or 0.12) for Rate and the range of cells containing the cash flows, C362:G362, for Value 1. Be very careful when entering the range of cash flows. With a financial calculator, you begin by entering the Time 0 cash flow. With *Excel*, you do *not* include the Time 0 cash flow; instead, you begin with the Year 1 cash flow. Now, when you click OK, you get the PV of the stream, $1,016.35. Note that you can use the PV function if the payments are constant but you must use the NPV function if the cash flows are not constant. Note too that one of the advantages of spreadsheets over financial calculators is that you can see the cash flows, which makes it easy to spot any typing errors.

CONCEPT REVIEW

1. Could you use Equation 4-3, once for each cash flow, to find the PV of an uneven stream of cash flows?

2. What is the present value of a 5-year ordinary annuity of $100 plus an additional $500 at the end of Year 5 if the interest rate is 6%? How would the PV change if the $100 payments occurred in Years 1 through 10 and the $500 came at the end of Year 10? (Check Figures: $794.87; $1,015.21)

3. What is the present value of the following uneven cash flow stream: $0 at Time 0, $100 in Year 1 (or at Time 1), $200 in Year 2, $0 in Year 3, and $400 in Year 4 if the interest rate is 8%? (Check Figure: $558.07)

4. Would a typical common stock provide cash flows more like an annuity or more like an uneven cash flow stream?

4.13 Future Value of an Uneven Cash Flow Stream

The future value of an uneven cash flow stream (sometimes called the *terminal*, or *horizon*, *value*) is found by compounding each payment to the end of the stream and then summing the future values:

$$FV = CF_0(1 + I)^N + CF_1(1 + I)^{N-1} + CF_2(1 + I)^{N-2} + \cdots + CF_{N-1}(1 + I) + CF_N$$

$$= \sum_{t=0}^{N} CF_t(1 + I)^{N-t} \tag{4-11}$$

The future value of our illustrative uneven cash flow stream is $1,791.15, as shown in Figure 4-8.

FIGURE
4-8   FV of an Uneven Cash Flow Stream

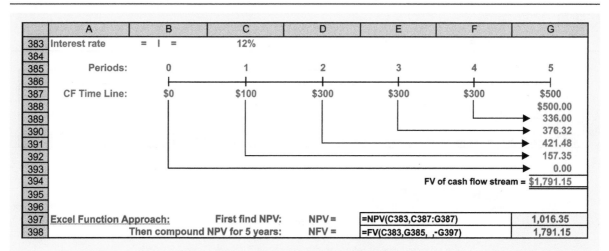

	A	B	C	D	E	F	G
383	Interest rate	= I =	12%				
384							
385	Periods:	0	1	2	3	4	5
386							
387	CF Time Line:	$0	$100	$300	$300	$300	$500
388							$500.00
389							336.00
390							376.32
391							421.48
392							157.35
393							0.00
394						FV of cash flow stream =	$1,791.15
395							
396							
397	**Excel Function Approach:**		First find NPV:	NPV =	=NPV(C383,C387:G387)		1,016.35
398		Then compound NPV for 5 years:		NFV =	=FV(C383,G385, ,-G397)		1,791.15

Some financial calculators have a net future value (NFV) key that, after the cash flows and interest rate have been entered, can be used to obtain the future value of an uneven cash flow stream. Even if your calculator doesn't have the NFV feature, you can use the cash flow stream's net present value to find its net future value: $NFV = NPV(1 + I)^N$. Thus, in our example, you could find the PV of the stream, then find the FV of that PV, compounded for N periods at I%. In the illustrative problem, find PV = 1,016.35 using the cash flow register and I = 12. Then enter N = 5, I = 12, PV = −1016.35, and PMT = 0. Press FV to find FV = 1,791.15, which equals the NFV shown on the time line in Figure 4-8. A similar procedure can be used in *Excel*: First find the NPV, then find its FV. See ***Ch 04 Tool Kit.xls*** for details.

See ***Ch 04 Tool Kit.xlsx***
for all calculations.

ⓒNCEPT REVIEW

1. What is the future value of this cash flow stream: $100 at the end of 1 year, $150 due after 2 years, and $300 due after 3 years if the appropriate interest rate is 15%? (Check Figure: $604.75)

4.14 Solving for I with Uneven Cash Flows

See ***Ch 04 Tool Kit.xlsx***
for all calculations.

Before financial calculators and spreadsheets existed, it was *extremely difficult* to find I if the cash flows were uneven. With spreadsheets and financial calculators, though, it's relatively easy to find I. If you have an annuity plus a final lump sum, you can input values for N, PV, PMT, and FV into the calculator's TVM registers and then press the I/YR key. Here is the setup for Stream 1 from Section 4.12, assuming we must pay $927.90 to buy the asset. The rate of return on the $927.90 investment is 12%, as shown below:

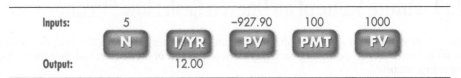

Inputs:	5		−927.90	100	1000
	N	I/YR	PV	PMT	FV
Output:		12.00			

Finding the interest rate for an uneven cash flow stream is a bit more complicated. Figure 4-9 shows Stream 2 from Section 4.12, assuming CF_0 is −$1,000. First, note that there is no simple procedure for finding the rate of return—finding the rate requires a trial-and-error process, which means that one really needs a financial calculator or a spreadsheet. With a calculator, we would enter the CFs into the cash flow register and then press the IRR key to get the answer. IRR stands for "internal rate of return," and it is the rate of return the investment provides. The investment is the cash flow at Time 0, and it must be entered as a negative number. When we enter those cash flows in the calculator's cash flow register and press the IRR key, we get the rate of return on the $1,000 investment, 12.55%.

You would get the same answer using *Excel's* IRR function, as shown in Figure 4-9. Notice that with the IRR function, you must include all cash flows, including the Time 0 cash flow; with the NPV function, you do not include the Time 0 cash flow.

FIGURE 4-9 IRR of an Uneven Cash Flow Stream

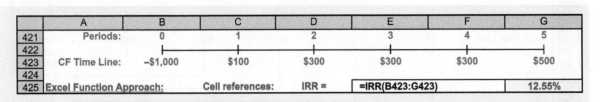

	A	B	C	D	E	F	G
421	Periods:	0	1	2	3	4	5
422							
423	CF Time Line:	−$1,000	$100	$300	$300	$300	$500
424							
425	Excel Function Approach:		Cell references:	IRR =	=IRR(B423:G423)		12.55%

ⓒNCEPT REVIEW

1. An investment costs $465 and is expected to produce cash flows of $100 at the end of each of the next 4 years, then an extra lump sum payment of $200 at the end of the 4th year. What is the expected rate of return on this investment? (Check Figure: 9.05%)

2. An investment costs $465 and is expected to produce cash flows of $100 at the end of Year 1, $200 at the end of Year 2, and $300 at the end of Year 3. What is the expected rate of return on this investment? (Check Figure: 11.71%)

4.15 Semiannual and Other Compounding Periods

In almost all of our examples thus far, we have assumed that interest is compounded once a year, or annually. This is called *annual compounding*. Suppose, however, that you put $100 into a bank that states it pays a 6% annual interest rate but that interest is credited each 6 months. This is called *semiannual compounding*. How much would you have accumulated at the end of 1 year, 2 years, or some other period under semiannual compounding? Note that virtually all bonds pay interest semiannually; most stocks pay dividends quarterly; and most mortgages, student loans, and auto loans require monthly payments. Therefore, it is essential that you understand how to deal with nonannual compounding.

Types of Interest Rates

When we move beyond annual compounding, we must deal with the following four types of interest rates:

- Nominal annual rates, given the symbol I_{NOM}
- Annual percentage rates, termed **APR**
- Periodic rates, denoted as I_{PER}
- Effective annual rates, given the symbol **EAR** or **EFF%**

Nominal, or Quoted, Rate, I_{NOM}[12] This is the rate that is quoted by banks, brokers, and other financial institutions. So, if you talk with a banker, broker, mortgage lender, auto finance company, or student loan officer about rates, the nominal rate is the one he or she will normally quote you. However, to be meaningful, the quoted nominal rate must also include the number of compounding periods per year. For example, a bank might offer 6%, compounded quarterly, on GICs; or a mutual fund might offer 5%, compounded monthly, on its money market account.

The nominal rate on loans to consumers is also called the **Annual Percentage Rate (APR).** For example, if a credit card issuer quotes an annual rate of 18%, this is the APR.

Note that the nominal rate is never shown on a time line, and it is never used as an input in a financial calculator, unless compounding occurs only once a year. If more frequent compounding occurs, you should use the periodic rate as discussed below.

Periodic Rate, I_{PER} This is the rate charged by a lender or paid by a borrower each period. It can be a rate per year, per 6-month period, per quarter, per month, per day, or per any other time interval. For example, a bank might charge 1.5% per month on its credit card loans, or a finance company might charge 3% per quarter on installment loans. We find the periodic rate as follows:

$$\text{Periodic rate, } I_{PER} = I_{NOM}/M \qquad \text{(4-12)}$$

which implies that

$$\text{Nominal annual rate} = I_{NOM} = (\text{Periodic rate})(M) \qquad \text{(4-13)}$$

Here I_{NOM} is the nominal annual rate and M is the number of compounding periods per year. To illustrate, consider a finance company loan at 3% per quarter:

$$\text{Nominal annual rate} = I_{NOM} = (\text{Periodic rate})(M) = (3\%)(4) = 12\%$$

---

[12]The term "nominal rate" as it is used here has a different meaning from the way it was used in Chapter 1. There, nominal interest rates referred to stated market rates as opposed to real (zero inflation) rates. In this chapter, the term "nominal rate" means the stated, or quoted, annual rate as opposed to the effective annual rate, which we explain later. In both cases, though, "nominal" means "stated," or "quoted," as opposed to some adjusted rate.

or

$$\text{Periodic rate} = I_{NOM}/M = 12\%/4 = 3\% \text{ per quarter}$$

If there is only one payment per year, or if interest is added only once a year, then M = 1, and the periodic rate is equal to the nominal rate.

The periodic rate is the rate that is generally shown on time lines and used in calculations.[13] To illustrate, suppose you invest $100 in an account that pays a nominal rate of 12%, compounded quarterly, or 3% per period. How much would you have after 2 years?

For compounding more frequently than annually, we use the following modification of Equation 4-1:

$$FV_N = PV(1 + I_{PER})^{\text{Number of periods}} = PV\left(1 + \frac{I_{NOM}}{M}\right)^{MN} \qquad (4\text{-}14)$$

For the example of $100 compounded quarterly at an annual nominal rate of 12% for 2 years, the time line is

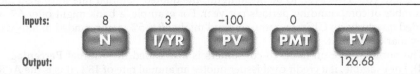

Using Equation 4-14,

$$FV = \$100(1 + 0.03)^8$$

$$= \$126.68$$

With a financial calculator, we work the problem with inputs N = 2 × 4 = 8, I = 12/4 = 3, PV = −100, and PMT = 0. The result is FV = $126.68.[14]

Inputs:	8	3	−100	0	
	N	I/YR	PV	PMT	FV
Output:					126.68

Effective (or Equivalent) Annual Rate (EAR or EFF%) This is the annual rate that produces the same result as if we had compounded at a given periodic rate M times per year. The EAR, also called EFF% (for effective percentage), is found as follows:

$$\text{Effective annual rate (EFF\%)} = (1 + I_{PER})^M - 1.0$$

$$= \left(1 + \frac{I_{NOM}}{M}\right)^M - 1.0 \qquad (4\text{-}15)$$

You could also use the interest conversion feature of a financial calculator.[15]

---

[13]The only exception is in situations where (1) annuities are involved and (2) the payment periods do not correspond to the compounding periods. If an annuity is involved and if its payment periods do not correspond to the compounding periods—for example, if you are making quarterly payments into a bank account to build up a specified future sum, but the bank pays interest on a daily basis—then the calculations are more complicated. For such problems, one can proceed in two alternative ways. (1) Determine the periodic (daily) interest rate by dividing the nominal rate by 365 (or 360 if the bank uses a 360-day year), then compound each payment over the exact number of days from the payment date to the terminal point, and then sum the compounded payments to find the future value of the annuity. This is what would generally be done in the real world, because with a computer it would be a simple process. (2) Calculate the EAR, as defined later in this section, based on daily compounding, then find the corresponding nominal rate based on quarterly compounding (because the annuity payments are made quarterly), then find the quarterly periodic rate, and use that rate with standard annuity procedures. The second procedure is faster with a calculator, but hard to explain and generally not used in practice given the ready availability of computers.

[14]Most financial calculators have a feature that allows you to set the number of payments per year and then use the nominal annual interest rate. However, in our experience, students make fewer errors when using the periodic rate with their calculators set for one payment per year (i.e., per period), so this is what we recommend.

[15]Most financial calculators are programmed to find the EFF% or, given the EFF%, to find the nominal rate. This is called "interest rate conversion." You enter the nominal rate and the number of compounding periods per year and then press the EFF% key to find the effective annual rate. However, we generally use Equation 4-15 because it's as easy to use as the interest conversion feature is, and the equation reminds us of what we are really doing. If you use the interest rate conversion feature on your calculator, don't forget to reset your calculator settings. Interest conversion is discussed in the tutorials.

In the EAR equation, I_{NOM}/M is the periodic rate, and M is the number of periods per year. For example, suppose you could borrow using either a credit card that charges 1% per month or a bank loan with a 12% quoted nominal interest rate that is compounded quarterly. Which should you choose? To answer this question, the cost rate of each alternative must be expressed as an EAR:

$$\text{Credit card loan: EFF\%} = (1 + 0.01)^{12} - 1.0 = (1.01)^{12} - 1.0$$
$$= 1.126825 - 1.0 = 0.126825 = 12.6825\%$$
$$\text{Bank loan: EFF\%} = (1 + 0.03)^{4} - 1.0 = (1.03)^{4} - 1.0$$
$$= 1.125509 - 1.0 = 0.125509 = 12.5509\%$$

See *Ch 04 Tool Kit.xlsx* for all calculations.

Thus, the credit card loan is slightly more costly than the bank loan. This result should have been intuitive to you—both loans have the same 12% nominal rate, yet you would have to make monthly payments on the credit card versus quarterly payments under the bank loan.

The EFF% rate should be used to compare the effective cost or rate of return on loans or investments when payment periods differ, as in the credit card versus bank loan example.

The Result of Frequent Compounding

Suppose you plan to invest $100 for 5 years at a nominal annual rate of 12%. What will happen to the future value of your investment if interest is compounded more frequently than once a year? Because interest will be earned on interest more often, you might expect the future value to increase as the frequency of compounding increases. Similarly, you might also expect the effective annual rate to increase with more frequent compounding. As Table 4-1 shows, you would be correct—the future value and EAR do in fact increase as the frequency of compounding increases. Notice that the biggest increases in FV and EAR occur when compounding goes from annual to semiannual, and that moving from monthly to daily compounding has a relatively small impact. Although Table 4-1 shows daily compounding as the smallest interval, it is possible to compound even more frequently. At the limit, one can have *continuous compounding*. This is explained in **Web Extension 4B** at the textbook's website.

TABLE 4-1   Effect on $100 of Compounding More Frequently Than Once a Year

Frequency of Compounding	Nominal Annual Rate	Number of Periods per Year (M)[a]	Periodic Interest Rate(I_{PER})	Effective Annual Rate (EFF%)[b]	Future Value[c]	Percentage Increased in FV
Annual	12%	1	12.0000%	12.0000%	$112.00	
Semiannual	12%	2	6.0000%	12.3600%	$112.36	0.32%
Quarterly	12%	4	3.0000%	12.5509%	$112.55	0.17%
Monthly	12%	12	1.0000%	12.6825%	$112.68	0.12%
Daily	12%	365	0.0329%	12.7475%	$112.75	0.06%

[a]We used 365 days per year in the calculations.
[b]The EFF% is calculated as $(1 + I_{PER})^M$.
[c]The future value is calculated as $\$100(1 + \text{EFF\%})$.

CONCEPT REVIEW

1. Would you rather invest in an account that pays 7% with annual compounding or 7% with monthly compounding? Would you rather borrow at 7% and make annual or monthly payments? Why?

2. What is the *future value* of $100 after 3 years if the appropriate interest rate is 8%, compounded annually? Compounded monthly? (Check Figures: $125.97; $127.02)

3. What is the *present value* of $100 due in 3 years if the appropriate interest rate is 8%, compounded annually? Compounded monthly? (Check Figures: $79.38; $78.73)

4. Define the terms "Annual Percentage Rate, or APR," "effective annual rate, or EFF%," and "nominal interest rate, I_{NOM}."

5. A bank pays 5% with daily compounding on its savings accounts. Should it advertise the nominal or effective rate if it is seeking to attract new deposits?

4.16 Fractional Time Periods

Thus far we have assumed that payments occur at either the beginning or the end of periods, but not *within* periods. However, we often encounter situations that require compounding or discounting over fractional periods. For example, suppose you deposited $100 in a bank that pays a nominal rate of 10%, compounded daily, based on a 365-day year. How much would you have after 9 months? The answer is $107.79, found as follows:[16]

$$\text{Periodic rate} = I_{PER} = 0.10/365 = 0.000273973 \text{ per day}$$
$$\text{Number of days} = (9/12)(365) = 0.75(365)$$
$$= 273.75 \text{ rounded to } 274$$
$$\text{Ending amount} = \$100(1.000273973)^{274} = \$107.79$$

Now suppose you borrow $100 from a bank whose nominal rate is 10% per year "simple interest," which means that interest is not earned on interest. If the loan is outstanding for 274 days, how much interest will you have to pay? Here we calculate a daily interest rate, I_{PER}, as above, but multiply it by 274 rather than use the 274 as an exponent:

$$\text{Interest owed} = \$100(0.000273973)(274) = \$7.51 \text{ interest}$$

FINANCE: IN FOCUS

What You Know Is What You Get: Not in Payday Lending

When money runs low toward the end of a month, many individuals turn to payday lenders. If a borrower's application is approved, the payday lender makes a short-term loan, which will be repaid with the next paycheque. In fact, on the next payday the lender actually transfers the repayment from the borrower's bank account. This repayment consists of the amount borrowed plus a fee.

How costly are payday loans? In Ontario, most lenders charge a fee of $21 per $100 borrowed. A typical loan is for about $300, so the typical fee is $63. A typical borrower gets paid every two weeks, so the loan is for a very short amount of time. With a big fee and a short time until repayment, the typical payday loan has an APR of over 540%!

Do borrowers actually realize the interest rate they are paying? Two professors at the University of Chicago set out to answer this question. When loans are approved, borrowers receive a form to sign that shows the APR. However, subsequent telephone surveys of borrowers show that over 40% of borrowers thought their APR was around 15%; perhaps not coincidentally, these are similar numerals to the fee schedules that are posted prominently in the lender's office.

The professors then did an experiment (with the agreement of 77 payday loan stores) in which they provided more information than just the APR. One group of borrowers received information about the APR of the payday loan as compared to the APRs of other loans, such as car loans. A second group received information about the dollar cost of the payday loan as compared to the dollar cost of other loans, such as car loans. A third group received information about how long it takes most payday borrowers to repay their loans (which is longer than the next payday; borrowers tend to extend the loan for additional pay periods, accruing additional fees).

Compared to a control group with no additional information, the results show that some borrowers with additional information decided not to take the loan; other borrowers reduced the amount that they borrow. These findings suggest that better information helps borrowers make less costly decisions. The more you know, the less you get, at least when it comes to costly payday loans.

Sources: Marianne Bertrand and Adair Morse, "Information Disclosure, Cognitive Biases, and Payday Borrowing," *Journal of Finance*, Vol. 66, No. 6, December 2011, pp. 1865–1893; Newsroom: Ontario's Payday Lending Industry, http://news.ontario.ca, accessed June 25, 2014.

---

[16]Bank loan contracts specifically state whether they are based on a 360- or a 365-day year. If a 360-day year is used, then the daily rate is higher, so the effective rate is also higher. Here we assumed a 365-day year.

You will owe the bank a total of $107.51 after 274 days. This is the procedure most banks actually use to calculate interest on loans, except that they require borrowers to pay the interest on a monthly basis rather than after 274 days. This more frequent compounding raises the EFF% and thus the total amount of interest paid.

⊙NCEPT REVIEW

1. Suppose a company borrowed $1 million at a rate of 9%, simple interest, with interest paid at the end of each month. The bank uses a 360-day year. How much interest would the firm have to pay in a 30-day month? What would the interest be if the bank used a 365-day year? [Check Figures: (0.09/360)(30)($1,000,000) = $7,500 interest for the month. For the 365-day year, (0.09/365) (30)($1,000,000) = $7,397.26 of interest. The use of a 360-day year raises the interest cost by $102.74. That's why banks like to use it on loans.]

2. Suppose you deposited $1,000 in a credit union that pays 7% with daily compounding and a 365-day year. What is the EFF%, and how much could you withdraw after 7 months, assuming this is 7/12 of a year? [Check Figure: EFF% = $(1 + 0.07/365)^{365} - 1 = 0.07250098 =$ 7.250098%. Thus, your account would grow from $1,000 to $1,000(1.07250098)^{0.583333} =$ $1,041.67, and you could withdraw that amount.]

4.17 Amortized Loans

An important application of compound interest involves loans that are paid off in installments over time. Included are automobile loans, home mortgage loans, student loans, and many business loans. A loan that is to be repaid in equal amounts on a monthly, quarterly, or annual basis is called an **amortized loan.**[17]

See *Ch 04 Tool Kit.xlsx* for all calculations.

Table 4-2 illustrates the amortization process. A homeowner borrows $100,000 on a mortgage loan, and the loan is to be repaid with equal monthly payments over a 25-year period. The lender charges 6%, compounded semiannually.[18] The mortgage term is for 5 years. Our first task is to determine the EFF%. Since the payments are monthly but the compounding period is twice per year, we must modify Equation 4-15:

$$\text{Effective monthly rate (EFF\%}_M) = \left(1 + \frac{I_{NOM}}{M}\right)^{\frac{M}{12}} - 1.0$$

$$\text{EFF\%}_M = \left(1 + \frac{0.06}{2}\right)^{\frac{2}{12}} - 1.0. = 0.00493862$$

It is possible to use the annuity formula in Equation 4-7, but it is much easier to use a financial calculator or spreadsheet. With a financial calculator, we insert values into a calculator as shown below to get the required payments of $639.81:

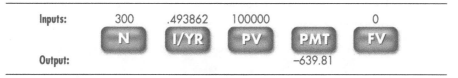

Inputs:	300	.493862	100000		0
	N	I/YR	PV	PMT	FV
Output:				−639.81	

Therefore, the borrower must pay the lender $639.81 per month for the next 25 years. With *Excel*, you would use the PMT function: =PMT(I,N,PV,FV) =PMT(0.00493862, 300,100000,0) = −$639.81.

There are two points worth noting. First, notice that N = 300. We adjusted the number of periods by multiplying the number of payments per year, 12, by the amortization period, 25. Second, do not get confused between the amortization period and the mortgage term. The term is the length of time the mortgage's terms and conditions, including its interest rate, are agreed upon under contract. After the term expires, the mortgage is renewed with a new current interest rate.

---

[17]The word "amortized" comes from the Latin *mors*, meaning "death," so an amortized loan is one that is "killed off" over time.
[18]In Canada the Interest Rate Act requires mortgages to be compounded semiannually.

TABLE 4-2   Monthly Loan Amortization Schedule, $100,000 at 6% for 25 years (first 6 months only)

Month	Beginning Amount (1)	Payment (2)	Interest[a] (3)	Repayment of Principal[b] (2) − (3) = (4)	Ending Balance (1) − (4) = (5)
1	$100,000.00	$639.81	$493.86	$145.95	$99,854.05
2	99,854.05	639.81	493.14	146.67	99,707.38
3	99,707.38	639.81	492.42	147.39	99,559.99
4	99,559.99	639.81	491.69	148.12	99,411.87
5	99,411.87	639.81	490.96	148.85	99,263.02
6	99,263.02	639.81	490.22	149.59	99,113.43
⋮	⋮	⋮	⋮	⋮	⋮
299	1,268.08	639.81	6.26	633.55	634.53
300	634.53	637.66	3.13	634.53	$0

[a]Interest in each period is calculated by multiplying the loan balance at the beginning of the year by the EFF%M. Therefore, interest in Month 1 is $100,000(0.00493862) = $493.86; in Month 2 it is $99,854.05(0.00493862) = $493.14; and so on.
[b]Repayment of principal is equal to the payment of $639.81 minus the interest charged for the month.

Amortization Schedules

Each payment will consist of two parts—interest and repayment of principal. This breakdown is shown on an **amortization schedule** such as the one in Table 4-2. This table shows only the first 6 of 300 payments to be made on the loan. The interest component is relatively high in the early payments, then declines as the loan balance decreases.

Mortgage Interest Payments

Continuing with our previous mortgage example, how much interest will the borrower pay over the life of the loan? How much in the first year?

We have already calculated the monthly payments of $639.81, therefore the total payments are 300($639.81) = $191,943. The borrower pays back the borrowed $100,000 over the life of the loan, so the total interest paid is $191,943 − $100,000 = $91,943.

To find the amount of interest paid in the first year, begin by finding the amount the borrower owes at the end of the first year. We know the number of remaining payments (300 − 12 = 288) and the amount of each payment ($631.81), so we can solve for the PV:

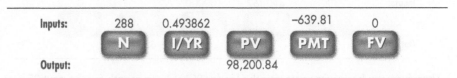

Inputs:	288	0.493862		−639.81	0
	N	I/YR	PV	PMT	FV
Output:			98,200.84		

The amount of principal repaid in the first year is $100,000 − $98,200.84 = $1,799.16. The total payments during the year are 12($639.81) = $7,677.72. So the total interest paid in the year is $7,677.72 − $1,799.16 = $5,878.56. Over three-quarters of the amount paid in the first year goes to interest!

Now consider a 15-year mortgage. Assume that all other variables, the principal, interest rate, and payment frequency (monthly) remain the same. Changing N to 180, the new payment is $839.88. The total amount of payments is 180($839.88) = $151,178 and the total interest paid is $151,178 − $100,000 = $51,178, a big decrease from the $91,943 on the 25-year mortgage. As this example shows, increasing the monthly payment can dramatically reduce the total interest paid and the time required to pay off the mortgage.

CONCEPT REVIEW

1. Suppose you borrowed $30,000 on a student loan at a rate of 8% and now must repay it in three equal installments at the end of each of the next 3 years. How large would your payments be, how much of the first payment would represent interest, how much would be principal, and what would your ending balance be after the first year? (Check Figures: PMT = $11,641.01; Interest = $2,400; Principal = $9,241.01; Balance at end of Year 1 = $20,758.99)

4.18 Growing Annuities

Normally, an annuity is defined as a series of *constant* payments to be received over a specified number of periods. However, the term *growing annuity* is used to describe a series of payments that grow at a constant rate.

Example 1: Finding a Constant Real Income

Growing annuities are often used in the area of financial planning, where a prospective retiree wants to determine the maximum constant *real*, or *inflation-adjusted*, withdrawals he or she can make over a specified number of years. For example, suppose a 65-year-old is contemplating retirement, expects to live for another 20 years, has a $1 million nest egg, expects to earn 8% on his or her investments, expects inflation to average 3% per year, and wants to withdraw a constant *real* amount annually over the next remaining 20 years. If the first withdrawal is to be made today, what is the amount of this initial withdrawal?

This problem can be solved in three ways. (1) Set up a spreadsheet model that is similar to an amortization table, where the account earns 8% per year, withdrawals rise at the 3% inflation rate, *Excel*'s Goal Seek function is used to find the initial inflation-adjusted withdrawal, and a zero balance remains at the end of the 20th year. (2) Use a financial calculator, where we first calculate the real rate of return, adjusted for inflation, and use it for I/YR when finding the payment for an annuity due. (3) Use a relatively complicated and obtuse formula to find this same amount.[19] We illustrate the first two procedures in the chapter model, *Ch 04 Tool Kit. xlsx.* The financial calculator approach is easiest to use, but the spreadsheet model provides the clearest picture of what is happening. It shows the value of the retirement portfolio, the earning, and each withdrawal over the 20-year planning horizon. Also, the spreadsheet model creates graphs that make it easy to explain things to people who are planning their financial futures.

To implement the calculator approach, we first find the expected real, or inflation adjusted, rate of return, where r_r is the real rate of return and r_{NOM} the nominal rate of return:

See *Ch 04 Tool Kit.xlsx* for all calculations.

$$\text{Real rate} = r_r = [(1 + r_{NOM})/(1 + \text{Inflation})] - 1.0$$

$$= [1.08/1.03] - 1.0 = 0.048543689 = 4.8543689\%$$

(4-16)

Next, we set the calculator to Begin Mode, after which we input N = 20, I = real rate = 4.8543689, PV = −1,000,000, and FV = 0, then press PMT to get $75,585.53. This is the value at Time 0, today, and the initial withdrawal will increase at the inflation rate, 3%. With this initial withdrawal, the retiree will have a constant real income over the next 20 years.

In our example we assumed that the first withdrawal would be made immediately. The procedure would be slightly different if we wanted to make end-of-year withdrawals. First, we would find the real rate the same way and enter the same inputs into the calculator as shown above. Second, we would set the calculator to End Mode. The calculated PMT would be $79,254.73. However, that value is in beginning-of-year terms, and since inflation of 3% will occur during the year, we must make the following adjustment to find the inflation-adjusted initial payment:

$$\text{Initial withdrawal} = \$79{,}254.73(1 + \text{Inflation})$$

$$= \$79{,}254.73(1.03)$$

$$= \$81{,}632.38$$

---

[19]For example, the formula used to find the payment for a growing ordinary annuity is shown below. If g = annuity growth rate and I = rate of return on investment, then

$$\text{PVIF of a growing annuity} = \text{PVIFGA} = [1 - [(1 + g)/(1 + 1)]^N]/[(I - g)/(1 + g)]$$

$$\text{PMT} = \text{PV/PVIFGA}$$

The first withdrawal, at the end of the year, would thus be \$81,632.38, it would grow by 3% per year, and after the 20th withdrawal (at the end of the 20th year) the balance in the retirement fund would be zero.

The end-of-year payment is also analyzed in *Ch 04 Tool Kit.xlsx*. There we set up an amortization table that shows the beginning balance, the annual withdrawals, the annual earnings, and the ending balance for each of the 20 years. This analysis confirms the \$81,632.38 initial withdrawal found above.

Example 2: Initial Deposit to Accumulate a Future Sum

As another example of a growing annuity, suppose you need to accumulate \$100,000 in 10 years. You plan to make a deposit now, at Time 0, and then to make 9 more deposits at the beginning of the following 9 years, for a total of 10 deposits. The bank pays 6% interest, and you expect to increase your initial deposit amount by the 2% inflation rate each year. How much would you need to deposit initially? First, we calculate the real rate:

$$\text{Real rate} = r_r = [1.06/1.02] - 1.0 = 0.0392157 = 3.92157\%$$

Next, since inflation is expected to be 2% per year, in 10 years the target \$100,000 will have a purchasing power of:

$$\$100,000/(1 + 0.02)^{10} = \$82,034.83$$

Now we can find the size of the required initial payment by setting a financial calculator to the "BEG" mode and then inputting N = 10, I/YR = 3.92157, PV = 0, and FV = 82,034.83. Then, when we press the PMT key, we get PMT = −6,598.87. Thus, a deposit of \$6,598.87 made at time zero and growing by 2 percent per year will accumulate to \$100,000 by Year 10 if the interest rate is 6%. Again, this result is confirmed in the chapter's *Tool Kit*. The key to this analysis is to express I/YR, FV, and PMT in real, not nominal, terms.

ⒸNCEPT REVIEW

1. Differentiate between a "regular" and a growing annuity.
2. What three methods can be used to deal with growing annuities?
3. If the nominal interest rate is 10% and the expected inflation rate is 5%, what is the expected real rate of return? (Check Figure: 4.7619%)

Summary

Most financial decisions involve situations in which someone pays money at one point in time and receives money at some later time. Dollars paid or received at two different points in time are different, and this difference is recognized and accounted for by *time value of money (TVM) analysis*.

- **Compounding** is the process of determining the **future value (FV)** of a cash flow or a series of cash flows. The compounded amount, or future value, is equal to the beginning amount plus the interest earned.
- Future value of a single payment: $FV_N = PV(1 + I)^N$.
- **Discounting** is the process of finding the **present value (PV)** of a future cash flow or a series of cash flows; discounting is the reciprocal, or reverse, of compounding.
- Present value of a single payment: $PV = \dfrac{FV_N}{(1 + I)^N}$.
- An **annuity** is defined as a series of equal periodic payments (PMT) for a specified number of periods.
- Future value of an annuity:

$$FVA_N = PMT\left[\frac{(1 + I)^N}{I} - \frac{1}{I}\right]$$

- Present value of an annuity:

$$PVA_N = PMT\left[\frac{1}{I} - \frac{I}{I(1 + I)^N}\right]$$

- An annuity whose payments occur at the *end* of each period is called an **ordinary annuity.** The formulas above are for ordinary annuities.
- If each payment occurs at the beginning of the period rather than at the end, then we have an **annuity due.** The PV of each payment would be larger, because each payment would be discounted back 1 year less, so the PV of the annuity would also be larger. Similarly, the FV of the annuity due would also be larger because each payment would be compounded for an extra year. The following formulas can be used to convert the PV and FV of an ordinary annuity to an annuity due:

$$PVA \text{ (annuity due)} = PVA \text{ of an ordinary annuity} \times (1 + I)$$

$$FVA \text{ (annuity due)} = FVA \text{ of an ordinary annuity} \times (1 + I)$$

- A **perpetuity** is an annuity with an infinite number of payments.

$$\text{Value of a perpetuity} = \frac{PMT}{I}$$

- To find the PV or FV of an uneven series, find the PV or FV of each individual cash flow and then sum them.
- If you know the cash flows and the PV (or FV) of a cash flow stream, you can **determine the interest rate.**
- When compounding occurs more frequently than once a year, the nominal rate must be converted to a periodic rate, and the number of years must be converted to periods.

$$I_{PER} = \text{Nominal annual rate/Periods per year}$$

$$\text{Periods} = \text{Years} \times \text{Periods per year}$$

The periodic rate and number of periods would be used for calculations and shown on time lines.

- If comparing the costs of loans that require payments more than once a year, or the rates of return on investments that pay interest more frequently, then the comparisons should be based on **equivalent** (or **effective**) rates of return using this formula:

$$\text{Effective annual rate (EFF\%)} = \left(1 + \frac{I_{NOM}}{M}\right)^M - 1.0$$

- The general equation for finding the future value for any number of compounding periods per year is

$$FV_N = PV(1 + I_{PER})^{\text{Number of periods}} = PV\left(1 + \frac{I_{NOM}}{M}\right)^{MN}$$

where

$$I_{NOM} = \text{Nominal quoted interest rate}$$

$$M = \text{Number of compounding periods per year}$$

$$N = \text{Number of years}$$

- An **amortized loan** is one that is paid off in equal payments over a specified period. An **amortization schedule** shows how much of each payment constitutes interest, how much is used to reduce the principal, and the unpaid balance at each point in time.
- A **growing annuity** is a stream of cash flows that grows at a constant rate for a specified number of years.

Questions

4-1 Define each of the following terms:
a. PV; I; INT; FV_N; PVA_N; FVA_N; PMT; M; I_{NOM}
b. Opportunity cost rate
c. Annuity; lump sum payment; cash flow; uneven cash flow stream
d. Ordinary (deferred) annuity; annuity due
e. Perpetuity; consol
f. Outflow; inflow; time line; terminal value
g. Compounding; discounting
h. Annual, semiannual, quarterly, monthly, and daily compounding
i. Effective annual rate (EAR); nominal (quoted) interest rate; APR; periodic rate
j. Amortization schedule; principal versus interest component of a payment; amortized loan

4-2 What is an *opportunity cost rate?* How is this rate used in discounted cash flow analysis, and where is it shown on a time line? Is the opportunity cost rate a single number that is used in all situations?

4-3 An *annuity* is defined as a series of payments of a fixed amount for a specific number of periods. Thus, $100 a year for 10 years is an annuity, but $100 in Year 1, $200 in Year 2, and $400 in Years 3 through 10 does *not* constitute an annuity. However, the second series *contains* an annuity. Is this statement true or false?

4-4 If a firm's earnings per share grew from $1 to $2 over a 10-year period, the *total growth* would be 100%, but the *annual growth rate* would be *less than* 10%. True or false? Explain.

4-5 Would you rather have a savings account that pays 5% interest compounded semiannually or one that pays 5% interest compounded daily? Explain.

Concept Review Problems

Full solutions are provided at www.nelson.com/brigham3ce.

CR-1
Future Value
Assume that 1 year from now, you will deposit $5,000 into a savings account that pays 4%.
a. If the bank compounds interest annually, how much will you have in your account 4 years from now?
b. What would your balance 4 years from now be if the bank used quarterly compounding rather than annual compounding?
c. Suppose you deposited the $5,000 in four payments of $1,250 each at Year 1, Year 2, Year 3, and Year 4. How much would you have in your account at Year 4, based on 4% annual compounding?
d. Suppose you deposited four equal payments in your account at Year 1, Year 2, Year 3, and Year 4. Assuming an 4% interest rate, how large would each of your payments have to be for you to obtain the same ending balance as you calculated in part a?

CR-2
Time Value of Money
Assume that 4 years from now you will need $1,000. Your bank compounds interest at an 8% annual rate.
a. How much must you deposit 1 year from now to have a balance of $1,000 four years from now?
b. If you want to make equal payments at Years 1 through 4 to accumulate the $1,000, how large must each of the four payments be?
c. If your father were to offer either to make the payments calculated in part b ($221.92) or to give you a lump sum of $750 one year from now, which would you choose?
d. If you have only $750 one year from now, what interest rate, compounded annually, would you have to earn to have the necessary $1,000 four years from now?
e. Suppose you can deposit only $186.29 each at Years 1 through 4, but you still need $1,000 at Year 4. What interest rate, with annual compounding, must you seek out to achieve your goal?
f. To help you reach your $1,000 goal, your father offers to give you $400 one year from now. You will get a part-time job and make six additional payments of equal amounts each 6 months thereafter. If all of this money is deposited in a bank that pays 8%, compounded semiannually, how large must each of the six payments be?
g. What is the effective annual rate being paid by the bank in part f?

CR-3
Effective Annual Rates

Bank A pays 8% interest, compounded quarterly, on its money market account. The managers of Bank B want its money market account to equal Bank A's effective annual rate, but interest is to be compounded on a monthly basis. What nominal, or quoted, rate must Bank B set?

Problems

Easy
Problems 1–8

Answers to odd-numbered problems appear in Appendix A.

4-1
Future Value of a Single Payment

How much money will you have in your bank account in 5 years if it pays 4% annually and you start with the following amounts. (*Hint:* If you are using a financial calculator, you can enter the known values and then press the appropriate key to find the unknown variable. Then, without clearing the TVM register, you can "override" the variable that changes by simply entering a new value for it and then pressing the key for the unknown variable to obtain the second answer. This procedure can be used in parts b through d, and in many other situations, to see how changes in input variables affect the output variable.)

a. $5,000.
b. $10,000.
c. $15,000.
d. $20,000.

4-2
Present Value of a Single Payment

What is the present value of a security that will pay the amounts shown below in 20 years? Securities of equal risk pay 7% annually.

a. $20,000.
b. $30,000.
c. $40,000.
d. $50,000.

4-3
Interest Rate of a Single Payment

Your parents will retire in 18 years and they think they will need $1,000,000 at retirement. What annual interest rate must they earn to reach their goal, based on the starting amounts shown below? Assume they don't save any additional funds.

a. $50,000.
b. $100,000.
c. $200,000.
d. $300,000.

4-4
Number of Periods for a Single Payment

If you deposit money in an account today, how long will it take to triple your money based on the annual interest rates below?

a. 2.5%.
b. 4%.
c. 7%.
d. 10%.

4-5
Number of Periods for an Annuity

You have $42,180.53 in a brokerage account, and you plan to deposit an additional $5,000 at the end of every future year until your account totals $250,000. You expect to earn 12% annually on the account. How many years will it take to reach your goal?

4-6
Future Value: Annuity versus Annuity Due

What is the future value of a 9%, 5-year ordinary annuity that pays $300 each year? If this were an annuity due, what would be its future value?

4-7
Present and Future Value of an Uneven Cash Flow Stream

An investment will pay $100 at the end of each of the next 3 years, $200 at the end of Year 4, $300 at the end of Year 5, and $500 at the end of Year 6. If other investments of equal risk earn 8% annually, what is its present value? Its future value?

4-8
Annuity Payment and EAR

You want to buy a car, and a local bank will lend you $20,000. The loan would be fully amortized over 5 years (60 months), and the nominal interest rate would be 12%, with interest paid monthly. What would be the monthly loan payment? What would be the loan's EAR?

Intermediate
Problems 9–34

4-9
Present and Future Values of Single Cash Flows for Different Periods

Find the following values, *using the equations,* and then work the problems using a financial calculator to check your answers. Disregard rounding differences.

a. An initial $9,500 compounded for 1 year at 7%.
b. An initial $9,500 compounded for 2 years at 7%.
c. The present value of $9,500 due in 1 year at a discount rate of 7%.
d. The present value of $9,500 due in 2 years at a discount rate of 7%.

4-10
Present and Future Values of Single Cash Flows for Different Interest Rates

Use equations and a financial calculator to find the following values.

a. An initial $500 compounded for 10 years at 6%
b. An initial $500 compounded for 10 years at 12%.
c. The present value of $500 due in 10 years at a 6% discount rate.
d. The present value of $500 due in 10 years at a 12% discount rate.

4-11   To the closest year, how long will it take $200 to double if it is deposited and earns the fol-

Time for a Lump   lowing rates? [Note: This problem cannot be solved exactly with some financial calculators.

Sum to Double   For example, if you enter PV = −200, PMT = 0, FV = 400, and I = 7 in an HP-12C, and then
press the N key, you will get 11 years for part a. The correct answer is 10.2448 years, which
rounds to 10, but the calculator rounds up. However, the HP-10B gives the correct answer.]

   a.   7%.   c.   18%.
   b.   10%.   d.   100%.

4-12   Find the *future value* of the following annuities. The first payment in these annuities is made

Future Value of   at the *end* of Year 1; that is, they are *ordinary annuities*. [Note: You can leave values in the TVM

an Annuity   register, switch to "BEG," press FV, and find the FV of the annuity due.]

   a. $600 per year for 10 years at 8%.
   b. $300 per year for 5 years at 4%.
   c. $600 per year for 5 years at 0%.
   d.   Now rework parts a, b, and c assuming that payments are made at the *beginning* of each
        year; that is, they are *annuities due*.

4-13   Find the *present value* of the following *ordinary annuities*:

Present Value of   a. $400 per year for 10 years at 10%.

an Annuity   b. $200 per year for 5 years at 5%.

   c. $400 per year for 5 years at 0%.
   d.   Now rework parts a, b, and c assuming that payments are made at the *beginning* of each
        year; that is, they are *annuities due*.

4-14   a.   Find the present values of the following cash flow streams. The appropriate interest

Uneven Cash Flow   rate is 14%. (*Hint:* It is fairly easy to work this problem dealing with the individual cash

Stream   flows. However, if you have a financial calculator, read the section of the manual that
        describes how to enter cash flows such as the ones in this problem. This will take a little
        time, but the investment will pay huge dividends throughout the course. Note, if you do
        work with the cash flow register, then you must enter $CF_0 = 0$.)

Year	Cash Stream A	Cash Stream B
1	$800	$100
2	300	300
3	300	300
4	300	300
5	100	800

   b.   What is the value of each cash flow stream at a 0% interest rate?

4-15   Find the interest rates, or rates of return, on each of the following:

Effective Rate of   a.   You *borrow* $700 and promise to pay back $749 at the end of 1 year.

Interest   b.   You *lend* $700 and receive a promise to be paid $749 at the end of 1 year.

   c.   You borrow $85,000 and promise to pay back $201,229 at the end of 10 years.
   d.   You borrow $9,000 and promise to make payments of $2,684.80 per year for 5 years.

4-16   Find the amount to which $2,000 will grow under each of the following conditions:

Future Value for   a.   8% compounded annually for 5 years.

Various   b.   8% compounded semiannually for 5 years.

Compounding   c.   8% compounded quarterly for 5 years.

Periods   d.   8% compounded monthly for 5 years.

4-17   Find the present value of $2,000 due in the future under each of the following conditions:

Present Value for   a.   8% nominal rate, semiannual compounding, discounted back 5 years.

Various   b.   8% nominal rate, quarterly compounding, discounted back 5 years.

Compounding   c.   8% nominal rate, monthly compounding, discounted back 1 year.

Periods

4-18   Find the future values of the following ordinary annuities:

Future Value of an   a.   FV of $750 each 6 months for 4 years at a nominal rate of 10%, compounded semiannually.

Annuity for Various   b.   FV of $375 each 3 months for 4 years at a nominal rate of 10%, compounded quarterly.

Compounding   c.   The annuities described in parts a and b have the same total amount of money paid into

Periods   them during the 4-year period and both earn interest at the same nominal rate, yet the
        annuity in part b earns $105.75 more than the one in part a over the 4 years. Why does
        this occur?

4-19
Effective versus
Nominal Interest
Rates

Universal Bank pays 7% interest, compounded annually, on time deposits. Regional Bank pays 6% interest, compounded quarterly.
a.   Based on effective interest rates, in which bank would you prefer to deposit your money?
b.   Could your choice of banks be influenced by the fact that you might want to withdraw your funds during the year as opposed to at the end of the year? In answering this question, assume that funds must be left on deposit during the entire compounding period in order for you to receive any interest.

4-20
Amortization
Schedule

a.   Set up an amortization schedule for a $15,000 loan to be repaid in equal installments at the end of each of the next 4 years. The interest rate is 10%.
b.   How large must each annual payment be if the loan is for $30,000? Assume that the interest rate remains at 10% and that the loan is paid off over 4 years.
c.   How large must each payment be if the loan is for $30,000, the interest rate is 10%, and the loan is paid off in equal installments at the end of each of the next 8 years? This loan is for the same amount as the loan in part b, but the payments are spread out over twice as many periods. Why are these payments not half as large as the payments on the loan in part b?

4-21
Growth Rates

Hanebury Corporation's current sales were $4 million. Sales were $2 million 4 years earlier.
a.   To the nearest percentage point, at what rate have sales been growing?
b.   Suppose someone calculated the sales growth for Hanebury Corporation in part a as follows: "Sales doubled in 4 years. This represents a growth of 100% in 4 years, so, dividing 100% by 4, we find the growth rate to be 25% per year." Explain what is wrong with this calculation.

4-22
Expected Rate of
Return

Alberta-Timber invests $4 million to clear a tract of land and to set out some young pine trees. The trees will mature in 10 years, at which time Alberta-Timber plans to sell the forest at an expected price of $8 million. What is Alberta-Timber's expected rate of return?

4-23
Effective Rate of
Interest

A bank offers to lend your company $70,000, and the loan calls for payments of $8,273.59 per year for 20 years. What interest rate is the bank charging you?

4-24
Required Lump
Sum Payment

To complete your last year in business school and then go through law school, you will need $10,000 per year for 4 years, starting next year (i.e., you will need to withdraw the first $10,000 one year from today). Your rich uncle offers to put you through school, and he will deposit in a bank paying 7% interest a sum of money that is sufficient to provide the four payments of $10,000 each. His deposit will be made today.
a.   How large must the deposit be?
b.   How much will be in the account immediately after you make the first withdrawal? After the last withdrawal?

4-25
Repaying a Loan

While Lisa was a student at the University of Ottawa, she borrowed $12,000 in student loans at an annual interest rate of 8%. If Lisa repays $1,600 per year, how long, to the nearest year, will it take her to repay the loan?

4-26
Reaching a
Financial Goal

You need to accumulate $10,000. To do so, you plan to make deposits of $1,250 per year, with the first payment being made a year from today, in a bank account that pays 12% annual interest. Your last deposit will be less than $1,250 if less is needed to round out to $10,000. How many years will it take you to reach your $10,000 goal, and how large will the last deposit be?

4-27
Present Value of
a Perpetuity

What is the present value of a perpetuity of $10,000 per year if the appropriate discount rate is 5%? If interest rates in general were to double and the appropriate discount rate rose to 10%, what would happen to the present value of the perpetuity?

4-28
PV and Effective
Annual Rate

You inherited some money. A friend of yours is working as an unpaid intern at a local brokerage firm, and her boss is selling securities that call for five payments, $50 at the end of each of the next 3 years, plus a payment of $1,050 at the end of Year 4. Your friend says she can get you some of these securities at a cost of $900 each. Your money is now invested in a bank that pays an 8% nominal (quoted) interest rate but with quarterly compounding. You regard the securities as being just as safe, and as liquid, as your bank deposit, so your required effective annual rate of return on the securities is the same as that on your bank deposit. You must calculate the value of the securities to decide whether they are a good investment. What is their present value to you?

4-29
Loan Amortization
Assume that your aunt sold her house on December 31 and that she took a mortgage in the amount of $10,000 as part of the payment. The mortgage has a quoted (or nominal) interest rate of 10%, but it calls for payments every 6 months, beginning on June 30, and the mortgage is to be amortized over 10 years. Now, 1 year later, your aunt must inform the tax department of the interest that was included in the two payments made during the year. (This interest will be income to your aunt.) To the closest dollar, what is the total amount of interest that was paid during the first year?

4-30
Loan Amortization
Your company is planning to borrow $1,000,000 on a 5-year, 15%, annual payment, fully amortized term loan. What fraction of the payment made at the end of the second year will represent repayment of principal?

4-31
Mortgage
You have decided to become a homeowner with the purchase of a condominium in a newly redeveloped part of town. The condo costs $300,000 and you have a down payment of $90,000, so you will be carrying a mortgage of $210,000. If you take on a 5-year mortgage with a 25-year amortization period at a rate of 4.5% (compounded semiannually), with monthly payments, determine the following:
a. Your monthly payment.
b. The total interest and total principal paid over the first 5 years.

4-32
Mortgage
Based on Problem 4-31, what would be your monthly payments if your mortgage amortization period was 20 years? 15 years?

4-33
Annual
Percentage Rate
Jane Doe has two borrowing alternatives. Loan A is offered at a rate of 1.1% per month. Her second alternative, loan B, uses quarterly compounding. What must be the annual percentage rate (APR) on loan B, so that it is equivalent in cost to loan A?

4-34
Nonannual
Compounding
Alex Leggatt made an initial deposit of $15,000 into a savings program. He plans on making additional payments of $2,500 each year for the next 5 years. If Alex earns 6% per annum, compounded semiannually, how much will he have at the end of 5 years?

**Challenging
Problems 35–40**

4-35
Nonannual
Compounding
a. It is now January 1. You plan to make five deposits of $100 each, one every 6 months, with the first payment being made *today*. If the bank pays a nominal interest rate of 8% but uses semiannual compounding, how much will be in your account after 8 years?
b. You must make a payment of $2,200 10 years from today. To prepare for this payment, you will make five equal deposits, beginning today and for the next four quarters, in a bank that pays a nominal interest rate of 12%, quarterly compounding. How large must each of the five payments be?

4-36
Nominal Rate of
Return
Jenny Lin, manager of Boutique Clothing, wants to sell on credit, giving customers 3 months in which to pay. However, Jenny will have to borrow from her bank to carry the accounts receivable. The bank will charge a nominal 8%, but with monthly compounding. Jenny wants to quote a nominal rate to her customers (all of whom are expected to pay on time) that will exactly cover her financing costs. What nominal annual rate should she quote to her credit customers?

4-37
Required Annuity
Payments
Assume that your father is now 50 years old, that he plans to retire in 10 years, and that he expects to live for 25 years after he retires, that is, until he is 85. He wants his first retirement payment to have the same purchasing power at the time he retires as $40,000 has today. He wants all his subsequent retirement payments to be equal to his first retirement payment (do not let the retirement payments grow with inflation: he realizes that the real value of his retirement income will decline year by year after he retires). His retirement income will begin the day he retires, 10 years from today, and he will then get 24 additional annual payments. Inflation is expected to be 5% per year from today forward; he currently has $100,000 saved up; and he expects to earn a return on his savings of 8% per year, annual compounding. To the nearest dollar, how much must he save during each of the next 10 years (with equal deposits being made at the end of each year) to meet his retirement goal? (*Hint:* Neither the amount he saves nor the amount he withdraws upon retirement is a growing annuity.)

4-38
Growing Annuity
Payments
You wish to accumulate $1 million by your retirement date, which is 25 years from now. You will make 25 deposits in your bank, with the first occurring today. The bank pays 6% interest, compounded annually. Because of expected inflation, you anticipate an annual raise of 2%,

so you will let the amount you deposit each year also grow by 2% (i.e., your second deposit will be 2% greater than your first, the third will be 2% greater than the second, and so on.). How much must your first deposit be to meet your goal?

4-39
Present Value

It is now December 31, 2014, and a jury just found in favour of a woman who sued the city for injuries sustained in a January 2013 accident. She requested recovery of lost wages, plus $100,000 for pain and suffering, plus $20,000 for her legal expenses. Her doctor testified that she has been unable to work since the accident and that she will not be able to work in the future. She is now 62, and the jury decided that she would have worked for another 3 years. She was scheduled to have earned $34,000 in 2013, and her employer testified that she would probably have received raises of 3% per year. The actual payment will be made on December 31, 2015. The judge stipulated that all dollar amounts are to be adjusted to a present value basis on December 31, 2015, using a 7% annual interest rate, using compound, not simple, interest. Furthermore, he stipulated that the pain and suffering and legal expenses should be based on a December, 31, 2014, date. How large a cheque must the city write on December 31, 2015?

4-40
Required Annuity
Payments

A father is planning a savings program to put his daughter through university. She is 13, she plans to enroll in 5 years, and she should graduate after 4 years. Currently, the annual cost (for everything—food, clothing, tuition, books, transportation, and so forth) is $15,000, but these costs are expected to increase by 5% annually. Assume that all amounts will be paid at the start of the year. She now has $7,500 in a university savings account that pays 6% annually. The father will make six equal annual deposits into her account; the first deposit today, and the sixth on the day she starts university. How large must each of the six payments be?

 # Spreadsheet Problem

4-41
Build a Model:
The Time Value
of Money

Start with the partial model in the file **Ch 04 Build a Model.xlsx** from the textbook's website. Answer the following questions, using a spreadsheet model to do the calculations.

a. Find the FV of $1,000 invested to earn 10% after 5 years. Answer this question by using a math formula and also by using the *Excel* function wizard.

b. Now create a table that shows the FV at 0%, 5%, and 20% for 0, 1, 2, 3, 4, and 5 years. Then create a graph with years on the horizontal axis and FV on the vertical axis to display your results.

c. Find the PV of $1,000 due in 5 years if the discount rate is 10%. Again, work the problem with a formula and also by using the function wizard.

d. A security has a cost of $1,000 and will return $2,000 after 5 years. What rate of return does the security provide?

e. Suppose Canada's population is 30 million people, and its population is expected to grow by 2% per year. How long will it take for the population to double?

f. Find the PV of an annuity that pays $1,000 at the end of each of the next 5 years if the interest rate is 15%. Then find the FV of that same annuity.

g. How would the PV and FV of the annuity change if it were an annuity due rather than an ordinary annuity?

h. What would the FV and PV for parts a and c be if the interest rate were 10% with semi-annual compounding rather than 10% with annual compounding?

i. Find the PV and FV of an investment that makes the following end-of-year payments. The interest rate is 8%.

Year	Payment
1	$500
2	600
3	800

j. Suppose you bought a house and took out a mortgage for $50,000. The interest rate is 8%, and you must amortize the loan over 10 years with equal end-of-year payments. Set up an amortization schedule that shows the annual payments and the amount of each payment that goes to pay off the principal and the amount that constitutes interest expense to the borrower and interest income to the lender. Remember that interest rates on mortgage loans are compounded semiannually.

(1) Create a graph that shows how the payments are divided between interest and principal repayment over time.

(2) Suppose the loan called for 10 years of monthly payments, with the same original amount and the same nominal interest rate. What would the amortization schedule show now?

MINI CASE

Assume that you are nearing graduation and that you have applied for a job with a local bank. As part of the bank's evaluation process, you have been asked to take an examination that covers several financial analysis techniques. The first section of the test addresses discounted cash flow analysis. See how you would do by answering the following questions.

a. Draw time lines for (1) a $100 lump sum cash flow at the end of Year 2, (2) an ordinary annuity of $100 per year for 3 years, and (3) an uneven cash flow stream of −$50, $100, $75, and $50 at the end of Years 0 through 3.

b. (1) What is the future value of an initial $100 after 3 years if it is invested in an account paying 10% annual interest?

(2) What is the present value of $100 to be received in 3 years if the appropriate interest rate is 10%?

c. We sometimes need to find how long it will take a sum of money (or anything else) to grow to some specified amount. For example, if a company's sales are growing at a rate of 20% per year, how long will it take sales to double?

d. If you want an investment to double in 3 years, what interest rate must it earn?

e. What is the difference between an ordinary annuity and an annuity due? What type of annuity is shown below? How would you change it to the other type of annuity?

f. (1) What is the future value of a 3-year ordinary annuity of $100 if the appropriate interest rate is 10%?

(2) What is the present value of the annuity?

(3) What would the future and present values be if the annuity were an annuity due?

g. What is the present value of the following uneven cash flow stream? The appropriate interest rate is 10%, compounded annually.

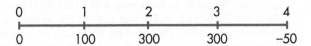

h. (1) Define (a) the stated, or quoted, or nominal rate (I_{NOM}) and (b) the periodic rate (I_{PER}).

(2) Will the future value be larger or smaller if we compound an initial amount more often than annually, for example, every 6 months, or *semiannually*, holding the stated interest rate constant? Why?

(3) What is the future value of $100 after 5 years under 12% annual compounding? Semiannual compounding? Quarterly compounding? Monthly compounding? Daily compounding?

(4) What is the effective annual rate (EFF%)? What is the EFF% for a nominal rate of 12%, compounded semiannually? Compounded quarterly? Compounded monthly? Compounded daily?

i. Will the effective annual rate ever be equal to the nominal (quoted) rate?

j. (1) Construct an amortization schedule for a $1,000, 10% annual rate loan with 3 equal installments.

(2) What is the annual interest expense for the borrower, and the annual interest income for the lender, during Year 2?

k. Suppose on January 1 you deposit $100 in an account that pays a nominal, or quoted, interest rate of 11.33463%, with interest added (compounded) daily. How much will you have in your account on October 1, or after 9 months?

l. (1) What is the value at the end of Year 3 of the following cash flow stream if the quoted interest rate is 10%, compounded semiannually?

(2) What is the PV of the same stream?

(3) Is the stream an annuity?

(4) An important rule is that you should never show a nominal rate on a time line or use it in calculations unless what condition holds? (*Hint:* Think of annual compounding, when I_{NOM} = EFF% = I_{PER}.) What would be wrong with your answer to Questions l-(1) and l-(2) if you used the nominal rate (10%) rather than the periodic rate ($I_{NOM}/2$ = 10%/2 = 5%)?

m. Suppose someone offered to sell you a note calling for the payment of $1,000 15 months from today. They offer to sell it to you for $850. You have $850 in a bank time deposit that pays a 6.76649% nominal rate with daily compounding, which is a 7% effective annual interest rate, and you plan to leave the money in the bank unless you buy the note. The note is not risky—you are sure it will be paid on schedule. Should you buy the note? Check the decision in three ways: (1) by comparing your future value if you buy the note versus leaving your money in the bank, (2) by comparing the PV of the note with your current bank account, and (3) by comparing the EFF% on the note versus that of the bank account.

chapter 5

Financial Planning and Forecasting Financial Statements

The need for companies to plan ahead—to forecast–would seem intuitive to most people. Estimating future product demand, competition and technological trends are a few variables that feed into forecasting a company's future sales. Companies must also estimate input costs, to ensure operations are profitable. Moreover, a company must determine how much money, if any, it must seek from investors to carry out its planned business. Perhaps, it will need none; the firm may actually generate sufficient free cash flows. In that case, management should plan how it intends to use the free cash flows in a manner that serves its shareholders best.

With the speed and volatility of business change in recent years, one might reasonably assume that CFOs have made their forecasting practices a priority. But just how far have companies ensured their forecasting methods are up to date? A 2013 survey by the Association for Financial Professionals shows a wide difference between where leaders say their companies should be and where many of them actually are. While over half the survey respondents reported that earnings volatility is greater today than five years ago, only 13% reported that they've made significant changes to their forecasting and planning systems.

To help address these shortcomings, CFOs report their number one priority in the next two years is improving their business planning and forecasting. Examples of new initiatives some companies are using include rolling forecasting, in which companies make 1- and 5-year forecasts but then modify the 1-year forecast each month as new operating results become available. Another initiative, the *Beyond Budgeting* concept, looks at replacing traditional top-down planning and budgeting systems, which are considered inflexible with a more decentralized model that uses resources closer to the company's customers and marketplace. A third initiative, activity-based budgeting, allocates costs and revenues by products and services rather than by traditional departments.

High-performance companies focus on the links among forecasting, planning, and business strategy rather than on just cost management and cost accounting. While some of these issues are often thought of as "management" rather than "finance," this is a false distinction. Much of finance is numbers oriented, but as any CFO will tell you, his or her primary job is to help the firm as a whole achieve good results. The procedures discussed in this chapter can help firms improve their operations and results.

Source: Adapted from "Forecasting: Best Practices for Common Challenges," Association for Financial Professionals, 2013, pp. 1–4.

Managers use **pro forma**, or **projected, financial statements** in four ways: (1) By looking at projected statements, they can assess whether the firm's anticipated performance is in line with the firm's own general targets and with investors' expectations. (2) Pro forma statements can be used to estimate the effect of proposed operating changes, enabling managers to conduct "what if" analyses. (3) Managers use pro forma statements to anticipate the firm's future financing needs. (4) Managers forecast free cash flows under different operating plans, forecast their capital requirements, and then choose the plan that maximizes shareholder value. Security analysts make the same types of projections, forecasting future earnings, cash flows, and stock prices.

The texbook's website contains an *Excel* file that will guide you through the chapter's calculations. The file for this chapter is ***Ch 05 Tool Kit.xlsx,*** and we encourage you to open the file and follow along as you read the chapter. **www.nelson.com/ brigham3ce**

5.1 Overview of Financial Planning

Our primary objective in this book is to explain what managers can do to make their companies more valuable. However, value creation is impossible unless the company has a well-articulated plan. As Yogi Berra once said, "You've got to be careful if you don't know where you're going, because you might not get there."

Strategic Plans

Strategic plans usually begin with a statement of the overall *corporate purpose.* Many companies are very clear about their corporate purpose: "Our mission is to maximize shareowner value over time."

This corporate purpose is increasingly common for Canadian companies, but that has not always been the case. Before the economic crisis of 2008 and 2009, many companies forgot about the "over time" part, focusing instead on maximizing short-term stock prices. Shareholders and directors have, fortunately, brought "over time" back into focus.

A corporate focus on creating wealth for the company's owners is not as common abroad as it is in North America. For example, Veba AG, one of Germany's largest companies, created a stir when it stated in its annual report that "Our commitment is to create value for you, our shareholders." This was quite different from the usual German model, in which companies have representatives from labour on their boards of directors and explicitly state their commitments to a variety of stakeholders. As one might expect, Veba's stock has consistently outperformed the average German stock. As the trend in

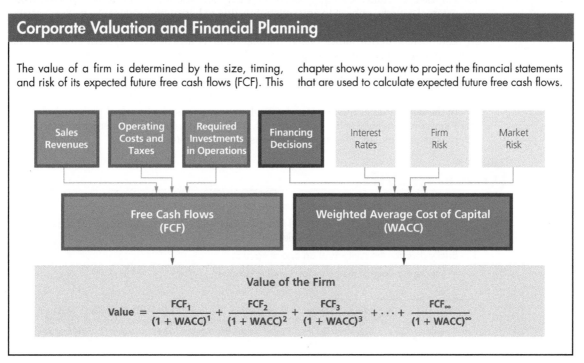

international investing continues, more and more companies are adopting a corporate purpose similar to that of Veba.

Corporate scope defines a firm's lines of business and geographic area of operations. For example, Coca-Cola limits its products to soft drinks, but on a global scale. PepsiCo recently followed Coke's lead—it restricted its scope by spinning off its food service businesses. In 2001, Canadian Pacific Limited decided to split itself into five different companies as a means to improve shareholder value. There had often been comments that its stock was underpriced, suffering from a "holding company discount."[1] In fact, several studies have found that the market tends to value focused firms more highly than diversified firms.[2]

The corporate purpose states the general philosophy of the business, but it does not provide managers with operational objectives. The *statement of corporate objectives* sets forth specific goals to guide management. Most organizations have both qualitative and quantitative objectives. A typical quantitative objective might be attaining a 50% market share, a 20% ROE, a 10% earnings growth rate, or a $100 million Economic Value Added (EVA).

Once a firm has defined its purpose, scope, and objectives, it must develop a strategy for achieving its goals. *Corporate strategies* are broad approaches rather than detailed plans. For example, one airline may have a strategy of offering no-frills service among a limited number of cities, while another's strategy may be to offer "staterooms in the sky." Any such strategy should be compatible with the firm's purpose, scope, and objectives.

Operating Plans

Operating plans provide detailed implementation guidance to help meet the corporate objectives. These plans can be developed for any time horizon, but most companies use a 5-year horizon. A 5-year plan is detailed for the first year, with each succeeding year's plan becoming less specific. The plan explains who is responsible for each particular function, when specific tasks are to be accomplished, sales and profit targets, and the like.

The Financial Plan

The financial planning process has five steps:

1. Project financial statements to analyze the effects of the operating plan on projected profits and financial ratios.
2. Determine the funds needed to support the 5-year plan.
3. Forecast the funds to be generated internally and identify those to be obtained from external sources, subject to any constraints due to borrowing covenants, such as restrictions on the debt ratio, the current ratio, and the coverage ratios.
4. Establish a performance-based management compensation system that rewards employees for creating shareholder wealth.
5. Monitor operations after implementing the plan, identify the cause of any deviations, and take corrective actions.

In the remainder of this chapter, we explain how to create a financial plan, including its three key components: (1) the sales forecast, (2) pro forma financial statements, and (3) the external financing plan. We discuss compensation in Chapter 22.

CONCEPT REVIEW

1. What are four ways that managers use pro forma statements?
2. Briefly explain the following terms: (1) corporate purpose, (2) corporate scope, (3) corporate objectives, and (4) corporate strategies.
3. Briefly describe the contents of an operating plan.
4. What are the steps of the financial planning process?

[1]Carlton Osakwe and Peggy Hedges, "The Diversification Discount: The Case of Canadian Pacific Limited," Working Paper no. 2002–17, University of Calgary, November 2002, http://www.haskayne.ucalgary.ca, accessed April 11, 2008.
[2]See, for example, Philip G. Berger and Eli Ofek, "Diversification's Effect on Firm Value," *Journal of Financial Economics*, 1995, 39–66; and Larry Lang and René Stulz, "Tobin's Q, Corporate Diversification, and Firm Performance," *Journal of Political Economy*, 1994, 1248–80.

5.2 Sales Forecast

The *sales forecast* generally starts with a review of sales during the past 5 years, expressed in a graph such as that in Figure 5-1. The first part of the graph shows 5 years of historical sales for MicroDrive.

See *Ch 05 Tool Kit.xlsx* at the textbook's website for details.

   Entire courses are devoted to forecasting sales, so we can only touch on the basic elements here. However, forecasting the future sales growth rate always begins with a look at past growth. For example, the average of MicroDrive's recent annual growth rates is 10.3%. However, the compound growth rate from 2012 to 2016 is the solution value for g in the equation

$$\$2,058(1 + g)^4 = \$3,000$$

and it can be found by solving the equation or with a financial calculator, entering N = 4, PV = −2,058, PMT = 0, FV = 3,000, and then pressing I/YR to get g = 9.9%.[3]

   The preceding approaches are simple, but both can be poor representations of past growth. First, the arithmetic average procedure generally produces numbers that are too high. To illustrate why, suppose sales grew by 100% one year and then fell by 50% the next year. There would actually be zero growth over the 2 years, but the calculated average growth rate would be 25%. Similarly, the point-to-point procedure is not reliable because if either the beginning or ending year is an "outlier" in the sense of being above or below the trend line shown in Figure 5-1, then the calculated growth rate will not be representative of past growth. The solution to these problems is to use a regression approach, where a curve is fitted to the historic sales data and then the slope of that curve is used to measure historic growth. If we expect a constant growth rate (as opposed to a constant dollar amount, which would mean a declining growth rate), then the regression should be based on the natural log of sales, not sales itself. With a spreadsheet, this is not a difficult calculation, and by far

FIGURE

MicroDrive Inc.: Historical Sales (Millions of Dollars)

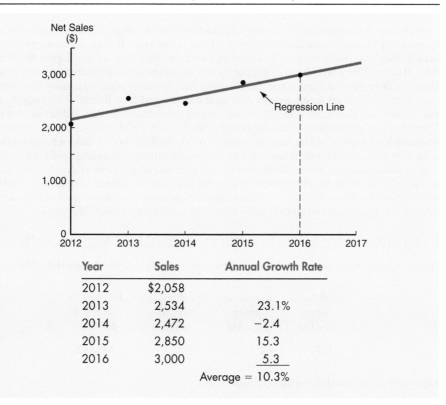

Year	Sales	Annual Growth Rate
2012	$2,058	
2013	2,534	23.1%
2014	2,472	−2.4
2015	2,850	15.3
2016	3,000	5.3
	Average =	10.3%

---

[3]Unless we state differently, we will report values from MicroDrive's financial statements in units of a million dollars, as shown in Figure 5-1.

These approaches are demonstrated in the **Ch 05 Tool Kit.xlsx** at the textbook's website. Also, **Web Extension 5B** illustrates these approaches when estimating dividend growth rates.

the easiest way to calculate the growth rate is with *Excel*'s LOGEST function. Simply type the years and sales into a spreadsheet, click f_x on the menu bar, select Statistical functions, and then choose the LOGEST function. Highlight the sales range for the Y variable and the years range for X in the function dialog box, and then click OK. The result will be $1 + g$, so you finish by subtracting 1 to get the growth rate. For MicroDrive, the growth rate is 9.1%.

Although it is useful to calculate the past growth rate in sales, much more is involved in estimating future sales. Future sales will depend on the economy (both domestic and global), the industry's prospects, the company's current product line, proposed products that are in the pipeline, and marketing campaigns. When MicroDrive incorporated these issues into its analysis, it estimated 10% expected growth for the upcoming year.

If the sales forecast is off, the consequences can be serious. First, if the market expands by *more* than MicroDrive has anticipated, the company will not be able to meet demand. Its customers will end up buying competitors' products, and MicroDrive will lose market share. On the other hand, if its projections are overly optimistic, MicroDrive could end up with too much plant, equipment, and inventory, which hurts free cash flow and stock prices. If MicroDrive had financed an unnecessary expansion with debt, high interest charges would compound its problems. Thus, an accurate sales forecast is critical to the firm's well-being.

After much discussion and analysis, MicroDrive's managers decided to forecast a 10% increase in sales. How will MicroDrive's managers incorporate this increased level of sales into the financial plan? In particular, will MicroDrive have to raise any additional external funds in order to implement the plan? We will answer this question using two approaches: (1) the additional funds needed (AFN) formula and (2) the forecasted financial statement method.

ⓒONCEPT REVIEW

1. List some factors that should be considered when developing a sales forecast.
2. Explain why an accurate sales forecast is critical to profitability.

5.3 Additional Funds Needed (AFN) Equation Method

If we assume that none of a firm's ratios will change (a heroic assumption!), we can use a simple approach to forecast financial requirements. Here is the logic. If sales increase, firms usually have to purchase assets (such as inventories, machines, etc.) in order to support the increased level of sales. Where will the firm get the money to purchase the projected increase in assets? There are three sources. First, some liabilities (such as accounts payable) usually increase when sales increase. Balance sheets require that total assets equal total liabilities and equity, which also means that the increase in assets must equal the increase in total liabilities and equity. Therefore, this spontaneous increase in liabilities is a source of funds—that is, spontaneous financing for the projected increase in assets. Second, the firm should make a profit on the new sales. Part of this profit will be used to pay dividends, but the remaining profit can be used to help purchase the new assets. Recall that the net income not paid out as dividends is an addition to retained earnings. Therefore, this increase in equity is a source of financing for the projected increase in assets. Finally, any remaining increase in assets must be financed by additional external funds, such as additional bank loans, long-term debt, or stock issuances.

Using MicroDrive's Data to Implement the AFN Equation Method

Equation 5-1 summarizes the logic and defines the **additional funds needed AFN method:**

$$\begin{matrix} \text{Additional} \\ \text{funds} \\ \text{needed} \end{matrix} = \begin{matrix} \text{Required} \\ \text{asset} \\ \text{increase} \end{matrix} - \begin{matrix} \text{Spontaneous} \\ \text{liabilities} \\ \text{increase} \end{matrix} - \begin{matrix} \text{Increase in} \\ \text{retained} \\ \text{earnings} \end{matrix} \qquad (5\text{-}1)$$

$$\text{AFN} = (A^*/S_0)\Delta S - (L^*/S_0)\Delta S - MS_1(RR)$$

The symbols in Equation 5-1 are defined below:

AFN = Additional funds needed.

A^* = Assets that are tied directly to sales, hence must increase if sales are to increase. Note that A designates total assets and A^* designates those assets that must increase if sales are to increase. When the firm is operating at full capacity, as is the case here, $A^* = A$. Often, though, A^* and A are not equal, and either the equation must be modified or we must use the projected financial statement method.

S_0 = Sales during the last year.

A^*/S_0 = Percentage of required assets to sales, which also shows the required dollar increase in assets per \$1 increase in sales.

L^* = Liabilities that increase spontaneously. L^* is normally much less than total liabilities (L). Spontaneous liabilities include accounts payable and accruals, but not bank loans and bonds.

L^*/S_0 = Liabilities that increase spontaneously as a percentage of sales, or spontaneously generated financing per \$1 increase in sales.

S_1 = Total sales projected for next year.

ΔS = Change in sales.

M = Profit margin, or profit per \$1 of sales.

RR = Retention ratio, which is the percentage of net income that is retained. The payout ratio is the percentage of net income paid out to shareholders. Because the retention ratio and the payout ratio must total to 1, RR is also equal to $1 -$ payout ratio.

Recall from the previous section that MicroDrive's managers forecast a 10% increase in sales, from \$3,000 million to \$3,300 million. Based on this projection, S_1 = \$3,300 million and ΔS = \$300 million. In the previous year, MicroDrive had \$2,000 million in assets, which means that A^*/S_0 = \$2,000/\$3,000 = 0.6667.[4] If this ratio remains constant, as assumed in the AFN formula, assets must increase by about 67 cents for every \$1 increase in sales.

In the previous year MicroDrive had \$60 million in accounts payable and \$140 million in accruals, for a total spontaneous liabilities, L^*, of \$60 + \$140 = \$200 million. Therefore, L^*/S_0 = \$200/\$3,000 = 0.0667, which means that MicroDrive generates about 7 cents of spontaneous financing for every \$1 increase in sales.

MicroDrive had \$113.5 million in net income, for a profit margin of M = \$113.5/\$3,000 = 0.0378, which means that MicroDrive earns almost 3.8 cents on each dollar of sales. MicroDrive paid out \$57.5 million in common dividends and retained \$56 million, so RR = \$56/\$113.5 = 0.493.

Inserting MicroDrive's values into Equation 5-1, we find the additional funds needed to be \$118 million:

$$\begin{matrix} \text{Additional} \\ \text{funds} \\ \text{needed} \end{matrix} = \begin{matrix} \text{Projected} \\ \text{increase in} \\ \text{assets} \end{matrix} - \begin{matrix} \text{Spontaneous} \\ \text{increase in} \\ \text{liabilities} \end{matrix} - \begin{matrix} \text{Increase in} \\ \text{retained} \\ \text{earnings} \end{matrix}$$

$$= 0.667(\Delta S) - 0.067(\Delta S) - 0.0378(S_1)(0.493)$$

$$= 0.667(\$300\,\text{million}) - 0.067(\$300\,\text{million})$$
$$- 0.0378(\$3,300\,\text{million})(0.493)$$

$$= \$200\,\text{million} - \$20\,\text{million} - \$61.58\,\text{million}$$

$$= \$118.42\,\text{million}[5]$$

The formula suggests that to increase sales by \$300 million, MicroDrive must increase assets by \$200 million. The \$200 million of new assets must be financed in some manner. Of the total, \$20 million will come from a spontaneous increase in liabilities, while another \$61.58 million will be obtained from retained earnings. The remaining \$118.42 million must be raised from external sources.

Factors in the AFN Equation

The AFN equation shows that external financing requirements depend on five factors:

1. **Sales growth (ΔS).** Rapidly growing companies require large increases in assets and more external financing, other things held constant.

---

[4]For MicroDrive's financial statements, look back to Chapter 2 or look ahead to Tables 5-2 or 5-3.
[5]All calculations are done in the *Excel* file, **Ch 05 Tool Kit.xlsx**, available at the textbook's website. Because *Excel* doesn't round values in intermediate steps, there may be slight differences between the values from *Excel* and calculations based on the rounded intermediate values in the textbook.

2. **Capital intensity ($A*/S_0$).** The amount of assets required per dollar of sales, $A*/S_0$ in Equation 5-1, is called the **capital intensity ratio**. This ratio has a major impact on capital requirements. Companies with higher assets-to-sales ratios require more assets for a given increase in sales, hence a greater need for external financing.

3. **Spontaneous liabilities-to-sales ratio ($L*/S_0$).** Companies that spontaneously generate a large amount of liabilities from accounts payable and accruals will have a relatively lower need for external financing.

4. **Profit margin (M).** The higher the profit margin, the larger the net income available to support increases in assets, hence the lower the need for external financing.

5. **Retention ratio (RR).** Companies that retain more of their earnings as opposed to paying them out as dividends will generate more retained earnings and thus have less need for external financing.

The logic behind the AFN formula and the insights above are important, but the AFN formula provides an accurate forecast only for companies whose ratios are all expected to remain constant. The AFN formula is useful for quickly obtaining a "back of the envelope" estimate of external financing requirements, but the percent of sales method, explained in the next section, is used by most companies for their more detailed financial planning.

The Self-Supporting Growth Rate

One interesting question is: "What is the maximum growth rate the firm could achieve if it had no access to external capital?" This rate is called the "self-supporting growth rate," and it can be found as the value of g that, when used in the AFN equation, results in an AFN of zero. We first replace ΔS in the AFN equation with gS_0 and S_1 with $(1 + g)S_0$ so that the only unknown is g; then we then solve for g to obtain the following equation for the self-supporting growth rate:

$$\text{Self-supporting } g = \frac{M(RR)(S_0)}{A* - L* - M(RR)(S_0)} \tag{5-2}$$

If the firm has any positive earnings and pays out less than 100% in dividends, then it will have some additions to retained earnings, and those additions could be combined with spontaneous funds to enable the company to grow at some rate without having to raise external capital. For MicroDrive, the self-supporting growth rate is 3.21%; this means it could grow at that rate even if capital markets dried up completely, with everything else held constant.

CONCEPT REVIEW

1. If all ratios are expected to remain constant, a formula can be used to forecast AFN. Give the formula and briefly explain it.

2. How do the following factors affect external capital requirements: (1) retention ratio, (2) capital intensity, and (3) profit margin?

3. Suppose MicroDrive's growth rate in sales is forecast as 15%. If all ratios stay the same, what is the AFN? (Check Figure: $205.62 million)

5.4 The Forecasted Financial Statement (FFS) Method

Unlike the AFN formula, the **forecasted financial statement (FFS) approach** actually forecasts the complete set of financial statements. However, the logic of this approach is similar to that of the AFN formula. Before going into the details, let's take a look at the big picture. Just as with the AFN formula, we begin with the sales forecast. Similarly, we also forecast the assets that are required to support the sales. The AFN formula assumes that all assets grow by the same proportion, but the forecasted financial statement approach allows different asset classes to grow at different rates. This additional level of detail makes this approach more realistic. In addition, the result is a forecast of the entire asset side of the balance sheet, whereas the AFN formula shows only the net increase in assets.

Similar to the AFN formula, we forecast the spontaneous liabilities in the FFS approach. The AFN formula assumes that each spontaneous liability grows at the same rate, but the FFS approach allows each spontaneous liability to grow at a different rate, providing a more realistic forecast. The AFN formula provides a forecast of the addition to retained earnings, based on the profit margin and the dividend retention ratio. In the FFS approach, we also forecast the addition to retained earnings, but we do this by first forecasting the entire income statement and dividend payment. We define the *specified sources of financing* as the total of spontaneous liabilities, existing financing (i.e., the current levels of debt and common equity), and the addition to retained earnings.

At this point in the process, we have a forecast of the projected income statements, a forecast of the asset side of the balance sheets, and a forecast of the liabilities and equity side of the balance sheets. If we are extraordinarily lucky, the balance sheets balance, which means that sources of financing (i.e., the liabilities and equity side of the balance sheets) are exactly equal to the required assets (i.e., the asset side of the balance sheets). If so, we have exactly enough financing to acquire the assets needed to support the forecasted level of sales. But in all our years of forecasting, we have never had this happen, and you probably won't be any luckier.

To make the balance sheets balance (ensuring enough financing to purchase the required assets), the FFS approach uses the **plug technique**. To use this technique, we define the AFN as the required assets minus the specified sources of financing, based on the projected balance sheets. If the AFN is positive, then we need to raise additional funds, so we "plug" this amount into the balance sheet as additional financing in the form of new notes payable, long-term debt, or equity.[6] For example, suppose the required assets equal $2,500 million and the specified sources of financing total $2,400 million. The required additional financing is $2,500 − $2,400 = $100 million. The firm might choose to raise this $100 million as new notes payable, thus increasing the old notes payable by $100 million.

If the AFN is negative, then the forecast has more financing (i.e., liabilities and equity) than needed to support the required assets. The firm could reduce its financing by paying off some debt, by repurchasing stock, or by paying higher dividends (which reduces the addition to retained earnings). However, many firms use short-term investments as a temporary repository for any extra cash, or as a "slush fund" for use in times when operating cash flows are lower than expected. Therefore, in our initial forecast, often we assume that any extra funds will be used to purchase additional short-term investments. We "plug" the amount of extra financing (the absolute value of the AFN) into short-term investments on the asset side of the balance sheet.

Keep the big picture in mind as we forecast MicroDrive's financial statements.

Step 1. Analyze the Historical Ratios

The first step is to analyze the historical ratios that will be used in the projections (see Table 5-1). This differs somewhat from the ratio analysis of Chapter 3, since the objective here is to forecast the future, or pro forma, financial statements. The next sections explain exactly why we need these particular ratios, but for now we will just describe the ratios and how to use them. Our illustration has only 2 years of data for MicroDrive, but a thorough analysis should have at least 5 years of historical data. In addition to MicroDrive's actual year-by-year ratios, the table also shows the historical average, which in this case is the average of the two prior years. The last column of the table shows the ratio for the industry composite, which is the sum of the financial statements for all firms in the industry.

Forecasting is as much art as science, but here are a few basic guidelines. First, are there trends in the ratios? In our experience, simple trends can help predict the future, because most companies, especially large ones, cannot turn on a dime. Second, how does a ratio compare with its historical average? Is any aberration caused by temporary factors, which means the ratio might revert back toward its average? Third, how does a ratio compare to the industry average? For example, in competitive industries, it is very difficult for a company to maintain a cost/sales ratio too much better than its peers. Fourth, what is happening in the economy and the firm's industry? For example, if a firm depends on oil as an input, then wars in the Middle East might drive up its costs. Fifth, what are the company's operating plans? For example, if the company is planning a major expansion, then its projected costs

See ***Ch 05 Tool Kit.xlsx*** at the textbook's website for details.

---

[6]We could even raise this additional financing by reducing dividend payments, which increases the addition to retained earnings. If the company has short-term investments, it might satisfy the AFN by selling some. But notice that if the company sells (or chooses not to purchase) operating assets, then the company will not be able to support the forecast sales. We'll discuss these issues later in the section.

TABLE 5-1   Historical Ratios for MicroDrive Inc.

	Actual 2015	Actual 2016	Historical Average	Industry Average
COGS (excl. dep.) to sales	70.2%	70.0%	70.1%	77.6%
Depreciation to net plant and equipment	10.3	10.0	10.2	10.2
Other operating exp. to sales	17.4	17.2	17.3	10.0
Cash to sales	0.5	0.3	0.4	1.0
Accounts receivable to sales	11.1	12.5	11.8	10.0
Inventory to sales	14.6	20.5	17.6	11.1
Net plant and equipment to sales	30.5	33.3	31.9	33.3
Accounts payable to sales	1.1	2.0	1.6	1.0
Accruals to sales	4.6	4.7	4.7	2.0

might be temporarily high as it will have larger than normal advertising campaigns. Only after thinking about these questions and issues should a forecaster move on to the next step.

Step 2. Forecast the Income Statement

In this section we explain how to forecast the income statement and in the following section we forecast the balance sheet. Although we cover these topics in two separate sections, the forecasted financial statements are actually integrated with one another and with the previous year's statements. For example, the following sections show that the income statement item "depreciation" depends on net plant and equipment, which is a balance sheet item. The balance sheet item "retained earnings" depends on the previous year's retained earnings, the forecasted net income, and the firm's dividend policy. Keep this interrelatedness in mind as you go through the forecast.

Forecast Sales   Table 5-2 shows the forecasted income statement. Management forecasts that sales will grow by 10%. Thus, forecasted sales, shown in Row 1, Column 3, is the product of the prior year's sales of $3,000 million and (1 + g): $3,000(1.1) = $3,300 million.

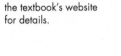

See **Ch 05 Tool Kit.xlsx** at the textbook's website for details.

Forecast Earnings Before Interest and Taxes (EBIT)   Table 5-1 shows that MicroDrive's ratio of costs of goods sold except depreciation to sales for the most recent year was 70.0% ($2,100/$3,000 = 0.70). Thus, to get a dollar of sales, MicroDrive had to incur 70.0 cents of costs. Initially, we assume that the cost structure will remain unchanged. Later on, we explore the impact of changes in the cost structure, but for now we assume that forecasted COGS will equal 70.0% of forecasted sales. See Row 2 of Table 5-2.[7]

Because depreciation depends on the asset base, it is more reasonable to forecast depreciation as a percent of net plant and equipment rather than sales. The most recent ratio of depreciation to net plant and equipment was 10% ($100/$1,000 = 0.10). As we show later in Table 5-3, the forecasted net plant and equipment is $1,100 million. Therefore, forecasted depreciation is 0.10($1,100) = $110 million.

MicroDrive's other operating expenses include items such as executive salaries, insurance fees, and marketing costs. These items tend to be related to a company's size, which is related to sales. MicroDrive's projection is 17.2%($3,300) = $567.6 million.

Total operating costs, shown on Row 5, are the sum of all costs including depreciation. EBIT is then found by subtraction.

Forecast Interest Expense   How should we forecast the interest charges? The actual net interest expense is the sum of a firm's daily interest charges less its daily interest income,

---

[7]Notice that we don't forecast the growth rate in costs. Instead, we forecast the growth rate in sales and specify costs as a percent of sales.

TABLE 5-2	MicroDrive Inc.: Actual and Projected Income Statements (Millions of Dollars Except Per-Share Data)

	Actual 2016 (1)	Forecast Basis (2)	Forecast for 2017 (3)
1. Sales	$3,000.0	110% × 2016 Sales =	$3,300.0
2. COGS except depreciation	2,100.0	70.0% × 2017 Sales =	2,310.0
3. Depreciation expense	100.0	10% × 2017 Net plant =	110.0
4. Other operating expenses	516.2	17.2% × 2017 Sales =	567.6
5. Total operating costs	2,716.2		2,987.6
6. EBIT	283.8		312.4
7. Less interest	88.0	(See text for explanation)	92.8
8. Earnings before taxes (EBT)	195.8		219.6
9. Taxes (40%)	78.3		87.8
10. Net income	117.5		131.8
11. Preferred dividends	4.0	Dividend rate × 2017 Pref. stk. =	4.0
12. NI available to common	$ 113.5		$ 127.8
13. Shares of common equity	50.0		50.0
14. Dividends per share	$ 1.15	108% × 2016 DPS =	$ 1.25
15. Dividends to common	$ 57.5	2017 DPS × Number of shares =	$ 62.5
16. Additions to retained earnings	$ 56.0		$ 65.3

if any, from short-term investments. Most companies have a variety of different debt obligations with different fixed interest rates and/or floating interest rates. For example, bonds issued in different years generally have different fixed rates, while most bank loans have rates that vary with interest rates in the economy. Given this situation, it is impossible to forecast the exact interest expense for the upcoming year, so we make two simplifying assumptions.

Assumption 1: Specifying the Balance of Debt for Computing Interest Expense. If the amount of debt were expected to remain constant throughout the year, the correct balance to use when forecasting the annual interest expense would be the amount of debt at the beginning of the year, which is the same as the debt shown on the balance sheet at the end of the previous year. Unfortunately, for most companies the amount of debt usually does change during the year. Another option would be to base the interest expense on the debt balance shown at the end of the forecasted year. However, by charging a full year's interest on the additional debt, you imply that the debt was added on January 1. In many cases this would also not be true; you would most likely be overstating the interest expense. Your debt assumption would also cause circularity in the calculation. We discuss this in detail in *Web Extension 5A,* but the short explanation is that additional debt causes additional interest expense, which reduces the addition to retained earnings, which in turn requires a higher level of debt, which causes still more interest expense, and the cycle keeps repeating. This is called **financing feedback.** Spreadsheets can deal with this problem (see *Web Extension 5A,* available at the textbook's website), but add complexity to the model that might not be worth the benefits.

A similar approach would be to base the interest expense on the average of the debt at the beginning and end of the year. This approach would produce the correct interest expense only if debt were added evenly throughout the year, which is a big assumption. In addition, it also results in a circular model with all its complexity.

A third approach, which we illustrate below, works well for most situations. We base the interest expense on the amount of debt at the beginning of the year as shown on the previous year's balance sheet. However, since this will underestimate the true interest expense if debt increases throughout the year, as it usually does for most companies, we use an interest rate that is about 0.5% higher than the rate we actually expect. This approach provides reasonably

See ***Ch 05 Tool Kit.xlsx*** at the textbook's website for details.

accurate forecasts without greatly increasing the model's complexity. Keep in mind, though, that this simple approach might not work well in all situations, so see *Web Extension 5A* if you want to implement the more complex modelling technique.

Assumption 2: Specifying Interest Rates. As noted earlier, different loans have different interest rates. Rather than trying to specify the rate on each separate debt issue, we usually specify only two rates, one for short-term notes payable and one for long-term bonds. The interest rate on short-term debt usually floats, and because the best estimate of future rates is generally the current rate, it is most reasonable to apply the current market rate to short-term loans. For MicroDrive, the appropriate short-term rate is about 8.5%, which we rounded up to 9% because we will apply it to the debt balance at the beginning of the year.

For long-term debt we average the rates on currently outstanding long-term bonds and the rate on any new long-term debt. The average rate for MicroDrive is 10.5%, which we round up to 11% because we are going to apply it to the debt at the beginning of the year, as explained above.

Calculating Interest Expense. The forecasted interest expense is the net interest paid on short-term financing plus the interest on long-term bonds. We estimate the net interest on short-term financing by first finding the interest expense on notes payable and then subtracting any interest income from short-term investments. We base interest charges on the amount of short-term debt at the beginning of the year (which is the debt at the end of the previous year), and we note that MicroDrive had no short-term investments. Therefore, MicroDrive's net short-term interest is 0.09($110) − 0.09($0) = $9.9 million. The interest on long-term bonds is 0.11($754.0) = $82.94, rounded to $82.9 million. Therefore, the total interest expense is $9.9 + $82.9 = $92.8 million.

Complete the Income Statement Earnings before taxes (EBT) is calculated by subtracting interest from EBIT and then deducting taxes calculated at a 40% rate. The resulting net income for 2017, which is $131.8 million, is shown in Row 10 of Table 5-2. MicroDrive's preferred stock pays a dividend of 10%. Based on the amount of preferred stock at the beginning of the year, the preferred dividends are 0.10($40) = $4 million. Thus, MicroDrive's forecasted net income available to common stock is $127.8 million, shown in Row 12.

Row 13 shows the number of common shares and Row 14 shows the most recent dividend per share, $1.15. MicroDrive does not plan to issue any new shares, but it does plan to increase the dividend by 8%, resulting in a forecasted dividend of 1.08($1.15) = $1.242, rounded up to $1.25 per share. With 50 million shares, the total forecasted dividend is 50($1.25) = $62.5 million. The forecasted addition to retained earnings is equal to the net income available to common shareholders minus the total dividends: $127.8 − $62.5 = $65.3 million, as shown in Row 16.

Step 3. Forecast the Balance Sheet

Let's start with the assets required to support sales.

Forecast Operating Assets As noted earlier, MicroDrive's assets must increase if sales are to increase. MicroDrive writes and deposits cheques every day. Because its managers don't know exactly when all of the cheques will clear, they can't predict exactly what the balance in their chequing accounts will be on any given day. Therefore, they must maintain a balance of cash and cash equivalents (such as very short-term marketable securities) to avoid overdrawing their accounts. We discuss the issue of cash management in Chapter 18, but for now we simply assume that the cash required to support a company's operations is proportional to its sales. MicroDrive's most recent ratio of cash to sales was approximately 0.33% ($10/$3,000 = 0.003333), and management believes this ratio should remain constant. Therefore, the forecasted cash balance, shown in Row 1 of Table 5-3, is 0.003333($3,300) = $11 million.[8]

Unless a company changes its credit policy or has a change in its customer base, accounts receivable should be proportional to sales. The ratio of accounts receivable to sales was $375/$3,000 = 0.125 = 12.5%. For now we assume that the credit policy and customers' paying patterns will remain constant, so the forecast for accounts receivable is 0.125($3,300) = $412.5 million, as shown in Row 3.

---

[8]Notice that we do not specify a growth rate for cash. Instead, we specify a growth rate for sales and let cash equal a percentage of sales. So the growth rate in cash depends on the sales growth rate and its percentage of sales. If this percentage of sales differs from the percentage in the previous year, then its growth rate will differ from the sales growth rate. Thus, items on the balance sheet may have different growth rates than the sales growth rate.

**TABLE
5-3**   MicroDrive Inc.: Actual and Projected Balance Sheets (Millions of Dollars)

	Actual 2016 (1)	Forecast Basis (2)	Forecast for 2017 (3)
Assets			
1. Cash	$ 10.0	0.33% × 2017 Sales =	$ 11.0
2. Short-term investments	0.0	Previous plus "plug" if needed	0.0
3. Accounts receivable	375.0	12.50% × 2017 Sales =	412.5
4. Inventories	615.0	20.50% × 2017 Sales =	676.5
5. Total current assets	1,000.0		1,100.0
6. Net plant and equipment	1,000.0	33.33% × 2017 Sales =	1,100.0
7. Total assets	$2,000.0		$2,200.0
Liabilities and Equity			
8. Accounts payable	$ 60.0	2.00% × 2017 Sales =	$ 66.0
9. Accruals	140.0	4.67% × 2017 Sales =	154.0
10. Notes payable	110.0	Previous plus "plug" if needed	224.7
11. Total current liabilities	310.0		444.7
12. Long-term bonds	754.0	Same: no new issue	754.0
13. Total liabilities	1,064.0		1,198.7
14. Preferred stock	40.0	Same: no new issue	40.0
15. Common stock	130.0	Same: no new issue	130.0
16. Retained earnings	766.0	2016 RE + 2017 Additions to RE =	831.3
17. Total common equity	896.0		961.3
18. Total liabilities and equity	$2,000.0		$2,200.0
19. Required assets[a]			$2,200.0
20. Specified sources of financing[b]			2,085.3
21. Additional funds needed (AFN)			$ 114.7
22. Required additional notes payable			$ 114.7
23. Additional short-term investments			0.0

[a]Required assets include all of the forecasted operating assets, plus short-term investments from the previous year.
[b]Specified sources of financing include forecasted operating current liabilities, forecasted long-term bonds, forecasted preferred stock, forecasted common equity, and the amount of notes payable from the previous year.

As sales increase, firms generally must carry more inventories. Chapter 18 discusses inventory management in detail, but for now we assume that inventory will also be proportional to sales. The most recent inventory-to-sales ratio was $615/$3,000 = 0.205 = 20.5%. Assuming no change in MicroDrive's inventory policy, the forecasted inventory is 0.205($3,300) = $676.5 million, as shown in Row 4.

It might be reasonable to assume that cash, accounts receivable, and inventories will be proportional to sales, but will the amount of net plant and equipment go up and down as sales go up and down? The correct answer could be either yes or no. When companies acquire plant and equipment, they often install more capacity than they currently need due to economies of scale in building capacity. Moreover, even if a plant is operating at its maximum rated capacity, most companies can produce additional units by reducing downtime for scheduled maintenance, by running machinery at a higher than optimal speed, or by adding a second or third shift. Therefore, at least in the short run, companies may not have a very close relationship between sales and net plant and equipment.

However, some companies do have a fixed relationship between sales and net plant and equipment, even in the short term. For example, new stores in many retail chains achieve the same sales during their first year as the chain's existing stores. The only way such retailers can grow (beyond inflation) is by adding new stores. Such companies therefore have a strong proportional relationship between fixed assets and sales.

Finally, in the long term there is a strong relationship between sales and net plant and equipment for virtually all companies: Few companies can continue to increase sales unless they eventually add capacity. Therefore, as a first approximation it is reasonable to assume that the long-term ratio of net plant and equipment to sales will be constant.

For the first years in a forecast, managers generally build in the actual planned expenditures on plant and equipment. If those estimates are not available, it is generally best to assume a constant ratio of net plant and equipment to sales.

For MicroDrive, the ratio of net plant and equipment to sales was $1,000/$3,000 = 0.3333 = 33.33\%$. MicroDrive's net plant and equipment have grown fairly steadily in the past, and its managers expect steady future growth. Therefore, they forecast that they will need net plant and equipment of $0.3333(\$3,300) = \$1,100$ million.

For now, we make the temporary assumption that short-term investments will remain at their current level. We will return to this point after we forecast the rest of the balance sheet.

Forecast Operating Current Liabilities

As sales increase, so will purchases of raw materials, and those additional purchases will spontaneously lead to a higher level of accounts payable. MicroDrive's most recent ratio of accounts payable to sales was $60/$3,000 = 0.02 = 2\%$. Assuming that the payables policy will not change, the forecasted level of accounts payable is $0.02(\$3,300) = \$66$ million, as shown in Row 8.

Higher sales require more labour, and higher sales normally result in higher taxable income and thus taxes. Therefore, accrued wages and taxes both increase as sales increase. MicroDrive's most recent ratio of accruals to sales was $140/$3,000 = 0.0467 = 4.67\%$. There is no reason to expect a change in this ratio, so the forecasted level of accruals is $0.0467(\$3,300) = \$154$ million.

Forecast Items Determined by Financial Policy Decisions

Forecasting the remaining liability and equity depends on a firm's financial policies, which vary widely from firm to firm. We explain one fairly typical set of financial policies below, and we go through the calculations in detail in the chapter spreadsheet model, *Ch 5 Tool Kit.xlsx*. However, there are many other possible policies. *Web Extension 5B* describes a procedure that can be used to develop a model to fit any set of financial policies. Following is a brief discussion of financial policy decisions.

First, most mature companies rarely issue new common stock, so the forecast for common stock is usually the previous year's common stock; see Chapter 12 for more discussion. Second, most firms increase their dividends at a fairly steady rate, which allows us to forecast dividend payments; see Chapter 13 for a discussion of dividend policy. Subtracting forecasted dividends from forecasted net income gives the additions to retained earnings, which affects total common equity. Third, most firms do not use preferred stock, and those that already have preferred stock issue new preferred stock infrequently. Fourth, issuing more long-term bonds is a major event for most firms, and it often requires approval from the board of directors. Chapter 12 discusses long-term debt financing in detail. Fifth, many firms use short-term bank loans as a financial "shock absorber." When extra funding is needed, they draw down their lines of credit, thus increasing notes payable, until their short-term debt has risen to an unacceptably high level, at which point they arrange long-term financing. When they secure the long-term financing, they pay off some of their short-term debt to bring it down to an acceptable level.

With these typical financial policies in mind, let's turn back to MicroDrive. Initially we assume that MicroDrive will simply maintain its current level of notes payable; we will explain how to forecast the final level of notes payable shortly. In its initial financial plan, MicroDrive will keep long-term debt at the 2016 level, as shown in Row 12 of Table 5-3. The company's policy is not to issue any additional shares of preferred or common stock barring extraordinary circumstances. Therefore, its forecasts for preferred and common stock, shown in Rows 14 and 15, are the 2016 levels. MicroDrive plans to increase its dividend per share by about 8% per year. As shown in Row 15, this policy, when combined with the forecasted level of net income, results in a $65.3 million addition to retained earnings. On the balance sheet, the forecasted level of retained earnings is equal to the 2016 retained earnings plus the forecasted addition to retained earnings, or

$766.0 + $65.3 = $831.3 million. Again, note that we make the temporary assumption that notes payable remain at their 2016 level.

Step 4. Raise the Additional Funds Needed

Based on the forecasted balance sheet, MicroDrive will need $2,200 million of operating assets to support its forecasted $3,300 million of sales. We define required assets as the sum of its forecasted operating assets plus the previous amount of short-term investments. Since MicroDrive had no short-term investments in 2016, its required assets are simply $2,200 million, as shown in Row 19 of Table 5-3.

We define the specified sources of financing as the sum of forecasted levels of operating current liabilities, long-term debt, preferred stock, and common equity, plus notes payable carried over from the previous year:

Accounts payable	$ 66.0
Accruals	154.0
Notes payable (carryover)	110.0
Long-term bonds	754.0
Preferred stock	40.0
Common stock	130.0
Retained earnings	831.3
Total	$2,085.3

Based on its required assets and specified sources of financing, MicroDrive's AFN is $2,200 − $2,085.3 = $114.7 million, as shown in Rows 19, 20, and 21 of Table 5-3. Because the AFN is positive, MicroDrive needs $114.7 million of additional financing, and its initial financial policy is to obtain these funds as notes payable. Therefore, we add $114.7 million into notes payable (Row 10 of Table 5-3), bringing the forecasted total to $110 + $114.7 = $224.7 million.

The plug approach that we used specifies the additional amount of *either* notes payable *or* short-term investments, but not both. If the AFN is positive, we assume that the firm will add to notes payable but leave short-term investments at their current level. If the AFN is negative, it will add to short-term investments but not to notes payable. Because we added notes payable, we don't add any short-term investment, so this completes the initial forecast. Now it is time to analyze the plan and consider potential changes.

Analysis of the Forecast

The 2017 forecast as developed above is only the first part of MicroDrive's total forecasting process. We must next examine the projected statements and determine whether the forecast meets the financial targets as set forth in the 5-year financial plan. If the statements do not meet the targets, then elements of the forecast must be changed.

Table 5-4 shows MicroDrive's most recent actual ratios, its projected ratios, and the latest industry average ratios. (The table also shows a "Revised Forecast" in the third column, which we will discuss later. Disregard the revised data for now.) The firm's financial condition at the close of 2016 was weak, with many ratios being well below the industry averages. For example, MicroDrive's current ratio, based on Column 1 of Table 5-4, was only 3.2 versus 4.2 for an average competitor.

The "Inputs" section shown on the top three rows of the table provides data on three of the model's key drivers: (1) costs (excluding depreciation) as a percentage of sales, (2) accounts receivable as a percentage of sales, and (3) inventory as a percentage of sales. The preliminary forecast in Column 2 assumes that these variables remain constant. While MicroDrive's cost-to-sales ratio is only slightly worse than the industry average, its ratios of accounts receivable to sales and inventory to sales are significantly higher than those of its competitors. Its investment in inventories and receivables is too high, causing its returns on assets, equity, and invested capital as shown in the lower part of the table to be too low. Therefore, MicroDrive should make operational changes designed to reduce its current assets.

The "Ratios" section of Table 5-4 provides more details regarding the firm's weaknesses. MicroDrive's asset management ratios are much worse than the industry averages.

TABLE 5-4   Model Inputs, AFN, and Key Ratios (Millions of Dollars)

	Actual 2016 (1)	Preliminary Forecast for 2017 (2)	Revised Forecast for 2017 (3)	Industry Average 2016 (4)
Model Inputs				
Costs (excluding depreciation) as percentage of sales	87.2%	87.2%	86.0%	87.1%
Accounts receivable as percentage of sales	12.5	12.5	11.8	10.0
Inventory as percentage of sales	20.5	20.5	16.7	11.1
Model Outputs				
NOPAT (net operating profit after taxes)[a]	$170.3	$187.4	$211.2	
Net operating working capital[b]	$800.0	$880.0	$731.5	
Total operating capital[c]	$1,800.0	$1,980.0	$1,831.5	
Free cash flows (FCF)[d]	$(174.7)	$7.4	$179.7	
AFN		$114.7	$(57.5)	
Ratios				
Current ratio	3.2×	2.5×	3.1×	4.2×
Inventory turnover	3.6×	3.6×	6.0×	8.0×
Days sales outstanding	45.6 days	45.6 days	43.1 days	36.0 days
Total assets turnover	1.5×	1.5×	1.6×	1.8×
Debt ratio	43.2%	44.5%	41.0%	30.0%
Profit margin	3.8%	3.9%	4.6%	5.0%
Return on assets	5.7%	5.8%	7.2%	9.0%
Return on equity	12.7%	13.3%	15.4%	15.0%
Return on invested capital (NOPAT/Total operating capital)	9.5%	9.5%	11.5%	11.4%

[a]NOPAT = EBIT × (1 − T) from Table 5-2.
[b]Net operating working capital = Cash + Accounts receivable + Inventories − Accounts payable − Accruals from Table 5-3.
[c]Total operating capital = Net operating working capital + Net plant and equipment from Table 5-3.
[d]Free cash flow = NOPAT − Investment in total operating capital.

For example, its total assets turnover ratio is 1.5 versus an industry average of 1.8. Its poor asset management ratios drag down the return on invested capital (9.5% for MicroDrive versus 11.4% for the industry average). Furthermore, MicroDrive must carry more than the average amount of debt to support its excessive assets, and the extra interest expense reduces its profit margin to 3.9% versus 5.0% for the industry. Much of the debt is short term, and this results in a current ratio of 2.5 versus the 4.2 industry average. These problems will persist unless management takes action to improve things.

After reviewing its preliminary forecast, management decided to take three steps to improve its financial condition: (1) It decided to lay off some workers and close certain operations. It forecasted that these steps would lower operating costs (excluding depreciation) from the current 87.2% to 86% of sales as shown in Column 3 of Table 5-4. (2) By screening credit customers more closely and being more aggressive in collecting past-due accounts, the company believes it can reduce the ratio of accounts receivable to sales from 12.5% to 11.8%.

(3) Finally, management thinks it can reduce the inventory-to-sales ratio from 20.5% to 16.7% through the use of tighter inventory controls.[9]

These projected operational changes were then used to create a revised set of forecasted statements for 2017. We do not show the new financial statements, but the revised ratios are shown in the third column of Table 5-4. You can see the details in the chapter spreadsheet model, *Ch 05 Tool Kit.xlsx.* Here are the highlights of the revised forecast:

1. The reduction in operating costs improved the 2017 NOPAT, or net operating profit after taxes, by $23.8 million. Even more impressive, the improvements in the receivables policy and in inventory management reduced receivables and inventories by $148.5 million. The net result of the increase in NOPAT and the reduction of operating current assets was a very large increase in free cash flow for 2017, from a previously estimated $7.4 million to $179.7 million.
2. The profit margin improved to 4.6%. However, the firm's profit margin still lagged the industry average because its high debt ratio resulted in higher than average interest payments.
3. The increase in the profit margin resulted in an increase in projected retained earnings. More important, by tightening inventory controls and reducing the days' sales outstanding, MicroDrive projected a reduction in inventories and receivables. Taken together, these actions resulted in a *negative* AFN of $57.5 million, which meant that MicroDrive would actually generate $57.5 million more from internal operations and its financing plan than it needed for new assets. Under its current financial policy, MicroDrive would have $110 million in notes payable (the amount it carried over from the previous year) and $57.5 million in short-term investments. (*Note:* MicroDrive's managers considered using the $57.5 million to pay down some of the debt but decided instead to keep it as a liquid asset, which gave them the flexibility to quickly fund any new projects created by their R&D department.) The net effect was a significant reduction in MicroDrive's debt ratio, although it was still above the industry average.
4. These actions also raised the rate of return on assets from 5.8% to 7.2%. They also boosted the return on equity from 13.3% to 15.4%, which was even higher than the industry average.

Although MicroDrive's managers believed that the revised forecast was achievable, they were not sure of this. Accordingly, they wanted to know how variations in sales would affect the forecast. Therefore, they ran a spreadsheet model using several different sales growth rates and analyzed the results to see how the ratios would change under different growth scenarios. To illustrate, if the sales growth rate increased from 10% to 20%, the AFN would change dramatically, from a $57.5 million *surplus* to an $89.8 million *shortfall* because more assets would be required to finance the additional sales.

The spreadsheet model was also used to evaluate dividend policy. If MicroDrive decided to reduce its dividend growth rate, then additional funds would be generated, and those funds could be invested in plant, equipment, and inventories; used to reduce debt; or used to repurchase stock.

We see, then, that forecasting is an iterative process. For planning purposes, the financial staff develop a preliminary forecast based on a continuation of past policies and trends. This provides a starting point, or "baseline" forecast. Next, the projections are modified to see what effects alternative operating plans would have on the firm's earnings and financial condition. This results in a revised forecast. Then alternative operating plans are examined under different sales growth scenarios, and the model is used to evaluate both dividend policy and capital structure decisions.

Finally, the projected statements can be used to estimate the effects of different plans on MicroDrive's stock price. This is called value-based management and is covered in Chapter 22.

CONCEPT REVIEW

1. List some factors that should be considered when developing a sales forecast.
2. What is the AFN, and how is the forecasted financial statements method used to estimate it?
3. Why do accounts payable and accruals provide "spontaneous funds" to a growing firm?

---

[9]We will discuss receivables and inventory management in detail in Chapter 18.

5.5 Forecasting Financial Requirements When the Balance Sheet Ratios Are Subject to Change

Both the AFN formula and the projected financial statement method as we initially used it assume that the ratios of assets and liabilities to sales (A^*/S_0 and L^*/S_0) remain constant over time. This, in turn, requires the assumption that each "spontaneous" asset and liability item increases at the same rate as sales. In graph form, this implies the type of relationship shown in Panel a of Figure 5-2, a relationship that (1) is linear and (2) passes through the origin. Under those conditions, if the company's sales increase from $200 million to $400 million, or by 100%, inventory will also increase by 100%, from $100 million to $200 million.

The assumption of constant ratios and identical growth rates is appropriate at times, but there are times when it is incorrect. Three such conditions are described in the following sections.

Economies of Scale

There are economies of scale in the use of many kinds of assets, and when economies occur, the ratios are likely to change over time as the size of the firm increases. For example, retailers often need to maintain base stocks of different inventory items, even if current sales are quite low. As sales expand, inventories may then grow less rapidly than sales, so the ratio of inventory to sales (I/S) declines. This situation is depicted in Panel b of Figure 5-2. Here we see that the inventory/sales ratio is 1.5, or 150%, when sales are $200 million, but that the ratio declines to 1.0 when sales climb to $400 million.

The relationship in Panel b is linear, but nonlinear relationships often exist. Indeed, if the firm uses one popular model for establishing inventory levels (the EOQ model), its inventories will rise with the square root of sales. This situation is shown in Panel c of Figure 5-2, which shows a curved line whose slope decreases at higher sales levels. In this situation, very large increases in sales would require very little additional inventory.

See *Web Extension 5B* for more on forecasting when variables are not proportional to sales.

Lumpy Assets

In many industries, technological considerations dictate that if a firm is to be competitive, it must add fixed assets in large, discrete units; such assets are often referred to as **lumpy assets.** In the paper industry, for example, there are strong economies of scale in basic paper mill equipment, so when a paper company expands capacity, it must do so in large, lumpy increments. This type of situation is depicted in Panel d of Figure 5-2. Here we assume that the minimum economically efficient plant has a cost of $75 million and that such a plant can produce enough output to reach a sales level of $100 million. If the firm is to be competitive, it simply must have at least $75 million of fixed assets.

Lumpy assets have a major effect on the fixed assets/sales (FA/S) ratio at different sales levels and, consequently, on financial requirements. At Point A in Panel d, which represents a sales level of $50 million, the fixed assets are $75 million, so the ratio FA/S = $75/$50 = 1.5. Sales can expand by $50 million, out to $100 million, with no additions to fixed assets. At that point, represented by Point B, the ratio FA/S = $75/$100 = 0.75. However, since the firm is operating at capacity (sales of $100 million), even a small increase in sales would require a doubling of plant capacity, so a small projected sales increase would bring with it a very large financial requirement.[10]

Excess Capacity Adjustments

Consider again the MicroDrive example set forth in Tables 5-2 and 5-3, but now assume that excess capacity exists in fixed assets. Specifically, assume that fixed assets in 2016 were being

[10]Several other points should be noted about Panel d of Figure 5-2. First, if the firm is operating at a sales level of $100 million or less, any expansion that calls for a sales increase above $100 million would require a *doubling* of the firm's fixed assets. A much smaller percentage increase would be involved if the firm were large enough to be operating a number of plants. Second, firms generally go to multiple shifts and take other actions to minimize the need for new fixed asset capacity as they approach Point B. However, these efforts can go only so far, and eventually a fixed asset expansion will be required. Third, firms often make arrangements to share excess capacity with other firms in their industry. For example, the situation in the electric utility industry is very much like that depicted in Panel d. However, electric companies often build jointly owned plants, or else they "take turns" building plants, and then they buy power from or sell power to other utilities to avoid building new plants that would be underutilized.

FIGURE
5-2 Four Possible Ratio Relationships (Millions of Dollars)

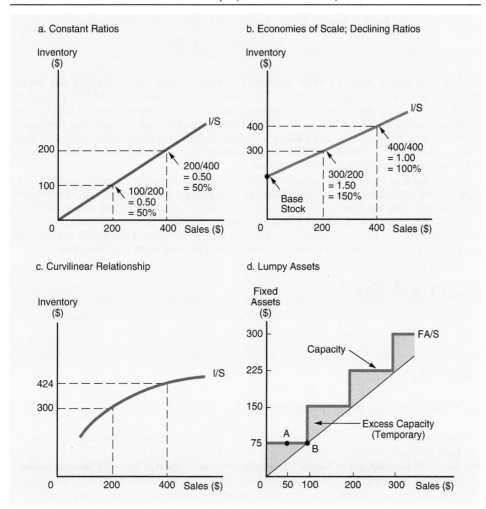

utilized to only 96% of capacity. If fixed assets had been used to full capacity, 2016 sales could have been as high as $3,125 million versus the $3,000 million in actual sales:

$$\text{Full capacity sales} = \frac{\text{Actual sales}}{\substack{\text{Percentage of capacity} \\ \text{at which fixed assets} \\ \text{were operated}}} \qquad (5\text{-}3)$$

$$= \frac{\$3,000\,\text{million}}{0.96} = \$3,125\,\text{million}$$

This suggests that MicroDrive's target fixed assets/sales ratio should be 32% rather than 33.3%:

$$\text{Target fixed assets/Sales} = \frac{\text{Actual fixed assets}}{\text{Full capacity sales}} \qquad (5\text{-}4)$$

$$= \frac{\$1,000}{\$3,125} = 0.32 = 32\%$$

Therefore, for sales to increase to $3,300 million, fixed assets will have to increase to $1,056 million:

$$\text{Required level of fixed assets} = (\text{Target fixed assets}/\text{Sales})(\text{Projected sales}) \tag{5-5}$$
$$= 0.32(\$3,300) = \$1,056 \text{ million}$$

We previously forecast that MicroDrive would need to increase fixed assets at the same rate as sales, or by 10%. That meant an increase from $1,000 million to $1,100 million, or by $100 million. Now we see that the actual required increase is only from $1,000 million to $1,056 million, or by $56 million. Thus, the capacity-adjusted forecast is $100 million − $56 million = $44 million less than the earlier forecast. With a smaller fixed asset requirement, the projected AFN would decline from an estimated $114.7 million to $114.7 million − $44 million = $70.7 million.

Note also that when excess capacity exists, sales can grow to the capacity sales as determined above with no increase in fixed assets, but sales beyond that level will require fixed asset additions as calculated in our example. The same situation could occur with respect to inventories, and the required additions would be determined in exactly the same manner as for fixed assets. Theoretically, the same situation could occur with other types of assets, but as a practical matter excess capacity normally exists only with respect to fixed assets and inventories.

ⓒNCEPT REVIEW

1. Explain how economies of scale and lumpy asset acquisition affect financial forecasting.

Summary

The key concepts covered are listed below:

- **Financial forecasting** generally begins with a forecast of the firm's sales, in terms of both units and dollars.
- Either the **forecast**, or **pro forma, financial statement method** or the **AFN formula method** can be used to forecast financial requirements. The financial statement method is more reliable, and it also provides ratios that can be used to evaluate alternative business plans.
- A firm can determine its **additional funds needed (AFN)** by estimating the amount of new assets necessary to support the forecast level of sales and then subtracting from that amount the spontaneous funds that will be generated from operations. The firm can then plan how to raise the AFN most efficiently.
- The **higher a firm's sales growth rate,** the **greater** will be its need for additional financing. Similarly, the **smaller its retention ratio,** the **greater** its need for additional funds.
- Adjustments must be made if **economies of scale** exist in the use of assets, if **excess capacity** exists, or if assets must be added in **lumpy increments**.
- **Linear regression** and **excess capacity adjustments** can be used to forecast asset requirements in situations where assets are not expected to grow at the same rate as sales.

Questions

5-1 Define each of the following terms:
   a. Operating plan; financial plan; sales forecast
   b. Pro forma financial statement; forecast financial statement method
   c. Spontaneously generated funds
   d. Additional funds needed (AFN); AFN formula; capital intensity ratio
   e. Lumpy assets; excess capacity; economies of scale
   f. Financing feedback effects

5-2 Certain liability and net worth items generally increase spontaneously with increases in sales. Put a tick mark (✓) by those items that typically increase spontaneously:

Accounts payable	_____	Mortgage bonds	_____
Notes payable to banks	_____	Common stock	_____
Accrued wages	_____	Retained earnings	_____
Accrued taxes	_____		

5-3 The following equation is sometimes used to forecast financial requirements:

$$AFN = (A^*/S_0)(\Delta S) - (L^*/S_0)(\Delta S) - MS_1(RR)$$

What key assumption do we make when using this equation? Under what conditions might this assumption not hold true?

5-4 Name the five factors that affect a firm's external financing requirements.

5-5 What is meant by the term "self-supporting growth rate"? How is this rate related to the AFN equation, and how can that equation be used to calculate the self-supporting growth rate?

5-6 Suppose a firm makes the following policy changes. If the change means that external, non-spontaneous financial requirements (AFN) will increase, indicate this by a (+); indicate a decrease by a (−); and indicate indeterminate or no effect by a (0). Think in terms of the immediate, short-run effect on funds requirements.
a. The dividend payout ratio is increased.   _____
b. The firm decides to pay all suppliers on delivery, rather than after a 30-day delay, to take advantage of discounts for rapid payment.   _____
c. The firm begins to sell on credit (previously all sales had been on a cash basis).   _____
d. The firm's profit margin is eroded by increased competition; sales are steady.   _____
e. The firm sells its manufacturing plants for cash to a contractor and simultaneously signs a contract to purchase from that contractor goods that the firm formerly produced.   _____
f. The firm negotiates a new contract with its union that lowers its labour costs without affecting its output.   _____

Concept Review Problems

Full solutions are provided at www.nelson.com/brigham3ce.

CR-1
Self-Supporting Growth Rate
The Barnsdale Corporation has the following ratios: $A^*/S_0 = 1.6$; $L^*/S_0 = 0.4$; profit margin = 0.10; and dividend payout ratio = 0.45, or 45%. Sales last year were $100 million. Assuming that these ratios will remain constant, use the AFN formula to determine the firm's self-supporting growth rate—in other words, the maximum growth rate Barnsdale can achieve without having to employ nonspontaneous external funds.

CR-2
Additional Funds Needed
Suppose Barnsdale's financial consultants (see Problem CR-1) report (1) that the sales-to-inventory ratio (sales/inventory) is three times versus an industry average of four times and (2) that Barnsdale could reduce inventories (and this ratio to 4) without affecting sales, the profit margin, or the other asset ratios. Under these conditions, use the AFN formula to determine the amount of additional funds Barnsdale would require during each of the next 2 years if sales grew at a rate of 20% per year.

CR-3 Holden Lumber's 2015 financial statements are shown below.

Excess Capacity

Holden Lumber: Balance Sheet as at December 31, 2015 (Thousands of Dollars)

Cash	$ 1,800	Accounts payable	$ 7,200
Receivables	10,800	Notes payable	3,472
Inventories	12,600	Accruals	2,520
Total current assets	25,200	Total current liabilities	13,192
Net fixed assets	21,600	Mortgage bonds	5,000
		Common stock	2,000
		Retained earnings	26,608
Total assets	$46,800	Total liabilities and equity	$46,800

Holden Lumber: Income Statement for December 31, 2015 (Thousands of Dollars)

Sales	$36,000
Operating costs	30,783
Earnings before interest and taxes	5,217
Interest	717
Earnings before taxes	4,500
Taxes (28%)	1,260
Net income	$ 3,240
Dividends (60%)	$ 1,944
Addition to retained earnings	$ 1,296

a. Assume that the company was operating at full capacity in 2015 with regard to all items *except* fixed assets; fixed assets in 2015 were being utilized to only 75% of capacity. By what percentage could 2016 sales increase over 2015 sales without the need for an increase in fixed assets?

b. Now suppose that 2016 sales increase by 25% over 2015 sales. Use the forecasted financial statement method to forecast a 12/31/16 balance sheet and 2016 income statement, assuming that (1) the historical ratios of operating cost/sales, cash/sales, receivables/sales, inventories/sales, accounts payable/sales, and accruals/sales remain constant; (2) Holden cannot sell any of its fixed assets; (3) any required financing is done at the *end* of 2016 as notes payable; (4) the firm earns no interest on its cash; and (5) the interest rate on all of its debt is 12%. Holden pays out 60% of its net income as dividends and has a tax rate of 28%. How much additional external capital will be required? (*Hints:* Base the forecasted interest expense on the amount of debt at the beginning of the year, because any new debt is added at the end of the year; also, use the forecasted income statement to determine the addition to retained earnings for use in the balance sheet.)

Problems

Easy   Answers to odd-numbered problems appear in Appendix A.
Problems 1–3

5-1   Broussard Skateboard's sales are expected to increase by 15% from $8 million in 2015 to $9.2 mil-
AFN Equation   lion in 2016. Its assets totalled $5 million at the end of 2015. Broussard is already at full capacity, so its assets must grow at the same rate as projected sales. At the end of 2015, current liabilities were $1.4 million, consisting of $450,000 of accounts payable, $500,000 of notes payable, and $450,000 of accruals. The after-tax profit margin is forecasted to be 6%, and the forecasted payout ratio is 40%. Use the AFN equation to forecast Broussard's additional funds needed for the coming year.

5-2   Refer to Problem 5-1. What would be the additional funds needed if the company's year-end 2015
AFN Equation   assets had been $7 million? Assume that all other numbers, including sales, are the same as in Problem 5-1 and that the company is operating at full capacity. Why is this AFN different from the one you found in Problem 5-1? Is the company's "capital intensity" ratio the same or different?

5-3   Refer to Problem 5-1. Return to the assumption that the company had $5 million in assets at
AFN Equation   the end of 2015, but now assume that the company pays no dividends. Under these assumptions, what would be the additional funds needed for the coming year? Why is this AFN different from the one you found in Problem 5-1?

**Intermediate
Problems 4–7
5-4**
Sales Increase

Maggie's Muffins Inc. generated $5,000,000 in sales during 2015, and its year-end total assets were $2,500,000. Also, at year-end 2015, current liabilities were $1,000,000, consisting of $300,000 of notes payable, $500,000 of accounts payable, and $200,000 of accruals. Looking ahead to 2016, the company estimates that its assets must increase at the same rate as sales, its spontaneous liabilities will increase at the same rate as sales, its profit margin will be 7%, and its payout ratio will be 80%. How large a sales increase can the company achieve without having to raise funds externally—that is, what is its self-supporting growth rate?

5-5
Long-Term
Financing Needed

At year-end 2015, Wallace Landscaping's total assets were $2.17 million and its accounts payable were $560,000. Sales, which in 2015 were $3.5 million, are expected to increase by 35% in 2016. Total assets and accounts payable are proportional to sales, and that relationship will be maintained. Wallace typically uses no current liabilities other than accounts payable. Common stock amounted to $625,000 in 2015, and retained earnings were $395,000. Wallace has arranged to sell $195,000 of new common stock in 2016 to meet some of its financing needs. The remainder of its financing needs will be met by issuing new long-term debt at the end of 2016. (Because the debt is added at the end of the year, there will be no additional interest expense due to the new debt.) Its net profit margin on sales is 5%, and 45% of earnings will be paid out as dividends.
a.   What were Wallace's total long-term debt and total liabilities in 2015?
b.   How much new long-term debt financing will be needed in 2016? (*Hint:* AFN – New stock = New long-term debt.)

5-6
Additional
Funds Needed

The Booth Company's sales are forecast to increase from $1,000 in 2015 to $2,000 in 2016. Here is the December 31, 2015, balance sheet:

Cash	$ 100	Accounts payable	$ 50
Accounts receivable	200	Notes payable	150
Inventories	200	Accruals	50
Net fixed assets	500	Long-term debt	400
		Common stock	100
		Retained earnings	250
Total assets	$1,000	Total liabilities and equity	$1,000

Booth's fixed assets were used to only 50% of capacity during 2015, but its current assets were at their proper levels. All assets except fixed assets increase at the same rate as sales, and fixed assets would also increase at the same rate if the current excess capacity did not exist. Booth's after-tax profit margin is forecasted to be 5%, and its payout ratio will be 60%. What is Booth's additional funds needed (AFN) for the coming year?

5-7
Additional
Funds Needed

Based on the information in Problem 5-6, assume that Booth has just completed a review of its net operating working capital policies and found that it can reduce its DSO to 60 and achieve an inventory turnover of 4.57× without impacting sales or profits, based on a cost of goods sold of $1,600.
a.   Recalculate the additional funds Booth requires to achieve its growth target.
b.   Assume Booth needed $360 in additional funds for Problem 5-6. Using your answer in part a, how much less will Booth pay in future interest costs, annually, given a 9% interest rate on all additional funds borrowed?

**Challenging
Problems 8–10
5-8**
Pro Forma
Statements and
Ratios

Cavuto makes bulk purchases of men's and women's shoes, stocks them in conveniently located warehouses, and ships them to its chain of retail stores. Cavuto's balance sheet as at December 31, 2015, is shown here (millions of dollars).

Cash	$ 3.5	Accounts payable	$ 9.0
Receivables	26.0	Notes payable	18.0
Inventories	58.0	Accruals	8.5
Total current assets	87.5	Total current liabilities	35.5
Net fixed assets	35.0	Mortgage loan	6.0
		Common stock	15.0
		Retained earnings	66.0
Total assets	$122.5	Total liabilities and equity	$122.5

Sales for 2015 were $350 million, while net income for the year was $14.35 million. Cavuto paid dividends of $5.74 million to common shareholders. The firm is operating at full capacity. Assume that all ratios remain constant.

a. If sales are projected to increase by $70 million, or 20%, during 2016, use the AFN equation to determine Cavuto's projected external capital requirements.

b. Using the AFN equation, determine Cavuto's self-supporting growth rate. That is, what is the maximum growth rate the firm can achieve without having to employ external funds?

c. Construct Cavuto's pro forma balance sheet for December 31, 2016. Assume that all external capital requirements are met by bank loans and are reflected in notes payable. Assume the company's profit margin and dividend payout ratio remain constant.

5-9
Additional
Funds Needed

Stevens Textile's 2015 financial statements are shown below.

Stevens Textile: Balance Sheet as at December 31, 2015 (Thousands of Dollars)

Cash	$ 1,080	Accounts payable	$ 4,320
Receivables	6,480	Accruals	2,880
Inventories	9,000	Notes payable	2,100
Total current assets	16,560	Total current liabilities	9,300
Net fixed assets	12,600	Mortgage bonds	3,500
		Common stock	3,500
		Retained earnings	12,860
Total assets	$29,160	Total liabilities and equity	$29,160

Stevens Textile: Income Statement for December 31, 2015 (Thousands of Dollars)

Sales	$36,000
Operating costs	32,440
Earnings before interest and taxes	3,560
Interest	460
Earnings before taxes	3,100
Taxes (40%)	1,240
Net income	$ 1,860
Dividends (45%)	$ 837
Addition to retained earnings	$ 1,023

a. Suppose that 2016 sales are projected to increase by 15% over 2015 sales. Use the forecasted financial statement method to forecast a balance sheet and income statement for December 31, 2016. The interest rate on all debt is 10%, and cash earns no interest income. Assume that all additional debt is added at the end of the year, which means that you should base the forecasted interest expense on the balance of debt at the beginning of the year. Assume that the company was operating at full capacity in 2015, that it cannot sell any fixed assets, and that any required financing will be borrowed as notes payable. Also, assume that assets, spontaneous liabilities, and operating costs are expected to increase by the same percentage as sales. Determine the additional funds needed.

b. In your answer to part a, you should not have charged any interest on the additional debt added during 2016 because it was assumed that the new debt was added at the end of the year. But now suppose that the new debt is added throughout the year. Don't do any calculations, but how would this change the answer to part a?

5-10
Additional
Funds Needed

Garlington Technologies Inc.'s 2015 financial statements are shown below.

Garlington Technologies Inc.: Balance Sheet as at December 31, 2015

Cash	$ 180,000	Accounts payable	$ 360,000
Receivables	360,000	Notes payable	156,000
Inventories	720,000	Accruals	180,000
Total current assets	1,260,000	Total current liabilities	696,000
Fixed assets	1,440,000	Common stock	1,800,000
		Retained earnings	204,000
Total assets	$2,700,000	Total liabilities and equity	$2,700,000

Garlington Technologies Inc.: Income Statement for December 31, 2015

Sales	$3,600,000
Operating costs	3,279,720
EBIT	320,280
Interest	18,280
EBT	302,000
Taxes (40%)	120,800
Net income	$ 181,200
Dividends	$ 108,000

a. Suppose that in 2016 sales increase by 10% over 2015 sales and that 2016 dividends will increase to $112,000. Construct the pro forma financial statements using the forecasted financial statement method. Assume the firm operated at full capacity in 2015. Use an interest rate of 13%, and assume that any new debt will be added at the end of the year (so forecast the interest expense based on the debt balance at the beginning of the year). Cash does not earn any interest income. Assume that the AFN will be in the form of notes payable.

b. Below is some additional information on Garlington:

	2015
Current ratio	1.81×
Return on equity	9%
Earnings per share	$1.68
Dividends per share	$1
Number of common shares outstanding	108,000
Common share price	$18

I. Calculate the company's 2016 current ratio, ROE, EPS, and DPS based on the expansion and financing as in part a.

II. Because of an agreement with their lender, Garlington's current ratio cannot drop below 1.7× or it will violate a debt covenant. How much can the company increase its notes payable and still not violate its minimum current ratio?

III. Assume that Garlington increases its notes payable to the maximum allowed under its current ratio restriction and issues stock to raise the remaining funds required. Calculate the company's ROE, EPS, and DPS.

IV. Recalculate Garlington's ROE, EPS, and DPS if *all* the additional financing was obtained through the sale of new common stock. Do you think the financing choice matters to the investors holding the common stock?

 # Spreadsheet Problem

5-11

Build a Model:
Forecasting
Financial Statements

Start with the partial model in the file *Ch 05 Build a Model.xlsx* from the textbook's website. Cumberland Industries' financial planners must forecast the company's financial results for the coming year. The forecast will be based on the forecasted financial statements method, and any additional funds needed will be obtained by using a mix of notes payable, long-term debt, and common stock. No preferred stock will be issued. Data for the problem, including Cumberland Industries' balance sheet and income statement, can be found in the spreadsheet problem for Chapter 2. Use these data to answer the following questions.

a. Cumberland Industries has had the following sales since 2010. Assuming the historical trend continues, what will sales be in 2016?

Year	Sales
2010	$129,215,000
2011	180,901,000
2012	235,252,000
2013	294,065,000
2014	396,692,000
2015	455,150,000

Base your forecast on a spreadsheet regression analysis of the 2010–2015 sales. By what percentage are sales predicted to increase in 2016 over 2015? Is the sales growth rate increasing or decreasing?

b.   Cumberland's management believes that the firm will experience a 20% increase in sales during 2016. Construct the 2016 pro forma financial statements. Cumberland will not issue any new stock or long-term bonds. Assume that Cumberland will carry forward its current amounts of short-term investments and notes payable, prior to calculating additional funds needed (AFN). Assume that any AFN will be raised as notes payable (if AFN is negative, Cumberland will purchase additional short-term investments). Use an interest rate of 9% for short-term debt (and for the interest income on short-term investments) and a rate of 11% for long-term debt. No interest is earned on cash. Use the beginning-of-year debt balances to calculate net interest expense. Assume dividends grow at an 8% rate.

c.   Now create a graph that shows the sensitivity of AFN to the sales growth rate. To make this graph, compare the AFN at sales growth rates of 5%, 10%, 15%, 20%, 25%, and 30%.

d.   Calculate net operating working capital (NOWC), total operating capital, NOPAT, and operating cash flow (OCF) for 2015 and 2016. Also, calculate the free cash flow (FCF) for 2016.

e.   Suppose Cumberland can reduce its inventory-to-sales ratio to 5% and its cost-to-sales ratio to 83%. What happens to AFN and FCF?

MINI CASE

Betty Simmons, the new financial manager of Okanagan Chemicals Ltd. (OCL), a B.C. producer of specialized chemicals for use in fruit orchards, must prepare a financial forecast for 2016. OCL's 2015 sales were $2 billion, and the marketing department is forecasting a 25% increase for 2016. Simmons thinks the company was operating at full capacity in 2015, but she is not sure about this. The 2015 financial statements, plus some other data, are shown below.

A. 2015 Balance Sheet (Millions of Dollars)

		Percent of Sales			Percent of Sales
Cash and securities	$ 20	1%	Accounts payable and accruals	$ 100	5%
Accounts receivable	240	12%	Notes payable	100	
Inventories	240	12%	Total current liabilities	200	
Total current assets	500		Long-term debt	100	
Net fixed assets	500	25%	Common stock	500	
			Retained earnings	200	
Total assets	$1,000		Total liabilities and equity	$1,000	

B. 2015 Income Statement (Millions of Dollars)

		Percent of Sales
Sales	$2,000.00	
Cost of goods sold (COGS)	1,200.00	60%
Sales, general, and administrative costs (SGA)	700.00	35%
Earnings before interest and taxes	100.00	
Interest	10.00	
Earnings before taxes	90.00	
Taxes (40%)	36.00	
Net income	$ 54.00	
Dividends (40%)	21.60	
Addition to retained earnings	$ 32.40	

C. Key Ratios

	OCL	Industry
Profit margin	2.70%	4.00%
Return on equity	7.71%	15.60%
Days sales outstanding (365 days)	43.80 days	32.00 days
Inventory turnover	5.00×	6.60×
Fixed assets turnover	4.00×	5.00×
Debt/assets	20.00%	24.00%
Times interest earned	10.00×	9.40×
Current ratio	2.50×	3.00×
Return on invested capital (NOPAT/Operating capital)	6.67%	14.00%

Assume that you have recently been hired as Simmons's assistant and that your first major task is to help her develop the forecast. She has asked you to begin by answering the following set of questions.

a.   Describe three ways that pro forma statements are used in financial planning.

b.   Explain the steps in financial forecasting.

c.   Assume (1) that OCL was operating at full capacity in 2015 with respect to all assets, (2) that all assets must grow proportionally with sales, (3) that accounts payable and accruals will also grow in proportion to sales, and (4) that the 2015 profit margin and dividend payout will be maintained. Under these conditions, what will the company's financial requirements be for the coming year? Use the AFN equation to answer this question.

d.   How would changes in the following items affect the AFN? (1) Sales increase; (2) the dividend payout ratio increases; (3) the profit margin increases; (4) the capital intensity ratio increases; (5) OCL begins paying its suppliers sooner. (Consider each item separately and hold all other things constant.)

e.   Briefly explain how to forecast financial statements using the forecast financial statements approach. Be sure to explain how to forecast interest expenses.

f.   Now estimate the 2016 financial requirements using the forecast financial statements approach. Assume (1) that each type of asset, as well as payables, accruals, and fixed and variable costs, will be the same percentage of sales in 2016 as in 2015; (2) that the payout ratio is held constant at 40%; (3) that external funds needed are financed 50% by notes payable and 50% by long-term debt (no new common stock will be issued); (4) that all debt carries an interest rate of 10%; and (5) that interest expenses should be based on the balance of debt at the beginning of the year.

g.   Why does the forecast financial statements approach produce somewhat different AFN than the equation approach? Which method provides the more accurate forecast?

h.   Calculate OCL's forecasted ratios, and compare them with the company's 2015 ratios and with the industry averages. Calculate OCL's forecast free cash flow and return on invested capital (ROIC).

i.   Based on comparisons between OCL's days sales outstanding (DSO) and inventory turnover ratios with the industry average figures, does it appear that OCL is operating efficiently with respect to its inventory and accounts receivable? Suppose OCL were able to bring these ratios into line with the industry averages and reduce its SGA/Sales ratio to 33%. What effect would this have on its AFN and its financial ratios? What effect would this have on free cash flow and ROIC?

j.   Suppose you now learn that OCL's 2015 receivables and inventories were in line with required levels, given the firm's credit and inventory policies, but that excess capacity existed with regard to fixed assets. Specifically, fixed assets were operated at only 75% of capacity.

(1)   What level of sales could have existed in 2015 with the available fixed assets?

(2)   How would the existence of excess capacity in fixed assets affect the additional funds needed during 2016?

k. The relationship between sales and the various types of assets is important in financial forecasting. The forecasted financial statements approach, under the assumption that each asset item grows at the same rate as sales, leads to an AFN forecast that is reasonably close to the forecast using the AFN equation. Explain how each of the following factors would affect the accuracy of financial forecasts based on the AFN equation: (1) economies of scale in the use of assets and (2) lumpy assets.

part 2

Securities and Their Valuation

chapter 6

Bonds, Bond Valuation, and Interest Rates

In 2013, Toronto-based Brookfield Asset Management had more than $46 billion worth of debt on its balance sheet, made up of bank loans, mortgages, and bonds. Despite Brookfield's size—in fact, despite any company's size—$46 billion is a large debt load, yet analysts are generally positive on the company. The company owns large hydro generation assets and commercial property in major centres, as well as infrastructure assets, many of which produce large, stable cash flows. Because of the nature of Brookfield's operations and assets, the company can issue bonds and borrow a significant amount of the capital it requires. The terms on Brookfield's bonds are designed to match the types of assets they need to finance.

Bonds are also used for very different purposes by technology companies. Successful and well-known high-tech companies are often cash rich and have no obvious need to issue bonds or take on debt. Yet companies such as Microsoft, Adobe, and SAP all have bonds outstanding, not to cover their cash needs or finance their R&D, but rather to build their "war chests" to purchase other companies should an opportunity arise. As a Goldman Sachs analyst states, it is "a good way to signal your intentions."

Bonds can also be used by riskier or smaller companies. For instance, when Air Canada came out of bankruptcy protection, the interest rate the company paid on new bonds was quite modest, considering the company's troubled financial history. Air Canada was able to pay a reasonable interest rate by making its bonds convertible into the company's common shares. In other words, if the shares went up in price, the bond investors would also benefit. Investors liked this feature and were willing to buy the bonds at a lower rate than they would have if the bonds had not been convertible.

Companies are also raising capital by selling bonds and then giving back the money to shareholders through share buybacks. Companies such as Tim Hortons, Home Depot, and U.S. pharmaceutical giant Amgen have all bought back their own shares with money raised by selling bonds.

The current low-interest-rate environment is enticing companies to raise money in the bond market. New bonds sold at lower rates are being used to pay off older debt that was issued when interest rates were higher. For some companies, this refinancing can save millions of dollars. TD Bank issued $1.25 billion in bonds at an interest rate 0.75% less than interest rates on their previous bonds. This action alone saved TD Bank about $9 million in annual interest costs.

Bonds provide an amazing flexibility to companies and investors alike. That flexibility extends to price, maturity term, collateral provided (if any), interest rate, payment terms, and conversion features. Keep this in mind as you go through the chapter.

Sources: Brookfield Asset Management 2013 Annual Report; Ben Worthen, "Tech Firms Bulk Up with Debt," *Silicon Investor*, April 4, 2010, http://www.siliconinvestor.com, accessed May 15, 2012; "Home Depot Conducts Offering and Share Buyback," *Businessweek*, March 28, 2011, http://www.businessweek.com, accessed May 14, 2012; Avi Salzman, "Amgen Stock Rises on New Buyback Plan, But How About the Debt?" *Barron's*, November 7, 2011, http://www.blogs.barrons.com, accessed May 15, 2012; Vatalyst, "5 Stock Buyback Candidates To Consider," *Seeking Alpha*, http://www.seekingalpha .com, accessed May 15, 2012.

Growing companies must acquire land, buildings, equipment, inventory, and other operating assets. The debt markets are a major source of funding for such purchases. Therefore, every manager should have a working knowledge of the types of bonds companies and government agencies issue, the terms that are contained in bond contracts, the types of risks to which both bond investors and issuers are exposed, and procedures for determining the values of and rates of return on bonds.

The textbook's website contains an *Excel* file that will guide you through the chapter's calculations. The file for this chapter is *Ch 06 Tool Kit.xlsx,* and we encourage you to open the file and follow along as you read the chapter.
www.nelson.com/ brigham3ce

6.1 Who Issues Bonds?

A **bond** is a long-term contract under which a borrower agrees to make payments of interest and principal, on specific dates, to the holders of the bond. For example, on January 5, 2016, MicroDrive Inc. borrowed $50 million by issuing $50 million of bonds. For convenience, we assume that MicroDrive sold 50,000 individual bonds for $1,000 each. Actually, it could have sold one $50 million bond, 10 bonds with a $5 million face value, or any other combination that totals $50 million. In any event, MicroDrive received the $50 million, and in exchange it promised to make annual interest payments and to repay the $50 million on a specified maturity date.

Investors have many choices when investing in bonds, but bonds are classified into three main types: government, corporate, and foreign. Each type differs with respect to expected return and degree of risk.

Government bonds are issued by the Canadian federal and provincial governments.[1] It is reasonable to assume that the federal government will make good on its promised payments, so these bonds have no default risk. While considered very low risk, provincial government

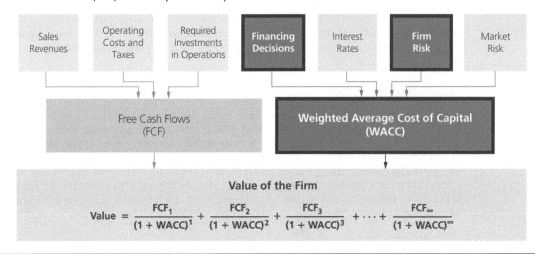

Corporate Valuation and Risk

In Chapter 1, we told you that managers should strive to make their firms more valuable and that the value of a firm is determined by the size, timing, and risk of its free cash flows (FCF). This chapter shows you how to measure a bond's risk and the return demanded by a firm's bondholders, which affect the firm's weighted average cost of capital, which in turn affects the firm's value.

Sales Revenues | Operating Costs and Taxes | Required Investments in Operations | Financing Decisions | Interest Rates | Firm Risk | Market Risk

Free Cash Flows (FCF)

Weighted Average Cost of Capital (WACC)

Value of the Firm

$$\text{Value} = \frac{\text{FCF}_1}{(1 + \text{WACC})^1} + \frac{\text{FCF}_2}{(1 + \text{WACC})^2} + \frac{\text{FCF}_3}{(1 + \text{WACC})^3} + \cdots + \frac{\text{FCF}_\infty}{(1 + \text{WACC})^\infty}$$

---

[1]The Canadian federal government actually issues two types of securities: "bills" and "bonds." A bond makes an equal payment every 6 months until it matures, at which time it makes an additional lump sum payment. A T-bill has a maturity of 52 weeks or less at the time of issue, and it makes no payments at all until it matures. Thus, bills are sold initially at a discount to their face, or maturity, value.

bonds are not considered as low risk as bonds issued by the federal government. However, government bond prices decline when interest rates rise, so they are not free of all risks.

Crown corporations—that is, companies owned by federal or provincial governments—also raise money by issuing bonds. These companies may carry on business much like a regular company, but their debt is ultimately guaranteed by the government; therefore they, too, have very little default risk.

Corporate bonds, as the name implies, are issued by corporations. Unlike federal government bonds, corporate bonds are exposed to default risk—if the issuing company gets into trouble, it may be unable to make the promised interest and principal payments. Different corporate bonds have different levels of default risk, depending on the issuing company's characteristics and the terms of the specific bond. Default risk often is referred to as "credit risk," and the larger the default or credit risk, the higher the interest rate the issuer must pay.

Foreign bonds are issued by foreign governments or foreign corporations. Foreign corporate bonds are, of course, exposed to default risk, and so are some foreign government bonds. An additional risk exists if the bonds are denominated in a currency other than that of the investor's home currency. For example, if a Canadian investor purchases a corporate bond denominated in Japanese yen and the yen subsequently falls relative to the dollar, then the investor will lose money, even if the company does not default on its bonds. When foreign corporate or government bonds are sold in Canadian dollars and in the Canadian market, they are called **Maple bonds.** These bonds do not carry the usual exchange rate risk for Canadian investors. The number of Maple bonds has grown substantially since 2006, although they are still a relatively small part of the overall bond market.[2]

CONCEPT REVIEW

1. What is a bond?
2. What are the three main types of bonds?
3. Why are Government of Canada bonds not riskless?
4. To what types of risk are investors of foreign bonds exposed?

6.2 Key Characteristics of Bonds

Although all bonds have some common characteristics, they do not always have identical contractual features, as described below.

Par Value

The **par value** is the stated *face value* of the bond; for illustrative purposes we generally assume a par value of $1,000, although any multiple of $1,000 (e.g., $5,000) can be used. The par value generally represents the amount of money the firm borrows and promises to repay on the maturity date.

Coupon Interest Rate

MicroDrive's bonds require the company to pay a fixed number of dollars of interest each year (or, more typically, each six months). When this **coupon payment,** as it is called, is divided by the par value, the result is the **coupon interest rate.** For example, MicroDrive's bonds have a $1,000 par value, and they pay $100 in interest each year. The bond's coupon interest is $100, so its coupon interest rate is $100/$1,000 = 10%. The coupon payment, which is fixed at the time the bond is issued, remains in force during the life of the bond.[3] Typically, at the time a bond is issued its coupon payment is set at a level that will enable the bond to be issued at or near its par value.

---

[2]For a good overview of Canadian fixed-income products, see Marlene K. Puffer, "Step 1 Back to Basics," *Canadian Investment Review,* Fall 2006, 22–27.

[3]At one time, bonds literally had a number of small (1/2- by 2-inch), dated coupons attached to them, and on each interest payment date the owner would clip off the coupon for that date and either cash it at his or her bank or mail it to the company's paying agent, who would then mail back a cheque for the interest. For example, a 30-year, semiannual bond would start with 60 coupons. Today, most new bonds are *registered*—no physical coupons are involved, and interest cheques are mailed automatically to the registered owners.

In some cases, a bond's coupon payment will vary over time. For these **floating-rate bonds,** the coupon rate is set for, say, the initial six-month period, after which it is adjusted every six months based on some market rate. Some corporate issues are tied to a government bond rate, while other issues are tied to other rates, such as LIBOR. Many additional provisions can be included in floating-rate issues. For example, some are convertible to fixed-rate debt, whereas others have upper and lower limits ("caps" and "floors") on how high or low the rate can go.

Floating-rate debt is popular with investors who are worried about the risk of rising interest rates, since the interest paid on such bonds increases whenever market rates rise. This causes the market value of the debt to be stabilized; it also provides institutional buyers, such as banks, with income that is better geared to their own obligations. Banks' deposit costs rise with interest rates, so the income on floating-rate loans they have made rises at the same time their deposit costs are rising. Moreover, floating-rate debt appeals to corporations that want to issue long-term debt without committing themselves to paying a historically high interest rate for the entire life of the loan.

Some bonds pay no coupons at all but are offered at a substantial discount below their par values and hence provide capital appreciation rather than interest income. These securities are called **zero coupon bonds** ("zeros") or *stripped bonds*. Investment dealers take regular government or corporate bonds and "strip" the coupon (or interest) payments from the principal. The coupons for the same payment period are bundled and sold as a zero coupon bond, as are the individual principal portions, which are called *residuals*. Investors are buying a bond with no regular interest payments. In fact there will be only one payment, at maturity, for its face value. As a result, zero coupon bonds are sold at deep discounts from their value at maturity. Zeros are available with a wide range of maturity dates, anywhere from 1 to 50 years. Zeros also retain the creditworthiness of the original bonds on which they were based. For instance, a Province of Ontario strip bond will retain the same guarantee and safety as the original full Ontario bond from which it was derived. Since no regular interest payments are made, there is no risk of having to reinvest interest payments. No reinvestment rate risk (something we'll look at later in this chapter) is one advantage that zero coupon bonds have over regular bonds. As an investment, zeros are typically best held in a tax-deferred account such as an RRSP, since taxes must be paid on yearly interest income accruing from the zero.

Some bonds have a step-up provision. Over time the coupon interest rate paid increases. The rate each year is specified on issuance. For instance, a company may issue a 5-year bond with a first-year rate of 3%, increasing $\frac{1}{4}$% each year for the next 2 years, and then increasing $\frac{1}{2}$% for the last two years. Step-up bonds typically have a provision that allows the issuer to buy (or call) the bonds back after the first year.

Maturity Date

Bonds generally have a specified **maturity date** on which the par value must be repaid. MicroDrive's bonds, which were issued on January 5, 2016, will mature on January 5, 2031; thus, they had a 15-year maturity at the time they were issued. Most bonds have *original maturities* (the maturity at the time the bond is issued) ranging from 10 to 40 years, but any maturity is legally permissible. Of course, the effective maturity of a bond declines each year after it has been issued. Thus, MicroDrive's bonds had a 15-year original maturity, but in 2017, a year later, they will have a 14-year maturity, and so on.

Provisions to Call or Redeem Bonds

Most corporate bonds contain a **call provision,** which gives the issuing corporation the right to call the bonds for redemption. The call provision generally states that the company must pay the bondholders an amount greater than the par value if they are called. The additional sum, which is termed a *call premium,* is often set equal to one year's interest if the bonds are called during the first year; the premium then declines each year thereafter. However, bonds are often not callable until several years after they are issued. This is known as a *deferred call*, and the bonds are said to have *call protection*. A common feature on Canadian corporate bonds is a "Doomsday call" or "Canada call." This call feature calculates the buy-back price based on the equivalent-maturity Government of Canada bond plus a premium. Since this feature makes it expensive to call a bond before maturity, it is not usually exercised.

Suppose a company sold bonds when interest rates were relatively high. Provided the issue is callable, the company could sell a new issue of low-yielding securities if and when interest rates drop. It could then use the proceeds of the new issue to retire the high-rate issue and thus reduce its interest expense. This process is called a **refunding operation.**

A call provision is valuable to the firm but potentially detrimental to investors. If interest rates go up, the company will not call the bond, and the investor will be stuck with the original coupon rate on the bond, even though interest rates in the economy have risen sharply. However, if interest rates fall, the company *will* call the bond and pay off investors, who then must reinvest the proceeds at the current market interest rate, which is lower than the rate they were getting on the original bond. In other words, the investor loses when interest rates go up, but he or she doesn't reap the gains when rates fall. To induce an investor to take this type of risk, a new issue of callable bonds must provide a higher interest rate than an otherwise similar issue of noncallable bonds. For example, Pacific Timber Company issued bonds yielding 9.5%; these bonds were callable immediately. On the same day, Northwest Milling Company sold an issue with similar risk and maturity that yielded 9.2%, but these bonds were noncallable for 10 years. Investors were willing to accept a 0.3% lower interest rate on Northwest's bonds for the assurance that the 9.2% interest rate would be earned for at least 10 years. Pacific, on the other hand, had to incur a 0.3% higher annual interest rate to obtain the option of calling the bonds in the event of a subsequent decline in rates.

Bonds that are **retractable** allow the holder to sell the bond back to the issuer before maturity at a pre-set price. This retraction privilege protects investors against a rise in interest rates. If rates rise, the price of a fixed-rate bond declines. However, if holders have the option of turning their bonds in and having them redeemed, say, at par, they are protected against rising rates.

In 2013 Sobeys announced an agreement to purchase the chain of Safeway stores across Canada. Sobey was to finance the majority of the transaction through the sale of assets as well as by issuing more debt. The same day a bond rating service, Dominion Bond Rating Service, placed Sobey's credit rating under review (with negative implications) and soon after downgraded the company's credit rating. The credit rating agency's rationale was that the additional debt Sobeys was taking on made the interest and principal cash flows to Sobey's bondholders more risky. This is an example of *event risk*, the risk that some sudden event will occur and increase the credit risk of the company, hence lowering the firm's bond rating and the value of its outstanding bonds. Investors' concern over event risk meant that those firms deemed most likely to face events that could harm bondholders had to pay dearly to raise new debt capital, if they could raise it at all. Earlier threats to the cost of raising funds led Wall Street to create a *super poison put*. This bond covenant enables a bondholder to turn in a bond—that is, "put" it back to the issuer—at par in the event of a takeover, merger, or major recapitalization.

Sinking Funds

Some bonds also include a **sinking fund** provision that facilitates the orderly retirement of the bond issue. On rare occasions the firm may be required to deposit money with a trustee, which invests the funds and then uses the accumulated sum to retire the bonds when they mature. Usually, though, the sinking fund is used to buy back a certain percentage of the issue each year. A failure to meet the sinking fund requirement causes the bond to be thrown into default, which may force the company into bankruptcy. Obviously, a sinking fund can constitute a significant cash drain on the firm.

In most cases, the firm is given the right to handle the sinking fund in either of two ways:

1. The company can call in for redemption (at par value) a certain percentage of the bonds each year; for example, it might be able to call 5% of the total original amount of the issue at a price of $1,000 per bond. The bonds are numbered serially, and those called for redemption are determined by a lottery administered by the trustee.
2. The company may buy the required number of bonds on the open market.

The firm will choose the least-cost method. If interest rates have risen, causing bond prices to fall, it will buy bonds in the open market at a discount; if interest rates have fallen, it will call the bonds. Note that a call for sinking fund purposes is quite different from a refunding call as discussed above. A sinking fund call typically requires no call premium, but only a small percentage of the issue is normally callable in any one year.[4]

Although sinking funds are designed to protect bondholders by ensuring that an issue is retired in an orderly fashion, you should recognize that sinking funds can work to the

---

[4]Some sinking funds require the issuer to pay a call premium.

detriment of bondholders. For example, suppose that the bond carries a 10% interest rate but that yields on similar bonds have fallen to 7.5%. A sinking fund call at par would require an investor to give up a bond that pays $100 of interest and then to reinvest in a bond that pays only $75 per year. This obviously harms those bondholders whose bonds are called. On balance, however, bonds that have a sinking fund are regarded as safer than those without such a provision, so at the time they are issued sinking fund bonds have lower coupon rates than otherwise similar bonds without sinking funds.

Other Features

Owners of **convertible bonds** have the option to convert the bonds into a fixed number of shares of common stock. Convertibles offer investors the chance to share in the upside if a company does well, so investors are willing to accept a lower coupon rate on convertibles than on otherwise identical but nonconvertible bonds.

Warrants are options that permit the holder to buy stock at a fixed price, thereby providing a gain if the price of the stock rises. Some bonds are issued with warrants. As with convertibles, bonds with warrants have lower coupon rates than straight bonds.

An **income bond** is required to pay interest only if earnings are high enough to cover the interest expense. If earnings are not sufficient, then the company is not required to pay interest and the bondholders do not have the right to force the company into bankruptcy. Therefore, from an investor's standpoint, income bonds are riskier than "regular" bonds.

Indexed bonds first became popular in Brazil, Israel, and a few other countries plagued by high inflation. The interest payments and maturity payments rise automatically when the inflation rate rises, thus protecting bondholders against inflation. In December 1991, the Canadian government began issuing indexed bonds called **real return bonds (RRBs)**.[5] See *Web Extension 6A* for a more detailed discussion of real return bonds.

*For more on real return bonds, see **Web Extension 6A** at the textbook's website.*

Bond Markets

Corporate bonds are traded primarily in the over-the-counter market rather than in organized exchanges. Most bonds are owned by and traded among the large financial institutions (e.g., life insurance companies, mutual funds, and pension funds, all of which deal in very large blocks of securities). It is relatively easy for over-the-counter bond dealers to arrange the transfer of large blocks of bonds among the relatively few holders of the bonds.

Information on Canadian bond prices and yields in the over-the-counter market is not widely published, but data are available at **http://www.financialpost.com.**

ⒸNCEPT REVIEW

1. Define "floating-rate bonds" and "zero coupon bonds."
2. Why is a call provision advantageous to a bond issuer?
3. What are the two ways a sinking fund can be handled? Which method will be chosen by the firm if interest rates have risen? If interest rates have fallen?
4. Are securities that provide for a sinking fund regarded as being riskier than those without this type of provision? Explain.
5. What are income bonds and real return bonds?
6. Why do bonds with warrants and convertible bonds have lower coupons than similarly rated bonds that do not have these features?

6.3 Bond Valuation

The value of any financial asset—a stock, a bond, a lease, or even a physical asset such as an apartment building or a piece of machinery—is simply the present value of the cash flows the asset is expected to produce. The cash flows from a specific bond depend on its contractual features as described above. For a standard coupon-bearing bond such as the one issued by

---

[5]These bonds are usually held in tax-deferred accounts because inflation-adjusted principal added is taxed yearly but is not actually received until the bond is sold.

MicroDrive, the cash flows consist of interest payments during the life of the bond, plus the amount borrowed when the bond matures (usually a $1,000 par value):

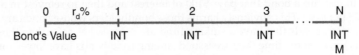

The notation in the time line is explained below:

r_d = The bond's required rate of return, which is the market rate of interest for that type of bond. This is the discount rate that is used to calculate the present value of the bond's cash flows. It is also called the "yield" or "going rate of interest." Note that r_d is *not* the coupon interest rate. It is equal to the coupon rate only if (as in this case) the bond is selling at par. Generally, most coupon bonds are issued at par, which implies that the coupon rate is set at r_d. Thereafter, interest rates, as measured by r_d, will fluctuate, but the coupon rate is fixed, so r_d will equal the coupon rate only by chance. We use the term "i" or "I" to designate the interest rate for many calculations because those terms are used on financial calculators but "r," with the subscript "d" to designate the rate on a debt security, is normally used in finance.

N = Number of years before the bond matures. Note that N declines each year after the bond was issued, so a bond that had a maturity of 15 years when it was issued (original maturity = 15) will have N = 14 after 1 year, N = 13 after 2 years, and so on. Note also that at this point we assume that the bond pays interest once a year, or annually, so N is measured in years. Later on, we will deal with semiannual payment bonds, which pay interest each 6 months.

INT = Dollars of interest paid each year = Coupon rate × Par value. For a bond with a 10% coupon and a $1,000 par value, the annual interest is 0.10($1,000) = $100. In calculator terminology, INT = PMT = 100. If the bond is a semiannual payment bond, the payment will be $50 every 6 months.

M = Par, or maturity, value of the bond. This amount must be paid off at maturity, and it is often equal to $1,000.

The following general equation, written in several forms, can be used to find the value of any bond, V_B:

$$V_B = \frac{INT}{(1+r_d)^1} + \frac{INT}{(1+r_d)^2} + \cdots + \frac{INT}{(1+r_d)^N} + \frac{M}{(1+r_d)^N}$$

$$= \sum_{t=1}^{N} \frac{INT}{(1+r_d)^t} + \frac{M}{(1+r_d)^N} \qquad (6\text{-}1)$$

$$= INT\left[\frac{1}{r_d} - \frac{1}{r_d(1+r_d)^N}\right] + \frac{M}{(1+r_d)^N}$$

Notice that the cash flows consist of an annuity of N years plus a lump sum payment at the end of Year N. Equation 6-1 can be solved by one of three procedures: (1) with a formula, (2) with a financial calculator, or (3) with a spreadsheet.

Solving for the Bond Price

Recall that MicroDrive issued a 15-year bond with an annual coupon rate of 10% and a par value of $1,000. To find the value of MicroDrive's bond with a formula, we insert values for MicroDrive's bond into Equation 6-1:

$$V_B = \sum_{t=1}^{15} \frac{\$100}{(1+0.10)^t} + \frac{\$1,000}{(1+0.10)^{15}}$$

$$= \$100\left[\frac{1}{0.10} - \frac{1}{0.10(1+0.10)^{15}}\right] + \frac{\$1,000}{(1+0.10)^{15}} \qquad (6\text{-}1a)$$

$$= \$1,000$$

We could use the first row of Equation 6-1a to discount each cash flow back to the present and then sum these PVs to find the bond's value; see Figure 6-1. But this procedure is not very efficient, especially if the bond has many years to maturity. Alternatively, you could use the formula in the second row of Equation 6-1a with a simple or scientific calculator, although this would still be somewhat cumbersome.

A financial calculator is ideally suited for finding bond values. Here is the setup for MicroDrive's bond:

Inputs:	15	10		100	1000
	N	I/YR	PV	PMT	FV
Output:			= −1,000		

Input N = 15, I/YR = r_d = 10, INT = PMT = 100, M = FV = 1,000, and then press the PV key to find the value of the bond, $1,000. Since the PV is an outflow to the investor, it is shown with a negative sign. The calculator is programmed to solve Equation 6-1. It finds the PV of an annuity of $100 per year for 15 years, discounted at 10%, then it finds the PV of the $1,000 maturity payment, and then it adds these two PVs to find the value of the bond. Notice that even though the time line in Figure 6-1 shows a total of $1,100 at Year 15, you should not enter FV = 1,100! When you entered N = 15 and PMT = 100, you told the calculator that there is a $100 payment at Year 15. Thus, the FV = 1,000 accounts for any *extra* payment at Year 15, above and beyond the $100 payment.

With *Excel*, it is easiest to use the same PV function that we used in Chapter 4: **=PV(I,N,PMT,FV,0)**. For MicroDrive's bond, the function is **=PV(0.10,15,100,1000,0)** with a result of −$1,000. Like the financial calculator solution, the bond value is negative because PMT and FV are positive.

Excel also provides specialized functions for bond prices based on actual dates. For example, in *Excel* you could find the MicroDrive bond value as of the date it was issued by using the function wizard to enter this formula:

$$=PRICE(DATE(2016,1,5),DATE(2031,1,5),10\%,10\%,100,1,1)$$

The first two arguments in the function are *Excel's* DATE function. The DATE function takes the year, month, and date as inputs and converts them into a date. The first argument is the date on which you want to find the price, and the second argument is the maturity date. The third argument in the PRICE function is the bond's coupon rate, followed by the

See ***Ch 06 Tool Kit.xlsx*** at the textbook's website.

FIGURE 6-1   Time Line for MicroDrive Inc.'s Bonds, 10% Interest Rate

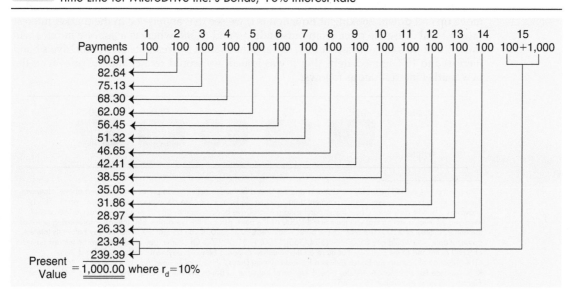

required return on the bond, r_d. The fifth argument, 100, is the redemption value of the bond at maturity per $100 of face value; entering "100" means that the bond pays 100% of its face value when it matures. The sixth argument is the number of payments per year. The last argument, 1, tells the program to base the price on the actual number of days in each month and year. This function produces a result based upon a face value of $100. In other words, if the bond pays $100 of face value at maturity, then the PRICE function result is the price of the bond. Because MicroDrive's bond pays $1,000 of face value at maturity, we must multiply the PRICE function's result by 10. In this example, the PRICE function returns a result of $100. When we multiply it by 10, we get the actual price of $1,000. This function is essential if a bond is being evaluated between coupon payment dates. See *Ch 06 Tool Kit.xlsx* at the textbook's website for the actual *Excel* spreadsheet.[6]

Zero Coupon Bond Prices

Calculating the price of a zero coupon bond is very straightforward. In fact, it is easier than for a regular bond. Remember that a zero pays no periodic interest; therefore, there is no constant annuity stream to discount. A zero coupon bond's cash flow in fact is the face value paid at maturity, so the price of a zero is the present value of the principal payment at maturity. Thus we can take Equation 6-1, eliminate the present value of the interest payment portion, and use the remaining equation:

$$V_{\text{zero coupon bond}} = \frac{M}{(1 + r_d)^N} \qquad (6\text{-}1b)$$

Notice that the cash flow consists of a single lump sum payment at the end of year N.

Using a financial calculator, let's find the price of a 15-year $1,000 zero coupon bond with a nominal (quoted) interest rate of 6.5%, assuming annual compounding:

Inputs:	15	6.5		0	1000
	N	I/YR	PV	PMT	FV
Output:			= −388.83		

Interest Rate Changes and Bond Prices

In the previous example using Equation 6-1a the bond is selling at a price equal to its par value. Whenever the going market rate of interest, r_d, is equal to the coupon rate, a *fixed-rate* bond will sell at its par value. Normally, the coupon rate is set at the going rate when a bond is issued, causing it to sell at par initially.

The coupon rate remains fixed after the bond is issued, but interest rates in the market move up and down. Looking at Equation 6-1, we see that an *increase* in the market interest rate (r_d) will cause the price of an outstanding bond to *fall*, whereas a *decrease* in rates will cause the bond's price to *rise*. For example, if the market interest rate on MicroDrive's bond increased to 15% immediately after it was issued, we would recalculate the price with the new market interest rate as follows:

Inputs:	15	15		100	1000
	N	I/YR	PV	PMT	FV
Output:			= −707.63		

---

[6]The bond prices quoted by brokers in Canada and the United States are called *clean prices,* as described above. However, if you bought a bond between interest payment dates, you would have to pay the clean price plus accrued interest. This is known as a bond's *dirty price.* Thus, if you purchased a MicroDrive bond 6 months after it was issued, your broker would send you an invoice stating that you must pay $1,000 as the basic price of the bond plus $50 interest, representing one-half the annual interest of $100. The seller of the bond would receive $1,050. If you bought the bond the day before its interest payment date, you would pay $1,000 + (364/365)($100) = $1,099.73. Of course, you would receive an interest payment of $100 at the end of the next day. For more on the valuation of bonds between payment dates, see Richard Taylor, "The Valuation of Semiannual Bonds between Interest Payment Dates," *Financial Review,* August 1988, 365–368; and K. S. Maurice Tse and Mark A. White, "The Valuation of Semiannual Bonds between Interest Payment Dates: A Correction," *Financial Review,* November 1990, 659–662.

The price would fall to $707.63. Notice that the bond would then sell at a price below its par value. Whenever the going rate of interest *rises above* the coupon rate, a fixed-rate bond's price will fall *below* its par value, and it is called a **discount bond.**

On the other hand, bond prices rise when market interest rates fall. For example, if the market interest rate on MicroDrive's bond decreased to 5%, we would once again recalculate its price:

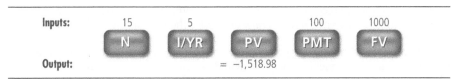

In this case the price rises to $1,518.98. In general, whenever the going interest rate *falls below* the coupon rate, a fixed-rate bond's price will *rise above* its par value, and it is called a **premium bond.**

CONCEPT REVIEW

1. Why do the prices of fixed-rate bonds fall if expectations for inflation rise?
2. What is a "discount bond"? A "premium bond"?
3. A bond that matures in 6 years has a par value of $1,000, an annual coupon payment of $80, and a market interest rate of 9%. What is its price? (Check Figure: $955.14)
4. A bond that matures in 18 years has a par value of $1,000, an annual coupon of 10%, and a market interest rate of 7%. What is its price? (Check Figure: $1,301.77)

6.4 Bond Yields

Unlike the coupon interest rate, which is fixed, the bond's *yield* varies from day to day depending on current market conditions. Moreover, the yield can be calculated in three different ways, and three "answers" can be obtained. These different yields are described in the following sections.

Yield to Maturity

Suppose you were offered a 14-year, 10% annual coupon, $1,000 par value bond at a price of $1,494.93. What rate of interest would you earn on your investment if you bought the bond and held it to maturity? This rate is called the bond's **yield to maturity (YTM),** and it is the interest rate generally discussed by investors when they talk about rates of return. The yield to maturity is usually the same as the market rate of interest, r_d, and to find it, all you need to do is solve Equation 6-1 for r_d:

$$V_B = \$1{,}494.93 = \frac{\$100}{(1 + r_d)^1} + \cdots + \frac{\$100}{(1 + r_d)^{14}} + \frac{\$1{,}000}{(1 + r_d)^{14}}$$

You can substitute values for r_d until you find a value that "works" and forces the sum of the PVs on the right side of the equal sign to equal $1,494.93. Alternatively, you can substitute values of r_d into the third form of Equation 6-1 until you find a value that works.

Finding r_d = YTM by trial and error would be a tedious, time-consuming process, but as you might guess, it is easy with a financial calculator. Here is the setup:

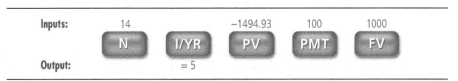

Simply enter N = 14, PV = −1,494.93, PMT = 100, and FV = 1,000, and then press the I/YR key. The answer, 5%, will then appear.

See **Ch 06 Tool Kit.xlsx** at the textbook's website.

You could also find the YTM with a spreadsheet. In *Excel*, you would use the RATE function for this bond, inputting N = 14, PMT = 100, PV = −1,494.93, FV = 1,000, 0 for Type, and leave Guess blank: **=RATE(14,100,−1494.93,1000,0)**. The result is 5%. The RATE function works only if the current date is immediately after either the issue date or a coupon payment date. To find bond yields on other dates, use *Excel's* YIELD function. See the **Ch 06 Tool Kit.xlsx** file for an example.

The yield to maturity can be viewed as the bond's *promised rate of return*, which is the return that investors will receive if all the promised payments are made. However, the yield to maturity equals the *expected rate of return* only if (1) the probability of default is zero and (2) the bond cannot be called. If there is some default risk, or if the bond may be called, then there is some probability that the promised payments to maturity will not be received, in which case the calculated yield to maturity will differ from the expected return.

The YTM for a bond that sells at par consists entirely of an interest yield, but if the bond sells at a price other than its par value, the YTM will consist of the interest yield plus a positive or negative capital gains yield. Note also that a bond's yield to maturity changes whenever interest rates in the economy change, and this is almost daily. One who purchases a bond and holds it until it matures will receive the YTM that existed on the purchase date, but the bond's calculated YTM will change frequently between the purchase date and the maturity date.

Yield to Call

If you purchased a bond that was callable and the company called it, you would not have the option of holding the bond until it matured. Therefore, the yield to maturity would not be earned. For example, if MicroDrive's 10% coupon bonds were callable, and if interest rates fell from 10% to 5%, then the company could call in the 10% bonds, replace them with 5% bonds, and save $100 − $50 = $50 interest per bond per year. This would be beneficial to the company but not to its bondholders.

If current interest rates are well below an outstanding bond's coupon rate, then a callable bond is likely to be called, and investors will estimate its expected rate of return as the **yield to call (YTC)** rather than as the yield to maturity. To calculate the YTC, solve this equation for r_d:

$$\text{Price of bond} = \sum_{t=1}^{N} \frac{\text{INT}}{(1 + r_d)^t} + \frac{\text{Call price}}{(1 + r_d)^N} \qquad (6\text{-}2)$$

Here N is the number of years until the company can call the bond; call price is the price the company must pay in order to call the bond (it is often set equal to the par value plus one year's interest); and r_d is the YTC.

To illustrate, suppose MicroDrive's bonds had a provision that permitted the company, if it desired, to call the bonds 10 years after the issue date at a price of $1,100. Suppose further that interest rates had fallen, and one year after issuance the going interest rate had declined, causing the price of the bonds to rise to $1,494.93. Here is the time line and the setup for finding the bond's YTC with a financial calculator:

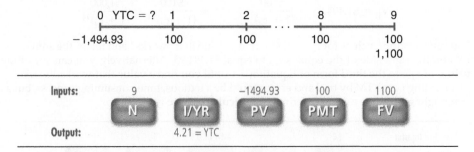

The YTC is 4.21%—this is the return you would earn if you bought the bond at a price of $1,494.93 and it was called 9 years from today. (The bond could not be called until 10 years after issuance, and 1 year has gone by, so there are 9 years left until the first call date.)

Do you think MicroDrive *will* call the bonds when they become callable? MicroDrive's actions would depend on what the going interest rate is when the bonds become callable. If the going rate remains at $r_d = 5\%$, then MicroDrive could save $10\% - 5\% = 5\%$, or $50 per bond per year, by calling them and replacing the 10% bonds with a new 5% issue. There would be costs to the company to refund the issue, but the interest savings would probably be worth the cost, so MicroDrive would probably refund the bonds. Therefore, you would probably earn YTC = 4.21% rather than YTM = 5% if you bought the bonds under the indicated conditions.

In the balance of this chapter, we assume that bonds are not callable unless otherwise noted. Some of the end-of-chapter problems, however, deal with yield to call.

Current Yield

If you examine brokerage house reports on bonds, you will often see reference to a bond's **current yield.** The current yield is the annual interest payment divided by the bond's current price. For example, if MicroDrive's bonds with a 10% coupon were currently selling at $985, the bond's current yield would be 10.15% ($100/$985).

Unlike the yield to maturity, the current yield does not represent the rate of return that investors should expect on the bond. The current yield provides information regarding the amount of cash income that a bond will generate in a given year, but since it does not take account of capital gains or losses that will be realized if the bond is held until maturity (or call), it does not provide an accurate measure of the bond's total expected return.

The fact that the current yield does not provide an accurate measure of a bond's total return can be illustrated with a zero coupon bond. Since zeros pay no annual income, they always have a current yield of zero. This indicates that the bond will not provide any cash interest income, but since the bond will appreciate in value over time, its total rate of return clearly exceeds zero.

CONCEPT REVIEW

1. Explain the difference between the yield to maturity and the yield to call.
2. How does a bond's current yield differ from its total return?
3. Could the current yield exceed the total return?
4. A bond currently sells for $850. It has an 8-year maturity, an annual coupon of $80, and a par value of $1,000. What is its yield to maturity? (Check Figure: 10.90%) What is its current yield? (Check Figure: 9.41%)
5. A bond currently sells for $1,250. It pays a $110 annual coupon and has a 20-year maturity, but it can be called in 5 years at $1,110. What are its YTM and its YTC? (Check Figures: 8.38%, 6.85%) Is it likely to be called if interest rates don't change?

6.5 Changes in Bond Values Over Time

At the time a coupon bond is issued, the coupon is generally set at a level that will cause the market price of the bond to equal its par value. If a lower coupon were set, investors would not be willing to pay $1,000 for the bond, while if a higher coupon were set, investors would clamour for the bond and bid its price up over $1,000. Investment bankers can judge quite precisely the coupon rate that will cause a bond to sell at its $1,000 par value.

A bond that has just been issued is known as a *new issue*. (Investment bankers classify a bond as a new issue for about one month after it has first been issued. New issues are usually actively traded and are called "on-the-run" bonds.) Once the bond has been on the market for a while, it is classified as an *outstanding bond*, also called a *seasoned issue*. Newly issued bonds generally sell very close to par, but the prices of seasoned bonds vary widely from par. Except for floating-rate bonds, coupon payments are constant, so when economic conditions change, a bond with a $100 coupon that sold at par when it was issued will sell for more or less than $1,000 thereafter.

MicroDrive's bonds with a 10% coupon rate were originally issued at par. If r_d remained constant at 10%, what would be the value of the bond 1 year after it was issued? Now the term to maturity is only 14 years—that is, N = 14. With a financial calculator, just override N = 15 with N = 14, press the PV key, and you find a value of $1,000. If we continued, setting N = 13, N = 12, and so forth, we would see that the value of the bond will remain at $1,000 as long as the going interest rate remains constant at the coupon rate, 10%.

Now suppose interest rates in the economy fell after the MicroDrive bonds were issued, and, as a result, r_d *fell below the coupon rate*, decreasing from 10% to 5%. Both the coupon interest payments and the maturity value remain constant, but now 5% would have to be used for r_d in Equation 6-1. The value of the bond at the end of the first year would be $1,494.93:

$$V_B = \sum_{t=1}^{14} \frac{\$100}{(1 + 0.05)^t} + \frac{\$1,000}{(1 + 0.05)^{14}}$$

$$= \$100\left[\frac{1}{0.05} - \frac{1}{0.05(1 + 0.05)^{14}}\right] + \frac{\$1,000}{(1 + 0.05)^{14}}$$

$$= \$1,494.93$$

With a financial calculator, just change r_d = I/YR from 10 to 5, and then press the PV key to get the answer, $1,494.93. Thus, if r_d fell *below* the coupon rate, the bond would sell above par, or at a *premium*.

The arithmetic of the bond value increase should be clear, but what is the logic behind it? The fact that r_d has fallen to 5% means that if you had $1,000 to invest, you could buy new bonds like MicroDrive's, except that these new bonds would pay $50 of interest each year rather than $100. Naturally, you would prefer $100 to $50, so you would be willing to pay more than $1,000 for a MicroDrive bond to obtain its higher coupons. All investors would react similarly, and as a result, the MicroDrive bonds would be bid up in price to $1,494.93, at which point they would provide the same 5% rate of return to a potential investor as the new bonds.

Assuming that interest rates remain constant at 5% for the next 14 years, what would happen to the value of a MicroDrive bond? It would fall gradually from $1,494.93 at present to $1,000 at maturity, when MicroDrive will redeem each bond for $1,000. This point can be illustrated by calculating the value of the bond 1 year later, when it has 13 years remaining to maturity. With a financial calculator, simply input the values for N, I, PMT, and FV, now using N = 13, and press the PV key to find the value of the bond, $1,469.68. Thus, the value of the bond will have fallen from $1,494.93 to $1,469.68, or by $25.25. If you were to calculate the value of the bond at other future dates, the price would continue to fall as the maturity date approached.

Note that if you purchased the bond at a price of $1,494.93 and then sold it 1 year later with r_d still at 5%, you would have a capital loss of $25.25, or a total return of $100.00 − $25.25 = $74.75. Your percentage rate of return would consist of an **interest yield** (also called a current yield) plus a **capital gains yield**, calculated as follows:

$$\text{Interest, or current, yield} = \$100/\$1,494.93 \quad = \quad 0.0669 \quad = \quad 6.69\%$$
$$\text{Capital gains yield} = -\$25.25/\$1,494.93 \quad = \quad -0.0169 \quad = \quad -1.69\%$$
$$\text{Total rate of return, or yield} = \$74.75/\$1,494.93 \quad = \quad 0.0500 \quad = \quad \underline{\underline{5.00\%}}$$

Had interest rates risen from 10% to 15% during the first year after issue rather than fallen from 10% to 5%, then you would enter N = 14, I/YR = 15, PMT = 100, and FV = 1,000, and then press the PV key to find the value of the bond, $713.78. In this case, the bond would sell below its par value, or at a discount. The total expected future return on the bond would again consist of a current yield and a capital gains yield, but now the capital gains yield would be *positive*. The total return would be 15%. To see this, calculate the price of the bond with 13 years left to maturity, assuming that interest rates remain at 15%. With a calculator, enter N = 13, I = 15, PMT = 100, and FV = 1,000, and then press PV to obtain the bond's value, $720.84.

Note that the capital gain for the year is the difference between the bond's value at Year 2 (with 13 years remaining) and the bond's value at Year 1 (with 14 years remaining), or $720.84 − $713.78 = $7.06. The interest yield, capital gains yield, and total yield are calculated as follows:

$$\text{Interest, or current, yield} = \$100/\$713.78 \quad = 0.1401 = 14.01\%$$
$$\text{Capital gains yield} = \$7.06/\$713.78 \quad = 0.0099 = \underline{0.99\%}$$
$$\text{Total rate of return, or yield} = \$107.06/\$713.78 \quad = 0.1500 = \underline{\underline{15.00\%}}$$

FIGURE 6-2 Time Path of the Value of a 10% Coupon, $1,000 Par Value Bond When Interest Rates Are 5%, 10%, and 15%

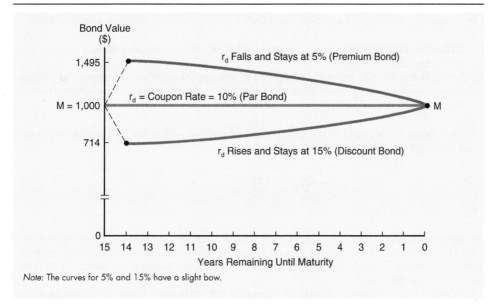

Note: The curves for 5% and 15% have a slight bow.

See *Ch 06 Tool Kit.xlsx* for all calculations.

Figure 6-2 graphs the value of the bond over time, assuming that interest rates in the economy (1) remain constant at 10%, (2) fall to 5% and then remain constant at that level, or (3) rise to 15% and remain constant at that level. Of course, if interest rates do *not* remain constant, then the price of the bond will fluctuate. However, regardless of what future interest rates do, the bond's price will approach $1,000 as it nears the maturity date (barring bankruptcy, in which case the bond's value might fall dramatically).

Figure 6-2 illustrates the following key points:

1. Whenever the going rate of interest, r_d, is equal to the coupon rate, a *fixed-rate* bond will sell at its par value. Normally, the coupon rate is set equal to the going rate when a bond is issued, causing it to sell at par initially.
2. Interest rates do change over time, but the coupon rate remains fixed after the bond has been issued. Whenever the going rate of interest *rises above* the coupon rate, a fixed-rate bond's price will *fall below* its par value. Such a bond is called a discount bond.
3. Whenever the going rate of interest *falls below* the coupon rate, a fixed-rate bond's price will *rise above* its par value. Such a bond is called a premium bond.
4. Thus, an *increase* in interest rates will cause the prices of outstanding bonds to *fall*, whereas a *decrease* in rates will cause bond prices to *rise*.
5. The market value of a bond will always approach its par value as its maturity date approaches, provided the firm does not go bankrupt.

These points are very important, for they show that bondholders may suffer capital losses or make capital gains, depending on whether interest rates rise or fall after the bond is purchased.

CONCEPT REVIEW

1. What is meant by the terms "new issue" and "seasoned issue"?
2. Last year a firm issued 30-year, 8% annual coupon bonds at a par value of $1,000. (1) Suppose that one year later the going rate drops to 6%. What is the new price of the bonds, assuming that they now have 29 years to maturity? (Check Figure: $1,271.81) (2) Suppose instead that one year after issue the going interest rate increases to 10% (rather than falling to 6%). What is the price? (Check Figure: $812.61)

6.6 Bonds with Semiannual Coupons

Although some bonds pay interest annually, the vast majority actually pay interest semiannually. To evaluate semiannual payment bonds, we must modify the valuation model as follows:

1. Divide the annual coupon interest payment by 2 to determine the dollars of interest paid each 6 months.
2. Multiply the years to maturity, N, by 2 to determine the number of semiannual periods.
3. Divide the nominal (quoted) interest rate, r_d, by 2 to determine the periodic (semiannual) interest rate.

By making these changes, we obtain the following equation for finding the value of a bond that pays interest semiannually:

$$V_B = \sum_{t=1}^{2N} \frac{INT/2}{(1 + r_d/2)^t} + \frac{M}{(1 + r_d/2)^{2N}} \qquad (6\text{-}3)$$

To illustrate, assume now that MicroDrive's bonds pay $50 interest each 6 months rather than $100 at the end of each year. Thus, each interest payment is only half as large, but there are twice as many of them. The coupon rate is thus "10%, semiannual payments." This is the nominal, or quoted, rate.[7]

When the going (nominal) rate of interest is 5% with semiannual compounding, the value of this 15-year bond is found as follows:

Inputs:	30	2.5		50	1000
	N	I/YR	PV	PMT	FV
Output:			= −1,523.26		

Enter N = 30, r_d = I/YR = 2.5, PMT = 50, FV = 1,000, and then press the PV key to obtain the bond's value, $1,523.26. The value with semiannual interest payments is slightly larger than $1,518.98, the value when interest is paid annually. This higher value occurs because interest payments are received somewhat faster under semiannual compounding.

Semiannual compounding periods are *also* used for zero coupon bonds. Therefore, we must also divide the quoted interest rate, r_d, by 2 and multiply the years to maturity, N, by 2. We don't worry about any annual interest, as there is none. Making this change results in the following equation:

$$V_{\text{zero coupon bond}} = \frac{M}{(1 + r_d/2)^{2N}} \qquad (6\text{-}3a)$$

CONCEPT REVIEW

1. Describe how the annual bond valuation formula is changed to evaluate semiannual coupon bonds. Then write out the revised formula.
2. A bond has a 25-year maturity, an 8% annual coupon paid semiannually, and a face value of $1,000. The going nominal annual interest rate (r_d) is 6%. What is the bond's price? (Check Figure: $1,257.30)

---

[7] In this situation, the coupon rate of "10% paid semiannually," is the rate that bond dealers, corporate treasurers, and investors generally would discuss. Of course, if this bond were issued at par, its effective annual rate would be higher than 10%:

$$EAR = EFF\% = \left(1 + \frac{r_{NOM}}{M}\right)^M - 1 = \left(1 + \frac{0.10}{2}\right)^2 - 1 = (1.05)^2 - 1 = 10.25\%$$

Since 10% with annual payments is quite different from 10% with semiannual payments, we have assumed a change in effective rates in this section from the situation in Section 6.3, where we assumed 10% with annual payments.

6.7 The Determinants of Market Interest Rates

Up until now we have given you r_d, the going market rate. But as we showed in Chapter 1, different debt securities often have very different market rates. What explains these differences? In general, the quoted (or nominal) interest rate on a debt security, r_d, is composed of a real risk-free rate of interest, r^*, plus several premiums that reflect inflation, the risk of the security, and the security's marketability (or liquidity). A conceptual framework is shown below:

$$\text{Quoted market interest rate} = r_d = r^* + IP + DRP + LP + MRP$$
$$= r_{RF} + DRP + LP + MRP \qquad \text{(6-4)}$$

Here are definitions of the variables in Equation 6-4:

r_d = Quoted, or nominal, rate of interest on a given security.[8] There are many different securities, hence many different quoted interest rates.

r^* = Real risk-free rate of interest. r^* is pronounced "r-star," and it is the rate that would exist on a riskless security if zero inflation were expected.

IP = Inflation premium. IP is equal to the average expected inflation rate over the life of the security. The expected future inflation rate is not necessarily equal to the current inflation rate, so IP is not necessarily equal to current inflation.

r_{RF} = $r^* + IP$, and it is the quoted risk-free rate of interest on a security such as a Government of Canada Treasury bill, which is very liquid and also free of most risks. Note that r_{RF} includes the premium for expected inflation, because $r_{RF} = r^* + IP$.

DRP = Default risk premium. This premium reflects the possibility that the issuer will not pay interest or principal at the stated time and in the stated amount. DRP is zero for Government of Canada securities, but it rises as the riskiness of issuers increases.

LP = Liquidity, or marketability, premium. This is a premium charged by lenders to reflect the fact that some securities cannot be converted to cash on short notice at a "reasonable" price. LP is very low for Government of Canada securities and for securities issued by large provinces and firms, but it is relatively high on securities issued by very small firms.

MRP = Maturity risk premium. As we will explain later, longer-term bonds, even government bonds, are exposed to a significant risk of price declines, and a maturity risk premium is charged by lenders to reflect this risk.

We discuss the components whose sum makes up the quoted, or nominal, rate on a given security in the following sections.

ⓒNCEPT REVIEW

1. Write out an equation for the nominal interest rate on any debt security.

6.8 The Real Risk-Free Rate of Interest, r*

The **real risk-free rate of interest, r***, is defined as the interest rate that would exist on a riskless security if no inflation were expected, and it may be thought of as the rate of interest on *short-term* Government of Canada T-bills in an inflation-free world. The real risk-free rate is not static—it changes over time depending on economic conditions, especially (1) on the rate of return corporations and other borrowers expect to earn on productive assets and (2) on people's time preferences for current versus future consumption.

---

[8]The term "nominal" as it is used here means the *stated* rate as opposed to the real rate, which is adjusted to remove inflation effects. Suppose you bought a 10-year government bond with a quoted, or nominal, rate of about 4.6%. If inflation averages 2.5% over the next 10 years, the real rate would be about 4.6% − 2.5% = 2.1%. To be technically correct, we should find the real rate by solving for r^* in the following equation: $(1 + r^*)(1 + 0.025) = (1 + 0.046)$. Solving the equation, we find $r^* = 2.05\%$. Since this is very close to the 2.1% calculated above, we will continue to approximate the real rate in this chapter by subtracting inflation from the nominal rate.

In November 2007, the yield on a 30-day T-bill was 3.88%, while inflation was 2.3%. The real risk-free rate of return in Canada was (3.88% − 2.3%) = 1.58%.[9] However, as of November 2012, T-bills yielded 0.93% while inflation expectations were 1.6%, resulting in a real risk-free rate of return of −0.67%. This negative return may be explained (as at the time of writing) by the ongoing financial difficulties in the United States as well as by the financial crisis in Europe. Investors are looking for the safest investments—namely, T-bills—thus bidding up their prices and pushing down their yields.

CONCEPT REVIEW

1. Define the real risk-free rate of interest.

6.9 The Inflation Premium (IP)

Inflation has a major effect on interest rates because it erodes the purchasing power of the dollar and lowers the real rate of return on investments. To illustrate, suppose you saved $1,000 and invested it in a bond that matures in 1 year and pays a 5% interest rate. At the end of the year, you will receive $1,050—your original $1,000 plus $50 of interest. Now suppose the inflation rate during the year is 10% and that it affects all items equally. If gas costs $1.25 per litre at the beginning of the year, it will cost $1.38 at the end of the year. Therefore, your $1,000 buys $1,000/$1.25 = 800 litres at the beginning of the year, but only $1,050/$1.38 = 761 litres at the end. In *real terms*, you are worse off—you have received $50 of interest, but it will not be sufficient to offset inflation. You would have been better off buying 1,000 litres of gas (or some other storable asset) than buying the bond.

Investors are well aware of inflation's effects on interest rates, so when they lend money, they build in an **inflation premium (IP)** equal to the average expected inflation rate over the life of the security. For a short-term, default-free Treasury bill, the actual interest rate charged, $r_{T\text{-bill}}$, will be the real risk-free rate, r^*, plus the inflation premium (IP):

$$r_{T\text{-bill}} = r_{RF} = r^* + IP.$$

Therefore, if the real short-term risk-free rate of interest were $r^* = 0.6\%$, and if inflation were expected to be 1.0% (and hence IP = 1.0%) during the next year, then the quoted rate of interest on 1-year T-bills would be 0.6% + 1.0% = 1.6%.

It is important to note that the inflation rate built into interest rates is *the inflation rate expected in the future*, not the rate experienced in the past. Thus, the latest reported figures might show an annual inflation rate of 2%, but that is for the *past* year. If people on average expect a 6% inflation rate in the future, then 6% will be built into the current interest rate.

Note also that the inflation rate reflected in the quoted interest rate on any security is the *average rate of inflation expected over the security's life*. Thus, the inflation rate built into a 1-year bond is the expected inflation rate for the next year, but the inflation rate built into a 30-year bond is the average rate of inflation expected over the next 30 years.

Japan and Switzerland have, over the past several years, had lower inflation rates than Canada, so their interest rates have generally been lower than ours. South Africa and most South American countries have experienced higher inflation, and that is reflected in their interest rates.

CONCEPT REVIEW

1. Is the inflation premium built into nominal rates based on past, current, or expected inflation? Over what time frame?

---

[9]CPI percentage change from Statistics Canada, Table 326-020 – Consumer Price Index (CPI), CANSIM, using E-STAT; T-bill yields and inflation expectation from Bank of Canada, www.bankofcanada.ca, accessed July 4, 2014.

6.10 The Nominal, or Quoted, Risk-Free Rate of Interest, r_{RF}

The **nominal, or quoted, risk-free rate, r_{RF},** is the real risk-free rate plus a premium for expected inflation: $r_{RF} = r^* + IP$. To be strictly correct, the risk-free rate should mean the interest rate on a totally risk-free security—one that has no risk of default, no maturity risk, no liquidity risk, no risk of loss if inflation increases, and no risk of any other type. There is no such security, so there is no observable truly risk-free rate. If the term "risk-free rate" is used without either the modifier "real" or the modifier "nominal," people generally mean the quoted (nominal) rate, and we will follow that convention in this book. Therefore, when we use the term "risk-free rate, r_{RF}," we mean the nominal risk-free rate, which includes an inflation premium equal to the average expected inflation rate over the life of the security. In general, we use the T-bill rate to approximate the short-term risk-free rate, and the Government of Canada bond rate to approximate the long-term risk-free rate (even though it also includes a maturity premium). So whenever you see the term "risk-free rate," assume that we are referring either to the quoted Canadian T-bill rate or to the quoted bond rate.

Since $r_{RF} = r^* + IP$, we can rewrite Equation 6-4 as follows:

$$\text{Nominal, or quoted, rate} = r_d = r_{RF} + DRP + LP + MRP \qquad (6\text{-}5)$$

Therefore, when discussing the rate on a bond, we often start with the short-term risk-free rate and make adjustments for the default risk premium, the liquidity premium, and the maturity risk premium.

CONCEPT REVIEW

1. What security is a good approximation of the nominal risk-free rate?

6.11 The Default Risk Premium (DRP)

If the issuer defaults on a payment, investors receive less than the promised return on the bond. The quoted interest rate includes a default risk premium (DRP)—the greater the default risk, the higher the bond's yield to maturity.[10] The default risk on Government of Canada bonds is zero, but default risk can be substantial for corporate bonds. In this section we consider some issues related to default risk.

Bond Contract Provisions That Influence Default Risk

Default risk is affected by both the financial strength of the issuer and the terms of the bond contract, especially whether collateral has been pledged to secure the bond. Several types of contract provisions are discussed below.

Bond Indentures An **indenture** is a legal document that spells out the rights of both bond-holders and the issuing corporation, and a trustee is an official (usually a bank) who represents the bondholders and makes sure the terms of the indenture are carried out. The indenture may be several hundred pages in length, and it will include *restrictive covenants* that cover points such as the conditions under which the issuer can pay off the bonds prior to maturity, the levels at which certain ratios must be maintained if the company is to issue additional debt, and restrictions against the payment of dividends unless earnings meet certain specifications.

Mortgage Bonds Under a **mortgage bond,** the corporation pledges certain assets as security for the bond. To illustrate, in 2012 Billingham Corporation needed $10 million to build a

---

[10]Suppose two bonds have the same promised cash flows, coupon rate, maturity, liquidity, and inflation exposure, but one bond has more default risk than the other. Investors will naturally pay less for the bond with the greater chance of default. As a result, bonds with higher default risk will have higher interest rates.

major regional distribution centre. Bonds in the amount of $4 million, secured by a *first mortgage* on the property, were issued. (The remaining $6 million was financed with equity capital.) If Billingham defaults on the bonds, the bondholders can foreclose on the property and sell it to satisfy their claims.

If Billingham were to choose, it could issue *second mortgage bonds* secured by the same $10 million of assets. In the event of liquidation, the holders of these second mortgage bonds would have a claim against the property, but only after the first mortgage bondholders had been paid off in full. Thus, second mortgages are sometimes called *junior mortgages*, because they are junior in priority to the claims of *senior mortgages*, or *first mortgage bonds*.

All mortgage bonds are subject to an indenture. The amount of new bonds that can be issued is virtually always limited to a specified percentage of the firm's total "bondable property," which generally includes all land, plant, and equipment.

Debentures and Subordinated Debentures A **debenture** is an unsecured bond, and as such it provides no lien against specific property as security for the obligation. Debenture holders are, therefore, general creditors whose claims are protected by property not otherwise pledged. Extremely strong companies often use debentures; they simply do not need to put up property as security for their debt. Debentures are also issued by weak companies that have already pledged most of their assets as collateral for mortgage loans. In this latter case, the debentures are quite risky, and they will bear a high interest rate.

The term *"subordinate"* means "below," or "inferior to," and, in the event of bankruptcy, subordinated debt has claims on assets only after senior debt has been paid off. **Subordinated debentures** may be subordinated either to designated notes payable (usually bank loans) or to all other debt. In the event of liquidation or reorganization, holders of subordinated debentures cannot be paid until all senior debt, as named in the debentures' indentures, has been paid.

Agency Bonds Companies created and owned by the federal or provincial governments (Crown corporations) often finance their operations through bond issues. Since the ultimate guarantor is a high-level government, interest and principal payments on these bonds are considered very safe. In fact, Crown corporations carry the same credit rating as their owner government. However, since their bond issues tend to be smaller in size, they are less liquid and provide a higher return than other equivalent rated bonds. The Canadian Mortgage and Housing Corporation (CMHC), and the Export Development Corporation (EDC), are both examples of federal Crown corporations active in the bond market. Canada Mortgage Trust, a relatively new agency holding residential mortgages, is a large issuer of agency bonds. These bonds are backed by the federal government. They are liquid but still pay a premium to Government of Canada bonds.

Bond Ratings

Since the early 1900s, bonds have been assigned quality ratings that reflect their probability of going into default. The three major rating agencies in the United States are Moody's Investors Service (Moody's), Standard & Poor's Corporation (S&P), and Fitch Ratings, while in Canada it is the Dominion Bond Rating Service (DBRS).

As shown in Columns (3) and (4) of Table 6-1, triple-A and double-A bonds are extremely safe, with none defaulting even within 5 years of being assigned a rating. Single-A and triple-B bonds are also strong enough to be called **investment-grade bonds** and are the lowest-rated bonds that many banks and other institutional investors are permitted by law to hold. Double-B and lower bonds are speculative, or **junk bonds.** These bonds have a significant probability of defaulting.

Bond Rating Criteria, Upgrades, and Downgrades

Bond ratings are based on both quantitative and qualitative factors, as we describe below.

1. *Financial Ratios.* Many ratios potentially are important, but the return on assets, interest coverage, and operating margin are particularly valuable for predicting financial distress. For example, Columns 5 and 6 in Table 6-1 show a strong relationship between

TABLE 6-1   Bond Ratings, Default Risk, and Yields

Rating Agencies[a]		Percent Defaulting Within[b]		Median Ratios[c]		Percent Upgraded or Downgraded in 2013[b]		
S&P and DBRS	Moody's	1 Year	5 Years	EBITA Avg Assets	EBITA Int Exp	Down	Up	Yield[d]
(1)	(2)	(3)	(4)	(5)	(6)	(7)	(8)	(9)
Investment-grade bonds								
AAA	Aaa	0.0%	0.0%	22.2%	21.2x	9.5%	NA	1.6%
AA	Aa	0.0	0.0	16.7	12.3	2.5	0.0	2.2
A	A	0.0	0.0	14.0	8.1	3.7	1.2	2.4
BBB	Baa	0.0	0.0	10.6	4.5	2.5	3.9	2.7
Junk bonds								
BB	Ba	0.1	3.6	9.8	3.2	4.7	5.1	4.7
B	B	1.6	19.6	7.0	1.4	6.0	5.8	5.9
CCC	C	25.7	68.5	2.8	0.4	23.4	10.1	13.5

Notes:
[a]The ratings agencies also use "modifiers" for bonds rated below triple-A. S&P uses a plus-and-minus system; thus, A+ designates the strongest A-rated bonds and A– the weakest. Moody's uses a 1, 2, or 3 designation, with 1 denoting the strongest and 3 the weakest; thus, within the double-A category, Aa1 is the best, Aa2 is average, and Aa3 is the weakest. DBRS uses a high-and-low system; thus AA Low designates the weakest AA-rated bonds.
[b]"Default, Transition, and Recovery: 2013 Annual Global Corporate Default Study And Rating Transitions," Standard & Poor's, March 19, 2014, http://www.standardandpoors.com, accessed July 14, 2014.
[c]"Key Ratios by Rating for North American Non-Financial Corporations: December 2009," Moody's Investors Service, December 2009, http://www.moodys.com, accessed December 2, 2011.
[d]Yields for AAA, AA, A, and BBB from Bloomberg LLP. Representative yields for BB, B, and CCC adapted from iShares Canadian Hybrid Corporate Bond Index ETF Holdings, http://www.ca.ishares.com, accessed July 15, 2014.

ratings and EBITA/assets (a return on assets measure) and EBITA/Interest expense (an interest coverage ratio).
2. *Bond Contract Terms.* Important provisions for determining the bond's rating include whether the bond is secured by a mortgage on specific assets, whether the bond is subordinated to other debt, any sinking fund provisions, guarantees by some other party with a high credit ranking, and *restrictive covenants* such as requirements that the firm keep its debt ratio below a given level or that it keep its times-interest-earned ratio above a given level.
3. *Qualitative Factors.* Included here would be factors such as sensitivity of the firm's earnings to the strength of the economy, how it is affected by inflation, whether it is having or is likely to have labour problems, the extent of its international operations (including the stability of the countries in which it operates), potential environmental problems, potential antitrust problems, and so on.

Ratings agencies review outstanding bonds on a periodic basis and re-rate if necessary. Columns (7) and (8) in Table 6-1 show the percentages of companies in each rating category that were downgraded or upgraded in 2013 by Standard and Poor's.

Over the long run, ratings agencies have done a reasonably good job of measuring average credit risk of bonds and of changing ratings whenever there is a significant change in credit quality. However, it is important to understand that ratings do not adjust immediately to changes in credit quality, and in some cases there can be a considerable lag between a change in credit quality and a change in rating. Abrupt rating downgrades occurred in 2007 and 2008, after credit problems surfaced, leading some to call for changes in rating agencies and how they rate bonds. Clearly, improvements can be made, but there will always be occasions when completely unexpected information about a company is released, leading to a sudden change in its rating.

Bond Ratings and the Default Risk Premium

Why are bond ratings so important? First, most bonds are purchased by institutional investors rather than by individuals, and many institutions are restricted to investment-grade securities. Thus, if a firm's bonds fall below BBB, it will have a difficult time selling new bonds because many potential purchasers will not be allowed to buy them. Second, many bond covenants stipulate that the coupon rate on the bond automatically increases if the rating falls below a specified level. Third, because a bond's rating is an indicator of its default risk, the rating has a direct, measurable influence on the bond's yield. Column (9) of Table 6-1 shows that a AAA bond has a yield of 1.6% and that yields increase as the rating falls. In fact, an investor will earn 13.5% on a CCC bond if it doesn't default!

A *bond spread* is the difference between a bond's yield and the yield on some other security of the same maturity. Unless specified differently, the term "spread" generally means the difference between a bond's yield and the yield on a Government of Canada bond of similar maturity.

Figure 6-3 shows the spread between a 5-year Government of Canada bond and an index of BBB-rated Canadian corporate bonds. Notice that the yield spread is always positive, that is, the riskier BBB bonds always pay a higher yield to investors as compensation for their extra risk. Also note that the spreads are not constant over time. For example, the spread was exceptionally low during the boom years of 2005 and 2006 but rose dramatically as the economy declined.

Also, spreads increase as maturity increases. This should make sense. If a bond matures soon, investors are able to forecast the company's performance fairly well. But if a bond has a long time until it matures, investors have a difficult time forecasting the likelihood that the company will fall into financial distress. This extra uncertainty creates additional risk, so investors demand a higher required return.

FIGURE 6-3   Bond Spreads, Canada AAA–BBB

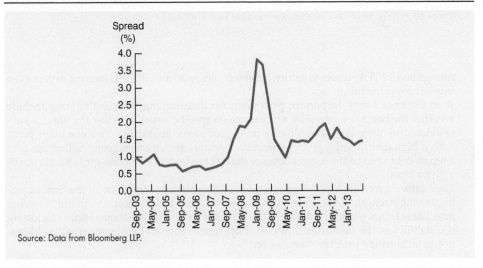

Source: Data from Bloomberg LLP.

CONCEPT REVIEW

1. Differentiate between mortgage bonds and debentures.
2. Name the major rating agencies, and list some factors that affect bond ratings.
3. What is a bond spread?
4. How do bond ratings affect the default risk premium?
5. A 10-year Government of Canada bond has a yield of 6%. A corporate bond with a rating of AA has a yield of 7.5%. If the corporate bond has excellent liquidity, what is an estimate of the corporate bond's default risk premium? (Check Figure: 1.5%)

Canadian Bond Investors Look for Better Protection

Foregoing their traditional silence, influential fixed-income investors are publicly lobbying for changes that would offer bond investors additional protection. Institutional bond market investors such as Canso Investment Counsel and Manulife Financial came together to create the Canadian Bond Investors' Association (CBIA), which advocates for the interest of bondholders. The basis for their concerns is the fact that while bondholders have a contractual relationship with corporate borrowers, shareholders control the votes on important manners. Bondholders have no such voice.

The CBIA has come out with a policy document arguing for changes to be made to debt covenants within a bond contract—the indenture. Debt covenants are rules that restrict what a company can do after it has issued bonds. The first concern relates to a "change of control" or a switch in company ownership. Currently, companies can have multiple bonds that come with different rules on how they will be treated in an ownership change. For example, Safeway, Inc., the giant U.S. grocery chain that was the target of a $9 billion buyout, had a number of bonds outstanding, and each had different change-of-control provisions. Some bondholders were allowed to sell their bonds back to the acquirer, Cerebus, for full value, while others could not.

Bond investors are also asking for what is known as a "coupon step-up" should the bonds' credit rating be downgraded for unusual reasons. For instance, this clause could be triggered if a company decides to borrow money to pay a special dividend to shareholders, and loses its investment-grade rating for putting its balance sheet at greater risk—a move that benefits shareholders but punishes debtholders. Such a downgrade is common. In 2010, Tim Hortons Inc. issued its very first series of bonds, rated A (low) by DBRS. Three years later, Tim Hortons management announced plans to borrow money to fund a share buyback, which resulted in a ratings downgrade to BBB, almost pushing the company out of investment-grade status. To address this inequity, bond investors want issuers to be required to increase their coupon payments by a preset amount—it could be 1 or 2 percent—in similar situations in the future, but only if a company loses its investment-grade rating.

While fixed-income investors aren't expecting quick changes, they do plan to meet with issuers, investment banks, lawyers, and regulators to start the discussion. Their hope is that over time some of these measures will be widely adopted.

Source: Adapted from Tim Kiladze, "Bond Investors Lobby for Reforms After Years of Frustration," *The Globe and Mail*, March 9, 2014.

6.12 The Liquidity Premium (LP)

A "liquid" asset can be converted to cash quickly and at a "fair market value." Financial assets are generally more liquid than real assets. Because liquidity is important, investors include **liquidity premiums (LPs)** when market rates of securities are established. Although it is difficult to accurately measure liquidity premiums, a differential of at least two and probably four or five percentage points exists between the least liquid and the most liquid financial assets of similar default risk and maturity. Corporate bonds issued by small companies are traded less frequently than those issued by large companies, so small company bonds tend to have a higher liquidity premium.[11]

CONCEPT REVIEW

1. Which bond usually will have a higher liquidity premium, one issued by a large company or one issued by a small company?

6.13 The Maturity Risk Premium (MRP)

All bonds, even Government of Canada bonds, are exposed to two additional sources of risk: interest rate risk and reinvestment risk. The net effect of these two sources of risk upon a

[11]For more on liquidity premium, see Long Chen, David A. Lesmond, and Jason Wei, "Corporate Yield Spreads and Bond Liquidity," *Journal of Finance* 62, no. 1 (2007), 119–49.

bond's yield is called the **maturity risk premium, MRP.** The following sections explain how interest rate risk and reinvestment risk affect a bond's yield.

Interest Rate Risk

For more on bond risk, including duration analysis, see **Web Extension 6B** at the textbook's website.

Interest rates go up and down over time, and an increase in interest rates leads to a decline in the value of outstanding bonds. This risk of a decline in bond values due to rising interest rates is called **interest rate risk.** To illustrate, suppose you bought some 10% MicroDrive bonds at a price of $1,000, and interest rates in the following year rose to 15%. As we saw earlier, the price of the bonds would fall to $713.78, so you would have a loss of $286.22 per bond.[12] Interest rates can and do rise, and rising rates cause a loss of value for bondholders. Thus, people or firms who invest in bonds are exposed to risk from changing interest rates.

One's exposure to interest rate risk is higher on bonds with long maturities than on those maturing in the near future.[13] This point can be demonstrated by showing how the value of a 1-year bond with a 10% annual coupon fluctuates with changes in r_d, and then comparing these changes with those on a 25-year bond. The 1-year bond's value for $r_d = 5\%$ is shown below:

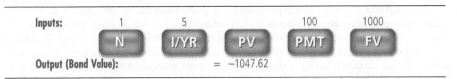

Inputs:	1	5		100	1000
	N	I/YR	PV	PMT	FV
Output (Bond Value):			= −1047.62		

Using either a calculator or a spreadsheet, you could calculate the bond values for a 1-year and 25-year bonds at several current market interest rates; these results are summarized and plotted in Figure 6-4. Note how much more sensitive the price of the 25-year bond is to changes in interest rates. At a 10% interest rate, both the 25-year and the 1-year bonds are valued at $1,000. When rates rise to 15%, the 25-year bond falls to $676.79, but the 1-year bond falls only to $956.52.

For bonds with similar coupons, this differential sensitivity to changes in interest rates always holds true—the longer the maturity of the bond, the more its price changes in response to a given change in interest rates. Thus, even if the risk of default on two bonds is exactly the same, the one with the longer maturity is exposed to more risk from a rise in interest rates.

The explanation for this difference in interest rate risk is simple. Suppose you bought a 25-year bond that yielded 10%, or $100 a year. Now suppose interest rates on comparable-risk bonds rose to 15%. You would be stuck with only $100 of interest for the next 25 years. On the other hand, had you bought a 1-year bond, you would have a low return for only 1 year. At the end of the year, you would get your $1,000 back, and you could then reinvest it and receive a 15% return ($150) for the next year. Thus, interest rate risk reflects the length of time one is committed to a given investment.

Reinvestment Rate Risk

As we saw in the preceding section, an *increase* in interest rates will hurt bondholders because it will lead to a decline in the value of a bond portfolio. But can a *decrease* in interest rates also hurt bondholders? The answer is yes, because if interest rates fall, a bondholder will probably suffer a reduction in his or her income. For example, consider a retiree who has a portfolio of bonds and lives off the income they produce. The bonds, on average, have a coupon rate of 10%. Now suppose interest rates decline to 5%. Many of the bonds will be called, and as calls occur, the bondholder will have to replace 10% bonds with 5% bonds. Even bonds that are not callable will mature, and when they do,

---

[12]You would have an *accounting* (and tax) loss only if you sold the bond; if you held it to maturity, you would not have such a loss. However, even if you did not sell, you would still have suffered a *real economic loss in an opportunity cost sense* because you would have lost the opportunity to invest at 15% and would be stuck with a 10% bond in a 15% market. In an economic sense, "paper losses" are just as bad as realized accounting losses.

[13]Actually, a bond's maturity and coupon rate both affect interest rate risk. Low coupons mean that most of the bond's return will come from repayment of principal, whereas on a high coupon bond with the same maturity, more of the cash flows will come in during the early years due to the relatively large coupon payments. A measurement called "duration," which finds the average number of years the bond's PV of cash flows remains outstanding, has been developed to combine maturity and coupons. A zero coupon bond, which has no interest payments and whose payments all come at maturity, has a duration equal to the bond's maturity. Coupon bonds all have durations that are shorter than maturity, and the higher the coupon rate, the shorter the duration. Bonds with longer duration are exposed to more interest rate risk. *Excel's* DURATION function provides an easy way to calculate a bond's duration. See **Web Extension 6B** and **Ch 06 Tool Kit.xlsx** for more on duration.

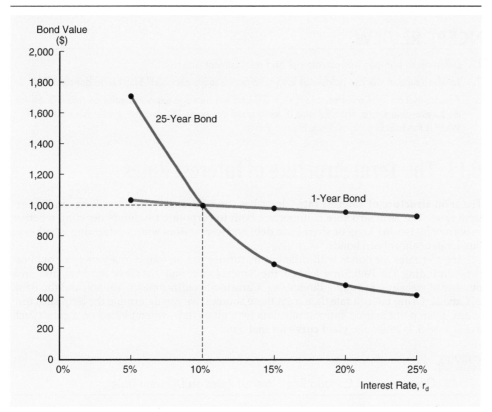

FIGURE 6-4 Value of Long- and Short-Term 10% Annual Coupon Bonds at Different Market Interest Rates

See *Ch 06 Tool Kit.xlsx* for all calculations.

they will have to be replaced with lower-yielding bonds. Thus, our retiree will suffer a reduction of income.

The risk of an income decline due to a drop in interest rates is called **reinvestment rate risk.** Reinvestment rate risk is obviously high on callable bonds. It is also high on short maturity bonds, because the shorter the maturity of a bond, the fewer the years when the relatively high old interest rate will be earned, and the sooner the funds will have to be reinvested at the new low rate. Thus, retirees whose primary holdings are short-term securities, such as bank GICs and short-term bonds, are hurt badly by a decline in rates, but holders of long-term bonds continue to enjoy their old high rates.

Comparing Interest Rate and Reinvestment Rate Risk: The Maturity Risk Premium

Note that interest rate risk relates to the *value* of the bonds in a portfolio, while reinvestment rate risk relates to the *income* the portfolio produces. If you hold long-term bonds, you will face a lot of interest rate risk because the value of your bonds will decline if interest rates rise, but you will not face much reinvestment rate risk, so your income will be stable. On the other hand, if you hold short-term bonds, you will not be exposed to much interest rate risk because the value of your portfolio will be stable, but you will be exposed to considerable reinvestment rate risk because your income will fluctuate with changes in interest rates. We see, then, that no fixed-rate bond can be considered totally riskless—even most Government of Canada bonds are exposed to both interest rate and reinvestment rate risk.[14]

Bond prices reflect the trading activities of the marginal investors, defined as those who trade often enough and with large enough sums to determine bond prices. Although one particular investor might be more averse to reinvestment risk than to interest rate risk, the data suggest that the marginal investor is more averse to interest rate risk than to reinvestment risk.

[14]Note, though, that real return bonds are almost riskless, but they pay a relatively low real rate. Also, risks have not disappeared—they are simply transferred from bondholders to taxpayers.

To induce the marginal investor to take on interest rate risk, long-term bonds must have a higher expected rate of return than short-term bonds. Holding all else equal, this additional return is the maturity risk premium (MRP).

CONCEPT REVIEW

1. Differentiate between interest rate risk and reinvestment rate risk.

2. To which type of risk are holders of long-term bonds more exposed? Short-term bondholders?

3. Assume that the real risk-free rate is $r^* = 3\%$ and the average expected inflation rate is 2.5% for the foreseeable future. The DRP and LP for a bond are each 1%, and the applicable MRP is 2%. What is the bond's yield? (Check Figure: 9.5%)

6.14 The Term Structure of Interest Rates

The **term structure of interest rates** describes the relationship between long- and short-term rates. The term structure is important both to corporate treasurers deciding whether to borrow by issuing long- or short-term debt and to investors who are deciding whether to buy long- or short-term bonds.

Interest rates for bonds with different maturities can be found in a variety of publications, including *The Wall Street Journal*, the *National Post*, and *The Globe and Mail*, and on a number of websites, including Bloomberg, CanadianFixedIncome.ca, Yahoo!, and the Bank of Canada. Using interest rate data from these sources, we can determine the term structure at any given point in time. Interest rate data for a given date, when plotted on a graph such as Figure 6-5, is called the **yield curve** for that date.

FIGURE
6-5   Government of Canada Bond Interest Rates on Different Dates

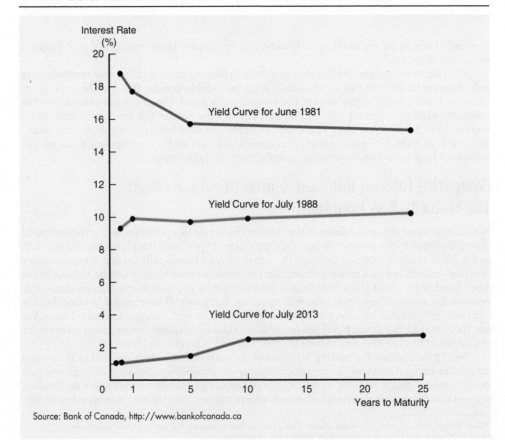

Source: Bank of Canada, http://www.bankofcanada.ca

As the figure shows, the yield curve changes both in position and in slope over time. In June 1981, all rates were quite high because high inflation was expected. However, the rate of inflation was expected to decline, so the inflation premium (IP) was larger for short-term bonds than for long-term bonds. This caused short-term yields to be higher than long-term yields, resulting in a *downward-sloping* yield curve. By July 1988, inflation had indeed declined and thus all rates were lower. The yield curve had become *flat*—short-, medium-, and long-term rates were almost the same. By July 2013, all rates had fallen below the 1988 levels, and because short-term rates had dropped below long-term rates, the yield curve was *upward sloping.*

Historically, long-term rates are generally above short-term rates because of the maturity risk premium, so the yield curve usually slopes upward. For this reason, people often call an upward-sloping yield curve a **"normal" yield curve** and a yield curve that slopes downward an **inverted, or "abnormal," curve.** Thus, in Figure 6-5 the yield curve for June 1981 was inverted, while for July 1988 and July 2013 the yield curves were flat and normal, respectively.

See *Ch 06 Tool Kit.xlsx* for all calculations.

A few academics and practitioners contend that large bond traders who buy and sell securities of different maturities each day dominate the market. According to this view, a bond trader is just as willing to buy a 30-year bond to pick up a short-term profit as to buy a 3-month security. Strict proponents of this view argue that the shape of the yield curve is therefore determined only by market expectations about future interest rates, a position that is called the **pure expectations theory,** or sometimes just the expectations theory. If this were true, then the maturity risk premium (MRP) would be zero, and long-term interest rates would simply be a weighted average of current and expected future short-term interest rates. See *Web Extension 6C* for a more detailed discussion of the expectations theory.

Go to the textbook's website for a discussion of the expectations theory in *Web Extension 6C.*

⃝NCEPT REVIEW

1. What is a yield curve, and what information would you need to draw this curve?

2. Distinguish among the shapes of a "normal" yield curve, an "abnormal" curve, and a "flat" curve.

3. If the interest rates on 1-, 5-, 20-, and 30-year bonds are 4%, 5%, 6%, and 7%, respectively, how would you describe the yield curve? If the rates were reversed, how would you describe it?

6.15 Junk Bonds

Recall that bonds rated less than BBB are noninvestment-grade debt, also called junk bonds or high-yield debt. These bonds are issued by companies with a high credit risk. Since junk bond investors are more likely to miss interest payments or return of their principal, issuing companies must pay high coupon rates to compensate investors for the added default risk. Junk bonds are used to finance distressed firms or as a method for financing leveraged buyouts. Another type of junk bond is one that was originally highly rated when issued, but whose rating has declined because the issuing corporation has fallen on hard times. These bonds are known as "fallen angels."

A study by Moody's estimated that average cumulative bond default rates over a 5-year period ranged from 1% for investment-grade bonds to 23% for junk bonds.[15] Looking at these figures, it should come as no surprise that many institutional bond funds have policies prohibiting investing in bonds related below A. While junk bonds are indeed risky, their default rates can vary significantly over the economic cycle. The large default variability combined with an appropriate risk-adjusted return creates the possibility for attractive returns. As a result, there are portfolio managers who specialize in junk bond investing. In addition, many major mutual fund companies such as AGF and RBC Global Asset Management manage high-yield funds on behalf of investors. Although the Canadian market has some notable junk bond names such as Air Canada, Bombardier, and Quebecor Media, that market is small—less than 4% of the comparable U.S. market.

⃝NCEPT REVIEW

1. What are junk bonds?

---

[15]"Default and Recovery Rates of Canadian Corporate Issuers, 1989–2009," Moody's Investors Services, April 2010, http://www.moodys.com, accessed December 2, 2010.

6.16 Bankruptcy and Reorganization

In recent times some well-known Canadian companies, including Nortel, Abitibi Bowater, and Canwest, filed for bankruptcy protection. The total assets of these companies, prior to filing for bankruptcy, were about $23 billion. A brief discussion of insolvency and bankruptcy follows.

When a business becomes *insolvent*, it does not have the ability to meet its financial obligations. Bankruptcy law in Canada provides insolvent companies with two options: dissolve through *liquidation*, or *reorganize* and stay alive. The decision to force a firm to liquidate rather than reorganize depends on whether the value of the reorganized firm is likely to be greater than the value of the firm's assets if they were sold off piecemeal. Two acts address bankruptcy and reorganization in Canada: the Bankruptcy and Insolvency Act (BIA) and the **Companies' Creditors Arrangements Act (CCAA)**. The CCAA is used when a company has liabilities exceeding $5 million.

A company may file for a *voluntary assignment in bankruptcy,* or a creditor may go to court to force it into bankruptcy through a *bankruptcy order*. On the assignment or order, the court appoints a *trustee in bankruptcy* whose role is to administer the process, manage, sell, and distribute any funds to the creditors. The alternative to bankruptcy is for the insolvent company to make a proposal to creditors for some mutually agreed upon alternative payment. Typically the company will offer to pay somewhat less to its creditors than what is actually owed, or payment will be made over a longer period. Before you think that creditors will reject such proposals out of hand, creditors may have good reasons to accept less than what they are actually owed. If the insolvent company is indeed economically viable, it may be worth keeping the company alive and as a customer. In addition, creditors may often receive more money through a proposal than through bankruptcy. One Canadian survey found that over 75% of unsecured creditors received no payment at all in bankruptcies. Besides that, administration costs, of which trustee fees are a large part, accounted on average for 44% of an insolvent company's asset value.[16] Proposals can be made informally outside the BIA or CCAA, but if they fail, the acts also provide a formal process for reaching settlements with creditors. The BIA sets procedures and time limits that the insolvent company must follow. The company must also work with an appointed trustee. Once the company comes up with a proposal, it is taken by the trustee to all the unsecured creditors, who will vote on whether to accept or reject it. The proposal will be accepted if at least 50% of the creditors representing at least two-thirds of what is owed vote in its favour. If the proposal is accepted, it is binding on all unsecured creditors. If either fewer than half the creditors, or creditors holding less than two-thirds of what is owed, vote in favour, the proposal is rejected and automatic bankruptcy occurs.[17]

If bankruptcy does occur, the trustee will sell off the assets and distribute the cash obtained as specified in the *BIA*. Here is a general priority of claims:[18]

- Those of suppliers, who can repossess goods delivered within 30-days prior to bankruptcy
- Costs for environmental damage
- Trustee expenses
- Unremitted payroll taxes and deductions
- Unpaid wages, up to $2,000 per worker
- Those of secured creditors whose loans are secured by some specific asset, mortgage, lien, etc.
- Bankruptcy administration costs
- Municipal taxes
- Those for rent, up to 3 months prior to bankruptcy
- Those of creditors who first filed claims
- Injury claim costs to employees not covered under Workers' Compensation
- Other unsecured creditors
- Preferred shareholders
- Common shareholders

CONCEPT REVIEW

1. When should a firm be reorganized rather than forced into bankruptcy and liquidated?

---

[16]Jocelyn Martel, "Commercial Bankruptcy and Financial Reorganization in Canada," *CIRANO* 94c-2, September 1994 p.12.
[17]The CCAA offers more flexibility than the BIA and is thus favoured by larger companies. The Companies' Creditors Arrangements Act allows greater protection from secured and unsecured creditors while the insolvent company restructures itself.
[18]Industry Canada, http://strategis.ic.gc.ca, accessed June 24, 2008.

Summary

This chapter described the different types of bonds that governments and corporations issue, explained how bond prices are established, and discussed how investors estimate the rates of return they can expect to earn. The rate of return required by debtholders is the company's pre-tax cost of debt, and this rate depends on the risk that investors face when they buy bonds.

- A **bond** is a long-term promissory note issued by a business or governmental unit. The issuer receives money in exchange for promising to make interest payments and to repay the principal on a specified future date.
- Some recent innovations in long-term financing include **zero coupon bonds,** which pay no annual interest, but sell at a discount; **floating-rate debt,** whose interest payments fluctuate with changes in the general level of interest rates; and **junk bonds,** which are high-risk, high-yield instruments issued by firms that use a great deal of financial leverage.
- A **call provision** gives the issuing corporation the right to redeem the bonds prior to maturity under specified terms, usually at a price greater than the maturity value (the difference is a **call premium**). A firm will typically call a bond if interest rates fall substantially below the coupon rate.
- A **retractable bond** gives the investor the right to sell the bond back to the issuing company at a previously specified price. This is a useful feature (for investors) if interest rates rise or if the company engages in unanticipated risky activities.
- A **sinking fund** is a provision that requires the corporation to retire a portion of the bond issue each year. The purpose of the sinking fund is to provide for the orderly retirement of the issue. A sinking fund typically requires no call premium.
- There are many different types of bonds with different sets of features. These include **convertible bonds, bonds with warrants, income bonds, real return bonds, mortgage bonds, debentures, subordinated debentures, agency bonds,** and **junk bonds.** The return required on each type of bond is determined by the bond's riskiness.
- The *value of a bond* is found as the present value of an **annuity** (the interest payments) plus the present value of a lump sum (the **principal**). The bond is evaluated at the appropriate periodic interest rate over the number of periods for which interest payments are made.
- The equation used to find the value of an annual coupon bond is

$$V_B = \sum_{t=1}^{N} \frac{INT}{(1 + r_d)^t} + \frac{M}{(1 + r_d)^N}$$

- An adjustment to the formula must be made if the bond pays interest **semiannually***:* divide INT and r_d by 2, and multiply N by 2.
- The return earned on a bond held to maturity is defined as the bond's **yield to maturity (YTM).** If the bond can be redeemed before maturity, it is **callable,** and the return investors receive if it is called is defined as the *yield to call (YTC).* The YTC is found as the present value of the interest payments received while the bond is outstanding plus the present value of the call price (the par value plus a call premium).
- The **nominal** (or **quoted**) **interest rate** on a debt security, r_d, is composed of the real risk-free rate, r*, plus premiums that reflect inflation (IP), default risk (DRP), liquidity (LP), and maturity risk (MRP):

$$r_d = r^* + IP + DRP + LP + MRP$$

- The **risk-free rate of interest, r_{RF},** is defined as the real risk-free rate, r*, plus an inflation premium, IP: $r_{RF} = r^* + IP$.
- **Real return bonds** are Government of Canada bonds with no inflation risks. *Web Extension 6A* discusses real return bonds.
- The longer the maturity of a bond, the more its price will change in response to a given change in interest rates; this is called **interest rate risk.** However, bonds with short maturities expose investors to high **reinvestment rate risk,** which is the risk that income from a bond portfolio will decline because cash flows received from bonds will be rolled over at lower interest rates.
- **Duration** is a measure of interest rate risk. See *Web Extension 6B* for a discussion on duration.

- Corporate bonds have **default risk.** If an issuer defaults, investors receive less than the promised return on the bond. Therefore, investors should evaluate a bond's default risk before making a purchase.
- Bonds are assigned **ratings** that reflect the probability of their going into default. The highest rating is AAA, and they go down to D. The higher a bond's rating, the lower its risk and therefore its interest rate.
- The relationship between the yields on securities and the securities' maturities is known as the **term structure of interest rates,** and the **yield curve** is a graph of this relationship.
- The shape of the yield curve depends on two key factors: (1) *expectations about future inflation* and (2) *perceptions about the relative risk of securities with different maturities.*
- The yield curve is normally *upward sloping*—this is called a *normal yield curve*. However, the curve can slope downward (an *inverted yield curve*) if the inflation rate is expected to decline. The yield curve also can be *flat*, which means that interest rates on short-, medium-, and long-term maturities are the same.
- The *expectations theory* states that yields on long-term bonds reflect expected future interest rates. **Web Extension 6C** discusses this theory.

Questions

6-1 Define each of the following terms:
  a. Bond; Government of Canada bond; corporate bond; foreign bond
  b. Par value; maturity date; coupon payment; coupon interest rate
  c. Floating-rate bond; zero coupon bond
  d. Call provision; retractable bond; sinking fund
  e. Convertible bond; warrant; income bond; real return bond
  f. Premium bond; discount bond
  g. Current yield (on a bond); yield to maturity (YTM); yield to call (YTC)
  h. Reinvestment risk; interest rate risk; default risk
  i. Indentures; mortgage bond; debenture; subordinated debenture
  j. Agency bond; junk bond; investment-grade bond
  k. Real risk-free rate of interest, r*; nominal risk-free rate of interest, r_{RF}
  l. Inflation premium (IP); default risk premium (DRP); liquidity; liquidity premium (LP)
  m. Interest rate risk; maturity risk premium (MRP); reinvestment rate risk
  n. Term structure of interest rates; yield curve
  o. "Normal" yield curve; inverted ("abnormal") yield curve

6-2 "The values of outstanding bonds change whenever the going rate of interest changes. In general, short-term interest rates are more volatile than long-term interest rates. Therefore, short-term bond prices are more sensitive to interest rate changes than are long-term bond prices." Is this statement true or false? Explain.

6-3 The rate of return you would get if you bought a bond and held it to its maturity date is called the bond's yield to maturity. If interest rates in the economy rise after a bond has been issued, what will happen to the bond's price and to its YTM? Does the length of time to maturity affect the extent to which a given change in interest rates will affect the bond's price?

6-4 If you buy a *callable* bond and interest rates decline, will the value of your bond rise by as much as it would have risen if the bond had not been callable? Explain.

6-5 A sinking fund can be set up in one of two ways. Discuss the advantages and disadvantages of each procedure from the viewpoint of both the firm and its bondholders.

Concept Review Problem

Full solutions are provided at www.nelson.com/brigham3ce.

CR-1
Bond Valuation
The Pennington Corporation issued a new series of bonds on January 1, 1991. The bonds were sold at par ($1,000), had a 12% coupon, and matured in 30 years, on December 31, 2020. Coupon payments are made semiannually (on June 30 and December 31).

a.   What was the YTM on January 1, 1991?

b.   What was the price of the bonds on January 1, 1996, 5 years later, assuming that interest rates had fallen to 10%?

c.   Find the current yield, capital gains yield, and total return on January 1, 1992, given the price as determined in part b.

d.   On July 1, 2014, $6\frac{1}{2}$ years before maturity, Pennington's bonds sold for $916.42. What were the YTM, the current yield, and the capital gains yield?

e.   Now, assume that you plan to purchase an outstanding Pennington bond on March 1, 2014, when the going rate of interest given its risk is 15.5%. How large a cheque must you write to complete the transaction?

Problems

Easy
Problems 1–6

Answers to odd-numbered problems appear in Appendix A.

6-1
Bond Valuation with Annual Payments

Jackson Corporation's bonds have 12 years remaining to maturity. Interest is paid annually, the bonds have a $1,000 par value, and the coupon interest rate is 8%. The bonds have a yield to maturity of 9%. What is the current market price of these bonds?

6-2
Yield to Maturity for Annual Payments

Temex bonds have 7 years remaining to maturity. Interest is paid annually, the bonds have a $1,000 par value, and the coupon interest rate is 8%. The bonds sell at a price of $930. What is their yield to maturity?

6-3
Current Yield for Annual Payments

Cold Stone's bonds have 12 years remaining to maturity. The bonds have a face value of $1,000 and a yield to maturity of 8%. They pay interest annually and have a 6% coupon rate. What is their current yield?

6-4
Determinant of Interest Rates

The real risk-free rate of interest is 4%. Inflation is expected to be 2% this year and 4% during the next 2 years. Assume that the maturity risk premium is zero. What is the yield on 2-year government securities? What is the yield on 3-year government securities?

6-5
Default Risk Premium

A government bond that matures in 10 years has a yield of 6%. A 10-year corporate bond has a yield of 9%. Assume that the liquidity premium on the corporate bond is 0.5%. What is the default risk premium on the corporate bond?

6-6
Maturity Risk Premium

The real risk-free rate is 2%, and inflation is expected to be 2.5% for the next 2 years. A 2-year government security yields 4.9%. What is the maturity risk premium for the 2-year security?

Intermediate
Problems 7–22

6-7
Bond Valuation with Semiannual Payments

Flipflop Footwear has issued bonds that have a 10% coupon rate, payable semiannually. The bonds mature in 6 years and have a face value of $1,000 and a yield to maturity of 5%. What is the price of the bonds?

6-8
Yield to Maturity and Call with Semiannual Payments

Digicomp's bonds will mature in 8 years. The bonds have a face value of $1,000 and a 7% coupon rate, paid semiannually. The price of the bonds is $1,110. The bonds are callable in 3 years at a call price of $1,050. What is their yield to maturity? What is their yield to call?

6-9
Zero Coupon Bond Valuation and Maturity Dates

Anthony has a choice of one of two bonds to purchase: a 5-year, $1,000 face value bond with 6% coupons, paid semiannually, or a 5-year, $1,000 face value zero coupon. Both have a yield to maturity of 5.5%.

a.   How much will each bond cost?

b.   How much would Anthony pay for similar bonds, assuming a flat yield curve, if they were available in maturity dates of 10 years? 15 years?

c.   Explain why the zero coupon bond prices change more than the regular bonds.

6-10
Yield to Maturity and Required Returns

The Brownstone Corporation bonds have 10 years remaining to maturity. Interest is paid annually; the bonds have a $1,000 par value; and the coupon interest rate is 9%.

a.   What is the yield to maturity at a current market price of (1) $875 or (2) $1,080?

b.   Would you pay $875 for one of these bonds if you thought that the appropriate rate of interest was 10%—that is, if r_d = 10%? Explain your answer.

6-11
Yield to Call and Realized Rates of Return

Four years ago, Guard Co. sold a 20-year bond issue with a 7% annual coupon rate and a 9% call premium. Today, Guard Co. called the bonds. The bonds originally were sold at their face value of $1,000. Compute the realized rate of return for investors who purchased the bonds when they were issued and who surrender them today in exchange for the call price.

6-12

Bond Yields and
Rates of Return

A 10-year, 12% semiannual coupon bond with a par value of $1,000 may be called in 4 years at a call price of $1,060. The bond sells for $1,100. (Assume that the bond has just been issued.)
a.   What is the bond's yield to maturity?
b.   What is the bond's current yield?
c.   What is the bond's capital gain or loss yield?
d.   What is the bond's yield to call?

6-13

Yield to Maturity
and Current Yield

You just purchased a bond that matures in 12 years. The bond has a face value of $1,000 and has an 6% annual coupon. The bond has a current yield of 6.4%. What is the bond's yield to maturity?

6-14

Current Yield with
Semiannual Payments

A bond that matures in 6 years sells for $1,090. The bond has a face value of $1,000 and a yield to maturity of 5.2328%. The bond pays coupons semiannually. What is the bond's current yield?

6-15

Yield to Call,
Yield to Maturity,
and Market Rates

Waterman's 14% coupon rate, semiannual payment, $1,000 par value bonds that mature in 22 years are callable 4 years from now at a price of $1,090. The bonds sell at a price of $1,410 and the yield curve is flat. Assuming that interest rates in the economy are expected to remain at their current level, what is the best estimate of the nominal interest rate on new bonds?

6-16

Interest Rate
Sensitivity

A bond trader purchased each of the following bonds at a yield to maturity of 9%. Immediately after she purchased the bonds, interest rates fell to 8%. What is the percentage change in the price of each bond after the decline in interest rates? Fill in the following table: (Assume semiannual compounding.)

	Price @ 9%	Price @ 8%	Percentage Change
10-year, 10% coupon	_____	_____	_____
10-year zero	_____	_____	_____
20-year zero	_____	_____	_____

6-17

Bond Value as
Maturity Approaches

An investor has two bonds in his portfolio. Each bond matures in 4 years, has a face value of $1,000, and has a yield to maturity equal to 6.5%. One bond, Bond C, has a 10% coupon (paid semiannually); the other bond, Bond Z, is a zero coupon bond. Assuming that the yield to maturity of each bond remains at 6.5% over the next 4 years, what will be the price of each of the bonds at the following time periods? Fill in the following table: (Assume semiannual compounding.)

t	Price of Bond C	Price of Bond Z
0	_____	_____
1	_____	_____
2	_____	_____
3	_____	_____
4	_____	_____

6-18

Determinants of
Interest Rates

The real risk-free rate is 2%. Inflation is expected to be 3% this year, 4% next year, and 3.5% thereafter. The maturity risk premium is estimated to be $0.0005 \times (t - 1)$, where t = number of years to maturity. What is the nominal interest rate on a 7-year government security? (*Hint:* Average the expected inflation rates to determine the inflation premium, IP.)

6-19

Maturity Risk
Premiums

Assume that the real risk-free rate, r*, is 3% and that inflation is expected to be 8% in Year 1, 5% in Year 2, and 4% thereafter. Assume also that all government securities are highly liquid and free of default risk. If 2-year and 5-year government bonds both yield 10%, what is the difference in the maturity risk premiums (MRPs) on the two notes; that is, what is MRP_5 minus MRP_2?

6-20

Capital Gain/Loss

Faber Overdrive Autoparts issued at par value a 15-year 6% semiannual coupon bond, face value $1,000. At the end of 2 years the market yield increased to 7%. One year later, the market yield was 8%. If you purchased the bond at the end of Year 2 and sold it one year later, how much was your capital gain or loss?

6-21
Zero Coupon Bond

Castle Company's pension fund projected that a significant number of its employees would take advantage of a retirement program the company plans to offer in 10 years. Anticipating the need to fund these pensions, the firm bought zero coupon Government of Canada bonds maturing in 10 years. When these instruments were originally issued, they were 6% semi-annual 30-year bonds. The stripped bonds are currently priced to yield 3.75%. Their total maturity value is $18,000,000. What is their total cost (price) to Castle today?

6-22
Bond Valuation

Bond X is noncallable, has 20 years to maturity, a 9% annual coupon, and a $1,000 par value. Your required return on Bond X is 10%, and if you buy it you plan to hold it for 5 years. You, and the market, have expectations that in 5 years the yield to maturity on a 15-year bond with similar risk will be 8.5%. How much should you be willing to pay for Bond X today?

**Challenging
Problems 23–26**

6-23
Bond Valuation

Maritime Construction needs to borrow $50 million for 5 years. The company estimates that the real rate of return is currently 2%, expected inflation per annum for the period is 3%, and the risk premium on its bonds is 2.5%. The nominal risk-free rate is currently 5%. The company has three financing options:
1.   5-year, 7% coupon rate bonds (paid annually);
2.   5-year zero coupon bonds; (annual compounding);
3.   5-year variable rate bonds (paid annually) at a coupon rate of LIBOR + 1.5%. Forecasted LIBOR rates are shown below. The variable rate bonds will be issued at par.

Year	LIBOR
1	3%
2	4%
3	4.5%
4	5%
5	5%

a.   What is the face value of the bonds (i.e., the total dollar amount of bonds) that need to be issued under the three options?
b.   What is the YTM on the variable rate bonds, assuming the above LIBOR rates?
c.   Why is the required rate of return different on the floating rate bonds than on both the fixed-rate bonds?
d.   Briefly describe the benefits and drawbacks of issuing each type of security from the company treasurer's perspective.

6-24
Bond Valuation and Changes in Maturity and Required Returns

Suppose Level 10 Systems sold an issue of bonds with a 15-year maturity, a $1,000 par value, a 6% coupon rate, and semiannual interest payments.
a.   Six years after the bonds were issued, the going rate of interest on bonds such as these fell to 5%. At what price would the bonds sell?
b.   Suppose that, 6 years after the initial offering, the going interest rate had risen to 8%. At what price would the bonds sell?
c.   Suppose that the conditions in part a existed—that is, interest rates fell to 5% 6 years after the issue date. Suppose further that the interest rate remained at 5% for the next 9 years. What would happen to the price of the bonds over time?

6-25
Yield to Maturity and Yield to Call

Arnot International's bonds have a current market price of $1,150. The bonds have a 7% annual coupon payment, a $1,000 face value, and 10 years left until maturity. The bonds may be called in 5 years at 107% of face value (call price = $1,070).
a.   What is the yield to maturity?
b.   What is the yield to call, if they are called in 5 years?
c.   Which yield might investors expect to earn on these bonds, and why?
d.   The bond's indenture indicates that the call provision gives the firm the right to call them at the end of each year beginning in Year 5. In Year 5, they may be called at 107% of face value, but in each of the next 4 years the call percentage will decline by 1 percentage point. Thus, in Year 6 they may be called at 106% of face value, in Year 7 they may be called at 105% of face value, and so on. If the yield curve is horizontal and interest rates remain at their current level, when is the latest that investors might expect the firm to call the bonds?

6-26 Suppose that you and most other investors expect the inflation rate to be 7% next year, to fall
Determinants of to 5% during the following year, and then to remain at a rate of 3% thereafter. Assume that
Interest Rates the real risk-free rate, r*, will remain at 2% and that maturity risk premiums on government
securities rise from zero on very short-term securities (those that mature in a few days) to
a level of 0.2 percentage point for 1-year securities. Furthermore, maturity risk premiums
increase 0.2 percentage point for each year to maturity, up to a limit of 1.0 percentage point
on 5-year or longer-term bonds.

a. Calculate the interest rate on 1-, 2-, 3-, 4-, 5-, 10-, and 20-year Treasury securities, and
plot the yield curve.

b. Now suppose Royal Bank bonds, rated A, have the same maturities as the government
bonds. As an approximation, plot a Royal Bank yield curve on the same graph with the
Government of Canada bond yield curve. (*Hint:* Think about the default risk premium
on Royal Bank's long-term versus its short-term bonds.)

c. Now plot the approximate yield curve of Rogers Communications, a more risky cable
company.

 # Spreadsheet Problem

6-27 Start with the partial model in the file *Ch06 Build a Model.xlsx* on the textbook's website.
Build a Model: A 20-year, 8% semiannual coupon bond with a par value of $1,000 may be called in 5 years at
Bond Valuation a call price of $1,040. The bond sells for $1,100. (Assume that the bond has just been issued.)

a. What is the bond's yield to maturity?

b. What is the bond's current yield?

c. What is the bond's capital gain or loss yield?

d. What is the bond's yield to call?

e. How would the price of the bond be affected by a change in the going market interest
rates? (*Hint:* Conduct a sensitivity analysis of price to changes in the going market
interest rate for the bond. Assume that the bond will be called if and only if the going
rate of interest *falls below* the coupon rate. That is an oversimplification, but assume it
anyway for purposes of this problem.)

f. Now assume the date is October 25, 2013. Assume further that a 12%, 10-year bond was
issued on July 1, 2013, pays interest semiannually (on January 1 and July 1), and sells for
$1,100. Use your spreadsheet to find the bond's yield.

MINI CASE

Sam Strother and Shawna Tibbs are vice presidents of Great White North Investment
Management and co-directors of the company's Pension Fund Management Division. An
important new client has requested that Great White North present an investment seminar
to its executive committee. Strother and Tibbs, who will make the actual presentation, have
asked you to help them by answering the following questions:

a. What are the key features of a bond?

b. What are call provisions and sinking fund provisions? Do these provisions make bonds
more or less risky?

c. How is the value of any asset whose value is based on expected future cash flows
determined?

d. How is the value of a bond determined? What is the value of a 10-year, $1,000 par value
bond with a 10% annual coupon if its required rate of return is 10%?

e. (1) What would be the value of the bond described in part d if, just after it had been
issued, the expected inflation rate rose by 3 percentage points, causing investors to
require a 13% return? Would we now have a discount or a premium bond?

(2) What would happen to the bond's value if inflation fell and r_d declined to 7%?
Would we now have a premium or a discount bond?

(3) What would happen to the value of the 10-year bond over time if the required rate
of return remained at 13%, or if it remained at 7%? (*Hint:* With a financial calculator,
enter PMT, I/YR, FV, and N, and then change [override] N to see what happens to
the PV as the bond approaches maturity.)

f. (1) What is the yield to maturity on a 10-year, 9%, annual coupon, $1,000 par value bond that sells for $887.00? That sells for $1,134.20? What does the fact that a bond sells at a discount or at a premium tell you about the relationship between r_d and the bond's coupon rate?

　　(2) What are the total return, the current yield, and the capital gains yield for the discount bond? (Assume that the bond is held to maturity and the company does not default on the bond.)

g. How does the equation for valuing a bond change if semiannual payments are made? Find the value of a 10-year, semiannual payment, 10% coupon bond if nominal $r_d = 13\%$.

h. Suppose a 10-year, 10%, semiannual coupon bond with a par value of $1,000 is currently selling for $1,135.90, producing a nominal yield to maturity of 8%. However, the bond can be called after 5 years for a price of $1,050.

　　(1) What is the bond's *nominal yield to call (YTC)?*

　　(2) If you bought this bond, do you think you would be more likely to earn the YTM or the YTC? Why?

i. Write a general expression for the yield on any debt security (r_d) and define these terms: real risk-free rate of interest (r^*), inflation premium (IP), default risk premium (DRP), liquidity premium (LP), and maturity risk premium (MRP).

j. Define the nominal risk-free rate (r_{RF}). What security can be used as an estimate of r_{RF}?

k. What is a bond spread and how is it related to the default risk premium? How are bond ratings related to default risk? What factors affect a company's bond rating?

l. What is *interest rate (or price) risk?* Which bond has more interest rate risk, an annual payment 1-year bond or a 10-year bond? Why?

m. What is *reinvestment rate risk?* Which has more reinvestment rate risk, a 1-year bond or a 10-year bond?

n. How are interest rate risk and reinvestment rate risk related to the maturity risk premium?

o. What is the term structure of interest rates? What is a yield curve?

p. At any given time, how would the yield curve facing an AA-rated company compare with the yield curve for Government of Canada bonds? At any given time, how would the yield curve facing a BB-rated company compare with the yield curve for Government of Canada bonds?

q. Briefly describe bankruptcy law. If a firm were to default on the bonds, would the company be immediately liquidated? Would the bondholders be assured of receiving all of their promised payments?

chapter 7

Risk, Return, and the Capital Asset Pricing Model

What a difference a year makes! At the beginning of 2013, many investors purchased shares in the Toronto Stock Exchange–traded companies Mitel Networks and Labrador Iron Mines. But by year-end, Mitel had gone up by 248% while Labrador Iron Mines had fallen by 79%. Big gains and losses weren't limited to small companies by any means. Investors in Air Canada were flying high with a 323% gain for the year. At the other extreme, construction materials company Armtec stock went down by 45%.

Did investors in Labrador Iron Mines and Armtec make bad decisions? Before you answer, suppose you were making the decision back in January 2013, with the information available then. You now know the decision's *outcome* was poor, but that doesn't mean the decision itself was badly made. Investors probably knew these stocks were risky, with a chance of gain or loss. However, given the information available to them, they invested with the expectation of a gain. What about the investors in Mitel and Air Canada? They also realized the stock prices could go down or up, but were probably pleasantly surprised that the stocks went up so much.

These examples show that what you expect to happen and what actually happens are often very different—the world is risky! Therefore, it is vital that you understand risk and the ways to manage it. As you read this chapter and think about risk, keep the examples of Air Canada and Armtec in mind.

In this chapter, we start from the basic premise that investors like returns and dislike risk. Therefore, people will invest in riskier assets only if they expect to receive higher returns. We define precisely what the term "*risk*" means as it relates to investments. We examine procedures managers use to measure risk, and we discuss the relationship between risk and return. In later chapters we extend these relationships to show how risk and return interact to determine security prices. Managers must understand and apply these concepts as they plan the actions that will shape their firms' future.

The textbook's website contains an *Excel* file that will guide you through the chapter's calculations. The file for this chapter is *Ch 07 Tool Kit.xlsx*, and we encourage you to open the file and follow along as you read the chapter. **www.nelson .com/brigham3ce**.

7.1 Investment Returns

With most investments, an individual or business spends money today with the expectation of earning even more money in the future. The concept of *return* provides investors with a convenient way to express the financial performance of an investment. To illustrate, suppose you buy 10 shares of a stock for $1,000. The stock pays no dividends, but at the end of one year, you sell the stock for $1,100. What is the return on your $1,000 investment?

One way to express an investment return is in *dollar terms*. The dollar return is simply the total dollars received from the investment less the amount invested:

$$\text{Dollar return} = \text{Amount received} - \text{Amount invested}$$
$$= \$1,100 - \$1,000$$
$$= \$100$$

If, at the end of the year, you sell the stock for only $900, your dollar return will be −$100.

Although expressing returns in dollars is easy, two problems arise: (1) To make a meaningful judgment about the return, you need to know the scale (size) of the investment; a $100 return on a $100 investment is a good return (assuming the investment is held for 1 year), but a $100 return on a $10,000 investment would be a poor return. (2) You also need to know the timing of the return; a $100 return on a $100 investment is a very good return if it occurs after one year, but the same dollar return after 20 years is not very good.

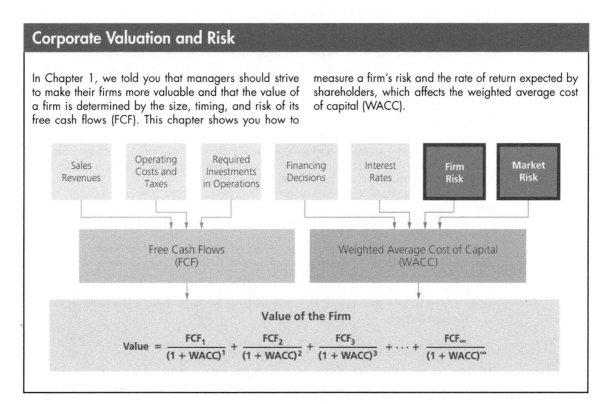

Corporate Valuation and Risk

In Chapter 1, we told you that managers should strive to make their firms more valuable and that the value of a firm is determined by the size, timing, and risk of its free cash flows (FCF). This chapter shows you how to measure a firm's risk and the rate of return expected by shareholders, which affects the weighted average cost of capital (WACC).

Sales Revenues — Operating Costs and Taxes — Required Investments in Operations — Financing Decisions — Interest Rates — **Firm Risk** — **Market Risk**

Free Cash Flows (FCF) — Weighted Average Cost of Capital (WACC)

Value of the Firm

$$\text{Value} = \frac{\text{FCF}_1}{(1 + \text{WACC})^1} + \frac{\text{FCF}_2}{(1 + \text{WACC})^2} + \frac{\text{FCF}_3}{(1 + \text{WACC})^3} + \cdots + \frac{\text{FCF}_\infty}{(1 + \text{WACC})^\infty}$$

The solution to the scale and timing problems is to express investment results as *rates of return*, or *percentage returns*. For example, the rate of return on the 1-year stock investment, when $1,100 is received after 1 year, is 10%:

$$\text{Rate of return} = \frac{\text{Amount received} - \text{Amount invested}}{\text{Amount invested}}$$

$$= \frac{\text{Dollar return}}{\text{Amount invested}} = \frac{\$100}{\$1,000}$$

$$= 0.10 = 10\%$$

The rate of return calculation "standardizes" the return by considering the annual return per unit of investment. Although this example has only one outflow and one inflow, the annualized rate of return can easily be calculated in situations where multiple cash flows occur over time by using time value of money concepts as discussed in Chapter 4.

CONCEPT REVIEW

1. Differentiate between dollar returns and rates of return.
2. Why are rates of return superior to dollar returns in terms of accounting for the size of investment and the timing of cash flows?
3. Suppose you pay $500 for an investment that returns $600 in 1 year. What is the annual rate of return? (Check Figure: 20%)

7.2 Stand-Alone Risk

Risk is defined in *Webster's* as "a hazard; a peril; exposure to loss or injury." Thus, risk refers to the chance that some unfavourable event will occur. If you go skydiving, you are taking a chance with your life—skydiving is risky. If you bet on the horses, you are risking your money. If you invest in speculative stocks (or, really, *any* stock), you are taking a risk in the hope of earning an appreciable return.

An asset's risk can be analyzed in two ways: (1) on a stand-alone basis, where the asset is considered in isolation, and (2) on a portfolio basis, where the asset is held as one of a number of assets in a portfolio. Thus, an asset's **stand-alone risk** is the risk an investor would face if he or she held only this one asset. Obviously, most assets are held in portfolios, but it is necessary to understand stand-alone risk in order to understand risk in a portfolio context.

To begin, suppose an investor buys $100,000 of short-term Treasury bills with an expected return of 5%. In this case, the rate of return on the investment, 5%, can be estimated quite precisely, and the investment is defined as being essentially *risk free*. However, if the $100,000 were invested in the stock of a company just being organized to prospect for oil in the mid-Atlantic, then the investment's return could not be estimated precisely. One might analyze the situation and conclude that the *expected* rate of return, in a statistical sense, is 20%, but the investor should recognize that the *actual* rate of return could range from, say, +1,000% to −100%. Because there is a significant danger of actually earning much less than the expected return, the stock would be relatively risky.

No investment should be undertaken unless the expected rate of return is high enough to compensate the investor for the perceived risk of the investment. In our example, it is clear that few if any investors would be willing to buy the oil company's stock if its expected return were the same as that of the T-bill.

Risky assets rarely actually produce their expected rates of return; generally, risky assets earn either more or less than was originally expected. Indeed, if assets always produced their expected returns, they would not be risky. Investment risk, then, is related to the probability of actually earning a low or negative return: The greater the chance of a low or negative return, the riskier the investment. However, risk can be defined more precisely, and we do so in the next section.

Probability Distributions

An event's *probability* is defined as the chance that the event will occur. For example, a weather forecaster might state, "There is a 40% chance of rain today and a 60% chance that it will not rain." If all possible events, or outcomes, are listed, and if a probability is assigned to each event, the listing is called a **probability distribution.** Keep in mind that the probabilities must sum to 1.0, or 100%.

With this in mind, consider the possible rates of return as a result of dividends and stock price changes that you might earn on a $10,000 investment in the stock of either Big Brewery Inc. or Micro Brewery Ltd. Big Brewery Inc. is a national brewer that distributes various brands of beer throughout the country. It also exports product to the United States. Because it has widespread distribution and has brands targeting different market niches, Big Brewery's earnings are less likely to be affected by changing market conditions. Micro Brewery, on the other hand, produces only a high-end dark beer for the discriminating beer drinker. Moreover, since it is small, Micro Brewery distributes only within its own province. Micro Brewery's earnings are more difficult to project. Losing just one distribution channel may appreciably affect sales; changing tastes among beer drinkers could potentially bankrupt the company.

The rate-of-return probability distributions for the two companies are shown in Table 7-1. There is a 30% chance of strong demand, in which case both companies will have high earnings, pay high dividends, and enjoy capital gains. There is a 40% probability of normal demand and moderate returns, and there is a 30% probability of weak demand, which will mean low earnings and dividends as well as capital losses. Notice, however, that Micro Brewery's rate of return could vary far more widely than that of Big Brewery. There is a fairly high probability that the value of Micro Brewery stock will drop substantially, resulting in a 70% loss, while there is a much smaller possible loss for Big Brewery.

Note that the following discussion of risk applies to all random variables, not just stock returns.

Expected Rate of Return

If we multiply each possible outcome by its probability of occurrence and then sum these products, as in Table 7-2, we have a *weighted average* of outcomes. The weights are the

TABLE 7-1 Probability Distributions for Big Brewery Inc. and Micro Brewery Ltd.

Demand for the Company's Products	Probability of This Demand Occurring	Rate of Return on Stock if This Demand Occurs	
		Micro Brewery	Big Brewery
Strong	0.3	100%	40%
Normal	0.4	15	15
Weak	0.3	(70)	(10)
	1.0		

TABLE 7-2 Calculation of Expected Rates of Return: Payoff Matrix

Demand for the Company's Products (1)	Probability of This Demand Occurring (2)	Micro Brewery		Big Brewery	
		Rate of Return (3)	Product: (2) × (3) = (4)	Rate of Return (5)	Product: (2) × (5) = (6)
Strong	0.3	100%	30%	40%	12%
Normal	0.4	15	6	15	6
Weak	0.3	(70)	(21)	(10)	(3)
	1.0		$\hat{r} = 15\%$		$\hat{r} = 15\%$

See **Ch 07 Tool Kit.xlsx** at the textbook's website for all calculations.

probabilities, and the weighted average is the **expected rate of return,** $\hat{r}$, called "r-hat."[1] The expected rates of return for both Micro Brewery and Big Brewery are shown in Table 7-2 to be 15%. This type of table is known as a *payoff matrix*.

The expected-rate-of-return calculation can also be expressed as an equation that does the same thing as the payoff matrix table:[2]

$$\text{Expected rate of return} = \hat{r} = P_1r_1 + P_2r_2 + \cdots + P_nr_n = \sum_{i=1}^{n} P_i r_i \qquad (7\text{-}1)$$

Here r_i is the return if outcome i occurs, P_i is the probability that outcome i occurs, and n is the number of possible outcomes. Thus, $\hat{r}$ is a weighted average of the possible outcomes (the r_i values), with each outcome's weight being its probability of occurrence. Using the data for Micro Brewery, we obtain its expected rate of return as follows:

$$\hat{r} = P_1(r_1) + P_2(r_2) + P_3(r_3)$$
$$= 0.3(100\%) + 0.4(15\%) + 0.3(-70\%)$$
$$= 15\%$$

Big Brewery's expected rate of return is also 15%:

$$\hat{r} = 0.3(40\%) + 0.4(15\%) + 0.3(-10\%)$$
$$= 15\%$$

We can graph the rates of return to obtain a picture of the variability of possible outcomes; this is shown in the Figure 7-1 bar charts. The height of each bar signifies the probability that a given outcome will occur. The range of probable returns for Micro Brewery is from −70 to +100%, with an expected return of 15%. The expected return for Big Brewery is also 15%, but its range is much narrower.

Thus far, we have assumed that only three situations can exist: strong, normal, and weak demand. Actually, of course, demand could range from a deep depression to a fantastic boom, and there are unlimited possibilities in between. Suppose we had the time and patience to assign a probability to each possible level of demand (with the sum of the

FIGURE 7-1   Probability Distributions of Micro Brewery Ltd.'s and Big Brewery Inc.'s Rates of Return

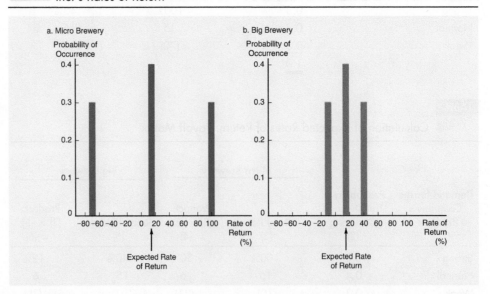

---

[1]In later chapters, we will use $\hat{r}_d$ and $\hat{r}_s$ to signify the returns on bonds and stocks, respectively. However, this distinction is unnecessary in this chapter, so we just use the general term, $\hat{r}$, to signify the expected return on an investment.
[2]This equation is valid for any random variable with a discrete probability distribution, not just for stock returns.

**FIGURE
7-2** Continuous Probability Distributions of Micro Brewery Ltd.'s and
Big Brewery Inc.'s Rates of Return

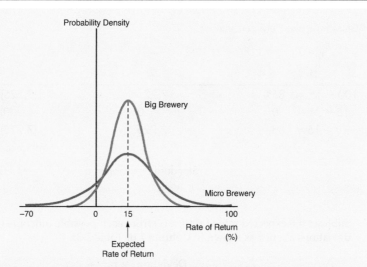

Note: The assumptions regarding the probabilities of various outcomes have been changed from those in Figure 7-1. There the probability of obtaining exactly 15% was 40%; here it is much smaller because there are many possible outcomes instead of just three. With continuous distributions, it is more appropriate to ask what the probability is of obtaining at least some specified rate of return than to ask what the probability is of obtaining exactly that rate. This topic is covered in detail in statistics courses.

probabilities still equalling 1.0) and to assign a rate of return to each stock for each level of demand. We would have a table similar to Table 7-1, except it would have many more entries in each column. This table could be used to calculate expected rates of return as shown previously, and the probabilities and outcomes could be approximated by continuous curves such as those presented in Figure 7-2. Here we have changed the assumptions so that there is essentially a zero probability that Micro Brewery's return will be less than −70% or more than 100%, or that Big Brewery's return will be less than −10% or more than 40%, but virtually any return within these limits is possible.

The tighter, or more peaked, the probability distribution, the more likely it is that the actual outcome will be close to the expected value, and, consequently, the less likely it is that the actual return will end up far below the expected return. Thus, the tighter the probability distribution, the lower the risk assigned to a stock. Since Big Brewery has a relatively tight probability distribution, its actual return is likely to be closer to its 15% expected return than that of Micro Brewery.

Measuring Stand-Alone Risk: The Standard Deviation

Risk is a difficult concept to grasp, and a great deal of controversy has surrounded attempts to define and measure it. However, a common definition, and one that is satisfactory for many purposes, is stated in terms of probability distributions such as those presented in Figure 7-2: *The tighter the probability distribution of expected future returns, the smaller the risk of a given investment.* According to this definition, Big Brewery Inc. is less risky than Micro Brewery Ltd. because there is a smaller chance that its actual return will end up far below its expected return.

To be most useful, any measure of risk should have a definite value—we need a measure of the tightness of the probability distribution. One such measure is the **standard deviation,** the symbol for which is σ, pronounced "sigma." The smaller the standard deviation, the tighter the probability distribution, and, accordingly, the less risky the stock. To calculate the standard deviation, we proceed as shown in Table 7-3, taking the following steps:[3]

1. Calculate the expected rate of return:

$$\text{Expected rate of return} = \hat{r} = \sum_{i=1}^{n} P_i r_i$$

For Micro Brewery, we previously found $\hat{r} = 15\%$.

---

[3]These equations are valid for any random variable from a discrete probability distribution, not just for returns.

See **Ch 07 Tool Kit.xlsx** at the textbook's website for all calculations.

TABLE 7-3   Calculating Micro Brewery Ltd.'s Standard Deviation

(Values for r_i and $\hat{r}$ are percentages.)

$r_i - \hat{r}$ (1)	$(r_i - \hat{r})^2$ (2)	$(r_i - \hat{r})^2 P_i$ (3)
$100 - 15 = \quad 85\%$	$7,225\%$	$(7,225)(0.3) = 2,167.5\%$
$15 - 15 = \quad 0$	0	$(0)(0.4) = \quad\quad 0.0$
$-70 - 15 = -85$	$7,225$	$(7,225)(0.3) = \underline{2,167.5}$
		Variance $= \sigma^2 = \underline{\underline{4,335.0\%}}$

Standard deviation $= \sigma = \sqrt{\sigma^2} = \sqrt{4,335\%} = 65.84\%$

2. Subtract the expected rate of return ($\hat{r}$) from each possible outcome (r_i) to obtain a set of deviations about $\hat{r}$ as shown in Column 1 of Table 7-3:

$$\text{Deviation}_i = r_i - \hat{r}$$

3. Square each deviation, as shown in Column 2. Then multiply the result by the probability of occurrence for its related outcome, and then sum these products to obtain the **variance** of the probability distribution as shown in Column 3 of the table:

$$\text{Variance} = \sigma^2 = \sum_{i=1}^{n}(r_i - \hat{r})^2 P_i \qquad (7\text{-}2)$$

4. Finally, find the square root of the variance to obtain the standard deviation:

$$\text{Standard deviation} = \sigma = \sqrt{\sum_{i=1}^{n}(r_i - \hat{r})^2 P_i} \qquad (7\text{-}3)$$

Thus, the standard deviation is essentially a weighted average of the deviations from the expected value, and it provides an idea of how far above or below the expected value the actual value is likely to be. Micro Brewery's standard deviation is seen in Table 7-3 to be $\sigma = 65.84\%$. Using these same procedures, we find Big Brewery's standard deviation to be 19.36%. Micro Brewery has the larger standard deviation, which indicates a greater variation of returns and thus a greater chance that the actual return may be substantially lower than the expected return. Therefore, Micro Brewery is a riskier investment than Big Brewery when held alone.[4]

If a probability distribution is normal, the *actual* return will be within ±1 standard deviation of the *expected* return 68.26% of the time. Figure 7-3 illustrates this point, and it also shows the situation for ±2 σ and ±3 σ. For Micro Brewery, $\hat{r} = 15\%$ and $\sigma = 65.84\%$, whereas for Big Brewery $\hat{r} = 15\%$ and $\sigma = 19.36\%$. Thus, if the two distributions were normal, there would be a 68.26% probability that Micro Brewery's actual return would be in the range of $15 \pm 65.84\%$, or from -50.84 to 80.84%. For Big Brewery's, the 68.26% range is $15 \pm 19.36\%$, or from -4.36 to 34.36%.

Using Historical Data to Measure Risk

In the previous example, we described the procedure for finding the mean and the standard deviation when the data are in the form of a known probability distribution. Suppose only

---

[4]Most financial calculators have no built-in formula for finding the expected value or variance for discrete probability distributions, except for the special case in which the probabilities for all outcomes are equal. Therefore, you must go through the processes outlined in Tables 7-2 and 7-3 (i.e., Equations 7-1 and 7-3). For an example of this process using a financial calculator, see Richard W. Taylor, "Discrete Probability Analysis with the BAII Plus Professional Calculator," *Journal of Financial Education,* Winter 2005, 100–06.

FIGURE
7-3 Probability Ranges for a Normal Distribution

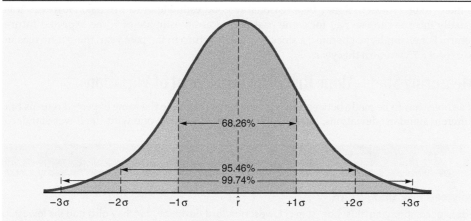

For more discussion of
probability distributions,
see **Web Extension 7A** at
the textbook's website.

Notes:
a. The area under the normal curve always equals 1.0, or 100%. Thus, the areas under any pair of normal curves drawn
    on the same scale, whether they are peaked or flat, must be equal.
b. Half of the area under a normal curve is to the left of the mean, indicating that there is a 50% probability that the actual
    outcome will be less than the mean, and half is to the right of $\hat{r}$, indicating a 50% probability that it will be greater than
    the mean.
c. Of the area under the curve, 68.26% is within $\pm 1\sigma$ of the mean, indicating that the probability is 68.26% that the actual
    outcome will be within the range $\hat{r} - \sigma$ to $\hat{r} + \sigma$.

sample returns data over some past period are available. The past **realized rate of return** in period t is denoted by $\bar{r}_t$ ("r bar t"). The average annual return over the last n years is $\bar{r}_{Avg}$:

$$\bar{r}_{Avg} = \frac{\sum\limits_{t=1}^{n} \bar{r}_t}{n} \qquad (7\text{-}4)$$

The standard deviation of a sample of returns can be estimated using this formula:

$$\text{Estimated } \sigma = S = \sqrt{\frac{\sum\limits_{t=1}^{n}(\bar{r}_t - \bar{r}_{Avg})^2}{n-1}} \qquad (7\text{-}5)$$

When estimated from past data, the standard deviation is often denoted by S. Here is an example:[5]

Year	$\bar{r}_t$
2013	15%
2014	−5
2015	20

$$\bar{r}_{Avg} = \frac{(15 - 5 + 20)}{3} = 10.0\%,$$

$$\text{Estimated } \sigma \text{(or S)} = \sqrt{\frac{(15 - 10)^2 + (-5 - 10)^2 + (20 - 10)^2}{3 - 1}}$$

$$= \sqrt{\frac{350}{2}} = 13.2\%$$

See **Ch 07 Tool Kit.xlsx** at
the textbook's website for
all calculations.

[5]Because we are estimating the standard deviation from a sample of observations, the denominator in Equation 7-5 is "n − 1"
and not just "n." Equations 7-4 and 7-5 are built into all financial calculators. For example, to find the sample standard
deviation, enter the rates of return into the calculator and press the key marked S (or S_x) to get the standard deviation.

In *Excel*, the average can be found using a built-in function: =**AVERAGE(0.15,−0.05,0.20)** = 10.0%. For the sample standard deviation, the function is =**STDEV(0.15,−0.05,0.20)** = 13.2%.

The historical σ is often used as an estimate of the future σ. Because past variability is likely to be repeated, S may be a reasonably good estimate of future risk. However, it is usually incorrect to use $\bar{r}_{Avg}$ for some past period as an estimate of $\hat{r}$, the expected future return. For example, just because a stock had a 75% return in the past year, there is no reason to expect a 75% return this year.

Measuring Stand-Alone Risk: The Coefficient of Variation

If a choice has to be made between two investments that have the same expected returns but different standard deviations, most people would choose the one with the lower standard

FINANCE: IN FOCUS

The Trade-Off between Risk and Return

The table and graph accompanying this box summarize the historical trade-off between risk and return for different classes of investments. Those assets that produced the highest average returns also had the highest standard deviations and the widest ranges of returns. For example, stocks had the highest average annual return, but the volatility (as shown in the graph and by its standard deviation) of their returns, was also the highest. By contrast, Treasury bills had the lowest standard deviation, but they also had the lowest average return.

Note that a T-bill is riskless *if you hold it until maturity*, but if you invest in a rolling portfolio of T-bills and hold the portfolio for a number of years, your investment income will vary, depending on what happens to the level of interest rates in each year. While you can be sure of the return you will earn on a T-bill, you cannot be sure of the return you will earn on a portfolio of T-bills over a number of years.

	Realized Returns, 1950–2013 (%)					
	Toronto Stock Exchange Stocks	**U.S. Stock Cdn $**	**Long-Term Corporate Bonds[b]**	**Long-Term Government Bonds**	**Government of Canada Treasury Bills**	**Inflation**
Average Return	11.7	12.6	9.4	7.0	5.7	3.7
Standard Deviation	17.1	17.6	10.1	9.9	4.1	3.3
Excess Return over Gov't. Bonds[a]	4.7	5.6	2.4			

Historical Yearly Returns for the Toronto Stock Exchange and Government of Canada T-bills, 1950–2013

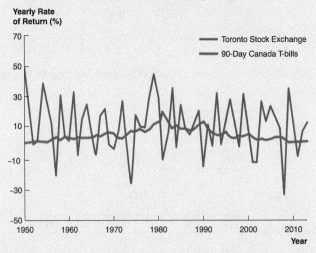

[a]The excess return over government bonds is called the "historical risk premium." If and only if investors expect returns in the future to be similar to returns earned in the past, the excess return will also be the current risk premium that is reflected in security prices.
[b]Calculated from data, 1993–2013.

Source: Data from Canadian Institute of Actuaries, "Report on Canadian Economic Statistics, 1924–2013," May 2014.

deviation and, therefore, the lower risk. Similarly, given a choice between two investments with the same risk (standard deviation) but different expected returns, investors would generally prefer the investment with the higher expected return. To most people, this is common sense—return is "good," risk is "bad," and consequently investors want as much return and as little risk as possible. But how do we choose between two investments if one has a higher expected return but the other a lower standard deviation? To help answer this question, we often use another measure of risk, the **coefficient of variation (CV),** which is the standard deviation divided by the expected return:

$$\text{Coefficient of variation} = \text{CV} = \frac{\sigma}{\hat{r}} \tag{7-6}$$

The coefficient of variation shows the risk per unit of return, and it provides a more meaningful basis for comparison than σ *when the expected returns on two alternatives are not the same.* Since Big Brewery and Micro Brewery have the same expected return, the coefficient of variation is not necessary in this case. The firm with the larger standard deviation, Micro Brewery, must have the larger coefficient of variation when the means are equal. In fact, the coefficient of variation for Micro Brewery is 65.84/15 = 4.39 and that for Big Brewery is 19.36/15 = 1.29. Thus, Micro Brewery is more than three times as risky as Big Brewery on the basis of this criterion. Because the coefficient of variation captures the effects of both risk and return, it is a better measure than just standard deviation for evaluating stand-alone risk in situations where two or more investments have substantially different expected returns.

Risk Aversion and Required Returns

Suppose you have worked hard and saved $1 million, which you now plan to invest. You can buy a 5% Government of Canada bond, and at the end of 1 year you will have a sure $1.05 million, which is your original investment plus $50,000 in interest. Alternatively, you can buy stock in Genetic Advances. If Genetic Advances' research programs are successful, your stock will increase in value to $2.1 million. However, if the research is a failure, the value of your stock will go to zero, and you will be penniless. You regard Genetic Advances' chance of success or failure as being 50–50, so the expected value of the stock investment is 0.5($0) + 0.5($2,100,000) = $1,050,000. Subtracting the $1 million cost of the stock leaves an expected profit of $50,000, or an expected (but risky) 5% rate of return: $50,000/$1,000,000 = 0.05 = 5%.

Thus, you have a choice between a sure $50,000 profit (representing a 5% rate of return) on the Government of Canada bond and a risky expected $50,000 profit (also representing a 5% expected rate of return) on the Genetic Advances stock. Which one would you choose? *If you choose the less risky investment, you are risk averse. Most investors are indeed risk averse, and certainly the average investor is risk averse with regard to his or her "serious money." Because this is a well-documented fact, we shall assume* **risk aversion** *throughout the remainder of the book.*

What are the implications of risk aversion for security prices and rates of return? The answer is that, other things held constant, the higher a security's risk, the lower its price and the higher its required return. To see how risk aversion affects security prices, consider again Big Brewery and Micro Brewery. Suppose each stock is expected to pay an annual dividend of $15 forever. Under these conditions, the price of each stock is just the present value of a perpetuity. If each stock had an expected return of 15%, then each stock's price would be P = $15/0.15 = $100. Investors are averse to risk, so under these conditions there would be a general preference for Big Brewery—it has the same expected return as Micro Brewery but less risk. People with money to invest would bid for Big Brewery rather than Micro Brewery stock, and Micro Brewery shareholders would start selling their stock and using the money to buy Big Brewery. Buying pressure would drive up Big Brewery's stock, and selling pressure would simultaneously cause Micro Brewery's price to decline.

These price changes, in turn, would cause changes in the expected rates of return on the two securities. Suppose, for example, that Big Brewery's stock price was bid up from $100 to $150, whereas Micro Brewery's stock price declined from $100 to $75. This would cause Big Brewery's expected return to fall to 10%, while Micro Brewery's expected return would rise to 20%.[6] The difference in returns, 20% − 10% = 10%, is a **risk premium, RP,** which represents the additional compensation investors require for assuming the additional risk of Micro Brewery stock.

---

[6]Recall that the present value of a perpetuity is P = PMT/I, where PMT is the constant annual cash flow of the perpetuity. For stocks, we use r for the expected rate of return. Solving for r, the expected return for Big Brewery is $15/$150 = 0.10 = 10%. The expected return for Micro Brewery is $15/$75 = 0.20 = 20%.

This example demonstrates a very important principle: *In a market dominated by risk-averse investors, riskier securities must have higher expected returns, as estimated by the marginal investor, than less risky securities. If this situation does not exist, buying and selling in the market will force it to occur.* We will consider the question of how much higher the returns on risky securities must be later in the chapter, after we see how diversification affects the way risk should be measured. Then, in later chapters, we will see how risk-adjusted rates of return affect the prices investors are willing to pay for bonds and stocks.

ⒸNCEPT REVIEW

1. What does "investment risk" mean?
2. Set up an illustrative probability distribution for an investment.
3. What is a payoff matrix?
4. Which of the two stocks graphed in Figure 7-2 is less risky? Why?
5. How does one calculate the standard deviation?
6. Which is a better measure of risk if assets have different expected returns: (1) the standard deviation or (2) the coefficient of variation? Why?
7. Explain the following statement: "Most investors are risk averse."
8. How does risk aversion affect rates of return?
9. An investment has a 30% chance of producing a 25% return, a 40% chance of producing a 10% return, and a 30% chance of producing a −15% return. What is its expected return? (Check Figure: 7%) What is its standard deviation? (Check Figure: 15.7%)
10. A stock's returns for the past 3 years are 10%, −15%, and 35%. What is the historical average return? (Check Figure: 10%) What is the historical sample standard deviation? (Check Figure: 25%)
11. An investment has an expected return of 15% and a standard deviation of 30%. What is its coefficient of variation? (Check Figure: 2.0)

7.3 Risk in a Portfolio Context

In the preceding section, we considered the risk of assets held in isolation. Now we analyze the risk of assets held in portfolios. As we shall see, an asset held as part of a **portfolio** is less risky than the same asset held in isolation. Accordingly, most financial assets are actually held as parts of portfolios. Banks, pension funds, insurance companies, mutual funds, and other financial institutions are required by law to hold diversified portfolios. Even individual investors—at least those whose security holdings constitute a significant part of their total wealth—generally hold portfolios, not the stock of only one firm. This being the case, from an investor's standpoint the fact that a particular stock goes up or down is not very important; *what is important is the return on his or her portfolio, and the portfolio's risk. Logically, then, the risk and return of an individual security should be analyzed in terms of how that security affects the risk and return of the portfolio in which it is held.*

To illustrate, Pay Up Inc. is a collection agency that operates nationwide through 37 offices. The company is not well known, its stock is not very liquid, its earnings have fluctuated quite a bit in the past, and it doesn't pay a dividend. All of this suggests that Pay Up is risky and that the required rate of return on its stock, r, should be relatively high. However, Pay Up's required rate of return in 2015, and all other years, was quite low in relation to those of most other companies. This indicates that investors regard Pay Up as a low-risk company in spite of its uncertain profits. The reason for this counterintuitive fact has to do with diversification and its effect on risk. Pay Up's earnings rise during recessions, whereas most other companies' earnings tend to decline when the economy slumps. The stock is like fire insurance—it pays off when other things go badly. Therefore, adding Pay Up to a portfolio of "normal" stocks tends to stabilize returns on the entire portfolio, thus making the portfolio less risky.

Portfolio Returns

The *expected return on a portfolio*, $\hat{r}_p$, is simply the weighted average of the expected returns on the individual assets in the portfolio, with the weights being the fraction of the total portfolio invested in each asset:

$$\hat{r}_p = w_1\hat{r}_1 + w_2\hat{r}_2 + \ldots + w_n\hat{r}_n$$

$$= \sum_{i=1}^{n} w_i\hat{r}_i \tag{7-7}$$

Here the $\hat{r}_i$'s are the expected returns on the individual stocks, the w_i's are the weights, and there are n stocks in the portfolio. Note that (1) w_i is the fraction of the portfolio's dollar value invested in Stock i (i.e., the value of the investment in Stock i divided by the total value of the portfolio) and (2) the w_i's must sum to 1.0.

Assume that in August 2015, a security analyst estimated that the following returns could be expected on the stocks of four large companies:

	Expected Return, $\hat{r}$
Air Canada	15.0%
Starbucks	12.0
Loblaws	10.0
Best Buy Co.	9.0

If we formed a $100,000 portfolio, investing $25,000 in each stock, the expected portfolio return would be 11.5%:

$$\hat{r}_p = w_1\hat{r}_1 + w_2\hat{r}_2 + w_3\hat{r}_3 + w_n\hat{r}_n$$

$$= 0.25(15\%) + 0.25(12\%) + 0.25(10\%) + 0.25(9\%)$$

$$= 11.5\%$$

Of course, the actual realized rates of return will almost certainly be different from their expected values, so the realized portfolio return, $\bar{r}_p$, will be different from the expected return. For example, Starbucks might double and provide a return of $+100\%$, whereas Best Buy might have a terrible year, fall sharply, and have a return of -75%. Note, though, that those two events would be somewhat offsetting, so the portfolio's return might still be close to its expected return, even though the individual stocks' actual returns were far from their expected returns.

Portfolio Risk

As we just saw, the expected return on a portfolio is simply the weighted average of the expected returns on the individual assets in the portfolio. However, unlike returns, the risk of a portfolio, σ_p is generally not the weighted average of the standard deviations of the individual assets in the portfolio; the portfolio's risk will almost always be smaller than the weighted average of the assets' σ's. In fact, it is theoretically possible to combine stocks that are individually quite risky as measured by their standard deviations to form a portfolio that is completely riskless, with $\sigma_p = 0$.

To illustrate the effect of combining assets, consider the situation in Figure 7-4. The bottom section gives data on rates of return for Stocks W and M individually, as well as for a portfolio invested 50% in each stock. The three graphs plot the data in a time series format. The two stocks would be quite risky if they were held in isolation, but when they are combined to form Portfolio WM, they are not risky at all. (*Note:* These stocks are called W and M because the graphs of their returns in Figure 7-4 resemble a W and an M.)

The reason Stocks W and M can be combined to form a riskless portfolio is that their returns move counter-cyclically to each other—when W's returns fall, those of M rise, and vice versa. The tendency of two variables to move together is called **correlation,** and the **correlation coefficient** measures this tendency.[7] The symbol for the correlation coefficient is the Greek letter rho, ρ (pronounced "roe"). In statistical terms, we say that the returns on Stocks W and M are *perfectly negatively correlated*, with $\rho = -1.0$.

The estimate of correlation from a sample of historical data is often called "R." Here is the formula to estimate the correlation between stocks i and j ($\bar{r}_{i,t}$ is the actual return for Stock

---

[7]The correlation coefficient, ρ, can range from $+1.0$, denoting that the two variables move up and down in perfect synchronization, to -1.0, denoting that the variables always move in exactly opposite directions. A correlation coefficient of zero indicates that the two variables are not related to each other—that is, changes in one variable are independent of changes in the other.

i in period t, and $\bar{r}_{i,Avg}$ is the average return during the n-period sample; similar notation is used for Stock j):

$$\text{Estimated } \rho = R = \frac{\displaystyle\sum_{t=1}^{n}(\bar{r}_{i,t} - \bar{r}_{i,Avg})(\bar{r}_{j,t} - \bar{r}_{j,Avg})}{\sqrt{\displaystyle\sum_{t=1}^{n}(\bar{r}_{i,t} - \bar{r}_{i,Avg})^2}\sqrt{\displaystyle\sum_{t=1}^{n}(\bar{r}_{j,t} - \bar{r}_{j,Avg})^2}} \tag{7-8}$$

Fortunately, it is easy to estimate the correlation coefficients with a financial calculator. Simply enter the returns on the two stocks and then press a key labelled "r."[8] In *Excel*, use the CORREL function. See *Ch 07 Tool Kit.xlsx* for the calculation of correlation between Stocks W and M.

The opposite of perfect negative correlation, with $\rho = -1.0$, is *perfect positive correlation*, with $\rho = +1.0$. Returns on two perfectly positively correlated stocks (M and M') would move up and down together, and a portfolio consisting of two such stocks would be exactly as risky as each individual stock. This point is illustrated in Figure 7-5, where we see that the portfolio's standard deviation is equal to that of the individual stocks. *Thus, diversification does nothing to reduce risk if the portfolio consists of perfectly positively correlated stocks.*

Figures 7-4 and 7-5 demonstrate that when stocks are perfectly negatively correlated ($\rho = -1.0$), all risk can be diversified away, but when stocks are perfectly positively correlated ($\rho = +1.0$), diversification does no good whatsoever. In reality, virtually all stocks are positively correlated, but not perfectly so. *Therefore, it is impossible to form completely riskless stock portfolios.* Past studies have estimated that on average the correlation coefficient for the monthly returns on two randomly selected stocks is about 0.3.[9] *Under this condition, combining stocks into*

FIGURE 7-4 Rates of Return for Two Perfectly Negatively Correlated Stocks ($\rho = -1.0$) and for Portfolio WM

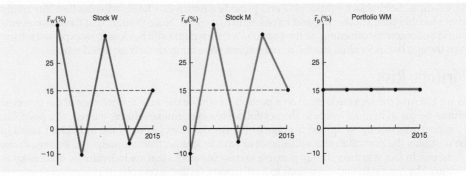

Year	Stock W ($\bar{r}_W$)	Stock M ($\bar{r}_M$)	Portfolio WM ($\bar{r}_p$)
2011	40.0%	(10.0%)	15.0%
2012	(10.0)	40.0	15.0
2013	35.0	(5.0)	15.0
2014	(5.0)	35.0	15.0
2015	15.0	15.0	15.0
Average return	15.0%	15.0%	15.0%
Standard deviation	22.6%	22.6%	0.0%

See *Ch 07 Tool Kit.xlsx* at the textbook's website for all calculations.

[8]See our tutorial or your calculator manual for the exact steps. Also note that the correlation coefficient is often denoted by the term "r." We use ρ here to avoid confusion with r as used to denote the rate of return.

[9]A study by Chan, Karceski, and Lakonishok (1999) estimated that the average correlation coefficient between two randomly selected stocks was 0.28, while the average correlation coefficient between two large-company stocks was 0.33. The time period of their sample was 1968 to 1998. See Louis K. C. Chan, Jason Karceski, and Josef Lakonishok, "On Portfolio Optimization: Forecasting Covariance and Choosing the Risk Model," *Review of Financial Studies* 12, no. 5, Winter 1999, 937–74. A study by Campbell, Lettau, Malkiel, and Xu found that the average correlation fell from around 0.35 in the late 1970s to less than 0.10 by the late 1990s; see John Y. Campbell, Martin Lettau, Burton G. Malkiel, and Yexiao Xu, "Have Individual Stocks Become More Volatile? An Empirical Exploration of Idiosyncratic Risk," *Journal of Finance*, February 2001, 1–43.

portfolios reduces risk but does not completely eliminate it. Figure 7-6 illustrates this point with two stocks whose correlation coefficient is $\rho = +0.35$. The portfolio's average return is 15%, which is exactly the same as the average return for our other two illustrative portfolios, but its standard deviation is 18.6%, which is below the other two portfolios' standard deviations.

FIGURE 7-5 Rates of Return for Two Perfectly Positively Correlated Stocks ($\rho = +1.0$) and for Portfolio MM′

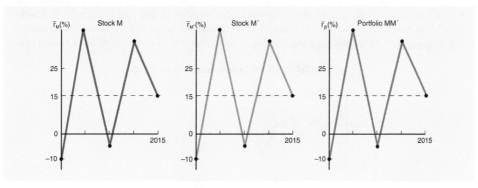

Year	Stock M ($\bar{r}_M$)	Stock M′ ($\bar{r}_{M'}$)	Portfolio MM′ ($\bar{r}_P$)
2011	(10.0%)	(10.0%)	(10.0%)
2012	40.0	40.0	40.0
2013	(5.0)	(5.0)	(5.0)
2014	35.0	35.0	35.0
2015	15.0	15.0	15.0
Average return	15.0%	15.0%	15.0%
Standard deviation	22.6%	22.6%	22.6%

See *Ch 07 Tool Kit.xlsx* at the textbook's website for all calculations.

FIGURE 7-6 Rates of Return for Two Partially Correlated Stocks ($\rho = +0.35$) and for Portfolio WY

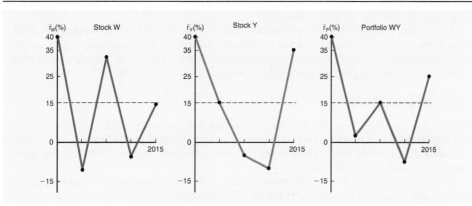

Year	Stock W ($\bar{r}_W$)	Stock Y ($\bar{r}_Y$)	Portfolio WY ($\bar{r}_P$)
2011	40.0%	40.0%	40.0%
2012	(10.0)	15.0	2.5
2013	35.0	(5.0)	15.0
2014	(5.0)	(10.0)	(7.5)
2015	15.0	35.0	25.0
Average return	15.0%	15.0%	15.0%
Standard deviation	22.6%	22.6%	18.6%

See *Ch 07 Tool Kit.xlsx*, at the textbook's website for all calculations.

FINANCE: IN FOCUS

How Risky Is a Large Portfolio of Stock?

Many investors buy "index" mutual funds that hold the same stocks that make up major indices such as the S&P/TSX 60. Such funds are quite well diversified. However, as you can see from the accompanying graph, diversification didn't help much when the market crashed in 2008. In just $2\frac{1}{2}$ months, the market in Canada lost more than 40% of its value. Investing in the much larger U.S. market didn't help either. The S&P500 index also fell 40% over the same time period. Someone with a $1 million nest egg invested in this "safe" portfolio suddenly experienced a $410,000 loss. Diversification helps, but it doesn't eliminate stock market risk.

S&P/TSX 60 Index, Sep.–Nov. 2008

What would happen if we included more than two stocks in the portfolio? *As a rule, the risk of a portfolio will decline as the number of stocks in the portfolio increases.* If we added enough partially correlated stocks, could we completely eliminate risk? In general, the answer is no, but the extent to which adding stocks to a portfolio reduces its risk depends on the *degree of correlation* among the stocks: The smaller the positive correlation coefficients, the lower the risk in a portfolio. If some stocks had correlations of −1.0, all risk could be eliminated. *In the real world, where the correlations among the individual stocks are generally positive but less than +1.0, some, but not all, risk can be eliminated.*

In general, there are higher correlations between the returns on two companies in the same industry than for two companies in different industries. There are also higher correlations among similar-"style" companies, such as large versus small and growth versus value. Thus to minimize risk, portfolios should be diversified across industries and styles.

See *Ch 07 Tool Kit.xlsx,* at the textbook's website for all calculations.

Efficient Portfolios

We just saw the important role that the correlation between assets plays in portfolio risk. One important use of portfolio risk concepts is to select **efficient portfolios,** defined as those portfolios that provide the highest expected return for any degree of risk, or the lowest degree of risk for any expected return.

Consider two assets, A and B. Suppose we have estimated the expected returns ($\hat{r}_A$ and $\hat{r}_B$), the standard deviations (σ_A and σ_B) of returns, and the correlation coefficient (ρ_{AB}) for returns. The expected return and standard deviation for a portfolio containing these two assets are

$$\hat{r}_p = w_A\hat{r}_A + (1 - w_A)\hat{r}_B$$

and

$$\text{Portfolio SD} = \sigma_p = \sqrt{w_A^2\sigma_A^2 + (1 - w_A)^2\sigma_B^2 + 2w_A(1 - w_A)\rho_{AB}\sigma_A\sigma_B} \qquad (7\text{-}9)$$

Note that the expected return formula is the same as Equation 7-7, though using only two assets. Here w_A is the fraction of the portfolio invested in Security A, so $(1 - w_A)$ is the fraction invested in Security B.

To illustrate, suppose we can allocate our funds between A and B in any proportion. Suppose Security A has an expected rate of return of $\hat{r}_A = 5\%$ and a standard deviation of returns $\sigma_A = 4\%$, while $\hat{r}_B = 8\%$ and $\sigma_B = 10\%$. Our first task is to determine the set of *attainable* portfolios, and then from this attainable set to select the *efficient* subset.

To construct the attainable set, we need data on the degree of correlation between the two securities' expected returns, ρ_{AB}. Let us work with three different assumed degrees of correlation, $\rho_{AB} = +1.0$, $\rho_{AB} = 0$, and $\rho_{AB} = -1.0$, and use them to develop the portfolios' expected returns, $\hat{r}_p$, and standard deviations, σ_p. (Of course, only one correlation can exist; our example simply shows three alternative situations that might exist.)

We can now calculate $\hat{r}_p$, for example, when w_A equals 0.75, then $\hat{r}_p = 5.75\%$:

$$\hat{r}_p = w_A\hat{r}_A + (1 - w_A)\hat{r}_B$$

$$= 0.75(5\%) + 0.25(8\%) = 5.75\%$$

Other values of $\hat{r}_p$ were found similarly, and they are shown in the $\hat{r}_p$ column of Table 7-4.

Next, we use Equation 7-9 to find σ_p. Substitute the given values for σ_A, σ_B, and ρ_{AB}, and then calculate σ_p for different values of w_A. For example, in the case where $\rho_{AB} = 0$ and $w_A = 0.75$, then $\sigma_p = 3.9\%$:

See **Ch 07 Tool Kit.xlsx** at the textbook's website for all calculations.

$$\sigma_p = \sqrt{w_A^2\sigma_A^2 + (1 - w_A)^2\sigma_B^2 + 2w_A(1 - w_A)\rho_{AB}\sigma_A\sigma_B}$$

$$= \sqrt{(0.5625)(0.0016) + (0.0625)(0.01) + 2(0.75)(0.25)(0)(0.04)(0.10)}$$

$$= \sqrt{0.0009 + 0.000625} = \sqrt{0.001525} = 0.039 = 3.9\%$$

Table 7-4 gives $\hat{r}_p$ and σ_p values for $w_A = 1.00, 0.75, 0.50, 0.25$, and 0.00, and Figure 7-7 plots $\hat{r}_p$, σ_p, and the attainable set of portfolios for each correlation. In both the table and the graphs, note the following points:

1. The three graphs across the top row of Figure 7-7 designate Case I, where the two assets are perfectly positively correlated; that is, $\rho_{AB} = +1.0$. The three graphs in the middle row are for the zero correlation case, and the three in the bottom row are for perfect negative correlation.
2. We rarely encounter $\rho_{AB} = -1.0, 0.0$, or $+1.0$. Generally, ρ_{AB} is in the range of $+0.5$ to $+0.7$ for most stocks. Case II (zero correlation) produces graphs which, pictorially, most closely resemble real-world examples.
3. The left column of graphs shows how the *expected portfolio returns* vary with different combinations of A and B. We see that these graphs are identical in each of the three cases: The portfolio return, $\hat{r}_p$, is a linear function of w_A, and it does not depend on the correlation coefficients. This is also seen from the single $\hat{r}_p$ column in Table 7-4.
4. The middle column of graphs shows how risk is affected by the portfolio mix. Starting from the top, we see that portfolio risk, σ_p, increases linearly in Case I, where $\rho_{AB} = +1.0$; it is nonlinear in Case II; and Case III shows that risk can be completely diversified away if $\rho_{AB} = -1.0$. Thus σ_p, unlike $\hat{r}_p$, *does* depend on correlation.

TABLE 7-4 $\hat{r}_p$ and σ_p under Various Assumptions

Proportion of Portfolio in Security A (Value of w_A)	Proportion of Portfolio in Security B (Value of $1 - w_A$)	$\hat{r}_p$	σ_p Case I ($\rho_{AB} = +1.0$)	Case II ($\rho_{AB} = 0$)	Case III ($\rho_{AB} = -1.0$)
1.00	0.00	5.00%	4.0%	4.0%	4.0%
0.75	0.25	5.75	5.5	3.9	0.5
0.50	0.50	6.50	7.0	5.4	3.0
0.25	0.75	7.25	8.5	7.6	6.5
0.00	1.00	8.00	10.0	10.0	10.0

FIGURE
7-7   Illustrations of Portfolio Returns, Risk, and the Attainable Set of Portfolios

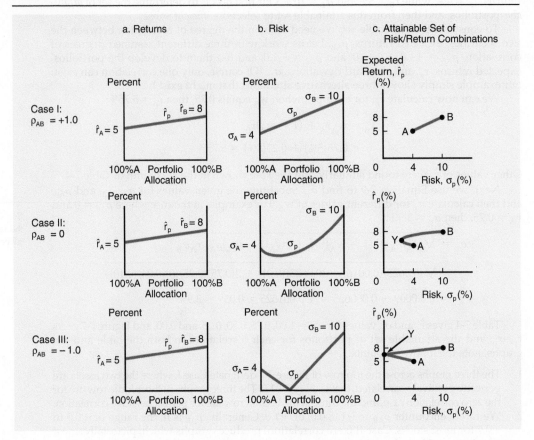

5. Note that in both Cases II and III, but not in Case I, someone holding only Stock A could sell some A, buy some B, and both increase his or her expected return and lower risk.
6. The right column of graphs shows the attainable, or feasible, set of portfolios constructed with different mixes of Securities A and B. Unlike the other columns, which plotted return and risk versus the portfolio's composition, each of the three graphs here was plotted from pairs of $\hat{r}_p$ and σ_p as shown in Table 7-4. For example, Point A in the upper-right graph is the point $\hat{r}_p = 5\%$, $\sigma_p = 4\%$ from the Case I data. All other points on the curves were plotted similarly. With only two securities in the portfolio, the attainable set is a curve or line, and we can achieve each risk/return combination on the relevant curve by some allocation of our investment funds between Securities A and B.
7. Are all combinations on the attainable set equally good? The answer is no. Only that part of the attainable set from Y to B in Cases II and III is defined to be efficient. The part from A to Y is inefficient because for any degree of risk on the line segment AY, a higher return can be found on segment YB. Thus, no rational investor would hold a portfolio that lies on segment AY. In Case I, however, the entire feasible set is efficient—no combination of the securities can be ruled out.

From these examples we see that in one extreme case ($\rho = -1.0$), risk can be completely eliminated, while in the other extreme case ($\rho = +1.0$), diversification does no good whatsoever. In between these extremes, combining two stocks into a portfolio reduces but does not eliminate the risk inherent in the individual stocks.

Diversifiable Risk versus Market Risk

As noted above, it is difficult if not impossible to find stocks whose expected returns are negatively correlated—most stocks tend to do well when the national economy is strong and badly when it is weak. Thus, even very large portfolios end up with a substantial amount of risk, but not as much risk as if all the money were invested in only one stock.

To see more precisely how portfolio size affects portfolio risk, consider Figure 7-8, which shows how portfolio risk is affected by forming larger and larger portfolios of randomly selected New York Stock Exchange (NYSE) stocks. Standard deviations are plotted for an average one-stock portfolio, a two-stock portfolio, and so on, up to a portfolio consisting of all 2,000-plus common stocks that were listed on the NYSE at the time the data were graphed. The graph illustrates that, in general, the risk of a portfolio consisting of large-company stocks tends to decline and to approach some limit as the size of the portfolio increases. According to data accumulated in recent years, σ_1, the standard deviation of a one-stock portfolio (or an average stock), is approximately 35%. A portfolio consisting of all stocks, which is called the **market portfolio,** would have a standard deviation, σ_M, of about 20%, which is shown as the horizontal dashed line in Figure 7-8.

Thus, almost half of the risk inherent in an average individual stock can be eliminated if the stock is held in a reasonably well diversified portfolio, which is one containing 40 or more stocks in a number of different industries. Some risk always remains, however, so it is virtually impossible to diversify away the effects of broad stock market movements that affect almost all stocks.

Generally speaking, the results in Figure 7-8 hold for stocks trading on the Toronto Stock Exchange. A study on portfolio size and diversification for Canadian stocks shows that a portfolio of more than 200 stocks reduces risk by 67%. Of the 67% reduction, 90% of it occurs by holding just 50 stocks. These results suggest that the S&P/TSX 60 Index, given its size and industry representation, is an appropriately diversified portfolio model.[10]

FIGURE
7-8   Effects of Portfolio Size on Portfolio Risk for Average Stocks

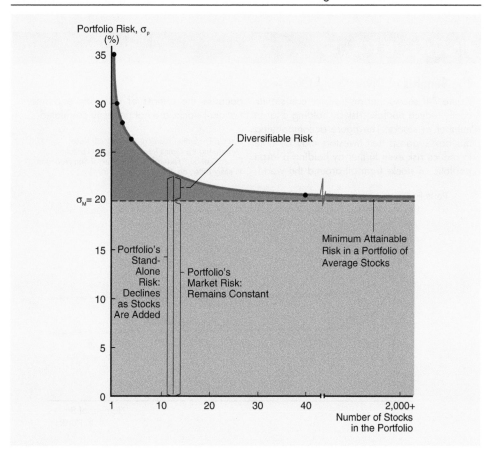

---

[10]Sean Cleary and David Copp, "Diversification with Canadian Stocks: How Much Is Enough?" *Canadian Investment Review,* Fall 1999. A recent study by Alexeev and Tapon on portfolio diversification for the Canadian market suggests more than 50 stocks are needed to maintain proper diversification. Vitali Alexeev and Francis Tapon, "Equity Portfolio Diversification: How Many Stocks are Enough? Evidence from Five Developed Markets," November 28, 2012, FIRN Research Paper. Available at SSRN: http://ssrn.com/abstract=2182295

The part of a stock's risk that *can* be eliminated is called *diversifiable risk*, while the part that *cannot* be eliminated is called *market risk*.[11] The fact that a large part of the risk of any individual stock can be eliminated is vitally important, because rational investors *will* eliminate it and thus render it irrelevant.

Diversifiable risk is caused by random events such as lawsuits, strikes, successful and unsuccessful marketing programs, the winning or losing of a major contract, and other events that are unique to a particular firm. Because these events are random, their effects on a portfolio can be eliminated by diversification—bad events in one firm will be offset by good events in another. **Market risk,** on the other hand, stems from factors that systematically affect most firms: war, inflation, recessions, and high interest rates. Since most stocks are negatively affected by these factors, market risk cannot be eliminated by diversification.

We know that investors demand a premium for bearing risk; that is, the higher the risk of a security, the higher its expected return must be to induce investors to buy (or to hold) it. However, if investors are primarily concerned with the risk of their *portfolios* rather than the risk of the individual securities in those portfolios, how should the risk of an individual stock be measured? One answer is provided by the **Capital Asset Pricing Model (CAPM),** an important tool used to analyze the relationship between risk and rates of return.[12] The primary conclusion of the CAPM is this: *The relevant risk of an individual stock is its contribution to the risk of a well-diversified portfolio.* A stock might be quite risky if held by itself, but if half of its risk can be eliminated by diversification, then its **relevant risk,** which is its *contribution to the portfolio's risk,* is much smaller than its stand-alone risk.

A simple example will help make this point clear. Suppose you are offered the chance to flip a coin once. If it's heads, you win $20,000, but if it's tails, you lose $16,000. This is a good bet—the expected return is 0.5($20,000) + 0.5(−$16,000) = $2,000. However, it is a highly risky proposition, because you have a 50% chance of losing $16,000. Thus, you might well refuse to make the bet. Alternatively, suppose you were offered the chance to flip a

---

FINANCE: IN FOCUS

The Benefits of Diversifying Overseas

Figure 7-8 shows that an investor can significantly reduce portfolio risk by holding a large number of stocks. The figure accompanying this box suggests that investors may be able to reduce risk even further by holding a large portfolio of stocks from all around the world, because the returns of domestic and international stocks are not perfectly correlated.

Source: For further reading, see Kenneth Kasa, "Measuring the Gains from International Portfolio Diversification," *Federal Reserve Bank of San Francisco Weekly Letter*, no. 94-14 (April 8, 1994).

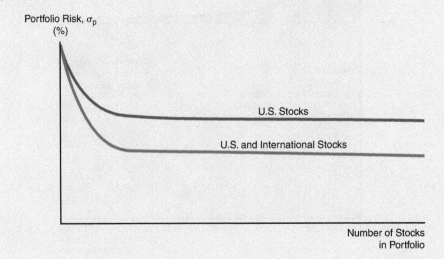

---

[11]Diversifiable risk is also known as *company-specific*, or *unsystematic*, risk. Market risk is also known as *nondiversifiable, systematic*, or *beta*, risk; it is the risk that remains after diversification.
[12]Indeed, the 1990 Nobel Prize was awarded to the developers of the CAPM, Professors Harry Markowitz and William F. Sharpe. The CAPM is a relatively complex theory, and only its basic elements are presented in this chapter.

coin 100 times, and you would win $200 for each head but lose $160 for each tail. It is theoretically possible that you would flip all heads and win $20,000, and it is also theoretically possible that you would flip all tails and lose $16,000, but the chances are very high that you would actually flip about 50 heads and about 50 tails, winning a net of about $2,000. Although each individual flip is a risky bet, collectively you have a low-risk proposition because most of the risk has been diversified away. This is the idea behind holding portfolios of stocks rather than just one stock, except that with stocks all of the risk cannot be eliminated by diversification—those risks related to broad, systematic changes in the stock market will remain.

Are all stocks equally risky in the sense that adding them to a well-diversified portfolio will have the same effect on the portfolio's riskiness? The answer is no. Different stocks will affect the portfolio differently, so different securities have different degrees of relevant risk. How can the relevant risk of an individual stock be measured? As we have seen, all risk except that related to broad market movements can, and presumably will, be diversified away. After all, why accept risk that can be easily eliminated? *The risk that remains after diversifying is market risk, or the risk that is inherent in the market, and it can be measured by the degree to which a given stock tends to move up or down with the market.* In a later section, we develop a measure of a stock's market risk; then we will introduce an equation for determining the required rate of return on a stock, given its market risk.

The Basic Assumptions of the Capital Asset Pricing Model

The Capital Asset Pricing Model specifies the relationship between risk and required rates of return on assets when they are held in well-diversified portfolios. The assumptions underlying the CAPM's development are summarized in the following list:[13]

1. All investors focus on a single holding period, and they seek to maximize the expected utility of their terminal wealth by choosing among alternative portfolios on the basis of each portfolio's expected return and standard deviation.
2. All investors can borrow or lend an unlimited amount at a given risk-free rate of interest, r_{RF}, and there are no restrictions on short sales of any asset.[14]
3. All investors have identical estimates of the expected returns, variances, and covariances among all assets (i.e., investors have homogeneous expectations).
4. All assets are perfectly divisible and perfectly liquid (i.e., marketable at the going price).
5. There are no transactions costs.
6. There are no taxes.
7. All investors are price takers (i.e., all investors assume that their own buying and selling activity will not affect stock prices).
8. The quantities of all assets are given and fixed.

Theoretical extensions in the literature have relaxed some of these assumptions, and in general these extensions have led to conclusions that are reasonably consistent with the basic theory. We will provide our own thoughts on CAPM's validity later in the chapter.

Contribution to Market Risk: Beta

As we noted above, the primary conclusion of the CAPM is that the relevant risk of an individual stock is the amount of risk the stock contributes to a well-diversified portfolio. The benchmark for a well-diversified stock portfolio is the market portfolio, which is a portfolio containing all stocks.[15] Therefore, the relevant risk of an individual stock, which is called its **beta coefficient,** is defined under the CAPM as the amount of risk that the stock contributes to the market portfolio. In CAPM terminology, ρ_{iM} is the correlation between the ith stock's return and the return on the market, σ_i is the standard deviation of the ith stock's return,

---

[13]The CAPM was originated by William F. Sharpe in his article "Capital Asset Prices: A Theory of Market Equilibrium under Conditions of Risk," which appeared in the September 1964 issue of the *Journal of Finance.* Note that Professor Sharpe won the Nobel Prize in economics for his capital asset pricing work. The assumptions inherent in Sharpe's model were spelled out by Michael C. Jensen in "Capital Markets: Theory and Evidence," *Bell Journal of Economics and Management Science,* Autumn 1972, 357–98.

[14]With no restrictions on short sales, an asset's weight in the portfolio may be negative or greater than 1 as long as the sum of all asset weights equals 1.

[15]In theory, the market portfolio should contain all assets. In practice, it usually contains only stocks. Many analysts use returns on the S&P 500 Index for the U.S. market and the S&P/TSX Composite Index for the Canadian market.

and σ_M is the standard deviation of the market's return. The beta coefficient of the ith stock, denoted by b_i, is defined as follows:

$$b_i = \left(\frac{\sigma_i}{\sigma_M}\right)\rho_{iM} \tag{7-10}$$

This tells us that a stock with a high standard deviation, σ_i, will tend to have a high beta, which means that it contributes a relatively large amount of risk to a well-diversified portfolio. This makes sense, because if all other things are equal, a stock with high stand-alone risk will contribute a lot of risk to the portfolio. Note too that a stock with a high correlation with the market, ρ_{iM}, will also have a large beta, and hence be risky. This also makes sense, because a high correlation means that diversification is not helping much; hence the stock contributes a lot of risk to the portfolio.

The *covariance between stock i and the market*, COV_{iM}, is defined as[16]

$$COV_{iM} = \rho_{iM}\sigma_i\sigma_M \tag{7-11}$$

Substituting Equation 7-11 into 7-10 provides another frequently used expression for beta:

$$b_i = \frac{COV_{iM}}{\sigma_M^2} \tag{7-12}$$

Calculators and spreadsheets can calculate the components of Equation 7-10 (ρ_{iM}, σ_i, and σ_M), which can then be used to calculate beta, but there is another way. Suppose you plotted the stock's returns on the y-axis of a graph and the market portfolio's returns on the x-axis, as shown in Figure 7-9. The formula for the slope of a regression line is exactly equal to the formula for beta in Equation 7-12. Therefore, to estimate beta for a security, you can just estimate a regression with the stock's returns on the y-axis and the market's returns on the x-axis. Appendix 7A of this chapter discusses how to calculate beta coefficients further.

Individual Stock Betas

The tendency of a stock to move up and down with the market is reflected in its beta coefficient. An *average-risk stock* is defined as one with a beta equal to 1.0. Such a stock's returns tend to move up and down, on average, with the market, which is measured by some index such as the S&P 500, or the S&P/TSX Composite Index. A portfolio of such b = 1.0 stocks will move up and down with the broad market indexes, and it will be just as risky as the indexes. A portfolio of b = 0.5 stocks will be half as risky as the market. On the other hand, a portfolio of b = 2.0 stocks will be twice as risky as the market.

Figure 7-9 shows a graph of the historical returns of three stocks and the market. The data below the graph assume that in Year 1 the "market," defined as a portfolio consisting of all stocks, had a total return (dividend yield plus capital gains yield) of $\bar{r}_M = 10\%$ and that Stocks H, A, and L (for High, Average, and Low risk) also all had returns of 10%. In Year 2, the market went up sharply, and the return on the market portfolio was $\bar{r} = 20\%$. Returns on the three stocks also went up: H soared to 30%; A went up to 20%, the same as the market; and L only went up to 15%. The market dropped in Year 3, and the market return was $\bar{r}_M = -10\%$. The three stocks' returns also fell, H plunging to -30%, A falling to -10%, and L going down to $\bar{r}_L = 0\%$. Thus, the three stocks all moved in the same direction as the market, but H was by far the most volatile; A was just as volatile as the market; and L was less volatile.

---

[16] Using historical data, the sample covariance can be calculated as

$$\text{Sample covariance from historical data} = COV_{iM} = \frac{\sum\limits_{t=1}^{n}(\bar{r}_{i,t} - \bar{r}_{i,Avg})(\bar{r}_{M,t} - \bar{r}_{M,Avg})}{n-1}$$

Calculating the covariance is somewhat easier than calculating the correlation. So if you have already calculated the standard deviations, then it is easier to calculate the covariance and then calculate the correlation as: $\rho_{iM} = COV_{iM}/(\sigma_i\sigma_M)$.

FIGURE 7-9 Relative Volatility of Stocks H, A, and L

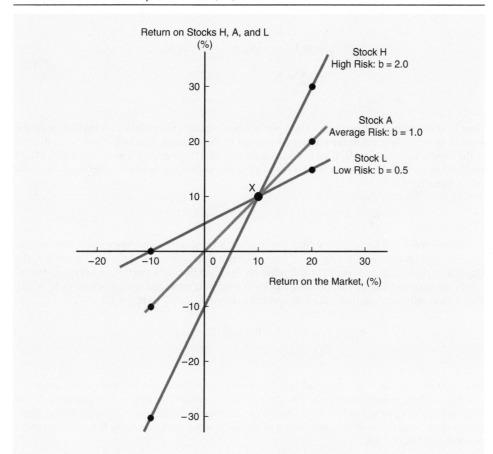

See *Ch 07 Tool Kit.xlsx,* at the textbook's website for all calculations.

		Historical Returns		
Year	Stock H	Stock A	Stock L	Market
1	10%	10%	10%	10%
2	30	20	15	20
3	(30)	(10)	0	(10)
Beta	2.0	1.0	0.5	

Notes: These three stocks plot exactly on their regression lines. This indicates that they are exposed only to market risk. Mutual funds that concentrate on stocks with betas of 2.0, 1.0, and 0.5 will have patterns similar to those shown in the graph.

Beta measures a stock's volatility relative to the market, which by definition has b = 1.0. As we noted above, the slope of a regression line shows how a stock moves in response to a movement in the general market. Most stocks have betas in the range of 0.40 to 1.60, and the average beta for all stocks is 1.0 by definition.

Theoretically, it is possible for a stock to have a negative beta. In this case, the stock's returns would tend to rise whenever the returns on other stocks fall. In practice, very few stocks have a negative beta. Keep in mind that a stock in a given period may move counter to the overall market, even though the stock's beta is positive. If a stock has a positive beta, we would *expect* its return to increase whenever the overall stock market rises. However, company-specific factors may cause the stock's realized return to decline, even though the market's return is positive.

Portfolio Betas

A very important feature of beta is that the beta of a portfolio is a weighted average of its individual securities' betas:

$$b_p = w_1 b_1 + w_2 b_2 + \dots + w_n b_n$$
$$= \sum_{i=1}^{n} w_i b_i \tag{7-13}$$

Here b_p is the beta of the portfolio, and it shows how volatile the portfolio is in relation to the market; w_i is the fraction of the portfolio invested in the ith stock; and b_i is the beta coefficient of the ith stock. For example, if an investor holds a $100,000 portfolio consisting of $33,333.33 invested in each of three stocks, and if each of the stocks has a beta of 0.7, then the portfolio's beta will be $b_p = 0.7$:

$$b_p = 0.3333(0.7) + 0.3333(0.7) + 0.3333(0.7) = 0.7$$

Such a portfolio will be less risky than the market, so it should experience relatively narrow price swings and have relatively small rate-of-return fluctuations. In terms of Figure 7-9, the slope of its regression line would be 0.7, which is less than that for a portfolio of average stocks.

Now suppose one of the existing stocks is sold and replaced by a stock with $b_i = 2.0$. This action will increase the beta of the portfolio from $b_{p1} = 0.7$ to $b_{p2} = 1.13$:

$$b_{p2} = 0.3333(0.7) + 0.3333(0.7) + 0.3333(2.0)$$
$$= 1.13$$

Had a stock with $b_i = 0.2$ been added, the portfolio beta would have declined from 0.7 to 0.53. Adding a low-beta stock, therefore, would reduce the risk of the portfolio. Consequently, adding new stocks to a portfolio can change the riskiness of that portfolio. *Thus, since a stock's beta measures its contribution to the risk of a portfolio, beta is the theoretically correct measure of the stock's risk.*

Key Points Related to Beta

The preceding analysis of risk in a portfolio context is part of the Capital Asset Pricing Model (CAPM), and we can highlight the key points as follows:

1. A stock's risk consists of two components, market risk and diversifiable risk.
2. Diversifiable risk can be eliminated by diversification, and most investors do indeed diversify, either by holding large portfolios or by purchasing shares in a mutual fund. We are left, then, with market risk, which is caused by general movements in the stock market and which reflects the fact that most stocks are systematically affected by events like war, recessions, and inflation. Market risk is the only risk relevant to a rational, diversified investor because such an investor would eliminate diversifiable risk.
3. Investors must be compensated for bearing risk—the greater the risk of a stock, the higher its required return. However, compensation is required only for risk that cannot be eliminated by diversification. If risk premiums existed on stocks due to diversifiable risk, well-diversified investors would start buying those securities (which would not be especially risky to such investors) and bidding up their prices. The stocks' final (equilibrium) expected returns would reflect only nondiversifiable market risk.
4. The market risk of a stock is measured by its beta coefficient, which is an index of the stock's relative volatility. If b equals 1.0, then the stock is about as risky as the market, if held in a diversified portfolio. If b is less than 1.0, the stock is less risky than the market. If beta is greater than 1.0, the stock is more risky.
5. The beta of a portfolio is a weighted average of the individual securities' betas.
6. *Since a stock's beta coefficient determines how the stock affects the risk of a diversified portfolio, beta is the most relevant measure of any stock's risk.*

ⓒNCEPT REVIEW

1. Explain the following statement: "An asset held as part of a portfolio is generally less risky than the same asset held in isolation."
2. What is meant by *perfect positive correlation, perfect negative correlation,* and *zero correlation?*
3. In general, can the risk of a portfolio be reduced to zero by increasing the number of stocks in the portfolio? Explain.
4. What is the beta of a stock that is as risky as the market?
5. Why is beta the theoretically correct measure of a stock's risk?
6. If you plotted the returns on a particular stock versus those on the Dow Jones Index over the past 5 years, what would the slope of the regression line you obtained indicate about the stock's market risk?
7. An investor has a three-stock portfolio with $25,000 invested in Agrium, $50,000 invested in Finning, and $25,000 invested in RONA. Assume Agrium's beta is estimated to be 1.20, Finning's beta is estimated to be 0.80, and RONA's beta is estimated to be 1.0. What is the estimated beta of the investor's portfolio? (Check Figure: 0.95)

7.4 The Relationship between Risk and Rates of Return

In the preceding section, we saw that under the CAPM theory, beta is the appropriate measure of a stock's relevant risk. Now we must specify the relationship between risk and return: For a given level of risk as measured by beta, what rate of return should investors require to compensate them for bearing that risk? To begin, let us define the following terms:

$\hat{r}_i$ = *expected* rate of return on the *i*th stock.

r_i = *required* rate of return on the *i*th stock. This is the minimum expected return that is required to induce an average investor to purchase the stock.

$\bar{r}$ = realized, after-the-fact return.

r_{RF} = risk-free rate of return. In this context, r_{RF} is generally measured by the expected return on long-term government bonds.

b_i = beta coefficient of the *i*th stock.

r_M = required rate of return on a portfolio consisting of all stocks, which is called the *market portfolio.*

RP_M = risk premium on "the market." $RP_M = (r_M - r_{RF})$ is the additional return over the risk-free rate required to induce an average investor to invest in the market portfolio.

RP_i = risk premium on the *i*th stock: $RP_i = (RP_M)b_i$.

The **market risk premium, RP_M,** shows the premium investors require for bearing the risk of an average stock, and it depends on the degree of risk aversion that investors on average have. Let us assume that government bonds yield $r_{RF} = 6\%$ and that the market has a required return of $r_M = 11\%$. The market risk premium is 5%:

$$RP_M = r_M - r_{RF} = 11\% - 6\% = 5\%$$

We can measure a stock's relative riskiness by its beta coefficient. The risk premium for the *i*th stock is

$$\text{Risk premium for Stock i} = RP_i = (RP_M)b_i \qquad (7\text{-}14)$$

If we know the market risk premium, RP_M, and the stock's risk as measured by its beta coefficient, b_i, we can find the stock's risk premium as the product $(RP_M)b_i$. For example, if $b_i = 0.5$ and $RP_M = 5\%$, then RP_i is 2.5%:

$$RP_i = (5\%)(0.5)$$

$$= 2.5\%$$

The required return for any investment can be expressed in general terms as

$$\text{Required return} = \text{Risk-free return} + \text{Premium for risk}$$

Here the risk-free return includes a premium for expected inflation, and we assume that the assets under consideration have similar maturities and liquidity. Under these conditions, the relationship between the required return and risk is called the **Security Market Line (SML):**

$$\text{SML Equation:} \quad \begin{array}{c}\text{Required return}\\\text{on Stock i}\end{array} = \begin{array}{c}\text{Risk-free}\\\text{rate}\end{array} + \left(\begin{array}{c}\text{Market risk}\\\text{premium}\end{array}\right)\left(\begin{array}{c}\text{Stock i's}\\\text{beta}\end{array}\right)$$

$$r_i = r_{RF} + (r_M - r_{RF})b_i \qquad (7\text{-}15)$$

$$= r_{RF} + (RP_M)b_i$$

The required return for Stock i can be written as follows:

$$r_i = 6\% + 5\%(0.5)$$

$$= 8.5\%$$

If some other Stock j were riskier than Stock i and had $b_j = 2.0$, then its required rate of return would be 16%:

$$r_j = 6\% + (5\%)2.0 = 16\%$$

An average stock, with $b = 1.0$, would have a required return of 11%, the same as the market return:

$$r_A = 6\% + (5\%)1.0 = 11\% = r_M$$

As noted above, Equation 7-15 is called the Security Market Line (SML) equation, and it is often expressed in graph form, as in Figure 7-10, which shows the SML when $r_{RF} = 6\%$ and $RP_M = 5\%$. Note the following points:

1. Required rates of return are shown on the vertical axis, while risk as measured by beta is shown on the horizontal axis. This graph is quite different from the one shown in Figure 7-9, where the returns on individual stocks were plotted on the vertical axis and returns on the market index were shown on the horizontal axis. The slopes of the three lines in Figure 7-9 were used to calculate the three stocks' betas, and those betas were then plotted as points on the horizontal axis of Figure 7-10.
2. Riskless securities have $b_i = 0$; therefore, r_{RF} appears as the vertical axis intercept in Figure 7-10. If we could construct a portfolio that had a beta of zero, it would have a required return equal to the risk-free rate.
3. The slope of the SML (5% in Figure 7-10) reflects the degree of risk aversion in the economy—the greater the average investor's aversion to risk, then (a) the steeper the slope of the line, (b) the greater the risk premium for all stocks, and (c) the higher the required rate of return on all stocks.[17] These points are discussed further in a later section.
4. The values we worked out for stocks with $b_i = 0.5$, $b_i = 1.0$, and $b_i = 2.0$ agree with the values shown on the graph for r_L, r_A, and r_H.
5. Negative betas are rare but can occur. For example, some stocks associated with gold, such as a mining operation, occasionally have a negative beta. Based on the SML, a stock with a negative beta should have a required return less than the risk-free rate. In fact, a stock with a very large but negative beta might have a negative required return! This means that when the market is doing well, this stock will do poorly. But it also implies the opposite: When the market is doing poorly, a negative beta stock should have a positive return. In other words, the negative beta stock acts as insurance. Therefore, an investor might be willing to accept a negative return on the stock during the good times if it is likely to provide a positive return in bad times.

---

[17]Students sometimes confuse beta with the slope of the SML. This is a mistake. The slope of any straight line is equal to the "rise" divided by the "run," or $(Y_1 - Y_0)/(X_1 - X_0)$. Consider Figure 7-10. If we let $Y = r$ and $X = $ beta, and we go from the origin to $b = 1.0$, we see that the slope is $(r_M - r_{RF})/(b_M - b_{RF}) = (11\% - 6\%)/(1 - 0) = 5\%$. Thus, the slope of the SML is equal to $(r_M - r_{RF})$, the market risk premium. In Figure 7-10, $r_i = 6\% + 5\%bi$, so an increase of beta from 1.0 to 2.0 would produce a 5 percentage point increase in r_i.

FIGURE
7-10   The Security Market Line (SML)

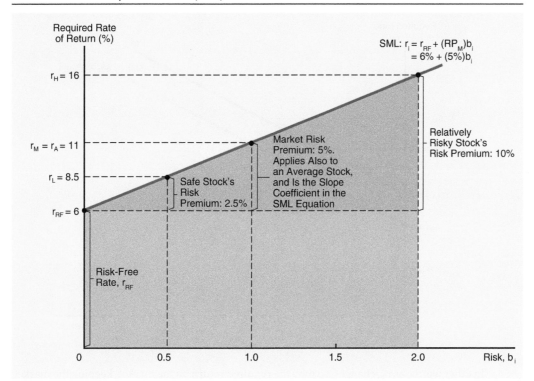

Both the Security Market Line and a company's position on it change over time due to changes in interest rates, investors' aversion to risk, and individual companies' betas. Such changes are discussed in the following sections.

The Impact of Changes in Inflation and Interest Rates

Interest is the same as "rent" on borrowed money, or the price of money. Thus, r_{RF} is the price of money to a riskless borrower. The risk-free rate as measured by the rate on Canadian government bonds is called the *nominal*, or *quoted, rate*, and it consists of two elements: (1) a *real inflation-free rate of return, r^**, and (2) an *inflation premium, IP*, equal to the anticipated rate of inflation.[18] Thus, $r_{RF} = r^* + IP$. The real rate on long-term bonds has historically ranged from 2% to 4%, with a mean of about 3%. Therefore, if no inflation were expected, long-term government bonds would yield about 3%. However, as the expected rate of inflation increases, a premium must be added to the real risk-free rate of return to compensate investors for the loss of purchasing power that results from inflation. Therefore, the 6% r_{RF} shown in Figure 7-10 might be thought of as consisting of a 3% real risk-free rate of return plus a 3% inflation premium: $r_{RF} = r^* + IP = 3\% + 3\% = 6\%$.

If the expected inflation rate rose by 2%, to 3% + 2% = 5%, this would cause r_{RF} to rise to 8%. Such a change is shown in Figure 7-11. Notice that under the CAPM, the increase in r_{RF} leads to an *equal* increase in the rate of return on all risky assets, because the same inflation premium is built into the required rate of return of both riskless and risky assets. For example, the rate of return on an average stock, r_M, increases from 11% to 13%. Other risky securities' returns also rise by 2 percentage points.

The discussion above also applies to any change in the nominal risk-free interest rate, whether it is caused by a change in expected inflation or in the real interest rate. The key point to remember is that a change in r_{RF} will not necessarily cause a change in the market risk premium, which is the required return on the market, r_M, minus the risk-free rate, r_{RF}.

---

[18]Long-term government bonds also contain a maturity risk premium, MRP. Here we include the MRP in r^* to simplify the discussion. See Chapter 6 for more on bond pricing and bond risk premiums.

FIGURE
7-11 Shift in the SML Caused by an Increase in Interest Rates

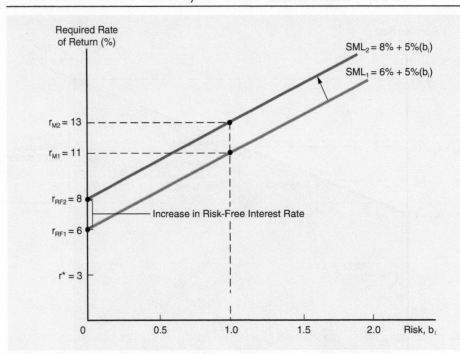

In other words, as r_{RF} changes, so may the required return on the market, keeping the market risk premium stable. Think of a sailboat floating in a harbour. The distance from the ocean floor to the ocean surface is like the risk-free rate, and it moves up and down with the tides. The distance from the top of the ship's mast to the ocean floor is like the required market return: it, too, moves up and down with the tides. But the distance from the mast-top to the ocean surface is like the market risk premium—it generally stays the same, even though tides move the ship up and down. In other words, a change in the risk-free rate also causes a change in the required market return, r_M, resulting in a relatively stable market risk premium, $r_M - r_{RF}$.

Changes in Risk Aversion

The slope of the Security Market Line reflects the extent to which investors are averse to risk—the steeper the slope of the line, the greater the average investor's risk aversion. Suppose investors were indifferent to risk; that is, they were not risk averse. If r_{RF} were 6%, then risky assets would also provide an expected return of 6%, because if there were no risk aversion, there would be no risk premium, and the SML would be plotted as a horizontal line. As risk aversion increases, so does the risk premium, and this causes the slope of the SML to become steeper.

Figure 7-12 illustrates an increase in risk aversion. The market risk premium rises from 5% to 7.5%, causing r_M to rise from $r_{M1} = 11\%$ to $r_{M2} = 13.5\%$. The returns on other risky assets also rise, and the effect of this shift in risk aversion is more pronounced on riskier securities. For example, the required return on a stock with $b_i = 0.5$ increases by only 1.25 percentage points, from 8.5% to 9.75%, whereas that on a stock with $b_i = 1.5$ increases by 3.75 percentage points, from 13.5% to 17.25%.

Changes in a Stock's Beta Coefficient

As we shall see later in the book, a firm can influence its market risk, hence its beta, through changes in the composition of its assets and also through its use of debt. A company's beta can also change as a result of external factors such as increased competition in its industry, the expiration of basic patents, and the like. When such changes occur, the required rate of return also changes.

FIGURE

7-12   Shift in the SML Caused by Increased Risk Aversion

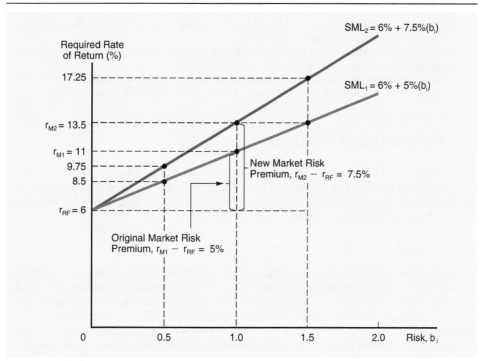

CONCEPT REVIEW

1. Differentiate among the expected rate of return ($\hat{r}$), the required rate of return (r), and the realized, after-the-fact return ($\bar{r}$) on a stock. Which would have to be larger to get you to buy the stock, $\hat{r}$ or r? Would $\hat{r}$, r, and $\bar{r}$ typically be the same or different for a given company?

2. What are the differences between the relative volatility graph (Figure 7-9), where "betas are made," and the SML graph (Figure 7-10), where "betas are used"? Discuss both how the graphs are constructed and the information they convey.

3. What happens to the SML graph in Figure 7-10 when inflation increases or decreases?

4. What happens to the SML graph when risk aversion increases or decreases? What would the SML look like if investors were indifferent to risk, that is, had zero risk aversion?

5. How can a firm influence its market risk as reflected in its beta?

6. A stock has a beta of 1.4. Assume that the risk-free rate is 5.5% and the market risk premium is 5%. What is the stock's required rate of return? (Check Figure: 12.5%)

Current Status of the CAPM

The CAPM is extremely appealing at an intellectual level: It is logical and rational, and once someone works through and understands the theory, his or her reaction is usually to accept it without question. However, doubts begin to arise when one thinks about the assumptions upon which the model is based, and these doubts are as much reinforced as reduced by the empirical tests. Our own views as to the current status of the CAPM are as follows:

1. The CAPM framework, with its focus on market as opposed to stand-alone risk, is clearly a useful way to think about the risk of assets. Thus, as a conceptual model, the CAPM is of truly fundamental importance.

2. When applied in practice, the CAPM appears to provide neat, precise answers to important questions about risk and required rates of return. However, the answers are

less clear than they seem. The simple truth is that we do not know precisely how to measure any of the inputs required to implement the CAPM. These inputs should all be ex ante, yet only ex post data are available. Furthermore, historical data on $\bar{r}_M$, r_{RF}, and betas vary greatly depending on the time period studied and the methods used to estimate them. Thus, although the CAPM appears precise, estimates of r_i found through its use are subject to potentially large errors.[19]

3. Because the CAPM is logical in the sense that it represents the way risk-averse people ought to behave, the model is a useful conceptual tool.

4. It is appropriate to think about many financial problems in a CAPM framework. However, it is important to recognize the limitations of the CAPM when using it in practice.

7.5 Behavioural Finance

A large body of evidence in the field of psychology shows that people often behave irrationally, but in predictable ways. The field of behavioural finance focuses on irrational, but predictable, financial decisions. The following sections examine applications of behavioural finance to market bubbles and to other financial decisions.

Market Bubbles and Behavioural Finance

Market bubbles such as the stock market bubble of 2008 occur when asset prices (stocks, houses, etc.) run up faster and much higher than economic conditions and models would normally predict. This price run-up is accompanied by larger than normal trading volumes and large numbers of new investors. Bubbles can persist for some time but, ultimately, they will burst and prices will fall very quickly and steeply, leaving investors with huge losses. Traditional finance has not provided any definitive explanations on why market bubbles form, but the field of behavioural finance offers some possible reasons, including overconfidence, anchoring bias, and herding.

Many psychological tests show that people are overconfident with respect to their own abilities relative to the abilities of others, which is the basis of Garrison Keillor's joke about a town where all the children are above average. Professor Richard Thaler and his colleague Nicholas Barberis address this phenomenon as it applies to finance:

> Overconfidence may in part stem from two other biases, self-attribution bias and hindsight bias. Self-attribution bias refers to people's tendency to ascribe any success they have in some activity to their own talents, while blaming failure on bad luck, rather than on their ineptitude. Doing this repeatedly will lead people to the pleasing but erroneous conclusion that they are very talented. For example, investors might become overconfident after several quarters of investing success [Gervais and Odean (2001)[20]]. Hindsight bias is the tendency of people to believe, after an event has occurred, that they predicted it before it happened. If people think they predicted the past better than they actually did, they may also believe that they can predict the future better than they actually can.[21]

Psychologists have learned that many people focus too closely on recent events when predicting future events, a phenomenon called **anchoring bias**. Therefore, when the market is performing better than average, people tend to think it will continue to perform better than average. When anchoring bias is coupled with overconfidence, investors can become convinced that their prediction of an increasing market is correct, thus creating even more demand for stocks. This demand drives up stock prices, which serves to reinforce the overconfidence and move the anchor even higher.

There is another way that an increasing market can reinforce itself. Studies have shown that gamblers who are ahead tend to take on more risks (i.e., they are playing with the

[19]For an article supporting a positive link between market risk and expected return, see Felicia Marston and Robert S. Harris, "Risk and Return: A Revisit Using Expected Returns," *Financial Review*, February 1993, 117–137.

[20]See Terrance Odean and Simon Gervais, "Learning to Be Overconfident," *Review of Financial Studies*, Spring 2001, pp. 1–27.

[21]See page 1066 in an excellent review of behavioural finance by Nicholas Barberis and Richard Thaler· A Survey of Behavioural Finance," in *Handbook of the Economics of Finance*, George Constantinides, Milt Harris, and Rene Stulz, eds. (Amsterdam: Elsevier/North-Holland, 2003), Chapter 18.

house's money), whereas those who are behind tend to become more conservative. If this is true for investors, we can get a feedback loop: when the market goes up, investors have gains, which can make them less risk averse, which increases their demand for stock, which leads to higher prices, which starts the cycle again.

Herding behaviour occurs when groups of investors emulate other successful investors and chase asset classes that are doing well. For example, high returns in mortgage-backed securities during 2004 and 2005 enticed other investors to move into that asset class. Herding behaviour can create excess demand for asset classes that have done well, causing price increases that induce additional herding behaviour. Thus, herding behaviour can inflate rising markets.

Sometimes herding behaviour occurs when a group of investors assumes that other investors are better informed—the herd chases the "smart" money. But in other cases herding can occur even when those in the herd suspect that prices are overinflated. For example, consider the situation of a portfolio manager who believes that bank stocks are overvalued even though many other portfolios are heavily invested in such stocks. If the manager moves out of bank stocks and they subsequently fall in price, then the manager will be rewarded for her judgment. But if the stocks continue to do well, the manager may well lose her job for missing out on the gains. If instead the manager follows the herd and invests in bank stocks, then the manager will do no better or worse than her peers. Thus, if the penalty for being wrong is bigger than the reward for being correct, it is rational for portfolio managers to herd even if they suspect the herd is wrong.

Researchers have shown that the combination of overconfidence and biased self-attribution can lead to overly volatile stock markets, short-term momentum, and long-term reversals.[22] We suspect that overconfidence, anchoring bias, and herding can contribute to market bubbles.

Other Applications of Behavioural Finance

Psychologists Daniel Kahneman and Amos Tversky show that individuals view potential losses and potential gains very differently[23] If you ask an average person whether he or she would rather have $500 with certainty or flip a fair coin and receive $1,000 if it comes up heads and nothing if it comes up tails, most would prefer the certain $500 gain, which suggests an aversion to risk—a *sure* $500 gain is better than a risky *expected* $500 gain. However, if you ask the same person whether he or she would rather pay $500 with certainly or flip a coin and pay $1,000 if it's heads and nothing if it's tails, most would indicate that they prefer to flip the coin, which suggests a preference for risk—a risky *expected* $500 loss is better than a *sure* $500 loss. In other words, losses are so painful that people will make irrational choices to avoid sure losses. This phenomenon is called "loss aversion."

One way that people avoid a loss is by not admitting that they have actually had a loss. For example, in many people's mental bookkeeping, a loss isn't really a loss until the losing investment is actually sold. Therefore, they tend to hold risky losers instead of accepting a certain loss, which is a display of loss aversion. Of course, this leads investors to sell losers much less frequently than winners even though this is suboptimal for tax purposes.[24]

Many corporate projects and mergers fail to live up to their expectations. In fact, most mergers end up destroying value in the acquiring company. Because this is well known, why haven't companies responded by being more selective in their investments? There are many possible reasons, but research by Ulrike Malmendier and Geoffrey Tate suggests that overconfidence leads managers to overestimate their abilities and the quality of their projects.[25] In other words, managers might know that the average decision to merge destroys value, but they are certain that their decision is above average.

Finance is a quantitative field, but good managers in all disciplines must also understand human behaviour.[26]

[22]See Terrance Odean, "Volume, Volatility, Price, and Profit When All Traders Are Above Average," *Journal of Finance*, December 1998, pp. 1887–1934; and Kent Danid, David Hirshleifer, and Avanidhar Subrahmanyam, "Investor Psychology and Security Market Under-and Overreactions," *Journal of Finance*, December 1998, pp. 1839–1885.
[23]Daniel Kahneman and Amos Tversky, "Prospect Theory: An Analysis of Decision under Risk," *Econometrica*, March 1979, pp. 263–292.
[24]See Terrance Odean, "Are Investors Reluctant to Realize Their Losses?" *Journal of Finance*, October 1998, pp. 1775–1798.
[25]See Ulrike Malmendier and Geoffrey Tate, "CEO Overconfidence and Corporate Investment," *Journal of Finance*, December 2005, pp. 2661–2700.
[26]Excellent reviews of behavioural finance are by Richard H. Thaler, Editor, *Advances in Behavioral Finance* (New York: Russell Sage Foundation. 1993); and Andrei Shleifer, *Inefficient Markets: An Introduction to Behavioral Finance* (New York: Oxford University Press, 2000).

CONCEPT REVIEW

1. What is behavioural finance?
2. What is anchoring bias? What is herding behaviour? How can these contribute to market bubbles?

Summary

In this chapter, we described the trade-off between risk and return. We began by discussing how to calculate risk and return for both individual assets and portfolios. In particular, we differentiated between stand-alone risk and risk in a portfolio context, and we explained the benefits of diversification. Finally, we developed the CAPM, which explains how risk affects rates of return. In the chapters that follow, we will give you the tools to estimate the required rates of return for bonds, preferred stock, and common stock, and we will explain how firms use these returns to develop their costs of capital. As you will see, the cost of capital is an important element in the firm's capital budgeting process. The key concepts covered in this chapter are listed below.

- **Risk** can be defined as the chance that some unfavourable event will occur.
- The risk of an asset's cash flows can be considered on a **stand-alone basis** (each asset by itself) or in a **portfolio context,** where the investment is combined with other assets and its risk is reduced through **diversification.**
- Most rational investors hold **portfolios of assets,** and they are more concerned with the riskiness of their portfolios than with the risk of individual assets.
- The **expected return** on an investment is the mean value of its probability distribution of returns.
- The **greater the probability** that the actual return will be far below the expected return, the **greater the stand-alone risk** associated with an asset.
- The average investor is **risk averse,** which means that he or she must be compensated for holding risky assets. Therefore, riskier assets have higher required returns than less risky assets.
- An **efficient portfolio** is one that offers the most return for a given amount of risk or the least risk for a given amount of return.
- An asset's risk consists of (1) **diversifiable risk,** which can be eliminated by diversification, plus (2) **market risk,** which cannot be eliminated by diversification.
- The **relevant risk** of an individual asset is its contribution to the riskiness of a well-diversified **portfolio,** which is the asset's **market risk.** Since market risk cannot be eliminated by diversification, investors must be compensated for bearing it.
- A stock's **beta coefficient, b,** is a measure of its market risk. Beta measures the extent to which the stock's returns move relative to the market.
- A **high-beta stock** is more volatile than an average stock, while a **low-beta stock** is less volatile than an average stock. An average stock has $b = 1.0$.
- The **beta of a portfolio** is a **weighted average** of the betas of the individual securities in the portfolio.
- The **Security Market Line (SML)** equation shows the relationship between a security's market risk and its required rate of return. The return required for any security i is equal to the **risk-free rate** plus the **market risk premium** times the security's beta: $r_i = r_{RF} + (RP_M)b_i$.
- Even though the expected rate of return on a stock is generally equal to its required return, a number of things can happen to cause the required rate of return to change: (1) **the risk-free rate can change** because of changes in either real rates or anticipated inflation, (2) **a stock's beta can change,** and (3) **investors' aversion to risk can change.**
- Because returns on assets in different countries are not perfectly correlated, **global diversification** may result in lower risk for multinational companies and globally diversified portfolios.
- **Behavioural finance** assumes that investors don't always behave rationally. **Anchoring bias** is the human tendency to "anchor" too closely on recent events when predicting future events. **Herding** is the tendency of investors to follow the crowd. When combined with overconfidence, anchoring and herding can contribute to market bubbles.

Questions

7-1 Define the following terms, using graphs or equations to illustrate your answers wherever feasible:
a. Stand-alone risk; risk; probability distribution
b. Expected rate of return, $\hat{r}$
c. Continuous probability distribution
d. Standard deviation, σ; variance, σ^2; coefficient of variation, CV
e. Risk aversion; realized rate of return, $\bar{r}$
f. Risk premium for Stock i, RP_i; market risk premium, RP_M
g. Capital Asset Pricing Model (CAPM)
h. Expected return on a portfolio, $\hat{r}_p$; market portfolio
i. Correlation coefficient, ρ; correlation
j. Market risk; diversifiable risk; relevant risk
k. Beta coefficient, b; average stock's beta, b_A
l. Security Market Line (SML); SML equation
m. Slope of SML as a measure of risk aversion

7-2 The probability distribution of a less risky return is more peaked than that of a riskier return. What shape would the probability distribution have for (a) completely certain returns and (b) completely uncertain returns?

7-3 Security A has an expected return of 7%, a standard deviation of returns of 35%, a correlation coefficient with the market of −0.3, and a beta coefficient of −1.5. Security B has an expected return of 12%, a standard deviation of returns of 10%, a correlation with the market of 0.7, and a beta coefficient of 1.0. Which security is riskier? Why?

7-4 Suppose you owned a portfolio consisting of $250,000 worth of long-term Government of Canada bonds.
a. Would your portfolio be riskless?
b. Now suppose you hold a portfolio consisting of $250,000 worth of 30-day Treasury bills. Every 30 days your bills mature, and you reinvest the principal ($250,000) in a new batch of bills. Assume that you live on the investment income from your portfolio and that you want to maintain a constant standard of living. Is your portfolio truly riskless?
c. Can you think of any asset that would be completely riskless? Could someone develop such an asset? Explain.

7-5 If investors' aversion to risk increased, would the risk premium on a high-beta stock increase more or less than that on a low-beta stock? Explain.

7-6 If a company's beta were to double, would its expected return double?

7-7 Is it possible to construct a portfolio of stocks that has an expected return equal to the risk-free rate?

Concept Review Problems

Full solutions are provided at www.nelson.com/brigham3ce.

CR-1 Stocks A and B have the following historical returns:

Realized Rates
of Return

Year	Stock A's Returns, $\bar{r}_A$	Stock B's Returns, $\bar{r}_B$
2011	(18)%	(24)%
2012	44	24
2013	(22)	(4)
2014	22	8
2015	34	56

a. Calculate the average rate of return for each stock during the 5-year period. Assume that someone held a portfolio consisting of 50% of Stock A and 50% of Stock B. What would have been the realized rate of return on the portfolio in each year? What would have been the average return on the portfolio during this period?

b. Now calculate the standard deviation of returns for each stock and for the portfolio.
c. Looking at the annual returns data on the two stocks, would you guess that the correlation coefficient between returns on the two stocks is closer to 0.8 or to −0.8?
d. If you added more stocks at random to the portfolio, which of the following is the most accurate statement of what would happen to σ_p?
   (1) σ_p would remain constant.
   (2) σ_p would decline to somewhere in the vicinity of 20%.
   (3) σ_p would decline to zero if enough stocks were included.

CR-2
Beta and Required Rate of Return

ECRI Corporation is a holding company with four main subsidiaries. The percentage of its business coming from each of the subsidiaries, and their respective betas, are as follows:

Subsidiary	Percentage of Business	Beta
Electric utility	60%	0.70
Cable company	25	0.90
Real estate	10	1.30
International/special projects	5	1.50

a. What is the holding company's beta?
b. Assume that the risk-free rate is 6% and the market risk premium is 5%. What is the holding company's required rate of return?
c. ECRI is considering a change in its strategic focus: it will reduce its reliance on the electric utility subsidiary, so the percentage of its business from this subsidiary will be 50%. At the same time, ECRI will increase its reliance on the international/special projects division, so the percentage of its business from that subsidiary will rise to 15%. What will be the shareholders' required rate of return if they adopt these changes?

Problems

Easy
Problems 1–3

Answers to odd-numbered problems appear in Appendix A.

7-1
Portfolio Beta

An individual has $35,000 invested in a stock that has a beta of 0.8 and $40,000 invested in a stock with a beta of 1.4. If these are the only two investments in her portfolio, what is her portfolio's beta?

7-2
Required Rate of Return

Assume that the risk-free rate is 6% and that the expected return on the market is 11%. What is the required rate of return on a stock that has a beta of 0.6?

7-3
Expected and Required Rates of Return

Assume that the risk-free rate is 5% and the market risk premium is 6%. What is the expected return for the overall stock market? What is the required rate of return on a stock that has a beta of 1.2?

Intermediate
Problems 4–14

7-4
Expected Return—Discrete Distribution

A stock's return has the following distribution:

Demand for the Company's Products	Probability of This Demand Occurring	Rate of Return if This Demand Occurs
Weak	0.1	(30)%
Below average	0.2	(5)
Average	0.4	10
Above average	0.2	16
Strong	0.1	40
	1.0	

Calculate the stock's expected return, standard deviation, and coefficient of variation.

7-5
Expected Returns—
Discrete Distribution

The market and Stock J have the following probability distributions:

Probability	r_M	r_J
0.3	12%	13%
0.4	5	4
0.3	15	12

a.   Calculate the expected rates of return for the market and Stock J.
b.   Calculate the standard deviations for the market and Stock J.
c.   Calculate the coefficients of variation for the market and Stock J.

7-6
Required Rate of Return

Suppose r_{RF} = 5%, r_M = 10%, and r_A = 12%.
a.   Calculate Stock A's beta.
b.   If Stock A's beta were 2.0, what would be A's new required rate of return?

7-7
Expected Rate of Return
and Risk

The following table shows the annual returns over time for two stocks.

Probability	A	B
0.10	–3%	–10%
0.20	2	1
0.40	7	8
0.20	12	16
0.10	17	24

Calculate each stock's expected return, standard deviation, and coefficient of variation.

7-8
Portfolio Expected Rate
of Return and Risk

Based on the information in Problem 7-7, if a portfolio is made up of 40% of stock A and 60% of stock B:
a.   Calculate the portfolio's expected rate of return.
b.   Calculate the portfolio's standard deviation. Assume the correlation between the two stocks is 0.40.

7-9
Required Rate of Return

Suppose r_{RF} = 9%, r_M = 14%, and b_i = 1.3.
a.   What is r_i, the required rate of return on Stock i?
b.   Now suppose r_{RF} (1) increases to 10% or (2) decreases to 8%. The slope of the SML remains constant. How would this affect r_M and r_i?
c.   Now assume r_{RF} remains at 9% but r_M (1) increases to 16% or (2) falls to 13%. The slope of the SML does not remain constant. How would these changes affect r_i?

7-10
Portfolio Beta

Suppose you hold a diversified portfolio consisting of a $10,000 investment in each of 20 different common stocks. The portfolio beta is equal to 1.20. Now, suppose you have decided to sell one of the stocks in your portfolio with a beta equal to 1.0 for $10,000 and to use these proceeds to buy another stock for your portfolio. Assume the new stock's beta is equal to 1.80. Calculate your portfolio's new beta.

7-11
SML

Assume that the risk-free rate is 2%, the market risk premium is 5%, and the beta of two stocks A and B are 1.4 and 0.8, respectively.
a.   Calculate both stocks' required rates of return.
b.   What would be the return on an "average" stock?
c.   Explain the significance of a security with a 0 beta. What would be this security's required return?
d.   Assume that the economy worsens and that investors correspondingly revise their attitudes toward stocks. Would this change be better reflected in a shift in the market risk premium to 3.5% or 6.5%?
e.   Based on your answer to (d), what would be the new required return for stocks A and B? Would you expect stock prices for A and B to fall or rise?
f.   Ignoring (d) and (e) above, assume that inflationary expectations were revised upward by 0.5%. What would be the change to required returns for stocks A and B? Would their prices fall or rise?

7-12
Two-Asset Portfolio

Stock A has an expected return of 12% and a standard deviation of 40%. Stock B has an expected return of 18% and a standard deviation of 60%. The correlation coefficient between

Stocks A and B is 0.2. What is the expected return and standard deviation of a portfolio invested 30% in Stock A and 70% in Stock B?

7-13
Portfolio Required Return

Suppose you are the money manager of a $4 million investment fund. The fund consists of four stocks with the following investments and betas:

Stock	Investment	Beta
A	$ 400,000	1.50
B	600,000	(0.50)
C	1,000,000	1.25
D	2,000,000	0.75

If the market required rate of return is 14% and the risk-free rate is 6%, what is the fund's required rate of return?

7-14
Expected Returns and SML

Karen has the following portfolio:

Stock	Amount Invested	Beta	Expected Return
Bio-Eng Inc.	$75,000	1.90	12.50%
Canada Pipelines Co.	$125,000	0.75	6.75
Industrial Auto Parts	$200,000	1.20	9.00

Upon further analysis, she determines that the current risk-free rate is 3%, while the market risk premium is 5%.

a. What return does Karen expect on her portfolio, based on the individual stocks' expected returns?

b. What is the required return on the portfolio? What do the answers in part (a) and (b) tell you about the stocks?

c. Karen is thinking of adding another stock, Offshore Oil Co., to her portfolio. Offshore has a beta of 2.3 and an expected return of 14%. Should she add this stock? Briefly explain why or why not.

d. Assuming that Offshore Oil does provide the expected return required and that Karen invests another $100,000 in Offshore Oil, what will be her portfolio's new expected return?

Challenging Problems 15–21

7-15
SML

You plan to invest in a hedge fund that has total capital of $200 million invested in five stocks:

Stock	Investment (in millions)	Stock's Beta
A	$70	0.7
B	50	1.4
C	30	2.5
D	30	2.6
E	20	2.8

The risk-free rate is 4%, and you believe that the following probability distribution for future market returns is realistic:

Probability	Market Return
0.1	5%
0.2	9%
0.4	12%
0.2	16%
0.1	20%

The hedge fund receives a proposal from a company seeking new capital. The amount needed to take a position on the stock is $50 million. The stock has an expected return of 15%, and its estimated beta is 1.2.

a. What is the expected return on the hedge fund?
b. Should the hedge fund invest in the new company?
c. At what expected rate of return should the fund be indifferent to purchasing the stock?

7-16
Portfolio Beta

You have an $8 million portfolio consisting of a $400,000 investment in each of 20 different stocks. The portfolio has a beta equal to 1.1. You are considering selling $400,000 worth of one stock that has a beta equal to 0.9 and using the proceeds to purchase another stock that has a beta equal to 1.9. What will be the new beta of your portfolio following this transaction?

7-17
Required Rate of Return

Stock R has a beta of 1.5, Stock S has a beta of 0.75, the expected rate of return on an average stock is 13%, and the risk-free rate of return is 7%. By how much does the required return on the riskier stock exceed the required return on the less risky stock?

7-18
Historical Realized
Rates of Return

Stocks A and B have the following historical returns:

Year	Stock A's Returns, $\bar{r}_A$	Stock B's Returns, $\bar{r}_B$
2011	(18)%	(14.50)%
2012	33.00	21.80
2013	15.00	30.50
2014	(0.50)	(7.60)
2015	27.00	26.30

a. Calculate the average rate of return for each stock during the 5-year period.
b. Assume that someone held a portfolio consisting of 50% of Stock A and 50% of Stock B. What would have been the realized rate of return on the portfolio in each year? What would have been the average return on the portfolio during this period?
c. Calculate the standard deviation of returns for each stock and for the portfolio.
d. Calculate the coefficient of variation for each stock and for the portfolio.
e. If you are a risk-averse investor, would you prefer to hold Stock A, Stock B, or the portfolio? Why?

7-19
Security Market Line

You are given the following information on five stocks:

	Expected Return	Beta
Five Star Properties	8%	0.8
Royal Paper Products	14%	1.6
Fairway Golf Products	10%	1.4
SPEC Engineering	14%	2.0
Diamond Technology	11%	1.2

The risk-free rate is 4% and the market risk premium is 5%.
a. Which stocks are (a) undervalued, (b) overvalued, and (c) correctly valued?
b. What would be the expected return and beta of a portfolio made up of only the stocks that are correctly valued and undervalued? Assume that each stock in the portfolio has an equal weighting.

7-20
Historical Returns:
Expected and Required
Rates of Return

You have observed the following returns over time:

Year	Stock X	Stock Y	Market
2011	14%	13%	12%
2012	19	7	10
2013	−16	−5	−12
2014	3	1	1
2015	20	11	15

Assume that the risk-free rate is 4%, the market risk premium is 5%, the beta for Stock X is 1.50, and the beta for Stock Y is 0.46:
a. What are the required rates of return for Stocks X and Y?
b. What is the required rate of return for a portfolio consisting of 40% of Stock X and 60% of Stock Y?
c. If Stock X's expected return is 13%, is Stock X under- or overvalued?

7-21
Security Market Line

You are given the following data:

	Historical Rates of Return	
Year	NYSE	Stock X
1	(26.5)%	(14.0)%
2	37.2	23.0
3	23.8	17.5
4	(7.2)	2.0
5	6.6	8.1
6	20.5	19.4
7	30.6	18.2

From the above data, assume that you calculated Stock X's beta coefficient to be 0.56.

a. Determine the arithmetic average rates of return for Stock X and the NYSE over the period given. Calculate the standard deviations of returns for both Stock X and the NYSE.

b. Assuming (1) that the situation during Years 1 to 7 is expected to hold true in the future (i.e., $\hat{r}_X = \bar{r}_X$; $\hat{r}_M = \bar{r}_M$; and both σ_X and b_X in the future will equal their past values), and (2) that Stock X is in equilibrium (i.e., it plots on the Security Market Line), what is the risk-free rate?

c. Plot the Security Market Line.

d. Suppose you hold a large, well-diversified portfolio and are considering adding to the portfolio either Stock X or another stock, Stock Y, that has the same beta as Stock X but a higher standard deviation of returns. Stocks X and Y have the same expected returns; that is, $\hat{r}_X = \hat{r}_Y = 10.6\%$. Which stock should you choose?

 # Spreadsheet Problem

7-22
Evaluating Risk and Return

Start with the partial model in the file *Ch07 P15 Build a Model.xls* on the textbook's website. The file contains hypothetical data for working this problem. Goodman Industries's and Landry Incorporated's stock prices and dividends, along with the Market Index, are shown below. Stock prices are reported for December 31 of each year, and dividends reflect those paid during the year. The market data are adjusted to include dividends.

	Goodman Industries		Landry Incorporated		Market Index
Year	Stock Price	Dividend	Stock Price	Dividend	Includes Dividends
2013	$25.88	$1.73	$73.13	$4.50	17,495.97
2012	22.13	1.59	78.45	4.35	13,178.55
2011	24.75	1.50	73.13	4.13	13,019.97
2010	16.13	1.43	85.88	3.75	9,651.05
2009	17.06	1.35	90.00	3.38	8,403.42
2008	11.44	1.28	83.63	3.00	7,058.96

a. Use the data given to calculate annual returns for Goodman, Landry, and the Market Index, and then calculate average annual returns for the two stocks and the index. (*Hint:* Remember, returns are calculated by subtracting the beginning price from the ending price to get the capital gain or loss, adding the dividend to the capital gain or loss, and then dividing the result by the beginning price. Assume that dividends are already included in the index. Also, you cannot calculate the rate of return for 2008 because you do not have 2007 data.)

b. Calculate the standard deviations of the returns for Goodman, Landry, and the Market Index. (*Hint:* Use the sample standard deviation formula given in the chapter, which corresponds to the STDEV function in *Excel*.)

c. Construct a scatter diagram graph that shows Goodman's returns on the vertical axis and the Market Index's returns on the horizontal axis. Construct a similar graph showing Landry's stock returns on the vertical axis.

d. Estimate Goodman's and Landry's betas as the slopes of regression lines with stock return on the vertical axis (y-axis) and market return on the horizontal axis (x-axis). (*Hint:* Use *Excel*'s SLOPE function.) Are these betas consistent with your graph?

e. The risk-free rate on long-term Treasury bonds is 6.04%. Assume that the market risk premium is 5%. What is the required return on the market? Now use the SML equation to calculate the two companies' required returns.

f. If you formed a portfolio that consisted of 50% Goodman stock and 50% Landry stock, what would be its beta and its required return?

g. Suppose an investor wants to include some Goodman Industries stock in his portfolio. Stocks A, B, and C are currently in the portfolio, and their betas are 0.769, 0.985, and 1.423, respectively. Calculate the new portfolio's required return if it consists of 25% Goodman, 15% Stock A, 40% Stock B, and 20% Stock C.

MINI CASE

Assume that you recently graduated with a major in finance and that you have just landed a job as a financial planner with Barney Smith Inc., a large financial services corporation. Your first assignment is to invest $100,000 for a client. Because the funds are to be invested in a business at the end of 1 year, you have been instructed to plan for a 1-year holding period. Furthermore, your boss has restricted you to the investment alternatives shown in the table with their probabilities and associated outcomes. The relatively high T-bill rate reflects significant inflationary expectations.

Barney Smith's economic forecasting staff have developed probability estimates for the state of the economy, and its security analysts have developed a sophisticated computer program that was used to estimate the rate of return on each alternative under each state of the economy. Alta Industries is an electronics firm; Repo Men Inc. collects past-due debts; and Canadian Foam manufactures mattresses and various other foam products. Barney Smith also maintains an "index fund" that owns a market-weighted fraction of all publicly traded stocks; you can invest in that fund, and thus obtain average stock market results. Given the situation as described, answer the following questions.

State of the Economy	Probability	T-Bills	Alta Industries	Repo Men	Canadian Foam	Market Portfolio	2-Stock Portfolio
				Returns on Alternative Investments			
				Estimated Rate of Return			
Recession	0.1	8.0%	(22.0)%	28.0%	10.0%[a]	(13.0)%	3.0%
Below average	0.2	8.0	(2.0)	14.7	(10.0)	1.0	
Average	0.4	8.0	20.0	0.0	7.0	15.0	10.0
Above average	0.2	8.0	35.0	(10.0)	45.0	29.0	
Boom	0.1	8.0	50.0	(20.0)	30.0	43.0	15.0
$\hat{r}$				1.7%	13.8%	15.0%	
σ		0.0		13.4	18.8	15.3	
CV				7.9	1.4	1.0	
b			1.29	−0.86	0.68		

[a]Note that the estimated returns of Canadian Foam do not always move in the same direction as the overall economy. For example, when the economy is below average, consumers purchase fewer mattresses than they would if the economy were stronger. However, if the economy is in a flat-out recession, a large number of consumers who were planning to purchase a more expensive inner spring mattress may purchase, instead, a cheaper foam mattress. Under these circumstances, we would expect Canadian Foam's stock price to be higher if there is a recession than if the economy was just below average.

a. What are investment returns? What is the return on an investment that costs $1,000 and is sold after 1 year for $1,100?

b. (1) Why is the T-bill's return independent of the state of the economy? Do T-bills promise a completely risk-free return? (2) Why are Alta Industries' returns expected to move with the economy whereas Repo Men's are expected to move counter to the economy?

c. Calculate the expected rate of return on each alternative and fill in the blanks in the row for r̂ in the table.

d. You should recognize that basing a decision solely on expected returns is appropriate only for risk-neutral individuals. Because your client, like virtually everyone, is risk averse, the riskiness of each alternative is an important aspect of the decision. One possible measure of risk is the standard deviation of returns. (1) Calculate this value for each alternative, and fill in the blank in the row for σ in the table. (2) What type of risk is measured by the standard deviation? (3) Draw a graph that shows *roughly* the shape of the probability distributions for Alta Industries, Canadian Foam, and T-bills.

e. Suppose you suddenly remembered that the coefficient of variation (CV) is generally regarded as being a better measure of stand-alone risk than the standard deviation when the alternatives being considered have widely differing expected returns. Calculate the missing CVs, and fill in the blanks in the row for CV in the table. Does the CV produce the same risk rankings as the standard deviation?

f. Suppose you created a 2-stock portfolio by investing $50,000 in Alta Industries and $50,000 in Repo Men. (1) Calculate the expected return ($\hat{r}_p$), the standard deviation (σ_p), and the coefficient of variation (CV_p) for this portfolio and fill in the appropriate blanks in the table. (2) How does the risk of this 2-stock portfolio compare with the risk of the individual stocks if they were held in isolation?

g. Suppose an investor starts with a portfolio consisting of one randomly selected stock. What would happen (1) to the risk and (2) to the expected return of the portfolio as more and more randomly selected stocks were added to the portfolio? What is the implication for investors? Draw a graph of the two portfolios to illustrate your answer.

h. (1) Should portfolio effects impact the way investors think about the risk of individual stocks? (2) If you decided to hold a 1-stock portfolio, and consequently were exposed to more risk than diversified investors, could you expect to be compensated for all of your risk? That is, could you earn a risk premium on that part of your risk that you could have eliminated by diversifying?

i. How is market risk measured for individual securities? How are beta coefficients calculated?

j. The expected rates of return and the beta coefficients of the alternatives as supplied by Barney Smith's computer program are as follows:

Security	Return (r̂)	Risk (Beta)
Alta Industries	17.4%	1.29
Market	15.0	1.00
Canadian Foam	13.8	0.68
T-bills	8.0	0.00
Repo Men	1.7	(0.86)

(1) Do the expected returns appear to be related to each alternative's market risk? (2) Is it possible to choose among the alternatives on the basis of the information developed thus far?

k. (1) Write out the Security Market Line (SML) equation, use it to calculate the required rate of return on each alternative, and then graph the relationship between the expected and required rates of return. (2) How do the expected rates of return compare with the required rates of return? (3) Does the fact that Repo Men has an expected return that is less than the T-bill rate make any sense? (4) What would be the market risk and the required return of a 50–50 portfolio of Alta Industries and Repo Men? Of Alta Industries and Canadian Foam?

l. (1) Suppose investors raised their inflation expectations by 3 percentage points over current estimates as reflected in the 8% T-bill rate. What effect would higher inflation have on the SML and on the returns required on high- and low-risk securities? (2) Suppose instead that investors' risk aversion increased enough to cause the market risk premium to increase by 3 percentage points. (Inflation remains constant.) What effect would this have on the SML and on returns of high- and low-risk securities?

appendix 7A

Calculating Beta Coefficients

The CAPM is an ex ante model, which means that all of the variables represent before-the-fact, *expected* values. In particular, the beta coefficient used by investors should reflect the expected volatility of a given stock's return versus the return on the market during some *future* period. However, people generally calculate betas using data from some *past* period, and then assume that the stock's relative volatility will be the same in the future as it was in the past.

Table 7A-1 shows the betas for some well-known companies, as provided by two different financial organizations, Value Line and Reuters. Notice that their estimates of beta usually differ, because they calculate beta in slightly different ways. Given these differences, many analysts choose to calculate their own betas.

Recall from Figure 7-9 how betas are calculated. The actual historical returns for a company are plotted on the *y*-axis and the market portfolio's returns are plotted on the *x*-axis. A regression line is then fitted through the points, and the slope of the regression line provides an estimate of the stock's beta. Although it is possible to calculate beta coefficients with a calculator, they are usually calculated with a computer, either with a statistical software program or a spreadsheet program. The file *Ch 07 Tool Kit.xlsx* shows how Imperial Oil's beta coefficient is calculated using *Excel's* regression function.[a]

The first step in a regression analysis is compiling the data. Most analysts use 4 to 5 years of monthly data, although some use 52 weeks of weekly data. We decided to use 4 years of monthly data, so we began by downloading 49 months of stock prices for Imperial Oil. from the Yahoo! Finance website. We used the S&P/TSX Composite Index as the market portfolio because it is representative of the market and because many analysts use this index. Table 7A-2 shows a portion of this data; the full data set is in the file *Ch 07 Tool Kit.xlsx*.

See *Ch 07 Tool Kit.xlsx* at the textbook's website for all calculations. www .nelson.com/brigham3ce

TABLE 7A-1 Beta Coefficients for Some Actual Companies

Stock (Ticker Symbol)	Value Line	Reuters
Barrick Gold (ABX)	0.8	0.2
Brookfield Asset Management (BAM)	1.1	1.0
Canadian National Railway (CNI)	1.0	1.0
Enbridge (ENB)	0.6	0.6
Magna International (MGA)	1.2	1.1
Potash Corporation (POT)	1.1	0.9
Manulife Financial (MFC)	1.5	1.8
Bank of Montreal (BMO)	0.8	1.0
Suncor Energy (SU)	1.3	1.7
Talisman Energy (TLM)	1.4	1.6

Sources: ValueLine.com and Reuters.com, accessed July 20, 2014.

---

[a]For an explanation of calculating beta with a financial calculator, see **Web Extension 7B** at the textbook's website.

The second step is to convert the stock prices into rates of return. For example, to find the June 2014 return for Imperial Oil, we find the percentage change from the previous month: ($56.23 − $53.26)/$53.26 = 5.6%.[b] We also find the percentage change of the S&P/TSX Composite Index level, and use this as the market return.

As Table 7A-2 shows, Imperial Oil had an average annual return of 11.8% during this 4-year period, while the market had an average annual return of 7.8%. As we noted before, it is usually unreasonable to think that the future expected return for a stock will equal its average historical return over a relatively short period, such as 4 years. However, we might well expect past volatility to be a reasonable estimate of future volatility, at least during the next couple of years. Note that the standard deviation for Imperial Oil's return during this period was 17.2% versus 9.8% for the market. Thus, the market's volatility is less than that of Imperial Oil. This is what we would expect, since the market is a well-diversified portfolio and thus much of its risk has been diversified away. The correlation between Imperial Oil's stock returns and the market returns is about 0.678, which is somewhat higher than the correlation between a typical stock and the market.

Figure 7A-1 shows a plot of Imperial Oil's returns against the market returns. As you will notice if you look in the file *Ch 07 Tool Kit.xlsx*, we used the *Excel* Chart feature to add a trend line and to display the equation and R^2 value on the chart itself. Alternatively, we could have used the *Excel* regression analysis feature, which would have provided more detailed data.

Figure 7A-1 shows that Imperial Oil's beta is about 1.19, as shown by the slope coefficient in the regression equation displayed on the chart. This means that Imperial Oil's beta is greater than the 1.0 average beta. Thus, Imperial Oil moves up and down more than the market. Note, however, that the points are not clustered very tightly around

TABLE 7A-2   Stock Return Data for Imperial Oil

Date	Market Level S&P/TSX Composite Index	Market Return (%)	Imperial Oil's Adjusted Stock Price	Imperial Oil's Return (%)
June 2014	15,146	3.7	56.23	5.6
May 2014	14,604	−0.3	53.26	−0.2
April 2014	14,652	2.2	53.39	4.0
March 2014	14,335	0.9	51.35	3.6
.	.	.	.	.
.	.	.	.	.
.	.	.	.	.
September 2010	12,369	3.8	37.46	−0.6
August 2010	11,914	1.7	37.67	−2.2
July 2010	11,713	3.7	38.53	3.7
June 2010	11,294	NA	37.15	NA
Average return (annual)		7.8		11.8
Standard deviation (annual)		9.8		17.2
Correlation between Imperial Oil and the market		0.678		

[b]The prices reported in Yahoo! Finance are adjusted for dividends and stock splits so we can calculate the return as the percentage change in the adjusted price. If you use a source that reports actual market prices, then you have to make the adjustment yourself when calculating returns. For example, suppose the stock price is $100 in July, the company has a 2-for-1 split, and the actual price is then $60 in August. The reported adjusted price for August would be $60, but the reported price for July would be lowered to $50 to reflect the stock split. This gives an accurate stock return of 20%: ($60 − $50)/$50 = 20%, the same as if there had not been a split, in which case the return would have been ($120 − $100)/$100 = 20%. Or suppose the actual price in September was $50, the company paid a $10 dividend, and the actual price in October was $60. Shareholders have earned a return of ($60 + $10 − $50)/$50 = 40%. Yahoo! Finance reports an adjusted price of $60 for October, and an adjusted price of $42.857 for September, which gives a return of ($60 − $42.857)/$42.857 = 40%. Again, the percentage change in the adjusted price accurately reflects the actual return.

FIGURE 7A-1 Calculating a Beta Coefficient for Imperial Oil Limited

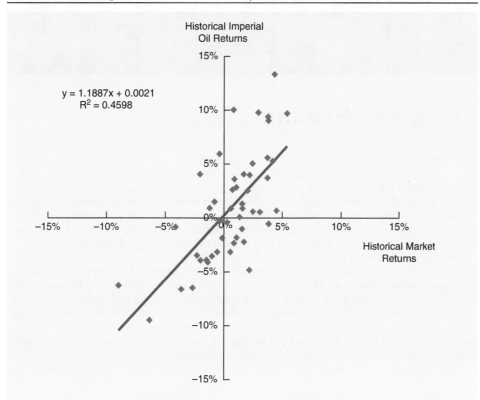

the regression line. Sometimes Imperial Oil does much better than the market, while at other times it does much worse. The R^2 value shown in the chart measures the degree of dispersion about the regression line. Statistically speaking, it measures the percentage of the variance that is explained by the regression equation. An R^2 of 1.0 indicates that all points lie exactly on the line, hence that all of the variance of the y-variable is explained by the x-variable. Imperial Oil's R^2 is about 0.46. This indicates that about 46% of the variance in Imperial Oil's returns is explained by the market returns. If we had done a similar analysis for a portfolio of 40 randomly selected stocks, then the points would probably have been clustered tightly around the regression line, and the R^2 would have probably been over 0.9.

Finally, note that the intercept shown in the regression equation on the chart is about 0.002. Since the regression equation is based on monthly data, this means that over this period Imperial Oil's stock earned about 0.2% more per month than an average stock as a result of factors other than a general change in stock prices.

CONCEPT REVIEW

1. What types of data are needed to calculate a beta coefficient for an actual company?
2. What does the R^2 measure?

appendix 7B

Arbitrage Pricing Theory

The CAPM is a single-factor model. That is, it specifies risk as a function of only one factor, the security's beta coefficient. Perhaps the risk/return relationship is more complex, with a stock's required return a function of more than one factor. For example, what if investors, because personal tax rates on capital gains are lower than those on dividends, value capital gains more highly than dividends? Then, if two stocks had the same market risk, the stock paying the higher dividend would have the higher required rate of return. In that case, required returns would be a function of two factors, market risk and dividend policy.

Furthermore, what if many factors are required to specify the equilibrium risk/return relationship rather than just one or two? Stephen Ross has proposed an approach called the **arbitrage pricing theory (APT).**[a] The APT can include any number of risk factors, so the required return could be a function of two, three, four, or more factors. We should note at the outset that the APT is based on complex mathematical and statistical theory that goes far beyond the scope of this text. Also, although the APT model is widely discussed in academic literature, practical use to date has been limited. However, use may increase, so students should at least have an intuitive idea of what the APT is all about.

The SML states that each stock's required return is equal to the risk-free rate plus the product of the market risk premium times the stock's beta coefficient. Assuming stocks are in equilibrium, the required return will be equal to the expected return:

$$\hat{r}_i = r_i = r_{RF} + (r_M - r_{RF})b_i.$$

The historical realized return, $\bar{r}_i$, which will generally be different from the expected return, can be expressed as follows:[b]

$$\bar{r}_i = \hat{r}_i + (\bar{r}_M - \hat{r}_M)b_i + e_i \qquad (7B\text{-}1)$$

Thus, the realized return, $\bar{r}_i$, will be equal to the expected return, $\hat{r}_i$, plus a positive or negative increment, $(\bar{r}_M - \hat{r}_M)b_i$, which depends jointly on the stock's beta and whether the market did better or worse than was expected, plus a random error term, e_i.

The market's realized return, $\bar{r}_M$, is in turn determined by a number of factors, including domestic economic activity as measured by gross domestic product (GDP), the strength of the world economy, the level of inflation, changes in tax laws, and so forth. Furthermore, different groups of stocks are affected in different ways by these fundamental factors. So, rather than specifying a stock's return as a function of one factor (return on the market), one could specify required and realized returns on individual stocks as a function of various fundamental economic factors. If this were done, we would transform Equation 7B-1 into 7B-2:

$$\bar{r}_i = \hat{r}_i + (\bar{F}_1 - \hat{F}_1)b_{i1} + \cdots + (\bar{F}_j - \hat{F}_j)b_{ij} + e_i \qquad (7B\text{-}2)$$

Here,

$\bar{r}_i$ = realized rate of return on Stock i

$\hat{r}_i$ = expected rate of return on Stock i

[a]See Stephen A. Ross, "The Arbitrage Theory of Capital Asset Pricing," *Journal of Economic Theory*, December 1976, 341–60.
[b]To avoid cluttering the notation, we have dropped the subscript t to denote a particular time period.

$\overline{F}_j$ = realized value of economic Factor j

$\hat{F}_j$ = expected value of Factor j

b_{ij} = sensitivity of Stock i to economic Factor j

e_i = effect of unique events on the realized return of Stock i

Equation 7B-2 shows that the realized return on any stock is equal to (1) the stock's expected return, (2) increases or decreases that depend on unexpected changes in fundamental economic factors times the sensitivity of the stock to these changes, and (3) a random term that reflects changes unique to the firm.

Certain stocks or groups of stocks are most sensitive to Factor 1, others to Factor 2, and so forth, and every portfolio's returns depend on what happened to the different fundamental factors. Theoretically, one could construct a portfolio such that (1) the portfolio was riskless and (2) the net investment in it was zero (some stocks would be sold short, with the proceeds from the short sales being used to buy the stocks held long). Such a zero investment portfolio must have a zero expected return, or else arbitrage operations would occur and cause the prices of the underlying assets to change until the portfolio's expected return was zero. Using some complex mathematics and a set of assumptions including the possibility of short sales, the APT equivalent of the CAPM's Security Market Line can be developed from Equation 7B-2:[c]

$$ r_i = r_{RF} + (r_1 - r_{RF})b_{i1} + \ldots + (r_j - r_{RF})b_{ij} \qquad \text{(7B-3)} $$

Here r_j is the required rate of return on a portfolio that is sensitive only to the *j*th economic factor ($b_{pj} = 1.0$) and has zero sensitivity to all other factors. Thus, for example, $(r_2 - r_{RF})$ is the risk premium on a portfolio with $b_{p2} = 1.0$ and all other $b_{pj} = 0.0$. Note that Equation 7B-3 is identical in form to the SML, but it permits a stock's required return to be a function of multiple factors.

To illustrate the APT concept, assume that all stocks' returns depend on only three risk factors: inflation, industrial production, and the aggregate degree of risk aversion (the cost of bearing risk, which we assume is reflected in the spread between the yields on Treasury and low-grade bonds). Furthermore, suppose (1) the risk-free rate is 8.0%; (2) the required rate of return is 13% on a portfolio with unit sensitivity ($b = 1.0$) to inflation and zero sensitivities ($b = 0.0$) to industrial production and degree of risk aversion; (3) the required return is 10% on a portfolio with unit sensitivity to industrial production and zero sensitivities to inflation and degree of risk aversion; and (4) the required return is 6% on a portfolio (the risk-bearing portfolio) with unit sensitivity to the degree of risk aversion and zero sensitivities to inflation and industrial production. Finally, assume that Stock i has factor sensitivities (betas) of 0.9 to the inflation portfolio, 1.2 to the industrial production portfolio, and -0.7 to the risk-bearing portfolio. Stock i's required rate of return, according to the APT, would be 16.3%:

$$ r_i = 8\% + (13\% - 8\%)0.9 + (10\% - 8\%)1.2 + (6\% - 8\%)(-0.7) $$

$$ = 16.3\% $$

Note that if the required rate of return on the market were 15.0% and Stock i had a CAPM beta of 1.1, then its required rate of return, according to the SML, would be 15.7%:

$$ r_i = 8\% + (15\% - 8\%)1.1 = 15.7\% $$

The primary theoretical advantage of the APT is that it permits several economic factors to influence individual stock returns, whereas the CAPM assumes that the effect of all factors, except those unique to the firm, can be captured in a single measure, the volatility of the stock with respect to the market portfolio. Also, the APT requires fewer assumptions than the CAPM and hence is more general. Finally, the APT does not assume that all investors hold the market portfolio, which is a CAPM requirement that clearly is not met in practice.

However, the APT faces several major hurdles in implementation, the most severe being that the APT does not identify the relevant factors. Thus, the APT does not tell us what factors influence returns, nor does it even indicate how many factors should appear in the

[c]See Thomas E. Copeland, J. Fred Weston, and Kuldeep Shastri, *Financial Theory and Corporate Policy*, 4th ed. (Reading, MA: Addison-Wesley, 2005).

model. There is some empirical evidence that only three or four factors are relevant: perhaps inflation, industrial production, the spread between low- and high-grade bonds, and the term structure of interest rates, but no one knows for sure.

The APT's proponents argue that it is not actually necessary to identify the relevant factors. Researchers use a statistical procedure called *factor analysis* to develop the APT parameters. Basically, they start with hundreds, or even thousands, of stocks and then create several different portfolios, where the returns on each portfolio are not highly correlated with returns on the other portfolios. Thus, each portfolio is apparently more heavily influenced by one of the unknown factors than are the other portfolios. Then, the required rate of return on each portfolio becomes the estimate for that unknown economic factor, shown as r_j in Equation 7B-3. The sensitivities of each individual stock's returns to the returns on that portfolio are the factor sensitivities (betas). Unfortunately, the results of factor analysis are not easily interpreted; hence it does not provide significant insights into the underlying economic determinants of risk.[d]

CONCEPT REVIEW

1. What is the primary difference between the APT and the CAPM?

2. What are some disadvantages of the APT?

3. An analyst has modelled the stock of Brown Kitchen Supplies using a two-factor APT model. The risk-free rate is 5%, the required return on the first factor (r_1) is 10%, and the required return on the second factor (r_2) is 15%. If $b_{i1} = 0.5$ and $b_{i2} = 1.3$, what is Brown's required return? (Check Figure: 20.5%)

---

[d] For additional discussion of the APT, see Edward L. Bubnys, "Simulating and Forecasting Utility Stock Returns: Arbitrage Pricing Theory vs. Capital Asset Pricing Model," *The Financial Review*, February 1990, 1–23; David H. Goldenberg and Ashok J. Robin, "The Arbitrage Pricing Theory and Cost-of-Capital Estimation: The Case of Electric Utilities," *Journal of Financial Research*, Fall 1991, 181–196; and Ashok Robin and Ravi Shukla, "The Magnitude of Pricing Errors in the Arbitrage Pricing Theory," *Journal of Financial Research*, Spring 1991, 65–82.

chapter 8

Stocks, Stock Valuation, and Stock Market Equilibrium

As sung by the Grateful Dead, "What a long, strange trip it's been!" The chart below provides some insights into the risks and returns for Canadian Tire Corporation's stock. From 1995 to 1999, Canadian Tire's stock rose almost 200%, but then, from 1999 to 2000, it experienced a large fall, losing over half its value. By 2007, not only had Canadian Tire recovered all its value, its stock had risen another 100%. From 2007 to 2009, Canadian Tire plummeted, again losing half its price. By 2013, the stock regained its previous high and has since (at the time of writing) continued to increase.

What led to those wild swings? In a nutshell, risk and expected cash flows. Until 1999, Canadian Tire was considered a low-risk company, capable of sustaining growing cash flows. Investors' perceptions of low risk and expected cash flow growth were behind the periods of the stock's growth, and investors' subsequent reduced expectations accounted for the stock's declines.

In this chapter we will see how stocks are valued in the marketplace. For the most part, professional security analysts do the work, using the techniques described in this chapter. "Sell side" analysts work for investment banks and brokerages. They write reports that are distributed to investors, generally through brokers. "Buy side" analysts work for mutual funds, hedge funds, pension funds, and other institutional investors. Those institutions obtain information from the buy-side analysts, but they also do their own research and ignore the buy side if they disagree.

The analysts on both sides generally focus on specific industries, and many of them were hired as analysts after working for a time in the industry they cover. Physics PhDs are often electronics analysts, biologists analyze biotech stocks, and so on. The analysts pore over financial statements, but they also go on the road and talk with company officials, companies' customers, and

companies' suppliers. The point of all this work is to try to predict corporate earnings, dividends, and free cash flow—and thus stock prices.

How good are analysts' predictions and hence their ability to forecast stock prices? A look back at the opening chart in Chapter 7 would suggest "not very good"—if they had seen the crash coming then they would have sold before the peaks and bought at the troughs, thus smoothing out the graphs. However, some analysts are better than others, and the material in this chapter can help you be better than average.

The textbook's website contains an *Excel* file that will guide you through the chapter's calculations. The file for this chapter is ***Ch 08 Tool Kit.xlsx,*** and we encourage you to open the file and follow along as you read the chapter. **www.nelson .com/brigham3ce**

In Chapter 7 we examined risk and required stock returns. In this chapter we will use those results to estimate the *intrinsic value* of a stock. The concepts and models developed here will also be used when we estimate the cost of capital in Chapter 9. In subsequent chapters, we will demonstrate how the cost of capital is used to help make many important decisions, especially the decision to invest or not invest in new assets.

Some companies are so small that their common stocks are not actively traded; they are owned by only a few people, usually the companies' managers. The stock in such firms is said to be **closely held.** In contrast, the stocks of most larger companies are owned by a large number of investors, most of whom are not active in management. Such stock is called **publicly held stock.** Institutions, such as pension plans, mutual funds, foreign investors, insurance companies, and brokerage firms, buy and sell relatively actively, accounting for about 75% of all transactions. Thus, institutional investors have a heavy influence on the valuation of individual stocks. But before plunging into stock valuation, we begin with a closer look at what it means to be a shareholder.

8.1 Legal Rights and Privileges of Common Shareholders

The common shareholders are the *owners* of a corporation, and as such they have certain rights and privileges, as discussed in this section.

Control of the Firm

A firm's common shareholders have the right to elect its directors, who, in turn, elect the officers who manage the business. In a small firm, the largest shareholder typically assumes the positions of president and chairperson of the board of directors. In a large, publicly owned firm, the managers typically have some stock, but their personal holdings are generally insufficient to give them voting control. Thus, the managers of most publicly owned firms can be removed by the shareholders if the management team is not effective.

Provincial and federal laws stipulate how shareholder control is to be exercised. First, corporations must hold an election of directors periodically, usually once a year, with the vote taken at the annual meeting. For instance, one-third of the directors may be elected each year for a 3-year term. Each share of stock has one vote; thus, the owner of 1,000 shares has 1,000 votes for each director.[1] Shareholders can appear at the annual meeting and vote in person, but typically they transfer their right to vote to a second party by means of a **proxy.** Management always solicits shareholders' proxies and usually gets them. However, if earnings are poor and shareholders are dissatisfied, an outside group may solicit the proxies in an effort to overthrow management and take control of the business. This is known as a **proxy fight.** Proxy fights are discussed in detail in Chapter 22.

The Preemptive Right

Common shareholders may have a right, called the **preemptive right,** to purchase any additional shares of stock sold by the firm. The preemptive right enables current shareholders to buy additional shares in the same proportion they currently hold in the firm. For instance, if

---

[1]In the situation described, a 1,000-share shareholder could cast 1,000 votes for each of three directors if there were three contested seats on the board. An alternative procedure that may be prescribed in the corporate charter calls for *cumulative voting*. Here the 1,000-share shareholder would get 3,000 votes if there were three vacancies, and he or she could cast all of them for one director. Cumulative voting helps small groups get representation on the board.

Corporate Valuation and Stock Risk

In Chapter 1, we told you that managers should strive to make their firms more valuable and that the value of a firm is determined by the size, timing, and risk of its free cash flows (FCF):

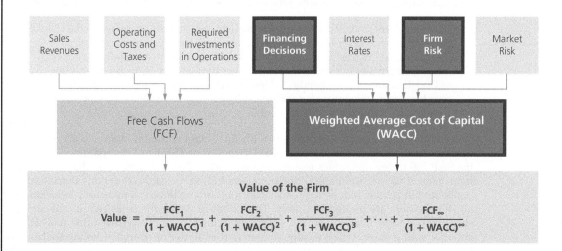

The FCFs are the cash flows available to all investors and the WACC is the return required by all investors, so the present value of the FCFs is the value of the firm to all investors. In Chapter 22 we will use the equation above to estimate the intrinsic value of stock, but in this chapter we use an alternative approach. Instead of discounting the cash flows to all investors at the rate of return required by all investors, we discount the cash flows to shareholders (dividends, D_t) at the rate required by shareholders (r_s). The result is the intrinsic value to shareholders:

$$V_{stock} = \frac{D_1}{(1 + r_s)^1} + \frac{D_2}{(1 + r_s)^2} + \cdots + \frac{D_\infty}{(1 + r_s)^\infty}$$

a company has 1,000 shares of stock outstanding and an investor holds 150 of them, a preemptive right gives that investor the right to buy 15% of the new shares the company may sell in an upcoming offering. This enables shareholders to maintain proportionate interest in the company and not suffer any dilution if the company issues more stock.

On the other hand, preemptive rights make it more difficult to raise equity capital. A company may sometimes find it advantageous to arrange financing with new large shareholders. However, obtaining waivers for the rights during a financing can be time consuming, and larger investors may not be able to buy the number of shares they seek as a result of such rights being exercised. This is why fewer Canadian companies are including preemptive rights in their articles of incorporation.

ⓒONCEPT REVIEW

1. What is a proxy fight?
2. What is a preemptive right?

8.2 Types of Common Stock

Not all common shares are created equal. While the basic premise "one share, one vote" holds true for most companies, some have classes of common shares with either superior or inferior voting rights. These **dual-class shares** are issued for two basic reasons: they allow (family) owners to obtain additional equity capital without giving up voting control of their firm; and they prevent takeover attempts. The voting rights can be granted or restricted in several ways.

Some shares with either no voting rights or very limited ones are referred to as *restricted* or *subordinate* voting shares; others, called *multiple* or *super-voting* shares, come with many votes per share. Roger Communications' Class-A shares carry 50 votes apiece, allowing the Rogers family to maintain control even though the family holds a very small portion of the company's equity. Other Canadian companies with restricted or multiple voting shares include Bombardier Inc., Canadian Tire, and Onex Corporation. Google's founders explicitly stated their intent for their Class-B shares, which carry 10 votes per share, in a letter to investors:

> The Class A common stock we are offering has one vote per share, while the Class B common stock held by many current shareholders has 10 votes per share . . .
> The main effect of this structure is likely to leave our team, especially Sergey and me, with increasingly significant control over the company's decisions and fate, as Google shares change hands . . . New investors will fully share in Google's long term economic future *but will have little ability to influence its strategic decisions through their voting rights.*[2] (italics added)

Though there are U.S. companies with dual-class common shares, such as Google, they are much more common in Canada. Up to 30% of TSX-listed companies versus 3% of the S&P 500 Index companies use dual-class shares.[3] Because dual-class shares can allow management to make unilateral decisions—including, possibly, decisions detrimental to noncontrolling shareholders, regulatory control is often viewed as necessary to ensure that all shareholders are treated equitably. The extent to which the rules require all common share classes to be treated equally will partly determine the price premium at which the superior voting shares will typically trade over the inferior or restricted voting shares. This premium varies widely, from approximately 6% in the United States to over 80% in Italy. The premium in Canada ranges from 7% to 20%. Other factors influencing the premium are the share's liquidity and dividend policies.[4]

The impact that dual-class shares have on stock performance is uncertain. The Jog, Zhu, and Dutta study reports that companies with subordinate or multiple voting class shares have more lax governance. They also have higher dividend payout ratios, as well as higher ROA and ROE, although their stocks underperform their peers and sector index. Other studies have reported varied results. Institutional investors such as the Canada Pension Plan and the Ontario Teachers' Pension Plan have written guidelines opposing the creation of dual-class share structures.[5]

CONCEPT REVIEW

1. Describe dual-class shares.

The Market Stock Price versus Intrinsic Value

We explained in Chapter 1 that managers should seek to maximize the value of their firms' shares. We also emphasized the difference between the market price and intrinsic value. Intrinsic value incorporates all *relevant available* information about expected cash flows and risk. This includes information about the company, the economic environment, and the political environment. In contrast to intrinsic value, market prices are based on investors' *selection and interpretation* of information. To the extent that investors don't select all relevant information and don't interpret it correctly, market prices can deviate from intrinsic values. Figure 8-1 illustrates this relationship between market prices and intrinsic value.

When market prices deviate from their intrinsic values, astute investors have profitable opportunities. For example, recall from Chapter 6 that the value of a bond is the present value of its cash flows when discounted at the bond's required return, which reflects the bond's risk. This is the intrinsic value of the bond because it incorporates all relevant available information. Notice that the intrinsic value is "fair" in the sense that it incorporates the bond's risk and investors' required returns for bearing the risk.

---

[2]Google Inc., "Amendment No. 9 to Form S-1 Registration Statement," Securities and Exchange Commission, http://www.sec.gov/, accessed May 12, 2008.
[3]Vijay Jog, PengCheng Zhu, and Shantanu Dutta, "One Share–One Vote," *Canadian Investment Review*, Fall 2006, 9–13.
[4]Samer Khalil and Michel Magnan, "Dual-Class Shares: Governance, Risks, and Rewards," *Ivey Business Journal*, May–June 2007.
[5]CPP Investment Board, "Proxy Voting Principles and Guidelines," February 5, 2008, http://www.cppib.ca/, accessed May 12, 2008; Ontario Teacher's Pension Plan, http://www.otpp.com/, accessed May 12, 2008.

FIGURE
8-1   Determinants of Intrinsic Values and Market Prices

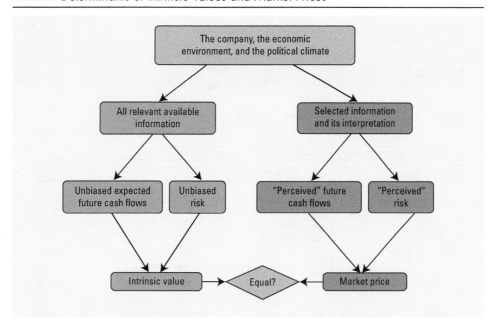

What would happen if a bond's market price were lower than its intrinsic value? In this situation, an investor could purchase the bond and receive a rate of return in excess of the required return. In other words, the investor would get more compensation than justified by the bond's risk. If all investors felt this way, then demand for the bond would soar as investors tried to purchase it, driving the bond's price up. But recall from Chapter 6 that as the price of a bond goes up, its yield goes down. This means that an increase in price would reduce the subsequent return for an investor purchasing (or holding) the bond at the new price.[6] It seems reasonable to expect that investors' actions would continue to drive the price up until the expected return on the bond equalled its required return. After that point, the bond would provide just enough return to compensate its owner for the bond's risk.

If the bond's price were too high compared to its intrinsic value, then investors would sell the bond, causing its price to fall and its yield to increase until its expected return equalled its required return.

A stock's future cash flows aren't as predictable as a bond's, but we show later in the chapter that a stock's intrinsic value is the present value of its expected future cash flows, just as a bond's intrinsic value is the present value of its cash flows. If the price of a stock is lower than its intrinsic value, then an investor would receive an expected return greater than the return required as compensation for risk. The same market forces we described for a mispriced bond would drive the mispriced stock's price up. If this process continues until its expected return equals it required return, then we say that there is market equilibrium:

Market equilibrium: Expected return = Required return

$$\hat{r} = r$$

We can also express market equilibrium in terms of prices:

Market equilibrium: Market price = Intrinsic value

8.3 Stock Market Reporting

Up until a few years ago, the best source of stock quotations was the business section of a daily newspaper, such as the *National Post*. One problem with newspapers, however, is

[6]The original owner of the bond when it was priced too low would reap a nice benefit as the price climbs, but the subsequent purchasers would receive only the now-lower yield.

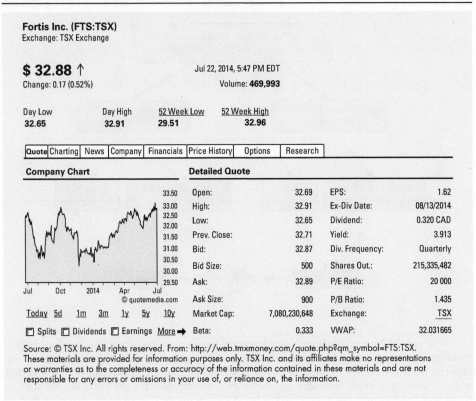

FIGURE 8-2 Stock Quote for Fortis Inc., July 22, 2014

Source: © TSX Inc. All rights reserved. From: http://web.tmxmoney.com/quote.php?qm_symbol=FTS:TSX. These materials are provided for information purposes only. TSX Inc. and its affiliates make no representations or warranties as to the completeness or accuracy of the information contained in these materials and are not responsible for any errors or omissions in your use of, or reliance on, the information.

that they are printed only once a day. Now it is possible to get quotes all during the day from a wide variety of Internet sources, including the TMX Group.[7] Figure 8-2 shows a quote from Fortis Inc., which is traded on the TSX under the symbol FTS. As Figure 8-2 shows, Fortis's stock last traded at $32.88 for a gain of $0.17, which was a 0.52% increase from the previous day. The data also show that Fortis reached a high during the day of $32.91, and fell as low as $32.65 that same trading day. A total of 469,993 shares traded during the day. The quote also provides the price ($32.89) a buyer would have to pay (the Ask) and the price ($32.87) someone could sell the stock for (the Bid). The screen with the stock quote information also gives the total market value of Fortis' common stock (the Market Cap); the dividend and dividend yield; and several market ratios. In addition, the tabs provide information and recent news on Fortis and its financial statements, along with analyst coverage and more.

CONCEPT REVIEW

1. What data are often provided in a stock quotation?

8.4 Valuing Common Stocks

Common stocks provide an expected future cash flow stream, and a stock's value is found in the same manner as the values of other financial assets—namely, as the present value of the expected future cash flow stream. The expected cash flows consist of two elements: (1) the dividends expected in each year and (2) the price investors expect to receive when they sell the stock. The expected final stock price includes the return of the original investment plus an expected capital gain.

---

[7] Most free sources actually provide quotes that are delayed by 15 to 20 minutes.

Definitions of Terms Used in Stock Valuation Models

We saw in Chapter 1 that managers seek to maximize the values of their firms' stocks. A manager's actions affect both the stream of income to investors and the riskiness of that stream. Therefore, managers need to know how alternative actions are likely to affect stock prices. At this point we develop some models to help show how the value of a share of stock is determined. We begin by defining the following terms:

D_t = Dividend the shareholder *expects* to receive at the end of Year t. D_0 is the most recent dividend, which has already been paid; D_1 is the first dividend expected, and it will be paid at the end of this year; D_2 is the dividend expected at the end of 2 years; and so forth. D_1 represents the first cash flow a new purchaser of the stock will receive. Note that D_0, the dividend that has just been paid, is known with certainty. However, all future dividends are expected values, so the estimate of D_t may differ among investors.[8]

P_0 = Actual market price of the stock today.

$\hat{P}_t$ = Expected price of the stock at the end of each Year t (pronounced "P hat t"). $\hat{P}_0$ is the **intrinsic, or fundamental, value** of the stock today as seen by the particular investor doing the analysis; $\hat{P}_1$ is the price expected at the end of one year; and so on.

D_1/P_0 = Expected **dividend yield** during the coming year. If the stock is expected to pay a dividend of $D_1 = \$1$ during the next 12 months, and if its current price is $P_0 = \$10$, then the expected dividend yield is $\$1/\$10 = 0.10 = 10\%$.

$\dfrac{\hat{P}_1 - P_0}{P_0}$ = Expected **capital gains yield** during the coming year. If the stock sells for \$10 today, and if it is expected to rise to \$10.50 at the end of one year, then the expected capital gain is $P_1 - P_0 = \$10.50 - \$10.00 = \$0.50$, and the expected capital gains yield is $\$0.50/\$10 = 0.05 = 5\%$.

g = Expected growth rate in dividends as predicted by a marginal investor. If dividends are expected to grow at a constant rate, g is also equal to the expected rate of growth in earnings and in the stock's price. Different investors may use different g's to evaluate a firm's stock, but the market price, P_0, is set on the basis of the g estimated by marginal investors.

r_s = Minimum acceptable, or **required, rate of return** on the stock, considering both its riskiness and the returns available on other investments. The primary determinants of r_s include the real rate of return, expected inflation, and risk.

$\hat{r}_s$ = **Expected rate of return** that an investor who buys the stock expects to receive in the future. $\hat{r}_s$ (pronounced "r hat s") could be above or below r_s, but one would buy the stock only if $\hat{r}_s \geq r_s$. Note that the expected return ($\hat{r}_s$) is equal to the expected dividend yield (D_1/P_0) plus expected capital gains yield $[(\hat{P}_1 - P_0)/P_0]$. In our example, $\hat{r}_s = 10\% + 5\% = 15\%$.

$\bar{r}_s$ = **Actual, or realized rate of return,** pronounced "r bar s." For a risky security, the actual return can differ considerably from the expected return.

Expected Dividends as the Basis for Stock Values

Like all financial assets, equilibrium stock prices are the present value of a stream of cash flows. What are the cash flows that corporations provide to their shareholders? First, think of yourself as an investor who buys a stock with the intention of holding it (in your family) forever. In this case, all that you (and your heirs) will receive is a stream of dividends, and the value of the stock today is calculated as the present value of an infinite stream of dividends:

$$\text{Value of stock} = \hat{P}_0 = \text{PV of expected future dividends}$$

$$= \frac{D_1}{(1 + r_s)^1} + \frac{D_2}{(1 + r_s)^2} + \cdots + \frac{D_\infty}{(1 + r_s)^\infty} \qquad \text{(8-1)}$$

$$= \sum_{t=1}^{\infty} \frac{D_t}{(1 + r_s)^t}$$

---

[8]Stocks generally pay dividends quarterly, so theoretically we should evaluate them on a quarterly basis. However, in stock valuation, most analysts work on an annual basis because the data generally are not precise enough to warrant refinement to a quarterly model. For additional information on the quarterly model, see Charles M. Linke and J. Kenton Zumwalt, "Estimation Biases in Discounted Cash Flow Analysis of Equity Capital Cost in Rate Regulation," *Financial Management*, Autumn 1984, 15–21. Also see Robert Brooks and Billy Helms, "An N-Stage, Fractional Period, Quarterly Dividend Discount Model," *Financial Review*, November 1990, 651–657.

What about the more typical case, where you expect to hold the stock for a finite period and then sell it—what is the value of P_0 in this case? Unless the company is likely to be liquidated or sold and thus to disappear, *the value of the stock is again determined by Equation 8-1*. To see this, recognize that for any individual investor, the expected cash flows consist of expected dividends plus the expected sale price of the stock. However, the sale price the current investor receives will depend on the dividends some future investor expects. Therefore, for all present and future investors in total, expected cash flows must be based on expected future dividends. Put another way, unless a firm is liquidated or sold to another concern, the cash flows it provides to its shareholders will consist only of a stream of dividends; therefore, the value of a share of its stock must be the present value of that expected dividend stream.

The general validity of Equation 8-1 can also be confirmed by asking the following question: Suppose I buy a stock and expect to hold it for 1 year. I will receive dividends during the year plus the value $\hat{P}_1$ when I sell out at the end of the year. But what will determine the value of P_1? The answer is that it will be determined as the present value of the dividends expected during Year 2 plus the stock price at the end of that year, which, in turn, will be determined as the present value of another set of future dividends and an even more distant stock price. This process can be continued ad infinitum, and the ultimate result is Equation 8-1.[9]

CONCEPT REVIEW

1. What are the two parts of most stocks' expected total return?
2. How does one calculate the capital gains yield and the dividend yield of a stock?
3. If D_1 = $3.00, P_0 = $50, and $\hat{P}_1$ = $52, what is the stock's expected dividend yield, capital gains yield, and total expected return for the coming year? (Check Figures: 6%, 4%, 10%)

8.5 Valuing a Constant Growth Stock

Equation 8-1 is a generalized stock valuation model in that the time pattern of D_t can be anything: D_t can be rising, falling, fluctuating randomly, or even zero for several years, yet Equation 8-1 will still hold. With a computer spreadsheet we can easily use this equation to find a stock's value for any pattern of dividends. However, if future dividends are expected to grow at a constant rate, we can use the constant growth model.

The Constant Growth Model

In the long run, dividends can't grow faster than earnings. A dollar used to pay dividends can't be used for reinvestment in the firm or to pay down debt, so everything else equal, higher dividends must be associated either with declining earnings growth due to a lack of reinvestment or with increasing debt levels. Growth in dividends can be supported by increasing debt for a while, but to avoid unacceptably high levels of debt, long-term dividend growth must be limited to long-term earnings growth.

Long-term earnings per share (EPS) growth depends on economy-wide factors (such as recessions and inflation), industry-wide factors (such as technological innovations), and firm-specific factors (management skill, brand identity, patent protection, etc.). For a firm to grow faster than the economy, either the industry must become a bigger part of the economy or the firm must take market share from its competitors. But as markets mature, competition and market saturation will tend to limit EPS growth to a constant long-term rate, approximately equal to the sum of population growth and inflation.

Some companies are in growing industries and won't hit their long-term constant growth rate for many years, but some mature firms in saturated industries are already at their constant long-term growth rate. We will address valuation of faster-growing firms later

---

[9]We should note that investors periodically lose sight of the long-run nature of stocks as investments and forget that in order to sell a stock at a profit, one must find a buyer who will pay the higher price. If you analyze a stock's value in accordance with Equation 8-1, conclude that the stock's market price exceeds a reasonable value, and then buy the stock anyway, then you would be following the "bigger fool" theory of investment—you think that you may be a fool to buy the stock at its excessive price, but you also think that when you get ready to sell it, you can find someone who is an even bigger fool. The bigger fool theory was widely followed in the spring of 2000, just before the Nasdaq market lost more than one-third of its value.

in the chapter, but for a mature company whose dividends are growing at a constant rate, Equation 8-1 can be rewritten as follows:

$$\hat{P}_0 = \frac{D_0(1 + g)^1}{(1 + r_s)^1} + \frac{D_0(1 + g)^2}{(1 + r_s)^2} + \cdots + \frac{D_0(1 + g)^\infty}{(1 + r_s)^\infty}$$

$$= D_0 \sum_{t=1}^{\infty} \frac{(1 + g)^t}{(1 + r_s)^t} \qquad (8\text{-}2)$$

$$= \frac{D_0(1 + g)}{r_s - g} = \frac{D_1}{r_s - g}$$

The last term in Equation 8-2 is derived in **Web Extension 8A,** available on the textbook's website.

The last term of Equation 8-2 is called the *constant growth model,* or the *Gordon model* after Myron J. Gordon, who did much to develop and popularize it.

A necessary condition for the validity of Equation 8-2 is that r_s be greater than g. Look back at the second form of Equation 8-2. If g is larger than r_s, then $(1 + g)^t/(1 + r_s)^t$ must always be greater than 1. In this case, the second line of Equation 8-2 is the sum of an infinite number of terms, with each term being a number larger than 1. Therefore, if the constant g were greater than r_s, the resulting stock price would be infinite! Since no company is worth an infinite price, it is impossible to have a constant growth rate that is greater than r_s. Occasionally, a student will plug a value for g greater than r_s into the last form of Equation 8-2 and report a negative stock price. This is nonsensical. The last form of Equation 8-2 is valid only when g is less than r_s. *If g is greater than r_s the constant growth model cannot be used and the answer you would get from using Equation 8-2 would be wrong and misleading.*

Illustration of a Constant Growth Stock

Assume that MicroDrive just paid a dividend of $1.15 (i.e., D_0 = $1.15). Its stock has a required rate of return, r_s, of 13.4%, and investors expect the dividend to grow at a constant 8% rate in the future. The estimated dividend 1 year hence would be D_1 = $1.15(1.08) = $1.24; D_2 would be $1.34; and the estimated dividend 5 years hence would be $1.69:

$$D_t = D_0(1 + g)^t = \$1.15(1.08)^5 = \$1.69$$

We could use this procedure to estimate each future dividend, and then use Equation 8-1 to determine the current stock value, $\hat{P}_0$. In other words, we could find each expected future dividend, calculate its present value, and then sum all the present values to find the intrinsic value of the stock.

Such a process would be time consuming, but we can take a short cut—just insert the illustrative data into Equation 8-2 to find the stock's intrinsic value, $23:

$$\hat{P}_0 = \frac{\$1.15(1.08)}{0.134 - 0.08} = \frac{\$1.242}{0.054} = \$23.00$$

The concept underlying the valuation process for a constant growth stock is graphed in Figure 8-3. Dividends are growing at the rate g = 8%, but because r_s > g, the present value of each future dividend is declining. For example, the dividend in Year 1 is $D_1 = D_0(1 + g)^1 = \$1.15(1.08) = \$1.242$. However, the present value of this dividend, discounted at 13.4%, is $PV(D_1) = \$1.242/(1.134)^1 = \$1.095$. The dividend expected in Year 2 grows to $1.242(1.08) = $1.341, but the present value of this dividend falls to $1.043. Continuing, D_3 = $1.449 and $PV(D_3)$ = $0.993, and so on. Thus, the expected dividends are growing, but the present value of each successive dividend is declining, because the dividend growth rate (8%) is less than the rate used for discounting the dividends to the present (13.4%).

If we summed the present values of each future dividend, this summation would be the value of the stock, $\hat{P}_0$. When g is a constant, this summation is equal to $D_1/(r_s - g)$, as shown in Equation 8-2. Therefore, if we extended the lower step function curve in Figure 8-3 on out to infinity and added up the present values of each future dividend, the summation would be identical to the value given by Equation 8-2, $23.00.

Although Equation 8-2 assumes that dividends grow to infinity, most of the value is based on dividends during a relatively short time period. In our example, 70% of the value

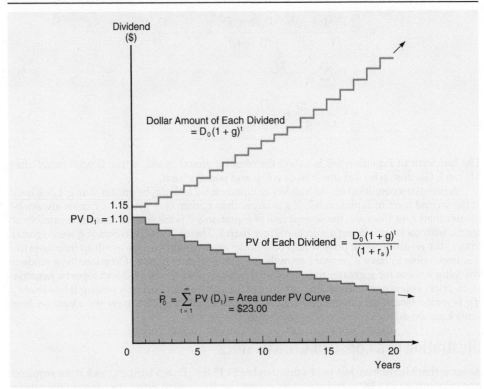

FIGURE 8-3 Present Value of Dividends of a Constant Growth Stock, Where $D_0 = \$1.15$, $g = 8\%$, $r_s = 13.4\%$

is attributed to the first 25 years, 91% to the first 50 years, and 99.4% to the first 100 years. So, companies don't have to live forever for the Gordon growth model to be used.

Do Stock Prices Reflect Long-Term or Short-Term Events?

Managers often complain that the stock market is shortsighted and that investors care only about next quarter's performance. Let's use the constant growth model to test this assertion. MicroDrive's most recent dividend was $1.15, and it is expected to grow at a rate of 8% per year. Since we know the growth rate, we can forecast the dividends for each of the next 5 years and then find their present values:

$$PV = \frac{D_0(1+g)^1}{(1+r_s)^1} + \frac{D_0(1+g)^2}{(1+r_s)^2} + \frac{D_0(1+g)^3}{(1+r_s)^3} + \frac{D_0(1+g)^4}{(1+r_s)^4} + \frac{D_0(1+g)^5}{(1+r_s)^5}$$

$$= \frac{\$1.15(1.08)^1}{(1.134)^1} + \frac{\$1.15(1.08)^2}{(1.134)^2} + \frac{\$1.15(1.08)^3}{(1.134)^3} + \frac{\$1.15(1.08)^4}{(1.134)^4} + \frac{\$1.15(1.08)^5}{(1.134)^5}$$

$$= \frac{\$1.242}{(1.134)^1} + \frac{\$1.341}{(1.134)^2} + \frac{\$1.449}{(1.134)^3} + \frac{\$1.565}{(1.134)^4} + \frac{\$1.690}{(1.134)^5}$$

$$= 1.095 + 1.043 + 0.993 + 0.946 + 0.901$$

$$\approx \$5.00$$

Recall that MicroDrive's stock price is $23.00. Therefore, only $5.00, or 22%, of the $23.00 stock price is attributable to short-term cash flows. This means that MicroDrive's managers will have a bigger effect on the stock price if they work to increase long-term cash flows rather than focus on short-term flows. This situation holds for most companies. Indeed, a number of professors and consulting firms have used actual company data to show that more than 80% of a typical company's stock price is due to cash flows expected more than 5 years in the future.

This brings up an interesting question. If most of a stock's value is due to long-term cash flows, why do managers and analysts pay so much attention to quarterly earnings? Part of the answer lies in the information conveyed by short-term earnings. For example, if actual quarterly earnings are lower than expected, not because of fundamental problems but only because a company has increased its research and development (R&D) expenditures, studies have shown that the stock price probably won't decline and may actually increase. This makes sense, because R&D should increase future cash flows. On the other hand, if quarterly earnings are lower than expected because customers don't like the company's new products, then this new information will have negative implications for future values of g, the long-term growth rate. As we show later in this chapter, even small changes in g can lead to large changes in stock prices. Therefore, quarterly earnings themselves might not be very important, but the information they convey about future prospects can be extremely important.

Another reason that many managers focus on short-term earnings is that some firms pay managerial bonuses on the basis of current earnings rather than stock prices (which reflect future earnings). For these managers, the concern with quarterly earnings is not due to their effect on stock prices—it's due to their effect on bonuses.[10]

When Can the Constant Growth Model Be Used?

The constant growth model is often appropriate for mature companies with a stable history of growth. Expected growth rates vary somewhat among companies, but dividend growth for most mature firms is generally expected to continue in the future at about the same rate as nominal gross domestic product (real GDP plus inflation). On this basis, one might expect the dividends of an average, or "normal," company to grow at a rate of 3% to 6% a year.

Note too that Equation 8-2 is sufficiently general to handle the case of a *zero growth stock,* where the dividend is expected to remain constant over time. If g = 0, Equation 8-2 reduces to Equation 8-3:

$$\hat{P}_0 = \frac{D}{r_s} \qquad\qquad (8\text{-}3)$$

This is essentially the equation for a perpetuity, and it is simply the dividend divided by the discount rate.

CONCEPT REVIEW

1. Write out and explain the valuation formula for a constant growth stock.
2. Are stock prices affected more by long-term or short-term events?
3. A stock is expected to pay a dividend of $2 at the end of the year. The required rate of return is $r_s = 12\%$. What would the stock's price be if the constant growth rate in dividends were 4%? What would the price be if g = 0%? (Check Figures: $25.00; $16.67)

8.6 Expected Rate of Return on a Constant Growth Stock

We can solve Equation 8-2 for r_s, again using the hat to indicate that we are dealing with an expected rate of return:[11]

$$\begin{array}{c}
\begin{matrix}
\text{Expected rate} \\ \text{of return}
\end{matrix}
=
\begin{matrix}
\text{Expected} \\ \text{dividend} \\ \text{yield}
\end{matrix}
+
\begin{matrix}
\text{Expected growth} \\ \text{rate, or capital} \\ \text{gains yield}
\end{matrix}
\\[2em]
\hat{r}_s = \dfrac{D_1}{P_0} + g
\end{array} \qquad\qquad (8\text{-}4)$$

---

[10]Many apparent puzzles in finance can be explained either by managerial compensation systems or by peculiar features of the Income Tax Act. So, if you can't explain a firm's behaviour in terms of economic logic, look to bonuses or taxes as possible explanations.

[11]The r_s value in Equation 8-2 is a *required* rate of return, but when we solve for r_s to obtain Equation 8-4, we are finding an *expected* rate of return. Obviously, the solution requires that $r_s = \hat{r}_s$. This equality holds if the stock market is in equilibrium, a condition that will be discussed later in the chapter.

Thus, if you buy a stock for a price $P_0 = \$23$, and if you expect the stock to pay a dividend $D_1 = \$1.242$ 1 year from now and to grow at a constant rate $g = 8\%$ in the future, then your expected rate of return will be 13.4%:

$$\hat{r}_s = \frac{\$1.242}{\$23} + 8\% = 5.4\% + 8\% = 13.4\%$$

In this form, we see that $\hat{r}_s$ is the *expected total return* and that it consists of an *expected dividend yield*, $D_1/P_0 = 5.4\%$, plus an *expected growth rate or capital gains yield*, $g = 8\%$.

Suppose this analysis had just been conducted, with the current price, P_0, equal to $23 and the Year 1 expected dividend, D_1, equal to $1.242. What is the expected price at the end of the first year, immediately after D_1 has been paid? We would again apply Equation 8-2, but this time we would use the Year 2 dividend, $D_2 = D_1(1 + g) = \$1.242(1.08) = \$1.3414$:

$$\hat{P}_1 = \frac{D_2}{r_s - g} = \frac{\$1.3414}{0.134 - 0.08} = \$24.84$$

Now, note that $24.84 is 8% larger than P_0, the $23 price found 1 year earlier:

$$\$23(1.08) = \$24.84$$

Thus, we would expect a capital gain of $24.84 − $23.00 = $1.84 during the year, which would provide a capital gains yield of 8%:

$$\text{Capital gains yield} = \frac{\text{Capital gain}}{\text{Beginning price}} = \frac{\$1.84}{\$23.00} = 0.08 = 8\%$$

We could extend the analysis, and in each future year the expected capital gains yield would always equal g, the expected dividend growth rate.

The dividend yield during the year could be estimated as follows:

$$\text{Dividend yield} = \frac{D_2}{\hat{P}_1} = \frac{\$1.3414}{\$24.84} = 0.054 = 5.4\%$$

The dividend yield for the next year could also be calculated, and again it would be 5.4%. Thus, *for a constant growth stock*, the following conditions must hold:

1. The dividend is expected to grow forever at a constant rate, g.
2. The stock price is expected to grow at this same rate.
3. The expected dividend yield is constant.
4. The expected capital gains yield is also constant, and it is equal to g.
5. The expected total rate of return, $\hat{r}_s$, is equal to the expected dividend yield plus the expected growth rate: $\hat{r}_s$ = dividend yield + g.

The term "expected" should be clarified—it means expected in a probabilistic sense, as the "statistically expected" outcome. Thus, if we say the growth rate is expected to remain constant at 8%, we mean that the best prediction for the growth rate in any future year is 8%, not that we literally expect the growth rate to be exactly 8% in each future year. In this sense, the constant growth assumption is a reasonable one for many large, mature companies.

CONCEPT REVIEW

1. What conditions must hold if a stock is to be evaluated using the constant growth model?
2. What does the term "expected" mean when we say "expected growth rate"?
3. If $D_0 = \$4.00$, $r_s = 9\%$, and $g = 5\%$ for a constant growth stock, what is the stock's expected dividend yield and capital gains yield for the coming year? (Check Figures: 4%, 5%)

8.7 Valuing Nonconstant Growth Stocks

For many companies, it is inappropriate to assume that dividends will grow at a constant rate. Firms typically go through *life cycles.* During the early part of their lives, their growth is much faster than that of the economy as a whole; then they match the economy's growth; and finally their growth is slower than that of the economy. Automobile manufacturers in the 1920s, computer software firms such as Microsoft in the 1990s, and technology firms such as Cisco in the 2000s are examples of firms in the early part of the cycle; these firms are called *supernormal,* or *nonconstant, growth* firms. Figure 8-4 illustrates nonconstant growth and also compares it with normal growth, zero growth, and negative growth.[12]

In Figure 8-4, the dividends of the supernormal growth firm are expected to grow at a 30% rate for 3 years, after which the growth rate is expected to fall to 8%, the assumed average for the economy. The value of this firm, like any other, is the present value of its expected future dividends as determined by Equation 8-1. When D_t is growing at a constant rate, we simplify Equation 8-1 to $\hat{P}_0 = D_1/(r_s - g)$. In the supernormal case, however, the expected growth rate is not a constant—it declines at the end of the period of supernormal growth.

Because Equation 8-2 requires a constant growth rate, we obviously cannot use it to value stocks that have nonconstant growth. However, assuming that a company currently enjoying supernormal growth will eventually slow down and become a constant growth stock, we can find its value. First, we assume that the dividend will grow at a nonconstant rate (generally a relatively high rate) for N periods, after which it will grow at a constant rate, g. N is often called the *terminal date,* or *horizon date.*

FIGURE 8-4 Illustrative Dividend Growth Rates

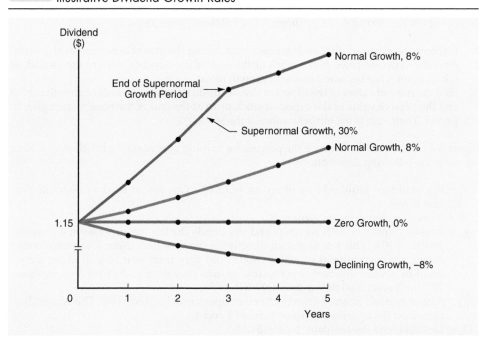

---

[12]A negative growth rate indicates a declining company. A mining company whose profits are falling because of a declining ore body is an example. Someone buying such a company would expect its earnings, and consequently its dividends and stock price, to decline each year, and this would lead to capital losses rather than capital gains. Obviously, a declining company's stock price will be relatively low, and its dividend yield must be high enough to offset the expected capital loss and still produce a competitive total return. Students sometimes argue that they would never be willing to buy a stock whose price was expected to decline. However, if the annual dividends are large enough to *more than offset* the falling stock price, the stock could still provide a good return.

We can use the constant growth formula, Equation 8-2, and what the stock's value will be at period N, to determine what the stock's **horizon, or terminal, value** will be N periods from today:

$$\text{Horizon value} = \hat{P}_N = \frac{D_{N+1}}{r_s - g} = \frac{D_N(1 + g)}{r_s - g} \tag{8-5}$$

The stock's intrinsic value today, $\hat{P}_0$, is the present value of the dividends during the non-constant growth period plus the present value of the horizon value:

$$\hat{P}_0 = \underbrace{\frac{D_1}{(1 + r_s)^1} + \frac{D_2}{(1 + r_s)^2} + \cdots + \frac{D_N}{(1 + r_s)^N}}_{\substack{\text{PV of dividends during the} \\ \text{nonconstant growth period} \\ t = 1, \ldots, N}} + \underbrace{\frac{D_{N+1}}{(1 + r_s)^{N+1}} + \cdots + \frac{D_\infty}{(1 + r_s)^\infty}}_{\substack{\text{PV of dividends during the} \\ \text{constant growth period} \\ t = N + 1, \ldots, \infty}}$$

$$\hat{P}_0 = \underbrace{\frac{D_1}{(1 + r_s)^1} + \frac{D_2}{(1 + r_s)^2} + \cdots + \frac{D_N}{(1 + r_s)^N}}_{\substack{\text{PV of dividends during the} \\ \text{nonconstant growth period} \\ t = 1, \ldots, N}} + \underbrace{\frac{\hat{P}_N}{(1 + r_s)^N}}_{\substack{\text{PV of horizon} \\ \text{value } \hat{P}_N: \\ \frac{[(D_{N+1})/(r_s - g)]}{(1 + r_s)^N}}} \tag{8-6}$$

To implement Equation 8-6, we go through the following three steps:

1. Estimate the expected dividends for each year during the period of nonconstant growth.
2. Find the expected price of the stock at the end of the nonconstant growth period, at which point it has become a constant growth stock.
3. Find the present values of the expected dividends during the nonconstant growth period and the present value of the expected stock price at the end of the nonconstant growth period. Their sum is the intrinsic value of the stock, $\hat{P}_0$.

Figure 8-5 can be used to illustrate the process for valuing nonconstant growth stocks. Here we make the following assumptions:

r_s = Shareholders' required rate of return = 13.4%. This rate is used to discount the cash flows.

N = Years of supernormal growth = 3.

g_s = Rate of growth in both earnings and dividends during the supernormal growth period = 30%. This rate is shown directly on the time line. (*Note:* The growth rate during the supernormal growth period could vary from year to year. Also, there could be several different supernormal growth periods, e.g., 30% for 3 years, then 20% for 3 years, and then a constant 8%.)

g_n = Rate of normal, constant growth after the supernormal period = 8%. This rate is also shown on the time line, between Periods 3 and 4.

D_0 = Last dividend the company paid = $1.15.

The valuation process as shown in Figure 8-5 is explained in the steps set forth below the time line. The estimated value of the supernormal growth stock is $39.21.

CONCEPT REVIEW

1. Explain how one would find the value of a supernormal growth stock.
2. Explain what is meant by "horizon (terminal) date" and "horizon (terminal) value."

3. Suppose D_0 = \$5.00 and r_s = 10%. The expected growth rate from Year 0 to Year 1 ($g_{0\ to\ 1}$) = 20%, the expected growth rate from Year 1 to Year 2 ($g_{1\ to\ 2}$) = 10%, and the constant rate beyond Year 2 is g_n = 5%. What are the expected dividends for Year 1 and Year 2? What is the expected horizon value price at Year 2 ($\hat{P}_2$)? What is $\hat{P}_0$? (Check Figure: \$6.00 and \$6.60; \$138.60; \$125.45)

Process for Finding the Value of a Supernormal Growth Stock

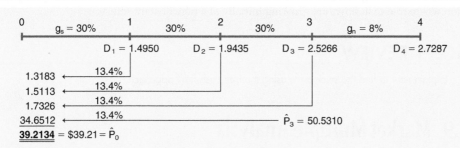

See **Ch 08 Tool Kit.xlsx** at the textbook's website for all calculations.

Notes:

Step 1.   Calculate the dividends expected at the end of each year during the nonconstant growth period. Calculate the first dividend, D_1 = $D_0(1 + g_s)$ = \$1.15(1.30) = \$1.4950. Here g_s is the growth rate during the 3-year supernormal growth period, 30%. Show the \$1.4950 on the time line as the cash flow at Time 1. Then, calculate D_2 = $D_1(1 + g_s)$ = \$1.4950(1.30) = \$1.9435, and then D_3 = $D_2(1 + g_s)$ = \$1.9435(1.30) = \$2.5266. Show these values on the time line as the cash flows at Time 2 and Time 3. Note that D_0 is used only to calculate D_1.

Step 2.   At Time 3, the stock becomes a constant growth stock. Therefore, we can use the constant growth formula to find $\hat{P}_3$, which is the PV of the dividends from Time 4 to infinity as evaluated at Time 3.

First, we determine D_4 = \$2.5266(1.08) = \$2.7287 for use in the formula, and then we calculate $\hat{P}_3$ as follows:

$$\hat{P}_3 = \frac{D_4}{r_s - g_n} = \frac{\$2.7287}{0.134 - 0.08} = \$50.5310$$

We show this \$50.5310 on the time line as a second cash flow at Time 3. The \$50.5310 is a Time 3 cash flow in the sense that the owner of the stock could sell it for \$50.5310 at Time 3 and also in the sense that \$50.5310 is the present value of the dividend cash flows from Time 4 to infinity.

Step 3.   Now that the cash flows have been placed on the time line, we can discount each cash flow at the required rate of return, r_s = 13.4%. This produces the PVs shown to the left below the time line, and the sum of the PVs is the value of the supernormal growth stock, \$39.21.

With a financial calculator, you can find the PV of the cash flows as shown on the time line with the cash flow register of your calculator. Enter 0 for CF_0 because you get no cash flow at Time 0, CF_1 = 1.495, CF_2 = 1.9435, and CF_3 = 2.5266 + 50.531 = 53.0576. Then enter I = 13.4, and press the NPV key to find the value of the stock, \$39.21.

8.8 Stock Valuation by the Free Cash Flow Approach

The box at the beginning of the chapter showed that the value of a firm is the present value of its future expected free cash flows (FCFs), discounted at the weighted average cost of capital (WACC). Following is a simple example illustrating this approach to stock valuation.

Suppose a firm had a free cash flow of \$200 million at the end of the most recent year. Chapter 5 showed how to forecast financial statements and free cash flows, but for simplicity let's assume that the firm's FCFs are expected to grow at a constant rate of 5% per year forever. Chapter 9 explains how to estimate the weighted average cost of capital, but for now let's assume that the firm's WACC is 9%. The present value of the expected future free cash flows is the PV of a growing annuity, so we can use a variation of Equation 8-2, the value of a constantly growing stream of dividends:

$$V = \frac{FCF(1 + g)}{WACC - g} = \frac{\$200(1.05)}{0.09 - 0.05} = \$5,250 \text{ million} \qquad (8\text{-}7)$$

FCFs are the cash flows available for distribution to *all* of the firm's investors, not just the shareholders. The WACC is the average rate of return required by *all* of the firm's investors, not just shareholders. Therefore, V is the value of the entire firm's operations, not just the value of its equity. If the firm had any nonoperating assets, such as short-term investments in marketable securities, we would add them to V to find the total value. The firm in this example has no nonoperating assets, so its total value is $5,250 million. To find the value of equity, subtract the value of claims held by all groups other than common shareholders, such as debtholders and preferred shareholders. If the value of debt and preferred stock equals $2,000 million, then the firm's equity has a value of $5,250 − $2,000 = $3,250 million. If 325 million shares of stock are outstanding, then the intrinsic stock value is $3,250/325 = $10 per share. This example should give you the general idea behind the free cash flow approach to stock valuation, but see Chapter 22 for a more comprehensive example, including the situation where free cash flows are growing initially at a nonconstant rate.

CONCEPT REVIEW

1. Explain how to find the stock price using the free cash flow approach.

8.9 Market Multiple Analysis

Another method of stock valuation is **market multiple analysis,** which applies a market-determined multiple to net income, earnings per share, sales, book value, or, for businesses such as cable TV or cellular telephone systems, the number of subscribers. While the discounted dividend method applies valuation concepts in a precise manner, focusing on expected cash flows, market multiple analysis is more judgmental. To illustrate the concept, suppose that a company's forecasted earnings per share are $7.70. The average price per share to earnings per share (P/E) ratio for similar publicly traded companies is 12.

To estimate the company's stock value using the market P/E multiple approach, simply multiply its $7.70 earnings per share by the market multiple of 12 to obtain the value of $7.70(12) = $92.40. This is its estimated stock price per share.

Another commonly used measure is *earnings before interest, taxes, depreciation, and amortization (EBITDA).* The EBITDA multiple is the total value of a company (the market value of equity plus debt) divided by EBITDA. This multiple is based on total value, since EBITDA measures the entire firm's performance. Therefore, it is called an **entity multiple.** The EBITDA market multiple is the average EBITDA multiple for similar publicly traded companies. Multiplying a company's EBITDA by the market multiple gives an estimate of the company's total value. To find the company's estimated stock price per share, subtract debt from total value, and then divide by the number of shares outstanding.

As noted above, in some businesses such as cable TV and mobile telephones, an important element in the valuation process is the number of customers a company has. For example, telephone companies have been paying about $2,000 per customer when acquiring mobile phone operators. Managed care companies such as U.S. HMOs have applied similar logic in acquisitions, basing their valuations on the number of people insured. Some Internet companies have been valued by the number of "eyeballs," which is the number of hits on the site.

CONCEPT REVIEW

1. What is market multiple analysis?
2. What is an entity multiple?

8.10 Preferred Stock

Preferred stock is similar to bonds in some respects and to common stock in other ways. Accountants classify preferred stock as equity and hence show it on the balance sheet as an equity account. However, from a finance perspective preferred stock lies somewhere between debt and common equity—it imposes a fixed charge and thus increases the firm's financial leverage, yet omitting the preferred dividend does not force a company into bankruptcy.

Also, unlike interest on debt, preferred dividends are not deductible by the issuing corporation, so preferred stock has a higher cost of capital than debt.

Basic Features

Preferred stock has a par (or liquidating) value, often $25. The dividend is stated as either a percentage of par, or as so many dollars per share, or both ways. For example, several years ago Klondike Paper Company sold 600,000 shares of $25 par value perpetual preferred stock for a total of $15 million. This preferred had a stated annual dividend of $2.25 per share, so the preferred dividend yield was $2.25/$25 = 0.09, or 9%, at the time of issue. The dividend was set when the stock was issued; it will not be changed in the future. Therefore, if the required rate of return on preferred, r_p, changes from 9% after the issue date—as it did—then the market price of the preferred stock will go up or down. Currently, r_p for Klondike Paper's preferred is 7%, and the price of the preferred has risen from $25 to $2.25/0.07 = $32.14.

If the preferred dividend is not earned, the company does not have to pay it. However, many preferred issues are *cumulative,* meaning that the cumulative total of unpaid preferred dividends must be paid before dividends can be paid on the common stock. Unpaid preferred dividends are called **arrearages.** Dividends in arrears do not earn interest; thus, arrearages do not grow in a compound interest sense—they grow only from additional nonpayments of the preferred dividend. The dividends in arrears continue in force until they are paid.

Preferred stock normally has no voting rights. However, most preferred issues stipulate that the preferred shareholders can elect a minority of the directors—say, three out of 10—if the preferred dividend is passed (omitted). Some preferreds even entitle their holders to elect a majority of the board.

Although nonpayment of preferred dividends will not trigger bankruptcy, corporations issue preferred with every intention of paying the dividend. Even if passing the dividend does not give the preferred shareholders control of the company, failure to pay a preferred dividend precludes payment of common dividends. In addition, passing the dividend makes it difficult to raise capital by selling bonds, and virtually impossible to sell more preferred or common stock except at rock bottom prices. However, having preferred stock outstanding does give a firm the chance to overcome its difficulties—if bonds had been used instead of preferred stock, a company could be forced into bankruptcy before it could straighten out its problems. *Thus, from the viewpoint of the issuing corporation, preferred stock is less risky than bonds.*

However, for an investor preferred stock is riskier than bonds: (1) preferred shareholders' claims are subordinated to those of bondholders in the event of liquidation, and (2) bondholders are more likely to continue receiving income during hard times than are preferred shareholders. Accordingly, investors require a higher after-tax rate of return on a given firm's preferred stock than on its bonds.

The after-tax return is important because dividends are taxed differently from interest income. For instance, Enbridge's Series 11 preferred shares were trading at $25.15 in mid-July 2014. Based on a dividend of $1.10, those shares have a pre-tax yield of 4.4%. These shares have a fixed dividend for 5 years, at which time they become callable. If not called, investors may choose to receive a new annual dividend fixed for 5 years based on a 2.64% yield over a 5-year Government of Canada bond; or they may convert their shares to a floating-rate series. Enbridge's bonds maturing around the same time yield 2.6%. The preferreds are riskier than bonds, and the pre-tax yield is greater. Once the after-tax returns are calculated the perferreds yield 4.0%, whereas the bonds return 1.8%, an even greater difference. The after-tax effect is also more pronounced if we repeat this exercise for a corporate investor, since Canadian companies don't pay taxes on dividends they receive from other Canadian companies. In this case the after-tax return would be 4.4% on the dividends and 1.9% on the interest.[13] For tax reasons, investing in preferred shares may be more advantageous for a company than for an individual.

Some preferred stocks are similar to perpetual bonds in that they have no maturity date; other issues have specified maturities. Preferred shares may have a sinking-fund provision that calls for the retirement of a certain percentage of the issue each year, meaning that the issue will have a maximum maturity date. Also, many preferred issues are callable by the issuing corporation, which can also limit their life.

Besides the "plain vanilla" variety of preferred shares, there are several variations. Floating-rate preferred shares pay dividends based on the prime rate—for example, 70% of prime.

---

[13]We are assuming an individual investor residing in Ontario with taxable income of $80,000 in 2014. Chapter 2 contained information on the dividend tax credit. For the corporation we are assuming an Ontario-based company for 2014 with a 26.5% tax rate.

Since the dividend reflects changing required market returns, the stock price will tend to be more stable. Another type is a preferred share convertible into common shares of the issuer, at a fixed price for a set period of time. Some preferred shares have a retraction feature, allowing investors to sell them back to the issuer, after a period of time, for their par value.

Advantages and Disadvantages of Preferred Stock

There are both advantages and disadvantages to financing with preferred stock. Here are the major advantages from the issuer's standpoint:

1. In contrast to bonds, the obligation to pay preferred dividends is not firm, and passing a preferred dividend cannot force a firm into bankruptcy.
2. By issuing preferred stock, the firm avoids the dilution of common equity that occurs when common stock is sold.
3. Since preferred stock sometimes has no maturity, and since preferred sinking-fund payments, if present, are typically spread over a long period, preferred issues reduce the cash flow drain from repayment of principal that occurs with debt issues.

There are two major disadvantages:

1. Preferred stock dividends are not normally deductible to the issuer; hence the after-tax cost of preferred is typically higher than the after-tax cost of debt. However, the tax advantage of preferreds to corporate purchasers lowers their pre-tax cost and thus their effective cost.
2. Although preferred dividends can be passed, investors expect them to be paid, and firms intend to pay the dividends if conditions permit. Thus, preferred dividends are considered to be a fixed cost. Therefore, their use, like that of debt, increases financial risk and thus the cost of common equity.

Preferred Stock Valuation

As noted above, a preferred stock entitles its owners to regular, fixed dividend payments. If the payments last forever, the issue is a perpetuity whose value, V_{ps}, is found as follows:

$$V_{ps} = \frac{D_{ps}}{r_{ps}} \tag{8-8}$$

V_{ps} is the value of the preferred stock, D_{ps} is the preferred dividend, and r_{ps} is the required rate of return. MicroDrive has preferred stock outstanding that pays a dividend of $10 per year. If the required rate of return on this preferred stock is 10%, then its value is $100, found by solving Equation 8-8 as follows:

$$V_{ps} = \frac{\$10.00}{0.10} = \$100.00$$

If we know the current price of a preferred stock and its dividend, we can solve for the expected rate of return as follows:

$$\hat{r}_{ps} = \frac{D_{ps}}{V_{ps}} \tag{8-8a}$$

Some preferred stocks have a stated maturity date, say, 20 years. If a firm's preferred stock matures in 20 years, pays a $2 annual dividend, has a par value of $25, and has a required return of 6%, then we can find its price as follows: Enter N = 20, I/YR = 6, PMT = 2, and FV = 25. Then press PV to find the price, V_{ps} = $30.73. If you know the price of a share of preferred stock, you can solve for I/YR to find the expected rate of return, $\hat{r}_{ps}$.

Most preferred stocks pay dividends quarterly. This is true for MicroDrive, so we could find the effective rate of return on its preferred stock (perpetual or maturing) as follows:

$$\text{EFF\%} = \text{EAR}_p = \left(1 + \frac{r_{\text{Nom}}}{m}\right)^m - 1 = \left(1 + \frac{0.10}{4}\right)^4 - 1 = 10.38\%$$

If an investor wanted to compare the returns on MicroDrive's bonds and its preferred stock, it would be best to convert the nominal rates on each security to effective rates and then compare these "equivalent annual rates."

CONCEPT REVIEW

1. Should preferred stock be considered equity or debt? Explain.
2. Is the equation used to value preferred stock more like the one used to evaluate a perpetual bond or the one used for common stock?
3. A preferred stock has an annual dividend of $5. The required return is 8%. What is the V_{ps}? (Check Figure: $62.50)

8.11 Stock Market Equilibrium

Recall that r_i, the required return on Stock i, can be found using the Security Market Line (SML) equation as it was developed in our discussion of the Capital Asset Pricing Model (CAPM) back in Chapter 7:

$$r_i = r_{RF} + (RP_M)b_i$$

If the risk-free rate of return is 8%, the market risk premium, RP_M, is 4%, and Stock i has a beta of 2, then its required rate of return is 16%:

$$r_i = 8\% + (4\%)2.0$$
$$= 16\%$$

The *marginal investor* will want to buy Stock i if its expected rate of return is more than 16%, will want to sell it if the expected rate of return is less than 16%, and will be indifferent, hence will hold but not buy or sell, if the expected rate of return is exactly 16%. Now suppose the investor's portfolio contains Stock i, and he or she analyzes the stock's prospects and concludes that its earnings, dividends, and price can be expected to grow at a constant rate of 5% per year. The last dividend was $D_0 = \$2.8571$, so the next expected dividend is

$$D_1 = \$2.8571(1.05) = \$3$$

Our investor observes that the present price of the stock, P_0, is $30. Should he or she purchase more of Stock i, sell the stock, or maintain the present position?

The investor can calculate Stock i's *expected rate of return* as follows:

$$\hat{r}_i = \frac{D_1}{P_0} + g = \frac{\$3}{\$30} + 5\% = 15\%$$

Because the expected rate of return is less than the required return of 16%, the investor would want to sell the stock, as would most other holders. However, few people would want to buy at the $30 price, so the present owners would be unable to find buyers unless they cut the price of the stock. Thus, the price would decline, and this decline would continue until the price reached $27.27, at which point the stock would be in **equilibrium,** defined as the price at which the expected rate of return, 16%, is equal to the required rate of return:

$$\hat{r}_i = \frac{\$3}{\$27.27} + 5\% = 11\% + 5\% = 16\% = r_i$$

Had the stock initially sold for less than $27.27, say, $25, events would have been reversed. Investors would have wanted to buy the stock because its expected rate of return would have exceeded its required rate of return, and buy orders would have driven the stock's price up to $27.27.

To summarize, in equilibrium two related conditions must hold:

1. A stock's expected rate of return as seen by the marginal investor must equal its required rate of return: $\hat{r}_i = r_i$.
2. The actual market price of the stock must equal its intrinsic value as estimated by the marginal investor: $P_0 = \hat{P}_0$.

Of course, some individual investors may believe that $\hat{r}_i > r_i$ and $\hat{P}_0 > P_0$; hence they would invest in the stock, while other investors may have an opposite view and would sell all of their shares. However, it is the marginal investor who establishes the actual market price, and for this investor, we must have $\hat{r}_i = r_i$ and $P_0 = \hat{P}_0$. If these conditions do not hold, trading will occur until they do.

Changes in Equilibrium Stock Prices and Market Volatility

Stock prices are not constant—as we showed earlier in this chapter and elsewhere, they undergo violent changes at times. Indeed, many stocks declined by 80% or more during 2008, and a few enjoyed gains of up to 200%. At the risk of understatement, the stock market is volatile!

To see how such changes can occur, assume that Stock i is in equilibrium, selling at a price of $27.27. If all expectations are exactly met, during the next year the price will gradually rise to $28.63, or by 5%. However, many different events may occur to cause a change in the equilibrium price. To illustrate, consider again the set of inputs used to develop Stock i's price of $27.27, along with a new set of assumed input variables:

	Variable Value	
	Original	New
Risk-free rate, r_{RF}	8%	7%
Market risk premium, $r_M - r_{RF}$	4%	3%
Stock i's beta coefficient, b_i	2.0	1.0
Stock i's expected growth rate, g_i	5%	6%
D_0	$2.8571	$2.8571
Price of Stock i	$27.27	?

Now give yourself a test: How would the indicated change in each variable, by itself, affect the price, and what is your guess as to the new stock price?

Every change, taken alone, would lead to an *increase* in the price. Taken together, the first three changes lower r_i, which declines from 16% to 10%:

$$\text{Original } r_i = 8\% + 4\%(2.0) = 16\%;$$

$$\text{New } r_i = 7\% + 3\%(1.0) = 10\%.$$

Using these values, together with the new g value, we find that $\hat{P}_0$ rises from $27.27 to $75.71:[14]

$$\text{Original } \hat{P}_0 = \frac{\$2.8571(1.05)}{0.16 - 0.05} = \frac{\$3}{0.11} = \$27.27$$

$$\text{New } \hat{P}_0 = \frac{\$2.8571(1.06)}{0.10 - 0.06} = \frac{\$3.0285}{0.04} = \$75.71$$

---

[14] A price change of this magnitude is by no means rare for an individual stock. The prices of many stocks double or halve during a year. For example, Teck Resources Corporation stock fell almost 90% in the last half of 2008, only to shoot up over 600% in 2009. Over 2010, Teck stock rose another 66%, yet subsequently fell by 50% between January and September 2011.

At the new price, the expected and required rates of return are equal:[15]

$$\hat{r}_i = \frac{\$3.0285}{\$75.71} + 6\% = 10\% = r_i$$

As this example illustrates, even small changes in the size or risk of expected future dividends can cause large changes in stock prices. What might cause investors to change their expectations about future dividends? It could be new information about the company, such as preliminary results for an R&D program, initial sales of a new product, or the discovery of harmful side effects from the use of an existing product. Or, new information that will affect many companies could arrive, such as a tightening of interest rates by the Bank of Canada. Given the existence of computers and telecommunications networks, new information hits the market on an almost constant basis, and it causes frequent and sometimes large changes in stock prices. In other words, *ready availability of information causes stock prices to be volatile!*

If a stock's price is stable, that probably means that little new information is arriving. But if you think it's risky to invest in a volatile stock, imagine how risky it would be to invest in a company that rarely released new information about its sales or operations. It may be bad to see your stock's price jump around, but it would be a lot worse to see a stable quoted price most of the time and then to see huge moves on the rare days when new information was released. Fortunately, in our economy timely information is readily available, and evidence suggests that stocks, especially those of large companies, adjust rapidly to new information. Consequently, equilibrium ordinarily exists for any given stock, and required and expected returns are generally equal. Stock prices certainly change, sometimes violently and rapidly, but this simply reflects changing conditions and expectations. There are, of course, times when a stock appears to react for several months to favourable or unfavourable developments. However, this does not signify a long adjustment period; rather, it simply indicates that as more new pieces of information about the situation become available, the market adjusts to them. The ability of the market to adjust to new information is discussed in the next section.

CONCEPT REVIEW

1. What two conditions must hold for a stock to be in equilibrium?
2. Why doesn't a volatile stock price imply irrational pricing?

8.12 The Efficient Markets Hypothesis

The **efficient markets hypothesis (EMH)** asserts that (1) stocks are always in equilibrium and (2) it is impossible for an investor to "beat the market" and consistently earn a higher rate of return than is justified by the stock's risk. In other words, a stock's market price is always equal to its intrinsic value. To put it a little more precisely, suppose a stock's market price is equal to the stock's intrinsic value but new information arrives that changes the stock's intrinsic value. The EMH asserts that the market price will adjust to the new intrinsic value so quickly that there isn't time for an investor to receive the new information, evaluate the information, take a position in the stock before the market price changes, and then profit from the subsequent change in price.

Here are three points to consider. First, almost every stock is under considerable scrutiny. With 100,000 or so full-time, highly trained, professional analysts and traders each following about 30 of the roughly 3,000 actively traded stocks (analysts tend to specialize in a specific industry), there are an average of about 1,000 analysts following each stock. Second, financial institutions, pension funds, money management firms, and hedge funds have billions of dollars available for portfolio managers to use in taking advantage of mispriced stocks. Third, disclosure requirements and electronic information networks cause new information about a stock to become available to all analysts virtually simultaneously and almost immediately. With so many analysts trying to take advantage of temporary mispricing due

---

[15]It should be obvious by now that *actual realized* rates of return are not necessarily equal to expected and required returns. Thus, an investor might have *expected* to receive a return of 15% if he or she had bought Teck stock, but after the fact, the realized return was far different from the 15% per annum in the years 2008–2011.

to new information, with so much money chasing the profits due to temporary mispricing, and with such widespread dispersal of information, a stock's market price should adjust quickly from its pre-news intrinsic value to its post-news intrinsic value, leaving only a very short amount of time that the stock is "mispriced" as it moves from one equilibrium price to another. That, in a nutshell, is the logic behind the efficient markets hypothesis.

The following sections discuss forms of the efficient markets hypothesis and empirical tests of the hypothesis.

Forms of the Efficient Markets Hypothesis

There are three forms of the efficient markets hypothesis, and each focuses on a different type of information availability.

Weak-Form Efficiency The **weak form of** the EMH asserts that all information contained in past price movements is fully reflected in current market prices. If this were true, then information about recent trends in stock prices would be of no use in selecting stocks—the fact that a stock has risen for the past three days, for example, would give us no useful clues as to what it will do today or tomorrow. In contrast, **technical analysts**, also called "chartists," believe that past trends or patterns in stock prices can be used to predict future stock prices.

To illustrate the arguments supporting weak-form efficiency, suppose that after studying the past history of the stock market, a technical analyst identifies the following historical pattern: If a stock has fallen for three consecutive days, its price rose by 10% (on average) the following day. The technician would then conclude that investors could make money by purchasing a stock whose price has fallen three consecutive days.

Weak-form advocates argue that if this pattern truly existed then other investors would soon discover it, and if so, why would anyone be willing to sell a stock after it had fallen for three consecutive days? In other words, why sell if you know that the price is going to increase by 10% the next day? For example, suppose a stock had fallen three consecutive days to $40. If the stock were really likely to rise by 10% to $44 tomorrow, then its price *today, right now,* would actually rise to somewhere close to $44, thereby eliminating the trading opportunity. Consequently, weak-form efficiency implies that any information that comes from past stock prices is too rapidly incorporated into the current stock price for a profit opportunity to exist.

Semistrong-Form Efficiency The **semistrong form** of the EMH states that current market prices reflect all *publicly available* information. Therefore, if semistrong-form efficiency exists, it would do no good to pore over annual reports or other published data because market prices would have adjusted to any good or bad news contained in such reports back when the news came out. With semistrong-form efficiency, investors should expect to earn returns commensurate with risk, but they should not expect to do any better or worse other than by chance.

Another implication of semistrong-form efficiency is that whenever information is released to the public, stock prices will respond only if the information is different from what had been expected. For example, if a company announces a 30% increase in earnings and if that increase is about what analysts had been expecting, then the announcement should have little or no effect on the company's stock price. On the other hand, the stock price would probably fall if analysts had expected earnings to increase by more than 30%, but it probably would rise if they had expected a smaller increase.

Strong-Form Efficiency The **strong form** of the EMH states that current market prices reflect all pertinent information, whether publicly available or privately held. If this form holds, even insiders would find it impossible to earn consistently abnormal returns in the stock market.

Is the Stock Market Efficient? The Empirical Evidence

Empirical studies are joint tests of the EMH and an asset pricing model, such as the CAPM. They are joint tests in the sense that they examine whether a particular strategy can beat the market, where "beating the market" means earning a return higher than that predicted by the particular asset pricing model. Before addressing tests of the particular forms of the EMH, let's take a look at market bubbles.

Market Bubbles The history of finance is marked by numerous instances in which (1) prices climb rapidly to heights that would have been considered extremely unlikely before the run-up; (2) the volume of trading is much higher than past volume; (3) many new investors (or speculators?) eagerly enter the market; and (4) prices suddenly fall precipitously, leaving many of the new investors with huge losses. These instances are called market bubbles.

The stock market bubbles that burst in 2000 and 2008 suggest that, at the height of these booms, the stocks of many companies—especially in the technology sector in 2000 and the financial sector in 2008—vastly exceeded their intrinsic values, which should not happen if markets are always efficient. Two questions arise. First, how are bubbles formed? Behavioural finance, which we discussed in Chapter 7, provides some possible answers. Second, why do bubbles persist when it is possible to make a fortune when they burst? For example, hedge fund manager Mark Spitznagel reputedly made billions for his Universa funds by betting against the market in 2008. The logic underlying market equilibrium suggests that everyone would bet against an overvalued market, and that their actions would cause market prices to fall back to intrinsic values fairly quickly. To understand why this doesn't happen, let's examine the strategies for profiting from a falling market: (1) Sell stocks (or the market index itself) short; (2) purchase a put option or write a call option; or (3) take a short position in a futures contract on the market index. Following is an explanation for how these strategies work (or fail).

Loosely speaking, selling a stock short means that you borrow a share from a broker and sell it. You get the cash (subject to collateral requirements required by the broker) but you owe a share of stock. For example, suppose you sell a share of Google short at a current price of $500. If the price falls to $400, you can buy a share of the stock at the now-lower $400 market price and return the share to the broker, pocketing the $100 difference between the higher price ($500) when you went short and the lower price ($400) when you closed the position. Of course, if the price goes up, say to $550, you lose $50 because you must replace the share you borrowed (at $500) with one that is now more costly ($550). Even if your broker doesn't require you to close out your position when the price goes up, your broker certainly will require that you put in more collateral.

Recall from the Chapter 1 Web Extension that a put option gives you the option to sell a share at a fixed strike price. For example, suppose you buy a put on Google for $60 with a strike price of $500. If the stock price falls below the strike price, say to $400, you can buy a share at the low price ($400) and sell it at the higher strike price ($500), making a net $40 profit from the decline in the stock price: $40 = −$60 −$400 + $500. However, if the put expires before the stock price falls below the strike price, you lose the $60 you spent buying the put. You can also use call options to bet on a decline. For example, if you write a call option, you receive cash in return for an obligation to sell a share at the strike price. Suppose you write a call option on Google with a strike price of $500 and receive $70. If Google's price stays below the $500 strike price, you keep the $70 cash you received from writing the call. But if Google goes up to $600 and the call you wrote is exercised, you must buy a share at the new high price ($600) and sell it at the lower strike price ($500), for a net loss of $30: $70 −$600 + $500 = −$30.[16]

With a short position in a futures contract on the market index (or a particular stock), you are obligated to sell a share at a fixed price. If the market price falls below the specified price in the futures contract, you make money because you can buy a share in the market and sell it at the higher price specified in the futures contract. But if the market price increases, you lose money because you must buy a share at the now higher price and sell it at the price fixed in the futures contract.[17]

Each of these strategies allows an investor to make a lot of money. And if all investors tried to capitalize on an overvalued market, their actions would soon drive the market back to equilibrium, preventing a bubble from forming. But here is the problem with these strategies. Even if the market is overvalued, it might takes months (or even years) before the market falls to its intrinsic value. During this period, an investor would have to spend a lot of cash maintaining the strategies described above, including margin calls, settling options, and daily marking to market for futures contracts. These negative cash flows could easily drive an investor into bankruptcy before the investor was eventually proven correct. Unfortunately, there aren't any low-risk strategies for puncturing a market bubble.

Notice that the problem of negative cash flows doesn't exist for the opposite situation of an undervalued market in which the intrinsic value is greater than the market

---

[16]Options are usually settled by cash rather than by actually buying and selling shares.
[17]Recall from Chapter 1 that futures contracts are actually settled daily and that they are usually settled for cash rather than the actual shares.

price. Investors can simply buy stock at the too-low market price and hold it until the market price eventually increases to the intrinsic value. Even if the market price continues to go down before eventually rising, the investor experiences only paper losses and not actual negative cash flows. Thus, we would not expect "negative" bubbles to persist very long.

Tests of Weak-Form Efficiency Most studies suggest that the stock market is highly efficient in the weak form, with two exceptions. The first exception is for long-term reversals, with studies showing that portfolios of stocks with poor past long-term performance (over the past five years, for example) tend to do slightly better in the long-term future than the CAPM predicts, and vice versa. The second is momentum, with studies showing that stocks with strong performance in the short-term past (over the past six to nine months, for example) tend to do slightly better in the short-term future than the CAPM predicts, and likewise for weak performance.[18] Strategies based on taking advantage of long-term reversals or short-term momentum produce returns that are in excess of those predicted by the CAPM. However, the excess returns are small, especially when transaction costs are considered.

Tests of Semistrong-Form Efficiency Most studies show that markets are reasonably efficient in the semistrong form: It is difficult to use publicly available information to create a trading strategy that consistently has returns greater than those predicted by the CAPM. In fact, the professionals who manage mutual fund portfolios, on average, do not outperform the overall stock market as measured by an index like the S&P/TSX 60 and tend to have returns lower than predicted by the CAPM, possibly because many mutual funds have high fees.[19]

However, there are two well-known exceptions to semistrong-form efficiency. The first is for small companies, which have had historical returns greater than predicted by the CAPM. The second is related to book-to-market ratios (B/M), defined as the book value of equity divided by the market value of equity (this is the inverse of the market-to-book ratio defined in Chapter 3). Companies with high B/M ratios have had higher returns than predicted by the CAPM.

Tests of Strong-Form Efficiency The evidence suggests that the strong form EMH does not hold, because those who possessed inside information could make and have (illegally) made abnormal profits. On the other hand, many insiders have gone to jail, so perhaps there is indeed a trade-off between risk and return!

CONCEPT REVIEW

1. What is the efficient markets hypothesis (EMH)?
2. What are the differences among the three forms of the EMH?
3. Why is it difficult to puncture a market bubble?
4. What violations of the EMH have been demonstrated?
5. What is short-term momentum? What are long-term reversals?

Summary

Corporate decisions should be analyzed in terms of how alternative courses of action are likely to affect a firm's value. However, it is necessary to know how stock prices are established before attempting to measure how a given decision will affect a specific firm's value. This chapter showed how stock values are determined, and also how

---

[18]For example, see N. Jegadeesh and S. Titman, "Returns to Buying Winners and Selling Losers: Implications for Stock Market Efficiency," *Journal of Finance*, March 1993, pp. 69-91, and W. F. M. DeBondt and R. H. Thaler, "Does the Stock Market Overreact?" *Journal of Finance*, July 1985, pp. 793–808.

[19]For a discussion of the performance of actively managed funds, see Jonathan Clements, "Resisting the Lure of Managed Funds," *The Wall Street Journal*, February 27, 2001, p. C1.

investors go about estimating the rates of return they expect to earn. The key concepts covered are listed below:

- A **proxy** is a document that gives one person the power to act for another, typically the power to vote shares of common stock. A **proxy fight** occurs when an outside group solicits shareholders' proxies in an effort to vote a new management team into office.
- A **takeover** occurs when a person or group succeeds in ousting a firm's management and takes control of the company.
- Shareholders often have the right to purchase any additional shares sold by the firm. This right, called the **preemptive right,** protects the control of the present shareholders and prevents dilution of their value.
- Although most firms have only one type of common stock, in some instances **dual-class stock** is used to meet the special needs of the company. Some classes of common stock may provide for multiple votes per share, while others may allow no voting or limited voting rights.
- **Closely held stock** is owned by a few individuals who are typically associated with the firm's management.
- **Publicly owned stock** is owned by a relatively large number of individuals who are not actively involved in the firm's management.
- The **intrinsic value of a share of stock** is calculated as the **present value of the stream of dividends** the stock is expected to provide in the future.
- The equation used to find the **intrinsic, or expected, value of a constant growth stock** is

$$\hat{P}_0 = \frac{D_1}{r_s - g}$$

- The **expected total rate of return** from a stock consists of an **expected dividend yield** plus an **expected capital gains yield**. For a constant growth firm, both the expected dividend yield and the expected capital gains yield are constant.
- The equation for $\hat{r}_s$, the **expected rate of return on a constant growth stock,** can be expressed as follows:

$$\hat{r}_s = \frac{D_1}{P_0} + g$$

- A **zero growth stock** is one whose future dividends are not expected to grow at all. A **supernormal growth** stock is one whose earnings and dividends are expected to grow much faster than the economy as a whole over some specified time period and then to grow at the "normal" rate.
- To find the **present value of a supernormal growth stock,** (1) find the dividends expected during the supernormal growth period, (2) find the price of the stock at the end of the supernormal growth period, (3) discount the dividends and the projected price back to the present, and (4) sum these PVs to find the current intrinsic, or expected, value of the stock, $\hat{P}_0$.
- The **horizon (terminal) date** is the date when individual dividend forecasts are no longer made because the dividend growth rate is assumed to be constant.
- The **horizon (terminal) value** is the value at the horizon date of all future dividends after that date.
- **Preferred stock** is a hybrid security having some characteristics of debt and some of equity.
- Most preferred stocks are **perpetuities,** and the value of a share of perpetual preferred stock is found as the dividend divided by the required rate of return:

$$V_{ps} = \frac{D_{ps}}{r_{ps}}$$

- **Preferred stock** that has a finite maturity is evaluated with a formula that is identical in form to the bond valuation formula.

- The **marginal investor** is a representative investor whose actions reflect the beliefs of those people who are currently trading a stock. It is the marginal investor who determines a stock's price.
- **Equilibrium** is the condition under which the expected return on a security as seen by the marginal investor is just equal to its required return, $\hat{r}_s = r_s$. Also, the stock's intrinsic value must be equal to its market price, $\hat{P}_0 = P_0$.
- The **efficient markets hypothesis (EMH)** holds (1) that stocks are always in equilibrium and (2) that it is impossible for an investor who does not have inside information to consistently "beat the market." Therefore, according to the EMH, stocks are always fairly valued ($\hat{P}_0 = P_0$), the required return on a stock is equal to its expected return ($r_s = \hat{r}_s$), and all stocks' expected returns plot on the SML.

Questions

8-1 Define each of the following terms:
a. Proxy; proxy fight; takeover; preemptive right; dual-class shares
b. Closely held stock; publicly owned stock
c. Intrinsic value ($\hat{P}_0$); market price (P_0)
d. Required rate of return, r_s; expected rate of return, $\hat{r}_s$; actual, or realized, rate of return, $\bar{r}_s$
e. Capital gains yield; dividend yield; expected total return
f. Normal, or constant, growth; supernormal, or nonconstant, growth; zero growth stock
g. Preferred stock
h. Equilibrium; efficient markets hypothesis (EMH); three forms of EMH

8-2 Two investors are evaluating Cogeco Cable's stock for possible purchase. They agree on the expected value of D_1 and also on the expected future dividend growth rate. Furthermore, they agree on the risk of the stock. However, one investor normally holds stocks for 2 years, while the other normally holds stocks for 10 years. On the basis of the type of analysis done in this chapter, they should both be willing to pay the same price for Cogeco Cable's stock. True or false? Explain.

8-3 A bond that pays interest forever and has no maturity date is a perpetual bond. In what respect is a perpetual bond similar to a no-growth common stock, and to a share of preferred stock?

Concept Review Problems

Full solutions are provided at www.nelson.com/brigham3ce.

CR-1
Constant Growth
Stock Valuation

Smith Co.'s current stock price is $84.80, and its last dividend was $3.20. In view of Smith's strong financial position and its subsequent low risk, its required rate of return is only 10%. If dividends are expected to grow at a constant rate, g, in the future, and if r_s is expected to remain at 10%, what is Smith's expected stock price 5 years from now?

CR-2
Supernormal Growth
Stock Valuation

Secure Systems Inc. is experiencing a period of rapid growth. Earnings and dividends are expected to grow at a rate of 18% during the next 2 years, at 14% in the third year, and at a constant rate of 5% thereafter. Snyder's last dividend was $1.15, and the required rate of return on the stock is 12%.
a. Calculate the value of the stock today.
b. Calculate $\hat{P}_1$ and $\hat{P}_2$.
c. Calculate the dividend yield and capital gains yield for Years 1, 2, and 3.

Problems

Easy Problems 1–6   Answers to odd-numbered problems appear in Appendix A.

8-1
DPS Calculation

Rident Corp. just paid a dividend of $1.50 a share (i.e., $D_0 = \$1.50$). The dividend is expected to grow 5% a year for the next 3 years, and then 10% a year thereafter. What is the expected dividend per share for each of the next 5 years?

8-2
Constant Growth
Valuation
Boehm Incorporated is expected to pay a $1.50 per share dividend at the end of the year (i.e., $D_1 = 1.50). The dividend is expected to grow at a constant rate of 6% a year. The required rate of return on the stock, r_s, is 13%. What is the value per share of the company's stock?

8-3
Constant Growth
Valuation
Addon Manufacturing's stock currently sells for $22 a share. The stock just paid a dividend of $1.20 a share (i.e., $D_0 = 1.20). The dividend is expected to grow at a constant rate of 10% a year. What stock price is expected 1 year from now? What is the required rate of return on the company's stock?

8-4
Preferred Stock
Valuation
Basil Pet Products has preferred stock outstanding that pays a dividend of $5 at the end of each year. The preferred stock sells for $50 a share. What is the preferred stock's required rate of return?

8-5
Nonconstant Growth
Valuation
A company currently pays a dividend of $2 per share, $D_0 = 2. It is estimated that the company's dividend will grow at a rate of 14% per year for the next 2 years, then the dividend will grow at a constant rate of 7% thereafter. The company's stock has a beta equal to 1.8, the risk-free rate is 4.5%, and the market risk premium is 4%. What is your estimate of the stock's current price?

8-6
Constant Growth
Valuation
A stock's most recent dividend was $1.80. The dividend is expected to grow by 6% and investors require an 11% return for holding the shares.
a. What is the value of the stock?
b. What proportion of the stock's value is derived from the first five years of dividends?

**Intermediate
Problems 7–20**

8-7
Constant Growth
Rate, g
A stock is trading at $28 per share. The stock is expected to have a year-end dividend of $0.84 per share, which is expected to grow at some constant rate g throughout time. The stock's required rate of return is 9%. If you are an analyst who believes in efficient markets, what is your forecast of g?

8-8
Constant Growth
Valuation
Crisp Cookware's common stock is expected to pay a dividend of $3 a share at the end of the year. The stock has a beta equal to 0.8. The risk-free rate is 5.2%, and the market risk premium is 6%. The stock's dividend is expected to grow at some constant rate g. The stock currently sells for $40 a share. Assuming the market is in equilibrium, what does the market believe will be the stock price at the end of 3 years? (That is, what is $\hat{P}_3$?)

8-9
Preferred Stock
Rate of Return
What will be the nominal rate of return on a preferred stock with a $25 par value, a stated dividend of 7% of par, and a current market price of (a) $16, (b) $21, (c) $25, and (d) $37?

8-10
Declining Growth Stock
Valuation
Brushy Mountain Mining Company's ore reserves are being depleted, so its sales are falling. Also, its pit is getting deeper each year, so its costs are rising. As a result, the company's earnings and dividends are declining at the constant rate of 4% per year. If $D_0 = 5 and $r_s = 15\%$, what is the value of Brushy Mountain's stock?

8-11
Constant Growth
Valuation
What must be a company's dividend growth rate for its stock to have an expected value of $13.25, assuming its most recently paid dividend was $0.50 and the stock's required return is 10%?

8-12
Nonconstant Growth
Valuation
Rosendale Clothiers has decided to make significant reinvestments in its operations. As a result it will be suspending dividend payments for 2 years. It anticipates paying a dividend again in year 3 in the amount of $0.80 per share. The dividend will then be expected to grow by 20% per year for the following 2 years, then growing at a long run rate of 4% thereafter. If the stock's required return is 11%, what is the value of Rosendale's stock at present?

8-13
Rates of Return and
Equilibrium
The beta coefficient for Stock C is $b_C = 0.4$, whereas that for Stock D is $b_D = -0.3$. (Stock D's beta is negative, indicating that its rate of return rises whenever returns on most other stocks fall. There are very few negative beta stocks, although collection agency stocks are sometimes cited as an example.)
a. If the risk-free rate is 4% and the expected rate of return on an average stock is 13%, what are the required rates of return on Stocks C and D?
b. For Stock C, suppose the current price, P_0, is $30; the next expected dividend, D_1, is $1.00; and the stock's expected constant growth rate is 4%. Is the stock in equilibrium? Explain, and describe what will happen if the stock is not in equilibrium.

8-14
Nonconstant Growth
Stock Valuation
Assume that the average firm in your company's industry is expected to grow at a constant rate of 6% and that its dividend yield is 7%. Your company is about as risky as the average firm in the industry, but it has just successfully completed some R&D work that leads you

to expect that its earnings and dividends will grow at a rate of 50% [$D_1 = D_0(1 + g) = D_0(1.50)$] this year and 25% the following year, after which growth should match the 6% industry average rate. The last dividend paid was $1. What is the value per share of your firm's stock?

8-15

Nonconstant Growth
Stock Valuation

Simpkins Ltd. is expanding rapidly, and it currently needs to retain all of its earnings; hence it does not pay any dividends. However, investors expect Simpkins to begin paying dividends, with the first dividend of $0.50 coming 3 years from today. The dividend should grow rapidly—at a rate of 80% per year—during Years 4 and 5. After Year 5, the company should grow at a constant rate of 7% per year. If the required return on the stock is 16%, what is the value of the stock today?

8-16

Preferred Stock Valuation

Rolen Riders issued preferred stock with a stated dividend of 6% of par. Preferred stock of this type currently yields 7%, and the par value is $25. Assume dividends are paid annually.
a. What is the value of Rolen's preferred stock?
b. Suppose interest rate levels rise to the point where the preferred stock now yields 9%. What would be the value of Rolen's preferred stock?

8-17

Return on
Common Stock

You buy a share of Bavarian Auto Parts Corp. stock for $33.44. You expect it to pay dividends of $3.01, $3.311, and $3.6421 in Years 1, 2, and 3, respectively, and you expect to sell it at a price of $44.51 at the end of 3 years.
a. Calculate the growth rate in dividends.
b. Calculate the expected dividend yield.
c. Assuming that the calculated growth rate is expected to continue, what is this stock's expected total rate of return?

8-18

Constant Growth
Stock Valuation

Investors require a 15% rate of return on Brooks Sisters' stock ($r_s = 15\%$).
a. What will be Brooks Sisters' stock value if the most recent dividend was $2 and if investors expect dividends to grow at a constant compound annual rate of (1) −5%, (2) 0%, (3) 5%, and (4) 10%?
b. Using data from part a, what is the Gordon (constant growth) model value for Brooks Sisters' stock if the required rate of return is 15% and the expected growth rate is (1) 15% or (2) 20%? Are these reasonable results? Explain.
c. Is it reasonable to expect that a constant growth stock would have $g > r_s$?

8-19

Equilibrium Stock
Price

The risk-free rate of return, r_{RF}, is 5%; the required rate of return on the market, r_M, is 8%; and Schuler Company's stock has a beta coefficient of 1.5.
a. If the dividend expected during the coming year, is $2.25, and if g = a constant 5%, at what price should Schuler's stock sell?
b. Now, suppose the Bank of Canada increases the money supply, causing the risk-free rate to drop to 4% and r_M to fall to 7%. What would this do to the price of the stock?
c. In addition to the change in part b, suppose investors' risk aversion declines; this fact, combined with the decline in r_{RF}, causes r_M to fall to 6.5%. At what price would Schuler's stock sell?
d. Now, suppose Schuler has a change in management. The new group institutes policies that increase the expected constant growth rate to 5.5%. Also, the new management stabilizes sales and profits, and thus causes the beta coefficient to decline from 1.5 to 1.3. Assume that r_{RF} and r_M are equal to the values in part c. After all these changes, what is Schuler's new equilibrium price? (*Note:* D_1 goes to $2.26.)

8-20

Nonconstant Growth

Mitts Cosmetics Co.'s stock price is $58.88, and it recently paid a $2 dividend. This dividend is expected to grow by 25% for the next 3 years, and then grow forever at a constant rate, g, and $r_s = 12\%$. At what constant rate is the stock expected to grow after Year 3?

**Challenging
Problems 21–24**

8-21

Constant Growth
Stock Valuation

You are analyzing Jillian's Jewellery (JJ) stock for a possible purchase. JJ just paid a dividend of $1.50 *yesterday*. You expect the dividend to grow at the rate of 6% per year for the next 3 years; if you buy the stock, you plan to hold it for 3 years and then sell it.
a. What dividends do you expect for JJ stock over the next 3 years? In other words, calculate D_1, D_2, and D_3.
b. JJ's stock has a required return of 13% and so this is the rate you'll use to discount dividends. Find the present value of the dividend stream; that is, calculate the PV of D_1, D_2, and D_3, and then sum these PVs.

c. JJ stock should trade for $27.05 3 years from now (i.e., you expect $\hat{P}_3 = \$27.05$). Discounted at a 13% rate, what is the present value of this expected future stock price? In other words, calculate the PV of $27.05.

d. If you plan to buy the stock, hold it for 3 years, and then sell it for $27.05, what is the most you should pay for it?

e. Use the constant growth model to calculate the present value of this stock. Assume that $g = 6\%$ and is constant.

f. f Is the value of this stock dependent on how long you plan to hold it? In other words, if your planned holding period were 2 years or 5 years rather than 3 years, would this affect the value of the stock today, $\hat{P}_0$? Explain your answer.

8-22
Nonconstant Growth
Stock Valuation

Reizenstein Technologies (RT) has just developed a solar panel capable of generating 200% more electricity than any solar panel currently on the market. As a result, RT is expected to experience a 15% annual growth rate for the next 5 years. By the end of 5 years, other firms will have developed comparable technology, and RT's growth rate will slow to 5% per year indefinitely. Shareholders require a return of 12% on RT's stock. The most recent annual dividend, which was paid yesterday, was $1.75 per share.

a. Calculate RT's expected dividends for $t = 1, t = 2, t = 3, t = 4$, and $t = 5$.

b. Calculate the estimated intrinsic value of the stock today, $\hat{P}_0$.

c. Calculate the expected dividend yield ($D_1/\hat{P}_0$), the capital gains yield expected during the first year, and the expected total return (dividend yield plus capital gains yield) during the first year. (Assume that $\hat{P}_0 = P_0$, and recognize that the capital gains yield is equal to the total return minus the dividend yield.) Also calculate these same three yields for $t = 5$ (e.g., $D_6/\hat{P}_5$).

8-23
Nonconstant Growth
Stock Valuation

Conroy Consulting Corporation (CCC) has been growing at a rate of 30% per year in recent years. This same nonconstant growth rate is expected to last for another 2 years.

a. If $D_0 = \$2.50$, $r_s = 12\%$, and $g_L = 7\%$, then what is CCCs stock worth today? What are its expected dividend yield and capital gains yield at this time?

b. Now assume that CCCs period of nonconstant growth is to last another 5 years rather than 2 years. How would this affect its price, dividend yield, and capital gains yield? Answer in words only.

c. What will CCCs dividend yield and capital gains yield be once its period of nonconstant growth ends? (*Hint:* These values will be the same regardless of whether you examine the case of 2 or 5 years of nonconstant growth, and the calculations are very easy.)

d. Of what interest to investors is the relationship over time between dividend yield and capital gains yield?

8-24
Corporate
Valuation Model

Assume that today is December 31, 2015, and the following information applies to Pacific Sky Airline:

• After-tax operating profit [EBIT(1-T), also called NOPAT] for 2016 is expected to be $500 million.

• The net capital expenditures for 2016 are expected to be $100 million (depreciation has already been deducted to arrive at the $100 million).

• No change is expected in net operating working capital.

• The free cash flow is expected to grow at a constant rate of 6% per year.

• The required rate of return on equity is 14%.

• The WACC is 10%.

• The market value of the company's debt is $3 billion.

• 200 million shares of stock are outstanding.

Using the free cash flow approach, what should the company's intrinsic stock price be today? (*Note:* Chapter 2 discussed how to calculate free cash flow.)

 Spreadsheet Problem

8-25
Build a Model:
Supernormal Growth
and Corporate
Valuation

Start with the partial model in the file *Ch 08 Build a Model.xlsx* from the textbook's website. Rework Problem 8-23, parts a, b, and c, using a spreadsheet model. For part b, calculate the price, dividend yield, and capital gains yield as called for in the problem.

MINI CASE

Sam Strother and Shawna Tibbs are senior vice presidents of First Strategies Investment Counsel (FSIC). They are co-directors of the company's pension fund management division, with Strother having responsibility for fixed income securities (primarily bonds) and Tibbs responsible for equity investments. A major new client has requested that FSIC present an investment seminar to its Executive Committee, and Strother and Tibbs, who will make the actual presentation, have asked you to help them.

To illustrate the common stock valuation process, Strother and Tibbs have asked you to analyze the Temp Force Company, an employment agency that supplies keyboarders and computer programmers to businesses with temporarily heavy workloads. You are to answer the following questions:

a. Describe briefly the legal rights and privileges of common shareholders.
b. (1) Write out a formula that can be used to value any stock, regardless of its dividend pattern.
   (2) What is a constant growth stock? How are constant growth stocks valued?
   (3) What happens if a company has a constant g that exceeds its r_s? Will many stocks have expected $g > r_s$ in the short run (i.e., for the next few years)? In the long run (i.e., forever)?
c. Assume that Temp Force has a beta coefficient of 1.2, that the risk-free rate (the yield on government bonds) is 5.0%, and that the market risk premium is 4%. What is the required rate of return on the firm's stock?
d. Assume that Temp Force is a constant growth company whose last dividend was $2.00 and whose dividend is expected to grow indefinitely at a 5% rate.
   (1) What is the firm's expected dividend stream over the next 3 years?
   (2) What is the firm's current stock price?
   (3) What is the stock's expected value 1 year from now?
   (4) What are the expected dividend yield, the capital gains yield, and the total return during the first year?
e. Now assume that the stock is currently selling at $43.75. What is the expected rate of return on the stock?
f. What would the stock price be if its dividends were expected to have zero growth?
g. Now assume that Temp Force is expected to experience supernormal growth of 30% for the next 3 years, then to return to its long-run constant growth rate of 5%. What is the stock's value under these conditions? What is its expected dividend yield and capital gains yield in Year 1? In Year 4?
h. Is the stock price based more on long-term or short-term expectations? Answer this by finding the percentage of Temp Force's current stock price based on dividends expected more than 3 years in the future, (using the original assumptions).
i. Suppose Temp Force is expected to experience zero growth during the first 3 years and then to resume its steady-state growth of 5% in the fourth year. What is the stock's value now? What is its expected dividend yield and its capital gains yield in Year 1? In Year 4?
j. Finally, assume that Temp Force's earnings and dividends are expected to decline by a constant 5% per year, that is, g = −5%. Why would anyone be willing to buy such a stock, and at what price should it sell? What would be the dividend yield and capital gains yield in each year?
k. What is market multiple analysis?
l. Temp Force recently issued preferred stock. It pays an annual dividend of $1.60, and the issue price was $25 per share. What is the expected return to an investor on this preferred stock?
m. Why do stock prices change? Suppose the expected D_1 is $2, the growth rate is 4%, and r_s is 12%. Using the constant growth model, what is the price? What is the impact on the stock price if g is 5% or 6%? If r_s is 11% or 13%?
n. What does market equilibrium mean?
o. If equilibrium does not exist, how will it be established?
p. What is the efficient markets hypothesis, what are its three forms, and what are its implications?

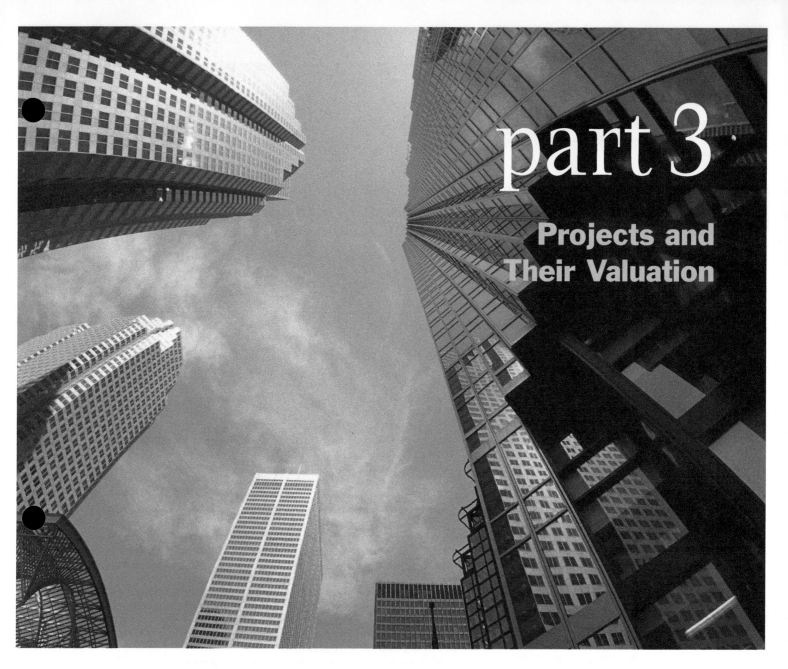

part 3

Projects and Their Valuation

chapter 9

The Cost of Capital

WestJet Airlines owns or operates aircraft and assets worth over $4 billion. From its economical turboprop aircraft designed for flying between small centres to its latest Boeing 737s on order, the company's reach is throughout North America (and beyond). Over its life, WestJet has raised a cumulative $1.5 billion in capital from shareholders; it has since turned that $1.5 billion into stock worth more than $3.6 billion. Its Market Value Added (MVA), which is the difference between its stock's market capitalization and the amount shareholders originally put up, is about $2.1 billion.

When investors provide a corporation with funds, they expect the company to generate an appropriate return on that capital. From the company's perspective, the investors' expected return is a cost of using the capital, and it is called the "cost of capital." A variety of factors influence a firm's cost of capital. Some, such as interest rates; taxation policies; regulations; and in WestJet's case, fuel prices, are outside the firm's control. However, the degree of risk in the projects it undertakes and the types of funds it raises are under the *company's* control, and both have a profound effect on its cost of capital. Indeed, with interest rates having declined over the past number of years, the cost of capital has fallen for many firms.

Before purchasing an aircraft or any other significant asset, WestJet must first determine whether that asset will help to provide a return that at least covers what investors require in order to invest in WestJet's securities. So every time WestJet decides to fly to a new destination, upgrade its technology, add to its fleet, or replace its existing aircraft, it must keep investors in mind.

WestJet has been expanding its existing business by adding additional routes throughout Canada and the United States. In 2013, the company also announced its first transatlantic destination of Dublin, Ireland. The company has been aggressive in upgrading its fleet, with an order to purchase 10 new Boeing 737s. Plans to expand its services have also led WestJet to place another order for 65 of the next-generation 737s. These purchases accounted for the large jump in investing activities, which increased from $269 million in 2012 to $715 million in 2013. Another $40 million was invested in new computer systems. When WestJet evaluates potential investments such as these, it must determine whether the return on the capital it invests in the project will exceed its cost of capital.

How has WestJet done with its investments? Over a five-year period, 2009–2013, its return on invested capital has ranged from 7.8% to 13.9%. While value creation may not occur evenly, investors over time have indeed been rewarded.

Source: WestJet Airlines Ltd., Annual Reports, 2013 and 2010.

Most important business decisions require capital, including decisions to develop new products, build factories and distribution centres, install information technology, expand internationally, and acquire other companies. For each of these decisions, a company must estimate the total investment required and decide whether the expected rate of return exceeds the cost of the capital. The cost of capital is also used in many compensation plans, with bonuses dependent on whether the company's return on invested capital exceeds the cost of capital. The cost of capital is also a key factor in choosing the mixture of debt and equity used to finance the firm and in decisions to lease rather than buy assets. As these examples illustrate, the cost of capital is a critical element in business decisions.[1]

The textbook's website contains an *Excel* file that will guide you through the chapter's calculations. The file for this chapter is *Ch 09 Tool Kit.xlsx,* and we encourage you to open the file and follow along as you read the chapter. **www.nelson .com/brigham3ce**

9.1 The Weighted Average Cost of Capital

What precisely do the terms "cost of capital" and "weighted average cost of capital" mean? To begin, note that it is possible to finance a firm entirely with common equity. However, most firms employ several types of capital, called *capital components,* with common and preferred stock, along with debt, being the three most frequently used types. All capital components have one feature in common: the investors who provided the funds expect to receive a return on their investment.

If a firm's only investors were common shareholders, then the cost of capital would be the required rate of return on equity. However, most firms employ different types of capital, and, due to differences in risk, these different securities have different required rates of return. The required rate of return on each capital component is called its *component cost,* and the cost of capital used to analyze capital budgeting decisions should be a *weighted average* of the various components' costs. We call this weighted average just that, the **weighted average cost of capital,** or **WACC**.

A firm's WACC has several important uses. Recall that firm value is based on the present value of its expected free cash flows. Since WACC is the discount rate, intuitively we know that the lower the WACC is, all other things equal, the greater the firm's value. Thus WACC and firm value are closely related. WACC is also used in evaluating new projects. Before a company commits to investing in a new long-term project, it must be confident that the returns generated will be at least as high, if not higher, than the company's WACC. If they are not, the project will not provide for sufficient returns and should not go ahead. Thus we also see that WACC and long-term investment decisions are related.

Most firms set target percentages for the different financing sources. For example, National Computer Corporation (NCC) plans to raise 30% of its required capital as debt, 10% as preferred stock, and 60% as common equity. This is its **target capital structure**. We discuss how targets are established in Chapter 12, but for now simply accept NCC's 30/10/60 debt, preferred, and common percentages as given.

The following sections discuss each of the component costs in more detail. Then we show how to combine them to calculate the weighted average cost of capital.

CONCEPT REVIEW

1. What are the three major capital components?
2. What is a component cost?
3. What is a target capital structure?

---

[1]The cost of capital is also an important factor in the regulation of electric, gas, and telephone companies. These utilities are natural monopolies in the sense that one firm can supply service at a lower cost than could two or more firms. Because it has a monopoly, your electric or telephone company could, if it were unregulated, exploit you. Therefore, regulators (1) determine the cost of the capital investors have provided the utility (2) and then set rates designed to permit the company to earn its cost of capital, no more and no less.

Corporate Valuation and the Cost of Capital

In Chapter 1, we told you that managers should strive to make their firms more valuable and that the value of a firm is determined by the size, timing, and risk of its free cash flows (FCF). In particular, a firm's value is the present value of its FCFs, discounted at the weighted average cost of capital (WACC). In the previous chapters, we examined the major sources of financing (stocks, bonds, and preferred stock) on an individual basis. In this chapter, we put those pieces together and estimate the WACC.

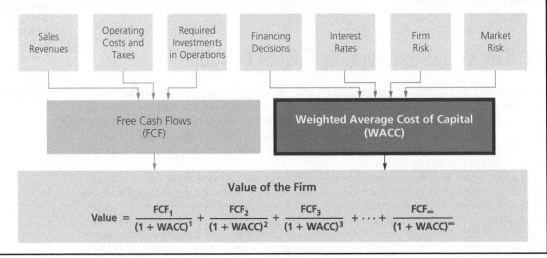

9.2 After-Tax Cost of Debt, $r_d(1 - T)$

The first step in estimating the cost of debt is to determine the rate of return lenders require.

The Before-Tax Cost of Short-Term Debt

Short-term debt should be included in the capital structure only if it is a permanent source of financing in the sense that the company plans to continually repay and refinance the short-term debt. NCC typically issues commercial paper to raise short-term money to finance working capital whose value can vary substantially throughout the year. In NCC's case, since it is not a permanent source of financing, NCC's treasurer will not include it in the WACC calculation.

The Before-Tax Cost of Long-Term Debt: r_d

For long-term debt, estimating r_d is conceptually straightforward, but some problems arise in practice. Companies use both fixed- and floating-rate debt, straight and convertible debt, and debt with and without sinking funds, and each form has a somewhat different cost.

It is unlikely that the financial manager will know at the start of a planning period the exact types and amounts of debt that will be used during the period. The type or types used will depend on the specific assets to be financed and on capital market conditions as they develop over time. Even so, the financial manager does know what types of debt are typical for his or her firm. For example, NCC typically issues 30-year bonds to raise long-term debt used to finance its capital budgeting projects. Since the WACC is used primarily in capital budgeting, NCC's treasurer uses the cost of 30-year bonds in her WACC estimate.

Assume that it is January 2016, and NCC's treasurer is estimating the WACC for the coming year. How should she calculate the component cost of debt? Most financial managers begin by discussing current and prospective interest rates with their investment bankers. Assume that NCC's bankers believe that a new 30-year, noncallable, straight bond issue will require an 8% coupon rate with semiannual payments, and that it can be offered to the public at its $1,000 par value. Therefore, their estimate of r_d is equal to 8%.[2]

---

[2]The effective annual rate is $(1 + 0.08/2)^2 - 1 = 8.2\%$, but NCC and most other companies use nominal rates for all component costs.

Note that the 8% is the cost of *new*, or *marginal, debt*, and it will probably not be the same as the average rate on NCC's previously issued debt, which is called the *historical*, or *embedded, rate*. The embedded cost is important for some decisions but not for others. For example, the average cost of all the capital raised in the past and still outstanding is used by regulators when they determine the rate of return a public utility should be allowed to earn. However, in financial management the WACC is used primarily to make investment decisions, and these decisions hinge on projects' expected future returns versus the cost of new, or marginal, capital. *Thus, for our purposes, the relevant cost is the marginal cost of new debt to be raised during the planning period.*

Suppose that NCC had issued debt in the past and that the bonds are publicly traded. The financial staff could use the market price of the bonds to find their yield to maturity (or yield to call if the bonds sell at a premium and are likely to be called). The yield is the rate of return the existing bondholders expect to receive, and it is also a good estimate of r_d, the rate of return that new bondholders will require.

For example, suppose NCC has outstanding bonds with a 7% annual coupon rate, 22 years remaining until maturity, and a face value of $1,000. The bonds make semiannual coupon payments and currently are trading in the market at a price of $897.26. We can find the yield to maturity using a financial calculator with these inputs: N = 44, PV = −897.26, PMT = 35, and FV = 1,000. Solving for the rate, we find I/YR = 4.000%. This is a semiannual periodic rate, so the annual rate is 8.00%. This is consistent with the investment bankers' estimated rate, so 8% is a reasonable estimate for r_d.

If NCC had no publicly traded debt, its staff could look at yields on publicly traded debt of similar firms. This too should provide a reasonable estimate of r_d.

The After-Tax Cost of Debt: $r_d (1 - T)$

The required return to debtholders, r_d, is not equal to the company's cost of debt because interest payments are deductible, which means the government in effect pays part of the total cost. As a result, the cost of debt to the firm is less than the rate of return required by debtholders.

The *after-tax cost of debt, $r_d(1 - T)$*, is used to calculate the weighted average cost of capital, and it is the interest rate on debt, r_d, less the tax savings that result because interest is deductible. This is the same as r_d multiplied by $(1 - T)$, where T is the firm's marginal tax rate.

$$\text{After-tax component cost of debt} = \text{Interest rate} - \text{Tax savings}$$
$$= r_d - r_d T \qquad \text{(9-1)}$$
$$= r_d(1 - T)$$

Suppose NCC has a federal-plus-provincial tax rate of 30%. NCC's after-tax cost of debt is 5.6%:

$$r_d(1 - T) = 8\%(1.0 - 0.3)$$
$$= 8\%(0.7)$$
$$= 5.6\%$$

Flotation Costs and the Cost of Debt

Most debt offerings have very low flotation costs, especially for privately placed debt. Because the flotation costs usually are low, most analysts ignore them when estimating the after-tax cost of debt. The following example illustrates the procedure for incorporating flotation costs and their impact on the after-tax cost of debt.

Suppose NCC can issue 30-year debt with an annual coupon rate of 8%, with coupons paid semiannually. The flotation costs, F, are equal to 1% of the value of the issue. Instead of finding the pre-tax yield based upon pre-tax cash flows and then adjusting it to reflect taxes, as we did in the example above, we can find the after-tax cost of debt based on after-tax cash flows using this formula:

$$M(1 - F) = \sum_{t=1}^{N} \frac{INT(1 - T)}{[1 + r_d(1 - T)]^t} + \frac{M}{[1 + r_d(1 - T)]^N} \qquad \text{(9-2)}$$

Here M is the bond's par value, F is the percentage flotation cost (i.e., the percentage of proceeds), N is the number of payments, T is the firm's tax rate, INT is the dollars of interest per period, and $r_d(1 - T)$ is the after-tax cost of debt adjusted for flotation costs. With a financial calculator, enter N = 60, PV = −1,000(1 − 0.01) = −990, PMT = 40(1 − 0.3) = 28, and FV = 1,000. Solving for I/YR, we find I/YR = $r_d(1 - T)$ = 2.83%, which is the semiannual after-tax component cost of debt. The nominal after-tax cost of debt is 5.66%. Note that this is quite close to the original 5.6% after-tax cost, so in this instance adjusting for flotation costs doesn't make much difference.

However, the flotation adjustment would be higher if F were larger or if the bond's life were shorter. For example, if F were 10% rather than 1%, then the nominal annual flotation-adjusted $r_d(1 - T)$ would be 6.35%. With N at 1 year rather than 30 years, and F still equal to 1%, then the nominal annual $r_d(1 - T)$ = 6.65%. Finally, if F = 10% and N = 1, then the nominal annual $r_d(1 - T)$ = 16.88%. In all of these cases, the differential would be too high to ignore.

CONCEPT REVIEW

1. Why is the after-tax cost of debt rather than the before-tax cost used to calculate the weighted average cost of capital?

2. Is the relevant cost of debt the interest rate on already *outstanding* debt or that on *new* debt? Why?

3. A company has outstanding long-term bonds with a face value of $1,000, a 10% coupon rate, 25 years remaining until maturity, and a current market value of $1,214.82. If it pays interest semiannually, what is the nominal annual pre-tax cost of debt? If the company's tax rate is 40%, what is the after-tax cost of debt? (Check Figures: 8%; 4.8%)

9.3 Cost of Preferred Stock, r_{ps}

A number of firms, including NCC, use preferred stock as part of their permanent financing mix. Preferred dividends are not tax deductible. Therefore, the company bears their full cost, and *no tax adjustment is used when calculating the cost of preferred stock*. Note too, although it is not mandatory that preferred dividends be paid, firms generally have every intention of doing so, because otherwise (1) they cannot pay dividends on their common stock, (2) they will find it difficult to raise additional funds in the capital markets, and (3) in some cases preferred stockholders can take control of the firm.

The *component cost of preferred stock, r_{ps},* is the cost used in the weighted average cost of capital calculation. For preferred stock with a stated maturity date, we use the same approach as in the previous section for the cost of debt, keeping in mind that a firm has no tax saving with preferred stock. For preferred stock without a stated maturity date, r_{ps} is

$$\text{Component cost of preferred stock} = r_{ps} = \frac{D_{ps}}{P_{ps}(1 - F)} \qquad (9\text{-}3)$$

where D_{ps} is the preferred dividend, P_{ps} is the preferred stock price, and F is flotation cost as a percentage of proceeds.

To illustrate the calculation, assume that NCC has preferred stock that pays a $1.75 dividend per share and sells for $25 per share. If NCC issued new shares of preferred, it would incur an underwriting (or flotation) cost of 2.5%, or $0.63 per share, so it would net $24.37 per share. Therefore, NCC's cost of preferred stock is 10.3%:

$$r_{ps} = \$1.75/\$24.37 = 7.2\%$$

If we had not incorporated flotation costs, we would have incorrectly estimated r_{ps} = $1.75/$25 = 7.0%, which is too big a difference to ignore. Therefore, analysts usually include flotation costs when estimating the cost of preferred stock.

ⓒNCEPT REVIEW

1. Does the component cost of preferred stock include or exclude flotation costs? Explain.
2. Why is no tax adjustment made to the cost of preferred stock?
3. A company's preferred stock currently trades at $27 per share and pays a $1.50 annual dividend per share. Flotation costs are equal to 3% of the proceeds. If the company issues preferred stock, what is the cost of the newly issued preferred stock? (Check Figure: 5.73%)

9.4 Cost of Common Stock, r_s

Companies can raise common equity in two ways: (1) by issuing new shares, and (2) by reinvesting, or retaining, earnings. If new shares are issued, what rate of return must the company earn to satisfy the new shareholders? In Chapter 7, we saw that investors require a return of r_s. However, a company must earn more than r_s on new external equity to provide this rate of return to investors because there are commissions and fees, called flotation costs, when a firm issues new equity.

Does new equity capital raised indirectly by retaining earnings have a cost? The answer is a resounding yes. If some earnings are retained, then shareholders will incur an **opportunity cost**—the earnings could have been paid out as dividends (or used to repurchase stock), in which case shareholders could then have reinvested the money in other investments. *Thus, the firm should earn on its reinvested earnings at least as much as its shareholders themselves could earn on alternative investments of equivalent risk.*

What rate of return can shareholders expect to earn on equivalent-risk investments? The answer is r_s, because they expect to earn that return by simply buying the stock of the firm in question or that of a similar firm. *Therefore, r_s is the cost of common equity raised internally by reinvesting earnings.* If a company cannot earn at least r_s on reinvested earnings, then it should pass those earnings on to its shareholders and let them invest the money themselves in assets that do provide r_s.

Whereas debt and preferred stock are contractual obligations that have easily determined costs, it is more difficult to estimate r_s. However, we can employ the principles described in Chapters 7 and 8 to produce reasonably good cost of equity estimates. Three methods typically are used: (1) the Capital Asset Pricing Model (CAPM), (2) the discounted cash flow (DCF) method, and (3) the bond-yield-plus-risk-premium approach. These methods are not mutually exclusive. When faced with the task of estimating a company's cost of equity, we generally use all three methods and then choose among them on the basis of our confidence in the input data available for the specific case at hand.

ⓒNCEPT REVIEW

1. What are the two sources of equity capital?
2. Explain why there is a cost to using reinvested earnings; that is, why aren't reinvested earnings a free source of capital?

9.5 The CAPM Approach

To estimate the cost of common stock using the Capital Asset Pricing Model (CAPM) as discussed in Chapter 7, we proceed as follows:

Step 1. Estimate the risk-free rate, r_{RF}.

Step 2. Estimate the current expected market risk premium, RP_M, which is the expected market return minus the risk-free rate.

Step 3. Estimate the stock's beta coefficient, b_i, which measures the stock's relative risk. The subscript i signifies stock i's beta.

Step 4. Use these three values in the CAPM equation to estimate the required rate of return on the stock in question:

$$r_s = r_{RF} + (RP_M)b_i \qquad (9\text{-}4)$$

Equation 9-4 shows that the CAPM estimate of r_s begins with the risk-free rate, r_{RF}, to which is added a risk premium set equal to the risk premium on the market, RP_M, scaled up or down to reflect the particular stock's risk as measured by its beta coefficient. The following sections explain how to implement the four-step process.

Estimating the Risk-Free Rate

The starting point for the CAPM cost of equity estimate is r_{RF}, the risk-free rate. There is really no such thing as a truly riskless asset in the Canadian economy. Federal government bonds are essentially free of default risk, but nonindexed long-term bonds will suffer capital losses if interest rates rise, and a portfolio of short-term T-bills will provide a volatile earnings stream because the rate earned on T-bills varies over time.

Since we cannot in practice find a truly riskless rate upon which to base the CAPM, what rate should we use? A survey of highly regarded companies shows that about two-thirds of the companies use the rate on long-term federal government bonds.[3] We agree with their choice, and here are our reasons:

1. Common stocks are long-term securities, and although a particular shareholder may not have a long investment horizon, most shareholders do invest on a long-term basis. Therefore, it is reasonable to think that stock returns embody long-term inflation expectations similar to those reflected in bonds rather than the short-term expectations in bills.
2. Treasury bill rates are more volatile than are longer-term government bond rates and, most experts agree, more volatile than r_s.[4]
3. In theory, the CAPM is supposed to measure the expected return over a particular holding period. When it is used to estimate the cost of equity for a project, the theoretically correct holding period is the life of the project. Since many projects have long lives, the holding period for the CAPM also should be long. Therefore, the rate on a long-term government bond is a logical choice for the risk-free rate.

Government bond rates can be found in the *National Post* or on the Bank of Canada website. Many analysts use the yield on a 10-year government bond as a proxy for the risk-free rate, although the yields on a 20-year or 30-year government bond are also reasonable proxies.

Estimating the Market Risk Premium

The market risk premium, RP_M, is the expected market return minus the risk-free rate. This is also called the **equity risk premium,** or just the *equity premium*. It is caused by investor risk aversion: since most investors are averse to risk, they require a higher expected return (a risk premium) to induce them to invest in risky equities versus relatively low-risk debt. The premium can be estimated on the basis of (1) historical data or (2) forward-looking data.

Historical Risk Premium The historical risk premium in Canada can be calculated from historical data on Canadian securities consisting of actual annual realized rates of return on stocks, federal government bonds, and T-bills. The historical market risk premium on common shares is the difference between the historical realized return on stocks and the return for long-term federal government bonds. For instance, the arithmetic average risk premium for Canadian stocks from 1924 to 2013 was 5.5%, while the geometric average was 4.5%.[5] If investor risk aversion had been variable during the sample period, the arithmetic average would be better for estimating next year's risk premium. The geometric average would be best for a longer-term risk premium estimate—say, 20 years.

Use of a historical risk premium to estimate the current risk premium assumes that the risk premium doesn't change over time. However, in 2000, 2001, and 2002, bonds had a higher return than stocks, resulting in a negative risk premium. In reality, though, the true equity risk premium actually increased over that time period. A higher risk premium led to a higher cost of equity, lower stock prices, and thus lower stock returns. The lower

---

[3]See Robert E. Bruner, Kenneth M. Eades, Robert S. Harris, and Robert C. Higgins, "Best Practices in Estimating the Cost of Capital: Survey and Synthesis," *Financial Practice and Education*, Spring–Summer 1998, 13–28.
[4]Economic events usually have a larger impact on short-term rates than on long-term rates. For example, see the analysis of the 1995–1996 federal debt limit disagreement between the White House and Congress provided in Srinivas Nippani, Pu Liu, and Craig T. Schulman, "Are Treasury Securities Free of Default?" *Journal of Financial and Quantitative Analysis*, June 2001, 251–266.
[5]Data taken from Canadian Institute of Actuaries, "Report on Canadian Economic Statistics, 1924–2013," May 2014.

stock returns reduced the average historical risk premium. Thus a greater risk aversion by investors leads to a lower historical risk premium—the exact opposite of its true effect! If indeed risk aversion does vary over time, the method of using historical data to estimate the current risk premium should be seriously questioned.

Forward-Looking Risk Premiums An alternative to the historical risk premium is to estimate a forward-looking, or ex ante, risk premium. The market risk premium, RP_M, can be estimated as $r_M - r_{RF}$. The risk-free rate is observable, so the key is to estimate the required return on the market. The most common approach is to use the discounted cash flow (DCF) model to estimate the expected market rate of return, $\hat{r}_M$. If the market is in equilibrium, then the expected return is equal to the required return: $\hat{r}_M = r_M$:

$$\frac{\text{Expected}}{\text{rate of return}} = \hat{r}_M = \frac{D_1}{P_0} + g = r_{RF} + RP_M = r_M = \frac{\text{Required}}{\text{rate of return}}$$

In words, the required return on the market is the sum of the expected dividend yield plus the expected growth rate. Note that the expected dividend yield, D_1/P_0, can be found using the current dividend yield and the expected growth rate: $D_1/P_0 = D_0(1 + g)/P_0$. Therefore, to estimate the required return on the market, all you need are estimates of the current dividend yield and the expected growth rate in dividends. Several data sources report the current dividend yield on the market, as measured by the S&P/TSX Composite. For example, as of mid-2014, the current dividend yield was 2.69% for the S&P/TSX Composite.

It is much more difficult to obtain an estimate of the expected dividend growth rate. What we really need is the long-run dividend growth rate that a marginal investor expects to obtain if he or she buys a broad portfolio of stocks. Since we cannot identify the marginal investors, let alone get inside their heads, it is impossible to obtain a direct estimate of the relevant growth rate. Faced with these data limitations, analysts usually estimate the expected dividend growth rate in one of two ways: (1) the historical dividend growth rate or (2) analysts' forecasts for earnings growth rates as an approximation for expected dividend growth.

For example, dividends on Toronto Stock Exchange stocks had a 5.1% average growth rate over the 20 years from 1991 to 2010. Using the current dividend yield of 2.69%, the estimated market return is

$$r_M = \left[\frac{D_0}{P_0} (1 + g) \right] + g$$
$$= [0.0269(1 + 0.051)] + 0.051$$
$$= 0.0793 = 7.93\%$$

Given a current (July 2014) long-term government bond rate of around 2.57%, the estimated forward-looking risk premium from this approach is about 7.93% − 2.57% = 5.36%. However, the problems here are similar to those encountered with historical risk premiums—there is no compelling reason to believe that investors expect future growth to be exactly like past growth, and past growth rates are extremely sensitive to the period over which growth is measured. In addition, many companies have small dividend payments but repurchase stock as a way to return free cash flow to investors. We discuss this more in Chapter 13, but the implication here is that historical dividend growth rates don't truly reflect the cash distributions to investors.

The second approach for estimating the expected dividend growth rate is to obtain published forecasts from security analysts. Unfortunately, analysts generally forecast earnings growth rates, not dividend growth rates, and the longest forecast period is typically 5 years.[6] One investment dealer forecasts a 5.7% earnings growth rate for the TSX. If we use this earnings growth rate as an approximation of the dividend growth rate, then the estimated market return is

$$r_M = \left[\frac{D_0}{P_0} (1 + g) \right] + g$$
$$= [0.0269(1 + 0.057)] + 0.057$$
$$= 0.085 = 8.5\%$$

---

[6]In theory, the constant growth rate for sales, earnings, and dividends ought to be equal. However, this has not been true for past growth rates.

Given a current long-term government bond rate of 2.57%, the estimated forward-looking risk premium from this approach is 8.5% − 2.57% = 5.93%. Notice that this is higher than our previous estimate based on the historical dividend growth rate.

Unfortunately, there are problems with this approach, too. (1) Earnings growth rates and dividend growth rates are not always identical. (2) The accuracy (and truthfulness) of analysts who work for investment banking firms has been questioned in recent years. This suggests that it might be better to use the forecasts of independent analysts, such as those who work for publications like *Value Line*, rather than those who work for the large investment banking firms. (3) Different analysts have different opinions, leading to very different growth rate estimates.

To muddy the waters a bit more, we see in Table 9-1[7] that the risk premium is quite dependent on the cutoff periods used. There is a marked reduction in the risk premium from 1957 onward. Others have come to very different estimates, ranging from 2.2% to 7.7%.[8]

Our View on the Market Risk Premium After reading the previous sections, you might well be confused about the correct market risk premium, since the different approaches give different results. Here is our opinion. The risk premium is driven primarily by investors' attitudes toward risk, and there are good reasons to believe that investors are less risk averse today than 50 years ago. The advent of company pension plans, the Canada Pension Plan, health insurance, and disability insurance means that people today can take more chances with their investments, which should make them less risk averse. Also, many households have dual incomes, which also allows investors to take more chances. Putting it all together, we conclude that the true risk premium in 2014 is lower than the long-term historical average.

But how much lower is the current premium? A risk premium of 4% to 5% for Canada is currently valid, though we would have a hard time arguing with someone who used a risk premium in the range of 3.0% to 6.0%. Canadian managers of utilities and pension plans have recently been using premiums within this range. We believe that investor risk aversion is relatively stable but not absolutely constant from year to year and is certainly not constant during periods of great stress, such as during the 2008–2009 financial crisis. When market prices are high, investors feel less risk averse, so a risk premium at the lower end of our range can be used. Conversely, a risk premium at the high end of our range can be used when market prices are relatively low. The bottom line is that there is no way to prove that a particular risk premium is either right or wrong, although one could be suspicious of an estimated market premium that is less than 3.0% or greater than 6.0%.

Estimating Beta

Recall from Chapter 7 that beta is usually estimated as the slope coefficient in a regression, with the company's stock returns on the y-axis and market returns on the x-axis. The resulting beta is called the *historical beta*, since it is based on historical data. Although this approach is conceptually straightforward, complications quickly arise in practice.

First, there is no theoretical guidance as to the correct holding period over which to measure returns. The returns for a company can be calculated using daily, weekly, or monthly time periods, and the resulting estimates of beta will differ. With too few observations, the regression loses statistical power, but with too many, the "true" beta may have changed during the sample period.

TABLE 9-1 Equity Risk Premium Estimates for the TSX

	1926–1956	1957–2000	1926–2000
Equity Risk Premium	8.6%	3.3%	5.5%

---

[7]Laurence Booth, "Equity Market Risk Premiums in the US and Canada," *Canadian Investment Review*, Fall 2001, 34–43.
[8]Jonathon Witmer and Lorie Zorn, "Estimating and Comparing the Implied Cost of Equity for Canadian and US Firms," Bank of Canada Working Paper no. 2007-48, September 2007; Elroy Dimson, Paul Marsh, and Mike Staunton, "Global Evidence on the Equity Risk Premium," *Journal of Applied Corporate Finance* 15, no. 4 (2003), 8–19.

Second, the market return should, theoretically, reflect every asset, even the human capital being built by students. In practice, however, it is common to use only an index of common stocks such as the S&P/TSX 60 or the S&P/TSX Composite Index for Canadian stocks.

Third, some organizations modify the calculated historical beta in order to produce what they deem to be a more accurate estimate of the "true" beta, where the true beta is the one that reflects the risk perceptions of the marginal investor.

Fourth, even the best estimates of beta for an individual company are statistically imprecise. The average company has an estimated beta of 1.0, but the 95% confidence interval ranges from about 0.6 to 1.4. For example, if your regression produces an estimated beta of 1.0, then you can be 95% sure that the true beta is in the range of 0.6 to 1.4.

The preceding discussion refers to conditions in Canada and other countries with well-developed financial markets, where relatively good data are available. Still, as we have seen, beta can be estimated only within a fairly wide range. When we move on to countries with less-developed financial markets, we are even less certain about the true size of a company's beta.

An Illustration of the CAPM Approach

To illustrate the CAPM approach for NCC, assume that $r_{RF} = 5\%$, $RP_M = 5.5\%$, and $b_i = 1.3$, indicating that NCC is riskier than average. Therefore, NCC's cost of equity is 12.2%:

$$
\begin{aligned}
r_s &= 5\% + (5.5\%)(1.3) \\
&= 5\% + 7.2\% \\
&= 12.2\%
\end{aligned}
$$

It should be noted that although the CAPM approach appears to yield an accurate, precise estimate of r_s, it is hard to know the correct estimates of the inputs required to make it operational because (1) it is hard to estimate precisely the beta that investors expect the company to have in the future, and (2) it is difficult to estimate the market risk premium. Despite these difficulties, surveys indicate that CAPM is the preferred choice for the vast majority of companies.

CONCEPT REVIEW

1. What is generally considered to be the most appropriate estimate of the risk-free rate, the yield on a short-term T-bill or the yield on a long-term government bond?
2. Explain the two methods for estimating the market risk premium, that is, the historical data approach and the forward-looking approach.
3. What are some of the problems encountered when estimating beta?
4. A company's beta is 1.4. The yield on a long-term government bond is 5%. If the market risk premium is 5.5%, what is r_s? (Check Figure: 12.7%)

9.6 Dividend-Yield-Plus-Growth-Rate, or Discounted Cash Flow (DCF), Approach

In Chapter 8, we saw that if dividends are expected to grow at a constant rate, then the price of a stock is

$$
P_0 = \frac{D_1}{r_s - g} \tag{9-5}
$$

Here P_0 is the current price of the stock, D_1 is the dividend expected to be paid at the end of Year 1, and r_s is the required rate of return. We can solve for r_s to obtain the required rate of return on common equity, which for the marginal investor is also equal to the expected rate of return:

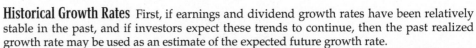

$$r_s = \hat{r}_s = \frac{D_1}{P_0} + \text{Expected } g \qquad (9\text{-}6)$$

Thus, investors expect to receive a dividend yield, D_1/P_0, plus a capital gain, g, for a total expected return of $\hat{r}_s$. In equilibrium this expected return is also equal to the required return, r_s. This method of estimating the cost of equity is called the **discounted cash flow, (DCF), method**. Henceforth, we will assume that markets are at equilibrium (which means that $r_s = \hat{r}_s$), so we can use the terms r_s and $\hat{r}_s$ interchangeably.

Estimating Inputs for the DCF Approach

Three inputs are required to use the DCF approach: the current stock price, the current dividend, and the expected growth in dividends. Of these inputs, the growth rate is by far the most difficult to estimate. The following sections describe the most commonly used approaches for estimating the growth rate: (1) historical growth rates, (2) the retention growth model, and (3) analysts' forecasts.

See **Web Extension 9A** at the textbook's website. The **Web 9A** worksheet in the file **Ch 09 Tool Kit.xlsx** shows all calculations.

Historical Growth Rates First, if earnings and dividend growth rates have been relatively stable in the past, and if investors expect these trends to continue, then the past realized growth rate may be used as an estimate of the expected future growth rate.

We explain several different methods for estimating historical growth rates in **Web Extension 9A**. For NCC, these different methods produce estimates of historical growth ranging from 4.6% to 11.0%, with most estimates fairly close to 7%.

As the **Tool Kit** shows, one can take a given set of historical data and, depending on the years and the calculation method used, obtain a large number of quite different growth rates. Now recall our purpose in making these calculations: we are seeking the future dividend growth rate that investors expect, and we reason that, if past growth rates have been stable, then investors may base future expectations on past trends. This is a reasonable proposition, but, unfortunately, we rarely find much historical stability. Therefore, the use of historical growth rates in a DCF analysis must be applied with judgment, and also be used (if at all) in conjunction with other growth estimation methods, as discussed next.

Retention Growth Model Most firms pay out some of their net income as dividends and reinvest, or retain, the rest. The payout ratio is the percentage of net income that the firm pays out as a dividend, defined as total dividends divided by net income; see Chapter 3 for more details on ratios. The retention ratio is the complement of the payout ratio: Retention ratio = (1 − Payout ratio). ROE is the return on equity, defined as net income available for common shareholders divided by common equity. We know that, other things held constant, the earnings growth rate depends on the amount of income the firm retains and the rate of return it earns on those retained earnings. Using this logic, we can write the **retention growth model**:

$$g = \text{ROE(Retention ratio)} \qquad (9\text{-}7)$$

Equation 9-7 produces a constant growth rate, but when we use it we are, by implication, making four important assumptions: (1) we expect the payout rate, and thus the retention rate, to remain constant; (2) we expect the return on equity on new investment to remain constant; (3) the firm is not expected to issue new common stock, or, if it does, we expect this new stock to be sold at a price equal to its book value; and (4) future projects are expected to have the same degree of risk as the firm's existing assets.

NCC has had an average return on equity of about 14.5% over the past 15 years. The ROE has been relatively steady, but even so it has ranged from a low of 11.0% to a high of 17.6%. In addition, NCC's dividend payout rate has averaged 0.52 over the past

15 years, so its retention rate has averaged $1.0 - 0.52 = 0.48$. Using Equation 9-7, we estimate g to be 7%:

$$g = 14.5\%(0.48) = 7\%$$

Analysts' Forecasts A third technique calls for using security analysts' forecasts. Analysts publish earnings' growth rate estimates for most of the larger publicly owned companies. For example, *Value Line* provides such forecasts on 1,700 companies, including large Canadian companies, and all of the larger brokerage houses provide similar forecasts. Furthermore, several companies compile analysts' forecasts on a regular basis and provide summary information such as the median and range of forecasts on widely followed companies. These growth rate summaries, such as those compiled by Reuters or Zack's, can be found on the Internet. These earnings' growth rates are often used as estimates of dividend growth rates.

However, these forecasts often involve nonconstant growth. For example, some analysts were forecasting that NCC would have a 10.4% annual growth rate in earnings and dividends over the next 5 years, but a growth rate after 5 years of 4.5%.

This nonconstant growth forecast can be converted to an approximate constant growth rate. Since the present value of dividends beyond 50 years is virtually zero, for practical purposes we can ignore anything beyond 50 years. If we consider only a 50-year horizon, we can develop a weighted average growth rate and use it as a constant growth rate for cost of capital purposes. In the NCC case, we assumed a growth rate of 10.4% for 5 years followed by a growth rate of 4.5% for 45 years. We weight the short-term growth by $5/50 = 10\%$ and the long-term growth by $45/50 = 90\%$. This produces an average growth rate of $0.10(10.4\%) + 0.90(4.5\%) = 5.1\%$.[9]

See **Web Extension 9B** at the textbook's website for an explanation of this approach; all calculations are in the worksheet **Web 9B** in the file **Ch 09 Tool Kit.xlsx.**

Illustration of the Discounted Cash Flow Approach

To illustrate the DCF approach, suppose NCC's stock sells for $32; its next expected dividend is $2.40; and its expected growth rate is 5%. NCC's expected and required rate of return, hence its cost of common stock, would then be 12.5%:

$$\hat{r}_s = r_s = \frac{\$2.40}{\$32.00} + 5.0\%$$
$$= 7.5\% + 5.0\%$$
$$= 12.5\%$$

Evaluating the Methods for Estimating Growth

Note that the DCF approach expresses the cost of common equity as the dividend yield (the expected dividend divided by the current price) plus the growth rate. The dividend yield can be estimated with a high degree of certainty, but uncertainty in the growth estimate induces uncertainty in the DCF cost estimate. We discussed three methods for estimating future growth: (1) historical growth rates, (2) retention growth model, and (3) analysts' forecasts. Of these three methods, studies have shown that analysts' forecasts usually represent the best source of growth rate data for DCF cost of capital estimates. We recommend a primary reliance on analysts' forecasts for the growth rate in DCF cost of capital estimates.[10]

(C)NCEPT REVIEW

1. What inputs are required for the DCF method?
2. What are the ways to estimate the dividend growth rate?
3. Which of these methods provides the best estimate?
4. A company's estimated growth rate in dividends is 6%. Its current stock price is $40 and its expected annual dividend is $2. Using the DCF approach, what is r_s? (Check Figure: 11%)

---

[9]Rather than convert nonconstant growth estimates into an approximate average growth rate, it is possible to use the nonconstant growth estimates to directly estimate the required return on common stock. See **Web Extension 9B** in the file **Ch09 Tool Kit.xlsx.**

[10]See Robert Harris, "Using Analysts' Growth Rate Forecasts to Estimate Shareholder Required Rates of Return," *Financial Management*, Spring 1986, 58–67. Analysts' forecasts are the best predictors of actual future growth, and also the growth rate investors say they use in valuing stocks. Also see Stephen G. Timme and Peter C. Eisemann, "On the Use of Consensus Forecasts of Growth in the Constant Growth Model: The Case of Electric Utilities," *Financial Management*, Winter 1989, 23–35.

9.7 Bond-Yield-Plus-Risk-Premium Approach

Some analysts use a subjective, ad hoc procedure to estimate a firm's cost of common equity: they simply add a judgmental risk premium of 3 to 5 percentage points to the interest rate on the firm's own long-term debt. It is logical to think that firms with risky, low-rated, and consequently high-interest-rate debt will also have risky, high-cost equity, and the procedure of basing the cost of equity on a readily observable debt cost utilizes this logic. In this approach,

$$r_s = \text{Bond yield} + \text{Risk premium} \qquad (9\text{-}8)$$

The bonds of NCC have a yield of 8.0%. If its risk premium is estimated as 3.7%, its estimated cost of equity is 11.7%:

$$r_s = 8.0\% + 3.7\% = 11.7\%$$

Because the 3.7% risk premium is a judgmental estimate, the estimated value of r_s is also judgmental. Empirical work suggests that the risk premium over a firm's own bond yield has generally ranged from 3 to 5 percentage points, with recent values close to 3%. With such a large range, this method is not likely to produce a precise cost of equity. However, it can get us "into the right ballpark."

CONCEPT REVIEW

1.   What is the reasoning behind the bond-yield-plus-risk-premium approach?
2.   A company's bond yield is 7%. If the appropriate bond risk premium is 3.5%, what is r_s, based on the bond-yield-plus-risk-premium approach? (Check Figure: 10.5%)

9.8 Comparison of the CAPM, DCF, and Bond-Yield-Plus-Risk-Premium Methods

We have discussed three methods for estimating the required return on common stock. For NCC, the CAPM estimate is 12.2%, the DCF constant growth estimate is 12.5%, and the bond-yield-plus-risk-premium is 11.7%. The overall average of these three methods is (12.2% + 12.5% + 11.7%)/3 = 12.1%. These results are consistent, so it would make little difference which one we used. However, if the methods produced widely varied estimates, then a financial analyst would have to use his or her judgment as to the relative merits of each estimate and then choose the estimate that seemed most reasonable under the circumstances.

People experienced in estimating the cost of equity recognize that both careful analysis and sound judgment are required. It would be nice to pretend that judgment is unnecessary and to specify an easy, precise way of determining the exact cost of equity capital. Unfortunately, this is not possible—finance is in large part a matter of judgment, and we simply must face that fact.

9.9 Adjusting the Cost of Stock for Flotation Costs

As explained earlier, most mature companies rarely issue new public equity. However, for those that do, the **cost of new common equity, r_e,** or external equity, is higher than the cost of equity raised internally by reinvesting earnings, r_s, because of **flotation costs** involved in issuing new common stock. What rate of return must be earned on funds raised by selling new stock to make issuing stock worthwhile? To put it another way, what is the cost of new common stock?

The answer for a constant growth stock is found by applying this formula:

$$r_e = \hat{r}_e = \frac{D_1}{P_0(1 - F)} + g \qquad (9\text{-}9)$$

In Equation 9-9, F is the percentage flotation cost incurred in selling the new stock, so $P_0(1 - F)$ is the net price per share received by the company.

Using the same inputs as before when we estimated NCC's cost of stock using the DCF approach, but assuming that NCC has a flotation cost of 12.5%, its cost of new outside equity is computed as follows:

$$r_e = \frac{\$2.40}{\$32(1 - 0.125)} + 5.0\%$$

$$= \frac{\$2.40}{\$28} + 5.0\%$$

$$= 8.6\% + 5.0\% = 13.6\%$$

As we calculated earlier using the DCF model but ignoring flotation costs, NCC's shareholders require a return of $r_s = 12.5\%$. However, because of flotation costs the company must earn *more* than 12.5% on the net funds obtained by selling stock if investors are to receive a 12.5% return on the money they put up. Specifically, if the firm earns 13.6% on funds obtained by issuing new stock, then earnings per share will remain at the previously expected level, the firm's expected dividend can be maintained, and, as a result, the price per share will not decline. If the firm earns less than 13.6%, then earnings, dividends, and growth will fall below expectations, causing the stock price to decline. If the firm earns more than 13.6%, the stock price will rise.

In an earlier section, we estimated NCC's CAPM cost of equity as 12.2%. How could the analyst incorporate flotation costs? In the example above, application of the DCF methodology gives a cost of equity of 12.5% if flotation costs are ignored and a cost of equity of 13.6% if flotation costs are included. Therefore, flotation costs add 1.1 percentage points to the cost of equity (13.6% − 12.5% = 1.1%). To incorporate flotation costs into the CAPM estimate, you would add the 1.1 percentage points to the 12.2% CAPM estimate, resulting in a 13.3% estimated cost of external equity. As an alternative, you could find the average of the CAPM, DCF, and bond-yield-plus-risk-premium costs of equity ignoring flotation costs, and then add to it the 1.1 percentage points due to flotation costs.

Table 9-2 shows the flotation cost for equity issued by Canadian companies. The common stock flotation costs are for IPOs. Notice that flotation costs (as a percentage of capital raised) fall as the amount of capital raised increases.

TABLE 9-2   Flotation Costs for Equity in Canada

Amount of Capital Raised (Millions of Dollars, US$)	Flotation Cost for Stock (% of Capital Raised)
1–9.9	15.98%
10.0–49.9	9.45%
50.0–99.9	8.00%
100 or more	7.28%
Average	11.78%

Source: Maher Kooli and Jean-Marc Suret, "How Cost-Effective Are Canadian IPO Markets?" *Canadian Investment Review* 16, no. 4 (Winter 2003). Reproduced with the permission of *Canadian Investment Review*.

ⓒONCEPT REVIEW

1. What are flotation costs?
2. A firm has common stock with $D_1 = \$3.00$; $P_0 = \$30$; $g = 5\%$; and $F = 4\%$. If the firm must issue new stock, what is its cost of external equity, r_e? (Check Figure: 15.42%)

9.10 Weighted Average Cost of Capital, WACC

As we will see in Chapter 12, each firm has an optimal capital structure, defined as that mix of debt, preferred, and common equity that causes its stock price to be maximized. Therefore, a value-maximizing firm will establish a *target (optimal) capital structure* and then raise new capital in a manner that will keep the actual capital structure on target over time. In this chapter, we assume that the firm has identified its optimal capital structure, that it uses this optimum as the target, and that it finances so as to remain constantly on target. How the target is established is examined in Chapter 12.

The target proportions of debt, preferred stock, and common equity, along with the component costs of capital, are used to calculate the firm's WACC. To illustrate, suppose NCC has a target capital structure calling for 30% debt, 10% preferred stock, and 60% common equity. Its before-tax cost of debt, r_d, is 8%; its after-tax cost of debt is $r_d(1 - T) = 8\%(0.7) = 5.6\%$; its cost of preferred stock, r_{ps}, is 7.2%; its cost of common equity, r_s, is 12.1%; its tax rate is 30%; and all of its new equity will come from retained earnings. We can calculate NCC's weighted average cost of capital, WACC, as follows:

$$\text{WACC} = w_d r_d (1 - T) + w_{ps} r_{ps} + w_{ce} r_s$$
$$= 0.3(8\%)(0.7) + 0.1(7.2\%) + 0.6(12.1\%) \qquad \text{(9-10)}$$
$$= 9.66\% \approx 9.7\%$$

Here w_d, w_{ps}, and w_{ce} are the weights used for debt, preferred, and common equity, respectively.

Every dollar of new capital that NCC obtains will on average consist of 30 cents of debt with an after-tax cost of 5.6%, 10 cents of preferred stock with a cost of 7.2%, and 60 cents of common equity with a cost of 12.1%. The average cost of each whole dollar, the WACC, is 9.7%.

Three points should be noted. First, the WACC is the cost the company would incur to raise each new, or *marginal*, dollar of capital—it is not the average cost of dollars raised in the past. Second, the percentages of each capital component, called *weights*, should be based on management's target capital structure, not on the particular sources of financing in any single year. Third, when management is setting the target weights, they should be based on market values and not on book values. The following sections explain these points.

Marginal Rates versus Historical Rates

The required rates of return for a company's investors, whether they are new or old, are always marginal rates. For example, a shareholder might have invested in a company last year when the risk-free interest rate was 6% and might have had a required return on equity of 12%. If the risk-free rate subsequently falls and is now 4%, then the investor's required return on equity is now 10% (holding all else constant). This is the same required rate of return that a new equity holder would have, whether the new investor bought stock in the secondary market or through a new equity offering. In other words, whether the shareholders are already equity holders or are brand new equity holders, all have the same required rate of return, which is the current required rate of return on equity. The same reasoning applies for the firm's bondholders. All bondholders, whether old or new, have a required rate of return equal to the yield on the firm's debt, which is based on current market conditions.

Because all investors have required rates of return based on *current* market conditions rather than the past market conditions at the investments' purchase dates, the cost of capital depends on current conditions, not on historic or past market conditions. It is in this sense that the cost of capital is a marginal cost, since it depends on current market rates, which are the rates the company would pay on any new capital (ignoring flotation costs, which we discuss later in the chapter).

Target Weights versus Annual Financing Choices

We have heard managers (and students!) say, "We are only raising debt this year, and it has a 5% after-tax cost, so we should use this, and not our 10% WACC, to evaluate this year's projects." Here is the flaw in that line of reasoning: Although some investors, such as debtholders, have higher-priority claims relative to other investors, *all* investors have claims on *all* future cash flows. For example, if a company raises debt and also invests in a new project that same year, the new debtholders don't normally have a specific claim on that specific project's cash flows. In fact, new debtholders receive a claim on the cash flows being generated by existing as well as new projects, while old debtholders (and equity holders) have claims on both new and existing projects. Thus, the decision to take on a new project should depend on the project's ability to satisfy all of the company's investors, not just the new debtholders, even if only debt is being raised that year.

Weights for Component Costs: Book Values versus Market Values versus Targets

An investor expects to receive a rate of return on the full amount that is at stake, which is the current market value of the investment. Therefore, the weights used in estimating the WACC should be based on market values, not book values. Recall from Chapter 3 that a firm's risk, as measured by its bond rating, affects its cost of debt. Recall also that the bond rating depends in part on the percentage of the firm that is financed with debt. As we show in Chapter 12, this also affects the cost of equity. In other words, the costs of debt and equity depend on the capital structure weights. However, these costs depend more on the future weights that investors expect than on the current weights, which fluctuate due to market conditions and the most recent form of external financing (debt or equity). Thus, the weights used in calculating the WACC should also be based on the expected future weights, which are the firm's target weights.

CONCEPT REVIEW

1. How is the weighted average cost of capital calculated? Write out the equation.
2. On what should the weights be based?
3. A firm has the following data: Target capital structure of 25% debt, 10% preferred stock, and 65% common equity; Tax rate = 30%; r_d = 7%; r_{ps} = 7.5%; and r_s = 11.5%. Assume the firm will not issue new stock. What is this firm's WACC? (Check Figure: 9.45%)

FINANCE: IN FOCUS

In Search of Capital? Head West

Economists have long called for trade liberalization between nations. And that call is just as true for the free flow of money as it is for the flow of goods. The figure below shows the cost of equity by region. Note that developing regions have higher costs of capital than do developed countries such as the United States or Canada. With higher costs of capital, foreign companies must forego investment opportunities, not because projects are not profitable, but because they are not profitable enough; that is, they do not meet the high cost of capital required by their domestic investors. Underinvestment negatively affects society in general. Reduced business investment means lower output, lower employment, lower taxes to government, and an overall lower standard of living. As we also know, higher costs of equity and debt are inversely

(continued)

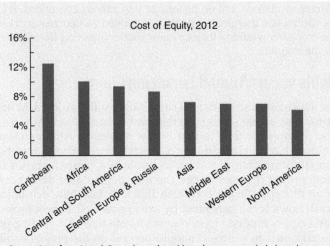

Source: Data from Aswath Damodaran, http://people.stern.nyu.edu/adamodar, Accessed July 26, 2014.

related to stock and bond prices, so investors also lose out. It would seem that if companies in emerging markets could lower their cost of capital, additional economic growth would result, benefiting both the labour force and investors.

The higher cost of capital in developing countries is partly due to one or more of the following causes: underdeveloped capital markets, limited liquidity, an uncompetitive banking sector, and a restrictive regulatory structure. If those domestic companies could tap into the capital markets in developed countries, their cost of capital would fall. This is the conclusion reached by Errunza and Miller[a] in a paper that studied the effect on foreign firms that raised equity capital in the United States. The authors found that foreign issuers of equity in the United States saw their cost of equity fall on average by 42%. As we would expect, with a fall in equity costs, stock prices in these companies shot up. The result of liberalizing international capital flows leads to greater investment in foreign markets, greater employment, and higher market values for the companies' investors. The benefits are also not just one-sided. U.S. investors get access to foreign corporation stock, which often has a lower correlation to their other portfolio assets. We know from Chapter 7 that lower-correlated securities in a portfolio provide investors with significantly greater portfolio diversification, resulting in reduced portfolio risk.

[a]Vihant R. Errunza and Darius P. Miller, "Market Segmentation and the Cost of Capital in International Equity Markets," *Journal of Financial and Quantitative Analysis*, Vol. 35, Issue 04, December 2000, pp. 577–600.

9.11 Factors That Affect the Weighted Average Cost of Capital

The cost of capital is affected by a number of factors. Some are beyond the firm's control, but others are influenced by its financing and investment policies.

Three Factors the Firm Cannot Control

The three most important factors that are beyond a firm's direct control are (1) the level of interest rates, (2) the market risk premium, and (3) tax rates.

The Level of Interest Rates If interest rates in the economy rise, the cost of debt increases because firms will have to pay bondholders a higher interest rate to obtain debt capital. Also, recall from our discussion of the CAPM that higher interest rates increase the costs of common and preferred equity. During the 1990s, interest rates in Canada declined significantly and are still low as of 2014. This reduced the cost of both debt and equity capital for all firms, which encouraged additional investment. Lower interest rates also enabled Canadian firms to compete more effectively with U.S. and German firms, which in the past had enjoyed relatively low costs of capital.

Market Risk Premium Investors' aversion to risk determines the market risk premium. Individual firms have no control over the RP_M, which affects the cost of equity and thus the WACC.

Tax Rates Tax rates, which are largely beyond the control of an individual firm (although firms do lobby for more favourable tax treatment), have an important effect on the cost of capital. Tax rates are used in the calculation of the cost of debt as used in the WACC, and there are other, less obvious ways in which tax policy affects the cost of capital. For example, lowering the capital gains tax rate relative to the rate on business income would make stocks more attractive, which would reduce the cost of equity relative to that of debt. That would, as we see in Chapter 12, lead to a change in a firm's optimal capital structure toward less debt and more equity.

Three Factors the Firm Can Control

A firm can affect its cost of capital through (1) its capital structure policy, (2) its dividend policy, and (3) its investment (capital budgeting) policy.

Capital Structure Policy In this chapter, we assume that a firm has a given target capital structure, and we use weights based on that target structure to calculate the WACC. It is clear, though, that a firm can change its capital structure and that such a change can affect its cost of capital. For example, the after-tax cost of debt is lower than the cost of equity, so, if the firm decides to use more debt and less common equity, then this increase in debt will tend to lower the WACC. However, an increase in the use of debt will increase the risk of debt and equity, offsetting to some extent the effect due to a greater weighting of debt. In Chapter 12 we discuss this in more depth, and we demonstrate that a firm's optimal capital structure is the one that minimizes its cost of capital.

Dividend Policy As we see in Chapter 13, the percentage of earnings paid out in dividends may affect a stock's required rate of return, r_s. Also, if a firm's payout ratio is so high that it must issue new stock to fund its capital budget, this will force it to incur flotation costs, and this too will affect its cost of capital.

Investment Policy When we estimate the cost of capital, we use as the starting point the required rates of return on the firm's outstanding stock and bonds. Those rates reflect the risk of the firm's existing assets. Therefore, we have implicitly been assuming that new capital will be invested in assets with the same degree of risk as existing assets. This assumption is generally correct, as most firms do invest in assets similar to those they currently use. However, it would be incorrect if a firm dramatically changed its investment policy. For example, if a firm invests in an entirely new line of business, its marginal cost of capital should reflect the risk of that new business. For instance, the Canadian oil company Talisman Energy purchased Arakis Energy along with its sizable oil resources in civil war–torn Sudan. All the controversy surrounding Talisman's investment in this troubled country undoubtedly increased the company's risk and cost of capital.

CONCEPT REVIEW

1. What three factors that affect the cost of capital are generally beyond the firm's control?
2. What three policies under the firm's control are likely to affect its cost of capital?
3. Explain how a change in interest rates in the economy would affect each component of the weighted average cost of capital.

9.12 Adjusting the Cost of Capital for Risk

As we have calculated it, the cost of capital reflects the average risk and overall capital structure of the entire firm. But what if a firm has divisions in several business lines that differ in risk? Or what if a company is considering a project that is much riskier than its typical project? It doesn't make sense for a company to use its overall cost of capital to discount divisional or project-specific cash flows that don't have the same risk as the company's average cash flows. The following sections explain how to adjust the cost of capital for divisions and for specific projects.

The Divisional Cost of Capital

Consider Starlight Sandwich Shops, a company with two divisions—a bakery operation and a chain of cafés. The bakery division is low risk and has a 10% cost of capital. The café division is riskier and has a 14% cost of capital. Each division is approximately the same size, so Starlight's overall cost of capital is 12%. The bakery manager has a project with an 11% expected rate of return, and the café division manager has a project with a 13% expected return. Should these projects be accepted or rejected? Starlight can create value if it accepts the bakery's project, since its rate of return is greater than its cost of capital (11% > 10%), but the café project's rate of return is less than its cost of capital (13% < 14%), so it should be rejected. However, if one simply compared the two projects' returns with Starlight's 12% overall cost of capital, then the bakery's value-adding project would be rejected while the café's value-destroying project would be accepted.

Many firms use the CAPM to estimate the cost of capital for specific divisions. To begin, recall that the Security Market Line equation expresses the risk/return relationship as follows:

$$r_s = r_{RF} + (RP_M)b_i$$

As an example, consider the case of Huron Steel Company, an integrated steel producer operating in the Great Lakes region. For simplicity, assume that Huron has only one division and uses only equity capital, so its cost of equity is also its corporate cost of capital, or WACC. Huron's beta = b = 1.1; r_{RF} = 4%; and RP_M = 5%. Thus, Huron's cost of equity is 9.5%:

$$r_s = 4\% + (5\%)1.1 = 9.5\%$$

This suggests that investors should be willing to give Huron money to invest in average-risk projects if the company expects to earn 9.5% or more on this money. By average risk we mean projects having risk similar to that of the firm's existing division.

Now suppose Huron creates a new transportation division consisting of a fleet of barges to haul iron ore and that barge operations have betas of 1.5 rather than 1.1. The barge division, with b = 1.5, has a 11.5% cost of capital:

$$r_{Barge} = 4\% + (5\%)1.5 = 11.5\%$$

On the other hand, if Huron adds a low-risk division, such as a new distribution centre with a beta of only 0.5, its divisional cost of capital will be 6.5%:

$$r_{Centre} = 4\% + (5\%)0.5 = 6.5\%$$

A firm itself may be regarded as a "portfolio of assets," and since the beta of a portfolio is a weighted average of the betas of its individual assets, adding the barge and distribution centre divisions will change Huron's overall beta. The exact value of the new beta will depend on the relative size of the investment in the new divisions versus Huron's original steel operations. If 70% of Huron's total value ends up in the steel division, 20% in the barge division, and 10% in the distribution centre, then its new corporate beta will be

$$\text{New beta} = 0.7(1.1) + 0.2(1.5) + 0.1(0.5) = 1.12$$

Thus, investors in Huron's stock will have a required return of

$$r_{Huron} = 4\% + (5\%)1.12 = 9.6\%$$

Even though the investors require an overall return of 9.6%, they expect a rate of return in each division at least as good as the division's required return based on the SML. In particular, they expect a return of at least 9.5% from the steel division, 11.5% from the barge division, and 6.5% from the distribution centre.

Techniques for Measuring Divisional Betas

In Chapter 7 we discussed the estimation of betas for stocks and indicated the difficulties in estimating beta. Estimating divisional betas is much more difficult because divisions do not have their own publicly traded stock.[11] Therefore, we must estimate the beta that the division would have if it were a separate publicly traded company. One approach used to estimate individual assets' beta is called the pure play method and is described below.

The Pure Play Method In the pure play method, the company tries to find several single-product companies in the same line of business as the division being evaluated. It then averages those companies' betas to determine the cost of capital for its own division. For example, suppose Huron finds three existing single-product firms that operate barges, and suppose also that Huron's management believes that its barge division will be subject to the same risks as those firms. Huron can then determine the betas of those firms, average them, and use this average beta as a proxy for the barge division's beta.[12]

Estimating the Cost of Capital for Individual Projects

Although it is intuitively clear that riskier projects have a higher cost of capital, it is difficult to estimate project risk. First, note that three separate and distinct types of risk can be identified:

1. *Stand-alone risk* is the variability of the project's expected returns.
2. *Corporate, or within-firm, risk* is the variability the project contributes to the corporation's returns, giving consideration to the fact that the project represents only one asset of the firm's portfolio of assets and so some of its risk will be diversified away.
3. *Market, or beta, risk* is the risk of the project as seen by a well-diversified shareholder. Market risk is measured by the project's effect on the firm's beta coefficient.

Taking on a project with a high degree of either stand-alone or corporate risk will not necessarily affect the firm's beta. However, if the project has highly uncertain returns, and if those returns are highly correlated with returns on the firm's other assets and with most other assets in the economy, then the project will have a high degree of all types of risk.

Of the three measures, market risk is theoretically the most relevant because of its direct effect on stock prices. Unfortunately, the market risk for a project is also the most difficult to estimate. In practice, most decision makers consider all three risk measures in a subjective manner.

The first step is to determine the divisional cost of capital before grouping divisional projects into subjective risk categories. Then, using the divisional WACC as a starting point, a *risk-adjusted cost of capital* is developed for each category. For example, a firm might establish three risk classes—high, average, and low—and then assign average-risk projects the divisional cost of capital, higher-risk projects an above-average cost, and lower-risk projects a below-average cost. Thus, if a division's WACC were 10%, its managers might use 10% to evaluate average-risk projects in the division, 12% for high-risk projects, and 8% for low-risk

---

[11]This same problem applies to privately held companies, which we discuss separately.
[12]If the pure play firms employ different capital structures than that of Huron, this fact must be dealt with by adjusting the beta coefficients. See Chapter 12 for a discussion of this aspect of the pure play method. For a technique that can be used when pure play firms are not available, see Yatin Bhagwat and Michael Ehrhardt, "A Full Information Approach for Estimating Divisional Betas." *Financial Management*, Summer 1991, 60–69.

projects. While this approach is better than ignoring project risk, these risk adjustments are necessarily subjective and somewhat arbitrary. Unfortunately, given the data, there is no completely satisfactory way to specify exactly how much higher or lower we should go in setting risk-adjusted costs of capital.

CONCEPT REVIEW

1. Based on the CAPM, how would one find the required return for a low-risk division and for a high-risk division?
2. Describe the pure play method for estimating divisional betas.
3. What are the three types of project risk?
4. Which type of risk is theoretically the most relevant? Why?
5. Describe a procedure firms can use to develop costs of capital for projects with differing degrees of risk.

9.13 Four Mistakes to Avoid

We often see managers and students make the following mistakes when estimating the cost of capital. Although we have discussed these errors previously at separate places in the chapter, they are worth repeating here:

1. *Never use the coupon rate on a firm's existing debt as the pre-tax cost of debt.* The relevant pre-tax cost of debt is the interest rate the firm would pay if it issued debt today.
2. *When estimating the market risk premium for the CAPM method, never use the historical average return on stocks in conjunction with the current risk-free rate.* The historical average return on

FINANCE: SMALL BUSINESS

Cost of Capital for Small and Privately Owned Businesses

Small and privately owned businesses face unique challenges in calculating their cost of capital. In the previous discussion we have used past stock prices to estimate beta, which in turn was used in the CAPM to calculate the company's cost of equity. But obviously, if shares of a small business don't trade publicly, the required historical stock data are not available. This poses a challenge to smaller businesses. How do they estimate their cost of equity? One method would be to identify one or more publicly traded firms that are in the same industry and that are approximately the same size as the privately owned firm. Betas are then estimated for the publicly traded companies; an average beta is taken and used as an estimated beta for the private company. Note that this is similar to the pure play method for estimating divisional beta that we discussed earlier. With an estimate of beta, the cost of equity can be estimated using the CAPM approach. There is, however, evidence that few small businesses actually calculate their cost of capital. Also, only a minority of small businesses surveyed calculate their WACC. They in fact find it hard to determine their cost of equity.[a]

The liquidity of owning stock in a privately held firm is less than the liquidity of publicly held stock. Just as the yield on a thinly traded bond has a liquidity premium, the required return on stock in a privately held firm should reflect a liquidity premium. An ad hoc adjustment can be made to reflect this lack of liquidity by adding 1 to 3 percentage points to the firm's cost of equity. This "rule of thumb" is not very satisfying theoretically because we don't know exactly how large a liquidity premium to add, but it is very common in practice.

There are also problems in estimating the capital structure weights. Capital structure weights should be based on the target market-value weights. However, a privately held firm can't observe its market value. If a firm doesn't know its current market weights, that makes it difficult for the firm to estimate its target weights. To resolve this problem, many analysts begin by making a trial guess as to the value of the firm's equity. The analysts then use this estimated value of equity to estimate the cost of capital, then use the cost of capital to estimate the value of the firm, and complete the circle by using the esti-

(continued)

mated value of the firm to estimate the value of its equity. If this newly estimated equity value is different from their trial guess, analysts repeat the process but start the iteration with the newly estimated equity value as the trial value of equity. After several iterations, the trial value of equity and the resulting estimated equity value usually converge. Although somewhat tedious, this process provides a good estimate of the weights and the cost of capital.

^aStanley Block, "Capital Budgeting Techniques Used by Small Business Firms in the 1990s," *Engineering Economist,* Summer 1997, 296. Also, see Chapter 22 of this book for more discussion on estimating the value of a firm.

bonds—that is, the historical risk-free rate—should be subtracted from the past average return on stocks to calculate the *historical market risk premium.* However, it is appropriate to subtract today's yield on federal government bonds from an estimate of the expected future return on stocks to obtain the *forward-looking market risk premium.* A case can be made for using either the historical or the current risk premium, but it would be wrong to take the *historical* rate of return on stocks, subtract from it the *current* rate on federal government bonds, and then use the difference as the market risk premium.

3. *Never use the book value of equity when estimating the capital structure weights for the WACC.* Your first choice should be to use the target capital structure to determine the weights. If you are an outside analyst and do not know the target weights, it is better to estimate weights based on the current market values of the capital components than on their book values. This is especially true for equity. For example, stocks in recent years have generally traded at 2 to 3 times their book values, so using book values for equity could lead to serious errors. If the company's debt is not publicly traded, then it is reasonable to use the book value of debt to estimate the weights, since book and market values of debt, especially short-term debt, are usually close to one another. To summarize, if you don't know the target weights, use market values of equity rather than book values to obtain the weights used to calculate WACC.

4. *Always remember that capital components are funds that come from investors.* If it's not from an investor, then it's not a capital component. Sometimes the argument is made that accounts payable and accruals are sources of funding and should be included in the calculation of the WACC. However, these accounts are due to operating relationships with suppliers and employees, and they are deducted when determining the investment requirement for a project. Therefore, they should not be included in the WACC. Of course, they are not ignored in either corporate valuation or capital budgeting. As we saw in Chapter 2, current liabilities do affect cash flow, hence they have an effect on corporate valuation. Moreover, in Chapter 11 we show that the same is true for capital budgeting, namely, that current liabilities affect the cash flows of a project, but not its WACC.

CONCEPT REVIEW

1. What are four common mistakes people make when estimating the WACC?

Summary

This chapter showed how the cost of capital is developed for use in capital budgeting. The key concepts covered are listed below.

- The cost of capital used in capital budgeting is a **weighted average** of the types of capital the firm uses, typically debt, preferred stock, and common equity.
- The **component cost of debt** is the **after-tax cost of new debt.** It is found by multiplying the cost of new debt by $(1 - T)$, where T is the firm's marginal tax rate: $r_d(1 - T)$.
- **Flotation cost adjustments** should be made for debt if the flotation costs are relatively large. Reduce the bond's issue price by the flotation expenses, reduce the bond's cash flows to reflect taxes, and then solve for the after-tax yield to maturity.
- The **component cost of preferred stock** is calculated as the preferred dividend divided by the net price the firm receives after deducting flotation costs: $r_{ps} = D_{ps}/[P_{ps}(1 - F)]$. Flotation costs are usually relatively large for preferred stock issues, so we typically include the impact of flotation costs when estimating r_{ps}.

- The **cost of common equity, r_s**, is also called the **cost of common stock.** It is the rate of return required by the firm's shareholders, and it can be estimated by three methods: (1) the **CAPM approach,** (2) the **dividend-yield-plus-growth-rate,** or **DCF, approach,** and (3) the **bond-yield-plus-risk-premium approach.**
- To use the **CAPM approach,** (1) estimate the firm's beta, (2) multiply this beta by the market risk premium to determine the firm's risk premium, and (3) add the firm's risk premium to the risk-free rate to obtain the cost of common stock: $r_s = r_{RF} + (RP_M)b_i$.
- The best proxy for the **risk-free rate** is the yield on long-term government bonds.
- To use the **dividend-yield-plus-growth-rate approach,** which is also called the **discounted cash flow (DCF) approach,** add the firm's expected growth rate to its expected dividend yield: $r_s = \hat{r}_s = D_1/P_0 + g$.
- The growth rate can be estimated from **historical earnings and dividends** or by use of the **retention growth model, g = (1 − Payout)(Return on equity),** or it can be based on **analysts' forecasts.**
- The **bond-yield-plus-risk-premium approach** adds a risk premium from 3 to 5 percentage points to the firm's cost of long-term debt: r_s = Bond yield + RP.
- When calculating the **cost of new common stock, r_e**, the DCF approach can be adapted to account for flotation costs. For a constant growth stock, this cost can be expressed as $r_e = \hat{r}_e = D_1/[P_0(1 − F)] + g$. Note that flotation costs cause r_e to be greater than r_s.
- Each firm has a **target capital structure,** defined as that mix of debt, preferred stock, and common equity that minimizes its **weighted average cost of capital (WACC):**

$$\text{WACC} = w_d r_d(1 − T) + w_{ps} r_{ps} + w_{ce} r_s.$$

- **Various factors affect a firm's cost of capital.** Some of these factors are determined by the financial environment, but the firm influences others through its financing, investment, and dividend policies.
- Many firms estimate a **divisional cost of capital** for each division that reflects that division's risk and capital structure.
- The **pure play method** can sometimes be used to estimate betas for large projects or for divisions.
- A project's **stand-alone risk** is the risk the project would have if it were the firm's only asset and if shareholders held only that one stock. Stand-alone risk is measured by the variability of the asset's expected returns.
- **Corporate,** or **within-firm, risk** reflects the effects of a project on the firm's risk, and it is measured by the project's effect on the firm's earnings variability.
- **Market,** or **beta, risk** reflects the effects of a project on the risk of shareholders, assuming they hold diversified portfolios. Market risk is measured by the project's effect on the firm's beta coefficient.
- Most decision makers consider all three risk measures in a judgmental manner and then classify projects into risk categories. Using the firm's WACC as a starting point, risk-adjusted costs of capital are developed for each category. The **risk-adjusted cost of capital** is the cost of capital appropriate for a given project, given the risk of that project. The greater the risk, the higher the cost of capital.
- Firms may be able to use the **CAPM** to estimate the cost of capital for specific projects or divisions. However, estimating betas for projects is difficult.

The cost of capital as developed in this chapter is used in the following chapters to determine the value of a corporation and to evaluate capital budgeting projects. In addition, we extend the concepts developed here in Chapter 12, where we consider the effect of the capital structure on the cost of capital.

Questions

9-1 Define each of the following terms:
a. Weighted average cost of capital, WACC; after-tax cost of debt, $r_d(1 - T)$
b. Cost of preferred stock, r_{ps}; cost of common equity (or cost of common stock), r_s
c. Target capital structure
d. Flotation cost, F; cost of new external common equity, r_e

9-2 In what sense is the WACC an average cost? A marginal cost?

9-3 How would each of the following affect a firm's cost of debt, $r_d(1 - T)$; its cost of equity, r_s; and its weighted average cost of capital, WACC? Indicate by a plus (+), a minus (−), or a zero (0) if the factor would raise, lower, or have an indeterminate effect on the item in question. Assume other things are held constant. Be prepared to justify your answer, but recognize that several of the parts probably have no single correct answer; these questions are designed to stimulate thought and discussion.

	Effect On		
	$r_d(1 - T)$	r_s	WACC
a. The corporate tax rate is lowered.	_____	_____	_____
b. The Bank of Canada tightens credit.	_____	_____	_____
c. The firm uses more debt.	_____	_____	_____
d. The firm doubles the amount of capital it raises during the year.	_____	_____	_____
e. The firm expands into a risky new area.	_____	_____	_____
f. Investors become more risk averse.	_____	_____	_____

9-4 Distinguish between beta (or market) risk, within-firm (or corporate) risk, and stand-alone risk for a potential project. Of the three measures, which is theoretically the most relevant, and why?

9-5 Suppose a firm estimates its cost of capital for the coming year to be 10%. What might be reasonable costs of capital for average-risk, high-risk, and low-risk projects?

Concept Review Problem

Full solutions are provided at www.nelson.com/brigham3ce.

CR-1
WACC
Brightview Utilities Inc. (BVU) has the following capital structure, which it considers to be optimal: debt = 35%, preferred stock = 15%, and common stock = 50%. BVU's tax rate is 30%, and investors expect earnings and dividends to grow at a constant rate of 3% in the future. BVU paid a dividend of $3.75 per share last year (D_0), and its stock currently sells at a price of $60 per share. Government bonds yield 4%, the market risk premium is 5%, and BVU's beta is 1.1. These terms would apply to new security offerings:

Preferred: New preferred shares could be sold to the public at a price of $25 per share, with a dividend of $1.75. Flotation costs of $2 per share would be incurred.
Debt: Debt could be sold at an interest rate of 6%.

a. Find the component costs of debt, preferred stock, and common stock. Assume BVU does not have to issue any additional common shares.
b. What is the WACC?

Problems

Answers to odd-numbered problems appear in Appendix A.

Easy Problems 1–8

9-1
After-Tax Cost of Debt

Calculate the after-tax cost of debt under each of the following conditions:
a.   Interest rate, 6%; tax rate, 0%.
b.   Interest rate, 6%; tax rate, 26%.
c.   Interest rate, 6%; tax rate, 30%.

9-2
After-Tax Cost of Debt

JR Oil Rigs' currently outstanding 13% coupon bonds have a yield to maturity of 9.5%. JR believes it could issue at par new bonds that would provide a similar yield to maturity. If its marginal tax rate is 30%, what is JR's after-tax cost of debt?

9-3
Cost of Preferred Stock

Long Haul Trucking can issue perpetual preferred stock at a price of $25 a share. The issue is expected to pay a constant annual dividend of $1.75 a share. Ignoring flotation costs, what is the company's cost of preferred stock, r_{ps}?

9-4
Cost of Preferred Stock with Flotation Costs

Burnwood Tech plans to issue some $25 par preferred stock with a 6% dividend. The stock is selling on the market for $27.00, and Burnwood must pay flotation costs of 4% of the market price. What is the cost of the preferred stock?

9-5
Cost of Equity: DCF

Summerdahl Resorts' common stock is currently trading at $36 a share. The stock is expected to pay a dividend of $3.00 a share at the end of the year, and the dividend is expected to grow at a constant rate of 5% a year. What is the cost of common equity?

9-6
Cost of Equity: CAPM

Booher Book Stores has a beta of 0.8. The yield on a 3-month T-bill is 4% and the yield on a 10-year government bond is 6%. The market risk premium is 5.5%, but the stock market return in the previous years was 15%. What is the estimated cost of common equity using the CAPM?

9-7
WACC

Shi Importers' balance sheet shows $300 million in debt, $50 million in preferred stock, and $250 million in total common equity. Shi faces a 30% tax rate and the following data: $r_d = 6\%$, $r_{ps} = 5.8\%$, and $r_s = 12\%$. If Shi has a target capital structure of 30% debt, 5% preferred stock, and 65% common stock, what is Shi's WACC?

9-8
WACC

Ridgeway Motors has a target capital structure of 30% debt and 70% equity. The yield to maturity on the company's outstanding bonds is 8%, and the company's tax rate is 30%. Ridgeway's CFO has calculated the company's WACC as 9.38%. What is the company's cost of equity capital?

Intermediate Problems 9–15

9-9
Bond Yield and After-Tax Cost of Debt

A company's 6% coupon rate, semiannual payment, $1,000 par value bond that matures in 30 years sells at a price of $821.97. The company's tax rate is 30%. What is the firm's component cost of debt for purposes of calculating the WACC? (*Hint:* Base your answer on the *nominal* rate.)

9-10
Cost of Equity

The earnings, dividends, and stock price of Motortech Inc. are expected to grow at 4% per year in the future. Motortech's common stock sells for $38 per share, its last dividend was $2.80, and the company will pay a dividend of $2.91 at the end of the current year.
a.   Using the discounted cash flow approach, what is its cost of equity?
b.   If the firm's beta is 1.3, the risk-free rate is 5.0%, and the expected return on the market is 9.0%, what will be the firm's cost of equity using the CAPM approach?
c.   If the firm's bonds earn a return of 8%, what will r_s be using the bond-yield-plus-risk-premium approach? (*Hint:* Use the midpoint of the risk premium range.)
d.   On the basis of the results of parts a through c, what would you estimate Motortech's cost of equity to be?

9-11
Cost of Equity

Maxon Construction's current EPS is $3.34. It was $2.75 4 years ago. The company pays out 30% of its earnings as dividends, and the stock sells for $26.25.
a.   Calculate the past growth rate in earnings. (*Hint:* This is a 4-year growth period.)
b.   Calculate the *next* expected dividend per share, D_1. Assume that the past growth rate will continue.
c.   What is the cost of equity, r_s, for Maxon?

9-12
Calculation of g and EPS

Skyline Aero stock is currently selling for $18 a share. The firm is expected to earn $1.98 per share this year and to pay a year-end dividend of $0.72.
a.   If investors require a 11% return, what rate of growth must be expected for Skyline Aero?
b.   If Skyline Aero reinvests earnings in projects with average returns equal to the stock's expected rate of return, what will be next year's EPS?

9-13
The Cost of Equity and Flotation Costs

Messman Manufacturing will issue common stock to the public for $30. The expected dividend and growth in dividends are $3.00 per share and 5%, respectively. If the flotation cost is 10% of the issue proceeds, what is the cost of external equity, r_e?

9-14
The Cost of Debt and Flotation Costs

Suppose a company will issue new 10-year debt with a par value of $1,000 and a coupon rate of 7.5%, paid annually. The tax rate is 30%. If the flotation cost is 2% of the issue proceeds, what is the after-tax cost of debt?

9-15
Component Costs

Assume that a company has a target debt-to-equity capital structure of 2. The company currently pays 8% annually on its bonds. There are 10 years until maturity, and the bonds currently trade at 93% of par. Bond flotation costs are 3%. The company's beta is 1.5, the $RP_M = 4\%$ and $r_{RF} = 5\%$. The company's tax rate = 30%.
a.   Calculate the WACC.
b.   Assume that the company changed its target capital structure to 47% long-term debt, 20% preferred stock, and 33% common stock. If preferreds are issued at $25, pay a dividend of 7%, and have flotation costs of 5%, recalculate the company's WACC.
c.   Briefly explain why the WACC has changed.

Challenging
Problems 16–20

9-16
WACC Estimation

On January 1, the total market value of Western Oil Co. was $100 million. During the year, the company plans to raise and invest $42 million in new projects. The firm's present market value debt-to-equity ratio is 1.8:1. Assume that there is no short-term debt. New bonds will have a 7% coupon rate, and they will be sold at par. Common stock is currently selling at $50 a share. Shareholders' required rate of return consists of a dividend yield of 2% and an expected constant growth rate of 6%. The corporate tax rate is 30%.
a.   To maintain the present capital structure, how much of the new investment must be financed by common equity?
b.   Assume that there is sufficient cash flow such that Western can maintain its target capital structure without issuing additional shares of equity. What is the WACC?
c.   Suppose now that there is not enough internal cash flow and that the firm must issue new shares of stock. Qualitatively speaking, what will happen to the WACC?

9-17
WACC Estimation

Your boss has asked you to estimate your company's WACC. You have assembled the following information:

Balance Sheet as at December 31, 2015 ($000s)

Current assets	$10,000	Current liabilities	$14,000
Net fixed assets	65,000	Long-term bonds	26,000
		Total liabilities	40,000
		Equity	35,000
Total assets	$75,000	Total liabilities and equity	$75,000

Additional company information:

Beta	0.9
Current stock price	$21
Most recent dividend	$1.50
Bonds issued 5 years ago: $26 million par value, 20-year, 9% semi-annual interest, currently priced at 103; flotation costs are 2%	
Shares outstanding	6 million
EPS and DPS past 5-year annual growth rate	10%
Common share flotation costs	6%
Target capital structure	60% equity/40% debt
Tax rate	30%
ROE, average past 5 years	18%
Dividend payout ratio	30%

Current liabilities consist of short-term par value bank debt at 3% to finance seasonal assets. This debt is paid off in the off-season.

Your company has been experiencing very rapid earnings and dividend growth, though the market for your products has matured, and going forward you expect growth to be tied to the overall economy's growth. You also realize that the market and your company's stock have risen dramatically recently, and you seriously question whether the stock price is sustainable. Any new equity needed comes from internal sources.

Market information:

Current 90-day T-bill rate	2.25%
Historical 90-day T-bill rate	3.9%
Historical average 10-year risk-free bond rate	7.75%
Current 10-year risk-free bond rate	5.0%
Expected market return	11.0%
Expected long-term annual GDP growth rate	2%

a. Determine whether the weighting for each component cost of capital should be based on the existing market values or the target weighting. Explain your answer.
b. Calculate the WACC.

Note: there is some subjective analysis to make in answering this question.

9-18
Market Value Capital Structure

Suppose Walker Company has this *book value* balance sheet:

Current assets	$ 30,000,000	Current liabilities	$ 20,000,000
		Notes payable	10,000,000
Fixed assets	70,000,000	Long-term debt	30,000,000
		Common stock (1 million shares)	1,000,000
		Retained earnings	39,000,000
Total assets	$100,000,000	Total liabilities and equity	$100,000,000

The notes payable are to banks, and the interest rate on this debt is 10%, the same as the rate on new bank loans. These bank loans are not used for seasonal financing but instead are part of the company's permanent capital structure. The long-term debt consists of 30,000 bonds, each with a par value of $1,000, an annual coupon interest rate of 6%, and a 20-year maturity. The going rate of interest on new long-term debt, r_d, is 10%, and this is the present yield to maturity on the bonds. The common stock sells at a price of $60 per share. Calculate the firm's *market value* capital structure.

9-19
WACC Estimation

The balance sheet for NickelBack-Hoe Equipment Implements Inc. (NHE) is provided below along with other selected financial data.

Balance Sheet as at December 31, 2015 ($000s)

Cash	$ 10,500	Accounts payable	$ 31,900
Accounts receivable	38,000	Short-term debt	3,300
Inventory	67,800	Other current liabilities	4,000
Total current assets	116,300	Total current liabilities	39,200
Plant and equip. (gross)	113,900	Long-term debt	35,700
Accumulated depreciation	56,900		
Plant and equipment (net)	57,000		
		Shareholders' equity	
		Common stock equity	98,400
Total assets	$173,300	Total liabilities and equity	$173,300

1. Short-term debt is permanent in nature. The company currently pays 6% and short-term borrowing costs are not expected to change over the next year. Short-term debt is valued at par.
2. Long-term debt is a 12-year 7.5% coupon bond paid semiannually. The bond currently trades for 102% of par.
3. The company has 25 million shares outstanding with a market price of $11. Based on forecasts, it is anticipated that any new equity capital required will come from internal sources. Net income for the most recent year is $20 million, and the company's tax rate is 35%.
4. Government 1-year Treasury bills are yielding 3%, while 10-year government bonds yield 5.5%. Inflation is currently running at 1.5%.
5. The beta for NickelBack-Hoe's stock is 1.2, and the market risk premium is 5%. Although the company has not paid a dividend on its common stock in the past, the company's new dividend policy calls for dividends to be paid starting next year. Dividends will be 40% of earnings, whereas growth in earnings is expected to be 8% per year.

Based on the above information, calculate NickelBack-Hoe's WACC.

9-20
WACC Estimation

A summary of the balance sheet of Travellers Inn Inc. (TII), a company that was formed by merging a number of regional motel chains and that hopes to rival Holiday Inn on the North American scene, is shown below:

Travellers Inn: December 31, 2015 (Millions of Dollars)

Cash	$10	Accounts payable	$10
Accounts receivable	20	Accruals	10
Inventories	20	Short-term debt	5
Current assets	50	Current liabilities	25
Net fixed assets	38	Long-term debt	20
		Preferred stock	3
		Common equity	
		Common stock	10
		Retained earnings	30
		Total common equity	$40
Total assets	$88	Total liabilities and equity	$88

These facts are also given for TII:

(1) Short-term debt consists of bank loans that currently cost 10%, with interest payable quarterly. These loans are used to finance receivables and inventories on a seasonal basis, so in the off-season, bank loans are zero.

(2) The long-term debt consists of 20-year, semiannual payment mortgage bonds with a coupon rate of 8%. Currently, these bonds provide a yield to investors of $r_d = 7\%$. If new bonds were sold, they would yield investors 7%.

(3) TII's perpetual preferred stock has a $25 par value, pays a quarterly dividend of $0.45, and has a yield to investors of 6.5%. New perpetual preferreds would have to provide the same yield to investors, and the company would incur a 5% flotation cost to sell them.

(4) The company has 4 million shares of common stock outstanding. $P_0 = \$20$, but the stock has recently traded in the range of $17 to $23. $D_0 = \$1$ and $EPS_0 = \$2$. ROE based on average equity was 24% in 2015, but management expects to increase this return on equity to 30%; however, security analysts are not aware of management's optimism in this regard.

(5) Betas, as reported by security analysts, range from 1.3 to 1.7; the government bond rate is 5%; and RP_M is estimated by various brokerage houses to be in the range of 2.5% to 3.5%. Brokerage house reports forecast growth rates in the range of 4% to 8% over the foreseeable future. However, some analysts do not explicitly forecast growth rates, but they indicate to their clients that they expect TII's historical trends, as shown in the table in fact (9), to continue.

(6) At a recent conference, TII's financial vice president polled some pension fund investment managers on the minimum rate of return they would have to expect on TII's common to make them willing to buy the common rather than TII bonds, when the bonds yielded 7%. The responses suggested a risk premium over TII bonds of 3 to 5 percentage points.

(7) TII is in the 30% tax bracket.

(8) TII's principal investment banker, Henry, Kaufman & Company, predicts a decline in interest rates, with r_d falling to 6% and the government bond rate to 4%, although Henry, Kaufman & Company acknowledges that an increase in the expected inflation rate could lead to an increase rather than a decrease in rates.

(9) Here is the historical record of EPS and DPS:

Year	EPS	DPS	Year	EPS	DPS
2001	$0.09	$0.00	2009	$0.78	$0.00
2002	–0.20	0.00	2010	0.80	0.00
2003	0.40	0.00	2011	1.20	0.20
2004	0.52	0.00	2012	0.95	0.40
2005	0.10	0.00	2013	1.30	0.60
2006	0.57	0.00	2014	1.60	0.80
2007	0.61	0.00	2015	2.00	1.00
2008	0.70	0.00			

Assume that you are a recently hired financial analyst and that your boss, the treasurer, has asked you to estimate the company's WACC; assume that no new equity will be issued. Your cost of capital should be appropriate for use in evaluating projects that are in the same risk class as the firm's average assets now on the books.

Spreadsheet Problem

9-21
Build a Model:
WACC

Start with the partial model in the file *Ch 09 Build a Model.xlsx* from the textbook's website. The stock of Gao Computing sells for $50, and last year's dividend was $2.10. A flotation cost of 10% would be required to issue new common stock. Gao's preferred stock pays a dividend of $3.30 per share, and new preferred could be sold at a price to net the company $30 per share. Security analysts are projecting that the common dividend will grow at a rate of 7% a year. The firm can also issue additional long-term debt at an interest rate (or before-tax cost) of 10%, and its marginal tax rate is 35%. The market risk premium is 6%, the risk-free rate is 6.5%, and Gao's beta is 0.83. In its cost-of-capital calculations, Gao uses a target capital structure with 45% debt, 5% preferred stock, and 50% common equity.

a. Calculate the cost of each capital component (i.e., the after-tax cost of debt), the cost of preferred stock (including flotation costs), and the cost of equity (ignoring flotation costs) with the DCF method and the CAPM method.

b. Calculate the cost of new stock using the DCF model.
c. What is the cost of new common stock, based on the CAPM? (*Hint:* Find the difference between r_e and r_s as determined by the DCF method and add that differential to the CAPM value for r_s.)
d. Assuming that Gao will not issue new equity and will continue to use the same target capital structure, what is the company's WACC?
e. Suppose Gao is evaluating three projects with the following characteristics:
   (1) Each project has a cost of $1 million. They will all be financed using the target mix of long-term debt, preferred stock, and common equity. The cost of the common equity for each project should be based on the beta estimated for the project. All equity will come from retained earnings.
   (2) Equity invested in Project A would have a beta of 0.5 and an expected return of 9.0%.
   (3) Equity invested in Project B would have a beta of 1.0 and an expected return of 10.0%.
   (4) Equity invested in Project C would have a beta of 2.0 and an expected return of 11.0%.

MINI CASE

During the past few years, Harry Davis Industries has been too constrained by the high cost of capital to make many capital investments. Recently, though, capital costs have been declining, and the company has decided to look seriously at a major expansion program that has been proposed by the marketing department. Assume that you are an assistant to Leigh Jones, the financial vice president. Your first task is to estimate Harry Davis's cost of capital. Jones has provided you with the following data, which she believes may be relevant to your task:

(1) The firm's tax rate is 35%.
(2) The current price of Harry Davis's 8% coupon, semiannual payment, noncallable bonds with 15 years remaining to maturity is $1,091.96. Harry Davis does not use short-term interest-bearing debt on a permanent basis. New bonds would be privately placed with no flotation cost.
(3) The current price of the firm's 6%, $25 par value, quarterly dividend, perpetual preferred stock is $19.74. Harry Davis would incur flotation costs equal to 5% of the proceeds on a new issue.
(4) Harry Davis's common stock is currently selling at $50 per share. Its last dividend (D_0) was $2.00, and dividends are expected to grow at a constant rate of 5% in the foreseeable future. Harry Davis's beta is 1.2, the yield on government bonds is 4%, and the market risk premium is estimated to be 5%. For the bond-yield-plus-risk-premium approach, the firm uses a 4 percentage point risk premium.
(5) Harry Davis's target capital structure is 30% long-term debt, 10% preferred stock, and 60% common equity.

To structure the task somewhat, Jones has asked you to answer the following questions.
a. (1) What sources of capital should be included when you estimate Harry Davis's weighted average cost of capital (WACC)?
   (2) Should the component costs be figured on a before-tax or an after-tax basis?
   (3) Should the costs be historical (embedded) costs or new (marginal) costs?
b. What is the market interest rate on Harry Davis's debt and its component cost of debt?
c. What is the firm's cost of preferred stock?
d. (1) What are the two primary ways companies raise common equity?
   (2) Why is there a cost associated with reinvested earnings?
   (3) Harry Davis doesn't plan to issue new shares of common stock. Using the CAPM approach, what is Harry Davis's estimated cost of equity?
e. (1) What is the estimated cost of equity using the discounted cash flow (DCF) approach?
   (2) Suppose the firm has historically earned 15% on equity (ROE) and retained 35% of earnings, and investors expect this situation to continue in the future. How could you use this information to estimate the future dividend growth rate, and what growth rate would you get? Is this consistent with the 5% growth rate given earlier?
   (3) Could the DCF method be applied if the growth rate was not constant? How?

f.   What is the cost of equity based on the bond-yield-plus-risk-premium method?

g.   What is your final estimate for the cost of equity, r_s?

h.   What is Harry Davis's weighted average cost of capital (WACC)?

i.   What factors influence a company's WACC?

j.   Should the company use the composite WACC as the hurdle rate for each of its divisions?

k.   What procedures are used to determine the risk-adjusted cost of capital for a particular division? What approach is used to measure a division's beta?

l.   What are three types of project risk? How is each type of risk used?

m.   Explain in words why new common stock that is raised externally has a higher percentage cost than equity that is raised internally by reinvesting earnings.

n.   (1)   Harry Davis estimates that if it issues new common stock, the flotation cost will be 15%. Harry Davis incorporates the flotation costs into the DCF approach. What is the estimated cost of newly issued common stock, taking into account the flotation cost?

     (2)   Suppose Harry Davis issues 30-year debt with a par value of $1,000 and a coupon rate of 7%, paid annually. If flotation costs are 2%, what is the after-tax cost of debt for the new bond issue?

o.   What four common mistakes in estimating the WACC should Harry Davis avoid?

chapter 10

The Basics of Capital Budgeting: Evaluating Cash Flows

Oil sands development in Canada has evolved over time, from its first commercial project in 1967 to its current world-scale operations involving extraction, upgrading, refining, and transportation. Already $160 billion has been invested in oil sands development, while another $207 billion will go into the sector over the next 10 years. The number of projects and dollars associated with each project are truly staggering. How are decisions made to effectively invest the funds required? How much should be invested in extraction? Should extraction projects be surfaced based or is it economical to go underground? Refineries, which process the bitumen (the product that is extracted) into products such as gas and diesel, must also be available. Should refineries be built close to the source, located on the coasts where the final product is loaded onto tankers, or located in export markets? How should the bitumen or the finished product be shipped? If transported by pipeline, is it economical to run the pipelines north-south, east-west, or even west-east? What are the most appropriate methods and technologies for protecting the environment? Evaluating all the alternatives and choosing the most profitable investments will have a huge impact on employment, government tax revenue, and of course investor returns! These are just a few of the large questions facing major Canadian companies such as Suncor, Athabasca Oil Sands, Syncrude Canada, and Canadian Oil Sands Ltd. which all operate in this sector.

The process of evaluating long-term investments is called capital budgeting. To increase share value, management must invest in projects that not only cover operating and financing costs but also create returns for shareholders. Clearly, making correct long-term investments will generate potentially huge returns for investors, along with major spin-off benefits to the economy as a whole. However, making incorrect decisions, given their size, will lead to large losses and in some cases bankruptcy for the companies involved. No wonder capital budgeting decisions are considered the most important financial decisions management takes.

The textbook's website contains an *Excel* file that will guide you through the chapter's calculations. The file for this chapter is *Ch 10 Tool Kit.xlsx,* and we encourage you to open the file and follow along as you read the chapter. **www .nelson.com/brigham3ce**

Capital budgeting is the process of evaluating a company's potential investments and deciding which ones to accept. This chapter provides an overview of the capital budgeting process and explains the basic techniques used to evaluate potential projects, given that their expected cash flows have already been estimated. Chapter 11 then explains how to estimate a project's cash flows and analyze its risk.

10.1 Overview of Capital Budgeting

Capital budgeting is the decision process that managers use to identify those projects that add to the firm's value, and as such it is perhaps the most important task faced by financial managers and their staffs. First, a firm's capital budgeting decisions define its strategic direction because moves into new products, services, or markets must be preceded by capital expenditures. Second, the results of capital budgeting decisions continue for many years, reducing flexibility. Third, poor capital budgeting can have serious financial consequences. If the firm invests too much, it will waste investors' capital on excess capacity. On the other hand, if it does not invest enough, its equipment and computer software may not be sufficiently modern to enable it to produce competitively. Also, if it has inadequate capacity, it may lose market share to rival firms, and regaining lost customers requires heavy selling expenses, price reductions, or product improvements, all of which are costly.

A firm's growth, and even its ability to remain competitive and to survive, depends on a constant flow of ideas for new products, for ways to make existing products better, and for ways to operate at a lower cost. Accordingly, a well-managed firm will go to great lengths to encourage good capital budgeting proposals from its employees. If a firm has capable and imaginative executives and employees, and if its incentive system is working properly, many ideas for capital investment will be advanced. Some ideas will be good

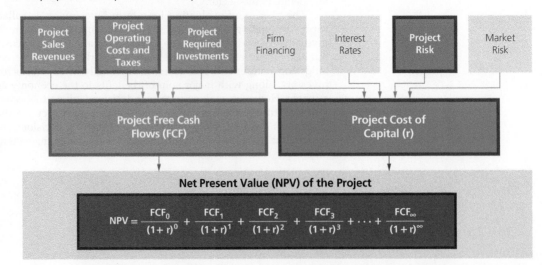

Corporate Valuation and Capital Budgeting

You can calculate the free cash flows (FCF) for a project in much the same way as for a firm. When the project's free cash flows are discounted at the appropriate risk-adjusted rate, the result is the project's value. One difference between valuing a firm and valuing a project is the rate that is used to discount cash flows. For a firm, it is the overall weighted cost of capital; for a project, it is r, the project's risk-adjusted cost of capital.

Subtracting the initial cost of the project gives the net present value (NPV). If a project has a positive NPV, then it adds value to the firm. In fact, the firm's market value added (MVA) is the sum of all its projects' NPVs. Therefore, the process for evaluating projects, called **capital budgeting,** is critical for a firm's success.

Project Sales Revenues   Project Operating Costs and Taxes   Project Required Investments   Firm Financing   Interest Rates   Project Risk   Market Risk

Project Free Cash Flows (FCF)   Project Cost of Capital (r)

Net Present Value (NPV) of the Project

$$NPV = \frac{FCF_0}{(1+r)^0} + \frac{FCF_1}{(1+r)^1} + \frac{FCF_2}{(1+r)^2} + \frac{FCF_3}{(1+r)^3} + \cdots + \frac{FCF_\infty}{(1+r)^\infty}$$

ones, but others will not. Therefore, companies must screen projects for those that add value, the primary topic of this chapter.

Firms generally categorize projects and analyze those in each category somewhat differently:

1. *Replacement needed to continue profitable operations.* An example would be an essential pump on a profitable offshore oil platform. The platform manager could make this investment without an elaborate review process.
2. *Replacement to reduce costs.* An example would be the replacement of serviceable but obsolete equipment in order to lower costs. A fairly detailed analysis would be needed, with more detail required for larger expenditures.
3. *Expansion of existing products or markets.* These decisions require a forecast of growth in demand, so a more detailed analysis is required. Go/no-go decisions are generally made at a higher level than are replacement decisions.
4. *Expansion into new products or markets.* These investments involve strategic decisions that could change the fundamental nature of the business. A detailed analysis is required, and the final decision is made by top officers, possibly with board approval.
5. *Contraction decisions.* Especially during bad recessions, companies often find themselves with more capacity than they are likely to need in the foreseeable future. Then, rather than continue to operate plants at, say, 50% of capacity and incur losses as a result of excessive fixed costs, they decide to downsize. That generally requires payments to laid-off workers and additional costs for shutting down selected operations. These decisions are made at the board level.
6. *Safety and/or environmental projects.* Expenditures necessary to comply with environmental orders, labour agreements, or insurance policy terms fall into this category. How these projects are handled depends on their size, with small ones being treated much like the Category 1 projects and large ones requiring expenditures that might even cause the firm to abandon the line of business.
7. *Other.* This catch-all includes items such as office buildings, parking lots, and executive aircraft. How they are handled varies among companies.
8. *Mergers.* Buying a whole firm (or division) is different from buying a machine or building a new plant. Still, basic capital budgeting procedures are used when making merger decisions.

Relatively simple calculations, and only a few supporting documents, are required for most replacement decisions, especially maintenance investments in profitable plants. More detailed analyses are required as we move on to more complex expansion decisions, especially for investments in new products or areas. Also, within each category projects are grouped by their dollar costs: Larger investments require increasingly detailed analysis and approval at higher levels. Thus, a plant manager might be authorized to approve maintenance expenditures up to $10,000 using a simple payback analysis, but the full board of directors might have to approve decisions that involve either amounts greater than $1 million or expansions into new products or markets.

Six key methods are used to evaluate projects and to decide whether they should be accepted: (1) net present value (NPV), (2) internal rate of return (IRR), (3) modified internal rate of return (MIRR), (4) profitability index (PI), (5) payback, and (6) discounted payback. We explain how each method is applied, and then we evaluate how well each performs in terms of identifying those projects that will maximize the firm's stock price.

The first and most difficult step in project analysis is estimating the relevant cash flows, a step that Chapter 11 explains in detail. Our present focus is on the different evaluation methods, so we provide the cash flows used in this chapter, starting with the expected cash flows of Projects S and L in Panel A of Figure 10-1 (we will explain Panel B when we discuss the evaluation methods shown in the next sections). These projects are equally risky, and the cash flows for each year, CF_t, reflect purchase cost, investments in working capital, taxes, depreciation, and salvage values. As we show in Chapter 11, this definition of project cash flows is equivalent to the definition of free cash flows as defined in Chapter 2, except that the cash flows are for the project and not the entire firm. Finally, we assume that all cash flows occur at the end of the designated year. Incidentally, the S stands for *short* and the L for *long*: Project S is a short-term project in the sense that its cash inflows come in sooner than L's.

Web Extension 10A at the textbook's website explains a seventh method, the accounting rate of return (ARR) approach. The ARR approach has major flaws, and the Web Extension explains why it should not be used.

See **Ch 10 Tool Kit.xlsx** at the textbook's website for all calculations.

FIGURE 10-1   Net Cash Flows and Selected Evaluation Criteria for Projects S and L (CF$_t$)

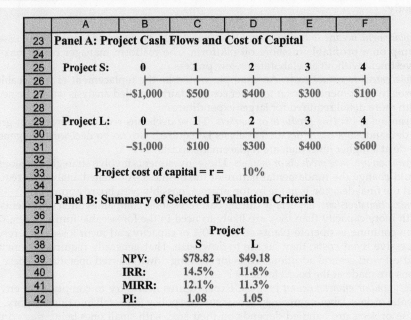

	A	B	C	D	E	F
23	**Panel A: Project Cash Flows and Cost of Capital**					
24						
25	**Project S:**	0	1	2	3	4
26						
27		–$1,000	$500	$400	$300	$100
28						
29	**Project L:**	0	1	2	3	4
30						
31		–$1,000	$100	$300	$400	$600
32						
33	**Project cost of capital = r =**		10%			
34						
35	**Panel B: Summary of Selected Evaluation Criteria**					
36						
37				**Project**		
38			**S**	**L**		
39		**NPV:**	$78.82	$49.18		
40		**IRR:**	14.5%	11.8%		
41		**MIRR:**	12.1%	11.3%		
42		**PI:**	1.08	1.05		

CONCEPT REVIEW

1.   Why are capital budgeting decisions so important?
2.   What are some ways firms get ideas for capital projects?
3.   Which types of projects receive the most analysis?

10.2   Net Present Value (NPV)

The **net present value (NPV) method** is based on the **discounted cash flow (DCF) technique.** To implement this approach, we proceed as follows:

1.   Find the present value of each cash flow, including the initial cash flow, discounted at the project's cost of capital, r.
2.   Sum these discounted cash flows; this sum is defined as the project's NPV.

The equation for the NPV is as follows:

$$NPV = CF_0 + \frac{CF_1}{(1 + r)^1} + \frac{CF_2}{(1 + r)^2} + ... + \frac{CF_N}{(1 + r)^N}$$

$$= \sum_{t=0}^{N} \frac{CF_t}{(1 + r)^t}$$

(10-1)

Here CF$_t$ is the expected net cash flow at Period t, r is the project's cost of capital, and N is its life. Cash outflows (expenditures such as the cost of buying equipment or building factories) are treated as *negative* cash flows. In evaluating Projects S and L, only CF$_0$ is negative, but for many large projects such as the Alaska Pipeline, an electric generating plant, or a new Boeing jet aircraft, outflows occur for several years before operations begin and cash flows turn positive.

Application of the NPV Method

At a 10% cost of capital, Project S's NPV is $78.82:

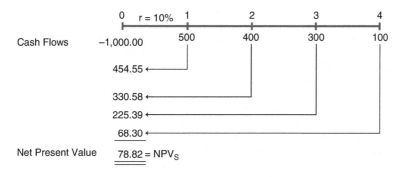

By a similar process, we find $NPV_L = \$49.18$.

If the projects were *mutually exclusive*, the one with the higher NPV should be accepted and the other rejected. S would be ranked over L and thus accepted because S has the higher NPV. **Mutually exclusive** means that if one project is taken on, the other must be rejected. For example, a conveyor belt system to move goods in a warehouse and a fleet of forklifts for the same purpose illustrates mutually exclusive projects—accepting one implies rejecting the other. **Independent projects** are those whose cash flows are independent of each other. If Loblaw's were considering a new store in Sarnia and another in Thunder Bay, those projects would be independent of each other. If our Projects S and L are independent, then both should be accepted because both have a positive NPV and thus add value to the firm. If they are mutually exclusive, then S should be chosen because it has the higher NPV.

Calculating the NPV by using a financial calculator or spreadsheet is straightforward. Different calculators are set up somewhat differently, but they all have a section of memory called the "cash flow register" that is used for uneven cash flows such as those in Projects S and L (as opposed to equal annuity cash flows). A solution process for Equation 10-1 is literally programmed into financial calculators, and all you have to do is enter the cash flows (being sure to observe the signs), along with the value of r = I/YR. At that point, you have (in your calculator) this equation:

$$NPV_S = -1,000 + \frac{500}{(1.10)^1} + \frac{400}{(1.10)^2} + \frac{300}{(1.10)^3} + \frac{100}{(1.10)^4}$$

Note that the equation has one unknown, NPV. Now all you need to do is ask the calculator to solve the equation for you, which you do by pressing the NPV button (and, on some calculators, the "compute" button). The answer, 78.82, will appear on the screen.

Most projects last for more than 4 years, and, as you will see in Chapter 11, we must go through quite a few steps to develop the estimated cash flows. Therefore, financial analysts generally use spreadsheets for project analysis. The cash flows for Projects S and L are shown in the spreadsheet in Panel A of Figure 10-1. In Panel B, we used the *Excel* NPV function to calculate the projects' NPVs. To access the NPV function in *Excel*, you can click the insert function, f_x, then type in *NPV* in the box that appears, and then GO. NPV will appear in the list immediately below—select it and press OK. Input D33 as the first argument in the NPV function; this is the rate for *Excel* to use in discounting the cash flows. Then input the range of future cash flows, C27:F27, in the NPV function as "Value 1." Click OK, and the result is $1,078.82. Despite its name, the NPV function actually finds the PV of future cash flows, not the NPV. To find the NPV, edit the cell by adding B27 to the NPV result. The resulting formula in Cell C39 is = **B27 + NPV(D33,C27:F27)**, and it gives a value of $78.82. Note that you cannot enter the initial cash flow of −$1,000 as part of the NPV range because the *Excel* NPV function assumes that the first cash flow in the range occurs at t = 1. Also be aware that if you input a value for the rate, it must be the actual number. For example, we could have entered a rate of "0.10" or "10%," but if we entered "10," *Excel* would interpret it as 1,000%. This is exactly opposite the convention used in financial calculators, where you would enter 10.

See *Ch 10 Tool Kit.xlsx* at the textbook's website for all calculations.

Rationale for the NPV Method

The rationale for the NPV method is straightforward. An NPV of zero signifies that the project's cash flows are exactly sufficient to repay the invested capital and to provide the required rate of return on that capital. If a project has a positive NPV, it is generating more cash than is needed to service the debt and to provide the required return to shareholders, and this excess cash accrues solely to the firm's shareholders. Therefore, if a firm takes on a project with a positive NPV, the wealth of the shareholders increases. In our example, shareholders' wealth would increase by $78.82 if the firm takes on Project S, but by only $49.18 if it takes on Project L. Viewed in this manner, it is easy to see why S is preferred to L, and it is also easy to see the logic of the NPV approach.[1]

There is also a direct relationship between NPV and EVA (Economic Value Added, as discussed in Chapter 2)—NPV is equal to the present value of the project's future EVAs. Therefore, accepting positive NPV projects should result in a positive EVA and a positive MVA (Market Value Added, or the excess of the firm's market value over its book value). So, a reward system that compensates managers for producing positive EVA is consistent with the use of NPV for making capital budgeting decisions.

CONCEPT REVIEW

1. Why is the NPV regarded as being the primary capital budgeting decision criterion?

2. What is the difference between "independent" and "mutually exclusive" projects?

3. A project has the following expected cash flows: $CF_0 = -\$500$, $CF_1 = \$200$, $CF_2 = \$200$, and $CF_3 = \$400$. If the project cost of capital is 9%, what is the NPV? (Check Figure: $160.70)

10.3 Internal Rate of Return (IRR)

In Chapter 6 we presented procedures for finding the yield to maturity, or rate of return, on a bond—if you invest in a bond, hold it to maturity, and receive all of the promised cash flows, you will earn the YTM on the money you invested. Exactly the same concepts are employed in capital budgeting when the **internal rate of return (IRR) method** is used. The IRR is defined as the discount rate that forces the NPV to equal zero:

$$CF_0 + \frac{CF_1}{(1 + IRR)^1} + \frac{CF_2}{(1 + IRR)^2} + \ldots + \frac{CF_N}{(1 + IRR)^N} = 0 \qquad (10\text{-}2)$$

$$NPV = \sum_{t=0}^{N} \frac{CF_t}{(1 + IRR)^t} = 0$$

Application of the IRR Method

For our Project S, here is the time-line setup:

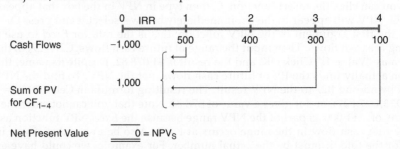

[1]This description of the process is somewhat oversimplified. Both analysts and investors anticipate that firms will identify and accept positive NPV projects, and current stock prices reflect these expectations. Thus, stock prices react to announcements of new capital projects only to the extent that such projects were not already expected.

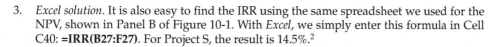

$$-1{,}000 + \frac{500}{(1 + IRR)^1} + \frac{400}{(1 + IRR)^2} + \frac{300}{(1 + IRR)^3} + \frac{100}{(1 + IRR)^4} = 0$$

Thus, we have an equation with one unknown, IRR, and we need to solve for IRR.
   Three methods can be used to find the IRR:

1. *Trial-and-error.* We could use a trial-and-error method: Try a discount rate, see if the equation solves to zero, and if it doesn't try a different rate. Continue until you find the rate that forces the NPV to zero, and that rate will be the IRR. This procedure is rarely done by hand calculations, however. IRR usually is calculated using either a financial calculator or *Excel* (or some other computer program) as described below.
2. *Calculator solution.* Enter the cash flows into the calculator's cash flow register just as you did to find the NPV, and then press the calculator key labelled "IRR." Instantly, you get the internal rate of return. Here are the values for Projects S and L:

$$IRR_S = 14.5\%$$
$$IRR_L = 11.8\%$$

3. *Excel solution.* It is also easy to find the IRR using the same spreadsheet we used for the NPV, shown in Panel B of Figure 10-1. With *Excel*, we simply enter this formula in Cell C40: **=IRR(B27:F27)**. For Project S, the result is 14.5%.[2]

See ***Ch 10 Tool Kit.xlsx*** at the textbook's website for all calculations.

   If both projects have a cost of capital, or **hurdle rate,** of 10%, then the internal rate of return rule indicates that if the projects are independent, both should be accepted—they are both expected to earn more than the cost of the capital needed to finance them. If they are mutually exclusive, S ranks higher and should be accepted, so L should be rejected. If the cost of capital is above 14.5%, both projects should be rejected.
   Notice that the internal rate of return formula, Equation 10-2, is simply the NPV formula, Equation 10-1, solved for the particular discount rate that forces the NPV to equal zero. Thus, the same basic equation is used for both methods, but in the NPV method the discount rate, r, is specified and the NPV is found, whereas in the IRR method the NPV is specified to equal zero, and the interest rate that forces this equality (the IRR) is calculated.
   Mathematically, the NPV and IRR methods will always lead to the same accept/reject decisions for independent projects. This occurs because if NPV is positive, IRR must exceed r. However, NPV and IRR can give conflicting rankings for mutually exclusive projects. This point will be discussed in more detail in a later section.

Rationale for the IRR Method

Why is the particular discount rate that equates a project's cost with the present value of its receipts (the IRR) so special? The reason is based on this logic: (1) The IRR on a project is its expected rate of return. (2) If the internal rate of return exceeds the cost of the funds used to finance the project, then the extra returns, that is, the surplus wealth, will remain after paying for the capital, and this surplus wealth will accrue to the firm's shareholders. (3) Therefore, taking on a project whose IRR exceeds its cost of capital increases shareholders' wealth. On the other hand, if the internal rate of return is less than the cost of capital, then taking on the project will impose a cost on current shareholders. It is this "break-even" characteristic that makes the IRR useful in evaluating capital projects.

CONCEPT REVIEW

1. In what sense is the IRR on a project related to the YTM on a bond?
2. A project has the following expected cash flows: $CF_0 = -\$500$, $CF_1 = \$200$, $CF_2 = \$200$, and $CF_3 = \$400$. What is the IRR? (Check Figure: 24.1%)

---

[2]Note that the full range is specified, because *Excel's* IRR function assumes that the first cash flow (the negative $1,000) occurs at t = 0. (This is in contrast to *Excel's* NPV function, where the first cash flow is assumed to be at t = 1.) You can use the insert function, f_x, if you don't have the formula memorized.

10.4 Comparison of the NPV and IRR Methods

In many respects the NPV method is better than IRR, so it is tempting to explain NPV only, to state that it should be used to select projects, and to go on to the next topic. However, the IRR is familiar to many corporate executives, it is widely entrenched in industry, and it does have some virtues. Therefore, it is important for you to understand the IRR method but also to be able to explain why, at times, a project with a lower IRR may be preferable to a mutually exclusive alternative with a higher IRR.

NPV Profiles

See *Ch 10 Tool Kit.xlsx* at the textbook's website for all calculations.

A graph that plots a project's NPV against the cost-of-capital rates is defined as the project's *net present value profile;* profiles for Projects L and S are shown in Figure 10-2. To construct NPV profiles, first note that at a zero cost of capital, the NPV is simply the total of the projects' undiscounted cash flows. Thus, at a zero cost of capital NPV$_S$ = $300 and NPV$_L$ = $400. These values are plotted as the vertical axis intercepts in Figure 10-2. Next, we calculate the projects' NPVs at three costs of capital, 5%, 10%, and 15%, and plot these values. The four points plotted on our graph for each project are shown at the bottom of the figure.

Recall that the IRR is defined as the discount rate at which a project's NPV equals zero. Therefore, *the point where its net present value profile crosses the horizontal axis indicates a project's internal rate of return.* Since we calculated IRR$_S$ and IRR$_L$ in an earlier section, we can confirm the validity of the graph.

See *Ch 10 Tool Kit.xlsx* at the textbook's website for all calculations.

FIGURE 10-2	Net Present Value Profiles: NPVs of Projects S and L at Different Costs of Capital

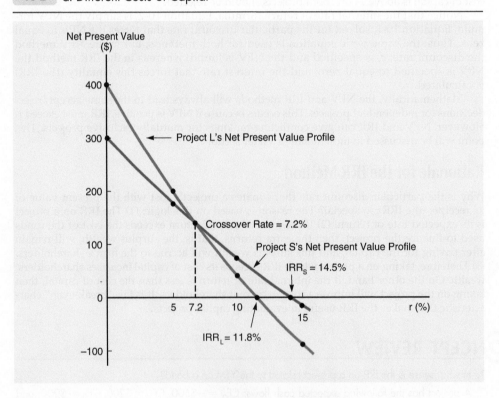

r	NPV$_S$	NPV$_L$
0%	$300.00	$400.00
5	180.42	206.50
10	78.82	49.18
15	(8.33)	(80.14)

When we plot a curve through the data points, we have the net present value profiles. NPV profiles can be very useful in project analysis, and we will use them often in the remainder of the chapter.

NPV Rankings Depend on the Cost of Capital

Figure 10-2 shows that the NPV profiles of both Project L and Project S decline as the cost of capital increases. But notice in the figure that Project L has the higher NPV when the cost of capital is low, while Project S has the higher NPV if the cost of capital is greater than the 7.2% crossover rate. Notice also that Project L's NPV is "more sensitive" to changes in the cost of capital than is NPV_S; that is, Project L's net present value profile has the steeper slope, indicating that a given change in r has a greater effect on NPV_L than on NPV_S.

Recall that a long-term bond has greater sensitivity to interest rates than a short-term bond. Similarly, if a project has most of its cash flows coming in the early years, its NPV will not decline very much if the cost of capital increases, but a project whose cash flows come later will be severely penalized by high capital costs. Accordingly, Project L, which has its largest cash flows in the later years, is hurt badly if the cost of capital is high, while Project S, which has relatively rapid cash flows, is affected less by high capital costs. Therefore, Project L's NPV profile has the steeper slope.

Evaluating Independent Projects

If *independent* projects are being evaluated, then the NPV and IRR criteria always lead to the same accept/reject decision: If NPV says accept, IRR also says accept. To see why this is so, assume that Projects L and S are independent, look at Figure 10-2, and notice (1) that the IRR criterion for acceptance for either project is that the project's cost of capital is less than (or to the left of) the IRR and (2) that whenever a project's cost of capital is less than its IRR, its NPV is positive. Thus, at any cost of capital less than 11.8%, Project L will be acceptable by both the NPV and the IRR criteria, while both methods reject Project L if the cost of capital is greater than 11.8%. Project S—and all other independent projects under consideration—could be analyzed similarly, and it will always turn out that if the IRR method says accept, then so will the NPV method.

Evaluating Mutually Exclusive Projects

Now assume that Projects S and L are *mutually exclusive* rather than independent. That is, we can choose either Project S or Project L, or we can reject both, but we cannot accept both projects. Notice in Figure 10-2 that as long as the cost of capital is *greater than* the crossover rate of 7.2%, then (1) NPV_S is larger than NPV_L and (2) IRR_S exceeds IRR_L. Therefore, if r is *greater than* the crossover rate of 7.2%, the two methods both lead to the selection of Project S. However, if the cost of capital is *less than* the crossover rate, the NPV method ranks Project L higher, but the IRR method indicates that Project S is better. *Thus, a conflict exists if the cost of capital is less than the crossover rate.*[3] NPV says choose mutually exclusive L, while IRR says take S. Which is correct? Logic suggests that the NPV method is better, because it selects the project that adds the most to shareholder wealth. But what causes the conflicting recommendations?

Two basic conditions can cause NPV profiles to cross, and thus conflicts to arise between NPV and IRR: (1) when *project size (or scale) differences* exist, meaning that the cost of one project is larger than that of the other, or (2) when *timing differences* exist, meaning that the timing of cash flows from the two projects differs such that most of the cash flows from one project come in the early years while most of the cash flows from the other project come in the later years, as occurred with our Projects L and S.

When either size or timing differences are present, the firm will have different amounts of funds to invest in the various years, depending on which of the two mutually exclusive projects it chooses. For example, if one project costs more than the other, then the firm will have more money at t = 0 to invest elsewhere if it selects the smaller project. Similarly, for

---

[3]The crossover rate is easy to calculate. Simply go back to Figure 10-1, where we set forth the two projects' cash flows, and calculate the difference in those flows in each year. The differences are $CF_S - CF_L = \$0, +\$400, +\$100, -\$100$, and $-\$500$, respectively. Enter these values in the cash flow register of a financial calculator, press the IRR button, and the crossover rate, $7.17\% \approx 7.2\%$, appears. Be sure to enter $CF_0 = 0$, or you will not get the correct answer.

projects of equal size, the one with the larger early cash inflows—in our example, Project S—provides more funds for reinvestment in the early years. Given this situation, the rate of return at which differential cash flows can be invested is a critical issue.

The key question in resolving conflicts between mutually exclusive projects is this: How useful is it to generate cash flows sooner rather than later? The value of early cash flows depends on the return we can earn on those cash flows, that is, the rate at which we can reinvest them. *The NPV method implicitly assumes that the rate at which cash flows can be reinvested is the cost of capital, whereas the IRR method assumes that the firm can reinvest at the IRR.* These assumptions are inherent in the mathematics of the discounting process. The cash flows may actually be withdrawn as dividends by the shareholders and spent on beer and pizza, but the NPV method still assumes that cash flows can be reinvested at the cost of capital, while the IRR method assumes reinvestment at the project's IRR.

Which is the better assumption—that cash flows can be reinvested at the cost of capital, or that they can be reinvested at the project's IRR? The best assumption is that projects' cash flows can be reinvested at the cost of capital, which means that the NPV method is more reliable.

We should reiterate that, when projects are independent, the NPV and IRR methods both lead to exactly the same accept/reject decision. However, *when evaluating mutually exclusive projects, especially those that differ in scale and/or timing, the NPV method should be used.*

CONCEPT REVIEW

1. Describe how NPV profiles are constructed, and define the crossover rate.
2. How does the "reinvestment rate" assumption differ between the NPV and IRR methods?
3. If a conflict exists, should the capital budgeting decision be made on the basis of the NPV or the IRR ranking? Why?

10.5 Multiple IRRs

There is another instance in which the IRR approach may not be reliable—when projects have non-normal cash flows. A project has **normal cash flows** if it has one or more cash outflows (costs) followed by a series of cash inflows.

Normal: $-+++$ or $--+++$ or $++--$

Notice that normal cash flows have only one change in sign—they begin as negative cash flows, change to positive cash flows, and then remain positive.[4] **Non-normal cash flows** occur when there is more than one change in sign. For example, a project may begin with negative cash flows, switch to positive cash flows, and then switch back to negative cash flows.

Non-normal: $-++++-$ or $-+++-+++$

If a project's cash flows have a non-normal pattern (that is, the cash flows have more than one sign change), it is possible for the project to have more than one positive real IRR—that is, *multiple IRRs!*

To illustrate, suppose a firm is considering the expenditure of $1.6 million to develop a strip mine (Project M). The mine will produce a cash flow of $10 million at the end of Year 1. Then, at the end of Year 2, $10 million must be expended to restore the land to its original condition. Therefore, the project's expected net cash flows are as follows (in millions of dollars):

Expected Net Cash Flows

Year 0	End of Year 1	End of Year 2
−$1.6	+$10	−$10

These values can be substituted into Equation 10-2 to derive the IRR for the investment:

$$\text{NPV} = \frac{-\$1.6\,\text{million}}{(1 + \text{IRR})^0} + \frac{\$10\,\text{million}}{(1 + \text{IRR})^1} + \frac{-\$10\,\text{million}}{(1 + \text{IRR})^2} = 0$$

---

[4]Normal cash flows can also begin with positive cash flows, switch to negative cash flows, and then remain negative. The key is that there is only one change in sign.

FIGURE
10-3 NPV Profile for Project M

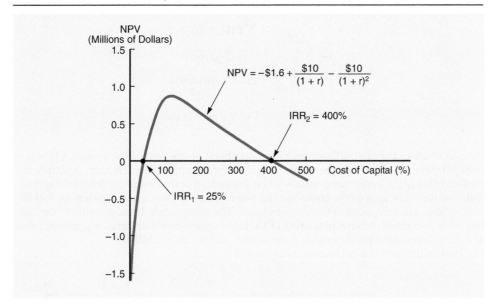

When solved, we find that NPV = 0 when IRR = 25% and also when IRR = 400%.[5] Therefore, the IRR of the investment is both 25% and 400%. This relationship is depicted graphically in Figure 10-3. Note that no dilemma would arise if the NPV method were used; we would simply use Equation 10-1, find the NPV, and use the result to evaluate the project. If Project M's cost of capital were 10%, then its NPV would be −$0.77 million, and the project should be rejected. If r were between 25 and 400%, the NPV would be positive.

The example illustrates how multiple IRRs can arise when a project has non-normal cash flows. In contrast, the NPV criterion can easily be applied, and this method leads to conceptually correct capital budgeting decisions.

See **Ch 10 Tool Kit.xlsx** at the textbook's website for all calculations.

ⓒNCEPT REVIEW

1. Explain the difference between normal and non-normal cash flows, and their relationship to the "multiple IRR problem."

10.6 Modified Internal Rate of Return (MIRR)

In spite of a strong academic preference for NPV, surveys indicate that many executives prefer IRR over NPV. Apparently, managers find it intuitively more appealing to evaluate investments in terms of percentage rates of return than dollars of NPV. Given this fact, can we devise a percentage evaluator that is better than the regular IRR? The answer is yes—we can modify the IRR and make it a better indicator of relative profitability, hence better for

---

[5]If you attempted to find the IRR of Project M with many financial calculators, you would get an error message. This same message would be given for all projects with multiple IRRs. However, you can still find Project M's IRR by first calculating its NPV using several different values for r and then plotting the NPV profile. The intersection with the x-axis gives a rough idea of the IRR value. Finally, you can use trial and error to find the exact value of r that forces NPV = 0.

The IRR function in spreadsheets begins its trial-and-error search for a solution with an initial guess. If you omit the initial guess, the *Excel* default starting point is 10%. Now suppose the values −1.6, +10, and −10 were in Cells A1:C1. You could use this *Excel* formula, **=IRR(A1:C1,10%)**, where 10% is the initial guess, and it would produce a result of 25%. If you used a guess of 300%, you would have this formula, **=IRR(A1:C1,300%)**, and it would produce a result of 400%.

use in capital budgeting. The new measure is called the **modified IRR, or MIRR,** and it is defined as follows:

$$\sum_{t=0}^{N} \frac{COF_t}{(1 + r)^t} = \frac{\sum_{t=0}^{N} CIF_t(1 + r)^{N-t}}{(1 + MIRR)^N}$$

$$PV \text{ of costs} = \frac{\text{Terminal value}}{(1 + MIRR)^N} \qquad \text{(10-3)}$$

$$= PV \text{ of terminal value}$$

Here COF refers to cash outflows (negative numbers) or the cost of the project, CIF refers to cash inflows (positive numbers), and r is the cost of capital. The left term is simply the present value of the investment outlays when discounted at the cost of capital, and the numerator of the right term is the compounded future value of the inflows, assuming that the cash inflows are reinvested at the cost of capital. The compounded future value of the cash inflows is also called the **terminal value (TV).** The discount rate that forces the present value of the TV to equal the present value of the costs is defined as the MIRR.[6]

We can illustrate the calculation with Project S:

See *Ch 10 Tool Kit.xlsx* at the textbook's website for all calculations.

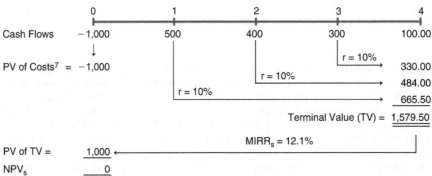

Using the cash flows as set out on the time line, first find the terminal value by compounding each cash inflow at the 10% cost of capital. Then enter N = 4, PV = −1,000, PMT = 0, FV = 1,579.5, and then press the I/YR button to find $MIRR_S$ = 12.1%. Similarly, we find $MIRR_L$ = 11.3%.

Excel has a function for the MIRR. Using the cash flows in Panel A of Figure 10-1, the formula in C41 is **=MIRR(B27:F27,D33,D33).** The first argument in the function is the range of cash flows, beginning with CF_0. The second argument is the cost of capital used for discounting cash outflows, and the third argument is the rate used for compounding inflows (i.e., the reinvestment rate). In our definition of the MIRR, we assume that reinvestment is at the cost of capital, so we enter the project cost of capital percent twice. The result is an MIRR of 12.1%.

The modified IRR has a significant advantage over the regular IRR. MIRR assumes that cash flows from all projects are reinvested at the cost of capital, while the regular IRR assumes that the cash flows from each project are reinvested at the project's own IRR. Because reinvestment at the cost of capital is generally more correct, the modified IRR is a better indicator of a project's true profitability. The MIRR also eliminates the multiple IRR problem caused by projects with more than one cash flow sign change. If Project M (the strip mine project) has a cost of capital of 10%, we then calculate the project's MIRR to be 5.6%. Since the MIRR < the cost of capital, the project should be rejected. This is consistent with the decision based on the NPV method, because at r = 10%, NPV = −$0.77 million.

---

[6]There are several alternative definitions for the MIRR. The differences primarily relate to whether negative cash flows that occur after positive cash flows begin should be compounded and treated as part of the TV or discounted and treated as a cost. A related issue is whether negative and positive flows in a given year should be netted or treated separately. For a complete discussion, see William R. McDaniel, Daniel E. McCarty, and Kenneth A. Jessell, "Discounted Cash Flow with Explicit Reinvestment Rates: Tutorial and Extension," *Financial Review*, August 1988, 369–85; and David M. Shull, "Interpreting Rates of Return: A Modified Rate of Return Approach," *Financial Practice and Education*, Fall 1993, 67–71.

[7]In this example, the only negative cash flow occurs at t = 0, so the PV of costs is equal to CF_0.

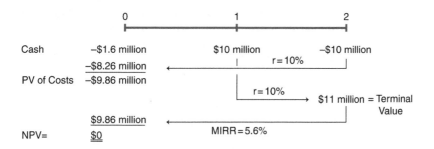

Is MIRR as good as NPV for choosing between mutually exclusive projects? If two projects are of equal size and have the same life, then NPV and MIRR will always lead to the same decision. Thus, for any set of projects like our Projects S and L, if $NPV_S > NPV_L$, then $MIRR_S > MIRR_L$, and the kinds of conflicts we encountered between NPV and the regular IRR will not occur. Also, if the projects are of equal size, but differ in lives, the MIRR will always lead to the same decision as the NPV if the MIRRs are both calculated using as the terminal year the life of the longer project. (Just fill in zeros for the shorter project's missing cash flows.) However, if the projects differ in size, then conflicts can still occur. For example, if we were choosing between a large project and a small mutually exclusive one, then we might find that $NPV_L > NPV_S$, but $MIRR_S > MIRR_L$.

Our conclusion is that the MIRR is superior to the regular IRR as an indicator of a project's "true" rate of return, or "expected long-term rate of return," but the NPV method is still the best way to choose among competing projects because it provides the best indication of how much each project will add to the value of the firm.

CONCEPT REVIEW

1. Describe how the modified IRR (MIRR) is calculated.
2. What are the primary differences between the MIRR and the regular IRR?
3. What condition can cause the MIRR and NPV methods to produce conflicting rankings?
4. A project has the following expected cash flows: $CF_0 = -\$500$, $CF_1 = \$200$, $CF_2 = \$200$, and $CF_3 = \$400$. Using a 10% discount rate and reinvestment rate, what is the MIRR? (Check Figure: 19.9%)

10.7 Profitability Index

Another method used to evaluate projects is the **profitability index (PI):**

$$PI = \frac{\text{PV of future cash flows}}{\text{Initial cost}} = \frac{\sum_{t=1}^{N} \frac{CF_t}{(1+r)^t}}{CF_0} \qquad (10\text{-}4)$$

Here CF_t represents the expected future cash flows, and CF_0 represents the initial cost. The PI shows the *relative* profitability of any project, or the present value per dollar of initial cost. The PI for Project S, based on a 10% cost of capital, is 1.08:

$$PI_s = \frac{\$1,078.82}{\$1,000} = 1.08$$

Thus, on a present value basis, Project S is expected to produce $1.08 for each $1 of investment. Project L, with a PI of 1.05, should produce $1.05 for each dollar invested.

In Panel B of Figure 10-1, we calculate the PI using the NPV function. Our formula in Cell C42 is **=NPV(D33,C27:F27)/(−B27).**

A project is acceptable if its PI is greater than 1.0, and the higher the PI, the higher the project's ranking. Therefore, both S and L would be accepted by the PI criterion if they were independent, and S would be ranked ahead of L if they were mutually exclusive.

See **Ch 10 Tool Kit.xlsx** at the textbook's website for all calculations.

Mathematically, the NPV, IRR, MIRR, and PI methods will always lead to the same accept/reject decisions for *normal, independent* projects: If a project's NPV is positive, its IRR and MIRR will always exceed r, and its PI will always be greater than 1.0. However, these methods can give conflicting rankings for *mutually exclusive* projects, for the same reasons that IRR can give conflicting rankings.

CONCEPT REVIEW

1. Explain how the PI is calculated. What does it measure?
2. A project has the following expected cash flows: $CF_0 = -\$500$, $CF_1 = \$200$, $CF_2 = \$200$, and $CF_3 = \$400$. If the project's cost of capital is 9%, what is the PI? (Check Figure: 1.32)

10.8 Payback Methods

NPV and IRR are the most widely used methods today, but the earliest selection criteria were the payback methods. We now discuss the regular payback period and the discounted payback period.

Payback Period

The **payback period,** defined as the expected number of years required to recover the original investment, was the first formal method used to evaluate capital budgeting projects. The basic idea is to start with the project's cost, determine the number of years prior to full recovery of the cost, and then determine the fraction of the next year that is required for full recovery, assuming that cash flows occur evenly during the year:

$$\text{Payback} = \begin{array}{c}\text{Number of}\\\text{years prior to}\\\text{full recovery}\end{array} + \frac{\text{Unrecovered cost at start of year}}{\text{Cash flow during full recovery year}} \quad (10\text{-}5)$$

The payback calculation for Project S is diagrammed in Figure 10-4 and is explained below.

The cumulative net cash flow at t = 0 is just the initial cost of −$1,000. At Year 1 the cumulative net cash flow is the previous cumulative of −$1,000 plus the Year 1 cash flow of $500: −$1,000 + $500 = −$500. Similarly, the cumulative for Year 2 is the previous cumulative of −$500 plus the Year 2 inflow of $400, resulting in −$100. We see that by the end of Year 3 the cumulative inflows have more than recovered the initial outflow. Thus,

FIGURE 10-4   Payback Period for Projects S and L

	A	B	C	D	E	F	G	H
398	Project S		Year:	0	1	2	3	4
399								
400			Cash flow:	−1,000	500	400	300	100
401			Cumulative cash flow:	−1,000	−500	−100	200	300
402			Percent of year required for payback:		1.00	1.00	0.33	0.00
403			Payback =	2.33				
404								
405	Project L		Year:	0	1	2	3	4
406								
407			Cash flow:	−1,000	100	300	400	600
408			Cumulative cash flow:	−1,000	−900	−600	−200	400
409			Percent of year required for payback:		1.00	1.00	1.00	0.33
410			Payback =	3.33				

See **Ch 10 Tool Kit.xlsx** at the textbook's website for all calculations.

the payback occurred during the third year. If the $300 of inflows comes in evenly during Year 3, then the exact payback period can be found as follows:

$$\text{Payback}_s = 2 + \frac{\$100}{\$300} = 2.33 \text{ years}$$

Applying the same procedure to Project L, we find $\text{Payback}_L = 3.33$ years.

The shorter the payback period, the better. If the projects were mutually exclusive, S would be ranked over L because S has the shorter payback.

The payback has three main flaws: (1) Dollars received in different years are all given the same weight—a dollar in Year 4 is assumed to be just as valuable as a dollar in Year 1. (2) Cash flows beyond the payback year are given no consideration whatsoever, regardless of how large they might be. (3) Unlike the NPV, which tells us by how much the project should increase shareholder wealth, and the IRR, which tells us how much a project yields over the cost of capital, the payback merely tells us when we get our investment back. There is no necessary relationship between a given payback and investor wealth maximization, so we don't know how to set the "right" payback.

Discounted Payback Period

Some firms use a variant of the regular payback, the **discounted payback period,** which is similar to the regular payback period except that the expected cash flows are discounted by the project's cost of capital. Thus, the discounted payback period is defined as the number of years required to recover the investment from *discounted* net cash flows. Figure 10-5 contains the discounted net cash flows for Projects S and L, assuming that both projects have a cost of capital of 10%. To construct Figure 10-5, each cash inflow is divided by $(1 + r)^t = (1.10)^t$, where t is the year in which the cash flow occurs and r is the project's cost of capital. After 3 years, Project S will have generated $1,011 in discounted cash inflows. Because the cost is $1,000, the discounted payback is just under 3 years, or, to be precise, $2 + (\$214.9/\$225.4) =$ 2.95 years. Project L's discounted payback is 3.88 years:

$$\text{Discounted payback}_S = 2.0 + \$214.9/\$225.4 = 2.95 \text{ years}$$

$$\text{Discounted payback}_L = 3.0 + \$360.6/\$409.8 = 3.88 \text{ years}$$

For Projects S and L, the rankings are the same regardless of which payback method is used; that is, Project S is preferred to Project L. Often, however, the regular and the discounted paybacks produce conflicting rankings.

FIGURE 10-5   Projects S and L: Discounted Payback Period (r = 10%)

	A	B	C	D	E	F	G	H
422								
423								
424	Project S		Year:	0	1	2	3	4
425								
426			Cash flow:	(1,000)	500	400	300	100
427			Discounted cash flow:	(1,000)	455	331	225	68
428			Cumulative discounted CF:	(1,000)	(545)	(215)	11	79
429			Percent of year required for payback:		1.00	1.00	0.95	0.00
430			Discounted Payback:	2.95				
431								
432	Project L		Year:	0	1	2	3	4
433								
434			Cash flow:	(1,000)	100	300	400	600
435			Discounted cash flow:	(1,000)	91	248	301	410
436			Cumulative discounted CF:	(1,000)	(909)	(661)	(361)	49
437			Percent of year required for payback:		1.00	1.00	1.00	0.88
438			Discounted Payback:	3.88				

See **Ch 10 Tool Kit.xlsx** at the textbook's website for all calculations.

Evaluating Payback and Discounted Payback

The discounted payback approach corrects the first flaw of the regular payback method because it considers the time value of the cash flows. However, it too fails to consider cash flows occurring after the payback year and, as with regular payback, there is no relationship between discounted payback and wealth maximization.

Although the payback methods have serious faults as ranking criteria, they do provide information on *liquidity* and *risk*. The shorter the payback period, other things held constant, the greater the project's liquidity. Also, since cash flows expected in the distant future are generally riskier than near-term cash flows, the payback is often used as an indicator of a project's risk.

ⓒNCEPT REVIEW

1. What two pieces of information do the payback methods convey that are absent from the other capital budgeting decision methods?

2. What three flaws does the regular payback method have? Does the discounted payback method correct these flaws?

3. A project has the following expected cash flows: $CF_0 = -\$500$, $CF_1 = \$200$, $CF_2 = \$200$, and $CF_3 = \$400$. If the project's cost of capital is 9%, what are the project's payback period and discounted payback period? (Check Figures: 2.25; 2.48)

10.9   Conclusions on Capital Budgeting Methods

We have discussed six capital budgeting decision methods, compared the methods with one another, and highlighted their relative strengths and weaknesses. In the process, we probably created the impression that "sophisticated" firms should use only one method in the decision process, NPV. However, virtually all capital budgeting decisions are analyzed by computer, so it is easy to calculate and list all the decision measures: payback and discounted payback, NPV, IRR, modified IRR (MIRR), and profitability index (PI). In making the accept/reject decision, most large, sophisticated firms calculate and consider all of the measures, because each one provides decision makers with a somewhat different piece of relevant information.

A Comparison of the Methods

NPV is important because it gives a direct measure of the dollar benefit of the project to shareholders. Therefore, we regard NPV as the best single measure of *profitability*. IRR also measures profitability, but here it is expressed as a percentage rate of return, which many decision makers prefer. Further, IRR contains information concerning a project's "safety margin." To illustrate, consider the following two projects: Project S (for small) costs $10,000 and is expected to return $16,500 at the end of one year, while Project L (for large) costs $100,000 and has an expected payoff of $115,500 after one year. At a 10% cost of capital, both projects have an NPV of $5,000, so by the NPV rule we should be indifferent between them. However, Project S has a much larger margin for error. Even if its realized cash inflow were 39% below the $16,500 forecast, the firm would still recover its $10,000 investment. On the other hand, if Project L's inflows fell by only 13% from the forecasted $115,500, the firm would not recover its investment. Furthermore, if no inflows were generated at all, the firm would lose only $10,000 with Project S, but $100,000 if it took on Project L.

The modified IRR has all the virtues of the IRR, but (1) it incorporates a better reinvestment rate assumption, and (2) it avoids the multiple rate of return problem. So if decision makers want to know a project's rate of return, the MIRR is a better indicator than the regular IRR.

The PI measures profitability relative to the cost of a project—it shows the "bang per buck." Like the IRR, it gives an indication of the project's risk, because a high PI means that cash flows could fall quite a bit and the project would still be profitable.

Payback and discounted payback provide an indication of both the *risk* and the *liquidity* of a project: A long payback means (1) that the investment dollars will be locked up for many years—hence the project is relatively illiquid—and (2) that the project's cash flows must be forecast far out into the future—hence the project is probably quite risky. A good analogy for this is the bond valuation process. An investor should never compare the yields to maturity on two bonds without also considering their terms to maturity, because a bond's risk is affected by its maturity.

In summary, the different measures provide different types of information. It is easy to calculate all of them, and all should be considered in the decision process. For any specific decision, more weight might be given to one measure than another, but it would be foolish to ignore the information provided by any of the methods.

The Decision Process: What Is the Source of a Project's NPV?

Just as it would be foolish to ignore these capital budgeting methods, it would also be foolish to make decisions based *solely* on them. One cannot know at Time 0 the exact cost of future capital, or the exact future cash flows. These inputs are simply estimates, and if they turn out to be incorrect, then so will be the calculated NPVs and IRRs. *Thus, quantitative methods provide valuable information, but they should not be used as the sole criteria for accept/reject decisions* in the capital budgeting process. Rather, managers should use quantitative methods in the decision-making process but also consider the likelihood that actual results will differ from the forecasts. Qualitative factors, such as the chances of a tax increase, or a war, or a major product liability suit, should also be considered. *In summary, quantitative methods such as NPV and IRR should be considered as an aid to informed decisions but not as a substitute for sound managerial judgment.*

In this same vein, managers should ask sharp questions about any project that has a large NPV, a high IRR, or a high PI. In a perfectly competitive economy, there would be no positive NPV projects—all companies would have the same opportunities, and competition would quickly eliminate any positive NPV. Therefore, positive NPV projects must be predicated on some imperfection in the marketplace, and the longer the life of the project, the longer that imperfection must last. Therefore, managers should be able to identify the imperfection and explain why it will persist before accepting that a project will really have a positive NPV. Valid explanations might include patents or proprietary technology, which is how pharmaceutical and software firms create positive NPV projects. Valeant's Wellbutrin® (an antidepression medicine) is an example. Companies can also create positive NPV by

FINANCE: SMALL BUSINESS

Capital Budgeting and Small Business

We've discussed in this chapter that the best way to evaluate long-term investments is by carrying out a discounted cash flow analysis—specifically, by calculating a project's NPV. We've further observed that large companies use DCF (including NPV and IRR) as their primary means for evaluating capital projects. Small businesses face the same long-term investment decisions. In fact, capital budgeting may well be more important to a small firm, for a mistake in choosing a long-term project can lead to bankruptcy. Small companies often can neither access additional capital to make up for the loss of an investment nor compensate for losses in one project against other more successful projects, as can larger businesses. Small businesses need proper decision-making processes, yet the evidence suggests that they do not follow capital budgeting theory and do not use NPV as an analytical method.

The table below shows the capital budgeting methods used by small firms, based on two recent studies. Stanley Block (1997) reported that less than 28% of respondents were using discounted cash flow (DCF) analysis. More recently, Danielson and Scott (2006) have reported that only 12% of small business respondents use DCF. Payback and Accounting rate of return (ARR) at 19% and 14% each were more widely used than DCF.

Primary Capital Budgeting Tools Used by Small Firms (in %)

	Payback	ARR	Other, Not Specified	Discounted Cash Flow[a]
Block	42.7	22.4	7.3	27.6
Danielson and Scott	19	14	37[b]	12

[a]Represents sum of IRR and NPV.
[b]Gut feel 26%, and a combination of methods 11%.

(continued)

If the capital budgeting decision is at least as important to small businesses as to their larger counterparts, why don't small companies use the best techniques to improve their chances for success? Is there something specific to small businesses that warrants an alternative evaluation methodology? There are a number of possible explanations why small businesses may not adhere to capital budgeting theory.

Company Size and Resources

Small companies are typically resource deprived. They may simply not have the time and/or the human resources to undertake a proper DCF analysis.

The differences in the analytical process between large and small firms may also play a role. In a large firm, decision making is often separate from analysis. Lower-level staff will gather the data, do the number crunching, and prepare a report for the decision makers to consider. With smaller firms, the decision maker may already have significant first-hand knowledge of the project and the market. He or she can make a rational decision, bypassing the formal analysis that managers of large companies rely on.

Another possible explanation is that small companies face a different decision outcome. The capital budgeting decision to be made may be whether to invest in the project or wind up the business. The project *is* the business. Maximizing an NPV may not be a consideration at this point.

Manager/Owner Objectives

Traditional finance theory, including capital budgeting, is based on maximizing the firm's value. However, small business owners may have other primary goals, such as self-employment and independence, commercializing a new product idea, or trying to minimize overall taxation between personal and corporate taxes.

Liquidity

Because of their size, limited collateral, lack of track record, and overall riskiness, small businesses often have a difficult time raising debt or equity capital. Add the fact that small businesses can experience high growth rates, and we see that liquidity—specifically, having sufficient cash on hand—can be a real problem for a small business manager. This preoccupation with cash affects a manager's outlook on capital projects. The liquidity of a capital investment may well be a key concern for a small business. Calculating the NPV of a project will not measure liquidity. However, estimating that the project will return its initial investment in one or two years does give an estimate of liquidity. So it should not be surprising that when liquidity is a concern, calculations such as payback period are given importance. Block summarizes this point well:

When the small business owner approaches his banker for a loan to finance a capital investment, he better be prepared to demonstrate his capacity to repay the loan within a set period of time rather than specify the project has a positive net present value or that the internal rate of return exceeds the weighted average cost of capital.

Liquidity and financing pressures may explain the use of payback period, but they do not explain the payback period that companies use as a cutoff criterion. Block found that the average payback period cutoff point was 2.8 years but that projects typically generated cash flows for more than 7 years. This suggests that cash flows beyond the 2.8 years were not being considered and that profitable projects were disregarded as a result.

Sophistication

Danielson and Scott found that over 50% of small business owners surveyed did not have a university degree. Education levels were positively correlated with the likelihood of making cash flow projections, using DCF analysis, writing business plans, and accounting for taxes. Lack of training in appropriate analytical tools may partially explain low DCF usage.

Even more troubling are the methods used by small business managers when they do calculate project NPVs. Block states that only 15% of those managers who calculated NPVs used a discount rate that was similar to their company's weighted average cost of capital. Most used the borrowing rate for the project being considered. Others used subjective or past target costs of capital. Managers tended not to consider the use of retained earnings and other corporate resources in the project. Small businesses may have difficulty even estimating their cost of equity. CAPM or dividend discount models typically are not practical tools for calculating cost of equity for a small private company with no established dividend policy.

Conclusion

Small businesses do not appear to use the tools for analyzing long-term projects as prescribed by capital budgeting concepts. Possible reasons include their small size, limited resources, and difficulty both accessing capital and estimating their cost of capital. There is also evidence that lack of training in analysis may be a factor. Ongoing concerns about liquidity very likely play a significant role in the continued reliance on payback period calculations. Given these constraints, many small businesses may well be acting logically in their decision making. At this point, however, we cannot definitively state whether the issue is a lack of understanding of how to use the analytical tools or whether capital budgeting theory must adapt itself to serve small businesses better.

Sources: Stanley Block, "Capital Budgeting Techniques Used by Small Business Firms in the 1990s," *Engineering Economist*, Summer 1997, 289–302; Morris G. Danielson and Jonathan A. Scott, "Capital Budgeting Decisions of Small Businesses," *Journal of Applied Finance*, Fall–Winter 2006, 45–56; L. R. Runyon, "Capital Expenditure Decision Making in Small Firms," *Journal of Business Research*, September 1983, 389–97.

being the first entrant into a new market or by creating new products that meet previously unidentified consumer needs. Apple's iPad tablet product is a good example. Similarly, Dell developed procedures for direct sales of microcomputers and in the process created projects with enormous NPV. Also, companies such as WestJet Airlines have managed to train and motivate their workers better than their competitors, and this has led to positive NPV projects. In all of these cases, the companies developed some source of competitive advantage, and that advantage resulted in positive NPV projects.

This discussion suggests three things: (1) If you can't identify the reason a project has a positive projected NPV, then its actual NPV will probably not be positive. (2) Positive NPV projects don't just happen—they result from hard work to develop some competitive advantage. At the risk of oversimplification, the primary job of a manager is to find and develop areas of competitive advantage. (3) Some competitive advantages last longer than others, with their durability depending on competitors' ability to replicate them. Patents, the control of scarce resources, or large size in an industry where strong economies of scale exist can keep competitors at bay. However, it is relatively easy to replicate nonpatentable features on products. The bottom line is that managers should strive to develop nonreplicable sources of competitive advantage, and if such an advantage cannot be demonstrated, then you should question projects with high NPV, especially if they have long lives.

CONCEPT REVIEW

1. Describe the advantages and disadvantages of the six capital budgeting methods discussed in this chapter.
2. Should capital budgeting decisions be made solely on the basis of a project's NPV?
3. What are some possible reasons that a project might have a large NPV?

10.10 Business Practices in Canada

Surveys designed to uncover which capital budgeting criteria Canadian managers actually use have been undertaken over the years. All of the surveys, except for the one given in 2000, asked companies to indicate their primary decision tool or the method they used most often. In several of these surveys, managers often selected more than one method primarily or often used. The 2000 survey asked respondents to rank criteria in order of importance. The summary of the results, provided in Table 10-1, reveals some interesting trends.

TABLE 10-1 Capital Budgeting Methods Used in Practice

	Primary Criterion Used, 1966[a]	Primary Criterion Used, 1988[b]	Technique Most Often Used, 1995[c]	Rank Order of Importance, 2000[d]	Often or Always Used, 2011[e]
NPV	4%	25%	43%	1	75%
IRR	24%	40%	64%	2	68%
Payback	32%	19%	52%	3	67%
Acct. Rate of Return	32%	9%	17%	4	40%
Other/None	8%	7%	n/a	n/a	n/a[f]

[a]John T. Nicholson and J.D. Ffolliott, "Investment Evaluation Criteria of Canadian Companies," *Business Quarterly*, Summer 1966, 54–62.
[b]J.D. Blazouske, Ian Carlin, and Suk H. Kim, "Current Capital Budgeting Practices in Canada," *CMA Magazine*, March 1988, 51–54. 1985 data reported.
[c]Vijay M. Jog and Ashwani K. Srivastava, "Capital Budgeting Practices in Corporate Canada," *Financial Practice and Education*, Fall–Winter 1995, 37–43. Method used for expansion of existing operations. More than one technique was often used.
[d]Janet D. Payne, Will Carrington Heath, and Lewis R. Gale, "Comparative Financial Practice in the US and Canada: Capital Budgeting and Risk Assessment Techniques," *Financial Practice and Education*, Spring–Summer 1999, 16–24. Discounted and regular payback treated singularly.
[e]H. Kent Baker, Shantanu Dutta, and Samir Saadi, "Corporate Finance Practices in Canada" Where Do We Stand?," *Multinational Finance Journal*, Vol. 15, No. 3/4, 157–192.
[f]Less commonly used methods reported include discounted payback, adjusted present value, profitability index, MIRR, and real options.

The discounted cash flow (DCF) criterion (that is, NPV or IRR) was not used significantly prior to 1970. By 1995, however, the majority of firms had adopted DCF methods. Payback, though still used significantly, was not considered as important as DCF. Since payback is easy to calculate and provides information on project liquidity, it is still used as a secondary method. The most recent study showed NPV to be the single most important method, but all were being used (along with judgment and common sense) because they provide useful information and are easy to calculate.[8]

10.11 Special Applications of Cash Flow Evaluation

Misapplication of the NPV method can lead to errors when two mutually exclusive projects have unequal lives. There are also situations in which an asset should not be operated for its full life. The following sections explain how to evaluate cash flows in these situations.[9]

Comparing Projects with Unequal Lives

When choosing between two mutually exclusive alternatives with significantly different lives, an adjustment is necessary. For example, suppose a company is planning to modernize its production facilities, and it is considering either a conveyor system (Project C) or some forklift trucks (Project F) for moving materials. The first two sections of Figure 10-6 show the expected net cash flows, NPVs, and IRRs for these two mutually exclusive alternatives. We see that Project C, when discounted at the firm's 11.5% cost of capital, has the higher NPV and thus appears to be the better project.

Although the NPV shown in Figure 10-6 suggests that Project C should be selected, this analysis is incomplete, and the decision to choose Project C is actually incorrect. If we choose Project F, we will have an opportunity to make a similar investment in 3 years, and if cost and revenue conditions continue at the Figure 10-6 levels, this second investment will also be profitable. However, if we choose Project C, we cannot make this second investment.

Equivalent Annual Annuities (EAA) Electrical engineers designing power plants and distribution lines were the first to encounter the unequal life problem. They could use transformers

See *Ch 10 Tool Kit.xlsx* at the textbook's website for all calculations.

FIGURE 10-6 Analysis of Projects C and F (r = 11.5%)

	A	B	C	D	E	F	G	H
465	**Project C:**							
466								
467	**Year (t)**	**0**	**1**	**2**	**3**	**4**	**5**	**6**
468	**CF$_t$ for C**	($40,000)	$8,000	$14,000	$13,000	$12,000	$11,000	$10,000
469								
470			**NPV$_C$ =**	**$7,165**		**IRR$_C$ =**	**17.5%**		
471								
472	**Project F:**							
473								
474	**Year (t)**	**0**	**1**	**2**	**3**			
475	**CF$_t$ for F**	($20,000)	$7,000	$13,000	$12,000			
476								
477			**NPV$_F$ =**	**$5,391**		**IRR$_F$ =**	**25.2%**		
478								

[8]For additional articles that discuss capital budgeting methods used in practice, see Suk H. Kim, Trevor Crick, and Seung H. Kim, "Do Executives Practice What Academics Preach?" *Management Accounting*, November 1986, 49–52; Tarun K. Mukherjee, "Capital Budgeting Surveys: The Past and the Future," *Review of Business and Economic Research*, Spring 1987, 37–56.; Tarun K. Mukherjee, "The Capital Budgeting Process of Large U.S. Firms: An Analysis of Capital Budgeting Manuals," *Managerial Finance*, Number 2/3, 1988, 28–35; Marc Ross, "Capital Budgeting Practices of Twelve Large Manufacturers," *Financial Management*, Winter 1986, 15–22; L. R. Runyan, "Capital Expenditure Decision Making in Small Firms," *Journal of Business Research*, September 1983, 389–397; and Samuel C. Weaver, Donald Peters, Roger Cason, and Joe Daleiden, "Capital Budgeting," *Financial Management*, Spring 1989, 10–17.

[9]For additional discussion of other special applications, see Paul K. Chaney, "Moral Hazard and Capital Budgeting," *Journal of Financial Research*, Summer 1989, 113–128; Edward M. Miller, "Safety Margins and Capital Budgeting Criteria," *Managerial Finance*, Number 2/3, 1988, 1–8; and John C. Woods and Maury R. Randall, "The Net Present Value of Future Investment Opportunities: Its Impact on Shareholder Wealth and Implications for Capital Budgeting Theory," *Financial Management*, Summer 1989, 85–92.

and other equipment that had relatively low initial costs but short lives, or they could use equipment that had higher initial costs but longer lives. The services would be required on into the indefinite future, so this was the issue: Which choice would result in the higher NPV in the long run? The engineers converted the annual cash flows under the alternative investments into a constant cash flow stream whose NPV was equal to, or equivalent to, the NPV of the initial stream. This was called the **equivalent annual annuity (EAA) method**. To apply the EAA method to Projects C and F, for each project we simply find the constant payment that has the same NPV as the project's traditional NPV. Using a financial calculator to find Project C's EAA, we enter N = 6, I/YR = 11.5, PV = −7,165, and FV = 0; solving for PMT, we find an EAA of $1,718. For Project F, we enter N = 3, I/YR = 11.5, PV = −5,391, and FV = 0; solving for PMT, we find an EAA of $2,225. Project F has the higher EAA, so it is the better project.

Conclusions About Unequal Lives   When should we worry about unequal life analysis? The unequal life issue (1) does not arise for independent projects, but (2) it can arise if mutually exclusive projects with significantly different lives are being compared. However, even for mutually exclusive projects, it is not always appropriate to extend the analysis to a common life. This should be done only if there is a high probability that the projects will actually be repeated at the end of their initial lives.

We should note several potentially serious weaknesses inherent in this type of analysis: (1) If inflation is expected, then replacement equipment will have a higher price. Moreover, both sales prices and operating costs will probably change. Thus, the static conditions built into the analysis would be invalid. (2) Replacements that occur down the road would probably employ new technology, which in turn might change the cash flows. (3) It is difficult enough to estimate the lives of most projects, and even more so to estimate the lives of a series of projects.

In view of these problems, no experienced financial analyst would be too concerned about comparing mutually exclusive projects with lives of, say, 8 years and 10 years. Given all the uncertainties in the estimation process, such projects would, for all practical purposes, be assumed to have the same life. Still, it is important to recognize that a problem exists if mutually exclusive projects have substantially different lives.

Economic Life versus Physical Life

Projects are normally analyzed under the assumption that the firm will operate the asset over its full physical life. However, this may not be the best course of action—it may be best to terminate a project before the end of its potential life, and this possibility can materially affect the project's estimated profitability. The situation in Table 10-2 can be used to illustrate this concept and its effects on capital budgeting. The salvage values listed in the third column are after taxes, and they have been estimated for each year of Project A's life.

Using a 10% cost of capital, the expected NPV based on 3 years of operating cash flows and the zero abandonment (salvage) value is −$14.12:

```
 0      10%     1           2           3
 |---------------|-----------|-----------|
$(4,800)      $2,000      $2,000      $1,750
                                         0
                                      -------
                                      $1,750
```

$$NPV = -\$4,800 + \$2,000/(1.10)^1 + \$2,000/(1.10)^2 + \$1,750/(1.10)^3$$
$$= -\$14.12$$

TABLE 10-2   Project A: Investment, Operating, and Salvage Cash Flows

Year (t)	Initial (Year 0) Investment and After-Tax Operating Cash Flows	Net Salvage Value at End of Year t
0	$(4,800)	$4,800
1	2,000	3,000
2	2,000	1,650
3	1,750	0

Thus, Project A would not be accepted if we assume that it will be operated over its full 3-year life. However, what would its NPV be if the project were terminated after 2 years? In this case, we would receive operating cash flows in Years 1 and 2, plus the salvage value at the end of Year 2, and the project's NPV would be $34.71:

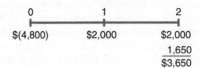

$$NPV = -\$4,800 + \$2,000/(1.10)^1 + \$3,650/(1.10)^2$$
$$= \$34.71$$

Thus, Project A would be profitable if we operate it for 2 years and then dispose of it. To complete the analysis, note that if the project were terminated after 1 year, its NPV would be −$254.55. Thus, the optimal life for this project is 2 years.

This type of analysis can be used to determine a project's *economic life*, which is the life that maximizes the NPV and thus maximizes shareholder wealth. For Project A, the economic life is 2 years versus the 3-year *physical*, or *engineering, life*. Note that this analysis is based on the expected cash flows and the expected salvage values and should always be conducted as a part of the capital budgeting evaluation if salvage values are relatively high.

ⒸNCEPT REVIEW

1. Briefly describe the equivalent annual annuities approach.
2. Define the economic life of a project (as opposed to its physical life).

10.12 The Optimal Capital Budget

The **optimal capital budget** is the set of projects that maximizes the value of the firm. Finance theory states that all projects with positive NPVs should be accepted, and the optimal capital budget consists of these positive NPV projects. However, two complications arise in practice: (1) an increasing marginal cost of capital and (2) capital rationing.

An Increasing Marginal Cost of Capital

See **Web Extension 10B** at the textbook's website for a discussion of the optimal budget with an increasing marginal cost of capital.

The cost of capital may depend on the size of the capital budget. As we discussed in Chapter 9, the flotation costs associated with issuing new equity or public debt can be quite high. This means that the cost of capital jumps after a company invests all of its internally generated cash and must sell new common stock. In addition, investors often perceive extremely large capital investments to be riskier, which may also drive up the cost of capital as the size of the capital budget increases. As a result, a project might have a positive NPV if it is part of a "normal size" capital budget, but the same project might have a negative NPV if it is part of an unusually large capital budget. Fortunately, this problem occurs very rarely for most firms, and it is unusual for an established firm to require new outside equity. Still, *Web Extension 10B* contains a more detailed discussion of this problem and shows how to deal with the existence of an increasing marginal cost of capital.

Capital Rationing

Armbrister Pyrotechnics, a manufacturer of fireworks and lasers for light shows, has identified 40 potential independent projects, with 15 having a positive NPV based on the firm's 12% cost of capital. The total cost of implementing these 15 projects is $75 million. Based on finance theory, the optimal capital budget is $75 million, and Armbrister should accept the 15 projects with positive NPVs. However, Armbrister's management has imposed a limit of $50 million for capital expenditures during the upcoming year. Due to this restriction, the company must forgo a number of value-adding projects. This is an example of *soft capital rationing*, defined as a situation in which a firm limits its capital expenditures to less than the amount required to fund the optimal capital budget. Despite being at odds with finance theory, this practice is quite common.

Why would any company forgo value-adding projects? Here are some potential explanations, along with some suggestions for better ways to handle these situations:

1. *Reluctance to issue new stock.* Many firms are extremely reluctant to issue new stock, so all of their capital expenditures must be funded out of debt and internally generated cash. Also, most firms try to stay near their target capital structure, and, combined with the limit on equity, this limits the amount of debt that can be added during any one year. The result can be a serious constraint on the amount of funds available for investment in new projects.

    This reluctance to issue new stock could be based on some sound reasons: (a) flotation costs can be very expensive; (b) investors might perceive new stock offerings as a signal that the company's equity is overvalued; and (c) the company might have to reveal sensitive strategic information to investors, thereby reducing some of its competitive advantages. To avoid these costs, many companies simply limit their capital expenditures.

    However, rather than placing a somewhat artificial limit on capital expenditures, a company might be better off explicitly incorporating the costs of raising external capital into its cost of capital. If there still are positive NPV projects even using this higher cost of capital, then the company should go ahead and raise external equity and accept the projects. See **Web Extension 10B** for more details concerning an increasing marginal cost of capital.

2. *Constraints on nonmonetary resources.* Sometimes a firm simply does not have the necessary managerial, marketing, or engineering talent to immediately accept all positive NPV projects. In other words, the potential projects are not really independent, because the firm cannot accept them all. To avoid potential problems due to spreading existing talent too thinly, many firms simply limit the capital budget to a size that can be accommodated by their current personnel.

    A better solution might be to employ a technique called *linear programming.* Each potential project has an expected NPV, and each potential project requires a certain level of support by different types of employees. A linear program can identify the set of projects that maximizes NPV, subject to the constraint that the total amount of support required for these projects does not exceed the available resources.[10]

3. *Controlling estimation bias.* Many managers become overly optimistic when estimating the cash flows for a project. Some firms try to control this estimation bias by requiring managers to use an unrealistically high cost of capital. Others try to control the bias by limiting the size of the capital budget. Neither solution is generally effective since managers quickly learn the rules of the game and then increase their own estimates of project cash flows, which might have been biased upward to begin with.

    A better solution is to implement a **post audit** program and to link the accuracy of forecasts to the compensation of the managers who initiated the projects.

    Another form of **capital rationing** exists when a company is unable to raise the necessary funds to undertake all positive NPV projects. Using the above example, assume that Armbrister Pyrotechnics wishes to undertake all 15 projects. The company, however, must raise the extra $25 million through new debt or equity. If market conditions are poor, Armbrister may not find willing investors to finance the $25 million. Though efficient capital markets ought to be able to find investors willing to invest in positive NPV projects, *hard capital rationing* can occur during periods of significant market uncertainty or volatility.

CONCEPT REVIEW

1. What factors can lead to an increasing marginal cost of capital? How might this affect capital budgeting?
2. What is capital rationing?
3. Briefly describe the two types of capital rationing.

---

[10]See Stephen P. Bradley and Sherwood C. Frey, Jr., "Equivalent Mathematical Programming Models of Pure Capital Rationing," *Journal of Financial and Quantitative Analysis*, June 1978, 345–361.

Summary

This chapter has described six techniques (NPV, IRR, MIRR, PI, payback, and discounted payback) that are used in capital budgeting analysis. Each approach provides a different piece of information, so in this age of computers, managers often look at all of them when evaluating projects. However, NPV is the best single measure, and almost all firms now use NPV. The key concepts covered in this chapter are listed below:

- **Capital budgeting** is the process of analyzing potential projects. Capital budgeting decisions are probably the most important ones managers must make.
- The **net present value (NPV) method** discounts all cash flows at the project's cost of capital and then sums those cash flows. The project should be accepted if the NPV is positive.
- The **internal rate of return (IRR)** is defined as the discount rate that forces a project's NPV to equal zero. The project should be accepted if the IRR is greater than the cost of capital.
- The NPV and IRR methods make the same accept/reject decisions for **independent projects**, but if projects are **mutually exclusive**, then ranking conflicts can arise. If conflicts arise, the NPV method should be used. The NPV and IRR methods are both superior to the payback, but NPV is superior to IRR.
- The NPV method assumes that cash flows will be reinvested at the firm's cost of capital, while the IRR method assumes reinvestment at the project's IRR. **Reinvestment at the cost of capital is generally a better assumption** because it is closer to reality.
- The **modified IRR (MIRR) method** corrects some of the problems with the regular IRR. MIRR involves finding the **terminal value (TV)** of the cash inflows, compounded at the firm's cost of capital, and then determining the discount rate that forces the present value of the TV to equal the present value of the outflows.
- The **profitability index (PI)** shows the dollars of present value divided by the initial cost, so it measures relative profitability.
- The **payback period** is defined as the number of years required to recover a project's cost. The regular payback method ignores cash flows beyond the payback period, and it does not consider the time value of money. The payback does, however, provide an indication of a project's risk and liquidity, because it shows how long the invested capital will be "at risk."
- The **discounted payback method** is similar to the regular payback method except that it discounts cash flows at the project's cost of capital. It considers the time value of money, but it ignores cash flows beyond the payback period.
- If mutually exclusive projects have **unequal lives,** it may be necessary to adjust the analysis to put the projects on an equal-life basis. This can be done using the **equivalent annual annuity (EAA) approach.**
- A project's true value may be greater than the NPV based on its **physical life** if it can be **terminated** at the end of its **economic life**.
- Flotation costs and increased riskiness associated with unusually large expansion programs can cause the **marginal cost of capital** to rise as the size of the capital budget increases.
- **Soft capital rationing** occurs when management places a constraint on the size of the firm's capital budget during a particular period. **Hard capital rationing** occurs when capital markets are unwilling to invest in securities of a company that wishes to raise capital for positive NPV investments.

Questions

10-1   Define each of the following terms:
   a.   Capital budgeting; regular payback period; discounted payback period
   b.   Independent projects; mutually exclusive projects
   c.   DCF techniques; net present value (NPV) method; internal rate of return (IRR) method
   d.   Modified internal rate of return (MIRR) method; profitability index
   e.   NPV profile; crossover rate
   f.   Non-normal cash flow projects; normal cash flow projects; multiple IRRs
   g.   Hurdle rate; reinvestment rate assumption
   h.   Economic life; capital rationing

10-2   What types of projects require more detailed analysis in the capital budgeting process?

10-3   Explain why the NPV of a relatively long-term project, defined as one for which a high percentage of its cash flows are expected in the distant future, is more sensitive to changes in the cost of capital than is the NPV of a short-term project.

10-4   Explain why, if two mutually exclusive projects are being compared, the short-term project might have the higher ranking under the NPV criterion if the cost of capital is high, but the long-term project might be deemed better if the cost of capital is low. Would changes in the cost of capital ever cause a change in the IRR ranking of two such projects?

10-5   In what sense is a reinvestment rate assumption embodied in the NPV, IRR, and MIRR methods? What is the assumed reinvestment rate of each method?

10-6   Suppose a firm is considering two mutually exclusive projects. One has a life of 6 years and the other a life of 10 years. Would the failure to employ equivalent annual annuity analysis bias an NPV analysis against one of the projects? Explain.

Concept Review Problem

Full solutions are provided at www.nelson.com/brigham3ce.

CR-1
Project Analysis

You are a financial analyst for the Hittle Company. The director of capital budgeting has asked you to analyze two proposed capital investments, Projects X and Y. Each project has a cost of $10,000, and the cost of capital for each project is 12%. The projects' expected net cash flows are as follows:

	Expected Net Cash Flows	
Year	Project X	Project Y
0	$(10,000)	$(10,000)
1	6,500	3,500
2	3,000	3,500
3	3,000	3,500
4	1,000	3,500

a.   Calculate each project's payback period, net present value (NPV), internal rate of return (IRR), and modified internal rate of return (MIRR).
b.   Which project or projects should be accepted if they are independent?
c.   Which project should be accepted if they are mutually exclusive?
d.   How might a change in the cost of capital produce a conflict between the NPV and IRR rankings of these two projects? Would this conflict exist if r were 5%? (*Hint:* Plot the NPV profiles.)
e.   Why does the conflict exist?

Problems

Easy Problems
1–7

Answers to odd-numbered problems appear in Appendix A.

10-1
NPV

A project has an initial cost of $40,000, expected net cash inflows of $9,000 per year for 7 years, and a cost of capital of 11%. What is the project's NPV? (*Hint:* Begin by constructing a time line.)

10-2
IRR

Refer to Problem 10-1. What is the project's IRR?

10-3
MIRR

Refer to Problem 10-1. What is the project's MIRR?

10-4
Profitability Index

Refer to Problem 10-1. What is the project's PI?

10-5
Payback

Refer to Problem 10-1. What is the project's payback period?

10-6
Discounted Payback

Refer to Problem 10-1. What is the project's discounted payback period?

10-7
NPV

Your division is considering two investment projects, each of which requires an up-front expenditure of $15 million. You estimate that the investments will produce the following net cash flows:

Year	Project A	Project B
1	$ 5,000,000	$20,000,000
2	10,000,000	10,000,000
3	20,000,000	6,000,000

a. What are the two projects' net present values, assuming the cost of capital is 10%? 5%? 15%?
b. What are the two projects' IRRs?

Intermediate Problems 8–20

10-8
NPVs, IRRs, and MIRRs for Independent Projects

Edelman Engineering is considering including two pieces of equipment, a truck and an overhead pulley system, in this year's capital budget. The projects are independent. The cash outlay for the truck is $39,500, and that for the pulley system is $94,800. The firm's cost of capital is 14%. After-tax cash flows, including depreciation, are as follows:

Year	Truck	Pulley
1	$12,500	$31,000
2	12,500	31,000
3	12,500	31,000
4	12,500	31,000
5	12,500	31,000

Calculate the IRR, the NPV, and the MIRR for each project, and indicate the correct accept/reject decision for each.

10-9
NPVs and IRRs for Mutually Exclusive Projects

Davis Industries must choose between a gas-powered and an electric-powered forklift truck for moving materials in its factory. Since both forklifts perform the same function, the firm will choose only one. (They are mutually exclusive investments.) The electric-powered truck will cost more, but it will be less expensive to operate; it will cost $22,000, whereas the gas-powered truck will cost $17,500. The cost of capital that applies to both investments is 12%. The life for both types of truck is estimated to be 6 years, during which time the net cash flows for the electric-powered truck will be $6,290 per year and those for the gas-powered truck will be $5,000 per year. Annual net cash flows include depreciation expenses. Calculate the NPV and IRR for each type of truck, and decide which to recommend.

10-10
Capital Budgeting Methods

Project A has a cost of $22,000 and is expected to produce benefits (cash flows) of $7,000 per year for 5 years. Project B costs $70,000 and is expected to produce cash flows of $20,000 per year for 5 years. Calculate the two projects' NPVs, IRRs, MIRRs, and PIs, assuming a cost of capital of 10%. Which project would be selected, assuming they are mutually exclusive, using each ranking method? Which should actually be selected?

10-11
MIRR and NPV

Your company is considering two mutually exclusive projects, J and K, whose costs and cash flows are shown below:

Year	J	K
0	$(5,000)	$(5,000)
1	1,000	4,500
2	1,500	1,500
3	2,000	1,000
4	4,000	500

The projects are equally risky, and their cost of capital is 12%. You must make a recommendation, and you must base it on the modified IRR (MIRR). What is the MIRR of the better project?

10-12
NPV and IRR
Analysis

After discovering a new gold vein in central Ontario, CTC Mining Corporation must decide whether to mine the deposit. The most cost-effective method of mining gold is sulfuric acid extraction, a process that results in environmental damage. To go ahead with the extraction, CTC must spend $900,000 for new mining equipment and pay $165,000 for its installation. The gold mined will net the firm an estimated $350,000 each year over the 5-year life of the vein. CTC's cost of capital is 14%. For the purposes of this problem, assume that the cash inflows occur at the end of the year.

a. What are the NPV and IRR of this project?
b. Should this project be undertaken, ignoring environmental concerns?
c. How should environmental effects be considered when evaluating this, or any other, project? How might these effects change your decision in part b?

10-13
NPV and IRR
Analysis

DHT International is considering two mutually exclusive investments. The projects' expected net cash flows are as follows:

	Expected Net Cash Flows	
Year	Project A	Project B
0	$ (400)	$(650)
1	(528)	210
2	(219)	210
3	(150)	210
4	1,100	210
5	820	210
6	990	210
7	(325)	210

a. Construct NPV profiles for Projects A and B.
b. If you were told that each project's cost of capital was 10%, which project should be selected? If the cost of capital was 17%, what would be the proper choice?
c. What is each project's MIRR at a cost of capital of 10%? At 17%? (*Hint:* Consider Period 7 as the end of Project B's life.)
d. What is the crossover rate, and what is its significance?

10-14
Timing Differences

Ewert Exploration Company is considering two mutually exclusive plans for extracting oil on property for which it has mineral rights. Both plans call for the expenditure of $10,000,000 to drill development wells. Under Plan A, all the oil will be extracted in 1 year, producing a cash flow at t = 1 of $12,000,000, while under Plan B, cash flows will be $1,750,000 per year for 20 years.

a. What are the annual incremental cash flows that will be available to Ewert Exploration if it undertakes Plan B rather than Plan A? (*Hint:* Subtract Plan A's flows from B's.)
b. If the firm accepts Plan A, then invests the extra cash generated at the end of Year 1, what rate of return (reinvestment rate) would cause the cash flows from reinvestment to equal the cash flows from Plan B?
c. Suppose a company has a cost of capital of 10%. Is it logical to assume that it would take on all available independent projects (of average risk) with returns greater than 10%? Furthermore, if all available projects with returns greater than 10% have been taken, would this mean that cash flows from past investments would have an opportunity cost of only 10%, because all the firm could do with these cash flows would be to replace money that has a cost of 10%? Finally, does this imply that the cost of capital is the correct rate to assume for the reinvestment of a project's cash flows?
d. Construct NPV profiles for Plans A and B, identify each project's IRR, and indicate the crossover rate of return.

10-15
Scale Differences

The Pinkerton Publishing Company is considering two mutually exclusive expansion plans. Plan A calls for the expenditure of $50 million on a large-scale, integrated plant that will provide an expected cash flow stream of $8 million per year for 20 years. Plan B calls for the expenditure of $15 million to build a somewhat less efficient, more labour-intensive plant that has an expected cash flow stream of $3.4 million per year for 20 years. The firm's cost of capital is 10%.

a. Calculate each project's NPV and IRR.
b. Set up a Project Δ by showing the cash flows that will exist if the firm goes with the large plant rather than the smaller plant. What are the NPV and the IRR for this Project Δ?

c. Graph the NPV profiles for Plan A, Plan B, and Project Δ.

d. Give a logical explanation, based on reinvestment rates and opportunity costs, as to why the NPV method is better than the IRR method when the firm's cost of capital is constant at some value such as 10%.

10-16
Unequal Lives

Seacraft Carriers is considering two alternative cargo ships. Ship A has an expected life of 7 years, will cost $60 million, and will produce net cash flows of $17 million per year. Ship B has a life of 14 years, will cost $75 million, and will produce net cash flows of $15 million per year. Seacraft plans to serve the route for 14 years. Inflation in operating costs, ship costs, and cargo rates is expected to be zero, and the company's cost of capital is 12%. What is the equivalent annual annuity for each ship? Which ship should be accepted?

10-17
Unequal Lives

Contec Systems has the opportunity to invest in one of two mutually exclusive machines that will produce a product it will need for the foreseeable future. Machine A costs $2.5 million and realizes after-tax inflows of $900,000 per year for 5 years. Machine B costs $3.4 million and realizes after-tax inflows of $800,000 per year for 9 years. Assume that machine prices are not expected to rise because inflation will be offset by cheaper components used in the machines. The cost of capital is 12%. What is the equivalent annual annuity for each machine? Which machine should be chosen?

10-18
Unequal Lives

Filkins Fabric Company is considering the replacement of its old, fully depreciated knitting machine. Two new models are available: Machine 190-3, which has a cost of $190,000, a 3-year expected life, and after-tax cash flows of $87,000 per year; and Machine 360-6, which has a cost of $360,000, a 6-year life, and after-tax cash flows of $98,300 per year. Knitting machine prices are not expected to rise, because inflation will be offset by cheaper components (microprocessors) used in the machines. Assume that Filkins's cost of capital is 14%. Should the firm replace its old knitting machine, and, if so, which new machine should it use? What is the equivalent annual annuity for each machine?

10-19
Multiple Rates of Return

The Ulmer Uranium Company is deciding whether it should open a strip mine, the net cost of which is $4.4 million. Net cash inflows are expected to be $27.7 million, all coming at the end of Year 1. The land must be returned to its natural state at a cost of $25 million, payable at the end of Year 2.

a. Plot the project's NPV profile.

b. Should the project be accepted if r = 8%? If r = 14%? Explain your reasoning.

c. Can you think of some other capital budgeting situations where negative cash flows during or at the end of the project's life might lead to multiple IRRs?

d. What is the project's MIRR at r = 8%? At r = 14%? Does the MIRR method lead to the same accept/reject decision as the NPV method?

10-20
MIRR

Project X costs $1,000 and its cash flows are the same in Years 1 through 10. Its IRR is 12%, and its WACC is 10%. What is the project's MIRR?

Challenging Problems 21–24

10-21
Present Value of Costs

The Aubey Coffee Company is evaluating the within-plant distribution system for its new roasting, grinding, and packing plant. The two alternatives are (1) a conveyor system with a high initial cost but low annual operating costs, and (2) several forklift trucks, which cost less but have considerably higher operating costs. The decision to construct the plant has already been made, and the choice here will have no effect on the overall revenues of the project. The cost of capital for the plant is 10%, and the projects' expected net costs are listed in the table:

| | Expected Net Cost | |
Year	Conveyor	Forklift
0	$(250,000)	$(120,000)
1	(65,000)	(90,000)
2	(65,000)	(90,000)
3	(65,000)	(90,000)
4	(65,000)	(90,000)
5	(65,000)	(90,000)

What is the present value of costs of each alternative? Which method should be chosen?

10-22

Payback, NPV, and MIRR

Your division is considering two investment projects, each of which requires an up-front expenditure of $25 million. You estimate that the cost of capital is 10% and that the investments will produce the following after-tax cash flows (in millions of dollars):

Year	Project A	Project B
1	5	20
2	10	10
3	15	8
4	20	6

a. What is the regular payback period for each of the projects?
b. What is the discounted payback period for each of the projects?
c. If the two projects are independent and the cost of capital is 10%, which project or projects should the firm undertake?
d. If the two projects are mutually exclusive and the cost of capital is 5%, which project should the firm undertake?
e. If the two projects are mutually exclusive and the cost of capital is 15%, which project should the firm undertake?
f. What is the crossover rate?
g. If the cost of capital is 10%, what is the modified IRR (MIRR) of each project?

10-23

Economic Life

The Scampini Supplies Company recently purchased a new delivery truck. The new truck cost $31,000, and it is expected to generate net after-tax operating cash flows, of $8,300 per year. The truck has a 5-year expected life. The expected proceeds upon sale after tax adjustments for the truck are given below. The company's cost of capital is 11%.

Year	Annual Operating Cash Flow	Proceeds upon Sale
0	$(31,000)	$31,000
1	8,300	24,000
2	8,300	19,200
3	8,300	15,500
4	8,300	8,500
5	8,300	0

a. Should the firm operate the truck until the end of its 5-year physical life? If not, what is its optimal economic life?
b. Would including the proceeds from selling an asset, in addition to operating cash flows, ever *reduce* the expected NPV and/or IRR of a project?

10-24

NPV and IRR

A store has 5 years remaining on its lease in a mall. Rent is $2,000 per month, 60 payments remain, and the next payment is due in 1 month. The mall's owner plans to sell the property in a year and wants rent at that time to be high so that the property will appear more valuable. Therefore, the store has been offered a "great deal" (mall owner's words) on a new 5-year lease. The new lease calls for no rent for 9 months, then payments of $2,600 per month for the next 51 months. The lease cannot be broken, and the store's WACC is 12% (or 1% per month).
a. Should the new lease be accepted? (*Hint:* Be sure to use 1% per month.)
b. If the store owner decided to bargain with the mall's owner over the new lease payment, what new lease payment would make the store owner indifferent between the new and old leases? (*Hint:* Find the FV of the old lease's original cost at t = 9, then treat this as the PV of a 51-period annuity whose payments represent the rent during months 10 to 60).
c. The store owner is not sure of the 12% WACC—it could be higher or lower. At what *nominal* WACC would the store owner be indifferent between the two leases? (*Hint:* Calculate the differences between the two payment streams, and then find IRR.)

Spreadsheet Problem

10-25

Build a Model:
Capital Budgeting
Tools

Start with the partial model in the file *Ch 10 Build a Model.xlsx* from the textbook's website. Gardial Fisheries is considering two mutually exclusive investments. The projects' expected net cash flows are as follows:

	Expected Net Cash Flows	
Year	Project A	Project B
0	$(375)	$(575)
1	(300)	190
2	(200)	190
3	(100)	190
4	600	190
5	600	190
6	926	190
7	(200)	0

a.   If you were told that each project's cost of capital was 12%, which project should be selected? If the cost of capital was 18%, what would be the proper choice?
b.   Construct NPV profiles for Projects A and B.
c.   What is each project's IRR?
d.   What is the crossover rate, and what is its significance?
e.   What is each project's MIRR at a cost of capital of 12%? At r = 18%? (*Hint:* Consider Period 7 as the end of Project B's life.)
f.   What is the regular payback period for these two projects?
g.   At a cost of capital of 12%, what is the discounted payback period for these two projects?
h.   What is the profitability index for each project if the cost of capital is 12%?

MINI CASE

You have just graduated with a business degree from a large university, and one of your favourite courses was "Today's Entrepreneurs." In fact, you enjoyed it so much you have decided you want to "be your own boss." While you were studying, your grandfather died and left you $1 million to do with as you please. You are not an inventor, and you do not have a trade skill that you can market; however, you have decided that you would like to purchase at least one established franchise in the fast-food area, maybe two (if profitable). The problem is that you have never been one to stay with any project for too long, so you figure that your time frame is 3 years. After 3 years you will go on to something else.

You have narrowed your selection down to two choices: (1) Franchise L, Lisa's Soups, Salads, & Stuff, and (2) Franchise S, Sam's Fabulous Fried Chicken. The net cash flows shown below include the price you would receive for selling the franchise in Year 3 and the forecast of how each franchise will do over the 3-year period. Franchise L's cash flows will start off slowly but will increase rather quickly as people become more health conscious, while Franchise S's cash flows will start off high but will trail off as other chicken competitors enter the marketplace and as people become more health conscious and avoid fried foods. Franchise L serves breakfast and lunch, while Franchise S serves only dinner, so it is possible for you to invest in both franchises. You see these franchises as perfect complements to each other: You could attract both the lunch and dinner crowds and the health-conscious and not so health-conscious crowds without the franchises directly competing against each other.

Here are the net cash flows (in thousands of dollars):

	Expected Net Cash Flow	
Year	Franchise L	Franchise S
0	$(100)	$(100)
1	10	70
2	60	50
3	80	20

Depreciation, salvage values, net working capital requirements, and tax effects are all included in these cash flows.

You also have made subjective risk assessments of each franchise, and concluded that both franchises have risk characteristics that require a return of 10%. You must now determine whether one or both of the franchises should be accepted.

a. What is capital budgeting?
b. What is the difference between independent and mutually exclusive projects?
c. (1) Define the term "*net present value (NPV)*." What is each franchise's NPV?
    (2) What is the rationale behind the NPV method? According to NPV, which franchise or franchises should be accepted if they are independent? Mutually exclusive?
    (3) How would the NPVs change if the cost of capital changed?
d. (1) Define the term "*internal rate of return (IRR)*." What is each franchise's IRR?
    (2) How is the IRR on a project related to the YTM on a bond?
    (3) What is the logic behind the IRR method? According to IRR, which franchises should be accepted if they are independent? Mutually exclusive?
    (4) How would the franchises' IRRs change if the cost of capital changed?
e. (1) Draw NPV profiles for Franchises L and S. At what discount rate do the profiles cross?
    (2) Look at your NPV profile graph without referring to the actual NPVs and IRRs. Which franchise or franchises should be accepted if they are independent? Mutually exclusive? Explain. Are your answers correct at any cost of capital less than 23.6%?
f. (1) What is the underlying cause of ranking conflicts between NPV and IRR?
    (2) What is the "reinvestment rate assumption," and how does it affect the NPV versus IRR conflict?
    (3) Which method is the best? Why?
g. (1) Define the term "*modified IRR (MIRR)*." Find the MIRRs for Franchises L and S.
    (2) What are the MIRR's advantages and disadvantages vis-à-vis the regular IRR? What are the MIRR's advantages and disadvantages vis-à-vis the NPV?
h. As a separate project (Project P), you are considering sponsoring a pavilion at the upcoming World's Fair. The pavilion would cost $800,000, and it is expected to result in $5 million of incremental cash inflows during its first year of operation. However, it would then take another year, and $5 million of costs, to demolish the site and return it to its original condition. Thus, Project P's expected net cash flows look like this (in millions of dollars):

Year	Net Cash Flows
0	$(0.8)
1	5.0
2	(5.0)

The project is estimated to be of average risk, so its cost of capital is 10%.
    (1) What are normal and non-normal cash flows?
    (2) What is Project P's NPV? What is its IRR? Its MIRR?
    (3) Draw Project P's NPV profile. Does Project P have normal or non-normal cash flows? Should this project be accepted?
i. What does the profitability index (PI) measure? What are the PIs of Franchises S and L?
j. (1) What is the payback period? Find the regular and discounted paybacks for Franchises L and S.
    (2) What is the rationale for the payback method? According to the payback criterion, which franchise or franchises should be accepted if the firm's maximum acceptable payback is 2 years, and if Franchises L and S are independent? If they are mutually exclusive?
    (3) What is the difference between the regular and discounted payback periods?
    (4) What is the main disadvantage of discounted payback? Is the payback method of any real usefulness in capital budgeting decisions?
k. In an unrelated analysis, you have the opportunity to choose between the following two mutually exclusive projects:

	Expected Net Cash Flows	
Year	Project S	Project L
0	$(100,000)	$(100,000)
1	60,000	33,500
2	60,000	33,500
3	—	33,500
4	—	33,500

The projects provide a necessary service, so whichever one is selected is expected to be repeated into the foreseeable future. Both projects have a 10% cost of capital.

(1) What is each project's initial NPV?

(2) What is each project's equivalent annual annuity?

l. You are also considering another project that has a physical life of 3 years; that is, the machinery will be totally worn out after 3 years. However, if the project were terminated prior to the end of 3 years, the machinery would have a positive salvage value. Here are the project's estimated cash flows:

Year	Initial Investment and Operating Cash Flows	End-of-Year Net Salvage Value
0	$(5,000)	$5,000
1	2,100	3,100
2	2,000	2,000
3	1,750	0

Using the 10% cost of capital, what is the project's NPV if it is operated for the full 3 years? Would the NPV change if the company planned to terminate the project at the end of Year 2? At the end of Year 1? What is the project's optimal (economic) life?

m. After examining all the potential projects, you discover that there are many more projects this year with positive NPVs than in a normal year. What two problems might this extra-large capital budget cause?

chapter 11

Cash Flow Estimation and Risk Analysis

In the previous chapter we discussed the Canadian oil sands industry, its size, and the huge amounts of money, human resources, and material it needs. We also discussed just a few of the many decisions companies must make regarding investments in mining, processing, and transportation projects. Let's now take a closer look at a "typical" oil sands project and some of the cash flows that must be estimated to evaluate its economic potential. The project we'll consider is an oil sands mine that extracts and ships bitumen. The size of the mine must first be determined. Three hundred million recoverable barrels of oil over a 30-year period might be typical for such a project. The capital costs for plant and equipment to mine and process the bitumen must also be calculated. Oil sands operations are capital intensive (and very large); therefore an investment of $1.3 billion might be realistic. Yearly operating costs for labour, natural gas, and bitumen transportation would also have to be forecast. Royalties must also be paid to government. We would need to forecast oil prices for the project. As well, since oil sands oil typically trades at a discount to conventional oil, the discount (or differential) would have to be accounted for. Foreign exchange rates would need to be forecast as revenue from sales are in U.S. dollars while many costs are in Canadian dollars. A discount rate would have to be chosen. Ten percent is a rule-of-thumb rate for such projects.

Project evaluation is always difficult, but it is even more so when there is a high degree of uncertainty in key cash flows. For example, capital costs for large projects such as a mine are notorious for exceeding budget, due to the limited availability of skilled workers as well as upward price pressures for steel and cement. Project delays are also a concern. A 2-year construction delay in our project could reduce its NPV by over $70 million. Oil prices are difficult to determine since they are influenced by international events. If actual prices were 10% lower than our forecast, over $200 million of our project's value would be lost. A 5% swing in exchange rates against our forecast could lower the project's value by another $100 million. A 1%–2% increase in the discount rate could add or subtract hundreds of millions of dollars from our project's NPV. In this chapter, we describe techniques for estimating a project's cash flows and their associated risk. As you read this chapter, think about how companies might use these techniques to evaluate their capital budgeting decisions.

Source: Adapted from BMO Capital Markets, "Valuation Review," May 10, 2013.

The basic principles of capital budgeting were covered in Chapter 10. Given a project's expected cash flows, it is easy to calculate its NPV, IRR, MIRR, PI, payback, and discounted payback. Unfortunately, cash flows are rarely just given—rather, managers must estimate them based on information collected from sources both inside and outside the company. Moreover, uncertainty surrounds the cash flow estimates, and some projects are riskier than others. In the first part of this chapter, we develop procedures for estimating the cash flows associated with capital budgeting projects. Then, in the second part, we discuss techniques used to measure and take account of project risk.

11.1 Estimating Cash Flows

The textbook's website contains an *Excel* file that will guide you through the chapter's calculations. The file for this chapter is **Ch 11 Tool Kit.xlsx,** and we encourage you to open the file and follow along as you read the chapter. **www .nelson.com/brigham3ce**

The most important, but also the most difficult, step in capital budgeting is estimating **project cash flows.** Many variables are involved, and many individuals and departments participate in the process. For example, the forecasts of unit sales and sales prices are normally made by the marketing group, based on their knowledge of price elasticity, advertising effects, the state of the economy, competitors' reactions, and trends in consumers' tastes. Similarly, the capital outlays associated with a new product are generally obtained from the engineering and product development staffs, while operating costs are estimated by cost accountants, production experts, personnel specialists, purchasing agents, and so forth.

A proper analysis includes (1) obtaining information from various departments such as engineering and marketing, (2) ensuring that everyone involved with the forecast uses a consistent set of realistic economic assumptions, and (3) making sure that no biases are inherent in the forecasts. This last point is extremely important, because some managers become emotionally involved with pet projects, and others seek to build empires. Both problems cause cash flow forecast biases that make bad projects look good—on paper!

It is vital to identify the *relevant cash flows*, defined as the specific set of cash flows that should be considered in the decision at hand. Analysts often make errors in estimating cash flows, but two cardinal rules can help you minimize mistakes: (1) Capital budgeting decisions must be based on *cash flows*, not accounting income. (2) Only *incremental cash flows* are relevant.

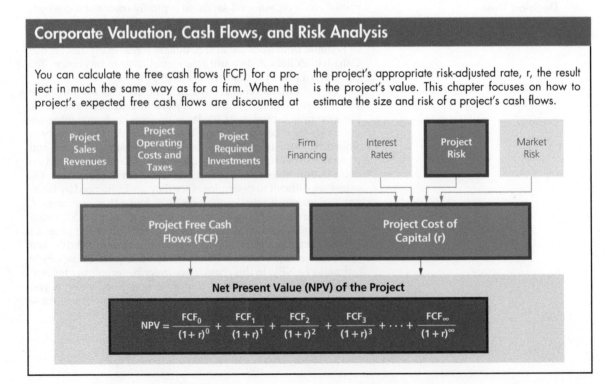

Corporate Valuation, Cash Flows, and Risk Analysis

You can calculate the free cash flows (FCF) for a project in much the same way as for a firm. When the project's expected free cash flows are discounted at the project's appropriate risk-adjusted rate, r, the result is the project's value. This chapter focuses on how to estimate the size and risk of a project's cash flows.

Project Sales Revenues · Project Operating Costs and Taxes · Project Required Investments · Firm Financing · Interest Rates · Project Risk · Market Risk

Project Free Cash Flows (FCF)

Project Cost of Capital (r)

Net Present Value (NPV) of the Project

$$\text{NPV} = \frac{\text{FCF}_0}{(1+r)^0} + \frac{\text{FCF}_1}{(1+r)^1} + \frac{\text{FCF}_2}{(1+r)^2} + \frac{\text{FCF}_3}{(1+r)^3} + \cdots + \frac{\text{FCF}_\infty}{(1+r)^\infty}$$

Incremental cash flows are the differences between the cash flows the firm will have if it goes ahead with the project versus the cash flows it will have if it rejects the project:

$$\begin{matrix} \text{Incremental} \\ \text{cash flows} \end{matrix} = \begin{matrix} \text{Company's cash} \\ \text{flows } with \text{ the project} \end{matrix} - \begin{matrix} \text{Company's cash flows} \\ without \text{ the project} \end{matrix}$$

Recall from Chapter 2 that free cash flow (FCF) is the cash flow available for distribution to investors. In a nutshell, the relevant cash flow for a project is the *additional* free cash flow that the company can expect if it implements the project. This is also called the **incremental cash flow,** and it is the cash flow above and beyond what the company could expect if it doesn't implement the project. It is common in capital budgeting analysis to break down the project's free cash flow into the components shown in Equation 11-1:

$$\text{FCF} = \begin{matrix} \text{Investment outlay} \\ \text{cash flow} \end{matrix} + \begin{matrix} \text{Operating} \\ \text{cash flow} \end{matrix} + \begin{matrix} \text{NOWC} \\ \text{cash flow} \end{matrix} + \begin{matrix} \text{Salvage} \\ \text{cash flow} \end{matrix} \qquad (11\text{-}1)$$

The investment outlay cash flow captures the cash that is used to invest in the project's gross fixed assets. Although some projects require expenditures on fixed assets at different times during their lives, most require only an initial investment outlay. The operating cash flow component consists of the project's cash inflows from revenues and outflows from cash operating expenses. It is also an after-tax cash flow. And although depreciation is not a cash expense, it does affect cash flows by lowering taxes; therefore, the effect of depreciation is also included. The net operating working capital (NOWC) cash flow accounts for any change in working capital resulting from the project. For example, inventory, accounts receivable, and accounts payable values may all change and those cash flows are all captured in the NOWC component. Finally, the salvage value cash flow recognizes that a project's fixed assets may have some value upon project completion and thus must also be accounted for.

It is worth mentioning that project analysis focuses on expected cash flows, not accounting net income. Accounting net income is based on the depreciation rate the firm's accountants choose, not necessarily the depreciation rates allowed by the Canada Revenue Agency. Also, net income is measured after the deduction of interest expenses, whereas net cash flow focuses on operating cash flow. Moreover, the investment in working capital is not deducted from accounting income. For these and other reasons, net income is generally different from cash flow. Each has a role in financial management, *but for capital budgeting purposes it is the project's net cash flow, not its accounting net income, that is relevant.*

Changes in Net Operating Working Capital

Normally, additional inventories are required to support a new operation, and expanded sales tie up additional funds in accounts receivable. However, payables and accruals also increase as a result of the expansion, and this reduces the cash needed to finance inventories and receivables. The difference between the required increase in operating current assets and the increase in operating current liabilities is the change in net operating working capital. If this change is positive, as it generally is for expansion projects, then additional financing, over and above the cost of the fixed assets, will be needed.

Toward the end of a project's life, inventories will be used but not replaced, and receivables will be collected without corresponding replacements. As these changes occur, the firm will receive cash inflows, and as a result, the investment in net operating working capital will be returned by the end of the project's life.

Interest Expenses Are Not Included in Project Cash Flows

Interest is a cash expense, so at first glance it would seem that interest on any debt used to finance a project should be deducted when we estimate the project's net cash flows. However, this is not correct. Recall from Chapter 10 that we discount a project's cash flows by its risk-adjusted cost of capital, which is a weighted average (WACC) of the costs of debt, preferred shares, and common equity, adjusted for the project's risk and debt capacity. This project cost of capital is the rate of return necessary to satisfy *all* of the firm's investors, including shareholders and debtholders. A common mistake made by many students and financial managers is to subtract interest payments when estimating a project's cash flows.

This is a mistake because the cost of debt is already embedded in the cost of capital, so subtracting interest payments from the project's cash flows would amount to double-counting interest costs. Therefore, *you should not subtract interest expenses when finding a project's cash flows.*

Sunk Costs

A **sunk cost** is a cash outlay related to the project that was incurred in the past and that cannot be recovered in the future regardless of whether or not the project is accepted. Therefore, sunk costs are *not incremental costs* and thus are not relevant in a capital budgeting analysis. For example, suppose Hudson's Bay spent $1 million to investigate sites for a potential new store in a given area. That $1 million is a sunk cost—the money is gone, and it won't come back regardless of whether or not a new store is built. Therefore, the $1 million should not be included in a capital budgeting decision.

Marketing or feasibility reports are often carried out before a decision is made to invest in a new product or to expand distribution into a new market. If the NPV analysis takes place after the marketing study, those cash expenses should not be included for capital budgeting purposes. Some may argue that since the study's costs were directly related to the project, they ought to be included in the NPV calculation. That is incorrect. No matter what decision is made regarding the project, those expenses have already occurred—they are *sunk*, and nothing you can do now (i.e., go ahead or don't go ahead) will change that.

Opportunity Costs

Another issue relates to **opportunity costs** related to assets the firm already owns. Suppose Hudson's Bay estimates it will cost $54 million for land and construction costs to build a new store. However, the company owns land with a current market value of $5 million that can be used for the new store if it decides to build the store. If Hudson's Bay goes forward with the project, only another $49 million will be required, not the full $54 million, because it will not need to buy the required land. Does this mean that Hudson's Bay should use the $49 million incremental cost as the cost of the new store? The answer is definitely "no." If the new store is *not* built, then Hudson's Bay could sell the land and receive cash flow of $5 million. This $5 million is an *opportunity cost*— it is cash that Hudson's Bay would not receive if the land is used for the new store. Therefore, the $5 million must be charged to the new project, and failing to do so would cause the new project's calculated NPV to be too high.

Effects on Other Parts of the Firm: Externalities

Economists define **externalities** as the effects a project has on other parts of the firm or on the environment. For example, Apple's introduction of the iPad caused some people who were planning to purchase a regular iPod touch to switch to an iPad. The iPad generates positive cash flows, but it also reduces some of the company's current cash flows. This type of externality is called a *cannibalization effect*, because the new business eats into the company's existing business. The lost cash flows should be charged to the new project. However, it often turns out that if the one company does not produce a new product, some other company will, so the old cash flows would be lost anyway. In this case, no charge should be assessed against the new project. All of this makes determining the cannibalization effect difficult, because it requires estimates of changes in sales and costs, and also of the timing of when those changes will occur. Still, cannibalization can be important, so its potential effects should be considered.

Note that externalities can be positive as well as negative. For example, Apple's music iPods were profitable products. Then, when Apple considered investing in its music store, it realized that the store would boost sales of iPods. So even if an analysis of the proposed music store indicated a negative NPV, the analysis would not be complete unless the incremental cash flows that would occur in the iPod division were credited to the music store. Consideration of positive externalities often changes a project's NPV from negative to positive.

Firms must also be concerned with *environmental externalities*. For example, a manufacturer may be planning a new plant that would give off noxious fumes that, while not severe enough to trigger governmental actions, would still cause ill feelings in the plant's neighbourhood. Those ill feelings might not show up in the cash flow analysis, but they should still be considered. Perhaps a relatively small expenditure could correct the problem and keep the firm from suffering future ill will that might be costly in some hard-to-measure way.

Rather than focusing narrowly on the project at hand, analysts must anticipate the project's impact on the rest of the firm. This requires imagination and creative thinking. It is critical to identify and account for all externalities when evaluating a proposed project.

Expansion Projects and Replacement Projects

Two types of projects can be distinguished: (1) *expansion projects*, in which the firm makes an investment; for example, a company building a new call centre in Mississauga; and (2) *replacement projects*, in which a company replaces existing assets, generally to reduce costs. In expansion projects, the cash expenditures on buildings, equipment, and required working capital are obviously incremental, as are the sales revenues and operating costs associated with the project. The incremental costs associated with replacement projects are not so obvious. In a replacement analysis, the company is comparing its value if it takes on the new project to its value if it continues to use the existing one. For example, the fuel bill for a more efficient truck might be $10,000 per year versus $15,000 for the old truck. Here, the $5,000 fuel savings would be an incremental cash flow associated with the replacement decision. We analyze an expansion and replacement decision later in the chapter.

Timing of Cash Flows

We must account properly for the timing of cash flows. Accounting income statements are for periods such as years or months, so they do not reflect exactly when during the period cash revenues or expenses occur. Because of the time value of money, capital budgeting cash flows should in theory be analyzed exactly as they occur. Of course, there must be a compromise between accuracy and feasibility. A time line with daily cash flows would in theory be most accurate, but daily cash flow estimates would be costly to construct, unwieldy to use, and probably no more accurate than annual cash flow estimates because we simply cannot forecast well enough to warrant this degree of detail. Therefore, in most cases, we simply assume that all cash flows occur at the end of every year. However, for some projects, it may be useful to assume that cash flows occur at mid-year, or even quarterly or monthly.

Adjusting for Inflation

Inflation (or deflation) occurs in Canada and other countries, so it should be considered in a capital budgeting analysis. Individual cash flow components should be adjusted to reflect expected inflation. For instance, it is possible for a company to increase product prices at a rate different than their component input costs. Forgetting to include inflation in a capital budgeting analysis normally causes the estimated NPV to be lower than the true NPV; this could cause a company to reject a project it should have accepted.[1] Our analysis of an expansion project example later in the chapter illustrates incorporating inflation into our cash flows.

CONCEPT REVIEW

1. What is the most important step in a capital budgeting analysis?
2. What are the major components of a project's free cash flows?
3. What is net operating working capital, and how does it affect a project's cash flows in capital budgeting?
4. Explain the following terms: sunk cost, opportunity cost, externality, and cannibalization.

---

[1] The market's estimate of expected inflation is already incorporated into the cost of debt (via the inflation premium) and the cost of equity (via the risk-free rate in the CAPM), so the project's cost of capital includes the effect of expected inflation. If you don't also include the effect of inflation in projected cash flows, then the cash flows will be too low relative to the cost of capital, leading to a downward-biased NPV estimate.

11.2 Capital Cost Allowance

Since we are concerned with estimating after-tax project cash flows, it is important to understand how depreciation affects taxes, which represents a cash outflow. Let's assume that there are two companies in the same industry, with identical sales and expenses. In fact, the only difference is that Company B claims depreciation whereas Company A does not. We will also assume that all sales and expenses are for cash. Table 11-1 summarizes their earnings and cash flows. As we would expect, Company B has lower earnings since it has higher expenses. But we also see that B has higher cash flow than A. Given that both had exactly the same sales, expenses, and tax rate, and that depreciation is *not* a cash expense, how do we account for the difference in cash flows? Although depreciation is indeed a noncash item, it is tax deductible, and therefore Company B pays less tax. In effect, depreciation shields some earnings from taxes, and since taxes are a cash expense, it indirectly increases cash flows. You will also notice that the difference in cash flows of $3,000 is the same as the difference in taxes.

Companies will try to claim as much depreciation—that is, CCA (as you recall from Chapter 2, capital cost allowance, CCA, is depreciation for tax purposes)—as allowed when calculating their taxes. There is a simple method for calculating how much of a tax shield, and therefore cash flow, CCA will generate for a company.

$$\text{CCA tax shield} = \text{CCA amount} \times \text{Tax rate} \qquad (11\text{-}2)$$

For the example in Table 11-1, using Equation 11-2, the CCA tax shield for company B is $10,000 \times 30\% = \$3,000$.

Canada Revenue Agency (CRA) publishes specific rules and rates that companies must use when calculating CCA. Capital assets fall into one of more than 40 CCA asset groups or "classes." The asset classes determine the maximum CCA rate a company may claim per year. These rates vary widely, from 4% to 100%. Most CCAs are calculated on a declining balance basis—that is, each year's CCA is based on the year-end **undepreciated capital cost (UCC)**. Several classes, though, are calculated "straight line" on the original capital cost. Table 11-2 lists some of the more commonly used asset classes.

For example, let's say that a company has a $250,000 capital asset with a 20% CCA rate whose year-end UCC is $150,000. If the 20% is a declining balance rate, the current CCA for the year will be $150,000 \times 20\% = \$30,000$. However, if the 20% is a straight-line rate, the company will be able to claim $250,000, \times 20\% = \$50,000$.

Included in capital costs are costs (if any) related to delivery, installation, and staff training that pertain to the capital asset. Also, there is a **half-year rule** whereby companies may claim only half the capital cost in the first year they acquired the asset. Thus, a company

TABLE 11-1 Effect of Depreciation on Income and Cash Flow

	Company A	Company B
Sales	$100,000	$100,000
Cost of goods sold	30,000	30,000
Gross profit	70,000	70,000
Operating expenses	50,000	50,000
Depreciation	0	10,000
Earnings before tax	20,000	10,000
Tax (30%)	6,000	3,000
Net income	14,000	7,000
Add back depreciation	0	10,000
Cash flow	14,000	17,000

11-2   Common Asset Classes

Class	Description	Rate
1[a]	Buildings	4%
8	Machinery, equipment, furniture	20%
10	Vehicles	30%
12	Computer software	100%
13	Leasehold improvements	Straight line; use lesser of 5 years or the lease term
43	Manufacturing assets	30%
50	Computer hardware	55%

[a] Like most everything else with taxes, it's never straightforward. In the 2007 federal budget, the government changed the rate to 10%, but *only* for buildings used primarily for manufacturing.

with an asset (CCA rate of 30%) costing $10,000 will for the first year be able to claim CCA of 50% × $10,000 × 30% = $1,500. The rationale behind the half-year rule is that companies normally try to claim as much CCA as possible in order to lower taxes; the rule discourages companies from purchasing assets right before year-end and then taking a full year of CCA.

Companies calculate CCA not on individual assets, but rather by asset class. Thus, if a company currently has three assets in the same asset class with a total UCC of $50,000 (CCA rate of 20%), and another asset is purchased during the year at a cost of $10,000, the company can claim CCA for the year of ($50,000 × 20%) + (50% × $10,000 × 20%) = $11,000. The UCC at year-end for all four assets will be $60,000 − $11,000 = $49,000.

It is not uncommon for companies to purchase and dispose of assets within the same class during the year in the normal course of business. For purposes of calculating CCA, when there is a purchase and sale of assets within the same asset class in the same year, CCA is calculated on the capital cost of the new asset minus the lesser of the original capital cost *or* the net proceeds from the asset disposed. This is called the **net acquisition.** If the net acquisition is positive, the half-year rule will again apply.

When a company disposes of the last asset in an asset class and the disposition value is greater than the UCC remaining, the asset class will be in a negative balance. The company closes the asset class and calculates **CCA recapture.** A company generates recapture when the proceeds from the asset sale are greater than the undepreciated amount remaining. The company has in fact claimed too much CCA, resulting in too little tax being paid, and now it must add back the extra CCA (which is fully taxable) to income to pay back the extra tax it had previously saved.

If, however, the proceeds from the asset sale are less than the remaining UCC in the asset class, and there are no other assets in that class, that asset class will have a positive UCC remaining balance. The asset class will be closed and the company will claim a **terminal loss**, which allows the remaining UCC to be deducted against income. For our purposes, we usually assume that the asset classes remain open, thus avoiding terminal losses or recaptures. This is reasonable, given that most companies have ongoing operations and maintain multiple assets per class even when certain assets are sold off.

Let's look at a company that incorporated on February 25, 2012, and purchased a truck for $30,000 on April 14, 2012. The company purchased two small excavators for $20,000 each on June 1, 2014. The following year, on March 20, 2015, the company traded the truck and, with an additional $12,000 cash, purchased a bulldozer. Finally, consider the tax consequences if on November 1, 2015, the company sold one excavator for (a) $10,000 or (b) $22,000. All the above assets fall into Class 10, which has a 30% CCA rate.

Because the company had just started business, it had no other assets in this class, so the beginning UCC was $0. The truck purchase added $30,000 to the company's Class 10 asset pool. For the year, the company was able to claim CCA of 50% × $30,000 × 30% = $4,500 (the 50% reflecting the half-year rule). For 2013, the company started with UCC of $30,000 − $4,500 = $25,500. The company did not add or dispose of any Class 10 assets during 2013, so the CCA could be claimed on UCC of $25,500.

TABLE 11-3	Example of Asset Purchases and Sales				
Year	Beginning UCC	Additions or Disposals to Asset Class	Proceeds	UCC Before CCA	CCA Taken
2012	$ 0	$30,000	–	$30,000	$ 4,500
2013	25,500	–	–	25,500	7,650
2014	17,850	40,000	–	57,850	11,355
2015	46,495	12,000	(a) $10,000	48,495	14,249
		12,000	(b) 20,000	38,495	11,549

For 2014, there was a beginning UCC balance of $17,850. The company then purchased two excavators at a total cost of $40,000. The UCC balance was now $17,850 + $40,000 = $57,850; thus, CCA for the year was ($17,850 × 30%) + (50% × $40,000 × 30%) = $11,355.

In 2015, the company traded the truck plus $12,000 for a bulldozer. It also (a) sold one excavator for $10,000. CCA could now be taken on the beginning UCC $46,495 × 30% = $13,949, and CCA could also be taken on the net acquisition—that is, the difference between the incremental purchase of $12,000 and the $10,000 excavator sale ($12,000 − $10,000) × 50% × 30% = $300. The total CCA for 2015 (a) was thus $13,949 + $300 = $14,249.

In (b), the excavator sold for $22,000. Since the original cost was $20,000, we use $20,000 as the deemed proceeds—that is, the original capital cost or proceeds of disposition, whichever is less. The company has reduced its UCC by $8,000, so the total is now $38,495. The CCA for 2015 is $38,495 × 30% = $11,549. In addition, there is a $2,000 capital gain to be claimed, of which 50% × $2,000 must be included in income. Table 11-3 summarizes the transactions.

11.3 Analysis of an Expansion Project

We illustrate the principles of capital budgeting analysis by examining a new project being considered by Regency Integrated Chips (RIC), a large Ottawa-based technology company. This is a *new expansion project*, defined as one where the firm invests in new assets to increase sales. Following is some background information on the project.

Background on the Project

RIC's research and development department has been applying its expertise in microprocessor technology to develop a small computer designed to control home appliances. Once programmed, the computer will automatically control the heating and air-conditioning systems, security system, hot water heater, and even small appliances such as a coffeemaker. By increasing a home's energy efficiency, the computer can cut costs enough to pay for itself within a few years. Development has now reached the stage where a decision must be made about whether to go forward with full-scale production.

RIC's marketing vice president believes that annual sales would be 20,000 units if the units were priced at $3,000 each, so annual sales are estimated at $60 million. RIC expects no growth in unit sales, and it believes that the unit price will rise by 2% each year. The engineering department has reported that the project will require additional manufacturing space, and RIC currently has an option to purchase an existing building, at a cost of $12 million, that would meet this need. The building would be bought and paid for on December 31, 2016. The building falls into Class 1 (4%) for CCA purposes.

The necessary equipment would be purchased and installed in late 2016, and it would be paid for on December 31, 2016. The equipment falls into CCA Class 43 (30%). The equipment would cost $7.8 million and would require $0.2 million for shipping and installation. CCA may be claimed on the purchase price of an asset plus any shipping and installation costs.

The project's estimated economic life is 4 years. At the end of that time, the building is expected to have a resale value of $10 million; the equipment will have a salvage value of $2 million.

The production department has estimated that variable manufacturing costs would be $2,100 per unit and that fixed overhead costs would be $8 million a year. They expect variable costs to rise by 2% per year and fixed costs to rise by 1% per year.

RIC's tax rate is 30%; its cost of capital is 12%; and, for capital budgeting purposes, the company's policy is to assume that operating cash flows occur at the end of each year. Because the plant would begin operations on January 1, 2017, the first full year of operating cash flows would end on December 31, 2017.

Several other points should be noted: (1) RIC is a relatively large corporation, with sales of more than $4 billion, and it takes on many investments each year. Thus, if the computer control project does not work out, it will not bankrupt the company—management can afford to take a chance on the computer control project. (2) If the project is accepted, the company will be contractually obligated to operate it for its full 4-year life. Management must make this commitment to its component suppliers. (3) Returns on this project would be positively correlated with returns on RIC's other projects and also with the stock market—the project should do well if other parts of the firm and the general economy are strong.

Assume that you have been assigned to conduct the capital budgeting analysis. For now, assume that the project has the same risk as an average project and use the corporate weighted average cost of capital, 12%.

Estimation of the Cash Flows

Most projects are analyzed using a spreadsheet program such as *Excel*, and this one is no exception. The analysis is shown in Table 11-4 and is divided into four parts: (1) Input Data, (2) CCA Schedule, (3) Projected Net Cash Flows, and (4) Key Output. Note that numbers in the printed table are rounded from the actual numbers in the spreadsheet, although the spreadsheet uses unrounded numbers for all calculations.

See **Ch 11 Tool Kit.xlsx** at the textbook's website for all calculations.

TABLE 11-4   Analysis of a New (Expansion) Project: Parts 1 and 2 (Dollars in Thousands)

	A	B	C	D	E	F	G	H	I
21									
22									
23									
24	**Part 1. Input Data**								
25							Key Output: NPV	=	$9,122
26	Building cost (Capital cost)			$12,000					
27	Equipment cost (Capital cost)			$8,000		Salvage value of building			$10,000
28	Net operating WC/Sales			10%		Salvage value of equipment			$2,000
29	First year sales (in units)			20,000		Tax rate			30%
30	Growth rate in units sold			0.0%		WACC			12.0%
31	Sales price per unit			$3.00		Inflation: growth in sales price			2.0%
32	Variable cost per unit			$2.10		Inflation: growth in VC per unit			2.0%
33	Fixed costs			$8,000		Inflation: growth in fixed costs			1.0%
34	Building CCA rate (Class 1)			4%					
35	Equipment CCA rate (Class 43)			30%					
36									
37	**Part 2. CCA Schedules**								
38	Building					Equipment			
39	Years	UCC before CCA	CCA	UCC after CCA		Years	UCC before CCA	CCA	UCC after CCA
40	2017	$12,000	$240	$11,760		2017	$8,000	$1,200	$6,800
41	2018	$11,760	$470	$11,290		2018	$6,800	$2,040	$4,760
42	2019	$11,290	$452	$10,838		2019	$4,760	$1,428	$3,332
43	2020	$10,838	$434	$10,404		2020	$3,332	$1,000	$2,332
44									
45									

(continued)

TABLE
11-4 Analysis of a New (Expansion) Project: Part 3 (Dollars in Thousands) (continued)

	A	B	C	D	E	F	G	H	I
46									
47	Part 3. Projected Net Cash Flows						Years		
48					0	1	2	3	4
49					2016	2017	2018	2019	2020
50	*Investment Outlays: Long-Term Assets*								
51	Building				($12,000)				
52	Equipment				(8,000)				
53									
54	*Operating Cash Flows over the Project's Life*								
55	Units sold					20,000	20,000	20,000	20,000
56	Sales price					$3.00	$3.06	$3.12	$3.18
57	Sales revenue					$60,000	$61,200	$62,424	$63,672
58	Variable costs					42,000	42,840	43,697	44,571
59	Fixed operating costs					8,000	8,080	8,161	8,242
60	CCA (building)					240	470	452	434
61	CCA (equipment)					1,200	2,040	1,428	1,000
62	Oper. income before taxes (EBIT)					8,560	7,770	8,687	9,426
63	Taxes on operating income (30%)					2,568	2,331	2,606	2,828
64	Net operating profit after taxes (NOPAT)					5,992	5,439	6,081	6,598
65	Add back CCA					1,440	2,510	1,880	1,433
66	Operating cash flow					$7,432	$7,949	$7,960	$8,031
67									
68	*Cash Flows Due to Net Operating Working Capital*								
69	Net operating working capital (based on sales)				$6,000	$6,120	$6,242	$6,367	$0
70	Cash flow due to investment in NOWC				($6,000)	($120)	($122)	($125)	$6,367
71									
72	*Salvage Cash Flows: Long-Term Assets*								
73	Salvage value cash flow: Building								$10,000
74	Salvage value cash flow: Equipment								2,000
75	Total salvage value cash flows								$12,000
76									
77	Net cash flow (Time line of cash flows)				($26,000)	$7,312	$7,827	$7,836	$26,399
78									

(continued)

Input Data (Part 1) Part 1 of Table 11-4, the Input Data section, provides the basic data used in the analysis. The inputs are really "assumptions"—thus, in the analysis we *assume* that 20,000 units can be sold at a price of $3 per unit (the sales price is actually $3,000, but for convenience we show all dollars in thousands). Some of the inputs are known with near certainty—for example, the 30% tax rate is not likely to change. Others are more speculative— units sold and the variable cost percentage are in this category. Obviously, if sales or costs are different from the assumed levels, then profits and cash flows, hence NPV and IRR, will differ from their projected levels. Later in the chapter, we discuss how changes in the inputs affect the results. We usually show a key output, such as NPV, in the same section as the inputs, so that we can quickly see how a change in an input affects the output.

CCA Schedules (Part 2) Columns B and G show the undepreciated capital cost before the CCA is taken each year for the building and equipment, respectively. Columns C and H show the annual CCA amount the company may claim on each asset. As previously discussed, the CCA is calculated based on the asset's CCA rate times the UCC. Finally, Columns D and I show the UCC balance for each asset after CCA is taken. Note that the UCC after CCA balance for any given year becomes the UCC before CCA balance for the next year.

Projected Net Cash Flows (Part 3) This section of Table 11-4 uses the information developed in Parts 1 and 2 to find the projected cash flows over the project's life. Five periods are shown, from Year 0 to Year 4, in Columns E through I.

The initial investment outlays for long-term assets are shown as negative cash flows in Cells E51 and E52 for Year 0. Had there been additional fixed assets purchased during the project's life, their cash flows also would have been shown.

TABLE 11-4 Analysis of a New (Expansion) Project: Part 4 (Dollars in Thousands) (continued)

	A	B	C	D	E	F	G	H	I
79									
80	Part 4. Key Output and Appraisal of the Proposed Project (WACC = 12%)								
81									
82	Net Present Value			$9,122					
83	IRR			24.45%					
84	MIRR			20.75%					
85	PI			1.35					
86									
87							Years		
88					0	1	2	3	4
89	Cumulative cash flow for payback					(18,688)	(10,861)	(3,026)	23,373
90	Part of year required for payback:					1.00	1.00	1.00	0.11
91	Payback =			3.11					
92									
93							Years		
94					0	1	2	3	4
95	Discounted cash flow for payback:					6,529	6,239	5,577	16,777
96	Cumulative discounted cash flow					(19,471)	(13,232)	(7,655)	9,122
97	Part of year required for payback:					1.00	1.00	1.00	0.46
98	Discounted Payback =			3.46					
99									
100									

Rows 55 through 66 show the calculations for the operating cash flows. We begin with sales revenues, found as the product of units sold and the sales price. Next, we subtract variable costs, which are assumed to be $2.10 per unit. We then deduct fixed operating costs and CCA to obtain taxable operating income, or EBIT, in Row 62. When taxes (at a 30% rate) are subtracted, we are left with net operating profit after taxes, or NOPAT, in Row 64. We add back CCA to obtain annual values for operating cash flow, as shown in Row 66.

RIC must purchase raw materials and replenish them each year as they are used. In Part 1 we assume that RIC must have an amount of NOWC on hand equal to 10% of the upcoming year's sales. For example, sales in Year 1 are $60,000, so RIC must have $6,000 in NOWC at Year 0, as shown in Cell E69. Because RIC had no NOWC prior to Year 0, it must make a $6,000 investment in NOWC at Year 0, as shown in Cell E70. Sales increase to $61,200 in Year 2, so RIC must have $6,120 of NOWC at Year 1. Because it already had $6,000 in NOWC on hand, its net investment at Year 1 is just $120, shown in Cell F70. Note that RIC will have no sales after Year 4, so it will require no NOWC at Year 4. Thus, it has a positive cash flow of $6,367 at Year 4 as working capital is sold but not replaced.

When the project's life ends, the company will receive the "Salvage Cash Flows" as shown in the column for Year 4 in Rows 73 and 74. Thus, the total salvage cash flow amounts to $12,000 as shown in Row 75.

We sum the subtotals in Part 3 to obtain the net cash flows shown in Row 77. Those cash flows constitute a *cash flow time line*, and they are evaluated in Part 4 of Table 11-4.

Making the Decision

Part 4 of Table 11-4 shows the standard evaluation criteria—NPV, IRR, MIRR, PI, payback, and discounted payback—based on the cash flows shown in Row 77. The NPV is positive, the IRR and MIRR both exceed the 12% cost of capital, and the PI is greater than 1.0. Therefore, on the basis of the analysis thus far, it appears that the project should be accepted. Note, though, that we have been assuming that the project is about as risky as the company's average project. If the project were judged to be riskier than average, it would be necessary to increase the cost of capital, which might cause the NPV to become negative and leave the IRR and MIRR below the new WACC. Therefore, we cannot make a final decision until we evaluate the project's risk, the topic of a later section.

CONCEPT REVIEW

1. Refer to Table 11-4 and answer these questions:
   a. If the WACC is 15%, what is the new NPV? (Check Figure: $6,522)
   b. If the equipment's CCA rate was 5% rather than 30%, but other aspects of the project were unchanged, would the NPV increase or decrease? Why?

11.4 An Alternative Approach for Calculating Project Cash Flows

In the previous example we calculated the CCA every year that the company claimed for each capital asset used in the project. The CCA was then included with other expenses to determine taxable income and taxes. Finally, the CCA was added back to calculate operating cash flows. The net cash flows contain two distinct cash flows: those from the operating project, and those (tax savings) from the CCA.

Equation 11-2 showed a simple way to calculate the tax shield generated by CCA. We can use Equation 11-2 to determine RIC's annual tax shield created from its two capital assets. Table 11-5 shows the yearly CCA tax shield based on the annual CCA as calculated in part 2 of Table 11-4.

Obviously, if we remove the cash flow effects due to CCA, the project cash flows must be recalculated. Table 11-6 recalculates the after-tax cash flows solely from the project's operations. Notice that if we add the cash flow for 2017 of $7,000 with the CCA tax shield of $432, the total $7,432 is the same as our original 2017 operating cash flow value in Part 3 of Table 11-4.

TABLE 11-5 Annual CCA Tax Shield (Dollars in Thousands)

Year	Building CCA (1)	Equipment CCA (2)	Total CCA (1) + (2) = (3)	Tax Rate (4)	Tax Shield (3) × (4) = (5)
2017	$240	$1,200	$1,440	30%	$432
2018	470	2,040	2,510	30	753
2019	452	1,428	1,880	30	564
2020	434	1,000	1,434	30	430

TABLE 11-6 After-Tax Cash Flow Due to the Project's Operations (Dollars in Thousands)

	2017	2018	2019	2020
Sales revenue	$60,000	$61,200	$62,424	$63,672
Variable costs	42,000	42,840	43,697	44,571
Fixed operating costs	8,000	8,080	8,161	8,242
Project cash flows before tax	10,000	10,280	10,566	10,859
Taxes (30%)	3,000	3,084	3,170	3,258
Project cash flows after tax	$ 7,000	$ 7,196	$ 7,396	$ 7,601

TABLE 11-7   Calculating the Present Value of the Project's Component Cash Flows (Dollars in Thousands)

	2016	2017	2018	2019	2020	Present Value
Initial investment	$(20,000)					$(20,000)
Project cash flows after tax		$7,000	$7,196	$7,396	$ 7,601	22,082
CCA tax shield		432	753	564	430	1,661
Net operating working capital	(6,000)	(120)	(122)	(125)	6,367	(2,247)
Salvage values					12,000	7,626
					NPV =	$ 9,122

There are three other sets of cash flows in this project. We had to estimate the initial investment. For RIC this was the building at $12 million, the equipment at $7.8 million, and the $0.2 million for shipping and installation. Another set of cash flows arose from working capital requirements. There was an initial investment of $6 million; followed by yearly investments of $120,000, $122,000, and $125,000; and, finally, recovery of the cumulative amount, which was $6.367 million at the end of the project. The last set of cash flows was from the salvage values realized when the assets were sold. For RIC, these were estimated at $12 million in total.

We can calculate the present value of each set of cash flows independently, sum them, and get the same NPV as calculated in Table 11-4, Part 4. Table 11-7 summarizes each set of cash flows along with their present values.

Likely one of the most time-consuming parts of this process is calculating the present value of the CCA tax shield. First, the CCA schedules are set up; then the annual tax shield is calculated; and finally, the present value can be calculated. This can get quite tedious when the cash flows go out a number of years and multiple capital assets are used. There is a way, however, to simplify the CCA tax shield calculation. We begin by defining the following terms:

Tax shield = Annual tax shield created from claiming CCA

$\quad$ C = Capital cost of the asset

$\quad$ S = Salvage value of the asset

$\quad$ d = the CCA rate for the asset class

$\quad$ T = the corporate tax rate

$\quad$ r = discount rate

When calculating declining balance rates, we know the annual tax shield declines over time, that is, the next year's tax shield = this year's tax shield $\times$ (1 − CCA rate). The tax shield in two years = this year's tax shield $\times$ (1 − CCA rate)^2, and so on. What we wish to calculate, the present value of cash flows declining at a constant rate, is conceptually identical to the Gordon Model we used in Chapter 8 for calculating the present value of stock with a constant growing dividend stream. The primary difference is that instead of the cash flow growing each year, it is declining at a constant rate. You can think of the "growth" rate as being negative. If we ignore the half-year rule for now we can calculate the PV of the CCA tax shield for an asset held in perpetuity as follows:

$$= \frac{\text{tax shield}_1}{(1 + r)^1} + \frac{\text{tax shield}_1(1 - d)}{(1 + r)^2} + \frac{\text{tax shield}_1(1 - d)^2}{(1 + r)^3} + \cdots + \frac{\text{tax shield}_1(1 - d)^{n-1}}{(1 + r)^n} = \frac{\text{tax shield}_1}{r - (-d)}$$

$$= \frac{\text{tax shield}_1}{(r + d)}$$

Substituting the variables that determine the tax shield, the formula can be rewritten as follows:

$$\text{Present value of the CCA tax shield} = \frac{CdT}{r + d}$$

We know that only one-half of the asset is used to claim CCA in the first year, so the formula can be adjusted for the one-half year rule:

$$\left(\frac{CdT}{r + d}\right) \times \left(\frac{1 + 0.5r}{1 + r}\right)$$

Finally, our formula must calculate the *net* tax shield benefits once we sell the asset. After all, once the asset is sold we no longer derive any tax shield benefits. Therefore we need to determine the present value of the tax shield we have lost and deduct it from the perpetual tax shield value. To do this, first calculate the present value at the time of the asset sale—that is, the tax shield benefits we lost by selling the asset. That calculation is identical to the first part of our formula:

$$\frac{SdT}{r + d}$$

where S equals the salvage value of the asset. These lost or foregone tax shields are then discounted back to time zero, where they are subtracted from the full tax shield:

$$\left(\frac{SdT}{r + d}\right) \times \left(\frac{1}{(1 + r)^n}\right)$$

Putting it all together, our formula becomes:

$$\text{Present value of the CCA tax shield} = \left(\frac{CdT}{r + d}\right) \times \left(\frac{1 + 0.5r}{1 + r}\right) - \left(\frac{SdT}{r + d}\right) \times \left(\frac{1}{(1 + r)^n}\right) \quad (11\text{-}3)$$

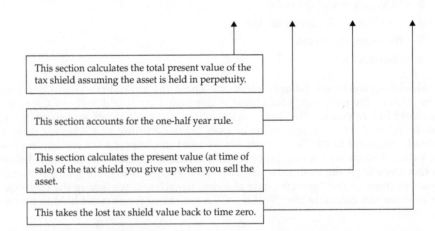

This section calculates the total present value of the tax shield assuming the asset is held in perpetuity.

This section accounts for the one-half year rule.

This section calculates the present value (at time of sale) of the tax shield you give up when you sell the asset.

This takes the lost tax shield value back to time zero.

Our formula approach assumes that the asset class remains open after the asset is sold— that is, that the asset class UCC is positive. As mentioned earlier, this is a reasonable assumption for companies disposing of old assets and reinvesting in their business. Our formula approach would not be used if a company's asset class were to close. In such a case we would also have to calculate and include in our last-year cash flows any terminal loss or CCA recapture there might be. An advantage to using the formula arises when the salvage value and UCC are different. Using our previous example, when we calculate the present value of the CCA tax shield we get:

PV of the CCA tax shield for the building:

$$\left(\frac{CdT}{r + d}\right) \times \left(\frac{1 + 0.5r}{1 + r}\right) - \left(\frac{SdT}{r + d}\right) \times \left(\frac{1}{(1 + r)^n}\right)$$

$$\left(\frac{12{,}000 \times 0.04 \times 0.30}{0.12 + 0.04}\right) \times \left(\frac{1 + 0.5 \times 0.12}{1 + 0.12}\right) - \left(\frac{10{,}000 \times 0.04 \times 0.30}{0.12 + 0.04}\right) \times \left(\frac{1}{(1 + 0.12)^4}\right) = \$375$$

PV of the CCA tax shield for the equipment:

$$\left(\frac{CdT}{r + d}\right) \times \left(\frac{1 + 0.5r}{1 + r}\right) - \left(\frac{SdT}{r + d}\right) \times \left(\frac{1}{(1 + r)^n}\right)$$

$$\left(\frac{8{,}000 \times 0.30 \times 0.30}{0.12 + 0.30}\right) \times \left(\frac{1 + 0.5 \times 0.12}{1 + 0.12}\right) - \left(\frac{2{,}000 \times 0.30 \times 0.30}{0.12 + 0.30}\right) \times \left(\frac{1}{(1 + 0.12)^4}\right) = \$1{,}350$$

Therefore the present value of the total tax shield is $375 + $1,350 = $1,725. This is different by $64 from the CCA tax shield we calculated in Table 11-7. The discrepancy is due to the salvage value being different from the UCC. For the building, the difference of $404 will continue to generate tax shields, as will the $332 for the equipment. The present value of those tax shields equals the difference between the $1,661 and $1,725.[2]

11.5 Project Risk Analysis: Techniques for Measuring Stand-Alone Risk

Recall from Chapter 9 that there are three distinct types of risk: stand-alone risk, corporate risk, and market risk. Why should a project's stand-alone risk be important to anyone? In theory, this type of risk should be of little or no concern. However, it is actually of great importance for two reasons:

1.   It is easier to estimate a project's stand-alone risk than its corporate risk, and it is far easier to measure stand-alone risk than market risk.
2.   In the vast majority of cases, all three types of risk are highly correlated—if the general economy does well, so will the firm, and if the firm does well, so will most of its projects. Because of this high correlation, stand-alone risk is generally a good proxy for hard-to-measure corporate and market risk.

   The starting point for analyzing a project's stand-alone risk involves determining the uncertainty inherent in its cash flows. To illustrate what is involved, consider again Regency Integrated Chips' appliance control computer project that we discussed above. Many of the key inputs shown in Part 1 of Table 11-4 are subject to uncertainty. For example, sales were projected at 20,000 units to be sold at a net price of $3,000 per unit. However, actual unit sales will almost certainly be somewhat higher or lower than 20,000, and the sales price will probably turn out to be different from the projected $3,000 per unit. *In effect, the sales quantity and price estimates are really expected values based on probability distributions, as are many of the other values that were shown in Part 1 of Table 11-4.* The distributions could be relatively "tight," reflecting small standard deviations and low risk, or they could be "wide," denoting a great deal of uncertainty about the actual value of the variable in question and thus a high degree of stand-alone risk.

---

[2] $\dfrac{(\$10{,}404 - \$10{,}000) \times 0.04 \times 0.30}{0.12 + 0.04} \times \dfrac{1}{(1 + 0.12)^4} = \$19$ equals the present value CCA tax shield difference between

the salvage value and the UCC for the building, while it is $\dfrac{(\$2{,}332 - \$2{,}000) \times 0.04 \times 0.30}{0.12 + 0.04} \times \dfrac{1}{(1 + 0.12)^4} = \$45$ for the

equipment. The two values $19 + $45 = $64, which is the difference between the table and formula PV CCA values.

The nature of the individual cash flow distributions, and their correlations with one another, determine the nature of the NPV probability distribution and, thus, the project's stand-alone risk. In the following sections, we discuss three techniques for assessing a project's stand-alone risk: (1) sensitivity analysis, (2) scenario analysis, and (3) Monte Carlo simulation.

Sensitivity Analysis

Intuitively, we know that many of the variables that determine a project's cash flows could turn out to be different from the values used in the analysis. We also know that a change in a key input variable, such as units sold, will cause the NPV to change. **Sensitivity analysis** is a technique that indicates how much NPV will change in response to a given change in an input variable, other things held constant.

Sensitivity Tables and Graphs Sensitivity analysis begins with a *base-case* situation, which is developed using the *expected* values for each input. To illustrate, consider the data given back in Table 11-4, where projected cash flows for RIC's computer project were shown. The values used to develop the table, including unit sales, sales price, fixed costs, and variable costs, are all most likely, or base-case values, and the resulting $9.122 million NPV shown in Table 11-4 is called the *base-case NPV*. Now we ask a series of "what if" questions: What if unit sales fall 15% below the most likely level? What if the sales price per unit falls? What if variable costs are $2.50 per unit rather than the expected $2.10? Sensitivity analysis is designed to provide decision makers with answers to questions such as these.

In a sensitivity analysis, each variable is changed by several percentage points above and below the expected value, holding all other variables constant. Then a new NPV is calculated using each of these values. Finally, the set of NPVs is plotted to show how sensitive NPV is to changes in each variable. Figure 11-1 shows the computer project's sensitivity graphs for six of the input variables. The table below the graph gives the NPVs that were used to construct the graph. The slopes of the lines in the graph show how sensitive NPV is to changes in each of the inputs: *The steeper the slope, the more sensitive the NPV is to a change in the variable.* From the figure and the table, we see that the project's NPV is very sensitive to changes in the sales price and variable costs, fairly sensitive to changes in the growth rate and units sold, and not very sensitive to changes in either fixed costs or the cost of capital.

If we were comparing two projects, the one with the steeper sensitivity lines would be riskier, because for that project a relatively small error in estimating a variable such as unit sales would produce a large error in the project's expected NPV. Thus, sensitivity analysis can provide useful insights into the risk of a project.

See *Ch 11 Tool Kit.xlsx* for all calculations.

Spreadsheet computer programs such as *Excel* are ideally suited for sensitivity analysis. We used the Data Table feature in the file *Ch 11 Tool Kit.xlsx* to generate the data for the graph in Figure 11-1. To conduct such an analysis by hand would be extremely time consuming.

See *Ch 11 Tool Kit.xlsx* at the textbook's website.

NPV Breakeven Analysis A special application of sensitivity analysis is called *NPV breakeven analysis*. In a breakeven analysis, we find the level of an input that produces an NPV of exactly zero. We used *Excel's* Goal Seek feature to do this.

Table 11-8 shows the values of the inputs discussed above that produce a zero NPV. For example, the unit sales price can drop to $2.79 before the project's NPV falls to zero. Breakeven analysis is helpful in determining how bad things can get before the project has a negative NPV.

Scenario Analysis

Although sensitivity analysis is probably the most widely used risk analysis technique, it does have limitations. For example, we saw earlier that the computer project's NPV is highly sensitive to changes in the sales price and the variable cost per unit. Those sensitivities suggest that the project is risky. Suppose, however, that Staples or Best Buy was anxious to get the new computer product and would sign a contract to purchase 20,000 units per year for 4 years at $3,000 per unit. Moreover, suppose Intel would agree to provide the principal component at a price that would ensure that the variable cost per unit would not exceed $2,100. Under these conditions, there would be a low probability of high or low sales prices and input costs, so the project would not be at all risky in spite of its sensitivity to those variables.

FIGURE
11-1 Evaluating Risk: Sensitivity Analysis (Dollars in Thousands)

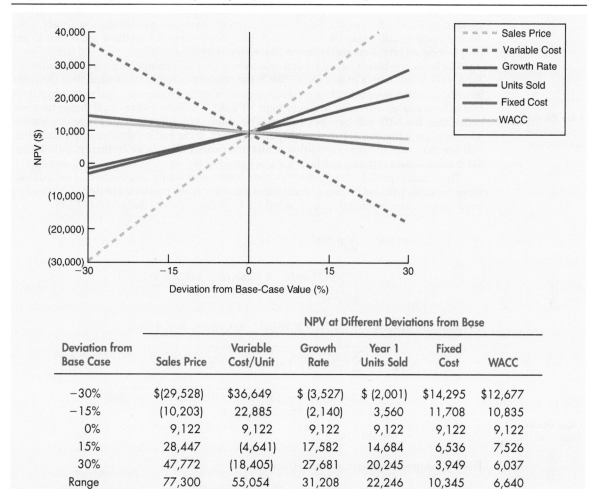

NPV at Different Deviations from Base

Deviation from Base Case	Sales Price	Variable Cost/Unit	Growth Rate	Year 1 Units Sold	Fixed Cost	WACC
−30%	$(29,528)	$36,649	$ (3,527)	$ (2,001)	$14,295	$12,677
−15%	(10,203)	22,885	(2,140)	3,560	11,708	10,835
0%	9,122	9,122	9,122	9,122	9,122	9,122
15%	28,447	(4,641)	17,582	14,684	6,536	7,526
30%	47,772	(18,405)	27,681	20,245	3,949	6,037
Range	77,300	55,054	31,208	22,246	10,345	6,640

**TABLE
11-8**   NPV Breakeven Analysis (Dollars in Thousands)

Input	Input Value that Produces Zero NPV
Sales price	$2.79
Variable cost/unit	$2.31
Growth rate	−20.3%
Year 1 units sold	15,079
Fixed cost	$12,233
WACC	24.4%

We see, then, that we need to extend sensitivity analysis to deal with the *probability distributions* of the inputs. In addition, it would be useful to vary more than one variable at a time so we could see the combined effects of changes in the variables. Scenario analysis provides these extensions—it brings in the probabilities of changes in the key variables, and it allows us to change more than one variable at a time. In a scenario analysis, the financial analyst begins with the *base case*, or most likely set of values for the input variables. Then, he or she asks marketing, engineering, and other operating managers to specify a *worst-case scenario* (low unit sales, low sales price, high variable costs, and so on) and a *best-case scenario*. Often, the best case and worst case are set so as to have a 25% probability of conditions being that good or bad, and a 50% probability is assigned to the base-case conditions. Obviously, conditions could actually take on other values, but parameters such as these are useful to get people focused on the central issues in risk analysis.

See *Ch 11 Tool Kit.xlsx* for a scenario analysis using *Excel's* Scenario Manager.

The best-case, base-case, and worst-case values for RIC's computer project are shown in Table 11-9, along with a plot of the NPVs. If the product is highly successful, then the combination of a high sales price, low production costs, high first-year sales, and a strong growth rate in future sales will result in a very high NPV, $173 million. However, if things turn out badly, then the NPV will be −$41 million. The graph shows a very wide range of possibilities, indicating that this is indeed a very risky project. If the bad conditions materialize, this will not bankrupt the company—this is just one project for a large company. Still, losing $41 million would certainly not help the stock price or the career of the project's manager.

The scenario probabilities and NPVs constitute a probability distribution of returns like those we dealt with in Chapter 7, except that the returns are measured in dollars instead of percentages (rates of return). The expected NPV (in thousands of dollars) is $37,583:[3]

$$\text{Expected NPV} = \sum_{i=1}^{N} P_i(\text{NPV}_i)$$

$$= 0.25(\$173,463) + 0.50(\$9,122) + 0.25(-\$41,376)$$

$$= \$37,583$$

The standard deviation of the NPV is $81,114 (in thousands of dollars):

See *Ch 11 Tool Kit.xlsx* at the textbook's website.

$$\sigma_{\text{NPV}} = \sqrt{\sum_{i=1}^{N} P_i(\text{NPV}_i - \text{Expected NPV})^2}$$

$$= \sqrt{\begin{array}{l}0.25(\$173,463 - \$37,583)^2 + 0.50(\$9,122 - \$37,583)^2 \\ +0.25(-\$41,376 - \$37,583)^2\end{array}}$$

$$= \$81,114$$

Finally, the project's coefficient of variation is

$$CV_{\text{NPV}} = \frac{\sigma_{\text{NPV}}}{E(\text{NPV})} = \frac{\$81,114}{\$37,583} = 2.16$$

The project's coefficient of variation can be compared with the coefficient of variation of RIC's "average" project to get an idea of the relative risk of the proposed project. RIC's existing projects, on average, have a coefficient of variation of about 1.0, so, on the basis of this stand-alone risk measure, we conclude that this project is much riskier than an "average" project.

Scenario analysis provides useful information about a project's stand-alone risk. However, it is limited in that it considers only a few discrete outcomes (NPVs), even though there are an infinite number of possibilities. We briefly introduce a more complete method of assessing a project's stand-alone risk in the next section.

Monte Carlo Simulation

Monte Carlo simulation ties together sensitivities and probability distributions. It grew out of work in the Manhattan Project to build the first atomic bomb and was so named because it utilized the mathematics of casino gambling. While Monte Carlo simulation is considerably more complex than scenario analysis, simulation software packages make this process manageable. Many of these packages are included as add-ons to spreadsheet programs such as *Excel*.

---

[3]Note that the expected NPV, $37,583, is *not* the same as the base-case NPV, $9,122 (in thousands). This is because the two uncertain variables, sales volume and sales price, are multiplied together to obtain dollar sales, and this process causes the NPV distribution to be skewed to the right. A big number times another big number produces a very big number, which, in turn, causes the average, or expected value, to increase.

TABLE
11-9   Scenario Analysis (Dollars in Thousands)

Scenario	Probability	Sales Price	Unit Sales	Variable Costs	Growth Rate	NPV
Best case	25%	$3.90	26,000	$1.47	30%	$173,463
Base case	50	3.00	20,000	2.10	0	9,122
Worst case	25	2.10	14,000	2.73	−30	(41,376)

Expected NPV = $ 37,583

Standard deviation = $ 81,114

Coefficient of variation = Standard deviation/Expected NPV = 2.16

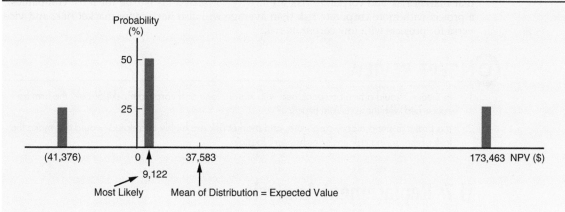

Note: The scenario analysis calculations were performed in the *Excel* model, **Ch 11 Tool Kit.xlsx**.

In a simulation analysis, the computer begins by picking at random a value for each variable—sales in units, the sales price, the variable cost per unit, and so on. Then those values are combined, and the project's NPV is calculated and stored in the computer's memory. Next, a second set of input values is selected at random, and a second NPV is calculated. This process is repeated perhaps 1,000 times, generating 1,000 NPVs. The mean and standard deviation of the set of NPVs is determined. The mean, or average value, is used as a measure of the project's expected NPV, and the standard deviation (or coefficient of variation) is used as a measure of risk. More information about Monte Carlo simulation can be found in **Web Extension 11A**.

CONCEPT REVIEW

1. List two reasons that, in practice, a project's stand-alone risk is important.
2. Differentiate between sensitivity and scenario analyses. What advantage does scenario analysis have over sensitivity analysis?
3. What is Monte Carlo simulation?

11.6 Project Risk Conclusions

We have discussed the three types of risk normally considered in capital budgeting analysis—stand-alone risk, within-firm (or corporate) risk, and market risk—and we have discussed ways of assessing each. However, two important questions remain: (1) Should firms be concerned with stand-alone or corporate risk in their capital budgeting decisions? (2) What do we do when the stand-alone, within-firm, and market risk assessments lead to different conclusions?

These questions do not have easy answers. From a theoretical standpoint, well-diversified investors should be concerned only with market risk, and managers should be concerned only with stock price maximization, and this should lead to the conclusion that market (beta) risk ought to be given virtually all the weight in capital budgeting decisions. However, if investors are not well diversified, if the CAPM does not operate exactly as theory says it should, or if measurement problems keep managers from having confidence in the CAPM approach in capital budgeting, it may be appropriate to give stand-alone and corporate risk more weight than financial theory suggests. Note also that the CAPM ignores bankruptcy costs, even though such costs can be substantial, and that the probability of bankruptcy depends on a firm's corporate risk, not on its beta risk. Therefore, even well-diversified investors should want a firm's management to give at least some consideration to a project's corporate risk instead of concentrating entirely on market risk.

Although it would be nice to reconcile these problems and to measure project risk on some absolute scale, the best we can do in practice is to estimate project risk in a somewhat nebulous, relative sense. For example, we can generally say with a fair degree of confidence that a particular project has more or less stand-alone risk than the firm's average project. Then, assuming that stand-alone and corporate risk are highly correlated (which is typical), the project's stand-alone risk will be a good measure of its corporate risk. Finally, assuming that market risk and corporate risk are highly correlated (as is true for most companies), a project with more corporate risk than average will also have more market risk, and vice versa for projects with low corporate risk.[4]

CONCEPT REVIEW

1. In theory, should a firm be concerned with stand-alone and corporate risk? Should the firm be concerned with these risks in practice?
2. If a project's stand-alone, corporate, and market risk are highly correlated, would this make the task of measuring risk easier or harder? Explain.

11.7 Replacement Analysis

In the previous sections we assumed that RIC's computer control system was an entirely new project, so that all of its cash flows were incremental—they would occur if and only if the new project were accepted. However, for replacement projects we must find the cash flow *differentials* between the new and old projects, and these differentials are the *incremental cash flows* that we must analyze.

We can illustrate a replacement decision with another RIC example, this time from the company's research and development (R&D) division. The R&D manager reports that a new special-purpose machine can be purchased and that over its 5-year life it will reduce labour and raw materials use sufficient to cut annual operating costs from $9,000 to $4,000. This reduction in costs will cause before-tax profits to rise by $9,000 − $4,000 = $5,000 per year. All the other relevant information on the new and old machine is shown in Table 11-10.

Let's take a look at the calculation. In Part II the incremental investment outlay consists of the cash outflow from the new machine purchase, less the inflow from selling the old machine and a one-time investment in working capital.

In Part III we see that every year the new machine can save $5,000 in operating costs, which is equivalent to a $5,000 cash inflow. Since we deal with after-tax cash flows, we compute an incremental annual after-tax operating savings of $3,500.

Part IV shows the terminal year cash flows associated with the project. The first item shows the new machine's estimated salvage value at the end of its 5-year life of $2,000. In this analysis, the old machine's salvage value is zero. However, if the old machine were expected to have a positive salvage value at the end of 5 years, replacing the old machine now would eliminate this cash flow. Therefore, the salvage value of the old machine would represent an opportunity cost to the firm, and it would be included as a Year 5 cash outflow in the terminal cash flow section of the worksheet. Finally, the $1,000 investment in net operating working capital that was made initially, that is at time 0, is recovered when the project terminates at the end of Year 5. In this case, inventories will be drawn down and not replaced, with a resulting inflow of $1,000 at Year 5.

---

[4]The traditional tools used to analyze project risk have come under critical review. Nassim Nicholas Taleb argues, in *The Black Swan: The Impact of the Highly Improbable* (New York: Random House, 2007), that very unlikely outcomes, which are not taken into account in traditional financial modelling, do sometimes occur, with serious financial consequences.

TABLE 11-10   Analysis of a Replacement Project

	A	B	C	D	E	F	G	H	I	J
1										
2										
3	*Part I. Input Data*									
4										
5	Cost of the new machine					$12,000				
6	Reduction in operating costs					$ 5,000				
7	New machine's salvage value at end of Year 5					$ 2,000				
8	Old machine's current market value					$ 1,000				
9	Old machine's salvage value at end of Year 5					$ 0				
10	Capital cost allowance rate					20%				
11	Increase in Net Operating WC					$ 1,000				
12	Tax rate					30%				
13	WACC					11.5%				
14	Number of Years					5				
15										
16	Replacement Project Net Cash Flow Schedule									Present
17				Time:	0	1	2	3	4	5	Value
18	*Part II. Investment Outlay*									
19	Cost of new equipment			$(12,000)						
20	Market value of old equipment			1,000						
21	Increase in net operating WC			(1,000)						
22	Total investment			$(12,000)						$(12,000)
23										
24										
25	*Part III. Operating Inflows over the Project's Life*									
26										
27	Decrease in operating costs				$5,000	$5,000	$5,000	$5,000	$5,000	
28	Taxes				1,500	1,500	1,500	1,500	1,500	
29	Project cash flows after tax				$3,500	$3,500	$3,500	$3,500	$3,500	$12,775
30										
31	*Part IV. Terminal Year Cash Flows*									
32	Estimated salvage value of new machine								$2,000	
33	Less salvage value of old machine								$0	
34	Recovery of net operating WC								1,000	
35	Total terminal cash flows								$3,000	$1,741
36										
37	*Part V. Present Value of the CCA Tax Shield*									$1,766
38							Key Output: NPV	=		$4,281

Part V of the table calculated the "Present Value of the CCA Tax Shield." Though very similar to Equation 11-3, which we used in the expansion project example, we must also take into account the CCA lost as a result of selling the old equipment. Instead of calculating CCA on the capital cost "C" in our formula, we calculate it on the net acquisition amount "C_{net}." This is the difference between the new capital cost and proceeds from disposing of the old capital asset. Likewise, the salvage value lost (if any) from our original asset is deducted from the salvage value of our replacement asset "S_{net}." Our formula can be slightly rewritten to account for these changes, as shown in Equation 11-4. This is the calculation we used to obtain $1,766. With a resulting NPV of $4,281, replacing the old machine appears to be a good decision.

$$\left(\frac{C_{net}dT}{r+d}\right) \times \left(\frac{1+0.5r}{1+r}\right) - \left(\frac{S_{net}dT}{r+d}\right) \times \left(\frac{1}{(1+r)^n}\right)$$

$$\left(\frac{(12,000-1,000) \times 0.20 \times 0.30}{0.115+0.20}\right) \times \left(\frac{1+0.5 \times 0.115}{1+0.115}\right) - \tag{11-4}$$

$$\left(\frac{(2,000-0) \times 0.20 \times 0.30}{0.115+0.20}\right) \times \left(\frac{1}{(1+0.115)^5}\right) = \$1,766$$

11.8 Incorporating Project Risk into Capital Budgeting

As we described in Chapter 9, many firms calculate a cost of capital for each division, based on the division's market risk and capital structure. This is the first step towards incorporating risk analysis into capital budgeting decisions, but it is limited because it encompasses only market risk. Instead of directly estimating the corporate risk of a project, the risk management departments at many firms regularly assess the entire firm's likelihood of financial distress, based on current and proposed projects.[5] In other words, they assess a firm's corporate risk, given its portfolio of projects. This screening process will identify those projects that significantly increase corporate risk.

Suppose a proposed project doesn't significantly affect a firm's likelihood of financial distress, but it does have greater stand-alone risk than the typical project in a division. Two methods are used to incorporate this project risk into capital budgeting. One is called the *certainty equivalent* approach. Here every cash inflow that is not known with certainty is scaled down, and the riskier the flow, the lower its certainty equivalent value. The other method, and the one we focus on here, is the **risk-adjusted discount rate** approach, under which differential project risk is dealt with by changing the discount rate. Average-risk projects are discounted at the firm's average cost of capital, higher-risk projects are discounted at a higher cost of capital, and lower-risk projects are discounted at a rate below the firm's average cost of capital. Unfortunately, there is no good way of specifying exactly *how much* higher or lower these discount rates should be. Given the present state of the art, risk adjustments are necessarily judgmental and somewhat arbitrary.[6]

ⓒONCEPT REVIEW

1. How are risk-adjusted discount rates used to incorporate project risk into the capital budget decision process?

11.9 Managing Risk through Phased Decisions: Decision Trees

Up to this point we have focused primarily on techniques for estimating a project's stand-alone risk. Although this is an integral part of capital budgeting, managers are generally more interested in *reducing* risk than in *measuring* it. For example, sometimes projects can be structured so that expenditures do not have to be made all at one time, but, rather, can be made in stages over a period of years. This reduces risk by giving managers the opportunity to re-evaluate decisions using new information and then either invest additional funds or terminate the project. Such projects can be evaluated using *decision trees*.

The Basic Decision Tree

Suppose United Robotics is considering the production of an industrial robot for the television manufacturing industry. The net investment for this project can be broken down into stages, as set forth in Figure 11-2:

STAGE 1. At t = 0, which in this case is sometime in the near future, conduct a $500,000 study of the market potential for robots in television assembly lines.

STAGE 2. If it appears that a sizable market does exist, then at t = 1 spend $1,000,000 to design and build a prototype robot. This robot would then be evaluated by television engineers, and their reactions would determine whether the firm should proceed with the project.

STAGE 3. If reaction to the prototype robot is good, then at t = 2 build a production plant at a net cost of $10,000,000. If this stage were reached, the project would generate either high, medium, or low net cash flows over the following 3 years.

---

[5]These processes also measure the magnitude of the losses, which is often called *value at risk*.
[6]For more on risk adjustments, see Tarun K. Mukherjee, "Reducing the Uncertainty-Induced Bias in Capital Budgeting Decisions—A Hurdle Rate Approach," *Journal of Business Finance and Accounting*, September 1991, 747–753; J. S. Butler and Barry Schachter, "The Investment Decision: Estimation Risk and Risk Adjusted Discount Rates," *Financial Management*, Winter 1989, 13–22; and Samuel C. Weaver, Peter J. Clemmens III, Jack A. Gunn, and Bruce D. Danneburg, "Divisional Hurdle Rates and the Cost of Capital," *Financial Management*, Spring 1989, 18–25.

FIGURE
11-2 United Robotics: Decision Tree Analysis (Thousands of Dollars)

Time						Joint		Product:
t = 0	t = 1	t = 2	t = 3	t = 4	t = 5	Probability	NPV	Prob. × NPV
			$18,000	$18,000	$18,000	0.144	$25,635	$ 3,691
		$(10,000) 0.3 0.4	8,000	8,000	8,000	0.192	6,149	1,181
	$(1,000) 0.6	③	(2,000) 0.3	Stop		0.144	(10,883)	(1,567)
$(500) 0.8	② 0.4	Stop	④			0.320	(1,397)	(447)
① 0.2	Stop					0.200	(500)	(100)
						1.000	Expected NPV =	$ 2,758
								σ = $10,584

STAGE 4. At t = 3 market acceptance will be known. If demand is low, the firm will terminate the project and avoid the negative cash flows in Years 4 and 5.

A **decision tree** such as the one in Figure 11-2 can be used to analyze such multistage,
or sequential, decisions. Here we assume that 1 year goes by between decisions. Each circle
represents a decision point and is called a *decision node.* The dollar value to the left of each
decision node represents the net investment required at that decision point, and the cash
flows shown under t = 3 to t = 5 represent the cash inflows if the project is pushed on to
completion. Each diagonal line represents a *branch* of the decision tree, and each branch has
an estimated probability. For example, if the firm decides to "go" with the project at Decision
Point 1, it will spend $500,000 on a marketing study. Management estimates that there is a 0.8
probability that the study will produce favourable results, leading to the decision to move
on to Stage 2, and a 0.2 probability that the marketing study will produce negative results,
indicating that the project should be cancelled after Stage 1. If the project is cancelled, the
cost to the company will be the $500,000 for the initial marketing study, and it will be a loss.

If the marketing study yields positive results, then United Robotics will spend $1,000,000
on the prototype robot at Decision Point 2. Management estimates (before even making the
initial $500,000 investment) that there is a 60% probability that the television engineers will
find the robot useful and a 40% probability that they will not.

If the engineers like the robot, the firm will spend the final $10,000,000 to build the
plant and go into production. If the engineers do not like the prototype, the project will be
dropped. If the firm does go into production, the operating cash flows over the project's
4-year life will depend on how well the market accepts the final product. There is a 30%
chance that acceptance will be quite good and that net cash flows will be $18 million per
year, a 40% probability of $8 million each year, and a 30% chance of losing $2 million.
These cash flows are shown under Years 3 through 5.

In summary, the decision tree in Figure 11-2 defines the decision nodes and the
branches that leave the nodes. There are two types of nodes: decision nodes and outcome nodes. Decision nodes are the points at which management can respond to new
information. The first decision node is at t = 1, after the company has completed the
marketing study (Decision Point 1 in Figure 11-2). The second decision node is at t = 2,
after the company has completed the prototype study (Decision Point 2 in Figure 11-2).
The outcome nodes show the possible results if a particular decision is taken. There is
one relevant outcome node (Decision Point 3 in Figure 11-2), the one occurring at t =
3, and its branches show the possible cash flows if the company goes ahead with the
industrial robot project. There is one more decision node, Decision Point 4, at which
United Robotics terminates the project if acceptance is low. Note that the decision tree
also shows the probabilities of moving into each branch that leaves a node.

The column of joint probabilities in Figure 11-2 gives the probability of occurrence of
each branch, hence of each NPV. Each joint probability is obtained by multiplying together
all probabilities on a particular branch. For example, the probability that the company will, if
Stage 1 is undertaken, move through Stages 2 and 3, and that a strong demand will produce
$18,000,000 per year of inflows, is (0.8)(0.6)(0.3) = 0.144 = 14.4%.

The company has a cost of capital of 11.5%, and management assumes initially that the project is of average risk. The NPV of the top (most favourable) branch as shown in the next-to-last column is $25,635 (in thousands of dollars):

$$NPV = -\$500 - \frac{\$1,000}{(1.115)^1} - \frac{\$10,000}{(1.115)^2} + \frac{\$18,000}{(1.115)^3} + \frac{\$18,000}{(1.115)^4} + \frac{\$18,000}{(1.115)^5}$$

$$= \$25,635$$

The NPVs for other branches were calculated similarly.

The last column in Figure 11-2 gives the product of the NPV for each branch times the joint probability of that branch, and the sum of these products is the project's expected NPV. Based on the expectations set forth in Figure 11-2 and a cost of capital of 11.5%, the project's expected NPV is $2.758 million.

As this example shows, decision tree analysis requires managers to explicitly articulate the types of risk a project faces and to develop responses to potential scenarios. Note also that our example could be extended to cover many other types of decisions and could even be incorporated into a simulation analysis. All in all, decision tree analysis is a valuable tool for analyzing project risk.[7] We will discuss decision trees in more detail in Web Chapter 24.

CONCEPT REVIEW

1. What is a decision tree? A branch? A node?

11.10 Introduction to Real Options

According to traditional capital budgeting theory, a project's NPV is the present value of its expected future cash flows, discounted at a rate that reflects the riskiness of the expected future cash flows. Note, however, that this says nothing about actions that can be taken after the project has been accepted and placed in operation that might cause the cash flows to increase. In other words, traditional capital budgeting theory assumes that a project is like a roulette wheel. A gambler can choose whether or not to spin the wheel, but once the wheel has been spun, there is nothing he or she can do to influence the outcome. Once the game begins, the outcome depends purely on chance, with no skill involved.

Contrast roulette with other games, such as draw poker. Chance plays a role in poker, and it continues to play a role after the initial deal because players receive additional cards throughout the game. However, poker players are able to respond to their opponents' actions, so skillful players usually win.

Capital budgeting decisions have more in common with poker than roulette because (1) chance plays a continuing role throughout the life of the project but (2) managers can respond to changing market conditions and to competitors' actions. Opportunities to respond to changing circumstances are called **managerial options** because they give managers a chance to influence the outcome of a project. They are also called **strategic options** because they are often associated with large, strategic projects rather than routine maintenance projects. Finally, they are called **real options,** which are differentiated from financial options because they involve real rather than financial assets. The following sections describe several types of projects with **embedded options.**

Investment Timing Options

Conventional NPV analysis implicitly assumes that projects will either be accepted or rejected, which implies that they will be undertaken now or never. In practice, however, companies sometimes have a third choice—delay the decision until later, when more information is available. Such **investment timing options** can dramatically affect a project's estimated profitability and risk.

---

[7]In the United Robotics example we glossed over an important issue, namely, the appropriate cost of capital for the project. Adding decision nodes to a project clearly changes its risk, so we would expect the cost of capital for a project with few decision nodes to have a different risk from one with many nodes. If this were so, we would expect the projects to have different costs of capital. In fact, we might expect the cost of capital to change over time as the project moves to different stages, since the stages themselves differ in risk.

For example, suppose Sony plans to introduce a new interactive gaming-TV system, and your software company has two alternatives: (1) immediately begin full-scale production of game software for the new system, or (2) delay investment in the project until you get a better idea of the size of the market for Sony's interactive system. You might prefer delaying implementation. Keep in mind, though, that the *option to delay* is valuable only if it more than offsets any harm that might come from delaying. For example, if you delay, some other company might establish a loyal customer base that makes it difficult for your company to enter the market later. The option to delay is usually most valuable to firms with proprietary technology, patents, licences, or other barriers to entry, because these factors lessen the threat of competition. The option to delay is valuable when market demand is uncertain, but it is also valuable during periods of volatile interest rates, since the ability to wait can allow firms to delay raising capital for projects until interest rates are lower.

Growth Options

A **growth option** allows a company to increase its capacity if market conditions are better than expected. There are several types of growth options. One lets a company *increase the capacity of an existing product line*. A "peaking unit" power plant illustrates this type of growth option. Such units have high variable costs and are used to produce additional power only if demand and therefore prices are high.

The second type of growth option allows a company to *expand into new geographic markets*. Many companies are investing in Eastern Europe, Russia, and China even though standard NPV analysis produces negative NPVs. However, if these developing markets really take off, the option to open more facilities could be quite valuable.

The third type of growth option is the opportunity to *add new products*, including complementary products and successive "generations" of the original product. Toshiba probably lost money on its first laptop computers, but the manufacturing skills and consumer recognition it gained helped turn subsequent generations of laptops into money makers. In addition, Toshiba used its experience and name recognition in laptops as a springboard into the desktop computer market.

Abandonment Options

Many projects contain an **abandonment option.** When evaluating a potential project, standard DCF analysis assumes that the assets will be used over a specified economic life. While some projects must be operated over their full economic life, even though market conditions might deteriorate and cause lower than expected cash flows, others can be abandoned. For example, some contracts between automobile manufacturers and their suppliers specify the quantity and price of the parts that must be delivered. If a supplier's labour costs increase, then the supplier might well lose money on each part it ships. Including the option to abandon in such a contract might be quite valuable.

Note too that some projects can be structured so that they provide the option to *reduce capacity* or *temporarily suspend operations*. Such options are common in the natural resources industry, including mining, oil, and timber, and they should be reflected in the analysis when NPVs are being estimated.

Flexibility Options

Many projects offer **flexibility options** that permit the firm to alter operations depending on how conditions change during the life of the project. Typically, either inputs or outputs (or both) can be changed. Nissan's manufacturing plant in Canton, Mississippi, provides a good example of output flexibility. Nissan invested $1.4 billion in the plant, which can alter production to meet changing demand. The facility started out producing cars, pickups, minivans, and SUVs. With the drastic increase in gasoline prices, consumers quickly changed their buying behaviour. Trucks and large SUVs fell out of favour, while sales of more fuel-efficient cars increased. Nissan responded by reducing production of its pickup trucks while increasing production of its more fuel-efficient four-cylinder Altimas. The plant's cash flows will be much higher than they would have been without the flexibility option that Nissan "bought" by paying more to build a more flexible plant.

Electric power plants provide an example of input flexibility. Utilities can build plants that generate electricity by burning coal, oil, or natural gas. The prices of those fuels change over time, depending on events in the Middle East, changing environmental policies, and weather conditions. Some years ago, virtually all power plants were designed to burn just one type of fuel, because this resulted in the lowest construction cost. However, as fuel cost volatility increased, power companies began to build higher-cost but more flexible plants, especially ones that could switch from oil to gas and back again, depending on relative fuel prices.

Valuing Real Options

A full treatment of real option valuation is beyond the scope of this chapter, but there are some things we can say. First, if your project has an embedded real option, you should at least recognize and articulate its existence. Second, we know that a financial option is more valuable if it has a long time until maturity or if the underlying asset is very risky. If either of these characteristics applies to your real option, then you know that its value is relatively high, qualitatively speaking. Third, you might be able to model the real option along the lines of a decision tree. This will give you an approximate value, but keep in mind that you may not have a good estimate of the appropriate discount rate, because the real option changes the risk, and hence the required return, of the project.[8] We will discuss real options in more detail in Web Chapter 24.

CONCEPT REVIEW

1. Name some different types of real options.

Summary

In this chapter, we developed a framework for analyzing a project's cash flows and risk. The key concepts covered are listed below.

* The most important (and most difficult) step in analyzing a capital budgeting project is **estimating the incremental after-tax cash flows** the project will produce.
* **Project cash flow** is different from accounting income. Project cash flow reflects (1) **cash outlays for fixed assets,** (2) the **tax shield provided by capital cost allowance,** and (3) cash flows due to **changes in net operating working capital.** Project cash flow does not include interest payments.
* In determining incremental cash flows, **opportunity costs** (the cash flows foregone by using an asset) must be included, but **sunk costs** (cash outlays that have been made and that cannot be recouped) are not included. Any **externalities** (effects of a project on other parts of the firm) should also be reflected in the analysis.
* **Cannibalization** occurs when a new project leads to a reduction in sales of an existing product.
* **Tax laws** affect cash flow analysis in two ways: (1) they reduce operating cash flows, and (2) they determine the depreciation expense, CCA, that can be taken in each year.
* The **half-year rule** states that a company can claim only one-half the CCA in the first year the asset was purchased.
* **Undepreciated capital cost (UCC)** is the amount remaining to be claimed as CCA over time for an asset class.
* **Recapture** occurs when the sale of an asset creates a negative UCC balance. That amount must be added back to income and is taxed. If on the sale of the last asset in an asset class the UCC is positive, a **terminal loss** is created, which may be deducted from income.
* Capital projects often require additional investments in **net operating working capital (NOWC).**
* **Inflation effects** must be considered in project analysis. The best procedure is to build expected inflation into the cash flow estimates.
* Since shareholders are generally diversified, **market risk** is theoretically the most relevant measure of risk. Market, or beta, risk is important because beta affects the cost of capital, which in turn affects stock prices.

---

[8]For more on real option valuation, see M. Amram and N. Kulatilaka, *Real Options: Managing Strategic Investment in an Uncertain World* (Boston: Harvard Business School Press, 1999); and M. Brennan and L. Trigeorgis, *Project Flexibility, Agency, and Competition: New Developments in the Theory and Application of Real Options* (New York: Oxford University Press, 2000).

- **Corporate risk** is important because it influences the firm's ability to use low-cost debt, to maintain smooth operations over time, and to avoid crises that might consume management's energy and disrupt its employees, customers, suppliers, and community.
- **Sensitivity analysis** is a technique that shows how much a project's NPV will change in response to a given change in an input variable such as sales, other things held constant.
- **Scenario analysis** is a risk analysis technique in which the best- and worst-case NPVs are compared with the project's expected NPV.
- **Monte Carlo simulation** is a risk analysis technique that uses a computer to simulate future events and thus to estimate the profitability and riskiness of a project.
- The **risk-adjusted discount rate**, or **project cost of capital**, is the rate used to evaluate a particular project. It is based on the corporate WACC, which is increased for projects that are riskier than the firm's average project but decreased for less risky projects.
- **Decision tree analysis** shows how different decisions in a project's life affect its value.
- Opportunities to respond to changing circumstances are called **managerial options** because they give managers the option to influence the outcome of a project. They are also called **strategic options** because they are often associated with large, strategic projects rather than routine maintenance projects. Finally, they are also called *real options* because they involve "real" rather than "financial" assets. Many projects include a variety of **embedded options** that can dramatically affect the true NPV.
- An **investment timing option** involves not only the decision of *whether* to proceed with a project but also the decision of *when* to proceed with it. This opportunity to affect a project's timing can dramatically change its estimated value.
- A **growth option** occurs if an investment creates the opportunity to make other potentially profitable investments that would not otherwise be possible. These include (1) options to expand output, (2) options to enter a new geographical market, and (3) options to introduce complementary products or successive generations of products.
- The **abandonment option** is the ability to abandon a project if the operating cash flows and/or abandonment cost turn out to be lower than expected. It reduces the risk of a project and increases its value. Instead of total abandonment, some options allow a company to reduce capacity or temporarily suspend operations.
- A **flexibility option** is the option to modify operations depending on how conditions develop during a project's life, especially the type of output produced or the inputs used.

Questions

11-1 Define each of the following terms:
  a. Cash flow; accounting income
  b. Incremental cash flow; sunk cost; opportunity cost
  c. Net operating working capital changes; salvage value
  d. Externality; cannibalization
  e. Sensitivity analysis; scenario analysis; Monte Carlo simulation analysis
  f. Risk-adjusted discount rate; project cost of capital
  g. Real options; managerial options; strategic options; embedded options
  h. Investment timing option; growth option; abandonment option; flexibility option

11-2 Operating cash flows, rather than accounting profits, are listed in project analysis. What is the basis for this emphasis on cash flows as opposed to net income?

11-3 Why is it true, in general, that a failure to adjust expected cash flows for expected inflation biases the calculated NPV downward?

11-4 Explain why sunk costs should not be included in a capital budgeting analysis, but opportunity costs and externalities should be included.

11-5 Explain how net operating working capital is recovered at the end of a project's life, and why it is included in a capital budgeting analysis.

11-6 Define (a) simulation analysis, (b) scenario analysis, and (c) sensitivity analysis.

11-7 What are some differences in the analysis for a replacement project versus a new expansion project?

Concept Review Problems

Full solutions are provided at www.nelson.com/brigham3ce.

CR-1

New Project Analysis

You have been asked by the president of Starbrite Manufacturing to evaluate the proposed acquisition of a new industrial robot. The robot's basic price is $110,000, and it would cost another $10,000 to modify it for special use. Assume that the robot falls into Class 43, CCA 30%, that it would be sold after 3 years for $45,000, and that it would require an increase in net working capital (spare parts inventory) of $2,000. The industrial robot would have no effect on revenues, but it is expected to save the firm $40,000 per year in before-tax operating costs, mainly labour. The firm's tax rate is 30%.
a.   What is the investment in the project? (That is, what are the Time 0 cash flows?)
b.   What are the operating cash flows in Years 1, 2, and 3?
c.   What are the additional (nonoperating) cash flows in Year 3?
d.   If the project's cost of capital is 9%, should the robot be purchased?

CR-2

Corporate Risk Analysis

The staff of Porter Manufacturing has estimated the following net after-tax cash flows and probabilities for a new manufacturing process:

	Net After-Tax Cash Flows		
Year	P = 0.2	P = 0.6	P = 0.2
0	$(100,000)	$(100,000)	$(100,000)
1	20,000	30,000	40,000
2	20,000	30,000	40,000
3	20,000	30,000	40,000
4	20,000	30,000	40,000
5	20,000	30,000	40,000
5*	0	20,000	30,000

Line 0 gives the cost of the process, Lines 1 through 5 give operating cash flows, and Line 5* contains the estimated salvage values. Porter's cost of capital for an average-risk project is 10%.
a.   Assume that the project has average risk. Find the project's expected NPV.
b.   Find the best-case and worst-case NPVs. What is the probability of occurrence of the worst case if the cash flows are perfectly dependent (perfectly positively correlated) over time? If they are independent over time?
c.   Assume that all the cash flows are perfectly positively correlated, that is, there are only three possible cash flow streams over time: (1) the worst case, (2) the most likely, or base, case, and (3) the best case, with probabilities of 0.2, 0.6, and 0.2, respectively. These cases are represented by each of the columns in the table. Find the expected NPV, its standard deviation, and its coefficient of variation.

Problems

Answers to odd-numbered problems appear in Appendix A.

Easy Problems 1–7

11-1

Investment Outlay

Johnson Industries is considering an expansion project. The necessary equipment could be purchased for $9 million, and the project would also require an initial $3 million investment in net operating working capital. The company's tax rate is 40%. What is the project's initial investment outlay?

11-2

Investment Outlay

Talbot Industries is considering launching a new product. The new manufacturing equipment will cost $17 million, and production and sales will require an initial $5 million investment in net operating working capital. The company's tax rate is 30%.
a.   What is the initial investment outlay?
b.   The company spent and expensed $150,000 on research related to the new product last year. Would this change your answer to part a? Explain.
c.   Rather than building a new manufacturing facility, the company plans to install the equipment in a building it owns but is not now using. The building could be sold for $1.5 million after taxes and real estate commissions. How would this affect your answer to part a?

11-3

Operating Cash Flow

Zepplin Aerospace is trying to estimate the first-year operating cash flow (at t = 1) for a proposed project. The financial staff has collected the following information:

Projected sales	$18 million
Operating costs	$9 million
Capital cost allowance	$4 million
Interest expense	$3 million

The company faces a 30% tax rate. What is the project's operating cash flow for the first year (t = 1)?

11-4

Cash Flows

Fruity Fruits Ltd. currently sells $25 million annually of apple juice in 1 litre containers and $10 million of individually packaged dried fruit snacks. The company wants to introduce a 230 mL single-serving cranberry–apple juice product next year. A $200,000 feasibility study just completed estimated yearly sales of $12 million for the new juice. The study also forecast that sales of the company's existing apple juice would fall by $2 million as some existing customers would switch to the new beverage; however, sales of the snack product would increase by 10% due its complementary nature to the new product. The company has unused land it can use, which was purchased two years ago for $500,000. That land could currently be sold for $700,000. Building and equipment costs for the new project are $1,000,000. What is the initial investment *and* first-year cash inflow for this project?

11-5

Cash Flows

General Wireless has just completed market research on a new smartphone. This new phone is lighter and smaller, though more feature rich, than its existing product. New product sales are estimated at 1,000,000 units per year with a contribution margin of $40. However, if General Wireless introduces its new product, sales of its existing smartphone will fall from 600,000 to 250,000 units per year. Its existing product has a contribution margin of $30.

The market research on the new phone was $350,000. General Wireless will retool one of its existing manufacturing facilities to produce the new model. The one-time retooling cost is $3,700,000. There will also be $80,000 in retraining costs incurred for workers who lost their jobs manufacturing the existing product. The new facility is expected to increase fixed cash costs of $150,000 per year. Research and development on the new phone took 2 years at a cost of $1,900,000. The R&D group also paid an external company for use of their advanced testing facilities at a further cost of $100,000.

General Wireless has also spent $90,000 in the design of a new corporate headquarters. Building the headquarters will cost $4,000,000.

For capital budgeting purposes, calculate the project's:
a.   Initial cost.
b.   Annual cash flows before tax.

11-6

New Project Analysis

Marine Technologies has identified a project that will lower annual operating costs by $10,000 per year for 5 years. The equipment costs $30,000, installation and training is $5,000, and there is an initial investment in net operating working capital of $6,000. There is no expected salvage value in 5 years. Marine Technologies operates at break-even so it pays no taxes. If the company's cost of capital is 10%, what is the project's NPV?

11-7

CCV

A company has purchased a piece of equipment for $10,000 that has a 5-year useful life and no salvage value. The company's tax rate is 30% and its cost of capital is 10%.
a.   What is the present value of the CCA tax shield if the equipment has a 20% declining balance CCA rate? (Ignore the half-year rule.)
b.   What is the present value of the CCA tax shield if the CCA rate is 20% straight-line?

Intermediate Problems 8–16

c.   What accounts for the difference in the two present values?

11-8

Project Life

Assume the following information for Project X:

Initial investment:	$50,000
Annual after-tax cash flows:	$8,000
Salvage value:	$0

If the project's internal rate of return is 12.5%, what must be the life of the project (to the nearest year)?

11-9

New Project Analysis

Campbell Company is evaluating the proposed acquisition of a new milling machine. The machine's base price is $120,000, and it would cost another $9,500 to modify it for special use. The machine falls into Class 8 with a 20% CCA rate, and it would be sold after 4 years for $60,000. The machine would require an increase in net working capital (inventory) of $7,500. The milling machine would have no effect on revenues, but it is expected to save the firm $31,000 per year in before-tax operating costs, mainly labour. Campbell's marginal tax rate is 30%.

a.   What is the total initial investment for capital budgeting purposes? (That is, what is the Time 0 net cash flow?)

b.   What is the PV of the project cash flows using an 11% cost of capital?

c.   What is the PV of the CCA tax shield?

d.   What is the PV of the additional Year 4 cash flow?

e.   If the project's cost of capital is 11%, should the machine be purchased?

11-10

New Project Analysis

Red Rock Lobster (RRL) is looking to expand its business. The new business would generate $2.5 million per year in sales over the next 5 years. Annual costs would increase by $2.1 million. An investment in working capital of $50,000 would have to be made initially. The machinery (CCA rate of 30%) would cost $700,000, with additional costs of $10,000 and $20,000 to be incurred for setup and training. RRL estimates that it would be possible to sell the equipment for 10% of its initial value at the end of 5 years. The company would set up operations in a building it does not use but does rent out for $100,000 per year. If RRL's cost of capital is 12% and its tax rate is 28%, should it proceed with this new business?

11-11

Inflation Adjustments

Ever Sparkle Company is considering an average-risk investment in a mineral water spring project that has a cost of $150,000. The project will produce 1,000 cases of mineral water per year indefinitely. The current sales price is $138 per case, and the current cost per case (all variable) is $105. The firm is taxed at a rate of 34%. Both prices and costs are expected to rise at a rate of 6% per year. The firm uses only equity, and it has a cost of capital of 15%. Assume that cash flows consist only of after-tax profits, since the spring has an indefinite life and will not be depreciated.

a.   Should the firm accept the project?

b.   If total costs consisted of a fixed cost of $10,000 per year and variable costs of $95 per unit, and if only the variable costs were expected to increase with inflation, would this make the project better or worse? Continue with the assumption that the sales price will rise with inflation.

11-12

Sensitivity Analysis

Nexus Toy Company is looking to introduce a new line of high-end toy action figures. Below are the company's forecast financial data for the product:

Price per unit	$15
Quantity	450,000
Variable cost per unit	$8
Fixed cost	$1,400,000
CCA rate	20%
Tax rate	30%
Capital investment	$4,800,000
Cost of capital	11.5%

Calculate the project's NPV based on a 5-year life, using straight-line CCA. (Ignore the half-year rule.) How sensitive is the NPV to a 5% reduction in price, reduction in quantity, and increase in variable cost?

11-13

New Project Analysis

Central Drug Mart (CDM) is a drugstore chain operating in Ontario and Quebec. The company is contemplating a home delivery service for its prescription drug sales to customers who are unable to pick up their drugs in the stores. CDM is investigating whether to invest in small hybrid automobiles. The new delivery service is forecast to increase prescription drug sales by $500,000 per year. CDM's total variable costs are 60% of sales. CDM will also charge a nominal delivery fee of $3 per delivery.

The new hybrid fleet would cost $890,000 and would have an economic life of 7 years, after which time the salvage value would be $40,000. The company expects to make 13,000 deliveries per year.

On further investigation, CDM finds that the new vehicles would save $60,000 per year in fuel costs compared to regular gasoline-powered vehicles. Spare parts inventory of $30,000 would have to be purchased. Assume that the spare parts inventory is purchased at t = 0.

CDM typically uses a 12% cost of capital. Its tax rate is 30%, and the vehicles fall into a CCA class of 30%.

a. What is the NPV of this fleet delivery project?

b. If the federal government changed the CCA rate to 50% for hybrid vehicles to encourage their use, what would the NPV of the project now be?

11-14

Replacement Analysis

Saint John River Shipyards is considering replacing an old riveting machine with a new one that will increase earnings before depreciation from $34,500 to $54,000 per year. The new machine will cost $92,500, and it will have an estimated life of 8 years with an estimated salvage value of $6,500. The new machine falls into Class 43, which has a 30% CCA rate. The company is taxed at 30% and its WACC is 12%. If replaced today, the old machine could be sold for $4,000. If the old machine is kept, it will have no salvage value in 8 years. Should they replace the old riveting machine?

11-15

New Project Analysis

The marketing department has proposed selling your company's product line in a new export market. Production equipment (Class 43) with a CCA rate of 30% costing $100,000 will be needed, as will installation and training estimated at $10,000 each. These costs will all occur at time 0. Project cash flows before tax are forecast to be $40,000 per year over the 4-year project life. An initial investment in net working capital of $4,000 will be needed, and each year net working capital will increase by $2,000. The equipment will likely be obsolete at the end of the 4 years, so no salvage value is forecast. The company's tax rate is 25%, and its cost of capital is 11%.

a. Should the company sell into the new market?

b. What is the project's NPV if the equipment had a salvage value of $20,000?

c. Assuming no salvage value, what is the NPV if the CCA rate is 10%?

11-16

Replacement Analysis

Taylor Corporation currently uses an injection-moulding machine that was purchased 2 years ago. The CCA rate on this machine is 30%. Currently, it can be sold for $2,500. If this old machine is not replaced, it is not expected to have any value at the end of its useful life, estimated to be 6 years from now.

Taylor is offered a replacement machine that has a cost of $12,000, an estimated useful life of 6 years, and an estimated salvage value of $1,200. The CCA rate on this machine is also 30%. The replacement machine would permit an output expansion, so sales would rise by $1,400 per year; also, the new machine's much greater efficiency would reduce operating expenses by $1,500 per year. The new machine would require that inventories be increased by $3,000, but accounts payable would simultaneously increase by $1,000. Taylor's tax rate is 30% and its WACC is 12%. Should the company replace the old machine?

Challenging Problems 17–21

11-17

Scenario Analysis

Shao Industries is considering a proposed project for its capital budget. The company estimates that the project's NPV is $12 million. This estimate assumes that the economy and market conditions will be average over the next few years. The company's CFO, however, forecasts that there is only a 50% chance that the economy will be average. Recognizing this uncertainty, she has also performed the following scenario analysis:

Economic Scenario	Probability of Outcome	NPV
Recession	0.05	$(70 million)
Below average	0.20	(25 million)
Average	0.50	12 million
Above average	0.20	20 million
Boom	0.05	30 million

What is the project's expected NPV, its standard deviation, and its coefficient of variation?

11-18

CCA

Green Day Packers (GDP) purchased a computer for its back office operations in 2011 (assume 45% CCA) for $5,000. Because of expanding operations, GDP purchased two additional computers in 2013 for $4,000 each. By 2014, the original computer was considered to be too slow and was sold for $800. One year later the company decided to sell all its computer hardware for $1,500 and outsource its operations. Calculate GDP's UCC and maximum CCA for each year, from 2012 to 2015. Assume that the asset class is closed upon sale of the computers. If GDP's income is $50,000 before claiming CCA for 2015 and its tax rate is 30%, how much tax will the company have to pay?

11-19

Risky Cash Flows

Nicola Company (NC) must decide between two mutually exclusive investment projects. Each project costs $25,000 and has an expected life of 3 years. Annual net cash flows from each project begin 1 year after the initial investment is made and have the following probability distributions:

Project X		Project Y	
Probability	Net Cash Flows	Probability	Net Cash Flows
0.25	$22,000	0.25	$ 0
0.50	25,000	0.50	25,000
0.25	28,000	0.25	60,000

NC has decided to evaluate the riskier project at a 12% rate and the less risky project at a 9% rate.

a. What is the expected value of the annual net cash flows from each project? What is the coefficient of variation (CV)?

b. What is the risk-adjusted NPV of each project?

c. If it were known that Project Y was negatively correlated with other cash flows of the firm, whereas Project X was positively correlated, how would this knowledge affect the decision? If Project Y's cash flows were negatively correlated with gross domestic product (GDP), would that influence your assessment of its risk?

11-20

Replacement Analysis

Metro Bottling Company is contemplating replacing one of its bottling machines with a newer and more efficient one. A just completed consultant's report, which cost Metro $12,000, provided the following rationale for the purchase.

The old machine has a current value of $265,000 and a remaining useful life of 6 years. If Metro keeps the machine for another 6 years, it should be able to sell it at that time for $20,000. The new machine has a purchase price of $1,175,000, an estimated useful life of 6 years, and estimated salvage value of $145,000. Installation and training will cost $15,000. The new machine will economize on electric power usage and labour and repair costs, as well as reduce the number of defective bottles. A total annual savings of $264,000 will be realized if the new machine is installed. The new machine will initially free up $7,000 in working capital. Both machines fall into CCA asset class 43, which has a 30% CCA rate. The company's tax rate is 25%, and it has a WACC of 12%. Should the company purchase the new bottling machine?

11-21

Sequential Decisions

Yoran Yacht Company (YYC), a prominent sailboat builder in Victoria, B.C., is considering designing a new 30-foot sailboat based on the "winged" keels first introduced on the 12-metre yachts that raced for the America's Cup.

First, YYC would have to invest $10,000 at t = 0 for the design and model tank testing of the new boat. YYC's managers believe that there is a 60% probability that this phase will succeed and that the project will continue. If Stage 1 is not successful, the project will be abandoned with zero salvage value.

The next stage, if undertaken, would consist of making the moulds and producing two prototype boats. This would cost $500,000 at t = 1. If the boats test well, YYC would go into production. If they do not, the moulds and prototypes could be sold for $100,000. The managers estimate that the probability is 80% that the boats will pass testing and that Stage 3 will be undertaken.

Stage 3 consists of converting an unused production line to produce the new design. This would cost $1,000,000 at t = 2. If the economy is strong at this point, the net value of sales would be $3,000,000, while if the economy is weak, the net value would be $1,500,000. Both net values occur at t = 3, and each state of the economy has a probability of 0.5. YYC's corporate cost of capital is 12%.

a. Assume that this project has average risk. Construct a decision tree and determine the project's expected NPV.

b. Find the project's standard deviation of NPV and coefficient of variation (CV) of NPV. If YYC's average project had a CV of between 1.0 and 2.0, would this project be of high, low, or average stand-alone risk?

Spreadsheet Problem

11-22

Build a Model: Issues in
Capital Budgeting

Start with the partial model in the file *Ch 11 Build a Model.xlsx* from the textbook's website. Webmasters.com has developed a powerful new server that would be used for corporations' Internet activities. It would cost $10 million to buy the equipment necessary to manufacture the server, and it would require net operating working capital equal to 10% of sales. The servers would sell for $24,000 per unit, and Webmasters believes that variable costs would amount to $17,500 per unit. After the first year the sales price and variable costs would increase at the inflation rate of 3%. The company's nonvariable costs would be $1 million at Year 1 and would increase with inflation. It would take 1 year to buy the required equipment and set up operations, and the server project would have a life of 4 years. If the project is undertaken, it must be continued for the entire 4 years. Also, the project's returns are expected to be highly correlated with returns on the firm's other assets. The firm believes that it could sell 1,000 units per year.

The equipment would be depreciated over a 5-year period, using a CCA rate of 35%. The estimated market value of the equipment at the end of the project's 4-year life is $500,000. Webmasters' federal-plus-provincial tax rate is 40%. Its cost of capital is 10% for average-risk projects, defined as projects with a coefficient of variation of NPV between 0.8 and 1.2. Low-risk projects are evaluated with a WACC of 8%, and high-risk projects at 13%.

a. Develop a spreadsheet model and use it to find the project's NPV, IRR, and payback.
b. Now conduct a sensitivity analysis to determine the sensitivity of NPV to changes in the sales price, variable costs per unit, and number of units sold. Set these variables' values at 10% and 20% above and below their base-case values. Include a graph in your analysis.
c. Now conduct a scenario analysis. Assume that there is a 25% probability that best-case conditions, with each of the variables discussed in part b being 20% better than its base-case value, will occur. There is a 25% probability of worst-case conditions, with the variables 20% worse than base, and a 50% probability of base-case conditions.
d. If the project appears to be more or less risky than an average project, find its risk-adjusted NPV, IRR, and payback.
e. On the basis of information in the problem, would you recommend that the project be accepted?

MINI CASE

Shrieves Casting Company is considering adding a new line to its product mix, and the capital budgeting analysis is being conducted by Sidney Johnson, a recent business school graduate. The production line would be set up in unused space in Shrieves's main plant. The machinery's invoice price would be approximately $200,000, another $10,000 in shipping charges would be required, and it would cost an additional $30,000 to install the equipment. The machinery has an economic life of 4 years and would be in Class 8 with a CCA rate of 20%. The machinery is expected to have a salvage value of $25,000 after 4 years of use.

The new line would generate incremental sales of 1,250 units per year for 4 years at an incremental cost of $100 per unit in the first year, excluding depreciation. Each unit can be sold for $200 in the first year. The sales price and cost are both expected to increase by 3% per year due to inflation. Furthermore, to handle the new line, the firm's net operating working capital would have to increase by an amount equal to 12% of sales revenues. The firm's tax rate is 28%, and its overall weighted average cost of capital is 10%.

a. Define "incremental cash flow."
 (1) Should you subtract interest expense or dividends when calculating project cash flow?
 (2) Suppose the firm had spent $100,000 last year to rehabilitate the production line site. Should this be included in the analysis? Explain.
 (3) Now assume that the plant space could be leased out to another firm at $25,000 per year. Should this be included in the analysis? If so, how?
 (4) Finally, assume that the new product line is expected to decrease sales of the firm's other lines by $50,000 per year. Should this be considered in the analysis? If so, how?

b. Calculate the annual sales revenues and costs (other than CCA). Why is it important to include inflation when estimating cash flows?

c. Construct annual incremental project operating cash flows.

d. Estimate the required net operating working capital for each year and the cash flow due to investments in net operating working capital.

e. Calculate the present value of the CCA tax shield.

f. What is the after-tax salvage cash flows?

g. What is the project's NPV? Should the project should be undertaken?

h. What does the term "risk" mean in the context of capital budgeting? To what extent can risk be quantified? When risk is quantified, is the quantification based primarily on statistical analysis of historical data or on subjective, judgmental estimates?

i. (1) What are the three types of risk that are relevant in capital budgeting?

   (2) How is each of these risk types measured, and how do they relate to one another?

   (3) How is each type of risk used in the capital budgeting process?

j. (1) What is sensitivity analysis?

   (2) Perform a sensitivity analysis on the unit sales, salvage value, and cost of capital for the project. Assume that each of these variables can vary from its base-case, or expected, value by ±10% and ±20%. Include a sensitivity diagram, and discuss the results.

   (3) What is the primary weakness of sensitivity analysis? What is its primary usefulness?

k. Assume that Sidney Johnson is confident of her estimates of all the variables that affect the project's cash flows except unit sales and sales price. If product acceptance is poor, unit sales will be only 900 units a year and the unit price will be only $160; a strong consumer response will produce sales of 1,600 units and a unit price of $240. Johnson believes that there is a 25% chance of poor acceptance, a 25% chance of excellent acceptance, and a 50% chance of average acceptance (the base case).

   (1) What is scenario analysis?

   (2) What is the worst-case NPV? the best-case NPV?

   (3) Use the worst-, base-, and best-case NPVs and probabilities of occurrence to find the project's expected NPV, standard deviation, and coefficient of variation.

l. Are there problems with scenario analysis? Define simulation analysis, and discuss its principal advantages and disadvantages.

m. (1) Assume that Shrieves's average project has a coefficient of variation in the range of 0.7 to 0.9. Would the new line be classified as high risk, average risk, or low risk? What type of risk is being measured here?

   (2) Shrieves typically adds or subtracts 3 percentage points to the overall cost of capital to adjust for risk. Should the new line be accepted?

   (3) Are there any subjective risk factors that should be considered before the final decision is made?

n. What is a real option? What are some types of real options?

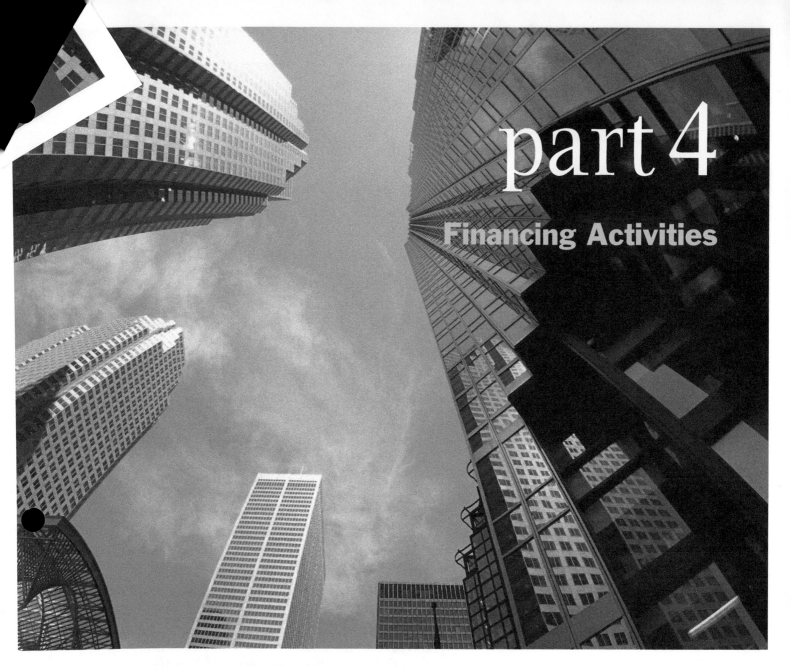

part 4

Financing Activities

chapter 12

Capital Structure Decisions

All companies need capital to finance their operations. To acquire that capital, funds must be raised, usually as a combination of debt and equity. While equity provides the most flexibility to managers, it is also the most expensive source of capital. Debt, on the other hand, is cheaper since creditors have a priority claim on the company's cash flows and assets and therefore require a lower rate of return. Moreover, a company's interest expenses are tax deductible, which further reduces debt's cost. However, debt also places a greater burden on the company. Interest payments must be made, regardless of the company's sales or profit levels, or creditors can force the company into bankruptcy. Therefore, during recessionary times, companies with significant debt levels often experience financial distress (or even worse) as they struggle to meet their legally binding interest obligations.

The above fact was quite evident during the most recent recession of 2008–2009, when Canadian resource companies were caught with too much debt on their balance sheets. One of the best-known examples was Teck Resources. In 2008 Teck reached an agreement to buy out Fording Coal in a $14 billion deal. Teck borrowed $10 billion to make the purchase. Since commodity prices had been high in the preceding years, Teck's strategy was to utilize the large cash flows that Fording and its own operations were producing in order to pay down the debt relatively quickly. However, as the 2008 financial crisis hit businesses globally, commodity prices fell quickly, significantly slashing Teck's ability to manage its huge debt. Over a 1-year period, from 2008 to 2009, Teck's debt-to-asset ratio rose from 16% to 54%, while its stock lost 90% of its value.

Teck made a series of bold steps to reduce and restructure its debt. The company stopped paying dividends, reduced its capital expenditures, sold off several mines, sold a share in a hydro dam, laid off workers, and sold 100 million of its shares to a Chinese investment fund. Teck's balance sheet is much stronger today, but the road to recovery has been difficult.

If we fast-forward to today, it appears that Canadian resource companies are now much more cautious about the amount of debt they use. Despite high commodity prices, growing profits, and large amounts of cash on hand, companies have been cautious about taking on projects or acquisitions that would aggressively leverage up their balance sheets. Should companies rely on more expensive equity to keep their debt levels low? Can some companies handle debt with less risk than others? Can a company make itself more valuable by altering the amount of debt it uses? Keep these questions in mind as you read this chapter.

Sources: Peter Koven, "Canadian Resource Companies Looking Like Winners," *National Post*, August 9, 2011, http://www.nationalpost.com, accessed January 9, 2012; "Teck Survives Fording Takeover," TSI Network, September 11, 2009, http://www.tsinetwork.ca, accessed January 9, 2012.

As we saw in Chapter 5, growth in sales requires growth in operating capital, often requiring that external funds be raised through a combination of debt and equity. The firm's mixture of debt and equity is called its **capital structure.** Although actual levels of debt and equity may vary somewhat over time, most firms try to keep their financing mix close to a **target capital structure.** A firm's *capital structure decision* includes its choice of a target capital structure, the average maturity of its debt, and the specific types of financing it decides to use at any particular time. As with operating decisions, managers should make capital structure decisions designed to maximize the firm's value.

The textbook's website contains an *Excel* file that will guide you through the chapter's calculations. The file for this chapter is *Ch 12 Tool Kit.xlsx*, and we encourage you to open the file and follow along as you read the chapter. **www .nelson.com/brigham3ce**

12.1 A Preview of Capital Structure Issues

The value of a firm's operations is the present value of its expected future free cash flows (FCF), discounted at its weighted average cost of capital (WACC):

$$V_{op} = \sum_{t=1}^{\infty} \frac{FCF_t}{(1 + WACC)^t} \qquad (12\text{-}1)$$

The WACC depends on the percentages of debt and equity (w_d and w_{ce}), the cost of debt (r_d), the cost of stock (r_s), and the corporate tax rate (T):

$$WACC = w_d(1 - T)r_d + w_{ce}\, r_s \qquad (12\text{-}2)$$

As these equations show, the only way any decision can change a firm's value is by affecting either free cash flows or the cost of capital. We discuss below some of the ways that a higher proportion of debt can affect WACC and/or FCF.

Debt Increases the Cost of Stock, r_s

Debtholders have a prior claim on the company's cash flows relative to shareholders, who are entitled only to any residual cash flow after debtholders have been paid. As we show later in a numerical example, the "fixed" claim of the debtholders causes the "residual" claim of the shareholders to become less certain, and this increases the cost of stock, r_s.

Debt Reduces the Taxes a Company Pays

Imagine that a company's cash flows are a pie and that three different groups get pieces of the pie. The first piece goes to the government in the form of taxes, the second goes to debtholders, and the third to shareholders. Companies can deduct interest expenses when calculating taxable income, which reduces the government's piece of the pie and leaves more pie available to debtholders and investors. This reduction in taxes reduces the after-tax cost of debt, as shown in Equation 12-2.

The Risk of Bankruptcy Increases the Cost of Debt, r_d

As debt increases, the probability of financial distress, or even bankruptcy, goes up. With higher bankruptcy risk, debtholders will insist on a higher promised return, which increases the pre-tax cost of debt, r_d.

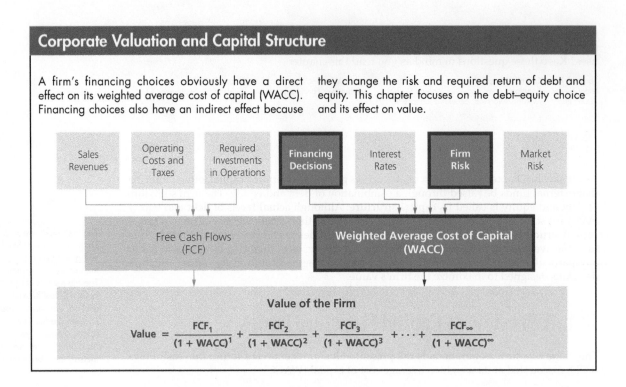

Corporate Valuation and Capital Structure

A firm's financing choices obviously have a direct effect on its weighted average cost of capital (WACC). Financing choices also have an indirect effect because they change the risk and required return of debt and equity. This chapter focuses on the debt–equity choice and its effect on value.

$$Value = \frac{FCF_1}{(1 + WACC)^1} + \frac{FCF_2}{(1 + WACC)^2} + \frac{FCF_3}{(1 + WACC)^3} + \cdots + \frac{FCF_\infty}{(1 + WACC)^\infty}$$

The Net Effect on the Weighted Average Cost of Capital

As Equation 12-2 shows, the WACC is a weighted average of relatively low-cost debt and high-cost equity. If we increase the proportion of debt, then the weight of low-cost debt (w_d) increases and the weight of high-cost equity (w_{ce}) decreases. If all else remained the same, the WACC would fall and the value of the firm in Equation 12-1 would increase. But the previous paragraphs show that all else doesn't remain the same: both r_d and r_s increase. While it should be clear that changing the capital structure affects all the variables in the WACC equation, it's not easy to say whether those changes increase the WACC, decrease it, or balance out exactly and leave the WACC unchanged. We'll return to this issue later, when we discuss capital structure theory.

Bankruptcy Risk Reduces Free Cash Flow

As the risk of bankruptcy increases, some customers may choose to buy from another company, which hurts sales. This, in turn, decreases net operating profit after taxes (NOPAT), thus reducing FCF. Financial distress also hurts the productivity of workers and managers, as they spend more time worrying about their next job rather than their current job. Again, this reduces NOPAT and FCF. Finally, suppliers tighten their credit standards, which reduces accounts payable and causes net operating working capital to increase, thus reducing FCF. Therefore, the risk of bankruptcy can decrease FCF and reduce the value of the firm.

Bankruptcy Risk Affects Agency Costs

Higher levels of debt may affect the behaviour of managers in two opposing ways. First, when times are good, managers may waste cash flow on perquisites and unnecessary expenditures. This is an agency cost, as described later in Chapter 22. The good news is that the threat of bankruptcy reduces such wasteful spending, which increases FCF.

But the bad news is that a manager may become gun-shy and reject positive NPV projects if they are risky. From the shareholder's point of view, it would be unfortunate if a risky project caused the company to go into bankruptcy, but note that other companies in the shareholder's portfolio may be taking on risky projects that turn out to be successful. Since most shareholders are well diversified, they can afford for a manager to take on risky but positive NPV projects. But a manager's reputation and wealth are generally tied to a single company, so the project may be unacceptably risky from the manager's point of view.

Thus, high debt can cause managers to forgo positive NPV projects unless they are extremely safe. This is called the **underinvestment problem,** and it is another type of agency cost. Notice that debt can reduce one aspect of agency costs (wasteful spending) but may increase another (underinvestment), so the net effect on value isn't clear.

Issuing Equity Conveys a Signal to the Marketplace

Managers are in a better position to forecast a company's free cash flow than are investors. Academics call this *informational asymmetry*. Suppose a company's stock price is $50 per share. If managers are willing to issue new stock at $50 per share, investors reason that no one would sell anything for less than its true value. Therefore, the true value of the shares as seen by the managers with their superior information must be less than or equal to $50. Thus, investors perceive an equity issue as a negative signal, and this usually causes the stock price to fall.[1]

CONCEPT REVIEW

1. Briefly describe some ways in which the capital structure decision can affect the WACC and FCF.

12.2 Business Risk and Financial Risk

Business risk and financial risk combine to determine the total risk of a firm's future return on equity, as we explain in the following sections.

Business Risk

Business risk is the risk a firm's common shareholders would face if the firm had no debt. Business risk arises from uncertainty in projections of the firm's cash flows, which in turn means uncertainty about its operating profit and its capital (investment) requirements. In other words, we do not know for sure how large operating profits will be, nor do we know how much we will have to invest to develop new products, build new plants, and so forth. The return on invested capital (ROIC) combines these two sources of uncertainty, and its variability can be used to measure business risk on a stand-alone basis:

$$\text{ROIC} = \frac{\text{NOPAT}}{\text{Capital}} = \frac{\text{EBIT}(1 - T)}{\text{Capital}}$$

$$= \frac{\text{Net income to common shareholders} + \text{After-tax interest payments}}{\text{Capital}}$$

Here NOPAT is net operating profit after taxes, and capital is the required amount of operating capital, which is numerically equivalent to the sum of the firm's debt and common equity. Business risk can then be measured by the standard deviation of ROIC, σ_{ROIC}. If the firm's capital requirements are stable, then we can use the variability in EBIT, σ_{EBIT}, as an alternative measure of stand-alone business risk.

Business risk depends on a number of factors, as described below:

1. *Demand variability.* The more stable the demand for a firm's products, other things held constant, the lower its business risk.
2. *Sales price variability.* Firms whose products are sold in highly volatile markets are exposed to more business risk than similar firms whose output prices are more stable.
3. *Input cost variability.* Firms whose input costs are highly uncertain are exposed to a high degree of business risk.
4. *Ability to adjust output prices for changes in input costs.* Some firms are better able than others to raise their own output prices when input costs rise. The greater the ability to adjust output prices to reflect cost conditions, the lower the business risk.

---

[1]An exception to this rule is any situation with little informational asymmetry, such as a regulated utility. Also, some companies, such as start-ups or high-tech ventures, are unable to find willing lenders and therefore must issue equity; we discuss this later in the chapter.

5. *Ability to develop new products in a timely and cost-effective manner.* Firms in high-tech industries such as drugs and computers depend on a constant stream of new products. The faster that products become obsolete, the greater the business risk.

6. *Foreign risk exposure.* Firms that generate a high percentage of their earnings overseas are subject to earnings declines due to exchange rate fluctuations. Also, if a firm operates in a politically unstable area, it may be subject to political risks. See Chapter 21 for a further discussion.

7. *The extent to which costs are fixed: operating leverage.* If a high percentage of its costs are fixed, and hence do not decline when demand falls, then the firm is exposed to a relatively high degree of business risk. This factor is called *operating leverage,* and it is discussed at length in the next section.

Each of these factors is determined partly by the firm's industry characteristics, but each of them is also controllable to some extent by management. For example, most firms can, through their marketing policies, take actions to stabilize both unit sales and sales prices. However, this stabilization may require spending a great deal on advertising and/or price concessions to get commitments from customers to purchase fixed quantities at fixed prices in the future. Similarly, firms can reduce the volatility of future input costs by negotiating long-term labour and materials supply contracts, but they may have to pay prices above the current spot price to obtain these contracts. Many firms are also using hedging techniques to reduce business risk.

Operating Leverage

In physics, leverage implies the use of a lever to raise a heavy object with a small force. In politics, if people have leverage, their smallest word or action can accomplish a lot. *In business terminology, a high degree of* **operating leverage,** *other factors held constant, implies that a relatively small change in sales results in a large change in EBIT.*

Other things held constant, the higher a firm's fixed costs, the greater its operating leverage. Higher fixed costs are generally associated with more highly automated, capital-intensive firms and industries. However, businesses that employ highly skilled workers who must be retained and paid even during recessions also have relatively high fixed costs, as do firms with high product development costs, because the amortization of development costs is an element of fixed costs.

Consider Strasburg Electronics Company, a debt-free (unlevered) firm. Figure 12-1 illustrates the concept of operating leverage by comparing the results that Strasburg could expect if it used different degrees of operating leverage. Plan A calls for a relatively small amount of fixed costs, $20,000. Here the firm would not have much automated equipment, so its depreciation, maintenance, property taxes, and so on would be low. However, the total operating costs line has a relatively steep slope, indicating that variable costs per unit are higher than they would be if the firm used more operating leverage. Plan B calls for a higher level of fixed costs, $60,000. Here the firm uses automated equipment (with which one operator can turn out a few or many units at the same labour cost) to a much larger extent. The break-even point is higher under Plan B—break-even occurs at 60,000 units under Plan B versus only 40,000 units under Plan A.

We can calculate the break-even quantity by recognizing that *operating break-even* occurs when earnings before interest and taxes (EBIT) = 0:[2]

See ***Ch 12 Tool Kit.xlsx*** at the textbook's website for all calculations.

$$EBIT = PQ - VQ - F = 0 \qquad (12\text{-}3)$$

Here P is average sales price per unit of output, Q is units of output, V is variable cost per unit, and F is fixed operating costs. If we solve for the break-even quantity, Q_{BE}, we get this expression:

$$Q_{BE} = \frac{F}{P - V} \qquad (12\text{-}4)$$

[2]This definition of break-even does not include any fixed financial costs because Strasburg is an unlevered firm. If there were fixed financial costs, the firm would suffer an accounting loss at the operating break-even point. We introduce financial costs shortly.

FIGURE 12-1 Illustration of Operating Leverage

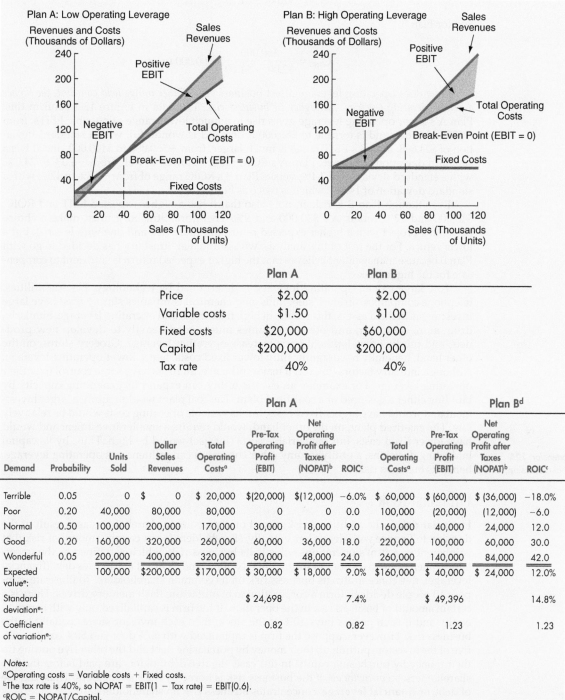

	Plan A	Plan B
Price	$2.00	$2.00
Variable costs	$1.50	$1.00
Fixed costs	$20,000	$60,000
Capital	$200,000	$200,000
Tax rate	40%	40%

				Plan A				Plan B[d]		
Demand	Probability	Units Sold	Dollar Sales Revenues	Total Operating Costs[a]	Pre-Tax Operating Profit (EBIT)	Net Operating Profit after Taxes (NOPAT)[b]	ROIC[c]	Total Operating Costs[a]	Pre-Tax Operating Profit (EBIT)	Net Operating Profit after Taxes (NOPAT)[b]	ROIC[c]
Terrible	0.05	0	$ 0	$ 20,000	$(20,000)	$(12,000)	−6.0%	$ 60,000	$ (60,000)	$ (36,000)	−18.0%
Poor	0.20	40,000	80,000	80,000	0	0	0.0	100,000	(20,000)	(12,000)	−6.0
Normal	0.50	100,000	200,000	170,000	30,000	18,000	9.0	160,000	40,000	24,000	12.0
Good	0.20	160,000	320,000	260,000	60,000	36,000	18.0	220,000	100,000	60,000	30.0
Wonderful	0.05	200,000	400,000	320,000	80,000	48,000	24.0	260,000	140,000	84,000	42.0
Expected value[e]:		100,000	$200,000	$170,000	$ 30,000	$ 18,000	9.0%	$160,000	$ 40,000	$ 24,000	12.0%
Standard deviation[e]:					$ 24,698		7.4%		$ 49,396		14.8%
Coefficient of variation[e]:					0.82		0.82		1.23		1.23

Notes:
[a]Operating costs = Variable costs + Fixed costs.
[b]The tax rate is 40%, so NOPAT = EBIT(1 − Tax rate) = EBIT(0.6).
[c]ROIC = NOPAT/Capital.
[d]The break-even sales level for Plan B is not shown in the table, but it is 60,000 units or $120,000.
[e]The expected value, standard deviations, and coefficients of variation were found using the procedures discussed in Chapter 7.

Thus for Plan A,

$$Q_{BE} = \frac{\$20,000}{\$2.00 - \$1.50} = 40,000 \text{ units}$$

and for Plan B,

$$Q_{BE} = \frac{\$60,000}{\$2.00 - \$1.00} = 60,000 \text{ units}$$

How does operating leverage affect business risk? *Other things held constant, the higher a firm's operating leverage, the higher its business risk.* The data in Figure 12-1 confirm this. Plan A's lower operating leverage gives rise to a much lower range of possible EBITs, from −$20,000 if demand is terrible to $80,000 if demand is wonderful, with a standard deviation of $24,698. Plan B's EBIT range is much larger, from −$60,000 to $140,000, and it has a standard deviation of $49,396. Plan A's ROIC range is lower as well, from −6.0% to 24.0%, with a standard deviation of 7.4%, versus Plan B's ROIC range of from −18% to 42%, with a standard deviation of 14.8%, which is twice as high as A's.

Even though Plan B is riskier, note also that it has a higher expected EBIT and ROIC: $40,000 and 12% versus A's $30,000 and 9%. Therefore, Strasburg must make a choice between a project with a higher expected return but more risk and one with less risk but a lower return. For the rest of this analysis, we assume that Strasburg has decided to go with Plan B because management believes that the higher expected return is sufficient to compensate for the higher risk.

To a large extent, operating leverage is determined by technology. Electric utilities, telephone companies, airlines, steel mills, and chemical companies simply *must* have large investments in fixed assets; this results in high fixed costs and operating leverage. Similarly, drug, auto, computer, and other companies must spend heavily to develop new products, and product development costs increase operating leverage. Grocery stores, on the other hand, generally have significantly lower fixed costs, hence lower operating leverage. Although industry factors do exert a major influence, all firms have some control over their operating leverage. For example, an electric utility can expand its generating capacity by building either a gas-fired or a coal-fired plant. The coal plant would require a larger investment and would have higher fixed costs, but its variable operating costs would be relatively low. The gas-fired plant, on the other hand, would require a smaller investment and would have lower fixed costs, but the variable costs (for gas) would be high. Thus, by its capital budgeting decisions, a utility (or any other company) can influence its operating leverage, hence its business risk.[3]

See **Web Extension 12A** for additional discussion.

Financial Risk

Financial risk is the additional risk placed on the common shareholders as a result of the decision to finance with debt. Conceptually, shareholders face a certain amount of risk that is inherent in a firm's operations—this is its business risk, which is defined as the uncertainty inherent in projections of future EBIT, NOPAT, and ROIC. If a firm uses debt (financial leverage), this concentrates its business risk on its common shareholders. To illustrate, suppose 10 people decide to form a corporation to manufacture flash memory drives. There is a certain amount of business risk in the operation. If the firm is capitalized only with common equity and if each person buys 10% of the stock, then each investor shares equally in the business risk. However, suppose the firm is capitalized with 50% debt and 50% equity, with five of the investors putting up their money by purchasing debt and the other five putting up their money by purchasing equity. In this case, the five debtholders are paid before the five shareholders, so *virtually all* of the business risk is borne by the shareholders. Thus, the use of debt, or **financial leverage,** concentrates business risk on shareholders.[4]

See **Ch 12 Tool Kit.xlsx** at the textbook's website for detailed calculations.

To illustrate the concentration of business risk, we can extend the Strasburg Electronics example. To date, the company has never used debt, but the treasurer is now considering a possible change in the capital structure. For now, assume that only two financing choices are being considered—remaining at zero debt, or shifting to $100,000 debt and $100,000 book equity.

---

[3]See **Web Extension 12A** for additional discussion of measuring the degree of operating leverage.
[4]Holders of corporate debt generally do bear some business risk, because they may lose some of their investment if the firm goes bankrupt. We discuss this in more depth later in the chapter.

First, focus on Section I of Table 12-1, which assumes that Strasburg uses no debt. Since debt is zero, interest is also zero; hence pre-tax income is equal to EBIT. Taxes at 40% are deducted to obtain net income, which is then divided by the $200,000 of book equity to calculate ROE. Note that Strasburg receives a tax credit if the demand is either terrible or poor (which are the two scenarios where net income is negative). Here we assume that Strasburg's losses can be carried back to offset income earned in the prior year. The ROE at each sales

TABLE 12-1 Effects of Financial Leverage: Strasburg Electronics Financed with Zero Debt or with $100,000 of Debt

Section I. Zero Debt

Debt   0
Book equity $200,000

Demand for Product (1)	Probability (2)	EBIT (3)	Interest (4)	Pre-Tax Income (5)	Taxes (40%) (6)	Net Income (7)	ROE (8)
Terrible	0.05	$ (60,000)	$0	$ (60,000)	$(24,000)	$(36,000)	−18.0%
Poor	0.20	(20,000)	0	(20,000)	(8,000)	(12,000)	−6.0
Normal	0.50	40,000	0	40,000	16,000	24,000	12.0
Good	0.20	100,000	0	100,000	40,000	60,000	30.0
Wonderful	0.05	140,000	0	140,000	56,000	84,000	42.0
Expected value:		$ 40,000	$0	$ 40,000	$ 16,000	$ 24,000	12.0%
Standard deviation:							14.8%
Coefficient of variation:							1.23

Section II. $100,000 of Debt

Debt $100,000
Book equity $100,000
Interest rate   10%

Demand for Product (1)	Probability (2)	EBIT (3)	Interest (4)	Pre-Tax Income (5)	Taxes (40%) (6)	Net Income (7)	ROE (8)
Terrible	0.05	$ (60,000)	$10,000	$ (70,000)	$(28,000)	$(42,000)	−42.0%
Poor	0.20	(20,000)	10,000	(30,000)	(12,000)	(18,000)	−18.0
Normal	0.50	40,000	10,000	30,000	12,000	18,000	18.0
Good	0.20	100,000	10,000	90,000	36,000	54,000	54.0
Wonderful	0.05	140,000	10,000	130,000	52,000	78,000	78.0
Expected value:		$ 40,000	$10,000	$ 30,000	$ 12,000	$ 18,000	18.0%
Standard deviation:							29.6%
Coefficient of variation:							1.65

Assumptions:

1. In terms of its operating leverage, Strasburg has chosen Plan B. The probability distribution and EBITs are obtained from Figure 12-1.
2. Sales and operating costs, hence EBIT, are not affected by the financing decision. Therefore, EBIT under both financing plans is identical, and it is taken from the EBIT column for Plan B in Figure 12-1.
3. All losses can be carried back to offset income in the prior year.

level is then multiplied by the probability of that sales level to calculate the 12% expected ROE. Note that this 12% is equal to the ROIC we found in Figure 12-1 for Plan B, since ROE is equal to ROIC if a firm has no debt.

Now let's look at the situation if Strasburg decides to use $100,000 of debt financing, shown in Section II of Table 12-1, with the debt costing 10%. Demand will not be affected, nor will operating costs; hence the EBIT columns are the same for the zero debt and $100,000 debt cases. However, the company will now have $100,000 of debt with a cost of 10%; hence its interest expense will be $10,000. This interest must be paid regardless of the state of the economy—if it is not paid, the company will be forced into bankruptcy, and shareholders will probably be wiped out. Therefore, we show a $10,000 cost in Column 4 as a fixed number for all demand conditions. Column 5 shows pre-tax income, Column 6 the applicable taxes, and Column 7 the resulting net income. When the net income figures are divided by the book equity—which will now be only $100,000 because $100,000 of the $200,000 total requirement was obtained as debt—we find the ROEs under each demand state. If demand is terrible and sales are zero, then a very large loss will be incurred, and the ROE will be −42.0%. However, if demand is wonderful, then ROE will be 78.0%. The probability-weighted average is the expected ROE, which is 18.0% if the company uses $100,000 of debt.

Typically, financing with debt increases the common shareholders' expected rate of return for an investment, but debt also increases the common shareholders' risk. This situation holds with our example—financial leverage raises the expected ROE from 12% to 18%, but it also increases the risk of the investment as seen by the increase in the standard deviation from 14.8% to 29.6% and the increase in the coefficient of variation from 1.23 to 1.65.[5]

We see, then, that using leverage has both good and bad effects: higher leverage increases expected ROE, but it also increases risk. The next section discusses how this trade-off between risk and return affects the value of the firm.[6]

CONCEPT REVIEW

1. What is business risk, and how can it be measured?
2. What are some determinants of business risk?
3. How does operating leverage affect business risk?
4. What is financial risk, and how does it arise?
5. Explain this statement: "Using leverage has both good and bad effects."
6. A firm has fixed operating costs of $100,000 and variable costs of $4 per unit. If it sells the product for $6 per unit, what is the break-even quantity? (Check Figure: 50,000)

12.3 Capital Structure Theory

In the previous section, we showed how capital structure choices affect a firm's ROE and its risk. For a number of reasons, we would expect capital structures to vary considerably across industries. For example, pharmaceutical companies generally have very different capital structures than airline companies. Moreover, capital structures vary among firms within a given industry. What factors explain these differences? In an attempt to answer this question, academics and practitioners have developed a number of theories, and these theories have been subjected to many empirical tests. The following sections examine several of these theories.[7]

---

[5]See Chapter 7 for a review of procedures for calculating the standard deviation and coefficient of variation. Recall that the advantage of the coefficient of variation is that it permits better comparisons when the expected values of ROE vary, as they do here for the two capital structures.
[6]For more on the links between market risk, operating risk, and financial leverage, see Carolyn M. Callahan and Rosanne M. Mohr, "The Determinants of Systematic Risk: A Synthesis," *Financial Review*, May 1989, 157–181; and Alexandros P. Prezas, "Effects of Debt on the Degrees of Operating and Financial Leverage," *Financial Management*, Summer 1987, 39–44.
[7]For additional discussion of capital structure theories, see John C. Easterwood and Palani-Rajan Kadapakkam, "The Role of Private and Public Debt in Corporate Capital Structures," *Financial Management*, Autumn 1991, 49–57; Gerald T. Garvey, "Leveraging the Underinvestment Problem: How High Debt and Management Shareholdings Solve the Agency Costs of Free Cash Flow," *Journal of Financial Research*, Summer 1992, 149–166; Milton Harris and Artur Raviv, "Capital Structure and the Informational Role of Debt," *Journal of Finance*, June 1990, 321–349; and Ronen Israel, "Capital Structure and the Market for Corporate Control: The Defensive Role of Debt Financing," *Journal of Finance*, September 1991, 1391–1409.

Modigliani and Miller: No Taxes

Modern capital structure theory began in 1958, when Professors Franco Modigliani and Merton Miller (hereafter MM) published what has been called the most influential finance article ever written.[8] As we explain in this chapter, MM employed the concept of **arbitrage** to develop their theory. Arbitrage occurs when two similar assets—in this case, levered and unlevered stocks—sell at different prices. Arbitrageurs will buy the undervalued stock and simultaneously sell the overvalued stock, earning a profit in the process, and will continue to do so until market forces of supply and demand cause the prices of the two assets to be equal. For arbitrage to work, the assets must be equivalent, or nearly so. MM show that under their assumptions, levered and unlevered stocks are sufficiently similar for the arbitrage process to operate.

No one, not even MM, believes that their assumptions are sufficiently correct to cause their models to hold exactly in the real world. However, their models do show how money can be made through arbitrage if one can find ways around problems with the assumptions. Here are the initial MM assumptions. Note that some of them were later relaxed:

1. There are no brokerage costs.
2. There are no taxes.
3. There are no bankruptcy costs.
4. Investors can borrow at the same rate as corporations.
5. All investors have the same information as management about the firm's future investment opportunities.
6. EBIT is not affected by the use of debt.

MM first analyzed leverage under the assumption that there are no corporate or personal income taxes. On the basis of their assumptions, they stated and algebraically proved two propositions:[9]

Proposition I The value of any firm is established by capitalizing its expected net operating income (EBIT) at a constant rate (r_{sU}) that is based on the firm's risk class:

$$V_L = V_U = \frac{EBIT}{WACC} = \frac{EBIT}{r_{sU}} \qquad (12\text{-}5)$$

Here the subscript L designates a levered firm and U designates an unlevered firm. Both firms are assumed to be in the same business risk class, and r_{sU} is the required rate of return for an unlevered, or all-equity, firm of this risk class when there are no taxes. For our purposes, it is easiest to think in terms of a single firm that has the option of financing either with all equity or with some combination of debt and equity. Hence, L designates the firm if it uses some amount of debt, and U designates the firm if it uses no debt.

Because V as established by Equation 12-5 is a constant, *then under the MM model, when there are no taxes, the value of the firm is independent of its leverage.* As we shall see, this also implies the following:

1. The weighted average cost of capital, WACC, to the firm, is completely independent of its capital structure.
2. Regardless of the amount of debt the firm uses, its WACC is equal to the cost of equity that it would have if it used no debt.

Proposition II When there are no taxes, the cost of equity to a levered firm, r_{sL}, is equal to (1) the cost of equity to an unlevered firm in the same risk class, r_{sU}, plus (2) a risk premium whose size depends on both the difference between an unlevered firm's costs of debt and equity and the amount of debt used:

$$r_{sL} = r_{sU} + \text{Risk premium} = r_{sU} + (r_{sU} - r_d)(D/S) \qquad (12\text{-}6)$$

---

[8]Franco Modigliani and Merton H. Miller, "The Cost of Capital, Corporation Finance, and the Theory of Investment," *American Economic Review*, June 1958, 261–297. Modigliani and Miller both won Nobel Prizes for their work.
[9]MM actually stated and proved three propositions, but the third one is not material to our discussion here.

Here D = market value of the firm's debt, S = market value of its equity, and r_d = the constant cost of debt. Equation 12-6 states that *as debt increases, the cost of equity also rises in a mathematically precise manner (even though the cost of debt does not rise)*.

Taken together, the two MM propositions imply that using more debt in the capital structure will not increase the value of the firm, because the benefits of cheaper debt will be exactly offset by an increase in the riskiness of the equity, hence in its cost. Thus, MM argue that, *in a world without taxes, both the value of a firm and its WACC would be unaffected by its capital structure.*

MM's Arbitrage Proof

MM used an *arbitrage proof* to support their propositions.[10] They showed that, under their assumptions, if two companies differed only (1) in the way they were financed and (2) in their total market values, then investors would sell shares of the higher-valued firm, buy those of the lower-valued firm, and continue this process until the companies had exactly the same market value. To illustrate, assume that two firms, L and U, are identical in all important respects except that Firm L has $4,000,000 of 7.5% debt while Firm U uses only equity. Both firms have EBIT = $900,000, and σ_{EBIT} is the same for both firms, so they are in the same business risk class.

MM assumed that all firms are in a zero-growth situation; that is, EBIT is expected to remain constant, which will occur if ROE is constant, all earnings are paid out as dividends, and there are no taxes. Under the constant EBIT assumption, the total market value of the common stock, S, is the present value of a perpetuity, which is found as follows:

$$S = \frac{\text{Dividends}}{r_{sL}} = \frac{\text{Net income}}{r_{sL}} = \frac{(\text{EBIT} - r_d D)}{r_{sL}} \qquad (12\text{-}7)$$

Equation 12-7 is merely the value of a perpetuity whose numerator is the net income available to common shareholders, all of which is paid out as dividends, and whose denominator is the cost of common equity. Since there are no taxes, the numerator is not multiplied by $(1 - T)$ as it would be if we calculated NOPAT as in Chapter 2.

Assume that initially, *before any arbitrage occurs*, both firms have the same equity capitalization rate: $r_{sU} = r_{sL} = 10\%$. Under this condition, according to Equation 12-7, the following situation would exist:

Firm U:

$$\text{Value of Firm U's stock} = S_U = \frac{\text{EBIT} - r_d D}{r_{sU}}$$

$$= \frac{\$900,000 - \$0}{0.10} = \$9,000,000$$

$$\text{The total market value of Firm U} = V_U = D_U + S_U = \$0 + \$9,000,000$$

$$= \$9,000,000$$

Firm L:

$$\text{Value of Firm L's stock} = S_L = \frac{\text{EBIT} - r_d D}{r_{sL}}$$

$$= \frac{\$900,000 - 0.075(\$4,000,000)}{0.10} = \frac{\$600,000}{0.10}$$

$$= \$6,000,000$$

---

[10]By *arbitrage* we mean the simultaneous buying and selling of essentially identical assets that sell at different prices. The buying increases the price of the undervalued asset, and the selling decreases the price of the overvalued asset. Arbitrage operations will continue until prices have adjusted to the point where the arbitrageur can no longer earn a profit, at which point the market is in equilibrium. In the absence of transaction costs, equilibrium requires that the prices of the two assets be equal.

$$\text{The total market value of Firm L} = V_L = D_L + S_L = \$4,000,000 + \$6,000,000$$

$$= \$10,000,000$$

Thus before arbitrage, and assuming that $r_{sU} = r_{sL}$ (which implies that capital structure has no effect on the cost of equity), the value of the levered Firm L exceeds that of the unlevered Firm U.

MM argued that this is a disequilibrium situation that cannot persist. To see why, suppose you owned 10% of L's stock, so that the market value of your investment was $0.10(\$6,000,000) = \$600,000$. According to MM, you could increase your income without increasing your exposure to risk. For example, suppose you (1) sold your stock in L for $600,000, (2) borrowed an amount equal to 10% of L's debt ($400,000), and then (3) bought 10% of U's stock for $900,000. Note that you would receive $1,000,000 from the sale of your 10% of L's stock plus your borrowing, and you would be spending only $900,000 on U's stock, so you would have an extra $100,000, which you could invest in riskless debt to yield 7.5%, or $7,500 annually.

Now consider your income positions:

Old Portfolio		**New Portfolio**	
10% of L's $600,000 equity income	$60,000	10% of U's $900,000 equity income	$90,000
		Less 7.5% interest on $400,000 loan	(30,000)
		Plus 7.5% interest on extra $100,000	7,500
Total income	$60,000	Total income	$67,500

Thus, your net income from common stock would be exactly the same as before, $60,000, but you would have $100,000 left over for investment in riskless debt, which would increase your income by $7,500. Therefore, the total return on your $600,000 net worth would rise to $67,500. Furthermore, your risk, according to MM, would be the same as before, because you would have simply substituted $400,000 of "homemade" leverage for your 10% share of Firm L's $4 million of corporate leverage. Thus, neither your "effective" debt nor your risk would have changed. Therefore, you would have increased your income without raising your risk, which is obviously desirable.

MM argued that this arbitrage process would actually occur, with sales of L's stock driving its price down and purchases of U's stock driving its price up, until the market values of the two firms were equal. Until this equality was established, gains could be obtained by switching from one stock to the other; hence the profit motive would force equality to be reached. When equilibrium was established, the values of Firms L and U, and their weighted average costs of capital, would be equal. Thus, according to Modigliani and Miller, both a firm's value and its WACC must be independent of capital structure.

Note that each of the assumptions listed at the beginning of this section is necessary for the arbitrage proof to work exactly. For example, if the companies did not have identical business risk, or if transactions costs were significant, then the arbitrage process could not be invoked. We discuss other implications of the assumptions later in the chapter.

Arbitrage with Short Sales

Even if you did not own any stock in L, you still could reap benefits if U and L did not have the same total market value. Your first step would be to sell short $600,000 of stock in L. To do this, your broker would let you borrow stock in L from another client. Your broker would then sell the stock for you and give you the proceeds, or $600,000 in cash. You would supplement this $600,000 by borrowing $400,000. With the $1 million total, you would buy 10% of the stock in U for $900,000, and have $100,000 remaining.

Your position would then consist of $100,000 in cash and two portfolios. The first portfolio would contain $900,000 of stock in U, and it would generate $90,000 of income. Because you own the stock, we'll call it the "long" portfolio. The other portfolio would consist of $600,000 of stock in L and $400,000 of debt. The value of this portfolio is $1 million, and it would generate $60,000 of dividends and $30,000 of interest. However, you would not own this second portfolio—you would "owe" it. Since you borrowed the $400,000, you would owe the $30,000 in interest. And since you borrowed the stock in L, you would

FINANCE: IN FOCUS

Yogi Berra on the MM Proposition

When a waitress asked Yogi Berra (Baseball Hall of Fame catcher for the New York Yankees) whether he wanted his pizza cut into four pieces or eight, Yogi replied: "Better make it four. I don't think I can eat eight."[a]

Yogi's quip helps convey the basic insight of Modigliani and Miller. The firm's choice of leverage "slices" the distribution of future cash flows in a way that is like slicing a pizza. MM recognized that if you fix a company's investment activities, it's like fixing the size of the pizza; no information costs means that everyone sees the same pizza; no taxes means the government gets none of the pie;

and no "contracting costs" means nothing sticks to the knife.

So, just as the substance of Yogi's meal is unaffected by whether the pizza is sliced into four pieces or eight, the economic substance of the firm is unaffected by whether the liability side of the balance sheet is sliced to include more or less debt, at least under the MM assumptions.

[a]Lee Green, *Sportswit* (New York: Fawcett Crest, 1984), p. 228.

Source: "The Determinants of Corporate Leverage and Dividend Policies," *Journal of Applied Corporate Finance*, Vol. 7, No. 4 (Winter 1995), p. 6. Reprinted by permission of John Wiley and Sons.

"owe the stock" to the client from whom it was borrowed. Therefore, you would have to pay your broker the $60,000 of dividends paid by L, which the broker would then pass on to the client from whom the stock was borrowed. So, your net cash flow from the second portfolio would be a negative $90,000. Because you would "owe" this portfolio, we'll call it the "short" portfolio.

Where would you get the $90,000 that you must pay on the short portfolio? The good news is that this is exactly the amount of cash flow generated by your long portfolio. Because the cash flows generated by each portfolio are the same, the short portfolio "replicates" the long portfolio.

Here is the bottom line. You started out with no money of your own. By selling L short, borrowing $400,000, and purchasing stock in U, you ended up with $100,000 in cash plus the two portfolios. The portfolios mirror each other, so their net cash flow is zero. This is perfect arbitrage: You invest none of your own money, you have no risk, you have no future negative cash flows, but you end up with cash in your pocket.

Not surprisingly, many traders would want to do this. The selling pressure on L would cause its price to fall, and the buying pressure on U would cause its price to rise, until the two companies' values were equal. To put it another way, *if the long and short replicating portfolios have the same cash flows, then arbitrage will force them to have the same value.*

This is one of the most important ideas in modern finance. Not only does it give us insights into capital structure, but it is the fundamental building block underlying the valuation of real and financial options and derivatives as discussed in Chapters 19 and 20. Without the concept of arbitrage, the options and derivatives markets we have today simply would not exist.

MM with Corporate Taxes

MM's original work, published in 1958, assumed zero taxes. In 1963, they published a second article that incorporated corporate taxes. With corporate income taxes, they concluded that leverage will increase a firm's value. This occurs because interest is a tax-deductible expense; hence more of a levered firm's operating income flows through to investors.

Later in this chapter we present the MM propositions when personal taxes as well as corporate taxes are allowed. The situation when corporations are subject to income taxes, but there are no personal taxes, is a special case of the situation with both personal and corporate taxes, so we only present results here.

Proposition I The value of a levered firm is equal to the value of an unlevered firm in the same risk class (V_U) *plus* the value of the interest tax shield ($V_{Tax\ shield}$) due to the tax deductibility of interest expenses. The value of the tax shield, which is often called the *gain from leverage*, is the present value of the annual tax savings. The annual tax saving is equal to the interest payment multiplied by the tax rate, T:

$$\text{Annual tax saving} = (r_d D)(T)$$

MM assume a no-growth firm, so the present value of the annual tax saving is the present value of a perpetuity. They assume that the appropriate discount rate for the tax shield is the interest rate on debt, so the value of the tax shield is

$$V_{\text{Tax shield}} = \frac{(r_d D)(T)}{r_d} = TD$$

Therefore, the value of a levered firm is

$$\begin{aligned} V_L &= V_U + V_{\text{Tax shield}} \\ &= V_U + TD \end{aligned} \tag{12-8}$$

The important point here is that when corporate taxes are introduced, the value of the levered firm exceeds that of the unlevered firm by the amount TD. Since the gain from leverage increases as debt increases, this implies that a firm's value is maximized at 100% debt financing.

Because all cash flows are assumed to be perpetuities, the value of the unlevered firm can be found by using Equation 12-7 and incorporating taxes. With zero debt (D = $0), the value of the firm is its equity value:

$$V_U = S = \frac{EBIT(1 - T)}{r_{sU}} \tag{12-9}$$

Note that the discount rate, r_{sU}, is not necessarily equal to the discount rate in Equation 12-5. The r_{sU} from Equation 12-5 is the required discount rate in a world with no taxes. The r_{sU} in Equation 12-9 is the required discount rate in a world with taxes.

Proposition II The cost of equity to a levered firm is equal to (1) the cost of equity to an unlevered firm in the same risk class plus (2) a risk premium whose size depends on the difference between the costs of equity and debt to an unlevered firm, the amount of financial leverage used, and the corporate tax rate:

$$r_{sL} = r_{sU} + (r_{sU} - r_d)(1 - T)(D/S) \tag{12-10}$$

Note that Equation 12-10 is identical to the corresponding without-tax equation, 12-6, except for the term (1 − T) in 12-10. Because (1 − T) is less than 1, corporate taxes cause the cost of equity to rise less rapidly with leverage than it would in the absence of taxes. Proposition II, coupled with the fact that taxes reduce the effective cost of debt, is what produces the Proposition I result—namely, that the firm's value increases as its leverage increases.

An increase in the debt ratio also increases the risk faced by shareholders, and this has an effect on the cost of equity, r_s. Recall from Chapter 7 that a stock's beta is the relevant measure of risk for diversified investors. Moreover, it has been demonstrated, both theoretically and empirically, that beta increases with financial leverage. Indeed, Robert Hamada developed the **Hamada equation** to specify the effect of financial leverage on beta:[11]

$$b = b_U[1 + (1 - T)(D/S)] \tag{12-11}$$

Here D is the market value of the debt and S is the market value of the equity. The Hamada equation shows how increases in the market value debt/equity ratio increase beta. Here $\mathbf{b_U}$ is the firm's *unlevered beta* coefficient—that is, the beta it would have if it had no debt. In that case, beta would depend entirely on business risk and thus be a measure of the firm's "basic business risk."

Note that beta is the only variable that can be influenced by management in the CAPM cost of equity equation, $r_s = r_{RF} + (RP_M)b$. The risk-free rate and market risk premium are determined by market forces that are beyond the firm's control. However, b is affected

---

[11]See Robert S. Hamada, "Portfolio Analysis, Market Equilibrium, and Corporation Finance," *Journal of Finance*, March 1969, 13–31. Note that Thomas Conine and Maurry Tamarkin extended Hamada's work to include risky debt. See "Divisional Cost of Capital Estimation: Adjusting for Leverage," *Financial Management*, Spring 1985, 54–58. For a comprehensive framework, see Robert A. Taggart, Jr., "Consistent Valuation and Cost of Capital Expressions with Corporate and Personal Taxes," *Financial Management*, Autumn 1991, 8–20.

(1) by the firm's operating decisions as discussed earlier in the chapter, which affect b_U, and (2) by its capital structure decisions as reflected in its D/S ratio.

As a starting point, a firm can take its current beta, tax rate, and debt/equity ratio and calculate its unlevered beta, b_U, simply by transforming Equation 12-11 as follows:

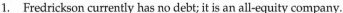

$$b_U = b/[1 + (1 - T)(D/S)] \qquad \text{(12-12)}$$

Then, once b_U is determined, the Hamada equation can be used to estimate how changes in the debt/equity ratio would affect the levered beta, b, and thus the cost of equity, r_s.

Illustration of the MM Models

To illustrate the MM models, assume that the following data and conditions hold for Fredrickson Water Company, an old, established firm that supplies water to residential customers in several no-growth Nova Scotia communities:

See ***Ch 12 Tool Kit.xlsx*** at the textbook's website for all calculations.

1. Fredrickson currently has no debt; it is an all-equity company.
2. Expected EBIT = $2,400,000. EBIT is not expected to increase over time, so Fredrickson is in a no-growth situation.
3. Needing no new capital, Fredrickson pays out all of its income as dividends.
4. If Fredrickson begins to use debt, it can borrow at a rate r_d = 8%. This borrowing rate is constant—it does not increase regardless of the amount of debt used. Any money raised by selling debt would be used to repurchase common stock, *so Fredrickson's assets would remain constant.*
5. The business risk inherent in Fredrickson's assets, and thus in its EBIT, is such that its beta is 0.80; this is called the unlevered beta, b_U, because Fredrickson has no debt. The risk-free rate is 8%, and the market risk premium (RP_M) is 5%. Using the Capital Asset Pricing Model (CAPM), Fredrickson's required rate of return on stock, r_{sU}, is 12% if no debt is used:

$$r_{sU} = r_{RF} + b_U(RP_M) = 8\% + 0.80(5\%) = 12\%$$

With Zero Taxes To begin, assume that there are no taxes, so T = 0%. At any level of debt, Proposition I (Equation 12-5) can be used to find Fredrickson's value in an MM world, $20 million:

$$V_L = V_U = \frac{EBIT}{r_{sU}} = \frac{\$2.4 \text{ million}}{0.12} = \$20.0 \text{ million}$$

If Fredrickson uses $10 million of debt, its stock's value must be $10 million:

$$S = V - D = \$20 \text{ million} - \$10 \text{ million} = \$10 \text{ million}$$

We can also find Fredrickson's cost of equity, r_{sL}, and its WACC at a debt level of $10 million. First, we use Proposition II (Equation 12-6) to find r_{sL}, Fredrickson's levered cost of equity:

$$
\begin{aligned}
r_{sL} &= r_{sU} + (r_{sU} - r_d)(D/S) \\
&= 12\% + (12\% - 8\%)(\$10 \text{ million}/\$10 \text{ million}) \\
&= 12\% + 4.0\% = 16.0\%
\end{aligned}
$$

Now we can find the company's weighted average cost of capital:

$$
\begin{aligned}
WACC &= (D/V)(r_d)(1 - T) + (S/L)r_{sL} \\
&= (\$10/\$20)(8\%)(1.0) + (\$10/\$20)(16.0\%) = 12.0\%
\end{aligned}
$$

Fredrickson's value and cost of capital based on the MM model without taxes at various debt levels are shown in Panel a on the left side of Figure 12-2. Here we see that in an MM world without taxes, financial leverage simply does not matter: *The value of the firm, and its overall cost of capital, are both independent of the amount of debt.*

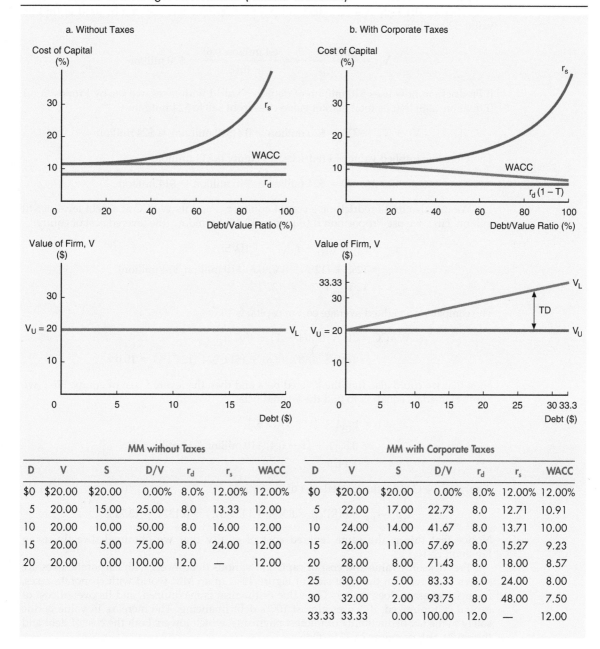

FIGURE
12-2 Effects of Leverage: MM Models (Millions of Dollars)

	MM without Taxes					
D	V	S	D/V	r_d	r_s	WACC
$0	$20.00	$20.00	0.00%	8.0%	12.00%	12.00%
5	20.00	15.00	25.00	8.0	13.33	12.00
10	20.00	10.00	50.00	8.0	16.00	12.00
15	20.00	5.00	75.00	8.0	24.00	12.00
20	20.00	0.00	100.00	12.0	—	12.00

	MM with Corporate Taxes					
D	V	S	D/V	r_d	r_s	WACC
$0	$20.00	$20.00	0.00%	8.0%	12.00%	12.00%
5	22.00	17.00	22.73	8.0	12.71	10.91
10	24.00	14.00	41.67	8.0	13.71	10.00
15	26.00	11.00	57.69	8.0	15.27	9.23
20	28.00	8.00	71.43	8.0	18.00	8.57
25	30.00	5.00	83.33	8.0	24.00	8.00
30	32.00	2.00	93.75	8.0	48.00	7.50
33.33	33.33	0.00	100.00	12.0	—	12.00

With Corporate Taxes To illustrate the MM model with corporate taxes, assume that all of the previous conditions hold except these two:

1. Expected EBIT = $4,000,000.[12]
2. Fredrickson has a 40% tax rate, so T = 40%.

---

[12]If we had left Fredrickson's EBIT at $2.4 million, the introduction of corporate taxes would have reduced the firm's value from $20 million to $12 million:

$$V_U = \frac{EBIT(1 - T)}{r_{sU}} = \frac{\$2.4 \text{ million}(0.6)}{0.12} = \$12.0 \text{ million}$$

Corporate taxes reduce the amount of operating income available to investors in an unlevered firm by the factor $(1 - T)$, so the value of the firm would be reduced by the same amount, holding r_{sU} constant.

Other things held constant, the introduction of corporate taxes would lower Fredrickson's net income, hence its value, so we increased EBIT from $2.4 million to $4 million to make the comparison between the two models easier.

When Fredrickson has zero debt but pays taxes, Equation 12-9 can be used to find its value, $20 million:

$$V_U = \frac{\text{EBIT}(1 - T)}{r_{sU}} = \frac{\$4 \text{ million}(0.6)}{0.12} = \$20 \text{ million}$$

If Fredrickson now uses $10 million of debt in a world with taxes, we see by Proposition I (Equation 12-8) that its total market value rises from $20 to $24 million:

$$V_L = V_U + TD = \$20 \text{ million} + 0.4(\$10 \text{ million}) = \$24 \text{ million}$$

Therefore, the implied value of Fredrickson's equity is $14 million:

$$S = V - D = \$24 \text{ million} - \$10 \text{ million} = \$14 \text{ million}$$

We can also find Fredrickson's cost of equity, r_{sL}, and its WACC at a debt level of $10 million. First, we use Proposition II (Equation 12-10) to find r_{sL}, the levered cost of equity:

$$
\begin{aligned}
r_{sL} &= r_{sU} + (r_{sU} - r_d)(1 - T)(D/S) \\
&= 12\% + (12\% - 8\%)(0.6)(\$10 \text{ million}/\$14 \text{ million}) \\
&= 12\% + 1.71\% = 13.71\%
\end{aligned}
$$

The company's weighted average cost of capital is 10%:

$$
\begin{aligned}
\text{WACC} &= (D/V)(r_d)(1 - T) + (S/L)r_{sL} \\
&= (\$10/\$24)(8\%)(0.6) + (\$14/\$24)(13.71\%) = 10.0\%
\end{aligned}
$$

Note that we could also find the levered beta and then the levered cost of equity. First, we apply Hamada's equation to find the levered beta:

$$
\begin{aligned}
b &= b_U[1 + (1 - T)(D/S)] \\
&= 0.80[1 + (1 - 0.4)(\$10 \text{ million}/\$14 \text{ million})] \\
&= 1.1429
\end{aligned}
$$

Applying the CAPM, the levered cost of equity is

$$r_{sL} = r_{RF} + b(RP_M) = 8\% + 1.1429(5\%) = 0.1371 = 13.71\%$$

Notice that this is the same levered cost of equity that we obtained directly using Equation 12-10.

Fredrickson's value and cost of capital at various debt levels with corporate taxes are shown in Panel b on the right side of Figure 12-2. In an MM world with corporate taxes, financial leverage does matter: The value of the firm is maximized, and its overall cost of capital is minimized, if it uses almost 100% debt financing. The increase in value is due solely to the tax deductibility of interest payments, which lowers both the cost of debt and the equity risk premium by $(1 - T)$.[13]

---

[13]In the limiting case, where the firm used 100% debt financing, the bondholders would own the entire company; thus, they would have to bear all the business risk. (Up until this point, MM assume that the shareholders bear all the risk.) If the bondholders bear all the risk, then the capitalization rate on the debt should be equal to the equity capitalization rate at zero debt, $r_d = r_{sU} = 12\%$.

The income stream to the shareholders in the all-equity case was $4,000,000(1 - T) = \$2,400,000$, and the value of the firm was

$$V_U = \frac{\$2,400,000}{0.12} = \$20,000,000$$

With all debt, the entire $4,000,000 of EBIT would be used to pay interest charges—r_d would be 12%, so $I = 0.12(\text{Debt}) = \$4,000,000$. Taxes would be zero, and investors (bondholders) would get the entire $4,000,000 of operating income; they would not have to share it with the government. Thus, at 100% debt, the value of the firm would be

$$V_L = \frac{\$4,000,000}{0.12} = \$33,333,333 = D$$

There is, of course, a transition problem in all this—MM assume that $r_d = 8\%$ regardless of how much debt the firm has until debt reaches 100%, at which point r_d jumps to 12%, the cost of equity. Realistically, r_d rises as the use of financial leverage increases.

To conclude this section, compare the "Without Taxes" and "With Corporate Taxes" sections of Figure 12-2. Without taxes, both WACC and the firm's value (V) are constant. With corporate taxes, WACC declines and V rises as more and more debt is used, so the optimal capital structure, under MM with corporate taxes, is 100% debt.

CONCEPT REVIEW

1. Is there an optimal capital structure under the MM zero-tax model?
2. What is the optimal capital structure under the MM model with corporate taxes?
3. How does the Proposition I equation differ between the two models?
4. How does the Proposition II equation differ between the two models?
5. Why do taxes result in a "gain from leverage" in the MM model with corporate taxes?
6. An unlevered firm has a value of $100 million. An otherwise identical but levered firm has $30 million in debt. Under the MM zero-tax model, what is the value of the levered firm? Under the MM corporate tax model, what is the value of a levered firm if the corporate tax rate is 40%? (Check Figures: $100 million; $112 million)

12.4 Miller: The Effect of Corporate and Personal Taxes

Merton Miller (this time without Modigliani) later brought in the effects of personal taxes.[14] He noted that all of the income from bonds is generally interest, which is taxed as personal income at rates (T_d), which is higher than income from stocks coming partly from dividends and partly from capital gains. Furthermore, tax on capital gains applies only when the stock is sold and the gain realized. In addition, only one-half of the capital gain is taxable. So, on average, returns on stocks are taxed at lower effective rates (T_s) than returns on debt.

Because of the tax situation, Miller argued that investors are willing to accept relatively low before-tax returns on stock relative to the before-tax returns on bonds. (The situation here is similar to that with preferred stocks held by investors as discussed in Chapter 8.) For example, an investor might require a return of 10% on Strasburg's bonds, and if stock income were taxed at the same rate as bond income, the required rate of return on Strasburg's stock might be 16% because of the stock's greater risk. However, in view of the favourable treatment of income on the stock, investors might be willing to accept a before-tax return of only 14% on the stock.

Thus, as Miller pointed out, (1) the *deductibility of interest* favours the use of debt financing, but (2) the *more favourable tax treatment of income from stock* lowers the required rate of return on stock and thus favours the use of equity financing.

Miller showed that the net impact of corporate and personal taxes is given by this equation:

$$V_L = V_U + \left[1 - \frac{(1 - T_c)(1 - T_s)}{(1 - T_d)} \right] D \qquad \text{(12-13)}$$

Here T_c is the corporate tax rate, T_s is the personal tax rate on income from stocks, and T_d is the tax rate on income from debt. Miller argued that the marginal tax rates on stock and debt balance out in such a way that the bracketed term in Equation 12-13 is zero, so $V_L = V_U$, but most observers believe that there is still a tax advantage to debt. For example, if we take a company whose tax rate is 33%, along with an individual investor at the marginal rate of 40% for income and half that amount (20%) for capital gains on stock, the advantage of debt financing is

$$V_L = V_U + \left[1 - \frac{(1 - 0.33)(1 - 0.20)}{(1 - 0.40)} \right] D \qquad \text{(12-13a)}$$

$$= V_U + 0.11D$$

---

[14]Merton H. Miller, "Debt and Taxes," *Journal of Finance*, May 1977, 261–275.

Thus it appears as though the presence of personal taxes reduces but does not completely eliminate the advantage of debt financing.

12.5 Criticisms of the MM and Miller Models

The conclusions of the MM and Miller models follow logically from their initial assumptions. However, both academicians and executives have voiced concerns about the validity of the MM and Miller models, and virtually no one believes they hold precisely. The MM zero-tax model leads to the conclusion that capital structure doesn't matter, yet we observe systematic capital structure patterns within industries. Furthermore, when used with "reasonable" tax rates, both the MM model with corporate taxes and the Miller model lead to the conclusion that firms should use 100% debt financing, but firms do not (deliberately) go to that extreme.

People who disagree with the MM and Miller theories generally attack them on the grounds that their assumptions are not correct. Here are the main objections:

1. Both MM and Miller assume that personal and corporate leverage are perfect substitutes. However, an individual investing in a levered firm has less loss exposure as a result of corporate *limited liability* than if he or she used "homemade" leverage. For example, in our earlier illustration of the MM arbitrage argument, it should be noted that only the $600,000 our investor had in Firm L would be lost if that firm went bankrupt. However, if the investor engaged in arbitrage transactions and employed "homemade" leverage to invest in Firm U, then he or she could lose $900,000—the original $600,000 investment plus the $400,000 loan less the $100,000 investment in riskless bonds. This increased personal risk exposure would tend to restrain investors from engaging in arbitrage, and that could cause the equilibrium values of V_L, V_U, r_{sL}, and r_{sU} to be different from those specified by MM. Restrictions on institutional investors, who dominate capital markets today, may also retard the arbitrage process, because many institutional investors cannot legally borrow to buy stocks, hence are prohibited from engaging in homemade leverage.

    Note, though, that while limited liability may present a problem to individuals, it *does not* present a problem to corporations set up to undertake **leveraged buyouts (LBOs).** Thus, after MM's work became widely known, literally hundreds of LBO firms were established, and their founders made billions recapitalizing underleveraged firms. "Junk bonds" were created to aid in the process, and the managers of underleveraged firms who did not want their firms to be taken over increased debt usage on their own. Thus, MM's work raised the level of debt in corporate America, and that probably raised the level of economic efficiency.

2. If a levered firm's operating income declined, it would sell assets and take other measures to raise the cash necessary to meet its interest obligations and thus avoid bankruptcy. If our illustrative unlevered firm experienced the same decline in operating income, it would probably take the less drastic measure of cutting dividends rather than selling assets. If dividends were cut, investors who employed homemade leverage would not receive cash to pay the interest on their debt. Thus, homemade leverage puts shareholders in greater danger of bankruptcy than does corporate leverage.

3. Brokerage costs were assumed away by MM and Miller, making the switch from L to U costless. However, brokerage and other transaction costs do exist, and they too impede the arbitrage process.

4. MM initially assumed that corporations and investors can borrow at the risk-free rate. Although risky debt has been introduced into the analysis by others, to reach the MM and Miller conclusions it is still necessary to assume that both corporations and investors can borrow at the same rate. While major institutional investors probably can borrow at the corporate rate, many institutions are not allowed to borrow to buy securities. Furthermore, most individual investors must borrow at higher rates than those paid by large corporations.

5. In his article, Miller concluded that an equilibrium would be reached, but to reach his equilibrium the tax benefit from corporate debt must be the same for all firms, and it must be constant for an individual firm regardless of the amount of leverage used. However, we know that tax benefits vary from firm to firm: highly profitable companies gain the maximum tax benefit from leverage, while the benefits to firms that are struggling are much smaller. Furthermore, some firms have other tax shields such as high depreciation, pension

plan contributions, and operating loss carryforwards, and these shields reduce the tax savings from interest payments.[15] It also appears simplistic to assume that the expected tax shield is unaffected by the amount of debt used. Higher leverage increases the probability that the firm will not be able to use the full tax shield in the future, because higher leverage increases the probability of future unprofitability and consequently lower tax rates. Note also that large, diversified corporations can use losses in one division to offset profits in another. Thus, the tax shelter benefit is more certain in large, diversified firms than in smaller, single-product companies. All things considered, it appears likely that the interest tax shield from corporate debt is more valuable to some firms than to others.

6. MM and Miller assume that there are no costs associated with financial distress, and they ignore agency costs. Furthermore, they assume that all market participants have identical information about firms' prospects, which is also incorrect.

These six points all suggest that the MM and Miller models lead to questionable conclusions, and that the models would be better if certain of their assumptions could be relaxed. In fact, in the next section we do discuss other theories behind capital structure decisions that relax some of MM's constrictive assumptions.

CONCEPT REVIEW

1. Should we accept that one of the models presented thus far (MM with zero taxes, MM with corporate taxes, or Miller) is correct? Why or why not?

2. Are any of the assumptions used in the models worrisome to you, and what does "worrisome" mean in this context?

12.6 Trade-Off Theory

MM's results depend on the assumption that there are no *bankruptcy costs*. However, in practice bankruptcy can be quite costly. Firms in bankruptcy have very high legal and accounting expenses, and they also have a hard time retaining customers, suppliers, and employees. Moreover, bankruptcy often forces a firm to liquidate or sell assets for less than they would be worth if the firm were to continue operating. For example, if a steel manufacturer goes out of business, it might be hard to find buyers for the company's blast furnaces, even though they were quite expensive. Assets are often illiquid because they are configured to a company's individual needs and also because they are difficult to disassemble and move.

Note, too, that the *threat of bankruptcy*, not just bankruptcy *per se*, produces these problems. Key employees jump ship, suppliers refuse to grant credit, customers seek more stable suppliers, and lenders demand higher interest rates and impose more restrictive loan covenants if potential bankruptcy looms.

Bankruptcy-related problems are most likely to arise when a firm includes a great deal of debt in its capital structure. Therefore, bankruptcy costs discourage firms from pushing their use of debt to excessive levels.

Bankruptcy-related costs have two components: (1) the probability of financial distress and (2) the costs that would be incurred if financial distress occurs. Firms whose earnings are more volatile, all else equal, face a greater chance of bankruptcy and, therefore, should use less debt than more stable firms. This is consistent with our earlier point that firms with high operating leverage, and thus greater business risk, should limit their use of financial leverage. Likewise, firms that would face high costs in the event of financial distress should rely less heavily on debt. For example, firms whose assets are illiquid and thus would have to be sold at "fire sale" prices should limit their use of debt financing.

The preceding arguments led to the development of what is called "the trade-off theory of leverage," in which firms trade off the benefits of debt financing (favourable corporate tax treatment) against higher interest rates and bankruptcy costs. In essence, the **trade-off theory** says that the value of a levered firm is equal to the value of an unlevered firm plus the

---

[15]For a discussion of the impact of tax shields, see Harry DeAngelo and Ronald W. Masulis, "Optimal Capital Structure under Corporate and Personal Taxation," *Journal of Financial Economics*, March 1980, 3–30; Thomas W. Downs, "Corporate Leverage and Nondebt Tax Shields: Evidence on Crowding-Out," *Financial Review*, November 1993, 549–583; John R. Graham, "Taxes and Corporate Finance: A Review," *Review of Financial Studies*, Winter 2003, 1075–1129; and Jeffrey K. Mackie-Mason, "Do Taxes Affect Corporate Financing Decisions?" *Journal of Finance*, December 1990, 1471–1493.

value of any side effects, which include the tax shield and the expected costs due to financial distress. A summary of the trade-off theory is expressed graphically in Figure 12-3. Here are some observations about the figure:

1. Under the assumptions of the MM model with corporate taxes, a firm's value will be maximized if it uses virtually 100% debt, and the line labelled "MM Result Incorporating the Effects of Corporate Taxation" in Figure 12-3 expresses the relationship between value and debt under their assumptions.
2. There is some threshold level of debt, labelled D_1 in Figure 12-3, below which the probability of bankruptcy is so low as to be immaterial. Beyond D_1, however, expected bankruptcy-related costs become increasingly important, and they reduce the tax benefits of debt at an increasing rate. In the range from D_1 to D_2, expected bankruptcy-related costs reduce but do not completely offset the tax benefits of debt, so the stock price rises (but at a decreasing rate) as the debt ratio increases. However, beyond D_2, expected bankruptcy-related costs exceed the tax benefits, so from this point on increasing the debt ratio lowers the value of the stock. Therefore, D_2 is the optimal capital structure. Of course, D_1 and D_2 vary from firm to firm, depending on their business risks and bankruptcy costs.
3. While theoretical and empirical work support the general shape of the curve in Figure 12-3, this graph must be taken as an approximation, not as a precisely defined function.

Signalling Theory

MM assumed that investors have the same information about a firm's prospects as its managers—this is called **symmetric information.** However, in fact managers often have better information than outside investors. This is called **asymmetric information,** and it has an important effect on the optimal capital structure. To see why, consider two situations, one in which the company's managers know that its prospects are extremely positive (Firm P) and one in which the managers know that the future looks negative (Firm N).

Suppose, for example, that Firm P's R&D labs have just discovered a nonpatentable cure for the common cold. They want to keep the new product a secret as long as possible to delay competitors' entry into the market. New plants must be built to make the new product, so capital must be raised. How should Firm P's management raise the needed capital? If it sells stock, then, when profits from the new product start flowing in, the price of the stock will rise sharply, and the purchasers of the new stock will make a bonanza. The current shareholders

FIGURE
12-3   Effect of Financial Leverage on Value

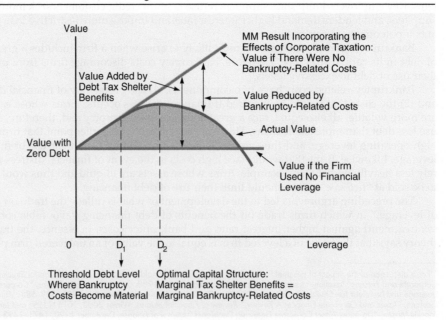

(including the managers) will also do well, but not as well as they would have done if the company had not sold stock before the price increased, because then they would not have had to share the benefits of the new product with the new shareholders. Therefore, *we should expect a firm with very positive prospects to avoid selling stock and, rather, to raise any required new capital by other means, including using debt beyond the normal target capital structure.*[16]

Now let's consider Firm N. Suppose its managers have information that new orders are off sharply because a competitor has installed new technology that has improved its products' quality. Firm N must upgrade its own facilities, at a high cost, just to maintain its current sales. As a result, its return on investment will fall (but not by as much as if it took no action, which would lead to a 100% loss through bankruptcy). How should Firm N raise the needed capital? Here the situation is just the reverse of that facing Firm P, which did not want to sell stock so as to avoid having to share the benefits of future developments. *A firm with negative prospects would want to sell stock, which would mean bringing in new investors to share the losses!*[17] The conclusion from all this is that firms with extremely bright prospects prefer not to finance through new stock offerings, whereas firms with poor prospects like to finance with outside equity. How should you, as an investor, react to this conclusion? You ought to say, "If I see that a company plans to issue new stock, this should worry me because I know that management would not want to issue stock if future prospects looked good. However, management *would* want to issue stock if things looked bad. Therefore, I should lower my estimate of the firm's value, other things held constant, if it plans to issue new stock."

If you gave the above answer, your views would be consistent with those of sophisticated portfolio managers. *All else equal, the announcement of a stock offering is generally taken as a signal that the firm's prospects as seen by its management are not good. Conversely, a debt offering is taken as a positive signal.* Notice that Firm N's managers cannot make a false signal to investors by mimicking Firm P and issuing debt. With its unfavourable future prospects, issuing debt could soon force Firm N into bankruptcy. Given the resulting damage to the personal wealth and reputations of N's managers, they cannot afford to mimic Firm P. All of this suggests that when a firm announces a new stock offering, more often than not the price of its stock will decline. Empirical studies have shown that this situation does indeed exist.[18]

Reserve Borrowing Capacity

Because issuing stock emits a negative signal and thus tends to depress the stock price, even if the company's prospects are bright, it should, in normal times, maintain a **reserve borrowing capacity** that can be used in the event that some especially good investment opportunity comes along. This means that *firms should, in normal times, use more equity and less debt than is suggested by the tax benefit/bankruptcy cost trade-off model expressed in Figure 12-3.*

The Pecking Order Hypothesis

The presence of flotation costs and asymmetric information may cause a firm to raise capital according to a **pecking order.** In this situation a firm first raises capital internally by reinvesting its net income and selling off its short-term marketable securities. When that supply of funds has been exhausted, the firm will issue debt and perhaps preferred stock. Only as a last resort will the firm issue common stock.[19]

Using Debt Financing to Constrain Managers

Agency problems may arise if managers and shareholders have different objectives. Such conflicts are particularly likely when the firm's managers have too much cash at their disposal. Managers often use excess cash to finance pet projects or for perquisites such as nicer offices, corporate jets, and sky boxes at sports arenas, all of which may do little to maximize stock prices. Even worse, managers may be tempted to pay too much for an acquisition— something that could cost shareholders hundreds of millions of dollars. By contrast, managers with limited "excess cash flow" are less able to make wasteful expenditures.

---

[16]It would be illegal for Firm P's managers to personally purchase more shares on the basis of their inside knowledge of the new product.

[17]Of course, Firm N would have to make certain disclosures when it offered new shares to the public, but it might be able to meet the legal requirements without fully disclosing management's worst fears.

[18]See Paul Asquith and David W. Mullins, Jr., "The Impact of Initiating Dividend Payments on Shareholders' Wealth," *Journal of Business*, January 1983, 77–96.

[19]For more, see Jonathon Baskin, "An Empirical Investigation of the Pecking Order Hypothesis," *Financial Management*, Spring 1989, 26–35.

Firms can reduce excess cash flow in a variety of ways. One way is to funnel some of it back to shareholders through higher dividends or stock repurchases. Another alternative is to shift the capital structure toward more debt in the hope that higher debt service requirements will force managers to be more disciplined. If debt is not serviced as required, the firm will be forced into bankruptcy, in which case its managers would likely lose their jobs. Therefore, a manager is less likely to buy an expensive new corporate jet if the firm has large debt service requirements that could cost the manager his or her job. In short, high levels of debt *bind the cash flow*, since much of it is precommitted to servicing the debt.

A leveraged buyout (LBO) is one way to bind cash flow. In an LBO, debt is used to finance the purchase of a company's shares, after which the firm "goes private." The first wave of LBOs was in the mid-1980s; private equity funds led the buyouts of the late 1990s and 2000s. Many of these LBOs were specifically designed to reduce corporate waste. As noted, high debt payments force managers to conserve cash by eliminating unnecessary expenditures.

Of course, increasing debt and reducing the available cash flow has its downside: it increases the risk of bankruptcy. One professor has argued that adding debt to a firm's capital structure is like putting a dagger into the steering wheel of a car.[20] The dagger—which points toward your stomach—motivates you to drive more carefully, but you may get stabbed if someone runs into you, even if you are being careful. The analogy applies to corporations in the following sense: higher debt forces managers to be more careful with shareholders' money, but even well-run firms could face bankruptcy (get stabbed) if some event beyond their control such as a war, an earthquake, a strike, or a recession occurs. To complete the analogy, the capital structure decision comes down to deciding how large a dagger shareholders should use to keep managers in line.

Finally, too much debt may overconstrain managers. A large portion of a manager's personal wealth and reputation is tied to a single company, so managers are not well diversified. When faced with a positive NPV project that is risky, a manager may decide that it's not worth taking on the risk, even when well-diversified shareholders would find the risk acceptable. As previously mentioned, this is an underinvestment problem. The more debt the firm has, the greater the likelihood of financial distress, and thus the greater the likelihood that managers will forego risky projects even if they have positive NPVs.

The Investment Opportunity Set and Reserve Borrowing Capacity

Bankruptcy and financial distress are costly, and, as noted above, this can discourage highly levered firms from undertaking risky new investments. If potential new investments, although risky, have positive net present values, then high levels of debt can be doubly costly—the expected financial distress and bankruptcy costs are high, and the firm loses potential value by not making some potentially profitable investments. On the other hand, if a firm has very few profitable investment opportunities, then high levels of debt can keep managers from wasting money by investing in poor projects. For such companies, increases in the debt ratio can increase the value of the firm.

Thus, in addition to the tax, signalling, bankruptcy, and managerial constraint effects discussed earlier, the firm's optimal capital structure is related to its set of investment opportunities. Firms with many profitable opportunities should maintain their ability to invest by using low levels of debt, which is also consistent with maintaining reserve borrowing capacity. Firms with few profitable investment opportunities should use high levels of debt and thus have substantial interest payments, which means imposing managerial constraint through debt.[21]

Windows of Opportunity

If markets are efficient, then security prices should reflect all available information, so that they are neither underpriced nor overpriced (except during the time it takes prices to move to a new equilibrium caused by the release of new information). The *windows of opportunity theory* states that managers don't believe this, but instead think that stock prices and interest rates are sometimes either too low or high relative to their true fundamental values. In particular, the theory suggests that managers issue equity when they believe that stock market prices are abnormally high and issue debt when they believe interest rates are abnormally low. In other words, they

[20]Ben Bernanke, "Is There Too Much Corporate Debt?" *Federal Reserve Bank of Philadelphia Business Review*, September–October 1989, 3–13.
[21]See Michael J. Barclay and Clifford W. Smith, Jr., "The Capital Structure Puzzle: Another Look at the Evidence," *Journal of Applied Corporate Finance*, Spring 1999, 8–20.

try to time the market.[22] Notice that this differs from signalling theory because no asymmetric information is involved: These managers aren't basing their beliefs on insider information, just on a difference of opinion with the market consensus.

CONCEPT REVIEW

1. Why does the MM theory with corporate taxes lead to 100% debt?
2. Explain how *asymmetric information* and *signals* affect capital structure decisions.
3. What is meant by *reserve borrowing capacity,* and why is it important to firms?
4. How can the use of debt serve to discipline managers?

12.7 Capital Structure Evidence and Implications

There have been hundreds, perhaps even thousands, of papers testing the capital structure theories described in the previous section. We can cover only the highlights here, beginning with the empirical evidence.[23]

Empirical Evidence

The Trade-Off Between Tax Benefits and Bankruptcy Costs Recent studies by Professors Van Binsbergen, Graham, and Yang and by Professor Korteweg suggest that the average net benefits of leverage (i.e., the value of the tax shield less the expected cost of financial distress) make up about 3% to 6% of a levered firm's value.[24] To put this into perspective, let's look at the impact of debt on an average company's value. The average company is financed with about 25% to 35% debt, so let's suppose that the company has $25 debt and $75 of equity, just to keep the arithmetic simple. The total net benefit of debt would be about $5, based on the recent research. This implies that each dollar of debt added (on average) about $0.20 of value ($5/$25 = 0.2) to the company. The first dollar of debt adds a bigger net benefit because bankruptcy risk is low when debt is low. By the time the 25th dollar of debt is added, its incremental net benefit was close to zero—the incremental expected costs of financial distress were about equal to the incremental expected tax shield.

These studies also showed that the net benefits of debt increase slowly until reaching the optimal level, but decline rapidly thereafter. In other words, it isn't very costly to be somewhat below the optimal level of debt, but it is costly to exceed it.

A particularly interesting study by Professors Mehotra, Mikkelson, and Partch examined the capital structure of firms that were spun off from their parent companies.[25] The financing choices of existing firms might be influenced by their past financing choices and by the costs of moving from one capital structure to another, but because spin-offs are newly created companies, managers can choose a capital structure without regard to these issues. The study found that more profitable firms (which have a lower expected probability of bankruptcy) and more asset-intensive firms (which have better collateral and thus a lower cost of bankruptcy should one occur) have higher levels of debt.

These findings support the trade-off theory.

A Dynamic Trade-Off Theory However, there is also evidence that is inconsistent with the static optimal target capital structure implied by the trade-off theory. For example, stock prices are volatile, which frequently causes a firm's actual market-based debt ratio to deviate from its target. However, such deviations don't cause firms to immediately return to their target by issuing or repurchasing securities. Instead, Professors Flannery and Rangan

---

[22]See Malcolm Baker and Jeffrey Wurgler, "Market Timing and Capital Structure," *Journal of Finance,* February 2002, 1–32.
[23]This section also draws heavily from Barclay and Smith, "The Capital Structure Puzzle," cited in footnote 21; Jay Ritter, ed., *Recent Developments in Corporate Finance* (Northampton, MA: Edward Elgar Publishing Inc., 2005); and a presentation by Jay Ritter at the 2003 EMA meeting, "The Windows of Opportunity Theory of Capital Structure."
[24]See Jules H. Van Binsbergen, John H. Graham, and Jie Yang, "The Cost of Debt," *Journal of Finance,* Vol. 65, No. 6, December, 2010, pp. 2089–2135; also see Arthur Korteweg, "The Net Benefits to Leverage," *Journal of Finance,* Vol. 65, No. 6, December, 2010, pp. 2137–2169.
[25]See V. Mehotra, W. Mikkelson, and M. Partch, "The Design of Financial Policies in Corporate Spin-offs," *Review of Financial Studies,* Winter 2003, pp. 1359–1388.

show that firms tend to make a partial adjustment each year, moving about 30% of the way toward their target capital structure. In a more recent study, Professors Faulkender, Flannery, Hankins, and Smith show that the speed of adjustment depends on a company's cash flows—companies with high cash flows adjust by about 50%. This effect is even more pronounced if the company's leverage exceeds its target—high cash flow companies in this situation have a 70% speed of adjustment. This is consistent with the idea that it is more costly to exceed the target debt ratio than to be lower than the target.[26]

Market Timing If a stock price has a big run-up, which reduces the debt ratio, then the trade-off theory suggests that the firm should issue debt to return to its target. However, firms tend to do the opposite, issuing stock after big run-ups. This is much more consistent with the market timing theory, with managers trying to time the market by issuing stock when they perceive the market to be overvalued. Furthermore, firms tend to issue debt when stock prices and interest rates are low. The maturity of the issued debt seems to reflect an attempt to time interest rates: Firms tend to issue short-term debt if the term structure is upward sloping but long-term debt if the term structure is flat. Again, these facts suggest that managers try to time the market.

Signalling and the Pecking Order Firms issue equity much less frequently than debt. On the surface, this seems to support both the pecking-order hypothesis and the signalling hypothesis. The pecking-order hypothesis predicts that firms with a high level of informational asymmetry, which causes equity issuances to be costly, should issue debt before issuing equity. Yet we often see the opposite, with high-growth firms (which usually have greater informational asymmetry) issuing more equity than debt. Also, many highly profitable firms could afford to issue debt (which comes before equity in the pecking order) but instead choose to issue equity. With respect to the signalling hypothesis, consider the case of firms that have large increases in earnings that were unanticipated by the market. If managers have superior information, then they will anticipate these upcoming performance improvements and issue debt before the increase. Such firms do, in fact, tend to issue debt slightly more frequently than other firms, but the difference isn't economically meaningful.

Reserve Borrowing Capacity Many firms have less debt than might be expected, and many have large amounts of short-term investments. This is especially true for firms with high market/book ratios (which indicate many growth options as well as informational asymmetry). This behaviour is consistent with the hypothesis that investment opportunities influence attempts to maintain reserve borrowing capacity. It is also consistent with tax considerations, because low-growth firms (which have more debt) are more likely to benefit from the tax shield. This behaviour is not consistent with the pecking-order hypothesis, where low-growth firms (which often have high free cash flow) would be able to avoid issuing debt by raising funds internally.

Summary of Empirical Tests To summarize these results, it appears that firms try to capture debt's tax benefits while avoiding financial distress costs. However, they also allow their debt ratios to deviate from the static optimal target ratio implied by the trade-off theory. In fact, Professors DeAngelo, DeAngelo, and Whited extend the dynamic trade-off model by showing that firms often deliberately issue debt to take advantage of unexpected investment opportunities, even if this causes them to exceed their target debt ratio.[27] Firms often maintain reserve borrowing capacity, especially firms with many growth opportunities or problems with informational asymmetry.[28] There is a little evidence that firms follow a pecking order and use security issuances as signals, but there is some evidence in support of the market timing theory.

---

[26]See Mark Flannery and Kasturi Rangan, "Partial Adjustment toward Target Capital Structures," *Journal of Financial Economics*, Vol. 79, 2006, pp. 469–506. Also see Michael Faulkender, Mark Flannery, Kristine Hankins, and Jason Smith, "Cash Flows and Leverage," *Journal of Financial Economics*, Vol. 103, 2012, pp. 632–646; also see Pravish K. Nunkoo and Agyenim Boateng, "The Empirical Determinants of Target Capital Structure and Adjustment to Long-Run Target: Evidence from Canadian Firms," *Applied Economics Letters*, Vol. 17, Issue 10, July 2010, pp. 983–990.

[27]See Harry DeAngelo, Linda DeAngelo, and Toni Whited, "Capital Structure Dynamics and Transitory Debt," *Journal of Financial Economics*, Vol. 99, 2011, pp. 235–261.

[28]For more on empirical tests of capital structure theory, see Gregor Andrade and Steven Kaplan, "How Costly Is Financial (Not Economic) Distress? Evidence from Highly Leveraged Transactions That Became Distressed," *Journal of Finance*, Vol. 53, 1998, pp. 1443–1493; Malcolm Baker, Robin Greenwood, and Jeffrey Wurgler, "The Maturity of Debt Issues and Predictable Variation in Bond Returns," *Journal of Financial Economics*, November 2003, pp. 261–291; Murray Z. Frank and Vidhan K. Goyal, "Testing the Pecking Order Theory of Capital Structure," *Journal of Financial Economics*, February 2003, pp. 217–248; and Michael Long and Ileen Malitz, "The Investment-Financing Nexus: Some Empirical Evidence," *Midland Corporate Finance Journal*, Fall 1985, pp. 53–59.

FINANCE: IN FOCUS

Capital Structure Differences in Canadian Firms

To what extent does capital structure vary across different industries? The table below shows the debt equity ratio for several industry sectors as well as selected companies within each sector. As you can see, not only is there considerable variation in capital structure between sectors but also within sectors. For instance, whereas Sears Canada has $0.03 of long-term debt for every $1 of equity, Hudson's Bay has $1.11 of debt for $1 of equity. In addition to industry characteristics, factors such as firm size, profitability, the market-to-book ratio as well as the ratio of fixed assets to total assets generally determines capital structure.

Sector and Company	Long-Term Debt-to-Equity Ratio	Sector and Company	Long-Term Debt-to-Equity Ratio
Telecommunications Services	87%	**Department Stores**	34%
Rogers Communications Inc.	260	Hudson's Bay Co.	111
Telus Corp.	92	Sears Canada Inc.	3
Energy	37	**Technology**	14
TransCanada Corp.	120	Constellation Software Inc.	66
Imperial Oil Ltd.	22	Descartes Systems Group Inc.	12
Consumer Non-Cyclicals	10	**Industrials**	51
Empire Company Ltd.	58	Toromont Industries Ltd.	22
Maple Leaf Foods Inc.	0	Finning International Inc.	71

Source: Data from www.reuters.com, accessed August 5, 2014.

Implications for Managers

Managers should explicitly consider tax benefits when making capital structure decisions. Tax benefits obviously are more valuable for firms with high tax rates. Firms can utilize tax loss carryforwards and carrybacks, but the time value of money means that tax benefits are more valuable for firms with stable, positive pre-tax income. Therefore, a firm whose sales are relatively stable can safely take on more debt and incur higher fixed charges than a company with volatile sales. Other things being equal, a firm with less operating leverage is better able to employ financial leverage because it will have less business risk and less volatile earnings.

Managers should also consider the expected cost of financial distress, which depends on the probability and cost of distress. Notice that stable sales and lower operating leverage provide tax benefits but also reduce the *probability* of financial distress. One *cost* of financial distress comes from lost investment opportunities. Firms with profitable investment opportunities need to be able to fund them, either by holding higher levels of marketable securities or by maintaining excess borrowing capacity. An astute corporate treasurer made this statement to the authors:

> Our company can earn a lot more money from good capital budgeting and operating decisions than from good financing decisions. Indeed, we are not sure exactly how financing decisions affect our stock price, but we know for sure that having to turn down a promising venture because funds are not available will reduce our long-run profitability.

Another cost of financial distress is the possibility of being forced to sell assets to meet liquidity needs. General-purpose assets that can be used by many businesses are relatively liquid and make good collateral, in contrast to special-purpose assets. Thus, real estate companies are usually highly levered, whereas companies involved in technological research are not.

Asymmetric information also has a bearing on capital structure decisions. For example, suppose a firm has just successfully completed an R&D program, and it forecasts higher earnings in the immediate future. However, the new earnings are not yet anticipated by investors and hence are not reflected in the stock price. This company should not issue stock—it should finance with debt until the higher earnings materialize and are reflected in the stock price. Then it could issue common stock, retire the debt, and return to its target capital structure.

Managers should consider conditions in the stock and bond markets. For example, during a recent credit crunch, the junk bond market dried up, and there was simply no market at a "reasonable" interest rate for any new long-term bonds rated below BBB. Therefore, low-rated companies in need of capital were forced to go to the stock market or to the short-term debt market, regardless of their target capital structures. When conditions eased, however, these companies sold bonds to get their capital structures back on target.

Finally, managers should always consider lenders' and rating agencies' attitudes. For example, one large utility was recently told by Moody's and Standard & Poor's that its bonds would be downgraded if it issued more debt. This influenced its decision to finance its expansion with common equity. This doesn't mean that managers should never increase debt if it will cause their bond rating to fall, but managers should always factor this into their decision making.[29]

CONCEPT REVIEW

1.   Which capital structure theories does the empirical evidence seem to support?
2.   What issues should managers consider when making capital structure decisions?

12.8   Capital Structure Theory: Our View

The great contribution of the capital structure models developed by MM, Miller, and their followers is that these models identified the specific benefits and costs of using debt—the tax benefits, financial distress costs, and so on. Prior to MM, no capital structure theory existed, so we had no systematic way of analyzing the effects of debt financing.

The trade-off model we discussed earlier is summarized graphically in Figure 12-4. The top graph shows the relationships between the debt ratio and the cost of debt, the cost of equity, and the WACC. Both r_s and $r_d(1 - T_c)$ rise steadily with increases in leverage, but the rate of increase accelerates at higher debt levels, reflecting agency costs and the increased probability of financial distress. The WACC first declines, then hits a minimum at D/V*, and then begins to rise. Note that the value of D in D/V* in the upper graph is D*, the level of debt in the lower graph that maximizes the firm's value. Thus, a firm's WACC is minimized and its value is maximized at the same capital structure. Note also that the general shapes of the curves apply regardless of whether we are using the modified MM with corporate taxes model, the Miller model, or a variant of these models.

Unfortunately, it is impossible to quantify accurately the costs and benefits of debt financing, so it is impossible to pinpoint D/V*, the capital structure that maximizes a firm's value. Most experts believe that such a structure exists for every firm, but that it changes over time as firms' operations and investors' preferences change. Most experts also believe that, as shown in Figure 12-4, the relationship between value and leverage is relatively flat over a fairly broad range, so large deviations from the optimal capital structure can occur without materially affecting the stock price.

Now consider signalling theory, which we discussed earlier. Because of asymmetric information, investors know less about a firm's prospects than its managers know. Furthermore, managers try to maximize value for *current* shareholders, not new ones. Therefore, if the firm has excellent prospects, management will not want to issue new shares, but if things look bleak, then a new stock offering would benefit current shareholders. Consequently, investors take a stock offering to be a signal of bad news, so stock prices tend to decline when new issues are announced. As a result, new equity financings are relatively expensive. The net effect of signalling is to motivate firms to maintain a reserve borrowing capacity designed to permit future investment opportunities to be financed by debt if internal funds are not available.

By combining the trade-off and asymmetric information theories, we obtain this explanation for firms' behaviour:

1.   Debt financing provides benefits because of the tax deductibility of interest, so firms should have some debt in their capital structures.

---

[29]For some insights into how practising financial managers view the capital structure decision, see John Graham and Campbell Harvey, "The Theory and Practice of Corporate Finance: Evidence from the Field," *Journal of Financial Economics*, 2001, 187–243; Ravindra R. Kamath, "Long-Term Financing Decisions: Views and Practices of Financial Managers of NYSE Firms," *Financial Review*, May 1997, 331–356; Edgar Norton, "Factors Affecting Capital Structure Decisions," *Financial Review*, August 1991, 431–446.

FIGURE 12-4 Effects of Leverage: The Trade-Off Models

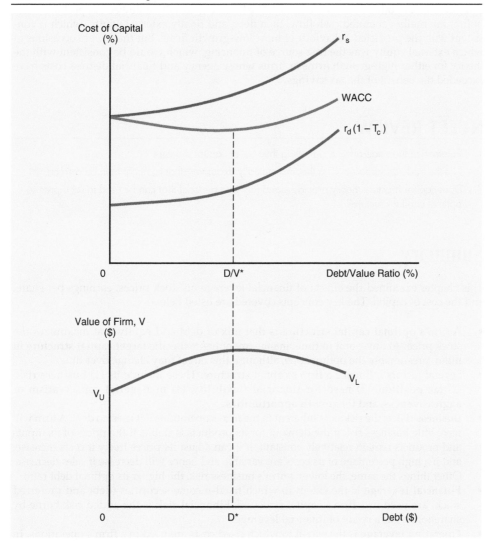

2. However, financial distress and agency costs place limits on debt usage—beyond some point, these costs offset the tax advantage of debt. The costs of financial distress are especially harmful to firms whose values consist primarily of intangible growth options, such as research and development. Such firms should have lower levels of debt than firms whose asset bases consist mostly of tangible assets.

3. Because of problems resulting from asymmetric information and flotation costs, low-growth firms should follow a pecking order, by raising capital first from internal sources, then by borrowing, and finally by issuing new stock. In fact, such low-growth firms rarely need to issue external equity. High-growth firms whose growth occurs primarily through increases in tangible assets, should follow the same pecking order, but usually they will need to issue new stock as well as debt. High-growth firms whose values consist primarily of intangible growth options may run out of internally generated cash, but they should emphasize stock rather than debt due to the severe problems that financial distress imposes on such firms.

4. Finally, because of asymmetric information, firms should maintain a reserve of borrowing capacity in order to be able to take advantage of good investment opportunities without having to issue stock at low prices. This reserve will cause the actual debt ratio to be lower than that suggested by the trade-off models.

There is some evidence that managers do attempt to behave in ways that are consistent with this view of capital structure. In a survey of CFOs, about two-thirds of the CFOs said that they follow a "hierarchy in which the most advantageous sources of funds are exhausted before other sources are used." The hierarchy usually followed the pecking order of first internally generated cash flow, then debt, and finally external equity, which is consistent with the predicted behaviour of most low-growth firms. But there were occasions in which external equity was the first source of financing, which would be consistent with the theory for either high-growth firms or firms whose agency and financial distress costs have exceeded the benefit of the tax savings.[30]

CONCEPT REVIEW

1. Summarize the trade-off and signalling theories of capital structure.
2. Are the trade-off and signalling theories mutually exclusive—that is, might both be correct?
3. Does capital structure theory provide managers with a model that can be used to set a precise optimal capital structure?

Summary

This chapter examined the effects of financial leverage on stock prices, earnings per share, and the cost of capital. The key concepts covered are listed below:

- A firm's **optimal capital structure** is that mix of debt and equity that maximizes the stock price. At any point in time, management has a specific **target capital structure** in mind, presumably the optimal one, although this target may change over time.
- Several factors influence a firm's capital structure. These include its (1) **business risk,** (2) **tax position,** (3) need for **financial flexibility,** (4) **managerial conservatism** or **aggressiveness,** and (5) **growth opportunities.**
- **Business risk** is the riskiness inherent in the firm's operations if it uses no debt. A firm will have little business risk if the demand for its products is stable, if the prices of its inputs and products remain relatively constant, if it can adjust its prices freely if costs increase, and if a high percentage of its costs are variable and hence will decrease if sales decrease. Other things the same, the lower a firm's business risk, the higher its optimal debt ratio.
- **Financial leverage** is the extent to which fixed-income securities (debt and preferred stock) are used in a firm's capital structure. **Financial risk** is the added risk borne by shareholders as a result of financial leverage.
- **Operating leverage** is the extent to which fixed costs are used in a firm's operations. In business terminology, a high degree of operating leverage, other factors held constant, implies that a relatively small change in sales results in a large change in ROIC.
- **Franco Modigliani** and **Merton Miller (MM)** proved that under a restrictive set of assumptions, including zero taxes, capital structure is irrelevant—that is, a firm's value is not affected by its financing mix.
- MM later added **corporate taxes** to their model and reached the conclusion that capital structure *does* matter. Indeed, their model led to the conclusion that firms should use 100% debt financing.
- MM's model with corporate taxes demonstrated that the primary benefits of debt stem from the **tax deductibility of interest payments.**
- Later, Miller extended the theory to include personal taxes. Personal taxes reduce but do not eliminate the benefits of debt financing.
- The **Hamada equation** shows the effect of financial leverage on beta as follows:

$$b = b_U[1 + (1 - T)(D/S)]$$

---

[30]For more on capital budgeting issues, see Ravindra R. Kamath, "Long-Term Financing Decisions: Views and Practices of Financial Managers of NYSE Firms," *Financial Review,* May 1997, 350–356; Michael T. Dugan and Keith A. Shriver, "An Empirical Comparison of Alternative Methods for Estimating the Degree of Operating Leverage," *Financial Review,* May 1992, 309–321; Dilip K. Ghosh, "Optimum Capital Structure Redefined," *Financial Review,* August 1992, 411–429.

Firms can take their current beta, tax rate, and debt/equity ratio to arrive at their **unlevered beta,** b_U, as follows:

$$b_U = b/[1 + (1 - T)(D/S)]$$

- **MM** and their followers developed a **trade-off theory of capital structure.** They showed that debt is useful because interest is **tax deductible,** but also that debt brings with it costs associated with actual or potential bankruptcy. The optimal capital structure strikes a balance between the tax benefits of debt and the costs associated with bankruptcy.
- An alternative (or, really, complementary) theory of capital structure relates to the **signals** given to investors by a firm's decision to use debt versus stock to raise new capital. A stock issue sets off a negative signal, while using debt is a positive, or at least a neutral, signal. As a result, companies try to avoid having to issue stock by maintaining a **reserve borrowing capacity,** and this means using less debt in "normal" times than the MM trade-off theory would suggest.
- A firm's owners may decide to use a relatively large amount of debt to constrain the managers. A **high debt ratio raises the threat of bankruptcy,** which not only carries a cost but also forces managers to be more careful and less wasteful with shareholders' money. Many of the corporate takeovers and leveraged buyouts in recent years were designed to improve efficiency by reducing the cash flow available to managers.

Although each firm has a theoretically optimal capital structure, as a practical matter we cannot estimate it with precision. Accordingly, financial executives generally treat the optimal capital structure as a range—for example, 40% to 50% debt—rather than as a precise point, such as 45%. The concepts discussed in this chapter help managers understand the factors they should consider when they set the target capital structure ranges for their firms.

Questions

12-1 Define each of the following terms:
  a. Capital structure; business risk; financial risk
  b. Operating leverage; financial leverage; break-even point
  c. Reserve borrowing capacity

12-2 What term refers to the uncertainty inherent in projections of future ROIC?

12-3 Firms with relatively high nonfinancial fixed costs are said to have a high degree of what?

12-4 "One type of leverage affects both EBIT and EPS. The other type affects only EPS." Explain this statement.

12-5 Why is the following statement true? "Other things being the same, firms with relatively stable sales are able to carry relatively high debt ratios."

12-6 Why do public utility companies usually have capital structures that are different from those of retail firms?

12-7 Why is EBIT generally considered to be independent of financial leverage? Why might EBIT actually be influenced by financial leverage at high debt levels?

12-8 If a firm went from zero debt to successively higher levels of debt, why would you expect its stock price to first rise, then hit a peak, and then begin to decline?

12-9 Define each of the following terms:
  a. MM Proposition I without taxes; with corporate taxes.
  b. MM Proposition II without taxes; with corporate taxes.
  c. Miller model.
  d. Financial distress costs.
  e. Agency costs.
  f. Trade-off model.
  g. Value of debt tax shield.

Concept Review Problems

Full solutions are provided at www.nelson.com/brigham3ce.

CR-1
Optimal Capital Structure

Rogers Company is currently in this situation: (1) EBIT = $4.7 million; (2) tax rate, T = 30%; (3) value of debt, D = $2 million; (4) r_d = 8%; (5) r_s = 15%; (6) shares of stock outstanding, n_0 = 600,000; and (7) stock price, P_0 = $30. The firm's market is stable, and it expects no growth, so all earnings are paid out as dividends. The debt consists of perpetual bonds.

a. What is the total market value of the firm's stock, S, and the firm's total market value, V?
b. What is the firm's weighted average cost of capital?
c. Suppose the firm can increase its debt so that its capital structure has 50% debt, based on market values (it will issue debt and buy back stock). At this level of debt, its cost of equity rises to 18.5% and its interest rate on all debt will rise to 10% (it will have to call and refund the old debt). What is the WACC under this capital structure? What is the total value?

CR-2
Hamada Equation

Lighter Industrial Corporation (LIC) is considering a large-scale recapitalization. Currently, LIC is financed with 25% debt and 75% equity. LIC is considering increasing its level of debt until it is financed with 60% debt and 40% equity. The beta on its common stock at the current level of debt is 1.5, the risk-free rate is 6%, the market risk premium is 4%, and LIC faces a 25% tax rate.

a. What is LIC's current cost of equity?
b. What is LIC's unlevered beta?
c. What will be the new beta and new cost of equity if LIC recapitalizes?

Problems

Easy
Problems 1–7

Answers to odd-numbered problems appear in Appendix A.

12-1
Break-even Quantity

J. Kirk Ltd. has fixed operating costs of $4,800,000 and variable costs of $75 per unit. If it sells the product for $95 per unit, what is the break-even quantity?

12-2
Unlevered Beta

Digital Design (DD) has a beta of 0.75. The tax rate is 30% and DD is financed with 40% debt. What is the company's unlevered beta?

12-3
Premium for
Financial Risk

Ethier Enterprise has an unlevered beta of 1.0. Ethier is financed with 50% debt and has a levered beta of 1.6. If the risk-free rate is 5.5% and the market risk premium is 6%, how much is the additional premium that Ethier's shareholders require to be compensated for financial risk?

12-4
Financial
Leverage

Gourmet Foods To Go has the following financial information:

Debt:	$0
Book Equity:	$4,000,000
Tax Rate:	26%
EBIT:	$500,000

Gourmet Foods decides to borrow $2,000,000 at a 7% interest rate and, with the proceeds, buy back $2,000,000 worth of their stock. Calculate return on equity before and after the loan and buy-back is made.

12-5
MM Model with
Zero Taxes

An unlevered firm has a value of $800 million. An otherwise identical but levered firm has $60 million in debt. Under the MM zero-tax model, what is the value of the levered firm?

12-6
MM Model with
Corporate Taxes

An unlevered firm has a value of $600 million. An otherwise identical but levered firm has $120 million in debt. If the corporate tax rate is 30%, what is the value of the levered firm using the MM corporate-tax model?

12-7
Miller Model with Corporate
and Personal Taxes

An unlevered firm has a value of $600 million. An otherwise identical but levered firm has $240 million in debt. Under the Miller model, what is the value of a levered firm if the corporate tax rate is 34%, the personal tax rate on equity is 10%, and the personal tax rate on debt is 35%?

Intermediate Problems 8–15

12-8
Break-Even Point

Quantum Computers Inc. produces mini super-computers that sell for $210,000 each. The firm's fixed costs, F, are $5 million; 200 super-computers are produced and sold each year; profits total $1.5 million and the firm's assets (all equity financed) are $10 million. The firm estimates that it can change its production process, adding $4 million to investment and $3 million to fixed operating costs. This change will (1) reduce variable costs per unit by $20,000 and (2) increase output by 40 units, but (3) the sales price on all units will have to be lowered to $200,000 to permit sales of the additional output. The firm has tax loss carry-forwards that cause its tax rate to be zero, its cost of equity is 16%, and it uses no debt.

a. What is the incremental profit? To get a rough idea of the project's profitability, what is the project's expected rate of return for the next year (defined as the incremental profit divided by the investment)? Should the firm make the investment?
b. Would the firm's break-even point increase or decrease if it made the change?
c. Would the new situation expose the firm to more or less business risk than the old one?

12-9
Business and Financial Risk

Here are the estimated ROE distributions for Firms A, B, and C:

	Probability				
	0.1	0.2	0.4	0.2	0.1
Firm A: ROE_A	0.0%	5.0%	10.0%	15.0%	20.0%
Firm B: ROE_B	(2.0)	5.0	12.0	19.0	26.0
Firm C: ROE_C	(5.0)	5.0	15.0	25.0	35.0

a. Calculate the expected value and standard deviation for Firm C's ROE. $ROE_A = 10.0\%$, $\sigma_A = 5.5\%$; $ROE_B = 12.0\%$, $\sigma_B = 7.7\%$.
b. Discuss the relative riskiness of the three firms' returns. (Assume that these distributions are expected to remain constant over time.)
c. Now suppose that all three firms have the same standard deviation of basic earning power (EBIT/Total assets), $\sigma_A = \sigma_B = \sigma_C = 5.5\%$. What can we tell about the financial risk of each firm?

12-10
Capital Structure Analysis

Fikse Gardening Supplies has no debt outstanding, and its financial position is given by the following data:

Assets (book = market)	$4,000,000
EBIT	$500,000
Cost of equity, r_s	8.75%
Stock price, P_0	$8
Shares outstanding, n_0	500,000
Tax rate, T	30%

The firm is considering selling bonds and simultaneously repurchasing some of its stock. If it moves to a capital structure with 30% debt based on market values, its cost of equity, r_s, will increase to 9.5% to reflect the increased risk. Bonds can be sold at a cost, r_d, of 7%. Fikse is a no-growth firm. Hence, all its earnings are paid out as dividends, and earnings are expected to be constant over time.

a. What effect would this use of leverage have on the value of the firm?
b. What would be the market value of Fikse's equity?
c. The $500,000 EBIT given previously is actually the expected value from the following probability distribution:

Probability	EBIT
0.10	$ (100,000)
0.20	200,000
0.40	500,000
0.20	800,000
0.10	1,100,000

Determine the times-interest-earned ratio for each probability. What is the probability of not covering the interest payment at the 30% debt level?

12-11
Business and Financial
Risk—MM Model

Air Kingston has just been incorporated, and its board of directors is currently grappling with the question of optimal capital structure. The company plans to offer commuter air services between Kingston and smaller surrounding cities. EagleAir has been around for a few years, and it has about the same basic business risk as Air Kingston would have. EagleAir's market-determined beta is 2.0, and it has a current market value debt ratio (total debt/total assets) of 50% and a tax rate of 30%. Air Kingston expects only to be marginally profitable at start-up; hence its tax rate would only be 15%. Air Kingston's owners expect that the total book and market value of the firm's stock, if it uses zero debt, will be $16 million. Air Kingston's CFO believes that the MM and Hamada formulas for the value of a levered firm and the levered firm's cost of capital should be used.

a. Estimate the beta of an unlevered firm in the commuter airline business based on EagleAir's market-determined beta.

b. Now assume that $r_d = r_{RF} = 6\%$ and the market risk premium, RP_M, is 5%. Find the required rate of return on equity for an unlevered commuter airline.

c. Air Kingston is considering three capital structures: (1) $2 million debt, (2) $6 million debt, and (3) $8 million debt. Estimate Air Kingston's r_s for these debt levels.

d. Calculate Air Kingston's r_s at $8 million debt assuming that its tax rate is now 30%. Compare this with your corresponding answer to part c.

12-12
Financial Leverage

Highridge Brewing Co. (HBC) wants to estimate next year's return on equity (ROE) under different financial leverage ratios. HBC's total capital is $14 million, it currently uses only common equity, it has no future plans to use preferred stock in its capital structure, and its tax rate is 30%. The CFO has estimated next year's EBIT for three possible states of the world: $4.2 million with a 0.2 probability, $2.8 million with a 0.5 probability, and $700,000 with a 0.3 probability. Calculate HBC's expected ROE, standard deviation, and coefficient of variation for each of the following debt-to-capital ratios; then evaluate the results:

Debt/Capital Ratio	Interest Rate
0%	—
10	9%
50	11
60	14

12-13
MM without Taxes

Companies U and L are identical in every respect except that U is unlevered while L has $10 million of 5% bonds outstanding. Assume that (1) all of the MM assumptions are met, (2) there are no corporate or personal taxes, (3) EBIT is $2 million, and (4) the cost of equity to Company U is 10%.

a. What value would MM estimate for each firm?

b. What is r_s for Firm U? For Firm L?

c. Find S_L, and then show that $S_L + D = V_L = \$20$ million.

d. What is the WACC for Firm U? For Firm L?

e. Suppose $V_U = \$20$ million and $V_L = \$22$ million. According to MM, do these values represent an equilibrium? If not, explain the process by which equilibrium would be restored.

12-14
MM with Corporate
Taxes

Companies U and L are identical in every respect except that U is unlevered while L has $10 million of 5% bonds outstanding. Assume that (1) all of the MM assumptions are met, (2) both firms are subject to a 40% corporate tax rate, (3) EBIT is $2 million, and (4) the unlevered cost of equity is 10%.

a. What value would MM now estimate for each firm? (Use Proposition I.)

b. What is r_s for Firm U? For Firm L?

c. Find S_L, and then show that $S_L + D = V_L$ results in the same value as obtained in Part a.

d. What is the WACC for Firm U? For Firm L?

12-15
Miller Model

Companies U and L are identical in every respect except that U is unlevered while L has $10 million of 5% bonds outstanding. Assume that (1) all of the MM assumptions are met, (2) both firms are subject to a 40% corporate tax rate, (3) EBIT is $2 million, (4) investors in both firms face a tax rate of $T_d = 28\%$ on debt income and $T_s = 20\%$, on average, on stock income, and (5) the unlevered cost of equity, r_{sU}, is 10%.

a. What is the value of the unlevered firm, V_U?

b. What is the value of V_L?

c.   What is the gain from leverage in this situation? Compare this with the gain from leverage in Problem 12–14.

d.   Set $T_c = T_s = T_d = 0$. What is the value of the levered firm? The gain from leverage?

e.   Now suppose $T_s = T_d = 0$, $T_c = 40\%$. What are the value of the levered firm and the gain from leverage?

f.   Assume that $T_d = 28\%$, $T_s = 28\%$, and $T_c = 40\%$. Now what are the value of the levered firm and the gain from leverage?

Challenging Problems 16–21

12-16
Break-Even and Leverage

Wingler Communications Corporation (WCC) produces premium stereo headphones that sell for $28.80 per set, and this year's sales are expected to be 450,000 units. Variable production costs for the expected sales under present production methods are estimated at $10,200,000, and fixed production (operating) costs at present are $1,560,000. WCC has $4,800,000 of debt outstanding at an interest rate of 8%. There are 240,000 common shares outstanding, and there is no preferred stock. The dividend payout ratio is 70%, and WCC is in the 30% tax bracket.

The company is considering investing $7,200,000 in new equipment. Sales would not increase, but variable costs per unit would decline by 20%. Also, fixed operating costs would increase from $1,560,000 to $1,800,000. WCC could raise the required capital by borrowing $7,200,000 at 10% or by selling 240,000 additional common shares at $30 per share.

a.   What would be WCC's EPS (1) under the old production process, (2) under the new process if it uses debt, and (3) under the new process if it uses common stock?

b.   At what unit sales level would WCC have the same EPS assuming it undertakes the investment and finances it with debt or with stock? {*Hint:* V = variable cost per unit = $8,160,000/450,000, and EPS = [(PQ − VQ − F − I)(1 − T)]/N. Set EPS_{Stock} = EPS_{Debt} and solve for Q.}

c.   At what unit sales level would EPS = 0 under the three production/financing setups—that is, under the old plan, the new plan with debt financing, and the new plan with stock financing? (*Hint:* Note that V_{Old} = $10,200,000/450,000 and use the hints for Part b, setting the EPS equation equal to zero.)

d.   On the basis of the analysis in Parts a through c and given that operating leverage is lower under the new setup, which plan is the riskiest, which has the highest expected EPS, and which would you recommend? Assume that there is a fairly high probability of sales falling as low as 250,000 units. Determine EPS_{Debt} and EPS_{Stock} at that sales level to help assess the riskiness of the two financing plans.

12-17
Capital Structure Analysis

Willard Pest Control (WPC) currently has a capital structure, based on market values, of 50% debt. The debt consists of 8% perpetual bonds selling at par. The company's EBIT is $7.25 million, and its tax rate is 15%. WPC can change its capital structure by either increasing its debt to 70% (based on market values) or decreasing it to 30%. If it decides to *increase* its use of leverage, it must call its old bonds and issue new ones with a 10% coupon. If it decides to *decrease* its leverage, it will call in its old bonds and replace them with new 7% coupon bonds. The company will sell or repurchase stock at the new equilibrium price to complete the capital structure change.

The firm pays out all earnings as dividends; hence, its stock is a zero-growth stock. Its current cost of equity, r_s, is 11%. If it increases leverage, r_s will be 13%. If it decreases leverage, r_s will be 10.5%. What is the firm's WACC and total corporate value under each capital structure?

12-18
Optimal Capital Structure with Hamada

Flex Logic System (FLS) is considering a change in its capital structure. FLS currently has $20 million in debt carrying a rate of 8%, and its stock price is $20 per share with 4 million shares outstanding. FLS is a zero-growth firm and pays out all of its earnings as dividends. EBIT is $15.262 million, and FLS has a 30% tax rate. The market risk premium is 4%, and the risk-free rate is 5%. FLS is considering increasing its debt level to a capital structure with 50% debt, based on market values, and repurchasing shares with the extra money that it borrows. FLS will have to retire the old debt in order to issue new debt, and the rate on the new debt will be 9.5%. FLS has a beta of 1.2.

a.   What is FLS's unlevered beta? Use market value D/S when unlevering.

b.   What are FLS's new beta and cost of equity if it has 50% debt?

c.   What are FLS's WACC and total value of the firm with 50% debt?

12-19
WACC and Optimal
Capital Structure

Elliott Athletics is trying to determine its optimal capital structure, which now consists of only debt and common equity. The firm does not currently use preferred stock in its capital structure, and it does not plan to do so in the future. To estimate how much its debt would cost at different debt levels, the company's treasury staff have consulted with investment bankers and, on the basis of those discussions, have created the following table:

Market Debt-to-Value Ratio (w_d)	Market Equity-to-Value Ratio (w_{ce})	Market Debt-to-Equity Ratio (D/S)	Bond Rating	Before-Tax Cost of Debt (r_d)
0.0	1.0	0.00	A	5.0%
0.2	0.8	0.25	BBB	6.0
0.4	0.6	0.67	BB	8.0
0.6	0.4	1.50	C	10.0
0.8	0.2	4.00	D	13.0

Elliott uses the CAPM to estimate its cost of common equity, r_s. The company estimates that the risk-free rate is 4%, the market risk premium is 5%, and its tax rate is 30%. Elliott estimates that if it had no debt, its "unlevered" beta, b_U, would be 1.2. Based on this information, what is the firm's optimal capital structure, and what would be the weighted average cost of capital at the optimal capital structure?

12-20
MM with Financial
Distress Costs

B. Gibbs Inc. is an unleveraged firm, and it has constant expected operating earnings (EBIT) of $2 million per year. The firm's tax rate is 40%, and its market value is V = S = $12 million. Management is considering the use of some debt financing. (Debt would be issued and used to buy back stock, so the size of the firm would remain constant.) Because interest expense is tax deductible, the value of the firm would tend to increase as debt is added to the capital structure, but there would be an offset in the form of a rising risk of financial distress. The firm's analysts have estimated, as an approximation, that the present value of any future financial distress costs is $8 million and that the probability of distress would increase with leverage according to the following schedule:

Value of Debt	Probability of Financial Distress
$ 2,500,000	0.00%
5,000,000	1.25
7,500,000	2.50
10,000,000	6.25
12,500,000	12.50
15,000,000	31.25
20,000,000	75.00

a.   What is the firm's cost of equity and weighted average cost of capital at this time?
b.   According to the "pure" MM with-tax model, what is the optimal level of debt?
c.   What is the optimal capital structure when financial distress costs are included? To account for financial distress, calculate the value of the firm for each level of debt and subtract the present value of financial distress multiplied by the probability of financial distress at each debt level.
d.   Plot the value of the firm, with and without distress costs, as a function of the level of debt.

12-21
MM with and
without Taxes

International Associates (IA) is just about to commence operations as an international trading company. The firm will have book assets of $15 million, and it expects to earn a 14% return on these assets before taxes. However, because of certain tax arrangements with foreign governments, IA will not pay any taxes; that is, its tax rate will be zero. Management is trying to decide how to raise the required $15 million. It is known that the capitalization rate for an all-equity firm in this business is 9%; that is, r_U = 9%. Further, IA can borrow at a rate r_d = 6%. Assume that the MM assumptions apply.

a. According to MM, what will be the value of IA if it uses no debt? If it uses $6 million of 6% debt?
b. What are the values of the WACC and r_s at debt levels of D = $0, D = $6 million, and D = $10 million? What effect does leverage have on firm value? Why?
c. Assume the initial facts of the problem (r_d = 6%, EBIT = $2.1 million, r_{sU} = 9%), but now assume that a 30% corporate tax rate exists. Find the new market values for IA with zero debt and with $6 million of debt, using the MM formulas.
d. What are the values of the WACC and r_s at debt levels of D = $0, D = $6 million, and D = $10 million, assuming a 30% corporate tax rate? Plot the relationships between the value of the firm and the debt ratio, and between capital costs and the debt ratio.
e. What is the maximum dollar amount of debt financing that can be used? What is the value of the firm at this debt level? What is the cost of this debt?
f. How would each of the following factors tend to change the values you plotted in your graph?
    (1) The interest rate on debt increases as the debt ratio rises.
    (2) At higher levels of debt, the probability of financial distress rises.

Spreadsheet Problem

12-22
Build a Model: WACC and Optimal Capital Structure

Start with the partial model in the file *Ch 12 Build a Model.xlsx* on the textbook's website. Reacher Technology has consulted with investment bankers and determined the interest rate it would pay for different capital structures, as shown in the following table. Data for the risk-free rate, the market risk premium, an estimate of Reacher's unlevered beta, and the tax rate are also shown. Based on this information, what is the firm's optimal capital structure, and what is the weighted average cost of capital at the optimal structure?

Percent Financed with Debt (w_d)	Before-Tax Cost of Debt (r_d)		Input Data	
0%	6.0%		Risk-free rate	4.5%
10	6.1		Market risk premium	5.5
20	7.0		Unlevered beta	0.8
30	8.0		Tax rate	40.0
40	10.0			
50	12.5			
60	15.5			
70	18.0			

MINI CASE

Assume that you have just been hired as business manager of PizzaPalace, a pizza restaurant located adjacent to campus. The company's EBIT was $500,000 last year, and since the university's enrollment is capped, EBIT is expected to remain constant (in real terms) over time. Since no expansion capital will be required, PizzaPalace plans to pay out all earnings as dividends. The management group owns about 50% of the stock, and the stock is traded in the over-the-counter market.

The firm is currently financed with all equity; it has 100,000 shares outstanding; and P_0 = $25 per share. When you took your corporate finance course, your instructor stated that most firms' owners would be financially better off if the firms used some debt. When you suggested this to your new boss, he encouraged you to pursue the idea. As a first step, assume that you obtained from the firm's investment banker the following estimated costs of debt for the firm at different capital structures:

Percent Financed with Debt, w_d	r_d
0%	—
20	6.0%
30	6.5
40	8.0
50	9.0

If the company were to recapitalize, debt would be issued, and the funds received would be used to repurchase stock. PizzaPalace is in the 30% corporate tax bracket, its beta is 1.0, the risk-free rate is 4%, and the market risk premium is 5%.

a.   Provide a brief overview of capital structure effects. Be sure to identify the ways in which capital structure can affect the weighted average cost of capital and free cash flows.

b.   (1) What is business risk? What factors influence a firm's business risk?
     (2) What is operating leverage, and how does it affect a firm's business risk? Show the operating break-even point if a company has fixed costs of $200, a sales price of $15, and variable costs of $10.

c.   Now, to develop an example that can be presented to PizzaPalace's management to illustrate the effects of financial leverage, consider two hypothetical firms: Firm U, which uses no debt financing, and Firm L, which uses $10,000 of 8% debt. Both firms have $20,000 in assets, a 30% tax rate, and an expected EBIT of $3,000.
     (1) Construct partial income statements, which start with EBIT, for the two firms.
     (2) Now calculate ROE for both firms.
     (3) What does this example illustrate about the impact of financial leverage on ROE?

d.   Explain the difference between financial risk and business risk.

e.   Now consider the fact that EBIT is not known with certainty, but rather has the following probability distribution:

Economic State	Probability	EBIT
Bad	0.25	$2,000
Average	0.50	3,000
Good	0.25	4,000

Redo the Part a analysis for Firms U and L, but add basic earnings power (BEP), return on invested capital (ROIC, defined as NOPAT/Capital = EBIT$(1 - T)$/TA for this company), and the times-interest-earned (TIE) ratio to the outcome measures. Find the values for each firm in each state of the economy, and then calculate the expected values. Finally, calculate the standard deviations. What does this example illustrate about the impact of debt financing on risk and return?

f.   What does capital structure theory attempt to do? What lessons can be learned from capital structure theory? Be sure to address the MM models.

g.   What does the empirical evidence say about capital structure theory? What are the implications for managers?

h.   With the above points in mind, now consider the optimal capital structure for PizzaPalace.
     (1) For each capital structure under consideration, calculate the levered beta, the cost of equity, and the WACC.
     (2) Now calculate the corporate value. What are the optimal capital structure and the greatest corporate value?

chapter 13

Distributions to Shareholders: Dividends and Repurchases

Apple's sales grew by over 65% in 2011 to $108 billion. One year later, Apple's sales topped $165 billion. With a stock price close to $600 per share, Apple's market capitalization was well over $500 billion and the company was sitting on about $110 billion in cash. To put that amount into perspective, Apple had almost enough cash to cover Ontario's provincial budget for the entire year of 2012!

Apple's founder and former CEO, Steve Jobs (who passed away in 2011), continually shocked the technology community with innovations such as the iPod, the MacBook Air, the iPhone, and the iPad. His successor, Timothy Cook, shocked the investment community by announcing that Apple would begin to pay a quarterly dividend of $2.65 per share. Apple had about 950 million shares outstanding, so this means that Apple paid about $10 billion in dividends. Apple also announced plans to repurchase about $10 billion of its stock, with much of the repurchased stock used to satisfy upcoming stock option exercises. The return of cash to shareholders did not end there. Since 2012, Apple has increased its dividend by 25% and its stock buyback program has ballooned to $46 billion. As of mid-2014, Apple had about $38 billion in cash and short-term investments on its balance sheet, so investors might expect more large cash distributions in the future.

As you read this chapter, think about Apple's decisions to initiate regular dividend payments, as well as its stock repurchase activities.

The textbook's website contains an *Excel* file that will guide you through the chapter's calculations. The file for this chapter is *Ch 13 Tool Kit.xlsx,* and we encourage you to open the file and follow along as you read the chapter. **www.nelson .com/brigham3ce**

Successful companies generate net operating profit after taxes (NOPAT). A company's growth opportunities and replacement requirements, identified through capital budgeting and financial planning, determine the amount that should be invested in operating capital. Subtracting the investment in operating capital from NOPAT results in free cash flow (FCF), which is the amount available for distribution to investors after paying expenses and taxes and making the necessary investments in operating capital. There are five potentially "good" uses for free cash flow: (1) to pay interest expenses, (2) to pay off debt, (3) to pay dividends, (4) to repurchase stock, and (5) to buy nonoperating assets such as Treasury bills or other marketable securities.[1] The capital structure choice determines the payments for interest expenses and debt principal, and the company's working capital policies (discussed in Chapter 17) determine its level of marketable securities. The remaining FCF should be distributed to shareholders, with the only choice being how much to distribute in the form of dividends versus stock repurchases.

Obviously, this is a simplification since companies (1) sometimes scale back their operating plans for sales and asset growth if such reductions are needed to maintain an existing dividend, (2) temporarily adjust their current financing mix in response to market conditions, and (3) often use marketable securities as shock absorbers for fluctuations in short-term cash flows. Still, there is interdependence among shareholder distributions, operating plans (which have the biggest impact on free cash flow), financing plans (which have the biggest impact on the cost of capital), and working capital policies (which determine the target level of marketable securities).

13.1 Cash Distributions and Firm Value

Shareholder distributions for a wealth-maximizing firm affect the value of operations only to the extent that they change the cost of capital or investors' perceptions regarding expected free cash flow.[2] Here are the central issues addressed in this chapter: Can a company increase its value through (1) its choice of **distribution policy,** defined as the *level* of distributions, (2) the *form* of distributions (cash dividends versus stock repurchases), and (3) the *stability* of distributions?

The answer depends in part on investors' preferences for returns as dividend yields versus capital gains. The mix of yield return versus gains return is determined by the **target distribution ratio,** which is the percentage of net income distributed to shareholders through cash dividends or stock repurchases, and the **target payout ratio,** which is the percentage of net income paid as a cash dividend. Notice that the payout ratio must be less than the distribution ratio since the distribution ratio includes stock repurchases as well as cash dividends.

A high distribution ratio and a high payout ratio mean that a company pays large dividends and has small, or zero, stock repurchases. In this situation, the dividend yield is relatively high and the expected capital gain is low. If a company has a large distribution ratio but a small payout ratio, then it pays low dividends but regularly repurchases stock, resulting in a low dividend yield but a relatively high expected capital gain yield. If a company has a low distribution ratio, then it must also have a relatively low payout ratio, again resulting in a low dividend yield and, it is hoped, a relatively high capital gain. Therefore, a firm's **optimal distribution policy** must strike a balance between cash dividends and capital gains so as to maximize the stock price.

In this section we examine three theories of investor preferences for dividend yield versus capital gains: (1) the dividend irrelevance theory, (2) the "bird-in-the-hand" theory, and (3) the tax preference theory.

Dividend Irrelevance Theory

It has been argued that dividend policy has no effect on either the price of a firm's stock or its cost of capital. If dividend policy has no significant effects, then it indeed is *irrelevant*. The principal proponents of the **dividend irrelevance theory** were Merton Miller and

---

[1]Recall from Chapter 2 that the company's cost of paying interest is on an after-tax basis. Recall also that a company doesn't spend FCF on operating assets (such as the acquisition of another company), because those expenditures were already deducted when calculating FCF. In other words, the purchase of an operating asset (even if it is another company) is not a use of FCF; instead, it is a source of FCF (albeit a "negative source"). Also, most growing companies actually issue new debt each year rather than repay debt. This "negative use" of FCF provides more FCF for the other uses.

[2]Shareholder distributions also affect the level of marketable securities, a nonoperating asset, which in turn affects the stock price.

Corporate Valuation and Distribution to Shareholders

Free cash flow is the amount of cash available for distribution to all investors (shareholders and debtholders) after paying expenses and taxes and making investments in the operating capital required to support the company's growth. This chapter focuses on the distributions of FCF to shareholders in the form of dividends and share repurchases.

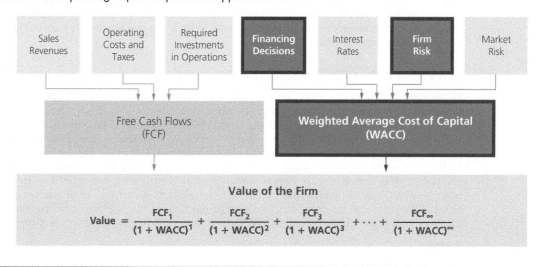

Value of the Firm

$$\text{Value} = \frac{\text{FCF}_1}{(1 + \text{WACC})^1} + \frac{\text{FCF}_2}{(1 + \text{WACC})^2} + \frac{\text{FCF}_3}{(1 + \text{WACC})^3} + \cdots + \frac{\text{FCF}_\infty}{(1 + \text{WACC})^\infty}$$

Franco Modigliani (MM).[3] They argued that the firm's value is determined only by its basic earning power and its business risk. In other words, they argued that the value of a firm depends only on the income produced by its assets, not on how this income is split between dividends and retained earnings.

To understand MM's argument, recognize that any shareholder can in theory construct his or her own dividend policy. For example, if a firm does not pay dividends, a shareholder who wants a 5% dividend can "create" it by selling 5% of his or her stock. Conversely, if a company pays a higher dividend than an investor desires, the investor can use the unwanted dividends to buy additional shares of the company's stock. If investors could buy and sell shares and thus create their own dividend policy without incurring costs, then the firm's dividend policy would truly be irrelevant. Note, though, that investors who want additional dividends must incur brokerage costs to sell shares and pay taxes on any capital gains. Investors who do not want dividends incur brokerage costs to purchase shares with their dividends. Because taxes and brokerage costs certainly exist, dividend policy may well be relevant.

In developing their dividend theory, MM made a number of assumptions, especially the absence of taxes and brokerage costs. Obviously, taxes and brokerage costs do exist, so the MM irrelevance theory may not be true. However, MM argued (correctly) that all economic theories are based on simplifying assumptions, and that the validity of a theory must be judged by empirical tests, not by the realism of its assumptions. We will discuss empirical tests of MM's dividend irrelevance theory shortly.

Bird-in-the-Hand Theory: Dividends Are Preferred

The principal conclusion of MM's dividend irrelevance theory is that dividend policy does not affect the required rate of return on equity, r_s. This conclusion has been hotly debated in academic circles. In particular, Myron Gordon and John Lintner argued that r_s *decreases* as the dividend payout is increased because investors are less certain of receiving the capital gains that are supposed to result from retaining earnings

[3]See Merton H. Miller and Franco Modigliani, "Dividend Policy, Growth, and the Valuation of Shares," *Journal of Business*, October 1961, 411–433. However, their conclusion is valid only if investors expect managers eventually to pay out the equivalent of the present value of all future free cash flows; see Harry DeAngelo and Linda DeAngelo, "The Irrelevance of the MM Dividend Irrelevance Theorem," *Journal of Financial Economics*, 2006, 293–315.

than they are of receiving dividend payments.[4] Gordon and Lintner said, in effect, that investors value a dollar of expected dividends more highly than a dollar of expected capital gains because the dividend yield component is less risky than the expected capital gain.

The possibility of agency costs leads to a similar conclusion. First, high payouts reduce the risk that managers will squander cash because there is less cash on hand. Second, a high-payout company must raise external funds more often than a low-payout company, all else held equal. If a manager knows that the company will receive frequent scrutiny from external markets, then the manager will be less likely to engage in wasteful practices. There-fore, high payouts reduce the risk of agency costs. With less risk, shareholders are willing to accept a lower required return on equity.

Tax Preference Theory: Capital Gains Are Preferred

Historically, investors in Canada and the United States have paid greater tax on dividend income than on capital gains. Recent changes in both countries (in 2006, the dividend tax credit in Canada was enhanced; and in 2003, the United States lowered the tax rate on dividends) have approximately equalized the taxes that investors pay on either source of income. How-ever, capital gains tax will still be effectively lower owing to (1) the time value of money and (2) the ability to time the capital gains. After all, dividends are typically distributed quarterly and taxed in the year received, whereas capital gains do not trigger taxation until an investor actually sells the stock, which may be in the distant future. Moreover, an investor may be able to time the sale of his or her stock so as to garner a lower tax rate (e.g., on retirement, or in between jobs or during a sabbatical). Because of these advantages, investors may prefer to

FIGURE 13-1   Dividend Irrelevance, Bird-in-the-Hand, and Tax Preference Dividend Theories

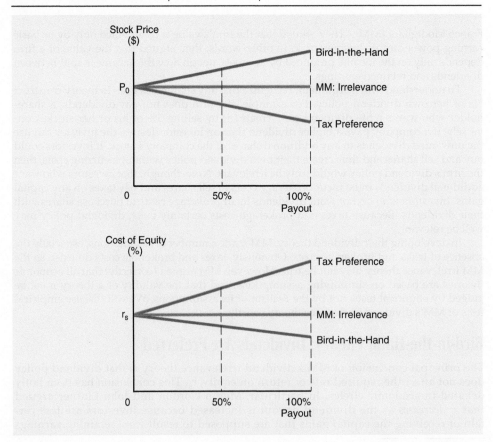

[4]Myron J. Gordon, "Optimal Investment and Financing Policy," *Journal of Finance*, May 1963, 264–272; and John Lintner, "Dividends, Earnings, Leverage, Stock Prices, and the Supply of Capital to Corporations," *Review of Economics and Statistics*, August 1962, 243–269.

FINANCE: IN FOCUS

Dividend Yields Around the World

Dividend yields vary considerably on stock markets around the world. In 2014, in Canada, dividend yields averaged 2.7%, whereas in the United States the yield was 2% on the broad-based S&P 500, but only 1.30% on the tech-heavy Nasdaq Index. In other countries the average dividend yield ranged from a high of 5.1% in Russia to 1.17% in Argentina. The accompanying graph summarizes the dividend picture in 2014.

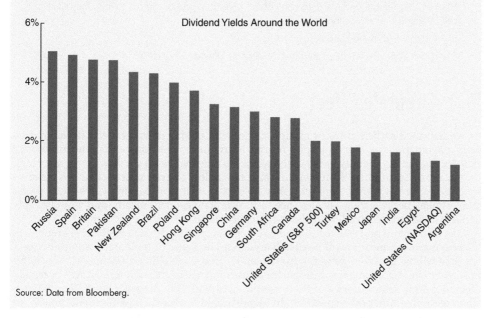

Dividend Yields Around the World

Source: Data from Bloomberg.

have companies minimize dividends. If so, investors would be willing to pay more for low-payout companies than for otherwise similar high-payout companies.

Empirical Evidence on Distribution Policies

As Figure 13-1 shows, these three theories offer contradictory advice to corporate managers, so which, if any, should we believe? The most logical way to proceed is to test the theories empirically. Many such tests have been conducted, but their results have been unclear. There are two reasons for this: (1) For a valid statistical test, things other than distribution level must be held constant—that is, the sample companies must differ only in their distribution levels. (2) We must be able to measure with a high degree of accuracy each firm's cost of equity. Neither of these two conditions holds: we cannot find a set of publicly owned firms that differ only in their distribution levels, nor can we obtain precise estimates of the cost of equity. Therefore, no one has yet identified a completely unambiguous relationship between distribution level and the cost of equity or firm value.

Although none of the empirical tests is perfect, recent evidence does suggest that firms with higher dividend payouts also have higher required returns.[5] This tends to support the tax effect hypothesis, although the size of the required return is too high to be fully explained by taxes.

Agency costs should be most severe in countries with poor investor protection. In such countries, companies with high dividend payouts should be more highly valued than those with low payouts because high payouts limit the extent to which managers can expropriate shareholder wealth. Recent research shows that this is the case, which supports the dividend preference hypothesis in the case of companies with severe agency problems.[6]

---

[5] See A. Naranjo, N. Nimalendran, and M. Ryngaert, "Stock Returns, Dividend Yields, and Taxes," *Journal of Finance*, December 1998, pp. 2029–2057.
[6] See L. Pinkowitz, R. Stulz, and R. Williamson, "Does the Contribution of Corporate Cash Holdings and Dividends to Firm Value Depend on Governance? A Cross-Country Analysis," *Journal of Finance*, December 2006, pp. 2725–2751.

Although investors in the aggregate cannot be shown to clearly prefer either higher or lower distribution levels, the evidence does show that individual investors have strong preferences. Evidence also shows that investors and managers who determine a company's dividend policy prefer stable, predictable dividend payouts (regardless of the payout level), and that both groups believe that dividend changes provide a signal about a firm's future prospects.[7] We discuss these issues in the next several sections.

CONCEPT REVIEW

1. What did Modigliani and Miller assume about taxes and brokerage costs when they developed their dividend irrelevance theory?
2. How did the bird-in-the-hand theory get its name?
3. What have been the results of empirical tests of the dividend theories?

13.2 Clientele Effect

As we indicated earlier, different groups, or *clienteles*, of shareholders prefer different dividend payout policies. For example, retired individuals, pension funds, and university endowment funds generally prefer cash income, so they may want the firm to pay out a high percentage of its earnings. Such investors are often in low or even zero tax brackets, so taxes are of no concern. On the other hand, shareholders in their peak earning years might prefer reinvestment, because they have less need for current investment income and would simply reinvest dividends received, after first paying income taxes on those dividends.

If a firm retains and reinvests income rather than paying dividends, those shareholders who need current income will be disadvantaged. The value of their stock might increase, but they will be forced to go to the trouble and expense of selling off some of their shares to obtain cash. Also, some institutional investors (or trustees for individuals) will be legally precluded from selling stock and then "spending capital." On the other hand, shareholders who are saving rather than spending dividends might favour the low dividend policy, for the less the firm pays out in dividends, the less these shareholders will have to pay in current taxes, and the less trouble and expense they will have to go through to reinvest their after-tax dividends. Therefore, investors who want current investment income should own shares in high dividend payout firms, while investors with no need for current investment income should own shares in low dividend payout firms. For example, investors seeking high cash income might invest in pipelines, which averaged a 42% payout in 2014, while those favouring growth could invest in the technology sector, which paid out only 19% during the same time period.

To the extent that shareholders can switch firms, a firm can change from one dividend payout policy to another and then let shareholders who do not like the new policy sell to other investors who do. However, frequent switching would be inefficient because of (1) brokerage costs, (2) the likelihood that shareholders who are selling will have to pay capital gains taxes, and (3) a possible shortage of investors who like the firm's newly adopted dividend policy. Thus, management should be hesitant to change its dividend policy, because a change might cause current shareholders to sell their stock, forcing the stock price down. Such a price decline might be temporary, but it might also be permanent—if few new investors are attracted by the new dividend policy, then the stock price will remain depressed. Of course, the new policy might attract an even larger clientele than the firm had before, in which case the stock price would rise.

Evidence from several studies suggests that there is in fact a **clientele effect.**[8] MM and others have argued that one clientele is as good as another, so the existence of a clientele effect does not necessarily imply that one dividend policy is better than any other. MM may be wrong, though, and neither they nor anyone else can prove that the aggregate makeup of investors permits firms to disregard clientele effects. This issue, like most others in the dividend arena, is still up in the air.

[7]H. Kent Baker, Samir Saadi, Shantanu Dutte, and Devinder Gandhi, "The Perception of Dividends by Canadian Managers: New Survey Evidence," *International Journal of Managerial Finance* 3, 2007, 70–91.

[8]For example, see R. Richardson Pettit, "Taxes, Transaction Costs and the Clientele Effect of Dividends," *Journal of Financial Economics,* December 1977, pp. 419–436; and William J. Moser and Andy Puckett, "Dividend Tax Clienteles: Evidence from Tax Law Changes," *Journal of the American Taxation Association,* Spring 2009, pp. 1–22.

CONCEPT REVIEW

1. Define the clientele effect and explain how it affects dividend policy.

13.3 Information Content, or Signalling, Hypothesis

When MM set forth their dividend irrelevance theory, they assumed that everyone—investors and managers alike—has identical information regarding a firm's future earnings and dividends. In reality, however, different investors have different views on both the level of future dividend payments and the uncertainty inherent in those payments, and managers have better information about future prospects than public shareholders.

It has been observed that an increase in the dividend is often accompanied by an increase in the price of a stock, while a dividend cut generally leads to a stock price decline. Some have argued that this indicates that investors prefer dividends to capital gains. However, MM argued differently. They noted the well-established fact that corporations are reluctant to cut dividends, and hence do not raise dividends unless they anticipate higher earnings in the future. Thus, MM argued that a higher-than-expected dividend increase is a signal to investors that the firm's management forecasts good future earnings. Conversely, a dividend reduction, or a smaller-than-expected increase, is a signal that management is forecasting poor earnings in the future. Thus, MM argued that investors' reactions to changes in dividend policy do not necessarily show that investors prefer dividends to retained earnings. Rather, they argue that price changes following dividend actions simply indicate that there is an important **information, or signalling, content** in dividend announcements.

The initiation of a dividend by a firm that formerly paid no dividend is certainly a significant change in distribution policy. It appears that initiating firms' future earnings and cash flows are less risky than before the initiation. However, the evidence is mixed regarding the future profitability of initiating firms: Some studies find slightly higher earnings after the initiation, while others find no significant change in earnings.[9] What happens when firms with existing dividends unexpectedly increase or decrease the dividend? Early studies, using small data samples, concluded that unexpected dividend changes did not provide a signal about future earnings.[10] However, more recent data with larger samples provide mixed evidence.[11] On average, firms that cut dividends have had poor earnings in the years directly preceding the cut but have actually improved earnings in subsequent years. Firms that increase dividends have had earnings increases in the years preceding the increase but don't appear to have had subsequent earnings increases. However, they don't have subsequent declines in earnings either, so it appears that the increase in dividends signals that past earnings increases were not temporary. Also, a relatively large number of firms that expect a large permanent increase in cash flow (as opposed to earnings) do in fact increase their dividend payouts in the year prior to the cash flow increase.

All in all, there is clearly some information content in dividend announcements: Stock prices tend to fall when dividends are cut, even if they don't always rise when dividends are increased. However, this doesn't necessarily validate the signalling hypothesis since it is difficult to tell whether any stock price changes that follow changes in dividends reflect only signalling effects or both signalling and dividend preferences.

CONCEPT REVIEW

1. Define information content, and explain how it affects dividend policy.

---

[9]See Edward Dyl and Robert Weigand, "The Information Content of Dividend Initiations: Additional Evidence," *Financial Management*, Autumn 1998, 27–35; P. Asquith and D. Mullins, "The Impact of Initiating Dividend Payments on Shareholders' Wealth," *Journal of Business*, January 1983, 77–96; and P. Healy and K. Palepu, "Earnings Information Conveyed by Dividend Initiations and Omissions," *Journal of Financial Economics*, September 1988, 149–175.

[10]For example, see N. Gonedes, "Corporate Signaling, External Accounting, and Capital Market Equilibrium: Evidence of Dividends, Income, and Extraordinary Items," *Journal of Accounting Research*, Spring 1978, 26–79; and R. Watts, "The Information Content of Dividends," *Journal of Business*, April 1973, 191–211.

[11]See Shlomo Benartzi, Roni Michaely, and Richard Thaler, "Do Changes in Dividends Signal the Future or the Past?" *Journal of Finance*, July 1997, 1007–1034; and Yaron Brook, William Charlton, Jr., and Robert J. Hendershott, "Do Firms Use Dividends to Signal Large Future Cash Flow Increases?" *Financial Management*, Autumn 1998, 46–57.

13.4 Implications for Dividend Stability

The clientele effect and the information content in dividend announcements definitely have implications regarding the desirability of stable versus volatile dividends. For example, many shareholders rely on dividends to meet expenses, and they would be seriously inconvenienced if the dividend stream were unstable. Furthermore, reducing dividends to make funds available for capital investment could send incorrect signals to investors, who might push down the stock price because they interpreted the dividend cut to mean that the company's future earnings prospects have been diminished. Thus, maximizing its stock price probably requires a firm to maintain a steady dividend policy. Because sales and earnings are expected to grow for most firms, a stable dividend policy means that a company's regular cash dividends should also grow at a steady, predictable rate.[12]

CONCEPT REVIEW

1. Why do the clientele effect and the information content hypotheses imply that investors prefer stable dividends?

13.5 Setting the Target Distribution Level: The Residual Distribution Model

When deciding how much cash to distribute to shareholders, two points should be kept in mind: (1) the overriding objective is to maximize shareholder value, and (2) the firm's cash flows really belong to its shareholders, so management should refrain from retaining income unless they can reinvest it to produce returns higher than shareholders could themselves earn by investing the cash in investments of equal risk. On the other hand, recall from Chapter 9 that internal equity (reinvested earnings) is cheaper than external equity (new common stock issues) because it avoids flotation costs. This encourages firms to retain earnings so as to avoid having to issue new stock.

When establishing a distribution policy, one size does not fit all. Some firms produce a lot of cash but have limited investment opportunities—this is true for firms in profitable but mature industries where few opportunities for growth exist. Such firms typically distribute a large percentage of their cash to shareholders, thereby attracting investment clienteles that prefer high dividends. Other firms generate little or no excess cash since they have many good investment opportunities. Such firms generally distribute little or no cash but enjoy rising earnings and stock prices, thereby attracting investors who prefer capital gains.

As Table 13-1 suggests, dividend payouts and dividend yields for large corporations vary considerably. Generally, firms in stable, cash-producing industries such as utilities, financial services, and tobacco pay relatively high dividends, whereas companies in rapidly growing industries such as computer software tend to pay lower dividends.

For a given firm, the optimal distribution ratio is a function of four factors: (1) investors' preferences for dividends versus capital gains, (2) the firm's investment opportunities, (3) its target capital structure, and (4) the availability and cost of external capital. The last three elements are combined in what we call the **residual distribution model.** Under this model a firm follows these four steps when establishing its target distribution ratio: (1) it determines the optimal capital budget; (2) it determines the amount of equity needed to finance that budget, given its target capital structure; (3) it uses reinvested earnings to meet equity requirements to the extent possible; and (4) it pays dividends or repurchases stock only if more earnings are available than are needed to support the optimal capital budget.

---

[12]For more on announcements and stability, see Jeffrey A. Born, "Insider Ownership and Signals—Evidence from Dividend Initiation Announcement Effects," *Financial Management*, Spring 1988, 38–45; Chinmoy Ghosh and J. Randall Woolridge, "An Analysis of Shareholder Reaction to Dividend Cuts and Omissions," *Journal of Financial Research*, Winter 1988, 281–294; C. Michael Impson and Imre Karafiath, "A Note on the Stock Market Reaction to Dividend Announcements," *Financial Review*, May 1992, 259–271; James W. Wansley, C. F. Sirmans, James D. Shilling, and Young-jin Lee, "Dividend Change Announcement Effects and Earnings Volatility and Timing," *Journal of Financial Research*, Spring 1991, 37–49; and J. Randall Woolridge and Chinmoy Ghosh, "Dividend Cuts: Do They Always Signal Bad News?" *Midland Corporate Finance Journal*, Summer 1985, 20–32.

| TABLE 13-1 | Dividend Payouts (August 2014) | | |

Company	Industry Group	Dividend Payout	Dividend Yield
Russel Metals (RUS)	Metals and mining	97%	4.0%
National Bank (NA)	Banking	39	4.0
TransCanada Corporation (TRP)	Utilities	78	3.6
Sun Life Financial Inc. (SLF)	Insurance	94	3.5
Enbridge Inc. (ENB)	Energy	85	2.6
Empire Company (EMP.A)	Retail	35	1.4
Barrick Gold (ABX)	Metals and mining	NM	1.1
Maple Leaf Foods (MFI)	Food and beverage	6.0	0.8
West Fraser Timber (WFT)	Materials and construction	8.0	0.6
Air Canada (AC.B)	Transportation	0	0

Source: http://www.financialpost.com, accessed August 8, 2014.

The word "residual" implies "leftover," and the residual policy implies that distributions are paid out of "leftover" earnings.

If a firm rigidly follows the residual distribution policy, then distributions paid in any given year can be expressed as follows:

$$
\begin{aligned}
\text{Distributions} &= \text{Net income} - \begin{array}{l}\text{Retained earnings needed} \\ \text{to finance new investments}\end{array} \\
&= \text{Net income} - [(\text{Target equity ratio}) \times (\text{Total capital budget})]
\end{aligned}
\tag{13-1}
$$

As an illustration, consider the case of Prairie and Western (P&W) Transport Company, which has $60 million in net income and a target capital structure of 60% equity and 40% debt.

If P&W forecasts poor investment opportunities, then its estimated capital budget will be only $40 million. To maintain the target capital structure, 40% ($16 million) of this capital must be raised as debt and 60% ($24 million) must be equity. If it followed a strict residual policy, P&W would retain $24 million of its $60 million earnings to help finance new investments and then distribute the remaining $36 million to shareholders:

$$
\begin{aligned}
\text{Distributions} &= \text{Net income} - [(\text{Target equity ratio})(\text{Total capital budget})] \\
&= \$60 - [(60\%)(\$40)] \\
&= \$60 - \$24 = \$36
\end{aligned}
$$

Under this scenario, the company's distribution ratio would be $36 million ÷ $60 million = 0.6 = 60%. These results are shown in Table 13-2.

In contrast, if the company's investment opportunities are average, its optimal capital budget will rise to $70 million. Here it will require $42 million of retained earnings, so distributions will be $60 − $42 = $ 18 million, for a ratio of $18/$60 = 30%. Finally, if investment opportunities are good then the capital budget will be $150 million, which will require 0.6($150) = $90 million of equity. In this case P&W will retain all of its net income ($60 million) and thus make no distributions. Moreover, since the required equity exceeds the retained earnings, the company will have to issue some new common stock to maintain the target capital structure.

Because investment opportunities and earnings will surely vary from year to year, a strict adherence to the residual distribution policy would result in unstable distributions.

TABLE 13-2 P&W's Distribution Ratio with $60 Million of Net Income and a 60% Target Equity Ratio When Faced with Different Investment Opportunities (Millions of Dollars)

	Investment Opportunities		
	Poor	Average	Good
Capital budget	$40	$70	$150
Net income	60	60	60
Required equity (0.6 × Capital budget)	24	42	90
Distributions paid (NI − Required equity)	$36	$18	−$ 30[a]
Distribution ratio (Dividend/NI)	60%	30%	0%

[a]With a $150 million capital budget, P&W would retain all of its earnings and also issue $30 million of new stock.

FINANCE: IN FOCUS

Berkshire Hathaway's Dividend Policy

Warren Buffett, often called the world's most successful investor, is frequently asked whether his company, Berkshire Hathaway, will pay a dividend. Buffett's response is that Berkshire Hathaway will not pay a dividend as long as it can create more than $1 of market value for every $1 of earnings retained. Buffett goes on to state that should Berkshire Hathaway ever declare a dividend, it will be substantial. His comments are consistent with the approach that earnings should be retained *only* if the company can invest them in positive NPV projects.

Sources: http://seekingalpha.com, accessed November 12, 2008; J.V. Bruni and Company, http://jvbruni.com, accessed November 11, 2008.

One year the firm might make no distributions because it needs the money to finance good investment opportunities, but the next year it might make a large distribution because investment opportunities are poor so it does not need to retain much. Similarly, fluctuating earnings could also lead to variable distributions, even if investment opportunities were stable. Until now, we have not said whether distributions should be in the form of dividends, stock repurchases, or some combination. The next sections discuss specific issues associated with dividend payments and stock repurchases; this is followed by a comparison of their relative advantages and disadvantages.

CONCEPT REVIEW

1. Explain the logic of the residual dividend model and the steps a firm would take to implement it.
2. Hamilton Corporation has a target equity ratio of 65%. Its capital budget is $2 million. If Hamilton has net income of $1.6 million and follows a residual distribution model, how much will its distribution be? (Check Figure: $300,000)

13.6 Distributions in the Form of Dividends

This section explains how the volatile distributions implied by the residual model affect the use of dividends as a form of distribution. It also describes some of the institutional features associated with dividend payments.

The Residual Distribution Model in Practice

If distributions were solely in the form of dividends, then rigidly following the residual policy would lead to fluctuating, unstable dividends. Since investors dislike volatile dividends, r_s would be high, and the stock price low. Therefore, firms should:

1. Estimate earnings and investment opportunities, on average, over the next five or so years.
2. Use this forecast information and the target capital structure to find the average residual model distributions and dollars of dividends during the planning period.
3. Set a *target payout ratio* based on the average projected data.

Thus, firms should use the residual policy to help set their long-run target distribution ratios, but not as a guide to the distribution in any one year.

Companies often use financial forecasting models in conjunction with the residual distribution model as discussed above to help understand the determinants of an optimal dividend policy. Most larger corporations forecast their financial statements over the next 5 to 10 years. Information on projected capital expenditures and working capital requirements is entered into the model, along with sales forecasts, profit margins, depreciation, and the other elements required to forecast cash flows. The target capital structure is also specified, and the model shows the amount of debt and equity that will be required to meet the capital budgeting requirements while maintaining the target capital structure. Then, dividend payments are introduced. Naturally, the higher the payout ratio, the greater the required external equity. Most companies use the model to find a dividend pattern over the forecast period (generally 5 years) that will provide sufficient equity to support the capital budget without forcing them to sell new common stock or move the capital structure ratios outside the optimal range.

Some companies set a very low "regular" dividend and then supplement it with an "extra" dividend when times are good. Canadian companies such as Husky Energy and Computer Modelling Group have followed the **regular-dividend-plus-extras policy** in the past. Each company announces a regular dividend that it will try to maintain. Then, when times are good and profits and cash flows are high, these companies either pay a specially designated extra dividend or repurchase shares of stock. Investors recognize that the extras may not be maintained in the future, so they do not interpret them as a signal that the companies' earnings are going up permanently, nor do they take the elimination of the extra as a negative signal.

In August 2009, faced with uncertain future profits and declining capital, Manulife Financial announced that it would be rolling back its dividend by half, from $0.26 per share to $0.13 per share. That same day, the market responded by cutting Manulife's market value by $6.8 billion. While the company's president had previously suggested that dividends from financial stocks might not be safe, the size of the cut surprised the market. Manulife said it wanted to build a "fortress"-like capital position. Figure 13-2 shows graphically the stock price before the dividend cut announcement and the sharp decline the day of the announcement.

FIGURE 13-2 Historical Share Price for Manulife Financial, May–November 2009

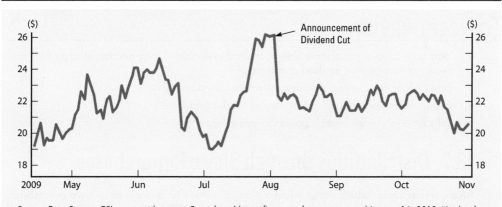

Source: Data Source: CSI, www.csidata.com. From: http://www.finance.yahoo.ca, accessed January 16, 2012. Used with permission of Commodity Systems, Inc.

Dividend Payment Procedures

Dividends are normally paid quarterly, and, if conditions permit, the dividend is increased once each year. For example, Katz Corporation paid $0.50 per quarter in 2015, or at an annual rate of $2.00. In common financial parlance, we say that in 2015, Katz's *regular quarterly dividend* was $0.50, and its *annual dividend* was $2.00. In late 2015, Katz's board of directors met, reviewed projections for 2016, and decided to keep the 2016 dividend at $2.00. The directors announced the $2 rate, so shareholders could count on receiving it unless the company experienced unanticipated operating problems.

The actual payment procedure is as follows:

1. *Declaration date.* On the **declaration date**—say, on November 12—the directors meet and declare the regular dividend, issuing a statement similar to the following: "On November 12, 2015, the directors of Katz Corporation met and declared the regular quarterly dividend of 50 cents per share, payable to holders of record on December 11, payment to be made on January 11, 2016." For accounting purposes, the declared dividend becomes an actual liability on the declaration date. If a balance sheet were constructed, the amount ($0.50)(Number of shares outstanding) would appear as a current liability, and retained earnings would be reduced by a like amount.

2. *Holder-of-record date.* At the close of business on the **holder-of-record date,** December 11, the company closes its stock transfer books and makes up a list of shareholders as of that date.

3. *Ex-dividend date.* Suppose Jean Buyer buys 100 shares of stock from John Seller on December 8. Will the company be notified of the transfer in time to list Buyer as the new owner and thus pay the dividend to her? To avoid conflict, the securities industry has set up a convention under which the right to the dividend remains with the stock until 2 business days prior to the holder-of-record date. Until the 2 business days prior to the holder-of-record date, the stock is said to trade **cum dividend** (with dividend). On the second day before that date, the right to the dividend no longer goes with the shares. The date when the right to the dividend leaves the stock is called the **ex-dividend date.** In this case, the ex-dividend date is 2 business days prior to December 11, or December 9:

Dividend goes with stock:	December 8
Ex-dividend date:	December 9
	December 10
Holder-of-record date:	December 11

Therefore, if Buyer is to receive the dividend, she must buy the stock *on or before* December 8. If she buys it on December 9 or later, Seller will receive the dividend because he will be the official holder of record.

Katz's dividend amounts to $0.50, so the ex-dividend date is important. Barring fluctuations in the stock market, we would normally expect the price of a stock to drop by approximately the amount of the dividend on the ex-dividend date. Thus, if Katz closed at $30.50 on December 8, it would probably open at about $30 on December 9.

4. *Payment date.* The company actually mails the cheques to the holders of record on January 11, the **payment date.**

CONCEPT REVIEW

1. Why is the residual model more likely to be used to establish a long-run payout target than to set the actual year-by-year dividend payout ratio?
2. How do firms use planning models to help set dividend policy?
3. Explain the procedures used to actually pay the dividend.
4. Why is the ex-dividend date important to investors?

13.7 Distributions through Share Repurchases

Share repurchases, which occur when a company buys back some of its own outstanding stock, have become an important part of the financial landscape.[13] While total cash

---

[13]Companies incorporated under the Canada Business Corporations Act must cancel any shares they repurchase.

distributions as a percentage of net income have remained fairly stable at around 26% to 28%, the mix of dividends and repurchases has changed.[14] The average dividend payout ratio fell from 22.3% in 1974 to 13.8% in 1998, while the average repurchase payout as a percentage of net income rose from 3.7% to 13.6%. Since 1985, large companies have repurchased more shares than they have issued. Since 1998, more cash has been returned to shareholders in repurchases than as dividend payments.[15]

Companies buy back their shares for a number of reasons. Perhaps a company wants to alter its capital structure (see Chapter 12) as a way to increase its value. Perhaps it offers stock options to its employees. In order to maintain the same number of shares outstanding, a company must repurchase its own shares to offset the number of new shares being made available to employees through their stock option. Perhaps it is assuming that its investors would rather receive capital gains over dividend income. Another hypothesis is that companies distribute cash through buybacks, as means of constraining managers from making wasteful or unproductive expenditures that would lower the share price (again, see Chapter 12). Finally, managers may buy back shares as a way of signalling to the market their belief that the company's growth opportunities are not fully reflected in the current share price.

A Canadian study[16] on open-market share repurchases suggests two principal reasons that companies initiate a repurchase plan. The biggest reason (69%) is that management thinks the company's shares are undervalued. This is consistent with the signalling hypothesis discussed earlier. The second reason (12%) is to offset the dilution resulting from employee stock option plans.

Share repurchases are usually made in one of three ways: (1) A publicly owned firm can buy back its own stock through a broker on the open market.[17] (2) The firm can make a tender offer, under which it permits shareholders to send in (i.e., "tender") shares in exchange for a specified price per share. In this case, the firm generally indicates that it will buy up to a specified number of shares within a stated time period (usually about 2 weeks). If more shares are tendered than the company wants to buy, purchases are made on a pro rata basis. (3) The firm can purchase a block of shares from one large holder on a negotiated basis.

The Effects of Stock Repurchases

Suppose a company has some extra cash, perhaps due to the sale of a division, and it plans to use that cash to repurchase stock. To keep the example simple, we assume that the company has no debt. The current stock price, P_0, is $20, and the company has 2 million outstanding shares, n_0, for a total market capitalization of $40 million. The company has $5 million in marketable securities (i.e., extra cash) from the recent sale of a division. It has no other financial assets.

As we saw in the diagram at the beginning of the chapter, the company's value of operations, V_{op}, is the present value of its expected future free cash flows, discounted at the WACC.[18] Notice that the repurchase will not affect the FCF or the WACC, so the repurchase doesn't affect the value of operations. The total value of the company is the value of operations plus the value of the nonoperating assets—the extra cash, in our case. We can find the price per share, P_0, by dividing the total value of the company by the number of shares outstanding, n_0:

$$P_0 = \frac{V_{op} + \text{Extra cash}}{n_0}$$

(13-2)

We can easily solve this for the value of operations: $V_{op} = P_0(n_0) - \text{Extra cash} = \$40 - \$5 = \$35$ million.

We can arrive at the same answer of $35 million by looking at a market value balance sheet for the company. Given the share price of $20 and 2 million shares outstanding, we

---

[14]See Gustavo Grullon and Roni Michaely, "Dividends, Share Repurchases, and the Substitution Hypothesis," *Journal of Finance*, August 2002, pp. 1649–1684; and Eugene Fama and Kenneth French, "Disappearing Dividends: Changing Firm Characteristics or Lower Propensity to Pay?" *Journal of Applied Corporate Finance*, Spring 2001, pp. 67–79.

[15]In Canada, share repurchases valued at $501 million in 1988 grew to $5.3 billion over a 12-year period.

[16]William J. McNally, "Open Market Share Repurchases in Canada," *Canadian Investment Review*, Winter 2002, 24–31.

[17]Although not all firms that announce their plans to repurchase stock on the open market do so, McNally found that 78% did repurchase at least some of their shares.

[18]The WACC is based on the company's capital used in operations and does not include any effects due to the extra cash.

know that the market value of the equity is $40 million. Since there is no debt, the left-hand side of the balance sheet must also total $40 million. As we know the company has $5 million in marketable securities, the value of the operating assets must equal $35 million.

Market Value Balance Sheet Before Repurchase (000s)

Assets		Equity	
Marketable securities	$ 5,000		
Operating assets	35,000	2,000 shares @ $20/share	$40,000
Market value of assets	$40,000	Market value of equity	$40,000

Now consider the repurchase. Below is a new market-value balance sheet showing the effect of the share purchase. All of the cash went to buy back the shares; thus, marketable securities are now $0. The operating asset value is not affected: it remains at $35 million, which is now the market value of the company. At $20 per share, the $5 million was used to repurchase and cancel 250,000 shares, leaving 1.75 million shares. The new market value of the equity is $35 million, $20 × 1.75 million (which it has to be, to equal the asset side of the balance sheet).

Market Value Balance Sheet After Repurchase (000s)

Assets		Equity	
Marketable securities	$ 0		
Operating assets	35,000	1,750 shares @ $20/share	$35,000
Market value of assets	$35,000	Market value of equity	$35,000

Notice that the total wealth of the shareholders didn't change. It was $40 million prior to the repurchase, and it is $40 million afterward ($35 million in stock and $5 million of cash in their pocket).

To summarize, the events leading up to a repurchase (the sale of a division, a recapitalization, or the generation of higher than normal free cash flows) can certainly change the stock price, but the repurchase itself doesn't change the stock price.

A Tale of Two Cash Distributions: Dividends versus Stock Repurchases

Suppose a company's current earnings are $400 million, that it has 40 million shares of stock, and that it pays out 50% of its earnings as dividends. Earnings are expected to grow at a constant rate of 5%, and the cost of equity is 10%. Its current dividend per share is 0.50($400/40) = $5. Using the dividend growth model, the current stock price is

$$P_0 = \frac{D_1}{r_s - g} = \frac{D_0(1 + g)}{r_s - g} = \frac{\$5(1 + 0.05)}{0.10 - 0.05} = \frac{\$5.25}{0.05} = \$105$$

As the year progresses, the stock should climb in price by 10% to $115.5, but then fall by the amount of the dividend ($5.25) to $110.25 when the dividend is paid at Year 1.[19] This process will be repeated each year, as shown in Figure 13-3. Notice that the shareholders experience a 10% total return each year, with 5% as a dividend yield and 5% as a capital gain. Also, the total expected market value of equity after paying the dividend at the end of Year 1 is the price per share multiplied by the number of shares:

$$S_1 = \$110.25(40 \text{ million}) = \$4,410 \text{ million}$$

Suppose the company decides to use 50% of its earnings to repurchase stock each year instead of paying dividends. To find the current price per share, we discount the total payments to shareholders and divide that by the current number of shares. These payments are exactly equal to the total dividend payments in the original scenario, so the current price is the same for both dividend policies, ignoring any taxes or signalling effects. But what happens when the end of the year arrives? The stock price has grown to $115.50, just as for the cash dividend policy. But unlike the case of cash dividends in which the stock price

---

[19]This assumes no tax effects.

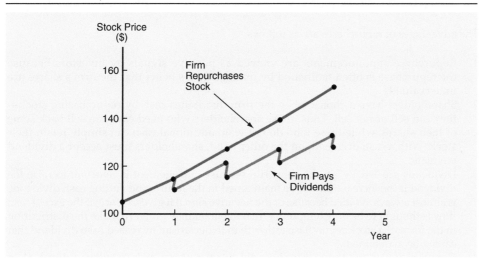

FIGURE

13-3   Stock Repurchases versus Cash Dividends

falls by the amount of the dividend, the price per share doesn't change when a company repurchases stock, as shown earlier in this section. This means that the total rate of return for a shareholder under the repurchase policy is 10%, with a zero dividend yield and a 10% capital gain.

Year 1 earnings will be $400(1.05) = $420 million, and the total amount of cash used to repurchase stock is 0.50($420 million) = $210 million. Since each share is now $115.50, we can calculate the number of repurchased shares: $210 million/$115.50 = 1.818 million. The remaining number of shares after the repurchase at Year 1 is 40 million − 1.818 million = 38.182 million. The total market value of equity at Year 1, S_1, is the price per share multiplied by the number of shares,

$$S_1 = \$115.5(38.182 \text{ million}) = \$4,410 \text{ million}$$

which is identical to the market value of equity if the firm pays dividends instead of repurchasing stock.

This example illustrates three key results: (1) Ignoring possible tax effects and signals, the total market value of equity will be the same whether a firm pays dividends or repurchases stock. (2) The repurchase itself does not change the stock price (compared with using the cash to buy marketable securities), although it does reduce the number of outstanding shares. (3) The stock price for a company that repurchases its stock will climb faster than if it pays a dividend, but the total return to the shareholders will be the same.[20]

CONCEPT REVIEW

1. Explain how a repurchase changes the number of shares but not the stock price.

2. A firm has 2 million shares outstanding, with a $20 per share market price. The firm has $4 million in extra cash that it plans to use in a stock repurchase; the firm has no other financial investments. What is the firm's value of operations, and how many shares will remain after the repurchase? (Check Figures: $36 million; 1.8 million)

---

[20]For more on repurchases, see David J. Denis, "Defensive Changes in Corporate Payout Policy: Share Repurchases and Special Dividends," *Journal of Finance*, December 1990, 1433–1456; Gerald D. Gay, Jayant R. Kale, and Thomas H. Noe, "Share Repurchase Mechanisms: A Comparative Analysis of Efficacy, Shareholder Wealth and Corporate Control Effects," *Financial Management*, Spring 1991, 44–59; Jeffry M. Netter and Mark L. Mitchell, "Stock-Repurchase Announcements and Insider Transactions after the October 1987 Stock Market Crash," *Financial Management*, Autumn 1989, 84–96; William Pugh and John S. Jahera, Jr., "Stock Repurchases and Excess Returns: An Empirical Examination," *Financial Review*, February 1990, pp. 127–142; and James W. Wansley, William R. Lane, and Salil Sarkar, "Managements' View on Share Repurchase and Tender Offer Premiums," *Financial Management*, Autumn 1989, 97–110.

13.8 The Pros and Cons of Dividends and Repurchases

The advantages of repurchases are as follows:

1. Repurchase announcements are viewed as positive signals by investors because the repurchase is often motivated by management's belief that the firm's shares are undervalued.
2. Shareholders have a choice when the firm distributes cash by repurchasing stock—they can sell or not sell. Thus, those shareholders who need cash can sell back some of their shares, while those who do not want additional cash can simply retain their stock. With a cash dividend, on the other hand, shareholders must accept a dividend payment.
3. Dividends are "sticky" in the short run because management is reluctant to raise the dividend if the increase cannot be maintained in the future, and cutting cash dividends is almost always avoided because of the negative signal it gives. Hence, if the excess cash flow is thought to be only temporary, management may prefer to make the distribution in the form of a stock repurchase rather than to declare an increased cash dividend that cannot be maintained.
4. Companies can use the residual model to set a *target cash distribution* level, then divide the distribution into a *dividend component* and a *repurchase component*. The dividend payout ratio will be relatively low, but the dividend itself will be relatively secure, and it will grow as a result of the declining number of shares outstanding. The company has more flexibility in adjusting the total distribution than it would if the entire distribution were in the form of cash dividends, because repurchases can be varied from year to year without giving off adverse signals. This procedure is one reason for the dramatic increase in the volume of stock repurchases.
5. Repurchases can be used to produce large-scale changes in capital structures. For example, several years ago Transat A.T. bought back 6.4 million shares, representing 15% of its common equity. In this way, Transat was able to quickly modify its capital structure.
6. Companies that use stock options as an important component of employee compensation can repurchase shares as a way of avoiding earnings dilution when employees exercise their options.

Disadvantages of repurchases include the following:

1. Shareholders may not be indifferent between dividends and capital gains, and the price of the stock might benefit more from cash dividends than from repurchases. Cash dividends are generally dependable, but repurchases are not.
2. The *selling* shareholders may not be fully aware of all the implications of a repurchase, or they may not have all the pertinent information about the corporation's present and future activities. However, firms generally announce repurchase programs before embarking on them.
3. The corporation may pay too much for the repurchased stock, to the disadvantage of remaining shareholders. If the firm seeks to acquire a relatively large amount of its stock, then the price may be bid above its equilibrium level and then fall after the firm ceases its repurchase operations.

When all the pros and cons of stock repurchases versus dividends have been totalled, where do we stand? Our conclusions may be summarized as follows:

1. Because of the deferred tax on capital gains, repurchases have a tax advantage over dividends as a way to distribute income to shareholders. This advantage is reinforced by the fact that repurchases provide cash to shareholders who want cash while allowing those who do not need current cash to delay its receipt. On the other hand, dividends are more dependable and are thus better suited for those who need a steady source of income.

2. Because of signalling effects, companies should not vary their dividends—that would lower investors' confidence in the company and adversely affect its cost of equity and its stock price. However, cash flows vary over time, as do investment opportunities, so the "proper" dividend in the residual model sense varies. To get around this problem, a company can set its dividend low enough to keep dividend payments from constraining operations and then use repurchases on a more or less regular basis to distribute excess cash. Such a procedure will provide regular, dependable dividends plus additional cash flow to those shareholders who want it.

3. Repurchases are also useful when a firm wants to make a large shift in its capital structure, wants to distribute cash from a one-time event such as the sale of a division, or wants to obtain shares for use in an employee stock option plan.

ⓒNCEPT REVIEW

1. What are some advantages and disadvantages of stock repurchases?
2. How can stock repurchases help a company operate in accordance with the residual distribution model?

13.9 Other Factors Influencing Distributions

In this section, we discuss several other factors that affect the dividend decision. These factors may be grouped into two broad categories: (1) constraints on dividend payments and (2) availability and cost of alternative sources of capital.

Constraints

1. *Bond indentures.* Debt contracts often limit dividend payments to earnings generated after the loan was granted. Also, debt contracts often stipulate that no dividends can be paid unless the current ratio, times-interest-earned ratio, and other safety ratios exceed stated minimums.

2. *Preferred stock restrictions.* Typically, common dividends cannot be paid if the company has omitted its preferred dividend. The preferred arrearages must be satisfied before common dividends can be resumed.

3. *Legal restrictions.* The Canada Business Corporations Act restricts dividend payments if a company is insolvent or if the dividend payment would cause the company to become insolvent. This rule is designed to protect creditors. Without the rule, a company that is in trouble might distribute most of its assets to shareholders and leave its debtholders out in the cold. (*Liquidating dividends* can be paid out of capital, but they must be indicated as such, and they must not reduce capital below the limits stated in debt contracts.)

4. *Availability of cash.* Cash dividends can be paid only with cash, so a shortage of cash in the bank can restrict dividend payments. However, the ability to borrow can offset this factor.

Alternative Sources of Capital

1. *Cost of selling new stock.* If a firm needs to finance a given level of investment, it can obtain equity by retaining earnings or by issuing new common stock. If flotation costs (including any negative signalling effects of a stock offering) are high, r_e will be well above r_s, making it better to set a low payout ratio and to finance through retention rather than through the sale of new common stock. On the other hand, a high dividend payout ratio is more feasible for a firm whose flotation costs are low. Flotation costs differ among firms—for example, the flotation percentage is generally higher for small firms, so they tend to set low payout ratios.

2. *Ability to substitute debt for equity.* A firm can finance a given level of investment with either debt or equity. As noted above, low stock flotation costs permit a more flexible dividend policy because equity can be raised either by retaining earnings or by selling new stock. A similar situation holds for debt policy: if the firm can adjust its debt ratio

without raising costs sharply, it can pay the expected dividend, even if earnings fluctuate, by increasing its debt ratio.

3. *Control.* If management is concerned about maintaining control, it may be reluctant to sell new stock; hence the company may retain more earnings than it otherwise would. However, if shareholders want higher dividends and a proxy fight looms, then the dividend will be increased.

⃝NCEPT REVIEW

1. What constraints affect dividend policy?
2. How does the availability and cost of outside capital affect dividend policy?

13.10 Summarizing the Distribution Policy Decision

In practice, the distribution decision is made jointly with capital structure and capital budgeting decisions. The underlying reason for joining these decisions is asymmetric information, which influences managerial actions in two ways:

1. In general, managers do not want to issue new common stock. First, new common stock involves issuance costs—commissions, fees, and so on—and those costs can be avoided by using retained earnings to finance equity needs. Second, as we discussed in Chapter 12, asymmetric information causes investors to view new common stock issues as negative signals and thus lowers expectations regarding the firm's future prospects. The end result is that the announcement of a new stock issue usually leads to a decrease in the stock price. Considering the total costs involved, including both issuance and asymmetric information costs, managers prefer to use retained earnings as the primary source of new equity.
2. Dividend changes provide signals about managers' beliefs as to their firms' future prospects. Thus, dividend reductions generally have a significant negative effect on a firm's stock price. Since managers recognize this, they try to set dollar dividends low enough that there is only a remote chance that the dividend will have to be reduced in the future.

The effects of asymmetric information suggest that, to the extent possible, managers should avoid both new common stock sales and dividend cuts, because both actions tend to lower stock prices. Thus, in setting distribution policy, managers should begin by considering the firm's future investment opportunities relative to its projected internal sources of funds. The target capital structure also plays a part, but because the optimal capital structure is a *range*, firms can vary their actual capital structures somewhat from year to year. Since it is best to avoid issuing new common stock, the target long-term payout ratio should be designed to permit the firm to meet all of its equity capital requirements with retained earnings. *In effect, managers should use the residual model to set dividends, but in a long-term framework.* Finally, the current dollar dividend should be set so that there is an extremely low probability that the dividend, once set, will ever have to be lowered or omitted.

Of course, the dividend decision is made during the planning process, so there is uncertainty about future investment opportunities and operating cash flows. Thus, the actual payout ratio in any year will probably be above or below the firm's long-range target. However, the dollar dividend should be maintained, or increased as planned, unless the firm's financial condition deteriorates to the point that the planned policy simply cannot be maintained. A steady or increasing stream of dividends over the long run signals that the firm's financial condition is under control. Furthermore, investor uncertainty is decreased by stable dividends, so a steady dividend stream reduces the negative effect of a new stock issue, should one become absolutely necessary.

In general, firms with superior investment opportunities should set lower payouts, hence retain more earnings, than firms with poor investment opportunities. The degree of uncertainty also influences the decision. If there is a great deal of uncertainty regarding the forecasts of free cash flows, which are defined here as the firm's operating cash flows minus mandatory equity investments, then it is best to be conservative and to set a lower current dollar dividend. Also, firms with postponable investment opportunities can afford to set a higher dollar dividend, because in times of stress, investments can be postponed for a year or two, thus increasing the cash available for dividends. Finally, firms whose cost of capital is largely unaffected by changes in the debt ratio can also afford to set a higher payout ratio, because they can, in times of stress, more easily issue additional debt to maintain the capital budgeting program without having to cut dividends or issue stock.

The net result of these factors is that many firms' dividend policies are consistent with the life cycle theory in which younger firms with many investment opportunities but relatively low cash flows reinvest their earnings so that they can avoid the large flotation costs associated with raising external capital.[21] As firms mature and begin to generate more cash flow, they tend to pay more dividends and issue more debt as a way to bond their cash flows and thereby reduce the agency costs of free cash flow.

What do executives think? Recent surveys indicate that financial executives believe that dividend policy does affect firm value. They also strongly think that dividends should not be reduced and that companies should maintain continuous dividend payments. Furthermore, dividends should be increased based on sustained earnings growth. Managers often repurchase shares when they are thought to be undervalued, believing that both dividends and repurchase announcements send a positive signal to investors. Managers believe in the life-cycle and signalling approaches to dividends, but do not agree with the tax-preference, bird-in-the-hand, or clientele arguments. Finally, they perceive dividend, financing, and investment decisions as interrelated.[22]

CONCEPT REVIEW

1. Describe the decision process for distribution policy and dividend payout. Be sure to discuss all the factors that influence the decision.

13.11 Stock Splits and Stock Dividends

Stock splits and stock dividends are related to the firm's cash dividend policy. The rationale for stock splits and dividends can best be explained through an example. We will use Porter Electronic Controls Inc., a $700 million electronic components manufacturer, for this purpose. Since its inception, Porter's markets have been expanding, and the company has enjoyed growth in sales and earnings. Some of its earnings have been paid out in dividends, but some are also retained each year, causing its earnings per share and stock price to grow. The company began its life with only a few thousand shares outstanding. After some years of growth, the stock price was so high that few people could afford to buy a "round lot" of 100 shares. Porter's CFO thought this limited the demand for the stock and thus kept the total market value of the firm below what it would have been if more shares, at a lower price, had been outstanding. To correct this situation, Porter "split its stock," as described in the next section.

Stock Splits

Although there is little empirical evidence to support the contention, there is nevertheless a widespread belief in financial circles that an *optimal price range* exists for stocks. "Optimal" means that if the price is within this range, the firm's value will be maximized. Many observers, including Porter's management, believe that the best range for most stocks is from $20 to $80 per share. Accordingly, if the price of Porter's stock rose to $80, management would probably declare a 2-for-1 **stock split,** thus doubling the number of shares outstanding, halving the earnings and dividends per share, and thereby lowering the stock price. Each shareholder would have more shares, but each share would be worth less. If the post-split price were $40, Porter's shareholders would be exactly as well off as before the split. However, if the stock price were to stabilize above $40, shareholders would be better

---

[21]For a test of the life cycle theory, see Harry DeAngelo, Linda DeAngelo, and René Stulz, "Dividend Policy and the Earned/Contributed Capital Mix: A Test of the Life-Cycle Theory," *Journal of Financial Economics*, August 2006, 227–254. For results on dividend policy, see Baker et al., "The Perception of Dividends"; for share repurchases, see McNally, "Open Market Share Repurchases in Canada."

[22]See Alon Brav, John R. Graham, Campbell R. Harvey, and Roni Michaely, "Payout Policy in the 21st Century," *Journal of Financial Economics*, September 2005, pp. 483–527; see also Baker et al., "The Perception of Dividends"; for share repurchases, see McNally, "Open Market Share Repurchases in Canada."

off. Stock splits can be of any size—for example, the stock could be split 2-for-1, 3-for-1, $1\frac{1}{2}$-for-1, or in any other way.

For example, Nortel Networks' (NT) common stock was trading in the $120 range in July 2000, prior to the dot.com crash. By September 2002, Nortel's stock had fallen to less than $1. It would never regain the values it reached in 2000. On December 1, 2006, the company carried out a 1:10 reverse stock split, with its shareholders exchanging 10 shares of stock for 1 new share. Nortel offered three reasons for the reverse split. First, with the higher share price, Nortel would again become an eligible investment among those institutional investors who are prohibited from buying stock below a certain price. Second, investor transactions costs would be reduced now that fewer shares could be purchased at a higher price. Third, the company's shares would be in full compliance with the NYSE's minimum $1 per share rule. The reverse stock split indicated that Nortel thought the stock price would not recover.

Stock Dividends

Stock dividends are similar to stock splits in that they "divide the pie into smaller slices" without affecting the fundamental position of the current shareholders. On a 5% stock dividend, the holder of 100 shares would receive an additional 5 shares (without cost); on a 20% stock dividend, the same holder would receive 20 new shares; and so on. Again, the total number of shares is increased, so earnings, dividends, and price per share all decline.

If a firm wants to reduce the price of its stock, should it use a stock split or a stock dividend? Stock splits are generally used after a sharp price run-up to produce a large price reduction. Stock dividends used on a regular annual basis will keep the stock price more or less constrained. For example, if a firm's earnings and dividends were growing at about 10% per year, its stock price would tend to go up at about that same rate, and it would soon be outside the desired trading range. A 10% annual stock dividend would maintain the stock price within the optimal trading range. Note, though, that small stock dividends create bookkeeping problems and unnecessary expenses, so firms today use stock splits far more often than stock dividends.[23]

Effect on Stock Prices

If a company splits its stock or declares a stock dividend, will this increase the market value of its stock? Many empirical studies have sought to answer this question. Here is a summary of their findings.

1. On average, the price of a company's stock rises shortly after it announces a stock split or dividend.
2. However, these price increases are more the result of the fact that investors take stock splits/dividends as signals of higher future earnings and dividends than of a desire for stock dividends/splits *per se*. Because only companies whose managements think things look good tend to split their stocks, the announcement of a stock split is taken as a signal that earnings and cash dividends are likely to rise. Thus, the price increases associated with stock splits/dividends are probably the result of signals of favourable prospects for earnings and dividends, not a desire for stock splits/dividends *per se*.
3. If a company announces a stock split or stock dividend, its price will tend to rise. However, if during the next few months it does not announce an increase in earnings and dividends, then its stock price will drop back to the earlier level.
4. As we noted earlier, brokerage commissions are generally higher in percentage terms on lower-priced stocks. This means that it is more expensive to trade low-priced than high-priced stocks, and this, in turn, means that stock splits may reduce the liquidity of a company's shares. This particular piece of evidence suggests that stock splits/dividends might actually be harmful, although a lower price does mean that more investors can afford to trade in round lots (100 shares), which carry lower commissions than do odd lots (less than 100 shares).

What do we conclude from all this? From a purely economic standpoint, stock dividends and splits are just additional pieces of paper. However, they provide management

---

[23]Accountants treat stock splits and stock dividends somewhat differently. For example, in a two-for-one stock split, the number of shares outstanding is doubled and the par value is halved, and that is about all there is to it. With a stock dividend, a bookkeeping entry is made transferring "retained earnings" to "common stock."

with a relatively low-cost way of signalling that the firm's prospects look good.[24] Furthermore, since few large, publicly owned stocks sell at prices above several hundred dollars, we simply do not know what the effect would have been if Imperial Oil or Scotia Bank or other highly successful firms had never split their stocks and consequently sold at prices in the thousands of dollars. All in all, it probably makes sense to employ stock dividends/splits when a firm's prospects are favourable, especially if the price of its stock has gone beyond the normal trading range.[25]

CONCEPT REVIEW

1. What are stock splits and stock dividends?
2. How do stock splits and dividends affect stock prices?
3. In what situations should managers consider the use of stock splits?
4. In what situations should managers consider the use of stock dividends?
5. Suppose you have 1,000 common shares of Burnside Bakeries. The EPS is $6.00, the DPS is $3.00, and the stock sells for $90 per share. Burnside announces a 3-for-1 split. Immediately after the split, how many shares will you have, what will the adjusted EPS and DPS be, and what would you expect the stock price to be? (Check Figures: 3,000; $2; $1; $30)

13.12 Dividend Reinvestment Plans

During the 1970s, most large companies instituted **dividend reinvestment plans (DRIPs),** under which shareholders can choose to automatically reinvest their dividends in the stock of the paying corporation. Today most larger companies offer DRIPs, and although participation rates vary considerably, about 25% of the average firm's shareholders are enrolled. There are two types of DRIPs: (1) plans that involve a "market purchase"—that is, of stock that is already outstanding and (2) plans that involve a "treasury purchase" of newly issued stock. In either case, the shareholder must pay taxes on the amount of the dividends, even though stock rather than cash is received.

Under both types of DRIPs, shareholders choose between continuing to receive dividend cheques or having the company use the dividends to buy more stock in the corporation. Under the "market purchase" type of plan, if a shareholder elects reinvestment, a bank, acting as trustee, takes the total funds available for reinvestment, purchases the corporation's stock on the open market, and allocates the shares purchased to the participating shareholders' accounts on a pro rata basis. The transaction costs of buying shares (brokerage costs) are low because of volume purchases, so these plans benefit small shareholders who do not need cash dividends for current consumption.

The "treasury purchase" type of DRIP uses the reinvested funds to buy newly issued stock; hence these plans raise new capital for the firm. Magna, Potash Corp., and other companies have had new stock plans in effect in recent years, using them to raise new equity capital. No fees are charged to shareholders, and many companies offer stock at a discount of up to 5% below the actual market price. The companies offer discounts as a trade-off against flotation costs that would have been incurred if new stock had been issued through investment bankers rather than through the dividend reinvestment plans.

One interesting aspect of DRIPs is that they are forcing corporations to reexamine their basic dividend policies. A high participation rate in a DRIP suggests that shareholders might be better off if the firm simply reduced cash dividends, which would save shareholders the current taxes they must pay on dividends. Quite a few U.S. firms are surveying their

---

[24]For more on stock splits and stock dividends, see Said Elfakhani and Trevor Lung, "The Effect of Split Announcements on Canadian Stocks," *Global Finance Journal*, July 2003, 197–217; Vijay Jog and PengCheng Zhu, "Thirty Years of Stock Splits, Reverse Stock Splits, and Stock Dividends in Canada," June 2004, available at http://ssrn.com/abstract5692941; H. Kent Baker, Aaron L. Phillips, and Gary E. Powell, "The Stock Distribution Puzzle: A Synthesis of the Literature on Stock Splits and Stock Dividends," *Financial Practice and Education*, Spring–Summer 1995, 24–37; Maureen McNichols and Ajay Dravid, "Stock Dividends, Stock Splits, and Signaling," *Journal of Finance*, July 1990, 857–879; David R. Peterson and Pamela P. Peterson, "A Further Understanding of Stock Distributions; The Case of Reverse Stock Splits," *Journal of Financial Research*, Fall 1992, 189–205.

[25]It is interesting to note that Berkshire Hathaway (controlled by billionaire Warren Buffett) has never had a stock split, and its stock (BRKa) sold on the NYSE for $196,253 per share in August 2014. But, in response to investment trusts that were being formed to sell fractional units of the stock, and thus, in effect, split it, Buffett himself created a new class of Berkshire Hathaway stock (Class B) worth about 1/30 of a Class A (regular) share.

shareholders to learn more about their preferences and to find out how they would react to a change in dividend policy. A more rational approach to basic dividend policy decisions may emerge from this research.

Note that companies can alter their DRIPs depending on their need for equity capital. Both EnCana and TD Bank have DRIPs that can switch between treasury and market purchase, as their need for equity capital changes.

Some companies have expanded their DRIPs by moving to "optional cash payments," whereby anyone can purchase additional stock directly and thus bypass brokers' commissions. In all of these plans, shareholders can invest more than the dividends they are forgoing—they simply send a cheque to the company and buy shares without a brokerage commission. There are currently about 160 Canadian companies offering DRIPs and/or optional cash payments.[26]

CONCEPT REVIEW

1. What are dividend reinvestment plans?
2. What are their advantages and disadvantages from both the shareholders' and the firm's perspectives?

Summary

- **Distribution policy** involves three issues: (1) What fraction of earnings should be distributed? (2) Should the distribution be in the form of cash dividends or stock repurchases? (3) Should the firm maintain a steady, stable dividend growth rate?
- The **optimal distribution policy** strikes a balance between current dividends and future growth so as to maximize the firm's stock price.
- Miller and Modigliani developed the **dividend irrelevance theory,** which holds that a firm's dividend policy has no effect on either the value of its stock or its cost of capital.
- The **bird-in-the-hand theory** holds that the firm's value will be maximized by a high dividend payout ratio, because investors regard cash dividends as less risky than potential capital gains.
- The **tax preference theory** states that because long-term capital gains are subject to somewhat less onerous taxes than dividends, investors prefer to have companies retain earnings rather than pay them out as dividends.
- **Empirical tests** of the three theories **have been inconclusive.** Therefore, academicians cannot tell corporate managers how a given change in dividend policy will affect stock prices and capital costs.
- Dividend policy should take account of the **information content of dividends (signalling)** and the **clientele effect.** The information content, or signalling, effect relates to the fact that investors regard an unexpected dividend change as a signal of management's forecast of future earnings. The clientele effect suggests that a firm will attract investors who like the firm's dividend payout policy. Both factors should be considered by firms that are considering a change in dividend policy.
- In practice, dividend-paying firms follow a policy of paying a **steadily increasing dividend.** This policy provides investors with stable, dependable income, and departures from it give investors signals about management's expectations for future earnings.
- The **residual distribution model** can be used to set the long-run target distribution ratio at a level that will permit the firm to meet its equity requirements with retained earnings.
- Under a **stock repurchase plan,** a firm buys back some of its outstanding stock, thereby decreasing the number of shares, but leaving the stock price unchanged.
- **Legal constraints, investment opportunities, availability and cost of funds from other sources,** and **taxes** are also considered when firms establish dividend policies.
- A **stock split** increases the number of shares outstanding. Normally, splits reduce the price per share in proportion to the increase in shares because splits merely "divide the

---

[26]For more on DRIPs, see Pamela P. Peterson, David R. Peterson, and Norman H. Moore, "The Adoption of New-Issue Dividend Reinvestment Plans and Shareholder Wealth," *Financial Review*, May 1987, 221–232.

pie into smaller slices." However, firms generally split their stocks only if (1) the price is quite high and (2) management thinks the future is bright. Therefore, stock splits are often taken as positive signals and thus boost stock prices.

- A **stock dividend** is a dividend paid in additional shares rather than in cash. Both stock dividends and splits are used to keep stock prices within an "optimal" trading range.
- A **dividend reinvestment plan (DRIP)** allows shareholders to have the company automatically use dividends to purchase additional shares. DRIPs are popular because they allow shareholders to acquire additional shares without brokerage fees.

Questions

13-1 Define each of the following terms:
   a. Optimal distribution policy
   b. Dividend irrelevance theory; bird-in-the-hand theory; tax preference theory
   c. Information content or signalling hypothesis; clientele effect
   d. Residual distribution model; extra dividend
   e. Declaration date; holder-of-record date; ex-dividend date; payment date
   f. Dividend reinvestment plan (DRIP)
   g. Stock split; stock dividend; stock repurchase

13-2 How would each of the following changes tend to affect aggregate (i.e., the average for all corporations) payout ratios, other things held constant? Explain your answers.
   a. An increase in the personal income tax rate
   b. A liberalization of depreciation for income tax purposes—that is, faster tax write-offs
   c. A rise in interest rates
   d. An increase in corporate profits
   e. A decline in investment opportunities
   f. Permission for corporations to deduct dividends for tax purposes as they now do interest charges
   g. A change in the Income Tax Act so that both realized and unrealized capital gains in any year were taxed at the same rate as dividends

13-3 What is the difference between a stock dividend and a stock split? As a shareholder, would you prefer to see your company declare a 100% stock dividend or a 2-for-1 split? Assume that either action is feasible.

13-4 One position expressed in the financial literature is that firms set their dividends as a residual after using income to support new investments.
   a. Explain what a residual policy implies (assuming all distributions as dividends), and show how different investment opportunities could lead to different dividend payout ratios.
   b. Think back to Chapter 12, in which we considered the relationship between capital structure and the cost of capital. If the WACC-versus-debt-ratio plot was shaped like a sharp V, would this have a different implication for the importance of setting dividends according to the residual policy than if the plot was shaped like a shallow bowl (or a flattened U)?

13-5 Indicate whether the following statements are true or false. If the statement is false, explain why.
   a. If a firm repurchases its stock in the open market, the shareholders who tender the stock are subject to capital gains taxes.
   b. If you own 100 shares in a company's stock and the company's stock splits 2-for-1, you will own 200 shares in the company following the split.
   c. Some dividend reinvestment plans increase the amount of equity capital available to the firm.
   d. The Income Tax Act encourages companies to pay a large percentage of their net income in the form of dividends.
   e. If your company has established a clientele of investors who prefer large dividends, the company is unlikely to adopt a residual dividend policy.
   f. If a firm follows a residual dividend policy, holding all else constant, its dividend payout will tend to rise whenever the firm's investment opportunities improve.

Concept Review Problem

Full solutions are provided at www.nelson.com/brigham3ce.

CR-1
Residual Dividend

Systems Analytics Inc. (SAI) has 1 million common shares outstanding. SAI has a target capital structure with 40% equity and 60% debt. The company projects net income of $5 million and investment projects requiring $6 million in the upcoming year.
a. SAI uses the residual distribution model and pays all distributions in the form of dividends. What is the projected DPS?
b. What is the projected payout ratio?

Problems

**Easy
Problems 1–5**

Answers to odd-numbered problems appear in Appendix A.

13-1
Residual Distribution
Model

Puckett Products is planning for $5 million in capital expenditures next year. Puckett's target capital structure consists of 60% debt and 40% equity. If net income next year is $3 million, and Puckett follows a residual distribution policy with all distributions as dividends, what will be its dividend payout ratio?

13-2
Residual Distribution
Policy

TDM Company has a capital budget of $1,125,000. The company wants to maintain a target capital structure that is 20% debt and 80% equity. The company forecasts that its net income this year will be $2,000,000. If the company follows a residual distribution model and pays all distributions as dividends, what will be its payout ratio?

13-3
Dividend Payout

Wei Corporation expects next year's net income to be $15 million. The firm's debt ratio is currently 40%. Wei has $12 million of profitable investment opportunities, and it wishes to maintain its existing debt ratio. According to the residual distribution model (assuming all payments are in the form of dividends), how large should Wei's dividend payout ratio be next year?

13-4
Stock Repurchase

A firm has 10 million shares outstanding, with a $20 per share market price. The firm has $25 million in extra cash that it plans to use in a stock repurchase; the firm has no other financial investments. What is the firm's value of operations and how many shares will remain after the repurchase?

13-5
Stock Split

Eastern Shipping stock trades at $120 a share. The company is contemplating a 5-for-2 stock split. Assuming that the stock split will have no effect on the total market value of its equity, what will be the company's stock price following the stock split?

**Intermediate
Problems 6–11**

13-6
External Equity Financing

Industrial Heating and Cooling Inc. has a 6-month backlog of orders for its patented solar heating system. To meet this demand, management plans to expand production capacity by 40% with a $15 million investment in plant and machinery. The firm wants to maintain a 0.43 debt–equity ratio in its capital structure; it also wants to maintain its past dividend policy of distributing 55% of last year's net income. In 2015, net income was $8 million. How much external equity must Saanich seek at the beginning of 2016 to expand capacity as desired?

13-7
Stock Split

Suppose you own 2,000 common shares of Laurence Incorporated. The EPS is $10.00, the DPS is $3.00, and the stock sells for $80 per share. Laurence announces a 2-for-1 split. Immediately after the split, how many shares will you have, what will the adjusted EPS and DPS be, and what would you expect the stock price to be?

13-8
Stock Split

After a 5-for-1 stock split, Strasburg Company paid a dividend of $0.75 per new share, which represents a 9% increase over last year's pre-split dividend. What was last year's dividend per share?

13-9
Residual
Distribution Policy

Burnaby Packers is considering three independent projects, each of which requires a $3 million investment. These projects have different levels of risk and therefore different costs of capital. Their projected IRRs and cost of capital are as follows:

Project A:	Cost of capital = 17%; IRR = 20%
Project B:	Cost of capital = 13%; IRR = 10%
Project C:	Cost of capital = 7%; IRR = 9%

The company's optimal capital structure calls for 35% debt and 65% common equity. The company expects to have net income of $4,750,000. If Burnaby bases its dividends on the residual model (all distributions are in the form of dividends), what will its payout ratio be?

13-10

Dividend versus Stock Repurchase

Titan Mining recently sold a piece of property for $15 million in cash. It wishes to return this money to shareholders and is contemplating either a special dividend or a repurchase of shares. Titan has net income of $5 million and 5,000,000 shares outstanding, and its stock trades at a P/E multiple of 12. Show the effect on shareholder wealth if either the special dividend or the repurchase takes place. What effect would each alternative have, if any, on Titan's capital structure?

13-11

Alternative Dividend Payouts

Peninsula Technology Corporation (PTC) has an all-common-equity capital structure. It has 200,000 shares of $2 par value common stock outstanding. When PTC's founder, who was also its research director and most successful inventor, retired unexpectedly to the South Pacific in late 2015, PTC was left suddenly and permanently with materially lower growth expectations and relatively few attractive new investment opportunities. Unfortunately, there was no way to replace the founder's contributions to the firm. Previously, PTC found it necessary to plow back most of its earnings to finance growth, which averaged 12% per year. Future growth at a 5% rate is considered realistic, but that level would call for an increase in the dividend payout. Further, it now appears that new investment projects with at least the 14% rate of return required by PTC's shareholders ($r_s = 14\%$) would amount to only $800,000 for 2016 in comparison to a projected $2,000,000 of net income. If the existing 20% dividend payout were continued, retained earnings would be $1,600,000 in 2016, but, as noted, investments that yield the 14% cost of capital would amount to only $800,000.

The one encouraging note is that the high earnings from existing assets are expected to continue, and net income of $2 million is still expected for 2016. Given the dramatically changed circumstances, PTC's management is reviewing the firm's dividend policy.

a. Assuming that the acceptable 2016 investment projects would be financed entirely by earnings retained during the year, calculate DPS in 2016, assuming that PTC uses the residual distribution model and pays all distributions in the form of dividends.

b. What payout ratio does your answer to Part a imply for 2016?

c. If a 60% payout ratio is maintained for the foreseeable future, what is your estimate of the present market price of the common stock? How does this compare with the market price that should have prevailed under the assumptions existing just before the news about the founder's retirement? If the two values of P_0 are different, comment on why.

Challenging Problems 12–15

13-12

Dividend Payout

Aqua Adventures currently generates net income of $500,000 every year, all of which is paid out in dividends, and expects no future growth. Aqua has 200,000 shares outstanding, and investors require an 8% return on the company's shares. Assume that new management is hired to grow the company. One plan for the company is to invest its earnings of $500,000 per year for 1 year in a new project. If Aqua goes with the new project it will not be able to pay a dividend for the next year. However, the new project will increase net income to $570,000 in the second year and onward, all which will be paid out as dividends.

a. Calculate the share price if the company maintains its current no-growth policy. Calculate the share price if the company goes with the new project. Briefly explain why the share price has gone higher or lower.

b. What must the minimum increase in net income be so that investors are equally well off between its current no-growth policy and its proposed new project?

13-13

Dividend versus Stock Repurchase

Anthony and Sarah both invested in the common shares of two very similar companies. In fact, the only difference was that Sarah's stock of Northern Petroleum paid a regular dividend while Anthony's stock of Southern Petroleum repurchased shares instead. On seeing her first (of many) dividend cheques, Sarah promptly declared to Anthony that the dividend meant her stock had superior returns. Based on the data below, show one year out whether Sarah is correct.

	Southern Petroleum	Northern Petroleum
Growth rate	6%	6%
Cost of equity	10%	10%
Earnings	$20,000,000	$20,000,000
Shares outstanding	25,000,000	25,000,000
Dividend payout ratio	0%	50%
Stock repurchase	50% of earnings	0%

13-14

Alternative Dividend Policies

In 2015, Sytek Environmental paid dividends totalling $2.6 million on net income of $9.8 million. 2015 was a normal year, and for the past 10 years, earnings have grown at a constant rate of 8%. However, in 2016, earnings are expected to jump to $12.6 million, and the firm expects to have profitable investment opportunities of $7.3 million. It is predicted that Sytek will not be able to maintain the 2016 level of earnings growth—the high 2016 earnings level is attributable to an exceptionally profitable new product line introduced that year—and the company will return to its previous 8% growth rate. Sytek's target debt ratio is 35%.

a. Calculate Sytek's total dividends for 2016 if it follows each of the following policies:
  (1) Its 2016 dividend payment is set to force dividends to grow at the long-run growth rate in earnings.
  (2) It continues the 2015 dividend payout ratio.
  (3) It uses a pure residual policy with all distributions in the form of dividends.
  (4) It employs a regular-dividend-plus-extras policy, with the regular dividend being based on the long-run growth rate and the extra dividend being set according to the residual policy.

b. Which of the preceding policies would you recommend? Restrict your choices to the ones listed, but justify your answer.

13-15

Residual Distribution Model

Landry Corporation is reviewing its capital budget for the upcoming year. It has paid a $2.00 dividend per share (DPS) for the past several years, and its shareholders expect the dividend to remain constant for the next several years. The company's target capital structure is 70% equity and 30% debt; it has 1,000,000 shares of common equity outstanding; and its net income is $11 million. The company forecasts that it would require $15 million to fund all of its profitable (i.e., positive NPV) projects for the upcoming year.

a. If Landry follows the residual model and makes all distributions as dividends, how much retained earnings will it need to fund its capital budget?

b. If Landry follows the residual model with all distributions in the form of dividends, what will be the company's dividend per share and payout ratio for the upcoming year?

c. If Landry maintains its current $2.00 DPS for next year, how much retained earnings will be available for the firm's capital budget?

d. Can the company maintain its current capital structure, maintain the $2.00 DPS, and maintain a $15 million capital budget *without* having to raise new common stock?

e. Suppose that Landry's management is firmly opposed to cutting the dividend; that is, it wishes to maintain the $2.00 dividend for the next year. Also assume that the company is committed to funding all profitable projects and is willing to issue more debt (along with the available retained earnings) to help finance the company's capital budget. Assume that the resulting change in capital structure has a minimal impact on the company's composite cost of capital, so that the capital budget remains at $15 million. What portion of this year's capital budget would have to be financed with debt?

f. Suppose once again that Landry's management wants to maintain the $2.00 DPS. In addition, the company wants to maintain its target capital structure (70% equity, 30% debt), and maintain its $15 million capital budget. What is the minimum dollar amount of new common stock that the company would have to issue in order to meet each of its objectives?

g. Now consider the case where Landry's management wants to maintain the $2.00 DPS and its target capital structure, but it wants to avoid issuing new common stock. The company is willing to cut its capital budget in order to meet its other objectives. Assuming that the company's projects are divisible, what will be the company's capital budget for the next year?

h. What actions can a firm that follows the residual distribution policy take when its forecast retained earnings are less than the retained earnings required to fund its capital budget?

Spreadsheet Problem

13-16

Build a Model: Distributions as Dividends or Repurchases

Start with the partial model in the file ***Ch 13 Build Model.xlsx*** on the textbook's website. J. Clark Inc. (JCI), a manufacturer and distributor of sports equipment, has grown until it has become a stable, mature company. Now JCI is planning its first distribution to shareholders. (See the file for the most recent year's financial statements and projections for the next year, 2014; JCI's fiscal year ends on June 30.) JCI plans to liquidate and distribute $500 million of its short-term securities on July 1, 2014, the first day of the next fiscal year, but has not yet decided whether to distribute with dividends or with stock repurchases.

a.   Assume first that JCI distributes the $500 million as dividends. Fill in the missing values in the file's balance sheet column for July 1, 2014, that is labelled Distribute as Dividends. (*Hint:* Be sure that the balance sheets balance after you fill in the missing items.) Assume that JCI did not have to establish an account for dividends payable prior to the distribution.

b.   Now assume that JCI distributes the $500 million through stock repurchases. Fill in the missing values in the file's balance sheet column for July 1, 2014, that is labelled Distribute as Repurchase. (*Hint:* Be sure that the balance sheets balance after you fill in the missing items.)

c.   Calculate JCI's projected free cash flow; the tax rate is 40%.

d.   What is JCI's current intrinsic stock price (the price on (June 30, 2013)? What is the projected intrinsic stock price for June 30, 2014?

e.   What is the projected intrinsic stock price on July 1, 2014 if JCI distributes the cash as dividends?

f.   What is the projected intrinsic stock price on July 1, 2014 if JCI distributes the cash through stock repurchases? How many shares will remain outstanding after the repurchase?

MINI CASE

Central Canada Steel (CCS) was formed 5 years ago to exploit a new continuous-casting process. CCS's founders, Donald Brown and Margo Lapointe, had been employed in the research department of a major integrated-steel company, but when that company decided against using the new process (which Brown and Lapointe had developed), they decided to strike out on their own. One advantage of the new process was that it required relatively little capital in comparison with the typical steel company, so Brown and Lapointe have been able to avoid issuing new stock, and thus they own all of the shares. However, CCS has now reached the stage where outside equity capital is necessary if the firm is to achieve its growth targets yet maintain its target capital structure of 60% equity and 40% debt. Therefore, Brown and Lapointe have decided to take the company public. Until now, Brown and Lapointe have paid themselves reasonable salaries but routinely reinvested all after-tax earnings in the firm, so dividend policy has not been an issue. However, before talking with potential outside investors, they must decide on a dividend policy.

Assume that you were recently hired by Pierce Westerfield Carney (PWC), a national consulting firm, which has been asked to help CCS prepare for its public offering. Martha Millon, the senior PWC consultant in your group, has asked you to make a presentation to Brown and Lapointe in which you review the theory of dividend policy and discuss the following questions.

a.   (1) What is meant by the term "distribution policy"?

(2) The terms "irrelevance," "bird-in-the-hand," and "tax preference" have been used to describe three major theories regarding the way dividend payouts affect a firm's value. Explain what these terms mean, and briefly describe each theory.

(3) What do the three theories indicate regarding the actions management should take with respect to dividend payouts?

(4) What results have empirical studies of the dividend theories produced? How does all this affect what we can tell managers about dividend payouts?

b.   Discuss (1) the information content, or signalling, hypothesis, (2) the clientele effect, and (3) their effects on distribution policy.

c.   (1) Assume that CCS has an $800,000 capital budget planned for the coming year. You have determined that its present capital structure (60% equity and 40% debt) is optimal, and its net income is forecast at $600,000. Use the residual distribution model approach to determine CCS's total dollar distribution. Assume for now that the distribution is in the form of a dividend. Then, explain what would happen if net income were forecast at $400,000, or at $800,000.

(2) In general terms, how would a change in investment opportunities affect the payout ratio under the residual distribution policy?

(3) What are the advantages and disadvantages of the residual policy? (*Hint:* Don't neglect signalling and clientele effects.)

d. What are stock repurchases? Discuss the advantages and disadvantages of a firm repurchasing its own shares.
e. Describe the series of steps that most firms take in setting dividend policy in practice.
f. What are stock splits and stock dividends? What are the advantages and disadvantages of stock splits and stock dividends?
g. What is a dividend reinvestment plan (DRIP), and how does it work?

chapter 14

Initial Public Offerings, Investment Banking, and Financial Restructuring

In any given month, many businesses go to the market to raise capital. Following are some examples of securities sold in 2014:

1. PrairieSky Royalty Ltd. is a company whose assets consist of mineral titles in lands primarily containing petroleum and natural gas. Encana Corporation, the sole owner of PrairieSky, sold 52 million common shares of PrairieSky in an initial public offering. Its underwriters, TD Securities and CIBC World Markets (along with eight others), anticipated that the stock could be sold in the range of $23 to $26.50. The actual offering was higher at $28, and the stock closed its first day of trading on the TSX at $37. Although the new investors paid $28 per share, Encana received only $26.60. The difference went to the underwriters as a fee for bringing the issue to market. Thus, out of the $1.456 billion paid by investors, Encana received $1.383 billion, and the underwriters and their sales force received $73 million.

2. Pembina Pipeline raised a total of $250 million by selling 10 million preferred shares with a dividend of 5%. The dividend is fixed for 5 years, after which the shares may be redeemed by the company. If not redeemed, investors have the option to reset the dividend to either a new fixed or floating-rate amount, based upon a specified formula. The proceeds will be used to partly fund the company's capital projects, to pay down some debt, and for general company purposes.

3. RioCan Real Estate Investment Trust sold $150 million of senior unsecured debentures. The debentures carry a coupon of 3.62% and mature in 2020. DBRS rated the debentures BBB (high). At the time of issue, the issue had a yield spread of 1.5 percentage points above the yield of a Government of Canada bond with a similar term to maturity. As part of the agreed-upon terms, RioCan agrees to maintain an EBITDA to interest expense ratio of 1.65 or greater.

These three issues represent an initial public offering, a preferred share offering, and a debt offering. After reading this chapter, you should have a better understanding of the procedures followed by these and other firms when issuing securities.

The previous two chapters described how a company makes capital structure and dividend policy decisions. Those decisions affect both the firm's need for new capital and the form or forms in which this capital is raised. We now discuss the actual process of raising capital, including the roles played by investment banks, secondary markets, and regulatory agencies.

14.1 The Financial Life Cycle of a Start-Up Company

The textbook's website contains an *Excel* file that will guide you through the chapter's calculations. The file for this chapter is *Ch 14 Tool Kit.xlsx*, and we encourage you to open the file and follow along as you read the chapter. **www .nelson.com/brigham3ce**

Most businesses begin life as proprietorships or partnerships, and if they succeed and grow, at some point they find it desirable to become corporations. Capital is initially provided by the owner, through personal savings and/or by borrowing against personal assets such as a house. Entrepreneurs often approach relatives and close friends for additional equity capital; this is sometimes referred to as "love money." In the beginning, most corporate stock is owned by the firm's founding managers and key employees and their relatives. Even start-up firms that ultimately succeed usually begin with negative free cash flow because of their high growth rates and product development costs; hence, they must turn to outside sources of capital. Start-up firms generally have high growth opportunities relative to assets in place, and they encounter especially serious problems with asymmetric information. As a consequence, as we discussed in Chapter 12, they must raise most of their external capital as equity rather than as debt.

Security regulation in Canada falls under provincial jurisdiction, which means that each province and territory has established a securities commission to govern sales of securities. The mandate of the Ontario Securities Commission (OSC) is to "provide protection to investors from unfair, improper and fraudulent practices and foster fair and efficient capital markets and confidence in their integrity."[1]

For most start-ups, the first round of external financing, outside the entrepreneur's circle of friends and relatives, involves a private placement of equity to one or two individual investors, called **angels.** In return for an investment (typically between $50,000 to $400,000), the angels receive stock and perhaps a seat on the board of directors. Because angels can influence the strategic direction of the company, it is best that they bring experience and industry contacts to the table, not just cash.

As the company grows, its financing requirements may exceed the resources of individual investors. **Venture capital funds** are one of the few sources of equity capital available for these companies. A venture capital fund is a private limited partnership, which typically

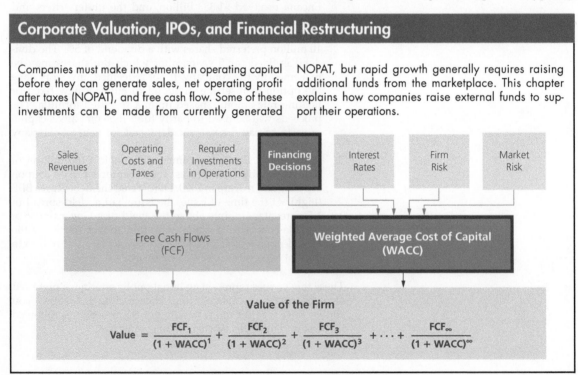

Corporate Valuation, IPOs, and Financial Restructuring

Companies must make investments in operating capital before they can generate sales, net operating profit after taxes (NOPAT), and free cash flow. Some of these investments can be made from currently generated NOPAT, but rapid growth generally requires raising additional funds from the marketplace. This chapter explains how companies raise external funds to support their operations.

Sales Revenues   Operating Costs and Taxes   Required Investments in Operations   Financing Decisions   Interest Rates   Firm Risk   Market Risk

Free Cash Flows (FCF)

Weighted Average Cost of Capital (WACC)

Value of the Firm

$$\text{Value} = \frac{FCF_1}{(1 + WACC)^1} + \frac{FCF_2}{(1 + WACC)^2} + \frac{FCF_3}{(1 + WACC)^3} + \cdots + \frac{FCF_\infty}{(1 + WACC)^\infty}$$

---

[1] Ontario Securities Commission, http://www.osc.gov.on.ca, accessed July 4, 2008.

raises $30 million to $80 million from a relatively small group of primarily institutional investors, including pension funds, university endowments, and corporations.[2] The managers of a venture capital fund, called **venture capitalist (VCs)**, are usually highly knowledgeable and experienced in a particular industry, such as telecommunications. They screen hundreds of companies and ultimately fund around a dozen, called *portfolio companies*. The venture fund buys shares of the portfolio companies, and the VCs sit on the companies' boards of directors. The venture capital fund usually has a prespecified life of 7 to 10 years, after which it is dissolved, either by selling the portfolio companies' stocks and distributing the proceeds to the funds' investors, or by directly distributing the stock to the investors.

CONCEPT REVIEW

1. What is an angel?
2. What is a venture capital fund? A VC?

14.2 Trading in Financial Markets

Because the primary objective of financial management is to maximize the firm's share price, knowledge of the stock market is important to anyone involved in managing a business. We can classify stock market transactions into three distinct types.

First, when stock is offered to the public for the first time, the company is said to be "going public." This primary transaction is carried out on the initial public offering (IPO) market. We will discuss IPOs in detail later in this chapter. *Second*, if a company decides to sell (or issue) additional shares to raise new equity capital, this is still a primary market, but it is called a **seasoned equity offering.** *Third,* and by contrast, trading in the outstanding shares of established, publicly owned companies is a *secondary* market transaction. For example, if the owner of 100 shares of publicly held stock sells his or her stock, the trade is said to have occurred in the secondary market. Thus, the market for outstanding shares, or used shares, is the secondary market. The company receives no new money when sales occur on this market.

The vast majority of trading occurs in the secondary markets. Although there are many secondary markets for a wide variety of securities, we can classify their trading procedures along two dimensions: location and method of matching orders.

A secondary market can be either a **physical location exchange** or a **computer/telephone network.** For example, the New York Stock Exchange, the Chicago Board of Trade (the CBOT trades futures and options), and the Tokyo Stock Exchange are all physical location exchanges. In other words, the traders actually meet and trade in a specific part of a specific building. By contrast, the Toronto Stock Exchange (TSX) is an electronic exchange, as it is automated and has no market floor or traders. Nasdaq, which trades U.S. stocks, is a network of linked computers. Other examples are the markets for Government of Canada bonds and foreign exchange, which are conducted via telephone and/or computer networks. In these electronic markets, the traders never see one another.

The second dimension is the way orders from sellers and buyers are matched. This can occur through an open outcry *auction* system, through dealers, or by automated order matching. An example of an outcry auction is the CBOT, where traders actually meet in a pit and sellers and buyers communicate with one another through shouts and hand signals.

In a **dealer market,** there are "market makers" who keep an inventory of the stock (or other financial instrument) in much the same way that any merchant keeps an inventory. These dealers list bid and asked quotes, which are the prices at which they are willing to buy or sell. Computerized quotation systems keep track of all bid and asked prices, but they don't actually match buyers with sellers. Instead, traders must contact a specific dealer to complete the transaction. Nasdaq (U.S. stocks) is one such market, as are the London SEAQ (UK stocks) and the Neuer Market (stocks of small German companies).

The third method of matching orders is through an **electronic communications network (ECN).** Participants in an ECN post their orders to buy and sell, and the ECN automatically

---

[2]The typical venture capital fund is a private limited partnership, with limited partners and a general partner. The limited partners contribute cash but are prohibited from being involved in the partnership's decision making. Because of their limited participation, they are not held liable for any of the partnership's liabilities, except to the extent of their original investment. The general partner usually contributes a relatively modest amount of cash, but acts as the partnership's manager. In return, the general partner normally receives annual compensation equal to 1% to 2% of the fund's assets plus a 20% share of the fund's eventual profits.

FINANCE: IN FOCUS

Crowdfunding and Raising Capital

Crowdfunding, a relatively new method for businesses to raise money, has caught the attention of securities regulators. Crowdfunding refers to funds being raised by small contributions from the general public (the crowd), using the Internet and social media. Money raised in 2013 totalled $9.7 billion, growing to $16.2 billion in 2014, and expectations for 2015 are $34.4 billion. Its success is partly based on the ability of social networking to harness the common goals and shared interests of online communities to fund projects of interest. There are three basic crowdfunding models. The first is donation-based, which currently raises the most money. Donors do not expect a return on the money they provide. Rather, the donors' return is the satisfaction received for funding something they deem important. Small nonmonetary incentives may also be provided. The second model is lending-based. Individuals provide small loans, which can have a variety of terms and conditions attached. There may be an agreement for interest as well as principal repayment; or the loan may be forgivable unless the project can produce profits; or the loan may be a pre-sales agreement, meaning that the lender will be reimbursed with the finished product. The third model is equity based, whereby investors buy shares in the business.

Companies seeking financing are typically developing technology and products in the music, film, and video game sectors. Regulators are concerned that without proper guidelines and rules the potential for investor fraud is high. Canada's provincial securities regulators have agreed on a general approach to managing crowd-sourced funding. The Internet portals, or websites, where the money is raised should be registered, they should maintain minimum capital and insurance requirements, and companies and their directors should be subject to background checks. Investors are also limited on how much they could invest per deal and per year, though the amounts vary by province.

Sources: Adapted from "Crowdfunding 101," National Crowdfunding Association of Canada, accessed August 30, 2014; Devin Thorpe, "Crowdfunding Entrepreneurs Predict More Good in the World in 2014," Forbes.com, December 24, 2013, http://www.forbes.com, accessed August 30, 2014.

matches orders. For example, someone might place an order to buy 1,000 shares of IBM stock (this is called a "market order" since it is to buy the stock at the current market price). Suppose another participant had placed an order to sell 1,000 shares of IBM at a price of $91 per share, and this was the lowest price of any "sell" order. The ECN would automatically match these two orders, execute the trade, and notify both participants that the trade had occurred. Participants can also post "limit orders," which might state that the participant is willing to buy 1,000 shares of IBM at $90 per share if the price falls that low during the next two hours. In other words, there are limits on the price and/or the duration of the order. The ECN will execute the limit order if the conditions are met—that is, if someone offers to sell IBM at a price of $90 or less during the next two hours. Two of the largest ECNs for trading U.S. stocks are Instinet (now owned by Nasdaq) and Archipelago (now owned by the NYSE). Two fledgling ECNs in Canada are Alpha and Chi-X.

CONCEPT REVIEW

1. What are the major differences between physical location exchanges and computer/telephone networks?
2. What are the differences among open outcry auctions, dealer markets, and ECNs?

14.3 The Secondary Stock Markets

The two leading U.S. stock markets today are the New York Stock Exchange and the Nasdaq stock market, while in Canada it is the Toronto Stock Exchange.

The Canadian Stock Exchanges

The trading of shares in Canadian companies began in 1832 in a Montreal coffeehouse. Twenty years later, informal trading also began in Toronto. Brokers formally incorporated the Montreal Stock Exchange (MSE) in 1874 and the Toronto Stock Exchange (TSE) four years later, in 1878. Members bought "seats" that allowed them to access the trading floor to buy and sell securities. Over time, the number of issues, along with trading volumes and values, grew with the Canadian economy. Other stock exchanges were created, such as the Vancouver Stock Exchange (VSE), the Alberta Stock Exchange (ASE), the Winnipeg Stock Exchange (WSE), the Standard Stock and Mining Exchange, and the Canadian Stock Exchange; these, however, mainly served the financing needs of the resource sector. By 1999, after a series of mergers and reorganizations, the Toronto Stock Exchange had become the only exchange in Canada to trade senior equities. The Montreal Exchange focused solely on trading derivative products, while the Canadian Venture Exchange (CDNX), formed through mergers of the VSE, ASE, and WSE, traded junior stocks. A year later, the TSE completed an IPO and became a for-profit publicly traded company.

In 2001, the TSE bought the CDNX. The entire business was then renamed the TSX Group, with the TSX Exchange (Toronto Stock Exchange) and the TSX Venture Exchange becoming the principal equity trading markets in Canada. In early 2008, agreement was reached for the TSX Group to purchase the Montreal Exchange for $1.1 billion. Reflecting this purchase, the company is now known as the TMX Group. As of 2013, the TMX ranked eighth worldwide in terms of market value, at $2,114 billion, and second in terms of number of listed companies, at 3,873. Canada's main commodity exchange, the Winnipeg Commodity Exchange (WCE), trades futures and options on crops such as canola, wheat, and barley. The WCE was purchased in 2007 by U.S.-based Intercontinental Exchange and has been renamed ICE Futures Canada.

The business of trading securities continues to evolve. A number of ECNs have entered the market to trade Canadian listed stocks. Two are worth mentioning. Chi-X is a global ECN that began Canadian operations in 2008. Alpha Trading Systems, formed by a consortium of Canada's largest investment dealers, also started trading Canadian listed securities in 2008. Both seek to take trading business from the TSX and TSX Venture exchanges. By mid-2014, Chi-X and Alpha accounted for 31% of the value of equities traded in Canada.[3]

The New York Stock Exchange

Before March 2006, the *New York Stock Exchange (NYSE)* was a privately held firm owned by its members. It then merged with Archipelago, a publicly traded company that was one of the world's largest ECNs. One year later, in 2007, the NYSE merged with Euronext, made up of several European exchanges; it is now known as NYSE-Euronext. The NYSE still has over 300 registered broker-dealer members. Member organizations may not conduct trading on the floor of the exchange unless they also hold a trading licence issued by the NYSE. Before the exchange went public, the equivalent to a trading licence was called a seat and sold for up to $4 million (in 2005). Trading licences are now leased by member organizations from the exchange, with an annual fee of $40,000 for 2012.

Most of the larger investment banks operate *brokerage departments* and are members of the NYSE with leased trading rights. The NYSE is open on all normal working days, with the members meeting in large rooms equipped with electronic equipment that enables each member to communicate with his or her firm's offices throughout the country. For example, Merrill Lynch might receive an order in its Atlanta office from a customer who wants to buy shares of AT&T. Simultaneously, Morgan Stanley's Denver office might receive an order from a customer wishing to sell shares of AT&T. Each broker communicates electronically with the firm's representative on the NYSE. Other brokers throughout the country are also communicating with their own exchange members. The exchange members with *sell orders* offer the shares for sale, and they are bid for by the members with *buy orders*. Thus, the NYSE operates as an *auction market*.[4]

---

[3]IIROC, "Market Share by Marketplace, June 30, 2014," http://www.iiroc.ca, accessed August 29, 2014.

[4]The NYSE is actually a modified auction market, wherein people (through their brokers) bid for stocks. Originally—about 200 years ago—brokers would literally shout, "I have 100 shares of Erie for sale; how much am I offered?" and then sell to the highest bidder. If a broker had a buy order, he or she would shout, "I want to buy 100 shares of Erie; who'll sell at the best price?" The same general situation still exists, although the exchanges now have members known as *specialists* who facilitate the trading process by keeping an inventory of shares of the stocks in which they specialize. If a buy order comes in at a time when no sell order arrives, the specialist will sell off some inventory. Similarly, if a sell order comes in, the specialist will buy and add to inventory. The specialist sets a *bid price* (the price the specialist will pay for the stock) and an *asked price* (the price at which shares will be sold out of inventory). The bid and asked prices are set at levels designed to keep the inventory in balance. If many buy orders start coming in because of favourable developments or sell orders come in because of unfavourable events, the specialist will raise or lower prices to keep supply and demand in balance. Bid prices are somewhat lower than asked prices, with the difference, or *spread*, representing the specialist's profit margin.

Special facilities are available to help institutional investors such as mutual funds or pension funds sell large blocks of stock without depressing their prices. In essence, brokerage houses that cater to institutional clients will purchase blocks (defined as 10,000 or more shares) and then resell the stock to other institutions or individuals. Also, when a firm has a major announcement that is likely to cause its stock price to change sharply, it will ask the exchanges to halt trading in its stock until the announcement has been made and digested by investors.

The Nasdaq Stock Market

The **National Association of Securities Dealers (NASD)** is a U.S. self-regulatory body that licenses brokers and oversees trading practices. The computerized network used by the NASD is known as the NASD Automated Quotation System, or Nasdaq. Nasdaq started as just a quotation system, but it has grown to become an organized securities market with its own listing requirements. Nasdaq lists about 5,000 stocks, although not all trade through the same Nasdaq system. For example, the Nasdaq National Market lists the larger Nasdaq stocks, such as Microsoft and Intel, while the Nasdaq SmallCap Market lists smaller companies with the potential for high growth. Nasdaq also operates the Nasdaq OTC Bulletin Board, which lists quotes for stock that is registered with the Securities and Exchange Commission (SEC) but that is not listed on any exchange, usually because the company is too small or too unprofitable. Finally, Nasdaq operates the Pink Sheets, which provide quotes on companies that are not registered with the SEC.

"Liquidity" is the ability to trade quickly at a net price (i.e., after any commissions) that is very close to the security's recent market value. In a dealer market, such as Nasdaq, a stock's liquidity depends on the number and quality of the dealers who make a market in the stock. Nasdaq has more than 400 dealers, most making markets in a large number of stocks.

FINANCE: IN FOCUS

Measuring the Market

A *stock index* is designed to show the performance of the stock market. Here are some leading indexes:

Dow Jones Industrial Average

Begun in 1896, the Dow Jones Industrial Average (DJIA) now includes 30 widely held stocks that represent almost one-fifth of the market value of all U.S. stocks. See http://www.dowjones.com for more information.

S&P 500 Index

Created in 1926, the S&P 500 Index is widely regarded as the standard for measuring large-cap U.S. stock market performance. It is value weighted, so the largest companies (in terms of value) have the greatest influence. The S&P 500 Index is used as a comparison benchmark by 97% of all U.S. money managers and pension plan sponsors. See http://www2 .standardand poors.com for more information.

S&P/TSX 60 Index

The S&P/TSX 60 is a widely used measure for tracking the performance of large-cap stocks trading on the Toronto Stock Exchange. This index is value weighted and is made up of 60 TSX-traded stocks whose total value accounts for over 70% of the equity traded in Canada. Criteria used for selecting companies for the index include their market capitalization, liquidity, proven history of sales and profits, and industry representation. Besides being used as a measure of market performance, the S&P/TSX 60 is used for benchmarking purposes, and also as a model for investing efficiently in the Canadian large-cap market. See

http://www2.standardandpoors.com for more information.

Trading the Market

Through the use of exchange-traded funds (ETFs), it is now possible to buy and sell the market in much the same way as an individual stock. For example, the Standard & Poor's depository receipt (SPDR) is a share of a fund composed of the stocks in the S&P 500. SPDRs trade during regular market hours, making it possible to buy or sell the S&P 500 any time during the day. Another example is Black Rock's iShares CDN 60 ETF, ticker symbol XIU. This large-cap index-traded fund provides investors with exposure to all 60 companies making up the S&P/TSX 60 Index. There are hundreds of other ETFs, including ones for the Nasdaq and the Dow Jones Industrial Average.

Recent Performance

Go to http://finance.yahoo.ca. Enter the symbol for any of the indexes (^SPTSE for the S&P/TSX 60, ^DJI for the Dow Jones, ^SPC for the S&P 500, ^IXIC for the Nasdaq, and ^NYA for the NYSE) and click GO. This will bring up the current value of the index, shown in a table. Click Basic Chart in the panel on the left; this will bring up a chart showing the historical performance of the index. Directly above the chart is a series of buttons that allows you to choose the number of years and to plot the relative performance of several indexes on the same chart. You can even download the historical data in spreadsheet form by clicking Historical Prices in the left panel.

The typical stock has about 10 market makers, but some stocks have more than 50 market makers. Obviously, there are more market makers, and liquidity, for the Nasdaq National Market than for the SmallCap Market. There is very little liquidity for stocks on the OTC Bulletin Board or the Pink Sheets.

CONCEPT REVIEW

1. What are the major differences between the TSX, TSX Venture Exchange, Montreal Exchange, and ICE Futures Canada?

14.4 The Decision to Go Public: Initial Public Offerings

Going public means selling some of a company's stock to outside investors in an **initial public offering (IPO)** and then letting the stock trade in public markets. Thirty Canadian issuers took this step in 2013.

Advantages of Going Public

1. *Increases liquidity and allows founders to harvest their wealth.* The stock of a private, or closely held, corporation is illiquid. It may be hard for one of the owners who wants to sell some shares to find a ready buyer, and even if a buyer is located, there is no established price on which to base the transaction.
2. *Permits founders to diversify.* As a company grows and becomes more valuable, its founders often have most of their wealth tied up in the company. By selling some of their stock in a public offering, they can diversify their holdings, thereby reducing the riskiness of their personal portfolios.
3. *Facilitates raising new corporate cash.* If a privately held company wants to raise cash by selling new stock, it must either go to its existing owners, who may not have any money or may not want to put more eggs in this particular basket, or else shop around for wealthy investors. However, it is usually quite difficult to get outsiders to put money into a closely held company, because if the outsiders do not have voting control (more than 50% of the stock), the inside shareholders/managers can take advantage of them. Going public, which brings with it both public disclosure of information and regulation by the securities commissions, greatly reduces this problem, and thus makes people more willing to invest in the company, which makes it easier for the firm to raise capital.
4. *Establishes a value for the firm.* A company that wants to give incentive stock options to key employees finds it useful to know the exact value of those options, and employees much prefer to own stock, or options on stock, that is publicly traded and therefore liquid.
5. *Facilitates merger negotiations.* Having an established market price helps when a company either is being acquired or is seeking to acquire another company where it will pay for the acquisition with stock.
6. *Increases potential markets.* Many companies find it easier to sell products and services to potential customers after they become publicly traded.
7. *Greater visibility.* A public listing improves the market recognition of a company. Enhanced corporate visibility through stock quotations, public press releases, and earnings announcements, and possible analyst coverage of the company's stock, together create greater investor awareness and thus a larger pool of investors for the company's stock.

Disadvantages of Going Public

1. *Cost of reporting.* A publicly owned company must file quarterly and annual reports with a securities commission. These reports can be a costly burden, especially for small firms. In addition, compliance with Sarbanes-Oxley and its Canadian equivalent often requires considerable expense and human resource.
2. *Continuous disclosure.* Public companies are obliged to provide an up-to-date public record of their activities and status. This information is for the benefit of its public shareholders; but anyone else, including competitors, can access such information. Besides the financial

statements, insider reports, quarterly management discussion and analysis (MD&A), and material changes to the company, other materials must be made public on a timely basis.

3. *Self-dealings.* The owners-managers of closely held companies have many opportunities for various types of questionable but legal self-dealings, including the payment of high salaries, nepotism, personal transactions with the business (such as leasing arrangements), and not-truly-necessary fringe benefits. Such self-dealings, which are often designed to minimize personal tax liabilities or to meet other personal needs, are much harder to arrange if a company is publicly owned.

4. *Inactive market/low price.* If the firm is very small, and if its shares are not traded frequently, its stock will not really be liquid, and the market price may not represent the stock's true value. Security analysts and stockbrokers simply will not follow the stock, because there will not be sufficient trading activity to generate enough brokerage commissions to cover the costs of following the stock.

5. *Control.* Because of possible tender offers and proxy fights, the managers of publicly owned firms who do not have voting control must be concerned about maintaining control. Furthermore, there is pressure on such managers to produce annual earnings gains, even when it might be in the shareholders' best long-term interests to adopt a strategy that reduces short-term earnings but raises them in future years. These factors have led a number of public companies to "go private" in "leveraged buyout" deals where the managers borrow the money to buy out the nonmanagement shareholders. We discuss the decision to go private in a later section.

6. *Investor relations.* Public companies must keep investors abreast of current developments. Many CFOs of newly public firms report that they spend two full days a week talking with investors and analysts.

Conclusions on Going Public

There are no hard-and-fast rules regarding if or when a company should go public. This is an individual decision that should be made on the basis of the company's and shareholders' own unique circumstances. If a company does decide to go public, either by selling newly issued stock to raise new capital or by the sale of stock by the current owners, the key issue is setting the price at which shares will be offered to the public. The company and its current owners should want to set the price as high as possible—the higher the offering price, the smaller the fraction of the company the current owners will have to give up to obtain any specified amount of money. On the other hand, potential buyers want the price set as low as possible. We return to the establishment of the offering price later in the chapter, after we describe some other aspects of common stock financing.

CONCEPT REVIEW

1. What are the major advantages of going public?
2. What are the major disadvantages?

14.5   The Process of Going Public

As the following sections show, the process of going public is a lot more complicated, expensive, and time consuming than simply making the decision to go public.

Selecting an Investment Bank

After a company decides to go public, it faces the problem of how to sell its stock to a large number of investors. While most companies know how to sell their products, few have experience in selling securities. To help in this process, the company will interview a number of different **investment banks,** also called *underwriters,* and select one to be the lead underwriter. To understand the factors that affect this choice, it helps to understand exactly what investment banks do.

First, the investment bank helps the firm determine the preliminary offering price, or price range, for the stock and the number of shares to be sold. The investment bank's reputation and experience in the company's industry are very important in convincing potential investors to purchase the stock at the offering price. In effect, the investment bank certifies that the stock is not overpriced, which obviously comforts investors. Second, the investment bank actually sells the shares to its existing clients, which include a mix of institutional investors and retail (i.e., individual) customers. Third, the investment bank, through its associated brokerage house, will have an analyst "cover" the stock after it is issued. This analyst will regularly distribute reports to investors describing the stock's prospects, which will help maintain an interest in the stock. Well-respected analysts increase the likelihood that there will be a liquid secondary market for the stock and that its price will reflect the company's true value.

The Underwriting Syndicate

The firm and its investment bank must next decide whether the bank will work on a **best efforts** basis or will **underwrite** the issue. In a best efforts sale, the bank does not guarantee that the securities will be sold or that the company will get the cash it needs—only that it will put forth its "best efforts" to sell the issue. The bank acts as an agent for the issuer. Best effort deals are usually used for small, unknown issuers, where the uncertainty of market acceptance for the stock is significant. On an underwritten issue, the company does get a guarantee, because the bank agrees to buy the entire issue and then resell the stock to its customers. That is, the bank acts as a principal. Therefore, the bank bears significant risks in underwritten offerings. For example, on one IBM bond issue, interest rates rose sharply and bond prices fell, after the deal had been set but before the investment banks could sell the bonds to the ultimate purchasers. The banks lost somewhere between $10 million and $20 million. Had the offering been on a best efforts basis, IBM would have been the loser.

Because they are exposed to large potential losses, investment banks typically do not handle the purchase and distribution of issues single-handedly unless the issue is a very small one. If the sum of money involved is large, investment banks form *underwriting syndicates* in an effort to minimize the risk each bank faces. The investment bank that sets up the deal is called the *lead*, or *managing, underwriter*. Syndicated offerings are usually covered by more analysts, which contributes to greater liquidity in the post-IPO secondary market. Thus, syndication provides benefits to both underwriters and issuers.

In addition to the underwriting syndicate, on larger offerings still more investment banks are included in a **selling group,** which handles the distribution of securities to individual investors. The selling group includes all members of the underwriting syndicate plus additional dealers who take relatively small percentages of the total issue from the members of the underwriting syndicate.

Regulation of Securities Sales

Sales of new securities, and also sales in the secondary markets, are regulated by the provincial securities commissions and by the Canada Business Corporations Act. Here are the primary elements governing securities sales:

1. An issuer must write a prospectus document and have it approved by a securities commission before the new securities (stocks and bonds) can be sold to the public. A **prospectus** is an in-depth legal document describing all material facts regarding the issuer, as well as the details regarding the securities being offered and the intended use of the proceeds. The prospectus is created to provide "full, true and plain disclosure" to investors. Issuers need an investment bank to guide them through the IPO process; they also require a law firm with experience in securities law, and an accounting firm to prepare audited financial statements for the past three years and to assist on the financial portions of the prospectus.
2. Once the *preliminary* or **"red herring" prospectus** is complete, it is filed with the securities commission for its review. Typically, the preliminary prospectus will have much of the information contained in the final prospectus, with the exception of the number of securities to be issued and their selling price. Several days later, the commission will provide a comment letter that states deficiencies, changes to be made, and additional information required. The issuer must address any concerns raised by the regulator. Since the prospectus has not yet been approved, the investment bank cannot yet sell any of the securities; it may, however, discuss the new issue with potential investors in order to determine market interest. The final selling price can be set as late as after the market closes the day before the new securities are actually offered to the public.
3. Once the securities commission has completed its review, a final prospectus is submitted to the regulators, at which time a "receipt" is provided to the issuer, acknowledging

that the prospectus has been approved. Each investor purchasing the security must receive a copy of the final prospectus. It is important to note that approval of the prospectus does *not* imply that the commission has accepted the security as a worthy investment. Approval simply means that the issuer has provided all the relevant information required in the prospectus. It is up to individual investors to determine whether the issue is a suitable investment.[5]

4. If the prospectus contains *misrepresentations* or *omissions* of material facts, any purchaser who suffers a loss may sue for damages. Significant penalties may be imposed on the issuer, accountant, engineers, appraisers, underwriters, and all others who participated in the preparation of the prospectus.

Figure 14-1 provides a description of the timing and activities associated with selling and listing new securities. Note that the timeline is an estimate and that actual issues may take longer to complete.

The Roadshow and Book Building

After the preliminary prospectus has been filed, the senior management team, the underwriter, and the company's lawyers go on a **roadshow.** The management team will make several presentations each day to potential institutional investors, as well as to groups of retail brokers. The institutional investors ask questions during the presentation, but the management team may not give any information that is not in the preliminary prospectus. The typical roadshow may last 10 to 14 days, with stops in 10 to 20 different cities. Occasionally, if investor interest is very high, the roadshow will be cut short.

After a presentation, the investment banks ask the investor for an indication of interest based on a price range provided by the investment bank. The investment bank records the number of shares that each investor is willing to buy, which is called *book building*. As the roadshow progresses, the investment bank's "book" shows how demand for the offering is building. Many IPOs are *oversubscribed*, with investors wishing to purchase more shares than are available. In such a case, the investment bank will allocate shares to the investors. If demand is high enough, sometimes they will increase the offering price. If demand is low, they will either reduce the offering price or withdraw the IPO. Sometimes low demand is specifically due to concern over the company's future prospects, but sometimes low demand

FIGURE 14-1   Activities and Timetable for the Prospectus and Listing Process

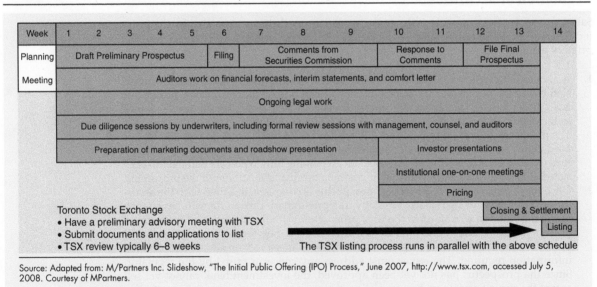

Source: Adapted from: M/Partners Inc. Slideshow, "The Initial Public Offering (IPO) Process," June 2007, http://www.tsx.com, accessed July 5, 2008. Courtesy of MPartners.

---

[5]The initial or final prospectus can be obtained at http://sedar.com for Canadian companies and at http://sec.gov for U.S. companies.

is caused by a fall in the general stock market. Thus, the timing of the roadshow and offering date are very important. As the old saying goes, sometimes it is better to be lucky than good.

The First Day of Trading

For many IPOs, there can be significant fluctuations in stock prices during the first day of trading. For instance, in 1991 during the dot.com boom, IPOs averaged a 71% gain on their first day of trading.[6] Some IPOs have a sharp run-up and then fall back by the end of the day. Others actually end their first day with a loss. Figure 14-2 shows the average first-day returns for IPOs in a number of countries.

There is an overall bias toward underpricing stocks on their IPO. A study of U.S. IPOs from 1990 to 1998 found an average overall positive return of 14.1% on the first day of trade. Moreover, three-quarters of all IPOs had a positive return. Canadian studies show similar though not so pronounced underpricing: Most first-day returns fall between 3.6% to 11.6%, with the trend generally becoming smaller over time.[7]

You're probably asking yourself two questions: (1) How can you get in on these deals? (2) Why is the offering price so low? First, you probably can't get the chance to buy a "hot" IPO at its offering price. To begin with, most of the shares go to institutional investors and preferred retail customers.

Various theories have been put forth to explain IPO underpricing. As long as issuing companies don't complain, investment banks have strong incentives to underprice the issue. First, underpricing increases the likelihood of oversubscription, which reduces the risk to the underwriter. Second, most investors who get to purchase the IPO at its offering price are preferred customers of the investment bank, and they became preferred customers because they generated lots of commissions in the investment bank's brokerage division. Therefore, the IPO is an easy way for the underwriter to reward customers for past and future commissions. Third, the underwriter needs an honest indication of interest when building the book prior to the offering, and underpricing is a possible way to secure this information from the institutional investors.

But why don't issuing companies object to underpricing? Some, such as Google do, and seek alternative ways to issue their securities.[8] However, most seem content to leave some money on the table. The best explanation seems to be that (1) the company wants to create

FIGURE 14-2 Average First-Day IPO Returns

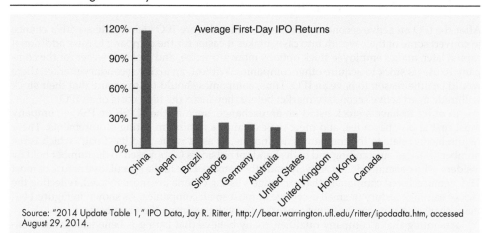

Source: "2014 Update Table 1," IPO Data, Jay R. Ritter, http://bear.warrington.ufl.edu/ritter/ipodadta.htm, accessed August 29, 2014.

---

[6]"The Risky Art of Going Public," CBC News Online, March 21, 2006, http://www.cbc.ca, accessed July 5, 2008.
[7]Nancy Ursel, "Priced to Sell: The Evolution of Underpricing in Canadian Initial Public Offerings," *Canadian Business Economics*, February, 2000, 15–20, http://www.cabe.ca, accessed July 5, 2008; Vijay M. Jog and Ashwani Srivastava, "The Mixed Results of Canadian IPOs," *Canadian Investment Review*, Winter 1997, 22–26. For the United States, see Tim Loughran and Jay R. Ritter, "Why Don't Issuers Get Upset About Leaving Money on the Table in IPOs?" *Review of Financial Studies*, 2002, 413–414.
[8]Google bypassed the traditional underwriting IPO process and instead used an auction to sell its shares. After receiving a prospectus, investors were able to bid on the price and number of shares they were willing to purchase. After bidding closed, Google's underwriters determined the share price that satisfied the company's financing requirements. All bidders whose bids were at or above the IPO price received the same IPO price.

excitement, and a price run-up on the first day does that; (2) only a small percentage of the company's stock is generally offered to the public, so current shareholders give away less due to underpricing than appears at first glance; and (3) IPO companies generally plan to have further offerings in the future, and the best way to ensure future success is to have a successful IPO, which underpricing guarantees.

Although IPOs on average provide large first-day returns, their long-term returns over the following 3 years are below average. For example, if you could not get in at the IPO price but purchased a portfolio of IPO stocks on their second day of trading, your 3-year return would have been lower than the return on a portfolio of similar but seasoned stocks. In summary, the offering price appears to be too low, but the first-day run-up is generally too high.

The Costs of Going Public

Investment banks in Canada on average have charged a 5.5% **spread** between the price they pay the issuing company and the price at which they sell shares to the public. Thus, they keep 5.5% of the offering price as their compensation. For example, in 2013 Saskatchewan-based Information Services Corporation sold 10.5 million shares at an offer price of $14 per share. In this IPO, the underwriters' direct compensation was $0.84 per share. For 10.5 million shares issued, these direct underwriting costs totalled $8.82 million.

But there are other direct costs, such as lawyers' fees, accountants' costs, printing, and so on. These fees can easily amount to several hundred thousand dollars, which can be a large percentage of a small IPO.

Last, but not least, are the indirect costs. The money left on the table, which is equal to the number of shares multiplied by the difference in the closing price and the offering price, can be quite large. Information Services Corp. experienced a first-day run-up to $15.87 from an offering price of $14, so the indirect costs totalled 10.5($15.87 − $14) = $19.635 million. In addition, senior managers spend an enormous amount of time working on the IPO rather than managing the business, which certainly carries a high cost, even if it cannot be easily measured.

Thus, Information Services Corp. received proceeds of $138.18 million, and the underwriter and its sales forces received $8.82 million, with $19.635 million left on the table. There were undoubtedly other direct costs of several hundred thousand dollars, and indirect costs due to the diversion of the management team. As you can see, an IPO is quite expensive.[9]

The Importance of the Secondary Market

After the IPO an active secondary market provides the pre-IPO shareholders with a chance to convert some of their wealth into cash, makes it easier for the company to raise additional capital later, makes employee stock options more attractive, and makes it easier for the company to use its stock to acquire other companies. Without an active secondary market, there would be little reason to have an IPO. Thus, companies should try to ensure that their stock will trade in an active secondary market before they incur the high costs of an IPO.

In order to have a stock listed on an exchange, such as the NYSE or TSX, a company must first apply, pay a fee, and meet the exchange's minimum listing requirements. These requirements relate to the company's net income, its asset value, and its "float," which is the number of shares outstanding and in the hands of outsiders (as opposed to the number held by insiders, who generally do not actively trade their stock). Due to the speculative nature of most TSX Venture–listed companies, that exchange's listing criteria are more relaxed, reflecting the lack of earnings history or small asset size of most small companies. As shown in Figure 14-1, the exchange's listing process runs concurrently with preparing the prospectus.

Assuming that a company qualifies, many believe that listing is beneficial to the company and to its shareholders. Listed companies receive a certain amount of free advertising and publicity, and their status as listed companies may enhance their prestige and reputation, which often leads to higher sales. Investors respond favourably to increased information, increased liquidity, and the confidence that the quoted price is not being manipulated.

---

[9]For more on IPOs, see Roger G. Ibbotson, Jody L. Sindelar, and Jay R. Ritter, "The Market's Problems with the Pricing of Initial Public Offerings," *Journal of Applied Corporate Finance*, Spring 1994, 66–74; Chris J. Muscarella and Michael R. Vetsuypens, "The Underpricing of 'Second' Initial Public Offerings," *Journal of Financial Research*, Fall 1989, 183–192; Jay R. Ritter, "The Long-Run Performance of Initial Public Offerings," *Journal of Finance*, March 1991, 3–27; Jay R. Ritter, "Initial Public Offerings," *Contemporary Finance Digest*, Spring 1998, 5–30; Maher Kooli and Jean-Marc Suret, "How Cost Effective Are Canadian IPO Markets?" *Canadian Investment Review*, Winter 2003, 20–28; Theresa Shutt and Hugh Williams, "Going to Market: The Cost of IPOs in Canada and the United States," Conference Board of Canada, June 2000.

Listing provides investors with these benefits, which may help managers lower their firms' cost of equity and increase the value of their stock.[10]

Regulating the Secondary Market

As we stated earlier, a liquid and crime-free secondary market is critical to the success of an IPO or any other publicly traded security. So, in addition to regulating the process for issuing securities, the 13 provincial and territorial securities commissions also have responsibilities in the secondary markets. The primary elements of regulation are set forth below.

1. *Continuous disclosure.* As mentioned earlier in the chapter, publicly traded companies in Canada must provide ongoing information to regulators and shareholders. This information can be easily obtained from **http://sedar.com** (a website operated by the Canadian Securities Association).[11]
2. *Enforcement.* The regulators have the authority to enforce securities laws. For example, the securities commissions can fine an insider found to have broken insider trading rules, or they can require a company to return monies raised on a prospectus offering if misleading information was given in the prospectus.
3. *Regulation of participants.* To maintain industry integrity and credibility, companies and individuals engaged in underwriting, trading, or providing investment advice are regulated and licensed by the regulators.[12] However, responsibility for disciplining the dealers and brokers is provided by self-regulatory organizations (SROs), such as the Investment Industry Regulatory Organization of Canada (IIROC). The IIROC also oversees market surveillance in real-time to ensure a fair and transparent trading system.

The fact that Canada's securities industry is not governed nationally creates the potential for a patchwork of multiple and inefficient rules and regulations. To partly address this concern, the 13 regulators have established the Canadian Securities Association (CSA), whose role is to simplify matters by reducing duplication and by harmonizing the regulation of capital markets. As part of this process, the CSA has created a series of "National Instruments" that are legally enforceable in all Canadian jurisdictions. Despite efforts to coordinate the various regulators, some in Canada—the federal government, some industry participants, and (at the time of writing) the securities commissions from Ontario, B.C., Saskatchewan, and New Brunswick are arguing in favour of a single national securities regulator, similar to the Securities and Exchange Commission (SEC) in the United States. They argue that the current system is inefficient and unresponsive to market needs.

In 2004, in response to these concerns, all regulators except the OSC signed a Memorandum of Understanding to create a passport system allowing a company to submit filings to one principal regulator; once the filing was approved, it would be automatically accepted in all other jurisdictions (except Ontario). Prospectus and continuous disclosure documents, as well as registration rules, are covered under the passport system. The debate over having one national regulator or a harmonized territorial system has yet to be settled in Canada.

(C)NCEPT REVIEW

1. What is the difference between "best efforts" and "underwriting"?
2. What are some regulations regarding sales of new securities?
3. What is a roadshow? What is book building?
4. What is underpricing? Leaving money on the table?
5. What are some of the costs of going public?
6. A company is planning an IPO. Its underwriters have said the stock will sell at $50 per share. The underwriters will charge a 7% spread. How many shares must the company sell to net $93 million, ignoring any other expenses? (Check Figure: 2 million)

---

[10]For additional discussion on the benefits of listing, see H. Kent Baker and Richard B. Edelman, "AMEX-to-NYSE Transfers, Market Microstructure, and Shareholder Wealth," *Financial Management*, Winter 1992, pp. 60–72; and Richard B. Edelman and H. Kent Baker, "Liquidity and Stock Exchange Listing," *Financial Review*, May 1990, pp. 231–249. For listing requirements on the TSX and TSX Venture exchange, go to http://www.tmx.com.
[11]Insider reports are available at http://www.sedi.com.
[12]Tara Gray and Andrew Kitching, "Reforming Canadian Securities Regulation," Library of Parliament, PRB 05-28E, September 19, 2005, 6–8.

FINANCE: IN FOCUS

Life in the Fast Lane: High-Frequency Trading!

In the time it takes to blink an eye, a high-frequency trader's computer could have made hundreds of bids, cancelled all but one, purchased stock, and then sold them for a profit of less than a penny. It may sound like a lot of work for such a small profit, but a million similar trades a day add up to big bucks. In fact high-frequency trading (HFT) firms made about $7.2 billion total profit in 2009.

Who are these traders? First, there are only about 400 HFT firms in the United States and 60 in Canada out of the 20,000 or so institutional traders, so there really aren't that many of them. Second, many of their employees have math and computer science backgrounds rather than trading experience. Third, they have access to the very best computer technology. Their demand for speed is so great that Hibernia Atlantic plans to lay a new underwater cable along a slightly shorter route from the United Kingdom to Canada in order to cut the transmission time from 65 to 60 milliseconds!

Despite the relatively small number of HFT firms, they have a large impact on the market, accounting for over 60% of the stock trading volume in the United States. In Canada, HFT trading has declined from 22% to 16% of total volume over the period 2011 to 2013. But are HFT firms good or bad for markets and other investors? The answer is not clear. On the one hand, other investors can trade much more quickly now, with execution time dropping from 10.1 seconds in 2005 to 0.7 seconds in 2010. The cost of trading, as measured by the spread in bid and ask prices, has also shrunk dramatically. On the other hand, some critics say that high-frequency trading distorts prices and makes markets less stable.

Canadian institutions have been at the forefront in addressing what they see as unfairness in HFT. Royal Bank's RBC Capital Markets developed trading software that eliminates the speed advantage of high frequency traders. They have since gone on to use their proprietary software to develop and co-invest in two alternative stock exchanges, one in Canada and one in the United States that attempt to level the playing field for all investors. It appears their efforts are being noticed. RBC is been given the name "RBC Nice" by Wall Street writers and RBC itself admits that business has picked up since becoming a leader against dubious HFT practices.

Sources: Doug Cameron and Jacob Bunge, "Underwater Options? Ocean Cable Will Serve High-Frequency Traders," *The Wall Street Journal*, October 1, 2010, p. C-3; Kambiz Foroohar, "Speed Geeks," *Bloomberg Markets*, November 2010, pp. 111–122; Barbara Shecter, "High-Frequency Trading Activity in Canada Appears to Have Declined: IIROC," *National Post*, November 21, 2013; Eric Lam and Doug Alexander, "'RBC Nice' Pays Off Amid High-Frequency-Trading Outcry," *Bloomberg Markets*, April 10, 2014.

14.6 Equity Carve-Outs: A Special Type of IPO

In 2013, Canadian Tire sold to the public about 17% of the equity in its wholly owned real estate subsidiary, CT REIT. In this transaction, the subsidiary, like the parent, became publicly owned, but the parent retained full control of the subsidiary by retaining about 83% of the subsidiary's common stock. This type of transaction is called an **equity carve-out** (or *partial public offering*, or *spin-out*). The market's response to Canadian Tire's carve-out announcement was very positive—the stock price rose 10%.[13] Equity carve-outs raise an interesting question: Why do carve-out announcements typically result in stock price increases while the announcements of new stock issues by parent corporations generally decrease stock prices?

One possible answer is that carve-outs facilitate the evaluation of corporate growth opportunities on a line-of-business basis. Thus, Canadian Tire enabled investors to separately value its real estate business, by offering its units to the public. Also, by creating a separate public market for CT REIT's units, Canadian Tire offered investors a "pure play" in the real estate sector.

Another potential advantage of carve-outs is that they can increase the effectiveness of capital allocation. Internally, the competition for capital is often waged on political rather

---

[13]For more information on equity carve-outs, see Roni Michaely and Wayne H. Shaw, "The Choice of Going Public: Spin-offs vs. Carve-outs," *Financial Management*, Autumn 1995, 5–21; Katherine Schipper and Abbie Smith, "Equity Carve-Outs," *Midland Corporate Finance Journal*, Spring 1986, 23–32; David M. Glassman, "Spin-Offs and Spin-Outs: Using 'Securitization' to Beat the Bureaucracy," *Journal of Applied Corporate Finance*, Fall 1988, 82–89; and Anand Vijh, "Long-Term Returns from Equity Carve-outs," *Journal of Financial Economics*, 1999, 273–308.

than economic grounds, and thus the use, and hence value, of new capital is very uncertain. After a carve-out, it is easier to measure the cost of capital for the different business units, and this can improve the capital budgeting process. Also, by selling an ownership interest in a narrowly focused line of business rather than offering a stake in the conglomerate parent, management can reduce the uncertainty faced by investors. This can lower the cost of capital for the various units and thus increase the aggregate value of the consolidated enterprise.

Equity carve-outs do have some associated costs. First, the underwriting commission involved in a carve-out is larger than for an equity offering by the parent. Second, because an equity carve-out is a type of IPO, there is a potential for underpricing the new offering. While CT REIT's first-day closing price was slightly higher ($0.06) than its IPO price, based on the 26 million units offered, less than $2 million was left on the table due to underpricing. Third, key managers of the subsidiary must spend a significant amount of time marketing the new stock. Fourth, there are costs associated with the minority interest that is created in the carve-out. For example, the subsidiary's new board of directors must monitor all transactions between the subsidiary and the parent to ensure that the minority investors are not being exploited. Finally, there are additional costs, including annual reports, regulatory filings, analyst presentations, and so on, that must now be borne by both the parent and the subsidiary.

In summary, there are costs to equity carve-outs, but there are also benefits, and the benefits may make the carve-out an attractive option in many situations. In essence, a carve-out is a form of corporate **securitization,** which is the issuance of public securities backed by assets that have been segregated from the remaining assets of the company. By creating such securities, and a liquid market for trading them, a corporation can potentially reduce investor risk and increase the value of the firm as a whole. We cover securitization in more depth in Chapter 16.

CONCEPT REVIEW

1. Explain what is meant by an equity carve-out.
2. On average, equity carve-outs have increased shareholder wealth. What is a potential explanation for this observed phenomenon?

14.7 Non-IPO Investment Banking Activities

In addition to helping with IPOs, investment banks also help public companies raise additional debt and equity capital. As shown in Table 14-1, the top 5 investment banks in Canada helped raise $201 billion during 2013. In this section we describe some of the ways that investment banks and public companies work together to raise capital.

See **Web Extension 14A** at the textbook's website for a discussion of rights offerings.

TABLE 14-1 Top Five Canadian Underwriters, Debt and Equity, 2013 (C$M)

Manager	Government Debt	Corporate Debt	Equity	Total[a]
RBC Capital Markets	$21,974	$28,266	$7,452	$57,692
TD Securities	24,415	14,964	3,645	43,024
CIBC World Markets	22,002	13,474	3,862	39,338
BMO Capital Markets	13,907	12,384	5,649	31,940
Scotia Capital Markets	14,299	10,351	4,382	29,032

[a]Totals may not equal due to rounding.

Source: "All the Tables for Dealmakers 2014," *National Post*, January 30, 2014, accessed August 29, 2014.

Preliminary Decisions

Before raising capital, the firm makes some initial preliminary decisions, including the following:

- *Dollars to be raised.* How much new capital is needed?
- *Type of securities used.* Should common, preferred, bonds, hybrid securities, or a combination be used?
- *Type of deal.* Should the financing be undertaken through a prospectus offering, a private placement, or a "bought deal"? Will a best efforts or firm commitment underwriting be most appropriate?
- *Selection of an investment bank.* Different investment banks are better suited for different types of companies. Resource companies may find boutique investment banks very useful. Since investment banks sell new issues largely to their own regular customers, the nature of these customers has a major effect on the bank's ability to do a good job for corporate customers.

Private Placements

Regulators under certain conditions allow companies an exemption from having to prepare a prospectus before selling securities. Private placements can be sold only to "accredited investors." This limits the potential investor market. The primary advantages of private placements are (1) lower flotation costs and (2) greater speed, since the securities do not have to be approved by the regulators.

The most common type of private placement is when a company places securities directly with an institutional investor, such as a pension fund or (sometimes) individuals with high net worth. An issuer creates a document called an **Offering Memorandum (OM),** which describes the company's business, use of funds, and key risk factors. An OM is provided to each investor and must also be filed with the securities regulator, although the regulator does not review or approve it. Putting together an OM requires much less time and effort on the part of the issuer and its legal and financial advisors. Also, the investor purchasing stock through a private placement faces a minimum hold period during which it is not allowed to sell the stock. The median financing raised through a private placement is about $3 million, compared to $15 million for a "seasoned" public offering. Private placements account for roughly 17% of all equity raised by public companies.[14]

Short-Form Prospectus Distribution (SFPD)

Companies whose stocks trade on a recognized Canadian exchange, that file electronically, and that are a reporting issuer may be eligible to issue new stock under SFPD. The rationale behind this simplified prospectus offering is that reporting issuers already make public much of the information required in a prospectus document. Thus, under SFPD, eligible companies need only prepare a prospectus containing information such as the type, amount, and price of the security being issued, as well as how the proceeds will be used. The short-form prospectus reduces both costs and the time required to issue new securities.

As an alternative, a company can file a **shelf prospectus,** which is another relatively quick way of raising capital. The term "shelf" is used because, in effect, the company places its new securities "on the shelf" and then sells them to investors when it feels the market is "right." Eligible companies submit in advance a base prospectus with regulators. Once approved, this prospectus remains open for 25 months. A company can then issue securities within this time period simply by providing a prospectus supplement to investors. Large companies, such as Loblaw, Canadian National Railway, and Toronto Dominion Bank, maintain current shelf prospectuses in order to maintain financial flexibility.

Bought Deals

First used in Canada, bought deal financing was introduced in response to the competitive nature of investment bank financing. Under a regular underwriting, the bank and the issuer sign off on the underwriting agreement *after* the prospectus has been submitted to regulators

---

[14]Cécile Carpentier, Jean-François L'Her, and Jean-Marc Suret, "The Costs of Issuing Private Versus Public Equity," CIRANO, 2005 s-14, March 2005, http://www.cirano.qc.ca, accessed July 10, 2008.

and market demand has been estimated. With a bought deal, the investment bank agrees on the price and quantity of the securities it will purchase *before* the prospectus is filed or *simultaneously* with its filing. In addition, there is normally no market-out clause.[15] These last two points increase the risk to the underwriters. Bought deals are used in conjunction with a short-form prospectus, as the investment bank must gain approval quickly in order to sell the securities to a small number of institutional investors before market demand changes. Overall, bought deals take 20 days to complete, compared to a regular short-form prospectus underwriting of 28 days. Bought deals carry lower underwriting fees, and the negative stock price reaction to new equity financing is typically lower.[16]

Seasoned Equity Offerings

When a company with publicly traded stock issues additional shares, this is called a seasoned equity offering, also known as a *follow-on offering*. Because the stock is already publicly traded, the offering price will be based on the existing market price of the stock.

As we discussed in Chapter 12, the announcement of a new stock offering by a mature firm is often taken as a negative signal—if the firm's prospects were good, management would not want to issue new stock and thus share the rosy future with new shareholders. Therefore, the announcement of a new offering is taken as bad news. Consequently, the price will probably fall when the announcement is made, so the offering price will probably have to be set at a price below the pre-announcement market price.

One final point is that *if negative signalling effects drive down the price of the stock, all shares outstanding, not just the new shares, are affected.* For instance, if a stock should fall from $28.60 to $25 per share as a result of financing, and if the price remains at the new level, then the company will incur a loss of $3.60 on each of the shares previously outstanding. If there were 25 million a shares outstanding, the total market value loss would be $90 million. This loss, like underwriting expenses, is a flotation cost, and it should be considered as a cost associated with the stock issue. However, if the company's prospects really were poorer than investors thought, then the price decline would have occurred sooner or later anyway. On the other hand, if the company's prospects are really not all that bad (the signal was incorrect), then over time the stock price should move back to its previous level. However, if the price does revert to its former level, there will have been a transfer of wealth from the original shareholders to the new shareholders. To prevent this, companies often sell additional shares of stock through a rights offering, which we explain in *Web Extension 14A*.

See **Web Extension 14A** at the textbook's website for a discussion of rights offerings.

Ⓞ NCEPT REVIEW

1. What is a private placement?
2. What is a shelf prospectus?

14.8 The Decision to Go Private

In a **going private** transaction, the entire equity of a publicly held firm is purchased by a small group of investors that may include the firm's current senior management.[17] In some of these transactions, the current management group acquires all of the equity of the company. In others, current management participates in the ownership with outside investors, who typically place directors on the firm's board and arrange for the financing needed to purchase the publicly held stock. When the financing involves substantial borrowing, as it usually does, it is known as a leveraged buyout (LBO). In some cases, the current management group raises the financing and acquires all of the equity of the company; this is referred to as a management buyout (MBO).

The outside equity in a buyout often comes from a **private equity (PE)** fund, which is created to own and manage investments in nontraded equity. Private equity funds raise

---

[15]Underwriting agreements often contain a market-out clause. This clause allows underwriters to terminate their obligations under certain circumstances, such as an adverse change in market conditions that would affect their ability to sell the securities.
[16]Ari Pandes, "Bought Deals: The Value of Underwriter Certification in Seasoned Equity Offerings," February 8, 2008, http://papers.ssrn.com/sol3/papers.cfm?abstract_id=1029745#PaperDownload, accessed July 11, 2008; Barry Critchley, "Bought deal gets high marks," National Post, October 17, 2007, FP2.
[17]See Harry DeAngelo, Linda DeAngelo, and Edward M. Rice, "Going Private: The Effects of a Change in Corporate Ownership," *Midland Corporate Finance Journal*, Summer 1984, 35–43, for a more complete discussion of going private. The discussion in this section draws heavily from their work.

money from wealthy investors and institutions such as university endowments, pension funds, and insurance companies. The PE funds then take public firms private or invest in firms that already are privately held. Most PE funds plan on improving the companies' performance and then harvesting their investments by selling the company, perhaps in an IPO.[18]

Regardless of the structure of the deal, going private initially affects the right-hand side of the balance sheet, the liabilities and capital, and not the assets—going private simply rearranges the ownership structure. Thus, going private involves no obvious operating economies, yet the new owners are generally willing to pay a large premium over the stock's current price in order to take the firm private. For example, a private equity fund offered to buy all the shares in the Canadian company Q9 Networks for $17.05, which represented a 31% premium to the $13 price that Q9's shares were trading at when the deal was announced.[19]

This suggests that going private can increase the value of some firms sufficiently to enrich both managers and public shareholders. Other large Canadian businesses that have gone private have included Softchoice, Viterra, and Atrium Innovations. There are five advantages of going private, which are discussed below.

1. *Administrative cost savings*. Because going private takes the stock of a firm out of public hands, it saves on costs associated with securities registration, continuous disclosure requirements, responding to shareholder inquiries, and so on. More important, the top managers of private firms are free from meetings with security analysts, government bodies, and other outside parties.

2. *Increased managerial incentives*. An even larger potential gain comes from the improvement in incentives for high-level managerial performance. Their increased ownership means that the firm's managers benefit more directly from their own efforts; hence managerial efficiency tends to increase after going private.

3. *Increased managerial flexibility*. Another source of value stems from the increased flexibility available to managers of private firms. These managers do not have to worry about what a drop in next quarter's earnings will do to the firm's stock price; hence they can focus on long-term, strategic actions that ultimately will have the greatest positive impact on the firm's value.

4. *Increased shareholder participation*. Going private typically results in replacing a dispersed, largely passive group of public shareholders with a small group of investors who take a much more active role in managing the firm. These new equity investors have a substantial position in the private firm; hence they have a greater motivation to monitor management and to provide incentives to management than do the typical shareholders of a public corporation.

5. *Increased financial leverage*. Going private usually entails a drastic increase in the firm's use of debt financing, which has two effects. First, the firm's taxes are reduced because of the increase in deductible interest payments, so more of the operating income flows through to investors. Second, the increased debt servicing requirements force managers to hold costs down to ensure that the firm has sufficient cash flow to meet its obligations—a highly leveraged firm simply cannot afford any fat.

One might ask why all firms are not privately held. The answer is that while there are real benefits to private ownership, there are also benefits to being publicly owned. Most notably, public corporations have access to large amounts of equity capital on favourable terms, and for most companies, the advantages of access to public capital markets dominate the advantages of going private. Also, note that most companies that go private end up going public again after several years of operation as private firms. For example, Yellow Pages, which went private in 2002, again went public in December 2003. During the private phase, management sheds inefficient businesses, cuts costs throughout the corporation, and, generally, rationalizes operations. These actions increase the value of the firm to investors. Once the company has been "straightened up," going public allows the private equity holders to recover their investment, take their profit, and move on to new ventures.

---

[18]For more information on private equity, see Steve Kaplan, "Private Equity: Past, Present, and Future," *Journal of Applied Corporate Finance*, Summer 2007, 8–16; "Morgan Stanley Roundtable on Private Equity and Its Import for Public Companies," *Journal of Applied Corporate Finance*, Summer 2006, 8–37.

[19]A. Willis, "Q9 the Latest Canadian Growth Stock Buyout," *Globe and Mail*, August 25, 2008, http://www.theglobeandmail.com, accessed January 26, 2012.

CONCEPT REVIEW

1. What is meant by the term "going private"?
2. What are the main benefits of going private?
3. Why don't all firms go private to capture these benefits?

14.9 Project Financing

Historically, many large projects such as the Confederation Bridge, which links Prince Edward Island with the mainland, have been financed by what is called **project financing.**[20] We can present only an overview of the concept, for in practice it involves very complicated provisions and can take on many forms.

Project financing is used to finance electricity generating plants, airports, and public infrastructure such as roads, hospitals, and transit systems. Generally, one or more firms will sponsor the project, putting up the required equity capital; the remainder of the financing is furnished by lenders or lessors.[21] Most often, a separate legal entity called a "special purpose entity" is formed to operate the project. Normally, the project's creditors do not have full recourse against the sponsors. In other words, the lenders and lessors must be paid from the project's cash flows plus the sponsors' equity in the project, because the creditors have no claims against the sponsors' other assets or cash flows. Often the sponsors write "comfort" letters, giving general assurances that they will strive diligently to make the project succeed. However, these letters are not legally binding, so in project financing the lenders and lessors must focus their analysis on the inherent merits of the project and on the equity cushion provided by the sponsors.

Project financings are generally characterized by large size and a high degree of complexity. However, because project financing is tied to a specific project, it can be tailored to meet the specific needs of both the creditors and the sponsors. In particular, the financing can be structured so that both the funds provided during the construction phase and the subsequent repayments match the timing of the project's projected cash outflows and inflows.

CONCEPT REVIEW

1. What is project financing?

Summary

- The 13 provincial and territorial securities regulators govern the securities markets in Canada.
- **Private placements** are securities offerings to a limited number of investors and are exempt from many rules governing general offerings.
- **Accredited investors** include financial institutions, pension plans, high-wealth individuals, and institutional investors. These investors are eligible to buy securities in private placements.
- An **angel** is a wealthy individual who makes an equity investment in a start-up company.
- The managers of a **venture capital fund** are called **venture capitalists,** or **VCs.** They raise money from investors and make equity investments in start-up companies, called **portfolio companies.**
- **Going public** in an **initial public offering (IPO)** facilitates shareholder diversification, increases liquidity of the firm's stock, makes it easier for the firm to raise capital, establishes a value for the firm, and makes it easier for a firm to sell its products. However, reporting costs are high, operating data must be disclosed, management self-dealings are harder to arrange, the price may sink to a low level if the stock is not traded actively, and public ownership may make it harder for management to maintain control.

---

[20]For an excellent discussion of project financing, see John W. Kensinger and John D. Martin, "Project Finance: Raising Money the Old-Fashioned Way," *Journal of Applied Corporate Finance*, Fall 1988, 69–81; and Benjamin C. Esty, "Petrozuata: A Case Study on the Effective Use of Project Finance," *Journal of Applied Corporate Finance*, Fall 1999, 26–42. For a good Canadian review on project financing, see Michael Davis et al., "Building Successful Alliances in Project Financing," 3rd Annual Project Financing and Direct Lending Forum, January 12–13, 2008, *http://www.osler.com*, accessed July 15, 2008.

[21]A lessor is an individual or firm that owns buildings and equipment and then leases them to another firm. Leasing is discussed in Chapter 15.

- **Investment banks** assist in issuing securities by helping the firm determine the size of the issue and the type of securities to be used, by establishing the selling price, by selling the issue, and, in some cases, by maintaining an after-market for the stock.
- An investment bank may sell a security issue on a **best efforts basis,** or may guarantee the sale by **underwriting** the issue.
- Before an IPO, the investment bank and management team go on a **roadshow** and make presentations to potential institutional investors.
- An IPO is **oversubscribed** if investors are willing to purchase more shares than are being offered at the IPO price.
- The **spread** is the difference between the price at which an underwriter sells a security and the proceeds that the underwriter gives to the issuing company. In recent years the spread for almost all IPOs has been around 5.5%.
- An **equity carve-out** (also called a **partial public offering** or **spin-out**) is a special IPO in which a publicly traded company converts a subsidiary into a separately traded public company by selling shares of stock in the subsidiary. The parent typically retains a controlling interest.
- A **shelf registration** allows a company to prepare a general prospectus and then sell the issue in pieces over time rather than all at once.
- Securities regulators allow some reporting issuers to use a **short-form prospectus,** which reduces the costs and time to sell new securities.
- **Bought deals** involve the underwriters buying the shares before the prospectus has been filed. Bought deals are typically sold to a small number of institutional investors.
- A **seasoned equity offering** occurs when a public company issues additional shares.
- A company **goes private** when a small group of investors, including the firm's senior management, purchases all of the equity in the company. Such deals usually involve high levels of debt and are commonly called **leveraged buyouts (LBOs).**
- In **project financing,** the payments on debt are secured by the cash flows of a particular project.

Questions

14-1 Define each of the following terms:
a. Going public; new issue market; initial public offering (IPO)
b. Public offering; private placement
c. Venture capitalists; roadshow; spread
d. Securities regulators
e. Prospectus; "red herring" prospectus
f. Best efforts arrangement; underwritten arrangement
g. Project financing

14-2 The securities commissions attempt to protect investors who are purchasing newly issued securities by ensuring that the information put out by a company and its investment banks is correct and is not misleading. However, they do not provide an opinion about the real value of the securities; hence, an investor might pay too much for some new stock and consequently lose heavily. Do you think the securities commission should, as a part of every new stock or bond offering, render an opinion to investors on the proper value of the securities being offered? Explain.

14-3 How do you think each of the following items would affect a company's ability to attract new capital and the flotation costs involved in doing so?
a. A decision of a privately held company to go public
b. The increasing institutionalization of the "buy side" of the stock and bond markets
c. The trend toward "financial conglomerates" as opposed to stand-alone investment banking houses
d. Reduction in use of the preemptive right
e. The introduction of shelf registrations

14-4 Before entering into a formal agreement, investment banks carefully investigate the companies whose securities they underwrite; this is especially true of the issues of firms going public for the first time. Since the banks do not themselves plan to hold the securities but intend to sell them to others as soon as possible, why are they so concerned about making careful investigations?

Concept Review Problem

Full solutions are provided at www.nelson.com/brigham3ce.

CR-1 House Mountain Breweries (HMB) is planning an IPO. Its underwriters have said the stock will sell at $20 per share. The direct costs (legal fees, printing, etc.) will be $800,000. The underwriters will charge a 6% spread.
a.   How many shares must HMB sell to net $30 million?
b.   If the stock price closes the first day at $22, how much cash has HMB left on the table?
c.   What are HMB's total costs (direct, indirect, and underwriting) for the IPO?

Problems

Answers to odd-numbered problems appear in Appendix A.

**Easy
Problems 1–4**

14-1
Profit or Loss on
New Stock Issue

Security Brokers Inc. completed a firm commitment underwriting for Beedles Inc. The terms were as follows:

Price to public	$12 per share
Number of shares	5 million
Proceeds to Beedles	$57,000,000

The out-of-pocket expenses incurred by Security Brokers in the design and distribution of the issue were $800,000. What profit or loss would Security Brokers incur if the issue were sold to the public at an average price of
a. $12 per share?
b. $13 per share?
c. $11 per share?

14-2
Underwriting and
Flotation Expenses

Tundra Engineering, whose stock price is now $32, needs to raise $40 million in common stock. Underwriters have informed the firm's management that they must price the new issue to the public at $31 per share because of signalling effects. The underwriters' compensation will be 6% of the issue price. The firm will also incur expenses in the amount of $110,000.

How many shares must the firm sell to net $40 million after underwriting and flotation expenses?

14-3
IPO Pricing

Assume a company just sold 15,000,000 shares in an IPO for $12 per share. If the underwriter took a 5% fee, and the company incurred $450,000 in legal and consulting costs:
a.   What net proceeds did the company and underwriters receive?
b.   How much money will be left on the table if at the end of the first day the stock closed at $15? at $11? Who benefits in each case?

14-4
New Stock Issue

J. Bourne Security Products (JBSP) is a successful company, but it needs $200,000 in additional funding to grow. JBSP and an angel investor agree the business is worth $800,000 and the angel has agreed to invest the $200,000 that is needed. There are currently 40,000 shares outstanding. What is a fair price per share and how many additional shares must JBSP sell to the angel? Because the stock will be sold directly to an investor, there is no spread; assume other flotation costs are insignificant.

**Intermediate
Problems 5–9**

14-5
Dilution

Elie's Concrete Co. (ECC) currently has sales of $30 million and a net profit margin of 5%. Management is contemplating expansion, which would lead to sales growth of 8% but would also require raising $4 million through an equity issue. ECC's shares currently trade at $14.75, and its underwriter believes that the market would be receptive to the offering at $14. The underwriter will charge 5.5%. If ECC currently has 3 million shares outstanding, calculate EPS before share issuance and after (assume that sales expansion occurs after share issuance). What if any dilution is there to EPS? What must the growth in earnings be for there to be no dilution in EPS?

14-6
New Stock Issue

Harbour Resources (HR) is contemplating an IPO. The company's investment banker has provided the following information. The current risk-free rate in the market is 3%, while the market risk premium is 5%. Publicly traded companies in the same industry have betas ranging from 1.9 to 2.3. HR has paid dividends over the past 8 years and on average they have grown 4% per year. The most recent annual dividend was $3.80. An IPO will provide HR with additional investment capital to expand, so a modest increase in dividend growth to 5% is assumed. Based on the above betas, what might be a suitable range of prices for HR's stock? What conditions would suggest a price at the high or low end of the price range?

14-7
New Stock Issue

Advanced Composites Inc. (ACI) will be undertaking an IPO. The company needs to raise $90,000,000 net of all costs. ACI estimates this year's annual EPS to be $3.50. EPS is expected to grow by 6% thereafter. Although the company does not currently pay a dividend, it will begin to pay dividends based on a 20% payout ratio. ACI estimates that the beta for its competitors' stock ranges from 1.7 to 2.1. The risk-free rate is currently 3%, the market risk premium is 4%, and inflation is expected to be 1.5%. Flotation costs on the IPO will be 5.5%. How many shares must ACI sell in the IPO to raise the required funds?

14-8
New Stock Issue

EastJet Airlines is an all-equity firm with a book value of $100,000,000 and 16,000,000 shares outstanding. Its stock currently trades at $9 per share, and EPS is $0.50. EastJet wishes to issue another 1,500,000 shares to finance the purchase of a new IT system. The new system will increase EBIT by $500,000. The company believes it would have to issue shares at $8.70 and that it would incur flotation costs of 6%. EastJet's tax rate is 30%, and the company assumes its P/E ratio will remain the same. Calculate whether the company will suffer any dilution (i.e., a decrease) to its EPS, book value per share, and market price if it goes ahead with the financing and the new system. How much must EBIT change so that there is no dilution to EPS and market price?

14-9
New Stock Issue

Edelman Gem Company, a small jewellery manufacturer, has been successful and has enjoyed a good growth trend. Now Edelman is planning to go public with an issue of common stock, and it faces the problem of setting an appropriate price on the stock. The company and its investment banks believe that the proper procedure is to select several similar firms with publicly traded common stock and to make relevant comparisons.

Several jewellery manufacturers are reasonably similar to Edelman with respect to product mix, asset composition, and debt/equity proportions. Of these companies, Kennedy Jewellers and Strasburg Fashions are most similar. When analyzing the following data, assume that 2010 and 2015 were reasonably "normal" years for all three companies—that is, these years were neither especially good nor especially bad in terms of sales, earnings, and dividends. At the time of the analysis, r_{RF} was 5% and RP_M was 4%. Kennedy is listed on the TSX and Strasburg is dual-listed on both the TSX and NYSE, while Edelman will be traded on the TSX.

	Kennedy	Strasburg	Edelman (Totals)
Earnings per share*			
2015	$4.50	$7.50	$1,200,000
2010	3.00	5.50	816,000
Price per share*			
2015	$36.00	$65.00	—
Dividends per share*			
2015	$2.25	$3.75	$600,000
2010	1.50	2.75	420,000
Book value per share, 2015*	$30.00	$55.00	$9 million
Market/book ratio, 2015	120%	118%	—
Total assets, 2015	$28 million	$82 million	$20 million
Total debt, 2015	$12 million	$30 million	$11 million
Sales, 2015	$41 million	$140 million	$37 million

*The data are on a per-share basis for Kennedy and Strasburg, but are totals for Edelman.

a. Assume that Edelman has 100 shares of stock outstanding. Use this information to calculate earnings per share (EPS), dividends per share (DPS), and book value per share for Edelman.

b. Calculate earnings and dividend growth rates for the three companies.

c. On the basis of your answer to Part a, do you think Edelman's stock would sell at a price in the same "ballpark" as that of Kennedy and Strasburg, that is, in the range of $36 to $65 per share?

d. Assuming that Edelman's management can split the stock so that the 100 shares could be changed to 1,000 shares, 100,000 shares, or any other number, would such an action make sense in this case? Why or why not?

e. Now assume that Edelman did split its stock and has 400,000 shares. Calculate new values for EPS, DPS, and book value per share.

f. Calculate ROEs for the three companies for 2015.

g. Calculate dividend payout ratios for the three companies for both years.

h. Calculate debt/total assets ratios for the three companies for 2015.

i. Calculate the P/E ratios for Kennedy and Strasburg for 2015. Are these P/Es reasonable in view of relative growth, payout, and ROE data? If not, what other factors might explain them?

j. Now determine a range of values for Edelman's stock price, with 400,000 shares outstanding, by applying Kennedy's and Strasburg's P/E ratios, price/dividends ratios, and price/book value ratios to your data for Edelman.

k. Using the equation $r_s = D_1/P_0 + g$, find approximate r_s values for Kennedy and Strasburg. Then use these values in the constant growth stock price model to find a price for Edelman's stock. (*Hint:* We averaged the EPS and DPS g's for Edelman.)

l. At what price do you think Edelman's shares should be offered to the public? You will want to select a price that will be low enough to induce investors to buy the stock but not so low that it will rise sharply immediately after it is issued. Think about relative growth rates, ROEs, dividend yields, and total returns ($r_s = D_1/P_0 + g$).

Spreadsheet Problem

14-10
Build a Model:
Bond Refunding

(This problem covers material discussed in this chapter's appendix.) Start with the partial model in the file ***Ch 14 Build a Model.xlsx*** from the textbook's website. Rework Problem 14A-2, Part a, using a spreadsheet model, and answer the following question: At what interest rate on the new debt is the NPV of the refunding no longer positive?

MINI CASE

Randy's, a family-owned restaurant chain operating in Montreal, has grown to the point where expansion throughout Quebec is feasible. The proposed expansion would require the firm to raise about $15 million in new capital. Because Randy's currently has a debt ratio of 50%, and also because the family members already have all their personal wealth invested in the company, the family would like to sell common stock to the public to raise the $15 million. However, the family does want to retain voting control. You have been asked to brief the family members on the issues involved by answering the following questions:

a. What agencies regulate securities markets?

b. How are start-up firms usually financed?

c. Differentiate between a private placement and a public offering.

d. Why would a company consider going public? What are some advantages and disadvantages?

e. What are the steps of an initial public offering?

f. Would the sale be on an underwritten or best efforts basis?

g. Without actually doing any calculations, describe how the preliminary offering range for the price of an IPO would be determined.

h. What is a roadshow? What is book building?

i. Describe the typical first-day return of an IPO and the long-term returns to IPO investors.

j. What are the direct and indirect costs of an IPO?

k. What are equity carve-outs?

l. In what other ways are investment banks involved in issuing securities?

m. What is meant by "going private"? What are some advantages and disadvantages?

n. Explain how firms manage the risk structure of their debt with project financing.

appendix 14A

Refunding Operations

Corporate debt sold during the late 1980s had interest rates in the 9% to 12% range. Because the call protection on much of this debt has ended, and because interest rates have fallen since the debt was issued, many companies are analyzing the pros and cons of bond refundings.

The decision to refund a security is analyzed in much the same way as a capital budgeting expenditure. The costs of refunding (the investment outlays) include (1) the call premium paid for the privilege of calling the old issue, (2) the costs of selling the new issue, (3) the tax savings from the flotation costs on the new issue, and (4) the net interest that must be paid while both issues are outstanding (the new issue is often sold prior to the refunding to ensure that the funds will be available). The annual cash flows, in a capital budgeting sense, are the interest payments that are saved each year. For example, if the interest expense on the old issue is $1,000,000, whereas that on the new issue is $700,000, the $300,000 reduction in interest savings constitutes an annual benefit.[1]

The net present value method is used to analyze the advantages of refunding: The future cash flows are discounted back to the present, and then this discounted value is compared with the cash outlays associated with the refunding. The firm should refund the bond only if the present value of the savings exceeds the cost—that is, if the NPV of the refunding operation is positive.

In the discounting process, the after-tax cost of the new debt, r_d, should be used as the discount rate. The reason is that there is relatively little risk to the savings—cash flows in a refunding decision are known with relative certainty, which is quite unlike the situation with cash flows in most capital budgeting decisions.

The easiest way to examine the refunding decision is through an example. Microchip Computer Company has a $60 million bond issue outstanding that has a 12% annual coupon interest rate and 20 years remaining to maturity. The bond has a call provision that makes it possible for the company to retire the issue at this time by calling the bonds in at a 10% call premium. Investment banks have assured the company that it could sell an additional $60 million to $70 million worth of new 20-year bonds at an interest rate of 7%. To ensure that the funds required to pay off the old debt will be available, the new bonds will be sold 1 month before the old issue is called, so for 1 month, interest will have to be paid on two issues. Current short-term interest rates are 4%. Predictions are that long-term interest rates are unlikely to fall below 7%. Flotation costs on a new refunding issue will amount to $2,650,000, and the firm's tax rate is 35%. Should the company refund the $60 million of 12% bonds?

The following steps outline the decision process; they are summarized in the spreadsheet in Table 14A-1. This spreadsheet is part of the spreadsheet model, *Ch 14 Tool Kit.xlsx*, developed for this chapter. The range of cells from A15 through H20 shows input data needed for the analysis, which were just discussed.

See *Ch 14 Tool Kit.xlsx* at the textbook's website for details. **www .nelson.com/brigham3ce.**

[1]During the early 1980s, there was a flurry of work on the pros and cons of refunding bond issues that had fallen to deep discounts as a result of rising interest rates. At such times, the company could go into the market, buy its debt at a low price, and retire it. The difference between the bonds' par values and the prices the company paid would be reported as income, and taxes would have to be paid on it. The results of the research on the refunding of discount issues suggest that bonds should not, in general, be refunded after a rise in rates. See Andrew J. Kalotay, "On the Structure and Valuation of Debt Refundings," *Financial Management*, Spring 1982, 41–42; and Robert S. Harris, "The Refunding of Discounted Debt: An Adjusted Present Value Analysis," *Financial Management*, Winter 1980, 7–12.

Step 1: Determine the Investment Outlay
Required to Refund the Issue

Row 26. *Call premium on old issue:*

$$Before\ tax:\ 0.10(\$60,000,000) = \$6,000,000$$

Microchip must spend $6 million on the call premium, which is a non-tax-deductible expense. This amount is shown in Row 26 of Table 14A-1.

Row 27. *Flotation costs on new issue:* Flotation costs on the new issue will be $2,650,000. For tax purposes, flotation costs are amortized straight line over 5 years.

Rows 29 and 30. *Additional interest:* One month's "extra" interest on the old issue, after taxes, costs $390,000:

$$(Dollar\ amount)(1/12\ of\ 12\%)(1 - T) = Interest\ cost$$
$$(\$60,000,000)(0.01)(0.65) = \$390,000$$

However, the proceeds from the new issue can be invested in short-term securities for 1 month. Thus, $60 million invested at a rate of 4% will return $130,000 in after-tax interest:

$$(\$60,000,000)(1/12\ of\ 4\%)(1 - T) = Interest\ earned$$
$$(\$60,000,000)(0.00333)(0.65) = \$130,000$$

The net after-tax additional interest cost is thus $180,000:

Interest paid on old issue	$(390,000)
Interest earned on short-term securities	130,000
Net additional interest	$(260,000)

These figures are reflected in Rows 29 and 30 of Table 14A-1.

Row 31. *Total after-tax investment:* The total investment outlay required to refund the bond issue, which will be financed by debt, is thus $8,910,000.[2]

Call premium	$(6,000,000)
Flotation costs, new	(2,650,000)
Net additional interest	(260,000)
Total investment	$(8,910,000)

This total is shown in Row 31 of Table 14A-1.

Step 2: Calculate the Annual Flotation Cost Tax Effects

Row 34. *Tax savings on flotation costs on the new issue:* Given that flotation costs are amortized over 5 years, the annual tax deduction is

$$\frac{\$2,650,000}{5} = \$530,000$$

---

[2]The investment outlay (in this case, $8,910,000) is usually obtained by increasing the amount of the new bond issue. In the example given, the new issue would be $68,910,000. However, the interest on the additional debt *should not* be deducted at Step 3 because the $8,910,000 itself will be deducted at Step 4. If additional interest on the $8,910,000 were deducted at Step 3, interest would, in effect, be deducted twice. The situation here is exactly like that in regular capital budgeting decisions. Even though some debt may be used to finance a project, interest on that debt is not subtracted when developing the annual cash flows. Rather, the annual cash flows are *discounted* at the project's cost of capital.

TABLE 14A-1   Spreadsheet for the Bond Refunding Decision

	A	B	C	D	E	F	G	H
12								
13	Input Data (in thousands of dollars)							
14								
15	Existing bond issue =			$60,000		New bond issue =		$60,000
16						New flotation cost =		$2,650
17	Maturity of original debt =			25		New bond maturity =		20
18	Years since old debt issue =			5		New cost of debt =		7.0%
19	Call premium (%) =			10.0%		Tax rate =		35.0%
20	Original coupon rate =			12.0%		Short-term interest rate =		4%
21	After-tax cost of new debt =			4.55%				
22								
23	Schedule of cash flows							
24						Before-tax	After-tax	
25	*Investment Outlay*							
26	Call premium on the old bond					($6,000.0)	($6,000.0)	
27	Flotation costs on new issue					($2,650.0)	($2,650.0)	
28								
29	Extra interest paid on old issue					($600.0)	($390.0)	
30	Interest earned on short-term investment					$200.0	$130.0	
31	Total after-tax investment						($8,910.0)	
32								
33	*Annual Flotation Cost Tax Effects: t=1 to 5*							
34	Annual tax savings from new issue flotation costs					$530.0	$185.5	
35								
36	Net flotation cost tax savings					$530.0	$185.5	
37								
38	*Annual Interest Savings Due to Refunding: t=1 to 20*							
39	Interest on old bond					$7,200.0	$4,680.0	
40	Interest on new bond					($4,200.0)	($2,730.0)	
41	Net interest savings					$3,000.0	$1,950.0	
42								
43	Calculating the annual flotation cost tax effects and the annual interest savings							
44								
45	Annual Flotation Cost Tax Effects					Annual Interest Savings		
46	Flotation cost amortization period (Nper)			5		Maturity of the new bond (Nper)		20
47	After-tax cost of new debt (Rate)			4.6%		After-tax cost of new debt (Rate)		4.6%
48	Annual flotation cost tax savings (Pmt)			$186		Annual interest savings (Pmt)		$1,950
49								
50	Since the annual flotation cost tax effects occur for the next 5 years, and the interest savings occur for the next 20 years, they							
51	represent annuities. To evaluate this project, we must find the present values of these savings. Using the function wizard							
52	and solving for present value, we find that the present values of these annuities are:							
53								
54	NPV of annual flotation cost savings			$813.207		NPV of annual interest savings		$25,255.935
55								
56	Hence, the net present value of this bond refunding project will be the sum of the initial outlay and the present values of the							
57	annual flotation cost tax effects and interest savings.							
58								
59	Bond Refunding NPV =	Initial Outlay			+	PV of flotation costs +	PV of interest savings	
60	Bond Refunding NPV =	($8,910.000)			+	$813.21	+	$25,255.935
61								
62	Bond Refund NPV =	$17,159.142						

Since our spreadsheet shows dollars in thousands, this number appears as $530 on the spreadsheet. Because the firm is in the 35% tax bracket, it has a tax savings of $530,000(0.35) = $185,500 a year for 5 years. This is an annuity of $185,500 for 5 years, and it is shown in Row 36.

Step 3: Calculate the Annual Interest Savings

Row 39. *Interest on old bond, after tax:* The annual after-tax interest on the old issue is $4.68 million:

$$\$60,000,000)(0.12)(0.65) = \$4,680,000$$

This is shown in Row 39 of Table 14A-1.

Row 40. *Interest on new bond, after tax:* The new issue has an annual after-tax cost of $2.73 million:

$$(\$60,000,000)(0.07)(0.65) = \$2,730,000$$

This is shown in Row 40.

Row 41. *Net annual interest savings:* Thus, the net annual interest savings is $1,950,000:

Interest on old bonds, after tax	$4,680,000
Interest on new bonds, after tax	2,730,000
Annual interest savings, after tax	$1,950,000

This is shown in Row 41.

Step 4: Determine the NPV of the Refunding

Row 54. *PV of the benefits:* The PV of the annual after-tax flotation cost benefit can be found with a financial calculator, with N = 5, I/YR = 4.55, PMT = 185,500, and FV = 0. Solving for PV shows the flotation cost savings have a present value equal to $813,207. The PV of the $1,950,000 annual after-tax interest savings can be found with a financial calculator, with N = 20, I/YR = 4.55, PMT = $1,950,000 and FV = 0. Solving for PV shows the present value of after-tax interest cost savings is $25,255,935.

These values are used in Row 60 when finding the NPV of the refunding operation:

PV of the tax shield	$ 813,207
PV of the interest savings	25,255,935
Net investment outlay	(8,910,000)
NPV from refunding	$ 17,159,142

Because the net present value of the refunding is positive, it would be profitable to refund the old bond issue.

We can summarize the data shown in Table 14A-1 using a time line (amounts in thousands) as shown below:

Time Period	0	4.55%	1	2	5	6	20
After-tax investment	−8,910						
Flotation cost tax effects			185.5	185.5 ...	185.5		
Interest savings			1,950	1,950 ...	1,950	1,950 ...	1,950
Net cash flows	−8,910		2,135.5	2,135.5 ...	2,135.5	1,950 ...	1,950

$NPV_{4.55\%} = \$17,159.$

FINANCE: IN FOCUS

Sherritt Calls and Offers to Exchange 9.875% 2010 Senior Notes

In 2005, Sherritt International decided it was in its best interests to call its 2010 senior unsecured notes, even at a hefty premium of $109.875. Noteholders were given a choice of cash or an exchange for new 7.875% 2012 senior unsecured debentures at a rate of $108.787 principal amount for each senior note exchanged. Making the offer more interesting was the fact that previously issued 7.875% debentures were trading at a value of $110.922 at the time of offering.

Of the $105 million face value notes being called, all but $14.4 million were exchanged. The remaining notes were paid out in cash. The offering was made under a shelf prospectus. The prospectus explicitly stated that any of the new debentures issued would go directly to refund the old notes.

Source: Sherritt International Corporation, "Prospectus Supplement," December 9, 2005; Sherritt International, "Sherritt Announces Redemption and Exchange Offer for 9.875% Senior Notes," Press Release, December 9, 2005, http://www.sherritt.com/, accessed July 14, 2008; Sherritt International, "Sherritt Announces Results of Exchange Offer of Senior Notes," Press Release, December 30, 2005, http://www.sherritt.com/, accessed July 14, 2008.

Several other points should be made. First, because the cash flows are based on differences between contractual obligations, their risk is the same as that of the underlying obligations. Therefore, the present values of the cash flows should be found by discounting at the firm's least risky rate—its after-tax cost of marginal debt. Second, since the refunding operation is advantageous to the firm, it must be disadvantageous to bondholders; they must give up their 12% bonds and reinvest in new ones yielding 7%. This points out the danger of the call provision to bondholders, and it also explains why noncallable bonds command higher prices than callable bonds. Third, although it is not emphasized in the example, we assumed that the firm raises the investment required to undertake the refunding operation (the $8,910,000 shown in Row 31 of Table 14A-1) as debt. This should be feasible because the refunding operation will improve the interest coverage ratio, even though a larger amount of debt is outstanding.[3] Fourth, we set up our example in such a way that the new issue had the same maturity as the remaining life of the old one. Often, the old bonds have a relatively short time to maturity (say, 5 to 10 years), whereas the new bonds have a much longer maturity (say, 25 to 30 years). In such a situation, the analysis should be set up similarly to an equivalent annual annuity (EAA) analysis in capital budgeting, which was discussed in Chapter 10. Finally, refunding decisions are well suited for analysis with a spreadsheet program. Spreadsheets such as the one shown in Table 14A-1 are easy to set up, and once the model has been constructed, it is easy to vary the assumptions (especially the assumption about the interest rate on the refunding issue) and to see how such changes affect the NPV.

CONCEPT REVIEW

1. How is bond refunding like a capital budgeting project?

Problems

Challenging Problems

14A-1
Refunding Analysis

Jan Volk, financial manager of Green Sea Services (GSS), has been asked by her boss to review GSS's outstanding debt issues for possible bond refunding. Five years ago, GSS issued $40,000,000 of 9%, 25-year debt. The issue, with semiannual coupons, is currently callable at a premium of 9%, or $90 for each $1,000 par value bond. Flotation costs on this issue were 6%, or $2,400,000.

Volk believes that GSS could issue 20-year debt today with a coupon rate of 6%. The firm has placed many issues in the capital markets during the past 10 years, and its debt flotation costs are currently estimated to be 4% of the issue's value. GSS's tax rate is 30%. Assume Volk will time the sale of the new bonds to match the refunding of the existing bonds (i.e., there is no overlap period).

Help Volk conduct the refunding analysis by answering the following questions:

a. What is the total dollar call premium required to call the old issue? Is it tax deductible? What is the net after-tax cost of the call?
b. What is the dollar flotation cost on the new issue? Is it immediately tax deductible? What is the after-tax flotation cost?
c. What is the cash outlay required to refund the old issue?
d. What is the annual tax savings that arises from amortizing the flotation costs on the new issue?
e. What is the semiannual after-tax interest savings that would result from the refunding?
f. Thus far, Volk has identified two future cash flows: (1) the new-issue flotation cost tax savings and (2) after-tax interest savings. What is the appropriate discount rate to apply to these future cash flows? What is the present value of the flotation cost tax shield and of the interest savings?
g. What is the NPV of refunding?

---

[3]See Aharon R. Ofer and Robert A. Taggart, Jr., "Bond Refunding: A Clarifying Analysis," *Journal of Finance*, March 1977, 21–30, for a discussion of how the method of financing the refunding affects the analysis.

14A-2
Refunding Analysis

South Tel Technologies is considering whether or not to refund a $90 million, 8% annual coupon, 30-year bond issue that was sold 5 years ago. South Tel's investment banks have indicated that the company could sell a new 25-year issue at an interest rate of 6.5 (annual payments) in today's market. Neither they nor South Tel's management anticipate that interest rates will fall below 6.5% any time soon, but there is a chance that rates will increase.

A call premium of 7% would be required to retire the old bonds, and flotation costs on the new issue would amount to $6 million. South Tel's tax rate is 30%. The new bonds would be issued 1 month before the old bonds are called, with the proceeds being invested in short-term government securities returning 2% annually during the interim period. Should South Tel refund its outstanding bond?

chapter 15

Lease Financing

The Forty-Year-Old Virgin, starring Steve Carell, cost $26 million to produce but grossed over $177 million at box offices worldwide. That's a lot of money, but there is a 28-year-old Virgin making even more: Virgin Atlantic, the airline, turned 28 in 2012.

Virgin is privately held by Sir Richard Branson's Virgin Group (with Singapore Airlines owning a 49% share), so we don't know exactly how much money Virgin is making, but in mid-2009 Virgin placed an order for 10 Airbus A330-300 jet airliners that cost about $2.1 billion. Virgin purchased 6 of the jets and then immediately sold them to AerCap Holdings NV, a Dutch company specializing in leasing aircraft. AerCap then leased the jets to back to Virgin. In addition, AerCap purchased 4 of the jets directly from Airbus and then leased them to Virgin. The bottom line is that Virgin didn't have to pony up $2.1 billion to get the 10 jets, but Virgin gets to operate the aircraft because it makes lease payments to AerCap.

Virgin had previously placed orders with Boeing, a U.S. company, for Boeing's 787 Dreamliner. Because Boeing experienced a series of production delays, Virgin turned to Airbus, which is owned by the European Aeronautic Defence and Space Company (EADS). EADS itself was formed in 2000 from a number of smaller companies at the encouragement of many European governments desiring a European company with the size and scope to be a major competitor in the global aviation and defense business.

Thus, the 10 Airbus jets will be produced in Europe by EADS, owned by the Dutch company AerCap, operated by the U.K. company Virgin Atlantic, and flown all over the world. As you read this chapter, think about the ways that leasing helps support global operations.

Firms generally own fixed assets and report them on their balance sheets, but it is the use of assets that is important, not their ownership *per se.* One way to obtain the *use* of facilities and equipment is to buy them, but an alternative is to lease them. Prior to the 1950s, leasing was generally associated with real estate—land and buildings. Today, however, it is possible to lease virtually any kind of fixed asset, and currently 30% of all new capital equipment is financed through lease arrangements.[1]

15.1 Types of Leases

The textbook's website contains an *Excel* file that will guide you through the chapter's calculations. The file for this chapter is *Ch 15 Tool Kit.xlsx,* and we encourage you to open the file and follow along as you read the chapter. **www.nelson.com/ brigham3ce**

Lease transactions involve two parties: the lessor, who owns the property, and the lessee, who obtains use of the property in exchange for one or more lease, or rental, payments. (Note that the term *lessee* is pronounced "less-ee," not "lease-ee," and *lessor* is pronounced "less-or.") Because both parties must agree before a lease transaction can be completed, this chapter discusses leasing from the perspectives of both the lessor and the lessee.

Leasing takes several different forms, the five most important being (1) operating leases, (2) financial, or capital, leases, (3) sale-and-leaseback arrangements, (4) combination leases, and (5) synthetic leases.

Operating Leases

Operating leases generally provide for both *financing* and *maintenance.* IBM was one of the pioneers of the operating lease contract, and computers and office copying machines, together with automobiles, trucks, and aircraft, are the primary types of equipment involved in operating leases. Ordinarily, operating leases require the lessor to maintain and service the leased equipment, and the cost of the maintenance is built into the lease payments.

Another important characteristic of operating leases is that they are *not fully amortized.* In other words, the rental payments required under the lease contract are not sufficient for the lessor to recover the full cost of the asset. However, the lease contract is written for a period considerably shorter than the expected economic life of the asset, so the lessor can expect to recover all costs either by subsequent renewal payments, by releasing the asset to another lessee, or by selling the asset.

A final feature of operating leases is that they often contain a *cancellation clause* that gives the lessee the right to cancel the lease and return the asset before the expiration of the

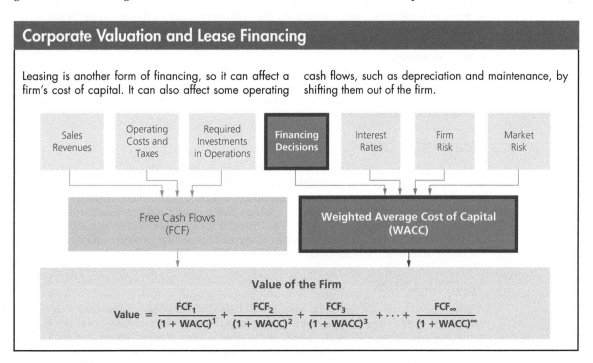

Corporate Valuation and Lease Financing

Leasing is another form of financing, so it can affect a firm's cost of capital. It can also affect some operating cash flows, such as depreciation and maintenance, by shifting them out of the firm.

Sales Revenues | Operating Costs and Taxes | Required Investments in Operations | Financing Decisions | Interest Rates | Firm Risk | Market Risk

Free Cash Flows (FCF)

Weighted Average Cost of Capital (WACC)

Value of the Firm

$$\text{Value} = \frac{FCF_1}{(1 + WACC)^1} + \frac{FCF_2}{(1 + WACC)^2} + \frac{FCF_3}{(1 + WACC)^3} + \cdots + \frac{FCF_\infty}{(1 + WACC)^\infty}$$

---

[1]For a detailed treatment of leasing, see James S. Schallheim, *Lease or Buy? Principles for Sound Decision Making* (Boston: Harvard Business School Press, 1994).

basic lease agreement. This is an important consideration to the lessee, for it means that the asset can be returned if it is rendered obsolete by technological developments or is no longer needed because of a change in the lessee's business.

Financial, or Capital, Leases

Financial leases, sometimes called **capital leases,** are differentiated from operating leases in that they (1) *do not* provide for maintenance service, (2) *are not* cancellable, and (3) *are* fully amortized (i.e., the lessor receives rental payments equal to the full price of the leased equipment plus a return on invested capital). In a typical arrangement, the firm that will use the equipment (the lessee) selects the specific items it requires and negotiates the price with the manufacturer. The user firm then arranges to have a leasing company (the lessor) buy the equipment from the manufacturer and simultaneously executes a lease contract. The terms of the lease generally call for full amortization of the lessor's investment, plus a rate of return on the unamortized balance that is close to the percentage rate the lessee would have paid on a secured loan. For example, if the lessee had to pay 10% for a loan, then a rate of about 10% would be built into the lease contract.

The lessee is generally given an option to renew the lease at a reduced rate upon expiration of the basic lease. However, the basic lease usually cannot be cancelled unless the lessor is paid in full. Also, the lessee generally pays the property taxes, and insurance on the leased property. Since the lessor receives a return *after*, or *net of*, these payments, this type of lease is often called a "net, net" lease.

Sale-and-Leaseback Arrangements

Under a **sale-and-leaseback** arrangement, a firm that owns land, buildings, or equipment sells the property to another firm and simultaneously executes an agreement to lease the property back for a stated period under specific terms. The capital supplier could be an insurance company, a commercial bank, a specialized leasing company, the finance arm of an industrial firm, a limited partnership, or an individual investor. The sale-and-leaseback plan is an alternative to a mortgage.

Note that the seller immediately receives the purchase price put up by the buyer. At the same time, the seller-lessee retains the use of the property. The parallel to borrowing is carried over to the lease payment schedule. Under a mortgage loan arrangement, the lender would normally receive a series of equal payments just sufficient to amortize the loan and to provide a specified rate of return on the outstanding loan balance. Under a sale-and-leaseback arrangement, the lease payments are set up exactly the same way—the payments are just sufficient to return the full purchase price to the investor, plus a stated return on the lessor's investment.

Sale-and-leaseback arrangements are almost the same as financial leases, the major difference being that the leased equipment is used, not new, and the lessor buys it from the user-lessee instead of a manufacturer or a distributor. A sale-and-leaseback is thus a special type of financial lease.

Combination Leases

Many lessors now offer leases under a wide variety of terms. Therefore, in practice leases often do not fit exactly into the operating lease or financial lease category but combine some features of each. Such leases are called **combination leases.** To illustrate, cancellation clauses are normally associated with operating leases, but many of today's financial leases also contain cancellation clauses. However, in financial leases these clauses generally include prepayment provisions whereby the lessee must make penalty payments sufficient to enable the lessor to recover the unamortized cost of the leased property.

Synthetic Leases

A fifth type of lease, the synthetic lease, should also be mentioned. These leases were first used in the early 1990s, and they became very popular in the mid- to late-1990s, when companies such as Enron and Tyco, as well as "normal" companies in Canada and the United States, discovered that synthetic leases could be used to keep debt off their balance sheets. In a typical *synthetic lease*, a corporation that wanted to acquire an asset—generally real estate, with a very long life—with debt would first establish a *special-purpose entity*, or SPE. The SPE would then obtain financing, typically 97% debt provided by a financial institution and 3% equity provided by a party other than the corporation itself.[2] The SPE would then use the funds to acquire the property, and the corporation would lease the asset from the SPE, generally for a term of 3 to 5 years but with an option to extend the lease, which the firm generally expected to exercise. Because of the relatively short term of the lease, it was deemed to be an operating lease and hence did not have to be capitalized and shown on the balance sheet.

A corporation that set up SPEs was required to do one of three things when the lease expired: (1) pay off the SPE's 97% loan, (2) refinance the loan at the currently going interest rate, if the lender was willing to refinance at all, or (3) sell the asset and make up any shortfall between the sale price and the amount of the loan. Thus, the corporate user was guaranteeing the loan, yet it did not have to show an obligation on its balance sheet.

Synthetic leases stayed under the radar until 2001. As we discuss in the next section, long-term leases must be capitalized and shown on the balance sheet. Synthetic leases were designed to get around this requirement, and neither corporations such as Enron and Tyco that used them nor accounting firms such as Arthur Andersen that approved them wanted to have anyone look closely at them. However, after the scandals of the early 2000s, the financial community began to seriously discuss SPEs and synthetic leases. Investors and bankers subjectively downgraded companies that made heavy use of them, and boards of directors began to tell their CFOs to stop using them and to close down the ones that existed. The International Financial Reporting Standards (IFRS) and FASB in the United States have updated their disclosure requirements for SPEs and synthetic leases, with the goal of giving investors and analysts more information on the profit and loss impact these structures may have on the reporting company.

CONCEPT REVIEW

1. Who are the two parties to a lease transaction?
2. What is the difference between an operating lease and a financial, or capital, lease?
3. What is a sale-and-leaseback transaction?
4. What is a combination lease?
5. What is a synthetic lease?

15.2 Tax Effects

The Canada Revenue Agency (CRA) allows leases to be fully tax deductible. Although it is possible to structure a lease contract to allow for accelerated tax deductions—that is, deductions greater than would be possible if CCA was being claimed on a purchased asset—companies must now watch out for the tax implications of a low-buyout option at lease end.[3] Under the Income Tax Act, if the purchase option is exercised, the CRA will for tax purposes deem the cost to the lessee to be the lesser of (1) the fair market value of the asset at the time of purchase and (2) the option purchase price plus all the lease payments previously made under the lease contract. The difference between the option purchase price and CRA's deemed cost is considered to have been claimed by the lessee as CCA and therefore eligible to be taxed as recapture if the asset is ever sold for a price greater than the purchase option. In effect, the tax savings from the previous lease payments are somewhat offset by the taxes paid on the recapture. The fact that most assets decline in value over time, however, mitigates the impact of this tax rule.

Also, the CRA restricts certain assets on which a lessor may claim full CCA. This change, introduced in 1989, stops nontaxable organizations such as hospitals from entering into sales-and-leaseback agreements for the sole purpose of transferring otherwise unusable

---

[2]Enron's CFO, Andy Fastow, and other insiders provided the equity for many of Enron's SPEs. Also, a number of Merrill Lynch's executives provided SPE equity, allegedly to enable Merrill Lynch to obtain profitable investment banking deals. The very fact that SPEs are so well suited to conceal what's going on helped those who used them engage in shady deals that would have at least raised eyebrows had they been disclosed. In fact, Fastow pled guilty to two counts of conspiracy in connection with Enron's accounting fraud and ultimate bankruptcy. For more on this subject, see W. R. Pollert and E. J. Glickman, "Synthetic Leases Under Fire," at http://www.strategicfinancemag.com, October 2002.

[3]The legal nature of the contract must still be considered. A "lease" contract could in fact be a disguised conditional sales contract, in which case a court would not recognize the contract as a lease arrangement.

CCA benefits to another taxable party (the lessor). Under this arrangement, the lessor passes on part of the tax savings to the hospital through lower lease payments. Assets for which lessors are still able to claim full CCA include office furniture and equipment, most computer equipment, cars and trucks, buildings, and railway cars.[4]

Leasing can be used only within limits to speed up the effective amortization schedule. Even so, there are still times when very substantial benefits can be derived from a leasing arrangement. For example, a leasing company may be able to buy assets in quantity, thus obtaining a better deal than if a firm bought a single or a small number of units. Likewise, leasing companies may be able to provide maintenance and servicing more cost-effectively than an individual company could by itself. In these cases, the leasing company could then share these benefits with the lessee by charging lower lease payments. This point will be discussed later in the chapter. Many other tax implications arise from leasing that are beyond the scope of this chapter but that are covered in specialized tax courses.[5]

15.3 Financial Statement Effects

Under certain conditions, neither the leased assets nor the liabilities under the lease contract appear directly on the firm's balance sheet. For this reason, leasing is often called **off–balance sheet financing.** This point is illustrated in Table 15-1 by the balance sheets of two hypothetical firms, B (for "borrow") and L (for "lease"). Initially, the balance sheets of both firms are identical, and they both have debt ratios of 50%. Next, each firm decides to acquire a fixed asset costing $100. Firm B borrows $100 and buys the asset, so both an asset and a liability go on its balance sheet, and its debt ratio rises from 50% to 75%. Firm L leases the equipment. The lease may call for fixed charges as high as or even higher than the loan, and the obligations assumed under the lease may be equally or more dangerous from the standpoint of potential bankruptcy, but the firm's debt ratio remains at only 50%.

To correct this problem, International Accounting Standards, (IAS 17), require that firms entering into financial (or capital) leases restate their balance sheets and report the leased asset as a fixed asset and the present value of the future lease payments as a liability.[6] This process is called **capitalizing the lease,** and its net effect is to cause Firms B and L to have similar balance sheets, both of which will, in essence, resemble the one shown for Firm B.

The logic behind IAS 17 is as follows. If a firm signs a financial lease contract, its obligation to make lease payments is just as binding as if it had signed a loan agreement—the

TABLE 15-1 Balance Sheet Effects of Leasing

	Before Asset Increase			After Asset Increase						
	Firms B and L			Firm B, Which Borrows and Buys				Firm L, Which Leases		
Current assets	$ 50	Debt	$ 50	Current assets	$ 50	Debt	$150	Current assets	$ 50	Debt	$ 50
Fixed assets	50	Equity	50	Fixed assets	150	Equity	50	Fixed assets	50	Equity	50
	$100		$100		$200		$200		$100		$100
Debt/assets ratio:			50%				75%				50%

[4]The "specified leasing property rules" categorize assets as exempt or nonexempt. Today, lessors may claim full CCA on exempt assets only. For nonexempt assets, Section 16.1 of the Income Tax Act allows both parties to agree that for tax purposes only, the lessee may treat the leased asset as capital property, in which case the lessee may claim the CCA and only the interest portion of the lease payment. For nonexempt assets, lessees often utilize this Section 16.1 allowance and are deemed to "own" the asset for tax purposes in order to claim CCA.
[5]For a review of the legal and tax aspects of leasing in Canada, see John J. Tobin, Jim Hong, and Richard Johnson, "Asset/Equipment Finance and Leasing," *2007/2008 Lexpert® CCCA/ACCJE Corporate Counsel Directory & Yearbook,* 162–165.
[6]IAS 17 on leases spells out in detail both the conditions under which the lease must be capitalized and the procedures for capitalizing it.

FINANCE: IN FOCUS

Capitalizing Leases and Financial Measures

A study from Georgia Tech's Financial Analysis Lab sheds some light regarding the financial impact that retail companies may face when the accounting bodies require all leases to be capitalized. The authors reworked the financial statements of 19 large retailers by placing operating leases on their balance sheets while also making any necessary changes to their income statements. The results were interesting.

Key Measure	Median Change (%)
EBITDA	+22.5
Earnings per Share	−5.3
Total Liabilities	+26.4
Liabilities/Equity	+26.4
ROA (before-tax)	−1.7
ROE (after-tax)	−0.6

EBITDA increases significantly as rents (lease payments) are deducted and replaced with interest and depreciation expenses, consistent with the capitalized

treatment of leases, both of which are not included in the EBITDA number. Earnings per share declines on average, for the depreciation and interest expenses from the capitalized leases are greater than the lease payments they replace. Perhaps the most significant impact is on liabilities—a median increase of 26%. The liabilities/equity ratio likewise shows the same increase. Profitability measures such as ROE and ROA show declines in both cases. Another point worth noting was the variation in changes between companies. For instance, Kohl's showed an increase in financial leverage of 135%, compared to a more modest increase of 8% for Wal-Mart. Likewise, Dollar Tree's ROE decreased 16%, while JC Penny had a slight increase! There is no doubt that the rule changes will impact companies, though the extent of the changes will vary widely. Although the changes are largely accounting based, they may well affect the debt covenants and performance measures that most companies have in place.

Source: Charles W. Mulford and Mark Gram, "The Effects of Lease Capitalization on Various Financial Measures: An Analysis of the Retail Industry," Georgia Tech Financial Analysis Lab, June 12, 2007, http://www.mgt.gatech.edu/finlab, accessed February 14, 2012.

failure to make lease payments can bankrupt a firm just as fast as the failure to make principal and interest payments on a loan. Therefore, for all intents and purposes, a financial lease is identical to a loan.[7] This being the case, if a firm signs a financial lease agreement, this has the effect of raising its true debt ratio, and thus its true capital structure is changed. Therefore, if the firm had previously established a target capital structure, and if there is no reason to think that the optimal capital structure has changed, then lease financing requires additional equity support, exactly like debt financing.

If disclosure of the lease in our Table 15-1 example were not made, then Firm L could deceive its investors into thinking that its financial position is stronger than it really is. Thus, even before IAS 17 was issued, firms were required to disclose the existence of long-term leases in footnotes to their financial statements. At that time, it was debatable whether or not investors recognized fully the impact of leases and, in effect, would see that Firms B and L were in essentially the same financial position. Some people argued that leases were not fully recognized, even by sophisticated investors. If this were the case, then leasing could alter the capital structure decision in a significant manner—a firm could increase its true leverage through a lease arrangement, and this procedure would have a smaller effect on its cost of conventional debt, r_d, and on its cost of equity, r_s, than if it had borrowed directly and reflected this fact on its balance sheet. These benefits of leasing would accrue to existing investors at the expense of new investors who would, in effect, be deceived by the fact that the firm's balance sheet did not reflect its true financial leverage.

The question of whether investors were truly deceived was debated but never resolved. Those who believed strongly in efficient markets thought that investors were not deceived and that footnotes were sufficient, while those who questioned market efficiency thought that all leases should be capitalized. IAS 17 represents a compromise between these two positions, though one that is tilted heavily toward those who favour capitalization.

---

[7]There are, however, certain legal differences between loans and leases. In the event of liquidation in bankruptcy, a lessor is entitled to take possession of the leased asset, and if the value of the asset is less than the required payments under the lease, the lessor can enter a claim (as a general creditor). Also, after bankruptcy has been declared but before the case has been resolved, lease payments may be continued, whereas all payments on debts are generally stopped. The lender under a secured loan arrangement has a security interest in the asset, meaning that if it is sold, the lender will be given the proceeds, and the full unsatisfied portion of the lender's claim will be treated as a general creditor obligation. It is not possible to state, as a general rule, whether a supplier of capital is in a stronger position as a secured creditor or as a lessor.

A lease is classified as a capital lease, and hence must be capitalized and shown directly on the balance sheet, if one or more of the following conditions exist:

1. The lease transfers ownership of the asset to the lessee by the end of the lease term.
2. The lessee has the option to purchase the asset at a price that is expected to be sufficiently lower than fair value at the date the option becomes exercisable that, at the inception of the lease, it is reasonably certain the option will be exercised.
3. The lease term is for the major part of the economic life of the asset, even if title is not transferred.
4. At the inception of the lease, the present value of the minimum lease payments amounts to at least substantially all of the fair value of the leased asset.[8]
5. The leased assets are of a specialized nature such that only the lessee can use them without major modifications.

These rules, together with strong footnote disclosure rules for operating leases, were supposed to be sufficient to ensure that no one would be fooled by lease financing.

Even with the above restrictions, the IAS is still planning (as of 2014) on treating all leases the same. If the changes are implemented, operating leases will in the future be capitalized. The leases will be shown as a "right-of-use" asset on the balance sheet, along with the rental liability the company faces for use of that asset. Placing all leases on a company's balance sheet is considered a significant change that could impact financial ratios, such as leverage and profits, which in turn would directly impact debt covenants and corporate performance measurements.

CONCEPT REVIEW

1. Why is lease financing sometimes referred to as off–balance sheet financing?
2. What is the difference in the balance sheet treatment of a lease that is capitalized versus one that is not?

15.4 Evaluation by the Lessee

See **Ch 15 Tool Kit.xlsx** at the textbook's website for all calculations.

See **Web Extension 15B** on the textbook's website for a discussion on leasing feedback.

Leases are evaluated by both the lessee and the lessor. The lessee must determine whether leasing an asset is less costly than buying it, and the lessor must decide whether the lease payments provide a satisfactory return on the capital invested in the leased asset. This section focuses on the lessee's analysis.

In the typical case, the events leading to a lease arrangement follow the sequence described below. We should note that a degree of uncertainty exists regarding the theoretically correct way to evaluate lease-versus-purchase decisions, and some very complex decision models have been developed to aid in the analysis. However, the simple analysis given here leads to the correct decision in all the cases we have ever encountered.

1. The firm decides to acquire a particular building or piece of equipment; this decision is based on regular capital budgeting procedures. Whether to acquire the asset is *not* part of the typical lease analysis—in a lease analysis, we are concerned simply with whether to obtain the use of the machine by lease or by purchase. Thus, for the lessee, the lease decision is typically just a financing decision. However, if the effective cost of capital obtained by leasing is substantially lower than the cost of debt, then the cost of capital used in the capital budgeting decision would have to be recalculated, and perhaps projects formerly deemed unacceptable might become acceptable. See *Web Extension 15B* at the textbook's website for more information on such feedback effects.
2. Once the firm has decided to acquire the asset, the next question is how to finance it. Well-run businesses do not have excess cash lying around, so capital to finance new assets must be obtained from some source.

---

[8]The discount rate used to calculate the present value of the lease payments must be (1) the rate used by the lessor to establish the lease payments (this rate is discussed later in the chapter) or if not practical (2) the rate of interest that the lessee would have to pay for new debt with a maturity equal to that of the lease. Also, note that any maintenance payments embedded in the lease payment must be stripped out prior to checking this condition.

3. Funds to purchase the asset could be obtained from internally generated cash flows, by borrowing, or by selling new equity. Alternatively, the asset could be leased. Because of the capitalization/disclosure provision for leases, leasing normally has the same capital structure effect as borrowing.

4. As indicated earlier, a lease is comparable to a loan in the sense that the firm is required to make a specified series of payments, and a failure to meet these payments could result in bankruptcy. If a company has a target capital structure, then $1 of lease financing displaces $1 of debt financing. Thus, the most appropriate comparison is lease financing versus debt financing. Note that the analysis should compare the cost of leasing with the cost of debt financing *regardless* of how the asset purchase is actually financed. The asset may be purchased with available cash or cash raised by issuing stock, but since leasing is a substitute for debt financing and has the same capital structure effect, the appropriate comparison would still be with debt financing.

To illustrate the basic elements of lease analysis, consider this simplified example (*Ch 15 Tool Kit.xlsx* at the textbook's website shows this analysis). The Thompson-Grammatikos Company (TGC) needs a 2-year asset that costs $100, and the company must choose between leasing and buying the asset. TGC's tax rate is 40%. If the asset is purchased, the bank would lend TGC the $100 at a rate of 10% on a 2-year, simple interest loan. Thus, the firm would have to pay the bank $10 in interest at the end of each year, plus return the $100 of principal at the end of Year 2. Assume (1) that the asset falls into asset Class 12 with a 100% CCA rate, and that (2) the asset has zero value left at the end of the second year. Below is a simple CCA schedule with the yearly tax savings arising from the CCA. TGC can realize tax savings of (tax rate × CCA) = $0.4 × $50 = $20 in each year. Note the half-year rule being applied for Year 1.

See *Ch 15 Tool Kit.xlsx* at the textbook's website for all calculations.

	UCC before CCA	CCA	UCC after CCA	Tax Savings from CCA
Year 1	$100	$50	$50	$20
Year 2	50	50	0	20

Alternatively, TGC could lease the asset for 2 years for a payment of $55 at the end of each year. The analysis for the lease-versus-borrow decision consists of (1) estimating the cash flows associated with borrowing and buying the asset, that is, the flows associated with debt financing; (2) estimating the cash flows associated with leasing the asset; and (3) comparing the two financing methods to determine which has the lower present value costs. Here are the borrow-and-buy flows, set up to produce a cash flow time line:

Cash Flows if TGC Buys	Year 0	Year 1	Year 2
Equipment cost	$(100)		
Inflow from loan	100		
Interest expense		$(10)	$(10)
Tax savings from interest		4	4
Principal repayment			(100)
Tax savings from CCA		20	20
Net cash flow (time line)	$ 0	$ 14	$(86)

The net cash flow is zero in Year 0, positive in Year 1, and negative in Year 2. The operating cash flows are not shown, but they must, of course, have a PV greater than the PV of the financing costs or else TGC would not want to acquire the asset. Because the operating cash flows will be the same regardless of whether the asset is leased or purchased, they can be ignored.

Here are the cash flows associated with the lease:

Cash Flows if TGC Leases	Year 0	Year 1	Year 2
Lease payment		$(55)	$(55)
Tax savings from payment		22	22
Net cash flow (time line)	$ 0	$(33)	$(33)

Note that the two sets of cash flows reflect the tax deductibility of interest and CCA if the asset is purchased, and the deductibility of lease payments if it is leased. Thus, the net cash flows include the tax savings from these items.

To compare the cost streams of buying versus leasing, we must put them on a present value basis. As we explain later, the correct discount rate is the after-tax cost of debt, which for TGC is $10\%(1 - 0.4) = 6.0\%$. Applying this rate, we find the present value cost of buying to be $63.33 versus a present value cost of leasing of $60.50. Since leasing has the lower present value of costs, the company should lease this particular asset.

Note what we've done here. We calculated the present value of borrowing and the present value of leasing and simply compared the two, choosing the lowest-cost alternative. We can actually simplify this calculation and still arrive at the same answer. TGC borrows at a 10% before-tax and 6% after-tax rate. We calculated the dollar interest payment that TGC had to make each year based on the 10% rate—that is, $10. However, since the interest payment is tax deductible, TGC's after-tax interest payment was $10(1 - 0.4) = $6, which is what we used in the numerator of our calculation. Our discount rate was our after-tax cost of borrowing: $10\%(1 - 0.4) = 6\%$. Both our numerator and our denominator are based on the same borrowing rate; thus the borrowing has no net effect on our present value calculation. If we ignore the actual dollar interest payments, since they have no incremental effect, and calculate the present value of buying, using the asset cost of $100 and the annual tax shields of $20, we get a PV = $63.33, which is exactly the same PV we got previously, when we included the interest payments in the numerator.

The $100 purchase price in the borrow-and-buy present value calculation is a cash outflow, since TGC is using $100 to buy the asset at time 0. However, if TGC leased instead it would not have to pay that $100 initially. That is an obvious advantage to leasing. The remaining item in the borrow-and-buy calculation is the tax shield that TGC can use by claiming CCA. As we know, if TGC leases the asset, it must give up those CCA tax shields. TGC can think of the CCA tax shields as an opportunity cost if it leases. We can now restate our leasing versus buying calculation in a single spreadsheet, shown below:

Cash Flows in TGC Lease/Buy Decision	Year 0	Year 1	Year 2
Equipment cost	$100		
Lease payment		$(55)	$(55)
Tax savings from payment		22	22
Foregone tax savings from CCA		(20)	(20)
Net cash flow (time line)	$100	$(53)	$(53)

Calculating the present value of the above net cash flows using the 6% discount rate gives a present value of $2.83, which is the same amount by which we found leasing to be better than buying in our earlier present value calculations for TGC ($63.33 − $60.50 = $2.83).

Now we examine a more realistic example, one from Anderson Company, which is conducting a lease analysis on some assembly line equipment that it will procure during the coming year (*Ch 15 Tool Kit.xlsx* at the textbook's website shows this analysis). The following data have been collected:

See **Ch 15 Tool Kit.xlsx** at the textbook's website for all calculations.

1. Anderson plans to acquire automated assembly line equipment at a cost of $10 million, delivered and installed. Anderson plans to use the equipment for 5 years and then discontinue the product line.
2. Anderson can borrow the required $10 million at a before-tax cost of 10%.
3. The equipment's estimated salvage value after 5 years of use is $2,000,000. Thus, if Anderson buys the equipment, it would expect to receive $2,000,000 when the equipment is sold in 5 years. Note that in leasing, the asset's value at the end of the lease is called its **residual value.** Since Anderson has other assets in CCA Class 43 (under which this asset falls), any difference between the asset's residual sales value and its undepreciated capital cost will not affect the company's taxes.[9]
4. Anderson can lease the equipment for 5 years for an annual rental charge of $2,600,000, payable at the beginning of each year, as is common in leasing, but the lessor will own

---

[9]If Anderson has no other assets in Class 43, that asset pool will be closed. In this case, if the asset's residual sales value exceeded the undepreciated capital cost (UCC), the difference would be considered recaptured CCA and would be included as taxable income for that year. On the other hand, if the asset's residual value was less than the UCC, the difference would be considered a terminal loss and that amount would be deducted from Anderson's income for that year.

the equipment upon the expiration of the lease. (The lease payment schedule is established by the potential lessor, as described in the next major section, and Anderson can accept it, reject it, or negotiate.)

5. The lease contract stipulates that the lessor will maintain the equipment at no additional charge to Anderson. However, if Anderson borrows and buys, it will have to bear the cost of maintenance, which will be done by the equipment manufacturer at a fixed contract rate of $500,000 per year. Maintenance cash flows are normally taken at year-end.

6. The equipment falls in asset Class 43 with a 30% CCA rate, Anderson's marginal tax rate is 35%, and the lease qualifies as an operating lease. As mentioned earlier, Anderson has other Class 43 assets and as a result the asset class pool will remain open even after the 5-year project life.

Table 15-2 shows the steps involved in the analysis. Part I, line 1, is the $10 million cost of the equipment. Since companies that lease save the up-front cash purchase, we treat the $10 million as a positive value. Anderson will ultimately compare this cost to all the leasing costs. Part II covers the cash flows associated with leasing. Line 2 shows the yearly lease payment incurred. As leases are paid at the beginning of the year, each lease payment is moved up by 1 time period. Line 3 shows the annual taxes saved through the tax deductibility of the lease payments: $2,600(0.35) = $910. Line 4 gives the annual maintenance fees required to operate the machine. Since the lessor covers the maintenance costs, Anderson saves $500 annually if it leases instead of purchasing. Therefore, in our leasing analysis we treat the "saved" maintenance fees as a cash inflow. Line 5 shows the taxes Anderson would have saved from the maintenance fees if it had purchased the equipment. Just as Anderson will not have to pay for maintenance if it leases, it will also lose out on any taxes saved from the deductibility of

TABLE 15-2   Anderson Company: Dollar Cost Analysis (Thousands of Dollars)

	Year 0	Year 1	Year 2	Year 3	Year 4	Year 5
I. Cost of owning						
1. Cost of equipment	$10,000					
II. Leasing cash flows						
2. Lease payment	(2,600)	$(2,600)	$(2,600)	$(2,600)	$(2,600)	
3. Tax savings from lease payment	910	910	910	910	910	
4. Maintenance costs saved		500	500	500	500	500
5. Taxes on maintenance costs		(175)	(175)	(175)	(175)	(175)
6. Residual value[a]						$(2,000)
7. Net cash flow[b] (lines 2–6)	$(1,690)	$(1,365)	$(1,365)	$(1,365)	$(1,365)	$(1,675)
8. PV net cash flow at 6.5%	$(7,589)					
9. PV of forgone CCA tax shield	(2,369)					
10. PV cost of leasing (lines 8–9)	$(9,958)					

III. Net advantage to leasing (NAL)

11. Net advantage to leasing[c,d] = Cost of equipment − | PV cost of leasing |

= $10,000 − $9,958

= $42

Notes:
[a]The residual value is $2,000, while the book value for taxes or UCC is $1,429. Since Anderson keeps the asset class open there is no recapture. If, however, Anderson had no other assets in this class, then the difference, $2,000 − $1,429 = $571, would be considered CCA recapture and would be added to taxable income. For lease evaluation purposes, the after-tax expense of $571 × 0.35 = $200 would be deducted in Year 5 cash flows.
[b]The net cash flows shown in Line 7 are discounted at the lessee's after-tax cost of debt, 6.5%.
[c]In the NAL equation in Line 11, the PV costs are stated in absolute values. Therefore, a positive result means that leasing is beneficial, while a negative result means that leasing in not beneficial.
[d]See **Ch15 Tool Kit.xlsx** at the textbook's website for all calculations.

See **Ch 15 Tool Kit. xlsx** at the textbook's website for all calculations.

maintenance costs; thus we show those lost tax savings as a cash outflow: $500(0.35) = $175. Line 6 contains the residual value cash flows. If Anderson leases, it does not own the asset and therefore cannot sell the asset after 5 years. The residual value is therefore treated as a lost benefit—that is, a cash outflow. Line 7 contains the net cash flows, and line 8 shows the present value of these flows, discounted at 6.5%. The 6.5% is Anderson's after-tax cost of debt, 10%(1 − 0.35) = 6.5%. Because leasing is a substitute for debt, most analysts recommend that the company's cost of debt be used, and this rate seems reasonable in our example. Furthermore, since the cash flows are after taxes, the *after-tax* cost of debt must be used. Line 9 of our lease calculation deals with the CCA tax ownership benefit. Since lessees do not own the asset, they cannot claim CCA; thus, they forgo the tax shield benefit from owning the asset. This foregone value is considered a cost to leasing. You might be wondering why we don't show the annual CCA tax shield in Table 15-2. Indeed, we could build the tax savings from CCA into the table; however, as we discussed in Chapter 11, the present value of the CCA tax shield formula (11-3) is a simple and accurate method for determining the tax shield benefit.

$$
\text{PV of the CCA tax shield} = \left(\frac{CdT}{r + d} \right) \times \left(\frac{1 + 0.5r}{1 + r} \right) - \left(\frac{SdT}{r + d} \right) \times \left(\frac{1}{(1 + r)^n} \right)
$$

$$
= \left(\frac{10{,}000 \times 0.30 \times 0.35}{0.065 + 0.30} \right) \times \left(\frac{1 + 0.5 \times 0.065}{1 + 0.065} \right) - \left(\frac{2{,}000 \times 0.30 \times 0.35}{0.065 + 0.30} \right) \times \left(\frac{1}{(1 + 0.065)^5} \right)
$$

$$
= \$2{,}369
$$

Line 10 is a total of all the present value of leasing cash flows. Part III, line 11, completes our lease analysis. We subtract the PV of the lease costs from the equipment purchase cost. If the total costs of leasing is greater than the equipment cost, the net advantage to leasing (NAL) will be negative and Anderson would be better off buying the equipment. If, however, the total costs of leasing are less than the equipment cost, the NAL will be positive and Anderson should lease. Based on the information provided, NAL = $10,000 − $9,958 = $42, and Anderson should lease.[10]

In this section, we focused on the dollar cost of leasing versus borrowing and buying, which is analogous to the NPV method used in capital budgeting. A second method that lessees can use to evaluate leases focuses on the percentage cost of leasing and is analogous to the IRR method used in capital budgeting. The percentage approach is discussed in *Web Extension 15A* on the textbook's website.

See **Web Extension 15A** on the textbook's website for a discussion on percentage cost analysis.

CONCEPT REVIEW

1. Explain how the cash flows are structured in order to estimate the net advantage to leasing.
2. What discount rate should be used to evaluate a lease? Why?
3. Define the term "net advantage to leasing, NAL."

15.5 Evaluation by the Lessor

Thus far we have considered leasing only from the lessee's viewpoint. It is also useful to analyze the transaction as the lessor sees it: Is the lease a good investment for the party who must put up the money? The lessor will generally be a specialized leasing company,

---

[10]The more complicated methods that exist for analyzing leasing generally focus on the issue of the discount rate that should be used to discount the cash flows. Conceptually, we could assign a separate discount rate to each individual cash flow component, then find the present values of each of the cash flow components, and finally sum these present values to determine the net advantage or disadvantage to leasing. This approach has been taken by Stewart C. Myers, David A. Dill, and Alberto J. Bautista (MDB) in "Valuation of Financial Lease Contracts," *Journal of Finance*, June 1976, 799–819, among others. MDB correctly note that the use of a single discount rate is valid only if (1) leases and loans are viewed by investors as being equivalent and (2) all cash flows are equally risky, hence appropriately discounted at the same rate. The first assumption is probably valid for most financial leases, and even where it is not, no one knows how to adjust properly for any capital structure effects that leases might have. Regarding the second assumption, advocates of multiple discount rates often point out that the residual value is less certain than are the other cash flows, and they thus recommend discounting it at a higher rate. However, there is no way of knowing precisely how much to increase the after-tax cost of debt to account for the increased riskiness of the residual value cash flow. Furthermore, in a market risk sense, all cash flows could be equally risky even though individual items such as the residual value might have more or less total variability than others. To complicate matters even more, the market risk of the residual value will usually be different than the firm's market risk. For more on residual value risk, see Schallheim, Chapter 8. For an application of option pricing techniques in the evaluation of the residual value, see Wayne Y. Lee, John D. Martin, and Andrew J. Senchack, "The Case for Using Options to Evaluate Salvage Values in Financial Leases," *Financial Management*, Autumn 1982, 33–41.

a bank or bank affiliate, an individual or group of individuals organized as a limited partnership or limited liability corporation, or a manufacturer such as IBM that uses leasing as a sales tool. The specialized leasing companies are often owned by profitable companies such as General Electric, which owns General Electric Capital, the largest leasing company in the world.

Any potential lessor needs to know the rate of return on the capital invested in the lease, and this information is also useful to the prospective lessee: Lease terms on large leases are generally negotiated, so the lessee should know what return the lessor is earning. The lessor's analysis involves (1) determining the net cash outlay, which is usually the invoice price of the leased equipment less any lease payments made in advance; (2) determining the periodic cash inflows, which consist of the lease payments minus both income taxes and any maintenance expense the lessor must bear; (3) estimating the residual value of the property when the lease expires; and (4) determining whether the rate of return on the lease exceeds the lessor's opportunity cost of capital or, equivalently, whether the NPV of the lease exceeds zero.

Analysis by the Lessor

To illustrate the lessor's analysis, we assume the same facts as for the Anderson Company lease, plus the following: (1) The potential lessor is a company whose marginal income tax rate, T, is 40%. (2) The lessor's pre-tax cost of capital is 9%, and its after-tax cost of capital is 9%(1 − 0.40) = 5.4%. This is the minimum return the company requires on the assets it leases. (3) The residual value is $2,000,000. Because the lessor specializes in leasing this type of equipment, its asset class pool will remain open after the lease expires, which means that CCA recapture or terminal losses will not be a factor.

See **Ch 15 Tool Kit.xlsx** for details.

The lessor's cash flows are developed in Table 15-3. Here we see that the lease as an investment has a net present value of $76,000. The lessor, on a present value basis, is better off by $76,000 by writing the lease rather than obtaining a return of 9% (5.4% after taxes),

TABLE 15-3   Lease Analysis from the Lessor's Viewpoint (Thousands of Dollars)

	Year 0	Year 1	Year 2	Year 3	Year 4	Year 5
I. Investment						
1. Cost of equipment	$(10,000)					
II. Leasing cash flows						
2. Lease payment	2,600	$2,600	$2,600	$2,600	$2,600	
3. Tax on lease payment	(1,040)	(1,040)	(1,040)	(1,040)	(1,040)	
4. Maintenance costs		(500)	(500)	(500)	(500)	(500)
5. Maintenance tax savings[a]		200	200	200	200	200
6. Residual value						$2,000
7. Net cash flow (lines 2–6)	$ 1,560	$1,260	$1,260	$1,260	$1,260	$1,700
8. PV net cash flows at 5.4%	$ 7,294					
9. PV of CCA tax shield	2,782					
10. PV leasing cash flows (lines 8–9)	$ 10,076					
III. Net present value of lease						
11. NPV of Lease = Cost of equipment + PV leasing cash flows						

$$= \$(10,000) \quad + \$10,076$$
$$= \$76$$

Note:
[a]Maintenance costs times the lessor's tax rate.

which is what could otherwise have been earned. As we saw earlier, the lease is also advantageous to Anderson Company, so the transaction should be completed.

Setting the Lease Payment

In the preceding sections, we evaluated the lease assuming that the lease payments had already been specified. However, in large leases the parties generally sit down and work out an agreement on the size of the lease payments, with these payments being set so as to provide the lessor with some specific rate of return. In situations in which the lease terms are not negotiated, which is often the case for small leases, the lessor must still go through the same type of analysis, setting terms that provide a target rate of return and then offering these terms to the potential lessee on a take-it-or-leave-it basis.

See **Ch 15 Tool Kit.xlsx** at the textbook's website for all calculations.

To illustrate all of this, suppose the potential lessor described earlier determines that its after-tax cost of capital is not 5.4% but rather 6%. What lease payment schedule would provide this return?

To answer this question, note again that Table 15-3 contains the lessor's cash flow analysis. If the basic analysis is computerized, it is easy to first change the discount rate to 6% and then change the lease payment—either by trial and error or by using the goal-seeking function—until the lease's NPV = $0. When we did this using **Ch 15 Tool Kit.xlsx**, we found that the lessor must set the lease payment at $2,623,000 to obtain an after-tax rate of return of 6.0%. If this lease payment is not acceptable to the lessee, Anderson Company, then it may not be possible to strike a deal. Naturally, competition among leasing companies forces lessors to build market-related returns into their lease payment schedules.[11]

See **Ch 15 Tool Kit.xlsx** at the textbook's website for all calculations.

If the inputs to the lessee and the lessor are identical, then a positive NAL to the lessee implies an equal but negative NPV to the lessor. *However, conditions are often such that leasing can provide net benefits to both parties. This situation arises because of differentials in taxes, in borrowing rates, in estimated residual values, or in the ability to bear the residual value risk.* We will explore these issues in detail in a later section.

See **Web Extension 15C** on the textbook's website for a discussion on leveraged leases.

Note that the lessor can, under certain conditions, increase the return on the lease by borrowing some of the funds used to purchase the leased asset. Such a lease is called a **leveraged lease.** Whether or not a lease is leveraged has no effect on the lessee's analysis, but it can have a significant effect on the cash flows to the lessor, hence on the lessor's expected rate of return. We discuss leveraged leases in more detail in **Web Extension 15C** at the textbook's website.

CONCEPT REVIEW

1. What discount rate is used in a lessor's NPV analysis?
2. What is the relationship between the lessor's IRR and the size of the lease payments?

15.6　Other Issues in Lease Analysis

The basic methods of analysis used by lessees and lessors were presented in the previous sections. However, some other issues warrant discussion.[12]

Estimated Residual Value

It is important to note that the lessor owns the property upon expiration of a lease; hence the lessor has claim to the asset's residual value. Superficially, it would appear that if residual values are expected to be large, owning would have an advantage over leasing. However, this apparent advantage does not hold up. If expected residual values are large—as they may be under inflation for certain types of equipment and also if real estate is involved—competition between leasing companies and other financing sources, as well as competition among leasing companies themselves, will force leasing rates down to the point where potential residual

---

[11]For a discussion of realized returns on lease contracts, see Ronald C. Lease, John J. McConnell, and James S. Schallheim, "Realized Returns and the Default and Prepayment Experience of Financial Leasing Contracts," *Financial Management*, Summer 1990, 11–20.

[12]For a description of lease analysis in practice, as well as a comprehensive bibliography of the leasing literature, see Tarun K. Mukherjee, "A Survey of Corporate Leasing Analysis," *Financial Management*, Autumn 1991, 96–107.

values are fully recognized in the lease contract. Thus, the existence of large residual values is not likely to result in materially higher costs for leasing.

Increased Credit Availability

As noted earlier, leasing is sometimes said to be advantageous for firms that are seeking the maximum degree of financial leverage. First, it is sometimes argued that firms can obtain more money, and for longer terms, under a lease arrangement than under a loan secured by a specific piece of equipment. Second, since some leases do not appear on the balance sheet, lease financing has been said to give the firm a stronger appearance in a *superficial* credit analysis and thus to permit the firm to use more leverage than would be possible if it did not lease.

There may be some truth to these claims for smaller firms, but since firms are required to capitalize financial leases and to report them on their balance sheets, this point is of questionable validity for any firm large enough to have audited financial statements. However, leasing can be a way to circumvent existing loan covenants. If restrictive covenants prohibit a firm from issuing more debt but fail to restrict lease payments, then the firm could effectively increase its leverage by leasing additional assets. Also, firms that are in very poor financial condition and facing possible bankruptcy may be able to obtain lease financing at a lower cost than comparable debt financing because (1) lessors often have a more favourable position than lenders should the lessee actually go bankrupt and (2) lessors that specialize in certain types of equipment may be in a better position to dispose of repossessed equipment than banks or other lenders.

Real Estate Leases

Most of our examples have focused on equipment leasing. However, leasing originated with real estate, and such leases still constitute a huge segment of total lease financing. (We distinguish between housing rentals and long-term business leases; our concern is with business leases.) Retailers lease many of their stores. In some situations, retailers have no choice but to

FINANCE: IN FOCUS

What You Don't Know *Can* Hurt You!

A leasing decision seems to be pretty straightforward, at least from a financial perspective: calculate the NAL for the lease and undertake it if the NAL is positive. Right? But tracking down all the financial implications from lease contract provisions can be difficult, requiring the lessee to make assumptions about future costs that are not explicitly spelled out in the lease contract. For example, consider the purchase option embedded in the lease that Rojacks Food Stores undertook with GE Capital for restaurant equipment. The lease allowed Rojacks either to purchase the equipment at the current market value when the lease expired, or return the equipment. When the lease expired, GE set a purchase price that was much higher than Rojacks expected. Rojacks needed the equipment for its day-to-day operations so it couldn't just return the equipment without disrupting its business. Ultimately, Rojacks hired an independent appraiser for the equipment and negotiated a lower purchase price, but without the appraiser, Rojacks would have been stuck with the price GE decided to set for the equipment.

The Rojacks-GE situation isn't that unusual. Lessors often use high expected residual values or high expected penalties to offset low lease payments. In addition, some contracts may require that (1) all of the equipment covered under a lease must either be purchased or returned in its entirety, (2) equipment that is moved must be purchased, (3) large fees must be paid even for minor damage or missing parts, and/or (4) equipment must be returned in its original packaging. These conditions impose costs on the lessee when the lease is terminated and should be considered explicitly when making the leasing decision. The moral of the story for lessees is to read the fine print and request changes to objectionable terms before signing the lease. Here are some ways to reduce the likelihood of unanticipated costs: (1) specify residual value as a percentage of the initial cost of the equipment, (2) allow for portions of the equipment to be returned and portions to be purchased at the end of the lease, and (3) specify that disagreements will be adjudicated by arbitration.

Source: Linda Corman, "{Don't} Look Deep Into My Lease," *CFO*, July 2006, pp. 71–75.

lease—this is true of locations in malls and certain office buildings. In other situations, they have a choice of building and owning versus leasing. Law firms and accounting firms, for example, can choose between buying their own facilities or leasing on a long-term basis (up to 20 or more years).

The type of lease-versus-purchase analysis we discussed in this chapter is just as applicable for real estate as for equipment—conceptually, there is no difference. Of course, such things as maintenance, who the other tenants will be, what alterations can be made, who will pay for alterations, and the like, become especially important with real property, but the analytical procedures upon which the lease-versus-buy decision is based are no different from any other lease analysis.

Vehicle Leases

Vehicle leasing is very popular today, both for large corporations and for individuals, especially professionals such as MBAs, doctors, lawyers, and accountants. For corporations, the key factor involved with transportation is often maintenance and disposal of used vehicles—the leasing companies are specialists here, and many businesses prefer to "outsource" services related to autos and trucks. For individuals, leasing is often more convenient, and it may be easier to justify tax deductions on leased than on owned vehicles. Also, most auto leasing to individuals is through dealers. These dealers (and manufacturers) use leasing as a sales

---

FINANCE: IN FOCUS

Leasing to Unlock Shareholder Value

What do Loblaw and Canadian Tire have in common? Neither of them directly owns the real estate and buildings that drive their operations. Loblaw was the first of the two to sell its properties for $7 billion to Choice Properties real estate investment trust and then lease them back on a long-term basis. Choice Properties then went on to raise $600 million through an IPO, $200 million through the sale of equity to George Weston Limited, and another $800 million through a debenture issue. Much of the funds were used to pay Loblaw for the assets.

More recently, Canadian Tire sold off its stores and land to CT REIT, which also went public soon after. By the two companies separating their real estate assets from their core retail operations, investors were able to value the real estate businesses separately (and higher) than when they were part of Loblaw's and Canadian Tire's overall corporate operations. The sale and leaseback of the properties also freed up cash to either reinvest in operations or to be distributed back to shareholders. While the effect on day-to-day operations was minimal, the effect on its stock price was not. The graph below shows the effect on the companies' share prices when they announced (Day 0) the restructuring. Loblaw's stock closed up over 13% while Canadian Tire's stock climbed about 10%. Over $4.8 billion in shareholder wealth was added by selling their properties to a REIT and leasing them back.

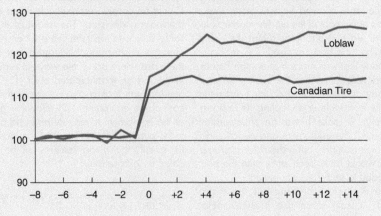

Stock Price Before and After Real Estate Announcement

tool, and they often make the terms quite attractive, especially when it comes to the down payment, which may be nonexistent in the case of a lease.

Vehicle leasing also permits many individuals to drive more expensive cars than would otherwise be possible. For example, the monthly payment on a new BMW might be $1,500 when financed with a 3-year loan, but the same car, if leased for 3 years, might cost only $749 a month. At first glance, it appears that leasing is less expensive than owning because the monthly payment is so much lower. However, such a simplistic analysis ignores the fact that payments end after the loan is paid off but continue indefinitely under leasing. By using the techniques described in this chapter, individuals can assess the true costs associated with auto leases and then rationally judge the merits of each type of auto financing.

15.7 Other Reasons for Leasing

Up to this point, we have noted that tax rate or other differentials are generally necessary to make leasing attractive to both the lessee and lessor. If the lessee and lessor are facing different tax rates, then it is often possible to structure a lease that is beneficial to both parties. However, there are other reasons firms might want to lease an asset rather than buy it.

More than half of all commercial aircraft are leased, and smaller airlines, especially in developing nations, lease an especially high percentage of their planes. One of the reasons is that airlines can reduce their risks by leasing. If an airline purchased all its aircraft, it would be hampered in its ability to respond to changing market conditions. Because they have become specialists at matching airlines with available aircraft, the aircraft lessors (which are multibillion-dollar concerns) are quite good at managing the changing demand for different types of aircraft. This permits them to offer attractive lease terms. In this situation, *leasing provides operating flexibility*. Leasing is not necessarily less expensive than buying, but the operating flexibility is quite valuable.

Leasing is also an attractive alternative for many high-technology items that are subject to rapid and unpredictable technological obsolescence. Say a hospital wants to buy a magnetic resonance imaging (MRI) device. If it buys the MRI equipment, it is exposed to the risk of technological obsolescence. In a short time some new technology may lower the value and usefulness of the current system. Since these devices are expensive and are meant to be used for a period of time, the hospital would bear a great deal of risk if it bought the MRI device. However, a lessor that specializes in state-of-the-art medical equipment would be exposed to significantly less risk. By purchasing and then leasing many different items, the lessor benefits from diversification. Of course, over time some items will probably lose more value than the lessor expected, but this will be offset by other items that retain more value than expected. Also, because such a leasing company will be especially familiar with the market for used medical equipment, it can refurbish the equipment and then get a better price in the resale market than could an individual hospital. For these reasons, leasing can reduce the risk of technological obsolescence.

Leasing can also be attractive when a firm is uncertain about the demand for its products or services and thus about how long the equipment will be needed. For instance, a company taking on contract manufacturing work could see the nature of its manufacturing change over time, due to new customers or changing customer requirements. If this happens, the original equipment may now be of little use. In this case, a lease with a cancellation clause would permit the contract manufacturer to simply return the equipment. The lessor would charge something for the cancellation, and this would lower the expected profitability of the company, but it would provide the company with an option to abandon the equipment, and the value of the option could easily exceed the incremental cost of the cancellation clause. The leasing company would be willing to write this option because it is in a better position to remarket the equipment, either by writing another lease or by selling it outright.

The leasing industry recently introduced a type of lease that even transfers some of a project's operating risk from the lessee to the lessor and that also motivates the lessor to maintain the leased equipment in good working order. Instead of making a fixed rental payment, the lessee pays a fee each time the leased equipment is used. This type of lease originated with copy machines, where the lessee pays so much per month plus an additional amount per copy made. If the machine breaks down, no copies are made, and the lessor's rental income declines. This motivates the lessor to repair the machine quickly.

This type of lease is also used in the U.S. health care industry, where it is called a "per-procedure lease." For example, a hospital might lease an X-ray machine for a fixed fee per X-ray, say, $5. If demand for the machine's X-rays is less than expected by the hospital, revenues will be lower than expected, but so will the machine's capital costs. Conversely, high demand would lead to higher than expected lease costs, but these would be offset by higher than expected revenues. By using a per-procedure lease, the hospital is converting a fixed cost for the equipment into a variable cost, and thereby reducing the machine's operating leverage and break-even point. The net effect is to reduce the project's risk. Of course, the expected cost of a per-procedure lease might be more than the cost of a conventional lease, but the risk reduction benefit could be worth the cost. Note too that if the lessor writes a large number of per-procedure leases, much of the riskiness inherent in such leases could be eliminated by diversification, so the risk premiums that lessors build into per-procedure lease payments could be low enough to attract potential lessees.

Some companies also find leasing attractive because the lessor is able to provide servicing on favourable terms. For example, Virco Manufacturing, a company that makes school desks and other furniture, recently leased 25 truck tractors and 140 trailers, which it uses to ship furniture from its plant. The lease agreement, with a large leasing company that specializes in purchasing, maintaining, and then reselling trucks, permitted the replacement of an aging fleet that Virco had built up over the years. "We are pretty good at manufacturing furniture, but we aren't very good at maintaining a truck fleet," said Virco's CFO.

There are other reasons that a firm might lease an asset rather than buy it. Often, these reasons are difficult to quantify; hence they cannot be easily incorporated into an NPV or IRR analysis. Nevertheless, a sound lease decision must begin with a quantitative analysis, and then qualitative factors can be considered before the final lease-or-buy decision is made.[13]

(C)NCEPT REVIEW

1. Describe some economic factors that might provide an advantage to leasing.

Summary

In Canada, 30% of all equipment is leased, as is a great deal of real estate. Consequently, leasing is an important financing vehicle. In this chapter, we discussed the leasing decision from the standpoints of both the lessee and the lessor. The key concepts covered are listed below:

- The five most important types of lease agreement are (1) **operating lease,** (2) **financial,** or **capital, lease,** (3) **sale-and-leaseback,** (4) **combination lease,** and (5) **synthetic lease.**
- The CRA has specific tax rules governing leases. If a lease contains a bargain purchase price option and the lessee subsequently sells the asset for a higher price, the lessee is deemed by the CRA to have claimed CCA and must claim CCA recapture on its income. The CRA also limits the types of assets on which lessors may claim CCA.
- International Accounting Standards 17 describes the conditions under which a lease must be capitalized (shown directly on the balance sheet) as opposed to shown only in the notes to the financial statements. Generally, leases that transfer ownership at term end, that have a bargain purchase price, that have a term covering the asset's useful life, or that cover an asset which is useful only to the lessee must be capitalized.
- The lessee's analysis consists basically of a comparison of the PV of costs associated with leasing versus the cost of buying. The difference in these costs is called the **net advantage to leasing (NAL).**
- One of the key issues in the lessee's analysis is the appropriate discount rate. Because a lease is a substitute for debt, because the cash flows in a lease analysis are stated on an after-tax basis, and because they are known with relative certainty, the appropriate discount rate is the **lessee's after-tax cost of debt.** A higher discount rate may be used on the **residual value** if it is substantially riskier than the other flows.
- The lessor evaluates the lease as an **investment.** If the lease's NPV is greater than zero, then the lease should be written.

---

[13]For more on leasing, see Thomas J. Finucane, "Some Empirical Evidence on the Use of Financial Leases," *Journal of Financial Research*, Fall 1988, 321–333; and Lawrence D. Schall, "The Evaluation of Lease Financing Opportunities," *Midland Corporate Finance Journal*, Spring 1985, 48–65.

- Leasing is motivated by various differences between lessees and lessors. Three of the most important reasons for leasing are (1) **tax rate differentials,** (2) the lessor is better able to bear the **residual value risk** than the lessee, and (3) the lessor can maintain the leased equipment more efficiently than the lessee.

Questions

15-1   Define each of the following terms:
  a.   Lessee; lessor
  b.   Operating lease; financial lease; sale-and-leaseback; combination lease; synthetic lease; SPE
  c.   Off–balance sheet financing; capitalizing
  d.   IAS 17
  e.   Residual value
  f.   Lessee's analysis; lessor's analysis
  g.   Net advantage to leasing (NAL)

15-2   Distinguish between operating leases and financial leases. Would you be more likely to find an operating lease employed for a fleet of trucks or for a manufacturing plant?

15-3   Are lessees more likely than lessors to be in high- or low-income tax brackets?

15-4   Will ROI, debt to equity, and net income become smaller or larger if a lease is considered an operating lease as opposed to a capital lease?

15-5   One alleged advantage of leasing voiced in the past is that it kept liabilities off the balance sheet, thus making it possible for a firm to obtain more leverage than it otherwise could have. This raised the question of whether both the lease obligation and the asset involved should be capitalized and shown on the balance sheet. Discuss the pros and cons of capitalizing leases and related assets.

15-6   Will a lessor likely charge higher or lower lease rates if the lessor's:
  a.   tax rate increases?
  b.   cost of borrowing increases?
  c.   residual value of the asset increases?
  d.   purchase price of the asset increases?
  Consider the impact of each separately.

15-7   In our Anderson Company example, we assumed that the lease could not be cancelled. What effect would a cancellation clause have on the lessee's analysis? On the lessor's analysis?

15-8   Suppose there were no CRA rules governing leases and taxes. Explain, in a manner that a federal MP might understand, why some restrictions should be imposed. Illustrate your answer with numbers.

Concept Review Problem

Full solutions are provided at www.nelson.com/brigham3ce.

CR-1
Lease Versus Buy
Cold Playground Products Co. (CPP) has decided to acquire a new truck. One alternative is to lease the truck on a 4-year contract for a lease payment of $10,000 per year, with payments to be made at the *beginning* of each year. The lease would include maintenance. Alternatively, CPP could purchase the truck outright for $40,000, financing the purchase by a 4-year bank loan for the net purchase price at an interest rate of 10% per year. Under the borrow-to-purchase arrangement, CPP would have to maintain the truck at a cost of $1,000 per year, payable at year-end. The truck is a Class 10, 30%, declining balance CCA rate asset. It has a residual value of $10,000, which is the expected market value after 4 years, when CPP plans to replace the truck irrespective of whether it leases or buys. CPP has a tax rate of 40%.
  a.   Should CPP buy or lease?
  b.   The appropriate discount rate for use in the analysis is the firm's after-tax cost of debt. Why?
  c.   The residual value is the least certain cash flow in the analysis. How might CPP incorporate the differential riskiness of this cash flow into the analysis?

Problems

Easy
Problems 1–2

Answers to odd-numbered problems appear in Appendix A.

15-1
Balance Sheet Effects

Minetello Construction needs a piece of equipment that costs $40,000. Minetello either can lease the equipment or borrow $40,000 from a local bank and buy the equipment. If the equipment is leased, the lease would *not* have to be capitalized. Minetello's balance sheet prior to the acquisition of the equipment is as follows:

Current assets	$15,000	Debt	$20,000
Net fixed assets	65,000	Equity	60,000
Total assets	$80,000	Total claims	$80,000

a. (1) What is Minetello's debt ratio at present?
    (2) What would be the company's debt ratio if it purchased the equipment?
    (3) What would be the debt ratio if the equipment were leased?
b. Would the company's financial risk be different under the leasing and purchasing alternatives?

15-2
Lease versus Buy

Assume in Problem 15-1 that Minetello's tax rate is 40% and that the equipment's CCA would be $20,000 per year. If the company leased the asset on a 2-year lease, the payment would be $22,000 at the beginning of each year. If Minetello borrowed and bought, the bank would charge 10% interest on the loan. In either case, the equipment is worth nothing after 2 years and will be discarded. Should Minetello lease or buy the equipment?

Intermediate
Problems 3–5

15-3
Balance Sheet Effects

Two companies, Shipton Ltd. and Falco Corporation, began operations with identical balance sheets. A year later, both required additional manufacturing capacity at a cost of $100,000. Shipton obtained a 5-year, $100,000 loan at a 7% interest rate from its bank. Falco, on the other hand, decided to lease the required $100,000 capacity for 5 years, and a 7% return was built into the lease. The balance sheet for each company, before the asset increases, follows:

		Debt	$100,000
		Equity	300,000
Total assets	$400,000	Total claims	$400,000

a. Show the balance sheets for both firms after the asset increases and calculate each firm's new debt ratio. (Assume that the lease is not capitalized.)
b. Show how Falco's balance sheet would look immediately after the financing if it capitalized the lease.
c. Would the rate of return (1) on assets and (2) on equity be affected by the choice of financing? How?

15-4
Lease versus Buy

Misty River Minerals must install $5.6 million of new machinery in its Ontario mine. It can obtain a bank loan for 100% of the purchase price, or it can lease the machinery. Assume that the following facts apply:
(1) The machinery falls into asset Class 38 with a declining balance CCA rate of 30%.
(2) Under either the lease or the purchase, Misty River must pay for insurance, property taxes, and maintenance.
(3) The firm's tax rate is 26%.
(4) The loan would have an interest rate of 10%.
(5) The lease terms call for $1,425,000 payments at the beginning of each of the next 4 years.
(6) Assume that Misty River Minerals has no use for the machine beyond the expiration of the lease. The machine has an estimated residual value of $1,000,000 at the end of the fourth year.

What is the NAL of the lease?

15-5
Lease versus Buy

Precision Graphics Ltd. (PGL) is looking at modernizing its facilities. As part of that process, PGL has decided to acquire new high-speed colour laser photocopiers. It has the option of buying the machines for $75,000 or leasing them for 5 years. PGL would be able to finance 100% of the purchase with a 5 year 7% loan. If purchased, PGL would also purchase a 5-year maintenance contract for $880 per year, payable at year-end. Annual lease payments, including maintenance, would cost $18,300. There is not expected to be any residual value at the end of the lease. PGL's tax rate is 28%, and the equipment falls into Class 8 with a 20% CCA rate.

a. Should PGL buy or lease the copiers?
b. If the copiers had a residual value of $10,000, what difference would that make to the leasing decision?
c. If the government changed the CCA rate for the machines to 50%, what would be the new NAL?
d. Should PGL lease if it can borrow at 5%?

Challenging Problem 6–7
15-6
Lease versus Buy

Alumco Industries must install $1 million of new computer equipment in its Ontario plant. It can obtain a bank loan for 100% of the required amount. Alternatively, Alumco believes that it can arrange for a lease financing plan. Assume that these facts apply:

(1) The computer equipment falls into asset Class 45 with a declining balance CCA rate of 45%.
(2) Estimated maintenance expenses are $50,000 per year.
(3) The firm's tax rate is 34%.
(4) If the money is borrowed, the bank loan will be at a rate of 14%.
(5) The tentative lease terms call for payments of $320,000 at the beginning of each year for 3 years.
(6) Under the proposed lease terms, the lessee must pay for insurance, property taxes, and maintenance.
(7) The best estimate of the market value at the end of 3 years is $200,000, but it could be much higher or lower under certain circumstances.

To assist management in making the proper lease-versus-buy decision, you are asked to answer the following questions:

a. Should the firm lease or borrow and buy the equipment? Explain.
b. Consider the $200,000 estimated residual value. Is it appropriate to discount it at the same rate as the other cash flows? What about the other cash flows—are they all equally risky?

15-7
Lease versus Buy

Technical Service Corp (TSC) requires advanced controller software for its network monitoring system. The software can be purchased for $900,000 or leased out by Vancouver Leasing Inc. (VLI) over 3 years at $335,000 per year. The software will be obsolete and will have no value after 3 years. Since TSC will be operating at approximately break-even for the foreseeable future, its tax rate will be close to 0. TSC can borrow at 13%. VLI can borrow at 7%, and its tax rate is 35%. Assume that the software falls into Class 12 with a CCA rate of 100%. (Note that the half-year rule applies for software.)

a. What is the NAL for TSC?
b. What is the NPV of the lease for VLI?
c. What is the minimum lease payment that VLI can charge and still wish to write the lease? (*Hint:* the minimum lease payment acceptable to VLI occurs when the NPV of the lease equals 0.)

 # Spreadsheet Problem

15-8
Build a Model:
Lessee's Analysis

Start with the partial model in the file *Ch 15 Build a Model.xlsx* at the textbook's website. As part of its overall plant modernization and cost reduction program, Western Fabrics' management has decided to install a new automated weaving loom. In the capital budgeting analysis of this equipment, the IRR of the project was found to be 20% versus the project's required return of 12%.

The loom has an invoice price of $250,000, including delivery and installation charges. The funds needed could be borrowed from the bank through a 4-year amortized loan at a 10% interest rate, with payments to be made at the end of each year. In the event the loom is purchased, the manufacturer will contract to maintain and service it for a fee of $20,000 per year paid at the end of each year. The loom has a CCA rate of 35%, and Western's tax rate is 40%.

Aubey Automation Inc., maker of the loom, has offered to lease the loom to Western for $70,000 upon delivery and installation (at t = 0) plus four additional annual lease payments of $70,000 to be made at the end of Years 1 to 4. (Note that there are five lease payments in total.) The lease agreement includes maintenance and servicing. Actually, the loom has an expected life of 8 years, at which time its expected salvage value is zero; however, after 4 years, its market value is expected to be $42,500. Western plans to build an entirely new plant in 4 years, so it has no interest in either leasing or owning the proposed loom for more than that period.

a. Should the loom be leased or purchased?
b. The salvage value is clearly the most uncertain cash flow in the analysis. What effect would a salvage value risk adjustment have on the analysis? (Assume that the appropriate salvage value pre-tax discount rate is 15%.)
c. Assuming that the after-tax cost of debt should be used to discount all anticipated cash flows, at what lease payment would the firm be indifferent to either leasing or buying?

MINI CASE

Big Beta Securities Inc. has decided to acquire a new market data and quotation system for its Vancouver home office. The system receives current market prices and other information from several online data services and then either displays the information on a screen or stores it for later retrieval by the firm's brokers. The system also permits customers to call up current quotes on terminals in the lobby.

The equipment costs $1,000,000, and, if it were purchased, Big Beta could obtain a term loan for the full purchase price at a 10% interest rate. The equipment falls into Class 45 with a declining balance CCA rate of 45%. If the system were purchased, a 4-year maintenance contract could be obtained at a cost of $20,000 per year, payable at the beginning of each year. The equipment would be sold after 4 years, and the best estimate of its residual value at that time is $200,000. However, since real-time display system technology is changing rapidly, the actual residual value is uncertain.

As an alternative to the borrow-and-buy plan, the equipment manufacturer informed Big Beta that Consolidated Leasing would be willing to write a 4-year lease on the equipment, including maintenance, for payments of $260,000 at the beginning of each year. Big Beta's tax rate is 35%. You have been asked to analyze the lease-versus-purchase decision, and in the process to answer the following questions:

a. (1) Who are the two parties to a lease transaction?
    (2) What are the five primary types of leases, and what are their characteristics?
    (3) What effect does leasing have on a firm's balance sheet?
    (4) What effect does leasing have on a firm's capital structure?
b. Explain the rationale for the discount rate you used to find the PV.
c. Calculate the net advantage to leasing (NAL). Does your analysis indicate that Big Beta should buy or lease the equipment? Explain.
d. Now assume that the equipment's residual value could be as low as $0 or as high as $400,000, but that $200,000 is the expected value. Since the residual value is riskier than the other cash flows in the analysis, this differential risk should be incorporated into the analysis. Describe how this could be accomplished. (No calculations are necessary, but explain how you would modify the analysis if calculations were required.) What effect would increased uncertainty about the residual value have on Big Beta's lease-versus-purchase decision?
e. The lessee compares the cost of owning the equipment with the cost of leasing it. Now put yourself in the lessor's shoes. In a few sentences, how should you analyze the decision to write or not write the lease?
f. (1) Assume that the lease payments were actually $280,000 per year, that Consolidated Leasing is also in the 35% tax bracket, and that it also forecasts a $200,000 residual value. Also, to furnish the maintenance support, Consolidated would have to purchase a maintenance contract from the manufacturer at the same $20,000 annual

cost, again paid in advance. Consolidated Leasing can obtain an expected 10% pre-tax return on investments of similar risk. What would Consolidated's NPV of leasing be under these conditions?

(2) What do you think the lessor's NPV would be if the lease payment were set at $260,000 per year? (*Hint:* The lessor's cash flows would be a "mirror image" of the lessee's cash flows.)

g. Big Beta's management has been considering moving to a new downtown location, and they are concerned that these plans may come to fruition prior to the expiration of the lease. If the move occurs, Big Beta would buy or lease an entirely new set of equipment, and hence management would like to include a cancellation clause in the lease contract. What effect would such a clause have on the riskiness of the lease from Big Beta's standpoint? From the lessor's standpoint? If you were the lessor, would you insist on changing any of the lease terms if a cancellation clause were added? Should the cancellation clause contain any restrictive covenants and/or penalties of the type contained in bond indentures or provisions similar to call premiums?

chapter 16

Capital Market Financing:
Hybrid and Other Securities

In earlier chapters, we discussed how companies raise money for their operations through a combination of debt and equity. Investment horizons, investors' differing preferences toward risk, and other factors determine whether they wish to be creditors or shareholders. There are, however, investors whose needs may not fit into either broad category. Additionally, at times market conditions may not be favourable for either straight debt or equity offerings. Financial markets have developed securities that combine features of debt and equity. The most obvious is preferred shares. Other securities such as convertible bonds and warrants also fit into this "hybrid" category. In fact, companies have been turning increasingly to convertible bonds for a variety of financing needs.

Convertible bonds that can be exchanged for common shares of the issuing corporation virtually always have coupon rates that are lower than rates on straight nonconvertible bonds. Therefore, if a company raises $100 million by issuing convertible bonds, its interest expense will be lower than if it financed with nonconvertible debt. But why would investors be willing to buy such a bond, given its lower interest payments? The answer lies in the conversion feature—if the price of the issuer's stock rises, the convertible bondholder can exchange it for stock and realize a capital gain. A convertible bond's value is based partly on interest rates in the economy, partly on the issuing company's regular bond risk, and partly on the price of the stock into which it is convertible. Therefore, convertibles' prices are more volatile than regular bonds' prices but not as risky as the company's common stock.

Convertible bonds are used somewhat differently in Canada than elsewhere. Canadian issuers tend to be small to mid-sized companies, often in the resource or real estate sectors. For instance, First Capital Realty's recent $70 million convertible offering with a 4.95% coupon and a 5-year term would be a typical Canadian offering. In total, there are more than 200 convertible bonds in Canada with a total value of about $15 billion. Contrast this with the $468 billion international market for convertible bonds, with an average issue size of more than $300 million. Internationally, companies of all sizes utilize convertibles, including Microsoft, Intel, and Deutsche Telecom. In 2011, Sinopec made a $3.6 billion convertible bond offering. Microsoft used the money it raised to repay short-term debt; Intel used the cash it raised to buy back its own shares; Sinopec used the $3.6 billion to finance new gas pipelines. After reading this chapter, you'll have a better understanding why companies use convertible securities for their financing requirements.

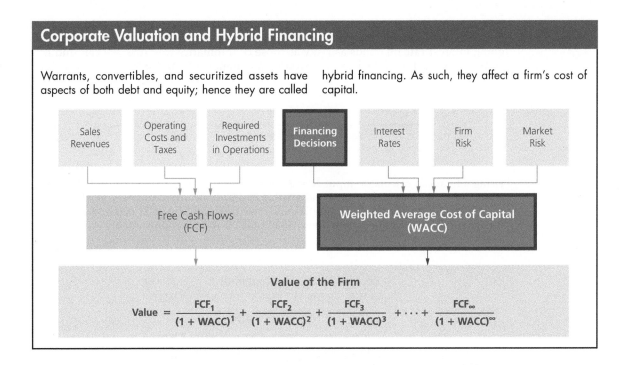

Corporate Valuation and Hybrid Financing

Warrants, convertibles, and securitized assets have aspects of both debt and equity; hence they are called hybrid financing. As such, they affect a firm's cost of capital.

Sales Revenues · Operating Costs and Taxes · Required Investments in Operations · **Financing Decisions** · Interest Rates · Firm Risk · Market Risk

Free Cash Flows (FCF)

Weighted Average Cost of Capital (WACC)

Value of the Firm

$$\text{Value} = \frac{\text{FCF}_1}{(1 + \text{WACC})^1} + \frac{\text{FCF}_2}{(1 + \text{WACC})^2} + \frac{\text{FCF}_3}{(1 + \text{WACC})^3} + \cdots + \frac{\text{FCF}_\infty}{(1 + \text{WACC})^\infty}$$

In previous chapters, we examined common stocks and various types of long-term debt. In this chapter, we examine other securities used to raise long-term capital: (1) *warrants*, which are derivative securities issued by firms to facilitate the sale of some other type of security; (2) *convertibles*, which combine the features of debt (or preferred stock) and warrants; and (3) *securitized assets*, a generic term used to describe how various kinds of debt are repackaged and sold to raise capital.

The textbook's website contains an *Excel* file that will guide you through the chapter's calculations. The file for this chapter is *Ch 16 Tool Kit.xlsx*, and we encourage you to open the file and follow along as you read the chapter. **www .nelson.com/brigham3ce**

16.1 Warrants

A **warrant** is a certificate issued by a company that gives the holder the right to buy a stated number of shares of the company's stock at a specified price for some specified length of time. Generally, warrants are issued along with debt or common shares. When packaged with debt, they are used to induce investors to buy long-term debt with a lower coupon rate than would otherwise be required. When warrants are sold with equity, often called a unit offering, they act as a **sweetener** to the deal. For example, when Infomatics Corporation, a rapidly growing high-tech company, wanted to sell $50 million of 20-year bonds in 2015, the company's investment bankers informed the financial vice president that the bonds would be difficult to sell and that a coupon rate of 10% would be required. However, as an alternative the bankers suggested that investors might be willing to buy the bonds with a coupon rate of only 8% if the company would offer 20 warrants with each $1,000 bond, each warrant entitling the holder to buy one share of common stock at a strike price (also called an exercise price) of $22 per share. The stock was selling for $20 per share at the time, and the warrants would expire in 2025 if they had not been exercised previously.

Why would investors be willing to buy Infomatics' bonds at a yield of only 8% in a 10% market just because warrants were also offered as part of the package? It is because the warrants are long-term *call options* that have value since holders can buy the firm's common stock at the strike price regardless of how high the market price climbs. This option offsets the low interest rate on the bonds and makes the package of low-yield bonds plus warrants attractive to investors. (See Chapter 19 for a discussion of options.)

Initial Market Price of a Bond with Warrants

The Infomatics bonds, if they had been issued as straight debt, would have carried a 10% interest rate. However, with warrants attached, the bonds were sold to yield 8%.

Someone buying the bonds at their $1,000 initial offering price would thus be receiving a package consisting of an 8%, 20-year bond plus 20 warrants. Because the going interest rate on bonds as risky as those of Infomatics was 10%, we can find the straight-debt value of the bonds, assuming an annual coupon for ease of illustration, as follows:

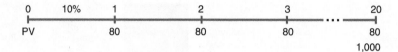

Using a financial calculator, input N = 20, I/YR = 10, PMT = 80, and FV = 1,000. Then press the PV key to obtain the bond's value, $829.73, or approximately $830. Thus, a person buying the bonds in the initial underwriting would pay $1,000 and receive in exchange a straight bond worth about $830 plus 20 warrants presumably worth about $1,000 − $830 = $170:

$$\frac{\text{Price paid for}}{\text{bond with warrants}} = \frac{\text{Straight-debt}}{\text{value of bond}} + \frac{\text{Value of}}{\text{warrants}} \tag{16-1}$$

$$\$1,000 = \$830 + \$170$$

Because investors receive 20 warrants with each bond, each warrant has an implied value of $170/20 = $8.50.

Use of Warrants in Financing

Warrants generally are used by small, rapidly growing firms as sweeteners when they sell debt or stock. Such firms frequently are regarded by investors as being highly risky, so their bonds can be sold only at extremely high coupon rates and with very restrictive indenture provisions. To avoid such restrictions, firms such as Infomatics often offer warrants along with the bonds.

Getting warrants along with bonds enables investors to share in the company's growth, assuming that it does in fact grow and prosper. Therefore, investors are willing to accept a lower interest rate and less restrictive indenture provisions. A bond with warrants has some characteristics of debt and some characteristics of equity. It is a hybrid security that provides the financial manager with an opportunity to expand the firm's mix of securities and thus to appeal to a broader group of investors.

Most warrants issued today are **detachable.** Thus, after a bond or stock with attached warrants is sold, the warrants can be detached and traded separately.[1]

The strike price on warrants is generally set some 20% to 30% above the market price of the stock on the date the bond is issued. If the firm grows and prospers, causing its stock price to rise above the strike price at which shares may be purchased, warrant holders can exercise their warrants and buy stock at the stated price. Warrants also often have **stepped-up exercise prices**, which prod owners into exercising them. For example, Paska Resources Inc. has warrants outstanding with an exercise price of $25 until December 31, 2018, at which time the exercise price will rise to $30. If the price of the common stock is over $25 just before December 31, 2018, many warrant holders will exercise their options before the stepped-up price takes effect and the value of the warrants falls.

A desirable feature of warrants is that they generally bring in funds only if funds are needed. If the company grows, it will probably need new equity capital. At the same time, growth will cause the price of the stock to rise and the warrants to be exercised; hence the firm will obtain the cash it needs. If the company is not successful, and it cannot profitably employ additional money, the price of its stock will probably not rise enough to induce exercise of the warrants.

---

[1] More recently with some smaller issues, the warrants detach from the common share, but they do not trade. Instead they are held in safekeeping for the investor by the brokerage firm.

Wheaton River Strikes Gold with Warrants

Resource-based companies are the largest users of warrants in Canada for financing purposes. Typically, a share is bundled with either a fraction or a full warrant and offered to investors at a single price. Known as unit offerings, these financings offer more attractive terms to investors than simply buying common stock. Probably no company has used warrants more successfully in recent times than Canadian-based Wheaton River Minerals before its takeover by Goldcorp. In just $1\frac{1}{2}$ years, Wheaton River successfully completed four financings, each consisting of a share plus a half or quarter warrant offering. Moreover, each financing was done at a higher price than the previous deal. In total, the company raised $680 million. Not bad, considering that Wheaton River reported only $14 million in revenue in its 2002 annual report. The company used the capital to purchase resource assets. Factoring in rising gold prices, both investors and the company did very well financially with the warrants.

Sources: Barry Critchley, "A Little Juice in Structured Product Mix," *National Post*, June 14, 2007, FP2; Wheaton River Minerals, 2002 and 2003 Annual Reports.

CONCEPT REVIEW

1. What is a warrant?
2. Describe how a new bond issue with warrants is valued.
3. How are warrants used in corporate financing?
4. Shanton Corporation could issue 15-year straight debt at a rate of 8%. Instead, Shanton issues 15-year debt with a coupon rate of 6%, but each bond has 25 warrants attached. The bonds can be issued at par ($1,000 per bond). Assuming annual interest payments, what is the implied value of each warrant? (Check Figure: $6.85)

16.2 Convertible Securities

Convertible securities are bonds or preferred stocks that, under specified terms and conditions, can be exchanged for (i.e., converted into) common stock at the option of the holder. Unlike the exercise of warrants, which brings in additional funds to the firm, conversion does not provide new capital; debt (or preferred stock) is simply replaced on the balance sheet by common stock. Of course, reducing the debt or preferred stock will improve the firm's financial strength and make it easier to raise additional capital, but that requires a separate action.

Conversion Ratio and Conversion Price

One of the most important provisions of a convertible security is the **conversion ratio, CR,** defined as the number of shares of stock a bondholder will receive upon conversion. Related to the conversion ratio is the **conversion price, P_c,** which is the effective price investors pay for the common stock when conversion occurs. The relationship between the conversion ratio and the conversion price can be illustrated by Silicon Valley Software Company's convertible debentures issued at their $1,000 par value in July 2015. At any time prior to maturity on July 15, 2035, a debenture holder can exchange bond for 20 common shares. Therefore, the conversion ratio, CR, is 20. The bond cost a purchaser $1,000, the par value, when it was issued. Dividing the $1,000 par value by the 20 shares received gives a conversion price of $50 a share:

See **Ch 16 Tool Kit.xlsx** at the textbook's website for details.

$$\text{Conversion price} = P_c = \frac{\text{Par value of bond given up}}{\text{Shares received}}$$

$$= \frac{\$1,000}{\text{CR}} = \frac{\$1,000}{20} = \$50 \qquad (16\text{-}2)$$

Conversely, by solving for CR, we obtain the conversion ratio:

$$\text{Conversion ratio} = \text{CR} = \frac{\$1,000}{P_c}$$

$$= \frac{\$1,000}{\$50} = 20 \text{ shares}$$ (16-3)

Once CR is set, the value of P_c is established, and vice versa.

Like a warrant's exercise price, the conversion price is typically set some 20% to 30% above the prevailing market price of the common stock on the issue date. Generally, the conversion price and conversion ratio are fixed for the life of the bond, although sometimes a stepped-up conversion price is used. For example, the 2015 convertible debentures for Breedon Industries are convertible into 12.5 shares until 2024; into 11.76 shares from 2025 until 2035; and into 11.11 shares from 2035 until maturity in 2045. The conversion price thus starts at $80, rises to $85, and then goes to $90. Breedon's convertibles, like most, have a 10-year call-protection period.

Clauses in the convertible's indenture may force a change in the conversion price and ratio to protect the bondholders against dilution in the event of a stock split, stock dividend, or sale of common stock below the conversion price. For example, if Breedon Industries were to have a 2-for-1 stock split during the first 10 years of its convertible's life, the conversion ratio would automatically be adjusted from 12.5 to 25, and the conversion price lowered from $80 to $40. If this protection were not contained in the contract, a company could completely thwart conversion through the use of stock splits and stock dividends. Warrants are similarly protected against dilution.

The Component Cost of Convertibles

See *Ch 16 Tool Kit.xlsx* at the textbook's website for details.

See *Web Extension 16A* on the textbook's website for a discussion on call strategies.

In the spring of 2015, Silicon Valley Software was evaluating the use of the convertible bond issue described earlier. The issue would consist of 20-year convertible bonds that would sell at a price of $1,000 per bond; this $1,000 would also be the bond's par (and maturity) value. The bonds would pay a 10% annual coupon interest rate, or $100 per year. Each bond would be convertible into 20 shares of stock, so the conversion price would be $1,000/20 = $50. The stock was expected to pay a dividend of $2.80 during the coming year, and it sold at $35 per share. Furthermore, the stock price was expected to grow at a constant rate of 8% per year. Therefore, $\hat{r}_s = D_1/P_0 + g = \$2.80/\$35 + 8\% = 8\% + 8\% = 16\%$. If the bonds were not made convertible, they would have to provide a yield of 13%, given their risk and the general level of interest rates. The convertible bonds would not be callable for 10 years, after which they could be called at a price of $1,050, with this price declining by $5 per year thereafter. If, after 10 years, the conversion value exceeds the call price by at least 20%, management will probably call the bonds.[2]

Figure 16-1 shows the expectations of both an average investor and the company.[3]

1. The horizontal line at M = $1,000 represents the par (and maturity) value. Also, $1,000 is the price at which the bond is initially offered to the public.
2. The bond is protected against a call for 10 years. It is initially callable at a price of $1,050, and the call price declines thereafter by $5 per year. Thus, the call price is represented by the solid section of the line V_0M''.
3. Since the convertible has a 10% coupon rate, and since the yield on a nonconvertible bond of similar risk is 13%, the expected "straight bond" value of the convertible, B_t, must be less than par. At the time of issue, assuming an annual coupon, B_0 is $789:

$$\begin{array}{l} \text{Pure-debt value} \\ \text{at time of issue} \end{array} = B_0 = \sum_{t=1}^{N} \frac{\text{Coupon interest}}{(1 + r_d)^t} + \frac{\text{Maturity value}}{(1 + r_d)^N}$$ (16-4)

$$= \sum_{t=1}^{20} \frac{\$100}{(1.13)^t} + \frac{\$1,000}{(1.13)^{20}} = \$789$$

---

[2]For a more detailed discussion of call strategies, see *Web Extension 16A* at the textbook's website.
[3]For a more complete discussion of how the terms of a convertible offering are determined, see M. Wayne Marr and G. Rodney Thompson, "The Pricing of New Convertible Bond Issues," *Financial Management*, Summer 1984, 31–37.

FIGURE 16-1 Silicon Valley Software: Convertible Bond Model

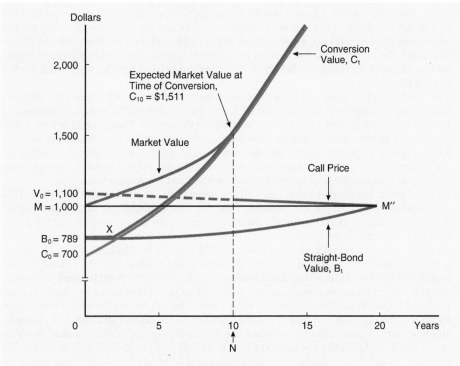

Year	Straight-Bond Value, B_t	Conversion Value, C_t	Maturity Value, M	Market Value	Floor Value	Premium
0	$ 789	$ 700	$1,000	$1,000	$ 789	$211
1	792	756	1,000	1,023	792	231
2	795	816	1,000	1,071	816	255
3	798	882	1,000	1,147	882	265
4	802	952	1,000	1,192	952	240
5	806	1,029	1,000	1,241	1,029	212
6	811	1,111	1,000	1,293	1,111	182
7	816	1,200	1,000	1,344	1,200	144
8	822	1,296	1,000	1,398	1,296	102
9	829	1,399	1,000	1,453	1,399	54
10	837	1,511	1,000	1,511	1,511	0
11	846	1,632	1,000	1,632	1,632	0
.	.	.	.	.	.	.
.	.	.	.	.	.	.
.	.	.	.	.	.	.
20	1,000	3,263	1,000	3,263	3,263	0

Note, however, that the bond's straight-debt value must be $1,000 at maturity, so the straight-debt value rises over time. B_t follows the line B_0M'' in the graph.

4. The bond's initial **conversion value, C_t,** or the value of the stock an investor would receive if the bonds were converted at t = 0, is $P_0(CR) = \$35(20 \text{ shares}) = \$700$. Since the stock price is expected to grow at an 8% rate, the conversion value should rise over time.

For example, in Year 5 it should be $P_5(CR) = \$35(1.08)^5(20) = \$1,029$. The conversion value given the expected stock price over time is given by the line C_t in Figure 16-1.

5. The actual market price of the bond can never fall below the higher of its straight-debt value and its conversion value. If the market price dropped below the straight-bond value, those who wanted bonds would recognize the bargain and buy the convertible as a bond. Similarly, if the market price dropped below the conversion value, people would buy the convertibles, exercise them to get stock, and then sell the stock at a profit. Therefore, the higher of the bond value and conversion value curves in the graph represents a *floor price* for the bond. In Figure 16-1, the floor price is represented by the thicker shaded line B_0XC_t.

6. The bond's market value will typically exceed its floor value. It will exceed the straight-bond value because the option to convert is worth something—a 10% bond with conversion possibilities is worth more than a 10% bond without this option. The convertible's price will also exceed its conversion value because holding the convertible is equivalent to holding a call option, and, prior to expiration, the option's true value is higher than its exercise (or conversion) value. We cannot say exactly where the market value line will lie, but as a rule it will be at or above the floor set by the straight-bond and conversion value lines.

7. At some point, the market value line will converge with the conversion value line. This convergence will occur for two reasons. First, the stock should pay higher and higher dividends as the years go by, but the interest payments on the convertible are fixed. For example, Silicon's convertibles would pay $100 in interest annually, while the dividends on the 20 shares received upon conversion would initially be $20(\$2.80) = \$56$. However, at an 8% growth rate, the dividends after 10 years would be up to $120.90, but the interest would still be $100. Thus, rising dividends will push against the fixed interest payments, causing the premium to disappear and investors to convert voluntarily. Second, once the bond becomes callable, its market value cannot exceed the higher of the conversion value and the call price without exposing investors to the danger of a call. For example, suppose that 10 years after issue (when the bonds become callable), the market value of the bond is $1,600, the conversion value is $1,500, and the call price is $1,050. If the company called the bonds the day after you bought 10 bonds for $16,000, you would be forced to convert into stock worth only $15,000, so you would suffer a loss of $100 per bond, or $1,000, in one day. Recognizing this danger, you and other investors would simply not pay a premium over the higher of the call price or the conversion value after the bond becomes callable. Therefore, in Figure 16-1, we assume that the market value line hits the conversion value line in Year 10, when the bond becomes callable.

8. Let N represent the year when investors expect conversion to occur, either voluntarily because of rising dividends or because the company calls the convertibles to strengthen its balance sheet by substituting equity for debt. In our example, we assume that $N = 10$, the first call date.

9. Since $N = 10$, the expected market value at Year 10 is $\$35(1.08)^{10} \times (20) = \$1,511$. An investor can find the expected rate of return on the convertible bond, r_c, by finding the IRR of the following cash flow stream:

The solution is $r_c = IRR = 12.8\%$.[4]

10. The return on a convertible is expected to come partly from interest income and partly from capital gains; in this case, the total expected return is 12.8%, with 10% representing interest income and 2.8% representing the expected capital gain. The interest component

---

[4]As in the case with warrants, the expected conversion value is not precisely equal to the expected stock price multiplied by the conversion ratio. Here is the reason. If after 10 years the stock price happens to be low so that the conversion value is less than the call price, then the bondholders would not choose to convert—instead, they would surrender their bonds if the company called them. In this example, nonconversion occurs if the stock price after 10 years is less than $1,050/20 = \$52.50$. Since the company makes a call to force conversion, the company won't call the bonds if the stock price is less than $52.50. Therefore, when there is a low stock price, the bondholders will keep the bonds, whose value will depend primarily on interest rates at that time. Finding the expected value in this situation is a very difficult problem (and is beyond the scope of this text)! However, if the expected stock price is much greater than the conversion price when the bonds are called (in this case, $35[1.08]^{10} = \$75.56$ is much bigger than $52.50), the difference between the true expected conversion value and the conversion value that we calculated using the expected stock price will be very small. Therefore, we can estimate the component cost very accurately using the approach in the example.

FINANCE: IN FOCUS

Warren Buffett Likes Warrants!

In August 2011, Warren Buffett's Berkshire Hathaway purchased $5 billion of 6% cumulative perpetual preferred stock from Bank of America. To sweeten the offer, Berkshire Hathaway also received 700 million warrants, which entitled Buffett's company to purchase Bank of America common stock at any time for a period of 10 years at a price of $7.14. As of September 2014, Bank of America was trading around $16, making Buffett more than $6.2 billion in paper profits.

During the height of the financial crisis in 2009, Berkshire Hathaway bought $5 billion worth of preferred stock in Goldman Sachs. As part of the purchase, Buffett also received 43 million warrants, allowing Berkshire Hathaway to purchase 43 million common shares in Goldman Sachs for $115 up until 2013. Although Berkshire Hathaway could have exercised its warrants earlier in 2011 and pocketed almost $2 billion in profit, Buffett stated his intention of waiting until 2013 to use the warrants. After the conversion, Buffett became the sixth largest Goldman Sachs external shareholder.

Also in 2009, Buffett purchased preferred stock in General Electric. Again, as a sweetener, his company received warrants entitling him to buy 135 million shares of GE at $22.25. When the warrants expired, GE stock was trading above the warrants' exercise price, netting Buffett a profit of about $260 million. In 2014 Warren Buffet agreed to help finance Burger King's takeover of Tim Hortons. And as you might have guessed, the deal included a purchase of preferred shares with warrants giving Buffet's company the option to purchase 1.75% of the combined fast-food company.

Sources: Dr. David Kass, "Bank of America Warrants Add Considerable Value to Berkshire Hathaway," January 13, 2012, http://www.blogs.rhsmith.umd.edu/davidkass/, accessed February 21, 2012; Becky Quick, "Berkshire Will Not Exercise Goldman Sachs Warrants Immediately," CNBC, March 20, 2011, http://www.cnbc.com/, accessed February 21, 2012; Alex Crippen, "Warren Buffett's Goldman Sachs Warrants Rebound From Deep Losses," CNBC, March 24, 2009, http://www.cnbc.com/, accessed February 21, 2012; Noah Buhayar, "Buffett's Burger King Deal Has Warrant for 1.75% Stake," Bloomberg.com, August 30, 2014, http://www.bloomberg.com/, accessed September 9, 2014; Alex Crippen, "Buffett's Berkshire Gets 'Only' $260 Million of GE Stock," CNBC, http://www.cnbc.com/, October 16, 2013, accessed September 9, 2014.

is relatively assured, while the capital gain component is more risky. Therefore, a convertible's expected return is more risky than that of a straight bond. This leads us to conclude that r_c should be larger than the cost of straight debt, r_d. Thus, it would seem that the expected rate of return on Silicon's convertibles, r_c, should lie between its cost of straight debt, $r_d = 13\%$, and its cost of common stock, $r_s = 16\%$.

11. Investment bankers use the type of model described here, plus a knowledge of the market, to set the terms on convertibles (the conversion ratio, coupon interest rate, and years of call protection) such that the security will just "clear the market" at its $1,000 offering price. In our example, the required conditions do not hold—the calculated rate of return on the convertible is only 12.8%, which is less than the 13% cost of straight debt. Therefore, the terms on the bond would have to be made more attractive to investors. Silicon Valley Software would have to increase the coupon interest rate on the convertible above 10%, raise the conversion ratio above 20 (and thereby lower the conversion price from $50 to a level closer to the current $35 market price of the stock), lengthen the call-protected period, or use a combination of these changes such that the resulting expected rate of return on the convertible is between 13% and 16%.[5]

Use of Convertibles in Financing

Convertibles have two important advantages from the issuer's standpoint: (1) Convertibles, like bonds with warrants, offer a company the chance to sell debt with a low interest rate in exchange for giving bondholders a chance to participate in the company's success if it does well. (2) In a sense, convertibles provide a way to sell common stock at prices higher than those currently prevailing. Some companies actually want to sell common stock, not debt, but feel that the price of their stock is temporarily depressed. Management may know, for example, that earnings are depressed because of start-up costs associated with a new project,

---

[5]In this discussion, we ignore the tax advantages to investors associated with capital gains. In some situations, tax effects could result in r_c being less than r_d.

but they expect earnings to rise sharply during the next year or so, pulling the price of the stock up with them. Thus, if the company sold stock now, it would be giving up more shares than necessary to raise a given amount of capital. However, if it set the conversion price 20% to 30% above the present market price of the stock, then 20% to 30% fewer shares would be given up when the bonds were converted than if stock were sold directly at the current time. Note, however, that management is counting on the stock's price to rise above the conversion price to make the bonds attractive in conversion. If earnings do not rise and pull the stock price up, conversion does not occur, and the company will be saddled with debt in the face of low earnings, which could be disastrous.

How can the company be sure that conversion will occur if the price of the stock rises above the conversion price? Typically, convertibles contain a call provision that enables the issuing firm to force holders to convert. Suppose the conversion price is $50, the conversion ratio is 20, the market price of the common stock has risen to $60, and the call price on a convertible bond is $1,050. If the company calls the bond, bondholders can either convert into common stock with a market value of 20($60) = $1,200 or allow the company to redeem the bond for $1,050. Naturally, bondholders prefer $1,200 to $1,050, so conversion would occur. The call provision thus gives the company a way to force conversion, provided the market price of the stock is greater than the conversion price. Note, however, that most convertibles have a fairly long period of call protection—10 years is typical. Therefore, if the company wants to be able to force conversion fairly early, then it will have to set a short call-protection period. This will, in turn, require that it set a higher coupon rate or a lower conversion price.

From the standpoint of the issuer, convertibles have three important disadvantages: (1) Although the use of a convertible bond may give the company the opportunity to sell stock at a price higher than the price at which it could be sold currently, if the stock greatly increases in price, the firm would have been better off if it had used straight debt in spite of its higher cost and then later sold common stock and refunded the debt. (2) Convertibles typically have a low coupon interest rate, and the advantage of this low-cost debt will be lost when conversion occurs. (3) If the company truly wants to raise equity capital, and if the price of the stock does not rise sufficiently after the bond is issued, then the company will be stuck with debt.[6]

Convertibles and Agency Costs

A potential agency conflict between bondholders and shareholders is asset substitution, also known as "bait and switch." Suppose a company has been investing in low-risk projects, and because risk is low, bondholders charge a low interest rate. What happens if the company is considering a highly risky but highly profitable venture—one that potential lenders don't know about? The company might decide to raise low-interest-rate debt without spelling out that the funds will be invested in the risky project. After the funds have been raised and the investment is made, the value of the debt should fall because the interest rate will be too low to compensate debtholders for the high risk they bear. This results in a wealth transfer from bondholders to shareholders.

If debtholders think that a company might employ the bait-and-switch tactic, they will charge a higher interest rate. This higher interest rate is an agency cost. Debtholders will charge this higher rate even if the company has no intention of engaging in bait-and-switch behaviour, since they don't know the company's true intentions. Therefore, they assume the worst and charge a higher interest rate.

Convertible securities are one way to mitigate this type of agency cost. Suppose the debt is convertible and the company does take on the high-risk project. If the value of the company turns out to be higher than expected, then bondholders can convert their debt to equity and benefit from the successful investment. Therefore, bondholders are willing to charge a lower interest rate on convertibles, which serves to minimize the agency costs.[7]

---

[6]For a list of Canadian convertible debentures, go to http://www.financialpost.com, and then click "Markets" and then "Market Data" and finally "Convertible Debentures."

[7]See Craig M. Lewis, Richard J. Rogalski, and James K. Seward, "Understanding the Design of Convertible Debt," *Journal of Applied Corporate Finance*, Spring 1998, 45–53. For more insights into convertible pricing and use, see Paul Asquith and David W. Mullins, Jr., "Convertible Debt: Corporate Call Policy and Voluntary Conversion," *Journal of Finance*, September 1991, 1273–1289; Randall S. Billingsley and David M. Smith, "Why Do Firms Issue Convertible Debt?" *Financial Management*, Summer 1996, 93–99; Douglas R. Emery, Mai E. Iskandor-Datta, and Jong-Chul Rhim, "Capital Structure Management as a Motivation for Calling Convertible Debt," *Journal of Financial Research*, Spring 1994, 91–104; T. Harikumar, P. Kadapakkam, and Ronald F. Singer, "Convertible Debt and Investment Incentives," *Journal of Financial Research*, Spring 1994, 15–29; Vahan Janjigian, "The Leverage Changing Consequences of Convertible Debt Financing," *Financial Management*, Autumn 1987, 15–21; and V. Sivarama Krishnan and Ramesh P. Rao, "Financial Distress Costs and Delayed Calls of Convertible Bonds," *Financial Review*, November 1996, 913–925.

FINANCE: IN FOCUS

Will Blackberry Be "Converting' Its Corporate Prospects?

Blackberry's struggle and dramatic fall from grace highlights the extremely competitive nature of the wireless industry. While Blackberry had significant cash on hand when the market for its products turned, it has been using up its cash reserves rapidly. In 2012 it used $2.3 billion in cash for investment purposes. By August 2013, it had consumed another $800 million in its efforts to turn itself around. To buy more breathing space, the company agreed to a $1 billion, 7-year convertible debenture financing. It had a limited number of options. The company's common stock had fallen from $69 in 2011 to about $6 in 2013, so investors would likely not have been receptive to a straight equity option. Although Blackberry had no long-term debt and could have issued straight bonds, its relatively bleak prospects would have required a high coupon rate. Instead, the interest rate on Blackberry's convertible debt was 6%, with an option to convert the debentures into common shares at $10, representing a 45% premium on its share price at the time.

What motivated the convertible debt investors? Well, (at the time of writing) the chance of Blackberry turning itself around is very uncertain. If it does, however, Blackberry's stock will climb sharply from its current levels, offering the convertible debenture holders significant upside potential. If the company fails and goes bankrupt, the convertible debenture holders will rank ahead of shareholders in being able to control the company's assets, technologies, and patents. Thus, the convertible debentures provide the investors downside protection with the possibility of benefiting from a successful turnaround.

CONCEPT REVIEW

1. What is a conversion ratio? A conversion price? A straight-bond value?
2. What is meant by a convertible's floor value?
3. What are the advantages and disadvantages of convertibles to issuers? To investors?
4. How do convertibles reduce agency costs?
5. A convertible bond has a par value of $1,000 and a conversion price of $25. The stock currently trades for $22 a share. What are the bond's conversion ratio and conversion value at t = 0? (Check Figures: 40; $880)

16.3 A Final Comparison of Warrants and Convertibles

Convertible debt can be thought of as straight debt with nondetachable warrants. Thus, at first blush, it might appear that debt with warrants and convertible debt are more or less interchangeable. However, a closer look reveals one major and several minor differences between these two securities.[8] First, as we discussed previously, the exercise of warrants brings in new equity capital, while the conversion of convertibles results only in an accounting transfer.

A second difference involves flexibility. Most convertibles contain a call provision that allows the issuer either to refund the debt or to force conversion, depending on the relationship between the conversion value and call price. However, most warrants are not callable, so firms must wait until maturity for the warrants to generate new equity capital. Generally, maturities also differ between warrants and convertibles. Warrants typically have much shorter maturities than convertibles, and warrants typically expire before their accompanying debt matures. Furthermore, warrants provide for fewer future common shares than do convertibles, because with convertibles all of the debt is converted to stock, whereas debt remains outstanding when warrants are exercised. Together, these facts

---

[8]For a more detailed comparison of warrants and convertibles, see Michael S. Long and Stephen F. Sefcik, "Participation Financing: A Comparison of the Characteristics of Convertible Debt and Straight Bonds Issued in Conjunction with Warrants," *Financial Management*, Autumn 1990, 23–34.

suggest that debt-plus-warrant issuers are actually more interested in selling debt than in selling equity.

In general, firms that issue debt with warrants are smaller and riskier than those that issue convertibles. One possible rationale for the use of option securities, especially the use of debt with warrants by small firms, is the difficulty investors have in assessing the risk of small companies. If a start-up with a new, untested product seeks debt financing, it is very difficult for potential lenders to judge the riskiness of the venture; hence it is difficult to set a fair interest rate. Under these circumstances, many potential investors will be reluctant to invest, making it necessary to set a very high interest rate to attract debt capital. By issuing debt with warrants, investors obtain a package that offers upside potential to offset the risks of loss.

Finally, there is a significant difference in issuance costs between debt with warrants and convertible debt. Bonds with warrants typically require issuance costs that are about 1.2 percentage points more than the flotation costs for convertibles. In general, bond-with-warrant financings have underwriting fees that approximate the weighted average of the fees associated with debt and equity issues, while underwriting costs for convertibles are more like those associated with straight debt.

CONCEPT REVIEW

1. What are some differences between debt-with-warrant financing and convertible debt?
2. Explain how bonds with warrants might help small, risky firms sell debt securities.

16.4 Reporting Earnings When Warrants or Convertibles Are Outstanding

If warrants or convertibles are outstanding, a firm can report earnings per share in one of two ways:

1. *Basic EPS*, calculated as earnings available to common shareholders divided by the weighted average number of shares actually outstanding during the period.
2. *Diluted EPS*, calculated as earnings available divided by the weighted average number of shares that would have been outstanding if all warrants and convertibles had actually been exercised or converted at the beginning of the year. When diluted EPS is being calculated, earnings are first adjusted by "backing out" the interest on the convertible bonds. The adjusted earnings are then divided by the adjusted number of shares.

Publicly traded companies in Canada must report both basic and diluted EPS. For firms with large amounts of option securities outstanding, there can be a substantial difference between the basic and diluted EPS figures. Keep in mind that diluted EPS is a hypothetical number, one that can assist in answering "what if" questions on the dilution of earnings by option securities.[9]

CONCEPT REVIEW

1. What are the possible methods for reporting EPS when warrants and convertibles are outstanding?
2. Why should investors be concerned about a firm's outstanding warrants and convertibles?

16.5 Securitization

As the term is generally used, a *security* refers to a publicly traded financial instrument, as opposed to a privately placed instrument. Thus, securities have greater liquidity than otherwise similar instruments that are not traded on an open market. In recent years, procedures

---

[9]Thomas H. Beechy and Joan E.D. Conrod, *Intermediate Accounting*, 4th ed. (Toronto: McGraw-Hill, 2008), 1142.

FIGURE
16-2   Asset Securitization Structure

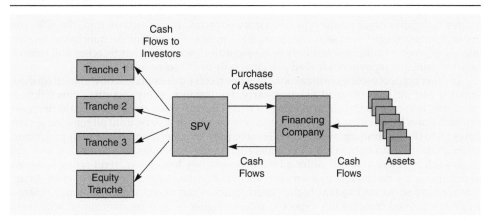

have been developed to **securitize** various types of debt instruments, thereby increasing their liquidity, lowering the cost of capital to borrowers, and generally increasing the efficiency of the financial markets.

Securitization has occurred in two major ways. First, some debt instruments that were formerly rarely traded are now actively traded, with the change being due to decisions by certain financial institutions to "make a market"—that is, stand willing to buy or sell the security and hold an inventory of the security in order to balance buy and sell orders. This occurred many years ago in the case of common stocks and investment-grade bonds. More recently, it occurred in the bankers' acceptance (BA) and commercial paper markets, in which large, financially strong firms issue short-term debt. The commercial paper market in Canada is relatively modest at less than $12 billion. By contrast, the market for BAs is about $60 billion.

The second major development in securitization involves the pledging of specific assets, *asset securitization,* or the creation of *asset-backed securities.* Assets such as automobile loans, credit card receivables, equipment leases, and residential mortgages are all assets with the potential to be combined into specific pools (such as a credit card or mortgage pool). Debt instruments of varying maturities are then created that use the pool of assets as collateral. The financial institution that originally held the assets generally continues to act as the servicing agent, but the assets themselves are sold to other investors. Figure 16-2 shows the structure and cash flows of a typical asset securitization. If the debt has a very short term, such as with asset-backed commercial paper (ABCP), it must be renewed frequently.

In 2007, there was a crisis of confidence over asset-backed securities, mainly due to "sub-prime" or risky U.S. residential mortgages being used as collateral by some ABCP. The concern was the default rate of the sub-prime mortgages brought on by declining residential housing prices in the United States. Although relatively few sub-prime mortgages were actually used as collateral for ABCP in Canada, the nature of these securities did not allow transparency into the specific assets being held. Investors became concerned about the quality of the assets backing up their ABCP, and when the securities had to be renewed, there were no buyers. This led to a $20 billion default in the Canadian ABCP market.[10]

The companies behind asset securitizations—often financial institutions such as banks and credit card or auto leasing companies—are called *originators.* In their regular business operations, these companies take on home mortgages, car loans and/or finance credit card receivables. Because they have a finite amount of available capital, financing companies are limited in the amount of lending they are able to do. However, if they could sell the mortgages they hold or the auto loans they have provided, these financing companies would then have additional capital to make further loans. So the financing company sets up a separate company, called a *special purpose vehicle* (SPV), that issues securities to investors and with the proceeds purchases the cash flow–producing assets that the financing company wishes to sell.

[10]Mortgage-backed securities (MBSs) for Canadian mortgages are quite different. MBSs are backed by conventional mortgages that are made on somewhat more conservative terms. In addition, payment is guaranteed by the CMHC, a federal Crown corporation. Default risk is comparable to Government of Canada bonds.

The financing company will continue to service and administer the assets: This includes collecting all regular payments such as the mortgage or car payments associated with the assets. These cash flows are passed through to the SPV, which in turn distributes them to investors. The cash flows, however, are not distributed uniformly to all investors. Investors receive cash flows based on the type of security or *tranche* they purchase from the SPV. For instance, in mortgage-based securitizations, it is common for some of the tranches to receive interest payments (called interest-only or IO securities), whereas other tranches will receive only the principal repayments (called principal-only or PO securities).

In other types of asset securitizations, tranches receive different cash flows based on their seniority and the level of credit risk they carry. For instance, many securitizations follow a "waterfall" payment schedule, according to which the top-rated tranches get paid first and any cash flows left over get passed on to the next tranche, and so on until all remaining cash flows go to the last tranche, which is called an equity tranche. If any of the cash-producing assets in the SPV do not make full or timely payments, the lower-rated tranches will not receive full payment and will suffer a loss. Investors rely heavily on credit rating agencies to determine the investment risk for each specific tranche. As to be expected, asset securitizations are structured so that higher-rated tranches can expect to receive lower returns while lower-rated tranches can expect to receive higher returns commensurate with their increased risk.

By selling assets such as mortgages or car loans to the SPVs, financing companies are able to replenish their capital and continue lending. For example, a car company can raise capital by packaging and selling its car leases and car loans through an asset securitization. The money raised allows the car company to offer additional car loans and leases, and at more attractive terms than it could otherwise. Likewise, a manufacturing company can securitize its accounts receivable, thereby generating financing to allow it to offer its customers credit terms at a better rate than it may otherwise be able to do. Additional financing capital benefits the general economy, allowing greater economic activity and growth.

Asset securitizations are extremely important to the housing market. By securitizing their home mortgages, banks free up capital to make more mortgages. The home mortgage securitization market is so central to the economy that governments have established special agencies to act as originators in this market. The Canada Mortgage and Housing Corporation (CMHC) is a Crown corporation that issues mortgage insurance to qualifying mortgages, working under the auspices of the National Housing Act to administer mortgage-backed securities for the Canadian market. In the United States, the Federal National Home Mortgage Association (FNMA, "Fannie Mae") is a public company established by the U.S. Congress, and the Federal Home Loan Mortgage Corporation (FHLMC, "Freddie Mac") is a government-sponsored enterprise. Both exist specifically to purchase mortgages from financial institutions and repackage them as mortgage-backed securities.

For investors, the main advantage of asset securitization is a function of the portfolio effect. A typical asset securitization has a portfolio of hundreds or even thousands of underlying assets. The payment risk on any one of those assets may be very difficult to determine and would likely be high; the portfolio effect of having so many assets allows for a more accurate and overall lower assessment of the risk, as the assets are presumed to have a low correlation of returns. Also, asset securitizations provide investors with access to financial assets such as car loans and home mortgages that would otherwise be very difficult to invest in and administer directly. A final advantage for investors relates to the choice of risk and return made available by the different tranches sold. That is, asset securitizations allow investors to broaden their choice of investable assets, to invest in more diverse portfolios, and to choose a specific level of investment risk.

ⓒNCEPT REVIEW

1. What are the benefits of securitization to investors?
2. Why is securitization important in the housing market?

16.6 Credit Derivatives

Credit derivatives are financial instruments that enable lenders such as banks to reduce the credit risks they take on when they loan money and thereby increase the amount they can lend. Credit derivatives also provide investors with yet another investment choice.

A **credit derivative** transfers credit risk from one counterparty (the protection buyer) to another counterparty (the protection seller). Figure 16-3 shows the structure and the cash flows of a basic credit derivative transaction called a **credit default swap**.

The protection buyer makes a quarterly payment, called the *credit default swap premium* or simply the *swap premium*, to the protection seller. The protection seller takes on the risk of default and in return makes a payment to the protection buyer, but only if the underlying company defaults on its obligations, declares bankruptcy, or suffers a similar type of negative credit event. The payment in response to a credit event is equal to the amount of the swap multiplied by the percentage loss in value of the underlying reference loan.

For example, Big City Bank (BCB) may have a $10 million loan outstanding to Widgets Manufacturing Company (WMC). To protect itself against a loss in the event that WMC defaults, BCB enters into a credit default swap with LifeCo Insurance (LCI), a large, highly rated insurance company. The amount of the swap, called the *notional* value, is $10 million and is based on the value of the underlying bank loan. The swap premium is 2.50% and the life of the swap is 5 years. This implies that each year, BCB will pay LCI a swap premium of 2.50% × $10 million or $250,000. If WCM does not default in the 5-year life of the swap, LCI will not make a payment to BCB. However, if WMC does default or declare bankruptcy, LCI will make a payment based on the severity of default. For instance, if WMC defaults, and the recovery value of the $10 million loan is only $3 million, LCI will make a payment to BCB of $7 million.

As the above example shows, credit derivatives are an effective way for a bank to hedge its credit risk. Starting in the mid-1990s, banks began using credit derivatives extensively to reduce their credit exposure, and this gave them the flexibility to make additional loans. Credit derivatives are yet another way for investors to invest in loan markets "synthetically," without having to fund the underlying loans or take physical ownership of the loans.

To make their credit hedges even more efficient, banks started bundling their loans together, using asset securitization techniques to pass the risk and return of large packages of corporate loans to investors. A security made up of corporate loans and credit default swaps is called a *collateralized debt obligation* or CDO.

Figure 16-4 shows the structure and cash flows for a CDO. In a typical CDO, a bank creates an SPV and enters into a large number of separate credit default swaps with the SPV based on different loans in the bank's loan portfolio. For example, the bank might enter into 200 different credit default swaps, each with a notional amount of $10 million, for a total amount of $2 billion. The bank pays a quarterly credit default swap (CDS) premium to the SPV, which in turn provides the bank with a payment based on the default on any of the underlying loans. The SPV sells notes or tranches of different credit quality to investors as in a traditional asset securitization and then uses the proceeds to buy high-quality securities such as government bonds. Investors in the different tranches receive periodic coupon payments that are based on the interest payments received from the government bonds as well as the payments the SPV receives from each of the credit default swap premiums. The SPV pays interest to the highest rated tranche first, then to the next

FIGURE 16-3   Credit Default Swap

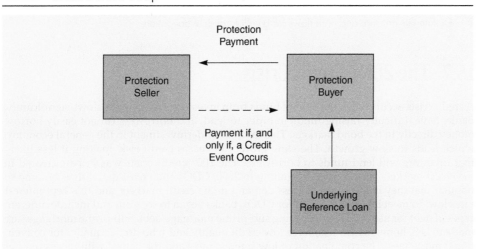

FIGURE
16-4   Collateralized Debt Obligation (CDO)

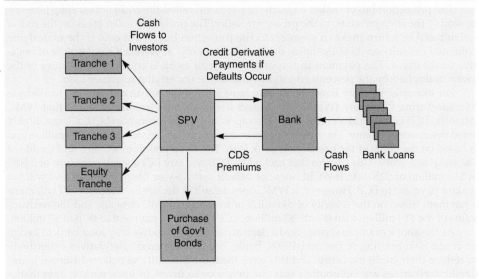

highest rated tranche, and so on until what is left is paid to the lowest rated tranche (the equity tranche). If there are any defaults in the basket of the 200 loans underlying the transaction, the SPV diverts funds from the trancheholders to the bank to make up for any loss on the loan. If the number and severity of the defaults is large enough, there may not be enough funds to pay the equity trancheholders anything. In that case, the equity holders will receive nothing back, and any further default payments will be taken out of the proceeds going to the next lowest rated tranche.

Higher yields and the ability to invest in very specific levels of risk made CDOs very popular investments with large institutional investors. Banks also liked CDOs, which allowed them to hedge a large amount of their credit risk in a very cost-effective and efficient manner. Indeed, the popularity of these instruments created a large demand in the market for credit-sensitive assets such as bonds and loans, which drove the prices of these securities higher and thereby lowered their yields. Although investors were receiving lower yields on their assets, the risk involved was considered lower because it could be hedged using credit derivatives and CDOs.

CONCEPT REVIEW

1.   Explain the structure and cash flows for a credit default swap.
2.   Explain the structure and cash flows for a collateral debt obligation.

16.7 The 2007 Credit Crisis

A credit crisis occurs when the flow of funds from investors to borrowers slows significantly. Banks have difficulty raising funds in order to lend, and borrowers cannot easily borrow money directly in the bond markets. This leads to underinvestment in the general economy, which leads to slow growth. The slow growth increases credit risk, making it less likely that investors will lend funds to borrowers. The 2007 credit crisis was in part created in the credit markets years earlier. Beginning in 2000, CDOs and credit derivatives became so popular that they helped create excess demand in the credit markets, and this kept interest rates low. To meet investor demand for CDOs, banks began to seek out and include different types of debt for use in CDOs, including sub-prime mortgage debt. Sub-prime mortgages are made to U.S. homeowners who have low credit quality and who do not qualify for conventional mortgages. The combination of low interest rates and the banks' willingness to offer sub-prime mortgages (both due in large part to meet investor demand for CDOs), helped push housing prices in the United States and globally to record high prices, setting the stage for a later dramatic fall. Low interest rates also provided investors with an incentive to take on riskier trades in their search for higher yields. Thus, the dramatic growth and widespread use of credit derivatives and CDOs is viewed as having contributed to the 2007 credit crisis.

CDOs were also becoming so large and complex that their diversification benefits were eroded. The pricing and risk of tranches depends on the riskiness of each individual loan and on the correlations among the various loans. Indeed, assessing correlations among loans is an especially difficult problem that is poorly understood by both theoreticians and practitioners. Assessing credit risks of conventional mortgage-backed securities is better understood, as the payment patterns of traditional mortgages have long been tracked. However, since the sub-prime mortgage market was relatively new, the default rate on these mortgages was difficult to estimate, and so was the degree of correlation of default between different sub-prime borrowers. However difficult it was to assess the underlying risks of CDOs, these instruments remained very popular with investors, who were attracted by the high returns relative to the perceived risk.

Problems in the CDO market began when a larger than predicted number of sub-prime mortgage holders began to default on their mortgages. Even though the CDOs were based on a geographically diversified pool of mortgages, there were uniformly high default rates across all regions. This suggested that the correlation assumptions built into the CDO pricing models were flawed and that investors were not realizing the expected benefits of portfolio diversification. Investors in the equity and low-rated tranches began to lose money on their investments as higher than expected mortgage defaults continued. This led to panic selling in CDOs, which in turn led to all of the tranches falling in value dramatically. As the demand for CDOs dried up, banks were unable to raise new funds to make additional loans. Banks responded by cutting back on their lending activity, which stalled economic growth and created a credit crisis.

One result of the credit crisis was a loss of investor confidence in financial institutions. By January 2009, several financial institutions had failed, with Lehman Brothers being the largest; others merged in order to prevent collapse (Bear Sterns, Wachovia, Merrill Lynch) or required significant government support (Citigroup, Bank of America, AIG). The entire banking industry of Iceland collapsed as a result of overinvestments in CDOs. Canadian financial institutions, while not immune from the global credit crisis, have been spared the extreme consequences suffered by other global banks, mainly because Canadian banks have more conservative lending policies and stronger retail banking businesses.

Credit derivatives and CDOs are considered one of the causes of the credit crisis; actually, though, they are simply one factor among many that created the conditions for that crisis. Overheated housing markets in Europe and the United States, a dramatic run-up in the price of oil, excessive individual and institutional leverage, inadequate regulatory oversight, poor lending practices, and the economic consequences of the Middle East conflict are just some of the other ingredients that contributed to the financial crisis. Economists, regulators, academics, and capital market pundits will no doubt research and debate for years the exact mix of causes of this very complex financial situation.[11]

There are several lessons we can learn from the rise and fall of the credit derivative and CDO markets. One lesson is that, while the benefits of diversification are real, flawed correlation forecasts can have disastrous results, as the sub-prime market showed. Another is that relatively risky illiquid assets can be combined into new, lower-risk securities that are easily traded on the markets. Asset securitizations, credit derivatives, and CDOs increase the availability of capital to borrowers, thus encouraging economic activity. A third lesson, and perhaps most important one, is that as securities become more complex, they can outpace the market's ability to properly assess the trade-off between risk and return, which may result in significant losses to capital as well as to investor confidence.

When properly used, credit derivatives and CDOs are powerful instruments that enable banks to hedge their credit risks and that provide investors with another asset class in which to invest. These products increased the willingness of investors to invest in bonds and loans, which made it easier for companies and individuals to borrow. However, their use—and

---

[11]For additional articles on securitization, see Martin Neil Baily, Robert E. Litan, and Matthew S. Johnson, "The Origins of the Financial Crisis," The Brookings Institution, Fixing Finance Series—Paper 3, November 2008; Adam B. Ashcraft and Til Schuermann, "Understanding the Securitization of Subprime Mortgage Credit," Wharton Financial Institutions Center Working Paper no. 07–43; Federal Reserve Bank of New York Staff Report no. 318, March 2008, available at http://ssrn.com/abstract51071189; and Joseph R. Mason and Josh Rosner, "How Resilient Are Mortgage Backed Securities to Collateralized Debt Obligation Market Disruptions?" February 13, 2007, available at http://ssrn.com/abstract51027472.

the dependence on expected diversification benefits that did not materialize as calculated—created excess risk and leverage in the economy, which led to the credit crisis. Until investors and financial institutions learn better ways to analyze and manage the risks of these instruments, their use will likely be limited.

CONCEPT REVIEW

1. What role did credit derivatives and CDOs play in creating the credit crisis of 2007?
2. What lessons from the credit crisis should be learned regarding the use of credit derivatives and CDOs?

Summary

While common stock and long-term debt provide most of the capital used by corporations, companies also use several forms of other securities. These include hybrids, such as convertibles, and warrants, that generally have some characteristics of debt and some of equity. We discussed the pros and cons of these hybrids from the standpoints of both issuers and investors, how to determine when to use them, and the factors that affect their values. The basic rationale for these securities, and the procedures used to evaluate them, are based on concepts developed in earlier chapters. The key concepts covered are listed below:

- A **warrant** is a long-term call option issued along with a bond. Warrants are generally detachable from the bond, and they trade separately in the market. When warrants are exercised, the firm receives additional equity capital, and the original bonds remain outstanding.
- A **convertible** security is a bond or preferred stock that can be exchanged for common stock at the option of the holder. When a security is converted, debt or preferred stock is replaced with common stock, and no money changes hands.
- Warrant and convertible issues are generally structured so that the **strike (exercise) price** or **conversion price** is 20% to 30% above the stock's price at time of issue.
- Although both warrants and convertibles are option securities, there are several differences between the two, including **separability, impact when exercised, callability, maturity,** and **flotation costs.**
- Warrants and convertibles are **sweeteners** used to make the underlying debt or preferred stock issue more attractive to investors. Although the coupon rate or dividend yield is lower when options are part of the issue, the overall cost of the issue is higher than the cost of straight debt or preferred, because option-related securities are riskier.
- **Asset securitization** occurs when assets such as mortgages or credit card receivables are bundled together. Securities, backed by this pool of assets, are then issued to investors. Cash flows, such as interest and principal payments from the underlying assets, are then bundled and passed through to the holders of the securitized assets.
- A **credit default swap** is a contract that transfers credit risk from one counterparty (the protection buyer) to another counterparty (the protection seller). Credit default swaps enable lenders such as banks to reduce the credit risks they take on when they loan money.

Questions

16-1 Define each of the following terms:
a. Warrant; detachable warrant
b. Stepped-up price
c. Convertible security
d. Conversion ratio; conversion price; conversion value
e. Sweetener

16-2 What effect does the trend in stock prices (subsequent to issue) have on a firm's ability to raise funds through (a) convertibles and (b) warrants?

16-3   If a firm expects to have additional financial requirements in the future, would you recommend that it use convertibles or bonds with warrants? What factors would influence your decision?

16-4   Evaluate the following statement: "Issuing convertible securities represents a means by which a firm can sell common stock at a price above the existing market."

16-5   Suppose a company simultaneously issues $50 million of convertible bonds with a coupon rate of 10% and $50 million of straight bonds with a coupon rate of 14%. Both bonds have the same maturity. Does the fact that the convertible issue has the lower coupon rate suggest that it is less risky than the straight bond? Is the cost of capital lower on the convertible than on the straight bond? Explain.

16-6   How will the protection payment of a credit default swap change as the following variables change? Will the default swap protection payment increase, decrease, or remain unchanged?
a.   The expected recovery values decrease
b.   The expected risk of default increases
c.   The company the swap is based on issues more debt
d.   The company the swap is based on issues more equity
e.   The company's bond prices increase
f.   The company's stock price increases

16-7   Pricing a CDO is very complicated and still not fully understood. What are some of the variables that you believe would be important in analyzing the price and the risk of a CDO?

Concept Review Problem

Full solutions are provided at www.nelson.com/brigham3ce.

CR-1   Connor Company recently issued two types of bonds. The first issue consisted of 10-year
Warrants   straight debt with a 6% annual coupon. The second issue consisted of 10-year bonds with a 4.5% annual coupon and attached warrants. Both issues sold at their $1,000 par values. What is the implied value of the warrants attached to each bond?

Problems

Easy   Answers to odd-numbered problems appear in Appendix A.
Problems 1–4

16-1   Newhouse Enterprises recently issued two types of bonds. The first issue consisted of 15-year
Warrants   straight debt with a 7% annual coupon. The second issue consisted of 15-year bonds with a 5% annual coupon and attached warrants. Both issues sold at their $1,000 par values. What is the implied value of the warrants attached to each bond?

16-2   Fisher Investments recently issued convertible bonds with a $1,000 par value. The bonds
Convertibles   have a conversion price of $50 a share. What is the convertible issue's conversion ratio?

16-3   Big City Bank enters into a credit default swap with LifeCo, a highly rated insurance com-
Credit Default Swap   pany. The notional amount of the swap is $20 million. The 5-year swap is based on a 5-year loan to ABC Corp. The size of the protection payment is 2.78% per year.
a.   How much does Big City Bank pay LifeCo for each year the swap is in place?
b.   If ABC does not suffer a credit event, how much does LifeCo pay Big City Bank over the 5-year life of the swap?
c.   Assume that ABC goes bankrupt before the swap matures and that the recovery value on the underlying loan is 45%. How much does LifeCo owe Big City Bank?

16-4   Complete the following table. Assume a bond with a $1,000 par value, 10-year maturity that
Warrants   pays interest annually.

Bond	Price per warrant	Number of warrants	Bond with warrant coupon rate	Straight bond YTM
A	$2.46	___	8%	10%
B	$4.49	40	4%	___
C	$3.68	20	___	6%

**Intermediate
Problems 5–7**

16-5

Warrants

Delphi Analytics has warrants outstanding that permit the holders to purchase one share of stock per warrant at a price of $15.

a. Calculate the exercise value of the firm's warrants if the common shares sell at each of the following prices: (1) $10, (2) $15, (3) $20, (4) $85. (*Hint:* A warrant's exercise value is the difference between the stock price and the purchase price specified by the warrant if the warrant were to be exercised.)

b. At what approximate price do you think the warrants would actually sell under each condition indicated above? What time value (price minus exercise value) is implied in your price? Your answer is a guess, but your prices and time values should bear reasonable relationships to one another.

c. How would each of the following factors affect your estimates of the warrants' prices and time values in part b?
   (1) The life of the warrant
   (2) Expected variability (σ_p) in the stock's price
   (3) The expected growth rate in the stock's EPS
   (4) The company announces a change in dividend policy: whereas it formerly paid no dividends, henceforth it will pay out all earnings as dividends.

d. Assume the firm's stock now sells for $10 per share. The company wants to sell some 10-year, annual interest, $1,000 par value bonds. Each bond will have attached 50 warrants, each exercisable into one share of stock at an exercise price of $13. The firm's straight bonds yield 8%. Regardless of your answer to Part b, assume that each warrant will have a market value of $2 when the stock sells at $10. What coupon interest rate, and dollar coupon, must the company set on the bonds with warrants if they are to clear the market?

16-6

Convertible Premiums

Tsetsekos Company was planning to finance an expansion. The principal executives of the company all agreed that an industrial company such as theirs should finance growth by means of common stock rather than by debt. However, they felt that the price of the company's common stock did not reflect its true worth, so they decided to sell a convertible security. They considered a convertible debenture but feared the burden of fixed interest charges if the common stock did not rise in price to make conversion attractive. They decided on an issue of convertible preferred stock, which would pay a dividend of $2.10 per share.

The common stock was selling for $42 a share at the time. Management projected earnings for 2015 at $3 a share and expected a future growth rate of 10%. It was agreed by the investment bankers and the management that the common stock would sell at 14 times earnings, the current price/earnings ratio.

a. The conversion ratio will be 1.0; that is, each share of convertible preferred can be converted into one share of common. Therefore, the convertible's par value (and also the issue price) will be equal to the conversion price, which, in turn, will be determined as a premium (i.e., the percentage by which the conversion price exceeds the stock price) over the current market price of the common stock. What will the conversion price be if it is set at a 10% premium? What will the conversion price be if it is set at a 30% premium?

b. Should the preferred stock include a call provision? Why?

16-7

**Convertible Bond
Analysis**

A company issues a 10-year convertible bond with a 6% coupon, paid annually. The bond is convertible into common shares at a conversion rate of 55. Straight bonds of similar risk currently yield 7.8%. The stock price is currently priced 25% less than the conversion price. The company's stock price is expected to grow by 8% per year, and the bond is callable at $1,100. The bonds will not be called until their price is 125% of the conversion value.

a. How many years do you expect it will take for the bonds to be called? (Round your answer up to a full year.)

b. What will be the overall return to the convertible bondholder?

**Challenging
Problems 8–11**

16-8

**Convertible
Calculations**

The table below provides market data from October 1, 2014, Solve for the unknown variables. The "Premium" column refers to the percentage extra an investor would pay for the stock if it purchased the bond at the market price and immediately converted at the conversion ratio. Assume that the bonds pay semiannually, that they mature at the end of the year shown, and that today is October 1, 2014. Thus the next payment will be in 3 months or 0.5 of a semiannual payment period. (Ignore any slight rounding.)

Issuer	Coupon (%)	Maturity	Price	Yield to Maturity (%)	Premium (%)	Conversion Ratio	Conversion Price	Price
H&R Real Estate	4.50	Dec 2016	_____	3.17	30.53	4.27	27.50	$21.67
Chemtrade Logistics	5.75	Dec 2018	111.75	2.79	_____	5.00	_____	$20.57
Cineplex Galaxy	4.50	Dec 2018	105.81	_____	44.56	1.79	56.00	$40.99
Rogers Sugar	5.75	Dec 2018	104.25	4.63	60.73	13.89	_____	_____
Canexus	5.75	Dec 2018	99.95	5.76	145.55	_____	_____	$4.62
Pembina Pipeline	5.75	Dec 2018	158.00	_____	0.04	_____	29.53	$46.64
Vicwest	5.25	Dec 2018	100.50	5.12	71.43	5.29	_____	_____

Source: Material adapted from *National Post*, http://www.financialpost.com/markets/data/bondsdebentures.html, accessed September 30, 2014.

16-9
Convertible Bond Analysis

Fifteen years ago, Caleb Industries sold $400 million of convertible bonds. The bonds had a 40-year maturity and a 5.75% coupon rate and paid interest annually. They were sold at their $1,000 par value. The conversion price was set at $62.75; the common stock price was $55 per share. The bonds were subordinated debentures, and they were given an A rating; straight nonconvertible debentures of the same quality yielded about 8.75% at the time Caleb's bonds were issued.

a. Calculate the premium on the bonds, that is, the percentage excess of the conversion price over the stock price at the time of issue.
b. What is Caleb's annual before-tax interest savings on the convertible issue versus a straight-debt issue?
c. At the time the bonds were issued, what was the value per bond of the conversion feature?
d. Suppose the price of Caleb's common stock fell from $55 on the day the bonds were issued to $32.75 now, 15 years after the issue date (also assume that the stock price never exceeded $62.75). Assume that interest rates remained constant. What is the current price of the straight-bond portion of the convertible bond? What is the current value if a bondholder converts a bond? Do you think it is likely that the bonds will be converted?
e. The bonds originally sold for $1,000. If interest rates on A-rated bonds had remained constant at 8.75% and the stock price had fallen to $32.75, what do you think would have happened to the price of the convertible bonds? (Assume no change in the standard deviation of stock returns.)
f. Now suppose that the price of Caleb's common stock had fallen from $55 on the day the bonds were issued to $32.75 at present, 15 years after the issue. Suppose also that the rate of interest had fallen from 8.75% to 5.75%. Under these conditions, what is the current price of the straight-bond portion of the convertible bond? What is the current value if a bondholder converts a bond? What do you think would have happened to the price of the bonds?

16-10
Warrant/Convertible Decisions

Rossi's Tile and Ceramic Company has grown rapidly during the past 5 years. Recently, its commercial bank urged the company to consider increasing its permanent financing. Its bank loan under a line of credit has risen to $600,000, carrying a 7% interest rate. Rossi has been 30 to 60 days late in paying trade creditors.

Discussions with an investment banker have resulted in the decision to raise $900,000 at this time. Investment bankers have assured the firm that the following alternatives are feasible (flotation costs will be ignored):
• *Alternative 1:* Sell common stock at $8.
• *Alternative 2:* Sell convertible bonds at a 7% coupon, convertible into 100 shares of common stock for each $1,000 bond (i.e., the conversion price is $10 per share).
• *Alternative 3:* Sell debentures at a 7% coupon, each $1,000 bond carrying 100 warrants to buy common stock at $10.

Aldo Rossi, the president, owns 68% of the common stock and wishes to maintain control of the company. Three hundred thousand shares are outstanding. The following are extracts from Rossi's latest financial statements:

Balance Sheet

		Current liabilities	$1,700,000
		Common stock, par $1	300,000
		Retained earnings	400,000
Total assets	$2,400,000	Total claims	$2,400,000

Income Statement		
Sales	$4,580,000	
All costs except interest	4,100,000	
EBIT	480,000	
Interest	22,000	
EBT	458,000	
Taxes (30%)	137,400	
Net income	$ 320,600	
Shares outstanding	300,000	
Earnings per share	$	1.07
Price/earnings ratio		8.0 ×
Market price of stock	$	8.55

a. Show the new balance sheet under each alternative. For Alternatives 2 and 3, show the balance sheet after conversion of the bonds or exercise of the warrants. Assume that some of the funds raised will be used to pay off the bank loan and the remainder to increase total assets.

b. Show Mr. Rossi's control position under each alternative, assuming that he does not purchase additional shares.

c. What is the effect on earnings per share of each alternative, if it is assumed that profits before interest and taxes will be 20% of total assets?

d. What will be the ratio of total liabilities to total assets under each alternative?

e. Which of the three alternatives would you recommend to Rossi, and why?

16-11
Convertible Bond Analysis

Memtech Ltd. needs to raise $15 million to construct production facilities for a new type of USB memory device. The firm's straight nonconvertible debentures currently yield 8%. Its stock sells for $23 per share, its most recent dividend (D_0) was $2.00, and the dividend has an expected constant growth rate of 6%. Investment bankers have tentatively proposed that the firm raise the $15 million by issuing convertible debentures. These convertibles would have a $1,000 par value, carry a coupon rate of 7%, have a 20-year maturity, and be convertible into 35 shares of stock. Coupon payments would be made annually. The bonds would be noncallable for 5 years, after which they would be callable at a price of $1,075; this call price would decline by $5 per year in Year 6 and each year thereafter. For simplicity, assume that the bonds may be called or converted only at the end of a year, immediately after the coupon and dividend payments. Assume that management would call eligible bonds if the conversion value exceeded 25% of par value (not 25% of call price).

a. At what year do you expect the bonds will be forced into conversion with a call? What is the bond's value in conversion when it is converted at this time? What is the cash flow to the bondholder when it is converted at this time? (*Hint:* The cash flow includes the conversion value and the coupon payment, because the conversion is immediately after the coupon is paid.)

b. What is the expected rate of return (i.e., before-tax component cost) on the proposed convertible issue?

Spreadsheet Problem

16-12

Build a Model:
Convertible Bond
Analysis

Start with the partial model in the file *Ch 16 Build a Model.xlsx* on the textbook's website. Maggie's Magazines (MM) has straight nonconvertible bonds that currently yield 9%. MM's stock sells for $22 per share, has an expected constant growth rate of 6%, and has a dividend yield of 4%. MM plans on issuing convertible bonds that will have a $1,000 par value, a coupon rate of 8%, a 20-year maturity, and a conversion ratio of 32 (i.e., each bond could be convertible into 32 shares). Coupon payments will be made annually. The bonds will be noncallable for 5 years, after which they will be callable at a price of $1,090; this call price would decline by $6 per year in Year 6 and each year thereafter. For simplicity, assume that the bonds may be called or converted only at the end of a year, immediately after the coupon and dividend payments. Management will call the bonds when their conversion value exceeds 25% of their par value (not their call price).

a. For each year, calculate (1) the anticipated stock price; (2) the anticipated conversion value; (3) the anticipated straight-bond price; and (4) the cash flow to the investor assuming conversion occurs. At what year do you expect the bonds will be forced into conversion with a call? What is the bond's value in conversion when it is converted at this time? What is the cash flow to the bondholder when it is converted at this time? (*Hint*: The cash flow includes the conversion value and the coupon payment, because the conversion occurs immediately after the coupon is paid.)

b. What is the expected rate of return (i.e., before-tax component cost) on the proposed convertible issue?

c. Assume that the convertible bondholders require a 9% rate of return. If the coupon rate remains unchanged, then what conversion ratio will give a bond price of $1,000?

MINI CASE

Paul Duncan, financial manager of EduSoft Inc., is facing a dilemma. The firm was founded 5 years ago to provide educational software for the rapidly expanding primary and secondary school markets. Although EduSoft has done well, the firm's founder believes that an industry shakeout is imminent. To survive, EduSoft must grab market share now, and this will require a large infusion of new capital.

Because he expects earnings to continue rising sharply and looks for the stock price to follow suit, Paul does not think it would be wise to issue new common stock at this time. On the other hand, interest rates are currently high by historical standards, and with the firm's B rating, the interest payments on a new debt issue would be prohibitive. Thus, he has narrowed his choice of financing alternatives to two securities: (1) bonds with warrants or (2) convertible bonds. As Paul's assistant, you have been asked to help in the decision process by answering the following questions:

a. How can a knowledge of call options help a financial manager better understand warrants and convertibles?

b. One of the firm's alternatives is to issue a bond with warrants attached. EduSoft's current stock price is $20, and its investment banker estimates that the cost of a 20-year, annual coupon bond without warrants would be 10%. The bankers suggest attaching 45 warrants, each with an exercise price of $25, to each $1,000 bond. It is estimated that each warrant, when detached and traded separately, would have a value of $3.

   (1) What coupon rate should be set on the bond with warrants if the total package is to sell for $1,000?

   (2) Suppose the bonds were issued and the warrants immediately traded on the open market for $5 each. What would this imply about the terms of the issue? Did the company "win" or "lose"?

   (3) When would you expect the warrants to be exercised? Assume that they have a 10-year life; that is, they expire 10 years after issue.

   (4) Will the warrants bring in additional capital when exercised? If so, how much, and what type of capital?

    c. As an alternative to the bond with warrants, Mr. Duncan is considering convertible bonds. The firm's investment bankers estimate that EduSoft could sell a 20-year, 8.5% annual coupon, callable convertible bond for its $1,000 par value, whereas a straight-debt issue would require a 10% coupon. The convertibles would be call protected for 5 years, the call price would be $1,100, and the company would probably call the bonds as soon as possible after their conversion value exceeds $1,200. Note, though, that the call must occur on an issue date anniversary. EduSoft's current stock price is $20, its last dividend was $1, and the dividend is expected to grow at a constant 8% rate. The convertible could be converted into 40 shares of EduSoft stock at the owner's option.

        (1) What conversion price is built into the bond?

        (2) What is the convertible's straight-debt value? What is the implied value of the convertibility feature?

        (3) What is the formula for the bond's expected conversion value in any year? What is its conversion value at Year 0? At Year 10?

        (4) What is meant by the "floor value" of a convertible? What is the convertible's expected floor value at Year 0? At Year 10?

        (5) Assume that EduSoft intends to force conversion by calling the bond as soon as possible after its conversion value exceeds 20% above its par value, or 1.2($1,000) = $1,200. When is the issue expected to be called? (*Hint:* Recall that the call must be made on an anniversary date of the issue.)

        (6) What is the expected cost of capital for the convertible to EduSoft? Does this cost appear to be consistent with the riskiness of the issue?

    d. Mr. Duncan believes that the costs of both the bond with warrants and the convertible bond are close enough to one another to call them even, and also consistent with the risks involved. Thus, he will make his decision based on other factors. What are some of the factors that he should consider?

    e. How do convertible bonds help reduce agency costs?

chapter 17

Working Capital Management and Short-Term Financing

What do WestJet Airlines, Postmedia Network Canada, and MacDonald Dettwiler & Associates have in common? Each led its industry in its working capital measurements. Each company was rated on its "days of working capital," which is the amount of net operating working capital required per dollar of daily sales:

$$\text{Days of working capital (DWC)} = \frac{\text{Receivables} + \text{Inventory} - \text{Payables}}{\text{Average daily sales}}$$

The median industry ratio varies significantly. For example, the median in the publishing and newspaper industry is 31, but the median in aerospace and defense is 91. The median airline holds –12; its payables are larger than its combined receivables and inventory. But even within an industry, there is considerable variation. For example, Macdonald Detwiler has 42 days but CAE has 68 days.

After being burned in the recent recession, many companies are holding record amounts of cash and have been accused by analysts of losing their focus on working capital. Not so Canadian company Thomson Reuters, a world leader in the news and data businesses. Thomson Reuters doesn't have much inventory and is hampered in reducing its receivables because it operates in so many different countries, so instead it focused on standardizing its global accounts payable policies and improved its DSO (days sales outstanding) by 3 days. When asked about the cash that other companies could possibly wring out of their working capital, Thomson Reuter's CFO Bob Daleo said, "Instead of giving it to their vendors and customers, why don't they give it back to their shareholders?" Keep this in mind as you read this chapter.

Source: See David Katz, "Easing the Squeeze: The 2011 Working Capital Scorecard," *CFO*, July/August 2011, www.cfo.com, accessed September 14, 2014.

The textbook's website contains an *Excel* file that will guide you through the chapter's calculations. The file for this chapter is **Ch 17 Tool Kit.xlsx,** and we encourage you to open the file and follow along as you read the chapter. **www .nelson.com/brigham3ce**

Working capital management involves two basic questions: (1) What is the appropriate amount of working capital, both in total and for each specific account, and (2) how should working capital be financed? Note that sound working capital management goes beyond finance. Indeed, improving the firm's working capital position generally comes from improvements in the operating divisions. For example, experts in logistics, operations management, and information technology often work with engineers and production specialists to develop ways to speed up the manufacturing process and thus reduce the goods-in-process inventory. Similarly, marketing managers and logistics experts cooperate to develop better ways to deliver the firm's products to customers. Finance comes into play in evaluating how effective the firm's operating departments are relative to other firms in its industry and also in evaluating the profitability of alternative proposals for improving working capital management. In addition, financial managers decide how much cash their companies should keep on hand and how much short-term financing should be used to finance their working capital

17.1 Overview of Working Capital Management

Consider some of the activities involved in a company's supply chain. The company places an order with a supplier. The supplier ships the order and bills the company. The company either pays immediately or waits, in which case the unpaid amount is called an account payable. The newly arrived shipment goes into inventory until it is needed. If the supplier shipped finished products, the company will distribute the goods to its warehouses or retail facilities. If instead the supplier shipped components or raw materials, the company will use the shipment in a manufacturing or assembly process, putting the final product into its finished goods inventory. Items from the finished goods inventory will be shipped either directly to customers or to warehouses for later shipments. When a customer purchases the product, the company bills the customer and often offers the customer credit. If the customer doesn't pay immediately, the unpaid balance is called an account receivable. During this process, the company has been accruing unpaid wages (because the company doesn't pay its employees daily) and unpaid taxes (because the company doesn't pay the Canada Revenue Agency daily).

Several current assets and current liabilities are involved in this process—cash is spent (when paying suppliers, employees, taxes, etc.) and collected (when customers pay), accounts receivable are created and collected, inventory ebbs and flows, accounts payable are generated

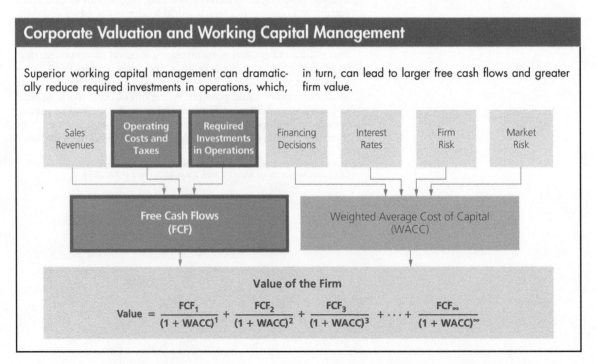

Corporate Valuation and Working Capital Management

Superior working capital management can dramatically reduce required investments in operations, which, in turn, can lead to larger free cash flows and greater firm value.

$$\text{Value} = \frac{\text{FCF}_1}{(1 + \text{WACC})^1} + \frac{\text{FCF}_2}{(1 + \text{WACC})^2} + \frac{\text{FCF}_3}{(1 + \text{WACC})^3} + \cdots + \frac{\text{FCF}_\infty}{(1 + \text{WACC})^\infty}$$

and paid, and accruals accumulate until paid. Notice that these are the same operating current assets (cash, accounts receivable, and inventories) and operating current liabilities (accounts payable and accruals) that are used in calculating **net operating working capital (NOWC)**, which is defined as operating current assets minus operating current liabilities.

In addition to operating current assets and operating current liabilities, there are two other current accounts related to working capital management: short-term investments and short-term debt. We discuss each current asset and liability later in the chapter, but it will be helpful if we first distinguish between cash and short-term investments because this can be a source of confusion.

Many dictionaries define cash as currency (coins and bills) and demand deposit accounts (such as a chequing account at a bank). Most companies have very little currency on hand, and most have relatively small chequing accounts. However, most companies own a wide variety of short-term financial assets. For example, Loblaw owns: (1) chequing accounts, (2) Government of Canada treasury bills and agency securities, (3) term deposits, (4) commercial paper and (5) bankers' acceptances. Most of these holdings can be converted into cash very quickly at prices identical or very close to their book values, so sometimes they are called cash equivalents.

Some of these financial assets are held to support current ongoing operations and some are held for future purposes, and this is the distinction we make when defining cash and short-term investments. In particular, we define cash as the total value of the short-term financial assets that are held to support ongoing operations because this is the definition of cash that is required to be consistent with the definition of cash used to calculate NOWC (which is used, in turn, to calculate free cash flow and the intrinsic value of the company). We define short-term investments as the total value of short-term financial assets held for future purposes. Keep these distinctions in mind when we discuss cash management and short-term investments later in the chapter.

We normally use the term NOWC, but the term *working capital* is also used for slightly different purposes, so be aware of this when you see it in the financial press. For example, the financial press defines **working capital,** sometimes called *gross working capital,* as current assets used in operations. The press also defines **net working capital** as all current assets minus all current liabilities.

17.2 Using and Financing Operating Current Assets

Operating current assets (CA) are used to support sales. Having too much invested in operating CA is inefficient, but having too little might constrain sales. Many companies have seasonal, growing sales, so they have seasonal growing operating CA, which has an implication for the pattern of financing that companies choose. The next sections address these issues.

Efficient Use of Operating Current Assets

Most companies can influence their ratios of operating current assets to sales. Some companies choose a relaxed policy and hold a lot of cash, receivables, and inventories relative to sales. This is a **relaxed policy.** On the other hand, if a firm has a **restricted policy,** holdings of current assets are minimized and we say that the firm's policy is *tight* or *"lean-and-mean."* A **moderate policy** lies between the two extremes.

We can use the basic DuPont equation to demonstrate how working capital management affects the return on assets:

$$\text{ROA} = \text{Profit margin} \times \text{Total assets turnover}$$

$$= \frac{\text{Net Income}}{\text{Sales}} \times \frac{\text{Sales}}{\text{Assets}}$$

A relaxed policy means a high level of assets and hence a low total assets turnover ratio; this results in a low ROA, other things held constant. Conversely, a restricted policy results in low current assets, a high turnover, and hence a relatively high ROA. However, the restricted policy exposes the firm to risk, because shortages can lead to work stoppages, unhappy customers, and serious long-run problems. The moderate policy falls between the two extremes. The optimal strategy is the one that management believes will maximize the firm's long-run free cash flow and thus the stock's intrinsic value.

Note that changing technologies can lead to changes in the optimal policy. For example, if a new technology makes it possible for a manufacturer to produce a given product in 5 rather than 10 days, then work-in-progress inventories can be cut in half. Similarly, many retailers have inventory management systems that use bar codes on all merchandise. These codes are read at the cash register; this information is transmitted electronically to a computer that adjusts the remaining stock of the item; and the computer automatically places an order with the supplier's computer when the stock falls to a specified level. This process lowers the "safety stocks" that would otherwise be necessary to avoid running out of stock. Such systems have dramatically lowered inventories and thus boosted profits.

Financing Operating Current Assets

Investments in operating current assets must be financed, and the primary sources of funds include bank loans, credit from suppliers (accounts payable), accrued liabilities, long-term debt, and common equity. Each of those sources has advantages and disadvantages, so a firm must decide which sources are best for it.

To begin, note that most businesses experience seasonal and/or cyclical fluctuations. For example, construction firms tend to peak in the summer, retailers peak around Christmas, and the manufacturers who supply both construction companies and retailers follow related patterns. Similarly, the sales of virtually all businesses increase when the economy is strong, so they increase operating current assets during booms but let inventories and receivables fall during recessions. However, current assets rarely drop to zero—companies maintain some **permanent operating current assets,** which are the operating current assets needed even at the low point of the business cycle. For a growing firm in a growing economy, permanent current assets tend to increase over time. Also, as sales increase during a cyclical upswing, current assets are increased; these extra current assets are defined as **temporary operating current assets** as opposed to permanent current assets. The way permanent and temporary current assets are financed is called the firm's **operating current assets** financing policy. Three alternative policies are discussed next.

Maturity Matching, or "Self-Liquidating," Approach The **maturity matching,** or "self-liquidating," approach calls for matching asset and liability maturities as shown in Panel a of Figure 17-1. All of the fixed assets plus the permanent current assets are financed with long-term capital, but temporary current assets are financed with short-term debt. Inventory expected to be sold in 30 days would be financed with a 30-day bank loan; a machine expected to last for 5 years would be financed with a 5-year loan; a 20-year building would be financed with a 20-year mortgage bond; and so on. Actually, two factors prevent exact maturity matching, uncertain asset lives and equity financing. For example, a firm might finance inventories with a 30-day bank loan, expecting to sell the inventories and use the cash to retire the loan. But if sales are slow, then the "life" of the inventories would exceed the original 30-day estimate and the cash from sales would not be forthcoming, perhaps causing the firm problems in paying off the loan when it comes due. In addition, some common equity financing must be used, and common equity has no maturity. Still, if a firm attempts to match or come close to matching asset and liability maturities, this is defined as a *moderate current asset financing policy.*

Aggressive Approach Panel b of Figure 17-1 illustrates the situation for a more aggressive firm that finances some of its permanent assets with short-term debt. Note that we used the term "relatively" in the title for Panel b because there can be different *degrees* of aggressiveness. For example, the dashed line in Panel b could have been drawn *below* the line designating fixed assets, indicating that all of the current assets—both permanent and temporary— and part of the fixed assets were financed with short-term credit. This policy would be highly aggressive and the firm would be subject to dangers from loan renewal as well as rising interest rate problems. However, short-term interest rates are generally lower than long-term rates, and some firms are willing to gamble by using a large amount of low-cost, short-term debt in hopes of earning higher profits.

A possible reason for adopting the aggressive policy is to take advantage of an upward sloping yield curve, for which short-term rates are lower than long-term rates. However, as many firms learned during the financial crisis of 2008, a strategy of financing long-term assets with short-term debt is really quite risky. As an illustration, suppose a company borrowed $1 million on a 1-year basis and used the funds to buy machinery that would lower

FIGURE

17-1 Alternative Operating Current Assets Financing Policies

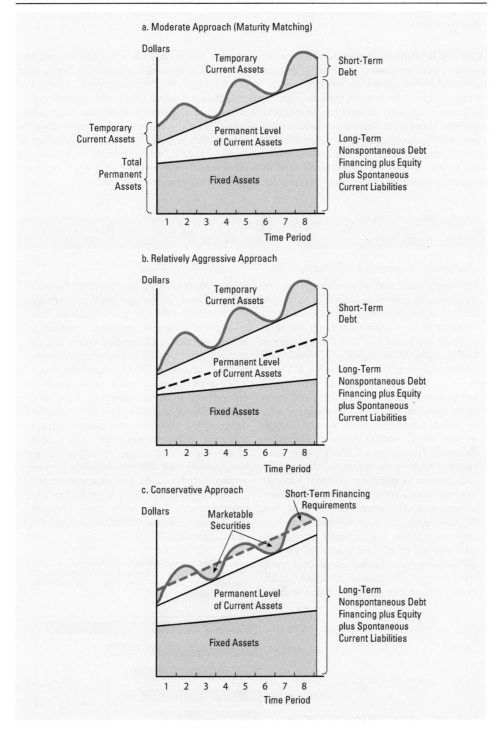

a. Moderate Approach (Maturity Matching)

b. Relatively Aggressive Approach

c. Conservative Approach

labour costs by $200,000 per year for 10 years[1]. Cash flows from the equipment would not be sufficient to pay off the loan at the end of only one year, so the loan would have to be

---

[1]We are oversimplifying here. Few lenders would explicitly lend money for 1 year to finance a 10-year asset. What would actually happen is that the firm would borrow on a 1-year basis for "general corporate purposes" and then actually use the money to purchase the 10-year machinery.

renewed. If the economy were in a recession like that of 2009, the lender might refuse to renew the loan, and that could lead to bankruptcy. Had the firm matched maturities and financed the equipment with a 10-year loan, then the annual loan payments would have been lower and better matched with the cash flows, and the loan renewal problem would not have arisen.

Conservative Approach Panel c of the figure shows the dashed line *above* the line designating permanent current assets, indicating that long-term capital is used to finance all permanent assets and also to meet some seasonal needs. In this situation, the firm uses a small amount of short-term credit to meet its peak requirements, but it also meets a part of its seasonal needs by "storing liquidity" in the form of marketable securities. The humps above the dashed line represent short-term financings, while the troughs below the dashed line represent short-term security holdings. This conservative financing policy is fairly safe, and the wisdom of using it was demonstrated in 2009—when credit dried up, firms with adequate cash holdings were able to operate more effectively than those that were forced to cut back their operations because they couldn't order new inventories or pay their normal workforce.

FINANCE: IN FOCUS

Electronic Payments in Canada: What's the Hold-Up?

The timely collection of receivables as well as payables control is essential to proper cash flow management. Cheques and wire transfers have traditionally been the dominant payment systems. With the widespread use of digital technologies, newer electronic payment methods include online bill payments, ATM payments, credit cards, and pre-authorized debit cards. Even more innovative methods are being developed, such as virtual currencies, PayPal, and Google Wallet. The Canadian Financial Executives Research Foundation (CFERF) prepared a report analyzing the adoption, demand for, and barriers to electronic payment methods. The most widely cited benefits are (1) business convenience, (2) improved cash flow, and (3) lower costs. Just over one-quarter of those surveyed say they use electronic payment for over one-half of all their payments, yet over 80% say they would rather use electronic payment methods. The most widely used types of transactions to process receivables are shown below. An interesting point is that the technology allows for various payment methods, which in turn makes it more difficult for businesses to standardize one or two methods to attain operational efficiencies. What are the primary obstacles to widespread electronic payment adoption? CFERF's report lists the difficulty in changing customer habits, suppliers not wanting to accept electronic payments, organizational priorities, lack of integration between the payment and accounting systems, and system development costs. In spite of the barriers to usage reported, survey respondents see the inevitability of new payment methods. As one executive stated, "...there's going to be a whole generation who have probably never come across cheques. They'll eventually ask: 'What is a cheque? I've never seen them.'"

Source: Adapted from "Electronic Payments in Canada: What's the Hold Up?," Canadian Financial Executives Research Foundation, 2011. https://portal.feicanada.org, accessed September 15, 2014.

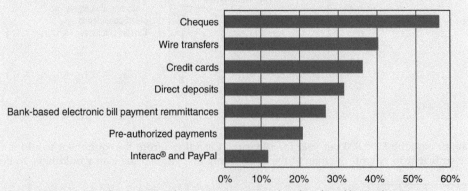

Source: FEI Canada, www.feicanada.org, "Electronic Payments in Canada: What's the Hold Up?" Chart 7, p. 18. Found at https://www.feicanada.org/do-resources/research-studies.

Choosing among the Approaches Because the yield curve is normally upward sloping, *the cost of short-term debt is generally lower than that of long-term debt.* However, *short-term debt is riskier for the borrowing firm* for two reasons: (1) If a firm borrows on a long-term basis then its interest costs will be relatively stable over time, but if it uses short-term credit, then its interest expense can fluctuate widely—perhaps reaching such high levels that profits are extinguished.[2] (2) If a firm borrows heavily on a short-term basis, then a temporary recession may adversely affect its financial ratios and render it unable to repay its debt. Recognizing this fact, the lender may not renew the loan if the borrower's financial position is weak, which could force the borrower into bankruptcy.

Note also that *short-term loans can generally be negotiated much faster* than long-term loans. Lenders need to make a thorough financial examination before extending long-term credit, and the loan agreement must be spelled out in great detail because a lot can happen during the life of a 10- to 20-year loan.

Finally, *short-term debt generally offers greater flexibility.* If the firm thinks that interest rates are abnormally high and due for a decline, it may prefer short-term credit because prepayment penalties are often attached to long-term debt. Also, if its needs for funds are seasonal or cyclical, then the firm may not want to commit itself to long-term debt because of its underwriting costs and possible prepayment penalties. Finally, long-term loan agreements generally contain provisions, or *covenants,* that constrain the firm's future actions in order to protect the lender, whereas short-term credit agreements generally have fewer restrictions.

All things considered, it is not possible to state that either long-term or short-term financing is generally better. The firm's specific conditions will affect its decision, as will the risk preferences of managers. Optimistic and/or aggressive managers will lean more toward short-term credit to gain an interest cost advantage, whereas more conservative managers will lean toward long-term financing to avoid potential renewal problems. The factors discussed here should be considered, but the final decision will reflect managers' personal preferences and subjective judgments.

⊙NCEPT REVIEW

1. Identify and explain three alternative current asset investment policies.
2. Use the DuPont equation to show how working capital policy can affect a firm's expected ROA.
3. What are the reasons for not wanting to hold too little working capital? For not wanting to hold too much?
4. Differentiate between permanent operating current assets and temporary operating current assets.
5. What does maturity matching mean, and what is the logic behind this policy?
6. What are some advantages and disadvantages of short-term versus long-term debt?

17.3 The Cash Conversion Cycle

Firms typically follow a cycle in which they purchase inventory, sell goods on credit, and then collect accounts receivable. This cycle is referred to as the *cash conversion cycle (CCC).*

Calculating the CCC

Consider Real Time Computer Corporation (RTC), which in early 2016 introduced a new supercomputer that will sell for $250,000. RTC expects to sell 40 computers in its first year of production. The effects of this new product on RTC's working capital position were analyzed in terms of the following five steps:

1. RTC will order and then receive the materials it needs to produce the 40 computers it expects to sell. Because RTC and most other firms purchase materials on credit, this transaction will create an account payable. However, the purchase will have no immediate cash flow effect.

---

[2]The prime interest rate—the rate banks charge very good customers—hit 22.75% in the early 1980s. This produced a level of business bankruptcies that was not seen again until 2009. The primary reason for the very high interest rate was that the inflation rate was up to 12.9%, and high inflation must be compensated by high interest rates. Also, the Bank of Canada was tightening credit in order to hold down inflation, and it was encouraging banks to restrict their lending.

2. Labour will be used to convert the materials into finished computers. However, wages will not be fully paid at the time the work is done, so, like accounts payable, accrued wages will also build up.
3. The finished computers will be sold, but on credit. Therefore, sales will create receivables, not immediate cash inflows.
4. At some point before receivables are collected, RTC must pay off its accounts payable and accrued wages. This outflow must be financed.
5. The cycle will be completed when RTC's receivables have been collected. At that time, the company can pay off the credit that was used to finance production, and it can then repeat the cycle.

The **cash conversion cycle model,** which focuses on the length of time between when the company makes payments and when it receives cash inflows, formalizes the steps outlined above. The following terms are used in the model:

1. **Inventory conversion period,** which is the average time required to convert materials into finished goods and then to sell those goods. Note that the inventory conversion period is calculated by dividing inventory by average daily cost of goods sold. For example, if average inventories are $1.6 million and cost of goods sold is $8 million, then the inventory conversion period is 73 days:

$$\text{Inventory conversion period} = \frac{\text{Inventory}}{\text{Average daily cost of goods sold}}$$

$$= \frac{\$1,600,000}{\$8,000,000/365} \tag{17-1}$$

$$= 73 \text{ days}$$

Thus, it takes an average of 73 days to convert materials into finished goods and then to sell those goods.

2. **Receivables collection period,** which is the average length of time required to convert the firm's receivables into cash; that is, to collect cash following a sale. The receivables collection period is also called the *days' sales outstanding (DSO),* and it is calculated by dividing accounts receivable by the average credit sales per day. If receivables are $657,534 and sales are $10 million, the receivables collection period is

$$\text{Receivables collection period} = \text{DSO} = \frac{\text{Receivables}}{\text{Sales}/365}$$

$$= \frac{\$657,534}{\$10,000,000/365} \tag{17-2}$$

$$= 24 \text{ days}$$

Thus, it takes 24 days after a sale to convert the receivables into cash.

3. **Payables deferral period,** which is the average length of time between the purchase of materials and labour, and the payment of cash for them. For example, if the firm on average has 30 days to pay for labour and materials, if its cost of goods sold is $8 million per year, and if its accounts payable average is $657,534, then its payables deferral period can be calculated as follows:

$$\text{Payables deferral period} = \frac{\text{Payables}}{\text{Purchases per day}}$$

$$= \frac{\text{Payables}}{\text{Cost of goods sold}/365} \tag{17-3}$$

$$= \frac{\$657,534}{\$8,000,000/365}$$

$$= 30 \text{ days}$$

The calculated figure is consistent with the stated 30-day payment period.

4. Cash conversion cycle, which nets out the three periods just defined and therefore equals the length of time between the firm's actual cash expenditures to pay for productive resources (materials and labour) and its own cash receipts from the sale of products (i.e., the length of time between paying for labour and materials and collecting on receivables). The cash conversion cycle thus equals the average length of time a dollar is tied up.

We can now use these definitions to analyze the cash conversion cycle. First, the concept is diagrammed in Figure 17-2. Each component is given a number, and the cash conversion cycle can be expressed by this equation:

$$
\begin{array}{ccccccc}
(1) & + & (2) & - & (3) & = & (4) \\
\text{Inventory} & & \text{Receivables} & & \text{Payables} & & \text{Cash} \\
\text{conversion} + & & \text{collection} & - & \text{deferral} & = & \text{conversion} \\
\text{period} & & \text{period} & & \text{period} & & \text{cycle}
\end{array}
\qquad (17\text{-}4)
$$

To illustrate, suppose it takes Real Time an average of 73 days to convert raw materials to computers and then to sell them, and another 24 days to collect on receivables. However, 30 days normally elapse between receipt of raw materials and payment for them. Therefore, the cash conversion cycle would be 67 days:

Days in cash conversion cycle = 73 days + 24 days − 30 days = 67 days

To look at it another way,

$$
\begin{array}{ll}
\text{Cash inflow delay} - \text{Payment delay} = \text{Net delay} \\
(73 \text{ days} + 24 \text{ days}) - 30 \text{ days} \qquad = 67 \text{ days}
\end{array}
$$

Shortening the Cash Conversion Cycle

Given these data, RTC knows when it starts producing a computer that it will have to finance the manufacturing costs for a 67-day period. The firm's goal should be to shorten its cash conversion cycle as much as possible without hurting operations. This would increase RTC's value, because the shorter the cash conversion cycle, the lower the required net operating working capital and the higher the resulting free cash flow.

The cash conversion cycle can be shortened (1) by reducing the inventory conversion period by processing and selling goods more quickly, (2) by reducing the receivables collection period by speeding up collections, or (3) by lengthening the payables deferral period by slowing down the firm's own payments. To the extent that these actions can be taken *without increasing costs or depressing sales*, they should be carried out.

Benefits

As we can see in Table 17-1, RTC currently has a CCC of 67 days, which results in $1.6 million being tied up in net operating working capital. Assuming that its cost of debt to carry

FIGURE 17-2   The Cash Conversion Cycle Model

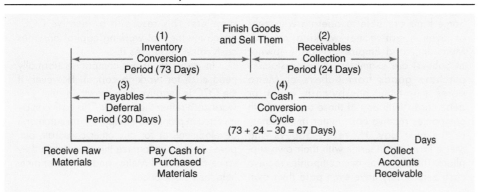

working capital is 10%, this means that the firm is incurring interest charges of $160,000 per year to carry its working capital. Now suppose RTC can improve its logistics and production processes so that its inventory conversion period drops to 65 days. The firm can also cut its receivable collection period to 23 days by billing customers daily rather than batching bills every other day as it now does. Finally, it can increase its payables deferral period by using remote disbursements, as discussed later in this chapter. Table 17-1 shows that the net effects of these improvements are a 10-day reduction in the cash conversion cycle and a $224,657 reduction in net operating capital, which saves $22,466 in interest.

Recall that free cash flow (FCF) is equal to NOPAT minus the net investments in operating capital. Therefore, if working capital decreases, FCF increases by that same amount. RTC's reduction in its cash conversion cycle would lead to a $224,657 increase in FCF. If sales stay at the same level, then the reduction in working capital would simply be a one-time

TABLE 17-1 Benefits from Improving the Cash Conversion Cycle

	Original	Improved
Annual sales	$10,000,000	$10,000,000
Cost of goods sold (COGS)	8,000,000	8,000,000
Inventory conversion period (days)	73	65
Receivables collection period (days)	24	23
Payable deferral period (days)	(30)	(31)
Cash conversion cycle (days)	67	57
Reduction in CCC		10
Inventory[a]	$ 1,600,000	$ 1,424,658
Receivables[b]	657,534	630,137
Payables[c]	(657,534)	(679,452)
Net operating working capital (NOWC)	$ 1,600,000	$ 1,375,343
Reduction in NOWC (Improvement in free cash flow)	$224,657	
Reduction in interest expense @ 10%	$ 22,466	

Notes:
[a]Inventory = (Inventory conversion period)(COGS/365)
[b]Receivables = (Receivables collection period)(Sales/365)
[c]Payables = (Payables deferral period)(COGS/365)

FINANCE: IN FOCUS

Some Firms Operate with Negative Working Capital!

Some firms are able to operate with zero or even negative net working capital. Metro Inc. and Empire Company (owner of Sobeys) are examples. When customers purchase goods from Sobeys or Metro stores, they either pay by cash, credit, or debit card. With any of these options, both companies receive cash either immediately or the next day. However, Sobeys and Metro have credit terms with their own suppliers. Therefore, the two companies receive cash before they have even paid their own suppliers. This results in a negative CCC, which means that working capital *provides* cash rather than uses it.

In order to grow, companies normally need cash for working capital. However, if the CCC is negative then growth in sales *provides* cash rather than *uses* it. This cash can be invested in plant and equipment, research and development, or for any other corporate purpose. Analysts recognize this point when they value Empire and Metro, and it can certainly help their stock prices.

cash inflow. However, suppose sales grow. When a company improves its working capital processes, they usually remain at their improved level. If the NOWC/Sales ratio remains at its new level, proportionately less working capital will be required to support the additional future sales, leading to an increase in projected FCF for each future year.

Thus, an improvement in working capital management creates a large one-time increase in FCF at the time of the improvement as well as higher FCF in future years. Therefore, an improvement in working capital management is a gift that keeps on giving.

The combination of the one-time cash inflow and the long-term improvement in free cash flow can add substantial value to a company. Two professors, Hyun-Han Shin and Luc Soenen, studied more than 2,900 companies for a 20-year period and found a strong relationship between a company's cash conversion cycle and its performance.[3] In particular, their results show that for the average company a 10-day improvement in the cash conversion cycle was associated with an increase in pre-tax operating profit margin from 12.7% to 13.02%. They also demonstrated that companies with a cash conversion cycle 10 days shorter than average also had an annual stock return that was 1.7 percentage points higher than that of an average company, even after adjusting for differences in risk. Given results like these, it's no wonder firms now place so much emphasis on working capital management![4]

CONCEPT REVIEW

1. Define the following terms: "inventory conversion period," "receivables collection period," and "payables deferral period". Give the equation for each term.

2. What is the cash conversion cycle? What is its equation?

3. What should a firm's goal be regarding the cash conversion cycle? Explain your answer.

4. What are some actions a firm can take to shorten its cash conversion cycle?

5. A company has $20 million in inventory, $5 million in receivables, and $4 million in payables. Its annual sales revenue is $80 million and its cost of goods sold is $60 million. What is its CCC? (Check Figure: 120.15)

17.4 The Cash Budget

The **cash budget** shows the firm's projected cash inflows and outflows over some specified period. Generally, firms use a monthly cash budget forecast over the next year, plus a more detailed daily or weekly cash budget for the coming month. The monthly cash budgets are used for planning purposes, and the daily or weekly budgets for actual cash control.

In Chapter 5, we saw that MicroDrive's projected sales were $3,300 million, resulting in a net cash flow from operations of $163 million. When all expenditures and financing flows were considered, its cash account was projected to increase by $1 million. Does this mean that it will not have to worry about cash shortages during the year? To answer this question, we must construct the cash budget.

To simplify the example, we will consider the cash budget for only the last half of the year. Also, we will not list every cash flow but instead will focus on the operating cash flows. Sales peak in September, and all sales are made on terms of 2/10, net 40, meaning that a 2% discount is allowed if payment is made within 10 days, and, if the discount is not taken, the full amount is due in 40 days. However, like most companies, MicroDrive finds that some of its customers delay payment up to 90 days. Experience has shown that payment on 20% of dollar sales is made during the month in which the sale is made—these are the discount sales. On 70% of sales, payment is made during the month immediately following the month of sale, and on 10% of sales, payment is made in the second month following the month of sale.

Costs average 70% of the sales prices of the finished products. Raw material purchases are generally made one month before the firm expects to sell the finished products, but MicroDrive's terms with its suppliers allow it to delay payments for 30 days. Accordingly, if July sales are forecast at $300 million, then purchases during June will amount to $210 million, and this amount will actually be paid in July.

---

[3]See Hyun-Han Shin and Luc Soenen, "Efficiency of Working Capital Management and Corporate Profitability," *Financial Practice and Education*, Fall–Winter 1998, 37–45.
[4]For more on the CCC, see James A. Gentry, R. Vaidyanathan, and Hei Wai Lee, "A Weighted Cash Conversion Cycle," *Financial Management*, Spring 1990, 90–9.

See *Ch 17 Tool Kit.xlsx* at the textbook's website for details.

Other cash expenditures such as wages and lease payments are also built into the cash budget, and MicroDrive must make estimated tax payments of $30 million on September 15 and $20 million on December 15. Also, a $100 million payment for a new plant must be made in October. Assuming that the **target cash balance** is $10 million, and that it projects $15 million to be on hand on July 1, what will MicroDrive's monthly cash surpluses or short-falls be for the period from July to December?

The monthly cash flows are shown in Table 17-2. Section I of the table provides a work-sheet for calculating both collections on sales and payments on purchases. Line 1 gives the sales forecast for the period from May through December. (May and June sales are necessary to determine collections for July and August.) Next, lines 2 through 5 show cash collections. Line 2 shows that 20% of the sales during any given month are collected during that month. Customers who pay in the first month, however, take the discount, so the cash collected in the month of sale is reduced by 2%; for example, collections during July for the $300 million of sales in that month will be 20% times sales times 1.0 minus the 2% discount = (0.20)($300) (0.98) ≈ $59 million. Line 3 shows the collections on the previous month's sales, or 70% of sales in the preceding month; for example, in July, 70% of the $250 million June sales, or $175 million, will be collected. Line 4 gives collections from sales 2 months earlier, or 10% of sales in that month; for example, the July collections for May sales are (0.10)($200) = $20 million. The collections during each month are summed and shown on line 5; thus, the July collections represent 20% of July sales (minus the discount) plus 70% of June sales plus 10% of May sales, or $254 million in total.

Next, payments for purchases of raw materials are shown. July sales are forecast at $300 million, so MicroDrive will purchase $210 million of materials in June (line 6) and pay for these purchases in July (line 7). Similarly, MicroDrive will purchase $280 million of materials in July to meet August's forecast sales of $400 million.

With Section I completed, Section II can be constructed. Cash from collections is shown on line 8. Lines 9 through 14 list payments made during each month, and these payments are summed on line 15. The difference between cash receipts and cash payments (line 8 minus line 15) is the net cash gain or loss during the month. For July there is a net cash loss of $11 million, as shown on line 16.

In Section III, we first determine the cash balance MicroDrive would have at the start of each month, assuming no borrowing is done. This is shown on line 17. MicroDrive would have $15 million on hand on July 1. The beginning cash balance (line 17) is then added to the net cash gain or loss during the month (line 16) to obtain the cumulative cash that would be on hand if no financing were done (line 18). At the end of July, MicroDrive forecasts a cumulative cash balance of $4 million in the absence of borrowing.

The target cash balance, $10 million, is then subtracted from the cumulative cash balance to determine the firm's borrowing requirements (shown in parentheses) or its surplus cash. Because MicroDrive expects to have cumulative cash, as shown on line 18, of only $4 million in July, it will have to borrow $6 million to bring the cash account up to the target balance of $10 million. Assuming that this amount is indeed borrowed, loans outstanding will total $6 million at the end of July. (MicroDrive did not have any loans outstanding on July 1.) The cash surplus or required loan balance is given on Line 20; a positive value indicates a cash surplus, whereas a negative value indicates a loan requirement. Note that the surplus cash or loan requirement shown on line 20 is a *cumulative amount*. MicroDrive must borrow $6 million in July. Then, it has an additional cash shortfall during August of $37 million as reported on line 16, so its total loan requirement at the end of August is $6 + $37 = $43 million, as reported on line 20. MicroDrive's arrangement with the bank permits it to increase its outstanding loans on a daily basis, up to a prearranged maximum, just as you could increase the amount you owe on a credit card. MicroDrive will use any surplus funds it generates to pay off its loans, and because the loan can be paid down at any time, on a daily basis, the firm will never have both a cash surplus and an outstanding loan balance.

This same procedure is used in the following months. Sales will peak in September, accompanied by increased payments for purchases, wages, and other items. Receipts from sales will also go up, but the firm will still be left with a $57 million net cash outflow during the month. The total loan requirement at the end of September will hit a peak of $100 million, the cumulative cash plus the target cash balance. The $100 million can also be found as the $43 million needed at the end of August plus the $57 million cash deficit for September.

Sales, purchases, and payments for past purchases will fall sharply in October, but col-lections will be the highest of any month because they will reflect the high September sales. As a result, MicroDrive will enjoy a healthy $44 million net cash gain during October. This

TABLE 17-2 MicroDrive Inc.: Cash Budget (Millions of Dollars)

	May	Jun	Jul	Aug	Sep	Oct	Nov	Dec
I. COLLECTIONS AND PURCHASES WORKSHEET								
(1) Sales (gross)[a]	$200	$250	$300	$400	$ 500	$350	$250	$200
Collections								
(2) During month of sale:								
(0.2)(0.98)(month's sales)			59	78	98	69	49	39
(3) During first month after sale:								
0.7(previous month's sales)			175	210	280	350	245	175
(4) During second month after sale:								
0.1(sales 2 months ago)			20	25	30	40	50	35
(5) Total collections (2 + 3 + 4)			$254	$313	$ 408	$459	$344	$249
Purchases								
(6) 0.7(next month's sales)		$210	$280	$350	$ 245	$175	$140	
(7) Payments (prior month's purchases)			$210	$280	$ 350	$245	$175	$140
II. CASH GAIN OR LOSS FOR MONTH								
(8) Collections (from Section I)			$254	$313	$ 408	$459	$344	$249
(9) Payments for purchases (from Section I)			$210	$280	$ 350	$245	$175	$140
(10) Wages and salaries			30	40	50	40	30	30
(11) Lease payments			15	15	15	15	15	15
(12) Other expenses			10	15	20	15	10	10
(13) Taxes					30			20
(14) Payment for plant construction						100		
(15) Total payments			$265	$350	$ 465	$415	$230	$ 215
(16) Net cash gain (loss) during month (line 8 − line 15)			$ (11)	$ (37)	$ (57)	$ 44	$114	$ 34
III. LOAN REQUIREMENT OR CASH SURPLUS								
(17) Cash at start of month if no borrowing is done[b]			$ 15	$ 4	$ (33)	$ (90)	$ (46)	$ 68
(18) Cumulative cash: cash at start if no borrowing + gain or − loss (line 16 + line 17)			$ 4	$ (33)	$ (90)	$ (46)	$ 68	$102
(19) Target cash balance			10	10	10	10	10	10
(20) Cumulative surplus cash or loans outstanding to maintain $10 target cash balance (line 18 − line 19)[c]			$ (6)	$ (43)	$(100)	$ (56)	$ 58	$ 92

Notes:

[a]Although the budget period is July through December, sales and purchases data for May and June are needed to determine collections and payments during July and August.

[b]The amount shown on Line 17 for July, the $15 balance (in millions), is on hand initially. The values shown for each of the following months on line 17 are equal to the cumulative cash as shown on line 18 for the preceding month; for example, the $4 shown on line 17 for August is taken from line 18 in the July column.

[c]When the target cash balance of $10 (line 19) is deducted from the cumulative cash balance (line 18), a resulting negative figure on Line 20 (shown in parentheses) represents a required loan, whereas a positive figure represents surplus cash. Loans are required from July through October, and surpluses are expected during November and December. Note also that firms can borrow or pay off loans on a daily basis, so the $6 borrowed during July would be done on a daily basis, as needed, and during October the $100 loan that existed at the beginning of the month would be reduced daily to the $56 ending balance, which, in turn, would be completely paid off during November.

net gain can be used to pay off borrowings, so loans outstanding will decline by $44 million, to $56 million.

MicroDrive will have an even larger cash surplus in November, which will permit it to pay off all of its loans. In fact, the company is expected to have $58 million in surplus cash by the month's end, and another cash surplus in December will swell the excess cash to $92 million.

With such a large amount of unneeded funds, MicroDrive's treasurer will certainly want to invest in interest-bearing securities or to put the funds to use some other way.

Cash budgets are an extremely useful tool for businesses and are used for a variety of planning purposes. Estimating short-term borrowing needs, assessing minimum cash balance requirements, and planning for business expansion are three cash budgeting applications. Bankers may request a cash budget in order to determine a company's ability to repay a loan. While we kept our cash budget relatively simple for illustrative purposes, it could easily incorporate items such as interest expenses, stock and bond issues, and dividend payments.

Cash Budgets versus Income Statements and Free Cash Flows

A cash budget looks similar to an income statement. However, the two statements are quite different. Here are some key differences: (1) In an income statement, the focus is on sales, not collections. (2) An income statement shows accrued taxes, wages, and so forth, not the actual payments. (3) An income statement shows depreciation as an expense but does not show expenditures on new fixed assets. (4) An income statement shows a cost for goods purchased when those goods are sold, not for when they are ordered or paid.

These are obviously large differences, so it would be a big mistake to confuse a cash budget with an income statement. Also, the cash flows shown on the cash budget are different from the firm's free cash flows, because FCF reflects after-tax operating income and the investments required to maintain future operations, whereas the cash budget reflects only the actual cash inflows and outflows during a particular period.

Cash budgets, income statements, and free cash flows are all important and are related to one another, but they are also quite different. Each is designed for a specific purpose, and the main purpose of the cash budget is to forecast the firm's liquidity position, not its profitability.

CONCEPT REVIEW

1. What is the purpose of the cash budget?
2. What are the three major sections of a cash budget?

17.5 Short-Term Financing

The three possible short-term financing policies described earlier were distinguished by the relative amounts of short-term debt used under each policy. The aggressive policy called for the greatest use of short-term debt, while the conservative policy called for the least. Maturity matching fell in between. Although short-term credit is generally riskier than long-term credit, using short-term funds does have some significant advantages. The pros and cons of short-term financing are considered in this section.

Advantages of Short-Term Financing

First, a short-term loan can be obtained much faster than long-term credit. Lenders will insist on a more thorough financial examination before extending long-term credit, and the loan agreement will have to be spelled out in considerable detail because a lot can happen during the life of a 10- to 20-year loan. Therefore, if funds are needed in a hurry, the firm should look to the short-term markets.

Second, if its needs for funds are seasonal or cyclical, a firm may not want to commit itself to long-term debt: (1) Flotation costs are higher for long-term debt than for short-term credit. (2) Although long-term debt can be repaid early, provided the loan agreement includes a prepayment provision, prepayment penalties can be expensive. Accordingly, if a firm thinks its need for funds will diminish in the near future, it should choose short-term debt. (3) Long-term loan agreements always contain provisions, or covenants, which constrain the firm's future actions. Short-term credit agreements are generally less restrictive.

Third, the yield curve is normally upward sloping, indicating that interest rates are generally lower on short-term debt. Thus, under normal conditions, interest costs at the time the funds are obtained will be lower if the firm borrows on a short-term rather than a long-term basis.

Disadvantages of Short-Term Debt

Even though short-term rates are often lower than long-term rates, short-term credit is riskier for two reasons: (1) If a firm borrows on a long-term basis, its interest costs will be relatively stable over time, but if it uses short-term credit, its interest expense will fluctuate widely, at times going quite high. For example, the rate banks charged large corporations for short-term debt more than doubled in just one year in the 1980s, rising from 9.9% to 20.0%. Many firms that had borrowed heavily on a short-term basis simply could not meet their rising interest costs, and as a result, bankruptcies hit record levels during that period. (2) If a firm borrows heavily on a short-term basis, a temporary recession may render it unable to repay this debt. If the borrower is in a weak financial position, the lender may not extend the loan, which could force the firm into bankruptcy.

CONCEPT REVIEW

1. What are the advantages and disadvantages of short-term debt over long-term debt?

17.6 Accruals and Accounts Payable (Trade Credit)

Accruals

Firms generally pay employees on a weekly, biweekly, or monthly basis, so the balance sheet will typically show some accrued wages. Similarly, the firm's own estimated income taxes, Canada Pension Plan and income taxes withheld from employee payrolls, and sales taxes collected are generally paid on a weekly, monthly, or quarterly basis; hence the balance sheet will typically show some accrued taxes along with accrued wages.

These *accruals* can be thought of as short-term, interest-free loans from employees and taxing authorities, and they increase automatically (that is, spontaneously) as a firm's operations expand. However, a firm cannot ordinarily control its accruals: The timing of wage payments is set by economic forces and industry custom, while tax payment dates are established by law. Thus, firms use all the accruals they can, but they have little control over the levels of these accounts.

Accounts Payable (Trade Credit)

Firms generally make purchases from other firms on credit, recording the debt as an *account payable*. Accounts payable, or **trade credit,** is the largest single category of operating current liabilities, representing about 40% of the current liabilities of the average nonfinancial corporation. The percentage is somewhat larger for smaller firms: Because small companies often do not qualify for financing from other sources, they rely especially heavily on trade credit.

Trade credit is a "spontaneous" source of financing in the sense that it arises from ordinary business transactions. For example, suppose a firm makes average purchases of $2,000 a day on terms of net 30, meaning that it must pay for goods 30 days after the invoice date. On average, it will owe 30 times $2,000, or $60,000, to its suppliers. If its sales, and consequently its purchases, were to double, then its accounts payable would also double, to $120,000. So, simply by growing, the firm would spontaneously generate an additional $60,000 of financing. Similarly, if the terms under which it bought were extended from 30 to 40 days, its accounts payable would expand from $60,000 to $80,000. Thus, lengthening the credit period, as well as expanding sales and purchases, generates additional financing.

The Cost of Trade Credit

Firms that sell on credit have a *credit policy* that includes certain *terms of credit*. For example, Microchip Electronics sells on terms of 2/10, net 30, meaning that it gives its customers a 2% discount if they pay within 10 days of the invoice date, but the full invoice amount is due and payable within 30 days if the discount is not taken.

Note that the true price of Microchip's products is the net price, or 0.98 times the list price, because any customer can purchase an item at that price as long as the customer pays within 10 days. Now consider Personal Computer Company (PCC), which buys its memory chips from Microchip. One commonly used memory chip is listed at $100, so the "true" price to PCC is $98. Now if PCC wants an additional 20 days of credit beyond the 10-day discount period, it must incur a finance charge of $2 per chip for that credit. Thus, the $100 list price consists of two components:

$$\text{List price} = \$98 \text{ true price} + \$2 \text{ finance charge}$$

The question PCC must ask before it turns down the discount to obtain the additional 20 days of credit from Microchip is this: Could we obtain credit under better terms from some other lender, say, a bank?

PCC buys an average of $11,923,333 of memory chips from Microchip each year at the net, or true, price. This amounts to $11,923,333/365 = $32,666.67 per day. For simplicity, assume that Microchip is PCC's only supplier. If PCC decides not to take the additional trade credit—that is, if it pays on the 10th day and takes the discount—its payables will average 10($32,666.67) = $326,667. Thus, PCC will be receiving $326,667 of credit from Microchip.

Now suppose PCC decides to take the additional 20 days' credit and thus must pay the finance charge. Since PCC will now pay on the 30th day, its accounts payable will increase to 30($32,666.67) = $980,000.[5] Microchip will now be supplying PCC with an additional $980,000 − $326,667 = $653,333 of credit, which PCC could use to build up its cash account, to pay off debt, to expand inventories, or even to extend credit to its own customers, hence increasing its own accounts receivable.

The additional trade credit offered by Microchip has a cost—PCC must pay a finance charge equal to the 2% discount it is foregoing. PCC buys $11,923,333 of chips at the true price, and the added finance charges increase the total cost to $11,923,333/0.98 = $12,166,666. Therefore, the annual financing cost is $12,166,666 − $11,923,333 = $243,333. Dividing the $243,333 financing cost by the $653,333 of additional credit, we find the nominal annual cost rate of the additional trade credit to be 37.2%:

$$\text{Nominal annual costs} = \frac{\$243,333}{\$653,333} = 37.2\%$$

If PCC can borrow from its bank (or from other sources) at an interest rate less than 37.2%, it should take the 2% discount and forgo the additional 20-day trade credit.

The following equation can be used to calculate the nominal cost, on an annual basis, of not taking discounts, illustrated with terms of 2/10, net 30:

$$\begin{array}{l}\text{Nominal} \\ \text{annual cost of} = \text{Cost per period} \times \text{Number of periods per year} \\ \text{trade credit}\end{array}$$

$$\begin{array}{l}\text{Nominal} \\ \text{annual} \\ \text{cost of} \\ \text{trade credit}\end{array} = \frac{\text{Discount percent}}{100 - \text{Discount percent}} \times \frac{365}{\text{Days credit is} - \text{Discount outstanding period}} \qquad (17\text{-}5)$$

$$= \frac{2}{98} \times \frac{365}{20} = 2.04\% \times 18.25 = 37.2\%$$

The numerator of the first term, Discount percent, is the cost per dollar of credit, while the denominator in this term, 100 − Discount percent, represents the funds made available by not taking the discount. Thus, the first term, 2.04%, is the cost per period for the trade credit. The denominator of the second term is the number of days of extra credit obtained by not taking the discount, so the entire second term shows how many times each year the cost is incurred—18.25 times in this example.

The nominal annual cost formula does not take account of compounding, and in effective annual interest terms, the cost of trade credit is even higher. The discount amounts to interest, and with terms of 2/10, net 30, the firm gains use of the funds for 30 − 10 = 20 days, so there

---

[5] A question arises here: Should accounts payable reflect gross purchases or purchases net of discounts? Generally accepted accounting principles permit either treatment if the difference is not material, but if the discount is material, then the transaction must be recorded net of discounts, or at "true" prices. Then, the higher payment that results from not taking discounts is reported as an additional expense called "discounts lost." *Thus, we show accounts payable net of discounts even if the company does not expect to take discounts.*

are $365/20 = 18.25$ "interest periods" per year. Remember that the first term in Equation 17-5, (Discount percent)/(100 − Discount percent) = $0.02/0.98 = 0.0204$, is the periodic interest rate. This rate is paid 18.25 times each year, so the effective annual cost of trade credit is

$$\text{Effective annual rate} = (1.0204)^{18.25} - 1.0 = 1.4459 - 1.0 = 44.6\%$$

Thus, the 37.2% nominal cost calculated with Equation 17-5 understates the true cost.

Note, however, that the cost of trade credit can be reduced by paying late. Thus, if PCC could get away with paying in 60 days rather than in the specified 30 days, then the effective credit period would become $60 - 10 = 50$ days, the number of times the discount would be lost would fall to $365/50 = 7.3$, and the nominal cost would drop from 37.2% to $2.04\% \times 7.3 = 14.9\%$. The effective annual rate would drop from 44.6% to 15.9%:

$$\text{Effective annual rate} = (1.0204)^{7.3} - 1.0 = 1.1589 - 1.0 = 15.9\%$$

In periods of excess capacity, firms may be able to get away with deliberately paying late, or **stretching accounts payable.** However, they will also suffer a variety of problems associated with being branded a "slow payer." These problems are discussed later in the chapter.

The costs of the additional trade credit from foregoing discounts under some other purchase terms are shown below:

Credit Terms	Cost of Additional Credit if the Cash Discount Is Not Taken	
	Nominal Cost	**Effective Cost**
1/10, net 20	36.9%	44.3%
1/10, net 30	18.4	20.1
2/10, net 20	74.5	109.0
3/15, net 45	37.6	44.9

As these figures show, the cost of not taking discounts can be substantial. Incidentally, throughout the chapter, we assume that payments are made either on the *last day* for taking discounts or on the *last day* of the credit period, unless otherwise noted. It would be foolish to pay, say, on the 5th day or on the 20th day if the credit terms were 2/10, net 30.[6]

On the basis of the preceding discussion, trade credit can be divided into two components: (1) **free trade credit,** which involves credit received during the discount period, and (2) **costly trade credit,** which involves credit in excess of the free trade credit and whose cost is an implicit one based on the forgone discounts. *Firms should always use the free component, but they should use the costly component only after analyzing the cost of this capital to make sure that it is less than the cost of funds that could be obtained from other sources.* Under the terms of trade found in most industries, the costly component is relatively expensive, so stronger firms will avoid using it.

CONCEPT REVIEW

1. What are accruals? How much control do managers have over accruals?
2. What is trade credit?
3. What is the difference between free trade credit and costly trade credit?
4. How does the cost of costly trade credit generally compare with the cost of short-term bank loans?
5. A company has credit terms of 2/12, net 28. What is the nominal annual cost of trade credit? The effective annual cost? (Check Figures: 46.6%; 58.5%)

---

[6]A financial calculator can also be used to determine the cost of trade credit. If the terms of credit are 2/10, net 30, this implies that for every $100 of goods purchased at the full list price, the customer has the choice of paying the full amount in 30 days or else paying $98 in 10 days. If a customer decides not to take the discount, then it is in effect borrowing $98, the amount it would otherwise have to pay, from Day 11 to Day 30, or for 20 days. It will then have to pay $100, which is the $98 loan plus a $2 financing charge, at the end of the 20-day loan period. To calculate the interest rate, enter N = 1, PV = 98, PMT = 0, FV = −100, and then press I/YR to obtain 2.04%. This is the rate for 20 days. To calculate the effective annual interest rate on a 365-day basis, enter N = 20/365 = 0.05479, PV = 98, PMT = 0, FV = −100, and then press I/YR to obtain 44.6%. The 20/365 = 0.05479 is the fraction of a year the "loan" is outstanding, and the 44.6% is the annualized cost of not taking discounts.

17.7 Short-Term Bank Loans

Short-term loans from commercial banks generally appear on balance sheets as notes payable. A bank's influence is actually greater than it appears from the dollar amounts it loans, because banks provide *nonspontaneous* financing. As a firm's financing needs increase, it requests additional funds from its bank. If the request is denied, the firm may be forced to abandon attractive growth opportunities. The key features of bank loans are discussed in the following paragraphs.

Banks in Canada divide the commercial lending market into three segments: small business lending may cover loans up to $250,000; mid-size market loans range from $250,000 to $20 million; and corporate lending covers amounts greater than $20 million.

Assessing Loan Applications

Lenders review multiple parts of a business before determining whether to provide financing. Typically required are historical financials for the past three years as well as pro forma financials for the upcoming year, broken down monthly. Bankers will look at levels of profitability (income and EBITDA) as well as their variability, since this is their primary source for repayment. High and/or stable EBITDA is preferred. Bankers will also look at the assets a business owns, for these would be a secondary source for repayment. Companies with assets that can be sold more easily at fair market value will be considered more favourably. Management ability and character will also be considered, as well as the industry in which the borrower operates. For example, as of August 2008, banks were actively reducing their exposure to loans in the real estate and forestry sectors in Canada. Finally, current economic factors such as inflation and economic growth are taken into account when loan applications are being evaluated.

Interest Rates

The cost of bank loans varies for different types of borrowers at any given point in time and for all borrowers over time. Interest rates are higher for riskier borrowers. Rates are also higher on smaller loans because of the fixed costs involved in making and servicing such loans. If a firm is large and is very financially sound, it can borrow at the **prime rate,** which is the lowest rate that banks generally charge their best customers.[7] Rates on other loans are generally scaled up from the prime rate—for example, prime plus 2%. The interest rate can be *fixed* or *floating*. If it floats, it is generally indexed to the bank's prime rate or for U.S. dollar loans to the London Interbank Offer Rate (LIBOR).

Bank rates vary widely over time depending on economic conditions and Bank of Canada policy. When the economy is weak, (1) loan demand is usually slack, (2) inflation is low, and (3) the Bank of Canada makes plenty of money available to the system to stimulate economic growth. As a result, rates on all types of loans are relatively low. Conversely, when the economy is booming, (1) loan demand is typically strong, (2) the Bank of Canada restricts the money supply to control inflation, and (3) interest rates rise. As mentioned earlier, the prime rate can swing quickly and significantly.

Interest Only versus Amortized

Loans are either *interest-only*, meaning that only interest is paid during the life of the loan, with the principal being repaid when the loan matures, or *amortized*, meaning that some of the principal is repaid on each payment date. In practice, interest-only loans are short term and are backed by sufficient assets. Amortized loans are called *installment loans*. Note, too, that loans can be fully or partly amortized. When most or all the principal is repaid at the end of the loan term, the final payment is referred to as a "balloon" or "bullet" repayment.

Other Cost Elements

There are often costs in addition to the interest charged on the loan. Compensating balance requirements, often used in the past but less so now, require borrowers to maintain an average demand deposit (chequing account) balance equal to 10% to 20% of the face amount

---

[7]Canadian banks sometimes offer commercial loans at less than prime—usually in highly competitive markets or when they are aggressively pursuing business in certain industry sectors.

of the loan. This raises the effective interest rate. For example, if a firm needs $80,000 to finance outstanding obligations, but if it must maintain a 20% compensating balance, then it must borrow $100,000 to obtain a usable $80,000. If the stated annual interest rate is 8%, the effective cost is actually 10%: $8,000 interest divided by $80,000 of usable funds equals 10%. Compensating balances are now offered to companies in lieu of regular bank service charges. Other costs such as commitment fees, renewal fees, and processing charges may also be included, and all raise the effective cost of a loan above its stated nominal rate.

Maturity

Although banks do make longer term loans, *the bulk of their lending is on a short-term basis*— about two-thirds of all bank loans mature within a year. Bank loans to businesses are often written as one year or less, which means that the loan must be repaid or renewed at the end of the year. Of course, if a borrower's financial position has deteriorated, the bank may refuse to renew the loan. This can mean serious trouble for the borrower. Instead of a specific maturity date, a loan may be "payable on demand," in which case the loan can remain outstanding as long as the borrower wants to continue using the funds and the bank agrees. Banks almost never call demand notes unless the borrower's creditworthiness deteriorates.

Collateral

If a short-term loan is secured by some specific collateral, this is indicated in the loan agreement. In most cases, banks have *a General Security Agreement* written into the agreement that covers all of the lender's assets. Any collateral used to cover a loan is registered under the Personal Property Security Act (PPSA) of the province in which the borrower is based.[8] This filing prevents the borrower from using the same collateral to secure loans from different lenders; it also spells out the conditions under which the lender can seize the collateral.

Loan Guarantees

If the borrower is a small corporation, its bank will probably insist that the largest shareholder *personally guarantee* the loan. Banks have often seen a troubled company's owner divert assets from the company to some other entity he or she owns, so banks protect themselves by insisting on personal guarantees. However, shareholder guarantees are virtually impossible to get in the case of larger corporations with many shareholders. For proprietorships or partnerships, guarantees are unnecessary because in these cases the owners are already personally liable for the business's debts.

Key Person Insurance

Often the success of a small company is linked to its owner or to a few important managers. It's a sad fact, but many small companies fail when one of these key individuals dies. Therefore, banks often require small companies to take out *key person insurance* on their most important managers as part of the loan agreement, with the bank being the beneficiary of the policy. Usually the loan becomes due and payable should there be an untimely demise, with the insurance benefits going directly to repay the loan. This makes the best of a bad situation—the bank gets its money, and the company reduces its debt burden without having to use any of its operating cash.

Covenants

In addition to the above requirements regarding collateral, guarantees, and insurance, a bank will write in additional terms that the company must adhere to for the loan to remain in good standing. These terms, or covenants, are designed to protect the lender. For instance, a typical covenant may require a borrower to maintain a minimum or better current ratio. Here, the borrower is forced to maintain adequate liquidity, which strengthens its ability to make payments on the loan. A liquidity covenant also inhibits the borrower from taking on too much additional short-term debt, for that would adversely affect the ratio's denominator. Other common covenants include a maximum leverage ratio such as Total liabilities/Tangible

---

[8]The Personal Property Security Act is based on the U.S. Uniform Commercial Code (UCC).

net worth, or a minimum interest coverage ratio such EBITDA/Interest payments. Covenant ratios vary based on the individual business and the industry in which it operates. Although a typical minimum current ratio may be 1.25× and a minimum EBITDA/Interest ratio may be 2×, borrowers with stable earnings and/or quality assets may face more lenient ratio restrictions than other borrowers.

Lenders set covenants at levels that allow them to call a loan back *before* the borrower's financial position has worsened to the point that the loan cannot be recovered. Other nonratio covenants may include limits on capital expenditures, distributions, and/or asset sales. Lenders will also require periodic financing statements and ask to monitor accounts receivables and payables for aging. While these types of covenants hold for loans in general, short-term loans tend to be less cumbersome and to have fewer restrictions than loans of a longer term.

Line of Credit

A **line of credit** is a one-year operating loan designed to finance seasonal working capital requirements. Although the contract will state a maximum amount that can be borrowed, a company may borrow any amount up to the maximum, when required, and can pay as little or as much off anytime during the year. Interest is paid only when funds are borrowed. The interest rate will be floating based on prime. In addition to interest charges, banks will charge a commitment fee[9] of 0.5% to 1% of the loan value. They may also charge between 0.25% and 0.5% on any unused portion of the credit line.

Earlier in the chapter we reviewed the cash flows for MicroDrive over a 6-month period. We saw that from July through October, MicroDrive had to borrow to cover its cash needs, while its November and December operations provided surplus cash. Under a line of credit arrangement, MicroDrive would borrow $6 million in July, $43 million in August, and $100 million in September. In October, MicroDrive's cash flows will enable the company to repay $44 million, and by the end of November the entire line of credit will have been repaid. Obviously, MicroDrive must forecast its cash needs for the upcoming year to ensure that it negotiates a line of credit in advance that is sufficient to meet its short-term borrowing needs. A **revolving line of credit,** (a "revolver") is similar to a standard line of credit except that it matures in 3 to 4 years. Revolving lines provide additional financing flexibility over standard lines of credit.

17.8 Commercial Paper

Commercial paper is a type of unsecured promissory note issued by large, strong firms and sold primarily to large institutional investors such as insurance companies, pension funds, and money market funds. Maturities can be up to three years, although most mature in 30 to 360 days. The interest rate on commercial paper fluctuates with supply and demand—it is determined by the marketplace and varies daily as conditions change. The use of commercial paper is restricted to a relatively small number of large concerns with investment-grade short-term credit ratings. Benefits include the opportunity to tap funds at a lower cost than traditional bank financing. The drawback is that in times of market turmoil and uncertainty, investors may have little appetite for short-term commercial paper, so companies relying on this financing source could run into trouble.

Commercial paper does not pay interest; rather, investors buy it at a discount from its face value. The difference between its purchase price and maturity value is the investment's return. Equation 17-6 is the same formula used to calculate the yield on Treasury bills and bankers' acceptances.

$$\text{Yield} = \frac{100 - P}{P} \times \frac{365}{d} \qquad (17\text{-}6)$$

Where P = Price of the commercial paper as a percentage of its face value
d = Number of days until it matures

---

[9]May also be called a setup fee or review fee.

17.9 Bankers' Acceptances

A significant source of short-term financing in Canada is bankers' acceptances (BAs). BAs are commonly used to finance goods sold with long payment terms—typically exports and imports. A BA is created when a company writes a term draft[10] for the purchase of merchandise, which is then "accepted" by a major bank. By accepting the term draft, the bank takes on the full obligation to pay the draft when it comes due. Since major banks have very good credit ratings, they can easily sell the accepted draft to investors at a discount from its full value. In fact, investors don't really care which company actually wrote the draft and must make good on it, because the bank is the ultimate guarantor for payment. The bank uses its good reputation and credit standing to make the draft marketable. Banks are paid 1% to "accept" such time drafts. BAs are popular in Canada as a financing source since few large Canadian companies have the creditworthiness and name recognition to issue commercial paper on their own.

FINANCE: IN FOCUS

Maturity Mismatching and the 2007 Canadian Credit Crisis

In 2007 the size of Canada's money market, where companies borrow short-term, was about $360 billion. Roughly one-third, or $115 billion of that borrowing, was through asset-backed commercial paper (ABCP). Commercial paper is a short-term security by definition, with maturities ranging from 30 to 365 days. However, the security or collateral behind ABCP—such as consumer and corporate loans, leases, and residential mortgages—was typically longer-term assets. Thus, there was a mismatch between the life of the asset being financed and the term of the financing used. As a result, ABCP had to be rolled over (renewed) every 90 days or so in order to continue financing the longer term assets.

The market for a portion ($32 billion) of the Canadian ABCP collapsed in 2007, when investors' demand dried up, owing to worries over the quality of their collateral. As the ABCP matured, investors chose not to renew the paper, and since no new investors wished to purchase the ABCP, the existing ABCP holders could not get their money back. This led to two major events. First, since the ABCP issuers were in default, the ABCP holders had the right to liquidate the assets to recover their money. However, selling $32 billion in loans could have led to chaos and major market turmoil. Second, borrowing difficulty spread to the money market as a whole, which greatly affected many companies' ability to finance and carry on their regular business. In the end, an outright liquidation was avoided, but at great cost to investors and borrowers alike. The ABCP was restructured with much longer terms, all the way out to 10 years. Now the assets were financed with securities of the same term as the assets' lives. When used cautiously, maturity mismatching can provide benefits in terms of cost and flexibility; however, the events of 2007 clearly illustrate the significant risks inherent in such a strategy.

17.10 Calculating Financing Costs

Regular, or Simple, Interest

In this and the following sections, we explain how to calculate the effective cost of different bank loans. For illustrative purposes, we assume a loan of $10,000 at a nominal interest rate of 12%, with a 365-day year.

For short-term business loans, the most common procedure is called *regular*, or *simple*, *interest*, based on an interest-only loan. We begin by dividing the nominal interest rate, 12% in this case, by 365 to get the rate per day[11]:

$$\text{Interest rate per day} = \frac{\text{Nominal rate}}{\text{Days in year}} \qquad (17\text{-}7)$$

$$= 0.12/365 = 0.00032876712$$

---

[10]A term draft can be thought of basically as a postdated cheque.
[11]Or 360 days, in some cases.

This rate is then multiplied by the number of days during the specific payment period, and then by the amount of the loan. For example, if the loan is interest-only, with monthly payments, then the interest payment for January would be $101.92:

$$\text{Interest charge for period} = (\text{Days in period})(\text{Rate per day})(\text{Amount of loan}) \tag{17-8}$$

$$= (31\,\text{days})(0.00032876712)(\$10{,}000) = \$101.92$$

If interest were payable quarterly, and if there were 91 days in the particular quarter, then the interest payment would be $299.18. The annual interest would be 365 × 0.00032876712 × $10,000 = $1,200.00.

The effective interest rate on a loan depends on how frequently interest must be paid—the more frequently, the higher the effective rate. We demonstrate this point with two time lines, one for interest paid once a year and one for quarterly payments:

Interest Paid Annually:

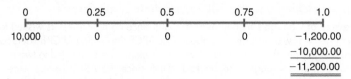

The borrower gets $10,000 at t = 0 and pays $11,200 at t = 1. With a financial calculator, enter N = 1, PV = 10,000, PMT = 0, and FV = −11,200, and then press I/YR to get the effective cost of the loan, 12%.

Interest Paid Quarterly:

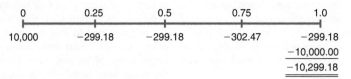

Note that the third quarter has 92 days. We enter the data in the cash flow register of a financial calculator (being sure to use the +/− key to enter −299.18), and we find the periodic rate to be 2.9999%. The effective annual rate is 12.55%:

$$\text{Effective annual rate, quarterly} = (1 + 0.029999)^4 - 1 = 12.55\%$$

Had the loan called for interest to be paid monthly, the effective rate would have been 12.68%, and if interest had been paid daily, the rate would have been 12.75%.

In these examples, we assumed that the loan matured in 1 year but that interest was paid at various times during the year. The rates we calculated would have been exactly the same as the ones above even if the loan had matured on each interest payment date. In other words, the effective rate on a monthly payment loan would be 12.68% regardless of whether it matured after 1 month, 6 months, 1 year, or 10 years, providing the stated rate remained at 12%.

Discount Interest

In a **discount interest** loan, the bank deducts the interest in advance (*discounts* the loan). Thus, the borrower receives less than the face value of the loan. On a 1-year, $10,000 loan with a 12% (nominal) rate, discount basis, the interest is $10,000(0.12) = $1,200. Therefore, the borrower obtains the use of only $10,000 − $1,200 = $8,800. If the loan were for less than a year, the interest charge (the discount) would be lower; in our example, it would be $600 if the loan were for 6 months; hence the amount received would be $9,400.

The effective rate on a discount loan is always higher than the rate on an otherwise similar simple interest loan. To illustrate, consider the situation for a discounted 12% loan for 1 year:

Discount Interest, Paid Annually:

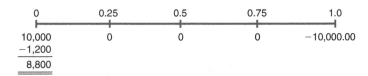

With a financial calculator, enter N = 1, PV = 8,800, PMT = 0, and FV = −10,000, and then press I/YR to get the effective cost of the loan, 13.64%.[12]

If a discount loan matures in less than a year—say, after one quarter—we have this situation:

Discount Interest, One Quarter:

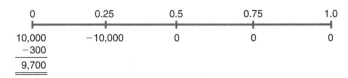

Enter N = 1, PV = 9,700, PMT = 0, and FV = −10,000, and then press I/YR to find the periodic rate, 3.092784% per quarter, which corresponds to an effective annual rate of 12.96%. Thus, shortening the period of a discount loan lowers the effective rate of interest. As mentioned earlier in the chapter, discount loans are usually provided only for terms of one year or less.

Effects of Compensating Balances

Banks have in the past sometimes required borrowers to maintain a deposit balance of 10% to 20% of a loan's face amount. This is called a compensating balance, and such balances raise the effective interest rate on loans. If the bank requires a compensating balance, and if the amount of the required balance exceeds the amount the firm would normally hold on deposit, then the excess must be deducted at t = 0 and then added back when the loan matures. This has the effect of raising the effective rate on the loan. To illustrate, here is the setup for a 1-year discount loan, with a 20% compensating balance that the firm would not otherwise hold on deposit:

Discount Interest, Paid Annually, with 20% Compensating Balance:

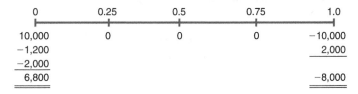

Note that the bank initially gives, and the borrower gets, $10,000 at time 0. However, the bank takes out the $1,200 of interest in advance, and the company must leave $2,000 in the bank as a compensating balance; hence the borrower's effective net cash flow at t = 0 is $6,800. At t = 1, the borrower must repay the $10,000, but $2,000 is already in the bank (the compensating balance), so the company must repay a net amount of $8,000.

---

[12]Note that the firm actually receives less than the face amount of the loan:

$$\text{Funds received} = (\text{Face amount of loan})(1.0 - \text{Nominal interest rate})$$

We can solve for the face amount as follows:

$$\text{Face amount of loan} = \frac{\text{Funds received}}{1.0 - \text{Nominal rate (decimal)}}$$

Therefore, if the borrowing firm actually requires $10,000 of cash, it must borrow $11,363.64:

$$\text{Face value} = \frac{\$10,000}{1.0 - 0.12} = \frac{\$10,000}{0.88} = \$11,363.64$$

Now, the borrower will receive $11,363.64 − 0.12($11,363.64) = $10,000. Increasing the face value of the loan does not change the effective rate of 13.64% on the $10,000 of usable funds.

With a financial calculator, enter N = 1, PV = 6,800, PMT = 0, and FV = −8,000, and then press I/YR to get the effective cost of the discount loan with a compensating balance, 17.65%.

Installment Loans: Add-On Interest

Lenders typically charge **add-on interest** on automobile and other types of installment loans. The term "add-on" means that the interest is calculated and then added to the amount received to determine the loan's face value. To illustrate, suppose you borrow $10,000 on an add-on basis at a nominal rate of 12% to buy a car, with the loan to be repaid in 12 monthly installments. At a 12% add-on rate, you will pay a total interest charge of $10,000(0.12) = $1,200. However, since the loan is paid off in monthly installments, you have the use of the full $10,000 for only the first month, and the outstanding balance declines until, during the last month, only 1/12 of the original loan will still be outstanding. Thus, you are paying $1,200 for the use of only about half the loan's face amount, as the average usable funds are only about $5,000.

To determine the effective rate of an add-on loan, we proceed as follows:

1. The total amount to be repaid is $10,000 of principal, plus $1,200 of interest, or $11,200.
2. The monthly payment is $11,200/12 = $933.33.
3. You are, in effect, paying off a 12-period annuity of $933.33 in order to receive $10,000 today, so $10,000 is the present value of the annuity. Here is the time line:

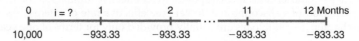

4. With a financial calculator, enter N = 12, PV = 10,000, PMT = −933.33, FV = 0, and then press I/YR to obtain 1.7880%. However, this is a monthly rate.
5. The effective annual rate is found as follows[13]:

$$\text{Effective annual rate}_{\text{Add-on}} = (1 + r_d)^n - 1.0$$
$$= (1.01788)^{12} - 1.0 \qquad (17\text{-}9)$$
$$= 1.2370 - 1.0 = 23.7\%$$

The **annual percentage rate (APR),** which the bank prints on all "consumer loan" agreements, would be 21.46%:

$$\text{APR} = (\text{Periods per year})(\text{Rate per period})$$
$$= 12(1.7880\%) = 21.46\%.$$

CONCEPT REVIEW

1. Name four different ways banks can calculate interest on loans.
2. What is a compensating balance? What effect does a compensating balance requirement have on the effective interest rate on a loan?

17.11 Secured Short-Term Financing

Below we discuss procedures for using accounts receivable and inventories as security for short-term loans. As noted earlier in the chapter, secured loans involve quite a bit of paperwork and other administrative costs, which make them relatively expensive. However, this is often the only type of financing available to weaker firms.

---

[13]Note that if an installment loan is paid off ahead of schedule, additional complications arise. For the classic discussion of this point, see Dick Bonker, "The Rule of 78," *Journal of Finance,* June 1976, 877–888.

Accounts Receivable Financing

Accounts receivable financing involves either pledging receivables or selling receivables (called *factoring*). **Pledging accounts receivable,** or putting accounts receivable up as security for a loan, is characterized by the fact that the lender not only has a claim against the receivables but also has *recourse* to the borrower. If the borrower does not pay back the loan, the lender may seize the receivables to collect what is owed. If the amount collected is insufficient, the lender may seek remaining payment directly from the borrower.

Factoring, or selling accounts receivable, involves the purchase of accounts receivable by the lender, generally without recourse to the borrower, which means that if the purchaser of the goods does not pay for them, the lender rather than the seller of the goods takes the loss. Under factoring, the buyer of the goods is typically notified of the transfer and is asked to make payment directly to the financial institution. Because the factoring firm assumes the risk of default on bad accounts, it must make the credit check. Accordingly, factors provide not only money, but also a credit department for the borrower.

- *Procedure for pledging accounts receivable.* The financing of accounts receivable is initiated by a legally binding agreement between the seller of the goods and the financing institution. The agreement sets forth in detail the procedures to be followed and the legal obligations of both parties. Once the working relationship has been established, the seller periodically takes a batch of invoices to the financing institution. The lender reviews the invoices and makes credit appraisals of the buyers. Invoices of companies that do not meet the lender's credit standards are not accepted for pledging.

    The financial institution seeks to protect itself at every phase of the operation. First, selection of sound invoices is one way the lender safeguards itself. Second, if the buyer of the goods does not pay the invoice, the lender still has recourse against the seller. Third, additional protection is afforded the lender because the loan will generally be less than 100% of the pledged receivables; for example, the lender may advance the selling firm only 75% of the amount of the pledged invoices.

- *Procedure for factoring accounts receivable.* The procedures used for factoring are somewhat different from those for pledging. Again, an agreement between the seller and the factor specifies legal obligations and procedural arrangements. When the seller receives an order from a buyer, a credit approval slip is written and immediately sent to the factoring company for a credit check. If the factor approves the credit, shipment is made and the invoice is stamped to notify the buyer to make payment directly to the factoring company. If the factor does not approve the sale, the seller generally refuses to fill the order; if the sale is made anyway, the factor will not buy the account.

    The factor normally performs three functions: (1) credit checking, (2) lending, and (3) risk bearing. However, the seller can select various combinations of these functions by changing provisions in the factoring agreement.

    Let's consider a typical situation in which the factor performs the lending, risk-bearing, and credit-checking functions. The goods are shipped, and even though payment is not due for 30 days, the factor immediately makes funds available to the seller. Suppose $10,000 worth of goods are shipped. Furthermore, assume that the factoring commission for credit checking and risk bearing is 2.5% of the invoice price, or $250, and that the interest expense is computed at a 9% annual rate on the invoice balance, or $75.[14] The selling firm's accounting entry is as follows:

Cash	$ 9,175
Interest expense	75
Factoring commission	250
Reserve due from factor on collection of account	500
Accounts receivable	$10,000

---

[14]Since the interest is only for 1 month, we multiply 1/12 of the quoted rate (9%) by the $10,000 invoice price:

$$(1/12)(0.09)(\$10,000) = \$75.$$

The effective annual interest rate is above 9% because (1) the term is for less than 1 year and (2) a discounting procedure is used and the borrower does not get the full $10,000. In many instances, however, the factoring contract calls for interest to be calculated on the invoice price minus the factoring commission and the reserve account.

The $500 due from the factor upon collection of the account is a reserve established by the factor to cover disputes between the seller and buyers over damaged goods, goods returned by the buyers to the seller, and the failure to make an outright sale of goods. The reserve is paid to the selling firm when the factor collects on the account. If the buyer defaults, the factor takes a loss on the $9,175 paid on the receivable.

Factoring is normally a continuous process instead of the single cycle just described. The firm that sells the goods receives an order; it transmits this order to the factor for approval; upon approval, the firm ships the goods; the factor advances the invoice amount minus withholdings to the seller; the buyer pays the factor when payment is due; and the factor periodically remits any excess in the reserve to the seller of the goods. Once a routine has been established, a continuous circular flow of goods and funds takes place between the seller, the buyers of the goods, and the factor. Thus, once the factoring agreement is in force, funds from this source are *spontaneous* in the sense that an increase in sales will automatically generate additional credit.

- *Cost of receivables financing.* Both accounts receivable pledging and factoring are convenient and advantageous, but they can be costly. The credit-checking and risk-bearing fee is 1% to 3% of the amount of invoices accepted by the factor, and it may be even more if the buyers are poor credit risks. The cost of money is reflected in the interest rate (usually 2 to 3 percentage points over the prime rate) charged on the unpaid balance of the funds advanced by the factor.

- *Evaluation of receivables financing.* It cannot be said categorically that accounts receivable financing is always either a good or a poor way to raise funds. Among the advantages is, first, the flexibility of this source of financing: As the firm's sales expand, more financing is needed, but a larger volume of invoices, and hence a larger amount of receivables financing, is generated automatically. Second, receivables can be used as security for loans that would not otherwise be granted. Third, factoring can provide the services of a credit department that might otherwise be available only at a higher cost.

  Accounts receivable financing also has disadvantages. First, when invoices are numerous and relatively small in dollar amount, the administrative costs involved may be excessive. Second, since receivables represent the firm's most liquid noncash assets, some trade creditors may refuse to sell on credit to a firm that factors or pledges its receivables on the grounds that this practice weakens the position of other creditors.

- *Future use of receivables financing.* We will make a prediction at this point: in the future, accounts receivable financing will increase in relative importance. Computer technology has advanced to the point where credit records of individuals and firms are instantly available. For example, one device used by retailers consists of a box that, when an individual's magnetic credit card is inserted, gives a signal that the credit is "good" and that a bank is willing to "buy" the receivable created as soon as the store completes the sale. The cost of handling invoices will be greatly reduced over present-day costs because the new systems will be so highly automated. This will make it possible to use accounts receivable financing for very small sales, and it will reduce the cost of all receivables financing. The net result will be a marked expansion of accounts receivable financing. In fact, when consumers use credit cards such as MasterCard or Visa, the seller is in effect factoring receivables. The seller receives the amount of the purchase, minus a percentage fee, the next working day. The buyer receives 30 days (or so) credit, at which time he or she remits payment directly to the credit card company or sponsoring bank.

Inventory Financing

A substantial amount of credit is secured by business inventories. If a firm is a relatively good credit risk, the mere existence of the inventory may be a sufficient basis for receiving an unsecured loan. However, if the firm is a relatively poor risk, the lending institution may insist upon security in the form of a *lien* against the inventory. Methods for using inventories as security are discussed in this section.

- *Blanket liens.* The **inventory blanket lien** gives the lending institution a lien against all the borrower's inventories. However, the borrower is free to sell inventories, and thus the value of the collateral can be reduced below the level that existed when the loan was granted.

- *Trust receipts.* Because of the inherent weakness of the blanket lien, another procedure for inventory financing has been developed—the **trust receipt,** which is an instrument acknowledging that the goods are held in trust for the lender. Under this method, the borrowing firm, as a condition for receiving funds from the lender, signs and delivers a trust receipt for the goods. The goods can be stored in a public warehouse or held on the premises of the borrower. The trust receipt states that the goods are held in trust for the lender or are segregated on the borrower's premises on the lender's behalf, and that any proceeds from the sale of the goods must be transmitted to the lender at the end of each day. Automobile dealer financing is one of the best examples of trust receipt financing.

  One disadvantage of trust receipt financing is the requirement that a trust receipt be issued for specific goods. For example, if the security is autos in a dealer's inventory, the trust receipts must indicate the cars by registration number. In order to validate its trust receipts, the lending institution must send someone to the borrower's premises periodically to see that the auto numbers are correctly listed because auto dealers who are in financial difficulty have been known to sell cars backing trust receipts and then use the funds obtained for other operations rather than to repay the bank. Problems are compounded if the borrower has a number of different locations, especially if they are separated geographically from the lender. To offset these inconveniences, *warehousing* has come into wide use as a method of securing loans with inventory.

- *Warehouse receipts.* **Warehouse receipt financing** is another way to use inventory as security. It is a method of financing that uses inventory as a security and that requires public notification, physical control of the inventory, and supervision by a custodian of the field warehousing concern. A *public warehouse* is an independent third-party operation engaged in the business of storing goods. Items that must age, such as tobacco and liquor, are often financed and stored in public warehouses. Sometimes a public warehouse is not practical because of the bulkiness of goods and the expense of transporting them to and from the borrower's premises. In such cases, a *field warehouse* may be established on the borrower's grounds. To provide inventory supervision, the lending institution employs a third party in the arrangement, the field warehousing company, that acts as its agent.

  Field warehousing can be illustrated by a simple example. Suppose a firm that has iron stacked in an open yard on its premises needs a loan. A field warehousing concern can place a temporary fence around the iron, erect a sign stating "This is a field warehouse supervised by the Smith Field Warehousing Corporation," and then assign an employee to supervise and control the fenced-in inventory.

  This example illustrates the three essential elements for the establishment of a field warehouse: (1) public notification, (2) physical control of the inventory, and (3) supervision by a custodian of the field warehousing concern. When the field warehousing operation is relatively small, the third condition is sometimes violated by hiring an employee of the borrower to supervise the inventory. This practice is viewed as undesirable by most lenders because there is no control over the collateral by a person independent of the borrowing firm.

- *Acceptable products.* Products that are relatively nonperishable and that are sold in well-developed, organized markets, provide a basis for field warehouse financing. Examples include lumber products, coal, and groceries such as canned foods. Nonperishability protects the lender if it should have to take over the security. For this reason, a bank would not make a field warehousing loan on perishables such as fresh fish, but frozen fish, which can be stored for a long time, can be field warehoused.

- *Cost of financing.* The fixed costs of a field warehousing arrangement are relatively high; such financing is therefore not suitable for a very small firm. If a field warehousing company sets up a field warehouse, it will typically set a minimum charge of about $5,000 per year, plus about 1% to 2% of the amount of credit extended to the borrower. Furthermore, the financing institution will charge an interest rate of 2 to 3 percentage points over the prime rate. An efficient field warehousing operation requires a minimum inventory of at least $1 million.

- *Evaluation of inventory financing.* The use of inventory financing, especially field warehouse financing, as a source of funds has many advantages. First, the amount of funds available is flexible because the financing is tied to inventory growth, which, in turn, is related directly to financing needs. Second, the field warehousing arrangement increases the acceptability of inventories as loan collateral; some inventories simply would not be accepted by a bank as security without such an arrangement. Third, the necessity for inventory control and safekeeping, as well as the use of specialists in warehousing, often results in improved warehouse practices, which, in turn, save handling costs, insurance charges, theft losses, and so on. Thus, field warehousing companies often save money for firms in spite of the costs of financing that we have discussed. The major disadvantages of field warehousing include the paperwork; physical separation requirements; and, for small firms, the fixed-cost element.

Summary

This chapter discussed working capital management and short-term financing. The key concepts covered are listed below.

- **Working capital** refers to current assets, and **net working capital** is defined as current assets minus current liabilities. **Net operating working capital** is defined as operating current assets minus operating current liabilities.
- The **cash conversion cycle model** focuses on the length of time between when the company makes payments and when it receives cash inflows.
- The **inventory conversion period** is the average time required to convert materials into finished goods and then to sell those goods.

$$\text{Inventory conversion period} = \text{Inventory/Cost of goods sold per day}$$

- The **receivables collection period** is the average length of time required to convert the firm's receivables into cash; that is, to collect cash following a sale.

$$\text{Receivables collection period} = \text{DSO} = \text{Receivables/(Sales/365)}$$

- The **payables deferral period** is the average length of time between the purchase of materials and labour and the payment of cash for them.

$$\text{Payables deferral period} = \text{Payables/Purchases per day}$$

- The **cash conversion cycle** equals the length of time between the firm's actual cash expenditures to pay for productive resources (materials and labour) and its own cash receipts from the sale of products (i.e., the length of time between paying for labour and materials and collecting on receivables).

$$\begin{array}{ccccc} \text{Cash} & & \text{Inventory} & \text{Receivables} & \text{Payables} \\ \text{conversion} & = & \text{conversion} & + \quad \text{collection} & - \quad \text{deferral} \\ \text{cycle} & & \text{period} & \text{period} & \text{period} \end{array}$$

- Under a **relaxed working capital policy,** a firm would hold relatively large amounts of each type of current asset. Under a **restricted working capital policy,** the firm would hold minimal amounts of these items.
- A **cash budget** is a schedule showing projected cash inflows and outflows over some period. The cash budget is used to predict cash surpluses and deficits, and it is the primary cash management planning tool.
- **Permanent net operating working capital** is the NOWC that the firm holds even during slack times, whereas **temporary NOWC** is the additional NOWC needed during seasonal or cyclical peaks. The methods used to finance permanent and temporary NOWC define the firm's **short-term financing policy.**
- A **moderate** approach to short-term financing involves matching, to the extent possible, the maturities of assets and liabilities, so that temporary NOWC is financed with short-term debt, and permanent NOWC and fixed assets are financed with long-term debt or equity. Under an **aggressive** approach, some permanent NOWC, and perhaps even

some fixed assets, are financed with short-term debt. A **conservative** approach would be to use long-term sources to finance all permanent operating capital and some of the temporary NOWC.

- The advantages of short-term credit are (1) the **speed** with which short-term loans can be arranged, (2) increased **flexibility,** and (3) the fact that short-term **interest rates** are generally **lower** than long-term rates. The principal disadvantage of short-term credit is the **extra risk** the borrower must bear because (1) the lender can demand payment on short notice and (2) the cost of the loan will increase if interest rates rise.
- **Accounts payable,** or **trade credit,** arises spontaneously as a result of credit purchases. Firms should use all the **free trade credit** they can obtain, but they should use **costly trade credit** only if it is less expensive than other forms of short-term debt. Suppliers often offer discounts to customers who pay within a stated discount period.
- A **line of credit** is an important short-term operating loan designed to finance seasonal working capital requirements. Any amount up to the stated maximum may be borrowed and repaid during the loan's life. A **revolving line of credit** is a multiyear line of credit.
- **Commercial paper** is a short-term promissory note issued by large, strong firms with investment-grade credit ratings and sold primarily to large institutional investors.
- A **bankers' acceptance (BA)** is a short-term note of a borrower (corporation), unconditionally guaranteed by a major bank. Because Canadian banks have high credit ratings, BAs are a popular Canadian money market instrument.
- Weaker companies can obtain financing by **pledging accounts receivable** as security against a loan or by **factoring** (selling) the receivables to a finance company.
- Inventory can be used to secure loans. Depending on the company's creditworthiness, an **inventory blanket lien**, a **trust receipt**, or **warehouse receipt financing** methods may be used.

Questions

17-1 Define each of the following terms:
  a. Working capital; net working capital; net operating working capital
  b. Inventory conversion period; receivables collection period; payables deferral period; cash conversion cycle
  c. Relaxed NOWC policy; restricted NOWC policy; moderate NOWC policy
  d. Cash budget
  e. Trade discounts
  f. Permanent NOWC; temporary NOWC
  g. Moderate short-term financing policy; aggressive short-term financing policy; conservative short-term financing policy
  h. Maturity matching, or "self-liquidating," approach
  i. Accruals
  j. Trade credit; stretching accounts payable; free trade credit; costly trade credit
  k. Line of credit; revolving credit agreement
  l. Commercial paper; bankers' acceptances

17-2 Is it true that when one firm sells to another on credit, the seller records the transaction as an account receivable while the buyer records it as an account payable and that, disregarding discounts, the receivable typically exceeds the payable by the amount of profit on the sale?

17-3 What are the advantages of matching the maturities of assets and liabilities? What are the disadvantages?

17-4 From the standpoint of the borrower, is long-term or short-term credit riskier? Explain. Would it ever make sense to borrow on a short-term basis if short-term rates were above long-term rates?

17-5 "Firms can control their accruals within fairly wide limits." Discuss.

17-6 Is it true that most firms are able to obtain some free trade credit and that additional trade credit is often available, but at a cost? Explain.

17-7 What kinds of firms use commercial paper?

Concept Review Problems

Full solutions are provided at www.nelson.com/brigham3ce.

CR-1

Working Capital Policy

Calgary Company is attempting to establish a current assets policy. Fixed assets are $600,000, and the firm plans to maintain a 50% debt-to-assets ratio. Calgary has no operating current liabilities. The interest rate is 10% on all debt. Three alternative current asset policies are under consideration: 40%, 50%, and 60% of projected sales. The company expects to earn 15% before interest and taxes on sales of $3 million. Calgary's effective tax rate is 40%. What is the expected return on equity under each alternative?

CR-2

Current Asset Financing

Safari Adventure Travels and Eco Touring Co. had the following balance sheets as at December 31, 2015 (thousands of dollars):

	Safari Adventure Travels	Eco Touring Co.
Current assets	$100,000	$ 80,000
Fixed assets (net)	100,000	120,000
Total assets	$200,000	$200,000
Current liabilities	$ 20,000	$ 80,000
Long-term debt	80,000	20,000
Common stock	50,000	50,000
Retained earnings	50,000	50,000
Total liabilities and equity	$200,000	$200,000

Earnings before interest and taxes for both firms are $20 million, and the effective tax rate is 30%.
a.   What is the return on equity for each firm if the interest rate on current liabilities is 6% and the rate on long-term debt is 8%?
b.   Assume that the short-term rate rises to 14%. While the rate on new long-term debt rises to 10%, the rate on existing long-term debt remains unchanged. What would be the return on equity for Safari Adventure Travels and Eco Touring Co. under these conditions?
c.   Which company is in a riskier position? Why?

Problems

Answers to odd-numbered problems appear in Appendix A.

Easy
Problems 1–3

17-1
Cost of Trade Credit

What is the nominal and effective cost of trade credit under the credit terms of 3/20, net 40?

17-2
Cost of Trade Credit

Jade Rabbit Imports obtains merchandise under the credit terms of 1/20, net 30, but routinely takes 50 days to pay its bills. Given that the retailer is an important customer, suppliers allow the firm to stretch its credit terms. What is the retailer's effective cost of trade credit?

17-3
Accounts Payable

A chain of appliance stores, APP Corporation, purchases inventory with a net price of $500,000 each day. The company purchases the inventory under the credit terms of 2/15, net 40. APP always takes the discount, but takes the full 15 days to pay its bills. What is the average accounts payable for APP?

Intermediate
Problems 4–12

17-4
Receivables Investment

Griswall Industries sells on terms of 2/10, net 30. Total sales for the year are $1,460,000. Thirty percent of the customers pay on the 10th day and take discounts; the other 70% pay, on average, 40 days after their purchases.
a.   What is the days' sales outstanding?
b.   What is the average amount of receivables?
c.   What would happen to average receivables if Griswall toughened up on its collection policy with the result that all nondiscount customers paid on the 30th day?

17-5
Cost of Trade Credit

Calculate the nominal annual cost of nonfree trade credit under each of the following terms.
a.   1/15, net 20
b.   2/10, net 60
c.   3/10, net 45
d.   2/10, net 45
e.   2/15, net 40

17-6
Cost of Trade Credit

a.   If a firm buys under terms of 3/15, net 45, but actually pays on the 20th day and *still takes the discount*, what is the nominal cost of its nonfree trade credit?
b.   Does it receive more or less credit than it would if it paid within 15 days?

17-7
Cost of Trade Credit

A wholesaler sells on terms of 1/15, net 45. Gross sales last year were $6,935,000, and accounts receivable averaged $665,000. Half of its customers paid on the 15th day and took discounts. What are the nominal and effective costs of trade credit to the wholesaler's non-discount customers?

17-8
Cash Conversion
Cycle

Sterling Enterprises has an inventory conversion period of 50 days, an average collection period of 35 days, and a payables deferral period of 25 days. Assume that cost of goods sold is 80% of sales.
a.   What is the length of the firm's cash conversion cycle?
b.   If Sterling's annual sales are $4,380,000 and all sales are on credit, what is the firm's investment in accounts receivable?
c.   How many times per year does Sterling Enterprises turn over its inventory?

17-9
Working Capital
Cash Flow Cycle

Qbit Technology is considering changes in its working capital policies to improve its cash flow cycle. Qbit's sales last year were $3,250,000 (all on credit), and its net profit margin was 7%. Its inventory turnover was 6.0 times during the year, and its DSO was 41 days. Its annual cost of goods sold was $1,800,000. The firm had fixed assets totalling $535,000. Qbit's payables deferral period is 45 days.
a.   Calculate the company's cash conversion cycle.
b.   Assuming Qbit holds negligible amounts of cash and marketable securities, calculate its total assets turnover and ROA.
c.   Suppose Qbit's managers believe the annual inventory turnover can be raised to 9 times without affecting sales. What would Qbit's cash conversion cycle, total assets turnover, and ROA have been if the inventory turnover had been 9 for the year?

17-10
Cost of Bank Loan

Alain Jones recently obtained an equipment loan from a local bank. The loan is for $15,000 with a nominal interest rate of 11%. However, this is an installment loan, so the bank also charges add-on interest. Alain must make monthly payments on the loan, and the loan is to be repaid in 1 year. What is the effective annual rate on the loan (assuming a 365-day year)?

17-11
Cost of Bank Loans

Del Hawley, owner of Hawley's Hardware, is negotiating with First City Bank for a 1-year loan of $50,000. First City has offered Hawley the following alternatives. Calculate the effective annual interest rate for each alternative. Which alternative has the lowest effective annual interest rate?
a.   A 12% annual rate on a simple interest loan, with no compensating balance required and interest due at the end of the year.
b.   A 9% annual rate on a simple interest loan, with a 20% compensating balance required and interest due at the end of the year.
c.   An 8.75% annual rate on a discounted loan, with a 15% compensating balance.
d.   Interest is figured as 8% of the $50,000 amount, *payable at the end of the year*, but the $50,000 is repayable in monthly installments during the year.

17-12
Effective Cost of
Short-Term Credit

Yonge Corporation must arrange financing for its working capital requirements for the coming year. Yonge can (a) borrow from its bank on a simple interest basis (interest payable at the end of the loan) for 1 year at a 12% nominal rate; (b) borrow on a 3-month, but renewable, loan basis at an 11.5% nominal rate; (c) borrow on an installment loan basis at a 6% add-on rate with 12 end-of-month payments; or (d) obtain the needed funds by no longer taking discounts and thus increasing its accounts payable. Yonge buys on terms of 1/15, net 60. What is the effective annual cost (*not* the nominal cost) of the *least expensive* type of credit, assuming 360 days per year?

Challenging
Problems 13–20
17-13
Working Capital Policy

Payne Products's sales last year were an anemic $1.6 million, but with an improved product mix it expects sales growth to be 25% this year, and Payne would like to determine the effect of various current assets policies on its financial performance. Payne has $1 million of fixed assets and intends to keep its debt ratio at its historical level of 60%. Payne's debt interest rate is currently 8%. You are to evaluate three different current asset policies: (1) a tight policy in which current assets are 45% of projected sales, (2) a moderate policy with 50% of sales tied up in current assets, and (3) a relaxed policy requiring current assets of 60% of sales. Earnings before interest and taxes is expected to be 12% of sales. Payne's tax rate is 26%.

a. What is the expected return on equity under each current asset level?
b. In this problem, we have assumed that the level of expected sales is independent of current asset policy. Is this a valid assumption? Why or why not?
c. How would the overall riskiness of the firm vary under each policy?

17-14
Cash Budgeting

Dorothy Koehl recently leased space in the Southside Mall and opened a new business, Koehl's Doll Shop. Business has been good, but Koehl has frequently run out of cash. This has necessitated late payment on certain orders, which, in turn, is beginning to cause a problem with suppliers. Koehl plans to borrow from the bank to have cash ready as needed, but first she needs a forecast of just how much she must borrow. Accordingly, she has asked you to prepare a cash budget for the critical period around Christmas, when needs will be especially high.

Sales are made on a cash basis only. Koehl's purchases must be paid for during the following month. Koehl pays herself a salary of $4,800 per month, and the rent is $2,000 per month. In addition, she must make a tax payment of $12,000 in December. The current cash on hand (on December 1) is $400, but Koehl has agreed to maintain an average bank balance of $6,000—this is her target cash balance. (Disregard till cash, which is insignificant because Koehl keeps only a small amount on hand in order to lessen the chances of robbery.)

The estimated sales and purchases for December, January, and February are shown below. Purchases during November amounted to $140,000.

	Sales	Purchases
December	$160,000	$40,000
January	40,000	40,000
February	60,000	40,000

a. Prepare a cash budget for December, January, and February.
b. Now, suppose Koehl were to start selling on a credit basis on December 1, giving customers 30 days to pay. All customers accept these terms, and all other facts in the problem are unchanged. What would the company's loan requirements be at the end of December in this case?

17-15
Cash Discounts

Suppose a firm makes purchases of $3.65 million per year under terms of 2/10, net 30, and takes discounts.

a. What is the average amount of accounts payable net of discounts? (Assume that the $3.65 million of purchases is net of discounts—that is, gross purchases are $3,724,489.80, discounts are $74,489.80, and net purchases are $3.65 million.)
b. Is there a cost of the trade credit the firm uses?
c. If the firm did not take discounts but it did pay on the due date, what would be its average payables and the cost of this nonfree trade credit?
d. What would its cost of not taking discounts be if it could stretch its payments to 40 days?

17-16
Trade Credit

Montgomery Corporation projects an increase in sales from $1.5 million to $2 million, but it needs an additional $300,000 of current assets to support this expansion. Montgomery can finance the expansion by no longer taking discounts, thus increasing accounts payable. Montgomery purchases under terms of 1/10, net 30, but it can delay payment for an additional 25 days—paying in 55 days and thus becoming 25 days past due—without a penalty because of its suppliers' current excess capacity problems. What is the effective, or equivalent, annual cost of the trade credit?

17-17
Bank Financing

Automated Dynamics had sales of $6.5 million last year, and it earned a 4% return, after taxes, on sales. Recently, the company has fallen behind in its accounts payable. Although its terms of purchase are net 30 days, its accounts payable represent 60 days' purchases. The company's treasurer is seeking to increase bank borrowings in order to become current in meeting its trade obligations (i.e., to have 30 days' payables outstanding). The company's balance sheet is as follows (thousands of dollars):

Cash	$ 200	Accounts payable	$ 900
Accounts receivable	500	Bank loans	1,100
Inventory	2,000	Accruals	400
Current assets	2,700	Current liabilities	2,400
Land and buildings	1,000	Mortgage on real estate	900
Equipment	1,300	Common stock	500
		Retained earnings	1,200
Total assets	$5,000	Total liabilities and equity	$5,000

a. How much bank financing is needed to eliminate the past-due accounts payable?
b. Would you as a bank loan officer make the loan? Why or why not?

17-18
Short-Term Financing
Analysis

Malone Feed and Supply Company buys on terms of 1/10, net 30, but it has not been taking discounts and has actually been paying in 60 rather than 30 days. Assume that the accounts payable are recorded at full cost, not net of discounts. Malone's balance sheet follows (thousands of dollars):

Cash	$ 50	Accounts payable	$ 500
Accounts receivable	450	Notes payable	50
Inventory	750	Accruals	50
Current assets	1,250	Current liabilities	600
		Long-term debt	150
Fixed assets	750	Common equity	1,250
Total assets	$2,000	Total liabilities and equity	$2,000

Now, Malone's suppliers are threatening to stop shipments unless the company begins making prompt payments (i.e., paying in 30 days or less). The firm can borrow on a 1-year note (call this a current liability) from its bank at a rate of 15%, discount interest, with a 20% compensating balance required. (Malone's $50,000 of cash is needed for transactions; it cannot be used as part of the compensating balance.)

a. How large would the accounts payable balance be if Malone takes discounts? If it does not take discounts and pays in 30 days?
b. How large must the bank loan be if Malone takes discounts? If Malone doesn't take discounts?
c. What are the nominal and effective costs of nonfree trade credit? What is the effective cost of the bank loan? Based on these costs, what should Malone do?
d. Assume that Malone foregoes the discount and borrows the amount needed to become current on its payables. Construct a pro forma balance sheet based on this decision. (*Hint:* You will need to include an account called "prepaid interest" under current assets.)
e. Now assume that the $500,000 shown on the balance sheet is recorded net of discounts. How much would Malone have to pay its suppliers to reduce its accounts payable to $250,000? If Malone's tax rate is 40%, what is the effect on its net income due to the lost discount when it reduces its accounts payable to $250,000? How much would Malone have to borrow? (*Hint:* Malone will receive a tax deduction due to the lost discount, which will affect the amount it must borrow.) Construct a pro forma balance sheet based on this scenario. (*Hint:* You will need to include an account called "prepaid interest" under current assets and adjust retained earnings by the after-tax amount of the lost discount.)

17-19
Cash Budgeting

Helen Bowers, owner of Helen's Fashion Designs, is planning to request a line of credit from her bank. She has estimated the following sales forecasts for the firm for parts of 2015 and 2016:

May 2015	$180,000
June	180,000
July	360,000
August	540,000
September	720,000
October	360,000
November	360,000
December	90,000
January 2016	180,000

Estimates regarding payments obtained from the credit department are as follows: collected within the month of sale, 10%; collected the month following the sale, 75%; collected the second month following the sale, 15%. Payments for labour and raw materials are made the month after these services were provided. Here are the estimated costs of labour plus raw materials:

May 2015	$ 90,000
June	90,000
July	126,000
August	882,000
September	306,000
October	234,000
November	162,000
December	90,000

General and administrative salaries are approximately $27,000 a month. Lease payments under long-term leases are $9,000 a month. Depreciation charges are $36,000 a month.

Miscellaneous expenses are $2,700 a month. Income tax payments of $63,000 are due in September and December. A progress payment of $180,000 on a new design studio must be paid in October. Cash on hand on July 1 will be $132,000, and a minimum cash balance of $90,000 should be maintained throughout the cash budget period.

a. Prepare a monthly cash budget for the last 6 months of 2015.
b. Prepare monthly estimates of the required financing or excess funds—that is, the amount of money Bowers will need to borrow or will have available to invest.
c. Now suppose receipts from sales come in uniformly during the month (that is, cash receipts come in at the rate of 1/30 each day), but all outflows must be paid on the 5th. Will this affect the cash budget? That is, will the cash budget you prepared be valid under these assumptions? If not, what could be done to make a valid estimate of the peak financing requirements? No calculations are required, although if you prefer, you can use calculations to illustrate the effects.
d. Bowers's sales are seasonal and her company produces on a seasonal basis, just ahead of sales. Without making any calculations, discuss how the company's current and debt ratios would vary during the year if all financial requirements were met with short-term bank loans. Could changes in these ratios affect the firm's ability to obtain bank credit? Explain.

17-20
Alternative Financing
Arrangements

High North Apparel Ltd. estimates that because of the seasonal nature of its business, it will require an additional $1.5 million of cash for the month of December. High North has the following four options available for raising the needed funds:
(1) Establish a 1-year line of credit for $1.5 million with a commercial bank. The commitment fee will be 0.5% per year on the unused portion, and the interest charge on the used funds will be 7% per annum. Assume that the funds are needed only in December and that there are 30 days in December.

(2) Forego the trade discount of 1/10, net 40, on $1.5 million of purchases during December.
(3) Issue $1.5 million of 30-day commercial paper at a 6% per annum interest rate. The total transaction fee, including the cost of a backup credit line, on using commercial paper is 0.5% of the amount of the issue.
(4) Issue $1.5 million of 60-day commercial paper at a 5.5% per annum interest rate, plus a transaction fee of 0.5%. Since the funds are required for only 30 days, the excess funds ($1.5 million) can be invested in 3% per annum marketable securities for the month of January.
  a. What is the dollar cost of each financing arrangement?
  b. Is the source with the lowest expected cost necessarily the one to select? Why or why not?

Spreadsheet Problem

17-21
Build a Model:
Cash Budgeting

Start with the partial model in the file **Ch17 Build a Model.xlsx** on the textbook's website. Rusty Spears, CEO of Rusty's Renovations, a custom building and repair company, is preparing documentation for a line of credit request from his commercial banker. Among the required documents is a detailed sales forecast for parts of 2015 and 2016:

	Sales	Labour and Raw Materials
May 2015	$60,000	$75,000
June	100,000	90,000
July	130,000	95,000
August	120,000	70,000
September	100,000	60,000
October	80,000	50,000
November	60,000	20,000
December	40,000	20,000
January 2016	30,000	NA

Estimates obtained from the credit and collection department are as follows: collections within the month of sale, 15%; collections during the month following the sale, 65%; collections the second month following the sale, 20%. Payments for labour and raw materials are typically made during the month following the one in which these costs were incurred. Total costs for labour and raw materials are estimated for each month as shown in the table.

General and administrative salaries will amount to approximately $15,000 a month; lease payments under long-term lease contracts will be $5,000 a month; depreciation charges will be $7,500 a month; miscellaneous expenses will be $2,000 a month; income tax payments of $25,000 will be due in both September and December; and a progress payment of $80,000 on a new office suite must be paid in October. Cash on hand on July 1 will amount to $60,000, and a minimum cash balance of $40,000 will be maintained throughout the cash budget period.
a. Prepare a monthly cash budget for the last 6 months of 2015.
b. Prepare an estimate of the required financing (or excess funds)—that is, the amount of money Rusty's Renovations will need to borrow (or will have available to invest)—for each month during that period.
c. Assume that receipts from sales come in uniformly during the month (i.e., cash receipts come in at the rate of 1/30 each day) but that all outflows are paid on the 5th of the month. Will this have an effect on the cash budget—in other words, would the cash budget you have prepared be valid under these assumptions? If not, what can be done to make a valid estimate of peak financing requirements? No calculations are required, although calculations can be used to illustrate the effects.
d. Rusty's Renovations produces on a seasonal basis, just ahead of sales. Without making any calculations, discuss how the company's current ratio and debt ratio would vary during the year assuming all financial requirements were met by short-term bank loans. Could changes in these ratios affect the firm's ability to obtain bank credit? Explain.

e. If its customers began to pay late, this would slow down collections and thus increase the required loan amount. Also, if sales dropped off, this would have an effect on the required loan amount. Perform a sensitivity analysis that shows the effects of these two factors on the maximum loan requirement.

MINI CASE

Dan Barnes, financial manager of Ski Equipment Inc. (SKI), is excited but apprehensive. The company's founder recently sold his 51% controlling block of shares to Kent Koren, who is a big fan of EVA (economic value added). EVA is found by taking the after-tax operating profit and then subtracting the dollar cost of all the capital the firm uses:

$$EVA = NOPAT - Capital\ costs$$

$$= EBIT(1 - T) - WACC(Capital\ employed)$$

If EVA is positive, then the firm is creating value. On the other hand, if EVA is negative, the firm is not covering its cost of capital, and shareholders' value is being eroded. Koren rewards managers handsomely if they create value, but those whose operations produce negative EVAs are soon looking for work. Koren frequently points out that if a company could generate its current level of sales with fewer assets, it would need less capital. That would, other things held constant, lower capital costs and increase its EVA.

Shortly after he took control of SKI, Kent Koren met with SKI's senior executives to tell them of his plans for the company. First, he presented some EVA data that convinced everyone that SKI had not been creating value in recent years. He then stated, in no uncertain terms, that this situation must change. He noted that SKI's designs of skis, boots, and clothing are acclaimed throughout the industry, but that something is seriously amiss elsewhere in the company. Costs are too high, prices are too low, or the company employs too much capital, and he wants SKI's managers to correct the problem or else.

Barnes has long felt that SKI's working capital situation should be studied—the company may have the optimal amounts of cash, securities, receivables, and inventories, but it may also have too much or too little of these items. In the past, the production manager resisted Barnes's efforts to question his holdings of raw materials inventories, the marketing manager resisted questions about finished goods, the sales staff resisted questions about credit policy (which affects accounts receivable), and the treasurer did not want to talk about her cash and securities balances. Koren's speech made it clear that such resistance would no longer be tolerated.

Barnes also knows that decisions about working capital cannot be made in a vacuum. For example, if inventories could be lowered without adversely affecting operations, then less capital would be required, the dollar cost of capital would decline, and EVA would increase. However, lower raw materials inventories might lead to production slowdowns and higher costs, while lower finished goods inventories might lead to the loss of profitable sales. So, before inventories are changed, it will be necessary to study operating as well as financial effects. The situation is the same with regard to cash and receivables. Barnes began collecting the ratios shown below.

	SKI	Industry
Current	1.75	2.25
Quick	0.83	1.20
Debt/assets	58.76%	50.00%
Turnover of cash and securities	16.67	22.22
Days' sales outstanding (365-day basis)	45.63	32.00
Inventory turnover	4.82	7.00
Fixed assets turnover	11.35	12.00
Total assets turnover	2.08	3.00
Profit margin	2.07%	3.50%
Return on equity (ROE)	10.45%	21.00%
Payables deferral period	30.00	33.00

	Nov	Dec	Jan	Feb	Mar	Apr
I. Collections and Purchases Worksheet						
(1) Sales (gross)	$71,218	$68,212	$65,213	$52,475	$42,909	$30,524
Collections						
(2) During month of sale (0.2)(0.98)(month's sales)			12,781.75	10,285.10		
(3) During first month after sale (0.7)(previous month's sales)			47,748.40	45,649.10		
(4) During second month after sale (0.1)(sales 2 months ago)			7,121.80	6,821.20		
(5) Total collections (Lines 2 + 3 + 4)			$67,651.95	$62,755.40		
Purchases						
(6) (0.85)(forecasted sales 2 months from now)		$44,603.75	$36,472.65	$25,945.40		
(7) Payments (1-month lag)			44,603.75	36,472.65		
II. Cash Gain or Loss for Month						
(8) Collections (from Section I)			$67,651.95	$62,755.40		
(9) Payments for purchases (from Section I)			44,603.75	36,472.65		
(10) Wages and salaries			6,690.56	5,470.90		
(11) Rent			2,500.00	2,500.00		
(12) Taxes						
(13) Total payments			$53,794.31	$44,443.55		
(14) Net cash gain (loss) during month (Line 8 – Line 13)			$13,857.64	$18,311.85		
III. Cash Surplus or Loan Requirement						
(15) Cash at beginning of month if no borrowing is done			$ 3,000.00	$16,857.64		
(16) Cumulative cash (cash at start + gain or − loss = Line 14 + Line 15)			16,857.64	35,169.49		
(17) Target cash balance			1,500.00	1,500.00		
(18) Cumulative surplus cash or loans outstanding to maintain $1,500 target cash balance (Line 16 – Line 17)			$15,357.64	$33,669.49		

a. Barnes plans to use the preceding ratios as the starting point for discussions with SKI's operating executives. He wants everyone to think about the pros and cons of changing each type of current asset and how changes would interact to affect profits and EVA. Based on the data, does SKI seem to be following a relaxed, moderate, or restricted working capital policy?

b. How can one distinguish between a relaxed but rational working capital policy and a situation in which a firm simply has a lot of current assets because it is inefficient? Does SKI's working capital policy seem appropriate?

c. Calculate the firm's cash conversion cycle.

d. What might SKI do to reduce its cash without harming operations?

In an attempt to better understand SKI's cash position, Barnes has developed a cash budget. Data for the first 2 months of the year are shown above. (Note that Barnes's preliminary cash budget does not account for interest income or interest expense.) He has the figures for the other months, but they are not shown.

e. Should depreciation expense be explicitly included in the cash budget? Why or why not?

f. In his preliminary cash budget, Barnes has assumed that all sales are collected and, thus, that SKI has no bad debts. Is this realistic? If not, how would bad debts be dealt with in a cash budgeting sense? (*Hint:* Bad debts will affect collections but not purchases.)

g. Barnes's cash budget for the entire year, although not given here, is based heavily on his forecast for monthly sales. Sales are expected to be extremely low between May and September but then increase dramatically in the fall and winter. November is typically the firm's best month, when SKI ships equipment to retailers for the holiday season. Interestingly, Barnes's forecasted cash budget indicates that the company's cash holdings will exceed the targeted cash balance every month except for October and November, when shipments will be high but collections will not be coming in until later. Based on the ratios shown earlier, does it appear that SKI's target cash balance is appropriate? In addition to possibly lowering the target cash balance, what actions might SKI take to better improve its cash management policies, and how might that affect its EVA?

h. What reasons might SKI have for maintaining a relatively high amount of cash?

i. Is there any reason to think that SKI may be holding too much inventory? If so, how would that affect EVA and ROE?

j. If the company reduces its inventory without adversely affecting sales, what effect should this have on the company's cash position (1) in the short run and (2) in the long run? Explain in terms of the cash budget and the balance sheet.

In addition to improving the management of its current assets, SKI is also reviewing the ways in which it finances its current assets. With this concern in mind, Dan is also trying to answer the following questions.

k. Is it likely that SKI could make significantly greater use of accruals?

l. Assume that SKI buys on terms of 1/10, net 30, but that it can get away with paying on the 40th day if it chooses not to take discounts. Also, assume that it purchases $506,985 of equipment per year, net of discounts. How much free trade credit can the company get, how much costly trade credit can it get, and what is the percentage cost of the costly credit? Should SKI take discounts?

m. SKI tries to match the maturity of its assets and liabilities. Describe how SKI could adopt either a more aggressive or more conservative financing policy.

n. What are the advantages and disadvantages of using short-term debt as a source of financing?

o. Would it be feasible for SKI to finance with commercial paper?

chapter 18

Current Asset Management

Vancouver-based Finning International is the world's largest dealer of Caterpillar heavy-duty machinery. Sales in 2013 were $6.8 billion and its operations span throughout Western Canada, the United Kingdom, Ireland, and a large part of South America. Increasing the return on invested capital, ROIC, is one of management's key goals. As you learned earlier, ROIC is net operating profit divided by operating capital. Finning chose to make improving its supply chain system and related working capital investments a priority. The thought was that improved supply chain efficiencies will increase operating profit while at the same time allowing the company to wring more productivity out of its working capital. Thus, improving its use of working capital—the focus of this chapter—will have two beneficial effects; it will help drive up EBIT and limit (or lower) any increase in operating capital, both of which will increase the company's ROIC.

So how does Finning's management view its current working capital? The company has no problem obtaining sufficient cash for operations. It has access to the commercial paper market as well as a $1.5 billion short-term credit line. Finning's accounts receivable are also not an issue. They are well diversified and not overly concentrated with any one customer, industry, or geographic market. It is inventory, which accounts for over one-half of Finning's current assets, which management sees a need to administer more effectively. The company plans to optimize delivery routes, reduce transfer points, and introduce centralized inventory management systems. As an example, one initiative is to reduce the delivery time to North American customers from 7 days to 12 hours! Improving inventory turnover by just 0.1 will reduce inventory levels by $50 million. Finning's goal is to improve inventory turnover at least by 0.5, potentially freeing up $250 million in operating capital. Will Finning be successful in its initiatives? Only time will tell, though in its latest quarterly report (as of the time of writing), the company had reduced operating capital by $80 million over the previous quarter despite an increase in sales.

To compete in today's business environment, strong working capital management practices are essential. Keep this in mind as you read how companies manage their current assets.

The textbook's website contains an *Excel* file that will guide you through the chapter's calculations. The file for this chapter is **Ch18 Tool Kit.xlsx,** and we encourage you to open the file and follow along as you read the chapter. **www.nelson.com/ brigham3ce**

Chapter 17 presented the basic elements of working capital management and short-term financing. Recall that net operating working capital (NOWC) consists of cash, inventory, and accounts receivable, minus accruals and accounts payable. Firms face a fundamental trade-off: Working capital is necessary to conduct business, and the greater the working capital, the smaller the danger of running short and the lower the firm's operating risk. However, holding working capital is costly—it reduces a firm's return on invested capital (ROIC), financing cost, and value. This chapter discusses the individual components of NOWC.

18.1 Cash Management

About 1.5% of the average industrial firm's assets are held in the form of cash. It is needed to pay for labour and raw materials, to buy fixed assets, to pay taxes, to service debt, to pay dividends, and so on. However, note the following: (1) cash is a "nonearning asset"; (2) it is an asset that appears on the left side of the balance sheet; (3) cash holdings must be financed by raising debt or equity; and (4) both debt and equity have a cost. If cash holdings could be reduced without hurting sales or other aspects of a firm's operations, this reduction would permit a reduction in either debt or equity, or both, which would in turn increase the return on capital and thus boost the value of the firm's stock. *Therefore, the general operating goal of the cash manager is to minimize the amount of cash held, subject to the constraint that enough cash must be held to enable the firm to operate efficiently.*

Reasons for Holding Cash

Firms hold cash for two primary reasons:

1. *Transactions.* Cash balances are necessary in business operations. Payments must be made in cash, and receipts are deposited in the cash account. Cash balances associated with routine payments and collections are known as **transactions balances.** Cash inflows and outflows are unpredictable, with the degree of predictability varying among firms and industries. Therefore, firms need to hold some cash in reserve for random, unforeseen fluctuations in inflows and outflows. These "safety stocks" are called **precautionary balances,** and the less predictable the firm's cash flows, the larger such balances should be.

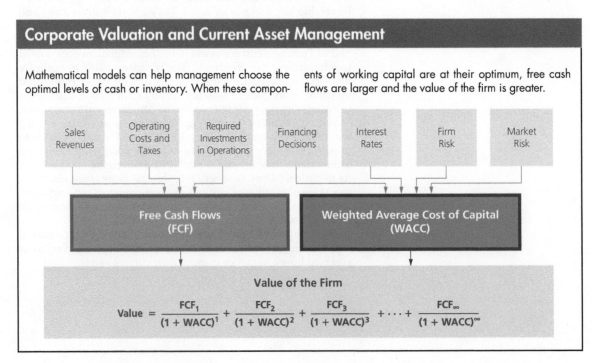

Corporate Valuation and Current Asset Management

Mathematical models can help management choose the optimal levels of cash or inventory. When these components of working capital are at their optimum, free cash flows are larger and the value of the firm is greater.

Sales Revenues | Operating Costs and Taxes | Required Investments in Operations | Financing Decisions | Interest Rates | Firm Risk | Market Risk

Free Cash Flows (FCF)

Weighted Average Cost of Capital (WACC)

Value of the Firm

$$\text{Value} = \frac{\text{FCF}_1}{(1 + \text{WACC})^1} + \frac{\text{FCF}_2}{(1 + \text{WACC})^2} + \frac{\text{FCF}_3}{(1 + \text{WACC})^3} + \cdots + \frac{\text{FCF}_\infty}{(1 + \text{WACC})^\infty}$$

Research confirms this and shows that companies with volatile cash flows do in fact hold higher cash balances.[1]

2. *Compensation to banks for providing loans and services.* A bank makes money by lending out funds that have been deposited with it, so the larger its deposits, the better the bank's profit position. If a bank is providing services to a customer, it may require the customer to leave a minimum balance on deposit to help offset the costs of providing the services. Also, banks may require borrowers to hold deposits at the bank. Both types of deposits are called **compensating balances.** In a 1979 survey, 84.7% of responding companies reported that they were required to maintain compensating balances to help pay for bank services.[2] Only 13.3% reported paying direct fees for banking services. By 1996 those findings were reversed: Only 28% paid for bank services with compensating balances, while 83% paid direct fees.[3] So, while the use of compensating balances to pay for services has declined, it is still a reason some companies hold so much cash.

In addition to holding cash for transactions, precautionary reasons, and compensating balances, it is essential that the firm have sufficient cash to take **trade discounts.** Suppliers frequently offer customers discounts for early payment of bills. As we saw in the previous chapter, the cost of not taking discounts is very high, so firms should have enough cash to permit payment of bills in time to take discounts. *Web Extension 18A* presents a model for determining a firm's optimal cash balance.

See **Web Extension 18A** on the textbook's website for a discussion on setting an optimal cash balance.

Finally, firms often hold short-term investments in excess of the cash needed to support operations. We discuss short-term investments later in the chapter.

CONCEPT REVIEW

1. Why is cash management important?
2. What are the two primary motives for holding cash?

18.2 Cash Management Techniques

Much business is conducted by large firms, many of which operate regionally, nationally, or even globally. They collect cash from many sources and make payments from a number of different cities or even countries. For example, companies such as Thomson Reuters and Magna International all have business units in many countries, even more sales offices, and bank accounts in almost every city where they do business. Their collection points follow sales patterns. Some disbursements are made from local offices, but most are made in the cities where their operations reside, or else from the home office. Thus, a major corporation might have hundreds or even thousands of bank accounts, and since there is no reason to think that inflows and outflows will balance in each account, a system must be in place to transfer funds from where they come in to where they are needed, to arrange loans to cover net corporate shortfalls, and to invest net corporate surpluses without delay. We discuss the most commonly used techniques for accomplishing these tasks in the following sections.[4]

Synchronizing Cash Flow

If you as an individual were to receive income once a year, you would probably put it in the bank, draw down your account periodically, and have an average balance for the year equal to about half of your annual income. If instead you received income weekly and paid rent,

---

[1]See Tim Opler, Lee Pinkowitz, René Stulz, and Rohan Williamson, "The Determinants and Implications of Corporate Cash Holdings," *Journal of Financial Economics,* 1999, pp 3–46; and Thomas Bates, Kathleen Kahle, and René Stulz, "Why Do U.S. Firms Hold So Much More Cash than They Used To?" *Journal of Finance,* October 2009, pp 1985–2021; for Canadian companies see Darcey McVanel and Nikita Perevalov, "Financial Constraints and the Cash-Holding Behaviour of Canadian Firms," Discussion Paper 2008-16, Bank of Canada, http://www.bankofcanada.ca.

[2]See Lawrence J. Gitman, E. A. Moses, and I. T. White, "An Assessment of Corporate Cash Management Practices," *Financial Management,* Spring 1979, 32–41.

[3]See Charles E. Maxwell, Lawrence J. Gitman, and Stephanie A. M. Smith, "Working Capital Management and Financial-Service Consumption Preferences of US and Foreign Firms: A Comparison of 1979 and 1996 Preferences," *Financial Practice and Education,* Fall–Winter 1998, 46–52.

[4]For more information on cash management, see Bernell K. Stone and Tom W. Miller, "Daily Cash Forecasting with Multiplicative Models of Cash Flow Patterns," *Financial Management,* Winter 1987, 45–54; and Keith C. Brown and Scott L. Lummer, "A Reexamination of the Covered Call Option Strategy for Corporate Cash Management," *Financial Management,* Summer 1986, 13–17.

tuition, and other charges on a weekly basis, and if you were confident of your forecasted inflows and outflows, then you could hold a small average cash balance.

Exactly the same situation holds for businesses—by improving their forecasts and by timing cash receipts to coincide with cash requirements, firms can hold their transactions balances to a minimum. Recognizing this, utility companies, oil companies, credit card companies, and so on, arrange to bill customers, and to pay their own bills, on regular "billing cycles" throughout the month. This **synchronization of cash flows** provides cash when it is needed and thus enables firms to reduce the cash balances needed to support operations.

Speeding Up the Cheque-Clearing Process

When a customer writes and mails a cheque, the funds are not available to the receiving firm until the **cheque-clearing process** has been completed. First, the cheque must be delivered through the mail. Cheques received from customers in distant cities are especially subject to mail delays.

When a customer's cheque is written upon one bank and a company deposits the cheque in its own bank, the company's bank must verify that the cheque is valid before the company can use those funds. Cheques are cleared through the Automated Clearing Settlement System, usually the same day as deposited.[5] Because of the automated clearing settlement system, and the fact that Canada's banks operate nationally, Canadian companies enjoy one of the most efficient cheque-clearing systems in the world.

Using Float

Float is defined as the difference between the balance shown in a firm's (or individual's) chequebook and the balance on the bank's records. Suppose a firm writes, on average, cheques in the amount of $5,000 each day, and it takes 6 days for its suppliers to receive and deposit the cheques and have them cleared and deducted from the firm's bank account. This will cause the firm's own chequebook to show a balance $30,000 smaller than the balance on the bank's records; this difference is called **disbursement float.** Now suppose the firm also receives cheques in the amount of $5,000 daily, but it loses 4 days while they are being deposited and cleared. This will result in $20,000 of **collections float.** In total, the firm's **net float**—the difference between the $30,000 positive disbursement float and the $20,000 negative collections float—will be $10,000.

Delays that cause float arise because it takes time for cheques (1) to travel through the mail (mail float), (2) to be processed by the receiving firm (processing float), and (3) to clear through the banking system (clearing, or availability, float). Basically, the size of a firm's net float is a function of its ability to speed up collections on cheques it receives and to slow down collections on cheques it writes as the clearing float is close to zero. Efficient firms go to great lengths to speed up the processing of incoming cheques, thus putting the funds to work faster, and they try to stretch their own payments out as long as possible, sometimes by disbursing cheques from banks in remote locations.

Speeding Up Receipts

Two major techniques are now used both to speed collections and to get funds where they are needed: (1) lockbox plans and (2) payment by wire or automatic debit.

Lockboxes A **lockbox plan** is one of the oldest cash management tools. In a lockbox system, incoming cheques are sent to post office boxes rather than to corporate headquarters. For example, a firm headquartered in Toronto might have its West Coast customers send their payments to a box in Vancouver, its customers in the Maritimes send their cheques to Halifax, and so on, rather than having all cheques sent to Toronto. Several times a day a local bank will collect the contents of the lockbox and deposit the cheques in the company's local account. In fact, some banks even have their lockbox operation located in the same facility as the post office. The bank then provides the firm with a daily record of the receipts collected, usually via an electronic data transmission system in a format that permits online updating of the firm's accounts receivable records.

A lockbox system reduces the time required for a firm to receive incoming cheques, to deposit them, and to get them cleared through the banking system so that the funds are

---

[5]For more information on cheque clearing in Canada, go to the Canadian Payments Association website at http://www.cdnpay.ca.

FINANCE: SMALL BUSINESS

Small Companies Providing Trade Credit

It is well known that small companies have difficulty raising capital and are often cash strapped. Indeed, for many small businesses, maintaining liquidity often takes precedence over maximizing profits or shareholder wealth. While small firms rely on trade credit as a financing source, they also, despite liquidity constraints, *provide* trade credit—they are in effect financing their (sometimes much larger) customers' businesses. Studies suggest that imperfections in the marketplace and asymmetric bargaining positions may explain why small companies tie up their limited financial resources in accounts receivable. In their paper on trade credit and small firms, Nicholas Wilson and Barbara Summers review the following possible rationales.

Imperfect markets and transaction costs. As part of their normal operations, sellers obtain detailed customer and industry knowledge and are able to evaluate and monitor customers at a lower cost than financing institutions. Sellers can also obtain higher value on reclaimed inventory (i.e., collateral) in the event of nonpayment. As a result, financial institutions such as banks are at a competitive disadvantage in short-term lending. Moreover, sellers do not specifically have to earn a profit on financing the sale, as a financing company must. As long as the combined product sale and trade credit provides an adequate return to the seller, the trade financing can go ahead.

Sellers can use two-part terms (e.g., 2/10, net 30) as a monitoring mechanism for their customers' financial health. Since the cost of forgoing the discount is so high, an early warning signal of financial difficulty is provided when buyers stop taking the discount. If discounts are not offered, then late payments on regular net terms would be a comparable early warning.

Use as a marketing tool. Trade credit can be used to hide price cuts from competitors, by permitting purchasers to take unearned discounts or to pay later than the stated net terms. This sort of masked price competition is not easy for a competitor to see and react to. Also, a small business can send a new buyer a "reputation" or "quality" signal by offering credit terms that enable it to inspect the goods before making the payment. This also protects the purchaser from sellers who are not living up to the contract terms. Finally, by offering generous terms, trade credit can be used to draw in new customers, making it a useful marketing tool for a growing business.

Asymmetric bargaining positions. Because of their weak bargaining position, and out of fear of losing large customers, small companies may be forced to offer trade credit. Moreover, those businesses that do offer such credit often do not enforce trade credit terms and late payment penalties. As a result, larger companies can take longer than agreed to pay, or they may take unearned early payment discounts. However, unearned discounts can be mitigated by a rebate offer. The buyer makes full payment to the seller, and if it is made within the discount period, a rebate for the discounted amount is sent back to the buyer.

Source: Adapted from Nicholas Wilson and Barbara Summers, "Trade Credit Terms Offered by Small Firms: Survey Evidence and Empirical Analysis," *Journal of Business Finance and Accounting*, April–May 2002, pp. 317–351.

available for use. Lockbox services can accelerate the availability of funds by 2 to 5 days over the "regular" system.

Payment by Wire or Automatic Debit Firms are increasingly demanding payments of larger bills by wire, or even by automatic electronic debits. Under an electronic debit system, funds are automatically deducted from one account and added to another. This is, of course, the ultimate in a speeded-up collection process, and computer technology is making such a process increasingly feasible and efficient, even for retail transactions.

ⓒONCEPT REVIEW

1.   What is float? How do firms use float to increase cash management efficiency?
2.   What are some methods firms can use to accelerate receipts?

18.3 Short-Term Investments: Marketable Securities

Realistically, the management of cash and marketable securities cannot be separated—management of one implies management of the other. In the first part of the chapter, we focused on cash management. Now, we turn to **marketable securities.**

Marketable securities typically provide much lower yields than operating assets. For example, recently Microsoft held approximately $41 billion in short-term marketable securities, in addition to the $10.6 billion it held in cash. Why would a company such as Microsoft have such large holdings of low-yielding assets?

In many cases, companies hold marketable securities for the same reasons they hold cash. Although these securities are not the same as cash, in most cases they can be converted to cash on very short notice (often just a few minutes) with a single telephone call. Moreover, while cash and most commercial chequing accounts yield nothing, marketable securities provide at least a modest return. For this reason, many firms hold at least some marketable securities in lieu of larger cash balances, liquidating part of the portfolio to increase the cash account when cash outflows exceed inflows. In such situations, the marketable securities could be used as a substitute for transactions balances or for precautionary balances. In most cases, the securities are held primarily for precautionary purposes—most firms prefer to rely on bank credit to make temporary transactions, but they may still hold some liquid assets to guard against a possible shortage of bank credit during difficult times.

There are both benefits and costs associated with holding marketable securities. The benefits are twofold: (1) the firm reduces risk and transactions costs because it won't have to issue securities or borrow as frequently to raise cash; and (2) it will have ready cash to take advantage of bargain purchases or growth opportunities. Funds held for the second reason are called *speculative balances*. The primary disadvantage is that the after-tax return on short-term securities is very low. Thus, firms face a trade-off between benefits and costs.

Recent research supports this trade-off hypothesis as an explanation for firms' cash holdings.[6] Firms with high growth opportunities suffer the most if they don't have ready cash to quickly take advantage of an opportunity, and the data show that these firms do hold relatively high levels of marketable securities. Firms with volatile cash flows are the ones most likely to run low on cash, so they tend to hold high levels of cash. In contrast, cash holdings are less important to large firms with high credit ratings, because they have quick and inexpensive access to capital markets. As expected, such firms hold relatively low levels of cash. Of course, there will always be outliers such as Microsoft, which is large, strong, and cash-rich, but volatile firms with good growth opportunities are still the ones with the most marketable securities, on average.

CONCEPT REVIEW

1. Why might a company hold low-yielding marketable securities when it could earn a much higher return on operating assets?

18.4 Receivables Management

Firms would, in general, rather sell for cash than on credit, but competitive pressures force most firms to offer credit. Thus, goods are shipped, inventories are reduced, and an **account receivable** is created.[7] Eventually, the customer will pay the account, at which time (1) the firm will receive cash and (2) its receivables will decline. Carrying receivables has both direct and indirect costs, but it also has an important benefit—increased sales.

Receivables management begins with the credit policy, but a monitoring system is also important. Corrective action is often needed, and the only way to know whether the situation is getting out of hand is with a good receivables control system.[8]

The credit manager is responsible for administering the firm's credit policy. However, because of the pervasive importance of credit, the credit policy itself is normally established by the executive committee, which usually consists of the president plus the vice presidents of finance, marketing, and production.

---

[6]See the study by Opler, Pinkowitz, Stulz, and Williamson cited in footnote 1.

[7]Whenever goods are sold on credit, two accounts are created—an asset item entitled *accounts receivable* appears on the books of the selling firm, and a liability item called *accounts payable* appears on the books of the purchaser. At this point, we are analyzing the transaction from the viewpoint of the seller, so we are concentrating on the variables under its control, in this case, the receivables. We examined the transaction from the viewpoint of the purchaser in Chapter 17, where we discussed accounts payable as a source of funds and considered their cost.

[8]For more on credit policy and receivables management, see George W. Gallinger and A. James Ifflander, "Monitoring Accounts Receivable Using Variance Analysis," *Financial Management*, Winter 1986, 69–76; Shehzad L. Mian and Clifford W. Smith, "Extending Trade Credit and Financing Receivables," *Journal of Applied Corporate Finance*, Spring 1994, 75–84; and Paul D. Adams, Steve B. Wyatt, and Yong H. Kim, "A Contingent Claims Analysis of Trade Credit," *Financial Management*, Autumn 1992, 104–112.

Credit Policy

The success or failure of a business depends primarily on the demand for its products—as a rule, the higher its sales, the larger its profits and the higher its stock price. Sales, in turn, depend on a number of factors, some exogenous but others under the firm's control. The major controllable determinants of demand are sales prices, product quality, advertising, and the firm's **credit policy.** Credit policy, in turn, consists of these four variables:

1. *Credit period,* which is the length of time buyers are given to pay for their purchases. For example, credit terms of "net 30," indicate that buyers may take up to 30 days to pay.
2. *Discounts* given for early payment, including the discount percentage and how rapidly payment must be made to qualify for the discount. The credit terms "2/10, net 30" allow buyers to take a 2% discount if they pay within 10 days. Otherwise, they must pay the full amount within 30 days.
3. *Credit standards,* which refer to the required financial strength of acceptable credit customers. Lower credit standards boost sales but also increase bad debts.
4. *Collection policy,* which is measured by its toughness or laxity in attempting to collect on slow-paying accounts. A tough policy may speed up collections, but it might also anger customers, causing them to take their business elsewhere.

Setting the Credit Period and Standards

A firm's regular **credit terms,** which include the **credit period** and **cash discount,** might call for sales on a 2/10, net 30 basis to all "acceptable" customers. Here customers are required to pay within 30 days, but they are given a 2% discount if they pay by the 10th day. The firm's credit standards would be applied to determine which customers qualify for the regular credit terms and the amount of credit available to each customer.

Credit Standards

Credit standards refer to the financial strength and creditworthiness a customer must exhibit in order to qualify for credit. If a customer does not qualify for the regular credit terms, it can still purchase from the firm, but under more restrictive terms. For example, a firm's "regular" credit terms might call for payment within 30 days, and these terms might be offered to all qualified customers. The firm's credit standards would be applied to determine which customers qualified for the regular credit terms and how much credit each should receive. The major factors considered when setting credit standards relate to the likelihood that a given customer will pay slowly or perhaps end up as a bad debt loss.

Setting credit standards requires a measurement of *credit quality,* which is defined in terms of the probability of a customer's default. The probability estimate for a given customer is, for the most part, a subjective judgment. Nevertheless, credit evaluation is a well-established practice, and a good credit manager can make reasonably accurate judgments of the probability of default by different classes of customers.

Managing a credit department requires fast, accurate, and up-to-date information. Several service bureaus provide this sort of information. For example, Dun and Bradstreet and Equifax both provide relevant financial and credit data on 1.5 million businesses in Canada. A typical business credit report would include the following pieces of information:

- General operating and historical corporate information.
- Public records regarding liens, lawsuits, and judgments.
- List of owners.
- Balance sheet information and trends.
- Information obtained from the firm's suppliers stating whether it pays promptly or slowly, and whether it has recently failed to make any payments.
- A summary rating on the company's credit risk.

Consumer credit is appraised similarly, using income, years of employment, ownership of home, and past credit history (pays on time or has defaulted) as criteria.

Although a great deal of credit information is available, it must still be processed in a judgmental manner. Computerized information systems can assist in making better credit decisions, but, in the final analysis, most credit decisions are really exercises in informed judgment.[9]

Setting the Collection Policy

Collection policy refers to the procedures the firm follows to collect past-due accounts. For example, a letter might be sent to customers when a bill is 10 days past due; a more severe letter, followed by a telephone call, would be sent if payment is not received within 30 days; and the account would be turned over to a collection agency after 90 days.

The collection process can be expensive in terms of both out-of-pocket expenditures and lost goodwill—customers dislike being turned over to a collection agency. However, at least some firmness is needed to prevent an undue lengthening of the collection period and to minimize outright losses. A balance must be struck between the costs and benefits of different collection policies.

Changes in collection policy influence sales, the collection period, and the bad debt loss percentage. All of this should be taken into account when setting the credit policy.

Cash Discounts

The last element in the credit policy decision, the use of **cash discounts** for early payment, is analyzed by balancing the costs and benefits of different cash discounts. For example, a firm might decide to change its credit terms from "net 30," which means that customers must pay within 30 days, to "2/10, net 30," where a 2% discount is given if payment is made in 10 days. This change should produce two benefits: (1) It should attract new customers who consider the discount to be a price reduction, and (2) the discount should lead to a reduction in the days' sales outstanding, because some existing customers will pay more promptly in order to get the discount. Offsetting these benefits is the dollar cost of the discounts. The optimal discount percentage is established at the point where the marginal costs and benefits are exactly offsetting.

If sales are seasonal, a firm may use *seasonal dating* on discounts. For example, Slimware Inc., a swimsuit manufacturer, sells on terms of 2/10, net 30, May 1 dating. This means that the effective invoice date is May 1, even if the sale was made back in January. The discount may be taken up to May 10; otherwise, the full amount must be paid on May 30. Slimware produces throughout the year, but retail sales of bathing suits are concentrated in the spring and early summer. By offering seasonal dating, the company induces some of its customers to stock up early, saving Slimware some storage costs and also "nailing down sales."

The Accumulation of Receivables

The total amount of accounts receivable outstanding at any given time is determined by two factors: (1) the volume of credit sales and (2) the average length of time between sales and collections. For example, suppose Sherbrooke Lumber Company (SLC), a wholesale distributor of lumber products, opens a warehouse on January 1 and, starting the first day, makes sales of $1,000 each day. For simplicity, we assume that all sales are on credit and that customers are given 10 days to pay. At the end of the first day, accounts receivable will be $1,000; they will rise to $2,000 by the end of the second day; and by January 10, they will have risen to 10($1,000) = $10,000. On January 11, another $1,000 will be added to receivables, but payments for sales made on January 1 will reduce receivables by $1,000, so total accounts receivable will remain constant at $10,000. Once the firm's operations have stabilized, the following situation will exist:

$$\frac{\text{Accounts}}{\text{receivable}} = \frac{\text{Credit sales}}{\text{per day}} \times \frac{\text{Length of}}{\text{collection period}}$$

$$= \$1,000 \times 10 \text{ days} = \$10,000. \tag{18-1}$$

---

[9]Credit analysts use procedures ranging from highly sophisticated, computerized "credit-scoring" systems, which actually calculate the statistical probability that a given customer will default, to informal procedures, which involve going through a checklist of factors that should be considered when processing a credit application. The credit-scoring systems use various financial ratios such as the current ratio and the debt ratio (for businesses) and income, years with the same employer, and the like (for individuals) to determine the statistical probability of default. Credit is then granted to those with low default probabilities. The informal procedures often involve examining the "5 C's of Credit": character, capacity, capital, collateral, and conditions. Character is obvious; capacity is a subjective estimate of ability to repay; capital means how much net worth the borrower has; collateral means assets pledged to secure the loan; and conditions refers to business conditions, which affect ability to repay.

If either credit sales or the collection period changes, such changes will be reflected in accounts receivable.

Monitoring the Receivables Position

Both investors and bank loan officers should pay close attention to accounts receivable, because what you see on a financial statement is not necessarily what you end up getting.

When a credit sale is made, the following events occur: (1) inventories are reduced by the cost of goods sold, (2) accounts receivable are increased by the sales price, and (3) the difference is profit, which is added to retained earnings. If the sale is for cash, then the cash from the sale has actually been received by the firm, but if the sale is on credit, the firm will not receive the cash from the sale unless and until the account is collected. Firms have been known to encourage "sales" to very weak customers in order to report high current profits. This could boost the firm's stock price, at least until credit losses begin to lower earnings, at which time the stock price will fall. Analyses along the lines suggested in the following sections will detect any such questionable practice, as well as any unconscious deterioration in the quality of accounts receivable. Such early detection helps both investors and bankers avoid losses.

Days' Sales Outstanding (DSO) Suppose Super Sets Inc., a television manufacturer, sells 200,000 television sets a year at a price of $198 each. Assume that all sales are on credit under the terms 2/10, net 30. Finally, assume that 70% of the customers take discounts and pay on Day 10, while the other 30% pay on Day 30.

Super Sets's **days' sales outstanding (DSO),** sometimes called the *average collection period (ACP)*, is 16 days:

$$DSO = ACP = 0.7(10 \text{days}) + 0.3(30 \text{days}) = 16 \text{days}$$

Super Sets's *average daily sales (ADS)* is $108,493:

$$ADS = \frac{\text{Annual sales}}{365} = \frac{(\text{Units sold})(\text{Sales price})}{365}$$

$$= \frac{200,000(\$198)}{365} = \frac{\$39,600,000}{365} = \$108,493$$

(18-2)

Super Sets's accounts receivable, assuming a constant, uniform rate of sales throughout the year, will at any point in time be $1,735,888:

$$\text{Receivables} = (ADS)(DSO)$$
$$= (\$108,493)(16) = \$1,735,888$$

(18-3)

Note also that its DSO, or average collection period, is a measure of the average length of time it takes Super Sets' customers to pay off their credit purchases, and that the DSO is often compared with an industry average DSO. For example, if all television manufacturers sell on the same credit terms, and if the industry average DSO is 25 days versus Super Sets's 16 days, then Super Sets has a higher percentage of discount customers; that, or its credit department is exceptionally good at ensuring prompt payment.

Finally, note that if you know both the annual sales and the receivables balance, you can calculate DSO as follows:

$$DSO = \frac{\text{Receivables}}{\text{Sales per day}} = \frac{\$1,735,888}{\$108,493} = 16 \text{ days}$$

The DSO can also be compared with the firm's own credit terms. For example, suppose Super Sets's DSO had been averaging 35 days. With a 35-day DSO, some customers would obviously be taking more than 30 days to pay their bills. In fact, if many customers were paying within 10 days to take advantage of the discount, the others must, on average, be taking much longer than 35 days. One way to check this possibility is to use an aging schedule as described in the next section.

TABLE
18-1 Aging Schedules

Age of Account (Days)	Super Sets		Wonder Vision	
	Value of Account	Percentage of Total Value	Value of Account	Percentage of Total Value
0–10	$1,215,122	70%	$ 815,867	47%
11–30	520,766	30	451,331	26
31–45	0	0	260,383	15
46–60	0	0	173,589	10
Over 60	0	0	34,718	2
Total receivables	$1,735,888	100%	$1,735,888	100%

Aging Schedules An **aging schedule** breaks down a firm's receivables by age of account. Table 18-1 contains the December 31, 2015, aging schedules of two television manufacturers, Super Sets and Wonder Vision. Both firms offer the same credit terms, and both show the same total receivables. However, Super Sets' aging schedule indicates that all of its customers pay on time—70% pay on Day 10 while 30% pay on Day 30. On the other hand, Wonder Vision's schedule, which is more typical, shows that many of its customers are not abiding by its credit terms—some 27% of its receivables are more than 30 days old, even though Wonder Vision's credit terms call for full payment by Day 30.

Aging schedules cannot be constructed from the type of summary data reported in financial statements; they must be developed from the firm's accounts receivable ledger. However, well-run firms have computerized their accounts receivable records, so it is easy to determine the age of each invoice, to sort electronically by age categories, and thus to generate an aging schedule.

Management should constantly monitor both the DSO and the aging schedule to detect trends, to see how the firm's collection experience compares with its credit terms, and to see how effectively the credit department is operating in comparison with other firms in the industry. If the DSO starts to lengthen, or if the aging schedule begins to show an increasing percentage of past-due accounts, then the firm's credit policy may need to be tightened.

Although a change in the DSO or the aging schedule should signal the firm to investigate its credit policy, a deterioration in either of these measures does not necessarily indicate that the firm's credit policy has weakened. In fact, if a firm experiences sharp seasonal variations, or if it is growing rapidly, then both the aging schedule and the DSO may be distorted. To see this point, note that the DSO is calculated as follows:

$$DSO = \frac{\text{Accounts receivable}}{\text{Sales}/365}$$

Since receivables at a given point in time reflect sales in the last month or so, but sales as shown in the denominator of the equation are for the past 12 months, a seasonal increase in sales will increase the numerator more than the denominator and hence will raise the DSO. This will occur even if customers are still paying exactly as before. Similar problems arise with the aging schedule if sales fluctuate widely. Therefore, a change in either the DSO or the aging schedule should be taken as a signal to investigate further, but not necessarily as a sign that the firm's credit policy has weakened.

CONCEPT REVIEW

1. Explain how a new firm's receivables balance is built up over time.
2. Define days' sales outstanding (DSO). What can be learned from it? How is it affected by sales fluctuations?

3. What is an aging schedule? What can be learned from it? How is it affected by sales fluctuations?

4. A company has annual sales of $730 million dollars. If its DSO is 35, what is its average accounts receivable? (Check Figure: $70 million)

18.5 Analyzing Proposed Changes in Credit Policy

In the last section we discussed credit policy, including setting the credit period, credit standards, collection policy, and discount percentage, as well as the factors that influence credit policy. A firm's credit policy is reviewed periodically, and policy changes may be proposed. However, before a new policy is adopted, it should be analyzed to determine whether it is indeed preferable to the existing policy. In this section, we discuss procedures for analyzing proposed changes in credit policy.

If a firm's credit policy is *eased* by such actions as lengthening the credit period, relaxing credit standards, following a less tough collection policy, or offering cash discounts, then sales should increase: *easing the credit policy stimulates sales*. Of course, if credit policy is eased and sales rise, then costs will also rise because more labour, materials, and so on, will be required to produce the additional goods. Additionally, receivables outstanding will also increase, which will increase carrying costs. Moreover, bad debts and/or discount expenses may also rise. Thus, the key question when deciding on a proposed credit policy change is this: Will sales revenues increase more than costs, including credit-related costs, causing cash flow to increase, or will the increase in sales revenues be more than offset by higher costs?

Table 18-2 illustrates the general idea behind the analysis of credit policy changes. Column 1 shows the projected 2016 income statement for Monroe Manufacturing under the assumption that the firm's current credit policy is maintained throughout the year. Column 2 shows the expected effects of easing the credit policy by extending the credit period, offering larger discounts, relaxing credit standards, and easing collection efforts. Specifically, Monroe is analyzing the effects of changing its credit terms from 1/10, net 30, to 2/10, net 40, relaxing

TABLE 18-2   Monroe Manufacturing Company: Analysis of Changing Credit Policy

	Projected 2016 Net Income under Current Credit Policy (1)	Effect of Credit Policy Change (2)	Projected 2016 Net Income under New Credit Policy (3)
Gross sales	$400,000	+$130,000	$530,000
Less discounts	2,000	+ 4,360	6,360
Net sales	398,000	+ 125,640	523,640
Production costs, including overhead	280,000	+ 91,000	371,000
Profit before credit costs and taxes	118,000	+ 34,640	152,640
Credit-related costs:			
Cost of carrying receivables	3,220	+ 1,660	4,880
Credit analysis and collection expense	5,000	− 3,000	2,000
Bad debt losses	10,000	+ 21,800	31,800
Profit before taxes	99,780	+ 14,180	113,960
Taxes (25%)	24,945	+ 3,545	28,490
Net income	$ 74,835	+$ 10,635	$ 85,470

Note: The above statements include only those cash flows incremental to the credit policy decision.

its credit standards, and putting less pressure on slow-paying customers. Column 3 shows the projected 2016 income statement incorporating the expected effects of an easing in credit policy. The generally looser policy is expected to increase sales and lower collection costs, but discounts and several other types of costs would rise. The overall, bottom-line effect is a $10,635 increase in projected net income. In the following paragraphs, we explain how the numbers in the table were calculated.

Monroe's annual sales are $400,000. Under its current credit policy, 50% of those customers who pay do so on Day 10 and take the discount, 40% pay on Day 30, and 10% pay late, on Day 40. Thus, Monroe's days' sales outstanding is $(0.5)(10) + (0.4)(30) + (0.1)(40) =$ 21 days, and discounts total $(0.01)($400,000)(0.5) = $2,000$.

The cost of carrying receivables is equal to the average receivables balance times the variable cost percentage times the cost of money used to carry receivables. The firm's variable cost ratio is 70%, and its pre-tax cost of capital invested in receivables is 20%. Thus, its annual cost of carrying receivables is $3,220:

$$(\text{DSO})\left(\frac{\text{Sales}}{\text{per day}}\right)\left(\frac{\text{Variable}}{\text{cost ratio}}\right)\left(\frac{\text{Cost of}}{\text{funds}}\right) = \text{Cost of carrying receivables}$$

$$(21)($400,000/365)(0.70)(0.20) = $3,222 \approx $3,220$$

Only variable costs enter this calculation because this is the only cost element in receivables that must be financed. We are seeking the cost of carrying receivables, and variable costs represent the firm's investment in the cost of goods sold.

Even though Monroe spends $5,000 annually to analyze accounts and to collect bad debts, 2.5% of sales will never be collected. Bad debt losses therefore amount to (0.025) $($400,000) = $10,000$.

Monroe's new credit policy would be 2/10, net 40 versus the old policy of 1/10, net 30, so it would call for a larger discount and a longer payment period, as well as a relaxed collection effort and lower credit standards. The company believes that these changes will lead to a $130,000 increase in sales, to $530,000 per year. Management believes that under the new terms, 60% of the customers who pay will take the 2% discount, so discounts will increase to $(0.02)($530,000)(0.60) = $6,360$. Half the nondiscount customers will pay on Day 40, and the remainder on Day 50. The new DSO is thus estimated to be 24 days:

$$(0.6)(10) + (0.2)(40) + (0.2)(50) = 24 \text{ days}$$

Also, the cost of carrying receivables will increase to $4,880.

$$(24)($530,000/365)(0.70)(0.20) = $4,879 \approx $4,880[10]$$

The company plans to reduce its annual credit analysis and collection expenditures to $2,000. The reduced credit standards and the relaxed collection effort are expected to raise bad debt losses to about 6% of sales, or to $(0.06)($530,000) = $31,800$, which is an increase of $21,800 from the previous level.

The combined effect of all the changes in credit policy is a projected $10,635 annual increase in net income. There would, of course, be corresponding changes on the projected balance sheet—the higher sales would necessitate somewhat larger cash balances, inventories, and, depending on the capacity situation, perhaps more fixed assets. Accounts receivable would, of course, also increase. Because these asset increases would have to be financed, certain liabilities and/or equity would have to be increased.

The $10,635 expected increase in net income is, of course, an estimate, and the actual effects of the change could be quite different. In the first place, there is uncertainty—perhaps quite a lot—about the projected $130,000 increase in sales. Indeed, if the firm's competitors

---

[10]Since the credit policy change will result in a longer DSO, the firm will have to wait longer to receive its profit on the goods it sells. Therefore, the firm will incur an opportunity cost due to not having the cash from these profits available for investment. The dollar amount of this opportunity cost is equal to the old sales per day times the change in DSO times the contribution margin (1 − Variable cost ratio) times the firm's cost of carrying receivables, or

$$\text{Opportunity cost} = (\text{Old sales}/365)(\Delta \text{DSO})(1 - V)(r)$$
$$= ($400,000/365)(3)(0.3)(0.20)$$
$$= $197$$

For simplicity, we have ignored this opportunity cost in our analysis.

matched its changes, sales might not rise at all. Similar uncertainties must be attached to the number of customers who would take discounts, to production costs at higher or lower sales levels, to the costs of carrying additional receivables, and to bad debt losses. In the final analysis, the decision will be based on judgment, especially concerning the risks involved, but the type of quantitative analysis set forth above is essential to the process.

ⓒNCEPT REVIEW

1.   Describe the procedure for evaluating a change in credit policy using the income statement approach.
2.   Do you think that credit policy decisions are made on the basis of numerical analysis or on judgmental factors?

18.6 Inventory

The twin goals of inventory management are (1) to ensure that the inventories needed to sustain operations are available, but (2) to hold the costs of ordering and carrying inventories to the lowest possible level. While analyzing improvements in the cash conversion cycle, we identified some of the cash flows associated with a reduction in inventory. In addition to the points made earlier, lower inventory levels reduce costs due to storage and handling, insurance, property taxes, and spoilage or obsolescence.

Consider Trane Corporation, which makes air conditioners, and recently adopted just-in-time inventory procedures. In the past, Trane produced parts on a steady basis, stored them as inventory, and had them ready whenever the company received an order for a batch of air conditioners. However, the company reached the point where its inventory covered an area equal to three football fields, and it still sometimes took as long as 15 days to fill an order. To make matters worse, occasionally some of the necessary components simply could not be located, while in other instances the components were located but found to have been damaged from long storage.

Then Trane adopted a new inventory policy—it began producing components only after an order was received, then sending the parts directly from the machines that made them to the final assembly line. The net effect: Inventories fell nearly 40% even as sales increased by 30%.

Such improvements in inventory management can free up considerable amounts of cash. For example, suppose a company has sales of $120 million and an inventory turnover ratio of 3. This means the company has an inventory level of

$$\text{Inventory} = \text{Sales}/(\text{Inventory turnover ratio})$$

$$= \$120/3 = \$40 \text{ million}$$

If the company can improve its inventory turnover ratio to 4, then its inventory will fall to

$$\text{Inventory} = \$120/4 = \$30 \text{ million}$$

This $10 million reduction in inventory boosts free cash flow by $10 million.

However, there are costs associated with holding too little inventory, and these costs can be severe. If a business lowers its inventories, then it must reorder frequently, which increases ordering costs. Even worse, if stocks become depleted then firms can miss out on profitable sales and also suffer lost goodwill, which may lead to lower future sales. Therefore, it is important to have enough inventory on hand to meet customer demands but not so much as to incur the costs we discussed previously.

Computerized Inventory Control

Most companies today employ *computerized inventory control systems*. The computer starts with an inventory count in memory. As withdrawals are made, they are recorded by the computer, and the inventory balance is revised. When the reorder point is reached, the computer automatically places an order, and when the order is received, the recorded balance is increased. As we noted earlier, retailers such as Wal-Mart have carried this system quite far—each item has a bar code, and, as an item is checked out, the code is read, a signal is sent to the computer, and the inventory balance is adjusted at the same time the price is fed into the cash register tape. When the balance drops to the reorder point, an order is placed. In Wal-Mart's case, the order goes directly from its computers to those of its suppliers.

A good inventory control system is dynamic, not static. A company such as Wal-Mart or General Motors stocks hundreds of thousands of different items. The sales (or use) of individual items can rise or fall quite separately from rising or falling overall corporate sales. As the usage rate for an individual item begins to rise or fall, the inventory manager must adjust its balance to avoid running short or ending up with obsolete items. If the change in the usage rate appears to be permanent, the safety stock level should be reconsidered, and the computer model used in the control process should be reprogrammed.

Just-in-Time Systems

An approach to inventory control called the **just-in-time (JIT) system** was developed by Japanese firms but is now used throughout the world. Toyota provides a good example of the just-in-time system. Eight of Toyota's ten factories, along with most of Toyota's suppliers, dot the countryside around Toyota City. Delivery of components is tied to the speed of the assembly line, and parts are generally delivered no more than a few hours before they are used. The just-in-time system reduces the need for Toyota and other manufacturers to carry large inventories, but it requires a great deal of coordination between the manufacturer and its suppliers, both in the timing of deliveries and in the quality of the parts. It also requires that component parts be perfect; otherwise, a few bad parts could stop the entire production line. Therefore, JIT inventory management has been developed in conjunction with total quality management (TQM).

Not surprisingly, automobile manufacturers were among the first North American firms to move toward just-in-time systems. Ford has restructured its production system with a goal of increasing its inventory turnover from 20 times a year to 30 or 40 times. Of course, just-in-time systems place considerable pressure on suppliers. GM formerly kept a 10-day supply of seats and other parts made by Lear Siegler; now GM sends in orders at 4- to 8-hour intervals and expects immediate shipment. A Lear Siegler spokesman stated, "We can't afford to keep things sitting around either," so Lear Siegler has had to be tough on its own suppliers.

The close coordination required among the parties using JIT procedures has led to an overall reduction of inventory throughout the production-distribution system and to a general improvement in economic efficiency. This point is borne out by economic statistics, which show that inventory as a percentage of sales has been declining since the use of just-in-time procedures began. Also, with smaller inventories in the system, economic recessions have become shorter and less severe.

Outsourcing

Another important development related to inventory is **outsourcing,** which is the practice of purchasing components rather than making them in-house. Thus, GM has been moving toward buying radiators, axles, and other parts from suppliers rather than making them itself, so it has been increasing its use of outsourcing. Outsourcing is often combined with just-in-time systems to reduce inventory levels. However, perhaps the major reason for outsourcing has nothing to do with inventory policy—a bureaucratic, unionized company like GM can often buy parts from a smaller, nonunionized supplier at a lower cost than it can make them itself.

The Relationship between Production Scheduling and Inventory Levels

A final point relating to inventory levels is *the relationship between production scheduling and inventory levels*. For example, a greeting card manufacturer has highly seasonal sales. Such a firm could produce on a steady, year-round basis, or it could let production rise and fall with sales. If it established a level production schedule, its inventory would rise sharply during periods when sales were low and then decline during peak sales periods, but its average inventory would be substantially higher than if production rose and fell with sales.

Our discussions of just-in-time systems, outsourcing, and production scheduling all point out the necessity of coordinating inventory policy with manufacturing/procurement policies. Companies try to minimize *total production and distribution costs,* and inventory costs are just one part of total costs. Still, they are an important cost, and financial managers should be aware of the determinants of inventory costs and how they can be minimized. *Web Extension 18B* discusses four methods of accounting for inventory and their impact on profits and ending inventory values.

See **Web Extension 18B** at the textbook's website for a discussion on the accounting for inventory.

FINANCE: IN FOCUS

Is There Too Much Dead Money in Canada?

The amount of cash and cash equivalents being held by Canadian companies have increased significantly over the past 26 years, from 3.1% to 5.3% of total assets. This apparent cash "hoarding" has led politicians and even the Governor of the Bank of Canada[a] to claim that companies are holding too much cash and are calling for businesses to invest in new plant and equipment. Are Canadian companies being inefficient and too conservative with their cash holdings? If we consider cash as just one element of current assets, the numbers suggest something different. Current assets in general produce zero income, therefore their levels should be carefully managed. However, they are still necessary to cover a company's short-term obligations. Moreover, cash and equivalents are also used as a precautionary balance, to carry companies through times of economic turmoil. The graph below shows cash, accounts receivable, and inventory as a percent of total assets over a 26-year period, 1988–2014. This period included the 1990s recession, the technology sector meltdown of 2000–2001, and the credit crisis of 2007–2009, all of which financially strained many companies. Note the long-run decline in inventory and receivables along with the corresponding increase in cash. We know over this time period that the use of information technology and improved logistic planning has led to a significant decline in the amount of inventory companies need to hold. Likewise, efficient payment processing has also sped up payments, causing the level of receivables to fall. It appears that companies have altered the *proportions* of current assets they use. Companies are using less inventory and receivables due to efficiency and operational reasons and instead relying more on cash and equivalents for their short-term and precautionary needs. Businesses may well be maintaining larger cash positions as protection against some future incident, due to their experiences of two recessions and the tech sector collapse over the past 26 years. Overall, non-income earning current assets have not grown as a proportion of total assets, but their mix has.

[a]John Shmuel, "Stop Sitting on Your Cash Piles, Carney Tells Corporate Canada," *Financial Post*, August 22, 2012, http://financialpost.com, accessed March 3, 2015.

Source: Adapted from Finn Poschmann, "Not Dead Yet: The Changing Role of Cash on Corporate Balance Sheets," C.D. Howe Institute, January 16, 2013, http://www.cdhowe.org/, accessed September 29, 2014.

Canadian Manufacturing Industries: Current Assets as a Percentage of Total Assets

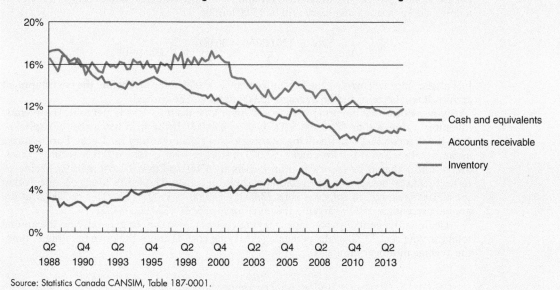

Source: Statistics Canada CANSIM, Table 187-0001.

CONCEPT REVIEW

1. What are just-in-time systems? What are their advantages? Why is quality especially important if a JIT system is used?
2. What is outsourcing?
3. Describe the relationship between production scheduling and inventory levels.

18.7 The Economic Ordering Quantity (EOQ) Model

As just discussed, inventories are obviously necessary, but it is equally obvious that a firm's profitability will suffer if it has too much or too little inventory. Most firms use a pragmatic approach to setting inventory levels, in which past experience plays a major role. However, as a starting point in the process, it is useful for managers to consider the insights provided by the **economic ordering quantity (EOQ) model.** The EOQ model first specifies the costs of ordering and carrying inventories and then combines these costs to obtain the total costs associated with inventory holdings. Finally, optimization techniques are used to find that order quantity, hence inventory level, that minimizes total costs. Note that a third category of inventory costs, the costs of running short (stock-out costs), is not considered in our initial discussion. These costs are dealt with by adding safety stocks, as we will introduce later. We more fully discuss safety stocks and introduce the effect of quantity discounts in *Web Extension 18C*. The costs that remain for consideration at this stage are carrying costs and ordering, shipping, and receiving costs.

See *Web Extension 18C* on the textbook's website for a discussion on safety stocks and the effect of quantity discounts.

Carrying Costs

Carrying costs generally rise in direct proportion to the average amount of inventory carried. Inventories carried, in turn, depend on the frequency with which orders are placed. To illustrate, if a firm sells S units per year, and if it places equal-sized orders N times per year, then S/N units will be purchased with each order. If the inventory is used evenly over the year, and if no safety stocks are carried, then the average inventory, A, will be

$$A = \frac{\text{Units per order}}{2} = \frac{S/N}{2} \tag{18-4}$$

For example, if S = 120,000 units in a year and N = 4, then the firm will order 30,000 units at a time, and its average inventory will be 15,000 units:

$$A = \frac{S/N}{2} = \frac{120,000/4}{2} = \frac{30,000}{2} = 15,000 \text{ units}$$

Just after a shipment arrives, the inventory will be 30,000 units; just before the next shipment arrives, it will be zero; and on average, 15,000 units will be carried.

Now assume that the firm purchases its inventory at a price P = $2 per unit. The average inventory value is thus (P)(A) = $2(15,000) = $30,000. If the firm has a cost of capital of 10%, it will incur $3,000 in financing charges to carry the inventory for 1 year. Furthermore, assume that each year the firm incurs $2,000 of storage costs (space, utilities, security, taxes, and so forth), that its inventory insurance costs are $500, and that it must mark down inventories by $1,000 because of depreciation and obsolescence. The firm's total cost of carrying the $30,000 average inventory is thus $3,000 + $2,000 + $500 + $1,000 = $6,500, and the annual percentage cost of carrying the inventory is $6,500/$30,000 = 0.217 = 21.7%.

Defining the annual percentage carrying cost as C, we can, in general, find the annual total carrying cost, TCC, as the percentage carrying cost, C, times the price per unit, P, times the average number of units, A:

$$\text{TCC} = \text{Total carrying cost} = (C)(P)(A) \tag{18-5}$$

In our example,

$$TCC = (0.217)(\$2)(15,000) \approx \$6,500$$

Ordering Costs

Although we assume that carrying costs are entirely variable and rise in direct proportion to the average size of inventories, *ordering costs* are often fixed. For example, the costs of placing and receiving an order—interoffice memos, long-distance telephone calls, setting up a production run, and taking delivery—are essentially fixed regardless of the size of an order, so this part of inventory cost is simply the fixed cost of placing and receiving orders times the number of orders placed per year.[11] We define the fixed costs associated with ordering inventories as F, and if we place N orders per year, the total ordering cost is given by Equation 18-6:

$$\text{Total ordering cost} = TOC = (F)(N) \qquad \text{(18-6)}$$

Here TOC = total ordering cost, F = fixed costs per order, and N = number of orders placed per year.

Equation 18-4 may be rewritten as N = S/2A and then substituted into Equation 18-6:

$$\text{Total ordering cost} = TOC = F\left(\frac{S}{2A}\right) \qquad \text{(18-7)}$$

To illustrate the use of Equation 18-7, if F = $100, S = 120,000 units, and A = 15,000 units, then TOC, the total annual ordering cost, is $400:

$$TOC = \$100\left(\frac{120,000}{30,000}\right) = \$100(4) = \$400.$$

Total Inventory Costs

Total carrying cost, TCC, as defined in Equation 18-5, and total ordering cost, TOC, as defined in Equation 18-7, may be combined to find *total inventory costs*, TIC, as follows:

$$\text{Total inventory costs} = TIC = \ TCC \ + \ TOC$$
$$= (C)(P)(A) + F\left(\frac{S}{2A}\right) \qquad \text{(18-8)}$$

Recognizing that the average inventory carried is A = Q/2, or one-half the size of each order quantity, Q, we may rewrite Equation 18-8 as follows:

$$TIC = TCC + TOC$$
$$= (C)(P)\left(\frac{Q}{2}\right) + (F)\left(\frac{S}{Q}\right) \qquad \text{(18-9)}$$

Here we see that total carrying cost equals average inventory in units, Q/2, multiplied by unit price, P, times the percentage annual carrying cost, C. Total ordering cost equals the

---

[11]Note that in reality both carrying and ordering costs can have variable and fixed-cost elements, at least over certain ranges of average inventory. For example, security and utilities charges are probably fixed in the short run over a wide range of inventory levels. Similarly, labour costs in receiving inventory could be tied to the quantity received and, hence, could be variable. To simplify matters, we treat all carrying costs as variable and all ordering costs as fixed. However, if these assumptions do not fit the situation at hand, the cost definitions can be changed. For example, one could add another term for shipping costs if there are economies of scale in shipping, such that the cost of shipping a unit is smaller if shipments are larger. However, in most situations shipping costs are not sensitive to order size, so total shipping costs are simply the shipping cost per unit times the units ordered (and sold) during the year. Under this condition, shipping costs are not influenced by inventory policy: hence they may be disregarded for purposes of determining the optimal inventory level and the optimal order size.

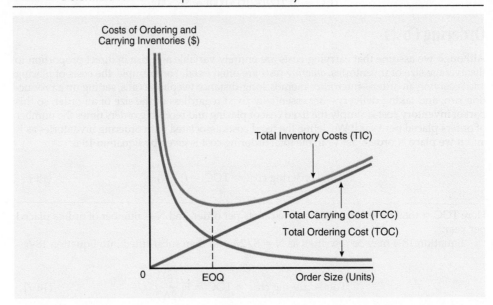

FIGURE
18-1 Determination of the Optimal Order Quantity

number of orders placed per year, S/Q, multiplied by the fixed cost of placing and receiving an order, F. Finally, total inventory costs equal the sum of total carrying cost plus total ordering cost. We will use this equation in the next section to develop the optimal inventory ordering quantity.

Derivation of the EOQ Model

Figure 18-1 illustrates the basic premise on which the EOQ model is built, namely, that some costs rise with larger inventories while other costs decline, and that there is an optimal order size (and associated average inventory) that minimizes the total costs of inventories. First, as noted earlier, the average investment in inventories depends on how frequently orders are placed and the size of each order—if we order every day, average inventories will be much smaller than if we order once a year. Furthermore, as Figure 18-1 shows, the firm's carrying costs rise with larger orders; larger orders mean larger average inventories, so warehousing costs, interest on funds tied up in inventory, insurance, and obsolescence costs will all increase. However, ordering costs decline with larger orders and inventories; the cost of placing orders, suppliers' production setup costs, and order handling costs will all decline if we order infrequently and consequently hold larger quantities.

If the carrying and ordering cost curves in Figure 18-1 are added, the sum represents total inventory costs, TIC. The point where the TIC is minimized represents the economic ordering quantity (EOQ), and this, in turn, determines the optimal average inventory level[12]:

$$Q = EOQ = \sqrt{\frac{2(F)(S)}{(C)(P)}} \qquad (18\text{-}10)$$

[12]The EOQ is found by differentiating Equation 18-9 with respect to ordering quantity, Q, and setting the derivative equal to zero:

$$\frac{d(TIC)}{dQ} = \frac{(C)(P)}{2} - \frac{(F)(S)}{Q^2} = 0$$

Now, solving for Q, we obtain:

$$\frac{(C)(P)}{2} = \frac{(F)(S)}{Q^2}$$

$$Q^2 = \frac{2(F)(S)}{(C)(P)}$$

$$Q = EOQ = \sqrt{\frac{2(F)(S)}{(C)(P)}}$$

Here:

EOQ = Economic ordering quantity, or the optimal quantity to be ordered each time an
order is placed
F = Fixed costs of placing and receiving an order
S = Annual sales in units
C = Annual carrying costs expressed as a percentage of average inventory value
P = Purchase price the firm must pay per unit of inventory

Equation 18-10 is the EOQ model.[13] The assumptions of the model, which will be relaxed shortly, include the following: (1) sales can be forecast perfectly, (2) sales are evenly distributed throughout the year, and (3) orders are received when expected.

EOQ Model Illustration

To illustrate the EOQ model, consider the following data supplied by Cotton Tops Limited, a distributor of budget-priced, custom-designed T-shirts, which it sells to concessionaires at various country fairs throughout Canada:

S = Annual sales = 26,000 shirts per year.
C = Percentage carrying cost = 25% of inventory value.
P = Purchase price per shirt = $4.92 per shirt. (The sales price is $9, but this is irrelevant
for our purposes here.)
F = Fixed cost per order = $1,000. Cotton Tops designs and distributes the shirts, but
the actual production is done by another company. The bulk of this $1,000 cost is the
labour cost for setting up the equipment for the production run, which the manufacturer bills separately from the $4.92 cost per shirt.

Substituting these data into Equation 18-10, we obtain an EOQ of 6,500 units:

$$EOQ = \sqrt{\frac{2(F)(S)}{(C)(P)}} = \sqrt{\frac{(2)(\$1,000)(26,000)}{(0.25)(\$4.92)}}$$

$$= \sqrt{42,276,423} \approx 6,500 \text{ units.}$$

With an EOQ of 6,500 shirts and annual usage of 26,000 shirts, Cotton Tops will place 26,000/6,500 = 4 orders per year. Note that average inventory holdings depend directly on the EOQ. This relationship is illustrated graphically in Figure 18-2, where we see that average inventory = EOQ/2. Immediately after an order is received, 6,500 shirts are in stock. The usage rate, or sales rate, is 500 shirts per week (26,000/52 weeks), so inventories are drawn down by this amount each week. Thus, the actual number of units held in inventory will vary from 6,500 shirts just after an order is received to zero just before a new order arrives. With a 6,500 beginning balance, a zero ending balance, and a uniform sales rate, inventories will average one-half the EOQ, or 3,250 shirts, during the year. At a cost of $4.92 per shirt, the average investment in inventories will be (3,250)($4.92) ≈ $16,000. If inventories are financed by bank loans, the loan will vary from a high of $32,000 to a low of $0, but the average amount outstanding over the course of a year will be $16,000.

Note that the EOQ, hence average inventory holdings, rises with the square root of sales. Therefore, a given increase in sales will result in a less-than-proportionate increase in inventories, so the inventory/sales ratio will tend to decline as a firm grows. For example, Cotton Tops's EOQ is 6,500 shirts at an annual sales level of 26,000, and the average inventory is 3,250 shirts, or $16,000. However, if sales were to increase by 100%, to 52,000 shirts per year, the EOQ would rise only to 9,195 units, or by 41%, and the average inventory would rise by this same percentage. This suggests that there are economies of scale in holding inventories.[14]

---

[13]The EOQ model can also be written as

$$EOQ = \sqrt{\frac{2(F)(S)}{C^*}}$$

where C* is the annual carrying cost per unit expressed in *dollars*.
[14]Note, however, that these scale economies relate to each particular item, not to the entire firm. Thus, a large distributor with $500 million of sales might have a higher inventory/sales ratio than a much smaller distributor if the small firm has only a few high-sales-volume items while the large firm distributes a great many low-volume items.

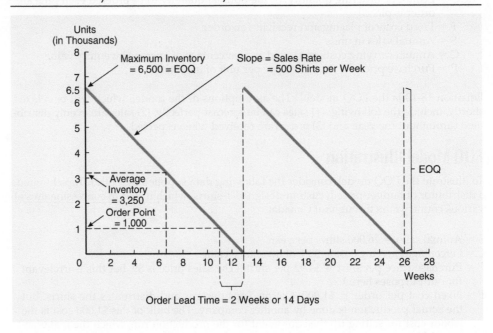

FIGURE 18-2   Inventory Position without Safety Stock

Finally, look at Cotton Tops's total inventory costs for the year, assuming that the EOQ is ordered each time. Using Equation 18-9, we find that total inventory costs are $8,000:

$$TIC = TCC + TOC$$

$$= (C)(P)\left(\frac{Q}{2}\right) + (F)\left(\frac{S}{Q}\right)$$

$$= 0.25(\$4.92)\left(\frac{6,500}{2}\right) + (\$1,000)\left(\frac{26,000}{6,500}\right)$$

$$\approx \$4,000 + \$4,000 = \$8,000$$

Note these two points: (1) The $8,000 total inventory cost represents the total of carrying costs and ordering costs, but this amount does *not* include the 26,000 ($4.92) = $127,920 annual purchasing cost of the inventory itself. (2) As we see both in Figure 18-1 and in the calculation above, at the EOQ, total carrying cost (TCC) equals total ordering cost (TOC). This property is not unique to our Cotton Tops illustration; it always holds.

Setting the Order Point

If a 2-week lead time is required for production and shipping, what is Cotton Tops's order point level? Cotton Tops sells 26,000/52 = 500 shirts per week. Thus, if a 2-week lag occurs between placing an order and receiving goods, Cotton Tops must place the order when there are 2(500) = 1,000 shirts on hand. During the 2-week production and shipping period, the inventory balance will continue to decline at the rate of 500 shirts per week, and the inventory balance will hit zero just as the order of new shirts arrives.

If Cotton Tops knew for certain that both the sales rate and the order lead time would never vary, it could operate exactly as shown in Figure 18-2. However, sales do change, and production and/or shipping delays are sometimes encountered. To guard against these events, the firm must carry additional inventories, or safety stocks, as discussed in the next section.

Safety Stock

Safety stock is, quite simply, extra inventory kept on hand to avoid shortages that can occur if sales increase more than was expected or if shipping delays are encountered on inventory ordered. If a stock-out occurs, production will stop or sales will be forfeited, all at significant cost to the company. However, carrying a safety stock has a cost. Average inventory will now be calculated as EOQ/2 plus the safety stock maintained.

The optimal level of safety stock varies, but in general, it *increases* (1) with the uncertainty of demand forecasts, (2) with the costs (in terms of lost sales and lost goodwill) that result from inventory shortages, and (3) with the probability that delays will occur in receiving shipments. The optimal safety stock *decreases* as the cost of carrying this additional inventory increases. **Web Extension 18C** further discusses safety stock and introduces the impact of quantity discounts on the setting of inventory levels.

*See **Web Extension 18C** at the textbook's website for a discussion on EOQ Model Extensions.*

CONCEPT REVIEW

1. What are some specific inventory carrying costs? As defined here, are these costs fixed or variable?
2. What are some inventory ordering costs? As defined here, are these costs fixed or variable?
3. What are the components of total inventory costs?
4. What is the concept behind the EOQ model?
5. What is the relationship between total carrying cost and total ordering cost at the EOQ?
6. What assumptions are inherent in the EOQ model as presented here?

Summary

This chapter discussed the management of current assets—specifically, cash, marketable securities, accounts receivable, and inventory. It also discussed motives for holding cash and marketable securities. The importance of monitoring receivables was reviewed, and an analysis of credit policy was undertaken, analyzing how a change in credit policy can affect asset levels, sales, and profits. Finally, the chapter covered how an optimal inventory policy might be identified using the economic ordering (EOQ) model. The key concepts covered are listed below:

- The **primary goal of cash management** is to minimize the amount of cash a firm holds while maintaining a sufficient **target cash balance** to conduct business.
- The **transactions balance** is the cash necessary to conduct day-to-day business, whereas the **precautionary balance** is a cash reserve held to meet random, unforeseen needs. A **compensating balance** is a minimum chequing account balance that a bank requires as compensation either for services provided or as part of a loan agreement.
- When a firm sells goods to a customer on credit, an **account receivable** is created.
- A firm can use an **aging schedule** and **days' sales outstanding (DSO)** to help keep track of its receivables position and to help avoid an increase in bad debts.
- The basic objective of the credit manager is to increase profitable sales by extending credit to worthy customers and thereby adding value to the firm.
- A firm's credit policy has four elements: (1) a **credit period**, (2) **discounts** given for early payment, (3) **credit standards**, and (4) a **collection policy.** The first two, when combined, are called the **credit terms.**
- If a firm **eases its credit policy** by lengthening the credit period, relaxing its credit standards and collection policy, and offering (or raising) a cash discount, its sales should increase. However, its costs will also increase. A firm should ease its credit policy only if the costs of doing so will be offset by higher expected revenues. In general, credit policy changes can be evaluated on the basis of incremental profits, by constructing pro forma income statements for both the current and proposed policies.
- The twin goals of **inventory management** are (1) to ensure that the inventories needed to sustain operations are available, but (2) to hold the costs of ordering and carrying inventories to the lowest possible level.
- **Just-in-time (JIT) systems** are used to hold down inventory costs and, simultaneously, to improve the production process. **Outsourcing** is the practice of purchasing components rather than making them in-house.

- **Inventory costs** can be divided into three parts: carrying costs, ordering costs, and stock-out costs. In general, **carrying costs** increase as the level of inventory rises, but **ordering costs** and **stock-out costs** decline with larger inventory holdings.
- **Total carrying cost (TCC)** is equal to the percentage cost of carrying inventory (C) times the purchase price per unit of inventory (P) times the average number of units held (A): TCC = (C)(P)(A).
- **Total ordering cost (TOC)** is equal to the fixed cost of placing an order (F) times the number of orders placed per year (N): TOC = (F)(N).
- **Total inventory costs (TIC)** equal total carrying cost (TCC) plus total ordering cost (TOC): TIC = TCC + TOC.
- The **economic ordering quantity (EOQ)** model is a formula for determining the order quantity that will minimize total inventory costs:

$$EOQ = \sqrt{\frac{2(F)(S)}{(C)(P)}}$$

Here F is the fixed cost per order, S is annual sales in units, C is the percentage cost of carrying inventory, and P is the purchase price per unit.
- The **order point** is the inventory level at which new items must be ordered.
- **Safety stocks** are held to avoid shortages, which can occur (1) if sales increase more than was expected or (2) if shipping delays are encountered on inventory ordered. The cost of carrying a safety stock, which is separate from that based on the EOQ model, is equal to the percentage cost of carrying inventory times the purchase price per unit times the number of units held as the safety stock.

Questions

18-1   What are the two principal reasons for holding cash? Can a firm estimate its target cash balance by summing the cash held to satisfy each of the reasons?

18-2   What are the four elements of a firm's credit policy? To what extent can firms set their own credit policies instead of having to accept policies that are dictated by "the competition"?

18-3   Suppose that a firm makes a purchase and receives the shipment on February 1. The terms of trade as stated on the invoice read "2/10, net 40, May 1 dating." What is the latest date on which payment can be made and the discount still be taken? What is the date on which payment must be made if the discount is not taken?

18-4   Firm A had no credit losses last year, but 1% of Firm B's accounts receivable proved to be uncollectible and resulted in losses. Should Firm B fire its credit manager and hire A's?

18-5   Indicate by a (+), (−), or (0) whether each of the following events would probably cause accounts receivable (A/R), sales, and profits to increase, decrease, or be affected in an uncertain manner:

	A/R	Sales	Profits
The firm tightens its credit standards.	_____	_____	_____
The terms of trade are changed from 2/10, net 30, to 3/10, net 30.	_____	_____	_____
The terms of trade are changed from 2/10, net 30, to 3/10, net 40.	_____	_____	_____
The credit manager gets tough with past due accounts.	_____	_____	_____

18-6   Indicate by a (+), (−), or (0) whether each of the following events would probably cause average annual inventory holdings to rise, fall, or be affected in an uncertain manner:
   a.   Our suppliers change from delivering by train to air freight.   _____
   b.   We change from producing just-in-time to meet seasonal demand to level, year-round production.   _____
   c.   Competition in the markets in which we sell increases.   _____

d. The general rate of inflation rises.   _____
e. Interest rates rise; other things are constant.   _____

18-7 Assuming that the firm's sales volume remained constant, would you expect it to have a higher cash balance during a tight money period or during an easy money period? Why?

18-8 Explain how each of the following factors would probably affect a firm's target cash balance if all other factors were held constant:
a. The firm institutes a new billing procedure that better synchronizes its cash inflows and outflows.
b. The firm develops a new sales forecasting technique that improves its forecasts.
c. The firm reduces its portfolio of Treasury bills.
d. The firm arranges to use an overdraft system for its chequing account.
e. The firm borrows a large amount of money from its bank and also begins to write far more cheques than it did in the past.
f. Interest rates on Treasury bills rise from 5% to 10%.

Concept Review Problem

Full solutions are provided at www.nelson.com/brigham3ce.

CR-1

Monitoring of Receivables

The Russ Fogler Company, a small manufacturer of cordless telephones, began operations on January 1, 2016. Its credit sales for the first 6 months of operations were as follows:

Month	Credit Sales
January	$ 50,000
February	100,000
March	120,000
April	105,000
May	140,000
June	160,000

Throughout this entire period, the firm's credit customers maintained a constant payments pattern: 20% paid in the month of sale, 30% paid in the month following the sale, and 50% paid in the second month following the sale.
a. What was Fogler's receivables balance at the end of March and at the end of June?
b. Assume 90 days per calendar quarter. What were the average daily sales (ADS) and days' sales outstanding (DSO) for the first quarter and for the second quarter? What were the cumulative ADS and DSO for the first half-year?
c. Construct an aging schedule as of June 30. Use account ages of 0–30, 31–60, and 61–90 days.

Problems

Easy
Problems 1–2

Answers to odd-numbered problems appear in Appendix A.

18-1

Cash
Management

Williams & Sons last year reported cost of sales of $10 million and an inventory turnover ratio of 2. The company is now adopting a new inventory system. If the new system is able to reduce the firm's inventory level and increase the firm's inventory turnover ratio to 5 while maintaining the same level of sales, how much cash will be freed up?

18-2

Receivables
Investment

Whitestone Corporation has a DSO of 26 days. The company averages $5,500 in credit sales each day. What is the company's average account receivable?

Intermediate
Problems 3–6

18-3

Relaxing
Collection Efforts

A-1 Electrical has annual credit sales of $2.2 million. Current expenses for the collection department are $42,000, bad debt losses are 1.5%, and days' sales outstanding is 25 days. The firm is considering easing its collection efforts in such a way that collection expenses will be reduced to $32,000 per year. The change is expected to increase bad debt losses to 2.5% and to increase days' sales outstanding to 45 days. In addition, sales are expected to increase to $2.3 million per year.

Should the firm relax its collection efforts if the opportunity cost of funds is 14%, the variable cost ratio is 75%, and taxes are 30%?

18-4
Tightening
Credit Terms

Kate Hansen, the new credit manager of the Farpoint Communications, was alarmed to find that Farpoint sells on credit terms of net 90 days while industry-wide credit terms have recently been lowered to net 30 days. On annual credit sales of $6 million, Farpoint currently averages 98 days of sales in accounts receivable. Hansen estimates that tightening the credit terms to 30 days would reduce annual sales to $5,580,000, but accounts receivable would drop to 37 days of sales and the savings on investment in them should more than overcome any loss in profit.

Farpoint's variable cost ratio is 80%, and taxes are 26%. If the interest rate on funds invested in receivables is 16%, should the change in credit terms be made?

18-5
Receivables
Investment

McDowell Industries sells on terms of 3/10, net 30. Total sales for the year are $912,500; 40% of the customers pay on the 10th day and take discounts, while the other 60% pay, on average, 40 days after their purchases.
a. What is the days' sales outstanding?
b. What is the average amount of receivables?
c. What are the (i) nominal and (ii) effective percentage costs of trade credit if customers do not take the discount and pay in 30 days?
d. What are the (i) nominal and (ii) effective percentage costs of trade credit to customers who do not take the discount and pay in 40 days?
e. What would happen to McDowell's accounts receivable if it toughened up on its collection policy with the result that all nondiscount customers paid on the 30th day?

18-6
Economic
Ordering Quantity

Gentry Garden Centre sells 90,000 bags of lawn fertilizer annually. The optimal safety stock (which is on hand initially) is 1,000 bags. Each bag costs the firm $1.50, inventory carrying costs are 20%, and the cost of placing an order with its supplier is $15.
a. What is the economic order quantity?
b. What is the maximum inventory of fertilizer?
c. What will be the firm's average inventory?
d. How often must the company order?

**Challenging
Problems 7–8**

18-7
Tightening Credit
Terms

Maxwell Corp. distributes the "Smart" brand of electronic controller systems. The company currently has a credit policy of 1/10, net 40, though on average only 20% of customers pay in 10 days and take the discount, while another 30% pay on average in 15 days yet still take the unearned discount. The company's remaining customers pay on average in 50 days. Bad debt losses are 3% of sales. The company's sales are currently $600,000 per month, all on credit. Maxwell is thinking of restructuring its credit and collections department, with the goal of eliminating all unearned discounts and reducing bad debt losses to 1.5%. With this new policy, the company believes that sales will fall by 5%, that 40% of customers will pay in 10 days and obtain the discount, and that the remaining customers will pay in 40 days. Maxwell's variable costs are 60% of sales, its monthly collections department expense is expected to rise by $6,000 to $20,000, and its opportunity cost on funds is 12%. Maxwell's tax rate is 30%.
a. Should the company implement the new policy?
b. What is the maximum percentage sales decline that the company could take and still proceed with the new policy?

18-8
Economic
Ordering Quantity

Lucas Mitchell, financial manager of Inland Industrial, has been asked by the firm's CEO to evaluate the company's inventory control techniques and to lead a discussion of the subject with the senior executives. Lucas plans to use as an example one of Inland's "big ticket" items, a customized high-pressure valve system. Each system costs Inlands $125 and in addition it must pay its supplier a $1,000 setup fee on each order. Furthermore, the minimum order size is 300 units; Inland's annual usage forecast is 4,000 units; and the annual carrying cost of this item is estimated to be 10% of the average inventory value.

Lucas plans to begin his session with the senior executives by reviewing some basic inventory concepts, after which he will apply the EOQ model to Inland's valve inventory. As his assistant, you have been asked to help him by answering the following questions:
a. What is the EOQ for custom valves? What are total inventory costs if the EOQ is ordered?

b. What is Inland's added cost if it orders 600 units at a time rather than the EOQ quantity? What if it orders 1000 units?

c. Suppose it takes 2 weeks for Inland's supplier to set up production, make and test the valves, and deliver them to Inland's plant. Assuming certainty in delivery times and usage, at what inventory level should Inland reorder? (Assume a 52-week year, and assume that Inland orders the EOQ amount.)

d. Of course, there is uncertainty in Inland's usage rate as well as in delivery times, so the company must carry a safety stock to avoid running out of valves and having to halt production. If a 200-unit safety stock is carried, what effect would this have on total inventory costs? What is the new reorder point? What protection does the safety stock provide if usage increases, or if delivery is delayed?

Spreadsheet Problem

18-9

Build a Model:
EOQ Sensitivity
Analysis

Open the file *Ch 18 Build a Model.xlsx* from the textbook's website. Rework Problem 18-8 using a spreadsheet, and do sensitivity analysis with respect to quantity ordered.

MINI CASE

Rich Jackson, a recent finance graduate, is planning to go into the wholesale building supply business with his brother, Jim, who majored in building construction. The firm would sell primarily to general contractors, and it would start operating next January. Due to the nature of the products, sales would be relatively constant with some fluctuations month to month. Sales estimates for the first 6 months are as follows (in thousands of dollars):

January	$190	March	$190	May	$190
February	210	April	210	June	210

The terms of sale are net 30, but because of special incentives, the brothers expect 30% of the customers (by dollar value) to pay on the 10th day following the sale, 50% to pay on the 40th day, and the remaining 20% to pay on the 70th day. No bad debt losses are expected, because Jim, the building construction expert, knows which contractors are having financial problems.

a. Discuss, in general, what it means for the brothers to set a credit and collections policy.

b. Assume that, on average, the brothers expect annual sales of 18,000 items at an average price of $100 per item. (Use a 365-day year.)

   (1) What is the firm's expected days sales outstanding (DSO)?

   (2) What is its expected average daily sales (ADS)?

   (3) What is its expected average accounts receivable level?

   (4) Assume that the firm's profit margin is 25%. How much of the receivables balance must be financed? What would the firm's balance sheet figures for accounts receivable, notes payable, and retained earnings be at the end of 1 year if notes payable are used to finance the investment in receivables? Assume that the cost of carrying receivables had been deducted when the 25% profit margin was calculated.

   (5) If bank loans have a cost of 12%, what is the annual dollar cost of carrying the receivables?

c. What are some factors that influence (1) a firm's receivables level and (2) the dollar cost of carrying receivables?

d. Assuming that the monthly sales forecasts given previously are accurate and that customers pay exactly as was predicted, what would the receivables level be at the end of each month? *To reduce calculations, assume that 30% of the firm's customers pay in the month of sale, 50% pay in the month following the sale, and the remaining 20% pay in the second month following the sale. Note that this is a different assumption than was made earlier. Also assume there are 91 days in each quarter. Use the following format to answer parts d and e:*

Month	Sales	End-of-Month Receivables	Quarterly Sales	ADS	DSO = (A/R)/(ADS)
January	$190	$133			
February	210	185			
March	190	175	$590	$6.48	27.0
April	210				
May	190				
June	210				

e. What is the firm's forecast average daily sales for the first 3 months? For the entire half-year? The days' sales outstanding is commonly used to measure receivables performance. What DSO is expected at the end of March? At the end of June? What does the DSO indicate about customers' payments?

f. Construct aging schedules for the end of March and the end of June (use the format given below).

Age of Account (Days)	March A/R	%	June A/R	%
0–30				
31–60				
61–90				

g. Assume now that it is several years later. The brothers are concerned about the firm's current credit terms, now net 30, which means that contractors buying building products from the firm are not offered a discount and are supposed to pay the full amount in 30 days. Gross sales are now running $1,000,000 a year, and 80% (by dollar volume) of the firm's *paying* customers generally pay the full amount on Day 30, while the other 20% pay, on average, on Day 40. Of the firm's gross sales, 2% end up as bad debt losses.

  The brothers are now considering a change in the firm's credit policy. The change would entail (1) changing the credit terms to 2/10, net 20, (2) employing stricter credit standards before granting credit, and (3) enforcing collections with greater vigour than in the past. Thus, cash customers and those paying within 10 days would receive a 2% discount, but all others would have to pay the full amount after only 20 days. The brothers believe that the discount would both attract additional customers and encourage some existing customers to purchase more from the firm—after all, the discount amounts to a price reduction. Of course, these customers would take the discount and, hence, would pay in only 10 days. The net expected result is for sales to increase to $1,100,000; for 60% of the paying customers to take the discount and pay on the 10th day; for 30% to pay the full amount on Day 20; for 10% to pay late on Day 30; and for bad debt losses to fall from 2% to 1% of gross sales. The firm's operating cost ratio will remain unchanged at 75%, and its cost of carrying receivables will remain unchanged at 12%.

  To begin the analysis, describe the four variables that make up a firm's credit policy, and explain how each of them affects sales and collections. Then use the information given in part g to answer parts h through m.

h. Under the current credit policy, what is the firm's days' sales outstanding (DSO)? What would the expected DSO be if the credit policy change were made?

i. What is the dollar amount of the firm's current bad debt losses? What losses would be expected under the new policy?

j. What would be the firm's expected dollar cost of granting discounts under the new policy?

k. What is the firm's current dollar cost of carrying receivables? What would it be after the proposed change?

l. What is the incremental after-tax profit associated with the change in credit terms? Should the company make the change? (Assume a tax rate of 40%.)

	New	Old	Difference
Gross sales		$1,000,000	
Less discounts	_____	0	_____
Net sales		1,000,000	
Production costs	_____	750,000	_____
Profit before credit costs and taxes		250,000	
Credit-related costs:			
Carrying costs		7,890	
Bad debt losses	_____	20,000	_____
Profit before taxes		222,110	
Taxes (40%)	_____	88,844	_____
Net income		$ 133,266	

m. Suppose the firm makes the change, but its competitors react by making similar changes to their own credit terms, with the net result being that gross sales remain at the current $1,000,000 level. What would the impact be on the firm's after-tax profitability?

part 5

Derivative Techniques

chapter 19

Financial Options and Applications in Corporate Finance

In early 2015, PyroGenesis Canada Inc., a high-tech maker of plasma torch systems, which are used in waste management and advanced materials processing, issued 2,680,000 options to its directors and officers as well as selected employees. The options gave the option grantees the right to buy PyroGenesis stock at a price of $0.30 per share. PyroGenesis shares are listed on the Toronto Venture Exchange. The granting of stock options gives PyroGenesis a way to both reward and retain key employees, while also potentially increasing its equity base. Whether your next job is with a high-tech firm, a financial service company, or a manufacturer, you will probably receive stock options, so it's important that you understand them.

In a typical grant, you receive options allowing you to purchase shares of stock at a fixed price, called the strike price or exercise price, on or before a stated expiration date. Most plans have a vesting period, during which you can't exercise the options. For example, suppose you are granted 1,000 options with a strike price of $50, an expiration date 10 years from now, and a vesting period of 3 years. Even if the stock price rises above $50 during the first 3 years, you can't exercise the options because of the vesting requirement. After 3 years, if you are still with the company, you have the right to exercise the options. For example, if the stock goes up to $110, you could pay the company $50(1,000) = $50,000 and receive 1,000 shares of stock worth $110,000. However, if you don't exercise the options within 10 years, they will expire and thus be worthless.

Even though the vesting requirement prevents you from exercising the options the moment they are granted to you, the options clearly have some immediate value. Therefore, if you are choosing between different job offers where options are involved, you will need a way to determine the value of the alternative options. This chapter explains how to value options, so read on.

There are two fundamental approaches to valuing assets. The first is the *discounted cashflow* (DCF) approach, which we covered in previous chapters: An asset's value is the present value of its cash flows. The second is the *option pricing* approach. It is important that every manager understands the basic principles of option pricing for the following reasons. First, many projects allow managers to make strategic or tactical changes in plans as market conditions change. The existence of these "embedded options" often means the difference between a successful project and a failure. Understanding basic financial options can help you manage the value inherent in these real options. Second, many companies use derivatives to manage risk; many derivatives are types of financial options, so an understanding of basic financial options is necessary before tackling derivatives. Third, option pricing theory provides insights into the optimal debt/equity choice, especially when convertible securities are involved. And fourth, knowing about financial options will help you understand any employee stock options that you receive.

The textbook's website contains an *Excel* file that will guide you through the chapter's calculations. The file for this chapter is *Ch 19 Tool Kit.xlsx*, and we encourage you to open the file and follow along as you read the chapter. **www.nelson.com/ brigham3ce**

19.1 Overview of Financial Options

In general, an **option** is a contract that gives its owner the right to buy (or sell) an asset at some predetermined price within a specified period of time. However, there are many types of options and option markets.[1] Consider the options reported in Table 19-1, which is an extract from a Listed Options Quotations table as it might appear on a Web site or in a daily newspaper.[2] The first column reports the closing stock price. For example, the table shows that BlackBerry Limited (BB) stock price closed at $12.44 on March 9, 2015.

A **call option** gives its owner the right to *buy* a share of stock at a fixed price, which is called the **strike price** (sometimes called the **exercise price** because it is the price at which you exercise the option). A **put option** gives its owner the right to *sell* a share of stock at a fixed strike price. For example, the first row in Table 19-1 is for BB's options that have a $12 strike price. Observe that the table has columns for call options and for put options with this strike price.

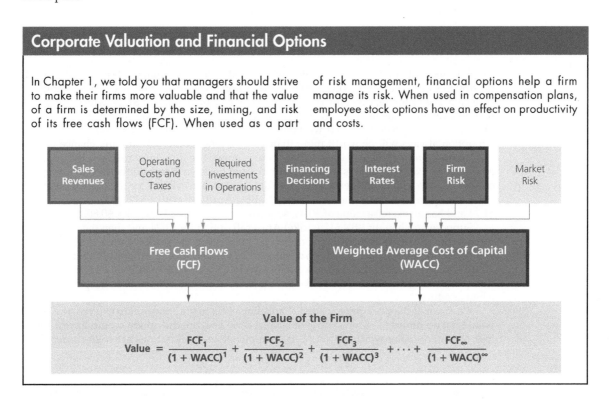

Corporate Valuation and Financial Options

In Chapter 1, we told you that managers should strive to make their firms more valuable and that the value of a firm is determined by the size, timing, and risk of its free cash flows (FCF). When used as a part of risk management, financial options help a firm manage its risk. When used in compensation plans, employee stock options have an effect on productivity and costs.

Value of the Firm

$$\text{Value} = \frac{FCF_1}{(1 + WACC)^1} + \frac{FCF_2}{(1 + WACC)^2} + \frac{FCF_3}{(1 + WACC)^3} + \cdots + \frac{FCF_\infty}{(1 + WACC)^\infty}$$

---

[1] For an in-depth treatment of options, see Don M. Chance and Robert Brooks, *An Introduction to Derivatives and Risk Management*, 8th ed. (Mason, OH: Southwestern, Cengage Learning, 2010), or John C. Hull, *Options, Futures, and Other Derivatives*, 9th ed. (Upper Saddle River, NJ: Pearson, 2015).
[2] For example at the TMX Montreal Exchange website www.m-x.ca.

TABLE 19-1   Listed Options Quotations for March 9, 2015

Closing Price	Strike Price	CALLS–LAST QUOTE			PUTS–LAST QUOTE		
		March	April	June	March	April	June
BlackBerry Limited (BB)							
12.44	12	0.72	1.24	1.71	0.24	0.77	1.32
12.44	13	0.23	0.75	1.27	0.80	1.32	1.82
12.44	14	0.15	0.45	0.95	1.70	2.03	2.36

Source: TMX Montreal Exchange www.m-x.ca

Each option has an **expiration date,** after which the option may not be exercised. Table 19-1 reports data for options that expire in March, April, and June.[3] If the option can be exercised any time before the expiration, it is called an **American option;** if it can be exercised only on its expiration date, it is a **European option.** All of BB's options are American options. The first row shows that BB has a call option with a strike price of $12 that expires on March 20 (the third Friday in March 2015 is the 20th). The quoted price for this option is $0.72.[4]

When the current stock price is greater than the strike price, the option is **in-the-money.** For example, BB's $12 (strike) March call option is in-the-money by $12.44 − $12 = $0.44. Thus, if the option were immediately exercised, it would have a payoff of $0.44. On the other hand, BB's $14 (strike) March call is **out-of-the-money** because the current $12.44 stock price is below the $14 strike price. Obviously, you currently would not want to exercise this option by paying the $14 strike price for a share of stock selling for $12.44. Therefore, the **exercise value,** which is any profit from immediately exercising an option, is[5]

$$\text{Exercise value} = \text{MAX}[\text{Current price of the stock} - \text{Strike price, 0}] \qquad (19\text{-}1)$$

An American option's price always will be greater than (or equal to) its exercise value. If the option's price were less, you could buy the option and immediately exercise it, reaping a sure gain. For example, BB's April call with a $12 strike price sells for $1.24, which is greater than its exercise value of $0.44. Also, BB's out-of-the-money April call with a strike price of $14 sells for $0.45 even though it would be worthless if it had to be exercised immediately. An option always will be worth more than zero as long as there is still any chance it will end up in-the-money: Where there is life, there is hope! The difference between the option's price and its exercise value is called the **time value** because it represents the extra amount over the option's immediate exercise value that a purchaser will pay for the chance the stock price will appreciate over time.[6] For example, BB's April call with a $12 strike price sells for $1.24 and has an exercise value of $0.44, so its time value is $1.24 − $0.44 = $0.80.

Suppose you bought BB's $12 (strike) April call option for $1.24 and then the stock price increased to $15. If you exercised the option by purchasing the stock for the $12 strike price, you could immediately sell the share of stock at its market price of $15, resulting in a payoff of $15 − $12 = $3. Notice that the stock itself had a return of 20.6% = ($15 − $12.44)/$12.44, but the option's return was 141.99% = ($3 − $1.28)/$1.28. Thus, the option offers the possibility of a higher return.

However, if the stock price fell to $11 and stayed there until the option expired, the stock would have a return of −$1.6% = ($11.00 − $12.44)/$12.44, but the option would have a 100% loss (it would expire worthless). As this example shows, call options are a lot riskier than

---

[3]The expiration date for listed stock options is the third Friday of the expiration month.
[4]Option contracts are generally written in 100-share multiples, but to reduce confusion we focus on the cost and payoffs of a single option.
[5]MAX means choose the maximum. For example, MAX[15, 0] = 15 and MAX[−10, 0] = 0.
[6]Among traders, an option's market price is also called its "premium." This is particularly confusing because for all other securities the word *premium* means the excess of the market price over some base price. To avoid confusion, we will not use the word *premium* to refer to the option price.

stocks. This works to your advantage if the stock price goes up but to your disadvantage if the stock price falls.

Suppose you bought BB's April put option (with a strike price of $12) for $0.77 and then the stock price fell to $10. You could buy a share of stock for $10 and exercise the put option, which would allow you to sell the share of stock at its strike price of $12. Your payoff from exercising the put would be $2 = $12 − $10. Shareholders would lose money because the stock price fell, but a put holder would make money. In this example, your rate of return would be 159.7% = ($2 − $0.77)/$0.77. So if you think a stock price is going to fall, you can make money by purchasing a put option. On the other hand, if the stock price doesn't fall below the strike price of $12 before the put expires, you would lose 100% of your investment in the put option.[7]

In Canada, options are traded on the TMX Montreal Exchange. Existing options can be traded in the secondary market in much the same way that existing shares of stock are traded in secondary markets. But unlike new shares of stock that are issued by corporations, new options can be "issued" by investors. This is called **writing** an option.

For example, you could write a call option and sell it to some other investor. You would receive cash from the option buyer at the time you wrote the option, but you would be obligated to sell a share of stock at the strike price if the option buyer later decided to exercise the option.[8] Thus, each option has two parties, the writer and the buyer, with the Montreal Exchange (or some other exchange) acting as an intermediary. Other than commissions, the writer's profits are exactly opposite those of the buyer. An investor who writes call options against stock held in his or her portfolio is said to be selling **covered options.** Options sold without the stock to back them up are called **naked options.**

In addition to options on individual stocks, options are also available on several stock indexes such as the S&P/TSX60 Index and the S&P TSX Energy Index. Index options permit investors to hedge (or bet) on a rise or fall in the general market as well as on individual stocks.

The leverage involved in option trading makes it possible for speculators with just a few dollars to make a fortune almost overnight. Also, investors with sizable portfolios can sell options against their stocks and earn the value of the option (less brokerage commissions) even if the stock's price remains constant. Most important, though, options can be used to create *hedges* that protect the value of an individual stock or portfolio.

Most options are generally written for 6 months or less, but some options are written that expire in one, two, or even three years. These long-term options are listed on exchanges and are available on both individual stocks as well as stock indexes. Options that expire in one year cost about twice as much as the matching 3-month option, but because of their much longer time to expiration, long-term options provide buyers with more potential for gains and offer better long-term protection for a portfolio.

Corporations on whose stocks the options are written have nothing to do with the option market. Corporations do not raise money in the option market, nor do they have any direct transactions in it. Moreover, option holders do not vote for corporate directors or receive dividends. There have been studies as to whether option trading stabilizes or destabilizes the stock market and whether this activity helps or hinders corporations seeking to raise new capital. The studies have not been conclusive, but research on the impact of option trading is ongoing.

CONCEPT REVIEW

1. What is an option? A call option? A put option?
2. Define a call option's exercise value. Why is the market price of a call option usually above its exercise value?
3. Brighton Memory's stock is currently trading at $50 a share. A call option on the stock with a $35 strike price currently sells for $21. What is the exercise value of the call option? (Check Figure: $15.00) What is the time value? (Check Figure: $6.00)

---

[7]Most investors don't actually exercise an option prior to expiration. If they want to cash in the option's profit or cut its losses, they sell the option to some other investor. As you will see later in the chapter, the cash flow from selling an American option before its expiration is always greater than (or equal to) the profit from exercising the option.
[8]Your broker would require collateral to ensure that you kept this obligation.

Financial Reporting for Employee Stock Options

When granted to executives and other employees, options are a "hybrid" form of compensation. At some companies, especially small ones, option grants may be a substitute for cash wages: Employees are willing to take lower cash salaries if they have options. Options also provide an incentive for employees to work harder. Whether issued to motivate employees or to conserve cash, options clearly have value at the time they are granted, and they transfer wealth from existing shareholders to employees to the extent that they do not reduce cash expenditures or increase employee productivity enough to offset their value at the time of issue.

Companies like the fact that an option grant requires no immediate cash expenditure, although it might dilute shareholder wealth if it is exercised later. Employees, and especially CEOs, like the potential wealth they receive when they are granted options. When option grants were relatively small, they didn't show up on investors' radar screens. However, as the high-tech sector began making mega-grants in the 1990s, and as other industries followed suit, shareholders began to realize that large grants were making some CEOs filthy rich at the shareholders' expense.

Before 2005, option grants were barely visible in companies' financial reports. Even though such grants are clearly a wealth transfer to employees, companies were required only to footnote the grants and could ignore them when reporting their income statements and balance sheets. The International Accounting Standards Board now requires companies to show option grants as an expense on the income statement. To do this, the value of the options is estimated at the time of the grant and then expensed during the vesting period, which is the amount of time the employee must wait before being allowed to exercise the options. For example, if the initial value is $100 million and the vesting period is 2 years, the company would report a $50 million expense for each of the next 2 years. This approach isn't perfect, because the grant is not a cash expense; nor does the approach take into account changes in the option's value after the initial grant. However, it does make the option grant more visible to investors, which is a good thing.

19.2 The Single-Period Binomial Option Pricing Approach

We can use a model like the Capital Asset Pricing Model (CAPM) to calculate the required return on a stock and then use that required return to discount its expected future cash flows to find its value. No such model exists for the required return on options, so we must use a different approach to find an option's value. In Section 19-3 we describe the Black-Scholes option pricing model, but in this section we explain the binomial option pricing model. The idea behind this model is different from that of the DCF model used for stock valuation. Instead of discounting cash flows at a required return to obtain a price, as we did with the stock valuation model, we will use the option, shares of stock, and the risk-free rate to construct a portfolio whose value we already know and then deduce the option's price from this portfolio's value.

The following sections describe and apply the binomial option pricing model to Western Fabrications, a manufacturer of plastic products. Call options exist that permit the holder to buy 1 share of Western at a strike price, X, of $35. Western's options will expire at the end of 6 months (t is the number of years until expiration, so t = 0.5 for Western's options). Western's stock price, P, is currently $40 per share. Given this background information, we will use the binomial model to determine the call option's value. The first step is to determine the option's possible payoffs, as described in the next section.

Payoffs in a Single-Period Binomial Model

In general, the time until expiration can be divided into many periods, with n denoting the number of periods. But in a single-period model, which we describe in this section, there is only one period. We assume that, at the end of the period, the stock's price can take on only one of two possible values, so this is called the **binomial approach.** For this example, Western's stock will either go up (u) by a factor of 1.25 or go down (d) by a factor of 0.80. If we were considering a riskier stock, then we would have assumed a wider range of ending prices; we will show how to estimate this range later in the chapter. If we let u = 1.25 and d = 0.80, then the ending stock price will be either P(u) = $40(1.25) = $50 or P(d) = $40(0.80) = $32. Figure 19-1 illustrates the stock's possible price paths and contains additional information about the call option that is explained in the text that follows.

When the option expires at the end of the year, Western's stock will sell for either $50 or $32. As shown in Figure 19-1, if the stock goes up to $50 then the option will have a payoff, C_u, of $15 at expiration because the option is in-the-money: $50 – $35 = $15. If the stock price goes down to $32, then the option's payoff, C_d, will be zero because the option is out-of-the-money.

*See **Ch19 Tool Kit.xls** on the textbook's website.*

The Hedge Portfolio Approach

Suppose we created a portfolio by writing 1 call option and purchasing 1 share of stock. As Figure 19-1 shows, if the stock price goes up then our portfolio's stock will be worth $50 but we will owe $15 on the option, so our portfolio's net payoff is $35 = $50 – $15. If the stock price goes down then our portfolio's stock will be worth only $32, but the amount we owe on the written option also will fall to zero, leaving the portfolio's net payoff at $32. The portfolio's end-of-period price range is smaller than if we had just owned the stock, so writing the call option reduces the portfolio's price risk. Taking this further: Is it possible for us to choose the number of shares held by our portfolio so that it will have the same net payoff whether the stock goes up or down? If so, then our portfolio is hedged and will have a riskless payoff when the option expires. Therefore, it is called a **hedge portfolio.**

We are not really interested in investing in the hedge portfolio, but we want to use it to help us determine the value of the option. Notice that if the hedge portfolio has a riskless net payoff when the option expires, then we can find the present value of this payoff by discounting it at the risk-free rate. Our current portfolio value must equal this present value, which allows us to determine the option's value. The following example illustrates the steps in this approach.

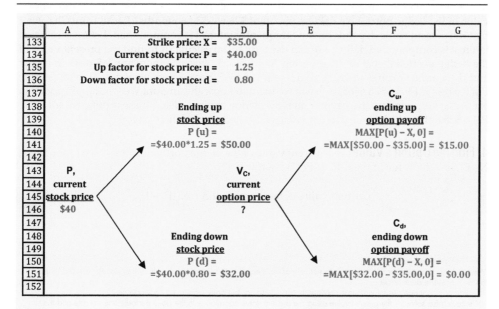

1. Find N$_s$, the Number of Shares of Stock in the Hedge Portfolio

We want the portfolio's payoff to be the same whether the stock goes up or down. If we write 1 call option and buy N$_s$ shares of stock, then the portfolio's stock will be worth N$_s$(P)(u) should the stock price go up, so its net payoff will be N$_s$(P)(u) - C$_u$. The portfolio's stock will be worth N$_s$(P)(d) if the stock price goes down, so its net payoff will be N$_s$(P)(d) - C$_d$. Setting these portfolio payoffs equal to one another and then solving for N$_s$ yields

$$N_s = \frac{C_u - C_d}{P(u) - P(d)} = \frac{C_u - C_d}{P(u - d)} \qquad (19\text{-}2)$$

For Western, the hedge portfolio has 0.83333 share of stock:[9]

$$N_s = \frac{C_u - C_d}{P(u) - P(d)} = \frac{\$15\ -\ \$0}{\$50\ -\ \$32} = 0.8333$$

2. Find the Hedge Portfolio's Payoff

Our next step is to find the hedge portfolio's payoff when the stock price goes up (you will get the same result if instead you find the portfolio's payoff when the stock price goes down). Recall that the hedge portfolio has N$_s$ shares of stock and that we have written the call option, so the call option's payoff must be subtracted:

$$
\begin{aligned}
\text{Hedge portfolio's payoff if stock is up} &= N_s P(u) - C_u \\
&= 0.83333(\$50) - \$15 \\
&= \$26.6665
\end{aligned}
$$

$$
\begin{aligned}
\text{Hedge portfolio's payoff if stock is down} &= N_s P(d) - C_d \\
&= 0.83333(\$32) - \$0 \\
&= \$26.6665
\end{aligned}
$$

Figure 19-2 illustrates the payoffs of the hedge portfolio.

3. Find the Present Value of the Hedge Portfolio's Payoff

Because the hedge portfolio's payoff is riskless, the current value of the hedge portfolio must be equal to the present value of its riskless payoff. Suppose the nominal annual risk-free rate, r$_{RF}$, is 8%. What is the present value of the hedge portfolio's riskless payoff of $26.6665 in 6 months? Recall from Chapter 4 that the present value depends on how frequently interest is compounded. Let's assume that interest is compounded daily.[10] We can use a financial calculator to find the present value of the hedge portfolio's payoff by entering N = 0.5(365), because there are 365 days in a year and the contract expires in half a year; I/YR = 8/365, because we want a daily interest rate; PMT = 0; and FV = –$26.6665, because we want to know the amount we would take today in exchange for giving up the payoff when the option expires. Using these inputs, we solve for PV = $25.6210, which is the present value of the hedge portfolio's payoff.[11]

*See **Ch19 Tool Kit.xlsx** on the textbook's website.*

4. Find the Option's Value

The current value of the hedge portfolio is the value of the stock, N$_S$(P), less the value of the call option we wrote:

$$\text{Current value of hedge portfolio} = N_S(P) - V_c$$

---

[9]An easy way to remember this formula is to notice that N$_s$ is equal to the range in possible option payoffs divided by the range in possible stock prices.

[10]Option pricing models usually assume continuous compounding, but daily compounding works well.

[11]We could also solve for the present value using the present value equation with the daily periodic interest rate and the number of daily periods: PV = $26.6665/(1 + 0.08/365)$^{0.5(365)}$ = $25.6210.

FIGURE 19-2 Hedge Portfolio with Riskless Payoffs

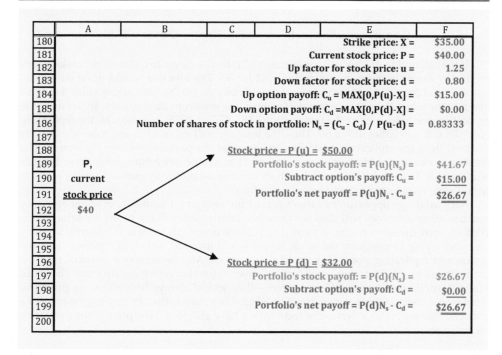

	A	B	C	D	E	F
180					**Strike price: X =**	$35.00
181					**Current stock price: P =**	$40.00
182					**Up factor for stock price: u =**	1.25
183					**Down factor for stock price: d =**	0.80
184					**Up option payoff: C_u = MAX[0,P(u)-X] =**	$15.00
185					**Down option payoff: C_d =MAX[0,P(d)-X] =**	$0.00
186			**Number of shares of stock in portfolio: N_s = (C_u - C_d) / P(u-d) =**			0.83333
187						
188			**Stock price = P (u) = $50.00**			
189	**P,**			**Portfolio's stock payoff: = P(u)(N_s) =**		$41.67
190	**current**			**Subtract option's payoff: C_u =**		$15.00
191	**stock price**			**Portfolio's net payoff = P(u)N_s - C_u =**		$26.67
192	**$40**					
193						
194						
195						
196			**Stock price = P (d) = $32.00**			
197				**Portfolio's stock payoff: = P(d)(N_s) =**		$26.67
198				**Subtract option's payoff: C_d =**		$0.00
199				**Portfolio's net payoff = P(d)N_s - C_d =**		$26.67
200						

Because the payoff is riskless, the current value of the hedge portfolio must also equal the present value of the riskless payoff:

$$\text{Current value of hedge portfolio} = \text{Present value of riskless payoff}$$

Substituting for the current value of the hedge portfolio, we get:

$$N_s(P) - V_C = \text{Present value of riskless payoff}$$

Solving for the call option's value, we get

$$V_C = N_s(P) - \text{Present value of riskless payoff}$$

For Western's option, this is

$$V_c = 0.83333(\$40) - \$25.621$$
$$= \$7.71$$

Hedge Portfolios and Replicating Portfolios

In our previous derivation of the call option's value, we combined an investment in the stock with writing a call option to create a risk-free investment. We can modify this approach and create a portfolio that replicates the call option's payoffs. For example, suppose we formed a portfolio by purchasing 0.83333 shares of Western's stock and borrowing $25.621 at the risk-free rate (this is equivalent to selling a T-bill short). In 6 months, we would repay the future value of a $25.621, compounded daily at the risk-free rate. Using a financial calculator, input N = 0.5(365), I/YR = 8/365, PV = –$25.621, and solve for FV = $26.6665.[12] If the stock goes up, our net payoff would be 0.83333($50) – $26.6665 = $15.00. If the stock goes down, our net payoff would be 0.83333($32) – $26.6665 = $0. The portfolio's payoffs are exactly equal to

---

[12]Alternatively, use the present value equation with daily compounding: $25.621(1 + 0.08/365)^{365(0.5/1)}$ = $26.6665.

the option's payoffs as shown in Figure 19-1, so our portfolio of 0.83333 shares of stock and the $25.621 that we borrowed would exactly replicate the option's payoffs. Therefore, this is called a **replicating portfolio.** Our cost to create this portfolio is the cost of the stock less the amount we borrowed:

$$\text{Cost of replicating portfolio} = 0.83333(\$40) - \$25.621 = \$7.71$$

If the call option did not sell for exactly $7.71, then a clever investor could make a sure profit. For example, suppose the option sold for $8. The investor would write an option, which would provide $8 of cash now but would obligate the investor to pay either $15 or $0 in 6 months when the option expires. However, the investor could use the $8 to create the replicating portfolio, leaving the investor with $8 − $7.71 = $0.29. In 6 months, the replicating portfolio will pay either $15 or $0. Thus, the investor isn't exposed to any risk—the payoffs received from the replicating portfolio exactly offset the payoffs owed on the option. The investor uses none of his own money, has no risk, has no net future obligations, but has $0.29 in cash. This is **arbitrage,** and if such an arbitrage opportunity existed then the investor would scale it up by writing thousands of options.[13]

Such arbitrage opportunities don't persist for long in a reasonably efficient economy because other investors will also see the opportunity and will try to do the same thing. With so many investors trying to write (i.e., sell) the option, its price will fall; with so many investors trying to purchase the stock, its price will increase. This will continue until the option and replicating portfolio have identical prices. And because our financial markets are really quite efficient, you would never observe the derivative security and the replicating portfolio trading for different prices—they would always have the same price and there would be no arbitrage opportunities. What this means is that, by finding the price of a portfolio that replicates a derivative security, we have also found the price of the derivative security itself!

CONCEPT REVIEW

1. Describe how a risk-free hedge portfolio can be created using stocks and options.
2. How can such a portfolio be used to help estimate a call option's value?
3. What is a replicating portfolio, and how is it used to find the value of a derivative security?
4. What is arbitrage?
5. Lett Incorporated's stock price is now $50, but it is expected either to rise by a factor of 1.5 or fall by a factor of 0.7 by the end of the year. There is a call option on Lett's stock with a strike price of $55 and an expiration date 1 year from now. What are the stock's possible prices at the end of the year? ($75 or $35) What is the call option's payoff if the stock price goes up? ($20) If the stock price goes down? ($0) If we sell 1 call option, how many shares of Lett's stock must we buy to create a riskless hedged portfolio consisting of the option position and the stock? (0.5) What is the payoff of this portfolio? ($17.50) If the annual risk-free rate is 6%, then how much is the riskless portfolio worth today (assuming daily compounding)? ($16.48) What is the current value of the call option? ($8.52)

19.3 The Black-Scholes Option Pricing Model (OPM)

The **Black-Scholes option pricing model (OPM),** developed in 1973, helped give rise to the rapid growth in options trading. This model has been programmed into many handheld and Web-based calculators, and it is widely used by option traders.

OPM Assumptions and Results

In deriving their model to value call options, Fischer Black and Myron Scholes made the following assumptions.

---

[13]If the option sold for less than the replicating portfolio, the investor would raise cash by shorting the portfolio and use the cash to purchase the option, again resulting in arbitrage profits.

1. The stock underlying the call option provides no dividends or other distributions during the life of the option.
2. There are no transaction costs for buying or selling either the stock or the option.
3. The short-term, risk-free interest rate is known and is constant during the life of the option.
4. Any purchaser of a security may borrow any fraction of the purchase price at the short-term, risk-free interest rate.
5. Short selling is permitted, and the short seller will receive immediately the full cash proceeds of today's price for a security sold short.
6. The call option can be exercised only on its expiration date.
7. Trading in all securities takes place continuously, and the stock price moves randomly.

The derivation of the Black-Scholes model rests on the same concepts as the binomial model, except time is divided into such small increments that stock prices change continuously. The Black-Scholes model for call options consists of the following three equations:

$$V_C = P[N(d_1)] - Xe^{-r_{RF}t}[N(d_2)] \tag{19-3}$$

$$d_1 = \frac{\ln(P/X) + [r_{RF} + (\sigma^2/2)]t}{\sigma\sqrt{t}} \tag{19-4}$$

$$d_2 = d_1 - \sigma\sqrt{t} \tag{19-5}$$

The variables used in the Black-Scholes model are explained below.

V_c = Current value of the call option.

P = Current price of the underlying stock.

$N(d_i)$ = Probability that a deviation less than d_i will occur in a standard normal distribution. Thus, $N(d_s)$ and $N(d_2)$ represent areas under a standard normal distribution function.

X = Strike price of the option.

$e \approx 2.7183$.

r_{RF} = Risk-free interest rate.[14]

t = Time until the option expires (the option period).

$\ln(P/X)$ = Natural logarithm of P/X.

σ = Standard deviation of the rate of return on the stock.

The value of the option is a function of five variables: (1) P, the stock's price; (2) t, the option's time to expiration; (3) X, the strike price; (4) σ, the standard deviation of the underlying stock; and (5) r_{RF}, the risk-free rate. We do not derive the Black-Scholes model—the derivation involves some extremely complicated mathematics that go far beyond the scope of this text. However, it is not difficult to use the model. Under the assumptions set forth previously, if the option price is different from the one found by Equation 19-3, then this would provide the opportunity for arbitrage profits, which would force the option price back to the value indicated by the model. As we noted earlier, the Black-Scholes model is widely used by traders because actual option prices conform reasonably well to values derived from the model.

---

[14]The correct process to estimate the risk-free rate for use in the Black-Scholes model for an option with 6 months to expiration is to find the annual nominal rate (compounded continuously) that has the same effective annual rate as a 6-month T-bill. For example, suppose a 6-month T-bill is yielding a 6-month periodic rate of 4.081%. The risk-free rate to use in the Black-Scholes model is $T_{RF} = \ln(1 + 0.0408)/0.5 = 8\%$. Under continuous compounding, a nominal rate of 8% produces an effective rate of yields $e^{0.08} - 1 = 8.33\%$. This is the same effective rate yielded by the T-bill: $(1+0.0408)^2 - 1 = 8.33\%$. The same approach can be applied for options with different expiration periods. We will provide the appropriate risk-free rate for all problems and examples.

Application of the Black-Scholes Option Pricing Model to a Call Option

The current stock price (P), the exercise price (X), and the time to maturity (t) can all be obtained from a newspaper, such as *The Wall Street Journal*, or from the Internet, such as the CBOE's website. The risk-free rate (r_{RF}) is the yield on a Treasury bill with a maturity equal to the option expiration date. The annualized standard deviation of stock returns (σ) can be estimated from daily stock prices. First, find the stock return for each trading day for a sample period, such as each trading day of the past year. Second, estimate the variance of the daily stock returns. Third, multiply this estimated daily variance by the number of trading days in a year, which is approximately 250.[15] Take the square root of the annualized variance, and the result is an estimate of the annualized standard deviation.

We will use the Black-Scholes model to estimate Western's call option, which we discussed previously. Here are the inputs:

$$P = \$40$$
$$X = \$35$$
$$t = 6 \text{ months (0.5 years)}$$
$$r_{RF} = 8.0\% = 0.080$$
$$\sigma = 31.557\% = 0.31557$$

See Ch19 Tool Kit.xls on the textbook's website.

Given this information, we first estimate d_1 and d_2 from Equations 19-4 and 19-5:

$$d_1 = \frac{\ln(\$40/\$35) + [0.08 + ((0.31557^2)/2)](0.5)}{0.31557\sqrt{0.5}}$$

$$= \frac{0.13353 + 0.064896}{0.22314} = 0.8892$$

$$d_2 = d_1 - 0.31557\sqrt{0.5} = 0.6661$$

Note that $N(d_1)$ and $N(d_2)$ represent areas under a standard normal distribution function. The easiest way to calculate this value is with *Excel*. For example, we can use the function **=NORMSDIST(0.8892),** which returns a value of $N(d_1) = N(0.8892) = 0.8131$. Similarly, the **NORMSDIST** function returns a value of $N(d_2) = 0.7473$.[16] We can use those values to solve Equation 19-3:

$$V_c = \$40[N(0.8892)] \ \$35e^{-(0.08)(0.5)}[N(0.6661)]$$
$$= \$7.39$$

Thus, the value of the option is $7.39.

The Five Factors That Affect Call Option Prices

See Ch19 Tool Kit.xls on the textbook's website.

The Black-Scholes model has five inputs, so there are five factors that affect call option prices. As we will see in the next section, these five inputs also affect put option prices. Figure 19-3 shows how three of Western Fabrication's call options are affected by Western's stock price (all three options have a strike price of $35). The three options expire in 1 year, in 6 months (0.5 years, like the option in our example), and in 3 months (or 0.25 years), respectively.

Figure 19-3 offers several insights regarding option valuation. Notice that for all stock prices in the figure, the call option prices are always above the exercise value.

---

[15]If stocks traded every day of the year, then each return covers a 24-hour period; you would simply estimate the variance of the 1-day returns with your sample of daily returns and then multiply this estimate by 365 for an estimate of the annual variance. However, stocks don't trade every day because of weekends and holidays. If you measure returns from the close of one trading day until the close of the next trading day (called "trading-day returns"), then some returns are for 1 day (such as Thursday close to Friday close) and some are for longer periods, like the 3-day return from Friday close to Monday close. It might seem reasonable that the 3-day returns have 3 times the variance of a 1-day return and should be treated differently when estimating the daily return variance, but that is not the case. It turns out that the 3-day return over a weekend has only slightly higher variance than a 1-day return (perhaps because of less new information on non-weekdays), and so it is reasonable to treat all of the trading-day returns the same. With roughly 250 trading days in a year, most analysts take the estimate of the variance of daily returns and multiply by 250 (or 252, depending on the year, to be more precise) to obtain an estimate of the annual variance.

[16]If you do not have access to *Excel*, then you can use the table in Appendix C. For example, the table shows that the value for $d_1 = 0.88$ is $0.5000 + 0.3106 = 0.8106$ and that the value for $d_1 = 0.89$ is $0.5000 + 0.3133 = 0.8133$, so $N(0.8892)$ lies between 0.8106 and 0.8133. You could interpolate to find a closer value, but we suggest using *Excel* instead.

FIGURE
19-3 Western Fabrication's Call Options with a Strike Price of $35

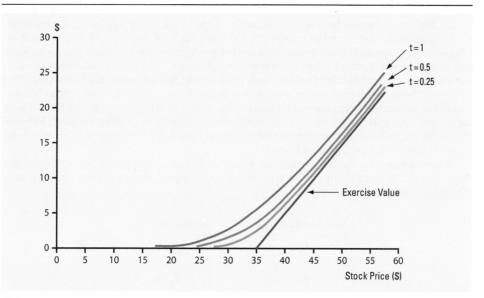

If this were not true, then an investor could purchase the call and immediately exercise it for a quick profit.[17]

Also, when the stock price falls far below the strike price, call option prices fall toward zero. In other words, calls lose value as they become more and more out-of-the-money. When the stock price greatly exceeds the strike price, call option prices fall toward the exercise value. Thus, for very high stock prices, call options tend to move up and down by about the same amount as does the stock price.

Call option prices increase if the stock price increases. This is because the strike price is fixed, so an increase in stock price increases the chance that the option will be in-the-money at expiration. Although we don't show it in the figure, an increase in the strike price would obviously cause a decrease in the call option's value because higher strike prices mean a lower chance of being in-the-money at expiration.

The 1-year call option always has a greater value than the 6-month call option, which always has a greater value than the 3-month call option; thus, the longer a call option has until expiration, the greater its value. Here is the intuition for that result. With a long time until expiration, the stock price has a chance to increase well above the strike price by the expiration date. Of course, with a long time until expiration, there is also a chance that the stock price will fall far below the strike price by expiration. But there is a big difference in payoffs for being well in-the-money versus far out-of-the-money. Every dollar that the stock price is above the strike price means an extra dollar of payoff, but no matter how far the stock price is below the strike price, the payoff is zero. When it comes to a call option, the gain in value due to the chance of finishing well in-the-money with a big payoff more than compensates for the loss in value due to the chance of being far out-of-the money.

How does volatility affect call options? Following are the Black-Scholes model prices for Western's call option with the original inputs except for different standard deviations:

*See **Ch19 Tool Kit.xls** on the textbook's website for all calculations.*

Standard Deviation (σ)	Call Option Price
0.001%	$ 6.37
10.000	6.38
31.557	7.39
40.000	8.07
60.000	9.87
90.000	12.70

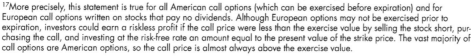

[17]More precisely, this statement is true for all American call options (which can be exercised before expiration) and for European call options written on stocks that pay no dividends. Although European options may not be exercised prior to expiration, investors could earn a riskless profit if the call price were less than the exercise value by selling the stock short, purchasing the call, and investing at the risk-free rate an amount equal to the present value of the strike price. The vast majority of call options are American options, so the call price is almost always above the exercise value.

The first row shows the option price if there is very little stock volatility. Notice that as volatility increases, so does the option price. Therefore, the riskier the underlying security, the more valuable the option. To see why this makes sense, suppose you bought a call option with a strike price equal to the current stock price. If the stock had no risk (which means $\sigma = 0$), then there would be a zero probability of the stock going up, hence a zero probability of making money on the option. On the other hand, if you bought a call option on a higher-volatility stock, there would be a higher probability that the stock would increase well above the strike price by the expiration date. Of course, with higher volatility there also would be a higher probability that the stock price would fall far below the strike price. But as we previously explained, an increase in the price of the stock helps call option holders more than a decrease hurts them: The greater the stock's volatility, the greater the value of the option. This makes options on risky stocks more valuable than those on safer, low-risk stocks. For example, an option on BlackBerry should have a greater value than an otherwise identical option on Royal Bank of Canada.

The risk-free rate also has a relatively small impact on option prices. Shown below are the prices for Western's call option with the original inputs except for the risk-free rate, which is allowed to vary.

See Ch19 Tool Kit.xls on the textbook's website for all calculations.

Risk-Free Rate (r_{RF})	Call Option Price
0%	$6.41
4	6.89
8	7.39
12	7.90
20	8.93

As the risk-free rate increases, the value of the option increases. The principal effect of an increase in r_{RF} is to reduce the present value of the exercise price, which increases the current value of the option. Option prices in general are not very sensitive to interest rate changes, at least not to changes within the ranges normally encountered.

Myron Scholes and Robert Merton (who also was a pioneer in the field of options) were awarded the 1997 Nobel Prize in Economics, and Fischer Black would have been a co-recipient had he still been living. Their work provided analytical tools and methodologies that are widely used to solve many types of financial problems, not just option pricing. Indeed, the entire field of modern risk management is based primarily on their contributions. Although the Black-Scholes model was derived for a European option that can be exercised only on its maturity date, it also applies to American options that don't pay any dividends prior to expiration. The textbooks by Don Chance and Robert Brooks, and John Hull (cited in footnote 1) show adjusted models for dividend-paying stocks.

CONCEPT REVIEW

1. What is the purpose of the Black-Scholes option pricing model?
2. Explain what a "riskless hedge" is and how the riskless hedge concept is used in the Black-Scholes OPM.
3. Describe the effect of a change in each of the following factors on the value of a call option: (1) stock price, (2) exercise price, (3) option life, (4) risk-free rate, and (5) stock return standard deviation (i.e., risk of stock).
4. Using an Excel worksheet, what is the value of a call option with these data: P = $35, X = $25, r_{RF} = 6%, t = 0.5 (6 months), and σ = 0.6? (Check Figure: $12.05)

19.4 The Valuation of Put Options

A put option gives its owner the right to sell a share of stock. Suppose a stock pays no dividends and a put option written on the stock can be exercised only upon its expiration date. What is the put's value? Rather than reinventing the wheel, we can establish the price of a put relative to the price of a call.

Put-Call Parity

Consider the payoffs for two portfolios at expiration date T, as shown in Table 19-2. The first portfolio consists of a put option and a share of stock; the second has a call option (with the same strike price and expiration date as the put option) and some cash. The amount of cash is equal to the present value of the strike price discounted at the continuously compounded risk-free rate, which is $Xe^{-r_{RF}t}$. At expiration, the value of this cash will equal the strike price, X.

If P_T, the stock price at expiration date T, is less than X, the strike price, when the option expires, then the value of the put option at expiration is $X - P_T$. Therefore, the value of Portfolio 1, which contains the put and the stock, is equal to X minus P_T plus P_T, or just X. For Portfolio 2, the value of the call is zero at expiration (because the call option is out-of-the-money), and the value of the cash is X, for a total value of X. Notice that both portfolios have the same payoffs if the stock price is less than the strike price.

What if the stock price is greater than the strike price at expiration? In this case, the put is worth nothing, so the payoff of Portfolio 1 is equal to P_T, the stock price at expiration. The call option is worth $P_T - X$, and the cash is worth X, so the payoff of Portfolio 2 is P_T. Hence the payoffs of the two portfolios are equal regardless of whether the stock price is below or above the strike price.

If the two portfolios have identical payoffs, then they must have identical values. This is known as the **put-call parity relationship:**

$$\text{Put option} + \text{Stock} = \text{Call option} + \text{PV of exercise price.}$$

If V_c is the Black-Scholes value of the call option, then the value of a put is[18]

$$\text{Put option} = V_c - P + Xe^{-r_{RF}t} \tag{19-6}$$

For example, consider a put option written on the stock discussed in the previous section. If the put option has the same exercise price and expiration date as the call, then its price is

$$\text{Put option} = \$7.39 - \$40 + \$35\,e^{-0.08(0.5)}$$
$$= \$7.39 - \$40 + \$33.63 = \$1.02$$

It is also possible to modify the Black-Scholes call option formula to obtain a put option formula:

$$\text{Put option} = P[N(d_1)-1] - Xe^{-r_{RF}t}[N(d_2)-1] \tag{19-7}$$

The only difference between this formula for puts and the formula for calls is the subtraction of 1 from $N(d_1)$ and $N(d_2)$ in the call option formula.

TABLE 19-2 Portfolio Payoffs

	Payoff at Expiration If:	
	$P_T < X$	$P_T \geq X$
Put	$X - P_T$	0
Stock	P_T	P_T
Portfolio 1:	X	P_T
Call	0	$P_T - X$
Cash	X	X
Portfolio 2:	X	P_T

---

[18]This model cannot be applied to an American put option or to a European option on a stock that pays a dividend prior to expiration. For an explanation of valuation approaches in these situations, see the books by Chance and Brooks or Hull cited in footnote 1.

The Five Factors That Affect Put Option Prices

Just like with call options, the exercise price, the underlying stock price, the time to expiration, the stock's standard deviation, and the risk-free rate affect the price of a put option. Because a put pays off when the stock price declines below the exercise price, the impact of the underlying stock price and exercise price and risk-free rate on the put are opposite that of the call option. That is, put prices are higher when the stock price is lower and when the exercise price is higher. Put prices are also lower when the risk-free rate is higher, mostly because a higher risk-free rate reduces the present value of the exercise price, which for a put is a payout to the option holder when the option is exercised.

On the other hand, put options are affected by the stock's standard deviation just like call options. Both put and call option prices are higher when the stock's standard deviation is higher. This is true for put options because the higher the standard deviation, the bigger the chance of a large stock price decline and a large put payoff. The effect of the time to maturity on the put option price is indeterminate. A call option is more valuable the longer the maturity, but some puts are more valuable the longer to maturity, and some are less valuable. For example, consider an in-the-money put option (the stock price is below the exercise price) on a stock with a low standard deviation. In this case a longer maturity put option is less valuable than a shorter maturity put option because the longer the time to maturity, the more likely the stock is to grow and erode the put's payoff. But if the stock's standard deviation is high, then the longer maturity put option will be more valuable because the likelihood of the stock declining even more and resulting in a high payoff to the put is greater.

ⓒNCEPT REVIEW

1. In words, what is put-call parity?

2. A put option written on the stock of Taylor Enterprises (TE) has an exercise price of $25 and 6 months remaining until expiration. The risk-free rate is 6%. A call option written on TE has the same exercise price and expiration date as the put option. TE's stock price is $35. If the call option has a price of $12.05, then what is the price (i.e., value) of the put option? (Check Figure: $1.31)

3. Explain why both put and call options are worth more if the stock return standard deviation is higher, but put and call options are affected oppositely by the stock price.

19.5 Applications of Option Pricing in Corporate Finance

Option pricing is used in four major areas of corporate finance: (1) real options analysis for project evaluation and strategic decisions, (2) risk management, (3) capital structure decisions, and (4) compensation plans.

Real Options

Suppose a company has a 1-year proprietary licence to develop a software application for use in a new generation of wireless cellular telephones. Hiring programmers and marketing consultants to complete the project will cost $30 million. The good news is that if consumers love the new cell phones, there will be a tremendous demand for the software. The bad news is that if sales of the new cell phones are low, the software project will be a disaster. Should the company spend the $30 million and develop the software?

Because the company has a licence, it has the option of waiting for a year, at which time it might have a much better insight into market demand for the new cell phones. If demand is high in a year, then the company can spend the $30 million and develop the software. If demand is low, it can avoid losing the $30 million development cost by simply letting the licence expire. Notice that the licence is analogous to a call option: It gives the company the right to buy something (in this case, software for the new cell phones) at a fixed price ($30 million) at any time during the next year. The licence gives the company a **real option,** because the underlying asset (the software) is a real asset and not a financial asset.

There are many other types of real options, including the option to increase capacity at a plant, to expand into new geographical regions, to introduce new products, to switch inputs (such as gas versus oil), to switch outputs (such as producing sedans versus SUVs), and to abandon a project. Many companies now evaluate real options with techniques that are similar to those described earlier in the chapter for pricing financial options.

Risk Management

Suppose a company plans to issue $400 million of bonds in 6 months to pay for a new plant now under construction. The plant will be profitable if interest rates remain at current levels, but if rates rise then it will be unprofitable. To hedge against rising rates, the company could purchase a put option on Government of Canada bonds. If interest rates go up then the company would "lose" because its bonds would carry a high interest rate, but it would have an offsetting gain on its put options. Conversely, if rates fall then the company would "win" when it issues its own low-rate bonds, but it would lose on the put options. By purchasing puts, the company has hedged the risk due to possible interest rate changes that it would otherwise face.

Another example of risk management is a firm that bids on a foreign contract. For example, suppose a winning bid means that the firm will receive a payment of 12 million euros in 9 months. At a current exchange rate of $1.57 per euro, the project would be profitable. But if the exchange rate falls to $1.10 per euro, the project would be a loser. To avoid exchange rate risk, the firm could take a short position in a forward contract that allows it to convert 12 million euros into Canadian dollars at a fixed rate of $1.50 per euro in 9 months, which would still ensure a profitable project. This eliminates exchange rate risk if the firm wins the contract, but what if the firm loses the contract? It would still be obligated to sell 12 million euros at a price of $1.50 per euro, which could be a disaster. For example, if the exchange rate rises to $1.75 per euro, then the firm would have to spend $21 million to purchase 12 million euros at a price of $1.75/€ and then sell the euros for $18 million = ($1.50/€) (€12 million), a loss of $3 million.

To eliminate this risk, the firm could instead purchase a currency put option that allows it to sell 12 million euros in 9 months at a fixed price of $1.50 per euro. If the company wins the bid, it will exercise the put option and sell the 12 million euros for $1.50 per euro if the exchange rate has declined. If the exchange rate hasn't declined, then it will sell the euros on the open market for more than $1.50 and let the option expire. On the other hand, if the firm loses the bid, it has no reason to sell euros and could let the option contract expire. Note, however, that even if the firm doesn't win the contract, it still is gambling on the exchange rate because it owns the put; if the price of euros declines below $1.50, the firm will still make some money on the option. Thus, the company can lock in the future exchange rate if it wins the bid and can avoid any net payment at all if it loses the bid. The total cost in either scenario is equal to the initial cost of the option. In other words, the cost of the option is like insurance that guarantees the exchange rate if the company wins the bid and guarantees no net obligations if it loses the bid.

Many other applications of risk management involve futures contracts and other complex derivatives rather than calls and puts. However, the principles used in pricing derivatives are similar to those used earlier in this chapter for pricing options. Thus, financial options and their valuation techniques play key roles in risk management.

Capital Structure Decisions

Decisions regarding the mix of debt and equity used to finance operations are quite important. One interesting aspect of the capital structure decision is based on option pricing. For example, consider a firm with debt requiring a final principal payment of $60 million in 1 year. If the company's value 1 year from now is $61 million, then it can pay off the debt and have $1 million left for shareholders. If the firm's value is less than $60 million, then it may well file for bankruptcy and turn over its assets to creditors, resulting in shareholders' equity of zero. In other words, the value of the shareholders' equity is analogous to a call option: The equity holders have the right to buy the assets for $60 million (which is the face value of the debt) in 1 year (when the debt matures).

Suppose the firm's owner-managers are considering two projects. One project has very little risk, and it will result in an asset value of either $59 million or $61 million. The other has high risk, and it will result in an asset value of either $20 million or $100 million. Notice that the equity will be worth zero if the assets are worth less than $60 million, so the shareholders will be no worse off if the assets end up at $20 million than if they end up at $59 million. On the other hand, the shareholders would benefit much more if the assets were worth $100 million rather than $61 million. Thus, the owner-managers have an incentive to choose risky projects, which is consistent with an option's value rising with the risk of the underlying asset. Potential lenders recognize this situation, so they build covenants into loan agreements that restrict managers from making excessively risky investments.

Not only does option pricing theory help explain why managers might want to choose risky projects and why debtholders might want restrictive covenants, but options also play a direct role in capital structure choices. For example, a firm could choose to issue convertible debt, which gives bondholders the option to convert their debt into stock if the value of the company turns out to be higher than expected. In exchange for this option, bondholders charge a lower interest rate than for nonconvertible debt. Because owner-managers must share the wealth with convertible-bond holders, they have a smaller incentive to gamble with high-risk projects.

Compensation Plans

Many companies use stock options as a part of their compensation plans. It is important for boards of directors to understand the value of these options before they grant them to employees. For instance, we began this chapter with the example of PyroGenesis, which issued options to its directors and selected employees.

CONCEPT REVIEW

1. Describe four ways that option pricing is used in corporate finance.

Summary

In this chapter we discussed option pricing topics, which included the following.

- **Financial options** are instruments that (1) are created by exchanges rather than firms, (2) are bought and sold primarily by investors, and (3) are of importance to both investors and financial managers.
- The two primary types of financial options are (1) **call options,** which give the holder the right to purchase a specified asset at a given price (the **exercise,** or **strike, price)** for a given period of time, and (2) **put options,** which give the holder the right to sell an asset at a given price for a given period of time.
- A call option's exercise value is defined as the maximum of zero or the current price of the stock less the strike price.
- The Black-Scholes option pricing model (OPM) or the binomial model can be used to estimate the value of a call option.
- The five inputs to the Black-Scholes model are (1) P, the current stock price; (2) X, the strike price; (3) r_{RF}, the risk-free interest rate; (4) t, the remaining time until expiration; and (5) α, the standard deviation of the stock's rate of return.
- A call option's value increases if P increases, X decreases, r_{RF} increases, t increases, or a increases.
- The put-call parity relationship states that

Put option + Stock = Call option + PV of exercise price.

Questions

19-1 Define each of the following terms:
  a. Option; call option; put option
  b. Exercise value; strike price
  c. Black-Scholes option pricing model

19-2   Why do options sell at prices higher than their exercise values?

19-3   Describe the effect on a call option's price that results from an increase in each of the following factors: (1) stock price, (2) strike price, (3) time to expiration, (4) risk-free rate, and (5) standard deviation of stock return.

Concept Review Problems

Full solutions are provided at www.nelson.com/brigham3ce.

CR-1
Binomial Option
Pricing

The current price of a stock is $40. In 1 year, the price will be either $60 or $30. The annual risk-free rate is 5%. Find the price of a call option on the stock that has an exercise price of $42 and that expires in 1 year. (*Hint:* Use daily compounding.)

CR-2
Black-Scholes Model

Use the Black-Scholes model to find the price for a call option with the following inputs: (1) current stock price is $22, (2) strike price is $20, (3) time to expiration is 6 months, (4) annualized risk-free rate is 5%, and (5) standard deviation of stock return is 0.7.

Problems

Answers to odd-numbered problems appear in Appendix A.

Easy Problems 1–2

19-1
Options

A call option on the stock of Cranberry Glass has a market price of $12. The stock sells for $45 a share, and the option has a strike price of $35 a share. What is the exercise value of the call option? What is the option's time value?

19-2
Options
**Intermediate
Problems 3–4**

The exercise price on one of Flanagan Company's options is $15, its exercise value is $22, and its time value is $5. What are the option's market value and the price of the stock?

19-3
Black-Scholes Model

Assume that you have been given the following information on Purcell Industries:

Current stock price = $25	Strike price of option = $25
Time to maturity of option = 6 months	Risk-free rate = 5%
Variance of stock return = 0.09	
$d_1 = 0.2239$	$N(d_1) = 0.5886$
$d_2 = 0.0118$	$N(d_2) = 0.5047$

According to the Black-Scholes option pricing model, what is the option's value?

19-4
Put-Call Parity

The current price of a stock is $33, and the annual risk-free rate is 6%. A call option with a strike price of $32 and with 1 year until expiration has a current value of $6.56. What is the value of a put option written on the stock with the same exercise price and expiration date as the call option?

**Challenging
Problems 5–8**

19-5
Black-Scholes Model

Use the Black-Scholes model to find the price for a call option with the following inputs: (1) current stock price is $30, (2) strike price is $35, (3) time to expiration is 4 months, (4) annualized risk-free rate is 5%, and (5) variance of stock return is 0.25.

19-6
Binomial Model

The current price of a stock is $28. In 1 year, the price will be either $35 or $23. The annual risk-free rate is 5%. Find the price of a call option on the stock that has a strike price of $30 and that expires in 1 year. (*Hint:* Use daily compounding.)

19-7
Binomial Model

The current price of a stock is $15. In 6 months, the price will be either $18 or $13. The annual risk-free rate is 6%. Find the price of a call option on the stock that has a strike price of $14 and that expires in 6 months. (*Hint:* Use daily compounding.)

19-8
Option Pricing

The current price of a stock is $100. A 1-year option on this stock has a strike price of $100.
(a) Find the price of this option using the Black-Scholes model given that the risk-free rate is 5% and that the variance of the stock return is 0.20.
(b) Find the price of the option using the binomial model and assuming that at the end of the year the stock price could be $122 or $82. Assume the annualized risk-free rate is 5%.

Spreadsheet Problem

19-9

Build a Model:
Black-Scholes Model

Start with the partial model in the file *Ch 19 Build a Model.xlsx* from the textbook's website. Rework Problem 19-3. Then work the next two parts of this problem given below.

a. Construct data tables for the exercise value and Black-Scholes option value for this option, and graph this relationship. Include possible stock price values ranging up to $30.00.

b. Suppose this call option is purchased today. Draw the profit diagram of this option position at expiration.

MINI CASE

You have just been hired as a financial analyst by Triple Trice Inc., a mid-sized Ontario company that specializes in creating exotic clothing. Because no one at Triple Trice is familiar with the basics of financial options, you have been asked to prepare a brief report that the firm's executives can use to gain at least a cursory understanding of the topic.

To begin, you gathered some outside materials on the subject and used these materials to draft a list of pertinent questions that need to be answered. In fact, one possible approach to the paper is to use a question-and-answer format. Now that the questions have been drafted, you have to develop the answers.

a. What is a financial option? What is the single most important characteristic of an option?
b. Options have a unique set of terminology. Define the following terms:
   (1) Call option
   (2) Put option
   (3) Exercise price
   (4) Striking, or strike, price
   (5) Option price
   (6) Expiration date
   (7) Exercise value
   (8) Covered option
   (9) Naked option
   (10) In-the-money call
   (11) Out-of-the-money call
c. In 1973, Fischer Black and Myron Scholes developed the Black-Scholes option pricing model (OPM).
   (1) What assumptions underlie the OPM?
   (2) Write out the three equations that constitute the model.
   (3) What is the value of the following call option according to the OPM?

   > Stock price = $27.00
   > Strike price = $25.00
   > Time to expiration = 6 months
   > Risk-free rate = 6.0%
   > Stock return variance = 0.11

d. What impact does each of the following call option parameters have on the value of a call option?
   (1) Current stock price
   (2) Strike price
   (3) Option's term to maturity
   (4) Risk-free rate
   (5) Variability of the stock price
e. What is put-call parity?
f. Explain four different ways that knowledge of financial options is useful in corporate finance.

chapter 20

Enterprise Risk Management

Clearwater Seafoods (Clearwater) is one of the world's leading seafood companies. Clearwater catches, processes, and sells seafood globally and as such is exposed to a wide variety of financial and operational risks.

Since most of its sales are transacted outside Canada, Clearwater is primarily exposed to foreign exchange rate risk. As exchange rates fluctuate, Clearwater's sales are affected as the local currency costs of its goods will likewise fluctuate, as will the proceeds in Canadian dollars that Clearwater receives. Clearwater estimated that a $0.01 change in the U.S./Canada exchange rate would change its gross profit by almost $2 million if the company does do not do something to hedge the exchange risk. Similar effects on sales and profits result from changes in the exchange rate between Canadian dollars and the euro as well as the Japanese yen.

Clearwater is also exposed to political risk in some of the countries in which it does business. For instance, its division in Argentina was prevented from repatriating dividends in 2012 by regulations imposed by the Government of Argentina. There is also the risk of expropriation of the company's capital and equipment that is domiciled in foreign countries.

By its very nature, fishing is a risky profession. The risk of operating a fishing boat is always top of mind for fishermen and by extension Clearwater needs to apply best practices in operational risk management. Environmental risk management and sustainability is also a concern.

Clearwater is exposed to a wide variety of risks, and how it manages and deals with these risks is a key factor in its success. Keep Clearwater and its need for risk management in mind as you read the rest of this chapter.

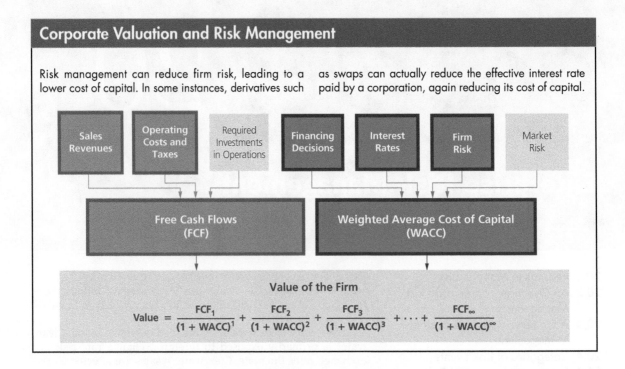

Corporate Valuation and Risk Management

Risk management can reduce firm risk, leading to a lower cost of capital. In some instances, derivatives such as swaps can actually reduce the effective interest rate paid by a corporation, again reducing its cost of capital.

| Sales Revenues | Operating Costs and Taxes | Required Investments in Operations | Financing Decisions | Interest Rates | Firm Risk | Market Risk |

Free Cash Flows (FCF)

Weighted Average Cost of Capital (WACC)

Value of the Firm

$$\text{Value} = \frac{\text{FCF}_1}{(1 + \text{WACC})^1} + \frac{\text{FCF}_2}{(1 + \text{WACC})^2} + \frac{\text{FCF}_3}{(1 + \text{WACC})^3} + \cdots + \frac{\text{FCF}_\infty}{(1 + \text{WACC})^\infty}$$

The textbook's website contains an *Excel* file that will guide you through the chapter's calculations. The file for this chapter is **Ch 20 Tool Kit.xlsx,** and we encourage you to open the file and follow along as you read the chapter.
www.nelson.com/ brigham3ce

Defining risk management is simple: Identify events that could have adverse consequences and then take actions to prevent or minimize the damage caused by these events. Applying risk management is more difficult, but it is vital for a company's success, and perhaps even its survival. In this chapter we explain how risk management adds value to a corporation, describe an enterprise risk management framework, identify different categories of risks, explain how to measure selected risks, and show how to manage those risks.[1] We also illustrate how companies can use **derivatives,** which are securities whose values are determined by the market price of some other asset, to manage certain types of risk.

20.1 Reasons to Manage Risk

Will reducing risk make a company more valuable? Consider Plastic Inc., which manufactures dashboards, interior door panels, and other plastic components used by auto companies. Petroleum is the key feedstock for plastic and thus makes up a large percentage of its costs. Plastic has a 3-year contract with an auto company to deliver 500,000 door panels each year at a price of $20 each. When the company recently signed this contract, oil sold for $100 per barrel and was expected to stay at that level for the next 3 years. If oil prices fell during this time, Plastic would have higher than expected profits and free cash flows, but if oil prices rose, profits would fall. Because Plastic's value depends on its profits and free cash flows, a change in the price of oil would cause shareholders to earn either more or less than they anticipated.

Now suppose that, shortly after signing the contract with its door panel supplier, Plastic announces that it plans to lock in a 3-year supply of oil at a guaranteed price of $100 per barrel *and* that the cost of this guarantee is zero. Would that cause its stock price to rise? At first glance, it seems the answer should be "yes," but that might not be correct. Recall that the value of a stock depends on the present value of its expected future free cash flows, discounted at the weighted average cost of capital (WACC). Locking in the cost of oil will cause an increase in Plastic's stock price if and only if (1) it causes the expected future free cash flows to increase or (2) it causes the WACC to decline.

[1]For excellent overviews of risk management, see Kenneth A. Froot, David S. Scharfstein, and Jeremy Stein, "A Framework for Risk Management," *Journal of Applied Corporate Finance,* Fall 1994, pp. 22–32; Brian Nocco and Rene Stultz, "Enterprise Risk Management, Theory and Practice," *Journal of Applied Corporate Finance,* Fall 2006, pp. 8–20; Walter Dolde, "The Trajectory of Corporate Financial Risk Management," *Journal of Applied Corporate Finance,* Fall 1993, pp. 33–41; and Marshall Blake and Nelda Mahady, "How Mid-Sized Companies Manage Risk," *Journal of Applied Corporate Finance,* Spring 1991, pp. 59–65.

Consider first the free cash flows. Before the announcement of guaranteed oil costs, investors had formed an estimate of the expected future free cash flows based on an expected oil price of $ 100 per barrel. Locking in the cost of oil at $ 100 per barrel will lower the *risk* of the expected future free cash flows, but it might not change the expected *size* of these cash flows because investors already expected a price of $100 per barrel. Of course, smaller than expected cash flows can disrupt a firm's operation and that disruption can, in turn, adversely affect cash flows.

Now what about the WACC? It will change only if locking in the cost of oil causes a change either in the cost of debt or equity or in the target capital structure. If the foreseeable increases in the price of oil are not enough to increase the threat of bankruptcy, then Plastic's cost of debt should not change and neither should its target capital structure. Regarding the cost of equity, recall from Chapter 7 that most investors hold well-diversified portfolios, which means that the cost of equity should depend only on systematic risk. Moreover, even though an increase in oil prices would have a negative effect on Plastic's stock price, it would not have a negative effect on all stocks. Indeed, oil producers should have higher than expected returns and stock prices. Assuming that Plastic's investors hold well-diversified portfolios that include stocks of oil-producing companies, we should have little reason to expect its cost of equity to decrease. The bottom line is this: If Plastic's expected future cash flows and WACC will not change significantly as a consequence of eliminating the risk of oil price increases, then neither should the value of its stock.

We discuss futures contracts and hedging in detail in the next section, but for now let's assume that Plastic has *not* locked in oil prices. Therefore, if oil prices increase, its stock price will fall. However, if its shareholders know this, they can build portfolios that contain oil futures whose values will rise or fall with oil prices and thus offset changes in the price of Plastic's stock. By choosing the correct amount of futures contracts, investors can thus "hedge" their portfolios and completely eliminate the risk due to changes in oil prices. There will be a cost to hedging, but that cost to large investors should be about the same as the cost to Plastic. Because shareholders can hedge away oil price risk themselves, why should they pay a higher price for Plastic's stock just because the company itself hedged away that risk?

The previous points notwithstanding, companies clearly believe that active risk management is important. A 2009 survey reported that 94% of the world's 500 largest firms engage in risk management.[2] A 2005 survey of CFOs reported that 90% of the international and domestic firms responding considered risk in the planning process. The average of the estimates of the contribution that risk management made to the market value of the firm was 3.8%.[3] There are many reasons that companies manage their risks.

1. *Debt capacity.* Risk management can reduce the volatility of cash flows, which decreases the probability of bankruptcy. As we discussed in Chapter 12, firms with lower operating risks can use more debt, and this can lead to higher share prices due to the interest tax savings.
2. *Maintaining the optimal capital budget over time.* Recall from Chapter 12 that firms are reluctant to raise external equity because of high flotation costs and market pressure. This means that the capital budget must generally be financed with a combination of debt and internally generated funds. In bad years, internal cash flows may be too low to support the optimal capital budget, causing firms to either slow investment below the optimal rate or else incur the high costs associated with external equity. By smoothing out the cash flows, risk management can alleviate this problem. This issue is most relevant for firms with large growth opportunities. A study by Professors Gerald Gay and Jouahn Nam found that such firms do in fact use derivatives more than low-growth firms.[4] Thus, maintaining an optimal capital budget is an important determinant of firms' risk management practices.
3. *Financial distress.* The stages of financial distress can range from shareholder concern and higher interest rates on debt to customer defections and bankruptcy. Any serious level of financial distress causes a firm to have lower cash flows than expected. Risk management can reduce the likelihood of low cash flows and hence of financial distress.

[2]Survey News Release, April 23, 2009, International Sweeps and Derivatives Association, www.isda.org/press/press 042309der.pdf
[3]See Henri Servaes, Ane Tamayo, and Peter Tufano, "The Theory and Practice of Corporate Risk Management," *Journal of Applied Corporate Finance*, Fall, 2009, pp. 60–78.
[4]See Gerald D. Gay and Jouahn Nam, "The Underinvestment Problem and Corporate Derivatives Use," *Financial Management*, Winter, 1998, pp. 53–69.

4. *Comparative advantages in hedging.* Most investors cannot hedge as efficiently as a company. First, firms generally incur lower transaction costs because of their larger volume of hedging activities. Second, there is the problem of asymmetric information: Managers know more about the firm's risk exposure than do outside investors, so managers can create more effective hedges. And third, effective risk management requires specialized skills and knowledge that firms are more likely to have.

5. *Borrowing costs.* As discussed later in the chapter, firms can sometimes reduce input costs—especially the interest rate on debt—through the use of derivative instruments called *swaps.* Any such cost reduction adds value to the firm.

6. *Tax effects.* The present value of taxes paid by companies with volatile earnings is higher than the present value of taxes paid by stable companies; this is because of the treatment of tax credits and the rules governing corporate loss carryforwards and carrybacks. Moreover, if volatile earnings cause a company to declare bankruptcy, then the company usually completely loses its tax loss carryforwards. Therefore, using risk management to stabilize earnings can reduce the present value of a company's tax burden.

7. *Compensation systems.* Many compensation systems establish "floors" and "ceilings" on bonuses and also reward managers for meeting targets. To illustrate, suppose a firm's compensation system calls for a manager to receive no bonus if net income is below $1 million, a bonus of $10,000 if income is between $1 million and $2 million, or a bonus of $20,000 if income is $2 million or more. The manager will also receive an additional $10,000 if actual income is at least 90% of the forecasted level, which is $1 million. Now consider the following two situations. First, if income is stable at $2 million each year then the manager receives a $30,000 bonus each year, for a 2-year total of $60,000. However, if income is zero the first year and $4 million the second, the manager gets no bonus the first year and $30,000 the second, for a 2-year total of $30,000. So, even though the company has the same total income ($4 million) over the two years, the manager's bonus is higher if earnings are stable. Therefore, even if hedging does not add much value for shareholders, it may still benefit managers.

There are regulatory and economically driven reasons to manage risk. The following section describes a typical enterprise risk management framework.

CONCEPT REVIEW

1. Explain why finance theory, combined with well-diversified investors and "homemade hedging," might suggest that risk management should not add much value to a company.

2. List and explain some reasons companies might employ risk management techniques.

20.2 An Overview of Enterprise Risk Management

The practice of enterprise risk management has evolved considerably over the past 20 years, due to advances in technology and regulatory changes. To better explain the framework for enterprise risk management, we begin with a brief history of risk management.

One of the earliest used tools in risk management is a futures contract, which is an agreement in which a buyer pledges to purchase a specific quantity of an item at a specific price on a specific future date from a seller who has pledged to provide the item at the agreed-upon terms. Written records show that commodity futures contracts were used and traded over 4,000 years ago in India, so risk management has been around a very long time. In North America, grain traders have used futures contracts as far back as the early 1800s.[5]

The history of insurance also dates back hundreds of years, with maritime insurance offered in Genoa in the 1300s and fire insurance offered in London in 1680, not long after the Great Fire of London. In fact, Benjamin Franklin and the Union Fire Company began a fire insurance company in 1752.

At the risk of oversimplification, not much new happened until the 1970s, probably because several sources of risk (interest rates, currency exchange rates, and oil prices) had been relatively stable, and perhaps because models for options and other derivatives had

---

[5]For a thorough treatment of the history of enterprise risk management, see Betty Simkins and Steven A. Ramirez, "Enterprise-Wide Risk Management and Corporate Governance", *Loyola University Chicago Law Journal*, Vol. 39, 2008, pp. 571–594.

not yet been developed. However, the 1970s saw the end of the monetary gold standard (which dramatically increased foreign exchange rate volatility), runaway inflation in North America, and a reversal in bargaining power between OPEC and oil companies during the Yom Kippur War between Egypt and Israel in 1973. These events, combined with the acceleration of international competition, exposed companies to much more risk than in the previous decades. In turn, these sources of risk made stocks, bonds, and other investments much more volatile.

With the development of pricing models for derivatives, most companies began to actively manage their exposures to interest rates, exchange rates, and a wide variety of commodities. However, few companies employed a systematic approach to risk management. Instead, most companies had a risk management group in charge of insurance-related issues, but different groups in charge of managing each of the other specific risks. For example, one group might manage foreign exchange risk and another might manage commodity risk.

The impetus for a more comprehensive and systematic approach to risk management came from several sources, including corporate bribery scandals in the 1970s, the S&L crisis in the early 1980s, the accounting scandals in the early 2000s (including Enron, WorldCom, and Nortel), and the financial crisis in the late 2000s. All of these events had several common factors, including accounting systems that lacked sufficient controls to identify improper activities.

In response to these risk management and governance failures, governments and regulators around the world started to impose guidelines to prevent the next crisis. The Toronto Stock Exchange formed a committee to examine the situation. The result was a report titled "Where Were the Directors?" This report, more commonly called the Dey Report after the committee's chair, Peter Dey, recommended 14 best practice guidelines. In 1995 the Toronto Stock Exchange required listed companies to annually disclose their corporate governance and risk management practices in accordance with these guidelines. In 2002, the U.S. Congress passed the Sarbanes-Oxley (SOX) Act to prevent accounting scandals like those that occurred at Enron, Arthur Andersen, and Tyco. Section 404 of SOX requires senior management to include a section in the annual report that addresses the internal control system, including the system's framework and an assessment of its ability to detect fraud.

Many major Canadian companies such as BCE Inc. and Royal Bank of Canada have their shares cross-listed on both the Toronto Stock Exchange and the New York Stock Exchange. Cross-listed companies must also comply with U.S. securities law and thus are subject to SOX.

In response to stinging criticism from regulators, five major accounting organizations formed the Committee of Sponsoring Organizations (COSO) and released several reports, including one in 1992 that provided a framework for an internal control system designed to prevent fraudulent accounting. The framework for the COSO accounting internal control system satisfied the reporting requirements made by the Foreign Corrupt Practices Act (FCPA) and SOX, so many companies adopted the framework. In 2004, COSO also issued a framework for enterprise risk management, which broadened the scope of the original internal control framework. Because many companies were already using the framework for internal controls, some adopted versions of the broader framework for enterprise risk management. Today, the COSO framework and similar frameworks are widely used.

COSO defines **enterprise risk management (ERM)** as follows:

> Enterprise risk management is a *process*, effected by an entity's *board of directors*, management and other personnel, applied in *strategy setting* and across the *enterprise*, designed to identify *potential events* that may affect the entity, and manage risk to be within its *risk appetite*, to provide reasonable *assurance* regarding the achievement of entity objectives.[6]

Notice how this definition differs from the traditional compartmentalization of risk management. The COSO framework is inclusive, starting with the board of directors in addition to managers and other employees; COSO is broad in defining risk, ranging from strategic choices to specific events; COSO is unambiguous, with the company explicitly choosing an acceptable level of risk; and COSO is transparent, requiring monitoring and reporting.

Before we describe ERM frameworks in more detail, you should know about the Basel Accords, another big regulatory wave that has had an impact on risk management. The Basel Committee, headquartered in Switzerland, is composed of the heads of the central banks from well-developed economies. In the past 25 years, the Committee has introduced three

---

[6]Italics added for emphasis. See page 2 of COSO, "Summary of Enterprise Risk Management—Integrated Framework," 2004, www.coso.org/documents/coso_erm_executivesummary.pdf.

major accords designed to control risk in the global financial system, Basel I (1988), Basel II (2004), and Basel III (introduced in 2010 and revised in 2011). There are similarities in all three accords, but we focus on Basel III because it is the most recent.

The essence of banking is raising funds (from sales of shares, issuances of debt, borrowing through short-term loans, and taking deposits) and then investing the funds in assets (such as business loans and derivatives). A bank experiences financial distress when its assets' cash flows and values aren't sufficient to cover its obligations to its creditors. To prevent a bank from experiencing financial distress (and then passing its problems on to taxpayers and the global financial system), Basel III seeks to ensure that a bank is not financed with too much debt relative to the risk of its assets. In addition to regulations regarding the types and proportions of capital a bank must maintain relative to its assets' risks, Basel III also requires adequate internal control systems to supervise a bank's risk and goes on to suggest particular techniques for measuring risk. We will describe several of these measures later in the chapter, including *value at risk* and *expected shortfall*.

CONCEPT REVIEW

1. Describe some regulatory actions that have influenced the evolution of risk management.
2. Define enterprise risk management.

20.3 A Framework for Enterprise Risk Management

No single framework is applicable to all companies, but the COSO framework (including modified versions) is widely used, so it provides an excellent example of an ERM framework.[7]

The Committee of Sponsoring Organizations' (COSO) Framework for Enterprise Risk Management (ERM)

COSO designed its enterprise risk management framework with three dimensions. The first dimension is the organizational level. The COSO framework applies ERM at all levels of an organization, including the corporate level, division levels, business units, and subsidiaries.

The second dimension is the category of objectives. Each organizational level should define its objectives in each of four categories: (1) *strategic objectives*, which are based on the company's mission and overall goals; (2) *operating objectives*, which focus on the selection, implementation, and ongoing execution of projects and other applications of corporate resources; (3) *reporting objectives*, which seek to disseminate accurate and up-to-date information to decision-makers inside the company and stakeholders outside the company (such as investors and regulators); and (4) *compliance objectives*, which seek to ensure the company complies with laws and regulatory requirements.

The third dimension is the process of risk management for an objective at a particular level within the organization. The risk management process for each objective has eight components, which we discuss in the following section.

The Components of the COSO Enterprise Risk Management Framework

The eight components of the COSO ERM process define the way in which an organization approaches and applies risk management.

Components 1 and 2: Internal Environment and Objective Setting
The first two components are related to a company's culture and mission, including the company's workplace environment, attitude toward risk, and goal-setting process. An important part of these processes is the identification of the amount of risk that a company is willing to take, which often is called the "risk appetite".

---

[7]For more on the COSO framework, see The Committee of Sponsoring Organizations of the Treadway Commission, *Enterprise Risk Management—Integrated Framework*, 2004, available at www.coso.org/guidance.htm. A summary of the framework is available for free at the same website. Another widely used framework is ISO 3100:2009, published by the International Organization for Standardization (ISO), headquartered in Switzerland.

Component 3: Event Identification You can't manage a source of risk if you don't recognize it. A risky event is defined as any uncertain outcome that affects a company's previously defined objectives.[8] For example, risky events include increases in the prices of raw materials, an explosion at a factory, or a loss of customers to a competitor. To prevent overlooking risky events, ERM systems typically define categories and then identify the potential events within those categories. We will take a much closer look at risk categories later.

Component 4: Risk Assessment After identifying a risk, a company should assess the risk. We will describe risk assessment in more detail later, but it always includes estimating both the probability that the event will occur and the resulting impact on the company's objectives. For example, an event might be an increase in interest rates, which would affect a company's cost when it issues debt. To assess this risk, the company would begin by forecasting the probabilities of different interest rates at the time it plans to issue the debt, and then estimate the cost of issuing debt at the different interest rates. As another example, an event might be a fire at a warehouse. In this case, a company would estimate the probability of a fire and the resulting cost. The insurance industry often uses the terms "loss frequency" and "loss severity" (the dollar value of each loss) for these concepts.

Component 5: Risk Response After identifying and assessing a risky event, the next steps are to choose a response to the risk and implement that choice. There are several different types of responses, including these:

Totally avoid the activity that gives rise to the risk. For example, a company might discontinue a product or service line because the risks outweigh the rewards. This often is the case with pharmaceutical products that have potentially harmful side effects or global expansion into countries with civil unrest.

Reduce the probability of occurrence of an adverse event. The expected loss arising from any risk is a function of both the probability of occurrence and the dollar loss if the adverse event occurs. In some instances, it is possible to reduce the probability that an adverse event will occur. For example, the probability that a fire will occur can be reduced by instituting a fire prevention program, by replacing old electrical wiring, and by using fire-resistant materials in areas with the greatest fire potential.

Reduce the magnitude of the loss associated with an adverse event. In some instances, companies can take actions to reduce losses even if the event occurs. Continuing with the previous example, the dollar cost associated with a fire can be reduced by actions such as installing sprinkler systems, designing facilities with self-contained fire zones, and locating facilities close to a fire station.

Transfer the risk to an insurance company. Often, it is advantageous to insure against risk by transferring it to an insurance company. Even though an insured item's expected loss is the same for its owner and for the insurance company, the insurance company benefits from diversification. For example, an insurance company might provide coverage for tractors, harvesters, and other types of agricultural equipment, which often cost several hundred thousand dollars or more. If the insurance company has a large number of customers, it can predict quite accurately the amounts it will pay in claims and then can set premiums high enough to pay the claims and provide the return required by its investors. In addition, insurance companies can themselves insure parts of their risk by purchasing reinsurance from another insurance company. Therefore, the potential loss of a harvester might be quite risky to a farmer, but it may not be risky to a large insurance company.

However, just because something can be insured does not mean that a company should insure it. In many instances, it might be better for the company to *self-insure,* which means bearing the risk directly rather than paying another party to bear it. In fact, many large companies choose to self-insure, or to insure only the part of an asset's loss that exceeds a certain amount, which is equivalent to an individual who has a large deductible on car or home insurance.

---

[8]COSO defines risk as an event that negatively affects an objective, and an opportunity as an event that can positively affect an objective. We don't make that distinction—we define risk as uncertainty, which can result in positive or negative outcomes.

Transfer the function that produces the risk to a third party. For example, suppose a furniture manufacturer is concerned about potential liabilities arising from its ownership of a fleet of trucks used to transfer products from its manufacturing plant to various points across the country. One way to eliminate this risk would be to contract with a trucking company to do the shipping, thus passing the risks to a third party.

Share or eliminate the risk by using derivative contracts. Many companies use derivative contracts to reduce or eliminate an event's risk. For example, a cereal company may use corn or wheat futures to hedge against increases in grain prices. Similarly, financial derivatives can be used to reduce risks that arise from changes in interest rates and exchange rates. As we will describe later, the risk doesn't disappear—it is just taken on by the other party in the derivative contract.

Accept the risk. In some instances, a company will decide to accept a risk because the expected benefits are greater than the expected costs and because the risk doesn't exceed the company's risk appetite. Indeed, accepting risk is the nature of most businesses—if they were riskless, then investors would expect to receive a return only equal to the risk-free rate. Also, some stand-alone risks may be quite large, but they may not contribute much to the total corporate risk if they are not highly correlated with the company's other risks.

Components 6, 7, and 8: Control Activities, Information and Communication, and Monitoring

The last three components focus on ensuring that risky events are in fact being treated according to the responses that were previously chosen—it doesn't do much good to develop strategies and tactics if employees don't follow them! For example, a single rogue trader lost £4.9 billion in 2008 at the French bank Société Générale, and another lost £1.5 billion in 2011 at the London branch of UBS (headquartered in Switzerland).

○NCEPT REVIEW

1. Define a risk event.
2. What are the two stages in risk assessment?
3. Describe some possible risk responses.
4. Should a firm insure itself against all of the insurable risks it faces? Explain.

20.4 Categories of Risk Events

Before addressing alternative risk responses to specific risk events, it will be helpful to describe ways to categorize risk.

Major Categories

Following is a typical list of major categories that are representative of those at several organizations.[9]

1. *Strategy and reputation.* A company's strategic choices simultaneously influence and respond to its competitors' actions; corporate social responsibilities; the public's perception of its activities; and its reputation among suppliers, peers, and customers. ERM addresses the risk inherent in these strategic choices.
2. *Control and compliance.* This category includes risk events related to regulatory requirements, litigation risks, intellectual property rights, reporting accuracy, and internal control systems.

---

[9]To see the way that several organizations have categorized risk and the ways that surveyors categorize risk, see the following: Mark L. Frigo and Hans Laessoe, "Strategic Risk Management at the LEGO Group," *Strategic Finance*, February, 2012, pp. 27–35; Henri Servaes, Ane Tamayo, and Peter Tufano, "The Theory and Practice of Corporate Risk Management," *Journal of Applied Corporate Finance*, Fall, 2009, pp. 60–78.

3. *Hazards.* These include fires, floods, riots, acts of terrorism, and other natural or man-made disasters. Notice that hazards have only negative outcomes—an earthquake might destroy a factory, but it isn't going to build one.

4. *Human resources.* Success often depends upon a company's employees. ERM addresses risk events related to employees, including recruiting, succession planning, employee health, and employee safety.

5. *Operations.* A company's operations include supply chains, manufacturing facilities, existing product lines, and business processes. Risk events include supply chain disruptions, equipment failures, product recalls, and changes in customer demand.

6. *Technology.* Technology changes rapidly and is a major source of risk, including risk events related to innovations, technological failures, and IT reliability and security.

7. *Financial management.* This category includes risk events related to (1) foreign exchange risk, (2) commodity price risk, (3) interest rate risk, (4) project selection risk (including major capital expenditures, mergers, and acquisitions), (5) liquidity risk, (6) customer credit risk, and (7) portfolio risk (the risk that a portfolio of financial assets will decrease in value). For the remainder of the chapter, we will focus on the risk events related to financial management, but first we need to describe several other ways to think about risk.

Dimensions of Risk

Sometimes it is helpful to think about risk events based on different dimensions. For example, several risk management systems classify risk by whether it is driven by external forces or by internal decisions and activities. This is especially helpful in risk identification because it forces managers to look at a broader range of risk events.

Sometimes it is useful to classify risk by whether it is a pure risk that has only a downside (e.g., a hazard, such as a fire) or a speculative risk that has potential positive as well as negative outcomes (e.g., the exchange rate between dollars and euros can go up or down, which would have a big impact on the cash flows of Canadian importers). Most pure risks can be reduced or eliminated with insurance products.

When choosing among different risk responses, it is helpful to determine whether the source of risk is linear or nonlinear. For example, consider an agricultural company with access to a low-cost source of water for irrigation. The company grows corn and can predict its costs and the size of its harvest, but it is exposed to volatility in the price of corn. Notice that this is a linear risk—the company loses money when prices are low and makes money when they are high. We discuss the details later, but the company can enter into derivative contracts that provide positive cash flows when prices are low but create negative cash flows when prices are high. The derivative also has a linear payout, but its payouts are opposite those of the company. The combination of the company's internally generated cash flows from the harvest and its externally generated cash flows from the derivative can reduce or eliminate the company's risk.

In contrast, consider a company in the oil exploration and extraction industry.[10] The company will incur fixed costs and negative cash flows associated with continuing operations when oil prices are too low to justify additional exploration. When oil prices are high, the company incurs fixed costs and also variable costs associated with expanded exploration and extraction. However, when oil prices are high, the company will generate enough positive cash flow to cover its fixed costs and also the new variable costs associated with the additional exploration and extraction. Therefore, the company is exposed to nonlinear risk—it needs additional cash flow to support its ongoing operations only when oil prices are low but not when prices are high. In this situation, the company might be willing to buy a derivative that pays out only when oil prices are low. In other words, the company reduces its nonlinear risk with a nonlinear hedging strategy.

ⒸNCEPT REVIEW

1. List and define the different major categories of risk events.

2. Explain the difference between a linear risk and a nonlinear risk.

---

[10]See Kenneth A. Froot, David S. Scharfstein, and Jeremy Stein, "A Framework for Risk Management," *Journal of Applied Corporate Finance*, Fall 1994, pp. 22–32; also see the paper by Servaes et al, cited in footnote 3.

20.5 Foreign Exchange (FX) Risk

Foreign exchange (FX) risk occurs when a company's cash flows are affected by changes in currency exchange rates. This can occur if a company imports materials from other countries or sells its products in other countries. Some smaller companies manage FX risk for each transaction, but most large companies aggregate their transactions and manage their exposures centrally. For example, if one division is selling goods denominated in U.S. dollars and another division is purchasing goods denominated in U.S. dollars, the company would net out the two transactions and just manage any remaining exposure.

The primary tool used to manage FX risk is a **forward contract,** which is an agreement in which one party agrees to buy an item at a specific price on a specific future date and another party agrees to sell the item at the agreed upon terms. *Goods are actually delivered under forward contracts.* In the case of foreign exchange, the goods are the amount of foreign currency specified in the contract, paid for with the other currency specified in the contract.

Most FX trading is directly between two parties using customized contracts with unique amounts and dates—there is no central market with standardized contracts. Unless both parties are morally and financially strong, there is a danger that one party will default on the contract—this is called **counterparty risk.** Major banks often act as counterparties for their customers. For example, a bank might agree to buy euros in 30 days at a price of 1.24 dollars per euro from one customer and agree to sell euros in 30 days at a price of 1.25 dollars per euro to another customer. Depending on the change in the euro exchange rate, the bank will make money on one of the contracts and lose money on the other, netting only the spread on the difference in prices. This matching of contracts allows banks to reduce their net exposure to exchange rate volatility, but the bank is still exposed to counterparty risk from the customers.

Because there is no central market, trading in FX is an OTC (over the counter) transaction. The amount of currency to be delivered is called the notional amount. At the end of June 2014, there was a total of about $60 *trillion* in the notional value of forward contracts outstanding globally.[11]

The failure to manage counterparty risk was one of the causes of the 2007 global financial crisis. For example, Lehman Brothers was a counterparty to many other financial institutions in a variety of derivative contracts, so Lehman's failure caused distress at financial institutions throughout the world.

To illustrate how foreign exchange contracts are used, suppose Magna International (Magna) arranges to buy electric motors from a European manufacturer on terms that call for Magna to pay 10 million euros in 180 days. Magna would not want to give up the free trade credit, but if the euro appreciated against the dollar during the next 6 months then the dollar cost of the 10 million euros would rise. Magna could hedge the transaction by buying a forward contract under which it agreed to buy the 10 million euros in 180 days at a fixed dollar price, which would lock in the dollar cost of the motors.

ⓒNCEPT REVIEW

1. What is a forward contract?
2. Explain how a company can use forward contracts to eliminate FX risk.
3. What is counterparty risk?

20.6 Commodity Price Risk

Many companies use or produce commodities, including agricultural products, energy, metals, and lumber. Because commodity prices can be quite volatile, many companies manage their exposure to commodity price risk. Before describing specific ways to manage commodity price risk, we begin with a brief overview of futures markets in North America.

One of the first formal markets for derivatives was the futures market for wheat. Farmers were concerned about the price they would receive for their wheat when they sold it in the fall, and millers were concerned about the price they would have to pay. Each party soon realized

---

[11]Bank for International Settlements Quarterly Review, June 2014; www.bis.org

that the risks they faced could be reduced if they established a price earlier in the year. Accordingly, mill agents began going out to the Wheat Belt with contracts that called for the farmers to deliver grain at a predetermined price, and both parties benefited from the transaction in the sense that their risks were reduced. The farmers could concentrate on growing their crop without worrying about the price of grain, and the millers could concentrate on their milling operations. Thus, *hedging with futures* lowered aggregate risk in the economy.

These early futures dealings were between two parties who arranged transactions between themselves. Soon, though, intermediaries came into the picture, and *trading* in futures was established. The Chicago Board of Trade, founded in 1848, and the Winnipeg Commodity Exchange, formed in 1887, were early marketplaces where *futures dealers* helped make a market in futures contracts. Thus, farmers could sell futures on the exchange, and millers could buy them there. This improved the efficiency and lowered the cost of hedging operations.[12]

A futures contract is similar to a forward contract in that two parties are involved, with one party taking a long position (which obligates the party to buy the underlying asset) and the other party taking a short position (which obligates the party to sell the asset). However, there are three key differences. First, futures contracts are **marked-to-market** on a daily basis, meaning that gains and losses are recognized daily and money must be put up to cover losses. This greatly reduces the risk of default that exists with forward contracts because daily price changes are usually smaller than the cumulative change over the contract's life. For example, if a corn futures contract has a price of $7.00 per bushel and the price goes up to $7.10 the next day, a party with a short position must pay the $0.10 difference, and a party with a long position would receive the difference. This marking-to-market occurs daily until the delivery date. To see that this procedure does in fact lock in the price, suppose that the price doesn't change again. On the delivery date, the party with the short position would sell corn at the current price of $7.10. Because the short seller had already paid $0.10 from daily marking-to-market, the short seller's net cash flow is $7.00. The party with the long position would have to buy corn at the current price of $7.10, but because the purchaser had already received $0.10 from cumulative daily marking-to-market, the net purchase price would be $7.00.

The second major difference between a forward contract and a futures contract is that physical delivery of the underlying asset in a futures contract is virtually never taken—the two parties simply settle up with cash for the difference between the contracted price and the actual price on the expiration date. The third difference is that futures contracts are generally standardized instruments that are traded on exchanges, whereas forward contracts are usually tailor-made, negotiated between two parties, and not traded after they have been signed. Figure 20-1 summarizes the differences between futures and forwards.

The needs of farmers and millers allowed a **natural hedge,** defined as a situation in which aggregate risk can be reduced by derivatives transactions between two parties. Natural hedges occur when futures are traded between cotton farmers and cotton mills, copper mines and copper fabricators, importers and foreign manufacturers for currency exchange rates, electric utilities and coal mines, and oil producers and oil users. In all such situations, hedging reduces aggregate risk and thus benefits the economy.

FIGURE 20-1   Summarizing the Difference Between Futures and Forwards

Differing Characteristics of Futures and Forwards	
Futures	**Forwards**
Created and traded on an exchange	Created by a financial institution and not traded after original agreement is signed
Marked-to-market on a daily basis with publicized prices	There is no public market and thus no transparent price for forward agreements
Limited default risk due to margin that must be posted with the exchange	Greater default risk if one of the counterparties fails to live up to the agreement
Standardized terms	Tailor-made contracts

---

[12]See the Montreal Exchange website at http://www.m-x.ca, and the ICE Futures Canada website at http://www.theice.com for a wealth of information on the history and operations of these two exchanges.

There are two basic types of hedges: (1) **long hedges,** in which futures contracts are *bought* (obligating the hedger to purchase the underlying asset), providing protection against price increases, and (2) **short hedges,** where a firm or individual *sells* futures contracts (obligating the hedger to sell the underlying asset), providing protection against falling prices.

Not all participants in the futures markets are hedgers. **Speculation** involves betting on future price movements, and futures are used instead of the commodities because of the leverage inherent in the contract. For example, a speculator might buy corn for $7 a bushel. If corn goes up to $7.70, the speculator has a 10% return (assuming rats don't eat the corn before it can be sold). Now consider a futures contract for 5,000 bushels at $7 per bushel. The exchange requires an investor to put up a **margin requirement** to ensure that the investor will not renege on the daily marking to market. However, the margin is quite small relative to the size of a contract—the margin is only $2,700, but the total amount of corn is valued at $35,000 = $7(5,000).[13] If the price goes up to $7.70, the profit is $3,500 = ($7.70 –$7.00)(5,000). The rate of return on the invested margin is 140% = $3,500/$2,500. Of course, any losses on the contract also would be magnified.

At first blush, one might think that the appearance of speculators would increase risk, but this is not necessarily true. Speculators add capital and players to the market. Thus, to the extent that speculators broaden the market and make hedging possible, they help decrease risk for those who seek to avoid it. Unlike the natural hedge, however, risk is not eliminated. Instead, it is transferred from the hedgers to the speculators.

Today, futures contracts are available on hundreds of real and financial assets traded on dozens of U.S. and international exchanges, the largest of which are the Chicago Board of Trade (CBOT) and the Chicago Mercantile Exchange (CME), both of which are now part of the CME Group. Futures contracts are divided into two classes, **commodity futures** and **financial futures.** Commodity futures include oil, various grains, oilseeds, livestock, meats, fibres, metals, and wood. Financial futures, which were first traded in 1975, include Treasury bills, notes, bonds, Banker's Acceptance Rate, Eurodollar deposits, foreign currencies, and stock indexes. We describe how financial futures can reduce interest rate risk in a later section.

Using Futures Contracts to Reduce Commodity Price Exposure

We will use Porter Electronics, which uses large quantities of copper, as well as several precious metals, to illustrate inventory hedging. Suppose that in May 2015, Porter foresaw a need for 100,000 pounds of copper in March 2016 for use in fulfilling a fixed-price contract to supply solar power cells to the Province of Ontario. Porter's managers are concerned that a strike by Chilean copper miners might occur, which would raise the price of copper in world markets and possibly turn Porter's expected profit into a loss.

Porter could go ahead and buy the copper it will need to fulfill the contract, but it would have to borrow money to pay for the copper and then pay for storage. As an alternative, the company could hedge against increasing copper prices in the futures market. The New York Commodity Exchange trades standard copper futures contracts of 25,000 pounds each. Thus, Porter could buy four contracts (go long) for delivery in March 2016. Assume these contracts were trading in May for about $4.10 per pound and that the spot price at that date was about $4.08 per pound. If copper prices rose appreciably over the next 10 months, then the value of Porter's long position in copper futures would increase, thus offsetting some of the price increase in the commodity itself. Of course, if copper prices fell, then Porter would lose money on its futures contracts, but the company would be buying the copper on the spot market at a cheaper price, so it would make a higher than anticipated profit on its sale of solar cells. Thus, hedging in the copper futures market locks in the cost of raw materials and removes some risk to which the firm would otherwise be exposed.

Many other companies, such as Barrick Gold with gold and Archer Daniels Midland with grains, routinely use the futures markets to reduce the risks associated with price volatility.

Options on Futures

Futures contracts and options are similar to one another—so similar that people often confuse the two. Therefore, it is useful to compare the two instruments. *A futures contract* is a definite agreement on the part of one party to buy something on a specific date and at a specific price, and the other party agrees to sell on the same terms. No matter how low or how high the price goes, the two parties must settle the contract at the agreed-upon price

---

[13]This is the margin requirement for hedgers. Speculators have a higher margin requirement.

and the losses of one party must exactly equal the gains of the other. In addition, a dollar increase in the futures price has exactly the opposite effect of a dollar decrease in the futures price. A hedge constructed using futures contracts is called a *symmetric hedge* because of this feature; the payoff from an increase in the futures price is exactly opposite the payoff from a decrease in the futures price. For this reason, symmetric hedges are typically used to provide a fixed transaction price at some date in the future and are ideal for managing a risk that is linear.

For example, suppose an agricultural company has access to a source of low-cost water for irrigation. The company can predict its costs and the size of its harvest but is exposed to price risk. The company could sell futures contracts (take a long position, which obligates it to sell corn) for delivery when the corn is harvested in 6 months. If the corn price (and hence the corn futures price) decreases over the 6 months, then the company will receive less when selling the corn but will make up the difference when closing out the futures contract. If instead the corn price increases, then the company will make more money when selling the corn in 6 months but will lose money when closing out the futures contract. In this way the ending value of the position doesn't depend on the corn price in 6 months, and so the amount received for selling the corn in 6 months is locked in.

An *option,* on the other hand, gives someone the right to buy (call) or sell (put) an asset, but the holder of the option does not have to complete the transaction. The payoff from a hedge constructed using options will be different from a futures hedge because of this option feature. As discussed in Chapter 19, the payoff from a call option increases as the price of the underlying asset increases, but if the underlying asset price decreases, then the most the option holder can lose is the amount invested in the option. That is, upside gains are unlimited but downside losses are capped at the amount invested in the option. For this reason, an option is said to create an *asymmetric hedge*—it hedges price changes in one direction more than price changes in the other. As such, options are ideal for managing nonlinear risks.

For example, suppose the agricultural company did not have access to irrigation but operated many farms in different provinces. A widespread drought would reduce the size of the harvest but probably would cause the price of corn to increase due to the lower supply. If this happened, the company's revenues would fall but would not be eliminated—the higher corn price would partially compensate for the smaller harvest. This means the company faces nonlinear risk with respect to corn prices. Instead of going long in a futures contract, the company might buy a put option on a corn futures contract, giving the company the right to sell a futures contract at a fixed price. If the price of corn decreased, the value of the put option would increase, and the profits on the option would offset the loss from selling the corn at the lower price. However, if corn prices increased, then the investor would let the put option expire and simply sell its smaller harvest at the higher price.

CONCEPT REVIEW

1. How does a futures contract differ from a forward contract?
2. What is a "natural hedge"? Give some examples of natural hedges.
3. Suppose a company knows the quantity of a commodity that it will produce. Describe how it might hedge using a futures contract.

20.7 Interest Rate Risk

Interest rates can be quite volatile, exposing a company to interest rate risk, especially if the company is planning to issue debt or if the company has floating rate debt. Interest rate futures and Interest rate swaps are key instruments for managing interest rate risk. The following sections describe these two situations.

Using Futures Contracts to Manage the Risk of Debt Issuances

To illustrate how interest rate futures contracts work, consider the Montreal Exchange's contract on Government of Canada Bonds, the CGB contract. The basic contract is for $100,000 of a hypothetical 6% Government of Canada bond with 10 years to maturity. Table 20-1 shows CGB bond futures data from the Montreal Exchange website.

| TABLE 20-1 | Futures Price (CGB Contract, $100,000 Government of Canada Bonds) |

Delivery Month	Last Price	Change	Volume
June 2015	141.28	0.01	47,080

Source: The Montreal Exchange, http://www.m-x.ca, March 11, 2015.

See *Ch 20 Tool Kit.xlsx* at the textbook's website for all calculations.

The first column of the table gives the delivery month, and the next two columns give the last price of the day and the change in price from the previous day. The prices given are as a percentage of the par value of the bonds. The volume is the number of contracts that traded that day. Most of the trading occurs in the contract with the nearest delivery date.

From Table 20-1, the price at which one could buy $100,000 face value of a 6%, 10-year Government of Canada bond to be delivered in June was 141.28% of par, or (141.28%) ($100,000) = $141,280. The contract price increased by 0.01% on this particular day. Why would the value of the bond futures increase? Bond prices increase when interest rates fall, so interest rates must have fallen slightly on this day. Moreover, we can calculate the implied rates inherent in the futures contracts. Recall that the contract relates to a hypothetical 10-year, semiannual payment, 6% coupon bond. The last price was 141.28% of par. We can solve for r_d by using the following equation:

$$\sum_{t=1}^{20} \frac{\$30}{(1 + r_d/2)^t} + \frac{\$1,000}{(1 + r_d/2)^{20}} = \$1,412.80$$

Using a financial calculator, input N = 20, PV = –1,412,80, PMT = 30, FV = 1,000, and solve for I/YR = 0.7660. This is the semiannual rate, which is the equivalent to a nominal annual rate of 1.5320%, or approximately 1.53%. The previous day's last price was 141.27. Setting N = 20, PV = −1,412.70, PMT = 30, FV = 1,000, and solving for I/YR = 0.7664 implies an annual yield of 1.5329%. Therefore, interest rates fell by only about 1/10 of a basis point from the previous day, but that was enough to increase the value of the contract by $10.

The fact that the change in value of the futures contract was $10 was not an accident. The futures contract on the 10-year Government of Canada bond is designed to change by $10 for each 0.01 change in the price of the futures contract. Thus, for example, a change in price of the futures contract from 141.27 to 141.28 would be an increase of 0.01 or a total change in value of the contract of $10. This feature makes working with futures contracts very simple.

When futures contracts are purchased, the purchaser does not have to put up the full amount of the purchase price; rather, the purchaser is required to post an initial *margin*, which for CGB bond contracts is $2,465 per $100,000 contract.[14] However, investors are required to maintain a certain value in the margin account, called a *maintenance margin*. If the value of the contract declines, then the owner may be required to add additional funds to the margin account, and the more the contract value falls, the more money must be added.[15] The value of the contract is checked at the end of every working day, and margin account adjustments are made at that time. This is called "marking-to-market." If an investor purchased our illustrative contract and then sold it later for $145,000, he or she would have made a profit of $3,720 on a $2,465 investment, or a return of 51% in only 3 months. It is clear, therefore, that futures contracts offer a considerable amount of leverage. Of course, if interest rates had risen, then the value of the contract would have fallen, and the investor could easily have lost his or her $2,465 or more. Futures contracts are rarely settled by delivery of the securities involved. Rather, the transaction is completed by reversing the trade, which amounts to selling the contract back to the

[14]This is the margin requirement for hedgers. Speculators have a different margin requirement.
[15]For current margin requirements on hedging investments, see http://www.m-x.ca.

original seller.[16] The actual gains and losses on the contract are realized when the futures contract is closed.[17,18]

Using Interest Rate Swaps: Managing Floating versus Fixed Rates

Suppose that Company S has a 20-year, $100 million floating-rate bond outstanding and that Company F has a $100 million, 20-year, fixed-rate issue outstanding. Thus, each company has an obligation to make a stream of interest payments, but one payment stream is fixed while the other will vary as interest rates change in the future. This situation is shown in the top part of Figure 20-1.

Now suppose that Company S has stable cash flows and wants to lock in its cost of debt. Company F has cash flows that fluctuate with the economy, rising when the economy is strong and falling when it is weak. Recognizing that interest rates also move up and down with the economy, Company F has concluded it would be better off with variable-rate debt. Suppose the companies agreed to swap their payment obligations. The bottom half of Figure 20-2 shows that the net cash flows for Company S are at a fixed rate and those for Company F are based on a floating rate. Company S would now have to make fixed payments, which are consistent with its stable cash inflows, and Company F would have a floating obligation, which for it is less risky.

A **swap** is just what the name implies—two parties agree to swap something, generally obligations to make specified payment streams.

The previous example illustrates how swaps can reduce risks by allowing each company to match the variability of its interest payments with that of its cash flows. However, there are also situations in which swaps can reduce both the risk and the effective cost of debt. For example, Antron Corporation, which has a high credit rating, can issue either floating-rate debt at LIBOR + 1% or fixed-rate debt at 10%.[19] Bosworth Industries is less creditworthy, so its cost for floating-rate debt is LIBOR + 1.5% and its fixed-rate cost is 10.4%. Owing to the nature of Antron's operations, its CFO has decided that the firm would be better off with fixed-rate debt; meanwhile, Bosworth's CFO prefers floating-rate debt. Paradoxically, both firms can benefit by issuing the type of debt they do not want and then swapping their payment obligations.

First, each company will issue an identical amount of debt, which is called the **notional principal.** Even though Antron wants fixed-rate debt, it issues floating-rate debt at LIBOR + 1%, and Bosworth issues fixed-rate debt at 10.4%. Next, the two companies enter into an interest rate swap.[20] Assume the debt maturities are 5 years, which means the length of this swap will also be 5 years. By convention, the floating-rate payments of most swaps are based on LIBOR, with the fixed rate adjusted upward or downward to reflect credit risk and the term structure. The riskier the company that will receive the floating-rate payments, the higher the fixed-rate payment it must make. In our example, Antron will be receiving floating-rate payments from Bosworth, and those payments will be set at LIBOR multiplied by the notional principal. Then, payments will be adjusted every 6 months to reflect changes in the LIBOR rate.

The fixed payment that Antron must make to Bosworth is set (that is, "fixed") for the duration of the swap at the time the contract is signed, and it depends primarily on two factors: (1) the level of fixed interest rates at the time of the agreement and (2) the relative creditworthiness of the two companies.

In our example, assume interest rates and creditworthiness are such that 8.95% is the appropriate fixed swap rate for Antron, so it will make 8.95% fixed-rate payments

---

[16]The buyers and sellers of most financial futures contracts do not actually trade with one another—each trader's contractual obligation is with a futures exchange. This feature helps to guarantee the fiscal integrity of the trade. Incidentally, commodities futures traded on the exchanges are settled in the same way as financial futures, but in the case of commodities much of the contracting is done off the exchange, between farmers and processors, as forward contracts, in which case actual deliveries occur.
[17]For additional insights into the use of financial futures for hedging, see Stanley B. Block and Timothy J. Gallagher, "The Use of Interest Rate Futures and Options by Corporate Managers," Financial Management, Autumn 1986, 73–8; and Mark G. Castelino, Jack C. Francis, and Avner Wolf, "Cross-Hedging: Basis Risk and Choice of the Optimal Hedging Vehicle," Financial Review, May 1991, 179–210.
[18]In this example, a 10-year bond was hedged with a matching maturity Government of Canada Bond futures contract. Rather than simply matching on maturity, it would be more accurate to match on duration (see Web Extension 6B, available on the textbook's website, for a discussion of duration).
[19]LIBOR stands for the London Interbank Offered Rate, the rate charged on interbank dollar loans in the Eurodollar market. LIBOR might possibly be the most important number reported in financial markets as so many financial contracts base payments on LIBOR. In Canada, the Canadian Dealer Offered Rate, CDOR, is sometimes used as a replacement for LIBOR for Canadian dollar–based contracts.
[20]Such transactions are generally arranged by large money centre banks, and payments are made to the bank, which in turn pays the interest on the original loans. The bank assumes the credit risk and guarantees the payments should one of the parties default. For its services, the bank receives a percentage of the payments as its fee.

FIGURE 20-2 Cash Flows under a Swap

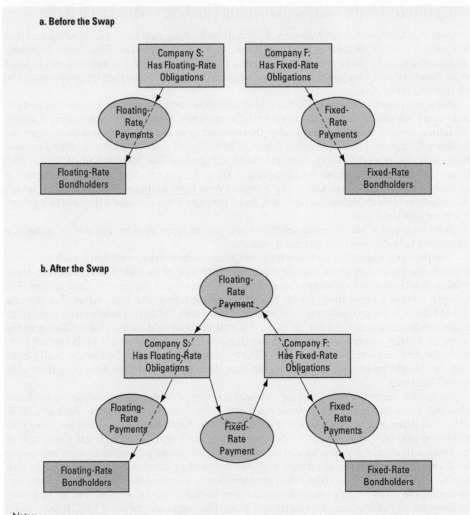

Notes:
In Panel a, Company S must make floating-rate payments out of its own internal cash flows, but in Panel b, it uses the floating payments from Company F to pay its bondholders. Company F has a reversed position. After the swap, S has de facto fixed payments, which are consistent with its stable internal flows, and F has floating payments, which are consistent with its fluctuating flows.

to Bosworth. In turn, Bosworth will pay the LIBOR rate to Antron. Table 20-2 shows the net rates paid by each participant, and Figure 20-3 graphs the flows. Note that Antron ends up making fixed payments, which it desires, but because of the swap the rate paid is 9.95% versus the 10% rate it would have paid had it issued fixed-rate debt directly. At the same time, the swap leaves Bosworth with floating-rate debt, which it wants, but at a rate of LIBOR + 1.45% versus the LIBOR + 1.50% it would have paid on directly issued floating-rate debt. As this example illustrates, swaps can sometimes lower the interest rate paid by each party.

Currency swaps are special types of interest rate swaps. To illustrate, suppose Company A, a Canadian firm, had issued $100 million of bonds in Canada to fund an investment in Germany. Meanwhile, Company G, a German firm, had issued $100 million of euro-denominated bonds in Germany to make an investment in Canada. Company A would earn euros but be required to make payments in dollars, and Company G would be in the opposite situation. Thus, both companies would be exposed to exchange rate risk. However, both companies' risks would be eliminated if they swapped payment obligations.

TABLE 20-2 Anatomy of an Interest Rate Swap

Antron's Payments: Borrows Floating, Swaps for Fixed		Bosworth's Payments: Borrows Fixed, Swaps for Floating	
Payment to lender	−(LIBOR + 1%)	Payment to lender	−10.40% fixed
Payment from Bosworth	+(LIBOR)	Payment from Antron	+8.95% fixed
Payment to Bosworth	−8.95% fixed	Payment to Antron	−(LIBOR)
Net payment by Antron	−9.95% fixed	Net payment by Bosworth	−(LIBOR + 1.45%)

FIGURE 20-3 The Antron/Bosworth Swap

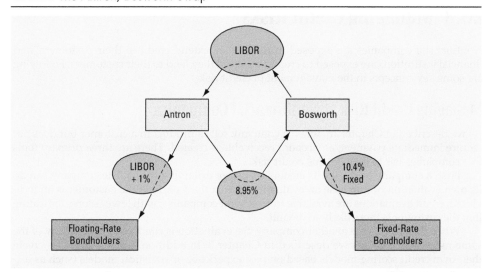

Originally, swaps were arranged between companies by money centre banks, which would match up counterparties. Such matching still occurs, but today most swaps are between companies and banks, with the banks then taking steps to ensure that their own risks are hedged. For example, Scotiabank might arrange a swap with Company A. Company A would agree to make specified payments in euros to Scotiabank, while Scotiabank made dollar payments to Company A. Scotiabank would charge a fee for setting up the swap, and those charges would reflect the creditworthiness of Company A. To protect itself against exchange rate movements, the bank would hedge its position, either by lining up a European company that needed to make dollar payments or else by using currency futures.[21]

Major changes have occurred over time in the swaps market. First, standardized contracts have been developed for the most common types of swaps, which has had two effects: (1) Standardized contracts lower the time and effort involved in arranging swaps, and this lowers transaction costs. (2) The development of standardized contracts has led to a secondary market for swaps, which has increased the liquidity and efficiency of the swaps market. A number of international banks now make markets in swaps and offer quotes on several standard types. Also, as noted previously, the banks now take counterparty positions in swaps, so it is not necessary to find another firm with mirror-image needs before a

---

[21]For more information on swaps, see Keith C. Brown and Donald J. Smith, "Default Risk and Innovations in the Design of Interest Rate Swaps," *Financial Management*, Summer 1993, pp. 94–105; Robert Einzig and Bruce Lange, "Swaps at Transamerica: Applications and Analysis," *Journal of Applied Corporate Finance*, Winter 1990, pp. 48–58; John F. Marshall, Vipul K. Bansal, Anthony F. Herbst, and Alan L. Tucker, "Hedging Business Cycle Risk with Macro Swaps and Options," *Journal of Applied Corporate Finance*, Winter 1992, pp. 103–108; and Laurie S. Goodman, "The Uses of Interest Rate Swaps in Managing Corporate Liabilities," *Journal of Applied Corporate Finance*, Winter 1990, pp. 35–47.

swap transaction can be completed. The bank would generally find a final counterparty for the swap at a later date, so its positioning helps make the swap market more operationally efficient.

Most swaps today involve either interest payments or currencies, but just about anything can be swapped, including equity swaps, credit spread swaps, and commodity swaps.[22]

CONCEPT REVIEW

1. Explain how a company can use Treasury bond futures to hedge against rising interest rates.

2. What is an interest rate swap? Describe the mechanics of a fixed-rate to floating-rate swap.

3. A CGB Treasury bond futures contract is trading for 103.52. What is the implied annual yield? (Check Figure: 5.54%)

4. Messman Corporation issues fixed-rate debt at a rate of 9.00%. Messman agrees to an interest rate swap in which it pays LIBOR to Moore Inc. and Moore pays 8.75% to Messman. What is Messman's resulting net payment? (Check Figure LIBOR + 0.25%)

20.8   Managing Credit Risks

Nonfinancial companies are exposed to risk if they extend credit to their customers, and financial institutions are exposed to credit risk when they lend to their customers. Following are some key concepts in the management of credit risk.

Managing Credit Risk at Nonfinancial Companies

As we described in Chapter 18, when a company sells a product to a customer but does not require immediate payment, an account receivable is created. There are three primary tools that companies use to manage this credit risk.

First, a company evaluates its customers before extending credit. The company can do its own evaluation or purchase an evaluation from a third party. If the customer is an individual, credit evaluations are available from several companies, with lower scores indicating that the customer is more likely to default.

When the customer is another company, the evaluation is conducted using many of the same ratios and analyses we described in Chapter 3. In addition, some companies create their own credit scoring models based on past experience or statistical models (such as discriminate analysis).

A company can mitigate its credit risk by selling its accounts receivable to a third party in a process called factoring. Of course, the price a company receives from selling its receivables depends on the receivables' risk, with riskier receivables purchased for much less than their nominal value. A company can also buy insurance for some or all of its receivables. Many companies, including the LEGO Group, use simulation to estimate the risk of their receivables so that they can better negotiate with insurers.

Managing Credit Risk at Financial Institutions

In addition to the same techniques used at nonfinancial corporations (credit scoring models and simulation), many financial institutions use credit default swaps (CDS), which were introduced in Chapter 16. Even though CDS are called swaps, they are like insurance. For example, an investor (which might be a financial institution) might purchase a CDS by making an annual payment to a counterparty to insure a particular bond or other security against default; if the bond defaults, the counterparty pays the purchaser the amount of the defaulted bond that was insured.

The CDS "price" is quoted in basis points and is called the CDS spread. For example, the spread on Barrick Gold Corp (Barrick) was 203 basis points in March 2015. An easy way to interpret the reported basis point spread is that it would be the annual fee in dollars to protect $10,000 of the bond. Therefore, it would cost $203 per year to insure $10,000 of Barrick's bonds.

---

[22]In an equity swap, the cash flow based on an equity index is swapped for some other cash flow. In a commodity swap, the swapped cash flow is based on commodity prices. In a credit swap, the cash flow usually is based on the spread between a risky bond and a U.S. Treasury bond.

To protect $10 million of Barrick's debt, a buyer would pay $203,000 = (0.0203) ($10 million) per year. In contrast, the spread on BCE was only 51 basis points, so insuring $10 million of BCE'S debt would cost only $51,000 per year. If the investors owned the bonds, then the purchase of the CDS would reduce the investor's risk.

There is an active secondary market for CDS and it is not necessary to own the underlying security. In fact, most participants in the CDS market don't own the underlying securities. For example, a speculator might purchase a CDS on Barrick for 203 basis points but purchase coverage for only 1 month, which would be a payment of $16,917 = $203,000/12. Now suppose that Barrick's credit worsened and drove Barrick's CDS spread up to 350 basis points. The investor could liquidate the position by selling 1-month credit protection for $29,167 = $350,000/12 and use the previously purchased CDS to offset the newly sold CDS. The investor's profit would be $12,250.

In addition to CDS for individual securities, there are CDS for indices. For example, the CDX.NA.IG is an index of 125 CDS for North American investment-grade debt. The index's movements are correlated with the overall level of default for many commercial loans—the index goes down as default rates increase. Therefore, a Canadian bank can protect itself from increasing default rates in its loan portfolio by taking short positions in the CDX.NA.IG, which pay off if the index goes up. This is a situation in which the CDS help reduce a financial institution's risk.

When banks and other major financial institutions take positions in swaps and CDS, they are themselves exposed to various risks, especially if their counterparties cannot meet their obligations. Furthermore, swaps are off-balance sheet transactions, making it impossible to tell just how large the swap market is or who has what obligation. Some estimate that the notional value of all CDS is over $9 trillion.[23] CDS are traded on government debt as well as corporate debt. Figure 20-4 shows the CDS prices for several countries. CDS prices range from 16 basis points for Germany to 1764 for a CDS on the debt of Greece. The extremely high CDS price for Greece's debt indicates the problems facing the country at the time of this writing (March 2015).

FIGURE 20-4 Credit Default Swap Spreads for Sovereign Debt (March 11, 2015)

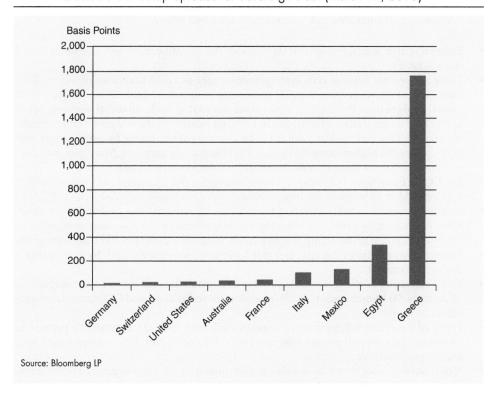

Source: Bloomberg LP

---

[23]Bank of International Settlements OTC derivatives statistics at end of June 2014, www.bis.org/publ/otc_hy 1411.pdf

CONCEPT REVIEW

1. Describe some ways to manage credit risk at a nonfinancial company.
2. What are credit default swaps?

20.9 Risk and Human Safety

Risk management decisions, like all corporate decisions, should begin with a cost-benefit analysis for each feasible alternative. For example, suppose it would cost $50,000 per year to conduct a comprehensive fire safety training program for all personnel in a high-risk plant. Presumably, this program would reduce the expected value of future fire losses. An alternative to the training program would be to place $50,000 annually in a reserve fund set aside to cover future fire losses. Both alternatives involve expected cash flows, and from an economic standpoint the choice should be made on the basis of the lowest present value of future costs.

However, suppose a fire occurs and a life is lost. In situations involving safety and health, the trade-off between expected profits and expected losses is not sufficient for making sound decisions. Companies must always consider the impact their decisions have on the safety of their employees and customers. Ignoring safety and health is an ethical mistake, but it also is a business mistake because many companies have been forced out of business or suffered debilitating losses when they produced unsafe products.

CONCEPT REVIEW

1. Describe a situation in risk management that involves ethical as well as financial issues.

Summary

The key concepts in enterprise risk management are listed below.

- **Enterprise risk management (ERM)** includes risk identification, risk assessment, and risk responses.
- There are several reasons **risk management** might increase the value of a firm. Risk management allows corporations (1) to increase their **use of debt,** (2) to maintain their **capital budget** over time, (3) to avoid costs associated with **financial distress,** (4) to utilize their **comparative advantages in hedging** relative to the hedging ability of individual investors, (5) to reduce both the risks and costs of borrowing by using **swaps,** and (6) to reduce the **higher taxes** that result from fluctuating earnings. Managers may also want to stabilize earnings in order to boost their own compensation.
- The COSO framework is a comprehensive enterprise risk management framework that applies ERM at all levels of the organization.
- Risk responses include (1) avoiding the activity, (2) reducing the probability of occurrence of an adverse event, (3) reducing the magnitude of the loss associated with an adverse event, (4) transferring the risk to an insurance company, (5) transferring the function that produces the risk to a third party, (6) sharing the risk by purchasing a derivative contract.
- Major categories of risk include (1) strategy and reputation, (2) control and compliance, (3) hazards, (4) human resources, (5) operation, (6) technology, and (7) financial management.
- Types of financial risk include (1) foreign exchange risk, (2) commodity price risk, (3) interest rate risk, (4) project selection risk, (5) liquidity risk, (6) customer credit risk, and (7) portfolio risk.
- A **derivative** is a security whose value is determined by the market price or interest rate of some other security.
- A **hedge** is a transaction that lowers risk. A **natural hedge** is a transaction between two **counterparties** whose risks are mirror images of each other.

- A **futures contract** is a standardized contract that is traded on an exchange and is marked-to-market daily, although physical delivery of the underlying asset usually does not occur.
- Under a **forward contract,** one party agrees to buy a commodity at a specific price and a specific future date and the other party agrees to make the sale; delivery does occur.
- A **swap** is an exchange of cash payment obligations. Swaps occur because the parties involved prefer the other's payment stream.
- **Financial futures** permit firms to create hedge positions to protect themselves against fluctuating interest rates, stock prices, and exchange rates.
- **Commodity futures** can be used to hedge against input price increases.
- **Long hedges** involve buying futures contracts to guard against price increases.
- **Short hedges** involve selling futures contracts to guard against price declines.
- **Symmetric hedges** protect against price increases and price decreases. Futures contracts are frequently used for symmetric hedges.
- **Asymmetric hedges** protect against price movements in one direction more than movements in another. Options are frequently used for asymmetric hedges.
- A **perfect hedge** occurs when the gain or loss on the hedged transaction exactly offsets the loss or gain on the unhedged position.

Questions

20-1 Define each of the following terms:
a. Derivative
b. Corporate risk management
c. Financial futures; forward contract
d. Hedging; natural hedge; long hedge; short hedge; perfect hedge
e. Swap; structured note
f. Commodity futures

20-2 Give two reasons shareholders might be indifferent between owning the stock of a firm with volatile cash flows and that of a firm with stable cash flows.

20-3 List six reasons risk management might increase the value of a firm.

20-4 Discuss some of the techniques available to reduce risk exposures.

20-5 Explain how the futures markets can be used to reduce interest rate and input price risk.

20-6 How can swaps be used to reduce the risks associated with debt contracts?

Concept Review Problem

Full solutions are provided at the www.nelson.com/brigham3ce.

CR-1 It is now March, and the current cost of debt for Wansley Construction is 12%. Wansley plans to issue $5 million in 10-year bonds (with coupons paid semiannually) in September, but is afraid that rates will climb even higher before then. The following data are available:

Futures Prices: Government of Canada Bonds—$100,000; Price in %

Delivery Month	Last Price	Change
Mar	99.16	0.04
June	98.78	−0.02
Sept	98.41	0.01

a. What is the implied interest rate on the September contract?
b. Construct a hedge for Wansley.
c. Assume all interest rates rise by 1 percentage point. What is the dollar value of Wansley's increased cost of issuing debt? What is Wansley's gain from the futures contract?

Problems

Easy
Problems 1–2

Answers to odd-numbered problems appear in Appendix A.

20-1
Swaps

Zhao Automotive issues fixed-rate debt at a rate of 7.00%. Zhao agrees to an interest rate swap in which it pays LIBOR to Lee Financial, and Lee pays 6.8% to Zhao. What is Zhao's resulting net payment?

20-2
Futures

A Government of Canada bond futures contract has a settlement price of 91.50. What is the implied annual yield?

Intermediate
Problems 3–4

20-3
Futures

What is the implied interest rate on a Government of Canada bond ($100,000) futures contract that settled at 112.75? If interest rates increased by 1%, what would be the contract's new value?

20-4
Swaps

Branger Ltd. has the choice of issuing floating-rate debt at LIBOR + 1% or fixed-rate debt at 6%. Likewise, Creeson Plastics can issue floating-rate debt at LIBOR + 2.5% or fixed-rate debt at 7.7%. Suppose Branger issues fixed-rate debt and Creeson issues floating-rate debt. The two companies are considering a swap where Branger will make LIBOR payments to Creeson in exchange for a fixed-rate payment of 5.1%. What are the net payments of Branger and Creeson if they engage in the swap? Is it better for Branger to issue fixed-rate debt and enter into the swap or to issue floating-rate debt? Is it better for Creeson to issue floating-rate debt and to enter into the swap or issue fixed-rate debt? What decision would each company make if the fixed-rate payment on the swap was 5.5%?

Challenging
Problems 5–7

20-5
Hedging

Zinn Company plans to issue $10,000,000 of 10-year bonds in June to help finance a new research and development laboratory. The bonds will pay interest semiannually. It is now November, and the current cost of debt to the high-risk biotech company is 9%. However, the firm's financial manager is concerned that interest rates will climb even higher in coming months. The following data are available:

Futures Prices: Government of Canada Bonds—$100,000; Price in%

Delivery Month	Price
Dec	102.16
Mar	102.78
June	102.53

a. Use the given data to create a hedge against rising interest rates.
b. Assume that interest rates in general increase by 200 basis points. How well did your hedge perform?
c. What is a perfect hedge? Are most real-world hedges perfect? Explain.

20-6
Hedging

DeWalden Resources Inc. plans to issue $30,000,000 of 10-year debt in September, and the chief financial officer is concerned that interest rates will rise over the next six months until the debt is raised. The current cost of debt for DeWalden Resources is 7.50%. The following futures prices are available.

Futures Prices: Government of Canada Bonds—$100,000; Price in %

Delivery Month	Price
June	96.58
September	97.61
December	97.24

a. Use the data given to hedge against rising interest rates.
b. Assume that interest rates increase by 250 basis points. How well did your hedge perform?
c. Assume that interest rates fall by 100 basis points. How well did your hedge perform?

20-7
Hedging

The following are data on August 2015 gold futures contracts:

Month	Last	Change	Prior Settle	Open	High	Low	Volume
Aug 2015	1,158.6	6.2	1,152.4	1,154.1	1,165.7	1,153.5	853

A mining company wishes to hedge against a decline in gold prices between now and August. The company has 2,500 oz. of gold to hedge (each futures contract is based on 100 oz.).
a. If gold prices decline by $0.25 per oz., what is the change in value of 1 contract?
b. How should the company hedge itself? What will be the value of the total futures position?
c. If closing prices for the next four days are 1,158.6; 1,176.1; 1,183.0 and 1,172.0, what are the losses and profits each day for the company? What was the company's net gain (loss) over the 4 days?
d. If the futures contract matured in August at 1,161.7, how much did the company gain or lose by hedging?

 # Spreadsheet Problem

20-8
Build a Model: Hedging

Start with the partial model in the file ***Ch 20 Build a Model.xlsx*** from the textbook's website. Use the information and data from Problem 20.5.
a. Create a hedge with the futures contract for Zinn Company's planned June debt offering of $10 million. What is the implied yield on the bond underlying the futures contract?
b. Suppose interest rates fall by 300 basis points. What are the dollar savings from issuing the debt at the new interest rate? What is the dollar change in value of the futures position? What is the total dollar value change of the hedged position?
c. Create a graph showing the effectiveness of the hedge if the change in interest rates, in basis points, is: −300, −200, −100, 0, 100, 200, or 300. Show the dollar cost (or savings) from issuing the debt at the new interest rates, the dollar change in value of the futures position, and the total dollar value change.

MINI CASE

You have just been hired as a financial analyst by Manitoba Sunshine Limited, a mid-sized Manitoba company that specializes in creating exotic sauces from imported fruits and vegetables. The firm's CEO, Bill Stooksbury, recently returned from an industry corporate executive conference in Vancouver, and one of the sessions he attended was on the pressing need for smaller companies to institute corporate risk management programs. Since no one at Manitoba Sunshine is familiar with the basics of derivatives and corporate risk management, Stooksbury has asked you to prepare a brief report that the firm's executives could use to gain at least a cursory understanding of the topics.

To begin, you gathered some outside materials on derivatives and corporate risk management and used these materials to draft a list of pertinent questions that need to be answered. In fact, one possible approach to the paper is to use a question-and-answer format. Now that the questions have been drafted, you have to develop the answers.
a. Why might shareholders be indifferent whether or not a firm reduces the volatility of its cash flows?
b. What are six reasons risk management might increase the value of a corporation?
c. What is corporate risk management? Why is it important to all firms?
d. Risks that firms face can be categorized in many ways. Define the following types of risk:
    (1) Speculative risks
    (2) Pure risks
    (3) Demand risks
    (4) Input risks
    (5) Financial risks
    (6) Property risks
    (7) Personnel risks
    (8) Environmental risks
    (9) Liability risks
    (10) Insurable risks

e. Explain how Manitoba Sunshine might benefit by implementing enterprise risk management and the COSO framework.

f. What are some actions that companies can take to minimize or reduce risk exposures?

g. What is financial risk exposure? Describe the following concepts and techniques that can be used to reduce financial risks:
    (1) Derivatives
    (2) Futures markets
    (3) Hedging
    (4) Swaps

h. Describe how commodity futures markets can be used to reduce input price risk.

i. It is January and Manitoba Sunshine is considering issuing $5 million in bonds in June to raise capital for an expansion. Currently, MS can issue 10-year bonds with a 7% coupon (with interest paid semiannually), but interest rates are on the rise and Stooksbury is concerned that long-term interest rates might rise by as much as 1% before June. You looked online and found that June T-bond futures are trading at 111.25. What are the risks of not hedging and how might MS hedge this exposure? In your analysis, consider what would happen if interest rates all increased by 1%.

part 6

Special Topics

Chapter 21 International Financial Management
Chapter 22 Corporate Valuation and Governance
Chapter 23 Mergers, Acquisitions, and Restructuring

chapter 21

International Financial Management*

Trading is vital to Canada. Exports account for 40% of our gross domestic product (GDP), and every day billions of dollars worth of goods and services are imported and exported. Trade will always be important to Canada as our economy is small and domestic companies must look to foreign markets to achieve economies of scale in order to remain competitive. Canadian aerospace companies generate only 20% of their sales domestically; the remaining 80% are exports. Even the insurance sector receives over half of its premiums from outside Canada.

While the above trade facts sound impressive, exports make up only part of overall globalization activity. Globalization now also encompasses production, including sourcing materials and components, assembling finished products in low-cost countries, and, finally, exporting them. Supply chains are now global and comparative advantages more fully utilized, resulting in improvements to productivity, profits, and wealth. Over half of China's exports are actually sold by *non-Chinese* multinationals operating out of China. Moreover, almost half of U.S. imports come from U.S. companies importing goods from their own subsidiaries! Distribution is the third globalization element. Foreign sales are realized by locating sales, service, and sometimes assembly operations in the export market itself. Canadian companies' sales from foreign affiliates total $400 billion annually—the same value of what we export annually.

Successful global companies must be sensitive to the many subtleties of different cultures and political systems. They find it useful to blend into the foreign landscape to win product acceptance and avoid political problems. Foreign-based multinationals such as Walmart, Home Depot, Toyota, and Honda are waging campaigns to fit in domestically, employ Canadians, and source products from local suppliers.

The emergence of multinational corporations raises a host of questions for governments. For example, should domestic firms be favoured, or does it make no difference what a company's nationality is as long as it provides domestic jobs? Should a company make an effort to keep jobs in its home country, or should it produce goods and services where costs are lowest? What nation controls the technology developed by a multinational, especially if the technology has military applications? Must a multinational company adhere to rules imposed in its home country with respect to its operations outside the home country? Keep these

*An earlier edition of this chapter benefited from the help of Professor Roy Crum of the University of Florida and Subu Venkataraman of Morgan Stanley.

questions in mind as you read this chapter. When you finish it, you should have a better appreciation of the problems facing governments and the difficult but profitable opportunities facing managers of multinational companies.

Sources: Stephen S. Poloz, "The New Global Trade Game: Will Canada Be a Player, or Just a Spectator?" Export Development Corporation, Speech given on January 20, 2005, http://www.edc.ca, accessed January 8, 2009; Government of Canada, http://www.investincanada.gc.ca, accessed August 19, 2008.

Managers of multinational companies must deal with a wide range of issues that are not present when a company operates in a single country. In this chapter, we highlight the key differences between multinational and domestic corporations, and we discuss the effects these differences have on the financial management of multinational businesses.

The textbook's website contains an *Excel* file that will guide you through the chapter's calculations. The file for this chapter is *Ch 21 Tool Kit.xlsx,* and we encourage you to open the file and follow along as you read the chapter. **www.nelson .com/brigham3ce**.

21.1 Multinational, or Global, Corporations

The term **multinational (global) corporation** is used to describe a firm that operates in an integrated fashion in a number of countries. International commercial activity has developed to greatly increase worldwide economic and political interdependence. Rather than merely buying resources from and selling goods to foreign nations, multinational firms now make direct investments in fully integrated operations, from extraction of raw materials, through the manufacturing process, to distribution to consumers throughout the world. Today, multinational corporate networks control a large and growing share of the world's technological, marketing, and productive resources.

Companies "go global" for many reasons, including the following:

1. *To broaden their markets.* After a company has saturated its home market, growth opportunities are often better in foreign markets. Thus, homegrown firms such as the Bank of Nova Scotia and the engineering firm SNC Lavalin are aggressively expanding into overseas markets, and foreign firms such as Sony and Toshiba now dominate the consumer electronics market. Also, as products become more complex, and development becomes more expensive, it is necessary to sell more units to cover overhead costs, so larger markets are critical. Thus, movie companies have "gone global" to get the volume necessary to support pictures such as *Lord of the Rings.*
2. *To seek raw materials.* Many resource companies, such as Barrick Gold, have major subsidiaries around the world to ensure access to the basic resources needed to sustain the companies' primary business lines.
3. *To seek new technology.* No single nation holds a commanding advantage in all technologies, so companies are scouring the globe for leading scientific and design ideas. For example, IBM acquired Canadian technology company Cognos Inc. for its unique business intelligence software product. IBM has bought 11 other Canadian companies since 2001. Magna International, a Canadian automotive systems supplier, has purchased 15 foreign companies since 2002. Versions of the superconcentrated detergent that Procter & Gamble first formulated in Japan in response to a rival's product are now being marketed in Europe and the United States.
4. *To seek production efficiency.* Companies in high-cost countries are shifting production to low-cost regions. For example, Canadian autoparts maker Linamar has production and assembly plants in Mexico, Hungary, and China, and Japanese manufacturers are shifting some of their production to lower-cost countries in the Pacific Rim. BMW, in response to high production costs in Germany, has built assembly plants in the United States. The ability to shift production from country to country has important implications for labour costs in all countries. For example, Alcan threatened to forego expansion of its Kitimat B.C. aluminum smelter in favour of projects in Iceland and South Africa if a settlement could not be reached with its union and the local governments over the sale of surplus electricity.
5. *To avoid political and regulatory hurdles.* The primary reason Japanese auto companies moved production to North America was to get around import quotas. Now Honda, Nissan, Toyota, Mazda, and Mitsubishi are all assembling vehicles in Canada and the United States. One factor that prompted the Canadian fertilizer company Agrium to sell its stake in a nitrogen production facility in Egypt was lobbying by local residents, which effectively stopped the project even after government approval had been provided.

Corporate Valuation and International Financial Management

The intrinsic value of a firm is determined by the size, timing, and risk of its expected future free cash flows (FCF). This is true for foreign as well as domestic operations. The FCF of a foreign operation is also affected by exchange rates, cultural differences, and the host country's regulatory environment. In addition, global financial markets and political risk can affect the cost of capital.

| Sales Revenues | Operating Costs and Taxes | Required Investments in Operations | | Financing Decisions | Interest Rates | Firm Risk | Market Risk |

Free Cash Flows (FCF)

Weighted Average Cost of Capital (WACC)

Value of the Firm

$$\text{Value} = \frac{FCF_1}{(1 + WACC)^1} + \frac{FCF_2}{(1 + WACC)^2} + \frac{FCF_3}{(1 + WACC)^3} + \cdots + \frac{FCF_\infty}{(1 + WACC)^\infty}$$

When Germany's BASF launched biotechnology research at home, it confronted legal and political challenges from the environmentally conscious Green movement. In response, BASF shifted its cancer and immune system research to two laboratories in the Boston suburbs. This location is attractive not only because of its large number of engineers and scientists but also because the Boston area has resolved controversies involving safety, animal rights, and the environment.

6. *To diversify.* By establishing worldwide production facilities and markets, firms can cushion the impact of adverse economic trends in any single country. For example, Bombardier can soften the blow of poor sales in the United States during a recession with strong sales in its European and Asian markets. In general, geographic diversification works because the economic ups and downs of different countries are not perfectly correlated.

There continues to be a large amount of investment in Canada by foreign corporations and in foreign nations by Canadian corporations. Given our population, such investment is necessary to ensure that Canadian companies remain competitive. However, even in the United States, the trend toward greater foreign investment has strengthened, eroding the Americans' traditional doctrine of independence and self-reliance. Just as U.S. corporations with extensive overseas operations are said to use their economic power to exert substantial economic and political influence over host governments, Americans fear that foreign corporations are gaining similar sway over U.S. policy. These developments suggest an overall increasing degree of mutual influence and interdependence among business enterprises and nations.

CONCEPT REVIEW

1. What is a multinational corporation?
2. Why do companies "go global"?

21.2 Multinational versus Domestic Financial Management

In theory, the concepts and procedures discussed in earlier chapters are valid for both domestic and multinational operations. However, six major factors distinguish financial management in firms operating entirely within a single country from that of firms operating globally:

1. *Different currency denominations.* Cash flows in various parts of a multinational corporate system will be denominated in different currencies. Hence, an analysis of exchange rates must be included in all financial analyses.

2. *Economic and legal ramifications.* Each country has its own unique economic and legal systems, and these differences can cause significant problems when a corporation tries to coordinate and control its worldwide operations. For example, differences in tax laws among countries can cause a given economic transaction to have strikingly different after-tax consequences, depending on where the transaction occurs. Similarly, differences in legal systems of host nations, such as the common law of Great Britain versus French civil law, complicate matters ranging from the simple recording of business transactions to the role played by the judiciary in resolving conflicts. Such differences can restrict multinational corporations' flexibility in deploying resources and can even make procedures that are required in one part of the company illegal in another part. These differences also make it difficult for executives trained in one country to move easily to another.

3. *Language differences.* The ability to communicate is critical in all business transactions. European and Japanese business people are usually fluent in several languages, including English, thus allowing them to enter our markets more easily than we can enter theirs.

4. *Cultural differences.* Even within geographic regions that are considered relatively homogeneous, different countries have unique cultural heritages that shape values and influence the conduct of business. Multinational corporations find that matters such as defining the appropriate goals of the firm, attitudes toward risk, dealings with employees, and the ability to curtail unprofitable operations vary dramatically from one country to the next.

5. *Role of governments.* Most financial models assume the existence of a competitive marketplace in which the terms of trade are determined by the participants. The government, through its power to establish basic ground rules, is involved in the process, but its role is minimal. Thus, the market provides the primary barometer of success, and it gives the best clues about what must be done to remain competitive. This view of the process is reasonably correct for Canada, the United States, and Western Europe, but it does not accurately describe the situation in most of the world. Frequently, the terms under which companies compete, the actions that must be taken or avoided, and the terms of trade on various transactions are determined not in the marketplace but by direct negotiation between host governments and multinational corporations. Such negotiation is essentially a political process, and it must be treated as such. Thus, our traditional financial models have to be recast to include political and other noneconomic aspects of the decision process.

6. *Political risk.* A nation might place constraints on the transfer of corporate resources or even appropriate assets within its boundaries. This is political risk, and it varies from country to country. Another aspect of political risk is terrorism against foreign firms and executives.

These six factors complicate financial management, and they increase the risks faced by multinational firms. However, the prospects for high returns, diversification benefits, and other factors make it worthwhile for firms to accept these risks and learn how to manage them.

CONCEPT REVIEW

1. Identify and briefly discuss six major factors that complicate financial management in multinational firms.

21.3 Exchange Rates

An **exchange rate** specifies the number of units of a given currency that can be purchased with one unit of another currency. Exchange rates appear daily in the financial sections of newspapers, such as the *Wall Street Journal*, the *National Post*, and at financial websites such as **http://www.bloomberg.com.** The values shown in Column 1 of Table 21-1 are the number of Canadian dollars required to purchase one unit of a foreign currency; this is called a **direct quotation.** Direct quotations have a dollar sign in their quotation and state the number of dollars per foreign currency unit, such as dollars per euro. Thus, the direct Canadian dollar quotation for the euro is $1.4116, because 1 euro can be bought for 1.4116 dollars.

The exchange rates given in Column 2 represent the number of units of a foreign currency that can be purchased for one Canadian dollar; these are called **indirect quotations.** Indirect quotations often begin with the foreign currency's equivalent to the dollar sign and express the foreign currency per dollar, such as euros per dollar. Thus, the indirect quotation for the euro is €0.7084. (The "€" stands for *euro* and is analogous to the symbol "$.")

Normal practice in currency trading centres is to use the indirect quotations (Column 2) for all currencies other than British pounds and euros, for which the direct quotations are given. Thus we speak of the pound as "selling at 1.7904 dollars, or at $1.7904," and the euro as "selling at $1.4116." For all other currencies, the normal convention is to use indirect quotations. For example, for the Japanese yen, we would quote the dollars as "being at ¥101.83," where the "¥" stands for *yen* and is analogous to the symbol "$." This convention eliminates confusion when comparing quotations from one trading centre—say, New York—with those from another—say, London or Zurich.

We can show how to work with exchange rates using the following example. Suppose an American tourist flies from New York to London, then to Paris, and then on to Geneva. She then flies to Montreal, and finally back to New York. Her tour includes lodging, food, and transportation, but she must pay for any other expenses. When she arrives at London's Heathrow Airport, she goes to the bank to check the foreign exchange listings. The rate she observes for US dollars is $1.5832; this means that £1 will cost US$1.5832. Assume that she exchanges US$3,000:

$$US\$3,000 = \frac{US\$3,000}{US\$1.5832 \text{ per pound}} = £1,894.90$$

She then enjoys a week's vacation in London, ending with £1,000.

After taking a train under the Channel to France, she realizes that she needs to exchange her 1,000 remaining pounds for euros. However, what she sees on the board is the quotation for US dollars per pound and the quotation for US dollars per euro (of $1.24825/euro). The exchange rate between any two currencies other than dollars is called a **cross rate.** Cross rates are actually calculated on the basis of various currencies relative to the US dollar. For example, the cross rate between British pounds and euros is computed as follows:

$$\text{Cross rate of euros per pound} = \frac{US\$1.5832 \text{ per pound}}{US\$1.24825 \text{ per euro}} = 1.2683 \text{ euros per pound}$$

TABLE 21-1 Selected Exchange Rates

	Direct Quotation: Canadian Dollars (CAD) Required to Buy One Unit of Foreign Currency (1)	Indirect Quotation: Number of Units of Foreign Currency per Canadian Dollar (CAD) (2)
US dollar (USD)	1.1309	0.8843
Japanese yen (JPY)	0.0098	101.83
Mexican peso (MXN)	0.0831	12.0347
Swiss franc (CHF)	1.1733	0.8523
UK (British) pound (GBP)	1.7904	0.5585
Euro (EUR)	1.4116	0.7084

Sources: "Financial Markets Daily," RBC Economics Research, Royal Bank of Canada, November 12 2014, http://www.rbc.com. Data from http://www.bankofcanada.ca/rates/interest-rates and http://www.federalreserve.gov/releases/h15/.

Therefore, for every British pound she would receive 1.2683 euros, so she would receive 1.2683(1,000) = 1,268.30 euros.

She has 800 euros remaining when she finishes touring in France and arrives in Geneva. She again needs to determine a cross rate, this time between euros and Swiss francs. The quotes she sees are a quote for euros (US$1.24825 per euro) and a quote for Swiss francs (CHF 0.9639 per US dollar). To find the cross rate for Swiss francs per euro, she makes the following calculation:

$$\text{Cross rate of Swiss francs per euro} = \left(\frac{\text{Swiss francs}}{\text{Dollar}}\right)\left(\frac{\text{Dollars}}{\text{Euro}}\right)$$

$$= (\text{CHF } 0.9639 \text{ per US dollar})(\$1.24825 \text{ per euro})$$

$$= 1.2032 \text{ Swiss francs per euro}$$

Therefore, for every euro she would receive 1.2032 Swiss francs, so she would receive 1.2032(800) = 962.56 Swiss francs.

She has 500 Swiss francs remaining when she leaves Geneva and arrives in Montreal. She again needs to determine a cross rate, this time between Swiss francs and Canadian dollars. The quotes she sees are a quote for Swiss francs (CHF 0.9639 per US dollar) and a quote for Canadian dollars (1.1309 Canadian dollars per US dollar). To find the cross rate for Canadian dollars per Swiss franc, she makes the following calculation:

$$\text{Cross rate of Canadian dollars per Swiss franc} = \frac{\left(\dfrac{\text{Canadian dollars}}{\text{US dollar}}\right)}{\left(\dfrac{\text{Swiss francs}}{\text{US dollar}}\right)}$$

$$= \frac{(1.1309 \text{ Canadian dollars per US dollar})}{(\text{CHF } 0.9639 \text{ per US dollar})}$$

$$= 1.1733 \text{ Canadian dollars per Swiss franc}$$

Therefore, she would receive 1.1733(500) = 586.65 Canadian dollars.

After leaving Montreal and arriving at New York, she has 100 Canadian dollars remaining. She sees the quote for Canadian dollars and converts the 100 Canadian dollars to US dollars as follows:

$$100 \text{ Canadian dollars} = \frac{100 \text{ Canadian dollars}}{1.1309 \text{ Canadian dollars per US dollar}} = \$88.43 \text{ US}$$

In this example, we made three assumptions. First, we assumed that our traveller had to calculate all of the cross rates. For retail transactions, it is customary to display the cross rates directly instead of as a series of dollar rates. Second, we assumed that exchange rates remain constant over time. Actually, exchange rates vary every day, often dramatically. We will have more to say about exchange rate fluctuations in the next section. Finally, we assumed that there were no transaction costs involved in exchanging currencies. In reality, small retail exchange transactions such as those in our example usually involve fixed and/ or sliding scale fees that can easily consume 5% or more of the transaction amount.

Major business publications, such as *The Globe and Mail*, and websites, such as **http:// www.bloomberg.com,** regularly report cross rates among key currencies. A set of cross rates is given in Table 21-2. When examining the table, note the following points:

1. Column 1 gives indirect quotes for Canadian dollars, that is, units of a foreign currency that can be bought with one Canadian dollar (CAD). Examples: $1 will buy 0.7084 euro (EUR) or 0.8523 Swiss francs (CHF). Note the consistency with Table 21-1, Column 2.
2. Other columns show number of units of other currencies that can be bought with 1 pound, 1 Swiss franc, and so on. For example, the euro column shows that 1 euro will buy 1.4116 Canadian dollars, 143.75 Japanese yen (JPY), or 1.24825 US dollars (USD).
3. The rows show direct quotes, that is, number of units of the currency of the country listed in the left column required to buy one unit of the currency listed in the top row. The top row is particularly important for Canadian companies, as it shows

TABLE 21-2	Key Currency Cross Rates						
	CAD	USD	JPY	MXN	CHF	GBP	EUR
CAD	1.0	1.1309	0.0098	0.0831	1.1733	1.7904	1.4116
USD	0.8843	1.0	0.008683	0.073475	1.037452	1.5832	1.24825
JPY	101.83	115.17	1.0	8.46	119.48	182.33	143.75
MXN	12.0347	13.6101	0.1182	1.0	14.1198	21.5474	16.9887
CHF	0.8523	0.9639	0.0084	0.0708	1.0	1.5260	1.2032
GBP	0.5585	0.6316	0.0055	0.0464	0.6553	1.0	0.7884
EUR	0.7084	0.8011	0.0070	0.0589	0.8311	1.2683	1.0

Sources: "Financial Markets Daily," *RBC Economics Research*, Royal Bank of Canada, November 12, 2014. http://www.rbc.com, accessed November 12, 2014. Data from http://www.bankofcanada.ca/rates/interest-rates and http://www.federalreserve.gov/releases/h15/.

the direct quotes for the Canadian dollar. This row is consistent with Column 1 of Table 21-1.

4. Note that the values on the top row of Table 21-2 are reciprocals of the corresponding values in the first column. For example, the Swiss franc row in the first column shows 0.8523 Swiss francs per Canadian dollar, and the Swiss franc column in the top row shows 1/0.8523 = 1.1733 dollars per Swiss franc.

The relationship with a common currency ensures that all currencies are related to one another in a consistent manner—if this consistency did not exist, currency traders could profit by buying undervalued and selling overvalued currencies. This process, known as **arbitrage**, works to bring about an equilibrium wherein the same relationship described earlier exists. Currency traders are constantly operating in the market, seeking small inconsistencies from which they can profit. The traders' existence enables the rest of us to assume that currency markets are in equilibrium and that, at any point in time, cross rates are all internally consistent.[1]

ⒸNCEPT REVIEW

1. What is an exchange rate?
2. Explain the difference between direct and indirect quotations.
3. What is a cross rate?
4. Assume that the indirect quote is for 10.0 Mexican pesos per Canadian dollar. What is the direct quote for dollars per peso? (Check Figure: 0.10 dollar/peso)
5. Assume there is a quote for 115 Japanese yen per Canadian dollar and another quote is for 1.25 Canadian dollars per euro. What is the yen per euro exchange rate? (Check Figure: 143.75 yen/euro)

21.4 Exchange Rates and International Trade

Just as the demand for consumer goods such as Tommy Hilfiger clothing and Nike shoes changes over time, so does the demand for currency. One factor affecting currency demand is the balance of trade between two countries. For example, Canadian importers must buy yen to pay for Japanese goods, whereas Japanese importers must buy Canadian dollars to pay for Canadian goods. If Canadian imports from Japan were to exceed Canadian exports to Japan,

---

[1]For more discussion of exchange rates, see Jongmoo Jay Choi and Anita Mehra Prasad, "Exchange Risk Sensitivity and Its Determinants: A Firm and Industry Analysis of U.S. Multinationals," *Financial Management*, Autumn 1995, 77–88; Jerry A. Hammer, "Hedging Performance and Hedging Objectives: Tests of New Performance Measures in the Foreign Currency Market," *Journal of Financial Research*, Winter 1990, 307–323; and William C. Hunter and Stephen G. Timme, "A Stochastic Dominance Approach to Evaluating Foreign Exchange Hedging Strategies," *Financial Management*, Autumn 1992, 104–112.

then Canada would have a **trade deficit** with Japan, and there would be a greater demand for yen than for Canadian dollars. Capital movements also affect currency demand. For example, suppose interest rates in Canada were higher than those in Japan. To take advantage of high Canadian interest rates, Japanese banks, corporations, and sophisticated individuals would buy Canadian dollars with yen and then use those dollars to purchase high-yielding Canadian securities. This would create greater demand for dollars than for yen.

Without any government intervention, the relative prices of yen and dollars would fluctuate in response to changes in supply and demand in much the same way that prices of consumer goods fluctuate. For example, if Canadian consumers were to increase their demand for Japanese electronic products, then the accompanying increase in demand for the yen would cause its value to increase relative to the dollar. In this situation, the strong yen would be due to fundamental economic forces.

However, governments can and do intervene. A country's central bank can artificially prop up its currency by using its reserves of gold or foreign currencies to purchase its own currency in the open market. This creates artificial demand for its own currency, thus causing its value to be artificially high. A central bank can also keep its currency at an artificially low value by selling its own currency in the open markets. This increases the currency's supply, which reduces its price.

Why might an artificially low currency be a problem? After all, a cheap currency makes it less expensive for other nations to purchase the country's goods, which creates jobs in the exporting country. However, an artificially low currency value raises the cost of imports, which increases inflation. In addition, high import prices allow competing domestic manufacturers to raise their prices as well, further boosting inflation. The government intervention that causes the artificially low value also contributes to inflation: When a government creates currency to sell in the open markets, this increases the money supply, and, all else held constant, an increasing money supply leads to still more inflation. Thus, artificially holding down the value of a currency stimulates exports but at the expense of potentially overheating and inflating the economy. Also, other countries—whose economies are being weakened because their manufacturers cannot compete against the artificially low prices—may retaliate and impose tariffs or other restrictions on the country that is holding its currency value down.

For example, China had for many years artificially held down the value of the yuan (also called the renminbi). This helped make China the world's largest exporter and greatly stimulated its economy. However, by 2004 the Chinese economy was growing at an unsustainably high rate, and inflation was rising rapidly. The United States and other nations began urging the Chinese government to allow the yuan to rise, which would help their economies by slowing Chinese exports and stimulating their own exports to China. On July 21, 2005, the Chinese government suddenly announced that it was changing the exchange rate to allow the yuan's value to rise by 2.1%. By November 2014, the yuan had risen about 33% against the US dollar.

A currency that is artificially high has the opposite effects: inflation will be held down, and citizens can purchase imported goods at low domestic prices, but exporting industries are hurt, as are domestic industries that compete with the cheap imports. Because there is relatively little external demand for the currency, the government will have to create demand by purchasing its own currency, paying with either gold or foreign currencies held by its central bank. Over time, supporting an inflated currency can deplete the gold and foreign currency reserves, making it impossible to continue propping up the currency.

The following sections describe ways that governments handle changes in currency demands.

CONCEPT REVIEW

1. What is the effect on a country's economy caused by an artificially low exchange rate? By an artificially high exchange rate?

21.5 The International Monetary System and Exchange Rate Policies

Every nation has a monetary system and a monetary authority. In Canada, the Bank of Canada is our monetary authority (in the United States, it is the Federal Reserve), and its task is to hold down inflation while promoting economic growth and raising our national standard of living. Moreover, if countries are to trade with one another, we must have some sort of system designed to facilitate payments between nations. The international monetary system is the framework within which exchange rates are determined. As we describe below, there are several different policies used by various countries to determine exchange rates.[2]

A Short History Lesson: The Bretton Woods Fixed Exchange Rate System

From the end of the Second World War until August 1971, most of the industrialized world operated under the Bretton Woods **fixed exchange rate system** administered by the International Monetary Fund (IMF). Under this system, the US dollar was linked to gold (at $35 per ounce), and other currencies were then tied to the dollar. The United States took actions to keep the price of gold at $35 per ounce, and central banks acted to keep exchange rates between other currencies and the dollar within narrow limits. For example, when the demand for pounds was falling, the Bank of England would step in and buy pounds to push up their price, offering gold or foreign currencies in exchange for pounds. Conversely, when the demand for pounds was too high, the Bank of England would sell pounds for dollars or gold. The Federal Reserve in the United States performed the same functions, and central banks of other countries operated similarly. These actions artificially matched supply and demand, keeping exchange rates stable, but they didn't address the underlying imbalance. For example, if the high demand for pounds occurred because British productivity was rising and British goods were improving in quality, then the underlying demand for pounds would continue in spite of central bank intervention. In such a situation the Bank of England would find it necessary to continually sell pounds indefinitely. If the central bank stopped selling pounds, their value would rise; that is, the pound would strengthen and exceed the agreed-upon limits.

Many countries found it difficult and economically painful to maintain the fixed exchange rates required by Bretton Woods. This system began to crumble in August 1971, and it was abandoned completely by the end of 1973. The following sections describe several modern exchange rate systems.

Freely, or Independently, Floating Rates

In the early 1970s, the US dollar was cut loose from the gold standard and, in effect, allowed to "float" in response to supply and demand caused by international trade and international investing activities. According to the IMF, about 36 countries currently operate under a system of **floating exchange rates,** whereby currency prices are allowed to seek their own levels, with only modest central bank intervention to smooth out extreme exchange rate fluctuations. According to the IMF, about 29 currencies have freely, or independently, floating exchange rates, including the US dollar, Canadian dollar, euro, pound, and yen.

Currency Appreciation and Depreciation Suppose the dollar cost of a pound is $1.7904 as shown in Table 21-1. If there were increased demand for pounds caused by a Canadian trade deficit with Great Britain, then the price of pounds might increase to $2.10. In this situation, the pound is said to be *appreciating*, because a pound now buys more dollars. In other words, a pound is now worth more than it previously was. This is called **currency appreciation.** Conversely, the dollar is *depreciating*, because the dollar now buys fewer pounds (a dollar would previously buy 1/1.7904 = 0.5585 pound, but afterward it buys only 1/2.10 = 0.4762 pound). This is called **currency depreciation.** Notice that the more costly pound makes British imports more expensive to Canadian consumers, which reduces imports—and, consequently, the demand for pounds—until the exchange rate reaches equilibrium.

Exchange Rate Risk Exchange rate fluctuations can have a profound effect on profits and trade. For example, in 2004 the euro exchange rate was about $1.59 (i.e., 1.59 Canadian dollars per euro). In 2014, the exchange rate was about $1.48. Consider the impact this has on profits and trade. For example, a hand-blown glass bowl from the Italian island of Murano cost about €50 in 2004. Ignoring shipping and taxes, a consumer in Canada could have purchased this glass

[2]For a comprehensive history of the international monetary system and details of how it has evolved, consult one of the many economics books on the subject, including Robert Carbaugh, *International Economics* 14th ed. (Mason, OH: South-Western, Cengage Learning, 2012); Mordechai Kreinin, *International Economics: A Policy Approach,* 10th ed. (Mason, OH: South-Western, 2006); Jeff Madura, *International Financial Management* 11th ed. (Mason, OH: Thomson/South-Western, 2012); and Joseph P. Daniels and David D. Van Hoose, *International Monetary and Financial Economics,* 3rd ed. (Mason, OH: South-Western, 2005).

for €50($1.59/€) = $79.50. Assuming the price in 2014 still was €50, it would cost €50($1.48/€) = $74.00. Thus the change in exchange rates would help Italian exports to Canada.

By contrast, Canadian producers were able to export maple syrup to Italy less profitably in 2014 than in 2004. For example, suppose a litre of maple syrup cost a Quebec producer $6 to produce in 2004 but could be sold for €5 in Italy. In 2004, the profit would have been €5($1.59/€) − $6 = $1.95. Assuming no change in production costs, the litre of maple syrup's profit in 2014 is €5($1.48/€) − $6 = $1.40. Thus, Canadian exporters to Europe have not done as well from the change in exchange rates.

The inherent volatility of exchange rates under a floating system increases the uncertainty of the cash flows for a multinational corporation. Because its cash flows are generated in many parts of the world, they are denominated in many different currencies. When exchange rates change, the dollar-equivalent value of the company's consolidated cash flows also fluctuates. This is known as **exchange rate risk,** and it is a major factor differentiating a global company from a purely domestic one.

Managed Floating Rates

In a **managed floating rate** system, there is significant government intervention to manage the exchange rate by manipulating the currency's supply and demand. The government rarely reveals its target exchange rate levels if it uses a managed-float regime because this would make it too easy for currency speculators to profit. According to the IMF, about 36 countries have a managed floating rate system, including Colombia, India, Turkey, and Brazil.

Pegged Exchange Rates

In a **pegged exchange rates** system, a country locks, or "pegs," its currency's exchange rate to another currency or basket of currencies. It is common for a country with a pegged exchange rate to allow its currency to vary within specified limits or bands (often set at ±1% of the target rate) before the country intervenes to force the currency back within the limits. Examples in which a currency is pegged to another country's currency include Bhutan's ngultrum, which is pegged to the Indian rupee; the Falkland Islands' pound, which is pegged to the British pound; and Barbados's dollar, which is pegged to the US dollar. An example of a currency being pegged to a basket is China, where the yuan is no longer just pegged to the US dollar but rather to a basket of currencies. Interestingly, the Chinese government will not reveal the currencies that make up the basket, but the US dollar, the euro, the yen, and the South Korean won are certainly components.

Currency Devaluation and Revaluation As indicated earlier, countries with pegged exchange rates establish a fixed exchange rate with some other major currency or basket of currencies. When a government lowers the target fixed exchange rate, this is called **devaluation,** and when it increases the rate it is called **revaluation.** For example, from 1991 through early 2002, Argentina had a fixed exchange rate of 1 peso per US dollar. Imports were high, exports were low, and the Argentinean government had to purchase huge amounts of pesos to maintain that artificially high exchange rate. The government borrowed heavily to finance these purchases, and eventually it was unable to continue supporting the peso. (Indeed, the government defaulted on some of its obligations.) As a result, the government had to devalue the peso to 1.4 pesos per dollar in early 2002. Notice that this made the peso weaker: Before the devaluation, 1 peso would buy 1 dollar, but afterward 1 peso would buy only 71 cents (1.4 pesos per dollar = 1/1.4 = 0.71 dollar per peso). The devaluation lowered the prices of Argentine goods on the world market, which helped its exporters, but prices rose for imported goods, including oil. The initial shock to the Argentine economy was severe, as employment fell in those industries that were not exporters. The problem was exacerbated because many Argentine companies and individuals had borrowed using debt denominated in dollars, which instantly cost much more to service. However, the economy gradually improved, with increased exports, tourism, and employment rates. Still, the initial pain caused by devaluation helps explain why many countries with fixed exchange rates tend to postpone needed measures until economic pressures build to explosive proportions.

Due to the expense of maintaining an artificially high exchange rate and the pain of large devaluations, many countries that once had pegged exchange rates now allow their currencies to float. For example, Mexico had a pegged exchange rate prior to 1994, but it depleted its foreign reserves trying to support the peso and was forced to devalue it. Mexico's currency now floats, as does that of Argentina.

Convertible versus Nonconvertible Securities A pegged exchange rate *per se* isn't necessarily a deterrent to direct investment in the country by foreign corporations, as long as the local government's central bank supports the currency and devaluations are unlikely. This was generally the case in the Bretton Woods era, and so those currencies were considered to be **convertible currencies** because the nations that issued them allowed them to be traded in the currency markets and was willing to redeem them at market rates. This is true today for all floating-rate currencies, which are also called **hard currencies** because of their convertibility. Some pegged currencies are also at least partially convertible, because their central banks will redeem them at market rates under specified conditions.

However, some countries set the exchange rate but do not allow their currencies to be traded on world markets. For example, the Chinese yuan is allowed to float in a very narrow band against a basket of securities. However, the yuan can be legally used and exchanged only within China. Furthermore, the Chinese government imposes restrictions on both residents and nonresidents from freely converting their holdings of yuans into another currency. Thus, the yuan is a *nonconvertible currency*, also called a **soft currency.** When official exchange rates differ from "market rates" or when there are restrictions on convertibility, a black market will often arise. For example, in September 2014, Venezuela's official exchange rate was about 6.3 bolivars per dollar, but black market prices were estimated to be around 100.7.

A nonconvertible currency creates problems for foreign companies looking to make direct investments. Consider the situation faced by Pizza Hut when it wanted to open a chain of restaurants in the former Soviet Union. The Russian ruble was not convertible, so Pizza Hut could not take the profits from its restaurants out of the Soviet Union in the form of dollars. There was no mechanism to exchange the rubles it earned in Russia for dollars; therefore, an investment in the Soviet Union was essentially worthless to a U.S. company. However, Pizza Hut arranged to use the ruble profit from the restaurants to buy Russian vodka, which it then shipped to the United States and sold for dollars. Pizza Hut managed to find a solution, but lack of convertibility significantly inhibits the ability of a country to attract foreign investment.

No Local Currency

A few countries don't have their own separate legal tender, but instead use the currency of another nation. For example, Ecuador has used the US dollar since September 2000. Other countries belong to a monetary union, such as the 19 European Monetary Union nations whose currency is the euro, which is allowed to float. In contrast, member nations of the Eastern Caribbean Currency Union, the West African Economic and Monetary Union (WAEMU), and the Central African Economic and Monetary Community (CAEMC) use their respective union's currency, which is itself pegged to some other currency. For example, the Eastern Caribbean dollar is pegged to the US dollar, and the CFA franc (used by both the WAEMU and CAEMC) is pegged to the euro.[3]

CONCEPT REVIEW

1. What is the difference between a fixed exchange rate system and a floating rate system?
2. What are pegged exchange rates?
3. What does it mean to say that the dollar is depreciating with respect to the euro?
4. What is a convertible currency?

21.6 Trading in Foreign Exchange

Importers, exporters, tourists, and governments buy and sell currencies in the foreign exchange market. For example, when a Canadian trader imports automobiles from Japan, payment will probably be made in Japanese yen. The importer buys yen (through its bank) in the foreign exchange market, much as one buys common stocks on the Toronto Stock Exchange or pork bellies on the Chicago Mercantile Exchange. However, whereas stock and commodity exchanges have a central location, the foreign exchange market consists of a

---

[3]A few countries, such as Bosnia and Herzegovina, have currency board arrangements. Under this system, a country technically has its own currency but commits to exchange it for a specified foreign money unit at a fixed exchange rate. This requires it to impose domestic currency restrictions unless it has the foreign currency reserves to cover requested exchanges.

network of brokers and banks based in New York, London, Tokyo, Toronto, and other financial centres. Most buy and sell orders are conducted by computer and telephone.

Spot Rates and Forward Rates

The exchange rates shown earlier in Tables 21-1 and 21-2 are known as **spot rates,** which means the rate paid for delivery of the currency "on the spot" or, in reality, no more than two days after the day of the trade. For most of the world's major currencies, it is also possible to buy (or sell) currencies for delivery at some agreed-upon future date, usually 30, 90, or 180 days from the day the transaction is negotiated. This rate is known as the **forward exchange rate.**

For example, suppose a Canadian firm must pay 500 million yen to a Japanese firm in 30 days, and the current spot rate is 101.83 yen per dollar. Unless spot rates change, the Canadian firm will pay the Japanese firm the equivalent of $4.910 million (500 million yen divided by 101.83 yen per dollar) in 30 days. But if the spot rate falls to 98 yen per dollar, for example, the Canadian firm will have to pay the equivalent of $5.102 million. The treasurer of the Canadian firm can avoid this risk by entering into a 30-day forward exchange contract. This contract promises delivery of yen to the Canadian firm in 30 days at a guaranteed price of 101.80 yen per dollar. No cash changes hands at the time the treasurer signs the forward contract, although the Canadian firm might have to put down some collateral as a guarantee against default. Because the firm can use an interest-bearing instrument for the collateral, though, this requirement is not costly. The counterparty to the forward contract must deliver the yen to the Canadian firm in 30 days, and the Canadian firm is obligated to purchase the 500 million yen at the previously agreed-upon rate of 101.80 yen per dollar. Therefore, the treasurer of the Canadian firm is able to lock in a payment equivalent to $4.912 million, no matter what happens to spot rates. This technique is called "hedging."

Forward rates for 30-, 90-, and 180-day delivery, along with the current spot rates for some commonly traded currencies, are given in Table 21-3. If you can obtain *more* of the foreign currency for a dollar in the forward than in the spot market, the forward currency is less valuable than the spot currency, and the forward currency is said to be selling at a *discount.* In other words, if the foreign currency is expected to depreciate (based on the forward rates), then the spot rate is at a discount. Conversely, since a dollar would buy *fewer* yen and US dollars in the forward than in the spot market, the forward yen and US dollars are selling at a *premium.*

ⒸNCEPT REVIEW

1. Differentiate between spot and forward exchange rates.
2. Explain what it means for a forward currency to sell at a discount and at a premium.

TABLE 21-3   Selected Spot and Forward Exchange Rates; Indirect Quotation: Number of Units of Foreign Currency per Canadian Dollar

		Forward Rates			
	Spot Rate	1 Month	3 Months	6 Months	Forward Rate at a Premium or Discount[a]
US (dollar)	0.8843	0.8839	0.8823	0.8800	Premium
Britain (pound)*	1.7904	1.7910	1.7935	1.7969	Premium
Japan (yen)	101.8348	101.80	101.52	101.12	Premium
Euro*	1.4116	1.4107	1.4145	1.4199	Premium

Notes:
* Inverted.
[a] When it takes more units of a foreign currency to buy one dollar in the future, the value of the foreign currency is less in the forward market than in the spot market; the forward rate is said to be at a *discount* to the spot rate.

Sources: "Financial Markets Daily," RBC Economics Research, Royal Bank of Canada, November 2014, http://www.rbc.com. Data from http://www.rbc.com. Data from http://www.bankofcanada.ca/rates/interest-rates and http://www.federalreserve.gov/releases/h15/.

21.7 Interest Rate Parity

Market forces determine whether a currency sells at a forward premium or discount, and the general relationship between spot and forward exchange rates is specified by a concept called "interest rate parity."

Interest rate parity means that investors should expect to earn the same return on security investments in all countries after adjusting for risk. It recognizes that when you invest in a country other than your home country, you are affected by two forces—returns on the investment itself and changes in the exchange rate. It follows that your overall return will be higher than the investment's stated return if the currency in which your investment is denominated appreciates relative to your home currency. Likewise, your overall return will be lower if the foreign currency you receive declines in value.

To illustrate interest rate parity, consider the case of a Canadian investor who can buy default-free 6-month US bonds that promise a 4% nominal annual return. The 6-month US interest rate, r_f, is $4\%/2 = 2\%$. Assume also that the indirect quotation for the spot exchange rate is 0.8843 US dollars per Canadian dollar, as shown in Table 21-3. Finally, assume that the 6-month forward exchange rate is 0.8800 US dollars per Canadian dollar, which means that in 6 months the investor can exchange 1 Canadian dollar for 0.8800 US dollars.

The Canadian investor could receive a 4% annualized return denominated in US dollars, but if he or she ultimately wants to consume goods in Canada, those US dollars must be converted to Canadian dollars. The dollar return on the investment depends, therefore, on what happens to exchange rates over the next 6 months. However, the investor can lock in the dollar return by selling the foreign currency in the forward market. For example, the investor could simultaneously:

1. Convert $1,000 Canadian to 884.30 US dollars in the spot market: $1,000(0.8843 US dollars per Canadian dollar) = 884.30 US dollars.
2. Invest the US dollars in a 6-month U.S. bond that has a 4% annual return or a 2% semi-annual return. This investment will pay 884.30(1.02) = 901.99 US dollars in 6 months.
3. Agree today to exchange the US dollars in 6 months at the rate of 0.8800 US dollars per Canadian dollar, for a total of (901.99 US dollars)/(0.8800 US dollars per Canadian dollar) = $1,024.99 Canadian.

This investment, therefore, has an expected 6-month return of $24.99/$1,000 = 2.499%, which translates into a nominal annual return of 2(2.499%) = 5.0%. In this case, 4% of the expected 5.0% return is coming from the bond itself, and 1.0% arises because the market believes that the US dollar will strengthen relative to the dollar. Note that by locking in the forward rate today, the investor has eliminated all exchange rate risk. And since the U.S. bond is assumed to be default-free, the investor is certain to earn a 5.0% annual dollar return.

Interest rate parity implies that an investment in Canada with the same risk as the U.S. bond should also have a return of 5.0%. We can express interest rate parity by the following equation:

$$\frac{\text{Forward exchange rate}}{\text{Spot exchange rate}} = \frac{(1 + r_h)}{(1 + r_f)} \qquad (21\text{-}1)$$

Here r_h is the periodic interest rate in the home country, r_f is the periodic interest rate in the foreign country, and the forward and exchange rates are expressed as direct quotations (i.e., dollars per foreign currency).

Using Table 21-3, the direct spot quotation is 1.1308 Canadian dollars per US dollar = (1/0.8843 US dollars per Canadian dollar), and the direct 6-month forward quotation is (1.1364 = 1/0.8800). Using Equation 21-1, we can solve for the equivalent home rate, r_h:

$$\frac{\text{Forward exchange rate}}{\text{Spot exchange rate}} = \frac{(1 + r_h)}{(1 + r_f)} = \frac{(1 + r_h)}{(1 + 0.02)} = \frac{1.1364}{1.1308}$$

$$(1 + r_h) = \left(\frac{1.1364}{1.1308}\right)(1 + 0.02) = 1.0250 \qquad (21\text{-}1a)$$

The periodic home interest rate is 2.50, and the annualized home interest rate is $(2.50\%)(2) =$ 5.0%, the same value we found above.

After accounting for exchange rates, interest rate parity states that bonds in the home country and the foreign country must have the same effective rate of return. In this example, the Canadian bond must yield 5.0% to provide the same return as the 4% U.S. bond. If one bond provides a higher return, investors will sell their low-return bond and flock to the high-return bond. This activity will cause the price of the low-return bond to fall (which pushes up its yield) and the price of the high-return bond to increase (driving down its yield). This will continue until the two bonds again have the same returns after accounting for exchange rates.

In other words, interest rate parity implies that an investment in Canada with the same risk as a U.S. bond should have a dollar value return of 5.0%. Solving for r_h in Equation 21-1, we indeed find that the predicted interest rate in Canada is 5.0%.

Interest rate parity shows why a particular currency might be at a forward premium or discount. Note that a currency is at a forward premium whenever domestic interest rates are higher than foreign interest rates. Discounts prevail if domestic interest rates are lower than foreign interest rates. If these conditions do not hold, then arbitrage will soon force interest rates and exchange rates back to parity.

⊙NCEPT REVIEW

1. What is interest rate parity?

2. Assume that interest rate parity holds. When a currency trades at a forward premium, what does that imply about domestic rates relative to foreign interest rates? What about when a currency trades at a forward discount?

3. Assume that 90-day Canadian T-bills have a 4.5% annualized interest rate, whereas 90-day Swiss securities have a 5% annualized interest rate. In the spot market, 1 Canadian dollar (CAD) can be exchanged for 1.2 Swiss francs (CHF). If interest rate parity holds, what is the 90-day forward rate exchange between Canadian dollars and Swiss francs? (Check Figures: 0.8323 CAD per CHF; 1.2015 CHF per CAD)

4. On the basis of your answer to the previous question, is the Swiss franc selling at a premium or discount on the forward rate? (Check Figure: Discount)

21.8 Purchasing Power Parity

We have discussed exchange rates in some detail, and we have considered the relationship between spot and forward exchange rates. However, we have not yet addressed the fundamental question: What determines the spot level of exchange rates in each country? While exchange rates are influenced by a multitude of factors that are difficult to predict, particularly on a day-to-day basis, over the long run market forces work to ensure that similar goods sell for similar prices in different countries after taking exchange rates into account. This relationship is known as "purchasing power parity."

Absolute purchasing power parity (PPP), sometimes referred to as the *law of one price,* implies that the levels of exchange rates and prices adjust so as to cause identical goods to cost the same amount in different countries. For example, if a pair of tennis shoes costs $150 in the Canada and 100 pounds in Britain, PPP implies that the exchange rate must be $1.50 per pound. Consumers could purchase the shoes in Britain for 100 pounds, or they could exchange their 100 pounds for $150 and then purchase the same shoes in Canada at the same effective cost, assuming no transaction or transportation costs. Here is the equation for pur-chasing power parity:

$$P_h = (P_f)(\text{Spot rate}) \qquad \text{(21-2)}$$

or

$$\text{Spot rate} = \frac{P_h}{P_f} \qquad \text{(21-3)}$$

FINANCE: IN FOCUS

Hungry for a Big Mac? Go to South Africa

Purchasing power parity (PPP) implies that the same product will sell for the same price in every country after adjusting for current exchange rates. One problem when testing to see if PPP holds is that it assumes that goods consumed in different countries are of the same quality. For example, if you find that a product is more expensive in Switzerland than it is in Canada, one explanation is that PPP fails to hold, but another explanation is that the product sold in Switzerland is of a higher quality and therefore deserves a higher price.

One way to test for PPP is to find goods that have the same quality worldwide. With this in mind, *The Economist* magazine occasionally compares the prices of a well-known good whose quality is the same in over 100 different countries: the McDonald's Big Mac hamburger.

The table on the next page provides partial information collected during July 2014. The first column shows the price of a Big Mac in local currency. For example, a Big Mac costs 89 rubles in Russia. The second column shows the cost in dollars (based on the actual exchange rate in the fourth column), which is the amount you would pay in that country if you exchanged US dollars for local currency and then purchased a Big Mac at the local price. For example, the exchange rate is 34.84 rubles per US dollar, which means that a Big Mac in Russia costs $2.55 = (89 rubles)/(34.84 rubles per US dollar).

The third column backs out the implied exchange rate that would hold under PPP. For example, the 89 ruble price of a Big Mac in Russia compared to the $4.80 price in the United States gives us the implied PPP exchange rate of (89 rubles per Big Mac)/ ($4.80 per Big Mac) = 18.5 rubles per dollar. The last column shows how much the local currency is over- or undervalued relative to the dollar. The ruble's implied PPP exchange rate of 18.5 rubles per dollar is 47% less than the actual exchange rate of 34.84 rubles per dollar, so the ruble is 47% undervalued relative to the dollar.

The evidence suggests that strict PPP does not hold, but the Big Mac test may shed some insights about where exchange rates are headed. Most Nordic currencies are overvalued against the dollar, while many Asian currencies are undervalued. The Big Mac 2014 test suggests that Asian currencies should rise over the next year or so but that Nordic currencies will fall. One last benefit of the Big Mac test is that it tells us the cheapest places to find a Big Mac. According to the data, if you are looking for a Big Mac, head to South Africa but avoid Norway.

Here

P_h = the price of the good in the home country ($150, assuming Canada is the home country).

P_f = the price of the good in the foreign country (100 pounds).

Note that the spot market exchange rate is expressed as the number of units of home currency that can be exchanged for one unit of foreign currency ($1.50 per pound).

PPP assumes that market forces will eliminate situations in which the same product sells at a different price overseas. For example, if the shoes cost $140 in Canada, importers/ exporters could purchase them in Canada for $140, sell them for 100 pounds in Britain, exchange the 100 pounds for $150 in the foreign exchange market, and earn a profit of $10 on every pair of shoes. Ultimately, this trading activity would increase the demand for shoes in Canada and thus raise P_h, increase the supply of shoes in Britain and thus reduce P_f, and increase the demand for dollars in the foreign exchange market and thus reduce the spot rate. Each of these actions works to restore PPP.

Note that PPP assumes that there are no transportation or transaction costs and no import restrictions, all of which limit the ability to ship goods between countries. In many cases, these assumptions are incorrect, which explains why PPP is often violated. An additional problem for empirical tests of the PPP theorem is that products in different countries are rarely identical. Frequently, there are real or perceived differences in quality, which can lead to price differences in different countries.

Still, the concepts of interest rate and purchasing power parity are critically important to those engaged in international activities. Companies and investors must anticipate changes

Big Mac Index Data

Country	Big Mac Prices in Local Currency (1)	Big Mac Prices in US Dollars (2)	Implied PPP[a] of the US Dollar (3)	Actual Exchange Rate, January 24, 2014 (4)	Under (−)/ Over (+) Valuation Against US Dollar, % (5)
United States[b]	$4.80	$4.80	–	–	–
Argentina	Peso 21	2.57	4.38	8.17	−46
Australia	A$5.10	4.81	1.06	1.06	0
Brazil	Real 13	5.86	2.71	2.22	22
Britain	£2.89	4.93	1.66[c]	1.70[c]	3
Canada	C$5.64	5.25	1.18	1.07	10
Chile	Peso 2,100	3.72	438	564	−22
China[d]	Yuan 16.9	2.73	3.52	6.20	−43
Euro area[e]	Euro 3.68	4.95	1.30[f]	1.35[f]	3
Hong Kong	HK$18.8	2.43	3.92	7.75	−49
Indonesia	Rupiah 27,939	2.43	5,827	11,505	−49
Israel	Shekel 17.5	5.13	3.65	3.41	7
Japan	Yen 370	3.64	77.16	101.53	−24
Malaysia	Ringgit 7.63	2.41	1.59	3.17	−50
Mexico	Peso 42	3.25	8.76	12.93	−32
Norway	Kroner 48	7.76	10.01	6.19	62
Russia	Rouble 89	2.55	18.56	34.84	−47
Saudi Arabia	Riyal 11	2.93	2.29	3.75	39
Singapore	S$4.7	3.80	0.98	1.24	−21
South Africa	Rand 24.5	2.33	5.11	10.51	−51
Sweden	Skr 40.7	5.95	8.49	6.84	24
Switzerland	SFr 6.16	6.83	1.28	0.90	42
Thailand	Baht 99	3.12	20.65	31.78	−35
Turkey	Lira 9.25	4.42	1.93	2.09	−8

Notes:
[a]Purchasing power parity; local price divided by price in United States
[b]Average of four cities
[c]Dollars per pound
[d]Average of five cities
[e]Weighted average of prices in euro area
[f]Dollars per euro

Source: Adapted from "The Big Mac Index," *The Economist*, July, 2014, http://www.economist.com/content/big-mac-index, accessed December 3, 2014. © The Economist Newspaper Limited, London (July 2014).

in interest rates, inflation, and exchange rates, and they often try to hedge the risks of adverse movements in these factors. The parity relationships are extremely useful when anticipating future conditions.

CONCEPT REVIEW

1. What is meant by purchasing power parity?
2. A computer sells for $1,500. In the spot market, $1 = 115 Japanese yen. If purchasing power parity holds, what should be the price (in yen) of the same computer in Japan? (Check Figure: ¥172,500)

21.9   Inflation, Interest Rates, and Exchange Rates

Relative inflation rates, or the rates of inflation in foreign countries compared with that in the home country, have many implications for multinational financial decisions. Obviously, relative inflation rates will greatly influence future production costs at home and abroad. Equally important, inflation has a dominant influence on relative interest rates and exchange rates. Both of these factors influence decisions by multinational corporations for financing their foreign investments, and both have an important effect on the profitability of foreign investments.

The currencies of countries with higher inflation rates than that of Canada by definition *depreciate* over time against the dollar. Countries where this has occurred include Mexico and all the South American nations. On the other hand, the currencies of Switzerland and Japan, which have had lower inflation than Canada, have generally *appreciated* against the dollar. In fact, *a foreign currency will, on average, depreciate or appreciate at a percentage rate approximately equal to the amount by which its inflation rate exceeds or is less than another country's rate.* The effect that differing inflation rates has on the *change* in exchange rates is known as **relative purchasing power parity** and is shown by the equation below:

$$\text{Expected spot rate} = \frac{(1 + i_h)}{(1 + i_f)} \times \text{Spot rate} \qquad (21\text{-}4)$$

Here

i_h = the inflation rate in the home country
i_f = the inflation rate in the foreign country

If the current exchange rate between the Swiss franc and Canadian dollar is $1.1733, while the inflation rate in Switzerland is 0.5%, and in Canada it is 2%, the Canadian dollar will expect to depreciate relative to the Swiss franc [(1 + 0.02)/(1 + 0.005) × 1.1733] = $1.1908.

Relative inflation rates also affect interest rates. The interest rate in any country is largely determined by its inflation rate. Therefore, countries currently experiencing higher rates of inflation than say, Canada, also tend to have higher interest rates. The reverse is true for countries with lower inflation rates.

It is tempting for a multinational corporation to borrow in countries with the lowest interest rates. However, this is not always a good strategy. Suppose, for example, that interest rates in Switzerland are lower than those in Canada because of Switzerland's lower inflation rate. A Canadian multinational firm could therefore save interest by borrowing in Switzerland. However, because of relative inflation rates, the Swiss franc will probably appreciate in the future, causing the dollar cost of annual interest and principal payments on Swiss debt to rise over time. Thus, *the lower interest rate could be more than offset by losses from currency appreciation.* Similarly, multinational corporations should not necessarily avoid borrowing in a country such as Brazil, where interest rates have been very high, because future depreciation of the Brazilian real could make such borrowing end up being relatively inexpensive.

ⓒNCEPT REVIEW

1. What effects do relative inflation rates have on relative interest rates?
2. What happens over time to the currencies of countries with higher inflation rates than that of Canada? To those with lower inflation rates?
3. Why might a multinational corporation decide to borrow in a country such as Brazil, where interest rates are high, rather than in a country like Switzerland, where interest rates are low?

21.10   International Money and Capital Markets

One way for U.S. citizens to invest in world markets is to buy the stocks of U.S. multinational corporations that invest directly in foreign countries. Another way is to purchase foreign securities—stocks, bonds, or money market instruments issued by foreign companies.

Security investments are known as *portfolio investments*, and they are distinguished from *direct investments* in physical assets by U.S. corporations.

From the Second World War through the 1960s, the U.S. capital markets dominated world markets. Today, however, the value of U.S. securities represents less than one-quarter the value of all securities while Canadian security values are modest by international standards. Given this situation, it is important for both corporate managers and investors to have an understanding of international markets. Moreover, these markets often offer better opportunities for raising or investing capital than are available domestically.

Eurocurrency Market

A **Eurocurrency** is simply a time deposit of a currency made in a bank account outside the country that issued the currency. For instance, a **Eurodollar** is a US dollar deposited in a bank outside the United States. (Although they are called Eurodollars because they originated in Europe, Eurodollars are really any US dollars deposited in any part of the world other than the United States.) The bank in which the deposit is made may be a non-U.S. bank, such as Barclays Bank in London; the foreign branch of a U.S. bank, such as Citibank's Paris branch; or even a foreign branch of a third-country bank, such as Barclays' Munich branch. Most Eurodollar deposits are for $500,000 or more, and they have maturities ranging from overnight to about one year. Euroswiss are bank deposits of Swiss Francs made outside Switzerland; Euroyen are bank deposits of yen made outside Japan; and Eurocanadian are Canadian dollars deposited in a bank outside Canada.

The major difference between Eurocurrency deposits and regular domestic time deposits is their geographic location. A deposit of a Eurocurrency such as Eurodollars does not involve different currencies—in both cases, US dollars are on deposit. However, Eurodollars are outside the direct control of the U.S. monetary authority, so U.S. banking regulations, including reserve requirements and deposit insurance premiums, do not apply. The absence of these costs means that the interest rate paid on Eurocurrencies can be higher than domestic rates on equivalent instruments.

Although the US dollar is the leading international currency, British pounds, euros, Swiss francs, Japanese yen, and other currencies are also deposited outside their home countries; these *Eurocurrencies* are handled in exactly same way as Eurodollars.

Eurodollars are borrowed by U.S. and foreign corporations for various purposes, but especially to pay for goods imported from the United States and to invest in U.S. security markets. Also, US dollars are used as an international currency, or international medium of exchange, and many Eurodollars are used for this purpose. It is interesting to note that Eurodollars were actually "invented" by the Soviets in 1946. International merchants did not trust the Soviets or their rubles, so the Soviets bought some dollars (for gold), deposited them in a Paris bank, and then used these dollars to buy goods in the world markets. Others found it convenient to use dollars this same way, and soon the Eurodollar market was in full swing.

Eurodollars are usually held in interest-bearing accounts. The interest rate paid on these deposits depends (1) on the bank's lending rate, as the interest a bank earns on loans determines its willingness and ability to pay interest on deposits, and (2) on rates of return available on U.S. money market instruments. If money market rates in the United States were above Eurodollar deposit rates, these dollars would be sent back and invested in the United States, whereas if Eurodollar deposit rates were significantly above U.S. rates—which is more often the case—more dollars would be sent out of the United States to become Eurodollars. Given the existence of the Eurodollar market and the electronic flow of dollars to and from the United States, it is easy to see why interest rates in the United States cannot be insulated from those in other parts of the world.

Interest rates on Eurodollar deposits (and loans) are tied to a standard rate known by the acronym **LIBOR,** which stands for *London Interbank Offer Rate.* LIBOR is the rate of interest offered by the largest and strongest London banks on dollar deposits of significant size. In December 2014, LIBOR rates were the same as domestic U.S. bank rates on time deposits of the same maturity—0.23% for 3-month deposit and 0.23% for a 3-month Eurodollar deposit. The Eurodollar market is essentially a short-term market; most loans and deposits are for less than 1 year.

International Bond Markets

Any bond sold outside the country of the borrower is called an *international bond.* However, there are two important types of international bonds: foreign bonds and Eurobonds.

Foreign bonds are bonds sold by a foreign borrower but denominated in the currency of the country in which the issue is sold. For instance, Canadian National Railway (CNR) may need US dollars to finance the operations of its business in the United States. If it decides to raise the needed capital in the United States, the bond would be underwritten by a syndicate of U.S. investment bankers, denominated in US dollars, and sold to U.S. investors in accordance with SEC and applicable state regulations. Except for the foreign origin of the borrower, this bond would be indistinguishable from those issued by equivalent U.S. corporations. Since CNR is a foreign corporation to the United States, the bond would be a foreign bond. Furthermore, because it is denominated in US dollars and sold in the United States under SEC regulations, it is also called a **Yankee bond.** In contrast, if CNR issued bonds in Mexico denominated in pesos, they would be a foreign bond, but not Yankee bonds. Bonds issued by foreign corporations or governments that are denominated in Canadian dollars and sold in Canada are known as Maple bonds. When Canada relaxed its foreign property rule, foreign corporations such as France Telecom and Telecom Corporation of New Zealand came in and issued Maple bonds in Canada.

The term **Eurobond** is used to designate any bond issued in one country but denominated in the currency of another country. Examples include a Ford Motor Company issue denominated in US dollars and sold in Germany, or a British firm's sale of euro-denominated bonds in Switzerland. The institutional arrangements by which Eurobonds are marketed are different than those for most other bond issues, with the most important distinction being a far lower level of required disclosure than is usually found for bonds issued in domestic markets, particularly in the United States. Governments tend to be less strict when regulating securities denominated in foreign currencies, because the bonds' purchasers are generally more "sophisticated." The lower disclosure requirements result in lower total transaction costs for Eurobonds.

Eurobonds appeal to investors for several reasons. Generally, they are issued in bearer form rather than as registered bonds, so the names and nationalities of investors are not recorded. Individuals who desire anonymity, whether for privacy reasons or for tax avoidance, like Eurobonds. Similarly, most governments do not withhold taxes on interest payments associated with Eurobonds. If the investor requires an effective yield of 6%, a Eurobond that is exempt from tax withholding would need a coupon rate of 6%. Another type of bond—for instance, a domestic issue subject to a 25% withholding tax on interest paid to foreigners—would need a coupon rate of 8% to yield an after-withholding rate of 6%. Investors who desire secrecy would not want to file for a refund of the tax, so they would prefer to hold the Eurobond.

More than half of all Eurobonds are denominated in US dollars. Bonds in Japanese yen and euros account for most of the rest. Although centred in Europe, Eurobonds are truly international. Their underwriting syndicates include investment bankers from all parts of the world, and the bonds are sold to investors not only in Europe but also in faraway places such as Bahrain and Singapore. Up to a few years ago, Eurobonds were issued solely by multinational firms, by international financial institutions, or by national governments. Today, however, the Eurobond market is also being tapped by purely domestic U.S. firms, because they often find that by borrowing overseas they can lower their debt costs.

International Stock Markets

New issues of stock are sold in international markets for a variety of reasons. For example, a Canadian firm might sell an equity issue in the United States because it can tap a much larger source of capital than in Canada alone. Also, a U.S. firm might tap a foreign market because it wants to create an equity market presence to accompany its operations in that country. Large multinational companies also occasionally issue new stock simultaneously in multiple countries. For example, Lululemon Athletica, a Canadian-based company, issued new stock in Canada and the United States simultaneously, using different underwriting syndicates in each market.

In addition to new issues, outstanding shares of large multinational companies are increasingly being listed on multiple international exchanges. For example, the stock of Thomson Reuters, a Canadian firm, trades on the London Stock Exchange, the NYSE, and the NASDAQ, as well as on the Toronto Stock Exchange. Some 500 foreign stocks are listed in the United States—an example here is Royal Dutch Petroleum, which is listed on the NYSE. U.S. investors can also invest in foreign companies through American Depository Receipts (ADRs), which are certificates representing ownership of foreign stock held in trust. About 1,700 ADRs are now available in the United States, with most of them traded on the

FINANCE: IN FOCUS

Stock Market Indices Around the World

Canada (^GSPTSE)

In Canada, the S&P/TSX Composite Index is a widely used measure for tracking the overall performance of the Toronto Stock Exchange. Similar indices exist for each major world financial centre. As shown in the table below, India's market has had the strongest performance, while Great Britain's has had the weakest.

United States (^GSPC)

In the United States, the S&P 500 is one of the best known stock market indices. The index is made up of 500 U.S. large cap industrial companies.

Hong Kong (^HSI)

In Hong Kong, the primary stock index is the Hang Seng. Created by HSI Services Limited, the Hang Seng index is composed of 33 large stocks.

Great Britain (^FTSE)

The FT-SE 100 Index (pronounced "footsie") is the most widely followed indicator of equity investments in Great Britain. It is a value-weighted index composed of the 100 largest companies on the London Stock Exchange.

Japan (^N225)

In Japan, the principal barometer of stock performance is the Nikkei 225 Index. The index consists of highly liquid equity issues thought to be representative of the Japanese economy.

India (^BSESN)

Of the 22 stock exchanges in India, the Bombay Stock Exchange (BSE) is the largest, with more than 6,000 listed stocks and approximately two-thirds of the country's total trading volume. Established in 1875, the exchange is also the oldest in Asia. Its yardstick is the BSE Sensex, an index of 30 publicly traded Indian stocks that account for one-fifth of the BSE's market capitalization.

Note: For easy access to world indices, see http://finance.yahoo.com/m2 and use the ticker symbols shown above in parentheses.

Relative 10-Year Performance (Starting Values = 100)

	Canada	United States	Great Britain	Hong Kong	India	Japan
December 2004	100	100	100	100	100	100
December 2014	157	174	142	171	449	164

Sources: Thomson ONE Banker and http://finance.yahoo.com

over-the-counter (OTC) market. However, more and more ADRs are being listed on the New York Stock Exchange, including England's British Airways, Japan's Honda Motors, and Italy's Fiat Group.[4]

CONCEPT REVIEW

1. Differentiate between foreign portfolio investments and direct foreign investments.
2. What are Eurodollars?
3. Has the development of the Eurodollar market made it easier or more difficult for the Federal Reserve to control U.S. interest rates?
4. Differentiate between foreign bonds and Eurobonds.
5. Why do Eurobonds appeal to investors?

21.11 Multinational Capital Budgeting

Up to now, we have discussed the general environment in which multinational firms operate. In the remainder of the chapter, we see how international factors affect key corporate

[4]For an interesting discussion of ADRs and the costs faced by listing companies when the ADR is underwritten by investment banks, see Hsuen-Chi Chen, Larry Fauver, and Pei-Ching Yang, "What Do Investment Banks Charge to Underwrite American Depository Receipts?" *Journal of Banking and Finance*, April 2009, 569–618.

decisions, beginning with capital budgeting. Although the same basic principles apply to capital budgeting for both foreign and domestic operations, there are some key differences, including types of risks the firm faces, cash flow estimation, and project analysis.[5]

Risk Exposure

Foreign projects may be more or less risky than equivalent domestic projects, and that can lead to differences in the cost of capital. Higher risk for foreign projects tends to result from two primary sources: (1) exchange rate risk and (2) political risk. However, international diversification might result in a lower risk.

Exchange rate risk relates to the value of the basic cash flows in the parent company's home currency. Foreign currency cash flows turned over to the parent must be converted into dollars, so projected cash flows must be translated to dollars at the expected future exchange rates. An analysis should be conducted to estimate the effects of exchange rate variations on dollar cash flows, and, on the basis of this analysis, an exchange rate risk premium should be added to the domestic cost of capital. It is sometimes possible to hedge against exchange rate risk, but it may not be possible to hedge completely, especially on long-term projects. If hedging is used, the costs of doing so must be subtracted from the project's operating cash flows.

Political risk refers to potential actions by a host government that would reduce the value of a company's investment. It includes at one extreme expropriation of the subsidiary's assets without compensation, but it also includes less drastic actions that reduce the value of the parent firm's investment in the foreign subsidiary.[6] Included here are higher taxes, tighter repatriation or currency controls, and restrictions on prices charged. The risk of expropriation is small in traditionally friendly and stable countries such as Great Britain and Switzerland. However, in Latin America, Africa, the Far East, Russia, and Eastern Europe, the risk may be substantial. Fairly recent expropriations include those of ExxonMobil, ConocoPhillips, and cement producers Lafarge, Holcim, and Cemex by the Venezuelan government.

Note that companies can take steps to reduce the potential loss from expropriation, including one or more of the following:

1. Finance the subsidiary with local capital.
2. Structure operations so that the subsidiary has value only as a part of the integrated corporate system.
3. Obtain insurance against economic losses from expropriation from a source such as the Export Development Corporation (EDC).

If EDC insurance is purchased, the premiums paid must be added to the project's cost.

Several organizations rate countries according to different aspects of risk. For example, Transparency International (TI) ranks countries based on perceived levels of public-sector corruption, which is an important part of political risk. Figure 21-1 shows selected countries. In 2014 TI rated Denmark, New Zealand, and Finland as the most honest countries, while North Korea and Somalia are the most dishonest. Canada is ranked 10th while the United States is ranked 17th.

Cash Flow Estimation

Cash flow estimation is more complex for foreign than domestic investments. Most multinational firms set up separate subsidiaries in each foreign country in which they operate, and the relevant cash flows for the parent company are the dividends and royalties paid by the subsidiaries to the parent, translated into dollars. Dividends and royalties are normally taxed by both foreign and home country governments, although the home country may allow credits for some or all of the foreign taxes paid. Furthermore, a foreign government may restrict the amount of the cash that may be *repatriated* to the parent company. For example, some governments place a ceiling, stated as a percentage of the company's net worth, on the amount of cash

---

[5]Many domestic companies form joint ventures with foreign companies; see Insup Lee and Steve B. Wyatt, "The Effects of International Joint Ventures on Shareholder Wealth," *Financial Review*, November 1990, 641–649. For a discussion of the Japanese cost of capital, see Jeffrey A. Frankel, "The Japanese Cost of Finance," *Financial Management*, Spring 1991, 95–127. For a discussion of financial practices in the Pacific basin, see George W. Kester, Rosita P. Chang, and Kai-Chong Tsui, "Corporate Financial Policy in the Pacific Basin: Hong Kong and Singapore," *Financial Practice and Education*, Spring–Summer 1994, 117–127.
[6]For an interesting article on expropriation, see Arvind Mahajan, "Pricing Expropriation Risk," *Financial Management*, Winter 1990, pp. 77–86.

The 2014 Transparency International Corruption Perceptions Index (CPI)

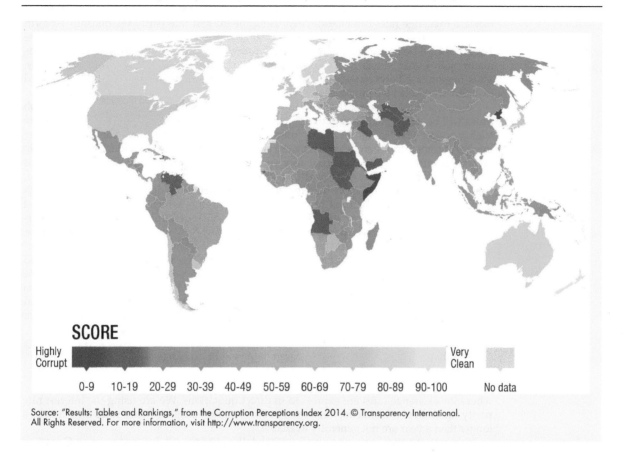

SCORE

Highly Corrupt										Very Clean		No data
0-9	10-19	20-29	30-39	40-49	50-59	60-69	70-79	80-89	90-100			No data

Source: "Results: Tables and Rankings," from the Corruption Perceptions Index 2014. © Transparency International. All Rights Reserved. For more information, visit http://www.transparency.org.

dividends that a subsidiary can pay to its parent. Such restrictions are normally intended to force multinational firms to reinvest earnings in the foreign country, although restrictions are sometimes imposed to prevent large currency outflows, which might disrupt the exchange rate.

Whatever the host country's motivation for blocking repatriation of profits, the result is that the parent corporation cannot use cash flows blocked in the foreign country to pay dividends to its shareholders or to invest elsewhere in the business. Hence, from the perspective of the parent organization, the cash flows relevant for foreign investment analysis are the cash flows that the subsidiary is actually expected to send back to the parent. Note, though, that if returns on investments in the foreign country are attractive, and if blockages are expected to be lifted in the future, then current blockages may not be bad, but dealing with this situation does complicate the cash flow estimation process.

Some companies attempt to circumvent repatriation restrictions (and also lower taxes paid) through the use of transfer pricing. For example, a foreign subsidiary might obtain raw materials or other input components from the parent. The price the subsidiary pays the parent is called a *transfer price*. If the transfer price is very high, then the foreign subsidiary's costs will be very high, leaving little or no profit to repatriate. However, the parent's profit will be higher because it sold to the subsidiary at an inflated transfer price. The net result is that the parent receives cash flows from the subsidiary via transfer pricing rather than as repatriated dividends. Transfer pricing can also be used to shift profits from high-tax to low-tax jurisdictions. Of course, governments are well aware of these possibilities, so governmental auditors are on guard to prevent abusive transfer pricing.

Project Analysis

First, consider a domestic project that requires foreign raw materials, or one where the finished product will be sold in a foreign market. Because the operation is based in Canada, any projected nondollar cash flows—costs in the first example and revenues in the second—should be converted into dollars. This conversion does not present much of a problem for cash flows to be paid or received in the short run, but there is a significant problem in estimating exchange rates for converting long-term foreign cash flows into dollars because forward exchange rates are usually not available for more than 180 days into the future. However, long-term expected forward exchange rates can be estimated using the interest rate parity relationship set forth in Equation 21-1. For example, if a foreign cash flow is expected to occur in 1 year, then the 1-year forward exchange rate can be estimated using domestic and foreign government bonds maturing in 1 year. Similarly, the 2-year exchange rate can be estimated using 2-year bonds. Thus, foreign cash flows can be converted into dollars and added to the project's other projected cash flows, and then the project's NPV can be calculated based on the project's cost of capital.

Now consider a project that will be based overseas, where most expected future cash flows will be denominated in a foreign currency. Two approaches can be used to estimate such a project's NPV. Both begin by forecasting the future cash flows denominated in the foreign currency and then determining the annual repatriations to Canada, denominated in the foreign currency. Under the first approach, we convert the expected future repatriations to dollars (as described earlier), and then find the NPV using the project's cost of capital. Under the second approach, we take the projected repatriations, denominated in the foreign currency, and discount them at the foreign cost of capital, which reflects foreign interest rates and relevant risk premiums. This produces an NPV denominated in the foreign currency, which can be converted into a dollar-denominated NPV using the spot exchange rate.

The following example illustrates the first approach. A Canadian company has the opportunity to lease a manufacturing facility in Great Britain for 3 years. The company must spend £20 million initially to refurbish the plant. The expected net cash flows from the plant for the next 3 years, in millions, are $CF_1 = £7$, $CF_2 = £9$, and $CF_3 = £11$. A similar project in Canada would have a risk-adjusted cost of capital of 10%. The first step is to estimate the expected exchange rates at the end of 1, 2, and 3 years using the multiyear interest rate parity equation:

$$\text{Expected t-year forward exchange rate} = \text{Spot exchange rate}\left(\frac{1 + r_h}{1 + r_f}\right)^t \quad \text{(21-1b)}$$

where the exchange rates are expressed in direct quotations. We are using the interest rate parity equation to calculate forward rates because market-based forward rates for maturities longer than a year are not generally available.

Suppose the spot exchange rate is 1.8000 dollars per pound. Interest rates on Canadian and U.K. government bonds are shown below, along with the expected forward rate implied by the interest rate parity relationship in Equation 21-1b:

Maturity (in Years)	r_h	r_f	Spot Rate ($/£)	Expected Forward Rate Based on Equation 21-1b ($/£)
1	2.0%	4.6%	1.8000	1.7553
2	2.8	5.0	1.8000	1.7254
3	3.5	5.2	1.8000	1.7141

TABLE 21-4   Net Present Value of International Investment (Cash Flows in Millions)

	Year			
	0	1	2	3
Cash flows in pounds	−£20	£7	£9	£11
Expected exchange rates	1.8000	1.7553	1.7254	1.7141
Cash flows in dollars	−$36.00	$12.29	$15.53	$18.86
Project cost of capital =	10%			
NPV =	$2.18			

The current dollar cost of the project is £20(1.8000 $/£) = $36 million. The Year 1 cash flow in dollars is £7(1.7553 $/£) = $12.29 million. Table 21-4 shows the complete time line and the net present value of $2.18 million.

CONCEPT REVIEW

1. List some key differences in capital budgeting as applied to foreign versus domestic operations.

2. What are the relevant cash flows for an international investment—the cash flow produced by the subsidiary in the country where it operates or the cash flows in dollars that it sends to its parent company?

3. Why might the cost of capital for a foreign project differ from that of an equivalent domestic project? Could it be lower?

4. What adjustments might be made to the domestic cost of capital for a foreign investment due to exchange rate risk and political risk?

21.12 International Capital Structures

Companies' capital structures vary among countries. For example, the Organisation for Economic Co-operation and Development (OECD) reported that, on average, Japanese firms use 85% debt to total assets (in book value terms), German firms use 64%, and U.S. firms use 55%. One problem, however, when interpreting these numbers is that different countries often use very different accounting conventions with regard to (1) reporting assets on a historical-versus a replacement-cost basis, (2) the treatment of leased assets, (3) pension plan funding, and (4) capitalizing versus expensing R&D costs. These differences make it difficult to compare capital structures.

A study by Raghuram Rajan and Luigi Zingales of the University of Chicago attempted to account for differences in accounting practices. In their study, Rajan and Zingales used a database that covered fewer firms than the OECD but that provided a more complete breakdown of balance sheet data. They concluded that differences in accounting practices can explain much of the cross-country variation in capital structures.

Rajan and Zingales's results are summarized in Table 21-5. There are a number of different ways to measure capital structure. One measure is the average ratio of total liabilities to total assets—this is similar to the measure used by the OECD, and it is reported in Column 1. Based on this measure, German and Japanese firms appear to be more highly levered than U.S. or Canadian firms. However, if you look at Column 2, where capital structure is measured by interest-bearing debt to total assets, it appears that German firms use less leverage than U.S., Canadian, and Japanese firms. What explains this difference? Rajan and Zingales argue that much of this difference is explained by the way German firms account for pension liabilities. German firms generally include all pension liabilities (and their offsetting assets) on the balance sheet, whereas firms in other countries (including Canada and the United States) generally "net out" pension assets and liabilities on their balance sheets. To see the importance of this difference, consider a firm with $10 million in liabilities (not including pension liabilities) and $20 million in assets (not including pension assets). Assume that the firm has $10 million in pension liabilities that are fully funded by $10 million in pension assets. Therefore, net pension liabilities are zero. If this firm were in Canada, it would report a ratio of total liabilities to total assets equal to 50% ($10 million/$20 million). By contrast, if this firm operated in Germany, both its pension assets and its liabilities would be reported on the balance sheet. The firm would have $20 million in liabilities and $30 million in assets—or a 67% ($20 million/$30 million) ratio of total liabilities to total assets. Total debt is the sum of short-term debt and long-term debt and excludes other liabilities including pension liabilities. Therefore, the measure of total debt to total assets provides a more comparable measure of leverage across different countries.

Rajan and Zingales also make a variety of adjustments that attempt to control for other differences in accounting practices. The effects of these adjustments are reported in Columns 3 and 4. Overall, the evidence suggests that companies in Germany and the United Kingdom tend to have less leverage, whereas firms in Canada appear to have more leverage, relative to firms in the United States, France, Italy, and Japan. This conclusion is supported by data in the final column, which shows the average times-interest-earned ratio for firms in a number of different countries. Recall from Chapter 3 that the times-interest-earned ratio is the ratio

TABLE 21-5   Median Capital Structures among Large Industrialized Countries (Measured in Terms of Book Value)

Country	Total Liabilities to Total Assets (Unadjusted for Accounting Differences) (1)	Interest-Bearing Debt to Total Assets (Unadjusted for Accounting Differences) (2)	Total Liabilities to Total Assets (Adjusted for Accounting Differences) (3)	Debt to Total Assets (Adjusted for Accounting Differences) (4)	Times-Interest-Earned (TIE) Ratio (5)
Canada	56%	32%	48%	32%	1.55×
France	71	25	69	18	2.64
Germany	73	16	50	11	3.20
Italy	70	27	68	21	1.81
Japan	69	35	62	21	2.46
United Kingdom	54	18	47	10	4.79
United States	58	27	52	25	2.41
Mean	64%	26%	57%	20%	2.69×
Standard deviation	8%	7%	10%	8%	1.07×

Source: "What Do We Know about Capital Structure? Some Evidence from International Data," Raghuram Rajan and Luigi Zingales, *Journal of Finance*, Vol. 50, No. 5, December 1995. Copyright © 1995. Reprinted by permission of John Wiley and Sons.

of operating income (EBIT) to interest expense. This measure indicates how much cash the firm has available to service its interest expense. In general, firms with more leverage have a lower times-interest-earned ratio. The data indicate that this ratio is highest in the United Kingdom and Germany and lowest in Canada.

CONCEPT REVIEW

1.   Do international differences in financial leverage exist? Explain.

21.13 Multinational Working Capital Management

Working capital management in a multinational setting involves more complexity than purely domestic working capital management. We discuss some of the differences below.

Cash Management

The goals of cash management in a multinational corporation are similar to those in a purely domestic corporation: (1) to speed up collections, slow down disbursements, and thus maximize net float; (2) to shift cash as rapidly as possible from those parts of the business where it is not needed to those parts where it is needed; and (3) to maximize the risk-adjusted, after-tax rate of return on temporary cash balances. Multinational companies use the same general procedures for achieving these goals as domestic firms, but because of longer distances and more serious mail delays, devices such as lockbox systems and electronic funds transfers are especially important.

Although multinational and domestic corporations have the same objectives and use similar procedures, multinational corporations face a far more complex task. As noted earlier in our discussion of political risk, foreign governments often place restrictions on transfers of funds out of the country, so although IBM can transfer money from its Salt Lake

City office to its New York concentration bank just by pressing a few buttons, a similar transfer from its Buenos Aires office is far more complex. Buenos Aires funds must be converted to dollars before the transfer. If there is a shortage of dollars in Argentina, or if the Argentinean government wants to conserve dollars so that they will be available for the purchase of strategic materials, then conversion, hence the transfer, may be blocked. Even if no dollar shortage exists in Argentina, the government may still restrict funds outflows if those funds represent profits or depreciation rather than payments for purchased materials or equipment, because many countries, especially those that are less developed, want profits reinvested in the country in order to stimulate economic growth.

Once it has been determined what funds can be transferred, the next task is to get those funds to locations where they will earn the highest returns. Whereas domestic corporations tend to think in terms of domestic securities, multinationals are more likely to be aware of investment opportunities all around the world. Most multinational corporations use one or more global concentration banks, located in money centres such as London, New York, Tokyo, Zurich, or Singapore, and their staffs in those cities, working with international bankers, are able to take advantage of the best rates available anywhere in the world.

Credit Management

Consider the international cash conversion cycle for a foreign company importing from Canada. The order is placed, the goods are shipped, an account payable is created for the importer and an account receivable is created for the exporter, the goods arrive in the foreign country, the importer sells them, and the importer collects on the sales. At some point in this process the importer pays off the account payable, which is usually before the importer collects on its own sales. Notice that the importer must finance the transaction from the time it pays the account payable until it collects on its sales. In many poorer, less-developed nations, the capital markets are not adequate to enable the importer to finance the cash conversion cycle. Even when foreign capital markets are available, the additional shipping time might lengthen the cash conversion cycle to such an extent that the importer can't afford the financing costs. Thus, there is enormous pressure on the exporter to grant credit, often with very lengthy payment periods.

But now consider the situation from the exporter's point of view. First, it is much more difficult for the exporter to perform a credit analysis on a foreign customer. Second, the exporter must also worry about exchange-rate fluctuations between the time of the sale and the time the receivable is collected. For example, if IBM sold a computer to a Japanese customer for 90 million yen when the exchange rate was 90 yen to the dollar, IBM would obtain $90,000,000/90 = \$1,000,000$ for the computer. However, if it sold the computer on terms of net/6 months, and if the yen fell against the dollar so that 1 dollar would now buy 112.5 yen, IBM would end up realizing only $90,000,000/112.5 = \$800,000$ when it collected the receivable. Hedging with forward contracts can reduce this exchange rate risk, but what about the credit risk?

One possibility is for the importer to obtain a letter of credit from its bank, whereby the bank certifies that the importer will meet the terms of the account payable or else the bank will pay. However, the importer often must pay the bank a relatively large fee for the letter of credit, and letters of credit might not be available to companies in developing countries.

A second option is for the importer to essentially write a cheque to the exporter at the time of the purchase, but one that is postdated so that it cannot be cashed until the account payable's due date. If the importer's bank promises that it will "accept" the cheque even if there are insufficient funds in the importer's account, then the cheque becomes a financial instrument that is called a **banker's acceptance.** If the bank is strong, then this virtually eliminates the credit risk. In addition, the exporter can then sell this banker's acceptance in the secondary market if it needs funds immediately. Of course, it must sell the banker's acceptance at a discount to reflect the time value of money because the banker's acceptance is essentially a short-term financial security that pays no interest, similar to a T-bill. Financing an international transaction via a banker's acceptance has many benefits for the exporter, but the importer often must pay the bank a relatively large fee, and this service might not be available to companies in developing countries.

A third alternative is for the exporter to purchase export credit insurance, in which an insurer makes a commitment to pay the exporter even if the importer defaults. Sometimes the "insurer" is a government agency, such as the Japanese Ministry of International Trade and Industry (MITI) or Canada's Export Development Corporation. Other times, the insurer is a private insurance company. These large insurance companies have developed expertise in international credit analysis and they can spread the risk over a large number of customers. These advantages allow them to offer credit insurance at rates that are competitive with either letters of credit or banker's acceptances.

Inventory Management

As with most other aspects of finance, inventory management for a firm in a multinational setting is similar to but more complex than for a purely domestic firm. First, there is the matter of the physical location of inventories. For example, where should Maple Leaf Foods keep its product inventory? It has food processing plants and bakeries in Canada, the United States, Britain, and Asia. One alternative is to keep items concentrated in a few strategic spots from which they can then be shipped as demand arises. Such a strategy might minimize the total amount of inventories needed and thus might minimize the investment in inventories. Note, though, that consideration will have to be given to potential delays in getting goods from central storage locations to user locations internationally. Both working stocks and safety stocks would have to be maintained at each user location. Problems such as commodity supply, livestock disease, tariffs, and foreign government protectionist policies complicate matters further.

Exchange rates also influence inventory policy. If a local currency, say, the Danish krone, were expected to rise in value against the dollar, a Canadian company operating in Denmark would want to increase stocks of local products before the rise in the krone, and vice versa if the krone were expected to fall.

Another factor that must be considered is the possibility of import or export quotas or tariffs. For example, Apple Computer Company was buying certain memory chips from Japanese suppliers at a bargain price. Then U.S. chipmakers accused the Japanese of dumping chips in the U.S. market at prices below cost, so they sought to force the Japanese to raise prices.[7] That led Apple to increase its chip inventory. Then computer sales slacked off, and Apple ended up with an oversupply of obsolete computer chips. Apple's profits were hurt and its stock price fell, demonstrating once more the importance of careful inventory management.

As mentioned earlier, another danger in certain countries is the threat of expropriation. If that threat is large, inventory holdings will be minimized, and goods will be brought in only as needed. Similarly, if the operation involves extraction of raw materials such as oil or bauxite, processing plants may be moved offshore rather than located close to the production site.

Taxes have two effects on multinational inventory management. First, countries often impose property taxes on assets, including inventories, and when this is done, the tax is based on holdings as of a specific date, say, January 1 or March 1. Such rules make it advantageous for a multinational firm (1) to schedule production so that inventories are low on the assessment date, and (2) if assessment dates vary among countries in a region, to hold safety stocks in different countries at different times during the year.

Finally, multinational firms may consider the possibility of at-sea storage. Oil, chemical, grain, and other companies that deal in bulk commodities that must be stored in some type of tank can often buy tankers at a cost not much greater—or perhaps even less, considering land cost—than land-based facilities. Loaded tankers can then be kept at sea or at anchor in some strategic location. This eliminates the danger of expropriation, minimizes the property tax problem, and maximizes flexibility with regard to shipping to areas where needs are greatest or prices highest.

This discussion has only scratched the surface of inventory management in the multinational corporation—the task is much more complex than for a purely domestic firm. However, the greater the degree of complexity, the greater the rewards from superior performance, so if you want challenge along with potentially high rewards, look to the international arena.

---

[7]The term "dumping" warrants explanation, because the practice is so potentially important in international markets. Suppose Japanese chipmakers have excess capacity. A particular chip has a variable cost of $25, and its "fully allocated cost," which is the $25 plus total fixed cost per unit of output, is $40. Now suppose the Japanese firm can sell chips in the United States at $35 per unit, but if it charges $40, it will not make any sales because U.S. chipmakers sell for $35.50. If the Japanese firm sells at $35, it will cover variable costs plus make a contribution to fixed overhead, so selling at $35 makes sense. Continuing, if the Japanese firm can sell in Japan at $40, but U.S. firms are excluded from Japanese markets by import duties or other barriers, the Japanese will have a huge advantage over U.S. manufacturers. This practice of selling goods at lower prices in foreign markets than at home is called "dumping." U.S. firms are required by antitrust laws to offer the same price to all customers and, therefore, cannot engage in dumping.

CONCEPT REVIEW

1. What are some factors that make cash management especially complicated in a multinational corporation?
2. Why is granting credit especially risky in an international context?
3. Why is inventory management especially important for a multinational firm?

Summary

Multinational companies have more opportunities but also face different risks than do companies that operate only in their home market. This chapter discussed many of the key trends affecting the global markets today, and it described the most important differences between multinational and domestic financial management. The key concepts are listed below:

- **International operations** are becoming increasingly important to individual firms and to the national economy. A **multinational,** or **global, corporation** is a firm that operates in an integrated fashion in a number of countries.
- Companies "go global" for six primary reasons: (1) **to expand their markets,** (2) **to obtain raw materials,** (3) **to seek new technology,** (4) **to lower production costs,** (5) **to avoid trade barriers,** and (6) **to diversify.**
- Six major factors distinguish financial management as practised by domestic firms from that practised by multinational corporations: (1) **different currency denominations,** (2) **different economic and legal structures,** (3) **languages,** (4) **cultural differences,** (5) **role of governments,** and (6) **political risk.**
- When discussing **exchange rates,** the number of Canadian dollars required to purchase one unit of a foreign currency is called a **direct quotation,** while the number of units of foreign currency that can be purchased for one Canadian dollar is called an **indirect quotation.**
- **Exchange rate fluctuations** make it difficult to estimate the dollars that overseas operations will produce.
- Prior to August 1971, the world was on a **fixed exchange rate system** whereby the US dollar was linked to gold, and other currencies were then tied to the dollar. After August 1971, the world monetary system changed to a **floating system** under which major world currency rates float with market forces, largely unrestricted by governmental intervention. The central bank of each country operates in the foreign exchange market, buying and selling currencies to smooth out exchange rate fluctuations, but only to a limited extent.
- **Pegged exchange rates** occur when a country establishes a fixed exchange rate with a major currency. Consequently, the values of pegged currencies move together over time.
- A **convertible currency** is one that may be readily exchanged for other currencies.
- **Spot rates** are the rates paid for delivery of currency "on the spot," while the **forward exchange rate** is the rate paid for delivery at some agreed-upon future date, usually 30, 90, or 180 days from the day the transaction is negotiated. The forward rate can be at either a **premium** or a **discount** to the spot rate.
- **Interest rate parity** holds that investors should expect to earn the same risk-free return in all countries after adjusting for exchange rates.
- **Purchasing power parity,** sometimes referred to as the **law of one price,** implies that the level of exchange rates adjusts so that identical goods cost the same in different countries.
- Granting credit is more risky in an international context because, in addition to the normal risks of default, the multinational firm must worry about **exchange rate changes** between the time a sale is made and the time a receivable is collected.
- Credit policy is important for a multinational firm for two reasons: (1) Much trade is with less-developed nations, and in such situations granting credit is a necessary condition for doing business. (2) The governments of nations such as Japan, whose economic health depends on exports, often help their firms compete by granting credit to foreign customers.
- Foreign investments are similar to domestic investments, but political risk and exchange rate risk must be considered. **Political risk** is the risk that the foreign government will take some action that will decrease the value of the investment, while **exchange rate risk**

is the risk of losses due to fluctuations in the value of the dollar relative to the values of foreign currencies.

- Investments in **international capital projects** expose firms to exchange rate risk and political risk. The relevant cash flows in international capital budgeting are the dollars that can be **repatriated** to the parent company.
- **Eurocurrencies** are deposits of money made in a bank account outside the country that issued the money.
- **Eurodollars** are US dollars deposited in banks outside the United States. Interest rates on Eurodollars are tied to **LIBOR,** the **London Interbank Offer Rate.**
- Canadian firms often find that they can raise long-term capital at a lower cost outside Canada by selling bonds in the **international capital markets.** International bonds may be either **foreign bonds,** which are exactly like regular domestic bonds except that the issuer is a foreign company, or **Eurobonds,** which are bonds sold in a foreign country but denominated in the currency of the issuing company's home country.

Questions

21-1   Define each of the following terms:
   a.   Multinational corporation
   b.   Exchange rate; fixed exchange rate system; floating exchange rates
   c.   Trade deficit; devaluation; revaluation
   d.   Exchange rate risk; convertible currency; pegged exchange rates
   e.   Interest rate parity; purchasing power parity
   f.   Spot rate; forward exchange rate; discount on forward rate; premium on forward rate
   g.   Repatriation of earnings; political risk
   h.   Eurodollar; Eurobond; international bond; foreign bond
   i.   The euro

21-2   Under the fixed exchange rate system, what was the currency against which all other currency values were defined? Why?

21-3   Exchange rates fluctuate under both the fixed exchange rate and floating exchange rate systems. What, then, is the difference between the two systems?

21-4   If the Swiss franc depreciates against the Canadian dollar, can a dollar buy more or fewer Swiss francs as a result?

21-5   If Canada imports more goods from abroad than it exports, foreigners will tend to have a surplus of Canadian dollars. What will this do to the value of the dollar with respect to foreign currencies? What is the corresponding effect on foreign investments in Canada?

21-6   Why do corporations build manufacturing plants abroad when they could build them at home?

21-7   Should firms require higher rates of return on foreign projects than on identical projects located at home? Explain.

21-8   What is a Eurodollar? If a French citizen deposits $10,000 in Chase Bank in New York, have Eurodollars been created? What if the deposit is made in Barclays Bank in London? Or in Chase's Paris branch? Does the existence of the Eurodollar market make the Federal Reserve's job of controlling U.S. interest rates easier or more difficult? Explain.

21-9   Does interest rate parity imply that interest rates are the same in all countries?

21-10   Why might purchasing power parity fail to hold?

Concept Review Problem

Full solutions are provided at www.nelson.com/brigham3ce.

CR-1   Suppose the exchange rate between US dollars and euros is EUR 0.80 = USD 1.00 and that
Cross Rates   the exchange rate between the US dollar and the Canadian dollar is USD $1.00 = CAD $1.14. What is the cross rate of euros to Canadian dollars?

Problems

Easy
Problems 1–4

21-1
Cross Rates

A currency trader observes that in the spot exchange market, one Canadian dollar can be exchanged for 12 Mexican pesos or for 102 Japanese yen. What is the cross rate between the yen and the peso? That is, how many yen would you receive for every peso exchanged?

21-2
Interest Rate Parity

Six-month T-bills have a nominal rate of 7%, while default-free Japanese bonds that mature in 6 months have a nominal rate of 5.5%. In the spot exchange market, one yen equals $0.012. If interest rate parity holds, what is the 6-month forward exchange rate?

21-3
Purchasing Power Parity

A computer costs $900 in Canada. The same computer costs 650 euros in France. If purchasing power parity holds, what is the spot exchange rate between the euro and the dollar?

21-4
Exchange Rate

If British pounds sell for $1.50 (Canadian) per pound, what should dollars sell for in pounds per dollar?

Intermediate
Problems 5–9

21-5
Currency Appreciation

Suppose that the exchange rate is $1.10 dollars per Swiss franc. If the franc appreciated 10% tomorrow against the dollar, how many francs would a dollar buy tomorrow?

21-6
Cross Rates

Suppose the exchange rate between US dollars and the Mexican peso is Ps 13.0 = 1 and that the exchange rate between the dollar and the British pound was £1 = $1.58. What is the cross rate between pesos and pounds?

21-7
Interest Rate Parity

Assume that interest rate parity holds. In both the spot market and the 90-day forward market one Japanese yen equals 0.0098 dollar. The 90-day risk-free securities yield 4.2% in Japan. What is the yield on 90-day risk-free securities in Canada?

21-8
Purchasing Power Parity

In the spot market 12.8 pesos can be exchanged for one Canadian dollar. A DVD costs $15 in Canada. If purchasing power parity holds, what should be the price of the same DVD in Mexico?

21-9
Spot and Forward Rates

A Canadian company is exporting lumber to Japan. The sales agreement calls for a payment of 7,000,000 yen to the Canadian company in 60 days. The current spot rate is 102 yen per dollar.
a.   Is the Canadian company worried that the yen may appreciate or depreciate in value over the next 60 days?
b.   If the Canadian company decides to hedge using a forward contract and the 60-day forward rate is 100.5 yen per dollar, how many dollars will it receive in 60 days?
c.   By how much is the Canadian company better or worse off if it does *not* hedge and the spot rate in 60 days is (i) 98 yen per dollar or (ii) 103 yen per dollar?

Challenging
Problems 10–16

21-10
Exchange Gains and Losses

You are the vice president of International InfoXchange, headquartered in Toronto. All shareholders of the firm live in Canada. Earlier this month, you obtained a loan of five million US dollars from a bank in Chicago to finance the construction of a new plant in St. Louis. At the time the loan was received, the exchange rate was $1.05 Canadian to the US dollar. By the end of the month, it has unexpectedly dropped to $0.98. Has your company made a gain or loss as a result, and by how much?

21-11
Results of Exchange Rate Changes

In September 1983, it took about 245 Japanese yen to equal $1. Thirty-one years later, in September 2014, the exchange rate had fallen to 98 yen to $1. Assume the price of a Japanese-manufactured automobile was $8,000 in September 1983 and that its price changes were in direct relation to exchange rates.
a.   Has the price, in dollars, of the automobile increased or decreased during the 31-year period because of changes in the exchange rate?
b.   What would the dollar price of the car be in September 2014, assuming the car's price changes only with exchange rates?
c.   What is the compound annual growth rate in the dollar automobile cost?

21-12
Spot and Forward
Rates

Neeves New Zealand Imports has agreed to purchase 16,000 cases of New Zealand wine for 3 million New Zealand dollars at today's spot rate. The firm's financial manager, Hinda Wilson, has noted the following current spot and forward rates:

	New Zealand Dollar/ Canadian Dollar
Spot	1.110
30-day forward	1.115
90-day forward	1.120
180-day forward	1.130

On the same day, Wilson agrees to purchase 16,000 more cases of wine in 3 months at the same price of 3 million New Zealand dollars.
a. What is the price of the wine in Canadian dollars if it is purchased at today's spot rate?
b. What is the cost in Canadian dollars of the second 16,000 cases if payment is made in 90 days and the spot rate at that time equals today's 90-day forward rate?
c. If the exchange rate for the New Zealand dollar is 1.06 to $1 in 90 days, how much will Wilson have to pay for the wine (in Canadian dollars)?

21-13
Interest Rate Parity

Assume that interest rate parity holds and that 90-day risk-free securities yield 5% in Canada and 5.3% in Germany. In the spot market, 1 euro equals $1.30.
a. Is the 90-day euro forward rate at a premium or discount relative to the spot rate?
b. What is the 90-day euro forward rate?

21-14
Spot and Forward Rates

A trader observes the following market information and sees an opportunity to make an arbitrage profit.
The spot rate is 82 yen per dollar, while the 1-year forward rate is 80.20 yen per dollar. The nominal risk-free rate is 1% in Japan and 2.5% in Canada.
a. Do the relevant calculation for each of the following steps. Calculate:
   (1) The number of yen the trader receives if he borrows $1,000,000 and converts it to yen at the current spot rate.
   (2) The interest received if he invests the yen at the Japanese 1 year risk-free rate.
   (3) The amount of yen (both principal and interest) he will lock into and exchange for dollars in 1 year, using a 1-year forward contract, and the amount of dollars received in 1 year.
   (4) The amount of dollars (both principal and interest) he will repay at year end.
   (5) The remaining profit.
b. Briefly explain how this arbitrage profit is possible.

21-15
Foreign Investment
Analysis

After all foreign and Canadian taxes, a Canadian corporation expects to receive 2 pounds of dividends per share from a British subsidiary this year. The exchange rate at the end of the year is expected to be $1.80 per pound, and the pound is expected to depreciate 3% against the dollar each year for an indefinite period. The dividend (in pounds) is expected to grow at 5% a year indefinitely. The parent Canadian corporation owns 7 million shares of the subsidiary. What is the present value in dollars of its equity ownership of the subsidiary? Assume a cost of equity capital of 12% for the subsidiary.

21-16
Foreign Capital
Budgeting

Solitaire Machinery is a Swiss multinational manufacturing company. Currently, Solitaire's financial planners are considering undertaking a 1-year project in Canada. The project's expected dollar-denominated cash flows consist of an initial investment of $1,000 and a cash inflow the following year of $1,200. Solitaire estimates that its risk-adjusted cost of capital is 14%. Currently, 1 Canadian dollar will buy 1.10 Swiss francs. In addition, 1-year risk-free securities in Canada are yielding 7.25%, while similar securities in Switzerland are yielding 4.5%.
a. If this project were instead undertaken by a similar Canadian-based company with the same risk-adjusted cost of capital, what would be the net present value and rate of return generated by this project?
b. What is the expected forward exchange rate 1 year from now?
c. If Solitaire undertakes the project, what is the net present value and rate of return of the project for Solitaire?

Spreadsheet Problem

21-17
Build a Model:
Multinational Financial
Management

Start with the partial model in the file *Ch 21 Build a Model. xlsx* from the textbook's website. Yohe Telecommunications is a multinational corporation that produces and distributes telecommunications technology. Although its corporate headquarters are located in Athabasca, Alberta, Yohe usually must buy its raw materials in several different foreign countries using several different foreign currencies. The matter is further complicated because Yohe usually sells its products in other foreign countries. One product in particular, the SY-20 radio transmitter, draws its principal components, Component X, Component Y, and Component Z, from Germany, Mexico, and England, respectively. Specifically, Component X costs 84 euros. Component Y costs 650 Mexican pesos, and Component Z costs 105 British pounds. The largest market for the SY-20 is in Japan, where it sells for 38,000 Japanese yen. Naturally, Yohe is intimately concerned with economic conditions that could adversely affect dollar exchange rates. You will find Tables 21-1, 21-2, and 21-3 useful for this problem.

a. How much, in dollars, does it cost for Yohe to produce the SY-20? What is the dollar sale price of the SY-20?
b. What is the dollar profit that Yohe makes on the sale of the SY-20? What is the percentage profit?
c. If the Canadian dollar were to weaken by 10% against all foreign currencies, what would be the dollar profit for the SY-20?
d. If the Canadian dollar were to weaken by 10% only against the Japanese yen and remain constant relative to all other foreign currencies, what would be the dollar and percentage profits for the SY-20?
e. Using the forward exchange information from Table 21-3, calculate the return on 90 days securities in England, if the rate of return on 90-day securities in Canada is 4.9%.
f. Assuming that purchasing power parity (PPP) holds, what would be the sale price of the SY-20 if it were sold in England rather than in Japan?

MINI CASE

Pure Juice Products Ltd. is a medium-sized producer of juice drinks with orchards in southern Ontario. Until now, the company has confined its operations and sales to Canada, but its CEO, George Gaynor, wants to expand into Europe. The first step would be to set up sales subsidiaries in Spain and Sweden, then to set up a production plant in Spain, and, finally, to distribute the product throughout the European common market. The firm's financial manager, Ruth Schmidt, is enthusiastic about the plan, but she is worried about the implications of the foreign expansion on the firm's financial management process. She has asked you, the firm's most recently hired financial analyst, to develop a 1-hour tutorial package that explains the basics of multinational financial management. The tutorial will be presented at the next board of directors' meeting. To get you started, Schmidt has supplied you with the following list of questions.

a. What is a multinational corporation? Why do firms expand into other countries?
b. What are the six major factors that distinguish multinational financial management from financial management as practised by a purely domestic firm?
c. Consider the following illustrative exchange rates.

	Canadian Dollars Required to Buy One Unit of Foreign Currency
Euro	1.5000
Swedish krona	0.1580

(1) Are these currency prices direct quotations or indirect quotations?
(2) Calculate the indirect quotations for euros and kronas.
(3) What is a cross rate? Calculate the two cross rates between euros and kronas.
(4) Assume Pure Juice Products can produce a litre of apple juice and ship it to Spain for $1.75. If the firm wants a 70% markup on the product, what should the apple juice sell for in Spain?
(5) Now, assume Pure Juice Products begins producing the same litre of apple juice in Spain. The product costs 1.8 euros to produce and ship to Sweden, where it can be sold for 20 kronas. What is the dollar profit on the sale?
(6) What is exchange rate risk?

d. Briefly describe the current international monetary system. How does the current system differ from the system that was in place prior to August 1971?

e. What is a convertible currency? What problems arise when a multinational company operates in a country whose currency is not convertible?

f. What is the difference between spot rates and forward rates? When is the forward rate at a premium to the spot rate? At a discount?

g. What is interest rate parity? Currently, you can exchange 1 euro for 1.5100 dollar in the 180-day forward market, and the risk-free rate on 180-day securities is 6% in Canada and 4% in Spain. Does interest rate parity hold? If not, which securities offer the higher expected return?

h. What is purchasing power parity? If grapefruit juice costs $2.00 a litre in Canada and purchasing power parity holds, what should be the price of grapefruit juice in Spain?

i. What effect does relative inflation have on interest rates and exchange rates?

j. Briefly discuss the international capital markets.

k. To what extent do average capital structures vary across different countries?

l. Briefly describe special problems that occur in multinational capital budgeting and describe the process for evaluating a foreign project. Now consider the following project: A Canadian company has the opportunity to lease a manufacturing facility in Japan for 2 years. The company must spend ¥1 billion initially to refurbish the plant. The expected net cash flows from the plant for the next 2 years, in millions, are $CF_1 = ¥500$ and $CF_2 = ¥800$. A similar project in Canada would have a risk-adjusted cost of capital of 10%. In Canada, a 1-year government bond pays 2% interest and a 2-year bond pays 2.8%. In Japan, a 1-year bond pays 0.05% and a 2-year bond pays 0.26%. The spot rate = 99 yen/dollar. What is the project's NPV?

m. Briefly discuss special factors associated with the following areas of multinational working capital management.
   (1) Cash management
   (2) Credit management
   (3) Inventory management

chapter 22

Corporate Valuation and Governance

If you had invested $1,000 in the S&P/TSX Composite Index 15 years ago, your investment would have grown to $2,165, resulting in a 5.3% annual rate of return. Had you put the $1,000 in WestJet Airlines when it went public, you would now have $7,425, which is a 14.3% annual return. And if you had been really smart (or lucky) and invested in Brookfield Asset Management, you would now have $8,399, which translates into a 15.2% annual return.

WestJet and Brookfield Asset Management compete in very different industries and utilize different strategies, yet both have beaten the market by sharing an operating philosophy: They have created value for shareholders by focusing on the free cash flows of their underlying businesses. Free cash flows are one of the most important variables to determining corporate value, which is one of the main themes of this chapter.

Brookfield's primary strategy has been to grow through acquisitions. The company's recent letter to shareholders states that Brookfield seeks to "[focus] . . . our investments on high quality, long-life, cash-generating real assets that require minimal sustaining capital expenditures . . . that lead to appreciation in the value of these assets over time." The letter further says that "the primary objective of the company continues to be generating increased cash flows on a per share basis, and as a result, higher intrinsic value over the longer term." Brookfield's growth strategy is governed by the principles of value-based management.

Instead of growing primarily through acquisitions, WestJet has chosen to grow "organically" by expanding its existing operations and routes. WestJet's route structure, flexible labour environment, and efficient fleet maintenance program enabled the company to generate cash flows of $506 million. It is now considered one of North America's top-performing airlines. In fact, during the past 5 years, WestJet has had outstanding performance in the drivers of increased corporate value: (1) its sales have grown faster than the industry average, (2) its profit margin has exceeded the industry average, and (3) its balance sheet has remained stronger than the industry average.

Keep Brookfield Asset Management's and WestJet's focus on cash flows in mind as you read this chapter.

Sources: 2011 annual reports for Brookfield Asset Management and WestJet Airlines.

The textbook's website contains an Excel file that will guide you through the chapter's calculations. The file for this chapter is **Ch 22 Tool Kit.xlsx,** and we encourage you to open the file and follow along as you read the chapter. **www.nelson.com/ brigham3ce**

As we have emphasized throughout the book, maximizing shareholder value should be management's primary objective. However, to maximize value, managers need a tool for estimating the effects of alternative strategies. In this chapter, we develop and illustrate such a tool—the **corporate valuation model,** which is the present value of expected future free cash flows, discounted at the weighted average cost of capital. In a sense, the corporate valuation model is the culmination of all the material covered thus far, because it pulls together financial statements, cash flows, financial projections, time value of money, risk, and the cost of capital. Finally, the decisions companies make regarding the above inputs into the corporate valuation model often depend on each company's *corporate governance,* which is the set of laws, rules, and procedures that influence its operations and the decisions made by its managers. This chapter addresses all of these topics, beginning with corporate valuation.

22.1 Overview of Corporate Valuation

As stated earlier, managers should evaluate the effects of alternative strategies on their firms' values. This really means forecasting financial statements under alternative strategies, finding the present value of each strategy's cash flow stream, and then choosing the strategy that provides the maximum value. The financial statements should be projected using the techniques and procedures discussed in Chapter 5, and the discount rate should be the risk-adjusted cost of capital as discussed in Chapter 9. But what model should managers use to discount the cash flows? One possibility is the dividend growth model from Chapter 8. However, that model is often unsuitable for managerial purposes. For example, suppose a start-up company is formed to develop and market a new product. Its managers will focus on product development, marketing, and raising capital. They will probably be thinking about an eventual IPO, or perhaps the sale of the company to a larger firm. For the managers of such a start-up, the decision to initiate dividend payments in the foreseeable future will be totally off the radar screen. Thus, the dividend growth model is not useful for valuing most start-up companies.

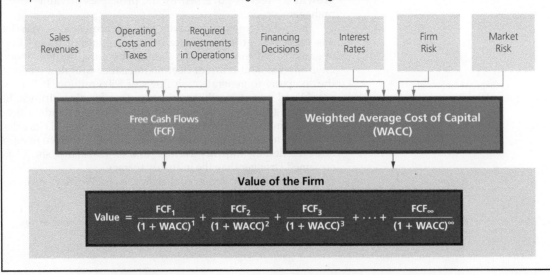

Corporate Valuation: Putting the Pieces Together

The value of a firm is determined by the size, timing, and risk of its expected future free cash flows (FCF). Chapter 5 showed how to project financial statements, and Chapter 2 showed how to calculate free cash flows. Chapter 9 explained how to estimate the weighted average cost of capital. This chapter puts the pieces together and shows how to calculate the value of a firm. It also shows how to use the valuation model as a guide for choosing among different corporate strategies and operating tactics.

Sales Revenues | Operating Costs and Taxes | Required Investments in Operations | Financing Decisions | Interest Rates | Firm Risk | Market Risk

Free Cash Flows (FCF)

Weighted Average Cost of Capital (WACC)

Value of the Firm

$$\text{Value} = \frac{FCF_1}{(1 + WACC)^1} + \frac{FCF_2}{(1 + WACC)^2} + \frac{FCF_3}{(1 + WACC)^3} + \cdots + \frac{FCF_\infty}{(1 + WACC)^\infty}$$

Also, many established firms pay no dividends. Investors may expect them to pay dividends sometime in the future, but when, and how much? As long as internal opportunities and acquisitions are so attractive, the initiation of dividends will be postponed, and this makes the dividend growth model of little use. Even Microsoft, one of the world's most successful companies, only started paying a dividend in 2003.

Finally, the dividend growth model is generally of limited use for internal management purposes, even for a dividend-paying company. If the firm consisted of just one big asset, and that asset produced all of the cash flows used to pay dividends, then alternative strategies could be judged through the use of the dividend growth model. However, most firms have several different divisions with many assets, so the corporation's value depends on the cash flows from many different assets, and on the actions of many managers. These managers need a way to measure the effects of their decisions on corporate value, but the discounted dividend model isn't very useful because individual divisions don't pay dividends.

Fortunately, the corporate valuation model does not depend on dividends, and it can be applied to divisions and subunits as well as to the entire firm.

The corporate valuation model shows how corporate decisions affect *shareholders*. However, corporate decisions are made by managers, not shareholders, and maximizing shareholder wealth is not the same as individual managers maximizing their own "satisfaction."[1] Thus, a key aspect is making sure that managers focus on the goal of shareholder wealth maximization. The laws, rules, and procedures that influence a company's operations and motivate its managers fall under the general heading of *corporate governance*.

This chapter discusses the corporate valuation model and corporate governance, beginning with the corporate valuation model.

CONCEPT REVIEW

1. Why is the corporate valuation model applicable in more circumstances than the dividend growth model?
2. What is corporate governance?

22.2 The Corporate Valuation Model

Corporate assets are of two types: *operating* and *nonoperating*. Operating assets, in turn, take two forms: **assets-in-place** and **growth options.** Assets-in-place include tangible assets such as land, buildings, machines, and inventory, plus intangible assets such as patents, customer lists, reputation, and general know-how. Growth options are opportunities to expand that arise from the firm's current operating knowledge, experience, and other resources. The assets-in-place provide an expected stream of cash flows, and so do the growth options. To illustrate, Shoppers Drug Mart owns stores, inventory, and other tangible assets; it has a well-known name and a good reputation; and it has a lot of business know-how. These assets produce current sales and cash flows, and they also provide opportunities for new investments that will produce additional cash flows in the future. Similarly, Teck Resources owns mines, a refinery, resource properties, and other real assets, and it has a knowledge base that facilitates the extraction and production of metals and minerals and thus new cash flow streams.

Most companies also own some nonoperating assets, which come in two forms. The first is a marketable securities portfolio over and above the cash needed to operate the business. For example, Barrick Gold had about $1.8 billion in term deposits and money market instruments as of December 31, 2013, and this was in addition to $648 million in cash. Second, Barrick also had $147 million of investments in other businesses, which were reported on the asset side of the balance sheet as "Equity in investees" and "Other investments." In total, Barrick had $0.65 + $1.8 + $0.15 = $2.6 billion of nonoperating assets, compared to its $37.4 billion of total assets, or 7% of the total. For most companies this percentage is closer to 1%.

---

[1]A distinction is sometimes made between "executives" and "managers," with executives being corporate officers and other members of the top management team. We do not make that distinction in this book—all people with important decision-making powers are designated "managers."

We see, then, that for most companies operating assets are far more important than nonoperating assets. Moreover, companies can influence the values of their operating assets, but the values of nonoperating assets are largely out of their direct control. Therefore, in this chapter, we focus more on operating assets.

Estimating the Value of Operations

Tables 22-1 and 22-2 contain the actual 2016 and projected 2017 to 2020 financial statements for MagnaVision Inc., which produces optical systems for use in medical photography. (See Chapter 5 for more details on how to project financial statements.) Growth has been rapid in the past, but the market is becoming saturated, so the sales growth rate is expected to decline from 21% in 2017 to a sustainable rate of 5% in 2020 and beyond. Profit margins are expected to improve as the production process becomes more efficient and because MagnaVision will no longer be incurring marketing costs associated with the introduction of a major product. All items on the financial statements are projected to grow at a 5% rate after 2020. Note that the company does not pay a dividend, but it is expected to start paying out about 75% of its earnings beginning in 2019.

Recall that free cash flow (FCF) is the cash from operations that is actually available for distribution to investors, including shareholders, bondholders, and preferred shareholders. The value of operations is the present value of the free cash flows the firm is expected to generate out into the future. Therefore, MagnaVision's value can be calculated as the present value of its expected future free cash flows from operations, discounted at its weighted average cost of capital, WACC, plus the value of its nonoperating assets. Here is the equation for the value of operations, which is the firm's value as a going concern:

TABLE 22-1   MagnaVision Inc.: Income Statements (Millions of Dollars, Except for Per-Share Data)

	Actual	Projected			
	2016	2017	2018[a]	2019	2020
Net sales	$700.0	$850.0	$1,000.0	$1,100.0	$1,155.0
Costs (except depreciation)	599.0	734.0	911.0	935.0	982.0
Depreciation	28.0	31.0	34.0	36.0	38.0
Total operating costs	627.0	765.0	945.0	971.0	1,020.0
Earnings before interest and taxes (EBIT)	73.0	85.0	55.0	129.0	135.0
Less: Net interest[b]	13.0	15.0	16.0	17.0	19.0
Earnings before taxes	60.0	70.0	39.0	112.0	116.0
Taxes (40%)	24.0	28.0	15.6	44.8	46.4
Net income before preferred dividends	36.0	42.0	23.4	67.2	69.6
Preferred dividends	6.0	7.0	7.4	8.0	8.3
Net income available for common dividends	$ 30.0	$ 35.0	$ 16.0	$ 59.2	$ 61.3
Common dividends	—	—	—	$ 44.2	$ 45.3
Addition to retained earnings	$ 30.0	$ 35.0	$ 16.0	$ 15.0	$ 16.0
Number of shares (in millions)	100	100	100	100	100
Dividends per share	—	—	—	$ 0.442	$ 0.453

Notes:

[a]Net income is projected to decline in 2018. This is due to the projected cost for a one-time marketing program in that year.

[b]"Net interest" is interest paid on debt less interest earned on marketable securities. Both items could be shown separately on the income statements, but for this example we combine them and show net interest. MagnaVision pays more interest than it earns; hence its net interest is subtracted.

TABLE
22-2 MagnaVision Inc.: Balance Sheets (Millions of Dollars)

	Actual	Projected			
	2016	2017	2018	2019	2020
Assets					
Cash	$ 17.0	$ 20.0	$ 22.0	$ 23.0	$ 24.0
Marketable securities[a]	63.0	70.0	80.0	84.0	88.0
Accounts receivable	85.0	100.0	110.0	116.0	121.0
Inventories	170.0	200.0	220.0	231.0	243.0
Total current assets	335.0	390.0	432.0	454.0	476.0
Net plant and equipment	279.0	310.0	341.0	358.0	376.0
Total assets	$614.0	$700.0	$773.0	$812.0	$852.0
Liabilities and Equity					
Accounts payable	$ 17.0	$ 20.0	$ 22.0	$ 23.0	$ 24.0
Notes payable	123.0	140.0	160.0	168.0	176.0
Accruals	43.0	50.0	55.0	58.0	61.0
Total current liabilities	183.0	210.0	237.0	249.0	261.0
Long-term bonds	124.0	140.0	160.0	168.0	176.0
Preferred stock	62.0	70.0	80.0	84.0	88.0
Common stock[b]	200.0	200.0	200.0	200.0	200.0
Retained earnings	45.0	80.0	96.0	111.0	127.0
Common equity	245.0	280.0	296.0	311.0	327.0
Total liabilities and equity	$614.0	$700.0	$773.0	$812.0	$852.0

Notes:
[a]All assets except marketable securities are operating assets required to support sales. The marketable securities are financial assets not required in operations.
[b]Par plus paid-in capital.

$$\text{Value of operations} = V_{op} = \text{PV of expected future free cash flow}$$

$$= \frac{FCF_1}{(1 + WACC)^1} + \frac{FCF_2}{(1 + WACC)^2} + \cdots + \frac{FCF_\infty}{(1 + WACC)^\infty} \quad (22\text{-}1)$$

$$= \sum_{t=1}^{\infty} \frac{FCF_t}{(1 + WACC)^t}$$

MagnaVision's cost of capital is 10.84%. To find its value of operations as a going concern, we use an approach similar to the nonconstant dividend growth model for stocks in Chapter 8, proceeding as follows:

1. Assume that the firm will experience nonconstant growth for N years, after which it will grow at some constant rate.
2. Calculate the expected free cash flow for each of the N nonconstant growth years.
3. Recognize that after Year N, growth will be constant, so we can use the constant growth formula to find the firm's value at Year N. This is the sum of the PVs for year N + 1 and all subsequent years, discounted back to Year N.

See **Ch 22 Tool Kit.xlsx** at the textbook's website for all calculations.

4. Find the PV of the free cash flows for each of the N nonconstant growth years. Also, find the PV of the firm's value at Year N.

5. Now sum all the PVs, those of the annual free cash flows during the nonconstant period plus the PV of the Year N value, to find the firm's value of operations.

Table 22-3 calculates free cash flow for each year, using procedures discussed in Chapter 2. Line 1, with data for 2016 from the balance sheets in Table 22-2, shows the required net operating working capital, or operating current assets minus operating current liabilities, for 2016:

$$\begin{matrix} \text{Required net} \\ \text{operating} \\ \text{working capital} \end{matrix} = \begin{pmatrix} \text{Cash} + \\ \text{Accounts receivable} \\ + \text{Inventories} \end{pmatrix} - \begin{pmatrix} \text{Accounts} \\ \text{payable} + \\ \text{Accruals} \end{pmatrix}$$

$$= (\$17.00 + \$85.00 + \$170.00) - (\$17.00 + \$43.00)$$

$$= \$212.00$$

Line 2 shows required net plant and equipment, and Line 3, which is the sum of Lines 1 and 2, shows the required net operating assets, also called total net operating capital, or just operating capital. For 2016, operating capital is $212 + $279 = $491 million.

Line 4 shows the required annual addition to operating capital, found as the change in operating capital from the previous year. For 2017, the required investment in operating capital is $560 − $491 = $69 million.

Line 5 shows NOPAT, or net operating profit after taxes. Note that EBIT is operating earnings *before* taxes, while NOPAT is operating earnings *after* taxes. Therefore, NOPAT = EBIT(1 − T). With 2017 EBIT of $85, as shown in Table 22-1, and a tax rate of 40%, NOPAT as projected for 2017 is $51 million:

$$\text{NOPAT} = \text{EBIT}(1 - \text{T}) = \$85(1.0 - 0.4) = \$51 \text{ million}$$

TABLE 22-3   Calculating MagnaVision's Expected Free Cash Flow (Millions of Dollars)

	Actual	Projected			
	2016	2017	2018	2019	2020
Calculation of Free Cash Flow					
1. Required net operating working capital	$212.00	$250.00	$275.00	$289.00	$303.00
2. Required net plant and equipment	279.00	310.00	341.00	358.00	376.00
3. Required total net operating capital[a]	$491.00	$560.00	$616.00	$647.00	$679.00
4. Required net new investment in operating capital = change in total net operating capital from previous year		$ 69.00	$ 56.00	$ 31.00	$ 32.00
5. NOPAT [Net operating profit after taxes = EBIT × (1 − Tax rate)][b]		$ 51.00	$ 33.00	$ 77.40	$ 81.00
6. Less: Required investment in operating capital		69.00	56.00	31.00	32.00
7. Free cash flow		$ (18.00)	$ (23.00)	$ 46.40	$ 49.00

Notes:
[a]The terms "total net operating capital," "operating capital," and "net operating assets" all mean the same thing.
[b]NOPAT declines in 2018 because of a marketing expenditure projected for that year. See Note a in Table 22-1.

Although MagnaVision's operating capital is projected to produce $51 million of after-tax profits in 2017, the company must invest $69 million in new operating capital in 2017 to support its growth plan. Therefore, the free cash flow for 2017, shown on Line 7, is a negative $18 million:

$$\text{Free cash flow (FCF)} = \$51 - \$69 = -\$18 \text{ million}$$

This negative free cash flow in the early years is typical for young, high-growth companies. Even though net operating profit after taxes (NOPAT) is positive in all years, free cash flow is negative because of the need to invest in operating assets. The negative free cash flow means the company will have to obtain new funds from investors, and the balance sheets in Table 22-2 show that notes payable, long-term bonds, and preferred stock all increase from 2016 to 2017. Shareholders will also help fund MagnaVision's growth—they will receive no dividends until 2019, so all of the net income from 2017 to 2018 will be reinvested. However, as growth slows, free cash flow will become positive, and MagnaVision plans to use some of its FCF to pay dividends beginning in 2019.[2]

A variant of the constant growth dividend model is shown below as Equation 22-2. This equation can be used to find the value of MagnaVision's operations at time N, when its free cash flows stabilize and begin to grow at a constant rate. This is the value of all FCFs beyond time N, discounted back to time N, which is 2020 for MagnaVision.

$$V_{op(at\ time\ N)} = \sum_{t=N+1}^{\infty} \frac{FCF_t}{(1 + WACC)^{t-N}}$$

$$= \frac{FCF_{N+1}}{WACC - g} = \frac{FCF_N(1 + g)}{WACC - g} \tag{22-2}$$

Based on a 10.84% cost of capital, $49 million of free cash flow in 2020, and a 5% growth rate, the value of MagnaVision's operations as of December 31, 2020, is forecast to be $880.99 million:

$$V_{op(12/31/20)} = \frac{FCF_{12/31/20}(1 + g)}{WACC - g}$$

$$= \frac{\$49(1 + 0.05)}{0.1084 - 0.05} = \frac{\$51.45}{0.1084 - 0.05} = \$880.99 \tag{22-2a}$$

See **Ch 22 Tool Kit.xlsx** at the textbook's website for all calculations.

This $880.99 million figure is called the company's **horizon, or terminal, value,** because it is the value at the end of the forecast period. It is also sometimes called a *continuing value.* It is the amount that MagnaVision could expect to receive if it sold its operating assets on December 31, 2020.

Figure 22-1 shows the free cash flow for each year during the nonconstant growth period, along with the horizon value of operations in 2020. To find the value of operations as of "today," December 31, 2016, we find the PV of each annual cash flow in Figure 22-1, discounting at the 10.84% cost of capital. The sum of the PVs is approximately $615 million, and it represents an estimate of the price MagnaVision could expect to receive if it sold its operating assets today, December 31, 2016.

Estimating the Price per Share

The total value of any company is the value of its operations plus the value of its nonoperating assets.[3] As the December 31, 2016, balance sheet in Table 22-2 shows, MagnaVision had $63 million of marketable securities. Unlike operating assets, we do not have to calculate a present value for marketable securities because short-term financial assets as reported on the balance sheet are at, or close to, their market value. Therefore, MagnaVision's total value on December 31, 2016, is $615.27 + $63.00 = $678.27 million.

---

[2]MagnaVision plans to increase its debt and preferred stock each year so as to maintain a constant capital structure. We discussed the importance of capital structure in Chapter 12.
[3]The total value also includes the value of growth options not associated with assets-in-place, but MagnaVision has none.

FIGURE
22-1
Process for Finding the Value of Operations for a Nonconstant Growth Company

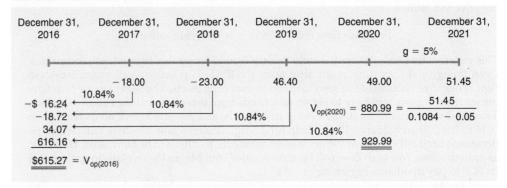

See **Ch 22 Tool Kit.xlsx** at the textbook's website for all calculations.

If the company's total value on December 31, 2016, is $678.27 million, what is the value of its common equity? First, the sum of notes payable and long-term debt is $123 + $124 = $247 million, and these securities have the first claim on assets and income. Accounts payable and accruals were netted out earlier when calculating free cash flow, so they have been accounted for. However, the preferred stock has a claim of $62 million, and it also ranks above the common. Therefore, the value left for common shareholders is $678.27 − $247 − $62 = $369.27 million.

Figure 22-2 is a bar chart that provides a breakdown of MagnaVision's value. The left bar shows the company's total value as the sum of its nonoperating assets plus its going concern value. Next, the middle bar shows the claim of each class of investors on that total value. Debtholders have the highest priority claim, and MagnaVision owes $123 million on notes payable and $124 million on long-term bonds, for a total of $247 million. The preferred shareholders have the next claim, $62 million. The remaining value belongs to the common equity, and it amounts to $678.27 − $247.00 − $62.00 = $369.27 million.[4]

FIGURE
22-2
MagnaVision's Value as of December 31, 2016

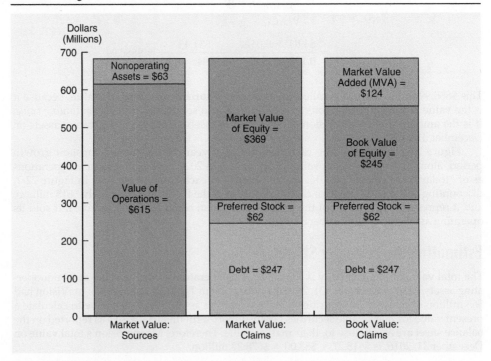

---

[4]When estimating the intrinsic market value of equity, it would be better to subtract the market values of debt and preferred stock rather than their book values. However, in most cases, including this one, the book values of fixed income securities are close to their market values. When this is true, one can simply use book values.

In Chapter 2, we defined the Market Value Added (MVA) as the difference between the market value of stock and the equity capital supplied by shareholders. Here, we assume that the estimated market value of equity is approximately equal to the actual market value of equity; in other words, the intrinsic value of MagnaVision is equal to its market value. The bar on the right side of Figure 22-2 divides the market value of the equity into two components, the book value of equity, which represents the equity capital supplied by shareholders, and the MVA.

Table 22-4 summarizes the calculations used to find MagnaVision's stock value. There are 100 million shares outstanding, and their total value is $369.27 million. Therefore, the value of a single share is $369.27/100 = $3.69.

The Dividend Growth Model Applied to MagnaVision

MagnaVision has not yet begun to pay dividends. However, as we saw in Table 22-1, a cash dividend of $0.442 per share is forecasted for 2019. The dividend is expected to grow by about 2.5% in 2020, and then at a constant 5% rate thereafter. MagnaVision's cost of equity is 14%. In this situation, we can apply the nonconstant dividend growth model as developed earlier in Chapter 8. Figure 22-3 shows that the value of MagnaVision's stock, based on this model, is $3.70 per share, which is the same as the value found using the corporate valuation model except for a rounding difference.

See **Ch 22 Tool Kit.xlsx** at the textbook's website for all calculations.

Comparing the Corporate Valuation and Dividend Growth Models

Because the corporate valuation and dividend growth models give the same answer, does it matter which model you choose? In general, it does. For example, if you were a financial analyst estimating the value of a mature company whose dividends are expected to grow

TABLE 22-4	Finding the Value of MagnaVision's Stock (Millions of Dollars, Except for Per-Share Data)	
1. Value of operations (present value of free cash flows)		$615.27
2. Plus value of nonoperating assets		63.00
3. Total market value of the firm		$678.27
4. Less: Value of debt		247.00
Value of preferred stock		62.00
5. Value of common equity		$369.27
6. Divide by number of shares (in millions)		100.00
7. Value per share		$ 3.69

See **Ch 22 Tool Kit.xlsx** at the textbook's website for all calculations.

FIGURE 22-3 Using the DCF Dividend Model to Find MagnaVision's Stock Value

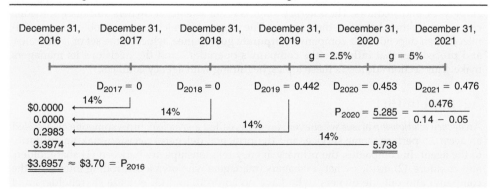

steadily in the future, it would probably be more efficient to use the dividend growth model. Here you would only need to estimate the growth rate in dividends, not the entire set of pro forma financial statements.

However, if a company is paying a dividend but is still in the high-growth stage of its life cycle, you would need to project the future financial statements before you could make a reasonable estimate of future dividends. Then, because you would have already estimated future financial statements, it would be a toss-up as to whether the corporate valuation model or the dividend growth model would be easier to apply. Canadian National Railway, which pays a dividend of about $1.00 per share versus earnings of about $3.30 per share, is an example of a company to which you could apply either model.

Now suppose you were trying to estimate the value of a company that has never paid a dividend, or a new firm that is about to go public, or a division that EnCana or some other large company is planning to sell. In all of these situations, you would have no choice: You would have to estimate future financial statements and use the corporate valuation model.

Actually, even if a company is paying steady dividends, much can be learned from the corporate valuation model; hence many analysts today use it for all types of valuations. The process of projecting the future financial statements can reveal quite a bit about the company's operations and financing needs, and can provide insights into actions that might be taken to increase the company's value.

CONCEPT REVIEW

1. Give some examples of assets-in-place, growth options, and nonoperating assets.
2. Write out the equation for the value of operations.
3. What is the terminal, or horizon, value? Why is it also called the continuing value?
4. Explain how to estimate the price per share using the corporate valuation model.
5. A company expects a FCF of −$10 million at Year 1 and a FCF of $20 million at Year 2. FCF is expected to grow at a 5% rate after Year 2. If the WACC is 10%, what is the horizon value of operations; i.e., $V_{op(Year\ 2)}$? What is the current value of operations; i.e., $V_{op(Year\ 0)}$? (Check Figures: $420 million; $354.55 million)
6. A company has a current value of operations of $800 million. The company has $100 million in short-term investments. If the company has $400 million in debt and has 10 million shares outstanding, what is the price per share? (Check Figure: $50.00)

22.3 Managerial Behaviour and Shareholder Wealth

There is no conflict at a one-person company—the owner makes all the decisions, does all the work, reaps all the rewards, and suffers all the losses. This situation changes as the owner begins hiring employees because the employees don't fully share in the owner's rewards and losses. The situation becomes more complicated if the owner sells some shares of the company to an outsider, and even more complicated if the owner hires someone else to run the company. In this situation, there are many potential conflicts between owners, managers, employees, and creditors. These *agency conflicts* occur whenever owners authorize someone else to act on their behalf as their agents. The degree to which agency problems are minimized often depends on a company's **corporate governance**, which is the set of laws, rules, and procedures that influence the company's operations and the decisions its managers make. This section addresses these topics, beginning with agency conflicts.

Agency Conflicts

An *agency relationship* arises whenever someone, called a *principal*, hires someone else, called an *agent*, to perform some service, and the principal delegates decision-making authority to the agent. In companies, the primary agency relationships are between (1) shareholders and creditors, (2) inside owner/managers (managers who own a controlling interest in the company) and outside owners (who have no control), and (3) outside shareholders and hired managers.[5] These conflicts lead to **agency costs**, which are the reductions in a company's value due to agency conflicts. The following sections describe the agency conflicts, the costs, and methods to minimize the costs.

Conflicts between Shareholders and Creditors

Creditors have a claim on the firm's earnings stream, and they have a claim on its assets in the event of bankruptcy. However, shareholders have control (through the managers) of decisions that affect the firm's riskiness. Therefore, creditors allocate decision-making authority to someone else, creating a potential agency conflict.

Creditors lend funds at rates based on the firm's perceived risk at the time the credit is extended, which in turn is based on (1) the risk of the firm's existing assets, (2) expectations concerning the risk of future asset additions, (3) the existing capital structure, and (4) expectations concerning future capital structure changes. These are the primary determinants of the risk of the firm's cash flows, hence the safety of its debt.

Suppose the firm borrows money, then sells its relatively safe assets and invests the proceeds in assets for a large new project that is far riskier. The new project might be extremely profitable, but it also might lead to bankruptcy. If the risky project is successful, most of the benefits go to the shareholders, because creditors' returns are fixed at the original low-risk rate. However, if the project is unsuccessful, the bondholders take a loss. From the shareholders' point of view, this amounts to a game of "heads, I win; tails, you lose," which obviously is not good for the creditors. Thus, the increased risk due to the asset change will cause the required rate of return on the debt to increase, which in turn will cause the value of the outstanding debt to fall. This is called asset switching or "bait-and-switch."

A similar situation can occur if a company borrows and then issues additional debt, using the proceeds to repurchase some of its outstanding stock, thus increasing its financial leverage. If things go well, the shareholders will gain from the increased leverage. However, the value of the debt will probably decrease, because now there will be a larger amount of debt backed by the same amount of assets. In both the asset switch and the increased leverage situations, shareholders have the potential for gaining, but such gains are made at the expense of creditors.

There are two ways that lenders address the potential of asset switching or subsequent increases in leverage. First, creditors may charge a higher rate to protect themselves in case the company engages in activities that increase risk. However, if the company doesn't increase risk, then its weighted average cost of capital (WACC) will be higher than is justified by the company's risk. This higher WACC will reduce the company's intrinsic value (recall that intrinsic value is the present value of free cash flows discounted at the WACC). In addition, the company will reject projects that it otherwise would have accepted at the lower cost of capital. Therefore, this potential agency conflict has a cost, which is called an agency cost.

The second way that lenders address the potential agency problems is by writing detailed debt covenants specifying what actions the company can and cannot take. Many debt covenants have provisions that (1) prevent the company from increasing its debt ratios beyond a specified level, (2) prevent the company from repurchasing stock or paying dividends unless profits and retained earnings are above a certain level, and (3) require the company to maintain liquidity ratios above a specified level. These covenants can cause agency costs if they restrict a company from value-adding activities. For example, a company may not be able to accept an unexpected but particularly good investment opportunity if it requires temporarily adding debt above the level specified in the bond covenant. In addition, the costs incurred to write the covenant and monitor the company to verify compliance also are agency costs.

Conflicts between Inside Owner/Managers and Outside Owners

If a company's owner also runs the company, the owner/manager will presumably operate it so as to maximize his or her own welfare. This welfare obviously includes the increased wealth due to increasing the value of the company, but it also includes perquisites (or "perks") such as more leisure time, luxurious offices, executive assistants, expense accounts, limousines, corporate jets, and generous retirement plans. However, if the owner/manager

---

[5]One of the first, and most important, papers in finance and economics to address agency conflicts was written by Michael Jensen and William Meckling and entitled "Theory of the Firm: Managerial Behavior, Agency Costs and Ownership Structure," *Journal of Financial Economics*, Vol. 3, 1976, pp. 305–360.

incorporates the business and then sells some of the shares to outsiders, a potential conflict of interest immediately arises. Notice that the value of the perquisites still accrues to the owner/manager, but the cost of the perquisites is now partially borne by the outsiders. This might even induce the owner/manager to increase consumption of the perquisites.

This agency problem causes outsiders to pay less for a share of the company and require a higher rate of return. This is exactly why dual class stock (see Chapter 1) that doesn't have voting rights has a lower price per share than voting stock.

Conflicts between Managers and Shareholders

Shareholders want companies to hire managers who are able and willing to take legal and ethical actions to maximize intrinsic stock prices.[6] This obviously requires managers with technical competence, but it also requires managers who are willing to put forth the extra effort necessary to identify and implement value-adding activities. However, managers are people, and people have both personal and corporate goals. Logically, therefore, managers can be expected to act in their own self-interests, and if their self-interests are not aligned with those of shareholders, then corporate value will not be maximized. There are six ways in which a manager's behaviour might harm a firm's intrinsic value.

1. Managers might not expend the time and effort required to maximize firm value. Rather than focusing on corporate tasks, they might spend too much time on external activities, such as serving on boards of other companies, or on nonproductive activities, such as golf, gourmet meals, and travel.
2. Managers might use corporate resources on activities that benefit themselves rather than shareholders. For example, they might spend company money on perquisites such as lavish offices, memberships at country clubs, museum-quality art for corporate apartments, large personal staffs, and corporate jets. Because these perks are not actually cash payments to the managers, they are called **nonpecuniary benefits**.
3. Managers might avoid making difficult but value-enhancing decisions that harm friends in the company. For example, a manager might not close a plant or terminate a project if the manager has personal relationships with those who are adversely affected by such decisions, even if termination is the economically sound action.
4. Managers might take on too much risk or they might not take on enough risk. For example, a company might have the opportunity to undertake a risky project with a positive NPV. If the project turns out badly, then the manager's reputation will be harmed and the manager might even be fired. Thus, a manager might choose to avoid risky projects even if they are desirable from a shareholder's point of view. On the other hand, a manager might take on projects with too much risk. Consider a project that is not living up to expectations. A manager might be tempted to invest even more money in the project rather than admit that the project is a failure. Or a manager might be willing to take on a second project with a negative NPV if it has even a slight chance of a very positive outcome, because hitting a home run with this second project might cover up the first project's poor performance. In other words, the manager might throw good money after bad.
5. If a company is generating positive free cash flow, a manager might "stockpile" it in the form of marketable securities instead of returning FCF to investors. This potentially harms investors because it prevents them from allocating these funds to other companies with good growth opportunities. Even worse, positive FCF often tempts a manager into paying too much for the acquisition of another company. In fact, most mergers and acquisitions end up as break-even deals, at best, for the acquiring company because the premiums paid for the targets are often very large.

    Why would a manager be reluctant to return cash to investors? First, extra cash on hand reduces the company's risk, which appeals to many managers. Second, a large distribution of cash to investors is an admission that the company doesn't have enough good investment opportunities. Slow growth is normal for a maturing company, but

---

[6]Notice that we said both legal and ethical actions. The accounting frauds perpetrated by Enron, WorldCom, and others that were uncovered in 2002 raised stock prices in the short run, but only because investors were misled about the companies' financial positions. Then, for example, when Enron finally revealed the correct financial information, the stocks tanked. Investors who bought shares based on the fraudulent financial statements lost tens of billions of dollars. Releasing false financial statements is illegal. Aggressive earnings management and the use of misleading accounting tricks to pump up reported earnings is unethical, and executives can go to jail as a result of their misconduct. When we speak of taking actions to maximize stock prices, we mean making operational or financial changes designed to maximize intrinsic stock value, not fooling investors with false or misleading financial reports.

this isn't very exciting for a manager to admit. Third, there is a lot of glamour associated with making a large acquisition, and this can provide a large boost to a manager's ego. Fourth, compensation usually is higher for executives at larger companies; cash distributions to investors make a company smaller, not larger.

6. Managers might not release all the information that investors desire. Sometimes, they might withhold information to prevent competitors from gaining an advantage. Other times, they might try to avoid releasing bad news. For example, they might "massage" the data or "manage the earnings" so that the news doesn't look so bad. If investors are unsure about the quality of information managers provide, they tend to discount the company's expected free cash flows at a higher cost of capital, which reduces the company's intrinsic value.

If senior managers believe there is little chance they will be removed, we say that they are *entrenched*. Such a company faces a high risk of being poorly run, because entrenched managers are able to act in their own interests rather than in the interests of shareholders.

CONCEPT REVIEW

1. What are agency conflicts? What groups can have agency conflicts?
2. Name six types of managerial behaviours that can reduce a firm's intrinsic value.

22.4 Corporate Governance

Agency conflicts can decrease the value of stock owned by outside shareholders. Corporate governance can mitigate this loss in value. Corporate governance can be defined as the laws, rules, and procedures that influence a company's operations and the decisions made by its managers. At the risk of oversimplification, most corporate governance provisions come in two forms, sticks and carrots. The primary stick is the *threat of removal*, either as a decision by the board of directors or as the result of a hostile takeover. If a firm's managers are maximizing the value of the resources entrusted to them, they need not fear the loss of their jobs. On the other hand, if managers are not maximizing value, they should be removed by their own boards of directors, by dissident shareholders, or by other companies seeking to profit by installing a better management team. The main carrot is *compensation*. Managers have greater incentives to maximize intrinsic stock value if their compensation is linked to their firm's performance rather than being strictly in the form of salary.

Almost all corporate governance provisions affect either the threat of removal or compensation. Some provisions are internal to a firm and are under its control.[7] These internal provisions and features can be divided into five areas: (1) monitoring and discipline by the board of directors; (2) charter provisions and bylaws that affect the likelihood of hostile takeovers; (3) compensation plans; (4) capital structure choices; and (5) accounting control systems.

In addition to the corporate governance provisions that are under a firm's control, there are also environmental factors outside a firm's control, such as the regulatory environment, block ownership patterns, competition in the product markets, the media, and litigation. Our discussion begins with the internal provisions.

Monitoring and Discipline by the Board of Directors

Shareholders are a corporation's owners and they elect the board of directors to act as agents on their behalf. In Canada and the United States, it is the board's duty to monitor senior managers and discipline them, either by removal or by a reduction in compensation, if the managers do not act in the interests of shareholders. This is not necessarily the case in other

---

[7]We have adapted this framework from the one provided by Stuart L. Gillan, "Recent Developments in Corporate Governance: An Overview," *Journal of Corporate Finance*, June 2006, pp. 381–402. Gillan provides an excellent discussion of the issues associated with corporate governance. We highly recommend this paper to the reader who is interested in an expanded discussion of the issues in this section. A highly regarded Canadian report on best practices in corporate governance for publicly traded companies was written in 1994 for the Toronto Stock Exchange by Peter Dey. The TSE adopted the report's recommendations the following year for its listed companies, though they were not made mandatory. "Where Were the Directors? Guidelines for Improved Corporate Governance in Canada: Report of the Toronto Stock Exchange Committee on Corporate Governance in Canada," Toronto Stock Exchange, 1994.

countries. For example, many companies in Europe are required to have employee representatives on the board. Also, many European and Asian companies have bank representatives on the board. But even in Canada and the United States, many boards fail to act in the shareholders' best interests. How can this be?

The Election Process The board of directors has a nominating committee. These directors choose the candidates for the open director positions, and the ballot for a board position usually lists only one candidate. Although outside candidates can run a "write-in" campaign, only those candidates named by the board's nominating committee are on the ballot.[8] At many companies, the CEO is also the chair of the board and has considerable influence on this nominating committee. This means that in practice it often is the CEO who in effect nominates candidates for the board. High compensation and prestige go with a position on the board of a major company, so board seats are prized possessions. Board members typically want to retain their positions, and they are grateful to whoever helped get them on the board. Thus, the nominating process often results in a board that is favourably disposed to the CEO.

Voting Procedures Directors of TSX-listed companies must be elected annually and receive a majority of votes cast. If any director receives less than 50% of the votes cast, he or she must normally resign. The company can retain the director only in exceptional circumstances. Voting procedures also affect the ability of outsiders to gain positions on the board. For example, boards can be elected by either cumulative or noncumulative voting. Under *cumulative voting*, each shareholder is given a number of votes equal to his or her shares times the number of board seats up for election. For example, the holder of 100 shares will receive 1,000 votes if 10 seats are to be filled. Then, the shareholder can distribute his or her votes however he or she sees fit. One hundred votes could be cast for each of 10 candidates, or all 1,000 votes could be cast for one candidate. If noncumulative voting is used, our hypothetical shareholder cannot concentrate his or her votes—no more than 100 votes can be cast for any one candidate.

With noncumulative voting, if management controls 51% of the shares, they can fill every seat on the board—dissident shareholders cannot put a representative on the board. With cumulative voting, however, if 10 seats are to be filled, dissidents can elect a representative, provided they have 10% plus one share. Though cumulative voting is not widely used by Canadian companies, it is generally considered to be beneficial to shareholders.

Board Make-Up Many board members are "insiders," that is, people who hold managerial positions within the company, such as the CFO. Because insiders report to the CEO, it may be difficult for them to oppose the CEO at a board meeting.

Even outside board members often have strong connections with the CEO through personal friendships, consulting, or other fee-generating activities (these people are known as "nonindependent outsiders"). In fact, outsiders sometimes have very little expert business knowledge but have "celebrity" status from nonbusiness activities. Some companies also have *interlocking boards of directors*, where Company A's CEO sits on Company B's board and B's CEO sits on A's board. In these situations, even the outside directors are not truly independent and impartial.

Large boards (those with more than 10 to 12 members) often are less effective than smaller boards. As anyone who has been on a committee can attest, individual participation tends to fall as committee size increases. Thus, there is a greater likelihood that members of a large board will be less active than those on smaller boards.

The compensation of board members has an impact on the board's effectiveness. When board members have extraordinarily high compensation, the CEO also tends to have extremely high compensation. This suggests that such boards tend to be too lenient with the CEO.[9] The form of board compensation also affects board performance. Rather than compensating board members with only salary, many companies now include restricted stock grants or stock options in an effort to better align board members with shareholders.

Studies show that corporate governance usually improves if (1) the CEO is not also the chair of the board; (2) the board has a majority of true outsiders who bring some type of business expertise to the board; (3) the board is not too large; and (4) board members are

---

[8]There is a movement underway in the United States to allow shareholders to also nominate candidates for the board, but only time will tell whether this movement is successful.
[9]See I. E. Brick, O. Palmon, and J. Wald, "CEO Compensation, Director Compensation, and Firm Performance: Evidence of Cronyism?" *Journal of Corporate Finance*, June 2006, 403–423.

compensated appropriately. The good news for the shareholder is that the boards at many companies have made significant improvements in these directions during the past decade. A 2012 survey found that in Canada, only 15% of CEOs are board chairs, that independent directors make up 80% of all seats, and that the median board size is 11. While board members are increasingly being compensated more with stock rather than straight salary, the proportion is still lower than for American companies.[10] These changes clearly have decreased the patience of boards with poorly performing CEOs. A study by consulting firm Booz Allen Hamilton found that the percentage of CEOs being replaced in North America increased from 10% to 16% over a 10-year period.[11] This would have been unheard of 30 years ago.

Charter Provisions and Bylaws That Affect the Likelihood of Hostile Takeovers

Hostile takeovers usually occur when managers have not been willing or able to maximize the profit potential of the resources under their control. In such a situation, another company can acquire the poorly performing firm, replace its managers, increase free cash flow, and improve MVA. The following paragraphs describe some provisions that can be included in a corporate charter to make it harder for poorly performing managers to remain in control.

A shareholder-friendly charter should ban **targeted share repurchases,** also known as **greenmail.** For example, suppose a company's stock is selling for $20 per share. Now a hostile bidder, or raider, who plans to replace management if the takeover is successful, buys 10% of the company's stock at the $20 price.[12] The raider then makes an offer to purchase the remainder of the stock for $30 per share. The company might offer to buy back the bidder's stock at a price of, say, $35 per share. This is called a targeted share repurchase since the stock will be purchased only from the bidder and not from any other shareholders. Because the bidder paid only $20 per share for the stock, he or she would be making a quick profit of $15 per share, which could easily total several hundred million dollars. As a part of the deal, the raider would sign a document promising not to attempt to take over the company for a specified number of years; hence the buyback also is called greenmail. Greenmail hurts shareholders in two ways. First, they are left with $20 stock when they could have received $30 per share. Second, the company purchased stock from the bidder at $35 per share, which represents a direct loss by the remaining shareholders of $15 for each repurchased share.

Managers who buy back stock in targeted repurchases typically argue that their firms are worth more than the raiders offered, and that in time the "true value" will be revealed in the form of a much higher stock price. This situation might be true if a company were in the process of restructuring itself, or if new products with high potential were in the pipeline. But if the old management had been in power for a long time, and if it had a history of making empty promises, then one should question whether the true purpose of the buyback was to protect shareholders or management.

Another characteristic of a shareholder-friendly charter is that it does not contain a **shareholder rights provision,** better described as a **poison pill.** These provisions give the shareholders of target firms the right to buy a specified number of shares in the company at a very low price if an outside group or firm acquires a specified percentage of the firm's stock. Therefore, if a potential acquirer tries to take over a company, its other shareholders will be entitled to purchase additional shares of stock at a bargain price, thus seriously diluting the holdings of the raider. For this reason, these clauses are called poison pills, because if they are in the charter, the acquirer will end up swallowing a poison pill if the acquisition is successful. Obviously, the existence of a poison pill makes a takeover more difficult, and this helps entrench management.

A third management entrenchment tool is a **restricted voting rights** provision, which automatically deprives a shareholder of voting rights if the shareholder owns more than a specified amount of stock. The board can grant voting rights to such a shareholder, but this is unlikely if the shareholder plans to take over the company.

---

[10]"Canadian Spencer Stuart Board Index: Board Trends and Practices at Leading Canadian Companies," Spencer Stuart, 2012.
[11]Chuck Lucier, Paul Kocourek, and Rolf Habbel, "CEO Succession 2005: The Crest of the Wave," Booz Allen Hamilton, 2005.
[12]Someone can, under the law, acquire up to 10% of a firm's stock without announcing the acquisition. Once the 10% limit has been hit, the acquirer must "announce" the acquisition by filing a report with the securities commission, and the report must list not only the acquirer's position but also his or her intentions, such as a passive investment or a takeover. These reports are monitored closely, so as soon as one is filed, management is alerted to the imminent possibility of a takeover.

Using Compensation to Align Managerial and Shareholder Interests

The typical CEO today receives a fixed salary, a cash bonus based on the firm's performance, and stock-based compensation, in the form of either stock grants or option grants. Cash bonuses often are based on short-run operating factors, such as this year's growth in earnings per share, or medium-term operating performance, such as earnings growth over the past 3 years.

Stock-based compensation is often in the form of options. Chapter 19 explains option valuation in detail, but we discuss here how a standard *stock option compensation plan* works. Suppose BMI Industries (BMI) decides to grant an option to an employee, allowing him or her to purchase a specified number of BMI shares at a fixed price, called the exercise price, regardless of the actual price of the stock. The exercise price is usually set equal to the current stock price at the time the option is granted. Thus, if BMI's current price were $100, then the option would have an exercise price of $100. Options usually cannot be exercised until after some specified period (the **vesting period**), which is usually 1 to 5 years. Moreover, they have an expiration date, usually 10 years after issue. For our BMI example, assume that the vesting period is 3 years and that the expiration date is 10 years. Thus, the employee can exercise the option 3 years after issue or wait as long as 10 years. Of course, the employee would not exercise unless BMI's stock is above the $100 exercise price, and if the price never rose above $100, the option would expire unexercised. However, if the stock price were above $100 on the expiration date, the option would surely be exercised.

Suppose the stock price had grown to $134 after 5 years, at which point the employee decided to exercise the option. He or she would buy stock from BMI for $100, so BMI would get only $100 for stock worth $134. The employee would (probably) sell the stock the same day he or she exercised the option, hence would receive in cash the $34 difference between the $134 stock price and the $100 exercise price. People often time the exercise of options to the purchase of a new home or some other large expenditure.

In theory, stock options should align a manager's interests with those of shareholders, influencing the manager to behave in a way that maximizes the company's value. But in practice there are two reasons this does not always occur.

First, suppose in the example above a CEO is granted options on 1 million shares. In this case, the executive would receive $34 for each option, or a total of $34 million. Keep in mind that this is in addition to an annual salary and cash bonuses. The logic behind employee options is that they motivate people to work harder and smarter, thus making the company more valuable and benefiting shareholders. But take a closer look at this example. If the risk-free rate is 5.5%, the market risk premium is 6%, and BMI's beta is 1.19, then the expected return, based on the CAPM, is 5.5% + 1.19(6%) = 12.64%. BMI's dividend yield is only 0.8%, so the expected annual price appreciation must be around 11.84% (12.64% − 0.8% = 11.84%). Now note that if BMI's stock price grew from $100 to $134 over 5 years, that would translate to an annual growth rate of only 6%, not the 11.84% shareholders expected. Thus, the executive would receive $34 million for helping run a company that performed below shareholders' expectations. As this example illustrates, standard stock options do not necessarily link executives' wealth with that of shareholders.

Even worse, the events of the early 2000s showed that some executives were willing to illegally falsify financial statements in order to drive up share prices just prior to exercising their stock options.[13] In some notable cases, the subsequent share price drop and loss of investor confidence forced firms into bankruptcy. This behaviour is certainly not in shareholders' best interests!

As a result, companies today are experimenting with different types of compensation plans, with different vesting periods and different measures of performance. For example, from a legal standpoint, it is more difficult to manipulate EVA (Economic Value Added) than it is to manipulate earnings per share.[14] Just as "all ships rise in a rising tide," so too do

---

[13]Several academic studies show that option-based compensation leads to a greater likelihood of earnings restatements and outright fraud. See A. Agrawal and S. Chadha, "Corporate Goverance and Accounting Scandals," *Journal of Law and Economics*, 2006, 371–406; N. Burns and S. Kedia, "The Impact of Performance-Based Compensation on Misreporting," *Journal of Financial Economics*, January 2006, 35–67; and D.J. Denis, P. Hanouna, and A. Sarin, "Is There a Dark Side to Incentive Compensation?" *Journal of Corporate Finance*, June 2006, 467–488.

[14]For a discussion of EVA, see Al Ehrbar, *EVA: The Real Key to Creating Wealth* (New York: John Wiley & Sons, 1998); and Pamela P. Peterson and David R. Peterson, *Company Performance and Measures of Value Added* (The Research Foundation of the Institute of Chartered Financial Analysts, 1996).

FINANCE: IN FOCUS

Corporate Governance in Canada

For the past 13 years *The Globe and Mail* has been surveying companies in the S&P/TSX Composite Index regarding their corporate governance practices. The table below shows some of the rankings from the 2014 survey. The survey is based on a series of questions, grouped by the following categories:

Board composition. The degree of director independence, whether the CEO and chairperson's positions are split, and whether the independent directors meet without management.

Shareholding and compensation. For example, disclosure of CEO bonus criteria, total executive compensation,

and whether directors and the CEO are required to own shares (not just stock options).

Shareholder rights. Company positions regarding the following: majority voting policy (where directors are asked to resign if they receive less than 50% of the votes in their favour), say-on-pay policy (shareholders provide feedback on executive pay), dual-class shares, and a policy for granting stock options.

Disclosure. Public disclosure of information on directors such as background, expertise, meeting attendance, and dollar value of their shareholdings.

The Globe and Mail's 2014 Canadian Company Corporate Governance Rankings

	Top-Ranked Companies			Bottom-Ranked Companies	
Rank	Company	Group	Rank	Company	Group
1	Bank of Montreal	Financials	237	Power Corp. of Canada	Financials
2	Sun Life Financial Inc.	Financials	238	BRP Inc.	Consumer discretionary
3 (tie)	Bank of Nova Scotia	Financials	239 (tie)	Birchcliff Energy Ltd.	Energy
	Emera Inc.	Utilities		RMP Energy Inc.	Energy
	Royal Bank of Canada	Financials		Tourmaline Oil Corp.	Energy
6 (tie)	Manulife Financial Corp.	Financials		Westshore Terminals Invest. Corp.	Industrial
	Potash Corp. of Sask. Inc.	Materials	243	OceanaGold Corp.	Materials
8 (tie)	Cameco Corp.	Energy	244	Avigilon Corp.	Technology
	Finning Int'l Inc.	Industrial	245	Bonterra Energy Corp.	Energy
	TransAlta Corp.	Utilities	246	Raging River Exploration Inc.	Energy
	Intact Financial Corp.	Financials	247	Fortuna Silver Mines Inc.	Materials

Sources: Board Games 2014 Corporate Governance Ranking, http://www.theglobeandmail.com/report-on-business/careers/management/board-games-2014/board-games-2014/article21525230/. Reprinted with permission of The Globe and Mail Inc. 2015.

most shares rise in a bull market such as that of 2003 to 2007. In a strong market, even the shares of companies whose performance ranks in the bottom 10% of their peer group can rise and thus trigger handsome executive bonuses. This situation is leading to compensation plans that are based on *relative* as opposed to *absolute* share price performance. For example, some compensation plans have indexed options, whose exercise prices depend on the performance of the market or of a subset of competitors.

Finally, the empirical results from academic studies show that the correlation between executive compensation and corporate performance is mixed. Some studies suggest that the type of compensation plan used affects company performance, while others suggest little if any effect. But we can say with certainty that managerial compensation plans will continue to receive lots of attention from researchers, the popular press, and boards of directors.

Capital Structure and Internal Control Systems

Capital structure decisions can affect managerial behaviour. As the debt level increases, so does the probability of bankruptcy. This increased threat of bankruptcy brings with it two effects on behaviour. First, when times are good, managers may waste cash flow on perquisites and unnecessary expenditures as described earlier in this chapter. The good news is that an increasing threat of bankruptcy reduces such wasteful spending.

But the bad news is that a manager may become gun-shy and reject positive NPV projects if they are risky. From a shareholder's point of view it would be unfortunate if a risky project caused the company to go into bankruptcy, but note that other companies in the shareholder's portfolio may be taking on risky projects that turn out successfully. Since most shareholders are well diversified, they can afford for a manager to take on risky but positive NPV projects. But a manager's reputation and wealth are generally tied to a single company, so the project may be unacceptably risky from the manager's point of view. Thus, high debt can cause managers to forego positive NPV projects unless they are extremely safe. This is called the **underinvestment problem,** and it is another type of agency cost. So increasing debt might increase firm value by reducing wasteful expenditures, but it also might reduce value by inducing underinvestment by managers. Empirical tests have not been able to establish exactly which effect dominates.

Internal control systems have become an increasingly important issue since the passage of the American Sarbanes-Oxley Act of 2002. Section 404 of the act requires companies to establish effective internal control systems. The Securities and Exchange Commission, which oversees Sarbanes-Oxley, defines an effective internal control system as one that provides "reasonable assurance regarding the reliability of financial reporting and the preparation of financial statements for external purposes in accordance with generally accepted accounting principles." In other words, investors should be able to trust a company's reported financial statements. The Canadian Securities Administrator's (CSA) introduced a Canadian equivalent in 2006.

Environmental Factors Outside a Firm's Control

As noted earlier, corporate governance is also affected by environmental factors that are outside a firm's control, including the regulatory/legal environment, block ownership patterns, competition in the product markets, the media, and litigation.

Regulations and Laws The regulatory/legal environment includes the agencies that regulate financial markets, such as the provincial securities commissions, the CSA, the stock exchanges, and the self-regulatory bodies. Even though the fines and penalties levied on firms for financial misrepresentation by the regulators are relatively small, the damage to a firm's reputation can have significant costs, leading to extremely large reductions in the firm's value.[15] Thus, the regulatory system has an enormous impact on corporate governance and firm value.

The regulatory/legal environment also includes the laws and legal system under which a company operates. These vary greatly from country to country. Studies show that firms located in countries with strong legal protection for investors have stronger corporate governance, and that this is reflected in better access to financial markets, a lower cost of equity, increases in market liquidity, and less "noise" in stock prices.[16]

Block Ownership Patterns Institutional investors such as pension plans and mutual funds have gained a larger share of investment capital over time and consequently control larger proportions of outstanding stock. The Canadian Coalition for Good Governance (CCGG) is an association made up of more than 48 institutional investors that collectively manage $2 trillion. The CCGG's mandate is to promote "corporate governance practices that best align the interests of boards and management with those of the shareholder." Given their large block holdings, it now makes sense for institutional investors to monitor management, and they have the clout to influence the board.

In general, activist investors with large blocks in companies have been good for all shareholders. They have searched for firms with poor profitability and then replaced management with new teams that are well-versed in value-based management techniques, thereby improving profitability. Not surprisingly, stock prices usually rise when the news comes out that a well-known activist investor has taken a major position in an underperforming company.

[15] For example, see Jonathan M. Karpoff, D. Scott Lee, and Gerald S. Martin, "The Cost to Firms of Cooking the Books," *Journal of Financial and Quantitative Analysis*, September 2008, pp. 581–612.
[16] For example, see R. La Porta, F. Lopez-de-Silanes, A. Shleifer, and R. Vishny, "Legal Determinants of External Finance," *Journal of Finance*, 1997, 1131–1150; Hazem Daouk, Charles M. C. Lee, and David Ng, "Capital Market Governance: How Do Security Laws Affect Market Performance?" *Journal of Corporate Finance*, June 2006, 560–593; and Li Jin and Stewart C. Myers, "R² Around the World: New Theory and New Tests," *Journal of Financial Economics*, 2006, 257–292.

FINANCE: IN FOCUS

Sarbanes-Oxley Act and C-SOX

Investor confidence was shattered with the accounting scandals at Enron and WorldCom. Financial statements that misstated profits, inflated assets, and hid debts resulted in investors, pensioners, and employees collectively losing billions of dollars. Accounting problems surfaced at other large companies, including Adelphia and Parmalat. In 2002, the U.S. Congress reacted swiftly, passing the Sarbanes-Oxley Act, known in the industry now as SOX, as a measure to restore investor confidence, improve transparency in financial accounting, and prevent fraud. SOX established wide-ranging new regulations for auditors, CEOs and CFOs, boards of directors, investment analysts, and investment banks. These regulations require (a) that companies performing audits be sufficiently independent of the companies they audit, (b) that a key executive in each company personally certify that the financial statements are complete and accurate, (c) that the board of directors' audit committee be relatively independent of management, (d) that financial analysts be relatively independent of the companies they analyze, and (e) that companies publicly and promptly release all important information about their financial condition.

This legislation is so significant that it has affected companies and capital markets beyond U.S. borders, reaching Canada, Europe, and Japan. For instance, 180 Canadian companies with dual listings in Canada and the United States must now conform to SOX. In a direct response to the new law, Ontario introduced Bill 198 in 2002, (sometimes called C-SOX), which covered many of the same regulatory issues. Since the TSX is in Ontario, Bill 198 effectively covers most publicly traded Canadian companies. While Bill 198 deals with many items covered by SOX, there are notable differences, as shown in the table below. Implementation and rules continue to evolve in order to balance the need to deter fraud and boost investor confidence with the expense and resources companies must expend in order to satisfy the requirements.

SOX	Bill 198	Differences
External auditors must offer an opinion on a company's internal controls.	External auditor opinion on a company's internal controls is not necessary.	Significantly higher auditing costs under SOX rules.
Companies must provide a "remote chance" that their internal controls will not result in misstatements.	Companies must provide a "reasonable assurance" that their internal controls will not result in misstatements.	Much higher standard must be met under SOX rules.
Significant financial penalties and prison time for violating SOX.	Financial penalties and prison time not as harsh.	Both provide a signal to the market and investors.

Sources: Michael A. Perino, "American Corporate Reform Abroad: Sarbanes-Oxley and the Foreign Private Issuer," http://papers.ssrn.com/sol3/papers.cfm?abstract_id5439501, accessed August 18, 2008; GFS Consulting, "Bill 198, MI52-109, 'C-SOX' and Its Impact on Canada," http://www.gfsconsulting.ca, accessed August 19, 2008.

Note that activist investors can improve performance even if they don't go so far as to take over a firm. More often, they either elect their own representatives to the board or simply point out the firm's problems to other board members. In such cases, boards often change their attitudes and become less tolerant when they realize that the management team is not necessarily undertaking actions that maximize value. The firm's top managers recognize what will happen if they don't whip the company into shape, and they go about doing just that.

Competition in the Product Markets The degree of competition in a firm's product market has an impact on its corporate governance. For example, companies in industries with lots of competition don't have the luxury of tolerating poorly performing CEOs. As might be expected, CEO turnover is more likely in competitive industries than in those with less competition.[17] When most firms in an industry are fairly similar, then you might expect it to be easier to find a qualified replacement from another firm for a poorly performing CEO. This is exactly what the evidence shows: as industry homogeneity increases, so does the likelihood of CEO turnover.[18]

---

[17]See M. De Fond and C. Park, "The Effect of Competition on CEO Turnover," *Journal of Accounting and Economics*, 1999, 35–56; and T. Fee and C. Hadlock, "Management Turnover and Product Market Competition: Empirical Evidence from the U.S. Newspaper Industry," *Journal of Business*, 2000, 205–243.
[18]See R. Parrino, "CEO Turnover and Outside Succession: A Cross-Sectional Analysis," *Journal of Financial Economics*, 1997, 165–197.

FINANCE: IN FOCUS

Corporate Governance and the Bell Canada Buyout

In 2007, Bell Canada reached an agreement to be bought out for $51.7 billion by an investors' group led by the Ontario Teachers' Pension Plan. The deal would be the largest leveraged buyout in corporate history. Considering that Bell Canada shares were trading around $30 before the talks became public, the $42.75 per share price put a smile on the face of shareholders. However, $34 billion of debt would have to be added to Bell's balance sheet as part of the leveraged buyout transaction. And that, unfortunately, was not in the best interests of the company's bondholders. Fearing dilution of collateral and lower interest coverage, the market wiped out 20% of the value of Bell Canada bonds.

In Canadian law, directors are told to act in the corporation's best interest. But you can legitimately ask, what is the corporation's best interest? Courts in Britain and the United States have equated the corporation's best interest with that of its owners. For instance, the often cited "Revlon Rule," named after the company in a previous U.S. court case, states that directors must work to the benefit of shareholders. A 2004 ruling by the Supreme Court of Canada stated that it may be reasonable for the board of directors, in determining the best interests of the corporation, to not only consider the interests of shareholders, but also those of "employees, suppliers, creditors, consumers, governments and the

environment." The best interests of the corporation in Canada need not be equated with the position of shareholders or any other stakeholders! Even if we ignore the stakeholder argument, things can still get confusing. After all, owners are typically shareholders, except when a company is bankrupt, when creditors take control. And the greater the financial leverage a company takes on, the greater the chance that creditors will assume control.

A group of bondholders went to court attempting to stop the takeover, arguing that Bell's board failed to adequately consider their interests. The first court ruling sided with Bell Canada, allowing the buyout to proceed. Bondholders then appealed the ruling to Quebec's Court of Appeal. The Appeal Court overturned the original ruling, stating that the transaction was not reasonable because it treated the bondholders unfairly. Bell Canada appealed the decision to the Supreme Court, and in June 2008, the Supreme Court ruled in favour of Bell Canada and allowed the sale to go forward. However, the Supreme Court also stated that in instances of change in ownership, directors must consider the interests of all stakeholders, consistent with the corporation's duties as a "good corporate citizen." It remains to be seen the actual impact this "good corporate citizenship" standard will have on future board decisions.

The Media and Litigation Corporate governance, especially compensation, is a hot topic in the media. The media can have a positive impact by discovering or reporting corporate problems, such as the Enron scandal. Another example was the coverage given to option backdating, in which the exercise prices of executive stock options are set *after* the options officially have been granted. Because the exercise prices are set at the lowest stock price during the quarter in which the options are granted, the options are in-the-money and more valuable when their "official" life begins.

However, the media can also hurt corporate governance by focusing too much attention on a CEO. Such "superstar" CEOs often command excessive compensation packages and spend too much time on activities outside the company, resulting in too much pay for too little performance.[19]

In addition to penalties and fines from regulatory bodies, civil litigation also occurs when companies are suspected of fraud. The recent research indicates that such suits lead to improvements in corporate governance.[20]

CONCEPT REVIEW

1. What are two primary forms of corporate governance (i.e., the carrot and the stick)?
2. What factors improve a board of directors' effectiveness?
3. What are three provisions in many corporate charters that deter takeovers?
4. Describe how a typical stock option plan works. What are some problems with a typical stock option plan?

[19]See U. Malmendier and G. A. Tate, "Superstar CEOs," *Quarterly Journal of Economics*, 4 no. 124 (2009), 1593–1638.
[20]For example, see D. B. Farber, "Restoring Trust after Fraud: Does Corporate Governance Matter?" *Accounting Review*, 2005, 539–561; and Stephen P. Ferris, Tomas Jandik, Robert M. Lawless, and Anil Makhija, "Derivative Lawsuits as a Corporate Governance Mechanism: Empirical Evidence on Board Changes Surrounding Filings," *Journal of Financial and Quantitative Analysis*, March 2007, 143–165.

Summary

- **Corporate assets** consist of operating assets and financial, or nonoperating, assets.
- **Operating assets** take two forms: assets-in-place and growth options.
- **Assets-in-place** include the land, buildings, machines, and inventory that the firm uses in its operations to produce products and services.
- **Growth options** refer to opportunities the firm has to increase sales. They include opportunities arising from R&D expenditures, customer relationships, and the like.
- **Financial,** or **nonoperating, assets** are distinguished from operating assets and include items such as investments in marketable securities and noncontrolling interests in the stock of other companies.
- The **value of nonoperating assets** is usually close to the figure reported on the balance sheet.
- The **value of operations** is the present value of all the future free cash flows expected from operations when discounted at the weighted average cost of capital:

$$V_{\text{op(at time 0)}} = \sum_{t=1}^{\infty} \frac{FCF_1}{(1 + WACC)^1}$$

- The **terminal,** or **horizon, value** is the value of operations at the end of the explicit forecast period. It is also called the **continuing value,** and it is equal to the present value of all free cash flows beyond the forecast period, discounted back to the end of the forecast period at the weighted average cost of capital:

$$\text{Continuing value} = V_{\text{op(at time N)}} = \frac{FCF_{N+1}}{WACC - g} = \frac{FCF_N(1 + g)}{WACC - g}$$

- The **corporate valuation model** can be used to calculate the total value of a company by finding the value of operations plus the value of nonoperating assets.
- The **value of equity** is the total value of the company minus the value of the debt and preferred stock. The **price per share** is the total value of the equity divided by the number of shares.
- **Expected return on invested capital (EROIC)** is equal to expected NOPAT divided by the amount of capital that is available at the beginning of the year.
- A company creates value when the spread between EROIC and WACC is positive, that is, when EROIC − WACC > 0.
- An **agency relationship** arises whenever an individual or group, called a **principal,** hires someone called an **agent** to perform some service and the principal delegates decision-making power to the agent.
- Important agency relationships include those between shareholders and creditors, owner/managers and outside shareholders, and shareholders and managers.
- An **agency conflict** refers to a conflict between principals and agents. For example, managers, as agents, may pay themselves excessive salaries, obtain unreasonably large stock options, and the like, at the expense of the principals, the shareholders.
- **Agency costs** are the reductions in a company's value due to actions by agents, including the costs principals incur (such as monitoring costs) in trying to modify their agents' behaviours.
- **Corporate governance** involves the manner in which shareholders' objectives are implemented, and it is reflected in a company's policies and actions.
- The two primary mechanisms used in corporate governance are (1) the threat of removal of a poorly performing CEO and (2) the type of plan used to compensate executives and managers.
- Poorly performing managers can be removed either by a takeover or by the company's own board of directors. Provisions in the corporate charter affect the difficulty of a successful takeover, and the composition of the board of directors affects the likelihood of a manager being removed by the board.
- **Managerial entrenchment** is most likely when a company has a weak board of directors coupled with strong anti-takeover provisions in its corporate charter. In this situation, the likelihood that badly performing senior managers will be fired is low.

- **Nonpecuniary benefits** are noncash perks such as lavish offices, memberships at country clubs, corporate jets, foreign junkets, and the like. Some of these expenditures may be cost effective, but others are wasteful and simply reduce profits. Such fat is almost always cut after a hostile takeover.
- With **cumulative voting** each shareholder is given a number of votes equal to his or her shares times the number of board seats up for election. The shareholder can then distribute his or her votes however he or she sees fit. That is, the shareholder can use all of his or her votes for one director or divide his or her votes over several board positions.
- **Targeted share repurchases,** also known as **greenmail,** occur when a company buys back stock from a potential acquirer at a higher than fair market price. In return, the potential acquirer agrees not to attempt to take over the company.
- **Shareholder rights provisions,** also known as **poison pills,** allow existing shareholders to purchase additional shares of stock at a lower than market value if a potential acquirer purchases a controlling stake in the company.
- A **restricted voting rights** provision automatically deprives a shareholder of voting rights if the shareholder owns more than a specified amount of stock.
- **Interlocking boards of directors** occur when the CEO of Company A sits on the board of Company B, and B's CEO sits on A's board.
- A **stock option** provides for the purchase of a share of stock at a fixed price, called the exercise price, no matter what the actual price of the stock is. Stock options have an expiration date, after which they cannot be exercised.

Questions

22-1 Define each of the following terms:
a. Assets-in-place; growth options; nonoperating assets
b. Net operating working capital; operating capital; NOPAT; free cash flow
c. Value of operations; horizon value; corporate valuation model
d. EROIC
e. Agent; principal; agency relationship
f. Agency cost
g. Basic types of agency conflicts
h. Managerial entrenchment; nonpecuniary benefits
i. Greenmail; poison pills; restricted voting rights
j. Stock option

22-2 Explain how to use the corporate valuation model to find the price per share of common equity.

22-3 What is the possible agency conflict between inside owner/managers and outside shareholders?

22-4 What are some possible agency conflicts between borrowers and lenders?

22-5 What are some actions an entrenched management might take that would harm shareholders?

22-6 How is it possible for an employee stock option to be valuable even if the firm's stock price fails to meet shareholders' expectations?

Concept Review Problem

Full solutions are provided at www.nelson.com/brigham3ce.

CR-1

Corporate Valuation

Watkins Inc. has never paid a dividend, and when it might begin paying dividends is unknown. Its current free cash flow is $100,000, and this FCF is expected to grow at a constant 7% rate. The weighted average cost of capital is 11%. Watkins currently holds $325,000 of nonoperating marketable securities. Its long-term debt is $1,000,000, but it has never issued preferred stock. Watkins has 50,000 shares outstanding.
a. Calculate Watkins' value of operations.
b. Calculate the company's total value.
c. Calculate the value of its common equity.
d. Calculate the per share stock price.

Problems

Easy
Problems 1–4

Answers to odd-numbered problems appear in Appendix A.

22-1
Free Cash Flow

Use the following income statements and balance sheets to calculate Garnet Inc.'s free cash flow for 2016.

Garnet Inc.	2016	2015
Income Statement		
Net sales	$530.0	$500.0
Costs (except depreciation)	400.0	380.0
Depreciation	30.0	25.0
Total operating costs	430.0	405.0
Earnings before interest and taxes (EBIT)	100.0	95.0
Less interest	23.0	21.0
Earnings before taxes	77.0	74.0
Taxes (30%)	23.1	22.2
Net income	$ 53.9	$ 51.8
Balance Sheet		
Assets		
Cash	$ 28.0	$ 27.0
Marketable securities	69.0	66.0
Accounts receivable	84.0	80.0
Inventories	112.0	106.0
Total current assets	293.0	279.0
Net plant and equipment	281.0	265.0
Total assets	$574.0	$544.0
Liabilities and Equity		
Accounts payable	$ 56.0	$ 52.0
Notes payable	138.0	130.0
Accruals	28.0	28.0
Total current liabilities	222.0	210.0
Long-term bonds	173.0	164.0
Common stock	100.0	100.0
Retained earnings	79.0	70.0
Common equity	179.0	170.0
Total liabilities and equity	$574.0	$544.0

22-2
Value of Operations of
Constant Growth Firm

Prester Corp. has never paid a dividend. Its current free cash flow is $900,000 and is expected to grow at a constant rate of 5%. The weighted average cost of capital is 12%. Calculate Prester's value of operations.

22-3
Horizon Value

Current and projected free cash flows for Radell Global Operations are shown below. Growth is expected to be constant after 2017. The weighted average cost of capital is 8%. What is the horizon, or continuing, value at 2017?

	Actual	Projected		
	2015	2016	2017	2018
Free cash flow (millions of dollars)	$606.82	$667.50	$707.55	$750.00

22-4
Value of Operations, Total
Value, and Equity Values

CAS Limited has free cash flow of $250,000 that is expected to grow on average at a 5% rate. The company holds $600,000 of long-term debt, and $80,000 in nonoperating short-term

investments. The company has 250,000 shares outstanding and its weighted average cost of capital is 10%. The company does not pay a dividend. Calculate CAS Limited's:
a. value of operations.
b. total company value.
c. value of common equity.
d. stock price.

Intermediate Problems 5–7

22-5
Value of Operations

Below is summary information for two companies. Which company has the higher value of operations? Briefly explain.

	A	B
NOPAT	$1,000,000	$1,200,000
Net investment in operating capital	370,000	700,000
WACC	10%	10%
Free cash flow growth rate	4%	5%

22-6
Value of Operations

Brooks Enterprises has never paid a dividend. Free cash flow is projected to be $80,000 and $100,000 for the next 2 years, respectively, and after the second year it is expected to grow at a constant rate of 8%. The company's weighted average cost of capital is 12%.
a. What is the terminal, or horizon, value of operations?
b. Calculate the value of Brooks' operations.

22-7
Corporate Valuation

Dozier Corporation is a fast-growing supplier of office products. Analysts project the following free cash flows (FCFs) during the next 3 years, after which FCF is expected to grow at a constant 7% rate. Dozier's WACC is 13%.

	Year		
	1	2	3
Free cash flow ($ millions)	−$20	$30	$40

a. What is Dozier's terminal, or horizon, value?
b. What is the current value of operations for Dozier?
c. Suppose Dozier has $10 million in marketable securities, $100 million in debt, and 10 million shares outstanding. What is the price per share?

Challenging Problems 8–11

22-8
Corporate Valuation

Use the financial statements from Garnet Inc. in problem 1. The 2015 financials are actuals, while 2016 shows projected financials. Garnet's WACC is 12%, and the company's free cash flows are expected to grow at 4% after 2016.
a. What is the company's horizon value as of December 31, 2016?
b. What is the company's value of operations as of December 31, 2015?
c. What is the total value of Garnet as of December 31, 2015?
d. If Garnet has 24 million shares outstanding, what is the share price for December 31, 2015?

22-9
Value of Equity

The balance sheet of Amico Chemical is shown below. If the December 31, 2015 value of operations is $220 million, what is the December 31, 2015 value of equity?

Balance Sheet, December 31, 2015 (Millions of Dollars)

Assets		Liabilities and Equity	
Cash	$ 20.0	Accounts payable	$ 19.0
Marketable securities	24.0	Notes payable	70.0
Accounts receivable	65.0	Accruals	51.0
Inventories	110.0	Total current liabilities	140.0
Total current assets	219.0	Long-term bonds	80.0
Net plant and equipment	225.0	Preferred stock	35.0
		Common stock	100.0
		Retained earnings	89.0
		Common equity	189.0
Total assets	$444.0	Total liabilities and equity	$444.0

22-10
Price per Share

The balance sheet of Roop Industries is shown below. The December 31, 2015 value of operations is $651 million and there are 10 million common shares. What is the price per share?

Balance Sheet, December 31, 2015 (Millions of Dollars)

Assets		Liabilities and Equity	
Cash	$ 20.0	Accounts payable	$ 19.0
Marketable securities	47.0	Notes payable	65.0
Accounts receivable	100.0	Accruals	51.0
Inventories	200.0	Total current liabilities	135.0
Total current assets	367.0	Long-term bonds	131.0
Net plant and equipment	279.0	Preferred stock	33.0
		Common stock	160.0
		Retained earnings	187.0
		Common equity	347.0
Total assets	$646.0	Total liabilities and equity	$646.0

22-11
Corporate Valuation

The financial statements of Can Cable Fabricators are shown below, with the actual results for 2015 and the projections for 2016. Free cash flow is expected to grow at a 5% rate after 2016. The weighted average cost of capital is 10%.
a.   If operating capital as of December 31, 2015 is $502.2 million, what is the free cash flow for December 31, 2016?
b.   What is the horizon value as of December 31, 2016?
c.   What is the value of operations as of December 31, 2015?
d.   What is the total value of the company as of December 31, 2015?
e.   What is the price per share for December 31, 2015?

Income Statements for the Year Ended December 31
(Millions of Dollars Except for Per-Share Data)

	Actual 2015	Projected 2016
Net sales	$500.0	$530.0
Costs (except depreciation)	360.0	381.6
Depreciation	37.5	39.8
Total operating costs	397.5	421.4
Earnings before interest and taxes	102.5	108.6
Less interest	13.9	16.0
Earnings before taxes	88.6	92.6
Taxes	26.6	27.8
Net income before preferred dividends	62.0	64.8
Preferred dividends	6.0	7.4
Net income available for common dividends	$ 56.0	$ 57.4
Common dividends	$ 49.6	$ 38.9
Addition to retained earnings	$ 6.4	$ 18.5
Number of shares (in millions)	12	12
Dividends per share	$ 4.13	$ 3.24

Balance Sheets for December 31 (Millions of Dollars)

	Actual 2015	Projected 2016
Assets		
Cash	$ 5.3	$ 5.6
Marketable securities	49.9	51.9
Accounts receivable	53.0	56.2
Inventories	106.0	112.4
Total current assets	214.2	226.1
Net plant and equipment	375.0	397.5
Total assets	$589.2	$623.6
Liabilities and Equity		
Accounts payable	$ 9.6	$ 11.2
Notes payable	69.9	74.1
Accruals	27.5	28.1
Total current liabilities	107.0	113.4
Long-term bonds	140.8	148.2
Preferred stock	35.0	37.1
Common stock	160.0	160.0
Retained earnings	146.4	164.9
Common equity	306.4	324.9
Total liabilities and equity	$589.2	$623.6

Spreadsheet Problem

22-12
Build a Model:
Corporate Valuation

Start with the partial model in the file *Ch 22 Build a Model.xlsx* from the textbook's website. Henley Corporation is a privately held company specializing in lawn care products and services. The most recent financial statements are shown below.

Income Statement for the Year Ended December 31
(Millions of Dollars Except for Per-Share Data)

	2015
Net sales	$800.0
Costs (except depreciation)	576.0
Depreciation	60.0
Total operating costs	636.0
Earnings before interest and taxes	164.0
Less interest	32.0
Earnings before taxes	132.0
Taxes (40%)	52.8
Net income before preferred dividends	79.2
Preferred dividends	1.4
Net income available for common dividends	$ 77.8
Common dividends	$ 31.1
Addition to retained earnings	$ 46.7
Number of shares (in millions)	10
Dividends per share	$ 3.11

Balance Sheet for December 31 (Millions of Dollars)

	2015		2015
Assets		**Liabilities and Equity**	
Cash	$ 8.0	Accounts payable	$ 16.0
Marketable securities	20.0	Notes payable	40.0
Accounts receivable	80.0	Accruals	40.0
Inventories	160.0	Total current liabilities	96.0
Total current assets	268.0	Long-term bonds	300.0
Net plant and equipment	600.0	Preferred stock	15.0
		Common stock	257.0
		Retained earnings	200.0
		Common equity	457.0
Total assets	$868.0	Total liabilities and equity	$868.0

The ratios and selected information for the current and projected years are shown below.

	Actual	Projected			
	2015	2016	2017	2018	2019
Sales growth rate		15%	10%	6%	6%
Costs/Sales	72%	72	72	72	72
Depreciation/Net PPE	10	10	10	10	10
Cash/Sales	1	1	1	1	1
Accounts receivable/Sales	10	10	10	10	10
Inventories/Sales	20	20	20	20	20
Net PPE/Sales	75	75	75	75	75
Accounts payable/Sales	2	2	2	2	2
Accruals/Sales	5	5	5	5	5
Tax rate	40	40	40	40	40
Weighted average cost of capital (WACC)	10.5	10.5	10.5	10.5	10.5

a. Forecast the parts of the income statement and balance sheets necessary to calculate free cash flow.
b. Calculate free cash flow for each projected year. Also calculate the growth rates of free cash flow each year to ensure that there is constant growth (i.e., the same as the constant growth rate in sales) by the end of the forecast period.
c. Calculate operating profitability (OP = NOPAT/Sales), capital requirements (CR = Operating capital/Sales), and expected return on invested capital (EROIC = Expected NOPAT/Operating capital at beginning of year). Based on the spread between EROIC and WACC, do you think that the company will have a positive Market Value Added (MVA = Market value of company − Book value of company = Value of operations − Operating capital)?
d. Calculate the value of operations and MVA. (*Hint:* First calculate the horizon value at the end of the forecast period, which is equal to the value of operations at the end of the forecast period. Assume that growth beyond the horizon is 6%.)
e. Calculate the price per share of common equity as of December 31, 2015.

MINI CASE

You have been hired as a consultant to Kulpa Fishing Supplies (KFS), a company that is seeking to increase its value. The company's CEO and founder, Mia Kulpa, has asked you to estimate the value of two privately held companies that KFS is considering acquiring. But first, the senior management of KFS would like you to explain how to value companies that don't pay any dividends. You have structured your presentation around the following questions:

a.   List the two types of assets that companies own.

b.   What are assets-in-place? How can their value be estimated?

c.   What are nonoperating assets? How can their value be estimated?

d.   What is the total value of a corporation? Who has claims on this value?

e.   The first acquisition target is a privately held company in a mature industry. The company currently has free cash flow of $20 million. Its WACC is 10% and it is expected to grow at a constant rate of 5%. The company has marketable securities of $100 million. It is financed with $200 million of debt, $50 million of preferred shares, and $210 million of book equity.

   (1)   What is its value of operations?

   (2)   What is its total corporate value? What is its value of equity?

   (3)   What is its MVA (MVA = Total corporate value − Total book value)?

f.   The second acquisition target is a privately held company in a growing industry. The target has recently borrowed $40 million to finance its expansion; it has no other debt or preferred shares. It pays no dividends and currently has no marketable securities. KFS expects the company to produce free cash flows of −$5 million in 1 year, $10 million in 2 years, and $20 million in 3 years. After 3 years, free cash flow will grow at a rate of 6%. Its WACC is 10% and it currently has 10 million shares outstanding.

   (1)   What is its horizon value (i.e., its value of operations at Year 3)? What is its current value of operations (i.e., at time zero)?

   (2)   What is its value of equity on a price per share basis?

g.   List six potential managerial behaviours that can harm a firm's value.

h.   The managers at KFS have heard that corporate governance can affect shareholder value. What is corporate governance? List five corporate governance provisions that are internal to a firm and are under its control.

i.   What characteristics of the board of directors usually lead to effective corporate governance?

j.   List three provisions in the corporate charter that affect takeovers.

k.   Briefly describe the use of stock options in a compensation plan. What are some potential problems with stock options as a form of compensation?

l.   What is block ownership? How does it affect corporate governance?

m.   Briefly explain how regulatory agencies and legal systems affect corporate governance.

chapter 23

Mergers, Acquisitions, and Restructuring

BCE Ltd. is Canada's largest communications company, operating wireless mobile networks, local and long-distance phone services, broadband Internet, and both satellite and broadband TV. BCE believes it is strategically important to control the content that is delivered over its networks. While the company could slowly and organically grow its programming and content business over time, it has chosen to purchase existing TV, radio, and digital content through a series of large acquisitions. In 2010, for $3.2 billion, BCE purchased CTVglobemedia, which included television and radio broadcasting and production assets. The following year, for $1.3 billion, BCE acquired (in conjunction with Rogers Communications) Maple Leaf Sports and Entertainment, which owns Toronto's professional hockey team (Maple Leafs), its basketball team (Raptors), and its soccer team (Toronto FC) in addition to other assets such as broadcasting rights and two sports channels. In 2012, BCE announced its intention to acquire Astral Media for $3.3 billion. Astral's business includes ownership of more than 20 TV channels and pay TV services, as well as 84 radio stations, throughout Canada. The three transactions, which have a combined value of $7.8 billion, have made BCE's Bell Media subsidiary Canada's largest media company.

The above acquisitions have produced several winners. When the deal was announced, Astral's shareholders saw the value of their stock rise by nearly 40%, while Torstar's (seller of CTV) shareholders saw their stock jump over 20%. Other winners include Astral's and Torstar's senior executives, who saw the value of their stock and options increase, and investment banks such as TD Securities, RBC Capital Markets, and National Bank Financial, which made millions from the transactions.

While some have applauded the deal, others believe that BCE will have to work hard to justify the acquisitions. Moreover, as we point out in this chapter, the track record for acquiring firms in large deals has not always been good. As we write this in January 2015, BCE's stock is up 74% since the first acquisition was announced, compared to a 20% increase in the S&P/TSX Composite. We can't say what BCE's performance would have been without the acquisitions, but it has certainly outperformed the overall stock market.

Sources: Euan Rocha, "Bell to Acquire Rival Astral Media," *Toronto Sun*, March 16, 2012, http://www.torontosun.com; "Acquisition of Astral Analyst Conference Call," March 16, 2012, http://www.bce.ca; "Bell to Acquire 100% of Canada's #1 Media Company CTV," News Release, September 10, 2010, http://www.bce.ca; "Teachers' Announces Sale of MLSE Majority Interest to Two Leading Canadian Corporations," News Release, Ontario Teachers' Pension Plan, December 9, 2011, http://www.otpp.com.

The textbook's website contains an *Excel* file that will guide you through the chapter's calculations. The file for this chapter is *Ch 23 Tool Kit.xlsx,* and we encourage you to open the file and follow along as you read the chapter. **www.nelson.com/ brigham3ce**

Most corporate growth occurs by *internal expansion,* which takes place when a firm's existing divisions grow through normal capital budgeting activities. However, the most dramatic examples of growth result from mergers, the first topic covered in this chapter. **Leveraged buyouts,** or *LBOs,* occur when a firm's stock is acquired by a small group of investors rather than by another operating company. Conditions change over time, causing firms to sell off, or divest, major divisions to other firms that can better utilize the divested assets discussed in the chapter. Thus we conclude the chapter with a discussion on divestitures.

23.1 Rationale for Mergers

Many reasons have been proposed by financial managers and theorists to account for the high level of merger activity. The primary motives behind corporate **mergers** are presented in this section.[1]

Synergy

The primary motivation for most mergers is to increase the value of the combined enterprise. If Companies A and B merge to form Company C, and if C's value exceeds that of A and B taken separately, then **synergy** is said to exist, and such a merger should be beneficial to both A's and B's shareholders.[2] Synergistic effects can arise from five sources: (1) *operating economies,* which result from economies of scale in management, marketing, production, or distribution; (2) *financial economies,* including lower transaction costs and better coverage by security analysts; (3) *tax effects,* where the combined enterprise pays less in taxes than the separate firms would pay; (4) *differential efficiency,* which implies that the management of one firm is more efficient and that the weaker firm's assets will be more productive after the merger; and (5) *increased market power* due to reduced competition. Operating and financial economies are socially desirable, as are mergers that increase managerial efficiency, but mergers that reduce competition are socially undesirable and illegal.

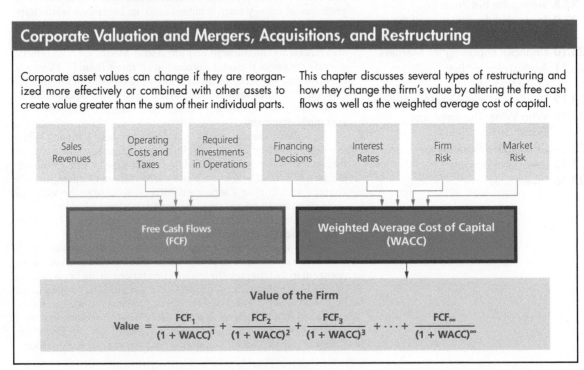

Corporate Valuation and Mergers, Acquisitions, and Restructuring

Corporate asset values can change if they are reorganized more effectively or combined with other assets to create value greater than the sum of their individual parts.

This chapter discusses several types of restructuring and how they change the firm's value by altering the free cash flows as well as the weighted average cost of capital.

Sales Revenues | Operating Costs and Taxes | Required Investments in Operations | Financing Decisions | Interest Rates | Firm Risk | Market Risk

Free Cash Flows (FCF)

Weighted Average Cost of Capital (WACC)

Value of the Firm

$$\text{Value} = \frac{FCF_1}{(1 + WACC)^1} + \frac{FCF_2}{(1 + WACC)^2} + \frac{FCF_3}{(1 + WACC)^3} + \cdots + \frac{FCF_\infty}{(1 + WACC)^\infty}$$

---

[1]As we use the term, "merger" means any combination that forms one economic unit from two or more previous ones. For legal purposes, there are distinctions among the various ways these combinations can occur, but our focus is on the fundamental economic and financial aspects of mergers.
[2]If synergy exists, then the whole is greater than the sum of the parts. Synergy is also called the "2 plus 2 equals 5 effect." The distribution of the synergistic gain between A's and B's shareholders is determined by negotiation. This point is discussed later in the chapter.

The merger a few years ago of TD Bank and U.S.-based Commerce Bancorp significantly expanded TD's branch network and illustrates the quest for synergies. The banks' operations overlapped in New Jersey, Philadelphia, and Metro New York, so closing neighbouring branches could cut costs and certain back office operations could be consolidated to further reduce costs. The acquisition has provided TD with a strong competitive presence in several major U.S. markets and provides a basis for it to grow its retail banking operations. Another synergistic merger was the 2011 acquisition of the Icelandic Group, a frozen seafood supplier, by Canadian-based High Liner Foods. This merger has created North America's largest value-added seafood supplier. High Liner optimized plant operations to improve economies of scale in production and distribution; rationalized procurement, manufacturing, and packaging; and eliminated duplication in selling and administrative functions. Annual synergies realized were $18 million. In addition, the acquisition provides High Liner with a larger international reach to source product as well as production facilities to support future growth.

Expected synergies are not always realized. For example, when U.S.-based AOL acquired Time Warner, it believed that Time Warner's extensive content library could be sold to AOL's Internet subscribers and that AOL subscribers could be shifted over to Time Warner's cable system. When the merger was announced, the new management estimated that such synergies would increase operating income by $1 billion per year. However, things didn't work out as expected, and in 2002 Time Warner had to write off $100 billion in lost value associated with the merger.

Tax Considerations

Tax considerations have stimulated a number of mergers. For example, a profitable firm in the highest tax bracket could acquire a firm with large accumulated tax losses. These losses could then be turned into immediate tax savings rather than carried forward and used in the future.[3]

Also, mergers can serve as a way of minimizing taxes when disposing of excess cash. For example, if a firm has a shortage of internal investment opportunities compared with its free cash flow, it could (1) pay an extra dividend, (2) invest in marketable securities, (3) repurchase its own stock, or (4) purchase another firm. If it paid an extra dividend, its shareholders would have to pay immediate taxes on the distribution. Marketable securities often provide a good temporary parking place for money, but they generally earn a rate of return less than that required by shareholders. A stock repurchase might result in a capital gain for the selling shareholders. However, using surplus cash to acquire another firm would avoid all these problems, and this has motivated a number of mergers. Still, as we discuss later, the tax savings are often less than the premium paid in the acquisition. Thus, mergers motivated only by tax considerations often reduce the acquiring shareholders' wealth.

Purchase of Assets Below Their Replacement Cost

Sometimes a firm is touted as an acquisition candidate because the cost of replacing its assets is considerably higher than its market value. This is especially true in the natural resource industry. For example, an oil company's reserves might be worth more on paper than the company's stock. (Of course, converting paper value to monetary value isn't always as easy as it sounds.)

Diversification

Managers often cite diversification as a reason for mergers. They contend that diversification helps stabilize a firm's earnings and thus benefits its owners. Stabilization of earnings is certainly beneficial to employees, suppliers, and customers, but its value to shareholders is less certain. Why should Firm A acquire Firm B to stabilize earnings when shareholders can simply buy the stocks of both firms? Indeed, research suggests that in most cases diversification does not increase the firm's value. In fact, many studies have found that diversified firms are worth significantly less than the sum of their individual parts.[4]

---

[3]Mergers undertaken only to use accumulated tax losses would probably be scrutinized by the Canada Revenue Agency to ensure the tax losses are eligible to be claimed by the acquiring company.
[4]See, for example, Philip Berger and Eli Ofek, "Diversification's Effect on Firm Value," *Journal of Financial Economics*, 1995, 37–65; and Larry Lang and René Stulz, "Tobin's Q, Corporate Diversification, and Firm Performance," *Journal of Political Economy*, 1994, 1248–1280.

Of course, if you were the owner-manager of a closely held firm, it might be nearly impossible to sell part of your stock to diversify. Also, selling your stock would probably lead to a large capital gains tax. So, a diversification merger might be the best way to achieve personal diversification for a privately held firm.

Managers' Personal Incentives

Financial economists like to think that business decisions are based only on economic considerations, especially maximization of firms' values. However, many business decisions are based more on managers' personal motivations than on economic analyses. Business leaders like power, and more power is attached to running a larger corporation than a smaller one. Most likely, no executive would admit that his or her ego was the primary reason behind a merger, but egos do play a prominent role in many mergers.[5]

It has also been observed that executive salaries are highly correlated with company size—the bigger the company, the higher the salaries of its top officers. This too could obviously cause unnecessary acquisitions.

Personal considerations deter as well as motivate mergers. After most takeovers, some managers of the acquired companies lose their jobs, or at least their autonomy. Therefore, managers who own less than 51% of their firms' stock look to devices that will lessen the chances of a takeover, and a merger can serve as such a device. For example, in 2005 MCI's board of directors, over the objection of large shareholders, turned down repeated acquisition offers from Qwest, at the time the United States' fourth largest local phone company, in favour of substantially smaller offers from Verizon, that country's largest phone company. MCI's management viewed Verizon as a stronger, more stable partner than Qwest even though Qwest's bid was at times 20% higher than Verizon's bid. In response to management's refusal to accept the higher bid, the holders of some 28% of MCI's stock withheld their votes to reelect the board of directors in protest. Nonetheless, management proceeded with merger negotiations with Verizon and the two companies merged in June 2006. In such cases management always argues that synergy, not a desire to protect their own jobs, is the motivation for the choice. However, it is difficult to rationalize rejecting a 20% larger bid for undocumented synergies, and some observers suspect that this and many mergers are ultimately designed to benefit managers rather than shareholders.

Breakup Value

Some takeover specialists estimate a company's **breakup value,** which is the value of the individual parts of the firm if they were sold off separately. If this value is higher than the firm's current market value, then a takeover specialist could acquire the firm at or even above its current market value, sell it off in pieces, and earn a profit.

CONCEPT REVIEW

1. Define synergy. Is synergy a valid rationale for mergers? Describe several situations that might produce synergistic gains.
2. Suppose your firm could purchase another firm for only half of its replacement value. Would that be a sufficient justification for the acquisition?
3. Discuss the pros and cons of diversification as a rationale for mergers.
4. What is breakup value?

23.2 Types of Mergers

Economists classify mergers into four types: (1) horizontal, (2) vertical, (3) congeneric, and (4) conglomerate. A **horizontal merger** occurs when one firm combines with another in its same line of business—the 2007 TSX–Montreal Exchange merger is an example. An example of a **vertical merger** would be a steel producer's acquisition of one of its own suppliers, such as an iron or coal mining firm, or an oil producer's acquisition of a petrochemical firm that

---

[5]See Randall Morck, Andrei Shleifer, and Robert W. Vishny, "Do Managerial Objectives Drive Bad Acquisitions?" *Journal of Finance,* March 1990, 31–48.

uses oil as a raw material. *Congeneric* means "allied in nature or action"; hence a **congeneric merger** involves related enterprises but not producers of the same product (horizontal) or firms in a producer–supplier relationship (vertical). Canadian graphics card maker ATI Technology's merger with Advanced Micro Devices is an example. A **conglomerate merger** occurs when unrelated enterprises combine.

Operating economies (and also anticompetitive effects) are at least partially dependent on the type of merger involved. Vertical and horizontal mergers generally provide the greatest synergistic operating benefits, but they are also the ones most likely to be reviewed carefully by the Competition Bureau.[6] In any event, it is useful to think of these economic classifications when analyzing prospective mergers.

CONCEPT REVIEW

1. What are the four economic types of mergers?

23.3 Level of Merger Activity

As can be seen from Table 23-1, some huge mergers have occurred in recent years. In general, recent mergers have been significantly different from those of the 1980s and 1990s. Most earlier mergers were financial transactions in which buyers sought companies that were selling at less than their true values as a result of incompetent or sluggish management. If a target company could be managed better, if redundant assets could be sold, and if operating and administrative costs could be cut, profits and stock prices would rise. In contrast, most recent mergers have been strategic in nature—companies are merging to gain economies of scale or scope and thus be better able to compete in the world economy. Indeed, many recent mergers have involved companies in the financial, defence, media,

TABLE 23-1 The Ten Largest Mergers Worldwide Through December 31, 2013

Lead Buyer	Target	Completion Date	Value ($ Billions)
Vodafone AirTouch	Mannesmann	April 12, 2000	$161
Verizon	Cellco	September 2, 2013	130
Pfizer	Warner-Lambert	June 19, 2000	116
America Online	Time Warner	January 11, 2001	106
Consortium led by Royal Bank of Scotland	ABN Amro Holding	October 10, 2007	95
Exxon	Mobil	November 30, 1999	81
Glaxo Wellcome	SmithKline Beecham	December 27, 2000	74
Royal Dutch Petroleum	Shell Transport and Trading	September 25, 2005	74
Citicorp	Travelers	October 8, 1998	74
ATT	BellSouth	December 29, 2006	73
SBC Communications	Ameritech	October 8, 1999	72

Sources: "A Look at the Top 10 Global Mergers," Associated Press Newswire, January 11, 2001; various issues of the Wall Street Journal's "Year-End Review of Markets and Finance World-Wide Deals"; and John Williamson, "Largest Mergers and Acquisitions by Corporations in 2007," CRS Report for Congress, February 14, 2008.

---

[6]For interesting insights into antitrust regulations and mergers, see B. Espen Eckbo, "Mergers and the Value of Antitrust Deterrence," *Journal of Finance*, July 1992, 1005–1029.

computer, telecommunications, and health care industries, all of which are experiencing structural changes and intense competition.

Recent deals also differ in the way they are financed and how the target firms' shareholders are compensated. In the 1980s, cash was the preferred method of payment, because large cash payments could convince even the most reluctant shareholder to approve the deal. However, the cash was generally obtained by borrowing, leaving the consolidated company with a heavy debt burden, which often led to difficulties. Through the mid-2000s, stock has replaced borrowed cash as the merger currency for two reasons: (1) Many of the 1980s mergers were financed with junk bonds that later went into default. These defaults, along with the demise of Drexel Burnham, the leading junk bond dealer, have made it difficult to arrange debt-financed mergers. (2) Most recent mergers have been strategic—as between the TSX Group and the Montreal Exchange, and between Royal Bank and money manager Phillips Hager and North—where the companies' managers realized they needed each other. Most of these mergers have been friendly, and stock swaps are easier to arrange in friendly mergers than in hostile ones. Also, both sets of managers have been concerned about the post-merger financial strength of the consolidated company, and the surviving company will obviously be stronger if the deal is financed with stock rather than debt.

There has also been an increase in cross-border mergers. For example, in the recent past, with the Canadian dollar rising relative to the U.S. dollar, so has the value of Canadian acquisitions abroad relative to foreign acquisitions of Canadian companies.

ⓒNCEPT REVIEW

1. What are some reasons for current mergers?

23.4 Hostile versus Friendly Takeovers

In the vast majority of merger situations, one firm (generally the larger of the two) simply decides to buy another company, negotiates a price with the management of the target firm, and then acquires the target company. Occasionally, the acquired firm will initiate the action, but it is much more common for a firm to seek companies to acquire than to seek to be acquired. Following convention, we call a company that seeks to acquire another firm the **acquiring company** and the one that it seeks to acquire the **target company.**

Once an acquiring company has identified a possible target, it must (1) establish a suitable price, or range of prices, and (2) decide on the terms of payment—will it offer cash, its own common stock, bonds, or some combination? Next, the acquiring firm's managers must decide how to approach the target company's managers. If the acquiring firm has reason to believe that the target's management will approve the merger, then one CEO will contact the other, propose a merger, and then try to work out suitable terms. If an agreement is reached, the two management groups will issue statements to their shareholders indicating that they approve the merger, and the target firm's management will recommend to its shareholders that they agree to the merger. Generally, the shareholders are asked to *tender* (or send in) their shares to a designated financial institution, along with a signed power of attorney that transfers ownership of the shares to the acquiring firm. The target firm's shareholders then receive the specified payment—either common stock of the acquiring company (in which case the target company's shareholders become shareholders of the acquiring company), cash, bonds, or some mix of cash and securities. This is a **friendly merger.** The BCE–Astral merger is an example.

Often, however, the target company's management resists the merger. Perhaps they feel that the price offered is too low, or perhaps they simply want to keep their jobs. In either case, the acquiring firm's offer is said to be **hostile** rather than friendly, and the acquiring firm must make a direct appeal to the target firm's shareholders. In a hostile merger, the acquiring company will again make a **tender offer,** and again it will ask the shareholders of the target firm to tender their shares in exchange for the offered price. This time, though, the target firm's managers will urge shareholders not to tender their shares, generally stating that the price offered (cash, bonds, or stocks in the acquiring firm) is too low.

While most mergers are friendly, recently there have been a number of interesting cases in which high-profile firms have attempted hostile takeovers. For example, in 2008, Yahoo! rejected a $44.6 billion hostile bid by Microsoft. Looking overseas, Olivetti successfully conducted a hostile takeover of Telecom Italia, and in another hostile telecommunications merger Britain's Vodafone AirTouch acquired its German rival, Mannesmann AG.

Perhaps not surprisingly, hostile bids often fail. However, an all-cash offer that is high enough will generally overcome any resistance by the target firm's management. A hostile merger often begins with a "preemptive" or "blowout" bid. The idea is to offer such a high premium over the preannouncement price that no other bidders will be willing to jump into the fray, and the target company's board cannot simply reject the bid. If a hostile bid is eventually accepted by the target's board, the deal ends up as "friendly," regardless of the acrimony during the hostile phase.

⊙NCEPT REVIEW

1. What is the difference between a hostile and a friendly merger?

23.5 Overview of Merger Analysis

An acquiring firm must answer two questions. First, how much would the target be worth after being incorporated into the acquirer? Notice that this may be quite different from the target's current value, which does not reflect any post-merger synergies or tax benefits. Second, how much should the acquirer offer for the target? Obviously, a low price is better for the acquirer, but the target won't take the offer if it is too low. Also, a higher offer price might scare off potential rival bidders. Later sections discuss setting the offer's price and structure (cash versus stock), but for now we focus on estimating the post-merger value of the target.

There are two basic approaches used in merger valuation: discounted cash flow techniques (DCF) and market multiple analysis.[7] Survey evidence shows that 49.3% of firms use only discounted cash flow techniques, 33.3% use DCF and market multiples, and 12.0% use only market multiples. The market multiple approach assumes that a target is directly comparable to the average firm in its industry. Therefore, this procedure provides at best a ballpark estimate. Because it is less accurate and less frequently used than DCF approaches, we will focus on DCF methods.[8]

Two widely used DCF methods are (1) the corporate valuation method and (2) the equity residual method, which is also called the free cash flow to equity method. Chapter 22 explained the corporate valuation model, and Section 23.6 explains the equity residual model.[9] Section 23.7 also provides a numerical illustration for a company with a constant capital structure and shows that the two models, when properly applied, produce identical valuations.

Web Extension 23A at the textbook's website explains a third DCF method, the adjusted present value method.

⊙NCEPT REVIEW

1. What are the two questions an acquirer must answer?
2. What are three methods for estimating a target's value?

23.6 The Free Cash Flow to Equity (FCFE) Approach

Free cash flow is the cash flow available for distribution to *all* investors. In contrast, **free cash flow to equity (FCFE)** is the cash flow available for distribution to *common shareholders*. Because FCFE is available for distribution only to shareholders, it should be discounted at the cost of equity. Therefore, the **free cash flow to equity approach**, also called the **equity residual model**, discounts the projected FCFE at the cost of equity to determine the value of the equity from operations.

---

[7]See Chapter 8 for an explanation of market multiple analysis.
[8]For recent survey evidence on merger valuation methods, see Tarun K. Mukherjee, Halil Kiymaz, and H. Kent Baker, "Merger Motives and Target Valuation: A Survey of Evidence from CFOs," *Journal of Applied Finance*, Fall–Winter 2004, 7–23. For evidence on the effectiveness of market multiples and DCF approaches, see S.N. Kaplan and R. S. Ruback, "The Market Pricing of Cash Flow Forecasts: Discounted Cash Flow vs. the Method of 'Comparables,'" *Journal of Applied Corporate Finance*, Winter 1996, 45–60. Also see Samuel C. Weaver, Robert S. Harris, Daniel W. Bielinski, and Kenneth F. MacKenzie, "Merger and Acquisition Valuation," *Financial Management*, Summer 1991, 85–96; and Nancy Mohan, M. Fall Ainina, Daniel Kaufman, and Bernard J. Winger, "Acquisition/Divestiture Valuation Practices in Major U.S. Firms," *Financial Practice and Education*, Spring 1991, 73–81.
[9]A third DCF method, the adjusted present value method, is described in *Web Extension 23A*.

Because FCFE is the cash flow available for distribution to shareholders, it may be used to pay common dividends, repurchase stock, purchase financial assets, or some combination of these methods. In other words, the uses of FCFE include all those of FCF except for distributions to debtholders. Therefore, one way to calculate FCFE is to start with FCF and reduce it by the net after-tax distributions to debtholders:

$$
\begin{aligned}
\text{FCFE} &= \frac{\text{Free}}{\text{cash flow}} - \frac{\text{After-tax}}{\text{interest expense}} - \frac{\text{Principal}}{\text{payments}} + \frac{\text{Newly issued}}{\text{debt}} \\
&= \frac{\text{Free}}{\text{cash flow}} - \frac{\text{Interest}}{\text{expense}} + \frac{\text{Interest}}{\text{tax savings}} + \frac{\text{Net change}}{\text{in debt}}
\end{aligned}
$$

(23-1)

Alternatively, the FCFE can be calculated as

$$
\text{FCFE} = \text{Net income} - \frac{\text{Net investment in}}{\text{operating capital}} + \frac{\text{Net change}}{\text{in debt}}
$$

(23-1a)

Both calculations provide the same value for FCFE, but Equation 23-1 is used more often because analysts don't always estimate the net income for a target after it has been acquired.

Given projections of FCFE, the value of a firm's equity due to operations, V_{FCFE}, is

$$
V_{\text{FCFE}} = \sum_{t=1}^{\infty} \frac{\text{FCFE}_t}{(1 + r_{sL})^t}
$$

(23-2)

Assuming constant growth beyond the horizon, the horizon value of the value of equity due to operations ($HV_{\text{FCFE,N}}$) is

$$
\frac{\text{Horizon value of equity}}{\text{due to operations } (HV_{\text{FCFE,N}})} = \frac{\text{FCFE}_{N+1}}{r_{sL} - g} = \frac{\text{FCFE}_N (1 + g)}{r_{sL} - g}
$$

(23-3)

The value of equity due to operations is the present value of the horizon value and the FCFE during the forecast period:

$$
V_{\text{FCFE}} = \sum_{t=1}^{N} \frac{\text{FCFE}_t}{(1 + r_{sL})^t} + \frac{HV_{\text{FCFE,N}}}{(1 + r_{sL})^N}
$$

(23-4)

The total value of a company's equity, S, is the value of the equity from operations plus the value of any nonoperating assets:

$$
S = V_{\text{FCFE}} + \text{Nonoperating assets}
$$

(23-5)

To get a per share price, simply divide the total value of equity by the shares outstanding.[10] Like the corporate valuation model, the FCFE model can be applied only when the capital structure is constant.

Table 23-2 summarizes the two cash flow valuation methods and their assumptions.

---

[10]The FCFE model is similar to the dividend growth model in that cash flows are discounted at the cost of equity. The cash flows in the FCFE model are those that are generated from operations, while the cash flows in the dividend growth model (i.e., the dividends) also contain cash flows due to interest earned on nonoperating assets.

TABLE
23-2   Summary of Cash Flow Approaches

	Approach	
	Corporate Valuation Model	**Free Cash Flow to Equity Model**
Cash flow definition:	FCF = NOPAT − Net investment in operating capital	FCFE = FCF − Interest expense + Interest tax shield + Net change in debt
Discount rate:	WACC	r_{sL} = Cost of equity
Result of present value calculation:	Value of operations	Value of equity due to operations
How to get equity value:	Value of operations + Value of nonoperating assets − Value of debt	Value of equity due to operations + Value of nonoperating assets
Assumption about capital structure during forecast period:	Capital structure is constant	Capital structure is constant
Requirement for analyst to project interest expense:	No interest expense projections needed	Projected interest expense must be based on the assumed capital structure
Assumption at horizon:	FCF grows at constant rate g	FCFE grows at constant rate g

CONCEPT REVIEW

1. What cash flows are discounted in the FCFE model and what is the discount rate?
2. How do the FCFE and corporate valuation models differ? How are they similar?

23.7 Illustration of the Two Valuation Approaches for a Constant Capital Structure

To illustrate the two valuation approaches, consider the analysis performed by Caldwell Inc., a large technology company, as it evaluates the potential acquisition of Tutwiler Controls. Tutwiler currently has a $62.5 million market value of equity and $27 million in debt, for a total market value of $89.5 million. Thus, Tutwiler's capital structure is composed of $27/($62.5 + $27) = 30.17% debt. Caldwell intends to finance the acquisition with this same proportion of debt and plans to maintain this constant capital structure throughout the projection period and thereafter. Tutwiler is a publicly traded company, and its market-determined pre-merger beta was 1.20. Given a risk-free rate of 7% and a 5% market risk premium, the Capital Asset Pricing Model produces a pre-merger required rate of return on equity, r_{sL}, of

$$r_{sL} = 7\% + 1.2(5\%) = 13\%$$

Tutwiler's cost of debt is 9% and has a tax rate of 40%. Its WACC is

$$\begin{aligned} WACC &= w_d(1 - T)r_d + w_s r_{sL} \\ &= 0.3017(0.60)(9\%) + 0.6983(13\%) \\ &= 10.707\% \end{aligned}$$

How much would Tutwiler be worth to Caldwell after the merger? The following sections illustrate the application of the corporate valuation model and the FCFE model. Both models produce an identical value of equity.

Projecting Post-Merger Cash Flows

The first order of business is to estimate the post-merger cash flows that Tutwiler will produce. This is by far the most important task in any merger analysis. In a **pure financial merger**, defined as one where no operating synergies are expected, the incremental post-merger cash flows are simply the target firm's expected cash flows. In an **operating merger,** where the two firms' operations are to be integrated, forecasting future cash flows is obviously more difficult, because potential synergies must be estimated. People from marketing, production, human resources, and accounting play leading roles here, with finance people focusing on financing the acquisition and doing an analysis designed to determine whether the projected cash flows are worth the cost. In this chapter, we take the projections as given and concentrate on how they are analyzed. See *Web Extension 23A,* available at the textbook's website, for a discussion focusing on projecting financial statements in a merger analysis.

See *Web Extension 23A* on the textbook's website for a discussion on projecting financial statements in a merger analysis.

Table 23-3 shows the post-merger projections for Tutwiler, taking into account all expected synergies and maintaining a constant capital structure. Both Caldwell and Tutwiler are in the 40% marginal tax bracket. The cost of debt after the acquisition will remain at 9%. The projections assume that growth in the post-horizon period will be 6%.

Panel A of Table 23-3 shows selected items from the projected financial statements. Panel B shows the calculations for free cash flow, which is used in the corporate valuation model. Row 9 shows net operating profit after taxes (NOPAT), which is equal to EBIT$(1 - T)$. Row 10 shows the net investment in operating capital, which is the annual change in the total net operating capital in Row 8. Free cash flow, shown in Row 11, is equal to NOPAT less the net investment in operating capital. Panel C provides the calculations for FCFE, based upon Equation 23-1.

Of course, the post-merger cash flows are extremely difficult to estimate, and in merger valuations, just as in capital budgeting analysis, sensitivity, scenario, and simulation analyses should be conducted.[11] Indeed, in a friendly merger the acquiring firm would send a team consisting of literally dozens of financial analysts, accountants, engineers, and so forth, to the target firm's headquarters. They would go over its books, estimate required maintenance expenditures, set values on assets such as real estate and petroleum reserves, and the like. Such an investigation, which is called *due diligence*, is an essential part of any merger analysis.

Following are valuations of Tutwiler using both methods, beginning with the corporate valuation model.

See *Ch 23 Tool Kit.xlsx* at the textbook's website for all calculations. Note that rounded intermediate values are shown in the text, but all calculations are performed in *Excel* using nonrounded values.

Valuation Using the Corporate Valuation Model

Because Caldwell does not plan on changing Tutwiler's capital structure, the post-merger WACC will be equal to the premerger WACC of 10.707% that we previously calculated. Tutwiler's free cash flows are shown in Row 11 of Table 23-3. The horizon value (HV) of Tutwiler's operations as of 2019 can be calculated with the constant growth formula that we used in Chapter 22:

$$HV_{\text{Operations,2019}} = \frac{FCF_{2020}}{(\text{WACC} - g)} = \frac{FCF_{2019}(1 + g)}{(\text{WACC} - g)}$$

$$= \frac{\$6.800(1.06)}{0.10707 - 0.06} = \$153.1 \text{ million}$$

---

[11]We purposely kept the cash flows simple in order to focus on key analytical issues. In actual merger valuations, the cash flows would be much more complex, normally including items such as tax loss carryforwards, tax effects of plant and equipment valuation adjustments, and cash flows from the sale of some of the subsidiary's assets.

TABLE

23-3 Post-Merger Projections for the Tutwiler Subsidiary (Millions of Dollars)

	Jan. 1, 2015	Dec. 31, 2015	Dec. 31, 2016	Dec. 31, 2017	Dec. 31, 2018	Dec. 31, 2019
Panel A: Selected Items from Projected Financial Statements[a]						
1. Net sales		$105.0	$126.0	$151.0	$174.0	$191.0
2. Cost of goods sold		80.0	94.0	113.0	129.3	142.0
3. Selling and administrative expenses		10.0	12.0	13.0	15.0	16.0
4. Depreciation		8.0	8.0	9.0	9.0	10.0
5. EBIT		$ 7.0	$ 12.0	$ 16.0	$ 20.7	$ 23.0
6. Interest expense[b]		3.0	3.2	3.5	3.7	3.9
7. Debt[c]	$ 33.2	35.8	38.7	41.1	43.6	46.2
8. Total net operating capital	116.0	117.0	121.0	125.0	131.0	138.0
Panel B: Corporate Valuation Model Cash Flows						
9. NOPAT = EBIT(1 − T)		$ 4.2	$ 7.2	$ 9.6	$ 12.4	$ 13.8
10. Less net investment in operating capital		1.0	4.0	4.0	6.0	7.0
11. Free cash flow		$ 3.2	$ 3.2	$ 5.6	$ 6.4	$ 6.8
Panel C: FCFE Model Cash Flows						
12. Free cash flow		$ 3.2	$ 3.2	$ 5.6	$ 6.4	$ 6.8
13. Less A-T interest = Interest(1 − T)		1.8	1.9	2.1	2.2	2.4
14. Plus change in debt[d]	6.2	2.6	2.9	2.5	2.5	2.6
15. FCFE	$ 6.2	$ 4.0	$ 4.1	$ 6.0	$ 6.7	$ 7.1

Notes:

[a]Rounded figures are presented here, but the full nonrounded values are used in all calculations. The tax rate is 40%.
[b]Interest payments are based on Tutwiler's existing debt, new debt to be issued to finance the acquisition, and additional debt required to finance annual growth.
[c]Debt is existing debt plus additional debt required to maintain a constant capital structure. Caldwell will increase Tutwiler's debt by $6.2 million from $27 million to $33.2 million at the time of the acquisition in order to keep the capital structure constant. This increase occurs because the post-merger synergies make Tutwiler more valuable to Caldwell than it was on a stand-alone basis. Therefore, it can support more dollars of debt and still maintain the constant debt ratio.
[d]The increase in debt at the time of acquisition is a source of free cash flow to equity.

The value of operations as of January 1, 2015, is the present value of the cash flows in the forecast period and the horizon value:

$$V_{\text{Operations}} = \frac{\$3.2}{(1 + 0.10707)} + \frac{\$3.2}{(1 + 0.10707)^2} + \frac{\$5.6}{(1 + 0.10707)^3}$$

$$+ \frac{\$6.4}{(1 + 0.10707)^4} + \frac{\$6.8 + \$153.1}{(1 + 0.10707)^5}$$

$$= \$110.1 \text{ million}$$

There are no nonoperating assets, so the value of equity to Caldwell if Tutwiler is acquired is equal to the value of operations less the value of Tutwiler's debt:

$$S = \$110.1 - \$27 = \$83.1 \text{ million}$$

Valuation Using the FCFE Model

The horizon value of Tutwiler's free cash flows to equity can be calculated using the constant growth formula of Equation 23-3:[12]

$$HV_{FCFE, 2019} = \frac{FCFE_{2019}(1 + g)}{(r_{sL} - g)} = \frac{\$7.06(1.06)}{0.13 - 0.06} = \$106.9 \text{ million}$$

Notice that this horizon value is different from the corporate valuation horizon value. That is because the FCFE horizon value is only for equity while the other horizon value is for the total value of operations. If the 2019 debt of $46.2 million shown in Row 7 of Table 23-3 is added to the $HV_{FCFE, 2019}$, the result is the same $153.1 million horizon value of operations obtained with the corporate valuation model.

Row 15 in Table 23-3 shows the yearly projections of FCFE. When discounted at the 13% cost of equity, the present value of these yearly FCFEs and the horizon value is the value of equity due to operations:[13]

$$V_{FCFE} = \$6.2 + \frac{\$4.0}{(1 + 0.13)} + \frac{\$4.1}{(1 + 0.13)^2} + \frac{\$6.0}{(1 + 0.13)^3}$$
$$+ \frac{\$6.7}{(1 + 0.13)^4} + \frac{\$7.1 + \$106.9}{(1 + 0.13)^5}$$
$$= \$83.1 \text{ million}$$

If Tutwiler had any nonoperating assets, we would add them to V_{FCFE} to determine the total value of equity. Since Tutwiler has no nonoperating assets, its total equity value is equal to the V_{FCFE} of $83.1 million. Notice that this is the same value given by the corporate valuation model.

Both models agree that estimated equity value is $83.1 million, which is more than the $62.5 million current market value of Tutwiler's equity, so Tutwiler is more valuable as a part of Caldwell than as a stand-alone corporation being run by its current managers.

See **Web Extension 23A**, available at the textbook's website, for a more detailed discussion. Also see **Ch 23 Tool Kit.xlsx** for all calculations. Note that rounded intermediate values are shown in the text, but all calculations are performed in Excel using nonrounded values.

CONCEPT REVIEW

1. What are the differences between the FCFE and corporate valuation approaches?

23.8 Setting the Bid Price

Under the acquisition plan, Caldwell would assume Tutwiler's debt, and it would take on additional short-term debt as necessary to complete the purchase. The valuation models show that $83.1 million is the most it should pay for Tutwiler's stock. If it paid more, then Caldwell's own value would be diluted. On the other hand, if it could get Tutwiler for less than $83.1 million, Caldwell's shareholders would gain value. Therefore, Caldwell should bid something less than $83.1 million when it makes an offer for Tutwiler.

Now consider the target company. As stated earlier, Tutwiler's value of equity as an independent operating company is $62.5 million. If Tutwiler were acquired at a price greater than $62.5 million, its shareholders would gain value, whereas they would lose value at any lower price.

The difference between $62.5 million and $83.1 million, or $20.6 million, represents *synergistic benefits* expected from the merger. If there were no synergistic benefits, the maximum

---

[12]Note that we report two decimal places for the 2019 FCFE even though Table 23-3 reports only one decimal place. All calculations are performed in *Excel*, which uses the full nonrounded valued.
[13]Row 14 in Table 23-3 shows that debt is forecast to increase from its pre-merger $27 million to $33.2 million at the acquisition date. This is because Tutwiler is more valuable after the merger, so it can support more dollars of debt while still maintaining 30% debt in its capital structure. The increase in debt of 33.2 − 27 = $6.2 million is a FCFE that is immediately available to Caldwell, and so is not discounted. See **Ch 23 Tool Kit.xlsx** for complete calculations and **Web Extension 23A** for a more detailed explanation.

FINANCE: IN FOCUS

Canadian Tech Companies in the Crosshairs

Foreign corporations are finding Canadian technology companies attractive investments. While it is normal for an acquiring company to offer a premium over a target company's stock price, the size of the premiums is indeed startling. Take a look at some of the premiums offered:

Target Company	Buyer	Premium over Trading Price	Year Acquired
RuggedCom	Siemens AG	142%	2012
Gennum	Semtech Corp	125%	2012
Mosaid	Sterling Partners	59%	2011
Zarlink	Microsemi Corp	67%	2011
Tundra	Integrated Device	104%	2009
Average of all Canadian deals for 2011		36%	

An obvious question is, why are foreign companies so willing to place so much greater a value on these companies than Canadian investors? One possible reason is the lack of a critical mass in publicly traded high-tech companies. If the sector size is too small in terms of market capitalization and number of companies, large institutional investors—and, as a consequence, analysts—don't pay much attention. That in turn adversely affects valuations, making those companies cheap to acquire. And if companies are bought up at a greater rate than they are replaced with new companies of similar size, the sector becomes even smaller, which perpetuates the downward spiral. Unfortunately, there has been only one Canadian high-tech IPO, Nexj Systems, of any size since 2011 to replace the above companies lost. Certainly, it's not a one-way street into Canada to buy up tech companies. Some Canadian companies are acquisitive—for example, Open Text Corp, SXC Health Solutions, and Constellation Software. However, if valuations remain low, relative to those of their peers in foreign markets, they will remain attractive takeover targets.

Source: Adapted from Boyd Erman, "We Undervalue Our Tech Stocks—and Pay the Price," *Globe and Mail*, January 30, 2012.

bid would be the current value of the target company. The greater the synergistic gains, the greater the gap between the target's current price and the maximum the acquiring company could pay.

The issue of how to divide the synergistic benefits is critically important. Obviously, both parties want to get the best deal possible. In our example, if Tutwiler's management knew the maximum price that Caldwell could pay, it would argue for a price close to $83.1 million. Caldwell, on the other hand, would try to get Tutwiler at a price as close to $62.5 million as possible.

Where, within the $62.5 to $83.1 million range, will the actual price be set? The answer depends on a number of factors, including whether Caldwell offers to pay with cash or securities, the negotiating skills of the two management teams, and, most important, the bargaining positions of the two parties as determined by fundamental economic conditions. Let's first consider bargaining power and then examine the mechanics of a cash offer versus a stock offer.

Relative Bargaining Power

To illustrate the relative bargaining power of the target and the acquirer, assume there are many companies similar to Tutwiler that Caldwell could acquire, but suppose that no company other than Caldwell could gain synergies by acquiring Tutwiler. In this case, Caldwell would probably make a relatively low, take–it–or–leave–it offer, and Tutwiler would probably take it because some gain is better than none. On the other hand, if Tutwiler has some unique technology or other asset that many companies want, then once Caldwell announces its offer, others would probably make competing bids and the final price would probably be close to (or even above) $83.1 million. A price above $83.1 million presumably would be paid by some other company with a better synergistic fit or with a management that is more optimistic about Tutwiler's cash flow potential.

Caldwell would, of course, want to keep its maximum bid secret, and it would plan its bidding strategy carefully. If Caldwell thought other bidders would emerge or that Tutwiler's management might resist in order to preserve their jobs, Caldwell might make a high preemptive bid in hopes of scaring off competing bids or management resistance. On the other hand, it might make a lowball bid in hopes of "stealing" the company[14]

Cash Offers versus Stock Offers

Most target shareholders prefer to sell their shares for cash rather than exchange them for stock in the post-merger company. Following is a brief description of each payment method.

Cash Offers Tutwiler's pre-merger equity is worth $62.5 million. With 10 million shares outstanding, Tutwiler's stock price is $62.5/10 = $6.25. If the synergies are realized, then Tutwiler's equity will be worth $83.1 million to Caldwell, so $83.1/10 = $8.31 is the maximum price per share that Caldwell should be willing to pay to Tutwiler's shareholders. For example, Caldwell might offer $7.75 cash for each share of Tutwiler stock.

Stock Offers In a stock offer, Tutwiler's shareholders exchange their Tutwiler shares for new shares in the post-merger company, which will be named CaldwellTutwiler. Targets typically prefer cash offers to stock offers, all else equal, but taxation of the offer prevents all else from being equal. We discuss taxation in more detail in Section 23.9, but for now you should know that stock offerings are taxed more favourably than cash offerings. In this case, perhaps Caldwell should offer a package worth $7.50 per share. With 10 million outstanding Tutwiler shares, the Tutwiler shareholders must end up owning $7.50 × 10 million = $75 million worth of stock in the post-merger company.

Suppose Caldwell has 20 million shares of stock outstanding (n_{Old}) prior to the merger and the stock price per share is $15. Then the total pre-merger value of Caldwell's equity is $15 × 20 million = $300 million. As calculated previously, the post-merger value of Tutwiler to Caldwell is $83.1 million. Therefore, the total post-merger value of CaldwellTutwiler will be $300 + $83.1 = $383.1 million.

After the merger, Tutwiler's former shareholders should own $75/$383.1 = 0.196 = 19.58% of the post-merger CaldwellTutwiler. With 20 million Caldwell shares outstanding, Caldwell must issue enough new shares, n_{New}, to the Tutwiler shareholders (in exchange for the Tutwiler shares) so that Tutwiler's former shareholders will own 19.6% of the shares of CaldwellTutwiler:

$$\text{Percent required by} \atop \text{target shareholders} = \frac{n_{New}}{n_{New} + n_{Old}}$$

$$19.58\% = \frac{n_{New}}{n_{New} + 20}$$

$$n_{New} = \frac{20 \times 0.1958}{1 - 0.1958} = 4.87 \text{ million}$$

Tutwiler's former shareholders will exchange 10 million shares of stock in Tutwiler for 4.87 million shares of stock in the combined CaldwellTutwiler. Thus, the exchange ratio is 4.87/10 = 0.487.

After the merger, there will be 4.87 million new shares for a total of 24.87 million shares. With a combined intrinsic equity value of $383.1 million, the resulting price per share will be $383.1/24.87 = $15.40. The total value owned by Tutwiler's shareholders is this price multiplied by their shares: $15.40 × 4.87 million = $75 million. Also notice that the price will increase from $15.00 per share before the merger to $15.40 after the merger, so the merger will benefit Caldwell's shareholders if the synergies are realized.

ⓒONCEPT REVIEW

1. Explain the issues involved in setting the bid price.

---

[14] For an interesting discussion of the aftereffects of losing a bidding contest, see Mark L. Mitchell and Kenneth Lehn, "Do Bad Bidders Become Good Targets?" *Journal of Applied Corporate Finance*, Summer 1990, pp. 60–69.

23.9   Taxes and the Structure of the Takeover Bid

In a merger, the acquiring firm can either buy the target's assets or buy shares of stock directly from the target's shareholders. If the offer is for the target's assets, the target's board of directors will make a recommendation to the shareholders, who will vote to accept or reject the offer. If they accept the offer, the payment goes directly to the target corporation, which pays off any debt not assumed by the acquiring firm, pays any corporate taxes that are due, and then distributes the remainder of the payment to the shareholders, often in the form of a liquidating dividend. In this situation, the target firm is usually dissolved and no longer continues to exist as a separate legal entity, although its assets and workforce may continue to function as a division or a wholly owned subsidiary of the acquiring firm. The acquisition of assets is a very common form of takeover for small and medium-sized firms, especially those that are not publicly traded. A major advantage of this method relative to the acquisition of the target's stock is that the acquiring firm simply acquires assets and is not saddled with any hidden liabilities. In contrast, if the acquiring firm buys the target's stock, then it is responsible for any legal contingencies against the target, even for those that might have occurred prior to the takeover.

An offer for a target's stock rather than its assets can be made either directly to the shareholders, as is typical in a hostile takeover, or indirectly through the board of directors, which, in a friendly deal, makes a recommendation to the shareholders to accept the offer. In a successful offer, the acquiring firm will end up owning a controlling interest, or perhaps even all of the target's stock. Sometimes the target retains its identity as a separate legal entity and is operated as a subsidiary of the acquiring firm, while sometimes its corporate status is dissolved and it is operated as one of the acquiring firm's divisions.

The payment offered by the acquiring firm can be in the form of cash, stock of the acquiring firm, debt of the acquiring firm, or some combination. The tax consequences of the merger depend on whether it is classified as a *taxable offer* or a *nontaxable offer*. In general, a nontaxable offer is one in which the form of payment is predominantly stock, although the application of this simple principle is much more complicated in practice. If the offer includes a significant amount of cash or bonds, then it is a taxable transaction, just like any other sale.

In a nontaxable deal, target shareholders who receive shares of the acquiring company's stock do not have to pay any taxes at the time of the merger. When they eventually sell their stock in the acquiring company, they must pay a tax on the gain. The amount of the gain is the sales price of their stock in the acquiring company minus the price at which they purchased their original stock in the target company. In a taxable offer, the gain between the offer price and the original purchase price of the target stock is taxed in the year of the merger.[15]

All other things equal, shareholders prefer nontaxable offers, since they may then postpone taxes on their gains. Furthermore, if the target firm's shareholders receive stock, they will benefit from any synergistic gains produced by the merger. Most target shareholders are thus willing to give up their stock for a lower price in a nontaxable offer than in a taxable one. As a result, one might expect nontaxable bids to dominate. However, this is not the case—roughly half of all mergers have been taxable. The reason for this is explained below.

Consider the following example. A target firm has assets with a book value of $100 million, but these assets have a fair market value (FMV) of $150 million. The offer by the acquiring firm is worth $225 million. The acquiring firm must choose between two tax treatments. Under the first alternative, it will record the assets at their taxable book value of $100 million (i.e., their undepreciated capital cost) and continue depreciating them according to their previous CCA schedules. When assets are transferred at their book value, no taxable income is created. Under the second alternative, it will record the assets at their FMV of $150 million and create $75 million of goodwill. The acquiring firm now has a larger cost base, from which it can claim higher CCA, thus lowering its future taxes. However, the increase in asset value triggers an immediate capital gain of $225 − $100 = $125 million for the selling company.

If you think this can become complicated, you are right! At this point you should be ready to delve into tax accounting texts, because merger taxation is too complex a subject to be covered thoroughly in a general finance textbook.

Each province manages its own securities legislation, including regulations governing mergers. That said, recent efforts through the Canadian Securities Administrators have made much of this regulation uniform across the country. Regulation is written mainly to

---

[15]Even in nontaxable deals, taxes must be paid in the year of the merger by any shareholders who receive cash.

FINANCE: IN FOCUS

Limits to Foreign Acquisitions

Almost all countries place certain restrictions (some much more than others) on acquisitions of their local companies and assets by foreign corporations. Canada is no exception. The Investment Canada Act requires the federal government to review foreign investments in companies considered culturally sensitive or of importance to national security. Moreover, the federal government reviews all potential foreign acquisitions over $369 million. During such reviews, the foreign investor must demonstrate that the investment is likely to be a "net benefit to Canada." With regard to national security, the federal government can reject any acquisition not seen as in the nation's security.

In 2012, state-owned enterprise (SOE) Petronas from Malaysia offered $6 billion for Progress Energy, while CNOOC from China offered $15.1 billion to purchase Nexen Inc. The prospect of foreign government–controlled companies buying large Canadian energy assets caused much debate in Canada. On the one hand, foreign SOEs control large amounts of capital and they are active in the resource sector. They offer significant capital needed to develop Canada's natural resources. On the other hand, there are concerns of potential foreign government interference in the private sector, especially controlling Canada's vast energy assets. While the federal government ultimately approved the above two acquisitions, going forward it signalled its apprehension for allowing foreign SOEs majority ownership in large Canadian assets. While the vast majority of acquisitions are approved, the government will step in, as shown in the table, and reject acquisitions it sees as not being in Canada's economic or political interests.

Source: Adapted from Michael Herman and David Campbell, "Mergers and Acquisitions," Lexpert, http://www.lexpert.ca, accessed April 24, 2012.

Selected Foreign Acquisitions of Canadian Companies since 2008

Year	Canadian Target	Acquirer	Value ($ billions)	Federal Government Ruling
2013	Manitoba Telecom	Accelero (Egypt)	$ 0.52	Rejected
2012	Viterra	Glencore (Switzerland)	6.1	Accepted
2012	Nexen	CNOOC (China)	15.1	Accepted
2012	Progress Energy	Petronas (Malaysia)	6.0	Accepted
2011	Daylight Energy	Sinopec (China)	2.2	Accepted
2010	Potash Corporation	BHP Billiton (Anglo/Australian)	38.6	Rejected
2008	Macdonald Detwiler & Associates	Alliant Techsystems (U.S.)	1.3	Rejected

ensure that all security holders (of the same security) are treated equally. Thus, whenever a corporation bids for control of another firm through the exchange of equity or debt, the entire process must follow the appropriate regulatory guidelines. The time required for such reviews allows the target company's management to implement defensive tactics, and other firms to make competing offers.

CONCEPT REVIEW

1. What are some alternative ways of structuring takeover bids?
2. How do taxes influence the payment structure?

23.10 Financial Reporting for Mergers

Although a detailed discussion of financial reporting is best left to accounting courses, the accounting implications of mergers cannot be ignored. Currently, mergers are handled using *acquisition accounting*. Keep in mind, however, that all larger companies are required

| TABLE 23-4 | Accounting for Mergers: A Acquires B |

	Firm A	Firm B		Firm A: Post-Merger		
	Book Value (1)	Book Value (2)	Fair Value (3)	$70 Paid (4)	$80 Paid (5)	$90 Paid (6)
Identifiable assets	$ 300	$ 100	$ 120	$ 350	$ 340	$ 330
Goodwill	0	0	0	0	0	10
Total assets	$ 300	$ 100	$ 120	$ 350	$ 340	$ 340
Liabilities	$ 120	$ 40	$ 40	$ 160	$ 160	$ 160
Equity	180	60	80	190	180	180
Total claims	$ 300	$ 100	$ 120	$ 350	$ 340	$ 340

to keep two sets of books. The first is for the Canada Revenue Agency (CRA) and reflects the tax treatment of mergers as described in the previous section. The second is for financial reporting and reflects the treatment described below. As you will see, the rules for financial reporting differ from those for the CRA.

Acquisition Accounting

Under the **acquisition method**, the acquiring company determines and reports the fair value—that is, the market value of the identifiable net assets (assets minus liabilities) of the acquired company, regardless of the amount actually paid for the net assets. Identifiable assets can include both tangible assets such as property, plant, and equipment and intangible assets such as trademarks, patents, and copyrights.[16] If the purchase price is greater than the fair value of the identifiable net assets, the difference is reported as goodwill (which is considered a nonidentifiable asset). If the purchase price is less than the fair value of the identifiable net assets, the deficiency is reported as a gain on purchase.

Table 23-4 illustrates the acquisition method. Here Firm A is assumed to have "bought" Firm B in much the same way as it would invest in any capital asset. In this example we assume that the book value of B's identifiable net assets is $60, while its fair value is $80. This $20 difference is called an "acquisition differential" and is allocated between B's various categories of identifiable assets and liabilities. Three situations are considered in this example. First, in Column 4 we assume that A pays cash of $70 to acquire the net assets (equity) of B. Notice that on A's post-merger balance sheet, the reported value of the identifiable assets is composed of the pre-merger book value of A's assets, plus the fair value of B's assets, minus the cash paid by A ($300 + $120 − $70 = $350). Notice also that no goodwill is reported but that A's equity has increased by $10, which represents the gain on the purchase of B's net assets ($80 of net assets purchased − $70 of cash paid). In this case, the acquisition of B is a "bargain purchase" for A since it is buying the net assets of B for less than their market value.

In Column 5 we assume that A pays $80, which exactly equals the fair value of B's identifiable net assets. Therefore, neither goodwill nor a gain on purchase arises from this transaction. This indicates that A's valuation of B is identical to the market's valuation of the firm. As in Column 4, the post-merger balance of the identifiable assets includes the fair value of B's assets ($300 + $120 − $80 = $340).

Finally, in Column 6 we assume that A pays $90 for B, giving rise to goodwill of $10. This represents the excess of the purchase price over the fair value of B's net assets ($90 − $80 = $10). Goodwill in a transaction such as this reflects a premium paid by the acquirer to achieve control of the target firm. It would include the value of nonidentifiable assets such as an assembled workforce, premium location, or reputation. It may also include the value of "synergistic benefits" that the acquiring firm hopes to realize from the merger.

---

[16]IFRS defines identifiable assets as assets that either are separable (i.e., capable of being separated from the entity and sold or otherwise transferred to another entity) or arise from contractual or other legal rights.

TABLE 23-5   Income Statement Effects

	Pre-Merger		Post-Merger: Firm A
	Firm A (1)	Firm B (2)	Merged (3)
Sales	$ 300.0	$ 100.0	$400.0
Depreciation	20.0	11.0	35.0[a]
Other operating expenses	193.0	60.0	253.0
	213.0	71.0	288.0
Operating income	87.0	29.0	112.0
Interest (10%)	12.0	4.0	16.0
Taxable income	75.0	25.0	96.0
Taxes (40%)	30.0	10.0	38.4
Net income	$ 45.0	$ 15.0	$ 57.6
EPS[b]	$ 1.50	$ 1.50	$ 1.44

Notes:
[a]Depreciation expense is $4 higher than it otherwise would be to reflect the amortization of the $20 "acquisition differential" relating to Firm B's depreciable assets.
[b]Firm A had 30 shares and Firm B had 10 shares before the merger. A gives 1 of its shares for each of B's, so A has 40 shares outstanding after the merger.

Income Statement Effects

A merger can have a significant effect on reported profits. First, the acquiring firm must expense any transaction costs related to the merger such as professional fees and organizational costs incurred to execute the merger. Second, if the fair values of the acquired firm's identifiable assets are greater than their book values, this acquisition differential may lead to higher depreciation charges (and also higher cost of sales if the value of inventories has been written up). Goodwill is not amortized; rather, it is subject to an "annual impairment test." If the fair value of goodwill has declined over the year, then the amount of the decline must be charged to earnings. If not, then there is no charge, but gains in goodwill cannot be added to earnings.

See **Ch 23 Tool Kit.xlsx** at the textbook's website for details.

Table 23-5 illustrates the income statement effect of the write-up of assets resulting from the application of the acquisition method. We assume that A purchased B for $90, creating $10 of goodwill. We also assume that the $20 acquisition differential relating to B's identifiable assets was entirely allocated to depreciable assets with a remaining life of five years. This results in additional annual depreciation charges of $4 ($20/5 = $4). As Column 3 indicates, the additional depreciation causes the reported profit of the consolidated firm to be lower than the sum of the individual companies' reported profits.

The additional depreciation expense is also reflected in earnings per share. In our hypothetical merger, we assume that A acquired B by issuing 10 shares so that 40 shares exist in the consolidated firm (30 owned by the original shareholders of A, and 10 owned by the former shareholders of B). The merged company's EPS is $1.44, while each of the individual companies had a pre-merger EPS of $1.50.

ⓒNCEPT REVIEW

1.   What is acquisition accounting for mergers?

2.   What is goodwill? What impact does goodwill have on the firm's balance sheet? On its income statement?

23.11 Analysis for a "True Consolidation"

Most of our analysis in the preceding sections assumed that one firm plans to acquire another. However, in many situations it is hard to identify an "acquirer" and a "target"—the merger appears to be a true "merger of equals," as was the case with the Molson–Coors merger. In such cases, how is the analysis handled?

The first step is to estimate the value of the combined enterprise, reflecting any synergies, tax effects, or capital structure changes. The second step is to decide how to allocate the new company's stock between the two sets of old shareholders. Normally, one would expect the consolidated value to exceed the sum of the pre-announcement values of the two companies because of synergy. For example, Company A might have had a pre-merger equity value of $10 billion, found as (Number of shares)(Price per share), and Company B might have had a pre-merger value of $15 billion. If the post-merger value of new Company AB is estimated to be $30 billion, then that value must be allocated. Company A's shareholders will have to receive enough shares to cause them to have a projected value of at least $10 billion, and Company B's shareholders will have to receive at least $15 billion. But how will the remaining $5 billion of synergistic-induced value be divided?

This is a key issue, requiring intense negotiation between the two management groups. There is no rule or formula that can be applied, but one basis for the allocation is the relative pre-announcement values of the two companies. For example, in our hypothetical merger of A and B to form AB, the companies might agree to give $10/$25 = 40% of the new stock to A's shareholders and 60% to B's shareholders. Unless a case could be made for giving a higher percentage of the shares to one of the companies because it was responsible for more of the synergistic value, then the pre-merger value proportions would seem to be a "fair" solution. In any event, the pre-merger proportions will probably be given the greatest weight in reaching the final decision.

It should also be noted that control of the consolidated company is always an issue. Generally, the companies hold a press conference and announce that the CEO of one firm will be chair of the new company, that the other CEO will be president, that the new board will consist of directors from both old boards, and that power will be shared. With huge mergers such as those we have been seeing lately, there is plenty of power to be shared.

CONCEPT REVIEW

1. How does merger analysis differ in the case of a large company acquiring a smaller one versus a "true merger of equals"?
2. Do you think the same guidelines for allocating synergistic gains would be used in both types of mergers?

23.12 The Role of Investment Bankers

Investment bankers are involved with mergers in a number of ways: (1) they help arrange mergers, (2) they help target companies develop and implement defensive tactics, (3) they help value target companies, (4) they help finance mergers, and (5) they invest in the stocks of potential merger candidates. These merger-related activities have been quite profitable.

Arranging Mergers

The major investment banking firms have merger and acquisition groups that operate within their corporate finance departments. (Corporate finance departments offer advice, as opposed to underwriting or brokerage services, to business firms.) Members of these groups identify firms with excess cash that might want to buy other firms, companies that might be willing to be bought, and firms that might, for a number of reasons, be attractive to others. Sometimes dissident shareholders of firms with poor track records work with investment bankers to oust management by helping to arrange a merger.

Developing Defensive Tactics

Target firms that do not want to be acquired generally enlist the help of an investment banking firm, along with a law firm that specializes in mergers. Defences include tactics such as (1) changing the bylaws so that only one-third of the directors are elected each year and/or so that a 75% approval (a *super majority*) versus a simple majority is required to approve a merger; (2) trying to convince the target firm's shareholders that the price being offered is too low; (3) raising antitrust issues in the hope that the Competition Bureau will intervene; (4) repurchasing stock in the open market in an effort to push the price above that being offered by the potential acquirer; (5) getting a **white knight** who is acceptable to the target firm's management to compete with the potential acquirer; (6) getting a **white squire** who is friendly to current management to buy enough of the target firm's shares to block the merger; and (7) taking a poison pill, as described next.

Poison pills—which occasionally really do amount to committing economic suicide to avoid a takeover—are tactics such as borrowing on terms that require immediate repayment of all loans if the firm is acquired, selling off at bargain prices the assets that originally made the firm a desirable target, granting such lucrative **golden parachutes** to their executives that the cash drain from these payments would render the merger infeasible, and planning defensive mergers that would leave the firm with new assets of questionable value and a huge debt load. Currently, the most popular poison pill is for a company to give its shareholders a *shareholder rights plan* allowing them to buy at half price the stock of an acquiring firm, should the firm itself be acquired. The blatant use of poison pills is constrained by directors' awareness that excessive use could trigger personal suits by shareholders against directors who voted for them, and, perhaps in the near future, bylaws that would further limit management's use of pills. Still, investment bankers and anti-takeover lawyers are busy thinking up new poison pill formulas, and others are just as busy trying to come up with antidotes.

Establishing a Fair Value

If a friendly merger is being worked out between two firms' managements, it is important to document that the agreed-upon price is a fair one; otherwise, the shareholders of either company may sue to block the merger. Therefore, in most large mergers each side will hire an investment banking firm to evaluate the target company and to help establish the fair price. Even if the merger is not friendly, investment bankers may still be asked to help establish a price. If a surprise tender offer is to be made, the acquiring firm will want to know the lowest price at which it might be able to acquire the stock, while the target firm may seek help in "proving" that the price being offered is too low.

Financing Mergers

To succeed in the mergers and acquisitions (M&A) business, an investment banker must be able to offer a financing package to clients, whether they are acquirers who need capital to take over companies or target companies trying to finance stock repurchase plans or other defences against takeovers. The fees that investment banks generate through issuing merger-related debt often dwarf their other merger-related fees.

Arbitrage Operations

Arbitrage generally means simultaneously buying and selling the same commodity or security in two different markets at different prices and pocketing a risk-free return. However, the major brokerage houses, as well as some wealthy private investors, are engaged in a different type of arbitrage called *risk arbitrage*. The *arbitrageurs*, or "arbs," speculate in the stocks of companies that are likely takeover targets. Vast amounts of capital are required to speculate in a large number of securities and thus reduce risk, and also to make money on narrow spreads. However, the large investment bankers have the wherewithal to play the game. To be successful, arbs need to be able to identify likely targets, assess the probability of offers reaching fruition, and move in and out of the market quickly and with low transactions costs.

CONCEPT REVIEW

1. What are some defensive tactics that firms can use to resist hostile takeovers?
2. What is the difference between pure arbitrage and risk arbitrage?

23.13 Who Wins: The Empirical Evidence

All the recent merger activity has raised two questions: (1) Do corporate acquisitions create value, and, (2) if so, how is the value shared between the parties?

Most researchers agree that takeovers increase the wealth of the shareholders of target firms, for otherwise they would not agree to the offer. However, there is a debate as to whether mergers benefit the acquiring firm's shareholders. In particular, managements of acquiring firms may be motivated by factors other than maximizing shareholder wealth. For example, they may want to merge merely to increase the size of the corporations they manage, because increased size usually brings larger salaries plus job security, perquisites, power, and prestige.

The question of who gains from corporate acquisitions can be tested by examining the stock price changes that occur around the time of a merger or takeover announcement.

FINANCE: IN FOCUS

KKR: The Leveraged Buyout Kings Look to Canada

KKR—the initials stand for Kohlberg Kravis Roberts & Co.—is the best-known private equity buyout firm in the world. If you've heard of leveraged buyouts—which involve the heavy use of borrowed money to engineer a takeover—it's probably because of KKR. It's been at the centre of some of the biggest buyouts in history, including several multibillion-dollar deals in Canada.

KKR's business template involves the search for undervalued firms with some combination of the following: little debt, steady cash flow, an industry-leading position, the potential to grow value, a languishing stock price, and/or unhappy institutional investors. When it finds such a firm, it often approaches management with a proposal to take the company private. KKR will then put together a deal with a consortium of other investors, which might include investment banks, private or corporate pension funds, university endowments, and even other private equity firms.

Sometimes KKR makes its money by buying conglomerates and then selling off the parts for a tidy profit. That's what happened in its takeover of Beatrice Cos. in 1986. Beatrice owned the Avis car rental firm, Tropicana juice, and Playtex, among others. KKR's analysts said that the market wasn't recognizing the true worth of Beatrice. They were right. In the following years, KKR sold off most of the big names in the Beatrice empire, making billions in profit by some estimates.

KKR's acquisition of the U.S. Safeway chain in 1986 was one of its most lucrative ever—and one of its most controversial. It saddled the company with billions of dollars in debt and slashed tens of thousands of jobs. It also made a fortune. KKR paid US$4.3 billion for Safeway, using only $130 million of its own money, *Fortune* later reported. KKR's total profit on the deal apparently came to more than $5 billion.

KKR has put together buyout deals all over the world. But its first international foray took place in Canada, when it bought Canadian General Insurance Group in 1995. Since then, it has made three other big investments in Canada.

Shoppers Drug Mart. In 2000, conglomerate Imasco said that KKR had won a seven-way bidding war for its Shoppers Drug Mart division, paying $2.55 billion for Canada's biggest drugstore chain. Shoppers went public in 2001, and KKR subsequently sold most of its shares, reaping a handsome profit.

BCE's directories business. In 2002, BCE sold its Bell Canada directories business for $3 billion to KKR, in partnership with the Ontario Teachers' Pension Plan. KKR and Teachers' later spun off the Yellow Pages directories into the Yellow Pages Income Fund and sold their investment, again for a profit.

Masonite International. In 2005, KKR paid $3.1 billion for all the stock of Masonite International, a building products company formed after Mississauga-based Premdor acquired Masonite. KKR still owns Masonite International.

In April 2007, BCE announced that it was talking to KKR and several Canadian pension plans about the possibility of taking the telecom giant private. A takeover of BCE would cost more than $32 billion, making it the biggest corporate takeover in Canadian history and one of the biggest buyouts ever. The takeover ultimately failed when accountants reported that BCE would fail certain solvency hurdles required for the purchase.

Source: Adapted from CBC, "KKR: The Leveraged Buyout Kings Look to Canada," CBC News, May 23, 2007, http://www.cbc.ca, accessed September 10, 2008. © CBC Licensing.

Changes in the stock prices of the acquiring and target firms represent market participants' beliefs about the value created by the merger and about how that value will be divided between the target and acquiring firms' shareholders. So, examining a large sample of stock price movements can shed light on the issue of who gains from mergers.

One cannot simply examine stock prices around merger announcement dates, because other factors influence stock prices. For example, if a merger was announced on a day when the entire market advanced, the fact that the target firm's price rose would not necessarily signify that the merger was expected to create value. Hence, studies examine *abnormal returns* associated with merger announcements, where abnormal returns are defined as that part of a stock price change caused by factors other than changes in the general stock market.

These "event studies" have examined both acquiring and target firms' stock price responses to mergers and tender offers. Jointly, they have covered nearly every acquisition involving publicly traded firms from the early 1960s to the present, and they are remarkably consistent in their results: On average, the stock prices of target firms increase by about 30% in hostile tender offers, while in friendly mergers the average increase is about 20%. However, for both hostile and friendly deals, the stock prices of acquiring firms, on average, remain constant. Thus, the event study evidence strongly indicates (1) that acquisitions do create value, but (2) that shareholders of target firms reap virtually all the benefits.

The event study evidence suggests that mergers benefit targets but not acquirers, hence that acquiring firms' shareholders should be skeptical of their managers' plans for acquisitions. This evidence cannot be dismissed out of hand, but neither is it entirely convincing. There are undoubtedly many good mergers, just as there are many poorly conceived ones. Like most of finance, merger decisions should be studied carefully, and it is best not to judge the outcome of a specific merger until the actual results start to come in.

CONCEPT REVIEW

1. Explain how researchers can study the effects of mergers on shareholder wealth.
2. Do mergers create value? If so, who profits from this value?
3. Do the research results discussed in this section seem logical? Explain.

23.14 Corporate Alliances

Mergers are one way for two companies to join forces, but many companies are striking cooperative deals, called **corporate,** or **strategic, alliances,** that stop far short of merging. Whereas mergers combine all of the assets of the firms involved, as well as their ownership and managerial expertise, alliances allow firms to create combinations that focus on specific business lines that offer the most potential synergies. These alliances take many forms, from simple marketing agreements to joint ownership of worldwide operations.

One form of corporate alliance is the **joint venture,** in which parts of companies are joined to achieve specific, limited objectives. A joint venture is controlled by a management team consisting of representatives of the two (or more) parent companies. Joint ventures have been used often by U.S., Japanese, European, and Canadian firms to share technology and/or marketing expertise. For example, Royal Bank of Canada announced a joint venture with China Minsheng Bank to manage and sell mutual funds to retail and institutional investors in China. By joining with their foreign counterparts, Canadian firms are gaining a stronger foothold in China. Although alliances are new to some firms, they are established practice to others. For example, CAE has undertaken numerous joint ventures with companies based in China, India, Dubai, the United Kingdom, and Brazil. The joint ventures CAE undertook were in addition to its teaming arrangements, alliances, and corporate acquisitions.

A recent study of 345 corporate alliances found that the stock prices of both partners in an alliance tended to increase when the alliance was announced, with an average abnormal return of about 0.64% on the day of the announcement.[17] About 43% of the alliances were marketing agreements, 14% were R&D agreements, 11% were for licensing technology, 7% for technology transfers, and 25% were for some combination of the four basic reasons. Although most alliances were for marketing agreements, the market reacted

---

[17]See Su Han Chan, John W. Kensinger, Arthur J. Keown, and John D. Martin, "When Do Strategic Alliances Create Shareholder Value?" *Journal of Applied Corporate Finance,* Winter 1999, 82–87.

most favourably when the alliance was for technology sharing between two firms in the same industry. The study also found that the typical alliance lasted at least 5 years and that the allied firms had better operating performance than their industry peers during this period.

CONCEPT REVIEW

1. What is the difference between a merger and a corporate alliance?
2. What is a joint venture? Give some reasons why joint ventures may be advantageous to the parties involved.

23.15 Leveraged Buyouts

In a leveraged buyout (LBO) a small group of investors, often led by a private equity fund, acquires a firm in a transaction financed largely by debt. The debt is serviced with funds generated by the acquired company's operations and often by the sale of some of its assets. Generally, the acquiring group keeps the current management team and provides them with incentive compensation plans. The objective is to run the acquired company for a number of years, boost its value, and then take it public again as a stronger company. In other instances, the acquiring firm plans to sell off divisions to other firms that can gain synergies. In either case, the acquiring group expects to make a substantial profit from the LBO, but the inherent risks are great due to the heavy use of financial leverage.[18]

CONCEPT REVIEW

1. What is an LBO?

23.16 Divestitures

There are four types of **divestitures.** *Sale to another firm* generally involves the sale of an entire division or unit, usually for cash but sometimes for stock in the acquiring firm. In a *spinoff*, the firm's existing shareholders are given new stock representing separate ownership rights in the division that was divested. The division establishes its own board of directors and officers and becomes a separate company. The shareholders end up owning shares of two firms instead of one, but no cash has been transferred. In a *carve-out*, a minority interest in a corporate subsidiary is sold to new shareholders, so the parent gains new equity financing yet retains control. Finally, in a *liquidation* the assets of a division are sold off piecemeal, rather than as an operating entity. To illustrate the different types of divestitures, we now present some examples.

Canadian Pacific Limited was a conglomerate holding a number of different businesses, ranging from hotels, railways, and mines to shipping and oil and gas production. In 2001 the company spun off its major businesses, arguing that a holding company strategy discounted the true worth of all its assets. Existing CP Limited shareholders received shares based in the spinoff companies, namely CP Ships, Canadian Pacific Railways, Fording Inc., and Pan Canadian Petroleum. The parent company kept its hotel operations under a new name: Fairmont Hotels and Resorts.

In 2007, Canadian-based Thomson Corporation sold Thomson Learning's Higher Education Division and Nelson Canada (the publisher of this textbook) to Apax Partners and the private equity arm of the Ontario Municipal Employees Retirement System (OMERS) for $7.6 billion. The sale was based on Thomson's restructuring to focus on electronic information solutions and its purchase of Reuters Group for US$18 billion in the same year. The company is now known as Thomson Reuters.

[18]For interesting discussions of highly leveraged takeovers, see Martin S. Fridson, "What Went Wrong with the Highly Leveraged Deals? (Or, All Variety of Agency Costs)," *Journal of Applied Corporate Finance*, Fall 1991, 47–57; Also see Jay R. Allen, "LBOs—The Evolution of Financial Strategies and Structures," *Journal of Applied Corporate Finance*, Winter 1996, 18–29; George P. Baker, "Beatrice: A Study in the Creation and Destruction of Value," *Journal of Finance*, July 1992, 1081–1119; George P. Baker and Karen H. Wruck, "Lessons from a Middle Market LBO: The Case of O. M. Scott," *Journal of Applied Corporate Finance*, Spring 1991, 46–58.

As these examples illustrate, the reasons for divestitures vary widely. Sometimes the market feels more comfortable when multiple businesses are not held under a single corporate entity; the CP Limited divestiture is an example. Sometimes companies need cash either to finance expansion in their primary business line as we saw with Thomson Corporation. The divestitures also show that running a business is a dynamic process—conditions change, corporate strategies change in response, and firms respond by altering their asset portfolios through acquisitions and/or divestitures. Some divestitures are to unload losing assets that would otherwise drag the company down.

In general, the empirical evidence shows that the market reacts favourably to divestitures, with the divesting company typically having a small increase in stock price on the day of the announcement. The announcement-day returns are largest for companies that "undo" previous conglomerate mergers by divesting businesses in unrelated areas.[19] Studies also show that divestitures generally lead to superior operating performance for both the parent and the divested company.[20]

CONCEPT REVIEW

1. What are some types of divestitures?
2. What are some motives for divestitures?

Summary

This chapter included discussions of mergers, divestitures, and LBOs. The majority of the discussion in this chapter focused on mergers. We discussed the rationale for mergers, different types of mergers, the level of merger activity, merger regulation, and merger analysis. We also showed how to use the free cash flow to equity method to value target firms. In addition, we explained how the acquiring firm can structure its takeover bid, the different ways accountants treat mergers, and investment bankers' roles in arranging and financing mergers. Furthermore, we discussed two cooperative arrangements that fall short of mergers: corporate (or strategic) alliances and joint ventures. The key concepts covered are listed below:

- A **merger** occurs when two firms combine to form a single company. The primary motives for mergers are (1) synergy, (2) tax considerations, (3) purchase of assets below their replacement costs, (4) diversification, (5) gaining control over a larger enterprise, and (6) breakup value.
- Mergers can provide economic benefits through **economies of scale** and through putting assets in the hands of **more efficient managers.** However, mergers also have the potential for reducing competition, and for this reason they are carefully regulated by government agencies.
- In most mergers, one company (the **acquiring company**) initiates action to take over another (the **target company**).
- A **horizontal merger** occurs when two firms in the same line of business combine.
- A **vertical merger** combines a firm with one of its customers or suppliers.
- A **congeneric merger** involves firms in related industries, but where no customer–supplier relationship exists.
- A **conglomerate merger** occurs when firms in totally different industries combine.
- In a **friendly merger,** the managements of both firms approve the merger, whereas in a **hostile merger,** the target firm's management opposes it.
- An **operating merger** is one in which the operations of the two firms are combined. A **financial merger** is one in which the firms continue to operate separately; hence, no operating economies are expected.

---

[19]For details, see Jeffrey W. Allen, Scott L. Lummer, John J. McConnell, and Debra K. Reed, "Can Takeover Losses Explain Spin-Off Gains?" *Journal of Financial and Quantitative Analysis*, December 1995, pp. 465–485.
[20]See Shane A. Johnson, Daniel P. Klein, and Verne L. Thibodeaux, "The Effects of Spin-Offs on Corporate Investment and Performance," *Journal of Financial Research*, Summer 1996, pp. 293–307. Also see Steven Kaplan and Michael S. Weisbach, "The Success of Acquisitions: Evidence from Divestitures," *Journal of Finance*, March 1992, pp. 107–138.

- In a typical **merger analysis,** the key issues to be resolved are (1) the price to be paid for the target firm and (2) the employment/control situation. If the merger is a consolidation of two relatively equal firms, at issue is the percentage of ownership each merger partner's shareholders will receive.
- Three methods commonly used to determine the **value of the target firm:** (1) **market multiple analysis,** (2) the **corporate valuation model,** and (3) the **free cash flow to equity (FCFE) model.** The cash flow models give the same value if implemented correctly.
- For accounting purposes, mergers are handled by the **acquisition method**.
- A **joint venture** is a **corporate alliance** in which two or more companies combine some of their resources to achieve a specific, limited objective.
- A **leveraged buyout (LBO)** is a transaction in which a firm's publicly owned stock is acquired in a mostly debt-financed tender offer, and a privately owned, highly leveraged firm results. Often, the firm's own management initiates the LBO.
- A **divestiture** is the sale of some of a company's operating assets. A divestiture may involve (1) selling an operating unit to another firm, (2) **spinning off** a unit as a separate company, (3) **carving out** a unit by selling a minority interest, and (4) the outright **liquidation** of a unit's assets.
- The **reasons for divestiture** include (1) to settle antitrust suits, (2) to clarify what a company actually does, (3) to enable management to concentrate on a particular type of activity, and (4) to raise the capital needed to strengthen the corporation's core business.

Questions

23-1 Define each of the following terms:
a. Synergy; merger
b. Horizontal merger; vertical merger; congeneric merger; conglomerate merger
c. Friendly merger; hostile merger; defensive merger; tender offer; target company; breakup value; acquiring company
d. Operating merger; financial merger
e. Free cash flow to equity
f. Acquisition accounting
g. White knight; poison pill; golden parachute; proxy fight
h. Joint venture; corporate alliance
i. Divestiture; spinoff; leveraged buyout (LBO)
j. Arbitrage; risk arbitrage

23-2 Four economic classifications of mergers are (1) horizontal, (2) vertical, (3) conglomerate, and (4) congeneric. Explain the significance of these terms in merger analysis with regard to (a) the likelihood of governmental intervention and (b) possibilities for operating synergy.

23-3 Firm A wants to acquire Firm B. Firm B's management agrees that the merger is a good idea. Might a tender offer be used?

23-4 Distinguish between operating mergers and financial mergers.

23-5 Distinguish between the FCFE and corporate valuation models.

Concept Review Problem

Full solutions are provided at www.nelson.com/brigham3ce.

CR-1 Green Mountain Breweries is considering an acquisition of Ritta Markets. Ritta currently has a cost of equity of 10%. Twenty-five percent of its financing is in the form of 6% debt, the rest in common equity. Its tax rate is 40%. After the acquisition, Green Mountain expects Ritta to have the following FCFs, interest payments, and new debt taken on for the next 5 years (in millions):

		Year 1	Year 2	Year 3	Year 4	Year 5
FCF		$3.0	$3.8	5.0	$7.8	$11.6
Interest expense		3.9	4.2	4.5	4.8	5.1
New debt	$8.7	4.8	5.0	5.1	4.8	4.3

After this, the free cash flows are expected to grow at a constant rate of 5%, and the capital structure will remain at 25% debt with an interest rate of 6%. Using the FCFE approach, what is Ritta's value of operations to Green Mountain?

Problems

Answers to odd-numbered problems appear in Appendix A.

Easy Problem 1

The following information is required to work Problems 23-1 through 23-3.

Bremer Corporation is interested in acquiring Quantix Corporation. Quantix has 1 million shares outstanding and a target capital structure consisting of 30% debt. Quantix's debt interest rate is 7%. Assume that the risk-free rate of interest is 4% and that the market risk premium is 5%. Both Quantix and Bremer face a 30% tax rate.

23-1
Valuation

Quantix's free cash flow (FCF_0) is $2.6 million per year and is expected to grow at a constant rate of 5% a year; its beta is 1.2. What is the value of Quantix's operations? If Quantix's has $12 million in debt, what is the current value of Quantix's stock? (*Hint:* Use the corporate valuation model of Chapter 22.)

**Intermediate
Problems 2–6**

23-2
Merger Valuation

Bremer estimates that if it acquires Quantix, the current target capital structure of 30% debt will be maintained. Synergies will cause the free cash flows to be $3.0 million, $3.3 million, $3.6 million, and then $3.9 million, in Years 1 through 4, after which the free cash flows will grow at a 5% rate. What is the per share value of Quantix to Bremer Corporation? Assume Quantix now has $12 million in debt.

23-3
Merger Bid

On the basis of your answers to Problems 23-1 and 23-2, if Bremer were to acquire Quantix, what would be the range of possible prices that it could bid for each share of Quantix common stock?

23-4
Merger Value

Greenback Sporting, a retailer of outdoor wear and sporting equipment, is investigating an opportunity to purchase Active Lifestyle Inc. An acquisition is expected to lower overhead costs, improve distribution efficiencies, and improve ordering volumes from the major manufacturers. Greenback's financial staff estimate that if those improvements (synergies) are implemented, incremental free cash flows will be $6 million, $7.2 million, and $8.2 million for the first three years. Free cash flows would grow at 5% thereafter. If Active Lifestyle's tax rate is 30% and its WACC is 12%, what is the most Greenback should pay for Active Lifestyle?

23-5
Synergy

Mistral Software is considering a merger with Amsted Technologies. Mistral has 1.2 million shares outstanding with a value of $22, while Amsted has 800,000 shares outstanding with a $23 value. The merged company's WACC will be 10%.
a. If Mistral believes the combined firm will have a market value of $50 million, what value of synergy is anticipated?
b. Assuming that synergy is estimated at $5.2 million and that $2 million of it is from cost savings expected in Year 1 due to the elimination of duplicate services, what must the remaining annual synergies be for the next 9 years to achieve the total expected synergies?
c. Based on the $50 million merged firm value, what is the maximum Mistral could pay for Amsted's shares in cash?
d. How much synergy will shareholders of Mistral and Amsted receive if a cash offering is made by Mistral to Amsted for (i) $23, (ii) $25, and (iii) $30 per share?

23-6
FCFE

Hiland Airways is planning to acquire Interstate Carriers. Interstate's cost of equity is 10%; it is financed 75% by common equity and the remainder by debt at 5%. Interstate's tax rate is 30%. Below is a 4-year forecast prepared by Hiland regarding Interstate's future free cash flows, interest expense, and new debt. After Year 4, growth is expected to be 3.5%. The capital structure and cost of debt is not expected to change.

		Year 1	Year 2	Year 3	Year 4
Free cash flows		$1,000,000	$1,140,000	$1,280,000	$1,420,000
Interest expense		85,000	92,500	100,500	109,000
New debt	$1,700,000	150,000	160,000	170,000	180,000

What is the maximum amount that Hiland Airways should pay for Interstate Carriers?

The following information is required to work Problems 23-7 through 23-9.

Brock Industries is contemplating whether to make a takeover bid for Dearborn Aerospace. Dearborn currently has $16 million of debt at 7%, and the market value of its equity is $34 million. Dearborn's tax rate is 35%. The following financial information, which includes all synergies, has been forecast for Dearborn Aerospace if the acquisition takes place. Dearborn's long-term growth rate is expected to be 4% per year.

$ Millions	1/1/16	12/31/16	12/31/17	12/31/18	12/31/19	12/31/20
Sales		$15.0	$19.0	$24.0	$29.0	$34.0
COGS		6.0	7.6	9.6	11.6	13.6
Selling and admin.		3.0	3.5	4.0	4.5	5.0
Depreciation		2.0	2.5	3.0	3.0	3.0
Interest expense		1.7	1.8	1.9	2.0	2.1
Debt	$23.8	25.6	27.2	28.9	30.5	31.7
Operating current assets	4.0	4.0	4.5	5.0	5.5	6.0
Operating long-term assets	40.0	42.0	45.0	48.0	52.0	56.0
Operating current liabilities	3.0	3.0	4.5	5.0	5.5	6.0

Additional market information is shown below:

Risk-free rate is 3%.

Market risk premium is 5%.

Dearborn's stock beta is 1.4.

Dearborn has 5 million shares outstanding.

Challenging Problems 7–10

23-7
Corporate Valuation Model

Calculate Dearborn's:
a.   yearly free cash flows.
b.   WACC.
c.   horizon value using the corporate valuation method.
d.   value of operations, value of equity, and maximum share price that Brock would be willing to pay.

23-8
FCFE Model

Calculate Dearborn's:
a.   yearly free cash flows to equity.
b.   cost of equity.
c.   horizon value using the free cash flow to equity model.
d.   value of equity and the maximum share price that Brock would be willing to pay.

23-9
Merger Bird

What is the market value of Dearborn's equity as a stand-alone company? What are the synergies valued at, assuming that Brock acquires Dearborn? If Brock has 10 million shares outstanding at a current price of $14, how much value is created for (a) Brock and (b) Dearborn shareholders if the acquisition price is $8? $10.25?

23-10
Merger Accounting

Company A has purchased Company T. Both companies' balance sheets (at book value) and income statements are shown below. Company A has identified the fair value of T's current assets to be $20 and its fixed assets to be $55. Any increase in fixed asset value is depreciated straight line over 5 years, and any increase in the current asset value is assumed to be inventory. Inventory turns over 2 times per year.

Balance Sheets

Company A		Company T	
Current assets	$ 55	Current assets	$ 15
Fixed assets	95	Fixed assets	50
Total assets	$150	Total assets	$ 65
Liabilities	$ 50	Liabilities	$ 25
Equity	100	Equity	40
Total liab. & equity	$150	Total liab. & equity	$ 65

Income Statements

Company A		Company T	
Sales	$100	Sales	$ 50
Costs	70	Costs	30
Taxable income	30	Taxable income	20
Taxes (30%)	9	Taxes (30%)	6
Net income	$ 21	Net income	$ 14

a. Create the balance sheet for the merged company, assuming that A acquired T for (i) $30 and (ii) $55 (both amounts in cash).

b. Assume that A has 100 shares outstanding before the merger and that T has 55 shares. Calculate the EPS for both companies.

c. Construct the income statement and calculate the EPS for the merged company based on a 1:1 share exchange.

Spreadsheet Problem

23-11
Build a Model:
Merger Analysis

Start with the partial model in the file *Ch 23 Build a Model.xlsx* from the textbook's website. Rework Problem 23-7. After completing parts a through d, answer the following related questions.

e. Calculate Dearborn's yearly free cash flow to equity from 2015 to 2020.

f. Calculate Dearborn's horizon value using the free cash flow to equity model.

g. Calculate Dearborn's value of equity and the maximum share price that Brock would be willing to pay based on the information in e and f.

h. What would be Dearborn's value of equity if the growth rate "g" varied ± 1%?

MINI CASE

Hager's Home Repair Company, a regional hardware chain that specializes in "do-it-yourself" materials and equipment rentals, is cash rich because of several consecutive good years. One of the alternative uses for the excess funds is an acquisition. Doug Zona, Hager's treasurer and your boss, has been asked to place a value on a potential target, Lyons Lighting (LL), a chain that operates in several provinces and he has enlisted your help.

The table below indicates Zona's estimates of LL's earnings potential if it came under Hager's management (in millions of dollars). The interest expense listed here includes the interest (1) on LL's existing debt, which is $55 million at a rate of 9%, and (2) on new debt expected to be issued over time to help finance expansion within the new "L division," the code name given to the target firm. If acquired, LL will face a 40% tax rate.

Security analysts estimate LL's beta to be 1.3. The acquisition would not change Lyons's capital structure, which is 20% debt. Zona realizes that Lyons Lighting's business plan also requires certain levels of operating capital and that the annual investment could be significant. The required levels of total net operating capital are listed below.

Zona estimates the risk-free rate to be 7% and the market risk premium to be 4%. He also estimates that free cash flows after 2020 will grow at a constant rate of 6%. Following are projections for sales and other items.

	2015	2016	2017	2018	2019	2020
Net sales		$ 60.00	$ 90.00	$112.50	$127.50	$139.70
Cost of goods sold (60%)		36.00	54.00	67.50	76.50	83.80
Selling/administrative expense		4.50	6.00	7.50	9.00	11.00
Interest expense		5.00	6.50	6.50	7.00	8.16
Total net operating capital	$150.00	150.00	157.50	163.50	168.00	173.00
Debt	55.55	72.22	72.22	77.78	90.67	96.1

Hager's management is new to the merger game, so Zona has been asked to answer some basic questions about mergers as well as to perform the merger analysis. To structure the task, Zona has developed the following questions, which you must answer and then defend to Hager's board.

a. Several reasons have been proposed to justify mergers. Among the more prominent are (1) tax considerations, (2) risk reduction, (3) control, (4) purchase of assets at below-replacement cost, (5) synergy, and (6) globalization. In general, which of the reasons are economically justifiable? Which are not? Which fit the situation at hand? Explain.
b. Briefly describe the differences between a hostile merger and a friendly merger.
c. What are the steps in valuing a merger?
d. Use the data developed in the table to construct LL's free cash flows to equity for 2016 through 2020. Why are investment in net operating capital and changes to debt included when calculating free cash flow to equity?
e. Conceptually, what is the appropriate discount rate to apply to the cash flows developed in part d? What is your actual estimate of this discount rate?
f. What is the estimated horizon, or continuing, value of the acquisition; that is, what is the estimated value of LL's cash flows beyond 2020? What is LL's value to Hager's shareholders? Suppose another firm were evaluating LL as an acquisition candidate. Would that company obtain the same value? Explain.
g. Assume that LL has 20 million shares outstanding. These shares are traded relatively infrequently, but the last trade, made several weeks ago, was at a price of $11 per share. Should Hager's make an offer for Lyons Lighting? If so, how much should it offer per share?
h. There has been considerable research undertaken to determine whether mergers really create value and, if so, how this value is shared between the parties involved. What are the results of this research?
i. What method is used to account for mergers?
j. What merger-related activities are undertaken by investment bankers?
k. What is a leveraged buyout (LBO)? What are some of the advantages and disadvantages of going private?
l. What are the major types of divestitures? What motivates firms to divest assets?

appendix a

Answers to End-of-Chapter Problems

We present here some inter-mediate steps and final answers to selected end-of-chapter prob-lems. Note that your answers may differ slightly from ours due to rounding differences. Also, although we hope not, some problems may have more than one correct solution, depending on what assumptions are made in working the problem. Finally, many of the problems involve some verbal discussion as well as numerical calculation; this verbal material is not presented here.

2-1 3.5%
2-3 $3,214,286
2-5 $20,000,000
2-7 Interest: $245.32
Capital gain: $322.66
2-9 NI = $450,000;
NCF = $650,000
2-11 No, $19,000,000 <
$22,000,000 of shares
2-13 a. MVA = $1,424, 000,000
b. EVA = –$102,245,000
2-15 Refund = $180,000
Future taxes = $0;
$40,000; $60,000; $60,000
3-1 AR = $945,000
3-3 M/B = 1.71
3-5 *Change* in AP = $46,026
3-7 CL = $2,000,000;
Inv = $2,200,000
3-9 $262,500; 1.19x
3-11 ROE_{13} = 25.9%
ROE_{14} = 27.7%
ROE_{15} = 28.5%
3-13 TIE = 3.5x
3-15 A/P = $110,000;
C/S = $140,000;
Sales = $600,000;
Inv = $120,000;
A/R = $60,000;
Cash = $28,000;

FA = $192,000;
COGS = $450,000
3-17 a. CR = 2.01x; DSO = 77;
Inv T. = 5.67x;
Fixed asset T. = 5.56x;
TAT = 1.75x;
PM = 1.8%;
ROA = 3.1;
ROE = 7.5%;
Debt ratio = 33%;
Liab/Assets = 59%
4-1 a. $6,083.27
b. $12,166.53
c. $18,249.80
d. $24,333.06
4-3 a. 18.11%
b. 13.65%
c. 9.35%
d. 6.92%
4-5 N = 11 years
4-7 PV = $923.98;
FV = $1,466.24
4-9 a. $10,165
b. $10,876.55
c. $8,878.50
d. $8,297.67
4-11 a. N = 10.24 ≈ 10 years
b. N = 7.27 ≈ 7 years
c. N = 4.19 ≈ 4 years
d. N = 1.00 ≈ 1 year
4-13 a. $2,457.83
b. $865.90
c. $2,000.00
d. (1) $2,703.61
(2) $909.19
(3) $2,000.00
4-15 a. 7%
b. 7%
c. 9%
d. 15%
4-17 a. $1,351.13
b. $1,345.94
c. $1,846.72
4-19 a. Universal, EAR = 7%
Regional,
EAR = 6.14%

4-21 a. I = 18.92% ≈ 19%
4-23 I = 10.1%
4-25 N = 11.91 ≈ 12 years
4-27 (1) $200,000
(2) $100,000
4-29 $984.88
4-31 a. $1,162.29
b. $25,628.10; $44,109.30
4-33 13.35%
4-35 a. $867.17
b. $142.97
4-37 PMT = $36,949.61
4-39 $309,014.91
5-1 AFN = $283,800
5-3 AFN = $63,000
5-5 a. L-T debt = $590,000
Total Liab. = $1,150,000
b. $238,562
5-7 a. $239
b. $10.89
5-9 a. AFN = $2,128
6-1 $928.39
6-3 7.06%
6-5 2.5%
6-7 $1,256.44
6-9 a. $1,021.60; $762.40
b. 10 year bond =
$1,038.07;
15 year bond =
$1,050.62;
10 year zero = $581.25;
15 year zero =
$443.14
6-11 8.97%
6-13 6.78%
6-15 YTC = 4.7%
6-17 C_0 = $1,121.56;
Z_0 = $774.25;
C_1 = $1,094.02;
Z_1 = $825.39;
C_2 = $1,064.66;
Z_2 = $879.91;
C_3 = $1,033.36;
Z_3 = $938.04;
C_4 = $1,000.00;
Z_4 = $1,000.00

6-19   1.5%

6-21 $12,414,238

6-23   a. Fixed cpn bd;
     $51,033,000
     Zero cpn bd;
     $71,782,000
     Float bd; $50,000,000
     b. 5.74%

6-25   a. 5.05%
     b. 4.82%

7-1   b = 1.12

7-3 $\hat{r}_M = 11\%$; $r_s = 12.2\%$

7-5   a. $\hat{r}_M = 10.1\%$;
     $\hat{r}_J = 9.1\%$
     b. $\sigma_M = 4.32\%$;
     $\sigma_J = 4.18\%$
     c. $CV_M = 0.43$;
     $CV_J = 0.46$

7-7 $\hat{r}_a = 7\%$;
     $\hat{r}_b = 8\%$;
     $\sigma_a = 5.48\%$;
     $\sigma_b = 8.98\%$;
     $CV_a = 0.78$;
     $CV_b = 1.12$

7-9   a. $r_i = 15.5\%$
     b. (1) $r_M = 15\%$;
       $r_i = 16.5\%$
     (2) $r_M = 13\%$;
       $r_i = 14.5\%$
     c. (1) $r_i = 18.1\%$
     (2) $r_i = 14.2\%$

7-11   a. Stock A: $r_i = 9\%$;
     Stock B: $r_i = 6\%$
     b. $r_i = 7\%$
     e. Stock A: $r_i = 11.1\%$
     Stock B: $r_i = 7.2\%$
     f. Stock A: $r_i = 9.5\%$
     Stock B: $r_i = 6.5\%$

7-13 $r_p = 12.1\%$

7-15   a. 17.61%
     b. Yes
     c. 14%

7-17   4.5%

7-19   a. FSP $\hat{r} = 8\%$
     correct value;
     RPP $\hat{r} = 14\%$
     under value;
     FGP $\hat{r} = 10\%$
     over value;
     SPEC $\hat{r} = 14\%$
     correct value;
     DT $\hat{r} = 11\%$
     under value;
     b. $b_P = 1.4$;
     $r_P = 11\%$

7-21   a. $\bar{r}_{Avg\,X} = 10.6\%$;
     $\bar{r}_{Avg\,M} = 12.1\%$
     $\sigma_X = 13.1\%$;
     $\sigma_M = 22.6\%$
     b. $r_{RF} = 8.6\%$

8-1 $D_1 = \$1.58$; $D_3 = \$1.74$;
     $D_5 = \$2.10$

8-3 $\hat{P}_1 = \$24.20$;
     $\hat{r}_s = 16\%$

8-5 $51.53

8-7   6%

8-9   a. 10.94%
     b. 8.33%
     c. 7.00%
     d. 4.73%

8-11   6%

8-13   a. $r_c = 7.6\%$;
     $r_d = 1.3\%$

8-15 $10.76

8-17   a. 10%
     b. 9%
     c. 19%

8-19   a. $50.00
     b. $64.29
     c. $81.82
     d. $129.14

8-21   a. $1.79
     b. $3.97
     c. $18.75
     d. $22.71
     e. $22.71
     f. $22.71

8-23   a. $P_0 = \$78.35$;
     Exp Div Yield = 4.15%;
     Cap Gain Yield = 7.85%;
     c. Cap Gain Yield = 7%;
     Div Yield = 5%;

9-1   a. 6%
     b. 4.4%
     c. 4.2%

9-3   7%

9-5   13.33%

9-7   9.35%

9-9   5.25%

9-11   a. 5%
     b. $1.05
     c. 9%

9-13   16.1%

9-15   a. 8.12%
     b. 8.26%

9-17   a. D : 40%;
     E : 60%
     b. 8.4%

9-19   10.5%

10-1   NPV = $2,409.77

10-3   MIRR = 11.93%

10-5   4.44 years

10-7   a. 5%:
     $NPV_A = \$16,108,952$;
     $NPV_B = \$18,300,939$
     10%:
     $NPV_A = \$12,836,213$;
     $NPV_B = \$15,594,170$
     15%:
     $NPV_A = \$10,059,587$;
     $NPV_B = \$13,897,838$
     b. $IRR_A = 43.97\%$;
     $IRR_B = 82.03\%$

10-9 $NPV_E = \$3,861$;
     $IRR_E = 18\%$;
     $NPV_G = \$3,057$;
     $IRR_G = 18\%$;
     Purchase electric-
     powered forklift; it has
     a higher NPV

10-11 $MIRR_J = 17.49\%$;
     $MIRR_K = 18.39\%$

10-13   b. 10%:
     $NPV_A = \$479$;
     $NPV_B = \$372$
     17%: $NPV_A = \$134$;
     $NPV_B = \$174$
     c. (1) $MIRR_A = 14.91\%$;
     $MIRR_B = 17.35\%$.
     (2) $MIRR_A = 18.76\%$;
     $MIRR_B = 21.03\%$
     d. 14.76%

10-15   a. $NPV_A = \$18,108,510$;
     $NPV_B = \$13,946,117$;
     $IRR_A = 15.03\%$;
     $IRR_B = 22.26\%$
     b. $NPV_\Delta = \$4,162,393$;
     $IRR_\Delta = 11.71\%$

10-17 $EAA_A = \$206,000$;
     $EAA_B = \$162,000$;
     Accept A

10-19   d. 7.61%; 15.58%

10-21 $NPV_C = -\$496,401$
     $NPV_F = -\$461,171$
     Choose the forklift.

10-23   NPV at year terminated;
     0: $0
     1: −$1,901
     2: −$1,203
     3: $616
     4: $350
     5: −$324
     Operate truck for 3 years

11-1 $12,000,000

11-3 $CF_1 = \$7,500,000$

11-5   a. −$3,780,000
     b. $29,350,000

11-7 a. $2,000
   b. $2,274
11-9 a. −$137,000
   b. $67,323
   c. $16,173
   d. $44,464
   e. −$9,040 Do not purchase
11-11 a. $106,537, Yes
11-13 a. $51,800
   b. $74,590
11-15 a. −$8,364
   b. $2,400
   c. −$15,649
11-17 $E(NPV) = \$3,000,000$;
   $\sigma_{NPV} = \$23,622,000$;
   $CV = 7.874$
11-19 a. Expected $CF_X = \$25,000$;
   Expected $CF_Y = \$27,500$;
   $CV_X = 0.0849$;
   $CV_Y = 0.7767$
   b. $NPV_X = \$38,282$;
   $NPV_Y = \$41,050$
11-21 $E(NPV) = \$117,779$;
   $\sigma_{NPV} = \$445,060$;
   $CV = 3.78$
12-1 240,000 units
12-3 3.6%
12-5 $800 million
12-7 $620.68 million
12-9 $ROE_c = 15\%$;
   $\sigma_c = 11\%$
12-11 a. $b_u = 1.18$
   b. $r_{sU} = 11.9\%$
   c. 12.60%; 14.66%; 16.26%
   d. 15.08%
12-13 a. $V_u = V_L = \$20,000,000$
   b. $r_{sU} = 10\%$; $r_{sL} = 15\%$
   c. $S_L = \$10,000,000$
   d. $WACC_u = WACC_L = 10\%$
12-15 a. $V_u = \$12,000,000$
   b. $V_L = \$15,330,000$
   c. Gain from leverage = $3,330,000
   d. $V_u = V_L = \$20,000,000$;
   Gain from leverage = $0
   e. $V_L = \$16,000,000$;
   Gain from leverage = $4,000,000
   f. $V_L = \$16,000,000$;
   Gain from leverage = $4,000,000

12-17 30% debt : WACC = 9.1% V = $67.72 M;
   50% debt : WACC = 8.9% V = $69.24 M;
   70% debt : WACC = 9.9% V = $62.24 M
12-19 9.72%; 20% debt, 80% equity
12-21 a. $V_L = V_u = \$23,333,333$
   b. D = $0 : WACC = $r_s = 9\%$; D = $6M : $r_{sL} = 10.04\%$; WACC = 9.0%; D = $10M: $r_{sL} = 11.25\%$; WACC = 9%
   c. $V_u = \$16,333,333$; $V_L = \$19,333,333$
   d. D = $0 : r_s = WACC = 9%; D = $6M : $r_{sL} = 10.04\%$; WACC = 8.1%; D = $10M : $r_{sL} = 11.25\%$; WACC = 7.6%
   e. $23,333,333; $r_d = 9\%$
13-1 Payout = 33%
13-3 Payout = 52%
13-5 $P_0 = \$48$
13-7 n = 4,000; EPS = $5.00; DPS = $1.50; P = $40.00
13-9 Payout = 18%
13-11 a. DPS = $6
   b. DPR = 60%
   c. 60% payout: $P_0 = \$66.67$; 20% payout: $P_0 = \$100$
13-15 a. $10,500,000
   b. DPS = $0.50; Payout = 4.55%
   c. $9,000,000
   d. No
   e. 40%
   f. $1,500,000
   g. $12,857,143
14-1 a. $2,200,000
   b. $7,200,000
   c. −$2,800,000
14-3 a. Company = $170,550,000;
   Underwriters = $9,000,000
   b. $15: $45,000,000 $11: −$15,000,000
14-5 EPS before = $0.50; EPS after = $0.491; No dilution if g = 10.1%
14-7 6,258,693 new shares

14-9 a. Edelman, 2015: EPS = $12,000; DPS = $6,000; BVPS = $90,000
   b. Edelman: $g_{eps} = 8.0\%$ $g_{dps} = 7.4\%$
   e. Edelman, 2015: EPS = $3,00; DPS = $1,50; BVPS = $22.50
   f. $ROE_{Kenn} = 15.00\%$ $ROE_{Stras} = 13.64\%$
   g. 2015: Kennedy, 50%; Strasburg, 50%;
   h. Kennedy, 43%; Strasburg, 37%;
   i. Kennedy, 8; Strasburg, 8.67.
14A-1 a. $3,600,000
   b. Dollar flotation cost = $1,600,000
   c. $5,200,000
   d. $96,000
   e. $420,000
   f. Discount rate = 4.2%; PV = $11,715,342
   g. $6,515,342 Refund
15-1 a. (1) 25%
   (2) 50%
   (3) 25%
15-3 a. Shipton: Debt/TA = 40%
   Falco: Debt/TA = 25%
15-5 a. NAL = $1,515, Lease
   b. NAL = −$4,556, Do not lease
   c. NAL = −$733 Do not Lease
   d. NAL = −$1,090 Do not Lease
15-7 a. NAL = $6,186
   b. NPV = $19,968
   c. $324,301
16-1 $182.16
16-3 a. $556,000 per year
   c. $11,000,000
16-5 a. $10: EV = $0;
   $15: EV = $0;
   $20: EV = $5;
   $85: EV = $70
   d. 6.5%, $65
16-7 a. 6 Years
   b. 9.53%
16-9 a. 14.1%
   b. $12 million (before-tax)

c. $330.89

d. Value as a straight
   bond = $669.25;
   Value in conversion
   = $521.91

f. Value as a straight
   bond = $1,000;
   Value in conversion
   = $521.91

16-11 a. Year = 8;
   CV_8 = $1,283.05;
   CF_8 = $1,353.0

b. 9.52%

17-1 r_{NOM} = 56.39%;
   EAR = 74.26%

17-3 $7,500,000

17-5 a. 73.74%

b. 14.90%

c. 32.25%

d. 21.28%

e. 29.80%

17-7 Nominal cost = 9.21%;
   Effective cost = 9.60%

17-9 a. 56.8 days

b. TAT = 2.71X;
   ROA = 18.97%;

c. CCC = 36.6 days
   TAT = 2.95X;
   ROA = 20.68%

17-11 a. 12%

b. 11.25%

c. 11.48%

d. 14.47%

17-13 a. Tight: 14.49%;
   Moderate: 13.32%;
   Relaxed: 11.30%

17-15 a. $100,000

b. No

c. $300,000; Nominal
   cost: 37.2%;
   Effective cost: 44.6%

d. Nominal rate: 24.8%
   Effective rate: 27.9%

17-17 a. $450,000

17-19 b. Cumulative cash
   surplus or loans:
   Jul: $111,300
   Aug: $297,600
   Sep: ($155,100)
   Oct: ($22,800)
   Nov: $118,500
   Dec: $187,800

18-1 $3,000,000

18-3 Current Policy: Profit =
   $321,425; New Credit
   Policy: Profit = $319,008.
   Do not change

18-5 a. 28 days

b. $70,000

c. Nominal cost: 56.4%;
   Effective cost: 74.3%

d. Nominal cost: 37.6%;
   Effective cost: 44.8%

e. $55,000

18-7 a. Current Policy:
   Profit = $1,690,683;
   New Policy:
   Profit = $1,629,783:
   Do not change.

b. 1.78%

19-1 $10; $2

19-3 $2.41

19-5 $1.90

19-7 $1.91

20-1 Net payment =
   LIBOR + 0.2%

20-3 4.41%, $104,511

20-5 Sell 98 June contracts
   If rates rise bond issues
   loses $1,195,038 but
   futures hedge gains
   $1.373,960

21-1 8.50 yen per peso

21-3 1 euro = $1.3846 or
   $1 = 0.7222 euros

21-5 0.826 SFr

21-7 $r_{NOM\ CAN}$ = 4.2%

21-9 a. Depreciate

b. $69,652

c. i $1,777 better off;
   ii $1,691 worse off

21-11 a. Increased

b. $20,000

c. 3.0%

21-13 a. Discount

b. $1.2990

21-15 $250,539,359

22-1 FCF = $47.0

22-3 V_{op} at 2017 = $37,500

22-5 A: $10,920,000;
   B: $10,500,000

22-7 a. $713.33

b. $527.89

c. $43.79

22-9 $59 million

22-11 a. $45.82 million

b. $962.22 million

c. $916.40 million

d. $966.30 million

e. $60.05

23-1 $66.67

23-3 $66.67 to $84.46

23-5 a. $5,200,000

b. $645,900

c. $23,600,000

d. At $23: Mistral: $5.2
   million, Amsted: $0;
   At $25: Mistral $3.6
   million, Amsted $1.6
   million; At $30:
   Mistral −$0.4 million
   Amsted $5.6 million

23-7 a. 2016: $0.60;
   2017: $1.51;
   2018: $1.81;
   2019: $2.44;
   2020: $4.06

b. 8.256%

c. $99.21 million

d. V_{op} = $74.5 million;
   V_{equity} = $58.50 million;
   Max price = $11.70

23-9 Stand-alone $34 million;
   Synergies = $24.55
   million;
   At $8: Value for
   Brock = $1.85;
   Value for
   Dearborn = $1.20;
   At $10.25: Value for
   Brock = $0.73; Value
   for Dearborn = $3.45.

**Online Chapter 24 (found at
www.nelson.com/brigham3ce)**

24-1 a. $1,074,000

b. $4,205,000

24-3 a. −$19,000,000

b. $9,098,100

24-5 a. $7,769

b. ENPV = $16,713;
   Value of growth
   option = $8,945

24-7 P = $10,479,000; X =
   $9,000,000; t = 2;
   r_{RF} = 0.06; σ^2 = 0.0111;
   V = $2,514,000

appendix b

Selected Equations and Data

Chapter 1

$$\text{Value} = \frac{FCF_1}{(1 + WACC)^1} + \frac{FCF_2}{(1 + WACC)^2} + \frac{FCF_3}{(1 + WACC)^3} + \cdots + \frac{FCF_\infty}{(1 + WACC)^\infty}$$

Chapter 2

EBIT = Earnings before interest and taxes = Sales revenues − Operating costs

EBITDA = Earnings before interest, taxes, depreciation, and amortization
= EBIT + Depreciation + Amortization

Net cash flow = Net income + Depreciation and amortization

NOWC = Net operating working capital
= Operating current assets − Operating current liabilities
= (Cash + Accounts receivable + Inventories)
− (Accounts payable + Accruals)

Total net operating capital = Net operating working capital
+ Operating long-term assets

NOPAT = Net operating profit after taxes = EBIT(1 − Tax rate)

Free cash flow (FCF) = NOPAT − Net investment in operating capital
= NOPAT − (Current year's total net operating capital
− Previous year's total net operating capital)

Operating cash flow = NOPAT + Depreciation and amortization

$$\text{Gross investment in operating capital} = \text{Net investment in operating capital} + \text{Depreciation}$$

FCF = Operating cash flow − Gross investment in operating capital

$$\text{Return on invested capital (ROIC)} = \frac{NOPAT}{\text{Total net operating capital}}$$

MVA = Market value of stock − Equity capital supplied by shareholders
= (Shares outstanding)(Stock price) − Total common equity

MVA = Total market value − Total investor-supplied capital
= (Market value of stock + Market value of debt)
− Total investor-supplied capital

$$\text{EVA} = \text{Net operating profit after taxes (NOPAT)}$$
$$\quad - \text{After-tax dollar cost of capital used to support operations}$$
$$= \text{EBIT}(1 - \text{Tax rate}) - (\text{Total net operating capital})(\text{WACC})$$

$$\text{EVA} = (\text{Total net operating capital})(\text{ROIC} - \text{WACC})$$

Chapter 3

$$\text{Current ratio} = \frac{\text{Current assets}}{\text{Current liabilities}}$$

$$\text{Quick, or acid test, ratio} = \frac{\text{Current assets} - \text{Inventories}}{\text{Current liabilities}}$$

$$\text{Inventory turnover ratio} = \frac{\text{Cost of goods sold}}{\text{Inventories}}$$

$$\text{DSO} = \text{Days sales outstanding} = \frac{\text{Receivables}}{\text{Average sales per day}} = \frac{\text{Reveivables}}{\text{Annual sales/365}}$$

$$\text{APP} = \text{Average payables period} = \frac{\text{Payables}}{\text{Annual operating costs/365}}$$

$$\text{Fixed assets turnover ratio} = \frac{\text{Sales}}{\text{Net fixed assets}}$$

$$\text{Total assets turnover ratio} = \frac{\text{Sales}}{\text{Total assets}}$$

$$\text{Debt ratio} = \frac{\text{Total debt}}{\text{Total assets}}$$

$$\text{Debt-to-equity ratio} = \frac{\text{Total debt}}{\text{Total common equity}}$$

$$\text{Equity multiplier} = \frac{\text{Total assets}}{\text{Common equity}}$$

$$\text{Times-interest-earned (TIE) ratio} = \frac{\text{EBIT}}{\text{Interest charges}}$$

$$\text{EBITDA coverage ratio} = \frac{\text{EBITDA} + \text{Lease payments}}{\text{Interest} + \text{Principal payments} + \text{Lease payments}}$$

$$\text{Net profit margin} = \frac{\text{Net income available to common shareholders}}{\text{Sales}}$$

$$\text{Return on total assets (ROA)} = \frac{\text{Net income available to common shareholders}}{\text{Total assets}}$$

$$\text{Basic earning power (BEP) ratio} = \frac{\text{EBIT}}{\text{Total assets}}$$

$$\text{ROA} = \text{Profit margin} \times \text{Total assets turnover}$$

$$\text{ROA} = \frac{\text{Net income}}{\text{Sales}} \times \frac{\text{Sales}}{\text{Total assets}}$$

$$\text{Return on common equity (ROE)} = \frac{\text{Net income available to common shareholders}}{\text{Common equity}}$$

$$\text{ROE} = \text{ROA} \times \text{Equity multiplier}$$

$$= \text{Profit margin} \times \text{Total assets turnover} \times \text{Equity multiplier}$$

$$= \frac{\text{Net income}}{\text{Sales}} \times \frac{\text{Sales}}{\text{Total assets}} \times \frac{\text{Total assets}}{\text{Common equity}}$$

$$\text{Price/earnings (P/E) ratio} = \frac{\text{Price per share}}{\text{Earnings per share}}$$

$$\text{Price/cash flow ratio} = \frac{\text{Price per share}}{\text{Cash flow per share}}$$

$$\text{Book value per share} = \frac{\text{Common equity}}{\text{Shares outstanding}}$$

$$\text{Market/book (M/B) ratio} = \frac{\text{Market price per share}}{\text{Book value per share}}$$

Chapter 4

$$\text{FV}_N = \text{PV}(1 + I)^N$$

$$\text{PV} = \frac{\text{FV}_N}{(1 + I)^N}$$

$$\text{FVA}_N = \text{PMT}\left[\frac{(1 + I)^N}{I} - \frac{1}{I}\right] = \text{PMT}\left[\frac{(1 + I)^N - 1}{I}\right]$$

$$\text{FVA}_{\text{due}} = \text{FVA}_{\text{ordinary}}(1 + I)$$

$$\text{PVA}_N = \text{PMT}\left[\frac{1}{I} - \frac{1}{I(1 + I)^N}\right] = \text{PMT}\left[\frac{1 - \dfrac{1}{(1 + I)^N}}{I}\right]$$

$$\text{PVA}_{N\,\text{due}} = \text{PVA}_{\text{ordinary}}(1 + I)$$

$$\text{PV of a perpetuity} = \frac{\text{PMT}}{I}$$

$$\text{PV}_{\text{Uneven stream}} = \sum_{t=1}^{N} \frac{\text{CF}_t}{(1 + I)^t}$$

$$\text{FV}_{\text{Uneven stream}} = \sum_{t=1}^{N} \text{CF}_t(1 + I)^{N-t}$$

$$I_{\text{PER}} = \frac{I_{\text{NOM}}}{M}$$

$$\text{APR} = (I_{\text{PER}})M$$

$$\text{Number of periods} = NM$$

$$\text{FV}_N = \text{PV}(1 + I_{\text{PER}})^{\text{Number of periods}} = \text{PV}\left(1 + \frac{I_{\text{NOM}}}{M}\right)^{MN}$$

$$\text{EFF\%} = \left(1 + \frac{I_{\text{NOM}}}{M}\right)^{M} - 1.0$$

Chapter 5

$$
\begin{array}{ccccc}
\text{Additional} & & \text{Required} & & \text{Spontaneous} & & \text{Increase in} \\
\text{funds} & = & \text{asset} & - & \text{liability} & - & \text{retained} \\
\text{needed} & & \text{increase} & & \text{increase} & & \text{earnings}
\end{array}
$$

$$AFN = (A^*/S_0)\Delta S - (L^*/S_0)\Delta S - MS_1(RR)$$

$$\begin{array}{c}\text{Full}\\ \text{capacity}\\ \text{sales}\end{array} = \dfrac{\text{Actual sales}}{\begin{array}{c}\text{Percentage of capacity}\\ \text{at which fixed assets}\\ \text{were operated}\end{array}}$$

$$\frac{\text{Target fixed assets}}{\text{Sales}} = \frac{\text{Actual fixed assets}}{\text{Full capacity sales}}$$

$$\text{Required level of fixed assets} = (\text{Target fixed assets/Sales})(\text{Projected sales})$$

Chapter 6

$$V_B = \sum_{t=1}^{N} \frac{INT}{(1 + r_d)^t} + \frac{M}{(1 + r_d)^N}$$

$$\text{Price of callable bond} = \sum_{t=1}^{N} \frac{INT}{(1 + r_d)^t} + \frac{\text{Call price}}{(1 + r_d)^N}$$

$$\text{Current yield} = \frac{\text{Annual interest}}{\text{Bond's current price}}$$

$$V_B = \sum_{t=1}^{2N} \frac{INT/2}{(1 + r_d/2)^t} + \frac{M}{(1 + r_d/2)^{2N}}$$

$$V_{\text{zero coupon bond}} = M/(1 + r_d/2)^{2N}$$

$$r_d = r^* + IP + DRP + LP + MRP$$

$$r_{RF} = r^* + IP$$

$$r_d = r_{RF} + DRP + LP + MRP$$

Chapter 7

$$\text{Expected rate of return} = \hat{r} = \sum_{i=1}^{n} P_i r_i$$

$$\text{Historical average, } \bar{r}_{Avg} = \frac{\sum_{t=1}^{n} \bar{r}_t}{n}$$

$$\text{Variance} = \sigma^2 = \sum_{i=1}^{n} (r_i - \hat{r})^2 P_i$$

$$\text{Standard deviation} = \sigma = \sqrt{\sum_{i=1}^{n} (r_i - \hat{r})^2 P_i}$$

$$\text{Historical estimated } \sigma = S = \sqrt{\frac{\sum_{t=1}^{n} (\bar{r}_t - \bar{r}_{Avg})^2}{n - 1}}$$

$$CV = \frac{\sigma}{\hat{r}}$$

$$\hat{r}_P = \sum_{i=1}^{n} w_i \hat{r}_i$$

$$\sigma_P = \sqrt{\sum_{i=1}^{n}(r_{pi} - \hat{r}_p)^2 P_i}$$

$$\text{Estimated } \rho = R = \frac{\sum_{t=1}^{n}(\bar{r}_{i,t} - \bar{r}_{i,Avg})(\bar{r}_{j,t} - \bar{r}_{j,Avg})}{\sqrt{\sum_{t=1}^{n}(\bar{r}_{i,t} - \bar{r}_{i,Avg})^2 \sum_{t=1}^{n}(\bar{r}_{j,t} - \bar{r}_{j,Avg})^2}}$$

$$\hat{r}_P = w_A \hat{r}_A + (1 + w_A)\hat{r}_B$$

$$\text{Portfolio SD} = \sigma_P = \sqrt{w_A^2\sigma_A^2 + (1 - w_A)^2\sigma_B^2 + 2w_A(1 - w_A)\rho_{AB}\sigma_A\sigma_B}$$

$$COV_{iM} = \rho_{iM}\sigma_i\sigma_M$$

$$b_i = \left(\frac{\sigma_i}{\sigma_M}\right)\rho_{iM} = \frac{COV_{iM}}{\sigma_M^2}$$

$$b_P = \sum_{i=1}^{n} w_i b_i$$

Required return on stock market $= r_M$

Market risk premium $= RP_M = r_M - r_{RF}$

$$RP_i = (r_M - r_{RF})b_i = (RP_M)b_i$$

$$SML = r_i = r_{RF} + (r_M - r_{RF})b_i = r_{RF} + RP_M b_i$$

$$r_i = r_{RF} + (r_1 - r_{RF})b_{i1} + \cdots + (r_j - r_{RF})b_{ij}$$

Chapter 8

$$\hat{P}_0 = \text{PV of expected future dividends} = \sum_{t=1}^{\infty}\frac{D_t}{(1 + r_s)^t}$$

$$\hat{P}_0 = \frac{D_0(1 + g)}{r_s - g} = \frac{D_1}{r_s - g}$$

$$\hat{r}_s = \frac{D_1}{P_0} + g$$

$$\text{Capital gains yield} = \frac{\hat{P}_1 - P_0}{P_0}$$

$$\text{Dividend yield} = \frac{D_1}{P_0}$$

For a zero growth stock, $\hat{P}_0 = \frac{D}{r_s}$

$$\text{Horizon value} = \hat{P}_N = \frac{D_{N+1}}{r_s - g}$$

$$V_P = \frac{D_P}{r_P}$$

$$\hat{r}_P = \frac{D_P}{V_P}$$

$\bar{r}_s$ = Actual dividend yield + Actual capital gains yield

Chapter 9

After-tax component cost of debt = $r_d(1 - T)$

$$M(1 - F) = \sum_{t=1}^{N} \frac{INT(1 - T)}{[1 + r_d(1 - T)]^t} + \frac{M}{[1 + r_d(1 - T)]^N}$$

$$r_{ps} = \frac{D_{ps}}{P_{ps}(1 - F)}$$

Market equilibrium: Expected rate of return = $\hat{r}_M = \dfrac{D_1}{P_0} + g = r_{RF} + RP_M$

$$= r_M = \text{Required rate of return}$$

CAPM: $r_s = r_{RF} + b_i (RP_M)$

DCF: $r_s = \hat{r}_s = \dfrac{D_1}{P_0} + \text{Expected } g$

Bond-yield-plus risk-premium: r_s = Bond yield + Bond risk premium

g = (Retention rate)(ROE) = (1.0 − Payout rate)(ROE)

$$r_e = \hat{r}_e = \frac{D_1}{P_0(1 - F)} + g$$

WACC = $w_d\, r_d(1 - T) + w_{ps}\, r_{ps} + w_{ce} r_s$

Chapter 10

$$NPV = CF_0 + \frac{CF_1}{(1 + r)^1} + \frac{CF_2}{(1 + r)^2} + \cdots + \frac{CF_N}{(1 + r)^N}$$

$$= \sum_{t=0}^{N} \frac{CF_t}{(1 + r)^t}$$

IRR: $CF_0 + \dfrac{CF_1}{(1 + IRR)^1} + \dfrac{CF_2}{(1 + IRR)^2} + \cdots + \dfrac{CF_N}{(1 + IRR)^N} = 0$

$$NPV = \sum_{t=0}^{N} \frac{CF_t}{(1 + IRR)^t} = 0$$

MIRR: PV of costs = PV of terminal value.

$$\sum_{t=0}^{N} \frac{COF_t}{(1 + r)^t} = \frac{\sum_{t=0}^{N} CIF_t(1 + r)^{N-t}}{(1 + MIRR)^N}$$

$$PV \text{ of costs} = \frac{\text{Terminal value}}{(1 + MIRR)^N}$$

$$PI = \frac{PV \text{ of future cash flows}}{\text{Initial cost}} = \frac{\sum_{t=1}^{N} \dfrac{CF_t}{(1 + r)^t}}{CF_0}$$

$$\text{Payback} = \begin{array}{c} \text{Number of} \\ \text{years prior to} \\ \text{full recovery} \end{array} + \frac{\begin{array}{c} \text{Unrecovered cost} \\ \text{at start of year} \end{array}}{\begin{array}{c} \text{Cash flow during} \\ \text{full recovery year} \end{array}}$$

Chapter 11

$$\text{FCF} = \frac{\text{Investment outlay}}{\text{cash flow}} + \frac{\text{Operating}}{\text{cash flow}} + \frac{\text{NOWC}}{\text{cash flow}} + \frac{\text{Salvage}}{\text{cash flow}}$$

$$\text{CCA tax shield} = \text{CCA amount} \times \text{Tax rate}$$

$$\text{PV of CCA tax shield} = \left(\frac{CdT}{r+d}\right) \times \left(\frac{1+0.5r}{1+r}\right) - \left(\frac{SdT}{r+d}\right) \times \left(\frac{1}{(1+r)^n}\right)$$

$$\text{NPV} = \sum_{t=0}^{N} \frac{NCF_t}{(1+r_{NOM})^t} = \sum_{t=0}^{N} \frac{RCF_t(1+i)^t}{(1+r_r)^t(1+i)^t} = \sum_{t=0}^{N} \frac{RCF_t}{(1+r_r)^t}$$

$$\text{Expected NPV} = \sum_{i=1}^{N} P_i(NPV_i)$$

$$\sigma_{NPV} = \sqrt{\sum_{i=1}^{N} P_i(NPV_i - \text{Expected NPV})^2}$$

$$CV_{NPV} = \frac{\sigma_{NPV}}{E(NPV)}$$

Chapter 12

$$V_{op} = \sum_{t=1}^{\infty} \frac{FCF_t}{(1+WACC)^t}$$

$$WACC = w_d(1-T)r_d + w_{ce}r_s$$

$$ROIC = \frac{NOPAT}{\text{Capital}} = \frac{EBIT(1-T)}{\text{Capital}}$$

$$EBIT = PQ - VQ - F$$

$$Q_{BE} = \frac{F}{P-V}$$

$$V_L = D + S$$

MM, no taxes:

$$V_L = V_U = \frac{EBIT}{WACC} = \frac{EBIT}{r_{sU}}$$

$$r_{sL} = r_{sU} + \text{Risk premium} = r_{sU} + (r_{sU} - r_d)(D/S)$$

MM, corporate taxes:

$$V_L = V_U + TD$$

$$V_U = S = \frac{EBIT(1-T)}{r_{sU}}$$

$$r_{sL} = r_{sU} + (r_{sU} - r_d)(1-T)(D/S)$$

Miller, corporate and personal taxes: $V_L = V_U + \left[1 - \dfrac{(1 - T_c)(1 - T_s)}{(1 - T_d)} \right] D$

$b = b_U[1 + (1 - T)(D/S)]$

$b_U = b/[1 + (1 - T)(D/S)]$

$r_s = r_{RF} + RP_M(b)$

$r_s = r_{RF} + \text{Premium for business risk} + \text{Premium for financial risk}$

If $g = 0$: $V_{op} = \dfrac{FCF}{WACC} = \dfrac{EBIT(1 - T)}{WACC}$

Total corporate value $= V_{op} + \text{Value of short-term investments}$

$S = \text{Total corporate value} - \text{Value of all debt}$

Chapter 13

Dividends $= \text{Net income} - [(\text{Target equity ratio})(\text{Total capital budget})]$

Chapter 14

Amount left on table $= (\text{Closing price} - \text{Offer price})(\text{Number of shares})$

Chapter 15

NAL $= \text{PV cost of owning} - \text{PV cost of leasing}$

Chapter 16

$\dfrac{\text{Price paid for}}{\text{bond with warrants}} = \dfrac{\text{Straight-debt}}{\text{value of bond}} + \dfrac{\text{Value of}}{\text{warrants}}$

Conversion price $= P_c = \dfrac{\text{Par value of bond given up}}{\text{Shares reveived}}$

$= \dfrac{\text{Par value of bond given up}}{CR}$

Conversion ratio $= CR = \dfrac{\text{Par value of bond given up}}{P_c}$

Chapter 17

Inventory conversion period $= \dfrac{\text{Inventory}}{\text{Cost of goods sold}/365}$

Receivables collection period $= DSO = \dfrac{\text{Receivables}}{\text{Sales}/365}$

Payables deferral period $= \dfrac{\text{Payables}}{\text{Cost of goods sold}/365}$

$$\begin{array}{c}\text{Inventory}\\\text{conversion}\\\text{period}\end{array} + \begin{array}{c}\text{Average}\\\text{collection}\\\text{period}\end{array} - \begin{array}{c}\text{Payables}\\\text{deferral}\\\text{period}\end{array} = \begin{array}{c}\text{Cash}\\\text{conversion}\\\text{cycle}\end{array}$$

$$\text{Yield} = \frac{100 - P}{P} \times \frac{365}{d}$$

Interest change per period = (Days in period) (Rate per day) (Amount of loan)

$$\text{Effective annual rate}_{\text{Add-on}} = (1 + r_d)^n - 1.0$$

$$\begin{array}{c}\text{Nominal annual cost}\\\text{of trade credit}\end{array} = \frac{\text{Discount\%}}{100 - \text{Discount\%}} \times \frac{365}{\begin{array}{c}\text{Days credit is} \\ \text{outstanding}\end{array} - \begin{array}{c}\text{Discount}\\\text{period}\end{array}}$$

Chapter 18

$$\begin{array}{c}\text{Accounts}\\\text{receivable}\end{array} = \begin{array}{c}\text{Credit sales}\\\text{per day}\end{array} \times \begin{array}{c}\text{Length of}\\\text{collection period}\end{array}$$

$$\text{ADS} = \frac{(\text{Units sold})(\text{Sales price})}{365} = \frac{\text{Annual sales}}{365}$$

Receivables = (ADS)(DSO)

$$(\text{DSO})\left(\frac{\text{Sales}}{\text{per day}}\right)\left(\begin{array}{c}\text{Variable}\\\text{cost ratio}\end{array}\right)\left(\begin{array}{c}\text{Cost of}\\\text{funds}\end{array}\right) = \text{Cost of carrying receivables}$$

Opportunity cost = (Old sales/365)(ΔDSO)(1 − V)(r)

$$A = \frac{\text{Units per order}}{2} = \frac{S/N}{2}$$

TCC = Total carrying cost = (C)(P)(A)

Total ordering cost = TOC = (F)(N)

TIC = TCC + TOC

$$Q = \text{EOQ} = \sqrt{\frac{2(F)(S)}{(C)(P)}}$$

Chapter 19

Exercise value = MAX[Current price of stock − Strike price, 0]

$$\text{Number of stock shares in hedged portfolio} = N = \frac{C_u - C_d}{P(u) - P(d)}$$

$$V = P[N(d_1)] - Xe^{-r_{RF}t}[N(d_2)]$$

$$d_1 = \frac{\ln(P/X) + [r_{RF} + (\sigma^2/2)]t}{\sigma\sqrt{t}}$$

$$d_2 = d_1 - \sigma\sqrt{t}$$

Put option $= V_C - P + Xe^{-r_{RF}t}$

Chapter 21

$$\frac{\text{Forward exchange rate}}{\text{Spot exchange rate}} = \frac{(1 + r_h)}{(1 + r_f)}$$

$$P_h = (P_f)(\text{Spot rate})$$

$$\text{Spot rate} = \frac{P_h}{P_f}$$

$$\text{Expected spot rate} = \frac{(1 + i_h)}{(1 + i_f)} \times \text{Spot rate}$$

Chapter 22

V_{op} = Value of operations

= Pv of expected future free cash flows

$$= \sum_{t=1}^{\infty} \frac{FCF_1}{(1 + WACC)^t}$$

Horizon value: $V_{op(\text{at time N})} = \dfrac{FCF_{N+1}}{WACC - g} = \dfrac{FCF_N(1 + g)}{WACC - g}$

Total value = V_{op} + Value of nonoperating assets

Value of equity = Total value − Preferred stock − Debt

Chapter 23

$$\text{FCFE} = \frac{\text{Free}}{\text{cash flow}} - \frac{\text{After-tax}}{\text{interest expense}} - \frac{\text{Principal}}{\text{payments}} + \frac{\text{Newly issued}}{\text{debt}}$$

$$= \frac{\text{Free}}{\text{cash flow}} - \frac{\text{Interest}}{\text{expense}} + \frac{\text{Interest}}{\text{tax shield}} + \frac{\text{Net change}}{\text{in debt}}$$

$$HV_{\text{FCFE,N}} = \frac{FCFE_{N+1}}{r_{sL} - g} = \frac{FCFE_N(1 + g)}{r_{sL} - g}$$

$$V_{\text{FCFE}} = \sum_{t=1}^{N} \frac{FCFE_t}{(1 + r_{sL})^t} + \frac{HV_{\text{FCFE, N}}}{(1 + r_{sL})^N}$$

$S = V_{\text{FCFE}}$ + Nonoperating assets

Online Chapter 24 (found at www.nelson.com/brigham3ce)

$$CV = \frac{\sigma(\text{PV of future CF})}{E(\text{PV of future CF})}$$

Variance of project's rate of return: $\sigma^2 = \dfrac{\ln(CV^2 + 1)}{t}$

appendix c

Values of the Areas under the Standard Normal Distribution Function

TABLE
C-1

Values of the Areas under the Standard Normal Distribution Function

Z	0.00	0.01	0.02	0.03	0.04	0.05	0.06	0.07	0.08	0.09
0.0	.0000	.0040	.0080	.0120	.0160	.0199	.0239	.0279	.0319	.0359
0.1	.0398	.0438	.0478	.0517	.0557	.0596	.0636	.0675	.0714	.0753
0.2	.0793	.0832	.0871	.0910	.0948	.0987	.1026	.1064	.1103	.1141
0.3	.1179	.1217	.1255	.1293	.1331	.1368	.1406	.1443	.1480	.1517
0.4	.1554	.1591	.1628	.1664	.1700	.1736	.1772	.1808	.1844	.1879
0.5	.1915	.1950	.1985	.2019	.2054	.2088	.2123	.2157	.2190	.2224
0.6	.2257	.2291	.2324	.2357	.2389	.2422	.2454	.2486	.2517	.2549
0.7	.2580	.2611	.2642	.2673	.2704	.2734	.2764	.2794	.2823	.2852
0.8	.2881	.2910	.2939	.2967	.2995	.3023	.3051	.3078	.3106	.3133
0.9	.3159	.3186	.3212	.3238	.3264	.3289	.3315	.3340	.3365	.3389
1.0	.3413	.3438	.3461	.3485	.3508	.3531	.3554	.3577	.3599	.3621
1.1	.3643	.3665	.3686	.3708	.3729	.3749	.3770	.3790	.3810	.3830
1.2	.3849	.3869	.3888	.3907	.3925	.3944	.3962	.3980	.3997	.4015
1.3	.4032	.4049	.4066	.4082	.4099	.4115	.4131	.4147	.4162	.4177
1.4	.4192	.4207	.4222	.4236	.4251	.4265	.4279	.4292	.4306	.4319
1.5	.4332	.4345	.4357	.4370	.4382	.4394	.4406	.4418	.4429	.4441
1.6	.4452	.4463	.4474	.4484	.4495	.4505	.4515	.4525	.4535	.4545
1.7	.4554	.4564	.4573	.4582	.4591	.4599	.4608	.4616	.4625	.4633
1.8	.4641	.4649	.4656	.4664	.4671	.4678	.4686	.4693	.4699	.4706
1.9	.4713	.4719	.4726	.4732	.4738	.4744	.4750	.4756	.4761	.4767
2.0	.4773	.4778	.4783	.4788	.4793	.4798	.4803	.4808	.4812	.4817
2.1	.4821	.4826	.4830	.4834	.4838	.4842	.4846	.4850	.4854	.4857
2.2	.4861	.4864	.4868	.4871	.4875	.4878	.4881	.4884	.4887	.4890
2.3	.4893	.4896	.4898	.4901	.4904	.4906	.4909	.4911	.4913	.4916
2.4	.4918	.4920	.4922	.4925	.4927	.4929	.4931	.4932	.4934	.4936
2.5	.4938	.4940	.4941	.4943	.4945	.4946	.4948	.4949	.4951	.4952
2.6	.4953	.4955	.4956	.4957	.4959	.4960	.4961	.4962	.4963	.4964
2.7	.4965	.4966	.4967	.4968	.4969	.4970	.4971	.4972	.4973	.4974
2.8	.4974	.4975	.4976	.4977	.4977	.4978	.4979	.4979	.4980	.4981
2.9	.4981	.4982	.4982	.4982	.4984	.4984	.4985	.4985	.4986	.4986
3.0	.4987	.4987	.4987	.4988	.4988	.4989	.4989	.4989	.4990	.4990

glossary

abandonment option Allows a company to reduce the capacity of its output in response to changing market conditions. This includes the option to contract production or abandon a project if market conditions deteriorate too much. *(p. 355)*

absolute purchasing power parity Implies that the level of exchange rates adjusts so that identical goods cost the same in different countries. Sometimes referred to as the "law of one price." *(p. 629)*

accounting profit A firm's net income as reported on its income statement. *(p. 36)*

account receivable Created when a good is shipped or a service is performed, and payment for that good is not made on a cash basis, but on a credit basis. *(p. 548)*

acquiring company A company that seeks to acquire another firm. *(p. 682)*

acquisition method Outlines the accounting when an acquirer obtains control of a business. Generally requires assets acquired and liabilities assumed to be measured at their fair values at the acquisition date. *(p. 693)*

actual, or realized, rate of return, $\bar{r}_s$ The rate of return that was actually realized at the end of some holding period. *(p. 243)*

additional funds needed (AFN) Those funds required from external sources to increase the firm's assets to support a sales increase. A sales increase will normally require an increase in assets. However, some of this increase is usually offset by a spontaneous increase in liabilities as well as by earnings retained in the firm. Those funds that are required but not generated internally must be obtained from external sources. *(p. 134)*

add-on interest Interest calculated over the life of the loan and then added on to the loan amount. This total amount is paid in equal installments. This raises the effective cost of the loan. *(p. 528)*

agency bond Bonds issued by Crown corporations to finance their operations. Canada Mortgage Trust is an issuer of agency bonds. Agency bonds are ultimately backed by the government that owns the Crown corporation. *(p. 176)*

agency costs Expenses, either direct or indirect, that are borne by a principal as a result of having delegated authority to an agent. An example is the costs borne by shareholders to encourage managers to maximize a firm's stock price rather than act in their own self-interests. These costs may also arise from lost efficiency and the expense of monitoring management to ensure that debtholders' rights are protected. *(p. 659)*

agency problem Can occur when owners authorize someone else to act on their behalf as their agents. For example, managers may make decisions that benefit themselves rather than making decisions to maximize the firm's fundamental stock price. *(p. 6)*

aging schedule Breaks down accounts receivable according to how long they have been outstanding. This gives the firm a more complete picture of the structure of accounts receivable than that provided by days' sales outstanding. *(p. 552)*

American option An option that can be exercised any time up to and including the expiration date. *(p. 574)*

amortization schedule A table that breaks down the periodic fixed payment of an installment loan into its principal and interest components. *(pp. 118, 121)*

amortized loan A loan repaid in equal periodic amounts (or "killed off" over time). *(pp. 117, 121)*

annual percentage rate (APR) The nominal annual interest rate is also called the annual percentage rate, or APR. *(pp. 113, 528)*

annuity A series of payments of a fixed amount for a specified number of periods. *(p. 101)*

annuity due An annuity with payments occurring at the beginning of each period. *(p. 121)*

arbitrage The simultaneous buying and selling of the same commodity or security in two different markets at different prices, thus pocketing a risk-free return. *(pp. 375, 580, 622, 696)*

arbitrage pricing theory (APT) An approach to measuring the equilibrium risk/return relationship for a given stock as a function of multiple factors, rather than the single factor (the market return) used by the Capital Asset Pricing Model. The APT which is based on complex mathematical and statistical theory, can account for several factors (such as GNP and the level of inflation) in determining the required return for a particular stock. *(p. 234)*

arrearages Preferred dividends that have not been paid, and hence are "in arrears." *(p. 253)*

asset management ratios A set of ratios that measure how effectively a firm is managing its assets. *(pp. 64, 81)*

assets-in-place The land, buildings, machines, and inventory that the firm uses in its operations to produce its products and services. Also known as operating assets. *(pp. 651, 669)*

asymmetric information Assumes managers have more complete information than investors about a firm's prospects—can have an important effect on capital structure. *(p. 386)*

average loss The average loss associated with a particular type of risk. *(Web Extension 20A-1)*

average payables period (APP) Used to appraise payables and indicates the length of time a company takes to pay its suppliers after it has made a purchase. It is found by dividing payables by average operating costs per day (or average cost of goods sold per day). *(p. 66)*

average tax rate The total amount of tax paid divided by taxable income. *(p. 48)*

balance sheets Statements of the firm's financial position at a specific point in time. A balance sheet specifically lists the firm's assets on the left-hand side of the balance sheet, while the right-hand side shows its liabilities and equity, or the claims against these assets. *(p. 27)*

banker's acceptance A short-term financing source used by large corporations; it is unconditionally guaranteed by a bank. *(p. 641)*

basic earning power (BEP) ratio Calculated by dividing earnings before interest and taxes by total assets. Shows the raw earning power of the firm's assets, before the influence of taxes and leverage. *(pp. 71, 81)*

benchmarking When a firm compares its ratios to other leading companies in the same industry. *(pp. 78, 81)*

best efforts A type of contract with an investment banker when issuing stock. In a best efforts sale, the investment banker is only committed to making every effort to sell the stock at the offering price. In this case, the issuing firm bears the risk that the new issue will not be fully subscribed. *(pp. 439, 450)*

beta coefficient, b A measure of a stock's market risk, or the extent to which the returns on a given stock move with the stock market. *(pp. 211, 222)*

binomial approach A method of pricing options that assumes the creation of a series of hedged option positions. *(p. 577)*

bird-in-the-hand theory Assumes that investors value a dollar of dividends more highly than a dollar of expected capital gains because the dividend yield component, D_1/P_0 is less risky than the g component in the total expected return equation $\bar{r}_s = D_1/P_0 + g$. *(p. 424)*

Black-Scholes option pricing model A model to estimate the value of a call option. It is widely used by option traders. *(p. 580)*

bond A promissory note issued by a business or a governmental unit. *(p. 159)*

breakup value A firm's value if its assets are sold off in pieces. *(p. 680)*

business risk The risk inherent in the operations of the firm, prior to the financing decision. Thus, business risk is the uncertainty inherent in a total risk sense, future operating income, or earnings before interest and taxes. Business risk is caused by many factors. Two of the most important are sales variability and operating leverage. *(p. 369)*

call option An option that allows the holder to buy the asset at some predetermined price within a specified period of time. *(p. 573)*

call provision Gives the issuing corporation the right to call the bonds for redemption. The call provision generally states that if the bonds are called, the company must pay the bondholders an amount greater than the par value, a call premium. Most bonds contain a call provision. *(pp. 161, 185)*

Capital Asset Pricing Model (CAPM) A model based on the proposition that any stock's required rate of return is equal to the risk-free rate of return plus a risk premium reflecting only the risk remaining after diversification. The CAPM equation is $r_i = r_{RF} + b_i(r_M - r_{RF})$. *(p. 210)*

capital budgeting The whole process of analyzing projects and deciding whether they should be included in the capital budget. *(p. 300)*

capital cost allowance (CCA) The Canada Revenue Agency's term for depreciation when calculating taxes. *(p. 47)*

capital gain The profit from the sale of a capital asset for more than its purchase price. *(p. 22)*

capital gains yield Results from changing prices and is calculated as $(P_1 - P_0)/P_0$, where P_0 is the beginning-of-period price and P_1 is the end-of-period price. *(pp. 170, 243)*

capital intensity ratio The dollar amount of assets required to produce a dollar of sales. The capital intensity ratio is the reciprocal of the total assets turnover ratio. *(p. 136)*

capitalizing the lease Incorporating the lease provisions into the balance sheet by reporting the leased asset under fixed assets and reporting the present value of future lease payments as debt. *(p. 464)*

capital leases Another name for financial leases. *(p. 462)*

capital loss The loss from the sale of a capital asset for less than its purchase price. *(pp. 49, 51)*

capital rationing Occurs when investors or management place a constraint on the size of the firm's capital budget during a particular period. *(p. 321)*

capital structure The manner in which a firm's assets are financed; that is, the right side of the balance sheet. Capital structure is normally expressed as the percentage of each type of capital used by the firm such as debt, preferred stock, and common equity. *(p. 367)*

cash budget A schedule showing cash flows (receipts, disbursements, and cash balances) for a firm over a specified period. *(p. 515)*

cash conversion cycle The length of time between the firm's actual cash expenditures on productive resources (materials and labour) and its own cash receipts from the sale of products (i.e., the length of time between paying for labour and materials and collecting on receivables). Thus, the cash conversion cycle equals the length of time the firm has funds tied up in current assets. *(p. 532)*

cash discounts The amount by which a seller is willing to reduce the invoice price in order to be paid immediately, rather than in the future. A cash discount might be 2/10, net 30, which means a 2% discount if the bill is paid within 10 days, otherwise the entire amount is due within 30 days. *(p. 550)*

cash flow (CF$_t$) Refers to uneven cash flows, where the t is the period in which the cash flow occurs. *(p. 109)*

cheque-clearing process When a customer's cheque is written upon one bank and a company deposits the cheque in its own bank, the company's bank must verify that the cheque is valid before the company can use those funds. Cheques are cleared through the Automated Clearing Settlement System in Canada. *(p. 546)*

clientele effect The attraction of companies with specific dividend policies to those investors whose needs are best served by those policies. Thus, companies with high dividends will have a clientele of investors with low marginal tax rates and strong desires for current income. Similarly, companies with low dividends will attract a clientele with little need for current income and who often have high marginal tax rates. *(pp. 408, 424)*

closely held Closely held companies are usually small, owned by a small number of people, typically managers and their common shares are not actively traded. *(pp. 238, 261)*

coefficient of variation, (CV) Equal to the standard deviation divided by the expected return; it is a standardized risk measure that allows comparisons between investments having different expected returns and standard deviations. *(p. 201)*

collections float Float created while funds from customers' cheques are being deposited and cleared through the cheque collection process. *(p. 546)*

combination leases Combines some aspects of both operating and financial leases. For example, a financial lease that contains a cancellation clause—normally associated with operating leases—is a combination lease. *(p. 462)*

commercial paper Unsecured, short-term promissory notes of large firms, usually issued in denominations of $100,000 or more and having an interest rate of somewhat below the prime rate. *(pp. 524, 533)*

commodity futures Futures contracts that involve the sale or purchase of various commodities, including grains, oilseeds, livestock, meats, fibre, metals, and wood. *(pp. 602, 611)*

Companies' Creditors Arrangements Act (CCAA) One of two federal acts governing bankruptcy and reorganization in Canada. The CCAA provides more flexibility than the BIA for insolvent companies. Only companies having liabilities over $5 million can use the CCAA. *(p. 184)*

compounding The process of finding the future value of a single payment or series of payments. *(p. 90)*

computer/telephone network A network, such as Nasdaq, that consists of all the facilities that provide for security transactions not conducted at a physical location exchange. These facilities are, basically, the communications networks that link buyers and sellers. *(p. 433)*

congeneric merger Involves firms that are interrelated but that do not have identical lines of business. One example is Advanced Micro Devices acquisition & ATI Technologies. *(pp. 681, 700)*

conglomerate merger Occurs when unrelated enterprises combine, such as Mobil Oil and Montgomery Ward. *(pp. 681, 700)*

consols Another term for perpetuity. Consols were originally bonds issued by England in 1815 to consolidate past debt. *(p. 108)*

conversion price, P$_c$ The effective price per share of stock if conversion occurs; the par value of the convertible security divided by the conversion ratio. *(pp. 485, 498)*

conversion ratio, CR The number of shares of common stock received upon conversion of one convertible security. *(p. 485)*

convertible bonds Security that is convertible into shares of common stock, at a fixed price, at the option of the bondholder. *(pp. 163, 185)*

convertible currencies Currencies that can be traded in the currency markets and that can be redeemed at current market rates. *(p. 626)*

convertible securities Bonds or preferred stocks that can be exchanged for (converted into) common stock, under specific terms, at the option of the holder. Unlike the exercise of warrants, conversion of a convertible security does not provide additional capital to the issuer. *(p. 485)*

corporate bonds Debt issued by corporations and exposed to default risk. Different corporate bonds have different levels of default risk, depending on the issuing company's characteristics and on the terms of the specific bond. *(p. 160)*

corporate governance The set of rules that controls a company's behaviour toward its directors, managers, employees, shareholders, creditors, customers, competitors, and community. *(p. 658)*

corporate (or strategic) alliances Cooperative deals that stop short of a merger; also called strategic alliances. *(p. 698)*

corporate valuation model Defines the total value of a company as the value of operations plus the value of nonoperating assets plus the value of growth options. *(pp. 650, 701)*

corporation A legal entity created by provincial or federal law. The corporation is separate and distinct from its owners and managers. *(p. 5)*

correlation The tendency of two variables to move together. *(p. 203)*

correlation coefficient, ρ (rho) A standardized measure of how two random variables covary. A correlation coefficient (ρ) of +1.0 means that the two variables move up and down in perfect synchronization, while a coefficient of −1.0 means the variables always move in opposite directions. A correlation coefficient of zero suggests that the two variables are not related to each other; that is, they are independent. *(p. 203)*

costly trade credit Credit taken in excess of free trade credit whose cost is equal to the discount lost. *(pp. 521, 533)*

cost of new common equity, r_e Projects financed with external equity must earn a higher rate of return, because the project must cover the flotation costs. Thus, the cost of new common equity is higher than that of common equity raised internally by reinvesting earnings. *(p. 280)*

counterparty risk The risk that the counterparty to a transaction will not be able to make required payments when due. *(p. 600)*

coupon interest rate Stated rate of interest on a bond, defined as the coupon payment divided by the par value. *(p. 160)*

coupon payment Dollar amount of interest paid to each bondholder on the interest payment dates. *(p. 160)*

covered option Occurs when a trader writes (sells) an option while having the underlying position to cover the position in the event that the option is exercised. *(p. 575)*

credit default swap A specific type of credit derivative where the underlying reference asset is a credit obligation such as a bond or a bank loan of a specific company. One counterparty (the protection buyer) makes a periodic payment (the credit default swap premium) to the second counterparty (the protection seller). If the underlying reference asset suffers a credit event such as bankruptcy, the protection seller will make a payment to the protection buyer. Credit default swaps allow protection buyers to hedge themselves against credit risk, and protection sellers to invest based on their assessment of credit risk. *(p. 495)*

credit derivative A derivative contract where the cash flows are contingent on the credit risk or credit events specific to a reference asset (such as a bond, bank loan, or mortgage) or a collection of reference assets. Two examples of credit derivatives are credit default swaps and collateralized debt obligations. *(p. 494)*

credit period The length of time for which credit is extended. If the credit period is lengthened, then sales will generally increase, as will accounts receivable. This will increase the firm's financing needs and possibly increase bad debt losses. A shortening of the credit period will have the opposite effect. *(p. 575)*

credit standards The financial strength and creditworthiness that qualifies a customer for a firm's regular credit terms. *(pp. 549, 563)*

credit terms Statements of the credit period and any discounts offered—for example, 2/10, net 30. *(pp. 549, 563)*

cross rate The exchange rate between two non–U.S. currencies. *(p. 620)*

cum dividend "With" dividend. A stock trades cum dividend up until two business days prior to the holder-of-record date. *(p. 414)*

currency appreciation Occurs to a particular currency when it increases in value relative to another particular currency. For example, if the exchange rate of 1.0 dollar per euro changes to 1.1 dollars per euro, then the euro has appreciated against the dollar by 10%. *(p. 624)*

currency depreciation Occurs to a particular currency when it decreases in value relative to another particular currency. For example, if the exchange rate of 1.0 dollar per euro changes to 0.9 dollars per euro, then the euro has depreciated against the dollar by 10%. *(p. 624)*

currency swaps Bilateral agreements to exchange periodic payments where the payments are based in two different currencies. *(p. 606)*

current ratio Indicates the extent to which current liabilities are covered by those assets expected to be converted to cash in the near future; it is found by dividing current assets by current liabilities. *(pp. 62, 81)*

current yield (on a bond) The annual coupon payment divided by the current market price. *(p. 169)*

days' sales outstanding (DSO) Used to appraise accounts receivable and indicates the length of time the firm must wait after making a sale before receiving cash. It is found by dividing receivables by average sales per day. *(pp. 551, 563)*

dealer market In a dealer market, a dealer holds an inventory of the security and makes a market by offering to buy or sell. Others who wish to buy or sell can see the offers made by the dealers and can contact the dealer of their choice to arrange a transaction. *(p. 433)*

debenture An unsecured bond; as such, it provides no lien against specific property as security for the obligation. Debenture holders are, therefore, general creditors whose claims are protected by property not otherwise pledged. *(pp. 176, 185)*

debt ratio The ratio of total debt to total assets, it measures the percentage of funds provided by investors other than preferred or common shareholders. Also called *debt-to-assets ratio*. *(p. 68)*

debt-to-equity (D/E) ratio Ratio of debt divided by equity. *(pp. 68, 81)*

decision tree A form of scenario analysis in which different actions are taken in different scenarios. *(p. W-19)*

declaration date The date on which a firm's directors issue a statement declaring a dividend. *(p. 414)*

default risk The risk that a borrower will not pay the interest and/or principal on a loan as it becomes due. If the issuer defaults, investors receive less than the promised return on the bond. Default risk is influenced by both the financial strength of the issuer and the terms of the bond contract, especially whether collateral has been

NEL

pledged to secure the bond. The greater the default risk, the higher the bond's yield to maturity. *(p. 186)*

degree of financial leverage (DFL) Defined as the percentage change in earnings per share that results from a given percentage change in earnings before interest and taxes (EBIT). *(Web Extension 12A-4)*

degree of operating leverage (DOL) Defined as the percentage change in operating income (or EBIT) that results from a given percentage change in sales. *(Web Extension 12A-1)*

degree of total leverage (DTL) Shows how a given change in sales will affect earnings per share. *(Web Extension 12A-5)*

derivatives Claims whose value depends on what happens to the value of some other asset. Futures and options are two important types of derivatives, and their values depend on what happens to the prices of other assets. Therefore, the value of a derivative security is derived from the value of an underlying real asset or other security. *(pp. 12, 592)*

detachable A warrant that can be detached and traded separately from the underlying security. Most warrants are detachable. *(p. 484)*

devaluation The lowering, by governmental action, of the price of its currency relative to another currency. For example, in 1967 the British pound was devalued from US$2.80 per pound to US$2.50 per pound. *(p. 625)*

direct losses Occur when property is destroyed, damaged, or lost. *(Web Extension 20A-2)*

direct quotation When discussing exchange rates, the number of units of home currency required to purchase one unit of a foreign currency. *(pp. 620, 643)*

disbursement float Float created before cheques written by a firm have cleared and been deducted from the firm's account. Disbursement float causes the firm's own cheque-book balance to be smaller than the balance on the bank's records. *(p. 546)*

discount bond Bond prices and interest rates are inversely related; that is, they tend to move in the opposite direction from each other. A fixed-rate bond will sell at par when its coupon interest rate is equal to the going rate of interest, r_d. When the going rate of interest is above the coupon rate, a fixed-rate bond will sell at a "discount" below its par value. If current interest rates are below the coupon rate, a fixed-rate bond will sell at a "premium" above its par value. *(p. 167)*

discounted cash flow (DCF) method A method of valuing a business that involves the application of capital budgeting procedures to an entire firm rather than to a single project. *(p. 278)*

discounted payback period The number of years it takes a firm to recover its project investment based on discounted cash flows. *(p. 313)*

discounting The process of finding the present value of a single payment or series of payments. *(p. 97)*

discount interest Interest that is calculated on the face amount of a loan but is paid in advance. *(p. 526)*

distribution policy The policy that sets the level of distributions and the form of the distributions (dividends and stock repurchases). *(p. 404)*

diversifiable risk Refers to that part of a security's total risk associated with random events not affecting the market as a whole. This risk can be eliminated by proper diversification. Also known as company-specific risk. *(pp. 210, 222)*

divestiture The opposite of an acquisition. That is, a company sells a portion of its assets, often a whole division, to another firm or individual. *(p. 699)*

dividend irrelevance theory Holds that dividend policy has no effect on either the price of a firm's stock or its cost of capital. *(p. 404)*

dividend reinvestment plan (DRIP) Allows shareholders to automatically purchase shares of common stock of the paying corporation in lieu of receiving cash dividends. There are two types of plans—one involves only stock that is already outstanding, while the other involves newly issued stock. In the first type, the dividends of all participants are pooled and the stock is purchased on the open market. Participants benefit from lower transaction costs. In the second type, the company issues new shares to the participants. Thus, the company issues stock in lieu of the cash dividend. *(p. 423)*

dividend yield Defined as either the end-of-period dividend divided by the beginning-of-period price, or the ratio of the current dividend to the current price. Valuation formulas use the former definition. *(p. 243)*

dual-class shares Sometimes created by a firm to meet special needs and circumstances. Generally, when special classifications of stock are used, one type is designated "Class A," another as "Class B," and so on. For example, Class A might be entitled to receive dividends before dividends can be paid on Class B stock. Class B might have the exclusive right to vote. *(p. 239)*

DuPont equation A formula which shows that the rate of return on equity can be found as the product of the profit margin times the total assets turnover times the equity multiplier. *(p. 77)*

EBITDA Earnings before interest, taxes, depreciation, and amortization. *(p. 29)*

EBITDA coverage ratio Similar to the times-interest-earned ratio, but it recognizes that many firms lease assets and also must make sinking fund payments. It is found by adding earnings before interest, taxes, depreciation, and amortization and lease payments, then dividing this total by interest charges, lease payments, and sinking fund payments over 1 minus the tax rate. *(pp. 69, 81)*

economic ordering quantity (EOQ) model A formula for determining the order quantity that will minimize total inventory costs. *(p. 558)*

economic perils Risks occurring through events in the broader economic landscape such a change in economic growth or changes in a competitor's strategy. *(Web Extension 20A-2)*

Economic Value Added (EVA) A method used to measure a firm's true profitability. EVA is found by taking the firm's after-tax operating profit and subtracting the annual cost of all the capital a firm uses. If the firm generates a positive EVA, its management has created value for its shareholders. If the EVA is negative, management has destroyed shareholder value. *(p. 43)*

efficient markets hypothesis (EMH) States (1) that stocks are always in equilibrium and (2) that it is impossible for an investor to consistently "beat the market." The EMH assumes that all important information regarding a stock is reflected in the price of that stock. *(p. 257)*

efficient portfolio Provide the highest expected return for any degree of risk. The efficient portfolio is that which provides the lowest degree of risk for any expected return. *(pp. 206, 222)*

electronic communications network (ECN) In an electronic communications network, orders from potential buyers and sellers are automatically matched and the transaction is automatically completed. *(p. 433)*

embedded options Options that are a part of another project. Also called real options, managerial options, and strategic options. *(pp. 354, 357)*

enterprise risk management (ERM) A term to describe managing all of the different types of risks that a firm may face in a holistic and integrated manner. Also called *integrated risk management. (pp. 595, 610)*

entity multiple A measure of stock valuation. Calculated by adding the firm's market value of debt and equity and then dividing it by the firm's earnings before interest, taxes, depreciation, and amortization (EBITDA). *(p. 252)*

equilibrium The condition under which the intrinsic value of a security is equal to its price; also, its expected return is equal to its required return. *(p. 255)*

equity carve-out When a parent company sells to the public a minority interest of shares in a wholly-owned subsidiary but retains full control of the subsidiary. Sometimes called a "partial public offering" or a "spin-out." *(p. 444)*

equity residual model Also called *free cash flow to equity approach.* Discounts the projected free cash flows to equity at the cost of equity to determine the value of equity from operations. *(p. 683)*

equity risk premium, RP$_M$ Expected market return minus the risk-free rate. Also called *market risk premium or equity premium. (p. 274)*

equivalent annual annuity (EAA) method A method for comparing mutually exclusive projects with unequal lives. The NPVs of the projects are converted into an annuity payment with a life equal to the life of the project. The project with the higher annuity should be selected. *(p. 322)*

Eurobond Any bond sold in some country other than the one in whose currency the bond is denominated.

Thus, a U.S. firm selling dollar bonds in Switzerland is selling Eurobonds. *(p. 635)*

Eurocurrency A time deposit of a currency made in a bank account outside the country that issued the currency. *(p. 633)*

Eurodollar A US dollar on deposit in a foreign bank or in a foreign branch of a U.S. bank. Eurodollars are used to conduct transactions throughout Europe and the rest of the world. *(p. 633)*

European option An option that can be exercised only on the maturity date or the expiration date. *(p. 574)*

euro The currency used by the nations in the European Monetary Union. *(p. 620)*

exchange rate Specifies the number of units of a given currency that can be purchased for one unit of another currency. *(p. 619)*

exchange rate risk The fluctuation in exchange rates between currencies over time. *(p. 643)*

ex-dividend date The date when the right to the dividend leaves the stock. This date was established by stockbrokers to avoid confusion and is two business days prior to the holder-of-record date. If the stock sale is made prior to the ex-dividend date, the dividend is paid to the buyer. If the stock is bought on or after the ex-dividend date, the dividend is paid to the seller. *(p. 414)*

exercise price The price stated in the option contract at which the security can be bought (or sold). Also called the strike price. *(p. 573)*

exercise value Equal to the current price of the stock (underlying the option) less the strike price of the option. *(p. 574)*

expected rate of return, r̂ The rate of return expected on a stock given its current price and expected future cash flows. If the stock is in equilibrium, the required rate of return will equal the expected rate of return. *(p. 196)*

expiration date The date that an option expires and the maturity value is calculated. Also known as the maturity date. *(p. 574)*

externalities Effects a project has on other parts of the firm or on the environment. *(p. 334)*

factoring Financing method where a firm sells its accounts receivables, usually to a specialized financing company, at a discount to their full value. *(p. 529)*

financial engineering The term used to describe using principles of finance to create new financial products. *(p. W-11)*

financial futures Provide for the purchase or sale of a financial asset at some time in the future, but at a price established today. Financial futures exist for Treasury bills, Treasury notes and bonds, certificates of deposit, Eurodollar deposits, foreign currencies, and stock indexes. *(p. 602)*

financial intermediary An intermediary that buys securities with funds that it obtains by issuing its own securities. An example is a common stock mutual fund that buys common stocks with funds obtained by issuing shares in the mutual fund. *(p. 12)*

financial leases Covers the entire expected life of the equipment; does not provide for maintenance service, is not cancellable, and is fully amortized. *(p. 462)*

financial leverage The extent to which fixed-income securities (debt and preferred stock) are used in a firm's capital structure. If a high percentage of a firm's capital structure is in the form of debt and preferred stock, then the firm is said to have a high degree of financial leverage. *(p. 67)*

financial risk The risk added by the use of debt financing. Debt financing increases the variability of earnings before taxes (but after interest); thus, along with business risk, it contributes to the uncertainty of net income and earnings per share. Business risk plus financial risk equals total corporate risk. *(p. 372)*

financing feedback Circularity created when additional debt causes additional interest expense, which reduces the addition to retained earnings, which in turn requires a higher level of debt, which causes still more interest expense, causing the cycle to be repeated. *(p. 139)*

fixed assets turnover ratio Measures how effectively the firm uses its plant and equipment. It is the ratio of sales to net fixed assets. *(p. 67)*

fixed exchange rate system The system in effect from the end of the Second World War until August 1971. Under the system, the US dollar was linked to gold at the rate of $35 per ounce, and other currencies were then tied to the dollar. *(p. 624)*

flexibility options Allows a company to alter operations depending on how conditions change during the life of a project. This usually includes the ability to change inputs or outputs (or both). *(p. 355)*

floating exchange rate System currently in effect where the forces of supply and demand are allowed to determine currency prices with little government intervention. *(p. 624)*

floating-rate bonds Bonds whose coupon payment may vary over time. The coupon rate is usually linked to the rate on some other security, such as a government bond, or to some other rate, such as the prime rate or LIBOR. *(p. 161)*

flotation costs Those costs occurring when a company issues a new security, including fees to an investment banker and legal fees. *(p. 280)*

forecasted financial statement (FFS) approach A method of forecasting financial statements to determine the additional funds needed. Many items on the income statement and balance sheet are assumed to increase proportionally with sales. As sales increase, these items that are tied to sales also increase, and the values of these items for a particular year are estimated as percentages of the forecasted sales for that year. *(p. 136)*

foreign bonds Bonds sold by a foreign borrower but denominated in the currency of the country in which the issue is sold. Thus, a Canadian firm selling bonds denominated in Swiss francs in Switzerland is selling foreign bonds. *(p. 634)*

foreign exchange risks The risk that currency fluctuations will change the realized cash flows from foreign operations. *(p. 600)*

foreign trade deficit Occurs when businesses and individuals in one country import more goods from foreign countries than are exported from the country. *(p. 15)*

forward contract A contract to buy or sell some item at some time in the future at a price established when the contract is entered into. *(p. 600)*

forward exchange rate The prevailing exchange rate for exchange (delivery) at some agreed-upon future date, usually 30, 90, or 180 days from the day the transaction is negotiated. *(p. 627)*

free cash flows (FCF) The cash flows actually available for distribution to all investors after the company has made all investments in fixed assets and working capital necessary to sustain ongoing operations. *(p. 10)*

free cash flow to equity approach Discounts the projected free cash flows to equity at the cost of equity to determine the value of equity from operations. *(p. 683)*

free cash flow to equity (FCFE) The cash flow available for distribution to common shareholders. *(p. 683)*

free trade credit Credit received during the discount period. *(p. 521)*

friendly merger Occurs when the target company's management agrees to the merger and recommends that shareholders approve the deal. *(p. 682)*

futures contract An exchange–traded contract that commits two counterparties to trade a specific asset at a specific price in the future. *(p. 611)*

future value of the annuity FVA$_N$ The ending value of a stream of equal payments, where N is the number of payments of the annuity. *(p. 101)*

going private A corporate transaction in which the entire equity of a publicly traded firm is purchased by a small group of investors. *(p. 447)*

Going public The act of selling stock to the public at large by a closely held corporation or its principal shareholders. *(p. 437)*

golden parachutes Payments made to executives who are forced out when a merger takes place. *(p. 696)*

greenmail Targeted share repurchases that occur when a company buys back stock from a potential acquirer at a higher than fair-market price. In return, the potential acquirer agrees not to attempt to take over the company. *(p. 663)*

gross profit margin Ratio of gross profit (sales minus cost of goods sold) divided by sales. *(p. 71)*

growth options Occurs if an investment creates the opportunity to make other potentially profitable investments that would not otherwise be possible, including options to expand output, options to enter a new geographical market, and options to introduce complementary products or successive generations of products. *(p. 355)*

half-year rule States that a company can claim only half the CCA in the first year the asset was purchased. *(p. 336)*

Hamada equation Shows the effect of debt on the beta coefficient—increases in debt increase beta, and decreases in debt reduce beta. *(p. 379)*

hard currencies Currencies considered to be convertible because the nation that issues them allows them to be traded in the currency markets and is willing to redeem them at market rates. *(p. 626)*

hedge portfolio A portfolio of the underlying asset that offsets the value of an option. Also called *replicating portfolio*. *(p. 577)*

holder-of-record date If a company lists the shareholder as an owner on the holder-of-record date, then the shareholder receives the dividend. *(p. 414)*

horizon, or terminal, value The value of operations at the end of the explicit forecast period. It is equal to the present value of all free cash flows beyond the forecast period, discounted back to the end of the forecast period at the weighted average cost of capital. *(pp. 250, 655)*

horizontal merger A merger between two companies in the same line of business. *(p. 680)*

hostile merger Occurs when the management of the target company resists the offer. *(p. 700)*

hurdle rate The project cost of capital, or discount rate. It is both the rate used in discounting future cash flows in the net present value method and the rate that is compared to the internal rate of return. *(p. 305)*

income bond Pays interest only if the interest is earned. These securities cannot bankrupt a company, but from an investor's standpoint, they are riskier than "regular" bonds. *(pp. 163, 185)*

incremental cash flow Those cash flows that arise solely from the asset that is being evaluated. *(p. 333)*

indenture A legal document that spells out the rights of both bondholders and the issuing corporation. *(p. 175)*

independent projects Projects that can be accepted or rejected individually. *(p. 303)*

indexed bonds The interest rate of such a bond is based on an inflation index such as the consumer price index (CPI), so the interest paid rises automatically when the inflation rate rises, thus protecting the bondholders against inflation. *(p. 163)*

indirect losses Losses that stem from direct losses, such as lost sales while damaged property is being repaired. *(Web Extension 20A-2)*

indirect quotations When discussing exchange rates, the number of units of foreign currency that can be purchased for one unit of home currency. *(p. 620)*

inflation premium (IP) The premium added to the real risk-free rate of interest to compensate for the expected loss of purchasing power. The inflation premium is the average rate of inflation expected over the life of the security. *(p. 174)*

information, or signalling, content A theory that holds that investors regard dividend changes as "signals" of management forecasts. Thus, when dividends are raised, this is viewed by investors as recognition by management of future earnings increases. Therefore, if a firm's stock price increases with a dividend increase, the reason may not be investor preference for dividends but expectations of higher future earnings. Conversely, a dividend reduction may signal that management is forecasting poor earnings in the future. *(p. 409)*

initial public offering (IPO) Occurs when a closely held corporation or its principal shareholders sell stock to the public at large. *(p. 20)*

interest rate parity Holds that investors should expect to earn the same return in all countries after adjusting for risk. *(pp. 628, 643)*

interest rate risk Arises from the fact that bond prices decline when interest rates rise. Under these circumstances, selling a bond prior to maturity will result in a capital loss; the longer the term to maturity, the larger the loss. *(p. 180)*

interest yield Calculated by dividing the coupon payment by the bond's current market price. Also called *current yield*. *(p. 170)*

internal rate of return (IRR) method The discount rate that equates the present value of the expected future cash inflows and outflows. IRR measures the rate of return on a project, but it assumes that all cash flows can be reinvested at the IRR rate. *(p. 304)*

international bond Any bond sold outside the country of the borrower. There are two types of international bonds: Eurobonds and foreign bonds. *(p. 633)*

in-the-money An option that, if exercised, would have a positive payoff to the option buyer. *(p. 574)*

intrinsic, or fundamental, value The present value of a firm's expected future free cash flows. *(p. 243)*

inventory blanket lien Gives a lending institution a claim against all of the borrower's inventories. *(p. 530)*

inventory conversion period The average length of time to convert materials into finished goods and then to sell them; calculated by dividing total inventory by sales per day. *(p. 532)*

inventory turnover ratio Sales divided by inventories. *(p. 64)*

inverted, or abnormal, yield curve A downward-sloping yield curve. *(p. 183)*

investment banks Firms that assist in the design of an issuing firm's corporate securities and in the sale of the new securities to investors in the primary market. *(p. 438)*

investment-grade bonds Securities with ratings of Baa/BBB or above. *(p. 176)*

investment timing option Gives companies the option to delay a project rather than implement it immediately.

This option to wait allows a company to reduce the uncertainty of market conditions before it decides to implement the project. *(p. 354)*

joint venture Involves the joining together of parts of companies to accomplish specific, limited objectives. Joint ventures are controlled by the combined management of the two (or more) parent companies. *(p. 698)*

junk bonds High-risk, high-yield bonds issued to finance leveraged buyouts, mergers, or troubled companies. *(p. 176)*

just-in-time (JIT) An inventory system used to hold down inventory costs and simultaneously improve the production process. *(p. 556)*

leveraged buyouts (LBOs) Transaction in which a firm's publicly owned stock is acquired in a mostly debt-financed tender offer, and a privately owned, highly leveraged firm results. Often, the firm's own management initiates the LBO. *(pp. 678, 384)*

leveraged lease The lessor borrows a portion of the funds needed to buy the equipment to be leased. *(p. 472)*

liability A cost when a corporate's responsibility has not been met. *(Web Extension 20A-3)*

LIBOR London Interbank Offered Rate; the rate that large banks in London charge one another. *(p. 633)*

limited liability partnership (LLP) A limited liability partnership (LLP) (sometimes called a limited liability company [LLC] in the United States) combines the limited liability advantage of a corporation with the tax advantages of a partnership. *(p. 5)*

limited partnership A partnership in which limited partners' liabilities, investment returns, and control are limited, while general partners have unlimited liability and control. *(p. 4)*

line of credit An arrangement in which a bank agrees to lend up to a specified maximum amount of funds during a designated period. *(p. 524)*

liquidity A firm's cash and marketable securities position, refers to its ability to meet maturing obligations. A liquid asset is any asset that can be quickly sold and converted to cash at its "fair" value. Active markets provide liquidity. *(p. 314)*

liquidity premiums (LPs) Premiums added to the real risk-free rate of interest, in addition to other premiums, if a security is not liquid. *(p. 179)*

liquidity ratio Shows the relationship of a firm's cash and other current assets to its current liabilities. *(pp. 62, 81)*

lockbox plan A cash management tool in which incoming cheques for a firm are sent to post office boxes rather than to corporate headquarters. A local bank will collect the contents of the lockbox and deposit the cheques into the company's local account. *(p. 546)*

long hedges Occur when futures contracts are bought in anticipation of (or to guard against) price increases. *(p. 602)*

loss frequency The probability or the frequency that a risk causing a loss occurs. *(Web Extension 20A-1)*

loss severity The dollar value of a loss (or potential loss). *(Web Extension 20A-1)*

lumpy assets Those assets that cannot be acquired smoothly, and that require large, discrete additions. For example, an electric utility that is operating at full capacity cannot add a small amount of generating capacity, at least not economically. *(p. 146)*

managed floating rate System used by some governments to manage the exchange rate by manipulating the currency's supply and demand to keep it within a pre-determined range. *(p. 625)*

managerial options Options that give opportunities to managers to respond to changing market conditions. Also called real options. *(pp. 354, 357)*

Maple bonds Foreign corporate or foreign government bonds issued in Canadian dollars to Canadian investors. Because maples are denominated in Canadian dollars, there is no currency or foreign interest rate risk. *(p. 160)*

margin requirement The margin is the percentage of a stock's price that an investor has borrowed in order to purchase the stock. The Investment Industry Regulatory Organization of Canada (IIROC) sets margin requirements, which are the maximum percentage of debt that can be used to purchase a stock. *(p. 602)*

marginal tax rate The tax rate on the last unit of income. *(p. 48)*

marked-to-market Occurs when the value of a security is valued at its current market value rather than its original price or its exercise value. *(p. 601)*

marketable securities Investments that can be converted to cash on very short notice and provide at least a modest return. *(p. 547)*

market/book (M/B) ratio Ratio of the company's stock price divided by its book value per share *(p. 73)*

market multiple analysis Applies a market-determined multiple to net income, earnings per share, sales, book value, or number of subscribers, and is a less precise method than discounted cash flow. *(pp. 252, 701)*

market portfolio A portfolio consisting of all stocks. *(p. 209)*

market risk That part of a security's total risk that cannot be eliminated by diversification; measured by the beta coefficient. *(p. 210)*

Market Value Added (MVA) The difference between the market value of the firm (i.e., the sum of the market value of common equity, the market value of debt, and the market value of preferred stock) and the book value of the firm's common equity, debt, and preferred stock. If the book values of debt and preferred stock are equal to their market values, then MVA is also equal to the difference between the market value of equity and the amount of equity capital that investors supplied. *(pp. 42, 51)*

market value ratios Relate the firm's stock price to its earnings and book value per share. (*p. 72*)

maturity date The date when the bond's par value is repaid to the bondholder. Maturity dates generally range from 10 to 40 years from the time of issue. (*p. 161*)

maturity matching Matching the maturities of debt used to finance assets with the lives of the assets themselves. The debt would be amortized such that the outstanding amount declined as the asset lost value due to depreciation. (*p. 508*)

maturity risk premiums (MRP) The premium that must be added to the real risk-free rate of interest to compensate for interest rate risk, which depends on a bond's maturity. Interest rate risk arises from the fact that bond prices decline when interest rates rise. Under these circumstances, selling a bond prior to maturity will result in a capital loss; the longer the term to maturity, the larger the loss. (*p. 180*)

maximum loss The dollar loss associated with a worst case scenario occurring. (*Web Extension 20A-1*)

merger The joining of two firms to form a single firm. (*p. 678*)

moderate policy Matches asset and liability maturities. Also referred to as the maturity matching, or self-liquidating, approach. (*p. 507*)

modified IRR or MIRR Assumes that cash flows from all projects are reinvested at the cost of capital as opposed to the project's own IRR. This makes the modified internal rate of return a better indicator of a project's true profitability. (*p. 310*)

money market A financial market for debt securities with maturities of less than 1 year (short term). The New York money market is the world's largest. (*p. 22*)

money market fund Mutual funds that invest in short-term debt instruments and that offer their investors cheque-writing privileges; thus, they are essentially interest-bearing chequing accounts. (*p. 18*)

Monte Carlo simulation A risk analysis technique in which a computer is used to simulate probable future events and thus to estimate the profitability and risk of a project. (*p. 348*)

mortgage bond A bond for which the corporation pledges certain assets as security. All such bonds are written subject to an indenture. (*p. 175*)

multinational (global) corporation A corporation that operates in two or more countries. (*p. 617*)

mutually exclusive Projects that cannot be performed at the same time. A company could choose either Project 1 or Project 2, or it can reject both, but it cannot accept both projects. (*p. 303*)

naked options Occur when a trader buys or sells options without any underlying hedge or position. A naked option is a purely speculative position. (*p. 575*)

National Association of Securities Dealers (NASD) A U.S. industry group primarily concerned with the operation of the over-the-counter (OTC) market. (*p. 436*)

natural hedge A transaction between two counterparties where both parties' risks are reduced. (*p. 601*)

net acquisition When there is a purchase and sale of assets (within the same asset class) in the same year, CCA is calculated on the capital cost of the new asset minus the lesser of the original capital cost or the net proceeds from the asset disposed. (*p. 337*)

net float The difference between a firm's disbursement float and collections float. (*p. 546*)

net operating working capital (NOWC) Operating current assets minus operating current liabilities. Operating current assets are the current assets used to support operations, such as cash, accounts receivable, and inventory. They do not include short-term investments. Operating current liabilities are the current liabilities that are a natural consequence of the firm's operations, such as accounts payable and accruals. They do not include notes payable or any other short-term debt that charges interest. (*p. 38*)

net present value (NPV) method The present value of the project's expected future cash flows, discounted at the appropriate cost of capital. NPV is a direct measure of the value of the project to shareholders. (*p. 302*)

net profit margin Calculated by dividing net income by sales; gives the profit per dollar of sales. (*p. 70*)

net working capital Current assets minus current liabilities. (*p. 507*)

nominal, or quoted, interest rate, I_{NOM} The rate of interest stated in a contract. If the compounding occurs annually, the effective annual rate and the nominal rate are the same. If compounding occurs more frequently, the effective annual rate is greater than the nominal rate. The nominal annual interest rate is also called the annual percentage rate, or APR. (*p. 113*)

nominal rate of return, r_{Nom} Includes an inflation adjustment (premium). Thus if nominal rates of return are used in the capital budgeting process, the net cash flows must also be nominal. (*p. 119*)

nominal risk-free rate of interest, r_{RF} The real risk-free rate plus a premium for expected inflation. The short-term nominal risk-free rate is usually approximated by the Treasury bill rate, while the long-term nominal risk-free rate is approximated by the rate on long-term federal government bonds. (*p. 175*)

non-normal cash flow Projects with a large cash outflow either sometime during or at the end of their lives. A common problem encountered when evaluating projects with non-normal cash flows is multiple internal rates of return. (*p. 308*)

nonoperating assets Include investments in marketable securities and noncontrolling interests in the stock of other companies. (*p. 669*)

nonpecuniary benefits Perks that are not actual cash payments, such as lavish offices, memberships at country clubs, corporate jets, and excessively large staffs. (*p. 660*)

NOPAT (net operating profit after taxes) The amount of profit a company would generate if it had no debt and no financial assets. *(p. 37)*

normal cash flow A project with one or more cash outflows (costs) followed by a series of cash inflows. *(p. 308)*

normal yield curve When the yield curve slopes upward, it is said to be "normal," because it is like this most of the time. *(p. 183)*

notional principle The numerical value that is used for calculating the payments of a derivative transaction. *(p. 605)*

off–balance sheet financing A financing technique in which a firm uses partnerships and other arrangements to effectively borrow money but avoid reporting the liability on its balance sheet. *(pp. 50, 464)*

operating current assets The current assets used to support operations, such as cash, accounts receivable, and inventory. It does not include short-term investments. *(p. 38)*

operating current liabilities The current liabilities that are a natural consequence of the firm's operations, such as accounts payable and accruals. It does not include notes payable or any other short-term debt that charges interest. *(pp. 38, 50)*

operating leases Provides for both financing and maintenance. Generally, the operating lease contract is written for a period considerably shorter than the expected life of the leased equipment and contains a cancellation clause; sometimes called a service lease. *(p. 461)*

operating leverage The extent to which fixed costs are used in a firm's operations. If a high percentage of a firm's total costs are fixed costs, then the firm is said to have a high degree of operating leverage. Operating leverage is a measure of one element of business risk, but does not include the second major element, sales variability. *(p. 370)*

operating merger Occurs when the operations of two companies are integrated with the expectation of obtaining synergistic gains. These may occur due to economies of scale, management efficiency, or a host of other reasons. *(p. 686)*

operating profit margin Ratio of earnings before interest and taxes divided by sales. *(p. 70)*

opportunity cost A cash flow that a firm must forego to accept a project. For example, if the project requires the use of a building that could otherwise be sold, the market value of the building is an opportunity cost of the project. *(p. 97)*

opportunity cost rate The rate of return available on the best alternative investment of similar risk. *(p. 122)*

optimal capital budget The set of projects that maximizes the value of the firm. *(p. 320)*

optimal distribution policy The distribution policy that maximizes the value of the firm by choosing the optimal level and form of distributions (dividends and stock repurchases). *(p. 404)*

option A contract that gives its holder the right to buy or sell an asset at some predetermined price within a specified period of time. *(p. 573)*

out-of-the-money An option that, if exercised, would have zero payoff. *(p. 574)*

outsourcing The practice of purchasing components rather than making them in-house. *(p. 556)*

partnership Exists when two or more persons associate to conduct a business. *(p. 4)*

par value The nominal or face value of a stock or bond. The par value of a bond generally represents the amount of money that the firm borrows and promises to repay at some future date. The par value of a bond is often $1,000 but can be $5,000 or more. *(p. 160)*

payables deferral period The average length of time between a firm's purchase of materials and labour and the payment of cash for them. It is calculated by dividing accounts payable by credit purchases per day (cost of goods sold / 365). *(p. 512)*

payback period The number of years it takes a firm to recover its project investment. Payback does not capture a project's entire cash flow stream and is thus not the preferred evaluation method. Note, however, that the payback does measure a project's liquidity, and hence many firms use it as a risk measure. *(p. 312)*

payment (PMT) Equal to the dollar amount of an equal, or constant cash flow (an annuity). *(p. 109)*

payment date The date on which a firm actually mails dividend cheques. *(p. 414)*

pecking order If flotation costs and asymmetric information exists, firms may raise capital according to a preferred "pecking order": (1) retained earnings, followed by (2) debt, and then (3) new common stock. *(p. 387)*

pegged exchange rates Refers to the rate fixed against a major currency such as the US dollar. Consequently, the values of the pegged currencies move together over time. *(p. 625)*

permanent operating current assets The minimum level of operating current assets a company keeps on its balance sheet. This level always requires financing and can be regarded as permanent. *(p. 508)*

perpetuity A series of payments of a fixed amount that last indefinitely. *(p. 108)*

personal property Assets that are not real property such as manufacturing equipment, corporate vehicles, furniture, or inventories. *(Web Extension 20A-2)*

physical location exchange Exchanges, such as the New York Stock Exchange, that facilitate trading of securities at a particular location. *(p. 433)*

physical perils Natural risks such as fires, floods, and windstorms. *(Web Extension 20A-2)*

pledging accounts receivable Using accounts receivable as security in order to get a loan. *(p. 529)*

plug technique Technique used in financial forecasting to "plug" in enough new liabilities or assets to make the balance sheet balance. *(p. 137)*

poison pill Shareholder rights provisions that allow existing shareholders in a company to purchase additional shares of stock at a lower than market value if a potential acquirer purchases a controlling stake in the company. *(p. 663)*

political risk The possibility of expropriation and the unanticipated restriction of cash flows to the parent by a foreign government. *(p. 636)*

portfolio A group of individual assets held in combination. An asset that would be relatively risky if held in isolation may have little, or even no risk, if held in a well diversified portfolio. *(p. 202)*

post audit The final aspect of the capital budgeting process. The post audit is a feedback process in which the actual results are compared with those predicted in the original capital budgeting analysis. The post audit has several purposes, the most important being to improve forecasts and improve operations. *(p. 321)*

precautionary balances Cash balances held in reserve for random, unforeseen fluctuations in cash inflows and outflows. *(p. 544)*

preemptive right Gives the current shareholders the right to purchase any new shares issued in proportion to their current holdings. The preemptive right enables current owners to maintain their proportionate share of ownership and control of the business. *(p. 238)*

preferred stock A security that is similar to bonds in some respects and to common stock in others. Preferred dividends are similar to interest payments on bonds in that they are fixed in amount and generally must be paid before common stock dividends can be paid. If the preferred dividend is not earned, the directors can omit it without throwing the company into bankruptcy. *(p. 252)*

premium bond Bond prices and interest rates are inversely related; that is, they tend to move in the opposite direction from each other. A fixed rate bond will sell at par when its coupon interest rate is equal to the going rate of interest, r_d. When the going rate of interest is above the coupon rate, a fixed rate bond will sell at a "discount" below its par value. If current interest rates are below the coupon rate, a fixed rate bond will sell at a "premium" above its par value. *(p. 167)*

price/cash flow ratio Calculated by dividing price per share by cash flow per share. This shows how much investors are willing to pay per dollar of cash flow. *(p. 72)*

price/earnings (P/E) ratio Calculated by dividing price per share by earnings per share. This shows how much investors are willing to pay per dollar of reported profits. *(p. 72)*

prime rate The lowest interest rate that banks generally charge their best customers. *(p. 522)*

private equity (PE) Funds from wealthy and institutional investors that are used to take public firms private or invest in firms that already are privately held. *(p. 447)*

probability distribution A listing, chart, or graph of all possible outcomes, such as expected rates of return, with a probability assigned to each outcome. *(p. 195)*

professional corporation (PC) Has most of the benefits of incorporation but the participants are not relieved of professional (malpractice) liability. *(p. 5)*

profitability index Found by dividing the project's present value of future cash flows by its initial cost. A profitability index greater than 1 is equivalent to a positive net present value project. *(p. 311)*

profitability ratios A group of ratios that show the combined effects of liquidity, asset management, and debt on operations. *(pp. 70, 81)*

project cash flows The incremental cash flows of a proposed project. *(p. 332)*

project financing Arrangements used to finance mainly large capital projects such as energy explorations, oil tankers, refineries, utility power plants, and so on. Usually, one or more firms (sponsors) will provide the equity capital required by the project, while the rest of the project's capital is supplied by lenders and lessors. The most important aspect of project financing is that the lenders and lessors do not have recourse against the sponsors; they must be repaid from the project's cash flows and the equity cushion provided by the sponsors. *(p. 449)*

prospectus Summarizes information about a new security issue and the issuing company. *(p. 439)*

proxy fight An attempt to take over a company in which an outside group solicits existing shareholders' proxies, which are authorizations to vote shares in a shareholders' meeting, in an effort to overthrow management and take control of the business. *(p. 261)*

publicly held stock Shares in a company whose stock is owned by a large number of investors, most of whom are not active in management. *(p. 238)*

pure expectations theory States that the slope of the yield curve depends on expectations about future inflation rates and interest rates. Thus, if the annual rate of inflation and future interest rates are expected to increase, the yield curve will be upward sloping; the curve will be downward sloping if the annual rates are expected to decrease. *(p. 183)*

pure financial merger A merger in which the companies will not be operated as a single unit and no operating economies are expected. *(p. 686)*

put-call parity relationship States that the value of a portfolio of buying a put option and the underlying stock is equivalent to a portfolio composed of buying a call option on the same stock and cash equal to the present value of the strike prices of the options. *(p. 585)*

put option Allows the holder to sell the asset at some predetermined price within a specified period of time. *(p. 573)*

quick, or acid test, ratio Found by taking current assets less inventories and then dividing by current liabilities. *(p. 64)*

realized rate of return, r̄ The actual return an investor receives on his or her investment. It can be quite different from the expected return. *(p. 199)*

real options Occur when managers can influence the size and risk of a project's cash flows by taking different actions during the project's life. They are referred to as real options because they deal with real as opposed to financial assets. They are also called managerial options because they give opportunities to managers to respond to changing market conditions. Sometimes they are called strategic options because they often deal with strategic issues. Finally, they are also called embedded options because they are a part of another project. *(p. 354)*

real property Assets that consist of physical property such as land and buildings. *(Web Extension 20A-2)*

real return bonds (RRBs) Bonds issued by the federal government that offer inflation protection to investors. *(p. 163)*

real risk-free rate of interest, r* That interest rate which equalizes the aggregate supply of, and demand for, riskless securities in an economy with zero inflation. The real risk-free rate could also be called the pure rate of interest since it is the rate of interest that would exist on very short-term, default-free Treasury bills if the expected rate of inflation were zero. *(p. 173)*

receivables collection period The average length of time required to convert a firm's receivables into cash. It is calculated by dividing accounts receivable by sales per day. *(p. 511)*

red herring (preliminary) prospectus A preliminary prospectus that may be distributed to potential buyers prior to approval of the registration statement by a securities commission. After the registration has become effective, the securities, accompanied by the prospectus, may be offered for sale. *(p. 439)*

refunding operation Occurs when a company issues debt at current low rates and uses the proceeds to repurchase one of its existing high coupon rate debt issues. Often these are callable issues, which means the company can purchase the debt at a lower than market price. *(p. 161)*

regular-dividend-plus-extras policy Dividend policy in which a company announces a regular dividend that it is sure can be maintained; if extra funds are available, the company pays a specially designated extra dividend or repurchases shares. *(p. 413)*

reinvestment rate risk Occurs when a short-term debt security must be "rolled over." If interest rates have fallen, the reinvestment of principal will be at a lower rate, with correspondingly lower interest payments and ending value. *(p. 181)*

relative purchasing power parity The change in the level of exchange rates based on the differing inflation rates of the two countries. *(p. 632)*

relaxed policy A policy under which relatively large amounts of cash, marketable securities, and inventories are carried and under which sales are stimulated by a liberal credit policy, resulting in a high level of receivables. *(p. 507)*

relevant risk The risk that an individual investment contributes to the overall portfolio's risk. *(p. 210)*

repatriation of earnings The cash flow, usually in the form of dividends or royalties, from the foreign branch or subsidiary to the parent company. These cash flows must be converted to the currency of the parent, and thus are subject to future exchange rate changes. A foreign government may restrict the amount of cash that may be repatriated. *(p. 636)*

replicating portfolio A portfolio of the underlying asset that offsets or replicates the value of an option. Also called *hedge portfolio*. *(p. 580)*

required rate of return The minimum acceptable rate of return considering both its risk and the returns available on other investments. *(p. 243)*

reserve borrowing capacity Exists when a firm uses less debt under "normal" conditions than called for by the trade-off theory. This allows the firm some flexibility to use debt in the future when additional capital is needed. *(p. 387)*

residual distribution model States that firms should pay dividends only when more earnings are available than needed to support the optimal capital budget. *(p. 410)*

residual value The market value of the leased property at the expiration of the lease. The estimate of the residual value is one of the key elements in lease analysis. *(p. 468)*

restricted policy A policy under which holdings of cash, securities, inventories, and receivables are minimized. *(p. 507)*

restricted voting rights A provision that automatically deprives a shareholder of voting rights if the shareholder owns more than a specified amount of stock. *(pp. 663, 670)*

retention growth model Calculates a company's growth rate by taking its return on equity and multiplying it by the proportion of earnings the company retains. *(pp. 278, 290)*

retractable A bond (or preferred shares) with a retractable feature allows the holder to sell the bond (or preferred shares) back to the issuer before maturity at a pre-set price. *(p. 185)*

return on common equity (ROE) Found by dividing net income by common equity. *(p. 71)*

return on invested capital (ROIC) Net operating profit after taxes divided by the operating capital. *(p. 41)*

return on total assets (ROA) The ratio of net income to total assets. *(p. 71)*

revaluation Occurs when the relative price of a currency is increased. It is the opposite of devaluation. *(p. 625)*

revolving line of credit A formal, committed line of credit extended by a bank or other lending institution. *(p. 524)*

rights offering Occurs when a corporation sells a new issue of common stock to its existing shareholders. Each shareholder receives a certificate called a stock purchase right giving the shareholder the option to purchase a specified number of the new shares. The rights are issued in proportion to the amount of stock that each shareholder currently owns. (*Web Extension 14A-1*)

risk-adjusted discount rate Incorporates the riskiness of the project's cash flows. The cost of capital to the firm reflects the average risk of the firm's existing projects. Thus, new projects that are riskier than existing projects should have a higher risk-adjusted discount rate. Conversely, projects with less risk should have a lower risk-adjusted discount rate. (*p. 357*)

risk identification Tthe process by which a business systematically identifies current and potential risks (*Web Extension 20A-1*)

risk premium, RP The extra return that an investor requires to hold risky Stock i instead of a risk-free asset. (*pp. 201, 215*)

roadshow Before an IPO, the senior management team and the investment banker make presentations to potential investors. They make presentations in 10 to 20 cities, with three to five presentations per day, over a 2-week period. (*p. 440*)

safety stocks Extra inventory held to avoid shortages. (*p. 564*)

sale-and-leaseback A type of financial lease in which the firm owning the property sells it to another firm, often a financial institution, while simultaneously entering into an agreement to lease the property back from the firm. (*p. 476*)

seasoned equity offering When a company with publicly traded shares issues additional shares. Also known as a "secondary" or "follow-on" offering. (*pp. 433, 450*)

Securities and Exchange Commission (SEC) A U.S. government agency that regulates the sales of new securities and the operations of securities exchanges. Along with other government agencies and sel-fregulation, the SEC helps ensure stable markets, sound brokerage firms, and the absence of stock manipulation. (*p. 33*)

securitization The process whereby financial instruments that were previously thinly traded are converted to a form that creates greater liquidity. Securitization also applies to the situation where specific assets are pledged as collateral for securities, and hence assetbacked securities are created. One example of the former is junk bonds; an example of the latter is mortgage-backed securities. (*p. 493*)

Security Market Line (SML) Represents, in a graphical form, the relationship between the risk of an asset as measured by its beta and the required rates of return for individual securities. The SML equation is essentially the Capital Asset Pricing Model, $r_i = r_{RF} + b_i(r_M - r_{RF})$. (*p. 216*)

semistrong form States that current market prices reflect all publicly available information. Therefore, the only way to gain abnormal returns on a stock is to possess inside information about the company's stock. (*p. 258*)

sensitivity analysis Indicates exactly how much net present value will change in response to a given change in an input variable, other things held constant. Sensitivity analysis is sometimes called "what if" analysis because it answers this type of question. (*p. 346*)

separation theorem States that a firm's investment decisions should be separate from the investment preferences of its investors. (*p. 7*)

shareholder rights provision Also known as a poison pill, it allows existing shareholders to purchase additional shares at a price that is lower than the market value if a potential acquirer purchases a controlling stake in the company. (*pp. 663, 670*)

share repurchases Occurs when a firm repurchases its own shares. (*p. 414*)

shelf prospectus Frequently, companies will file a prospectus and then update it with a short-form prospectus just before an offering. This procedure is termed a shelf prospectus because companies put new securities "on the shelf" and then later sell them when the market is right. (*p. 446*)

short hedges Occur when futures contracts are sold to guard against price declines. (*p. 602*)

sinking fund Facilitates the orderly retirement of a bond issue. This can be achieved in one of two ways: (1) the company can call in for redemption (at par value) a certain percentage of bonds each year or (2) the company may buy the required amount of bonds on the open market. (*pp. 162, 185*)

social perils Risks associated with the behaviour of people such as theft, strikes, or vandalism. (*Web Extension 20A-2*)

soft currency Currency of a country that sets the exchange rate but does not allow its currency to be traded on world markets. (*p. 626*)

sole proprietorship A business owned by one individual. (*p. 4*)

speculation The investment in an asset with the expectation of financial gain. (*p. 602*)

spontaneously generated funds Funds generated if a liability account increases spontaneously (automatically) as sales increase. An increase in a liability account is a source of funds; thus, funds have been generated. Two examples of spontaneous liability accounts are accounts payable and accrued wages. Note that notes payable, although a current liability account, is not a spontaneous source of funds since an increase in notes payable requires a specific action between the firm and a creditor. (*p. 135*)

spot rates The exchange rate that applies to "on the spot" trades, or, more precisely, exchanges that occur two days following the day of trade (in other words, current exchanges). (*p. 627*)

stand-alone risk The risk an investor takes by holding only one asset. (*p. 194*)

standard deviation, σ A statistical measure of the variability of a set of observations. It is the square root of the variance. (*p. 197*)

statement of cash flows Reports the impact of a firm's operating, investing, and financing activities on cash flows over an accounting period. *(pp. 33, 50)*

stepped-up exercise prices Provisions in a warrant that increases the strike price over time. These provisions are included to prod owners into exercising their warrants. *(p. 484)*

stock dividend Increases the number of shares outstanding, but at a slower rate than splits. Current shareholders receive additional shares on some proportional basis. Thus, a holder of 100 shares would receive 5 additional shares at no cost if a 5% stock dividend were declared. *(p. 422)*

stock split Current shareholders are given some number (or fraction) of shares for each share owned. Thus, in a three-for-one split, each shareholder would receive three new shares in exchange for each old share, thereby tripling the number of shares outstanding. Stock splits usually occur when the stock price is outside of the optimal trading range. *(p. 424)*

strategic options Options that often deal with strategic issues. Also called *real options, embedded options,* or *managerial options. (p. 354)*

stretching accounts payable The practice of deliberately paying accounts late. *(p. 521)*

strike price The price stated in the option contract at which the security can be bought (or sold). Also called the exercise price. *(p. 573)*

stripped bonds Zero coupon bonds created by investment dealers taking regular bonds and stripping the coupons from the principal. The same period coupons are bundled and sold as a zero coupon bond. The principal portion is also sold as a zero coupon bond. *(p. 161)*

strong form Assumes that all information pertaining to a stock, whether public or inside information, is reflected in current market prices. Thus, no investors would be able to earn abnormal returns in the stock market. *(p. 258)*

subordinated debentures Debentures that have claims on assets, in the event of bankruptcy, only after senior debt as named in the subordinated debt's indenture has been paid off. Subordinated debentures may be subordinated to designated notes payable or to all other debt. *(pp. 176, 185)*

sunk cost A cost that has already occurred and that is not affected by the capital project decision. Sunk costs are not relevant to capital budgeting decisions. *(p. 334)*

swap An exchange of cash payment obligations. Usually occurs because the parties involved prefer someone else's payment pattern or type. *(p. 605)*

sweetener A feature that makes a security more attractive to some investors, thereby inducing them to accept a lower current yield. Convertible features and warrants are examples of sweeteners. *(p. 483)*

symmetric information Assumes managers and investors have the same information about a firm's prospects. *(p. 386)*

synchronization of cash flows Occurs when firms are able to time cash receipts to coincide with cash requirements. *(p. 546)*

synergy Occurs when the whole is greater than the sum of its parts. When applied to mergers, a synergistic merger occurs when the postmerger earnings exceed the sum of the separate companies' pre-merger earnings. *(p. 678)*

target capital structure The relative amount of debt, preferred stock, and common equity that the firm desires. The weighted average cost of capital should be based on these target weights. *(pp. 269, 290)*

target cash balance The desired cash balance that a firm plans to maintain in order to conduct business. *(pp. 516, 563)*

target company A firm that another company seeks to acquire. *(p. 682)*

target distribution ratio Percentage of net income distributed to shareholders through cash dividends or share repurchases. *(p. 404)*

targeted share repurchases Also known as greenmail, occurs when a company selectively buys back stock from a potential acquirer at a price that is higher than the market price. In return, the potential acquirer agrees not to attempt to take over the company. *(p. 663)*

target payout ratio Percentage of net income paid as a cash dividend. *(p. 404)*

technical analysts Those who study past stock trends or patterns to predict future stock prices. Also called *chartists. (p. 258)*

temporary operating current assets The level of operating current assets required above the permanent level when the economy is strong and/or seasonal sales are high. *(p. 508)*

tender offer The offer of one firm to buy the stock of another by going directly to the shareholders, frequently over the opposition of the target company's management. *(p. 682)*

terminal loss The amount that can be deducted against income if, on the sale of the last asset in an asset class, the undepreciated capital cost is positive. *(pp. 337, 356)*

terminal value (TV) Value of operations at the end of the explicit forecast period; It is equal to the present value of all free cash flows beyond the forecast period, discounted back to the end of the forecast period at the weighted average cost of capital. *(p. 310)*

term structure of interest rates The relationship between yield to maturity and term to maturity for bonds of a single risk class. *(pp. 182, 186)*

time line A graphical representation used to show the timing of cash flows. *(p. 90)*

times-interest-earned (TIE) ratio Determined by dividing earnings before interest and taxes by the interest charges. This ratio measures the extent to which operating income can decline before the firm is unable to meet its annual interest costs. *(p. 68)*

time value The difference between the current value of the option and the value of the option if it were immediately exercised. *(p. 574)*

total assets turnover ratio Measures the turnover of all the firm's assets; it is calculated by dividing sales by total assets. *(p. 67)*

total investor-supplied capital Total amount of short-term debt, long-term debt, preferred shares, and total common equity shown on a balance sheet. It is the amount of financing that investors have provided to a company. Also called *investor-supplied capital*. *(p. 39)*

total investor-supplied operating capital The total amount of short-term debt, long-term debt, preferred shares, and total common equity shown on a balance sheet, less the amount of short-term investments shown on the balance sheet. It is the amount of financing used in operations that investors have provided to a company. Also called *investor-supplied operating capital*. *(p. 39)*

trade credit Debt arising from credit sales and recorded as an account receivable by the seller and as an account payable by the buyer. *(p. 519)*

trade deficit Occurs when a country imports more goods from abroad than it exports. *(p. 623)*

trade discounts Price reductions that suppliers offer customers for early payment of bills. *(p. 545)*

trade-off theory The addition of financial distress and agency costs to either the MM tax model or the Miller model. When trade-off is added to either model, the optimal capital structure can be visualized as a trade-off between the benefit of debt (the interest tax shield) and the costs of debt (financial distress and agency costs). *(p. 385)*

trend analysis An analysis of a firm's financial ratios over time. It is used to estimate the likelihood of improvement or deterioration in its financial situation. *(pp. 75, 81)*

trust receipt An instrument acknowledging that the goods are held in trust for the lender. *(pp. 531, 533)*

undepreciated capital cost (UCC) The amount remaining to be claimed as CCA over time for an asset class. *(pp. 336, 356)*

underinvestment problem A type of agency problem in which high debt can cause managers to forego positive NPV projects unless they are extremely safe. *(p. 666)*

underwrite A type of contract with an investment banker when issuing stock. An investment banker agrees to buy the entire issue at a set price and then resells the stock at the offering price. Thus, the risk of selling the issue rests with the investment banker. *(p. 439)*

variance A measure of the distribution's variability. It is the sum of the squared deviations about the expected value. *(p. 198)*

venture capitalists (VCs) Managers of a venture capital fund. The fund raises most of its capital from institutional investors and invests in start-up companies in exchange for equity. *(pp. 433, 449)*

vertical merger Occurs when a company acquires another firm that is "upstream" or "downstream"; for example, an automobile manufacturer acquires a steel producer. *(pp. 680, 700)*

vesting period Period during which employee stock options cannot be exercised. *(p. 664)*

warehouse receipt financing Financing method using inventory as security. Used when stronger control over the inventory is required by the lender. *(pp. 531, 533)*

warrants Call options issued by a company allowing the holder to buy a stated number of shares of stock from a company at a specified price. Warrants are generally distributed with debt, or preferred stock, to induce investors to buy those securities at lower cost. *(p. 163)*

weak form Assumes that all information contained in past price movements is fully reflected in current market prices. Thus, information about recent trends in a stock's price is of no use in selecting a stock. *(p. 258)*

weighted average cost of capital (WACC) The weighted average of the after-tax component costs of capital—debt, preferred stock, and common equity. Each weighting factor is the proportion of that type of capital in the optimal, or target, capital structure. *(pp. 10, 21)*

white knight A friendly competing bidder that a target management likes better than the company making a hostile offer; the target solicits a merger with the white knight as a preferable alternative. *(p. 696)*

white squire A competing bidder that is friendly to current management that buys enough of the target firm's shares to block a merger with a hostile bidder. *(p. 696)*

window dressing Techniques employed by firms to make their financial statements look better than they really are. *(p. 80)*

working capital A firm's investment in short-term assets—cash, marketable securities, inventory, and accounts receivable. *(p. 507)*

writing Writing an option is the same as selling an option. The option writer collects the premium for selling the option. *(p. 575)*

Yankee bond Bond denominated in U.S. dollars and sold in the United States under SEC regulations by a foreign borrower. *(p. 634)*

yield curve The curve that results when yield to maturity is plotted on the y-axis with term to maturity on the x-axis. *(pp. 182, 186)*

yield to call (YTC) The rate of interest earned on a bond if it is called. If current interest rates are well below an outstanding callable bond's coupon rate, the YTC may be a more relevant estimate of expected return than the YTM, since the bond is likely to be called. *(p. 168)*

yield to maturity (YTM) The rate of interest earned on a bond if it is held to maturity. *(pp. 167, 185)*

zero coupon bonds Pay no coupons at all, but are offered at a substantial discount below their par value and hence provides capital appreciation rather than interest income. Sometimes referred to as "stripped bonds." *(pp. 161, 185)*

name index

Note: Page numbers with "f" indicate figures, those with "t" indicate tables, and those with "n" indicate footnotes.

subject index

Note: Page numbers with "f" indicate figures, those with "t" indicate tables, and those with "n" indicate footnotes.

Corporate Valuation Framework

Financial Management: Theory and Practice emphasizes valuation and cash flow throughout the book. The Corporate Valuation Framework, such as the one shown below, is presented early in each of the book's chapters. Through the use of unique highlighting of the specific parts of the framework, the model explicitly shows how each chapter's material is related to corporate valuation. This practical, easy-to-use framework is intuitive and helps students keep the big picture in mind, even as they focus on a specific chapter's concepts.

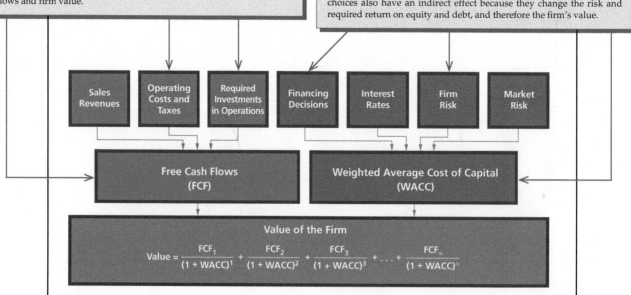

Efficient working capital management (Chapters 17 and 18) can reduce required investments in operations, which in turn can lead to larger cash flows and firm value.

Chapter 12, on capital structure, looks at a firm's financing choices and their effect on a company's weighted average cost of capital. Financing choices also have an indirect effect because they change the risk and required return on equity and debt, and therefore the firm's value.

| Sales Revenues | Operating Costs and Taxes | Required Investments in Operations | Financing Decisions | Interest Rates | Firm Risk | Market Risk |

Free Cash Flows (FCF)

Weighted Average Cost of Capital (WACC)

Value of the Firm

$$\text{Value} = \frac{FCF_1}{(1 + WACC)^1} + \frac{FCF_2}{(1 + WACC)^2} + \frac{FCF_3}{(1 + WACC)^3} + \ldots + \frac{FCF_\infty}{(1 + WACC)^\infty}$$

FOR STUDENTS

Through repeated use of the Corporate Valuation Framework, the connections between the various topics in the book are highlighted and brought together in one place. The framework shows how all of the individual concepts in each chapter relate back to a firm's value and why they are important.

FOR PROFESSORS

The Corporate Valuation Framework provides a useful visual tool to launch a lecture or plan the term around. The framework shows the connection between related concepts and the logical flow of material covered in class. The framework can also be used as a review, recapping the material taught and summarizing how it all fits together.